Cover Image:
African (Tanzania), Tinga Tinga school by Issa Monde Mlaponi (c. 1990s). Oil on wood panels.

Painted as a commission for the shop Kichaka, in Nairobi, Kenya, owned by Esther Ndisi-Bertolli.
Photo © Jason Lauré

Adventures in Literature

Where Timeless Becomes Timely

ATHENA EDITION
ATHENA EDITION
ATHENA EDITION
ATHENA EDITION
ATHENA EDITION
ATHENA EDITION
ATHENA EDITION
ATHENA EDITION

Classic Tales and

Classic literature is timeless and timely—
forever lifting time-bound travelers
beyond the boundaries of their ages
with supreme grace and beauty.

For nearly 70 years,
Adventures in Literature
has helped teachers to bring about
this transformation in their classrooms.

LITERATURE SOARS TO NEW HEIGHTS

Our Athena Edition ©1996, for grades 6 through 12, expands upon the traditional flight of the imagination and travels along some new and exciting paths.

You'll find

- Time-honored classics you love to teach and new selections to further enlighten and engage students
- Cross-cultural connections to elevate student awareness of literature's global reach
- Interdisciplinary bridges that make selections more relevant to students
- Stimulating activities to develop and improve students' writing skills
- Special critical-reading and thinking features to enhance students' literary insight

New Adventures

These well-organized support materials not only meet your students' needs, but also will save you valuable lesson planning time by enhancing students' learning experiences, integrating language arts skills, and offering multiple assessment options.

TIMELY MATERIALS FOR TODAY'S CLASSROOM

Pupil's Edition

Annotated Teacher's Edition

Teaching Resources with Organizer
- Teaching Resources Booklets
  - Teacher's Notes and Answer Keys
  - Reading Checks
  - Reading Focus Worksheets (Grade 6)
  - Study Guides
  - Language Skills Worksheets
  - Building Vocabulary Worksheets
  - Selection Vocabulary Tests
  - Selection Tests
  - Mastery Tests
  - Analogy Lessons
  - Analogy Tests
  - Revision Worksheets (Grade 6); Composition Tests (Grades 7-12)
- Portfolio Assessment and Professional Support Materials
- Teaching Resource Organizer

Test Generator
- IBM® PC and Compatibles
- Macintosh® Computers

Audiovisual Resources Binder
- Fine Art and Instructional Transparencies with Teacher's Notes and Blackline Masters
- Many Voices: Selection Audiocassettes with Teacher's Notes

ANNOTATED TEACHER'S EDITION

ATHENA EDITION

HOLT, RINEHART AND WINSTON
Harcourt Brace & Company

Austin • New York • Orlando • Atlanta • San Francisco • Boston • Dallas • Toronto • London

Copyright © 1996 by Holt, Rinehart and Winston, Inc.

All rights reserved. No part of this publication may be reproduced or transmitted in any form or by any means, electronic or mechanical, including photocopy, recording, or any information storage and retrieval system, without permission in writing from the publisher.

Requests for permission to make copies of any part of the work should be mailed to: Permissions Department, Holt, Rinehart and Winston, Inc., 6277 Sea Harbor Drive, Orlando, Florida 32887-6777.

Material from earlier edition: copyright © by Harcourt Brace & Company. All rights reserved.

For permission to reprint copyrighted material, grateful acknowledgment is made to the following sources:

BOA Editions, Ltd., 92 Park Avenue, Brockport, NY 14420: From "the 1st" from *good woman: poems and a memoir 1969–1980* by Lucille Clifton. Copyright © 1987 by Lucille Clifton.

Gwendolyn Brooks: From "Home" from *Maud Martha* by Gwendolyn Brooks. Copyright © 1993 by Gwendolyn Brooks. Published by Third World Press, Chicago.

Harvard University Press: From *One Writer's Beginnings* by Eudora Welty, Cambridge, Mass.: Harvard University Press. Copyright © 1983, 1984 by Eudora Welty.

Henry Holt and Company, Inc.: From "The Runaway" and from "Stopping by Woods on a Snowy Evening" from *The Poetry of Robert Frost,* edited by Edward Connery Lathem. Copyright 1951 by Robert Frost; copyright 1923, © 1969 by Henry Holt and Company, Inc.

Holt, Rinehart and Winston, Inc.: From "The Beginnings of African American Literature" from *African American Literature,* Teacher's Manual. Copyright © 1992 by Holt, Rinehart and Winston, Inc.

Mary Jarrell: From "The Chipmunk's Day" from *The Bat Poet* by Randall Jarrell. Copyright © 1963, 1964 by Macmillan Publishing Company.

Alfred A. Knopf, Inc.: From "In Time of Silver Rain" from *Selected Poems* by Langston Hughes. Copyright 1928 and renewed © 1966 by Langston Hughes.

Barbara S. Kouts on behalf of Joseph Bruchac: From "Birdfoot's Grampa" by Joseph Bruchac.

Liveright Publishing Corporation: From "maggie and milly and molly and may" from *Complete Poems, 1904–1962* by E. E. Cummings, edited by George J. Firmage. Copyright © 1923, 1925, 1926, 1931, 1935, 1938, 1939, 1940, 1944, 1945, 1946, 1947, 1948, 1949, 1950, 1951, 1952, 1953, 1954, 1955, 1956, 1957, 1958, 1959, 1960, 1961, 1962 by E. E. Cummings; copyright © 1961, 1963, 1966, 1967, 1968 by Marion Morehouse Cummings; copyright © 1972, 1973, 1974, 1975, 1976, 1977, 1978, 1979, 1980, 1981, 1982, 1983, 1984, 1985, 1986, 1987, 1988, 1989, 1990, 1991 by the Trustees for the E. E. Cummings Trust. From "Those Winter Sundays" from *Angle of Ascent, New and Selected Poems* by Robert Hayden. Copyright © 1975, 1972, 1970, 1966 by Robert Hayden.

Ashley D. Moss, Brett Deal, and Shane Townsend: From "Antaeus" by Borden Deal. Copyright © 1961 by Southern Methodist University.

The New Yorker: From "Phaethon" by Morris Bishop from *The Best of Bishop: Light Verse from The New Yorker and Elsewhere* (Cornell). Copyright © 1955 and renewed © 1983 by Alison Kinsbury Bishop. Originally in *The New Yorker.*

W. W. Norton & Company, Inc.: From "A Parrot" from *Collected Poems (1930–1973)* by May Sarton. Copyright © 1974 by May Sarton.

Marian Reiner: From "I must go begging" by Chiyo from *Cricket Songs: Japanese Haiku,* translated by Harry Behn. Copyright © 1964 by Harry Behn; copyright renewed © 1992 by Prescott Behn, Pamela Behn Adam, and Peter Behn.

The Sewanee Review: From "Sled" by Thomas E. Adams from *The Sewanee Review,* vol. 69, no. 1, Winter 1961. Copyright © 1961 by the University of the South.

Simon & Schuster, Inc.: From "The Spider" from *Collected Poems of Robert P. Tristram Coffin.* Copyright 1935 by Macmillan Publishing Company; copyright renewed © 1963 by Margaret Coffin Halvosa.

The Society of Authors as the literary trustees of Walter de la Mare: From "The Listeners" by Walter de la Mare.

Rosemary Thurber: From "What Happened to Charles" from *Further Fables for Our Time* by James Thurber. Copyright © 1956 by James Thurber; copyright renewed © 1987 by Helen Thurber. Published by Simon & Schuster, Inc. Text originally published in *The New Yorker.*

University of Arkansas Press: From "One of the Seven Has Somewhat to Say" from *Story Hour* by Sara Henderson Hay. Copyright © 1982 by the University of Arkansas Press.

Printed in the United States of America

ISBN 0-03-098629-X

2 3 4 5 041 97 96 95

Critical Readers and Contributors

H. Edward Deluzain
A. Crawford Mosley
High School
Panama City, Florida

Beverly Grossman
Austin, Texas

Annie Hartnett
Austin, Texas

Theresa Holloway
George Washington
Intermediate School
Honolulu, Hawaii

Carolee Lanier
Rockville, Maryland

Emily Orlando Licate
West Junior High School
Ashtabula, Ohio

Elizabeth McGonigal
Round Rock, Texas

Penny Dolison Nadeau
O'Donnell Middle School
Stoughton, Massachusetts

Nancy Nowlin
Austin, Texas

Donna Rawlins
McGuffey Intermediate School
Claysville, Pennsylvania

Barbara Scroggie
Austin, Texas

Donna Townsend
Austin, Texas

Trudy Williams
Austin, Texas

Contents

Annotated Teacher's Edition

To the Teacher T26

Part One Themes in Literature

Close Reading of a Selection 2
Guidelines for Close Reading 2
   Eudora Welty . . . . FROM One Writer's Beginnings 3
Looking at Yourself as a Reader 7

Unit 1

REFLECTIONS

Teaching Guide		7A

James Berry . . . . One 10
Gary Soto . . . . Seventh Grade 13
Jack London . . . . The King of Mazy May 19
Sherwood Anderson . . . . Stolen Day 27
**Virginia Driving
  Hawk Sneve** . . . . The Medicine Bag 32

▪▪ **Connecting Cultures: The Influence of American Indian Languages** . . . 40

Ruth McKenney . . . . Guinea Pig 41
Mark Twain . . . . The Cat and the Pain Killer
                                        FROM *The Adventures of Tom Sawyer* 48

Reading Skills Practice		51
Countee Cullen	Tableau	54
Ruskin Bond	The Fight	56

Connecting Cultures: Bazaars 62

Yoshiko Uchida	The Bracelet	63

Literature and History: The Internment of Japanese Americans 68

E. E. Cummings	maggie and milly and molly and may	69
Francisco Jiménez	The Circuit	71
Morley Callaghan	Luke Baldwin's Vow	77

Reading Skills Practice	81

Focus on Reading and Critical Thinking:
Making Generalizations About Theme 88

Focus on Writing: Writing a Personal Narrative 89

Unit 2

FAMILY ALBUM

Teaching Guide		91A
Merle Hodge	FROM Crick Crack, Monkey	94
■ **Connecting Cultures: Trickster Heroes**		99
Edna St. Vincent Millay	The Courage That My Mother Had	100
Harper Lee	One-Shot Finch FROM *To Kill a Mockingbird*	102
Robert Hayden	Those Winter Sundays	112
Thomas E. Adams	Sled	114
Reading Skills Practice		118
Monica Sone	FROM *Nisei Daughter*	122
Gwendolyn Brooks	Home FROM *Maud Martha*	127
Amy Ling	Grandma Ling	131
James Thurber	The Night the Bed Fell	133
■ **Focus on Writing: Writing a Description**		139

T6 Contents

Unit 3

THE NATURAL WORLD

Teaching Guide 141A		
Nina Otero	The Wind in the Mountains	 144
Edward Abbey	Desert Creatures	 147
Paul Annixter	Last Cover	 153
▪▪ **Literature and Science: Protective Coloration** 161		
Langston Hughes	In Time of Silver Rain	 162
Henry Wadsworth Longfellow	The Wreck of the *Hesperus*	. . . 164
Jim Kjelgaard	The Tiger's Heart	 170
Reading Skills Practice 173		
Robert Frost	The Runaway	 178
Michael McLaverty	The Wild Duck's Nest	 180
Joseph Bruchac	Birdfoot's Grampa	 186
Borden Deal	Antaeus	 187
▪▪ **Focus on Writing: Writing an Informative Paper** 196		

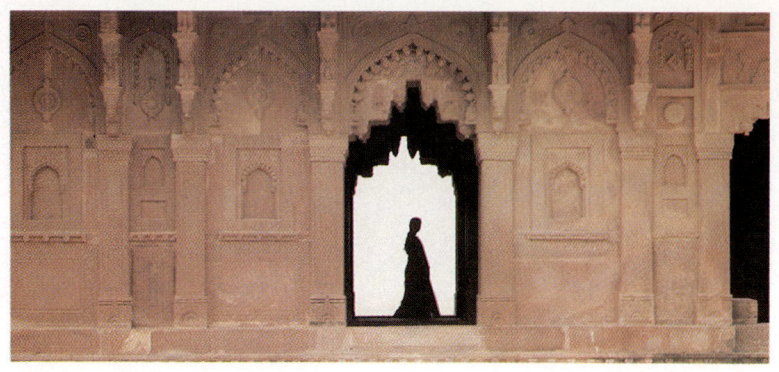

Part Two Forms of Literature

Unit 4

SHORT STORIES

Teaching Guide		199A
Close Reading of a Short Story		202
Guidelines for Close Reading		203
Mona Gardner	The Dinner Party	204
Looking at Yourself as a Reader		207
T. O. Beachcroft	The Erne from the Coast	208
Roald Dahl	The Landlady	220
Rudyard Kipling	Rikki-tikki-tavi	229
Connecting Cultures: Words of Indian Origin		241
Ernest Hemingway	A Day's Wait	242
Literature and Math: Prefixes Used in Measurement		246
Washington Irving	Rip Van Winkle	247
Reading Skills Practice		251
Literature and the Arts: Illustrated Editions		263
Eva-Lis Wuorio	You Can't Take It with You	264
Isaac Bashevis Singer	Zlateh the Goat	270
Charles Dickens	A Christmas Carol	276
Reading Skills Practice		281
Literature and the Arts: Adaptations of "A Christmas Carol"		302
Focus on Reading and Critical Thinking: Evaluating Short Stories		303
Focus on Writing: Writing a Short Story		304

Unit 5

DRAMA

Teaching Guide	305A
Close Reading of a Play	308
Guidelines for Close Reading	308
Milton Geiger . . . . In the Fog	309
Looking at Yourself as a Reader	317
Michael and	
Molly Hardwick . . . . The Mazarin Stone	318
Reading Skills Practice	324
Serafín and	
Joaquín Quintero . . . . A Sunny Morning	335
Neil Simon . . . . The Governess	343
Alice Childress . . . . When the Rattlesnake Sounds	347
James Ene Henshaw . . . . . . The Jewels of the Shrine	357
Reading Skills Practice	361
▪▪ **Connecting Cultures: The Trickster in Folk Tales**	372
▪▪ **Focus on Reading and Critical Thinking: Drawing Inferences**	376
▪▪ **Focus on Writing: Writing a Scene**	377

Contents **T9**

Unit 6

NONFICTION

Teaching Guide 379A

Close Reading of an Essay 382
Guidelines for Close Reading 382
    Barry Holstun Lopez .... FROM River Notes 383
Looking at Yourself as a Reader 385

Jane Goodall .... FROM In the Shadow of Man 386

Reading Skills Practice 388

Julia Alvarez .... Names/Nombres 393
**Marjorie Kinnan
    Rawlings** .... Rattlesnake Hunt
                                  FROM Cross Creek 398
Ved Mehta .... FROM Sound-Shadows of the New
                                    World 404

Reading Skills Practice 409

J. Frank Dobie .... When I Was A Boy on the Ranch ... 414

Reading Skills Practice 420

▪▪ **Focus on Reading and Critical Thinking:
Understanding Cause and Effect** 424
    **Elizabeth Marshall
       Thomas** .... FROM The Hidden Life of Dogs 424

▪▪ **Focus on Writing: Writing a Biographical Report** 425

Unit 7

POETRY

Teaching Guide	427A

Close Reading of a Poem	430
Guidelines for Close Reading	430
Sara Teasdale May Day	431
Looking at Yourself as a Reader	432

Language and Meaning

THE SPEAKER

Robert Graves	The Caterpillar	433
Sara Henderson Hay	One of the Seven Has Somewhat to Say	435

DICTION

Carl Sandburg	Fog	437
Lucille Clifton	The 1st	438
E.E. Cummings	in Just-	439
Randall Jarrell	The Chipmunk's Day	441
James Whitcomb Riley	When the Frost Is on the Punkin	443

Contents **T11**

IMAGERY

John Masefield	Trade Winds	447
May Sarton	A Parrot	448

FIGURATIVE LANGUAGE

May Swenson	Living Tenderly	450
Robert P. Tristram Coffin	The Spider	452

THE IDEAS IN A POEM

Robert Frost	Stopping by Woods on a Snowy Evening	455
Walter de la Mare	The Listeners	457

Sound and Meaning

REPETITION AND RHYME

Edgar Allan Poe	Annabel Lee	460
Vachel Lindsay	The Broncho That Would Not Be Broken	464
William Shakespeare	Full Fathom Five	466

ONOMATOPOEIA AND RHYTHM

Alfred Noyes	The Highwayman	468

Types of Poetry

NARRATIVE POETRY

Anonymous	The Golden Vanity	475
Robert Browning	The Pied Piper of Hamelin	478

LYRIC POETRY

Henry Wadsworth Longfellow	Snowflakes	488
James Stephens	Little Things	490
Emily Dickinson	I'm Nobody	490
Bashō, Chosu, Chiyo	Haiku	491

DRAMATIC POETRY

Lewis Carroll	Father William	493

COMIC VERSE

    Edward Lear . . . . The Bearded Man 496
    Carolyn Wells . . . . A Tutor 496
    Ogden Nash . . . . The Lama 496

▪▪ **Focus on Reading and Critical Thinking:**
   Relating Sound to Meaning 497
    Simon J. Ortiz . . . . My Father's Song 497

▪▪ **Focus on Writing: Writing a Poem** 498

Unit 8

THE NOVEL

| **Teaching Guide** . . . . 499A |

Guidelines for Close Reading 502
    Gary Soto . . . . Pacific Crossing 503

| **Reading Skills Practice** . . . . 514 |

▪▪ **Connecting Cultures: Games from Around the World** 530
▪▪ **Connecting Cultures: International Exchange** 531

| **Reading Skills Practice** . . . . 538 |

▪▪ **Connecting Cultures: Holidays** 564
▪▪ **Connecting Cultures: Japanese Culture** 564

▪▪ **Focus on Reading and Critical Thinking:**
   Using Analysis and Synthesis 566

▪▪ **Focus on Writing: Writing a Letter** 567

Part Three Literary Heritage

Unit 9

CLASSICAL MYTHOLOGY

| **Teaching Guide** | 571A |

Guidelines for Close Reading 574
    Olivia Coolidge . . . . The Gods and Goddesses of Mount
                                     Olympus 575
Classical Gods and Goddesses 576

■■ **Literature and Sports: The Olympic Games** 582

Jeremy Ingalls . . . . Prometheus the Fire-Bringer 583

■■ **Literature and Research: Sources of Information** 591

■■ **Connecting Cultures: Comparative Mythology** 591

Olivia Coolidge . . . . The Origin of the Seasons 592
Rex Warner . . . . Arachne 598
Sally Benson . . . . The Reward of Baucis and Philemon . . 602

■■ **Literature and Research: Entries in Reference Books**		605
Classical Mythology in Today's World		606
Edith Hamilton	Phaethon	608
Morris Bishop	Phaethon	613
Josephine Preston Peabody	Icarus and Daedalus	614
Reading Skills Practice		616
■■ **Literature and the Arts: Interpretations of a Myth**		617
Anne Sexton	To a Friend Whose Work Has Come to Triumph	618
■■ **Literature and Research: Allusions to Mythology**		619
Classical Mythology in Today's World		620
Edith Hamilton	The Adventures of Hercules	622
■■ **Literature and Research: Mythological Monsters**		628
Index of Names		629
■■ **Connecting Cultures: Myths from Different Lands**		632
■■ **Focus on Reading and Critical Thinking: Using Methods of Comparison and Contrast**		633
The Origin of Corn		633

Unit 10

NORSE MYTHOLOGY

Teaching Guide		633A
Names in Norse Mythology		636
Barbara Leonie Picard	The Norse Gods and Goddesses	640
Olivia Coolidge	The Fenris Wolf	644
Hamilton Wright Mabie	How Thor Found His Hammer	648
Olivia Coolidge	Thor and the Giant King	653
Reading Skills Practice		656
Edith Hamilton	The Death of Balder	660
Barbara Leonie Picard	The End of All Things	663

Unit 11

FABLES

Teaching Guide		665A
Guidelines for Close Reading		668
Fables by Aesop	Belling the Cat	669
	The Town Mouse and the Country Mouse	670
	The Ant and the Grasshopper	672
Reading Skills Practice		672
	The Fox and the Crow	673
Fables in Verse		
John Godfrey Saxe	The Blind Men and the Elephant	675
Marie de France	The Wolf and the Dog	677
Fables by James Thurber	The Fairly Intelligent Fly	679
	What Happened to Charles	680
	The Fox and the Crow	682

▪▪ Focus on Reading and Critical Thinking:
Distinguishing Between Facts and Opinions ... 685
   Edith Hamilton .... FROM Mythology 685

▪▪ Focus on Writing: Writing a Persuasive Paper 686

WRITING ABOUT LITERATURE

The Writing Process 689
Answering Examination Questions 690
    Using the Writing Process to Answer an Essay Question 693
    Sample Examination Questions and Answers 694
Writing on a Topic of Your Own 697
    Prewriting
        Choosing a Topic 697
        Gathering Evidence/Formulating Major Points 698
            James Stephens   The Wind 699
            Emily Dickinson   The Wind Tapped like a Tired Man .. 699
        Organizing Ideas 701
    Writing the Essay 702
    Evaluating and Revising Papers 703
    Proofreading and Publishing 705
Literary Terms and Techniques 706
Handbook for Revision 726
    Model Essays 727
    Sentence Structure 738
    Pronouns 739
    Verbs 740
    Word Order 744
    Comma Usage 744
    Style 746
    Glossary of Usage 749
    Grammar Reference Guide 757
    Mechanics 760
Glossary 768
Outline of Concepts and Skills 786
Index of Contents by Types 789
Index of Fine Art and Illustrations 791
Photo Credits 792
Index of Authors and Titles 794

Index of Titles by Themes

Reflections

from *One Writer's Beginnings,* Eudora Welty, 3
One, James Berry, 10
Seventh Grade, Gary Soto, 13
King of Mazy May, The, Jack London, 19
Stolen Day, Sherwood Anderson, 27
Medicine Bag, The, Virginia Driving Hawk Sneve, 32
Guinea Pig, Ruth McKenney, 41
Cat and the Pain Killer, The,
    from *The Adventures of Tom Sawyer,* Mark Twain, 48
Tableau, Countee Cullen, 54
Fight, The, Ruskin Bond, 56
Bracelet, The, Yoshiko Uchida, 63
maggie and milly and molly and may, E. E. Cummings, 69
Circuit, The, Francisco Jiménez, 71
Luke Baldwin's Vow, Morley Callaghan, 77
Wild Duck's Nest, The, Michael McLaverty, 180
Antaeus, Borden Deal, 188
Names/Nombres, Julia Alvarez, 393
When I Was a Boy on the Ranch, J. Frank Dobie, 414
Pacific Crossing, Gary Soto, 503

Family Album

from *Crick Crack, Monkey,* Merle Hodge, 94
Courage That My Mother Had, The, Edna St. Vincent Millay, 100
One-Shot Finch, from *To Kill a Mockingbird,* Harper Lee, 102
Those Winter Sundays, Robert Hayden, 112
Sled, Thomas E. Adams, 114
from *Nisei Daughter,* Monica Sone, 122
Home from *Maude Martha,* Gwendolyn Brooks, 127
Grandma Ling, Amy Ling, 131
Night the Bed Fell, The, James Thurber, 133
Erne from the Coast, The, T. O. Beachcroft, 208
A Day's Wait, Ernest Hemingway, 242
Zlateh the Goat, Isaac Bashevis Singer, 270
My Father's Song, Simon J. Ortiz, 497

The Natural World

Wind in the Mountains, The, Nina Otero, 144
Desert Creatures, Edward Abbey, 147
Last Cover, Paul Annixter, 153
In Time of Silver Rain, Langston Hughes, 162
Tiger's Heart, The, Jim Kjelgaard, 170
Runaway, The, Robert Frost, 178
Wild Duck's Nest, The, Michael McLaverty, 180
Birdfoot's Grampa, Joseph Bruchac, 186
Antaeus, Borden Deal, 188
Erne from the Coast, The, T. O. Beachcroft, 208
Zlateh the Goat, Isaac Bashevis Singer, 270
from *River Notes,* Barry Holstun Lopez, 383
from *In the Shadow of Man,* Jane Goodall, 386
Rattlesnake Hunt, from *Cross Creek,* Marjorie Kinnan Rawlings, 398
from *The Hidden Life of Dogs,* Elizabeth Marshall Thomas, 424
May Day, Sara Teasdale, 431
Caterpillar, The, Robert Graves, 433
Fog, Carl Sandburg, 437
in Just-, E. E. Cummings, 439
Chipmunk's Day, The, Randall Jarrell, 441
When the Frost Is on the Punkin, James Whitcomb Riley, 443
Parrot, A, May Sarton, 448
Living Tenderly, May Swenson, 450
Spider, The, Robert P. Tristram Coffin, 452
Stopping by Woods on a Snowy Evening, Robert Frost, 455
Broncho That Would Not Be Broken, The, Vachel Lindsay, 464
Snowflakes, Henry Wadsworth Longfellow, 488
Little Things, James Stephens, 490
Wind, The, James Stephens, 699
Wind Tapped like a Tired Man, The, Emily Dickinson, 699

On the Light Side

Stolen Day, A, Sherwood Anderson, 27
Guinea Pig, Ruth McKenney, 41
Cat and the Pain Killer, The,
    from *The Adventures of Tom Sawyer,* Mark Twain, 48
Night the Bed Fell, The, James Thurber, 133
Rip Van Winkle, Washington Irving, 247
You Can't Take It with You, Eva-Lis Wuorio, 264
Sunny Morning, A, Serafin and Joaquín Quintero, 335
Jewels of the Shrine, The, James Ene Henshaw, 357
One of the Seven Has Somewhat to Say, Sara Henderson Hay, 435
Pied Piper of Hamelin, The, Robert Browning, 478
I'm Nobody, Emily Dickinson, 490
Father William, Lewis Carroll, 493
Bearded Man, The, Edward Lear, 496
Lama, The, Ogden Nash, 496
Tutor, A, Carolyn Wells, 496
Belling the Cat, Aesop, 669
Town Mouse and the Country Mouse, The, Aesop, 670
Ant and the Grasshopper, The, Aesop, 672
Fox and the Crow, The, Aesop, 673
Blind Men and the Elephant, The, John Godfrey Saxe, 675
Fairly Intelligent Fly, The, James Thurber, 679
What Happened to Charles, James Thurber, 680
Fox and the Crow, The, James Thurber, 682

Call It Courage

King of Mazy May, The, Jack London, 19
Courage That My Mother Had, The, Edna St. Vincent Millay, 100
Tiger's Heart, The, Jim Kjelgaard, 170
Dinner Party, The, Mona Gardner, 203
Erne from the Coast, The, T. O. Beachcroft, 208
Rikki-tikki-tavi, Rudyard Kipling, 229
Day's Wait, A, Ernest Hemingway, 242
When the Rattlesnake Sounds, Alice Childress, 347
Rattlesnake Hunt, from *Cross Creek,* Marjorie Kinnan Rawlings, 398
from *Sound-Shadows of the New World,* Ved Mehta, 404
Golden Vanity, The, Anonymous, 475
Phaethon, Edith Hamilton, 608
Icarus and Daedalus, Josephine Preston Peabody, 614
Adventures of Hercules, The, Edith Hamilton, 622
Fenris Wolf, The, Olivia Coolidge, 644

The Power of Love

Luke Baldwin's Vow, Morley Callaghan, 77
Those Winter Sundays, Robert Hayden, 112
Birdfoot's Grampa, Joseph Bruchac, 186
Christmas Carol, A, Charles Dickens, 276
Annabel Lee, Edgar Allan Poe, 460
Highwayman, The, Alfred Noyes, 468

Mystery and Adventure

Tiger's Heart, The, Jim Kjelgaard, 170
Erne from the Coast, The, T. O. Beachcroft, 208
Landlady, The, Roald Dahl, 220
In the Fog, Milton Geiger, 309
Mazarin Stone, The, Michael and Molly Hardwick, 318
Listeners, The, Walter de la Mare, 457

Changes/Transformations

Christmas Carol, A, Charles Dickens, 276
Arachne, Rex Warner, 598
Reward of Baucis and Philemon, The, Sally Benson, 602
Thor and the Giant King, Olivia Coolidge, 653

Note to Teachers

EXCERPTED LITERARY WORKS USED IN THIS TEXT

The following selections are excerpts from larger works. Excerpts were chosen on the basis of key literary or thematic elements.

FROM *One Writer's Beginnings*
FROM *The Adventures of Tom Sawyer*
FROM *Crick Crack, Monkey*
FROM *To Kill a Mockingbird*
FROM *Nisei Daughter*
FROM *Maud Martha*
FROM *"Down to the Sea of Cortez"*
 from *Beyond the Wall*

FROM *The Good Doctor*
FROM *River Notes*
FROM *In the Shadow of Man*
FROM *Cross Creek*
FROM *Sound-Shadows of the New World*
FROM *The Hidden Life of Dogs*

BOOK ONE

ATHENA EDITION

HOLT, RINEHART AND WINSTON
Harcourt Brace & Company

Austin • New York • Orlando • Atlanta • San Francisco • Boston • Dallas • Toronto • London

Staff Credits

EDITORIAL
Project Director: Fannie Safier
Editorial Coordinator: Katie Vignery
Editorial Staff: Lynda Abbott, Sally Ahearn, Judith Austin-Mills, Laura Baci, Amanda Beard, Richard Blake, Susan Britt, Robert Carranza, Daniela Guggenheim, Scott Hall, Bobbi Hernandez, Constance D. Israel, Susan Lynch, Mary Malone, Jennifer Osborne, Marie Hoffman Price, Sara Schroeder, Amy D.D. Simpson, Atietie O. Tonwe
Editorial Support: Carla M. Beer, Ruth Hooker, Margaret Guerrero
Editorial Permissions: Carrie Jones
Software Development: Armin Gutzmer, Lydia Doty

DESIGN AND PHOTO RESEARCH
Design: Pun Nio, *Senior Art Director;* Richard Metzger, *Design Supervisor;* Diane Motz, *Senior Designer;* Stephen Sharpe, *Designer*
Photo: Debra Saleny, *Photo Research Manager;* V. Sing Griffin Bitzer, Shelley Boyd, Yvonne Gerin, Jeannie Taylor, *Photo Researchers*

PRODUCTION
Beth Prevelige, *Senior Production Manager;* Simira Davis, *Production Assistant;* Sergio Durante, *Secretary;* George Prevelige, *Production Manager;* Rose Degollado, *Production Coordinator*
Electronic Publishing: Carol Martin, *Electronic Publishing Manager;* Kristy Sprott, *Electronic Publishing Supervisor;* Debra Schorn, *Electronic Publishing Senior Coordinator;* Lana Castle, Denise Haney, David Hernandez, Maria Homic, Barbara Hudgens, Mercedes Newman, Monica Shomos, *Electronic Publishing Staff*

Cover Design: Design 5

Copyright © 1996 by Holt, Rinehart and Winston, Inc.

All rights reserved. No part of this publication may be reproduced or transmitted in any form or by any means, electronic or mechanical, including photocopy, recording, or any information storage and retrieval system, without permission in writing from the publisher.

Requests for permission to make copies of any part of the work should be mailed to: Permissions Department, Holt, Rinehart and Winston, Inc., 6277 Sea Harbor Drive, Orlando, Florida 32887-6777.

Material from earlier editions: copyright © by Harcourt Brace & Company.
All rights reserved.

Acknowledgments appear on pages iv–v, which are an extension of the copyright page.

Printed in the United States of America

ISBN 0-03-098628-1   2 3 4 5 040 97 96 95

Curriculum and Writing

V. Pauline Hodges
Forgan Public Schools
Forgan, Oklahoma

Carroll Moulton
Formerly of Duke University
Durham, North Carolina

Contributors and Critical Readers

Arlene Arthur
Loma Linda Academy
Loma Linda, California

Eleanor J. Brazell
Sandy Springs Middle School
Atlanta, Georgia

Charlene Couvillon
Fort Walton Beach High School
Fort Walton Beach, Florida

Jan Freeman
Florence, Massachusetts

Mae Holup
Lake Shore Middle School
Mequon, Wisconsin

Nancy Horvit
Welch Middle School
Houston, Texas

Maryann Hughes
Catonsville Middle School
Baltimore, Maryland

Emily Licate
West Junior High School
Ashtabula, Ohio

Ernest Ortiz
Frank M. Black Middle School
Houston, Texas

Acknowledgments

For permission to reprint copyrighted material, grateful acknowledgment is made to the following sources:

Andrews & McMeel, Inc.: From "River Notes" from *River Notes: The Dance of the Herons* by Barry Lopez. Copyright © 1979 by Barry Holstun Lopez. All rights reserved.

Elizabeth Barnett, Literary Executor: "The Courage That My Mother Had" from *Collected Poems* by Edna St. Vincent Millay. Copyright © 1954, 1982 by Norma Millay Ellis.

Susan Bergholz Literary Services, New York: "Names/Nombres" by Julia Alvarez. Copyright © 1985 by Julia Alvarez. First published in *Nuestro*, March 1985. Comment on "Names/Nombres" by Julia Alvarez. Copyright © 1996 by Julia Alvarez.

BOA Editions, Ltd., 92 Park Avenue, Brockport, NY 14420: "the 1st" from *good woman: poems and a memoir 1969–1980* by Lucille Clifton. Copyright © 1987 by Lucille Clifton.

Ruskin Bond: Comment on "The Fight" by Ruskin Bond. Copyright © 1996 by Ruskin Bond.

Gwendolyn Brooks: "Home" from *Maud Martha* by Gwendolyn Brooks. Copyright © 1993 by Gwendolyn Brooks. Published by Third World Press, Chicago.

Estate of Morley Callaghan: "Luke Baldwin's Vow" by Morley Callaghan from *The Saturday Evening Post*, March 15, 1947. Copyright 1947 by Saturday Evening Post; copyright renewed © 1974 by Morley Callaghan.

Coward-McCann, Inc.: *When the Rattlesnake Sounds* by Alice Childress. Copyright © 1975 by Alice Childress.

Andre Deutsch Ltd.: From *Crick Crack, Monkey* by Merle Hodge. Copyright © 1970 by Merle Hodge.

Devin-Adair, Publishers, Inc., Old Greenwich, CT 06870: "The Wild Duck's Nest" from *The Game Cock and Other Stories* by Michael McLaverty. Copyright 1947, © 1975 by Devin Adair, Publishers, Inc.

Dial Books for Young Readers, a division of Penguin Books USA Inc.: "The Reward of Baucis and Philemon" from *Stories of the Gods and Heroes* by Sally Benson. Copyright 1940 and renewed © 1968 by Sally Benson.

Dorothy Geiger: "In the Fog" by Milton Geiger.

The General Media Publishing Group: "The Dinner Party" by Mona Gardner from *Saturday Review of Literature*, vol. 25, no. 5, January 31, 1941. Copyright 1941 by Saturday Review Co. Inc.; copyright renewed © 1969 by Saturday Review, Inc.

Grafton Books, an imprint of HarperCollins Publishers Limited: "Arachne" from *Men and Gods* by Rex Warner.

GRM Associates, Inc., Agents for the Estate of Ida M. Cullen: "Tableau" from *Color* by Countee Cullen. Copyright © 1925 by Harper & Brothers; copyright renewed 1953 by Ida M. Cullen.

Harcourt Brace & Company: "One" from *When I Dance* by James Berry. Copyright © 1991, 1988 by James Berry. "Guinea Pig" from *My Sister Eileen* by Ruth McKenney. Copyright 1938 and renewed © 1966 by Ruth McKenney. "Seventh Grade" from *Baseball in April and Other Stories* by Gary Soto. Copyright © 1990 by Gary Soto. Adaptation of *Pacific Crossing* by Gary Soto. Copyright © 1992 by Gary Soto.

HarperCollins Publishers, Inc.: From *To Kill a Mockingbird* by Harper Lee. Copyright © 1960 and renewed © 1988 by Harper Lee. "Zlateh the Goat" from *Zlateh the Goat and Other Stories* by Isaac Bashevis Singer. Text copyright © 1966 by Isaac Bashevis Singer.

Harvard University Press: From *One Writer's Beginnings* by Eudora Welty, Cambridge, Mass.: Harvard University Press. Copyright © 1983, 1984 by Eudora Welty.

Hearst Corporation: "The Tiger's Heart" by Jim Kjelgaard from *Esquire*, April 1951. Copyright 1951 by Esquire Associates.

James Ene Henshaw: "The Jewels of the Shrine, A Play in One Act" from *This Is Our Chance, Plays from West Africa* by James Ene Henshaw. Copyright © 1956 by James E. Henshaw. Originally published by the University of London Press Ltd.

Richard H. Herdman: "The Wind in the Mountains" from *Old Spain in Our Southwest* by Nina Otero.

Lawrence Hill Books, New York, NY: "Last Cover" from *The Best Nature Stories of Paul Annixter*. Copyright © 1974 by Jane and Paul Annixter.

Henry Holt and Company, Inc.: From "Down to the Sea of Cortez" from *Beyond the Wall* by Edward Abbey. Copyright © 1971, 1976, 1977, 1979, 1984 by Edward Abbey. "The Runaway" and "Stopping by Woods on a Snowy Evening" from *The Poetry of Robert Frost*, edited by Edward Connery Lathem. Copyright 1951 by Robert Frost; copyright 1923, © 1969 by Henry Holt and Company, Inc.

Houghton Mifflin Company: Pronunciation key and entry, "Thursday," from *The American Heritage Dictionary of the English Language*. Copyright © 1981 by Houghton Mifflin Company. "The Gods and Goddesses of Mount Olympus" and "The Origin of the Seasons" from *Greek Myths* by Olivia E. Coolidge. Copyright 1949 and renewed © 1977 by Olivia E. Coolidge. All rights reserved. "The Fenris Wolf" and "Thor and the Giant King" from *Legends of the North* by Olivia E. Coolidge. Copyright 1951 and renewed © 1979 by Olivia E. Coolidge. All rights reserved. From "First Observations" from *In the Shadow of Man* by Jane Goodall. Copyright © 1971 by Hugo and Jane van Lawick-Goodall, revisions copyright © 1988 by Jane Goodall. All rights reserved. "To a Friend Whose Work Has Come to Triumph" from *All My Pretty Ones* by Anne Sexton. Copyright © 1962 by Anne Sexton; copyright renewed © 1990 by Linda G. Sexton. All rights reserved. From *The Hidden Life of Dogs* by Elizabeth Marshall Thomas. Copyright © 1993 by Elizabeth Marshall Thomas.

Jeremy Ingalls: "Prometheus the Fire-Bringer" from *A Book of Legends* by Jeremy Ingalls. Copyright © 1950, 1968 by Jeremy Ingalls.

Mary Jarrell: "The Chipmunk's Day" from *The Bat Poet* by Randall Jarrell. Copyright © 1963, 1964 by Macmillan Publishing Company.

Francisco Jiménez: "The Circuit" by Francisco Jiménez from *Cuentos Chicanos: A Short Anthology*, edited by Rudolfo A. Anaya and Antonio Marquez.

Alfred A. Knopf, Inc.: "The Landlady" from *Kiss, Kiss* by Roald Dahl. Copyright © 1959 by Roald Dahl. Originally appeared in *The New Yorker*. "In Time of Silver Rain" from *Selected Poems* by Langston Hughes. Copyright 1928 and renewed © 1966 by Langston Hughes.

Barbara S. Kouts on behalf of Joseph Bruchac: "Birdfoot's Grampa" by Joseph Bruchac.

Amy Ling: "Grandma Ling" by Amy Ling. Copyright © 1980 by Amy Ling. Originally published as "Grandma" in *Bridge: An Asian American Perspective*, vol. 7, no. 3, 1980. Comment on "Grandma Ling" by Amy Ling. Copyright © 1996 by Amy Ling.

Little, Brown and Company: From "Hercules," from the Introduction, from "The Norse Gods," and "Phaethon" from *Mythology* by Edith Hamilton. Copyright 1942 by Edith Hamilton; copyright renewed © 1969 by Dorian Fielding Reid and Doris Fielding Reid. "The Lama" from *Verses from 1929 On* by Ogden Nash. Copyright 1931 by Ogden Nash; copyright renewed © 1985 by Frances Nash, Isabel Nash Eberstadt, and Linell Nash Smith. First appeared in *The New Yorker*. From *Nisei Daughter* by Monica Sone. Copyright 1953 and renewed © 1981 by Monica Sone.

Liveright Publishing Corporation: Liveright Publishing Corporation: "in Just-" and "maggie and milly and molly and may" from *Complete Poems, 1904–1962* by E. E. Cummings, edited by George J. Firmage. Copyright © 1923, 1925, 1926, 1931, 1935, 1938, 1939, 1940, 1944, 1945, 1946, 1947, 1948, 1949, 1950, 1951, 1952, 1953, 1954, 1955, 1956, 1957, 1958, 1959, 1960, 1961, 1962 by E. E. Cummings; copyright © 1961, 1963, 1966, 1967, 1968 by Marion Morehouse Cummings; copyright © 1972, 1973, 1974, 1975, 1976, 1977, 1978, 1979, 1980, 1981, 1982, 1983, 1984, 1985, 1986, 1987, 1988, 1989, 1990, 1991 by the Trustees for the E. E. Cummings Trust. "Those Winter Sundays" from *Angle of Ascent, New and Selected Poems* by Robert Hayden. Copyright © 1975, 1972, 1970, 1966 by Robert Hayden.

Macmillan Publishing Company: "The Ant and the Grasshopper," "Belling the Cat," "The Fox and the Crow," and "The Town Mouse and the Country Mouse" from *Aesop's Fables,* translated and retold by Joseph Jacobs. Copyright © 1950 and renewed © 1978 by Macmillan Publishing Company. "The Spider" from *Collected Poems of Robert P. Tristram Coffin.* Copyright 1935 by Macmillan Publishing Company; copyright renewed © 1963 by Margaret Coffin Halvosa.

Ved Mehta and W. W. Norton & Company, Inc.: From *Sound-Shadows of the New World* by Ved Mehta. Copyright © 1985 by Ved Mehta.

Ashley D. Moss, Brett Deal, and Shane Townsend: "Antaeus" by Borden Deal. Copyright © 1961 by Southern Methodist University.

John Murray (Publishers) Ltd.: "The Mazarin Stone" from *Four Sherlock Holmes Plays,* dramatized by Michael and Mollie Hardwick.

Nina Nettell: "The Erne from the Coast" by T. O. Beachcroft. Copyright 1930 and renewed © 1966 by T. O. Beachcroft.

The New Yorker: "Phaethon" by Morris Bishop from *The Best of Bishop: Light Verse from The New Yorker and Elsewhere* (Cornell). Copyright © 1955 and renewed © 1983 by Alison Kinsbury Bishop. Originally in *The New Yorker*.

W. W. Norton & Company, Inc.: "A Parrot" from *Collected Poems (1930–1973)* by May Sarton. Copyright © 1974 by May Sarton.

Harold Ober Associates Incorporated: "Stolen Day" by Sherwood Anderson from *This Week Magazine,* 1941. Copyright 1941 by United Newspapers Magazine Corporation; copyright renewed © 1968 by Eleanor Copenhaver Anderson.

Marie O'Connell: "A Tutor" by Carolyn Wells.

Simon J. Ortiz: "My Father's Song" by Simon J. Ortiz.

Oxford University Press: "The Beginning of All Things" (Retitled: "The Norse Gods and Goddesses") and "The End of All Things" from *Tales of the Norse Gods and Heroes,* retold by Barbara Leonie Picard. Published by Oxford University Press, London, 1953.

Penguin Books India Pvt. Ltd. on behalf of Ruskin Bond: "The Fight" from *Time Stops at Shamli and Other Stories* by Ruskin Bond. Copyright © 1989 by Ruskin Bond.

Random House, Inc.: "The Owl and the Two Rabbits" from *Hesitant Wolf & Scrupulous Fox: Fables Selected from World Literature,* edited by Karen Kennerly. "The Governess" from *The Good Doctor* by Neil Simon. Copyright © 1974 by Neil Simon and Albert I. Da Silva as trustee. Entry, "Niobe," from *Random House College Dictionary.* Copyright © 1988, 1984, 1982, 1980, 1979, 1975 by Random House, Inc.

Lou Reda: "When I Was a Boy on the Ranch" by J. Frank Dobie.

Marian Reiner: "I must go begging" by Chiyo and "Broken and broken" by Chosu from *Cricket Songs: Japanese Haiku,* translated by Harry Behn. Copyright © 1964 by Harry Behn; copyright renewed © 1992 by Prescott Behn, Pamela Behn Adam, and Peter Behn.

Charles Scribner's Sons, an imprint of Macmillan Publishing Company: "A Day's Wait" from *Winner Take Nothing* by Ernest Hemingway. Copyright 1933 by Charles Scribner's Sons; copyright renewed © 1961 by Mary Hemingway. From *Cross Creek* (Retitled: "Rattlesnake Hunt") by Marjorie Kinnan Rawlings. Copyright 1942 by Marjorie Kinnan Rawlings; copyright renewed © 1970 by Norton Baskin. "The Bracelet" by Yoshiko Uchida from *The Scribner Anthology for Young People,* edited by Anne Diven. Copyright © 1976 by Yoshiko Uchida.

The Sewanee Review: "Sled" by Thomas E. Adams from *The Sewanee Review,* vol. 69, no. 1, Winter 1961. Copyright © 1961 by the University of the South.

Virginia Driving Hawk Sneve: "The Medicine Bag" by Virginia Driving Hawk Sneve.

The Society of Authors as the literary representative of the Estate of John Masefield: "Trade Winds" from *Poems* by John Masefield.

The Society of Authors as the literary trustees of Walter de la Mare: "The Listeners" by Walter de la Mare.

The Society of Authors on behalf of the copyright owner, Mrs. Iris Wise: "Little Things" from *Collected Poems, New, Revised, and Enlarged Edition* by James Stephens. Copyright 1926 by James Stephens; copyright renewed 1954 by Cynthia Stephens.

Gary Soto: Comments on "Seventh Grade" from *Baseball in April and Other Stories* by Gary Soto. Copyright © 1996 by Gary Soto. Comment on *Pacific Crossing* by Gary Soto. Copyright © 1996 by Gary Soto.

Literary Estate of May Swenson: "Living Tenderly" by May Swenson. Copyright © 1963 and renewed © 1991 by May Swenson.

Rosemary Thurber: "The Fairly Intelligent Fly" with drawing from *Fables for Our Time* by James Thurber. Copyright 1940 by James Thurber; copyright renewed © 1968 by Helen Thurber. Published by HarperCollins Publishers. "The Fox and the Crow" with drawing and "What Happened to Charles" with drawing from *Further Fables for Our Time* by James Thurber. Copyright © 1956 by James Thurber; copyright renewed © 1987 by Helen Thurber. Published by Simon & Schuster, Inc. Text originally published in *The New Yorker.* "The Night the Bed Fell" with drawing from *My Life and Hard Times* by James Thurber. Copyright © 1933 and renewed © 1961 by James Thurber. Published by HarperCollins Publishers.

University of Arkansas Press: "One of the Seven Has Somewhat to Say" from *Story Hour* by Sara Henderson Hay. Copyright © 1982 by the University of Arkansas Press.

University of Toronto Press: "The Wolf and the Dog" from *Marie de France: Fables,* edited and translated by Harriet Spiegal. Copyright © 1987 by University of Toronto Press.

Viking Penguin, a division of Penguin Books USA Inc.: "You Can't Take It with You" from *Escape If You Can* by Eva-Lis Wuorio. Copyright © 1977 by Eva-Lis Wuorio.

A. P. Watt Ltd. on behalf of The Trustees of the Robert Graves Copyright Trust: "The Caterpillar" from *Fairies and Fusiliers* by Robert Graves.

A few selections in public domain have been slightly abridged for greater readability.

To the Teacher—

This **Annotated Teacher's Edition** for *ADVENTURES FOR READERS: BOOK ONE* includes all the Pupil's Edition pages, slightly reduced in size to create top and side margins. Each unit of this Annotated Teacher's Edition includes a **Teaching Guide** at the beginning, **Teaching Features** in the top margins of every selection, and **Side-Margin Features** and **Annotations** that offer information about the content for all selections. The reduced pupil's pages contain notes for teachers.

Teaching Guides

Each unit begins with a Teaching Guide, which includes the following features:

- **Overview of the Unit**—offers information pertaining to the theme, genre, or other element used in grouping the selections into a cohesive unit as well as introductory notes about the selections.
- **Planning Guide Chart**—provides a list of ancillary material available for each selection to aid in developing daily lesson plans and in planning units of instruction.
- **Transparency Listing**—fine art and instructional transparencies from the *Audiovisual Resources Binder* are listed.
- **Objectives of the Unit**—lists specific student skills addressed in the unit.
- **Concepts and Skills**—lists the literary elements taught, language and vocabulary exercises, writing activities, and other study activities included in the unit.
- **Introducing the Unit**—provides teaching strategies for presenting the selections in the unit.
- **Student Learning Options**—suggests activities for the whole unit as well as for individual selections. Many of these activities may be suitable as projects that allow for alternative assessment.

Teaching Features

In the top margins of each selection, teacher's materials are included that give a preview of the selection; provide additional information about the selection, its genre, particular features, or author; and suggest how to conclude study of the selection, evaluate, and extend student learning. Additional teacher's materials in the top margin provide numerous suggestions for tailoring instruction to various learning styles.

- **Introduction**—in selections that include several works by one author, this feature provides information on the author's life and works.
- **Objectives**—identifies specific student skills to be developed in teaching the selection.
- **Vocabulary**—gives information on in-text vocabulary words and related vocabulary activities, and notes special vocabulary activities in the Pupil's Edition or the **Teacher's Notes.**
- **Focus/Motivation**—suggests ideas that may be used to increase student interest and involvement.
- **Motivational Summary**—provides a preview suitable for reading aloud in class to heighten student interest in a selection.
- **Presentation**—provides information useful in presenting the selection to students, such as suggested teaching approaches and commentary on specific literary elements in the selection.
- **Reading Skills Practice**—uses passages identified in the selection to allow students to apply specific reading skills (such as identifying the main idea, drawing logical conclusions, or identifying specific details) and includes suggestions on instructional presentation of the material to students.
- **Closure**—suggests activities to conclude the study of the selection and meet the stated objectives.
- **Extension and Enrichment**—suggests activities to encourage students to extend ideas or skills beyond study of the specific selection.

Teaching Features: *New to This Edition*

- **Meeting Individual Needs: ESL/LEP (English as a Second Language/Limited English Proficient)**—aids students for whom English is a second language or other students who may be challenged in understanding literature. Focuses upon idioms, dialect, and other aspects of the literature that students might have trouble with.
- **Meeting Individual Needs: Learning Styles**—provides activities appropriate to students with various learning styles (visual, auditory, kinesthetic).
- **Cultural Diversity**—explores the sociological, political, historical, literary, and other characteristics and achievements of various cultures as they relate to the literature being studied.
- **Curriculum/Community Link**—includes activities that link literature to other subjects in the curriculum or to the community.
- **Cooperative Learning**—provides suggestions for structured collaborative activities.
- **Portfolio Assessment**—suggests a variety of projects suitable for student portfolios.
- **Transparency Listing**—cross-references fine art and instructional transparencies from the *Audiovisual Resources Binder*.

Side-Margin Features and Annotations

In the side margin of each selection appear annotations that give specific, helpful information about material in the Pupil's Edition.

- **Unit Introduction**—explains the focus of student study materials for the unit.
- **Visual Connections**—gives information about artwork and illustrations; may include information about the artist or the subject of the artwork and may suggest student activities that could be generated by using the illustration as a catalyst.
- **Teaching Resources**—provides a listing of additional teaching materials and audiovisual resources.
- **Prereading Focus**—suggests ways to lead students into a selection and guide them in their study.
- **Selection Annotations**—provide glosses of specific passages in the selection. These may include explanations of an uncommon term or allusion, or an identification or comment on a literary technique. They may also identify passages that relate to questions in the **For Study and Discussion** exercise following each selection. In addition, questions intended to encourage student involvement are included (with probable student responses). *New to This Edition:* Reading and critical thinking skills associated with the side-margin questions are identified.
- **Answer Annotations**—provide brief, note-form responses placed for easy reference in the margin beside exercises and questions appearing in the pupil's pages.

Reduced Pupil's Pages

An exact, full-color reproduction of each pupil's page appears in this annotated teacher's edition. On these reduced-size pupil's pages, several different types of notations are added for ease of use. These include:

- **Vocabulary Underscores**—provide a quick locator for vocabulary words found in the Glossary.
- **Reference Numbers**—match material on pupil's pages to side annotations for quick referral.
- **Underscored Reading Skills Practice Passages**—identify, with underscores, passages to be used by students in applying a specific reading skill. The objective for that reading skill is explained in a footnote.

T28

PART I

THEMES IN LITERATURE

Unit One
REFLECTIONS
9

Unit Two
FAMILY ALBUM
93

Unit Three
THE NATURAL WORLD
143

THEMES IN LITERATURE
This part contains three thematically arranged units. The first unit, titled Reflections, features selections in which adolescents face the challenges of growing up. Although the selections are set in various times and places, the problems faced by the young protagonists are such that young people of any time or culture might easily relate to them.

In the second unit, titled Family Album, young protagonists again face the challenges of growing up and learning to interact with those around them. In this unit, however, family members—mothers, fathers, brothers, sisters, and other relatives—play a major role in this development.

The Natural World unit contains selections in which young people in various times and geographical areas come to terms with the natural world around them. Animals, both domestic and wild, are featured in many of the selections in this unit and are presented sometimes as friends, sometimes as magnificent and mysterious creatures in the wild, and sometimes as threatening adversaries.

FOCUS / MOTIVATION

Ask students to think about how they read different texts. Do they read science texts, novels, how-to articles, and TV schedules in the same way? Point out that people intuitively approach these materials in different ways.

TEACHING RESOURCES A

Teacher's Notes, p. 2
Reading Check, p. 3

CLOSE READING OF A SELECTION

1
A description of literal reading. Its purpose is to increase knowledge of specific facts or information.

2
A description of inferential reading. The writer's purpose may be to lead a reader to make a particular inference, but readers may come to different conclusions, based on their own interpretation of the evidence.

3
A description of critical reading. Critical judgments also depend, to some extent, on inference, so judgments may vary. However, readers should be able to provide logical arguments for their conclusions, based on what is in the story.

GUIDELINES FOR CLOSE READING

1. You may encourage such active reading by allowing time and creating an atmosphere in which students are comfortable with asking questions and discussing with others the inferences they have made.
2. Explain to students that when they make predictions, they look for clues left by the writer. They can also look for clues in illustrations.
3. You may want to discuss with students some examples of **similes**, **metaphors**, **personification**, and **imagery**.
4. Encourage students to listen to their inner voices and to respond without worrying what others might think.
5. Remind students that there are no right and wrong answers when they respond personally to the literature.

PRESENTATION

This **Close Reading** feature focuses on developing the special abilities and skills needed in approaching literary selections. Before students read the excerpt from Welty's *One Writer's Beginnings,* you may want to discuss the **Guidelines for Close Reading** in relation to this selection and the students' study of literature throughout the course. You may ask students to draw their own conclusions about the story. Or you might read the selection aloud, stopping where appropriate to ask questions that will

Close Reading OF A SELECTION

When you read a chapter in a social studies or science textbook, you usually read to get the facts. Your purpose may be to find out how a bill proposed in Congress becomes a law. You may wish to understand how bats capture their prey by using sonar. You read chiefly to
1 gather information that is stated directly on the page.

Reading literature calls for more than understanding what all the words mean and getting the facts straight. The meaning of a work may be stated indirectly. When you read literature, you depend a great deal
2 on inference, or drawing conclusions from different kinds of evidence. To read literature critically and to grasp its meaning, you have to be an active reader. You need to be aware of what the author is doing, how
3 the author is doing it, and why.

In order to enjoy literature, you need to practice asking yourself key questions as you read. You need to become aware of your reactions to what you read. Reading and responding to good literature can provide more than enjoyment. It can also give you a better understanding of yourself and others.

Guidelines for Close Reading

1. **Read actively,** asking yourself questions as you read. Respond to clues and draw inferences from them. Ask about unfamiliar words. Ask about situations or actions that puzzle you.
2. **Make predictions** as you read. Ask yourself, "What is going to happen next?"
3. **Take note of interesting comparisons or unusual associations.** Be aware of language that appeals to your senses and comparisons that are imaginative.
4. **Relate what you are reading to your own life and experience.** Put yourself in the character's place and think about how you might behave in a similar situation.
5. **Put together your responses.** Try to answer the questions you raised during reading. See if your predictions came true. Think of

2 THEMES IN LITERATURE

help students identify and analyze the elements of the selection.

how the selection relates to your own life. Try to determine the author's overall purpose or the main idea of the selection.

In the following selection, Eudora Welty, a well-known American writer, tells about one of the experiences that helped to shape her imagination. The comments in the margin show how one reader has responded to the selection. If you would like to record your own ideas on a separate sheet of paper, cover up these notes as you read.

FROM
One Writer's Beginnings
EUDORA WELTY

1 I had the window seat. Beside me, my father checked the progress of our train by moving his finger down the timetable and springing open his pocket watch. He explained to me what the position of the arms of the semaphore[1] meant; before we were to pass through a switch we would watch the signal lights change. Along our track, the mileposts could be read; he read them. Right on time by Daddy's watch, the next town sprang into view, and just as quickly was gone.

2 Side by side and separately, we each lost ourselves in the experience of not missing anything, of seeing everything, of knowing each time what the blows of the whistle meant. But of course it was not the same experience: what was new to me, not older than ten, was a landmark to him. My father knew our way mile by mile; by day or by night, he knew where we were. Everything that changed under our eyes, in the flying countryside, was the known world to him, the imagination to me.

3 Each in our own way, we hungered for all of this: my father and I were in no other respect or situation so congenial.[2]

4 In Daddy's leather grip was his traveler's drinking cup, collapsible; a lid to fit over it had a ring to carry it by; it traveled

5 in a round leather box. This treasure would be brought out at

1. **semaphore** (sĕm′ə-fôr′, -fōr′): a signaling apparatus with mechanically moving arms.
2. **congenial** (kən-jēn′yəl): agreeable; compatible.

ONE READER'S RESPONSE

I've seen these mechanical arms giving the engineer signals.

I've watched trains switch from one set of tracks to another.

I wonder if this is her first train ride? Her father must travel a lot.

A collapsible drinking cup? Were people expected to carry their own cups?

1
Inference. Details suggesting father was experienced traveler: checks timetable, understands semaphore, watches signal lights, knows how to read mileposts.

2
First and last sentences of paragraph stress shared experience of train ride; middle sentences describe how different the experience is for father and daughter.

3
Contrast between father and daughter points out the differences in their levels of experience. The father knows "the world"; the daughter does not know and must fill in with imagination.

4
Grip: valise or traveling bag.

5
Symbol. Cup is treasure because it is silver (valuable) and it is her father's (symbol of adulthood to her); it is the source of a pleasurable experience.

Close Reading OF A SELECTION

6
Light is unifying image in this paragraph: "sparkling dining car," flying sparks, "rose-red cinders," "light no bigger than a star."

7
Imagery. The image of the "sparks we made" refers to sparks from the burning coal flying out of the smoke stack.

8
Welty uses vivid and suggestive descriptions: "swaying," "just so," "green fishnet hammock," "ride along," "tight-made," "snowy," "eye of the reading lamp," "blades turn into gauze," "insect murmur," "theaterlike."

9
The phrase "crawl or dive head first" refers to crawling into top bunk or diving into bottom bunk.

10
Description. Cocoon-like darkness in berth amplifies rail clicks (vibration) but muffles sound (engine, whistle).

11
To child, each sound is not just a noise but distinctive, unique.

12
Possessive phrases "my own strip of the night," "our train," "our car" reflect personal significance of ride to narrator.

I know what this feels like. It really hurts. **6**

This must be an overnight trip.

I like to watch sparks fly. **7**

8

I guess they didn't have closets on those trains.

A fan? This must be before air conditioning.

I get it. The blades turn so fast that they look like gauze. An electric fan does make this kind of sound. **9**

10

She has a great memory. She remembers colors and smells and sounds. **11**

12

---

my request, for me to bear to the water cooler at the end of the Pullman car, fill to the brim, and bear back to my seat, to drink water over its smooth lip. The taste of silver could almost be relied on to shock your teeth.

After dinner in the sparkling dining car, my father and I walked back to the open-air observation platform at the end of the train and sat on the folding chairs placed at the railing. We watched the sparks we made fly behind us into the night. Fast as our speed was, it gave us time enough to see the rose-red cinders turn to ash, each one, and disappear from sight. Sometimes a house far back in the empty hills showed a light no bigger than a star. The sleeping countryside seemed itself to open a way through for our passage, then close again behind us.

The swaying porter would be making ready our berths for the night, pulling the shade down just so, drawing the green fishnet hammock across the window so the clothes you took off could ride along beside you, turning down the tight-made bed, standing up the two snowy pillows as high as they were wide, switching on the eye of the reading lamp, starting the tiny electric fan—you suddenly saw its blades turn into gauze and heard its insect murmur; and drawing across it all the pair of thick green theaterlike curtains—billowing, smelling of cigar smoke —between which you would crawl or dive headfirst to button them together with yourself inside, to be seen no more that night.

When you lay enclosed and enwrapped, your head on a pillow parallel to the track, the rhythm of the rail clicks pressed closer to your body as if it might be your heart beating, but the sound of the engine seemed to come from farther away than when it carried you in daylight. The whistle was almost too far away to be heard, its sound wavering back from the engine over the roofs of the cars. What you listened for was the different sound that ran under you when your own car crossed on a trestle, then another sound on an iron bridge; a low or a high bridge—each had its pitch, or drumbeat, for your car.

Riding in the sleeper rhythmically lulled me and waked me. From time to time, waked suddenly, I raised my window shade and looked out at my own strip of the night. Sometimes there was unexpected moonlight out there. Sometimes the perfect shadow of our train, with our car, with me invisibly included,

THEMES IN LITERATURE

A National Institution, a portrait of the Twentieth Century Limited by Walter L. Greene.

Arthur Detmers Dubin Collection

13
14

ran deep below, crossing a river with us by the light of the moon. Sometimes the encroaching³ walls of mountains woke me by clapping at my ears. The tunnels made the train's passage resound like the "loud" pedal of a piano, a roar that seemed to last as long as a giant's temper tantrum.

15

But my father put it all into the frame of regularity, predictability, that was his fatherly gift in the course of our journey. I saw it going by, the outside world, in a flash. I dreamed

This is exactly how a ten-year-old would react to the roar of a train.

To her father the trip was ordinary, but to her it was a dream.

3. **encroaching** (ĕn-krōch'əng): advancing.

VISUAL CONNECTIONS
About the Artwork
A National Institution was painted by artist Walter L. Greene. New York Central Lines hired Greene to create advertising and calendar art for the railroad during the 1920s and 1930s. The Twentieth Century Limited illustrated in this painting was used in the New York Central's 1926 calendar. The train is shown passing under the Alfred H. Smith Bridge, named after a railroad president.

13
The violent rush of air as the train goes into the tunnel and the intensity of the sound "clap" against her ears.

14
Simile. Welty compares forceful sound of the train's passing through the tunnel as echoing like a piano's "loud" pedal and as being long and noisy like a "giant's temper tantrum."

15
"Regularity" and "predictability" may also, to narrator, represent unimaginative, practical adulthood.

Close Reading of a Selection 5

Close Reading OF A SELECTION

16
Constant supply of new sights provides food for her imagination. Last remark suggests that her ability to fantasize about what she sees as well as what she imagines seeing will continue through her writings.

I understand what she means. This journey stimulated her imagination.

over what I could see as it passed, as well as over what I couldn't. Part of the dream was what lay beyond, where the path wandered off through the pasture, the red clay road climbed and went over the hill or made a turn and was hidden in trees, or toward a river whose bridge I could see but whose name I'd never know. A house back at its distance at night showing a light from an open doorway, the morning faces of the children who stopped still in what they were doing, perhaps picking blackberries or wild plums, and watched us go by—I never saw with the thought of their continuing to be there just the same after we were out of sight. For now, and for a long **16** while to come, I was proceeding in fantasy.

6 THEMES IN LITERATURE

PORTFOLIO ASSESSMENT
As students study the first three units, they may want to keep a "What did I learn?" journal in which they collect their reactions to the literature they read. Their journals may include a short summary of the selection, doodle art, and a statement telling what they learned from their reading. Journals may be kept in a spiral notebook or computer database, and later the collection of entries may be added to student portfolios. Consult with students to decide how their journals will be assessed. (See *Portfolio Assessment and Professional Support Materials* for additional information on student portfolios.)

LOOKING AT YOURSELF AS A READER
Discuss with students the value of responses that vary. The questions they ask about the literature and the conclusions they draw might differ greatly from the responses of their classmates or from those of the reader in the textbook. Remind students that there are no right or wrong answers in personal response.

Looking at Yourself as a Reader

Compare your own responses with those in the notes alongside the selection. Using the Guidelines on pages 2–3, evaluate the reader's responses. Do you agree or disagree with any of the reader's ideas?

Which of these statements do you think best expresses the overall purpose or main idea of the selection? After making your choice, discuss your reasons with a partner. You may wish to reconsider your answer before making a final decision.

1. A train journey can be a voyage of the imagination.
2. Writers draw on their personal experiences in both fictional and nonfictional work.
3. Adults take comfort in what is familiar and predictable, whereas children need to experience fantasy.
4. Writers do not need extraordinary experiences to stimulate their imaginations; they can find material in everyday, ordinary events.

Close Reading of a Selection 7

UNIT 1 ◆ TEACHING GUIDE

THEMES IN LITERATURE
REFLECTIONS

OVERVIEW OF THE UNIT

The selections featured in this unit provide variations on the theme of growing up. Some are funny; others, poignant. The young characters, who represent several different ethnic groups, grow up in different times and places. All provide points of identification for young adolescents. Headnotes, questions, and writing assignments invite self-examination as students study the images of adolescence shown in the selections.

Jack London's "The King of Mazy May" is an exciting "coming-of-age" adventure story. Using vivid description of the Yukon and intricate personal knowledge of the Alaskan gold rush, London tells the tale of a young man's willingness to risk all to thwart claim jumpers.

In "Luke Baldwin's Vow," Morley Callaghan turns what might have been a routine story about a boy and his dog into a revealing study of how the things or qualities that people value determine their characters and actions. When Luke's "practical" uncle attempts to have the boy's aging dog drowned, Luke learns a lesson in the importance of compromise.

Humor is also a large part of growing up, and this is reflected in the selections in this unit. Ruth McKenney's family sketch, "Guinea Pig," uses exaggeration and irony to turn a Red Cross lifesaving class into a hilarious setting for comedy. Mark Twain also uses comic exaggeration and vivid description of action in "The Cat and the Pain Killer," his classic account of Tom Sawyer sharing his "liquid fire" medicine with Peter, the unsuspecting cat. A more understated brand of humor is found in Gary Soto's "Seventh Grade" and in Sherwood Anderson's "Stolen Day." Both concentrate on motivation, Anderson to characterize a young boy who enjoys attention but who seeks to escape from responsibility for a day and Soto to portray a boy's efforts to impress a girl he likes. Using first-person narration and informal language, both manage to capture the workings of a young person's mind.

Several of the stories in the unit offer glimpses into worlds with which students may not be familiar. Virginia Driving Hawk Sneve's "The Medicine Bag" includes fascinating details of the heritage of the Sioux to illustrate that growing up often involves understanding, accepting, and having respect for the cultural traditions of one's own ethnic group. In "The Circuit," Francisco Jiménez uses the hopes and frustrations of a young Chicano boy to present an insider's view of the hard lives of migrant workers. Similarly, the young protagonist of Yoshiko Uchida's "The Bracelet" deftly reveals the pain and isolation experienced by a Japanese family forced to move to an internment camp during World War II. Finally "The Fight" by Ruskin Bond offers students a window into the lives of two Indian boys whose initial disdain for one another is transformed to respect.

In addition, though prose is emphasized in this unit, the poems of E. E. Cummings, Countee Cullen, and James Berry offer poetic interpretations of issues connected with growing up.

These selections, wide in range yet all dealing with interests and concerns of adolescents and young adults, offer a variety of perspectives on the theme of growing up. The characters, though sometimes fearful and confused, always attempt to face the challenges that confront them. The universality and timelessness of these challenges help make these works interesting and relevant to young people of any time and culture.

Throughout the unit, questions focus on the understanding of plot and character, the most fundamental elements of fiction. Students are led not only to examine plot line ("What happens in the story?") but also to infer cause and effect ("Why do you think this event happened?"). Students learn to recognize important ways in which authors develop character—direct description, dialogue, and the reporting of actions and thoughts—and to question why characters behave as they do. Developing these fundamental skills in discerning plot and character will provide students with a solid platform for building more complex interpretive skills later.

The vocabulary activities related to selections build skills such as using the Glossary, understanding synonyms and antonyms, analysis of word parts, using context as a clue to meaning, and recognizing special uses of words.

Opportunities for writing are carefully integrated into the unit and concentrate on writing a personal narrative. Although these assignments should be considered cumulative, the **Focus on Writing a Personal Narrative** section at the end of the unit summarizes and emphasizes the skills acquired throughout.

OBJECTIVES OF THE UNIT

The aims of the unit are for the student:
◆ To demonstrate an understanding of plot
◆ To demonstrate an understanding of literary elements such as theme and flashback
◆ To identify major character traits and ways in which authors develop characters
◆ To use the Glossary for vocabulary development
◆ To infer meaning from context
◆ To identify a character's motivation
◆ To recognize examples of humor in a story
◆ To write a personal narrative
◆ To make connections between literature and history and cultures

PLANNING GUIDE

FOR UNIT PLANNING
- Transparencies 1–5: *Audiovisual Resources Binder*
- Portfolio Assessment: *Professional Support Materials*
- Test Generator
- Mastery Tests: Teaching Resources A, pp. 153, 155
- Analogy Lessons 1–5: Teaching Resources A, pp. 158–168
- Analogy Test: Teaching Resources A, p. 169
- Composition Test: Teaching Resources A, p. 170

SELECTION (Pupil's Page)	TEACHING RESOURCES A (page numbers shown below)							AV BINDER
	Teacher's Notes	Reading Check	Study Guide	Language Skills	Building Vocabulary	Selection Vocab. Test	Selection Test	Audio-cassette
REFLECTIONS *Introduction* (p. 9)	1							
Close Reading of a Selection Eudora Welty *One Writer's Beginnings* (p. 2)	2	3						
James Berry *One* (p. 10)	4	5	7				27	
Gary Soto *Seventh Grade* (p. 13)	10	13	15	18, 23	26	41	27	TAPE 1 SIDE A
Jack London *The King of Mazy May* (p. 19)	29	32	33	35	39	41	43	
Sherwood Anderson *Stolen Day* (p. 27)	45	47	48				50	
Virginia Driving Hawk Sneve *The Medicine Bag* (p. 32)	52	55	56	58	61	76	64	
Ruth McKenney *Guinea Pig* (p. 41)	66	69	70	72	74	76	77	
Mark Twain *The Cat and the Pain Killer* (p. 48)	79	82	83		85	87	88	TAPE 1 SIDE A
Countee Cullen *Tableau* (p. 54)	89	91	93				97	
Ruskin Bond *The Fight* (p. 56)	98	101	102		105	109	111	TAPE 1 SIDE A
Yoshiko Uchida *The Bracelet* (p. 63)	113	115	116	119			122	
E. E. Cummings *maggie and milly and molly and may* (p. 69)	124		125					
Francisco Jiménez *The Circuit* (p. 71)	127	129	130	132			135	TAPE 1 SIDE B
Morley Callaghan *Luke Baldwin's Vow* (p. 77)	137	140	141	143	145	147	148	

CONCEPTS AND SKILLS

The following concepts and skills are treated in this unit:

CLOSE READING OF A SELECTION
Guidelines for Close Reading 2
One Reader's Response 3
Looking at Yourself as a Reader 7

LITERARY ELEMENTS/TERMS AND TECHNIQUES
Recognizing and Understanding Flashback 30

LANGUAGE AND VOCABULARY SKILLS
Tracing Origins of Words 17
Using the Glossary 25
Recognizing Informal Language 31
Analyzing Words with *dis–* 46
Getting Meaning from Context 52
Recognizing Special Uses of a Word 76
Forming Modifiers with *–ly* 86

WRITING OPPORTUNITIES

Writing About Literature
Interpreting a Poem 54
Supporting a Statement of Theme 87

Focus on Personal Narrative
Choosing a Topic 18
Gathering Details 31
Focusing on Your Senses 40
Telling an Anecdote 47
Using Vivid Action Verbs 53
Using Chronological Order 62
Reflecting on Meanings 67
Writing a Personal Narrative 89

ORAL RECITATION
Preparing a Reading of the Poem 70

CONNECTIONS
Connecting Cultures 40
Literature and History 68

FOCUS ON READING AND CRITICAL THINKING
Recognizing Humor in Situations 46
Drawing Conclusions 86
Making Generalizations About Theme 88

TRANSPARENCIES

The following unit support materials with specific correlations to literature selections are available in the **Fine Art and Instructional Transparencies with Teacher's Notes and Blackline Masters** section of your *Audiovisual Resources Binder*.

FINE ART TRANSPARENCIES

Theme: Self-Image
1 *Self-Portrait,* Erma Gordon
2 *Chambered Nautilus,* Andrew Wyeth

READER RESPONSE
3 Mirror, Mirror

LITERARY ELEMENTS
4 Plot

WRITING PROCESS
5 Writing a Personal Narrative

INTRODUCING THE UNIT

After calling attention to the introductory comments on page 1, you may wish to use one of the following activities to generate interest and involvement in the theme of growing up:

1. Ask students to name current television shows that depict characters in the process of growing up. How are these characters and their situations similar? How are they different? Which are most realistic? Why? As students move throughout the unit, they may wish to compare literary portrayals of adolescence with those on television.

2. Ask each student (or small group of students) to make a collage titled "Reflections of Growing Up." Explain briefly that a collage is an original arrangement of pictures (and perhaps other materials) designed to convey a theme. Provide a stack of discarded magazines and other supplies needed for making collages. After finished collages have been explained, keep them on display throughout the unit. If possible, illustrate with several examples made by former students. Then, as each selection is read, have students identify visual parallels to characters and situations described.

3. Read aloud Stephen Spender's poem "My Parents Kept Me From Children Who Were Rough" (*Collected Poems 1928–1953*). Stimulate response by asking such questions as these:

- What mental picture do you get of the "rough" children? How do they look? What kinds of things do they do?
- How do you know that the speaker is different? What mental picture do you have of him? Did he mind being different? How do you know? Do you think that most young people mind being different?
- How did the speaker feel about the "rough" children? About himself?
- Why wouldn't his parents let him play with these children? Do you think they were right or wrong? Why?
- How is being protected a part of growing up? Is it always pleasant?
- What other problems of growing up does the poem suggest?

Relate this discussion to the problems to be explored by various selections in the unit.

4. Begin by asking each student to complete an interest inventory, perhaps in the form of a fictional questionnaire from an anthologist planning a seventh-grade literature book. (See questionnaire that follows.) After responses have been compiled—perhaps by students working in small groups—use the composite profile to lead into an overview of the unit. Point out selections featuring the kinds of characters, settings, and situations requested by students. Note the emphasis on young characters facing problems of growing up. Throughout the unit, note elements that should appeal to special interests expressed by various students.

Dear Editor:

I understand that you are putting together a seventh-grade literature book with stories about growing up.

Here are some things that *this* seventh grader would like you to include:

THESE KINDS OF CHARACTERS (age, interests, etc.):
_____
_____

PROBLEMS AND SITUATIONS SUCH AS _____
_____
_____

STORIES THAT TAKE PLACE IN _____
_____

Here are a few things I hope you WON'T include:
_____
_____
_____

It might help you to know that my favorite TV show is
_____
and that I consider _____
the best book I ever read. In my spare time I like to
_____

PORTFOLIO ASSESSMENT

Suggestions for use of portfolios as support for this unit are described in the **Portfolio Assessment and Professional Support Materials** booklet accompanying this program. Specific suggestions are provided for a variety of student projects that may be suitable for inclusion in a portfolio. In addition, copying masters are provided for guides that may be used for evaluation and assessment of student projects.

Student Learning Options

REFLECTIONS

1. Producing a Television Newscast
Divide the class into groups, assigning each group a different story to summarize as part of a television newscast. Each story should take about one or two minutes to read aloud. After the writing is finished, the class can present its own television news program, with each group presenting its own story as one item of the news. Encourage the students to watch several news programs as models for their own writing. For a final production, select news anchors to provide transitions between stories.

2. Acting Out a Story
Ask students to write a script for "The Fight." Then ask for volunteers to act out the parts in a reader's theater format, with minimal body movement but realistic voices. An alternative exercise is to select two casts, one to read the script aloud and the other to act out the story as it unfolds.

3. Bringing Back Memories
Ask students to bring to class an item that holds special memories for them, an item like the bracelet in Yoshiko Uchida's story "The Bracelet." Then ask each student to show the memento and tell about it (what it is, why it is important, how it makes the student feel). Finally, ask students to write a one-page story about the memento, with the final drafts written or displayed on a colorful piece of paper. Assemble the collected stories to make a patchwork display.

4. Making Medicine Bags
Assist students in making medicine bags similar to the one described in "The Medicine Bag." (Or you could use brown paper bags decorated individually by the students.) Ask students to bring objects significant to them to place in their bags. Then students can exchange bags and guess why each object is significant. Finally, ask each student to orally explain or write about the meaning of each object. Students can continue to add objects to the medicine bags for the rest of the year.

5. Making a World Map
Perhaps working with a social studies teacher, place a small flag (or other indicator) on a world globe at the location of each of the stories. You may want to provide each student with a flat world map on which to mark the locations.

6. Illustrating Definitions
Encourage students to keep a list of new vocabulary words (in addition to those already defined in the text). Then ask each student to choose five words to define through illustration. For example, to illustrate the word "frail" (p. 35), a student might draw a very thin person holding on to a cane for support. A word definition should be written below each picture. Place these picture definitions around the room so that all students can share in the learning.

7. Writing Encyclopedia Entries
Ask students to write informative essays on topics found in the selections in this unit. For example, students might write on such topics as Sioux medicine bags, Japanese internment during World War II, the gold rush, the Yukon Territory, weather in Rajpur, and the daily lives of migrant workers. The class can compile these essays in a class encyclopedia which may be expanded during the year as they learn about other topics.

VISUAL CONNECTIONS
Ideas for Writing
Everyone, at one time, has faced problems that seemed insurmountable. Young people in particular may feel doubt and confusion as they deal with new situations or face an uncertain future.

With this in mind, students might write a fictional character sketch of Mrs. Chase based on their impressions of the painting. What events might cause a young lady to row alone to a secluded spot on a lake? What is she thinking? What attitude of mind is suggested by her posture and the position of her arm? Will she resolve her problems? If so, how? Might there be some ironic or symbolic meaning attached to the word "prospect" in the name "Prospect Park"? Another possibility is for students to use the painting as a springboard for a narrative about a time when they or someone they know overcame a personal dilemma.

About the Artist
William Chase (1849–1919) was an influential American painter famous for his landscapes, still lifes, and especially his portraits. (He did portraits of his well-known colleagues James Whistler and Frank Duveneck.) Though he worked and studied in Munich for several years, he finally settled in New York, where he taught, worked, and held the presidency of the Society of Amer   ⌐ Artists for ten years.

> **TRANSPARENCIES 1 & 2**
> **Fine Art**
> Theme: *Self-Image* – invites students to explore artworks depicting people in a process of self-discovery.

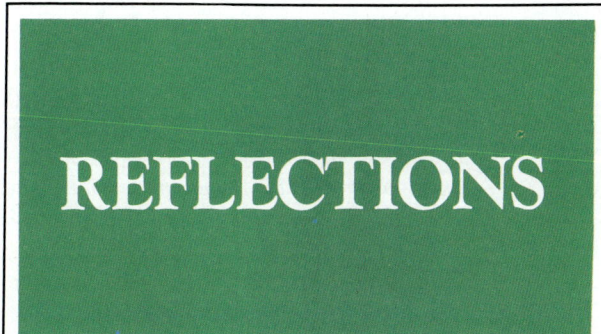

REFLECTIONS

The word *reflection* has several different meanings. What kinds of reflection are shown in this painting? Freewrite for a few minutes about what is happening in this scene. Would the word *Reflections* be a good title for the subject of this painting?

Consider how the word *reflection* might apply to a work of literature. Instead of reflecting light or heat or sound or an image from a surface, how does a story reflect, or give back, a likeness of people? Have you ever found characters in a book that seemed familiar? Have you ever recognized yourself in their thoughts and actions?

Mrs. Chase in Prospect Park by William Merritt Chase. Oil on panel.
The Metropolitan Museum of Art, Bequest of Chester Dale, 1962. The Chester Dale Collection. (63.138.2)

TEACHING RESOURCES A
Teacher's Notes, p. 1

REFLECTIONS
Each selection in the Reflections unit features a story about growing up. Each main character is young and provides points of identification for adolescent readers. This opening unit develops the fundamental skills of discerning plot and character. Questions lead students to infer cause and effect. These skills in drawing inferences are necessary before moving into more complex interpretive skills in later units.

The **Literary Elements** exercises in the unit deal with critical techniques such as recognizing unity, understanding flashback, recognizing humor in situations, identifying clues to later actions, and drawing conclusions about the meaning of a story.

Language and Vocabulary exercises offer practice in determining exact meaning, using a glossary, recognizing informal language, recognizing words of American Indian origin, analyzing the prefix *dis-*, determining meaning from context, learning words that come from names, recognizing special uses of the word *circuit*, and forming modifiers with *-ly*.

OBJECTIVES
The overall aim is for students to demonstrate an understanding of the **theme** of "One." For a complete list of objectives, see the **Teacher's Notes**.

VOCABULARY
The **Language and Vocabulary** section on p. 11 gives students practice in identifying synonyms and determining the exact meanings of words.

FOCUS / MOTIVATION
Ask students to consider some things about themselves that are unique—things that no one else can copy. Explain to students that this poem is about distinctness.

> **TEACHING RESOURCES A**
> Teacher's Notes, p. 4
> Reading Check, p. 5
> Study Guide, p. 7
> Selection Test, p. 27

PREREADING FOCUS
The headnote introduces the concept of uniqueness and ties it to identical twins. Students who do not know identical twins personally might be familiar with twins from books, television, or movies. Ask students to share their experiences.

One

1 Analyzing
What does speaker imply in first stanza? That he is an original that nobody can copy exactly.

2
Speaker says his emotional reactions (sadness, joy) are uniquely his own.

3
Metaphor. Compares playing with dog to dancing.

4
Metaphor. Speaker compares his singing to howling of a dog or other animal.

5
Just as speaker's emotional reactions in stanza two are uniquely his, so are his physical activities.

6 Analyzing
What does speaker imply by using "act"? That even though someone else can "stutter in a rage" as he does, the person will only be acting like him; he or she will not be the speaker.

One

JAMES BERRY

In this poem the author points out how unique each person is. Think about identical twins you may have known. Were they exactly alike in every way? Could you tell them apart?

Only one of me
and nobody can get a second one
1 from a photocopy machine.

Nobody has the fingerprints I have.
2 Nobody can cry my tears, or laugh my laugh   5
or have my expectancy when I wait.

3 But anybody can mimic my dance with my dog.
4 Anybody can howl how I sing out of tune.
And mirrors can show me multiplied
many times, say, dressed up in red   10
or dressed up in grey.

5 Nobody can get into my clothes for me
or feel my fall for me, or do my running.
Nobody hears my music for me, either.

I am just this one.   15
Nobody else makes the words
I shape with sound, when I talk.

6 But anybody can act how I stutter in a rage.
Anybody can copy echoes I make.
And mirrors can show me multiplied   20
many times, say, dressed up in green
or dressed up in blue.

10 REFLECTIONS

PRESENTATION

Write the word *one* on the board and ask students what image it suggests. Does it call up visions of seclusion and isolation or visions of strength and uniqueness? As students read the poem, ask them to look for things about the writer that he claims cannot be copied and things that he claims can.

CLOSURE

Ask students to discuss the meaning of James Berry's poem "One." Encourage students to support their discussion with words or lines from the poem.

For Study and Discussion

Analyzing and Interpreting the Poem

1. The word *identity* refers to the distinguishing character and personality of an individual. According to the speaker, what things about a person *cannot* be copied?

2. What are the things that *can* be imitated?

3a. How can mirrors show someone multiplied many times? **b.** What do mirrors have in common with *echoes*?

4. The words *anybody* and *nobody* are repeated several times. How does the contrast between these words emphasize the speaker's belief in individuality?

5. Do you think that "One" is a good title for this poem? Give reasons for your answer.

Language and Vocabulary

Determining Exact Meanings

A **synonym** is a word that has the same or nearly the same meaning as another word. Several words in Berry's poem are close in meaning to the word *copy*, but they are not exact synonyms. For example, the word *mimic* (line 7) means "to imitate closely."

Locate other words in the poem that are similar to *copy*. Check the exact meaning of each one in a college or an unabridged dictionary. Find additional words that you can add to this list and determine if any are exact synonyms.

About the Author

James Berry (1925–)

James Berry was born in Jamaica, and his short stories, poems, and children's fiction reflect his early years in a Caribbean village. He is the author of several poetry collections, including *Fractured Circles* (1979), *Lucy's Letters and Loving* (1982), and *Chain of Days* (1985). His poems are known for their reggae-inspired rhythms.

A Thief in the Village, Berry's best-known story collection, was a Coretta Scott King Honor Book in 1989. In *Spiderman Anancy* (1989), another of his story collections, he relates the antics of the popular West Indian prankster Anancy and his friends Bro Monkey, Bro Dog, and Bro Tiger.

Berry has done a great deal of work in the field of multicultural education. He was recognized for his accomplishments in literature when he received the Order of the British Empire in 1990.

FOR STUDY AND DISCUSSION

1. A person's fingerprints, tears, laugh, expectancy, way of getting dressed, the feel of falling, running, how one hears music and makes words.
2. A dance, a song, a raging stutter, echoes.
3a. Mirrors on facing walls reflect a scene repeatedly. 3b. Mirrors reflect images and echoes reflect sound.
4. Certain things about a person can be imitated by *anybody,* but uniqueness stems from those characteristics that *nobody* can imitate.
5. Responses will vary. Students will probably agree that "One" appropriately identifies an individual's uniqueness.

LANGUAGE AND VOCABULARY

Answers will vary. Below are some possible answers. Definitions are from *Webster's Ninth New Collegiate Dictionary.* **Photocopy** (line 3)—"a photographic reproduction"; **multiplied** (line 9)—"increased in number."

ABOUT THE AUTHOR

Not all of James Berry's works are set in the Caribbean. Because his second home is England, he also writes about the experiences of minorities there. The title story of his collection *The Girls and Yanga Marshall* (1987) depicts two kinds of education a young man named Yanga receives — that which he learns at school and that which he learns on the streets of London.

VISUAL CONNECTIONS

Ideas for Writing
Have students write a journal entry describing what the first day of school may have been like for the girl in this photo. Remind students that facial expressions and gestures may hide the true feelings a person is experiencing. Encourage students to look beyond the obvious characteristics of the girl in this photo.

Relating Expression Skills
Drawing on students' multicultural backgrounds and language studies, divide the class into small groups interested in a single ethnic heritage. Encourage each group to perform a short skit in another language, introducing themselves in that language to the class. Students could prepare for the assignment by conducting research through textbooks, interviewing relatives and language teachers, listening to foreign-language TV, and using the help of bilingual classmates.

OBJECTIVES
The overall aim is for students to analyze the change in the story's main character. For a complete list of objectives, see the **Teacher's Notes**.

VOCABULARY
The **Language and Vocabulary** exercise on p. 17 of the textbook helps give students an appreciation of the Spanish words that have become a part of English.

FOCUS / MOTIVATION
Ask students if they have ever embarrassed themselves by trying to impress someone. Explain that each time the main character in the story tries to impress the girl he likes, he embarrasses himself.

Seventh Grade

GARY SOTO

Victor has a chance to pick an elective class in seventh grade. Think about how you have decided which classes to take. Have you ever been influenced in your decisions by what your friends did? Have you ever regretted those decisions?

> **TEACHING RESOURCES A**
> Teacher's Notes, p. 10
> Reading Check, p. 13
> Study Guide, p. 15
> Language Skills, pp. 18, 23
> Building Vocabulary, p. 26
> Selection Vocabulary Test, p. 41
> Selection Test, p. 27
>
> **AV RESOURCES BINDER**
> Audiocassette 1, Side A

PREREADING FOCUS
As the headnote suggests, students' choice of classes can be subject to various influences. Ask students to write a brief narrative about how they chose their classes this year.

Seventh Grade

1
Earliest computers did not have keyboards. Information was input, using cards with small holes punched in them. Computer "read" cards.

2 Drawing Conclusions
Why does narrator give detail about "brown people"? To establish that Victor and his classmates are Mexican Americans.

3 Making Inferences
Why is Victor interested that Teresa is good at math? As narrator says later, math is Victor's weakest subject. Perhaps he hopes Teresa will be able to help him with his math homework.

4
In some cities public library has large vans, known as bookmobiles, that go into neighborhoods and check out books and magazines to people who hold library cards.

5
Fresno, in central California, is a center for fruit packing. Victor and Michael earn part of their living picking grapes that are dried to make raisins.

---

1 On the first day of school, Victor stood in line half an hour before he came to a wobbly card table. He was handed a packet of papers and a computer card on which he listed his one elective, French. He already spoke Spanish and English, but he thought some day he might travel to France, where it was cool; not like Fresno, where summer days reached 110 degrees in the shade. There were rivers in France, and huge churches, and fair-skinned people every-
2 where, the way there were brown people all around Victor.

Besides, Teresa, a girl he had liked since they were in catechism¹ classes at Saint Theresa's, was taking French, too. With any luck they would be in the same class. Teresa is going to be my girl this year, he promised himself as he left the gym full of students in their new fall clothes. She was
3 cute. And good at math, too, Victor thought as he walked down the hall to his homeroom. He ran into his friend, Michael Torres, by the water fountain that never turned off.

They shook hands, *raza*-style,² and jerked their heads at one another in a *saludo de vato*.³
"How come you're making a face?" asked Victor.

"I ain't making a face, *ese*.⁴ This *is* my face." Michael said his face had changed during the summer. He had read a *GQ*⁵ magazine that his
4 older brother borrowed from the Book Mobile and noticed that the male models all had the same look on their faces. They would stand, one arm around a beautiful woman, and *scowl*. They would sit at a pool, their rippled stomachs dark with shadow, and *scowl*. They would sit at dinner tables, cool drinks in their hands, and *scowl*.

"I think it works," Michael said. He scowled and let his upper lip quiver. His teeth showed along with the ferocity of his soul. "Belinda Reyes walked by a while ago and looked at me," he said.

Victor didn't say anything, though he thought his friend looked pretty strange. They talked about recent movies, baseball, their parents, and
5 the horrors of picking grapes in order to buy their fall clothes. Picking grapes was like living in Siberia, except hot and more boring.

"What classes are you taking?" Michael said, scowling.

---

1. **catechism** (kăt′ĭ-kĭz′əm): religious instruction.
2. ***raza*** (rä′sä)**-style:** The author says, "A *raza*-style handshake starts out like a normal handshake, but after a series of prescribed moves on the part of both handshakers' hands, it ends with a fist tap."
3. ***saludo de vato*** (sä-lōō′thō thā bä′tō): a greeting between friends.
4. ***ese*** (ĕ′sā): a slang term meaning "dude" or "guy."
5. ***GQ:*** Gentlemen's Quarterly.

Seventh Grade 13

MOTIVATIONAL SUMMARY

On the first day of school, Victor vows that this year Teresa will be his girl. However, throughout the day, his attempts to impress her only embarrass him. Still trying to impress her, he lies to the teacher in French class. Although the lie initially shames Victor, the teacher helps him recover with grace and confidence.

PRESENTATION

In "Seventh Grade," Gary Soto examines the first day of school through the eyes of a seventh-grade boy. The story's strength lies in Soto's ability to portray age-appropriate conversations, thoughts, and actions, thus making the

6
Victor and Michael punch one another lightly as a sign of friendship.

7
When Victor saw girl look at him, he scowled again but with more feeling and emphasis than before.

8
Students fill out *emergency cards* with name and phone number of person to contact in case students have emergencies at school.

9 Expressing an Opinion
Why do students ignore principal's announcement? Answers will vary. Some students may say students in story have heard message before and do not think it is important.

10
Metaphor. Compares students to herd of animals that are moved from place to place.

11 Analyzing
Why does narrator give detail about Teresa's asking the homeroom teacher about ballet? To suggest Teresa is self-confident and that she has sophisticated cultural interests.

12
Victor immediately regrets his silly attempt to be "cool," or clever.

13
Teresa's graceful walk suggests she has studied ballet.

14
Metaphor. Narrator compares teacher's walk to walk of a duck.

15 Finding Cause and Effect
Why does Victor blush again? He is self-conscious over fact that girls who giggle know he likes Teresa.

"French. How 'bout you?"

"Spanish. I ain't so good at it, even if I'm Mexican."

"I'm not either, but I'm better at it than math, that's for sure."

A tinny, three-beat bell propelled students to
6 their homerooms. The two friends socked each other in the arm and went their ways, Victor thinking, man, that's weird. Michael thinks making a face makes him handsome.

On the way to his homeroom, Victor tried a scowl. He felt foolish, until out of the corner of his eye he saw a girl looking at him. Umm, he
7 thought, maybe it does work. He scowled with greater conviction.

8 In homeroom, roll was taken, emergency cards were passed out, and they were given a bulletin to take home to their parents. The principal, Mr. Belton, spoke over the crackling loudspeaker, welcoming the students to a new year, new experiences, and new friendships. The stu-
9 dents squirmed in their chairs and ignored him. They were anxious to go to first period. Victor sat calmly, thinking of Teresa, who sat two rows away, reading a paperback novel. This would be his lucky year. She was in his homeroom, and would probably be in his English and math classes. And, of course, French.

10 The bell rang for first period, and the students herded noisily through the door. Only
11 Teresa lingered, talking with the homeroom teacher.

"So you think I should talk to Mrs. Gaines?" she asked the teacher. "She would know about ballet?"

"She would be a good bet," the teacher said. Then added, "Or the gym teacher, Mrs. Garza."

Victor lingered, keeping his head down and staring at his desk. He wanted to leave when she did so he could bump into her and say something clever.

He watched her on the sly. As she turned to leave, he stood up and hurried to the door, where he managed to catch her eye. She smiled and said, "Hi, Victor."

12 He smiled back and said, "Yeah, that's me." His brown face blushed. Why hadn't he said, "Hi, Teresa," or "How was your summer?" or something nice?

As Teresa walked down the hall, Victor walked the other way, looking back, admiring
13 how gracefully she walked, one foot in front of the other. So much for being in the same class, he thought. As he trudged to English, he practiced scowling.

In English they reviewed the parts of speech.
14 Mr. Lucas, a portly man, waddled down the aisle, asking, "What is a noun?"

"A person, place, or thing," said the class in unison.

"Yes, now somebody give me an example of a person—you, Victor Rodriguez."

"Teresa," Victor said automatically. Some of the girls giggled. They knew he had a crush on
15 Teresa. He felt himself blushing again.

"Correct," Mr. Lucas said. "Now provide me with a place."

Mr. Lucas called on a freckled kid who answered, "Teresa's house with a kitchen full of big brothers."

After English, Victor had math, his weakest subject. He sat in the back by the window, hoping that he would not be called on. Victor understood most of the problems, but some of the stuff looked like the teacher made it up as she went along. It was confusing, like the inside of a watch.

After math he had a fifteen-minute break, then social studies, and, finally, lunch. He bought a tuna casserole with buttered rolls, some fruit cocktail, and milk. He sat with Michael, who practiced scowling between bites.

Girls walked by and looked at him.

characters believable and identifiable. As students read the story, ask them to look for the various methods Soto uses to develop his characters (thoughts, actions, thoughts of others, conversation).

WRITING LINK
As students begin the study of literature, you might want to allow time for students to write in their journals responses to the literature. You might use the unit theme or an individual story to elicit students' reaction. Gary Soto's "Seventh Grade" is a good place to start, since it relates directly to students as they begin seventh grade. You might get students started by asking whether they have ever tried to impress someone only to have things turn out all wrong. How did they feel afterward? What did they learn about themselves as a result?

"See what I mean, Vic?" Michael scowled. "They love it."

"Yeah, I guess so."

16 They ate slowly, Victor scanning the horizon for a glimpse of Teresa. He didn't see her. She must have brought lunch, he thought, and is eating outside. Victor scraped his plate and left Michael, who was busy scowling at a girl two tables away.

The small, triangle-shaped campus bustled with students talking about their new classes. **17** Everyone was in a sunny mood. Victor hurried to the bag lunch area, where he sat down and opened his math book. He moved his lips as if **18** he were reading, but his mind was somewhere else. He raised his eyes slowly and looked **19** around. No Teresa.

He lowered his eyes, pretending to study, then looked slowly to the left. No Teresa. He turned a page in the book and stared at some math problems that scared him because he knew he would have to do them eventually. He looked to the right. Still no sign of her. He stretched out lazily in an attempt to disguise his snooping.

Then he saw her. She was sitting with a girlfriend under a plum tree. Victor moved to a table near her and daydreamed about taking her to a movie. When the bell sounded, Teresa looked up, and their eyes met. She smiled sweetly and gathered her books. Her next class was French, same as Victor's.

20 They were among the last students to arrive in class, so all the good desks in the back had already been taken. Victor was forced to sit near the front, a few desks away from Teresa, while Mr. Bueller wrote French words on the chalkboard. The bell rang, and Mr. Bueller wiped his

16
Metaphor. Narrator compares Victor's looking around cafeteria to watchman on a ship searching for other ships or objects of interest.

17
Metaphor. Mood of students compared to cheerful, happy sunny day.

18 Drawing Conclusions
Why does Victor pretend to be reading? He does not want to be too obvious in his search for Teresa.

19
Style. Short sentence fragments suggest Victor realizes quickly that Teresa is not around.

20 Analyzing
Why does narrator say desks in back are good ones? In back of room, students are farther away from teacher and less likely to be called on to answer questions.

Seventh Grade 15

Cultural Diversity

Explain to the class that when Victor and Michael discuss "picking grapes," the boys indicate they are from families of farm workers. Students may have heard the term *migrant farm worker*, referring to people who often move from place to place, following the harvest of various crops. The majority of farm workers who help with seasonal harvests in the western part of the United States, especially in California, are of Mexican origin. Most are U.S. citizens and are no longer migrant, but instead have settled in one location. Emphasize to students that much of the fresh fruit and vegetables on our tables is harvested by families such as Victor's and Michael's.

---

21 Finding Cause and Effect
Why does Victor whisper French word? He wants to impress Teresa, but he does not want to call attention to himself from rest of class.

22
Victor raises his hand without thinking of what might happen next.

23
Metaphor. Teacher's smile is like beam of sunshine.

24
Metaphor. Compares Victor's deep blushing to blooming red roses that start as small buds but gradually open to larger red flowers.

25
Exaggeration. Victor's perspiration called "river" to emphasize that he is sweating a lot.

26 Making Generalizations
What does fact that Mr. Bueller simply turns away suggest about his character? That he has good understanding of students. He knows Victor is not trying to create disturbance, and he does not want to embarrass him by telling everyone Victor does not know French.

27
Exaggeration. Victor is terribly embarrassed by what has happened, as though it were worst event of his life.

28 Drawing Conclusions
Why does Victor bite his thumb? Answers will vary. Some may say to punish himself, others to distract himself from his embarrassment.

29
Metaphor. Victor leaves quickly as a bullet would from a gun.

---

hands, turned to the class, and said, "*Bonjour.*"[6]

"*Bonjour*," braved a few students.

"*Bonjour*," Victor whispered. He wondered if Teresa heard him.

Mr. Bueller said that if the students studied hard, at the end of the year they could go to France and be understood by the populace.

One kid raised his hand and asked, "What's 'populace'?"

"The people, the people of France."

Mr. Bueller asked if anyone knew French. Victor raised his hand, wanting to impress Teresa.

The teacher beamed and said, "*Très bien. Parlez-vous français?*"[7]

Victor didn't know what to say. The teacher wet his lips and asked something else in French. The room grew silent. Victor felt all eyes staring at him. He tried to bluff his way out by making noises that sounded French.

"La me vava me con le grandma," he said uncertainly.

Mr. Bueller, wrinkling his face in curiosity, asked him to speak up.

Great rosebushes of red bloomed on Victor's cheeks. A river of nervous sweat ran down his palms. He felt awful. Teresa sat a few desks away, no doubt thinking he was a fool. Without looking at Mr. Bueller, Victor mumbled, "Frenchie oh wewe gee in September."

Mr. Bueller asked Victor to repeat what he had said.

"Frenchie oh wewe gee in September," Victor repeated.

Mr. Bueller understood that the boy didn't know French and turned away. He walked to the blackboard and pointed to the words on the board with his steel-edged ruler.

"*Le bateau*," he sang.

"*Le bateau*," the students repeated.

"*Le bateau est sur l'eau*,"[8] he sang.

"*Le bateau est sur l'eau*."

Victor was too weak from failure to join the class. He stared at the board and wished he had taken Spanish, not French. Better yet, he wished he could start his life over. He had never been so embarrassed. He bit his thumb until he tore off a sliver of skin.

The bell sounded for fifth period, and Victor shot out of the room, avoiding the stares of the other kids, but had to return for his math book. He looked sheepishly at the teacher, who was erasing the board, then widened his eyes in terror at Teresa who stood in front of him. "I didn't know you knew French," she said. "That was good."

Mr. Bueller looked at Victor, and Victor looked back. Oh please, don't say anything, Victor pleaded with his eyes. I'll wash your car, mow your lawn, walk your dog—anything! I'll be your best student, and I'll clean your erasers after school.

Mr. Bueller shuffled through the papers on his desk. He smiled and hummed as he sat down to work. He remembered his college years when he dated a girlfriend in borrowed cars. She thought he was rich because each time he picked her up he had a different car. It was fun until he had spent all his money on her and had to write home to his parents because he was broke.

Victor couldn't stand to look at Teresa. He was sweaty with shame. "Yeah, well, I picked up a few things from movies and books and stuff like that." They left the class together. Teresa asked him if he would help her with her French.

"Sure, anytime," Victor said.

"I won't be bothering you, will I?"

"Oh no, I like being bothered."

"*Bonjour*," Teresa said, leaving him outside her

---

6. **Bonjour** (boN-zhoor'): Good day.
7. **Très bien. Parlez-vous français?** (trĕ byĕn' pär-lā-voo' fräN-sā'): Very good. Do you speak French?
8. **Le bateau est sur l'eau** (lə bä-tō' ĕ sür lō'): The boat is on the water.

CLOSURE

Have students discuss how Victor changes in the story. Ask students to identify the events that lead to his change.

EXTENSION AND ENRICHMENT

Students might enjoy reading other short stories by Gary Soto. You could suggest his story collections, *Small Faces* (1986) or *Baseball in April* (1990). One of his novels for young readers, *Pacific Crossing* (1992), appears on pp. 503–560 of this volume.

---

next class. She smiled and pushed wisps of hair from her face.

"Yeah, right, *bonjour*," Victor said. He turned 30 and headed to his class. The rosebushes of shame on his face became bouquets of love. Teresa is a great girl, he thought. And Mr. Bueller is a good guy.

He raced to metal shop. After metal shop there was biology, and after biology a long sprint to the public library, where he checked out three French textbooks.

He was going to like seventh grade.

Reading Check

1. Why does Victor sign up for a French class?
2. Where did Victor first meet Teresa?
3. What does Victor's friend Michael do to attract girls?
4. Why does Victor pretend that he knows French?
5. How does Victor feel about seventh grade at the end of the story?

For Study and Discussion

Analyzing and Interpreting the Story

1. Soto's use of precise details helps readers visualize the setting of the story. Which of these details sound like descriptions of your school and classes?

2. Although Michael, Victor's friend, believes that girls find him more attractive when he scowls, why are they really staring at him?

3. Victor very much wants to impress Teresa, but each time he tries, he embarrasses himself. How would you explain his behavior?

4. Mr. Bueller decides not to add to Victor's embarrassment by revealing to Teresa that Victor doesn't know French. What does this action say about Mr. Bueller's character?

5a. How does Victor turn his embarrassment into a positive experience? b. How do you think he has changed at the end of the story?

6a. Do the characters in Soto's story remind you of people you know? b. How does Soto make his characters believable?

Focus on Reading

Evaluating a Character's Behavior

In order for characters in a story to be believable, they must behave in ways that are reasonable and convincing. A character who is shown to be weak and indecisive cannot suddenly become a bold, confident individual. If a character changes in some significant way, there has got to be a convincing explanation to prepare readers for the change. When you read a story, you should **evaluate,** or judge, whether the characters are believable.

Decide how Victor has changed at the end of the story. Then list the major events affecting Victor in the story. Ask yourself whether the change in his character is consistent with what has happened to him.

Language and Vocabulary

Tracing Origins of Words

Many military and food terms, words that describe nature, and place names are adopted from Spanish. Some of these words are *armada, armadillo, tortilla, plaza,* and *Rio Grande.* Add to this list other words of Hispanic origin (from Spain or Latin America) that have come into English. Trace the origin of these words in a dictionary. How do the words differ in spelling and meaning from their original Spanish forms?

Seventh Grade 17

30
Metaphor. Blushes of embarrassment are compared to rosebushes, but blushes of love are compared to a bouquet of flowers.

READING CHECK
1. He dreams of traveling to France, and a girl he likes is taking French (p. 13).
2. In catechism classes (p. 13).
3. He scowls, imitating models in *GQ* (p. 13).
4. Wants to impress Teresa (p. 16).
5. He is going to like it (p. 17).

FOR STUDY AND DISCUSSION
1. Responses will vary. Students might identify with "tinny, three-beat bell," "crackling loudspeaker," or "triangle-shaped campus."
2. Because he looks strange.
3. He is trying too hard.
4. He is compassionate and respects the feelings of his students.
5a. He agrees to help Teresa with her French. 5b. His confidence and spirits are boosted, and he is eager to learn French.
6a. Responses will vary. 6b. He includes familiar, precise details and the conversations, thoughts, and actions of characters are appropriate.

FOCUS ON READING
At end of story, Victor is more confident with Teresa and more enthusiastic about learning French. The events include Victor's first day of school and his anticipation of having a class with Teresa, his self-conscious response to her greeting, his lie to impress her and his resulting embarrassment, her admiration of him resulting in his boosted confidence. Students will probably agree that Victor's change is believable.

LANGUAGE AND VOCABULARY

Responses will vary. Some words of Spanish origin include *fiesta, burro, cargo, hammock, tomato, alligator, guerrilla,* and *embargo.*

FOCUS ON PERSONAL NARRATIVE

Like Gary Soto, students might want to focus on an experience that seemed horrible at the time, but in retrospect seems humorous.

ABOUT THE AUTHOR

Gary Soto's first book of poetry, in which he recalls his impoverished Mexican-American childhood, won the U.S. Award of the International Poetry Forum. Numerous other awards and honors followed, hailing his depiction of poverty, children, human relationships, and optimism.

Focus on Personal Narrative

Choosing a Topic

Do you think Victor is likely to remember his experience in French class? What kind of outlook might he have several years later about his experience?

A **personal narrative** tells about an experience of the writer. In this kind of writing, you tell about events in the order in which they happened. You not only give details about these events but also explain the meaning that the experience had for you.

Here are some guidelines to use when you choose a topic for a personal narrative:

1. Write about something you remember well.
2. Write about an experience that was important to you.
3. Write about an experience you're willing to share.

Explore some topics for a personal narrative by listing ideas and memories on a chart like the one below. You may change one or more of the column heads if you wish. Save your notes.

Victories	Scary Times	Friends	Funny Times
_____	_____	_____	_____
_____	_____	_____	_____
_____	_____	_____	_____
_____	_____	_____	_____

About the Author

Gary Soto (1952–   )

Gary Soto has written five collections of poetry and several books of essays, as well as short fiction, and autobiographical recollections. His poetry has been translated into German, Italian, Estonian, and Yugoslavian. He often writes of the experiences and feelings of Mexican Americans. Two popular collections of stories by Soto are *Small Faces* (1986) and *Baseball in April* (1990), from which "Seventh Grade" is taken. Soto has also edited a volume of Chicano fiction, *Pieces of the Heart* (1993).

The Author Comments on His Story

No, I'm not Victor in the story "Seventh Grade." I would never have volunteered in class. I was too shy and fearful of rejection. But, like Victor, I was already noticing girls. During my elementary-school years girls were the enemy because they were always telling on us boys, but by seventh grade I thought perhaps I'd been hasty in my judgment. Girls were cute! Girls were smart! So even though I never showed off in class, I do remember showing off to a five-year-old kid on my block. I told him that I was stronger than him and that if he wanted, he could run over my leg with his tricycle. He did. Wow, did it hurt. It left my leg purple. My suggestion for a happy school life is never to show off, especially if it's the first day of class and your name is Victor!

OBJECTIVES
The overall aim is for students to demonstrate an understanding of London's use of specific details to build suspense and excitement. For a complete list of objectives, see the **Teacher's Notes**.

VOCABULARY
The underlined words are in the Glossary. The **Language and Vocabulary** exercise on p. 25 of the textbook gives students practice in using the Glossary.

FOCUS / MOTIVATION
Ask students to recall the coldest weather they have ever experienced. Have them imagine racing through the night at a temperature of forty below zero.

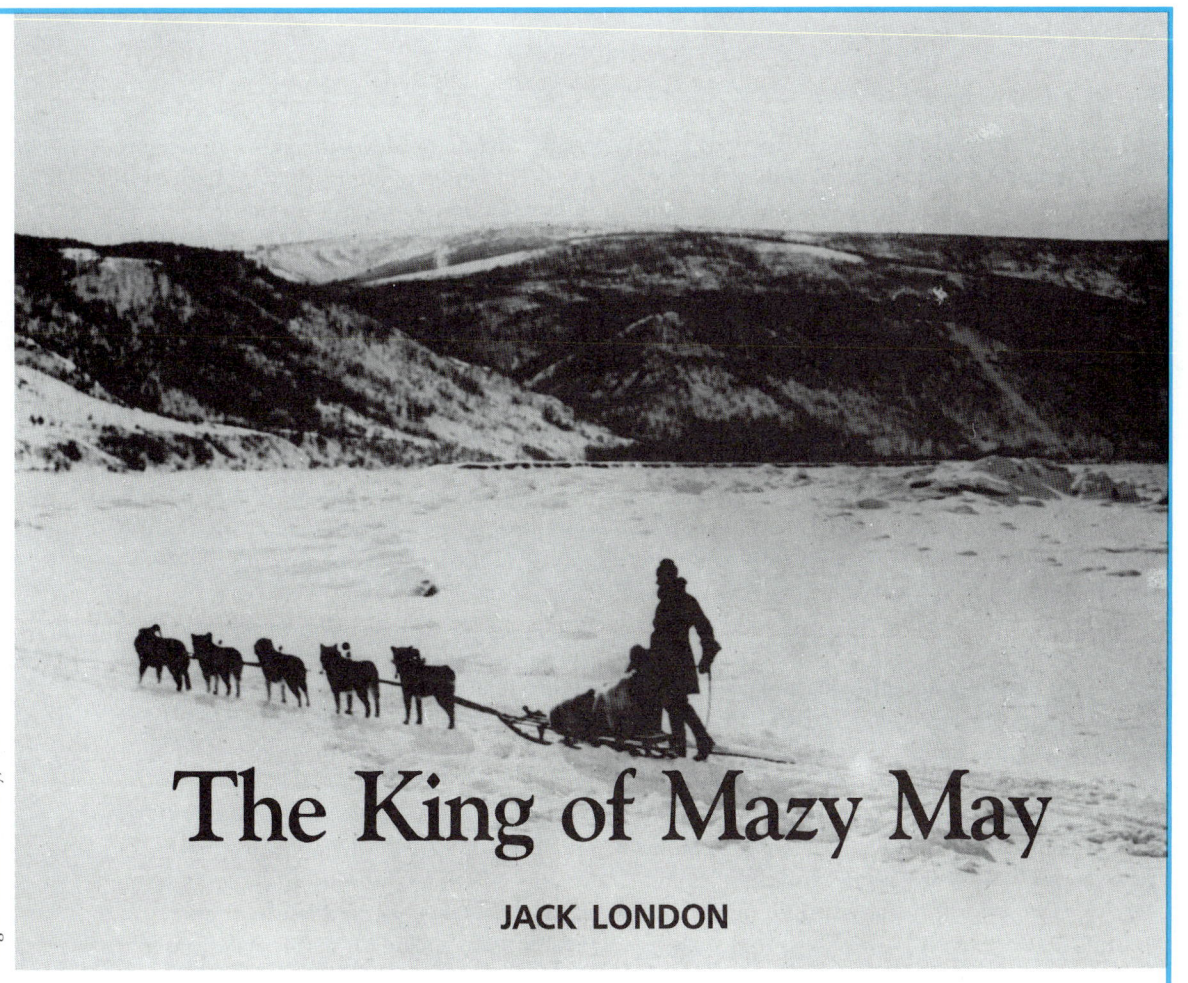

The King of Mazy May

JACK LONDON

On August 16, 1896, gold was discovered on Bonanza Creek in the Klondike, a region in the Yukon Territory, Canada, close to Alaska. This discovery led to a gold rush, and in 1897 Jack London went to seek his fortune in the Far North. How does London use his knowledge of the Yukon to make this exciting adventure story believable?

1 Walt was born a thousand miles or so down the Yukon, in a trading post below the Ramparts. After his mother died, his father and he came on up the river, step by step, from camp to camp, till they settled down on the Mazy May Creek in the Klondike country. They and several others had spent much toil and time on *2* the Mazy May, and endured great hardships; the creek, in turn, was just beginning to show up its richness and to reward them for their heavy labor. But with the news of their discoveries, strange men began to come and go through the short days and long nights, and *3* many unjust things they did to the men who had worked so long upon the creek.

Si Hartman had gone away on a moose hunt,

TEACHING RESOURCES A
Teacher's Notes, p. 29
Reading Check, p. 32
Study Guide, p. 33
Language Skills, p. 35
Building Vocabulary, p. 39
Selection Vocabulary Test, p. 41
Selection Test, p. 43

VISUAL CONNECTIONS
Ideas for Writing
Have students imagine they are the figure in the sled. Ask them to imagine the cold, the expansive wilderness, the wind, and quiet. Then have them write a short essay describing their feelings, using details that appeal to the senses.

PREREADING FOCUS
The headnote emphasizes London's use of personal knowledge of the Yukon to make his story believable. Ask students to list facts and details about some setting, building, hobby, job, or activity they know well enough to add believability to a story.

The King of Mazy May

1
The nonspecific measurement "a thousand miles or so" suggests the vast expanse of the Yukon. Distances are so great that exact numbers are meaningless; understatement of apparent hardship typical of these rugged prospectors.

2 Finding Details
What is the Mazy May? A creek.

3
Conflict. The strange men exploit hard work of others.

The King of Mazy May 19

MOTIVATIONAL SUMMARY

Walt Masters lives with his prospector father in the Klondike during the Gold Rush days. The Far North is cold and harsh, and the men who live there must be rugged and resourceful. Their chief enemies are the claim jumpers who try to steal their hard-worked claims. One day, when Walt's father is away and Walt has promised to keep an eye on a neighbor's claim, several strangers show up. Walt suspects they may be claim jumpers. Can he handle this alone?

PRESENTATION

Many of the best stories in literature are about ordinary people in extraordinary situations. Jack London's "The King of Mazy May" is such a story. Walt Masters is an ordinary boy, bound by nothing but his word and his sense of justice to

---

4 Since their claim is recorded, claim jumpers cannot steal it.

5 The agreement to watch neighbor's claim leads to **conflict**.

6 Hall cannot travel faster than claim jumpers.

7 Suspicion of newcomers aroused by rigs allowing fast travel.

8 Evidently, Walt is skilled: he is neither seen nor heard.

9 Drawing Conclusions
Why is the moonlight important? Moon shining on snow would give enough light to travel.

10 **Irony and Inference.** Leader's words are ironic (Walt is watching); also indicate claim jumpers' awareness that prospectors stick together.

11 Ease in obtaining list adds to hardships of gold prospecting by attracting claim jumpers.

12 Thirty-three is Loren Hall's claim.

---

to return and find new stakes driven and his claim jumped. George Lukens and his brother had lost their claims in a like manner, having delayed too long on the way to Dawson[1] to record them. In short, it was an old story, and quite a number of the earnest, industrious prospectors had suffered similar losses.

But Walt Masters' father had recorded his
4 claim at the start, so Walt had nothing to fear, now that his father had gone on a short trip up the White River prospecting for quartz. Walt was well able to stay by himself in the cabin, cook his three meals a day, and look after things. Not only did he look after his father's
5 claim, but he had agreed to keep an eye on the adjoining one of Loren Hall, who had started for Dawson to record it.

Loren Hall was an old man, and he had no dogs, so he had to travel very slowly. After he had been gone some time, word came up the river that he had broken through the ice at Rosebud Creek, and frozen his feet so badly that he would not be able to travel for a couple of weeks. Then Walt Masters received the news that old Loren was nearly all right again, and
6 about to move on afoot for Dawson, as fast as a weakened man could.

Walt was worried, however; the claim was liable to be jumped at any moment because of this delay, and a fresh stampede had started in
7 on the Mazy May. He did not like the looks of the newcomers, and one day, when five of them came by with crack dog teams and the lightest of camping outfits, he could see that they were prepared to make speed, and resolved to keep an eye on them. So he locked up the cabin and followed them, being at the same time careful to remain hidden.

He had not watched them long before he was sure that they were professional stampeders, bent on jumping all the claims in

1. **Dawson** (dô′sən): city which became the center of the Klondike mining region.

sight. Walt crept along the snow at the rim of the creek and saw them change many stakes, destroy old ones, and set up new ones.

In the afternoon, with Walt always trailing on their heels, they came back down the creek, unharnessed their dogs, and went into camp within two claims of his cabin. When he saw them make preparations to cook, he hurried home to get something to eat himself, and then hurried back. He crept so close that he could
8 hear them talking quite plainly, and by pushing the underbrush aside he could catch occasional glimpses of them. They had finished eating and were smoking around the fire.

"The creek is all right, boys," a large, black-bearded man, evidently the leader, said, "and I think the best thing we can do is to pull out tonight. The dogs can follow the trail; besides,
9 it's going to be moonlight. What say you?"

"But it's going to be beastly cold," objected one of the party. "It's forty below zero now."

The leader said, "If we can get to Dawson
10 and record, we're rich men; and there is no telling who's been sneaking along in our tracks, watching us, and perhaps now off to give the alarm. The thing for us to do is to rest the dogs a bit, and then hit the trail as hard as we can. What do you say?"

Evidently the men had agreed with their leader, for Walt Masters could hear nothing but the rattle of the tin dishes which were being washed. Peering out cautiously, he could see the leader studying a piece of paper. Walt knew what it was at a glance—a list of all the
11 unrecorded claims on Mazy May. Any man could get these lists by applying to the gold commissioner at Dawson.

"Thirty-two," the leader said, lifting his face to the men. "Thirty-two isn't recorded, and
12 this is thirty-three. Come on; let's take a look at it. I saw somebody had been working on it when we came up this morning."

Three of the men went with him, leaving

fulfill his agreement to oversee his neighbor's unstaked claim. Another boy might have found it easier to stay inside and risk nothing. Instead, Walt risks all and gains the respect of men throughout the Yukon as he becomes known as "The King of Mazy May."

one to remain in camp. Walt crept carefully after them till they came to Loren Hall's shaft. **13** One of the men went down and built a fire on the bottom to thaw out the frozen gravel, while the others built another fire on the dump and melted water in a couple of gold pans. This they poured into a piece of canvas stretched between two logs, used by Loren Hall in which to wash his gold.

In a short time a couple of buckets of dirt were sent up by the man in the shaft, and Walt could see the others grouped anxiously about their leader as he proceeded to wash it. When this was finished, they stared at the broad streak of black sand and yellow gold grains on the bottom of the pan, and one of them called excitedly for the man who had remained in **14** camp to come. Loren Hall had struck it rich, and his claim was not yet recorded. It was plain that they were going to jump it.

15 Walt lay in the snow, thinking rapidly. He was only a boy, but in the face of the threatened injustice against old lame Loren Hall he felt that he must do something. He waited and watched, with his mind made up, till he saw the men begin to square up new stakes. Then he crawled away till out of hearing, and broke into a run for the camp of the stampeders. Walt's father had taken their own dogs with him prospecting, and the boy knew how impossible it

13
Description. Details of preparation for gold-washing in the frozen mine: building fire to thaw gravel, melting snow for water, pouring water on canvas (filter to sift out big rocks).

14
Camp is now empty, leaving Walt free to act.

15
Characterization. Decision to help Hall by risking his own life proves he is mature despite youth.

VISUAL CONNECTIONS
Exploring the Subject
Imagine the two men in the photograph, after the picture has been taken, go to a local restaurant and order food. What do they talk about? Work? Sweethearts? Returning home? Think of the cold, the snow, and the relatively primitive housing.

From 1897 to 1900 miners "panned" (using metal dishes in which they washed gravel, sand, or other sediments away from gold) over $50 million in gold from the Klondike. The record reported for one pan of gold was $212.

Miners weighing gold during the gold rush of 1898.   The Granger Collection, New York

The King of Mazy May

MEETING INDIVIDUAL NEEDS
ESL/LEP • The author uses several expressions associated with a gold rush that may be confusing to students. Explain and discuss the following terms: *to prospect* (for gold), *to stake a claim*, *to jump a claim*, *to square up new stakes, prospector, claim jumper, stampeder.*

TRANSPARENCY 4
Literary Elements
Plot – explores a specific sequence of events that make up the plot of a narrative.

16
Evidence of "experienced eye": choosing best sled, best dogs, knowledge of head dog's importance.

17
Has to guess about head dog due to lack of time.

18
Author's stories about the Yukon made "Mush!" famous.

19
Suspense. Vivid action details help reader to share Walt's suspense.

20 Making Inferences
What would happen if they caught him? They might kill him.

21
These men are "desperate," "swearing," "threatening," but Walt is undaunted.

22
Dog trail is frozen creek bed.

23
Walt's bravery shows in his continuing despite threats, ignoring bullets.

24
Lying flat increases speed by reducing wind resistance; keeps him warmer by staying out of wind.

was for him to undertake the seventy miles to Dawson without the aid of dogs.

16 Gaining the camp, he picked out, with an experienced eye, the easiest running sled and started to harness up the stampeders' dogs. There were three teams of six each, and from these he chose ten of the best. Realizing how necessary it was to have a good head dog, he strove to discover a leader amongst them; but **17** he had little time in which to do it, for he could hear the voices of the returning men. By the time the team was in shape and everything ready, the claim jumpers came into sight in an open place not more than a hundred yards from the trail, which ran down the bed of the creek. They cried out to him, but he gave no heed, grabbing up one of their fur sleeping robes which lay loosely in the snow, and leaping upon the sled.

18 "Mush! Hi! Mush on!" he cried to the animals, snapping the keen-lashed whip among them.

19 The dogs sprang against the yoke straps, and the sled jerked under way so suddenly as to almost throw him off. Then it curved into the creek, poising perilously on one runner. He was almost breathless with suspense, when it finally righted with a bound and sprang ahead again. The creek bank was high and he could not see, although he could hear the cries of the men and knew they were running to cut him off. He did not dare to think what would happen **20** if they caught him; he only clung to the sled, his heart beating wildly, and watched the snow rim of the bank above him.

Suddenly, over this snow rim came the flying body of one of the men, who had leaped **21** straight for the sled in a desperate attempt to capture it; but he was an instant too late. Striking on the very rear of it, he was thrown from his feet, backward, into the snow. Yet, with the quickness of a cat, he had clutched the end of the sled with one hand, turned over, and was dragging behind on his breast, swearing at the boy and threatening all kinds of terrible things if he did not stop the dogs; but Walt cracked him sharply across the knuckles with the butt of the dog whip till he let go.

It was eight miles from Walt's claim to the Yukon—eight very crooked miles, for the creek wound back and forth like a snake, "tying knots in itself," as George Lukens said. **22** And because it was so crooked, the dogs could not get up their best speed, while the sled ground heavily on its side against the curves, now to the right, now to the left.

Travelers who had come up and down the Mazy May on foot, with packs on their backs, had declined to go around all the bends, and instead had made short cuts across the narrow necks of creek bottom. Two of his pursuers had gone back to harness the remaining dogs, but the others took advantage of these shortcuts, running on foot, and before he knew it they had almost overtaken him.

"Halt!" they cried after him. "Stop, or we'll shoot!"

But Walt only yelled the harder at the dogs, **23** and dashed round the bend with a couple of revolver bullets singing after him. At the next bend they had drawn up closer still, and the bullets struck uncomfortably near to him; but at this point the Mazy May straightened out and ran for half a mile as the crow flies. Here the dogs stretched out in their long wolf swing, and the stampeders, quickly winded, slowed down and waited for their own sled to come up.

Looking over his shoulder, Walt reasoned that they had not given up the chase for good, and that they would soon be after him again. So he wrapped the fur robe about him to shut out the stinging air, and lay flat on the empty **24** sled, encouraging the dogs, as he well knew how.

At last, twisting abruptly between two river

22   REFLECTIONS

SOCIAL STUDIES LINK
You might have interested students find out about the gold rushes in North America from 1849 to 1899. Students could report on what the lure of gold brought to the territories—the creation of cities in the wilderness, the building of railroads to connect the gold supply to industrial areas, the establishment of territories and states, and the advancement of technical knowledge and capital investment.

Another group of students might locate on a map or globe the Yukon Territory and other places of interest mentioned in the story. Have them note the location's distance from the United States and the proximity to the Arctic.

VISUAL CONNECTIONS
Exploring the Subject
Ask students to make a list of adjectives that might be used to describe Dawson City. (Examples: bustling, dirty, active, gloomy.) Police estimates show that only 4,000 miners were in the Klondike at the peak of the rush, but popular estimates have run as high as 40,000. Claim jumpers were a major hazard, but discovery of gold in the beach sands near Nome helped alleviate that problem. The sands could not be claimed, but could be worked by all.

Dawson City at the height of the gold rush in 1898.

islands, he came upon the mighty Yukon sweeping grandly to the north. He could not see from bank to bank, and in the quick-falling twilight it loomed a great white sea of frozen stillness. There was not a sound, save the breathing of the dogs, and the churn of the steel-shod sled.

No snow had fallen for several weeks, and the traffic had packed the main-river trail till it was hard and glassy as glare ice.[2] Over this the sled flew along, and the dogs kept the trail fairly well, although Walt quickly discovered that he had made a mistake in choosing the leader. As they were driven in single file, without reins, he had to guide them by his voice, and it was evident the head dog had never learned the meaning of "gee" and "haw."[3] He hugged the inside of the curves too closely, often forcing his comrades behind him into the soft snow, while several times he thus capsized the sled.

There was no wind, but the speed at which he traveled created a bitter blast, and with the thermometer down to forty below, this bit through fur and flesh to the very bones. Aware that if he remained constantly upon the sled he would freeze to death, and knowing the practice of Arctic travelers, Walt shortened up one

2. **glare ice:** ice with a smooth, slippery surface.

3. **gee** (jē): a command to turn to the right or to move ahead; **haw** (hô): a command to turn to the left.

25
Imagery. London appeals to senses with images of falling twilight, "a great white sea of frozen stillness," sounds of dogs and sled.

26
Walt's choice was forced by close pursuit; however, author often added details to stories showing that one human mistake could lead to disaster in wilderness.

27
Head dog's lack of ability causes loss of speed and time.

28
Immobility slows circulation, leads to freezing; knowledge of danger and what to do about it shows Walt's skill.

The King of Mazy May 23

SCIENCE LINK
You may have students who are interested in learning about the use of sled dogs in the Yukon Territory and Alaska. You could point out that the American Kennel Club classifies dogs by breed. Examples of working-dog breeds that have been used as sled dogs are the Alaskan Malamute and the Samoyed.

Students could find out what characteristics trainers look for in the dogs they select, how the dogs are trained, how a lead dog is chosen, and how long it takes to train a dog team.

29 Drawing Conclusions
Why does he hold onto the lashing thong? So he can pull himself back onto sled.

30
Pursuers have eight dogs, Walt ten; but because of bad head dog, they are gaining.

31
Contrast between their desperate, exhausting efforts and the unchanging distance between two sleds.

32
Before, they were using revolver; rifle is better suited to distance, but harder to aim from moving sled.

33
Making himself smaller target.

34
Apparently, their trying to shoot him twenty times with the rifle has slowed them up a little.

35
Walt's skill shown in knowledge of what to do, need for speed.

36
While they protect their faces, he thinks and acts quickly by grabbing their wheel dog.

---

29 of the lashing thongs, and whenever he felt chilled, seized hold of it, jumped off, and ran behind till warmth was restored. Then he would climb on and rest till the process had to be repeated. Looking back he could see the sled of his pursuers, drawn by eight dogs, rising and falling over the ice hummocks like a boat in a seaway.

Night fell, and in the blackness of the first **30** hour or so, Walt toiled desperately with his dogs. On account of the poor lead dog, they were constantly floundering off the beaten track into the soft snow, and the sled was as often riding on its side or top as it was in the proper way. This work and strain tried his strength sorely. Had he not been in such haste he could have avoided much of it, but he feared the stampeders would creep up in the darkness and overtake him. However, he could hear them occasionally yelling to their dogs, and knew from the sounds that they were coming up very slowly.

When the moon rose he was off Sixty Mile, and Dawson was only fifty miles away. He was almost exhausted, and breathed a sigh of relief as he climbed on the sled again. Looking back, he saw his enemies had crawled up within four hundred yards. At this space they remained, a black speck of motion on the white river breast. Strive as they would, they could not **31** shorten this distance, and strive as he would he could not increase it.

He had now discovered the proper lead dog, and he knew he could easily run away from them if he could only change the bad leader for the good one. But this was impossible, for a moment's delay, at the speed they were running, would bring the men behind upon him.

When he got off the mouth of Rosebud Creek, just as he was topping a rise, the ping of a bullet on the ice beside him, and the report of a gun, told him that they were this time **32** shooting at him with a rifle. And from then on, as he cleared the summit of each ice jam, he **33** stretched flat on the leaping sled till the rifle shot from the rear warned him that he was safe till the next ice jam.

Now it is very hard to lie on a moving sled, jumping and plunging and yawning like a boat before the wind, and to shoot through the deceiving moonlight at an object four hundred yards away on another moving sled performing equally wild antics. So it is not to be wondered at that the black-bearded leader did not hit him.

After several hours of this, during which, perhaps, a score of bullets had struck about him, their ammunition began to give out and their fire slackened. They took greater care, and only whipped a shot at him at the most favorable opportunities. He was also beginning **34** to leave them behind; the distance slowly increasing to six hundred yards.

Lifting clear on the crest of a great jam off Indian River, Walt Masters met his first accident. A bullet sang past his ears, and struck the bad lead dog.

The poor brute plunged in a heap, with the rest of the team on top of him.

Like a flash, Walt was by the leader. Cutting the traces with his hunting knife, he dragged the dying animal to one side and straightened out the team.

He glanced back. The other sled was coming **35** up like an express train. With half the dogs still over their traces, he cried, "Mush on!" and leaped upon the sled just as the pursuing team dashed abreast of him.

One of the men was just preparing to spring for him—they were so sure they had him that they did not shoot—when Walt turned fiercely upon them with his whip.

36 He struck at their faces, and men must save their faces with their hands. So there was no shooting just then. Before they could recover from the hot rain of blows, Walt reached out

24 REFLECTIONS

from his sled, catching their wheel dog by the forelegs in midspring, and throwing him heavily. This brought the whole team into a snarl, capsizing the sled and tangling his enemies up beautifully.

Away Walt flew, the runners of his sled fairly screaming as they bounded over the frozen surface. And what had seemed an accident, proved to be a blessing in disguise. The proper lead dog was now to the fore, and he stretched low to the trail and whined with joy as he jerked his comrades along.

By the time he reached Ainslie's Creek, seventeen miles from Dawson, Walt had left his pursuers, a tiny speck, far behind. At Monte Cristo Island he could no longer see them. And at Swede Creek, just as daylight was silvering the pines, he ran plump into the camp of old Loren Hall.

Almost as quick as it takes to tell it, Loren had his sleeping furs rolled up, and had joined Walt on the sled. They permitted the dogs to travel more slowly, as there was no sign of the chase in the rear, and just as they pulled up at the gold commissioner's office in Dawson, Walt, who had kept his eyes open to the last, fell asleep.

And because of what Walt Masters did on this night, the men of the Yukon have become very proud of him, and always speak of him now as the King of Mazy May.

Reading Check

1. Where has Walt Masters' father gone?
2. Why is Loren Hall's claim not safe?
3. What are professional stampeders?
4. Why does Walt jump off the sled periodically?
5. What is the only weapon Walt uses?

For Study and Discussion

Analyzing and Interpreting the Story

1a. Why is Walt at first suspicious of the newcomers at Mazy May Creek? **b.** How are his suspicions confirmed?

2. How do the claim jumpers test Loren Hall's mine?

3. How does Walt plan to stop the stampeders from jumping Loren Hall's claim?

4. The chase is the most exciting part of the story. **a.** What difficulties does Walt have in trying to outrace his pursuers? **b.** How do they nearly stop him? **c.** What accident saves him?

5. What details of life in the Yukon does London use to make his story convincing?

Language and Vocabulary

Using the Glossary

At the back of this book, you will find a list of words, together with their pronunciations and meanings, called a *glossary*. The words in this glossary are found in the selections that appear throughout the book. You can use this glossary as you would a dictionary—to find the pronunciations and meanings of words that are unfamiliar to you.

For example, take the word *poising* in this sentence from London's story:

Then it curved into the creek, *poising* perilously on one runner.

If you consult the glossary, you will find this entry for the word *poise*:

poise (poiz) *v.* To balance or steady.—**poised** *adj.*

The abbreviation *v.* tells you that the word *poise,* as used here, is a verb. You probably know that the ending *-ing* represents ongoing

The King of Mazy May **25**

CLOSURE

Ask students to identify scenes from the story that illustrate Walt's knowledge of life in the Yukon.

EXTENSION AND ENRICHMENT

Some students may want to read Jack London's adventure *The Call of the Wild* and report to the class. Students might research topics such as malamutes, dogsled racing, gold mining, or Alaska.

LANGUAGE AND VOCABULARY

1. *adjoining:* touching on line.
abruptly: unexpectedly or suddenly.
floundering: plunging awkwardly.
slackened: slowed down.

ABOUT THE AUTHOR

Since much of London's writing is based on his own experiences, accounts exist of many periods of his adventurous life. His experiences as an oyster pirate can be found in *Tales of the Fish Patrol* (1905); his life as a social protest marcher and as a hobo in *The Road* (1907); living in British slums in *The People of the Abyss* (1903); and sailing to the South Pacific in *The Cruise of the Snark* (1911). London taught himself how to write fiction, learning the narrative techniques of Rudyard Kipling (p. 241).

---

action. To get the meaning of *poising*, change the definition to "balancing."

To show how a word is pronounced, a dictionary uses special marks called *diacritical marks*. Accent marks show you which syllables are stressed. Other marks show how vowels are pronounced. In the glossary, the pronunciation of a word is given in parentheses. You can use the pronunciation key at the bottom of each right-hand page to determine which sounds the marks stand for.

1 Use the glossary to find the pronunciation and meaning of each italicized word in the following sentences from the story.

> Not only did he look after his father's claim, but he had agreed to keep an eye on the *adjoining* one of Loren Hall, who had started for Dawson to record it.
>
> At last, twisting *abruptly* between two river islands, he came upon the mighty Yukon sweeping grandly to the north.
>
> On account of the poor lead dog, they were constantly *floundering* off the beaten track into the soft snow, and the sled was as often riding on its side or top as it was in the proper way.
>
> After several hours of this, during which, perhaps, a score of bullets had struck about him, their ammunition began to give out and their fire *slackened*.

For more information about the words in the glossary, consult a dictionary.

About the Author

Jack London   (1876–1916)

Jack London, who became one of the most successful and popular writers in the world, was born in grim poverty in San Francisco. He never received much formal education. He educated himself by studying for hours at a time in public libraries.

In his teens he was a longshoreman, an oyster pirate, a seaman, and a hobo. When he was nineteen, he decided to finish high school. He condensed a four-year course into one year and was able to pass the entrance examination at the University of California in the following year. In 1897 he left college to seek gold in the Klondike. He found no gold and returned to San Francisco, sailing 1,900 miles (about 3,060 kilometers) in an open boat. His experiences in the Arctic gave him the material for many short stories and for his famous novels *The Call of the Wild* and *White Fang*.

London worked hard at being a writer. In seventeen years he produced fifty books. His popularity grew until he became the highest-paid writer in the United States. When he died at the age of forty, he had either spent or given away all his money. London's tales of rough adventure are widely read today. His books and short stories have been translated into many languages.

OBJECTIVES
The overall aim is for students to identify the main character's **motivation** for his actions. For a complete list of objectives, see the **Teacher's Notes**.

VOCABULARY
The **Language and Vocabulary** exercise on p. 31 in the textbook discusses the use of colloquial expressions and the role of conversational style to create believable characters.

FOCUS / MOTIVATION
Ask students to think about the intriguing title "Stolen Day." How might it be possible to "steal" a day? Have students discuss what they do when distracted by "spring fever."

Stolen Day

SHERWOOD ANDERSON

In order for a character in a story to be believable, there must be a purpose, or motivation, *for the character's actions. What motivates the narrator in this story to "steal" a day?*

1 It must be that all children are actors. The
2 whole thing started with a boy on our street named Walter, who had inflammatory rheumatism.[1] That's what they called it. He didn't have to go to school.

Still he could walk about. He could go fishing in the creek or the waterworks pond. There was a place up at the pond where in the spring the water came tumbling over the dam and formed a deep pool. It was a good place. Sometimes you could get some good big ones there.

3 I went down that way on my way to school one spring morning. It was out of my way but I wanted to see if Walter was there.

He was, inflammatory rheumatism and all. There he was, sitting with a fish pole in his hand. He had been able to walk down there all right.

It was then that my own legs began to hurt.
4 My back too. I went on to school but, at the recess time, I began to cry. I did it when the
5 teacher, Sarah Suggett, had come out into the schoolhouse yard.

She came right over to me.
"I ache all over," I said. I did, too.
I kept on crying and it worked all right.

---
1. **inflammatory rheumatism** (rōō′mə-tĭz′əm): a painful disease affecting the joints and muscles.

"You'd better go on home," she said.
So I went. I limped painfully away. I kept on limping until I got out of the schoolhouse street.

6 Then I felt better. I still had inflammatory rheumatism pretty bad but I could get along better.

I must have done some thinking on the way home.

"I'd better not say I have inflammatory rheumatism," I decided. "Maybe if you've got that you swell up."

I thought I'd better go around to where Walter was and ask him about that, so I did—but he wasn't there.

7 "They must not be biting today," I thought.

I had a feeling that, if I said I had inflammatory rheumatism, Mother or my brothers and
8 my sister Stella might laugh. They did laugh at me pretty often and I didn't like it at all.

"Just the same," I said to myself, "I have got it." I began to hurt and ache again.

I went home and sat on the front steps of our house. I sat there a long time. There wasn't anyone at home but Mother and the two little ones. Ray would have been four or five then and Earl might have been three.

It was Earl who saw me there. I had got tired

TEACHING RESOURCES A
Teacher's Notes, p. 45
Reading Check, p. 47
Study Guide, p. 48
Selection Test, p. 50

PREREADING FOCUS
As the headnote suggests, stories are more believable if characters have logical purposes or **motivations** for their actions. Ask students to write a paragraph about something they have done, explaining both the act and the motivation or purpose.

Stolen Day

1
Adult narrator looks back on childhood incident.

2
Sees relationship between illness and missing school.

3
Motivation. Narrator knows little about actual illness but sees Walter having a good time.

4
He convinces himself of illness.

5
Crying from "pain" timed to convince teacher.

6
Feels better as soon as he is away from school; he is still "sick" because he must convince mother.

7
Reader can infer that child does not understand the illness may be serious.

8 Making Inferences
Why does he think his family will laugh at him? Evidently, he has attempted such ruses in past.

Stolen Day 27

MOTIVATIONAL SUMMARY
On a lovely spring morning, a boy on his way to school passes his favorite fishing hole. There he sees Walter fishing. The boy thinks Walter, who has inflammatory rheumatism, is lucky. He wishes he did not have to go to school on such a nice day and could fish whenever he wanted. He wishes he were lucky enough to have inflammatory rheumatism. As he continues to think about it, some interesting symptoms begin to appear.

PRESENTATION
Sherwood Anderson's "Stolen Day" delves into the sometimes illogical workings of a child's mind. Behind the boy protagonist's self-deception that he suffers from inflammatory rheumatism lies the idea that if he actually

VISUAL CONNECTIONS
Ideas for Writing
Students might enjoy writing about a day they went fishing. Or they might write a fictional account of the thoughts that run through this boy's mind as he stands on the bank of a quiet fishing hole on a bright summer day.

9
Conflict. The narrator's conflict is internal. He begins to believe his own pretense; he worries about consequences of a disease he does not have.

10
Normal physical reaction now seems threatening to him; he is engrossed with pretense and his father's remark about heart effects.

11
It is no fun to lie in bed pretending to be sick when it is spring, thus his rapid recovery.

sitting and was lying on the porch. Earl was always a quiet, solemn little fellow.

He must have said something to Mother for presently she came.

"What's the matter with you? Why aren't you in school?" she asked.

I came pretty near telling her right out that I had inflammatory rheumatism but I thought I'd better not. Mother and Father had been speaking of Walter's case at the table just the day before. "It affects the heart," Father had 9 said. That frightened me when I thought of it. "I might die," I thought. "I might just suddenly die right here; my heart might stop beating."

On the day before I had been running a race with my brother Irve. We were up at the fairgrounds after school and there was a half-mile track.

"I'll bet you can't run a half-mile," he said. "I bet you I could beat you running clear around the track."

And so we did it and I beat him, but afterwards my heart did seem to beat pretty hard. I remembered that lying there on the porch. "It's a wonder, with my inflammatory rheumatism and all, I didn't just drop down dead," I thought. The thought frightened me a lot. I ached worse than ever.

"I ache, Ma," I said. "I just ache."

She made me go in the house and upstairs and get into bed.

11 It wasn't so good. It was spring. I was up there for perhaps an hour, maybe two, and then I felt better.

I got up and went downstairs. "I feel better, Ma," I said.

Mother said she was glad. She was pretty

28   28 REFLECTIONS

believes he is sick, then he cannot lie when he claims to be sick. In his mind, his pretense evolves into a reality that will justify his ulterior motive for playing hooky—a fishing expedition. It is this fishing expedition that rescues the boy from his "I'll show them" fantasy and plants him firmly in the real world, where he receives the attention he thinks he lacks.

---

12 busy that day and hadn't paid much attention to me. She had made me get into bed upstairs and then hadn't even come up to see how I was.

I didn't think much of that when I was up there but when I got downstairs where she was, and when, after I had said I felt better and she only said she was glad and went right on with her work, I began to ache again.

I thought, "I'll bet I die of it. I bet I do."

I went out to the front porch and sat down. I was pretty sore at Mother.

"If she really knew the truth, that I have the inflammatory rheumatism and I may just drop down dead any time, I'll bet she wouldn't care about that either," I thought.

I was getting more and more angry the more thinking I did.

"I know what I'm going to do," I thought; "I'm going to go fishing."

13 I thought that, feeling the way I did, I might be sitting on the high bank just above the deep pool where the water went over the dam, and suddenly my heart would stop beating.

And then, of course, I'd pitch forward, over the bank into the pool and, if I wasn't dead when I hit the water, I'd drown sure.

They would all come home to supper and they'd miss me.

"But where is he?"

Then Mother would remember that I'd come home from school aching.

She'd go upstairs and I wouldn't be there. One day during the year before, there was a child got drowned in a spring. It was one of the Wyatt children.

14 Right down at the end of the street there was a spring under a birch tree and there had been a barrel sunk in the ground.

Everyone had always been saying the spring ought to be kept covered, but it wasn't.

So the Wyatt child went down there, played around alone, and fell in and got drowned.

Mother was the one who had found the drowned child. She had gone to get a pail of water and there the child was, drowned and dead.

This had been in the evening when we were all at home, and Mother had come running up the street with the dead, dripping child in her arms. She was making for the Wyatt house as hard as she could run, and she was pale.

15 She had a terrible look on her face, I remembered then.

"So," I thought, "they'll miss me and there'll be a search made. Very likely there'll be someone who has seen me sitting by the pond fishing, and there'll be a big alarm and all the town will turn out and they'll drag the pond."

16 I was having a grand time, having died. Maybe, after they found me and had got me out of the deep pool, Mother would grab me up in her arms and run home with me as she **17** had run with the Wyatt child.

I got up from the porch and went around the house. I got my fishing pole and lit out for the pool below the dam. Mother was busy—she **18** always was—and didn't see me go. When I got there I thought I'd better not sit too near the edge of the high bank.

By this time I didn't ache hardly at all, but I thought.

"With inflammatory rheumatism you can't tell," I thought.

19 "It probably comes and goes," I thought.

"Walter has it and he goes fishing," I thought.

I had got my line into the pool and suddenly I got a bite. It was a regular whopper. I knew that. I'd never had a bite like that.

I knew what it was. It was one of Mr. Fenn's big carp.

Mr. Fenn was a man who had a big pond of his own. He sold ice in the summer and the pond was to make the ice. He had bought some big carp and put them into his pond and then,

---

12
Motivation. Clue that one thing he wants is attention.

13
Begins "she'll be sorry" fantasy in which he gets back at his mother for not taking him more seriously.

14
Flashback. Narrator remembers the drowning of a child. Perfunctory description shows narrator's inability to comprehend real effects of death as a child.

15
Child's point of view: he sees mother's reaction but does not understand; reflects his youthful innocent perspective.

16
Child's viewpoint: reacts to drama and excitement but does not understand real consequences.

17 Drawing Conclusions
Why does the narrator imagine dying? He wants same attention from his mother that she gave other child.

18
Irony. If he wanted to die, he would choose to sit near the bank. Indicates he does not really want to die; he only wants attention.

19
"Comes" when narrator wants attention; "goes" when he gets bored or forgets.

MEETING INDIVIDUAL NEEDS
Auditory Learners • The colloquial language and conversational style in this selection make it a good choice for oral reading. You might ask several students to prepare sections of the story for reading aloud to the class. When they read, encourage them to use a relaxed tone and familiar expression and to use a voice appropriate for the narrator.

Ask students to listen as the readers present the story. You might conclude the reading with discussion and interpretation to find out how well students are able to follow the story when their only method of study is auditory.

20
Engrossed in catch, he "tumbles" down bank he feared earlier; "struggles" and "wrestles" fish.

21
Forgets to worry about heart now.

22
Characterization. Highlight of day is attention for catching fish.

23
He must explain why he was fishing, not in school.

24 Synthesizing
Where do you think he aches? Perhaps his heart or stomach, symbolizing humiliation.

READING CHECK
1. Spring (p. 25).
2. Pond spot where water coming over dam formed deep pool (p. 27).
3. Faked aching symptoms (p. 25).
4. Struggled with it in water and got hand under gills (p. 28).
5. He told family he had rheumatism; family laughed (p. 28).

FOR STUDY AND DISCUSSION
1. Narrator wants excuse for fishing instead of attending school, so convinces himself he has same illness.
2. He complains she is too busy; imagines himself drowning and her sweeping up his body in her arms.
3. To save face after telling family.
4. The narrator has stolen a day to escape routine duties.

---

earlier in the spring when there was a freshet,[2] his dam had gone out.

So the carp had got into our creek and one or two big ones had been caught—but none of them by a boy like me.

The carp was pulling and I was pulling and 20 I was afraid he'd break my line, so I just tumbled down the high bank, holding onto the line and got right into the pool. We had it out, there in the pool. We struggled. We wrestled. Then I got a hand under his gills and got him out.

He was a big one all right. He was nearly half as big as I was myself. I had him on the bank and I kept one hand under his gills and I ran.

21   I never ran so hard in my life. He was slippery, and now and then he wriggled out of my arms; once I stumbled and fell on him, but I got him home.

22   So there it was. I was a big hero that day. Mother got a washtub and filled it with water. She put the fish in it and all the neighbors came to look. I got into dry clothes and went down to supper—and then I made a break that spoiled my day.

There we were, all of us, at the table, and suddenly Father asked what had been the matter with me at school. He had met the teacher, Sarah Suggett, on the street and she had told him how I had become ill.

23   "What was the matter with you?" Father asked, and before I thought what I was saying I let it out.

"I had the inflammatory rheumatism," I said—and a shout went up. It made me sick to hear them, the way they all laughed.

It brought back all the aching again, and like a fool I began to cry.

"Well, I *have* got it—I *have*, I *have*," I cried, and I got up from the table and ran upstairs.

2. **freshet:** a sudden overflowing of a stream from a heavy rain or thaw.

I stayed there until Mother came up. I knew it would be a long time before I heard the last of the inflammatory rheumatism. I was sick all 24 right, but the aching I now had wasn't in my legs or in my back.

Reading Check

1. During what season does this story take place?
2. What was the narrator's favorite fishing spot?
3. How did the narrator get himself sent home from school?
4. How did the narrator capture the carp?
5. What happened to spoil the narrator's day?

For Study and Discussion

Analyzing and Interpreting the Story

1. Why do you suppose the narrator's "symptoms" develop after he sees Walter fishing at the pond?
2. How do you know that the narrator wants his mother to pay more attention to him?
3. Why does he insist that he had "the inflammatory rheumatism"?
4. Explain the title of the story.

Literary Elements

Recognizing and Understanding Flashback

A writer usually tells the events of a story in the order in which they happen. However, sometimes the writer will interrupt the action to tell of something that happened in the past. In "Stolen Day," the narrator interrupts his

30 REFLECTIONS

own fantasy about dying to tell about a drowning accident the year before.

This interruption of action to tell something that happened in the past is called a **flashback.** A flashback is often used to clarify something that is happening in the present. How does the flashback help you to understand the narrator's feelings?

Language and Vocabulary

Recognizing Informal Language

In order for characters to be believable, they must act and speak appropriately. Anderson tells his story in a conversational style, using language that is natural to his character.

The narrator uses some informal, or **colloquial** (kə-lō′kwē-əl), expressions. He says that he became "sore" at his mother. Used in this way, the word *sore* means "angry" or "resentful." He tells us that he got his fishing pole and "lit out" for the pool. The phrase *light out* is a coloquial expression meaning "to leave suddenly."

1. What is the meaning of *whopper*? Check your answer in a dictionary.

Focus on Personal Narrative

Gathering Details

You can make your personal narrative lively and interesting by including vivid, specific **details** about your experience. For example, reread the second paragraph on page 30. Notice all the details the narrator of "Stolen Day" gives about how he caught the carp.

Choose one of the topics for the assignment on page 18 or select a new topic for a personal narrative. To collect details for your narrative, fill in a chart like the one below. Save your notes.

Topic of Narrative: _____

Events	Characters
1. _____	1. _____
2. _____	2. _____
3. _____	3. _____
4. _____	4. _____

Dialogue/Quotations _____

Thoughts/Feelings _____

About the Author

Sherwood Anderson (1876–1941)

The Granger Collection, New York

Sherwood Anderson was born in Camden, Ohio, and spent much of his youth in Clyde. He left school when he was fourteen and worked at a variety of odd jobs. He became successful as a businessman and organized a paint-manufacturing company. He was not happy, however, and gave up his business in order to devote himself to writing. Anderson is best known for his stories of small-town life in America. His stories, like "Stolen Day," are often told by a narrator who is recalling some incident from the past. Anderson developed a style based on the spoken American language. His style and subject matter have strongly influenced other twentieth-century writers.

Stolen Day 31

OBJECTIVES
The overall aim is for students to demonstrate an understanding of Martin's attitude change toward his cultural heritage and traditions. For a complete list of objectives, see the **Teacher's Notes.**

VOCABULARY
The underlined words are in the Glossary. Encourage students to notice the author's use of sensory details to paint vivid pictures.

FOCUS / MOTIVATION
Ask students to describe any historical sites they may have visited that reflect the lifestyles of early American Indians.

TEACHING RESOURCES A
Teacher's Notes, p. 52
Reading Check, p. 55
Study Guide, p. 56
Language Skills, p. 58
Building Vocabulary, p. 61
Selection Vocabulary Test, p. 76
Selection Test, p. 64

PREREADING FOCUS
The headnote may be used to initiate a discussion of character development. What might motivate believable change in a character? Possible techniques are interaction between characters that leads to growth, events that lead to new insight, change that is gradual and within the scope of the story.

The Medicine Bag

1
Martin uses Indian heritage to impress friends; does not yet value it for itself.

2
Grandpa's gifts are treated like souvenirs.

3
Conflict. Disparity between fantasy "TV Indian" and reality causes Martin's discomfort.

4
Reality of reservation life is not glamorous.

5
"Yippy poodles" and "fancy little dogs" represent affluent neighborhood; dogs barking at Grandpa represents **conflict** of values.

6 Analyzing
What does walking in middle of street say about Grandpa? Perhaps inexperienced or unconcerned with traffic; looking on both sides for address, and so on.

The Medicine Bag

VIRGINIA DRIVING HAWK SNEVE°

Characters are believable when they behave consistently. The reader must be prepared for any dramatic change in a character's actions or beliefs. How does the author of this story make the change in her narrator convincing?

My kid sister Cheryl and I always bragged about our Sioux grandpa, Joe Iron Shell. Our friends, who had always lived in the city and *1* only knew about Indians from movies and TV, were impressed by our stories. Maybe we exaggerated and made Grandpa and the reservation sound glamorous, but when we'd return home to Iowa after our yearly summer visit to Grandpa we always had some exciting tale to tell.

We always had some authentic Sioux article *2* to show our listeners. One year Cheryl had new moccasins that Grandpa had made. On another visit he gave me a small, round, flat, rawhide drum which was decorated with a painting of a warrior riding a horse. He taught me a real Sioux chant to sing while I beat the drum with a leather-covered stick that had a feather on the end. Man, that really made an impression.

We never showed our friends Grandpa's pic-*3* ture. Not that we were ashamed of him, but because we knew that the glamorous tales we told didn't go with the real thing. Our friends would have laughed at the picture, because Grandpa wasn't tall and stately like TV Indians. His hair wasn't in braids, but hung in stringy, gray strands on his neck and he was old. He was our great-grandfather, and he *4* didn't live in a tepee, but all by himself in a part log, part tar-paper shack on the Rosebud Reservation in South Dakota. So when Grandpa came to visit us, I was so ashamed and embarrassed I could've died.

There are a lot of yippy poodles and other *5* fancy little dogs in our neighborhood, but they usually barked singly at the mailman from the safety of their own yards. Now it sounded as if a whole pack of mutts were barking together in one place.

I got up and walked to the curb to see what the commotion was. About a block away I saw a crowd of little kids yelling, with the dogs yipping and growling around someone who was *6* walking down the middle of the street.

I watched the group as it slowly came closer and saw that in the center of the strange procession was a man wearing a tall black hat. He'd pause now and then to peer at something in his hand and then at the houses on either

°**Sneve** (snā′vē).

MOTIVATIONAL SUMMARY
Martin and his sister live in a big city, but every summer they visit Joe Iron Shell, their grandfather, a Sioux living on the Rosebud reservation in South Dakota. When they return to the city, they always tell their friends glamorized accounts of their grandfather and of the reservation. But one day, Martin's grandfather comes to the city. Martin is worried: will his friends make fun of him when they see that the real person is not as glamorous as Martin made him seem?

PRESENTATION
As Native Americans assimilate into mainstream America, valuable cultural traditions are weakened and eventually lost. "The Medicine Bag," by Virginia Driving Hawk Sneve, focuses on one boy's realization of the great significance of his

Sioux beaded buffalo robe.

VISUAL CONNECTIONS
About the Artwork
Like the one pictured here, buffalo robes were often brightly painted or beaded with geometric designs or pictographs of the owner's exploits. Men often did the painting, and women did sewing and beadwork. Color as well as pattern in design elements might have significance, but symbolic meanings varied from tribe to tribe. For example, black could signify "night" or "safe return from battle"; red could signify "thunder," "sunset," or "blood."

Buffalo robes were made from the hides of buffalo killed in winter when their fur was heavy. Buffalo robes were well suited for their use as blankets or overcoats because the skin was both tough and waterproof.

Exploring the Subject
The cultural identity of the Plains Indians was linked to the buffalo. Indians used buffalo for food, clothing, shelter, tools, utensils, fuel; and the hunt served as a focus for ritual. When Europeans first saw buffalo, they were overwhelmed by the number and size of the herds; buffalo seemed inexhaustible. In 1850, estimates set their number at 50,000,000, yet thirty-five years later they were almost extinct. Some whites, such as General Sheridan, favored wiping out the herds because they understood that to destroy the buffalo was to destroy the Plains Indian way of life. This was an accurate perception; disappearance of the buffalo drove Indians to the reservations.

rich cultural heritage. The shame Martin at first feels when his grandfather arrives is shame for his Indian ancestry. The old man's appearance is often shabby and he is not "tall and stately." Nor does he wear his hair in braids. However, his quiet dignity awes Martin's city friends, and Martin learns that a real Indian is much more impressive than the ones of Hollywood make-believe.

7
Martin's reaction to dogs hints at his true loyalty.

8
Characterization. He wants to hurry Grandpa, but Grandpa is not ashamed of who he is.

9 Finding Details
What details of Grandpa's appearance embarrass Martin? Hat, black suit, red satin shirt, and bolo tie.

10
Conflict. Martin's confusion shown by holding head down, pulling hand away, feeling like crying.

11
Mother's behavior results from concern for Grandpa, not shame.

VISUAL CONNECTIONS
Ideas for Writing
Martin is worried that his real grandfather will not impress his friends; grandfather is not an embodiment of the TV Indian. Ever since Europeans first arrived in America, they have dealt with Indians in terms of stereotype and myth. You might ask students to write a paragraph relating the picture of Hear Crow Dog to the ways in which Indians are portrayed in popular culture. Does he look the way he is "supposed" to look?

side of the street. I felt cold and hot at the same time as I recognized the man. "Oh, no!" I whispered. "It's Grandpa!"

I stood on the curb, unable to move even though I wanted to run and hide. Then I got 7 mad when I saw how the yippy dogs were growling and nipping at the old man's baggy pant legs and how wearily he poked them away with his cane. "Stupid mutts," I said as I ran to rescue Grandpa.

When I kicked and hollered at the dogs to get away, they put their tails between their legs and scattered. The kids ran to the curb where they watched me and the old man.

"Grandpa," I said and felt pretty dumb 8 when my voice cracked. I reached for his beat-up old tin suitcase, which was tied shut with a rope. But he set it down right in the street and shook my hand.

"*Hau, Takoza,* Grandchild," he greeted me formally in Sioux.

All I could do was stand there with the whole neighborhood watching and shake the hand of 9 the leather-brown old man. I saw how his gray hair straggled from under his big black hat, which had a drooping feather in its crown. His rumpled black suit hung like a sack over his stooped frame. As he shook my hand, his coat fell open to expose a bright-red, satin shirt with a beaded bolo tie[1] under the collar. His get-up wasn't out of place on the reservation, but it sure was here, and I wanted to sink right through the pavement.

10 "Hi," I muttered with my head down. I tried to pull my hand away when I felt his bony hand trembling, and looked up to see fatigue in his face. I felt like crying. I couldn't think of anything to say so I picked up Grandpa's suitcase, took his arm, and guided him up the driveway to our house.

Mom was standing on the steps. I don't know

1. **bolo tie:** a string tie held together by a sliding device.

Hear Crow Dog of the Sioux.

how long she'd been watching, but her hand was over her mouth and she looked as if she couldn't believe what she saw. Then she ran to us.

11 "Grandpa," she gasped. "How in the world did you get here?"

She checked her move to embrace Grandpa and I remembered that such a display of affec-

SOCIAL STUDIES LINK
Along with the reading of this story, you might have students research the Sioux or the Dakota. Some students might find out facts about the Sioux nation and use a map showing where it was historically located to present their finding. Other students might research the current location of Sioux reservations and try to find out information about current traditions.

---

tion is unseemly to the Sioux and would embarrass him.

"*Hau,* Marie," he said as he shook Mom's hand. She smiled and took his other arm.

As we supported him up the steps the door banged open and Cheryl came bursting out of 12 the house. She was all smiles and was so obviously glad to see Grandpa that I was ashamed of how I felt.

"Grandpa!" she yelled happily. "You came to see us!"

Grandpa smiled and Mom and I let go of him as he stretched out his arms to my ten-year-old sister, who was still young enough to be hugged.

"*Wicincala,* little girl," he greeted her and then collapsed.

He had fainted. Mom and I carried him into her sewing room, where we had a spare bed.

After we had Grandpa on the bed Mom stood there helplessly patting his shoulder.

"Shouldn't we call the doctor, Mom?" I suggested, since she didn't seem to know what to do.

"Yes," she agreed with a sigh. "You make Grandpa comfortable, Martin."

I reluctantly moved to the bed. I knew Grandpa wouldn't want to have Mom undress 13 him, but I didn't want to, either. He was so skinny and frail that his coat slipped off easily. When I loosened his tie and opened his shirt collar, I felt a small leather pouch that hung 14 from a thong around his neck. I left it alone and moved to remove his boots. The scuffed old cowboy boots were tight and he moaned as I put pressure on his legs to jerk them off.

I put the boots on the floor and saw why they fit so tight. Each one was stuffed with money. I 15 looked at the bills that lined the boots and started to ask about them, but Grandpa's eyes were closed again.

Mom came back with a basin of water. "The doctor thinks Grandpa is suffering from heat exhaustion," she explained as she bathed 16 Grandpa's face. Mom gave a big sigh, "*Oh hinh,* Martin. How do you suppose he got here?"

We found out after the doctor's visit. 17 Grandpa was angrily sitting up in bed while Mom tried to feed him some soup.

"Tonight you let Marie feed you, Grandpa," spoke my dad, who had gotten home from work just as the doctor was leaving. "You're not really sick," he said as he gently pushed Grandpa back against the pillows. "The doctor said you just got too tired and hot after your long trip."

Grandpa relaxed, and between sips of soup he told us of his journey. Soon after our visit to him Grandpa decided that he would like to see where his only living descendants lived and what our home was like. Besides, he admitted sheepishly, he was lonesome after we left.

18 I knew everybody felt as guilty as I did—especially Mom. Mom was all Grandpa had left. So even after she married my dad, who's a white man and teaches in the college in our city, and after Cheryl and I were born, Mom made sure that every summer we spent a week with Grandpa.

I never thought that Grandpa would be lonely after our visits, and none of us noticed how old and weak he had become. But Grandpa knew and so he came to us. He had ridden on buses for two and a half days. When he arrived in the city, tired and stiff from sitting for so long, he set out, walking, to find us.

He had stopped to rest on the steps of some building downtown and a policeman found 19 him. The cop, according to Grandpa, was a good man who took him to the bus stop and waited until the bus came and told the driver to let Grandpa out at Bell View Drive. After Grandpa got off the bus, he started walking again. But he couldn't see the house numbers on the other side when he walked on the sidewalk 20 walk so he walked in the middle of the street.

---

12 Characterization. Seeing the contrast between Cheryl and himself, Martin is shamed by her genuine feeling.

13 Martin's distaste may reflect that of many children who have never had to care for an elderly relative.

14 Grandpa's medicine bag.

15 Money put in boots to prevent theft.

16 Sioux words reflect her Indian heritage; translate as "Oh, dear."

17 Making Inferences
Why do you think Grandpa is angry? Responses will vary. His dignity may be offended; he may fear sickness.

18 Family has unintentionally neglected Grandpa's feelings; yearly visit to lonely old man is not much.

19 Policeman is "good man" because kind, helpful.

20 Explanation for walking in middle of street reveals cleverness rather than eccentricity.

The Medicine Bag

MEETING INDIVIDUAL NEEDS
Visual and Kinesthetic Learners • To foster students' understanding of how people pass on traditions to their descendants, you might ask students to bring to class something that represents their own family practices or traditions. You could suggest photographs, favorite gifts from relatives, items that have personal significance, and anything else that a family might pass along.

As students share their objects with the class, you might ask how the item they brought could be a part of a "medicine bag." How does the item make students feel about their family? Is it comforting to have the object around?

21
Foreshadowing. An early indication of Grandpa's approaching death.

22
Martin's father shows Grandpa proper respect.

23
Characterization. Reflects Grandpa's extraordinary sensitivity to feelings of others.

24
Purpose of visit: to pass on medicine bag to oldest male child before death.

25
Use to answer **study question 2, p. 37.**

26
He would take it out of duty, not pride.

27
"Not time" because Grandpa is not ready to die, also because Martin is not ready to accept it.

28 Drawing Conclusions
At whom, and why, does Martin think they will laugh? At Martin, because Grandpa is not as Martin has described.

29
Younger children see less discrepancy between the fantasy and the reality.

30
Martin's anxiety aroused by Hank's sarcasm.

That's when all the little kids and dogs followed him.

I knew everybody felt as bad as I did. Yet I was proud of this eighty-six-year-old man, who had never been away from the reservation, having the courage to travel so far alone.

"You found the money in my boots?" he asked Mom.

"Martin did," she answered, and roused herself to scold. "Grandpa, you shouldn't have carried so much money. What if someone had stolen it from you?"

Grandpa laughed. "I would've known if any- 21 one tried to take the boots off my feet. The money is what I've saved for a long time—a hundred dollars—for my funeral. But you take it now to buy groceries so that I won't be a burden to you while I am here."

22 "That won't be necessary, Grandpa," Dad said. "We are honored to have you with us and you will never be a burden. I am only sorry that we never thought to bring you home with us this summer and spare you the discomfort of a long trip."

23 Grandpa was pleased. "Thank you," he answered. "But do not feel bad that you didn't bring me with you, for I would not have come then. It was not time." He said this in such a way that no one could argue with him. To Grandpa and the Sioux, he once told me, a thing would be done when it was the right time to do it and that's the way it was.

"Also," Grandpa went on, looking at me, "I 24 have come because it is soon time for Martin to have the medicine bag."

We all knew what that meant. Grandpa thought he was going to die and he had to follow the tradition of his family to pass the medicine bag, along with its history, to the oldest male child.

"Even though the boy," he said still looking at me, "bears a white man's name, the medicine bag will be his."

I didn't know what to say. I had the same hot and cold feeling that I had when I first saw 25 Grandpa in the street. The medicine bag was the dirty leather pouch I had found around his neck. "I could never wear such a thing," I almost said aloud. I thought of having my friends see it in gym class, at the swimming pool, and could imagine the smart things they would say. But I just swallowed hard and took 26 a step toward the bed. I knew I would have to take it.

27 But Grandpa was tired. "Not now, Martin," he said, waving his hand in dismissal, "it is not time. Now I will sleep."

So that's how Grandpa came to be with us for two months. My friends kept asking to come see the old man, but I put them off. I told myself that I didn't want them laughing at 28 Grandpa. But even as I made excuses I knew it wasn't Grandpa that I was afraid they'd laugh at.

Nothing bothered Cheryl about bringing 29 her friends to see Grandpa. Every day after school started there'd be a crew of giggling little girls or round-eyed little boys crowded around the old man on the patio, where he'd gotten in the habit of sitting every afternoon. Grandpa would smile in his gentle way and patiently answer their questions, or he'd tell them stories of brave warriors, ghosts, animals, and the kids listened in awed silence. Those little guys thought Grandpa was great.

Finally, one day after school, my friends came home with me because nothing I said 30 stopped them. "We're going to see the great Indian of Bell View Drive," said Hank, who was supposed to be my best friend. "My brother has seen him three times so he oughta be well enough to see us."

When we got to my house Grandpa was sitting on the patio. He had on his red shirt, but today he also wore a fringed leather vest that was decorated with beads. Instead of his usual

36 REFLECTIONS

> **TRANSPARENCY 4**
> **Literary Elements**
> *Plot* – explores a specific sequence of events that make up the plot of a narrative.

> **TRANSPARENCIES 1 & 2**
> **Fine Art**
> Theme: *Self-Image* – invites students to explore artworks depicting people in a process of self-discovery.

Bandolier bag, worn across the chest. Sioux.

American Museum of Natural History

31 cowboy boots he had solidly beaded moccasins on his feet that stuck out of his black trousers. Of course, he had his old black hat on—he was seldom without it. But it had been brushed and the feather in the beaded headband was proudly erect, its tip a brighter white. His hair lay in silver strands over the red shirt collar.

I started just as my friends did and I heard one of them murmur, "Wow!"

32 Grandpa looked up and when his eyes met mine they twinkled as if he were laughing inside. He nodded to me and my face got all hot. I could tell that he had known all along I was afraid he'd embarrass me in front of my friends.

"*Hau, hoksilas*, boys," he greeted and held out his hand.

My buddies passed in a single file and shook
33 his hand as I introduced them. They were so polite I almost laughed. "How, there, Grandpa," and even a "How-do-you-do, sir."

"You look fine, Grandpa," I said as the guys sat on the lawn chairs or on the patio floor.

34 "*Hanh*, yes," he agreed. "When I woke up this morning it seemed the right time to dress in the good clothes. I knew that my grandson would be bringing his friends."

"You guys want some lemonade or something?" I offered. No one answered. They were listening to Grandpa as he started telling how he'd killed the deer from which his vest was made.

Grandpa did most of the talking while my friends were there. I was so proud of him and amazed at how respectfully quiet my buddies were. Mom had to chase them home at suppertime. As they left they shook Grandpa's hand again and said to me:

"Martin, he's really great!"

"Yeah, man! Don't blame you for keeping him to yourself."

"Can we come back?"

But after they left, Mom said, "No more visi-

31 Finding Details
What aspects of Grandpa's attire make him seem more impressive? Beaded vest and moccasins, brushed hat, brighter feather.

32
Characterization. Grandpa impresses boys to save Martin from embarrassment; Grandpa seems to understand Martin's ambivalent attitude toward his Indian heritage.

33
Boys' sarcastic attitudes disappear when they meet Grandpa.

34
Reflects Grandpa's Sioux belief in knowing the proper time to do things.

VISUAL CONNECTIONS
About the Artwork
The beadwork on this bandolier bag shows a blending of Indian and European design elements. Traditional Indian designs are geometric, but the use of an all-over pattern shows European influence. The flower design is clearly European; designs of this type are not seen in early artifacts. Beads of shell and bone had been in use long before the arrival of Europeans; however, the popular glass beads introduced by European traders generally replaced these.

The Medicine Bag

Cultural Diversity

The goal of the Sioux vision quest is to find a spirit guide. Ask students to name the necessary steps in a vision quest, as Grandpa's father undertook it.
    Taking a sweat bath (purification)
Being alone (solitude)
Going into the wilderness (communion with nature)
Not eating food (fasting)
Asking for guidance (praying)

Invite students to share similar traditions with which they might be familiar. What are the separate steps taken? What is the goal?

---

35 Grandpa knows his strength is failing.

36 Scared of unknown, of growing up, of Grandpa's dying.

37 Finding Cause and Effect **Why does Martin shiver?** Perhaps from fear, dawning awareness of importance of tradition, approaching manhood, and so on.

38 Grandpa also holds on to traditional ways.

39 Foreshadowing. Vision foretells increasing dependence on, and connection to, white culture.

40 His trade is a blessing; it allows him to survive on reservation.

41 Martin's "disbelief" because Grandpa's show of emotion uncharacteristic.

---

tors for a while, Martin. Grandpa won't admit it, but his strength hasn't returned. He likes having company, but it tires him."

35 That evening Grandpa called me to his room before he went to sleep. "Tomorrow," he said, "when you come home, it will be time to give you the medicine bag."

I felt a hard squeeze from where my heart is 36 supposed to be and was scared, but I answered, "OK, Grandpa."

All night I had weird dreams about thunder and lightning on a high hill. From a distance I heard the slow beat of a drum. When I woke up in the morning I felt as if I hadn't slept at all. At school it seemed as if the day would never end and, when it finally did, I ran home.

Grandpa was in his room, sitting on the bed. The shades were down and the place was dim and cool. I sat on the floor in front of Grandpa, but he didn't even look at me. After what seemed a long time he spoke.

"I sent your mother and sister away. What you will hear today is only for a man's ears. What you will receive is only for a man's 37 hands." He fell silent and I felt shivers down my back.

"My father in his early manhood," Grandpa began, "made a vision quest to find a spirit guide for his life. You cannot understand how it was in that time, when the great Teton Sioux were first made to stay on the reservation. 40 There was a strong need for guidance from *Wakantanka*, the Great Spirit. But too many of the young men were filled with despair and hatred. They thought it was hopeless to search for a vision when the glorious life was gone and only the hated confines of a reservation lay 41 38 ahead. But my father held to the old ways.

"He carefully prepared for his quest with a purifying sweat bath and then he went alone to a high butte top to fast and pray. After three days he received his sacred dream—in which he found, after long searching, the white man's 39 iron. He did not understand his vision of finding something belonging to the white people, for in that time they were the enemy. When he came down from the butte to cleanse himself at the stream below, he found the remains of a campfire and the broken shell of an iron kettle. This was a sign which reinforced his dream. He took a piece of the iron for his medicine bag, which he had made of elk skin years before, to prepare for his quest.

"He returned to his village, where he told his dream to the wise old men of the tribe. They gave him the name Iron Shell, but neither did they understand the meaning of the dream. This first Iron Shell kept the piece of iron with him at all times and believed it gave him protection from the evils of those unhappy days.

"Then a terrible thing happened to Iron Shell. He and several other young men were taken from their homes by the soldiers and sent far away to a white man's boarding school. He was angry and lonesome for his parents and the young girl he had wed before he was taken away. At first Iron Shell resisted the teachers' attempts to change him and he did not try to learn. One day it was his turn to work in the school's blacksmith shop. As he walked into the place he knew that his medicine had brought him there to learn and work with the white man's iron.

"Iron Shell became a blacksmith and worked at the trade when he returned to the reservation. All of his life he treasured the medicine bag. When he was old, and I was a man, he gave it to me, for no one made the vision quest anymore."

Grandpa quit talking and I stared in disbelief as he covered his face with his hands. His shoulders were shaking with quiet sobs and I looked away until he began to speak again.

"I kept the bag until my son, your mother's father, was a man and had to leave us to fight in the war across the ocean. I gave him the bag,

38 REFLECTIONS

PORTFOLIO ASSESSMENT

In the story "The Medicine Bag," Martin's feelings about his grandfather change as the story progresses. Students may have similar experiences where once they had been ashamed of older relatives but are now as proud of them and their heritage as Martin is. Students may want to write paragraphs in which they describe older relatives and how and why their opinions of them have changed in a positive way. Revised paragraphs may be included in student portfolios. (See *Portfolio Assessment and Professional Support Materials* for additional information on student portfolios.)

---

for I believed it would protect him in battle, 42 but he did not take it with him. He was afraid that he would lose it. He died in a faraway place."

Again Grandpa was still and I felt his grief around me.

"My son," he went on after clearing his throat, "had only a daughter and it is not proper for her to know of these things."

He unbuttoned his shirt, pulled out the leather pouch, and lifted it over his head. He held it in his hand, turning it over and over as if memorizing how it looked.

"In the bag," he said as he opened it and removed two objects, "is the broken shell of the iron kettle, a pebble from the butte, and a piece of the sacred sage."[2] He held the pouch upside down and dust drifted down.

"After the bag is yours you must put a piece of prairie sage within and never open it again 43 until you pass it on to your son." He replaced the pebble and the piece of iron, and tied the bag.

44 I stood up, somehow knowing I should. Grandpa slowly rose from the bed and stood upright in front of me, holding the bag before my face. I closed my eyes and waited for him to slip it over my head. But he spoke.

45 "No, you need not wear it." He placed the soft leather bag in my right hand and closed my other hand over it. "It would not be right to wear it in this time and place where no one will understand. Put it safely away until you are again on the reservation. Wear it then, when you replace the sacred sage."

Grandpa turned and sat again on the bed. Wearily he leaned his head against the pillow. 46 "Go," he said, "I will sleep now."

"Thank you, Grandpa," I said softly and left with the bag in my hands.

That night Mom and Dad took Grandpa to 47 the hospital. Two weeks later I stood alone on the lonely prairie of the reservation and put the sacred sage in my medicine bag.

---

2. **sage:** a plant with aromatic leaves, believed to have healing powers.

Reading Check

1. How are Joe Iron Shell and the narrator related?
2. What does Grandpa have in his boots?
3. What does the medicine bag contain?
4. How does Grandpa entertain Cheryl's friends?
5. Who was the first person to wear the medicine bag?

For Study and Discussion

Analyzing and Interpreting the Story

1. Martin says that he and his sister always bragged about Grandpa. Why, then, is Martin embarrassed when Grandpa arrives?

2. Grandpa explains that the purpose of his visit is to pass along the medicine bag and its history to Martin. Why is Martin miserable at the thought of wearing the medicine bag?

3. Martin is concerned about how his friends will react to Grandpa. What actually happens when they come to visit Grandpa?

4. When he feels it is time, Grandpa tells Martin the history of the medicine bag. Why does Grandpa treasure it?

5. Martin's feelings toward Grandpa begin to change after he sees how much his friends admire the old man. **a.** When do his feelings about the medicine bag change? **b.** How do you know at the end of the story that he understands and respects the tradition it represents?

---

42 Believes son would not have died if he had worn medicine bag.

43 Medicine bag binds generations; strengthens sense of identity.

44 Knowing proper time for action may indicate Martin is beginning to accept Sioux heritage.

45 Drawing Conclusions *Why does Grandpa tell Martin he need not wear the bag?* Grandpa understands ridicule Martin would face; medicine bag is too sacred to subject to mockery.

46 Knows it is time for him to die.

47 Plot. The resolution is complete with Martin's acceptance of his heritage.

READING CHECK
1. Joe is Martin's great-grandfather (p. 30).
2. $100 for his funeral (p. 34).
3. Part of iron kettle, pebble from butte, and sacred sage (p. 37).
4. Stories of warriors, ghosts, and animals (p. 34).
5. Grandpa's father (p. 36).

FOR STUDY AND DISCUSSION
1. Martin's glamorous tales do not fit Grandpa.
2. He is afraid friends will tease him if he wears it.
3. Grandpa has dressed impressively and tells about killing deer for his vest; boys are in awe.
4. Symbol of his father's vision quest to find a spirit guide; believes it has protective powers.
5a. After hearing Grandpa's story. 5b. Goes to reservation; puts sacred sage in medicine bag.

CLOSURE

Have students trace Martin's feelings toward his grandfather throughout the story. His feelings change from a false, bragging pride to a sincere pride and honor.

EXTENSION AND ENRICHMENT

Stage an informal debate over whether Martin will pass the medicine bag on to his son. Students might also discuss why families pass objects such as a family Bible or piece of furniture from generation to generation.

FOCUS ON PERSONAL NARRATIVE

Students often have difficulty including details about the sense of smell. You may want to brainstorm with students by asking them to share smells that come to mind. Start a list on the chalkboard with such phrases as *newly cut grass, musty cellar, exhaust fumes, sweaty socks,* and *overpowering perfume.* Add students' suggestions, and encourage students to refer to the list as they complete their sensory detail webs.

ABOUT THE AUTHOR

Sneve has said that one of her reasons for writing is to present an accurate portrayal of Indian life as she has known it, correcting myths and stereotypes about Indians.

CONNECTING CULTURES

1. *hogan:* earth-covered lodge of the Navajo.
kayak: skin-covered portable canoe.
mackinaw: heavy woolen cloth.
manitou: spirit dominating forces of nature.
pemmican: dried buffalo or venison pounded and mixed with fat.
sagamore: chief of secondary rank.
succotash: lima beans and green corn cooked together.
terrapin: freshwater turtle.
totem: a carved emblem of family and symbolic ancestry.
2. Another informative source about word origins is *The Encyclopedia of Word and Phrase Origins* by Robert Hendrickson.

Focus on Personal Narrative

Focusing on Your Senses

Sensory details are details that appeal to one of the five senses: sight, hearing, smell, taste, and touch. These details can make a narrative especially vivid.

Use a web like the one below to gather sensory details for your narrative. In the center of the web, write your topic. Then pick some specific moments of your experience. Try to visualize each moment in your mind. Then make notes on the web about what you observe with all your senses. Save your notes.

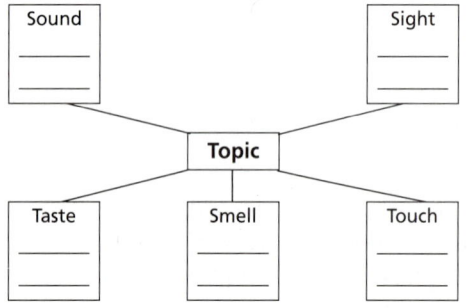

About the Author

Virginia Driving Hawk Sneve (1933–   )

Virginia Driving Hawk Sneve grew up on the Rosebud Sioux reservation in South Dakota. She has said, "I try to present an accurate portrayal of American Indian life as I have known it." Her books include *Jimmy Yellow Hawk* (1972) and *When Thunders Spoke* (1974). She has also edited *Dancing Teepees: Poems of American Indian Youth* (1989).

Connecting Cultures

The Influence of American Indian Languages

Many words in English are **loan words,** or words that have been borrowed from other languages. For example, the word *butte* comes from French, the word *patio* from Spanish, and the word *Indian* from Latin.

A number of words in English have been borrowed from American Indian languages. The word *moccasin* comes from a family of languages called Algonquian. The word *tepee* comes from a word in the Siouan language family. Loans from Nahuatl (nä′wät′l), a language spoken in central and western Mexico by Amerindian peoples, have generally come into English by way of Spanish. This is how we got the word *chocolate*.

Many place names come from Indian words. According to some sources, the city of Chicago derives its name from an Indian word meaning "the place of strong smells," presumably from the wild onions found growing there.

Making Connections: Activities

1. All the words in the following list come from American Indian languages. Give the meaning of each word, using a dictionary if necessary.

   hogan   manitou   succotash
   kayak   pemmican   terrapin
   mackinaw   sagamore   totem

2. Find out if your school or local library has a copy of *The American Language: Supplement I,* by H. L. Mencken (Knopf, 1961). Read Chapter 3, "The Beginnings of American." Working with a partner or a small group, choose some colorful examples of words borrowed from American Indian languages as the subject of a brief informative report. Trace the word histories on a chart or on a transparency. Indicate how the usage and spelling of the words changed as they passed into English.

OBJECTIVES	VOCABULARY	FOCUS / MOTIVATION
The overall aim is for students to demonstrate an understanding of the ironic humor within this story. For a complete list of objectives, see the Teacher's Notes.	The underlined words are in the Glossary. The Language and Vocabulary exercise on p. 46 of the textbook gives students practice in identifying selected prefixes, root words, and affixes. The exercise focuses on use of the prefix *dis-*.	Ask students to think about experiences that seemed frightening or embarrassing at the time, but that seemed funny later on. "Guinea Pig" presents near-tragic events that McKenney could later laugh at.

Guinea Pig

RUTH McKENNEY

A guinea pig is something or someone used in an experiment or a test of some kind. How does the narrator turn her experiences as a "guinea pig" into a hilarious story?

1 I was nearly drowned, in my youth, by a Red Cross Lifesaving Examiner, and I once suffered, in the noble cause of saving human life from a watery grave, a black eye which was a **2** perfect daisy and embarrassed me for days.
3 Looking back on my agonies, I feel that none of my sacrifices, especially the black eye, were in the least worthwhile. Indeed, to be brutally frank about it, I feel that the whole modern school of scientific lifesaving is a lot of hogwash.
4 Of course, I've had rather bad luck with lifesavers, right from the beginning. Long before I ever had any dealings with professional lifesavers my sister nearly drowned me, quite by mistake. My father once took us to a northern Michigan fishing camp, where we found the life very dull. He used to go trolling for bass on our little lake all day long, and at night come home to our lodge, dead beat and minus any bass. In the meantime Eileen and I, who were nine and ten at the time, used to take an old rowboat out to a shallow section of the lake **5** and, sitting in the hot sun, feed worms to an unexciting variety of small, undernourished fish called gillies. We hated the whole business.

Father, however, loved to fish, even if he didn't catch a single fish in three weeks, which on this trip he didn't. One night, however, he carried his enthusiasm beyond a decent pitch. He decided to go bass fishing after dark, and **6** rather than leave us alone in the lodge and up to heaven knows what, he ordered us to take our boat and row along after him.

Eileen and I were very bored rowing around in the dark, and finally, in desperation, we began to stand up and rock the boat, which resulted, at last, in my falling into the lake with a mighty splash.

When I came up, choking and mad as anything, Eileen saw me struggling, and, as she al-
7 ways says with a catch in her voice, she only meant to help me. Good intentions, however, are of little importance in a situation like that. For she grabbed an oar out of the lock, and with an uncertain gesture hit me square on the chin.

I went down with a howl of pain. Eileen, who could not see much in the darkness, was now

Guinea Pig **41**

TEACHING RESOURCES A

Teacher's Notes, p. 66
Reading Check, p. 69
Study Guide, p. 70
Language Skills, p. 72
Building Vocabulary, p. 74
Selection Vocabulary Test, p. 76
Selection Test, p. 77

PREREADING FOCUS
The headnote gives a definition of guinea pig. Ask students to discuss experience in which they or someone they know was used as a guinea pig with humorous or disastrous results.

Guinea Pig

1
Irony. First sentence sets up sardonic humor: the description of "nearly drowned" is ironic because acquired due to "lifesaver"; "black eye" because acquired in "noble cause."

2
"Perfect daisy" means "fine example."

3
Exaggerated language underscores humor: "agonies," "sacrifices," "brutally," "hogwash."

4
This digression adds humor and suggests type of physical comedy found in main **plot**.

5
Feeding worms to "undernourished" fish is humorous description of unsuccessful fishing.

6
Irony. They get into more trouble on lake than they would in lodge.

7
Narrator mockingly describes her sister.

MOTIVATIONAL SUMMARY
In the past, Ruth has not had much luck with lifesavers. Her sister Eileen once tried to save her from drowning by extending her an oar to hold onto, but she accidentally hit Ruth on the head with it and almost knocked her unconscious. Now, at a summer camp for girls, Ruth is enrolled in a course in lifesaving. When Miss Folgil, the no-nonsense instructor, decides that big-boned Ruth will make the perfect "drowning victim" for the other girls to practice on, Ruth starts to get worried.

PRESENTATION
Ruth McKenney turns what could have been disastrous situations into a humorous tale in "Guinea Pig." The tone of the story is ironic, even sardonic, as the older, wiser narrator remembers how her easily persuaded young self

VISUAL CONNECTIONS
Ideas for Writing
Students might write a descriptive paragraph giving their ideas about the photograph. Students might mention summer, possible location of pond (grandparent's farm?), relationship of girls, their conversation, and so on. Or students might write about a personal experience at a pool or beach, perhaps a humorous incident or a more serious event such as an injury or near-catastrophe.

8
Irony. Swimming to boat gives Eileen another chance to hit her.

9
Humor lies in contrast between Eileen's intentions and how her actions are perceived by Ruth.

10 Summarizing
What is the ironic outcome of the incident? Eileen is regarded as a heroine.

11
Plot. Transition back to main plot; prepares reader for subsequent events by comparing to previous action.

8 really frightened. The cold water revived me after the blow and I came up to the surface, considerably weakened but still able to swim over to the boat. Whereupon Eileen, in a noble attempt to give me the oar to grab, raised it once again, and socked me square on the top of the head. I went down again, this time without a murmur, and my last thought was a
9 vague wonder that my own sister should want to murder me with a rowboat oar.

As for Eileen, she heard the dull impact of the oar on my head and saw the shadowy figure of her sister disappear. So she jumped in the lake, screeching furiously, and began to flail around in the water, howling for help and looking for me. At this point I came to the surface and swam over to the boat, with the intention of killing Eileen.

Father, rowing hard, arrived just in time to pull us both out of the water and prevent me from attacking Eileen with the rowboat anchor. The worst part about the whole thing, as far as I was concerned, was that Eileen was considered a heroine and Father told everybody in the lake community that she had saved
10 my life. The postmaster put her name in for a medal.

11 After what I suffered from amateur lifesaving, I should have known enough to avoid even the merest contact with the professional

42   42 REFLECTIONS

was talked into "volunteering" as the perfect "victim" for Miss Folgil's lifesaving class to attempt to rescue. In their eagerness, the "little pupils" are more life-threatening than life-saving, but the author's humorous descriptions show that the challenges of growing up are often improved when seen from the vantage point of one who has safely survived the ordeal.

TRANSPARENCY 3
Reader Response
Mirror, Mirror – invites students to assess a character's personality traits as if they themselves were the character.

---

variety of water mercy. I learned too late that being socked with an oar is as nothing compared to what the Red Cross can think up.

From the very beginning of that awful lifesaving course I took the last season I went to a girls' camp, I was a marked woman. The rest of the embryo[1] lifesavers were little, slender maidens, but I am a peasant type, and I was monstrously big for my fourteen years. I approximated, in poundage anyway, the theoretical adult we energetic young lifesavers were scheduled to rescue, and so I was, for the teacher's purpose, the perfect guinea pig.

The first few days of the course were unpleasant for me, but not terribly dangerous. The elementary lifesaving hold, in case you haven't seen some hapless victim being rescued by our brave beach guardians, is a snakelike arrangement for supporting the drowning citizen with one hand while you paddle him in to shore with the other. You are supposed to wrap your arm around his neck and shoulders, and keep his head well above water by resting it on your collarbone.

This is all very well in theory, of course, but the trick that none of Miss Folgil's little pupils could master was keeping the victim's nose and mouth above the waterline. Time and again I was held in a viselike[2] grip by one of the earnest students with my whole face an inch or two under the billowing waves.

"No, no, Betsy," Miss Folgil would scream through her megaphone, as I felt the water rush into my lungs. "No, no, you must keep the head a little higher." At this point I would begin to kick and struggle, and generally the pupil would have to let go while I came up for air. Miss Folgil was always very stern with me.

"Ruth," she would shriek from her boat, "I insist! You must allow Betsy to tow you all the way in. We come to Struggling in Lesson 6."

This was but the mere beginning, however. A few lessons later we came to the section of the course where we learned how to undress under water in forty seconds. Perhaps I should say we came to the point where the *rest* of the pupils learned how to get rid of shoes and such while holding their breaths. I never did.

There was quite a little ceremony connected with this part of the course. Miss Folgil, and some lucky creature named as timekeeper and armed with a stopwatch, rowed the prospective victim out to deep water. The pupil, dressed in high, laced tennis shoes, long stockings, heavy bloomers, and a middy blouse, then stood poised at the end of the boat. When the timekeeper yelled "Go!" the future boon to mankind dived into the water and, while holding her breath under the surface, unlaced her shoes and stripped down to her bathing suit. Miss Folgil never explained what connection, if any, this curious rite had with saving human lives.

I had no middy of my own, so I borrowed one of my sister's. My sister was a slender little thing and I was, as I said, robust, which puts it politely. Eileen had some trouble wedging me into that middy, and once in it I looked like a stuffed sausage. It never occurred to me how hard it was going to be to get that middy off, especially when it was wet and slippery.

As we rowed out for my ordeal by undressing, Miss Folgil was snappish and bored.

"Hurry up," she said, looking irritated. "Let's get this over with quick. I don't think you're ready to pass the test, anyway."

I was good and mad when I jumped off the boat, and determined to Make Good and show that old Miss Folgil, whom I was beginning to dislike thoroughly. As soon as I was under water, I got my shoes off, and I had no trouble with the bloomers or stockings. I was just beginning to run out of breath when I held up

1. **embryo** (ĕm′brē-ō): here, beginning.
2. **viselike** (vīs′līk′): like a vise, or clamping device.

12
"Peasant type" means "big-boned," "of sturdy build."

13
Use to answer **study question 3**, p. 44.

14
Sarcasm based on contrast between theory and practice suggested by "hapless victim," "brave beach guardians," "supposed."

15
Not keeping volunteer's nose and mouth above waterline means that truly the volunteer was a victim being drowned.

16
Miss Folgil is more concerned with technique than with possible danger to Ruth.

17
Bloomers: loose, baggy pants, gathered at knees. *Middy blouse:* hip-length blouse with sailor collar. Both were popular in 1930s as women's sports clothing.

18
"Future boon to mankind" meaning "prospective lifesaver."

19
A *middy* fits over the head and is straight-sided, almost sacklike.

20
"Ordeal by undressing" is humorous allusion to medieval challenges like ordeal by combat, and so on.

Guinea Pig 43

MEETING INDIVIDUAL NEEDS
ESL/LEP • Discuss the meaning of the expression "dead beat" (p. 41) and explain that several English words may be preceded by the word *dead* to mean *complete(ly)*. Ask the class to name a few of these expressions and use them in sentences. Examples might include the following combinations:

You're *dead wrong*.
The car came to *a dead stop*.
The restaurant is *dead ahead*.

The class sat in *dead silence*.
He struck the target *dead center*.

21
She decides she had better save her own life.

22
Humorous since purpose of the class is to train lifesavers: given real victim, no one sees.

23
Irony. The professional lifesaver hates to save someone because suit will get wet.

24
Her thoughtfulness is for rest of class, at Ruth's expense.

25
Mocks absurdities sometimes found in textbooks and in "by the book" person like Miss Folgil.

26
Quitting for good reason is not a sign of weakness.

27
Her resolution is comic in light of perils she has already suffered.

---

my arms and started to pull off the middy.

Now, the middy, in the event you don't understand the principle of this girl-child garment, is made with a small head opening, long sleeves, and no front opening. You pull it on and off over your head. You do if you are lucky, that is. I got the middy just past my neck, so that my face was covered with heavy linen cloth, when it stuck.

I pulled frantically and my lungs started to burst. Finally I thought the heck with the test, the heck with saving other people's lives, anyway. I came to the surface, a curious sight, my head enfolded in a water-soaked middy blouse. I made a brief sound, a desperate glub-glub, a call for help. My arms were stuck in the middy and I couldn't swim. I went down. I breathed in large quantities of water and linen cloth.

I came up again, making final frantic appeals. Four feet away sat a professional lifesaver, paying absolutely no attention to somebody drowning right under her nose. I went down again, struggling with last panic-stricken feverishness, fighting water and a middy blouse for my life. At this point the timekeeper pointed out to Miss Folgil that I had been under water for eighty-five seconds, which was quite a time for anybody. Miss Folgil was very annoyed, as she hated to get her bathing suit wet, but, a thoughtful teacher, she picked up her megaphone, shouted to the rest of the class on the beach to watch, and dived in after me.

If I say so myself, I gave her quite a time rescuing me. I presented a new and different problem, and probably am written up in textbooks now under the heading "What to Do When the Victim Is Entangled in a Tight Middy Blouse." Miss Folgil finally towed my still-breathing body over to the boat, reached for her bowie knife, which she carried on a ring with her whistle, and cut Eileen's middy straight up the front. Then she towed me with Hold No. 2 right in to the shore and delivered me up to the class for artificial respiration. I will never forgive the Red Cross for that terrible trip through the water, when I might have been hoisted into the boat and rowed in except for Miss Folgil's overdeveloped sense of drama and pedagogy.

I tried to quit the lifesaving class after that, but the head counselor at the camp said I must keep on, to show that I was the kind of girl who always finished what she planned to do. Otherwise, she assured me, I would be a weak character and never amount to anything when I grew up.

So I stayed for Lesson 6: "Struggling." After that I didn't care if I never amounted to anything when I grew up. In fact, I hoped I wouldn't. It would serve everybody right, especially Miss Folgil. I came a little late to the class session that day and missed the discussion of theory, always held on the beach before the actual practice in the lake. That was just my hard luck. I was always a child of misfortune. I wonder that I survived my youth at all.

"We were waiting for you, Ruth," Miss Folgil chirped cheerily to me as I arrived, sullen and downcast, at the little group of earnest students sitting on the sand.

"What for?" I said warily. I was determined not to be a guinea pig any more. The last wave had washed over my helpless face.

"You swim out," Miss Folgil went on, ignoring my bad temper, "until you are in deep water—about twelve feet will do. Then you begin to flail around and shout for help. One of the students will swim out to you."

All of this sounded familiar and terrible. I had been doing that for days, and getting water in my nose for my pains.

"But when the student arrives," Miss Folgil went on, "you must not allow her to simply tow you away. You must struggle, just as hard as

MEETING INDIVIDUAL NEEDS
Auditory Learners • Students might appreciate the humor in this selection more if the story is read aloud. You might encourage several of your better readers to prepare a reading for the class. Suggest that they use appropriate expression and a humorous tone as they read.

---

you can. You must try to clutch her by the head, you must try to twine your legs about her, and otherwise hamper her in trying to save you."

28 Now, *this* sounded something like.[3] I was foolishly fired by the attractive thought of getting back at some of the fiends who had been ducking me in the name of science for the past two weeks. Unfortunately, I hadn't studied Chapter 9, entitled "How to Break Holds the Drowning Swimmer Uses." Worse, I hadn't

29 heard Miss Folgil's lecture on "Be Firm with the Panic-Stricken Swimmer—Better a Few Bruises Than a Watery Grave." This last was Miss Folgil's own opinion, of course.

30 So I swam out to my doom, happy as a lark. Maybelle Anne Pettijohn, a tall, lean girl who ordinarily wore horn-rimmed spectacles, was Miss Folgil's choice to rescue Exhibit A, the panic-stricken swimmer.

 I laughed when I saw her coming. I thought I could clean up Maybelle Anne easily enough,
31 but alas, I hadn't counted on Maybelle Anne's methodical approach to life. She had read Chapter 9 in our textbook, and she had listened carefully to Miss Folgil's inspiring words. Besides, Maybelle Anne was just naturally the kind of girl who ran around doing people dirty for their own good. "This may hurt your feelings," she used to say mournfully, "but I feel I have to tell you . . ."

 When Maybelle Anne got near me, I enthusiastically lunged for her neck and hung on with both hands while getting her around her waist with my legs. Maybelle Anne thereupon dug her fingernails into my hands with ferocious force, and I let go and swam away, hurt

---

3. **something like:** the way it should be.

---

and surprised. This was distinctly not playing fair.

 "What's the idea?" I called out.

 "It says to do that in the book," Maybelle Anne replied, treading water.

 "Well, you lay off of that stuff," I said, angered, book or no book. Maybelle Anne was a
32 Girl Scout, too, and I was shocked to think she'd go around using her fingernails in a fair fight.

 "Come on, struggle," Maybelle Anne said, getting winded from treading water. I swam over, pretty reluctant and much more wary. Believe it or not, this time Maybelle Anne, who was two medals from being a Beaver or whatever it is Girl Scouts with a lot of medals get to be, bit me.

 In addition to biting me, Maybelle Anne swung her arm around my neck, with the intention of towing me in to the shore. But I still had plenty of fight left and I had never been so mad in my life. I got Maybelle Anne underwater two or three times, and I almost thought I had her when suddenly, to my earnest surprise, she hauled off and hit me as hard as she could, right in the eye. Then she towed me in, triumphant as anything.

33 Maybelle Anne afterward claimed it was all in the book, and she wouldn't even apologize for my black eye. Eileen and I fixed her, though. We put a little garter snake in her bed and scared the daylights out of her. Maybelle Anne was easy to scare anyway, and really a very disagreeable girl. I used to hope that she would come to a bad end, which, from my point of view, at least, she did. Maybelle Anne grew up to be a Regional Red Cross Lifesaving Examiner.

 I'll bet she just loves her work.

---

28 Use to answer **study question 5, p. 44.**

29 Without Ruth's knowing it, Miss Folgil has told students to subdue "victim" at all costs.

30 Humor: she does not realize what will happen when she struggles.

31 Maybelle Anne's zeal apparently matches that of Miss Folgil.

32 Analyzing **What is ironic about Ruth's shock?** She thinks other "unfair" when she herself had planned to fight and struggle.

33 **Characterization.** Like Miss Folgil, Maybelle Anne goes "by the book."

Guinea Pig 45

MEETING INDIVIDUAL NEEDS
Kinesthetic Learners • If you have any students who like to pantomime, you might encourage them to act out scenes from the story as it is being read. Encourage them to divide the story into acting parts, determine the number of actors needed, assign characters to pantomime each part and practice their presentation with the readers. Then have the students plan a presentation of the story.

READING CHECK
1. Two sisters were standing and rocking boat; Ruth lost her balance (p. 39).
2. To "rescue" Ruth (p. 40).
3. Keeping victim's nose and mouth above waterline (p. 41).
4. She cut it with her bowie knife (p. 42).
5. She punched her in the eye (p. 43).

FOR STUDY AND DISCUSSION
1. Being nearly drowned by Lifesaving Examiner and getting black eye for volunteering for lifesaving class.
2. Responses will vary. Hitting Ruth on chin with oar; Ruth's wonder that her sister would want to murder her; Eileen's being a heroine.
3. Her size approximates an adult's.
4. It makes clear that middy is too small for Ruth and will be difficult to get off.
5. She sees opportunity to get back at girls in class.
6a. One in which she has all the advantages. 6b. She uses painful measures: scratching, biting, and hitting Ruth in the eye.
7a. She had to be to survive course. 7b. If a poor swimmer, struggles would be pathetic; as able swimmer, they are comic.

FOCUS ON READING
1. Eileen's rescue attempt misfires as she hurts Ruth instead of saving her.
2. Maybelle turns out to be a tough girl who does not fight fair.
3. Eileen "wedging" Ruth into middy, her frantic appeals for help, Miss Folgil's reaction.
4. Maybelle had read Chapter 9 and listened carefully to Miss Folgil.

Reading Check

1. What caused Ruth to fall out of the rowboat?
2. Why did Eileen jump into the lake?
3. In the elementary lifesaving hold, what trick were the pupils unable to master?
4. How did Miss Folgil remove the middy Ruth was wearing?
5. How did Maybelle Anne subdue Ruth during their struggle?

For Study and Discussion

Analyzing and Interpreting the Story

1. What two surprising events revealed in the first sentence tell you that this is a humorous story?

2. Ruth tells you that her sister once nearly drowned her. Which details of the "rescue" are particularly funny?

3. Why does Miss Folgil consider Ruth to be the perfect guinea pig for the lifesaving course?

4. Reread Ruth's description of being helped into Eileen's middy blouse (page 43). How does this passage prepare you for Ruth's underwater struggle with the middy?

5. Why does Ruth agree to be the guinea pig for the lesson on struggling?

6. Ruth expects a "fair fight" from Maybelle Anne. **a.** What kind of fight do you think she considers "fair"? **b.** What is "unfair" about Maybelle Anne's methods?

7a. Although Ruth says that she was nearly drowned on several occasions, how do you know that she is a good swimmer? **b.** How does this knowledge make the story even funnier?

Focus on Reading

Recognizing Humor in Situations

"Guinea Pig" begins like a serious story about a near-fatal accident: "I was nearly drowned, in my youth. . . ." Before you are midway through the first sentence, however, you realize that the author is going to treat the subject humorously. After all, who ever heard of being drowned by a Lifesaving Examiner, an expert in saving lives? And what a reward for serving a noble cause—a black eye! These unlikely events are surprising and funny.

Some of the funniest situations in the story occur when people's intentions misfire. Instead of helping, a character ends up hindering. Instead of winning, a character winds up losing. How is this humor shown when Eileen attempts to help Ruth back into the rowboat? How do Ruth's plans for Maybelle Anne misfire?

Some of the situations in the story are funny because they are exaggerated. Reread the description of the underwater test on page 43. Which details in this test are particularly silly?

You often enjoy a comic situation more if you know that it is coming. Before Ruth appears for the test, you know that she will have trouble with the middy blouse. How do you know that Maybelle Anne has some surprises in store for Ruth?

Language and Vocabulary

Analyzing Words with *dis-*

Many words in our language are made up of individual elements or parts. For example, the word **disagreeable** has three parts. The **root,** or main part of the word, is *agree*. The part that follows the root, *-able*, is a **suffix** that means "capable of" or "tending to." The part

46 REFLECTIONS

CLOSURE

Have students describe two of the episodes where Ruth was persuaded to do something that she had at first hesitated to do.

EXTENSION AND ENRICHMENT

Have students consider that maybe Miss Folgil was not such a bad person. How would she see her student, Ruth? How would Eileen describe Miss Folgil's "rescue" of Ruth? How would this point of view affect the story?

---

that stands in front of the root, *dis-*, is a **prefix** meaning "not" or "the lack of" or "the opposite of." When you put these meanings together, you get the definition of *disagreeable*: "not tending to agree." Ruth thinks Maybelle Anne is disagreeable because she is hard to get along with.

You can sometimes figure out the meaning of an unfamiliar word by analyzing its structure. Using the definitions of the prefix *dis-* given above, work out the meanings of the following words. Then check your answers in a dictionary.

| discontent | displease | disservice |
| disorder | disregard | disunion |

Focus on Personal Narrative

Telling an Anecdote

An **anecdote** is a very short story with a simple, usually amusing point. Ruth McKenney's story "Guinea Pig" contains a number of anecdotes about the narrator's experiences with lifesaving.

Most people love to laugh, and you've probably heard dozens of funny anecdotes from family members and friends. Make some notes now for a humorous anecdote about an event in your own experience. Here are some guidelines to help you prepare your anecdote:

1. Use your own point of view, with the pronouns *I, me, my,* and so on.
2. Tell the events in chronological (or time) order.
3. Try to end with a punch line: a joke, a clever saying, or an unexpected event.

After making your notes, practice telling your anecdote aloud. Then get together with a small group of classmates and trade anecdotes. After all the group members have told their anecdotes, hold a brief discussion. Offer your classmates suggestions about ways to make their anecdotes clearer, funnier, or more interesting. Save your notes.

About the Author

Ruth McKenney (1911–1972)

Ruth McKenney was an American writer, best known for the humorous family sketches she wrote for *The New Yorker*, collected and published in 1938 as *My Sister Eileen*. This book was the source for a hit play, a musical, and a movie. It was followed by *The McKenneys Carry On* (1940), *Loud Red Patrick* (1947), and *All About Eileen* (1952). "Guinea Pig" is one of the most popular selections from *My Sister Eileen*.

LANGUAGE AND VOCABULARY

1. Suggested answers:
discontent: unhappiness, unrest.
disorder: mess or confusion.
displease: annoy or irritate.
disregard: pay no attention to.
disservice: harmful act.
disunion: lack of unity.

FOCUS ON PERSONAL NARRATIVE

You may want to remind students to have a particular audience in mind when preparing their anecdotes. What is interesting and amusing to one group may not be to another.

ABOUT THE AUTHOR

The McKenneys Carry On and *Loud Red Patrick* also deal with McKenney's family. She also wrote nonfiction, including *Industrial Valley* (1939), about labor problems in Akron, Ohio.

Guinea Pig 47

OBJECTIVES

The overall aim is for students to identify the tongue-in-cheek humor and comic exaggeration Twain uses throughout the story. For a complete list of objectives, see the **Teacher's Notes**.

VOCABULARY

The underlined words are in the Glossary. The **Language and Vocabulary** exercise on pp. 52–53 of the textbook gives students practice in determining the meanings of words from their context.

FOCUS / MOTIVATION

Ask students to name young characters from books, television, and movies who have talked their way out of "sticky" situations. Explain that Tom Sawyer was one of the original fast-talkers.

TEACHING RESOURCES A

Teacher's Notes, p. 79
Reading Check, p. 82
Study Guide, p. 83
Building Vocabulary, p. 85
Selection Vocabulary Test, p. 87
Selection Test, p. 88

AV RESOURCES BINDER

Audiocassette 1, Side A

PREREADING FOCUS

The headnote emphasizes the use of exaggeration for comic effect. Ask students to invent (perhaps in groups) and tell to the rest of the class a brief story or anecdote in which they exaggerate to create humor.

The Cat and the Pain Killer

1
"Secret troubles": Tom and Huckleberry Finn have witnessed graveyard murder by Injun Joe.

2
Conflict. Tom tries to pretend he does not care, but he is clearly lovesick over Becky.

3
Use to answer **study question 1**, p. 50.

4
Irony. Word of the existence of a new medicine puts Aunt Polly into a "fever."

5
Various forms of pseudo-medicine were popular in the nineteenth century.

6
Characterization. Aunt Polly's innocence makes her gullible.

48

The Cat and the Pain Killer

MARK TWAIN

Mark Twain is generally thought to be one of the greatest humorists this country has produced. Note how he uses comic exaggeration in this excerpt from The Adventures of Tom Sawyer.

One of the reasons why Tom's mind had drifted away from its secret troubles was that it had found a new and weighty matter to interest itself about. Becky Thatcher had stopped coming to school. Tom had struggled with his pride a few days and tried to "whistle her down the wind,"¹ but failed. He began to find himself hanging around her father's house, nights, and feeling very miserable. She was ill. What if she should die! There was distraction in the thought. He no longer took an interest in war, nor even in piracy. The charm of life was gone; there was nothing but dreariness left. He put his hoop away, and his bat; there was no joy in them any more. His aunt was concerned. She began to try all manner of remedies on him. She was one of those people who are infatuated with patent medicines and all newfangled methods of producing health or mending it. She was an inveterate² experimenter in these things. When something fresh in this line came out she was in a fever, right away, to try it, not on herself, for she was never ailing, but on anybody else that came handy. She was a subscriber for all the "Health" periodicals and phrenological frauds;³ and the solemn ignorance they were inflated with was breath to her nostrils. All the "rot" they contained about ventilation, and how to go to bed, and how to get up, and what to eat, and what to drink, and how much exercise to take, and what frame of mind to keep one's self in, and what sort of clothing to wear, was all gospel to her, and she never observed that her health journals of the current month customarily upset everything they had recommended the month before. She was as simple-hearted and honest as the day was long, and so she was an easy victim. She gathered together her quack periodicals and her quack medicines, and thus armed with death, went about on her pale horse, metaphorically speaking,⁴ with "hell following after." But she never suspected that she was

---

1. **"whistle . . . wind":** forget about her.
2. **inveterate** (ĭn-vĕt′ər-ĭt): habitual.

3. **phrenological** (frĕn′ə-lŏj′ĭk-əl) **frauds:** claims that studying the bumps on a person's skull could reveal character, intelligence, and temperament.
4. **metaphorically** (mĕt′ə-fôr′ĭk-lē) **speaking:** to use a comparison. Twain humorously compares Aunt Polly to Death, who traditionally rides a pale horse. He is referring to a passage in the Bible (Revelation 6:8).

48 REFLECTIONS

MOTIVATIONAL SUMMARY

Tom Sawyer is a very active and imaginative boy, usually up to some mischief. He has just discovered the wonders of girls, particularly Becky Thatcher, and when she is ill and out of school for a few days, he finds his old pursuits have lost their attraction. His Aunt Polly decides that Tom must be ill. Being fond of medical experimentation, she welcomes the opportunity to try out her latest discovery, a patent-medicine pain killer she thinks just might cure him.

PRESENTATION

The Adventures of Tom Sawyer by Mark Twain is an episodic novel relating the exploits of the title **character.** The two main **plots,** involving the murderous Injun Joe and Tom's romance with Becky Thatcher, are interspersed with entertain-

VISUAL CONNECTIONS

About the Artist

Norman Rockwell (1894–1978) depicted nostalgic and somewhat idealized scenes from American life. It is estimated that more people have seen his work than have viewed the art of Michelangelo, Rembrandt, and Picasso combined. He illustrated 317 covers for the *Saturday Evening Post* magazine between 1916 and 1973, and a Rockwell cover could add an extra 50,000–75,000 copies in sales.

When Rockwell, a stickler for authenticity, illustrated editions of *Tom Sawyer* and of *The Adventures of Huckleberry Finn,* he traveled from his home in Massachusetts to Hannibal, Missouri, the site of Twain's boyhood, making sketches of the area and buying costumes of the period depicted in the novels.

Critics are sharply divided on the merits of his work. Some criticize his sentimental portraits of middle-class America. A few claim that ideas for his illustrations came not from him, but from editors. Defenders praise his technical ability and the power of his work to affect the emotions of millions of people.

Exploring the Subject

The Adventures of Tom Sawyer is an idyllic and nostalgic account of boyhood in Missouri, written in the popular "local color," regionalist tradition. Generally considered Twain's best book except for *Huckleberry Finn,* the tale of a mischievous but basically "good" boy retains its popularity with juvenile and adult audiences.

A scene from *The Adventures of Tom Sawyer,* illustrated around 1936 by Norman Rockwell (1894–1978).

The Cat and the Pain Killer

ing subplots of which "The Cat and the Pain Killer" is one. Tom Sawyer is a romantic who dreams of piracy and buried treasure, and his extreme case of lovesickness is but another manifestation of his dramatic tendencies.

MEETING INDIVIDUAL NEEDS

ESL/LEP • Tom's dialect may prove difficult for students to understand. Select several of Tom's statements from the story and write them on the chalkboard. As a whole-class activity, discuss how the sentences would be written if Tom used standard grammar. Write students' suggestions for grammatically correct versions of the sentences on the chalkboard.

---

7 Finding Details
What humorous exaggeration does Twain use in his description of Aunt Polly's water treatment? She "drowned him," "brought him to" (supposedly from unconsciousness), and "sweated his soul clean."

8
Irony. Aunt Polly's regimen worsens Tom's condition instead of curing him.

9
Tom's indifference is a result of melancholic stupor, so painful that he ignores the "persecution" of his aunt's cures.

10
Irony. In her attempt to cure him, Aunt Polly has finally caused Tom a pain so great that she has "broken up" his "indifference."

11
Sid is Tom's brother; in Aunt Polly's eyes, he is a paragon.

12
Tom pours medicine in a crack in the floor.

13
Tom pretends the cat understands him and is begging for the medicine.

14
Twain uses exaggerated, humorous descriptions of the cat's reactions: "war whoop," "frenzy of enjoyment," "unappeasable happiness."

---

not an angel of healing and the balm of Gilead[5] in disguise, to the suffering neighbors.

7 The water treatment was new, now, and Tom's low condition was a windfall to her. She had him out at daylight every morning, stood him up in the woodshed and drowned him with a deluge of cold water; then she scrubbed him down with a towel like a file, and so brought him to; then she rolled him up in a wet sheet and put him away under blankets till she sweated his soul clean and "the yellow stains of it came through his pores"—as Tom said.

8 Yet notwithstanding all this, the boy grew more and more melancholy and pale and dejected. She added hot baths, sitz baths,[6] shower baths, and plunges. The boy remained as dismal as a hearse. She began to assist the water with a slim oatmeal diet and blister plasters. She calculated his capacity as she would a jug's, and filled him up every day with quack cure-alls.

Tom had become indifferent to persecution by this time. This phase filled the old lady's **9** heart with consternation.[7] This indifference must be broken up at any cost. Now she heard of Pain Killer for the first time. She ordered a lot at once. She tasted it and was filled with gratitude. It was simply fire in a liquid form. She dropped the water treatment and everything else and pinned her faith to Pain Killer. **10** She gave Tom a teaspoonful and watched with the deepest anxiety for the result. Her troubles were instantly at rest, her soul at peace again, for the "indifference" was broken up. The boy could not have shown a wilder, heartier interest if she had built a fire under him.

Tom felt that it was time to wake up; this sort of life might be romantic enough, in his blighted condition, but it was getting to have too little sentiment and too much distracting variety about it. So he thought over various plans for relief and finally hit upon that of professing to be fond of Pain Killer. He asked for it so often that he became a nuisance, and his aunt ended by telling him to help himself and quit bothering her. If it had been Sid, she would have had no misgivings to alloy her delight, but since it was Tom, she watched the **12** bottle clandestinely.[8] She found that the medicine did really diminish, but it did not occur to her that the boy was mending the health of a crack in the sitting-room floor with it.

One day Tom was in the act of dosing the crack when his aunt's yellow cat came along, **13** purring, eyeing the teaspoon avariciously, and begging for a taste. Tom said:

"Don't ask for it unless you want it, Peter."

But Peter signified that he did want it.

"You better make sure."

Peter was sure.

"Now you've asked for it, and I'll give it to you, because there ain't anything mean about *me*; but if you find you don't like it, you mustn't blame anybody but your own self."

Peter was agreeable. So Tom pried his mouth open and poured down the Pain Killer. **14** Peter sprang a couple of yards in the air and then delivered a war whoop and set off round and round the room, banging against furniture, upsetting flowerpots, and making general havoc. Next he rose on his hind feet and pranced around, in a frenzy of enjoyment, with his head over his shoulder and his voice proclaiming his unappeasable[9] happiness. Then he went tearing around the house again spreading chaos and destruction in his path.

---

5. **balm** (bäm) **of Gilead** (gĭl′ē-əd): a reference to a passage in Jeremiah 8:22. In ancient times, the people of Gilead, a region in what is now Jordan, produced balm, an ointment used for healing.
6. **sitz** (sĭts) **baths:** baths taken sitting in shallow water.
7. **consternation** (kŏn′stər-nā′shən): alarm.

8. **clandestinely** (klăn-dĕs′tən-lē): secretly.
9. **unappeasable** (ŭn′ə-pēz′əb-əl): not capable of being reduced or quieted.

READING SKILLS PRACTICE
The underlined passage can be used to give students practice in the reading skill of identifying the main idea. Ask students to read the passage and choose the answer that is accurate and also encompasses the most important details.

A. Tom is sorry that he gave the medicine to the cat. (Unsupported by information in the passage.) **B.** Tom unrepentantly suggests that the medicine was good for the cat. (Correct.) **C.** Peter does not blame Tom for giving him the medicine. (Unsupported by information in the selection.) **D.** Tom accuses his aunt of trying to make him sick. (Contradicted by information in the selection.)

Aunt Polly entered in time to see him throw a few double somersaults, deliver a final mighty hurrah, and sail through the open window, carrying the rest of the flowerpots with him. The old lady stood petrified with astonishment, peering over her glasses; Tom lay on the floor expiring with laughter.

15 "Tom, what on earth ails that cat?"

"*I* don't know, Aunt," gasped the boy.

"Why, I never see anything like it. What *did* make him act so?"

"'Deed I don't know, Aunt Polly; cats always act so when they're having a good time."

"They do, do they?" There was something in the tone that made Tom <u>apprehensive</u>.

"Yes'm. That is, I believe they do."

"You *do*?"

"Yes'm."

16 The old lady was bending down, Tom watching, with interest emphasized by anxiety. Too late he <u>divined</u> her "drift." The handle of the telltale teaspoon was visible under the bed valance.[10] Aunt Polly took it, held it up. Tom winced and dropped his eyes. Aunt Polly raised him by the usual handle—his ear—and cracked his head soundly with her thimble.

"Now, sir, what did you want to treat that poor dumb beast so for?"

"I done it out of pity for him—because he hadn't any aunt."

"Hadn't any aunt!—you numskull. What has that got to do with it?"

17 "Heaps. Because if he'd 'a' had one she'd 'a' burnt him out herself! She'd 'a' roasted his bowels out of him 'thout any more feeling than if he was a human!"

Aunt Polly felt a sudden pang of remorse. This was putting the thing in a new light; what was cruelty to a cat *might* be cruelty to a boy, too. She began to soften; she felt sorry. Her eyes watered a little, and she put her hand on Tom's head and said gently:

"I was meaning for the best, Tom. And, Tom, it *did* do you good."

18 ▶ Tom looked up in her face with just a perceptible twinkle peeping through his gravity:[11]

"I know you was meaning for the best, Auntie, and so was I with Peter. It done *him* good, too. I never see him get around so since——" ◀

"Oh, go 'long with you, Tom, before you aggravate me again. And you try and see if you can't be a good boy, for once, and you needn't take any more medicine."

Tom reached school ahead of time. It was noticed that this strange thing had been occurring every day latterly. And now, as usual of **19** late, he hung about the gate of the schoolyard instead of playing with his comrades. He was sick, he said, and he looked it. He tried to seem to be looking everywhere but whither he really **20** was looking—down the road. Presently Jeff Thatcher hove in sight,[12] and Tom's face lighted; he gazed a moment, and then turned sorrowfully away. When Jeff arrived, Tom <u>accosted</u> him and "led up" <u>warily</u> to opportunities for remarks about Becky, but the giddy lad never could see the bait. Tom watched and **21** watched, hoping whenever a frisking frock came in sight, and hating the owner of it as soon as he saw she was not the right one. At last frocks ceased to appear, and he dropped hopelessly into the dumps; he entered the empty schoolhouse and sat down to suffer. Then one more frock passed in at the gate, **22** and Tom's heart gave a great bound. The next instant he was out and "going on," like an Indian; yelling, laughing, chasing boys, jumping over the fence at risk of life and limb, throwing

---

10. **valance** (văl'əns): drapery hanging from the edge of the bed.
11. **gravity:** here, seriousness.
12. **hove in sight:** came into view, like a ship on the horizon.

15
Aunt Polly's medication has, ironically, caused the cat's "ailment."

16
Inference. Aunt Polly, seeing the medicine spoon, has guessed correctly that Tom dosed the cat.

17
Tom's outburst is humorous; reverses the idea of treating a human with no more feeling than an animal; makes Aunt Polly feel guilty for having given the pain killer to Tom.

18
Twinkle in his eye, followed by pretended innocent comment, shows he is teasing his aunt.

19 Drawing Conclusions
Why does Tom hang around the schoolyard gate? He is waiting for Becky Thatcher to come to school.

20
Tom's joy ends as soon as he realizes Becky is not with Jeff, her brother.

21
Figurative Language. "Frisking frock" here means a girl; refers to a girl's short, petticoat-stiff dress which bounces energetically as she walks.

22
Tom's lovesickness is instantly cured when he sees Becky. His actions humorously parallel the cat's reactions to the Pain Killer.

The Cat and the Pain Killer

HEALTH LINK
During the time of Twain's story, many kinds of unusual patent medicines, folk remedies, and medical quackery abounded. Students might be interested in finding out about the health concerns of the people and the therapies used during the time the story was written (1876).

> **TRANSPARENCY 4**
> **Literary Elements**
> *Plot* – explores a specific sequence of events that make up the plot of a narrative.

23 Analyzing
Even though Becky does not look directly at Tom, how can you tell that she is very conscious of his actions? He is so boisterous that it is impossible not to be aware of them (he is yelling, jumping, and so on); her comment, made with nose in the air and after turning away from Tom, is nevertheless clearly directed at him.

READING CHECK
1. He loses interest in toys and games (p. 46).
2. Pouring cold water over Tom, scrubbing with towel, rolling in wet sheet, putting under blankets to sweat (p. 48).
3. Pours it down crack in floor (p. 48).
4. Sees teaspoon sticking out under bed (p. 49).
5. Becky Thatcher returns to school (p. 49).

FOR STUDY AND DISCUSSION
1. Loses interest in war and piracy, hangs around Becky's house, finds all charm of life gone.
2a. It causes greater pain. 2b. It rouses him out of melancholy.
3. Sees she was treating Tom as Tom was treating cat, although she had good intentions.
4. Yells, laughs, chases boys, stands on head, does handsprings.
5a. Feels his display is far more impressive than an unmanly declaration. 5b. Probably not. Her remarks show she did not ignore him.

---

handsprings, standing on his head—doing all the heroic things he could conceive of, and keeping a furtive eye out, all the while, to see if Becky Thatcher was noticing. But she seemed to be unconscious of it all; she never looked. **23** Could it be possible that she was not aware that he was there? He carried his exploits to her immediate vicinity, came war-whooping around, snatched a boy's cap, hurled it to the roof of the schoolhouse, broke through a group of boys, tumbling them in every direction, and fell sprawling, himself, under Becky's nose, almost upsetting her—and she turned, with her nose in the air, and he heard her say: "Mf! Some people think they're mighty smart—always showing off!"

Tom's cheeks burned. He gathered himself up and sneaked off, crushed and crestfallen.

Reading Check

1. Why does Tom's aunt become concerned about him?
2. What is the "water treatment"?
3. How does Tom secretly get rid of the medicine?
4. How does Aunt Polly find out that Tom has given the cat his medicine?
5. What finally cures Tom of his melancholy?

For Study and Discussion

Analyzing and Interpreting the Selection

1. Tom's condition might be described as "lovesickness." What are his symptoms?

2. A pain killer is supposed to relieve pain. **a.** What is unusual about the Pain Killer in this story? **b.** In what way is it "good" for Tom?

3. Tom's explanation of his treatment of Peter makes Aunt Polly see her own treatment of Tom in a "new light." Why does Aunt Polly suddenly become gentle with Tom?

4. Tom recovers as soon as Becky Thatcher returns to school. How does he show that he is cured?

5a. Why do you suppose Tom doesn't tell Becky that he is glad to see her? **b.** Do you believe Becky is really annoyed by Tom's behavior? Give reasons to support your answers.

Language and Vocabulary

Getting Meaning from Context

When you come across an unfamiliar word in your reading, you may be able to work out its meaning by looking at the **context**, that is, the

52 REFLECTIONS

CLOSURE
Ask students to give examples of the tongue-in-cheek humor used throughout the story. Also, ask them to identify examples of Twain's comic exaggeration.

EXTENSION AND ENRICHMENT
Some students may enjoy performing readers' theater presentations of selected scenes. Others may want to read *The Adventures of Tom Sawyer* and report to the class.

---

sentence or paragraph in which the word appears. You can probably guess the meaning of *avariciously* from its use in this sentence:

> One day Tom was in the act of dosing the crack when his aunt's yellow cat came along, purring, eyeing the teaspoon *avariciously*, and begging for a taste.

1 The word *avariciously* means "greedily." What other words in the sentence give clues to this meaning?

Look at the passage on page 50 in which Twain describes Peter's reaction to Pain Killer.
2 Can you guess the meaning of the words *havoc* and *chaos* from the context? Check your an-
3 swers in the glossary. How close did you come
4 to the precise meanings of these words? What is the difference in meaning between them?

Focus on Personal Narrative

Using Vivid Action Verbs

In "The Cat and the Pain Killer," Mark Twain uses **vivid action verbs** to bring the narrative to life. Look at the last paragraph on page 50, beginning "Peter was agreeable." Here are some of the vivid verbs that describe Peter's reaction: *sprang, banging, upsetting, pranced, proclaiming, tearing, spreading, throw, sail*.

Write a paragraph in which you describe an action-filled event from your own life. For example, you might choose a sports event, a family outing, or an event involving a pet. Use as many vivid action verbs as you can. Save your writing.

About the Author

Mark Twain (1835–1910)

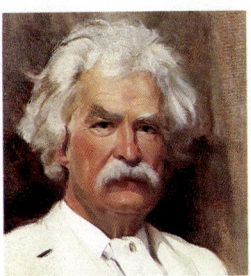

You may know that Mark Twain was the pen name of Samuel Langhorne Clemens. He began using the name Mark Twain after working as a steamboat pilot on the Mississippi River. He took the name from a cry of the riverboatmen, "By the mark, twain!" This cry meant that the depth of the river was two fathoms (twelve feet or about four meters), a depth that was safe for the riverboats.

Twain grew up in Hannibal, Missouri, a small town on the Mississippi River. Many of his own experiences as a boy are re-created in *The Adventures of Tom Sawyer* and *Adventures of Huckleberry Finn*, two of the best-known and best-loved books in American literature. When Twain was twelve, his father died. He had to leave school and go to work. After working for five years as a printer's apprentice, he left Missouri to see the world. He spent the next four years as an apprentice to a steamboat pilot. He later wrote about his experiences as a cub pilot in *Life on the Mississippi*.

When the Civil War broke out, he headed west and supported himself by writing for newspapers. Much of Twain's writing grew out of his experiences in the West. Some of his best stories are tall tales of the frontier, such as "The Notorious Jumping Frog of Calaveras County." A number of humorous sketches about life in mining camps are contained in *Roughing It*, an autobiographical account of his years in the West. As his writing became well known, he began to give lecture tours throughout America and abroad, entertaining audiences with his wonderful stories.

The Cat and the Pain Killer

LANGUAGE AND VOCABULARY

1. Clues to meaning of *avariciously*: "purring," "eyeing," "begging."
2. Clues to meaning of *havoc*: "sprang," "war whoop," "banging," "upsetting." Clues to meaning of *chaos*: "pranced," "frenzy," "unappeasable," "destruction."
3. Precise meaning of *havoc*: n., wide and general destruction. Precise meaning of *chaos*: n., utter confusion.
4. Difference in meaning: *havoc* can occur in orderly fashion, without confusion; *chaos* can occur without any destruction taking place.

FOCUS ON PERSONAL NARRATIVE
You may want to encourage students to use thesauruses to find appropriate synonyms for overused verbs. In addition, students could read each other's paragraphs and offer suggestions for additional vivid action verbs.

ABOUT THE AUTHOR
Mark Twain led an exciting life even before he established himself as an author. He was raised in Hannibal, Missouri on the Mississippi River, and so came into contact with riverboat men, circus performers, minstrel show performers, and other colorful characters. He worked on newspapers in St. Louis, New York, and Philadelphia, and for six years was a river pilot on the Mississippi. For a few weeks he was in the Confederate Army and then joined the gold rush in Nevada and California. In 1867, the same year he published his first book, he journeyed to France, Italy, Turkey, Greece, and the Holy Land. His humorous account of this trip to old world Europe, published as *Innocents Abroad* (1869), quickly sold 150,000 copies and established his career as a writer.

OBJECTIVES

The overall aim is for students to demonstrate an understanding of the **theme** of "Tableau." For a complete list of objectives, see the Teacher's Notes.

VOCABULARY

The underlined words are in the Glossary. Encourage students to notice the use of words that reflect the **themes** of prejudice and friendship.

FOCUS / MOTIVATION

Ask students if they know of a friendship that survived although family or friends might have warned against it. Tell students that the two boys in the poem are friends although the people around them do not approve.

TEACHING RESOURCES A
Teacher's Notes, p. 89
Reading Check, p. 91
Study Guide, p. 93
Selection Test, p. 97

PREREADING FOCUS

The headnote defines *tableau* and explains why the author chose this title. You may want to have students predict what kind of dramatic scene or picture they think the poet might portray.

Tableau

1

Metaphor. Compares white boy to beauty of sunny day and black boy to beauty of deep, clear night.

2 Making Inferences

Why are boys unaware of people's stares and comments about their friendship? They may be too young to be aware of racial prejudice. To them, their friendship is perfectly natural.

3

Metaphor. Compares boys' friendship to lightning, which comes before thunder of opposition—people's opposition to their friendship.

FOR STUDY AND DISCUSSION

1. The white boy and the black boy.
2. The boys are "opposite" in color, but they still share a close relationship.
3. Responses will include "lowered blinds," "dark folk stare," "fair folk talk," "Indignant," and "dare."
4. The boys' friendship is compared to brilliant lightning that precedes the thunder of opposition.

54

Tableau

(for Donald Duff)

COUNTEE° CULLEN

Tableau (tă-blō′) is a French word meaning "a striking or dramatic scene or picture." This poem paints a picture of two boys. The poem also points out how friendship overcomes racial prejudice.

Locked arm in arm they cross the way,
    The black boy and the white,
1 The golden splendor of the day,
    The sable pride of night.

From lowered blinds the dark folk stare,   5
    And here the fair folk talk,
Indignant that these two should dare
    In unison to walk.

2 Oblivious to look and word
    They pass, and see no wonder   10
3 That lightning brilliant as a sword
    Should blaze the path of thunder.

°**Countee** (coun′tā).

For Study and Discussion

Analyzing and Interpreting the Poem

1. Who is Cullen referring to in lines 3–4?

2. While "night" and "day" are opposites, they share a close relationship to one another. Why is this an important idea in the poem?

3. What words in the second stanza tell us that people who observe them together do not approve of the friendship between the two boys?

4. Which images in the last stanza highlight the importance and dramatic nature of the event described in the poem?

Writing About Literature

Interpreting a Poem

In a short essay give your interpretation of "Tableau." Consider how the themes of prejudice and friendship are treated in the poem. Support your interpretation with evidence from the poem.

54 REFLECTIONS

PRESENTATION
Write the word *prejudice* on the board and ask students to provide a definition. Lead them to understand that *prejudice* is "mistrust or irrational hatred of other groups such as races, religions, and occupations."

Although Countee Cullen's poem focuses on prejudice, it shows friendship rising above the suspicion and hatred. The poem's **rhythm** and **rhyme** invite oral reading.

CLOSURE
Ask students to discuss the meaning of Countee Cullen's poem "Tableau." Encourage students to support their discussion with words or lines from the poem.

The Wall (1989) by Hughie Lee-Smith. Oil on canvas, 36 x 40 in.

VISUAL CONNECTIONS
About the Artist
Hughie Lee-Smith's (1915–) childhood interest in art has led to a celebrated career. He was educated at Wayne State University, the Cleveland Institute of Art, the Art School of the Detroit Society of Arts and Crafts, and the John Huntington Polytechnic Institute. He often paints ghetto environments, with one or two figures like the one shown here. Although these works may seem to suggest desolation, Lee-Smith often instills optimism into the paintings with the addition of balloons or waving banners. In *The Wall* the unity of the two figures walking in the sunlight suggests solidarity against the isolation of the concrete wall.

WRITING ABOUT LITERATURE
Before students write, you may want to discuss with them some of the poetic devices used in the poem. Review **rhythm**, **rhyme**, **metaphor**, and **simile** and discuss with students how these devices affect the **themes** in the poem.

ABOUT THE AUTHOR
Countee Cullen focused on the life of black Americans without emphasizing dialect or stereotypes. In addition to his volumes of poetry, his works include a novel dealing with life in Harlem, *One Way to Heaven* (1931).

About the Author

Countee Cullen (1903–1946)

Countee Cullen's place of birth is unknown. It may have been Louisville, Kentucky, although he often claimed either New York City or Baltimore as his birthplace. He was probably the most popular poet of the Harlem Renaissance, a movement during the 1920s in which African American urban artists began to find their voices. Cullen believed that art had no racial boundaries. Although most of his poetry stems from racial issues, he wanted to be remembered as a poet, not just a black poet.

Cullen received his M.A. from Harvard in 1926, and in 1928 he was awarded a Guggenheim Fellowship to write poetry in France. He produced his best work while still in his twenties, and his several collections of poetry include *Color* (1925), *The Black Christ and Other Poems* (1929), and *On These I Stand* (1947). In his poetry Cullen adhered to a traditional style of careful meter and rhyme.

Tableau 55

OBJECTIVES
The overall aim is for students to demonstrate an understanding of the characters' motivation for their actions. For a complete list of objectives, see the **Teacher's Notes**.

VOCABULARY
The underlined words are in the Glossary. In addition, call students' attention to the vocabulary footnotes in their textbooks.

FOCUS / MOTIVATION
Ask students to think of fights or disagreements they have had. What caused the fights? Who started them? What was the outcome? Tell students that although the boys in the story fight, they do become friends.

TEACHING RESOURCES A
Teacher's Notes, p. 98
Reading Check, p. 101
Study Guide, p. 102
Building Vocabulary, p. 105
Selection Vocabulary Test, p. 109
Selection Test, p. 111

AV RESOURCES BINDER
Audiocassette 1, Side A

PREREADING FOCUS
The headnote identifies the **setting** of the story and discusses the rivalry that results when two boys from different regions meet. Ask students to discuss an experience in which they or someone they know befriended a rival.

The Fight

1
Metaphor. Compares year to object thrown into air. Height of summer is hottest time, and it is compared to highest point of object's flight.

2
In British and Indian usage, a *vest* is a man's sleeveless undershirt.

3
Personification. Compares day to a person who has been working hard in heat.

4
Personification. Desert town needs water in same way thirsty person does.

5
Tone. Narrator uses "threw off" and "leapt" to show Ranji's excitement at finding a place to swim.

6 Analyzing
What does "quench" suggest? That heat makes Ranji's whole body thirsty.

The Fight

RUSKIN BOND

This story takes place in Rajpur (räj'pōor) in northwestern India near the border of Pakistan. Look at a map and see if you can locate the setting of the story. Rivalry between different states is common in India. The two boys in the story consider themselves enemies because they come from different regions. Like many quarrels, this one has nothing to do with the two boys personally. Read to discover how these two, born as enemies, find a way to share and become friends.

Ranji[1] had been less than a month in Rajpur when he discovered the pool in the forest. It was the height of summer, and his school had not yet opened; and, having as yet made no friends in this semi-hill-station,[2] he wandered about a good deal by himself into the hills and forests that stretched away interminably on all sides of the town. It was hot, very hot, at that time of the year, and Ranji walked about in his vest and shorts, his brown feet white with the chalky dust that flew up from the ground. The earth was parched, the grass brown, the trees listless, hardly stirring, waiting for a cool wind or a refreshing shower of rain.

It was on such a day—a hot, tired day—that Ranji found the pool in the forest. The water had a gentle translucency, and you could see the smooth round pebbles at the bottom of the pool. A small stream emerged from a cluster of rocks to feed the pool. During the monsoon,[3] this stream would be a gushing torrent, cascading down from the hills, but during the summer it was barely a trickle. The rocks, however, held the water in the pool, and it did not dry up like the pools in the plains.

When Ranji saw the pool, he did not hesitate to get into it. He had often gone swimming, alone or with friends, when he had lived with his parents in a thirsty town in the middle of the Rajputana[4] desert. There, he had known only sticky, muddy pools, where buffaloes wallowed and women washed clothes. He had never seen a pool like this—so clean and cold and inviting. He threw off all his clothes, as he had done when he went swimming in the plains, and leapt into the water. His limbs were supple, free of any fat, and his dark body glistened in patches of sunlit water.

The next day he came again to quench his body in the cool waters of the forest pool. He was there for almost an hour, sliding in and out of the limpid green water, or lying stretched out on the smooth yellow rocks in the shade of broad-leaved *sal* trees. It was while he lay thus, naked on a rock, that he noticed another boy standing a little distance away, staring at him in a rather hostile manner. The other boy was a little older

---

1. **Ranji** (rän'jē).
2. **hill-station:** a government post situated in the hills and used as a health resort during the hot months.
3. **monsoon** (mŏn-sōon'): season of heavy rain.
4. **Rajputana** (räj'pōo-tä'nä): a region in northwest India.

MOTIVATIONAL SUMMARY
New to the village, Ranji spends much of his time alone. One hot day, he discovers a cool, refreshing pool and enjoys a secluded swim. He returns to the pool the next day, but his solitude is interrupted by a boy who claims the pool is his. Unkind words are exchanged as both boys assert their identities. A fight ensues, but neither boy is victorious, so they agree to fight again the next day. What actually takes place the next day makes friends of the two enemies.

PRESENTATION
Ruskin Bond's "The Fight" is a character study of two enemies who become friends. The two boys are quite different, not only in appearance but also in what motivates them. You may want to ask students to make a chart with the two

A fresco painted on a stone mansion in Rajasthan, India, showing a procession of camels, elephants, and horses.

than Ranji, taller, thick-set with a broad nose and thick, red lips. He had only just noticed Ranji, and he stood at the edge of the pool, wearing a pair of bathing shorts, waiting for Ranji to explain himself.

7 When Ranji did not say anything, the other called out, "What are you doing here, Mister?"

Ranji, who was prepared to be friendly, was taken aback at the hostility of the other's tone.

"I am swimming," he replied. "Why don't you join me?"

8 "I always swim alone," said the other. "This is my pool, I did not invite you here. And why are you not wearing any clothes?"

9 "It is not your business if I do not wear clothes. I have nothing to be ashamed of."

"You skinny fellow, put on your clothes."

"Fat fool, take yours off."

This was too much for the stranger to <u>tolerate</u>. He strode up to Ranji, who still sat on the rock and, planting his broad feet firmly on the sand, said (as though this would settle the matter once

10 and for all), "Don't you know I am a Punjabi?⁵ I do not take replies from villagers like you!"

"So you like to fight with villagers?" said Ranji. "Well, I am not a villager: I am a Rajput!"⁶

"I am a Punjabi!"

---
5. **Punjabi** (pŭn-jä′bē): He is from a region in northwest India.
6. **Rajput** (räj′p̄ oot): He is from another region in northwest India.

11 "I am a Rajput!"

They had reached an <u>impasse</u>. One had said he was a Punjabi, the other had <u>proclaimed</u> himself a Rajput. There was little else that could be said.

"You understand that I am a Punjabi?" said the stranger, feeling that perhaps this information had not penetrated Ranji's head.

"I have heard you say it three times," replied Ranji.

"Then why are you not running away?"

"I am waiting for *you* to run away!"

12 "I will have to beat you," said the stranger, assuming a violent attitude, showing Ranji the palm of his hand.

"I am waiting to see you do it," said Ranji.

"You will see me do it," said the other boy.

13 Ranji waited. The other boy made a strange, hissing sound. They stared each other in the eye for almost a minute. Then the Punjabi boy slapped Ranji across the face with all the force he could <u>muster</u>. Ranji staggered, feeling quite dizzy. There were thick red finger-marks on his cheek.

"There you are!" exclaimed his <u>assailant</u>. "Will you be off now?"

For answer, Ranji swung his arm up and pushed a hard, bony fist into the other's face.

14 And then they were at each other's throats, swaying on the rock, tumbling on to the sand, rolling over and over, their legs and arms locked

---

7
Irony. Boy addresses Ranji as "Mister," which is a term of respect, but his hostile tone of voice means he does not respect Ranji.

8 Finding Cause and Effect
Why does boy claim pool is his? He probably thinks he discovered it before Ranji, a stranger to him, did.

9
Ranji tries to be friendly, but he will not let other boy insult him.

10
Boy thinks he is superior to villagers because he is a Punjabi.

11
Ranji lets other boy know he is unimpressed by fact he is a Punjabi.

12 Summarizing
What is Punjabi boy's attitude toward Ranji? That he can easily beat him in a fight.

13 Making Inferences
Why does Punjabi boy make hissing sound? Answers will vary. Some students might say he is trying to frighten Ranji.

14
Style. Narrator uses words ending in *–ing* to emphasize that several things are happening at same time and that everything is happening very quickly.

The Fight 57

15 Analyzing Why does narrator describe fight as "unscientific"? Boys use no plan or method in fight. They just do whatever seems to make sense at moment. **16** Both boys are out of breath from struggle. **17** Each boy is convinced he is superior to other because of where each came from. **18** Punjabi boy implies he chose not to win fight by saying he showed Ranji mercy. **19** Expressing an Opinion Why does Ranji not want to tell his mother about fight? Answers will vary. Mother will disapprove and punish Ranji for fighting, or she will be worried about danger and not allow Ranji to go back to pool. **20** Expressing an Opinion Why do boys not fight at bazaar? Answers will vary. Perhaps boys are too tired to fight, or perhaps they do not want to fight in public for fear of getting into trouble. **21** Ranji thinks fight will have important consequences for rest of his life. **22** Oil Punjabi boy rubs on his skin may not be suntan lotion. He may be using oil to make it harder for Ranji to hold on to him in fight.	headings **Ranji the Rajput** and **Suraj the Punjabi**. As students read the story, ask them to use their charts to jot down notes about each of the boys. Then discuss the boys' similarities and differences. You may want to call students' attention to the author's style. His use of sensory details, figurative language, and realistic dialogue add to the story's appeal.

in a desperate, violent struggle. Gasping and cursing, clawing and slapping, they rolled right into the shallows of the pool.

Even in the water the fight continued as, spluttering and covered with mud, they groped for each other's heads and throats. But after five minutes of frenzied, unscientific struggle, neither boy had emerged victorious. Their bodies heaving with exhaustion, they stood back from each other, making tremendous efforts to speak.

"Now—now do you realize—I am a Punjabi?" gasped the stranger.

"Do you know I am a Rajput?" said Ranji with difficulty.

They gave a moment's consideration to each other's answers, and in that moment of silence there was only their heavy breathing and the rapid beating of their hearts.

"Then you will not leave the pool?" said the Punjabi boy.

"I will not leave it," said Ranji.

"Then we shall have to continue the fight," said the other.

"All right," said Ranji.

But neither boy moved, neither took the initiative.

Then the Punjabi boy had an inspiration.

"We will continue the fight tomorrow," he said. "If you dare to come here again tomorrow, we will continue this fight, and I will not show you mercy as I have done today."

"I will come tomorrow," said Ranji. "I will be ready for you."

They turned from each other then, and going to their respective rocks put on their clothes, and left the forest by different routes.

When Ranji got home, he found it difficult to explain his cuts and bruises that showed on his face, legs and arms. It was difficult to conceal the fact that he had been in an unusually violent fight, and his mother insisted on his staying at home for the rest of the day. That evening, though, he slipped out of the house and went to the bazaar,[7] where he found comfort and solace in a bottle of vividly coloured lemonade and a banana-leaf full of hot, sweet *jalebis*.[8] He had just finished the lemonade when he saw his adversary coming down the road. His first impulse was to turn away and look elsewhere; his second to throw the lemonade bottle at his enemy; but he did neither of these things. Instead, he stood his ground and scowled at his passing adversary. And the Punjabi boy said nothing either but scowled back with equal ferocity.

The next day was as hot as the previous one. Ranji felt weak and lazy and not at all eager for a fight. His body was stiff and sore after the previous day's encounter. But he could not refuse the challenge. Not to turn up at the pool would be an acknowledgement of defeat. From the way he felt just then, he knew he would be beaten in another fight; but he could not acquiesce in his own defeat; he must defy his enemy to the last, or outwit him, for only then could he gain his respect. If he surrendered now, he would be beaten for all time; but to fight and be beaten today left him free to fight and be beaten again. As long as he fought, he had a right to the pool in the forest.

He was half hoping that the Punjabi boy would have forgotten the challenge; but these hopes were dashed when he saw his opponent sitting, stripped to the waist, on a rock on the other side of the pool. The Punjabi boy was rubbing oil on his body, massaging it into his broad thighs. He saw Ranji beneath the *sal* trees, and called a challenge across the waters of the pool.

"Come over on this side, and fight!" he shouted.

But Ranji was not going to submit to any conditions laid down by his opponent.

---

7. **bazaar** (bə-zär′): a market with rows of stalls or shops.
8. *jalebis* (jä-lā′bēz): spangled sweetmeats, made from milk and sugar; very sweet and sticky [author's note].

58 REFLECTIONS

MEETING INDIVIDUAL NEEDS
ESL/LEP • The first part of the story contains four verbs that have been changed to nouns by adding the –*tion* suffix. Can students find them? (information, exhaustion, consideration, inspiration) Did all of the verbs go through the same process in changing from verb to noun? (They did not.) Write the following items on the chalkboard.

inform + *a* + *tion*
exhaust (delete *t*) + *tion*
consider + *a* + *tion*
inspire (delete *e*) + *a* + *tion*

What spelling patterns can students find?

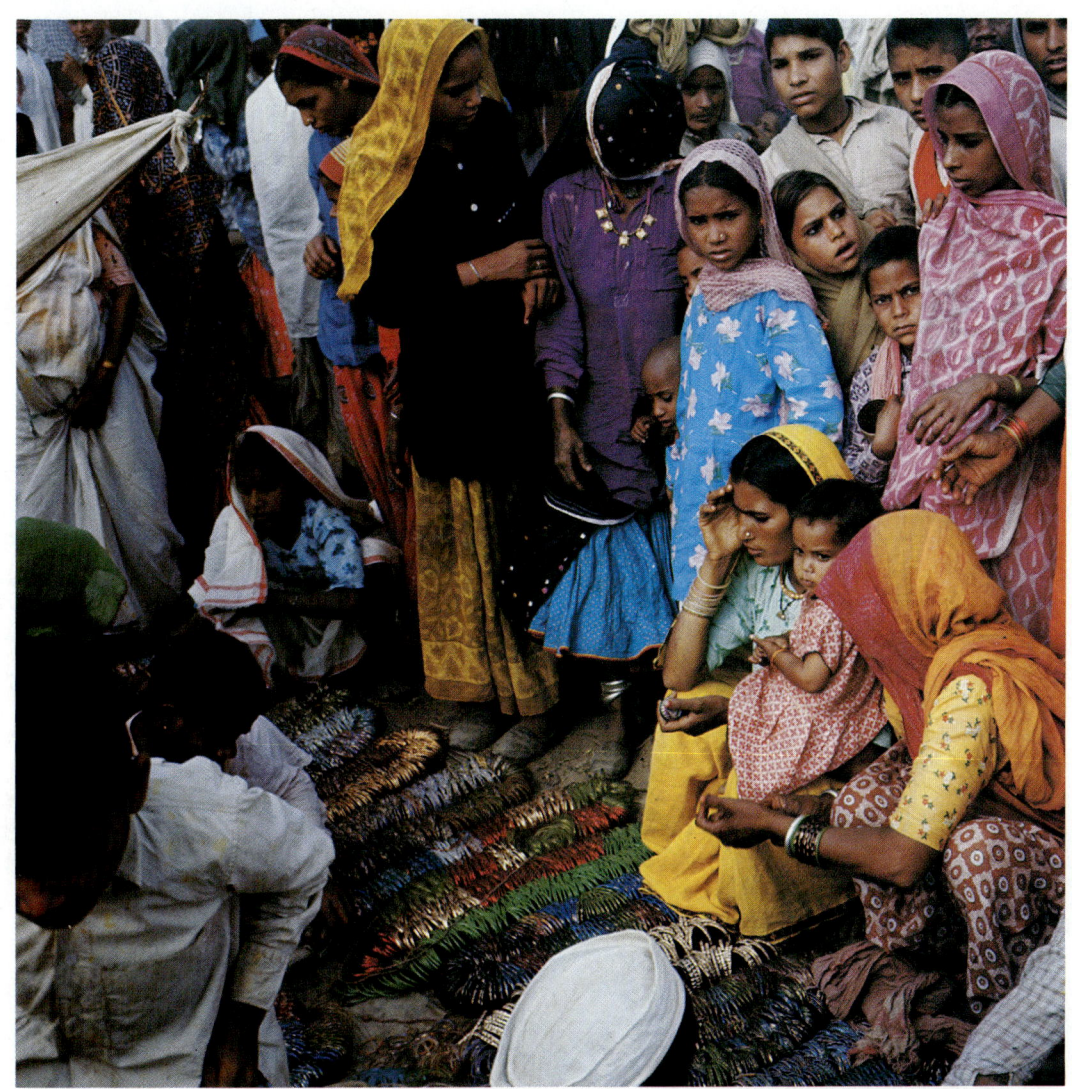

"Come *this* side and fight!" he shouted back with equal vigour.

"Swim across, and fight me here!" called the other. "Or perhaps you cannot swim the length of this pool?"

But Ranji could have swum the length of the pool a dozen times without tiring, and here he would show the Punjabi boy his superiority. So, slipping out of his vest and shorts, he dived straight into the water, cutting through it like a knife, and surfacing with hardly a splash. The Punjabi boy's mouth hung open in amazement.

"You can dive!" he exclaimed.

"It is easy," said Ranji, treading water, waiting for a further challenge. "Can't you dive?"

"No," said the other. "I jump straight in. But

23
Punjabi boy taunts Ranji by implying he cannot swim well.

24
Simile. Compares Ranji's clean dive to a sharp knife cutting through water scarcely disturbing it.

25
Tone. Punjabi boy's attitude changes from hostility to admiration.

26
By admitting he cannot dive, Punjabi boy acknowledges Ranji's superiority.

The Fight 59

PORTFOLIO ASSESSMENT
Pairs of students may want to write a **dialogue** in which two **characters** resolve a **conflict**. Remind the students to identify the speakers and the conflict early in the conversation and to show plausible changes in the characters' behaviors. Review with students how to punctuate quotations and how to appropriately change paragraphs when writing dialogue. Some pairs may want to present their revised dialogues to the class. (See *Portfolio Assessment and Professional Support Materials* for additional information on student portfolios.)

27 Drawing Conclusions
What does exchange about diving imply about how boys feel about one another now? Both boys are now ready to be friends.

28
Simile. Whales spout liquid through a hole in top of their heads. Narrator compares water spurting from boy to liquid spouting from a whale.

29
Simile. Compares boy to a duck feeding under water with its tail feathers stuck in air above surface.

30 Analyzing
Is Ranji frightened by boy's threat to beat him if he does not teach him how to dive and swim? No. Ranji realizes boy wants to be his friend and does not really mean what he says.

31
Ranji realizes his new friend needs to feel superior to him in some way, so he agrees with Suraj that he is strong.

32 Expressing an Opinion
Is it likely Suraj will ever be a world champion wrestler? Answers will vary. Most students will probably think there is not much chance of that happening.

---

if you will tell me how, I will make a dive."

27 "It is easy," said Ranji. "Stand on the rock, stretch your arms out and allow your head to displace your feet."

The Punjabi boy stood up, stiff and straight, stretched out his arms, and threw himself into the water. He landed flat on his belly, with a crash that sent the birds screaming out of the trees.

Ranji dissolved into laughter.

"Are you trying to empty the pool?" he asked, 28 as the Punjabi boy came to the surface, spouting water like a small whale.

"Wasn't it good?" asked the boy, evidently proud of his feat.

"Not very good," said Ranji. "You should have more practice. See, I will do it again."

And pulling himself up on a rock, he executed another perfect dive. The other boy waited for him to come up, but, swimming under water, Ranji circled him and came upon him from behind.

"How did you do that?" asked the astonished youth.

"Can't you swim under water?" asked Ranji.

"No, but I will try it."

The Punjabi boy made a tremendous effort to plunge to the bottom of the pool; and indeed, he 29 thought he had gone right down, though his bottom, like a duck's, remained above the surface.

Ranji, however, did not discourage him.

"It was not bad," he said. "But you need a lot of practice."

"Will you teach me?" asked his enemy.

"If you like, I will teach you."

30 "You must teach me. If you do not teach me, I will beat you. Will you come here every day and teach me?"

"If you like," said Ranji. They had pulled themselves out of the water, and were sitting side by side on a smooth grey rock.

"My name is Suraj,"[9] said the Punjabi boy. "What is yours?"

"It is Ranji."

"I am strong, am I not?" said Suraj, bending his arm so that a ball of muscle stood up stretching the white of his flesh.

31 "You are strong," said Ranji. "You are a real *pahelwan*."[10]

32 "One day I will be the world's champion wrestler," said Suraj, slapping his thighs, which shook with the impact of his hand. He looked critically at Ranji's hard, thin body. "You are quite strong yourself," he conceded. "But you are too bony. I know, you people do not eat enough. You must come and have your food with me. I drink one seer[11] of milk every day. We have

---

9. **Suraj** (sōō′räj).
10. **pahelwan** (pä′hāl-wän): a wrestler, usually the village wrestling champion.
11. **seer** (sēr, sĭr): an Indian unit of weight, a little over two pounds. Also *ser* or *sir*.

60 REFLECTIONS

Cultural Diversity

Invite students to give examples from their own backgrounds in which young people from different areas, like the two boys in this selection, tend to view each other as "enemies." (One example might be gangs that live in different neighborhoods of a city.) Why are people often afraid or mistrustful of each other? (People speak different languages or dialects, practice different religions, and have different customs.) In students' opinions, what can be done to establish friendship and understanding among people from different backgrounds? What strategies do the boys in the story use to become friends?

---

got our own cow! Be my friend, and I will make you a *pahelwan* like me! I know—if you teach me to dive and swim under water, I will make you a *pahelwan!* That is fair, isn't it?"

33 "That is fair!" said Ranji, though he doubted if he was getting the better of the exchange.

Suraj put his arm around the younger boy, and said, "We are friends now, yes?"

They looked at each other with honest, unflinching eyes, and in that moment love and understanding were born.

"We are friends," said Ranji.

The birds had settled again in their branches, and the pool was quiet and limpid in the shade of the *sal* trees.

"It is our pool," said Suraj. "Nobody else can come here without our permission. Who would dare?"

34 "Who would dare?" said Ranji, smiling with the knowledge that he had won the day.

Reading Check

1. Why does Ranji spend much of his time alone?
2. When the two boys meet, who tries first to intimidate the other?
3. What is the result of their fight?
4. What does Ranji agree to teach the other boy?
5. What does the Punjabi boy promise?

For Study and Discussion

Analyzing and Interpreting the Story

1. Reread the author's description of the pool in the summer and during the monsoon season. **a.** What are the pool's two different phases? **b.** How is the boys' relationship to one another like the pool?

2. The boys' rivalry centers on who owns the pool, but how do the boys' assertions about their identities as Rajput and Punjabi reveal another kind of rivalry?

3. Look at the dialogue that occurs at the boys' first meeting. How does the dialogue reveal differences in their personalities?

4. What kinds of feelings does Ranji experience when he returns to the pool on the following day?

5. How do the boys become friends?

6. At the end of the story, Ranji questions whether he has gotten "the better of the exchange," but why does he believe that he has "won the day"?

Focus on Reading

Drawing Inferences

When you draw an inference, you reach a conclusion about something from certain clues. To say that Ranji is Rajput is not an inference because this fact is clearly stated in the story. However, to say that a rivalry may exist between the Punjabi and Rajput peoples is an inference. This source of conflict is never clearly stated in the text but instead is suggested by the dialogue that takes place between the two boys. What else can you infer about the two boys based on clues in the story?

33
Ranji doubts Suraj will ever turn him into a wrestler.

34 Analyzing
Does Suraj realize Ranji has won day? Answers will vary. Probably not. He probably thinks he defeated Ranji by threatening to beat him.

READING CHECK
1. He has lived in the village less than a month, school has not yet started, and he has made no friends (p. 56).
2. Suraj (pp. 56–57).
3. Neither wins so they agree to continue fight next day (p. 58).
4. To dive and swim underwater (p. 61).
5. To make Ranji a wrestler (p. 61).

FOR STUDY AND DISCUSSION
1a. In summer, stream that feeds calm, refreshing pool is a trickle; but in monsoon season, stream becomes gushing torrent.
1b. Friendship becomes calm after torrential beginning.
2. Each boy comes from a different region in India, believing that his region is superior and showing distrust toward inhabitants of other regions.
3. Ranji is hopeful of gaining a friend, while Suraj is surly and aggressive.
4. He is not eager to fight, for he is sore and tired and knows Punjabi boy will win. But refusing challenge admits defeat, so he must defy enemy or outsmart him. He half hopes Punjabi boy has forgotten challenge.
5. Ranji impresses Suraj with diving and swimming ability and agrees to teach him both.
6. Had they fought again, Suraj would have won, for he is stronger. Instead, Ranji has outwitted his adversary and made a needed friend of him.

TRANSPARENCIES 1 & 2
Fine Art
Theme: *Self-Image* – invites students to explore artworks depicting people in a process of self-discovery.

CLOSURE
Ask students to discuss the motivation of each character to enter into a fight. Have students support their answers with passages from the story.

EXTENSION AND ENRICHMENT
The story mentions that Ranji used to go swimming with friends in his old village. Ask students to write a letter from Ranji to one of his friends describing how he met and became friends with Suraj.

FOCUS ON READING
Responses will vary. Possible answers include Ranji is basically peaceful, but Suraj is aggressive. Ranji probably makes friends more easily than Suraj. Neither boy backs down from a challenge nor gives up easily. Suraj needs to have his ego fed, but Ranji is self-assured.

FOCUS ON PERSONAL NARRATIVE
You may want to allow students to choose other subjects for their paragraphs. Suggest that they narrate an amusing, embarrassing, or inspiring experience. No matter what their subject, their focus should be on making the sequence of events clear.

ABOUT THE AUTHOR
For his novel, *The Room on the Roof* (1956), Ruskin Bond received the John Llewellyn Rhys Memorial Prize for most memorable work of 1957 by a writer under thirty. His works have been translated into French, German, Dutch, Danish, and Spanish.

CONNECTING CULTURES
As an alternative activity, encourage students to locate resource books in the library that describe and show pictures of Eastern bazaars. Encourage students to share their information with the rest of the class.

Focus on Personal Narrative

Using Chronological Order

Most narratives use **chronological** or **time order.** Here is a brief outline of a narrative:

Beginning
grabs the reader's attention
gives the background

Middle
tells the events in order

End
explains the outcome

You can help the readers of your narrative understand the connections of events and ideas by using **transitional words and phrases.** Here is a list of transitions that are useful for chronological order:

after	first, second, etc.	then
before	next	until
finally	often	when

Write a paragraph or two telling about an occasion when you faced a challenge at school. Use time order and transitions to make the sequence of events clear. Save your writing.

About the Author

Ruskin Bond (1934–   )

Ruskin Bond was born in Kasauli, a rural area of India, and writes about his experiences there. He has said: "My interests (children, mountains, folklore, nature) are embodied in [these books]....Once you have lived in the Himalayas, you belong to them and must come back again and again. There is no escape." He lives in Mussoorie, an area far removed from the large cities of India, and works as a full-time writer. Bond's books include *The Room on the Roof* (1956), *The Neighbor's Wife and Other Stories* (1967), and his best-known collection, *Time Stops at Shamli and Other Stories* (1989).

The Author Comments on His Story

A country like India has a tremendous diversity of language, culture, religion, and ethnic backgrounds. The two boys in this story belong to different regions, and their initial hostility towards each other mirrors the distrust that the people of one area feel towards those of another. But when they discover that they have much in common, as these boys do, a strong friendship is the result; for children are the same the world over.

Connecting Cultures

Bazaars

Bazaars originated in the Eastern part of the world as a kind of market where traders set up small stalls or shops to trade and sell their goods. Some bazaars occupy a single narrow street. The bazaar dates back to early times and was a place not only for trading and selling but also for people to meet and gossip. Many of the tales of *The Arabian Nights* are set in bazaars.

Making Connections: Activities

The illustration on page 59 shows a bazaar in modern-day India. Look for pictures and descriptions of bazaars in travel magazines and reference books. Imagine yourself as a tourist visiting one of these bazaars and describe in detail what you see. Share your impressions with your classmates.

The Bracelet

YOSHIKO UCHIDA°

On December 8, 1941, a day after the Japanese air attack on Pearl Harbor, President Roosevelt asked Congress to declare war against Japan. Because of strong anti-Japanese feeling and fear of an enemy attack on the California coast, all people of Japanese descent on the West Coast of the United States were evacuated to internment camps. This is the story of how one girl felt as she left her home, most of her possessions, and her best friend.

Have you ever lost a best friend because one of you moved? Did you ever forget how much your friend meant to you?

"Mama, is it time to go?"

I hadn't planned to cry, but the tears came suddenly, and I wiped them away with the back of my hand. I didn't want my older sister to see me crying.

"It's almost time, Ruri," my mother said gently. Her face was filled with a kind of sadness I had never seen before.

I looked around at my empty room. The clothes that Mama always told me to hang up in the closet, the junk piled on my dresser, the old rag doll I could never bear to part with; they were all gone. There was nothing left in my room, and there was nothing left in the rest of the house. The rugs and furniture were gone, the pictures and drapes were down, and the closets and cupboards were empty. The house was like a gift box after the nice thing inside was gone; just a lot of nothingness.

It was almost time to leave our home, but we weren't moving to a nicer house or to a new town. It was April 21, 1942. The United States and Japan were at war, and every Japanese per-

Detail of kimono showing chrysanthemums.

°**Yoshiko Uchida** (yō-shē′kō ōō-chē′dä).

MOTIVATIONAL SUMMARY
Because the United States and Japan are at war, Ruri and her family are being forced to abandon their home and move to a concentration camp with other Japanese Americans. As a farewell present, Ruri's best friend gives her a bracelet that Ruri promises never to take off. In the confusion of being herded to their new living quarters in a racetrack horse stable, Ruri loses her bracelet. Although deeply distressed, Ruri learns a valuable lesson from her loss.

PRESENTATION
This story is told from the perspective of an innocent young girl, who in the midst of tragedy can still be hopeful. You may want to point out to students the characteristics of personal narrative: the use of first person, the portrayal of

The Great Wave of Kanagawa, from *Thirty-six Views of Fuji.* Color woodblock print. Private collection.

4
A *concentration camp* is called that because a large number of people are concentrated in one place.

5 Drawing Conclusions
Why does Ruri want to answer door before her sister? She wants to be first to get good news.

6
Ruri's hope is so strong she can mentally picture man whom she imagines will bring good news.

7 Summarizing
Why is Ruri eager to hear from her father? She has not seen him in over four months, and apparently he has not been allowed to contact his family.

8
Japanese bombed Pearl Harbor in Hawaii on Sunday, December 7, 1941. Hawaii was then a U.S. possession but not yet a state.

son on the West Coast was being evacuated by the government to a concentration camp. Mama, my sister Keiko and I were being sent from our home, and out of Berkeley, and eventually, out of California.

The doorbell rang, and I ran to answer it before my sister could. I thought maybe by some miracle, a messenger from the government might be standing there, tall and proper and buttoned into a uniform, come to tell us it was all a terrible mistake; that we wouldn't have to leave after all. Or maybe the messenger would have a telegram from Papa, who was interned in a prisoner-of-war camp in Montana because he had worked for a Japanese business firm.

The FBI had come to pick up Papa and hundreds of other Japanese community leaders on the very day that Japanese planes had bombed Pearl Harbor. The government thought they were dangerous enemy aliens. If it weren't so

64 REFLECTIONS

thoughts and feelings, the arrangement of events in chronological order, and the inclusion of realistic details.

After students have read the story, discuss with them the hardships and indignities that Japanese American people faced in this period. You may want to focus on the narrator's mother and how she handles the family's uprooting. The narrator never tells what kind of person her mother is, but the reader can draw inferences from the mother's words and actions.

---

sad, it would have been funny. Papa could no more be dangerous than the mayor of our city, and he was every bit as loyal to the United States. He had lived here since 1917.

When I opened the door, it wasn't a messenger from anywhere. It was my best friend, Laurie Madison, from next door. She was holding a package wrapped up like a birthday present, but she wasn't wearing her party dress, and her face drooped like a wilted tulip.

"Hi," she said. "I came to say good-bye."

She thrust the present at me and told me it was something to take to camp. "It's a bracelet," she said before I could open the package. "Put it on so you won't have to pack it." She knew I didn't have one inch of space left in my suitcase. We had been instructed to take only what we could carry into camp, and Mama had told us that we could each take only two suitcases.

"Then how are we ever going to pack the dishes and blankets and sheets they've told us to bring with us?" Keiko worried.

"I don't really know," Mama said, and she simply began packing those big impossible things into an enormous duffel bag—along with umbrellas, boots, a kettle, hot plate, and flashlight.

"Who's going to carry that huge sack?" I asked.

But Mama didn't worry about things like that. "Someone will help us," she said. "Don't worry." So I didn't.

Laurie wanted me to open her package and put on the bracelet before she left. It was a thin gold chain with a heart dangling on it. She helped me put it on, and I told her I'd never take it off, ever.

"Well, good-bye then," Laurie said awkwardly. "Come home soon."

"I will," I said, although I didn't know if I would ever get back to Berkeley again.

I watched Laurie go down the block, her long blond pigtails bouncing as she walked. I wondered who would be sitting in my desk at Lincoln Junior High now that I was gone. Laurie kept turning and waving, even walking backwards for a while, until she got to the corner. I didn't want to watch anymore, and I slammed the door shut.

The next time the doorbell rang, it was Mrs. Simpson, our other neighbor. She was going to drive us to the Congregational church, which was the Civil Control Station where all the Japanese of Berkeley were supposed to report.

It was time to go. "Come on, Ruri. Get your things," my sister called to me.

It was a warm day, but I put on a sweater and my coat so I wouldn't have to carry them, and I picked up my two suitcases. Each one had a tag with my name and our family number on it. Every Japanese family had to register and get a number. We were Family Number 13453.

Mama was taking one last look around our house. She was going from room to room, as though she were trying to take a mental picture of the house she had lived in for fifteen years, so she would never forget it.

I saw her take a long last look at the garden that Papa loved. The irises beside the fish pond were just beginning to bloom. If Papa had been home, he would have cut the first iris blossom and brought it inside to Mama. "This one is for you," he would have said. And Mama would have smiled and said, "Thank you, Papa San,"[1] and put it in her favorite cut-glass vase.

But the garden looked shabby and forsaken now that Papa was gone and Mama was too busy to take care of it. It looked the way I felt, sort of empty and lonely and abandoned.

When Mrs. Simpson took us to the Civil Control Station, I felt even worse. I was scared, and

---

1. **Papa San:** The suffix *san* is added to a name as a mark of respect.

---

9 Analyzing
Why does Ruri give date of her father's arrival in United States? To emphasize fact that he has lived in America a long time.

10
Simile. Emphasizes sad look on Laurie's face by comparing her expression to a wilted flower.

11
Symbol. Bracelet represents girls' friendship. Bracelet is circular and never ends, just as they hope their friendship will last forever.

12
Style. Laurie's comment about packing causes a flashback in which Ruri remembers a previous conversation about packing.

13 Making Inferences
Why does Mama not worry? Answers will vary. Some may point out that she probably has too much on her mind to worry about details.

14 Drawing Conclusions
Why does Ruri not want to watch Laurie walk away? She is sad about having to leave her friend.

15
Friendliness of Laurie and Mrs. Simpson suggests Ruri's family is well liked and respected in their neighborhood.

16
Symbol. Iris symbolizes spring and Papa's love for Mama.

17
Irony. Garden is usually a cheerful place, but Ruri's mood changes the way she sees it.

18
Ruri is nervous about what is happening because she does not know what to expect.

HISTORY LINK
Remind students that before the bombing of Pearl Harbor, the United States had not been involved directly in WWII. Encourage students to find out about the bombing of Pearl Harbor, the U.S. entry into the war, and the wave of hysteria that caused suspicion and created a climate in which an executive order to evacuate Japanese American citizens was written. Encourage students to talk about this event in terms of the story's characters and the effect the move had on them.

19 Analyzing
Were people laughing out of happiness? Probably not. Their laughter could be an emotional reaction people have when they are scared or nervous.

20 Making Inferences
Why are soldiers armed? U.S. government was suspicious that Japanese Americans might be enemy agents.

21
Bus ride down Grove Street emphasizes ordinary life of Japanese Americans.

22
Ruri seems to grasp irony of situation, even though she does not use term to describe it.

23 Analyzing
Is Keiko's comment logical? No. If spies returned to Japan, they would no longer be spies and would be of no use to Japanese government.

24
Metaphor. Compares people getting off bus in a continuous line to a flowing stream.

25
Doctors want to make sure no one has a contagious disease, which could spread rapidly in close quarters of camp.

26 Making Generalizations
What does Ruri's excitement about living in an apartment suggest about her character? Answers will vary. Some may point out her innocence and inexperience in thinking ordinary apartments exist at racetrack. Others may point to her desire to make best of bad situation by finding something good in what they are experiencing.

27
Irony. Nice apartment Ruri expects is really a dirty horse stall.

---

for a minute I thought I was going to lose my breakfast right in front of everybody. There must have been over a thousand Japanese people gathered at the church. Some were old and some were young. Some were talking and laughing, and some were crying. I guess everybody else was scared too. No one knew exactly what was going to happen to us. We just knew we were being taken to the Tanforan Racetracks, which the army had turned into a camp for the Japanese. There were fourteen other camps like ours along the West Coast.

What scared me most were the soldiers standing at the doorway of the church hall. They were carrying guns with mounted bayonets. I wondered if they thought we would try to run away, and whether they'd shoot us or come after us with their bayonets if we did.

A long line of buses waited to take us to camp. There were trucks, too, for our baggage. And Mama was right; some men were there to help us load our duffel bag. When it was time to board the buses, I sat with Keiko and Mama sat behind us. The bus went down Grove Street and passed the small Japanese food store where Mama used to order her bean-curd cakes and pickled radish. The windows were all boarded up, but there was a sign still hanging on the door that read, "We are loyal Americans."

The crazy thing about the whole evacuation was that we were all loyal Americans. Most of us were citizens because we had been born here. But our parents, who had come from Japan, couldn't become citizens because there was a law that prevented any Asian from becoming a citizen. Now everybody with a Japanese face was being shipped off to concentration camps.

"It's stupid," Keiko muttered as we saw the racetrack looming up beside the highway. "If there were any Japanese spies around, they'd have gone back to Japan long ago."

"I'll say," I agreed. My sister was in high school and she ought to know, I thought.

When the bus turned into Tanforan, there were more armed guards at the gate, and I saw barbed wire strung around the entire grounds. I felt as though I were going into a prison, but I hadn't done anything wrong.

We streamed off the buses and poured into a huge room, where doctors looked down our throats and peeled back our eyelids to see if we had any diseases. Then we were given our housing assignments. The man in charge gave Mama a slip of paper. We were in Barrack 16, Apartment 40.

"Mama!" I said. "We're going to live in an apartment!" The only apartment I had ever seen was the one my piano teacher lived in. It was in an enormous building in San Francisco with an elevator and thick carpeted hallways. I thought how wonderful it would be to have our own elevator. A house was all right, but an apartment seemed elegant and special.

We walked down the racetrack looking for Barrack 16. Mr. Noma, a friend of Papa's, helped us carry our bags. I was so busy looking around, I slipped and almost fell on the muddy track. Army barracks had been built everywhere, all around the racetrack and even in the center oval.

Mr. Noma pointed beyond the track toward the horse stables. "I think your barrack is out there."

He was right. We came to a long stable that had once housed the horses of Tanforan, and we climbed up the wide ramp. Each stall had a number painted on it, and when we got to 40, Mr. Noma pushed open the door.

"Well, here it is," he said, "Apartment 40."

The stall was narrow and empty and dark. There were two small windows on each side of the door. Three folded army cots were on the dust-covered floor and one light bulb dangled from the ceiling. That was all. This was our apartment, and it still smelled of horses.

REFLECTIONS

PORTFOLIO ASSESSMENT
Students may want to react to "The Bracelet" by writing a short essay about a friend left behind or a treasured item lost. Suggest that students plan what they will write by developing an outline so that their thoughts are organized in a logical manner. From their outlines they can write and revise their essays. All phases of their writing project may be included in their portfolios as an example of how the writing process develops. (See *Portfolio Assessment and Professional Support Materials* for additional information on student portfolios.)

---

28 Mama looked at my sister and then at me. "It won't be so bad when we fix it up," she began. "I'll ask Mrs. Simpson to send me some material for curtains. I could make some cushions too, and . . . well . . . . " She stopped. She couldn't think of anything more to say.

Mr. Noma said he'd go get some mattresses for us. "I'd better hurry before they're all gone." He rushed off. I think he wanted to leave so that he wouldn't have to see Mama cry. But
29 he needn't have run off, because Mama didn't cry. She just went out to borrow a broom and began sweeping out the dust and dirt. "Will you girls set up the cots?" she asked.

30 It was only after we'd put up the last cot that I noticed my bracelet was gone. "I've lost Laurie's bracelet!" I screamed. "My bracelet's gone!"

We looked all over the stall and even down the ramp. I wanted to run back down the track and go over every inch of ground we'd walked on, but it was getting dark and Mama wouldn't let me.

I thought of what I'd promised Laurie. I wasn't ever going to take the bracelet off, not
31 even when I went to take a shower. And now I had lost it on my very first day in camp. I wanted to cry.

I kept looking for it all the time we were in Tanforan. I didn't stop looking until the day we were sent to another camp, called Topaz, in the middle of a desert in Utah. And then I gave up.

But Mama told me never mind. She said I didn't need a bracelet to remember Laurie, just as I didn't need anything to remember Papa or our home in Berkeley or all the people and things we loved and had left behind.
32 "Those are things we can carry in our hearts and take with us no matter where we are sent," she said.

And I guess she was right. I've never forgotten Laurie, even now.

Reading Check

1. Where does Ruri live?
2. What has Ruri's best friend, Laurie Madison, brought for her?
3. Why has Laurie given Ruri a gift?
4. Where is Ruri's new home going to be?

For Study and Discussion

Analyzing and Interpreting the Story

1. Why is the idea of Ruri's father being taken away by the F.B.I. both sad and funny to Ruri?

2. When Ruri reaches the camp, she is excited about living in an apartment. What clues lead you to believe that Ruri will be disappointed with her new home?

3. How does Ruri react when she discovers that she has lost Laurie's bracelet?

4. What important lesson does Ruri learn from the loss of the bracelet?

Focus on Personal Narrative

Reflecting on Meanings

What did Ruri learn from her experience with the bracelet? How do you think this incident may have changed her?

In a personal narrative, you should include an explanation showing the meaning that the experience you describe had for you. Before you write a first draft of your narrative, **reflect on the meaning** of your experience by asking yourself questions like these:

1. What was I like before the experience?
2. How did I change?
3. What did I learn from the experience about myself and others?

The Bracelet **67**

---

28 Mama is optimistic about their new home, perhaps to keep from crying in despair.

29 **Drawing Conclusions** *Why does Mama get busy so quickly?* Probably to take her mind off terrible family situation.

30 **Symbol.** Just as bracelet is symbol of friendship, losing bracelet symbolizes destruction of friendship by forces neither girl can understand or control.

31 Besides sadness of leaving home, Ruri now has to endure sadness of losing bracelet as well.

32 **Making Generalizations** *What does Mama's advice suggest about her character?* She is a woman of great strength and insight.

READING CHECK
1. In Berkeley, California (p. 64).
2. A bracelet (p. 65).
3. Because she and Ruri are best friends, and she does not want Ruri to forget her after she moves away (p. 65).
4. At a camp for the Japanese Americans at the Tanforan Racetracks (p. 66).

FOR STUDY AND DISCUSSION
1. Sad because he is gone, and funny because his harmlessness and loyalty make him an unlikely enemy.
2. Barracks have been built all around the racetrack and the entire grounds are encircled by barbed wire; the track leading to Barrack 16 is muddy; their barrack is a stable.
3. She screams and wants to retrace their steps; she wants to cry.
4. That she does not need objects to remind her of the people and places she loves.

CLOSURE
Ask students to identify how the narrator feels about being uprooted from her home and how she feels about losing her bracelet.

EXTENSION AND ENRICHMENT
The story is told from Ruri's **point of view.** How would it differ if it were told from her mother's point of view? Have students choose a section of the story to rewrite from the perspective of Ruri's mother.

FOCUS ON PERSONAL NARRATIVE
You may want to model filling in the chart before asking students to do so. Think of an experience you feel comfortable sharing with students, and then work through the chart on the chalkboard. Explain to students that although others might have shared your experience, you are writing from your **point of view,** so you will focus on what the event meant to you.

ABOUT THE AUTHOR
After the success of her first book, *The Dancing Kettle and Other Japanese Folk Tales,* Yoshiko Uchida visited Japan on a Ford Foundation grant. There she collected additional tales and became fascinated with Japanese arts and crafts. In her writing, she recognizes the importance of an awareness of the Japanese culture but also responds to the need for identity among third-generation Japanese Americans.

LITERATURE AND HISTORY
As an alternative activity you may want to have interested students debate the issue of internment of Japanese Americans during World War II. Divide students into two groups—one against internment and one for it. Provide enough research time for both groups to prepare their arguments.

Explore the meaning of a personal experience by filling out a chart like the one below. Save your notes.

```
Experience: _____
                  Before        After
     Thoughts: _____    _____
     Feelings: _____    _____
                _____    _____
Views of Self  _____    _____
 and Others:   _____    _____
```

About the Author

Yoshiko Uchida (1921–1992)

Like her character in "The Bracelet," Yoshiko Uchida was taken to an internment camp during World War II. On the day Pearl Harbor was bombed, her family was split apart—her father was taken away and interned. Yoshiko, her mother, and her brother were taken to a camp in Topaz, Utah, where they waited out the war. There she witnessed her grandfather's death; a guard who saw him looking for arrowheads assumed he was trying to escape and shot him. Uchida recounts her internment experience in *Journey to Topaz* (1971).

Uchida wrote many books for young people, among them *The Dancing Kettle and Other Japanese Folk Tales* (1949) and *The Invisible Thread: A Memoir* (1991). She hoped to increase Asian Americans' sense of personal history, but her concerns were universal. She wrote, she once said, "to celebrate our common humanity, for the basic elements of humanity are present in all our strivings."

Literature and History

The Internment of Japanese Americans

During World War II over 100,000 people of Japanese descent living in the United States were forced to relocate to internment camps. More than 70,000 of these people were American citizens. There was never any proof of actual wrongdoing, but they were imprisoned until the end of the war. In spite of this treatment, many Japanese Americans remained loyal to the United States and some even served in the U.S. Army during the war. Besides Uchida, Jeanne Wakatsuki Houston and James D. Houston wrote about this period in American history in a book called *Farewell to Manzanar.*

Making Connections: Activities

1. Choose an incident described in *Farewell to Manzanar,* Yoshiko Uchida's book *Journey to Topaz,* or another book about the same topic. Create a play based on this incident. Make sure to include a detailed description of the setting.

2. In a class report describe the events leading up to the release of Japanese Americans from internment camps. Include a section devoted to what Japanese Americans did to resume their normal lives.

OBJECTIVES
The overall aim is for students to identify major character traits the author conveys about each girl. For a complete list of objectives, see the **Teacher's Notes**.

FOCUS / MOTIVATION
Ask students what they like best about the beach or if any of them have collections of seashells or driftwood. Tell them that Cummings makes his own rules about the appearance of his poetry on the page.

PRESENTATION
The lyric and imaginative qualities of "maggie and milly and molly and may" belie the more serious and universal themes E. E. Cummings addresses in this poem. The reader learns the personality of each girl by the type of activity

TEACHING RESOURCES A
Teacher's Notes, p. 124
Study Guide, p. 125

PREREADING FOCUS
The headnote refers to Cummings' unusual punctuation and capitalization. Ask students to spell their full names with no capital letters and no spaces. Have them discuss why someone might choose to write his or her name that way all of the time, and whether there might be any drawbacks.

maggie and milly and molly and may

1
The lack of capitalization and the **alliteration** and **rhythm** of the names establish a playful, child-like mood.

2
Characterization. Maggie is explorer and dreamer.

3
She finds nature soothing; it calms her worldly worries.

4
Milly is kindhearted and unafraid of sea creatures; reader may infer she returns starfish to sea.

5 Drawing Conclusions
What is Molly chased by? Crab, but poem's light tone suggests her fear is part of her play.

6
Simile. This apparent contradiction suggests the "ourselves we find" and the "you or a me" we lose.

7
We lose our loneliness in something larger than ourselves, and in doing so we find who we are.

maggie and milly and molly and may
E. E. CUMMINGS

What makes this poem look unusual? Can you suggest the poet's reason for not using capitalization and standard punctuation?

1 maggie and milly and molly and may
   went down to the beach(to play one day)

2 and maggie discovered a shell that sang
3 so sweetly she couldn't remember her troubles,and

4 milly befriended a stranded star   5
   whose rays five languid fingers were;

5 and molly was chased by a horrible thing
   which raced sideways while blowing bubbles:and

   may came home with a smooth round stone
6 as small as a world and as large as alone.   10

7 For whatever we lose(like a you or a me)
   it's always ourselves we find in the sea

maggie and milly and molly and may **69**

FOR STUDY AND DISCUSSION
1a. Responses will vary. Many will say sounds of the seashore. **1b.** She escapes from the real world to her imagination as she listens to seashell.
2a. Starfish has five arms: "fingers." **2b.** She seems kind for befriending starfish.
3a. A crab. **3b.** Excitable and playful.
4a. Physically small, but no bound on ideas or feelings it might evoke; or immensely alone out of its element. **4b.** Responses will vary.
5. Each discovers a thing suitable to her temperament.
6a. Answers will vary. Perhaps girls represent all people. **6b.** Runs ideas together so there is unbroken flow. **6c.** Something childlike and mischievous in his avoidance of conventional style.

FOR ORAL RECITATION
1. Answers will vary. Most readers would say that some pause should occur between each stanza or each time the speaker talks about a different girl.
2. Answers will vary. Cummings uses punctuation so sparingly that most readers would assume any punctuation calls for a definite pause. Interestingly, there is no punctuation at the end of the last line.

ABOUT THE AUTHOR
In many of his poems, Cummings wrote with great faith in the ability of individuals, as long as they are guided by the instincts of their hearts. He satirized those who lived by mind alone, placing ideology above sensitivity and feeling. His prose book, *Elimi* (1933), detailing a trip to the Soviet Union, used the techniques of his poetry to attack the regimentation of that society.

---

with which she becomes involved at the seashore. However, a broader theme emerges, suggesting the unity of unselfishness that draws life on earth closer together and the loneliness of selfishness represented by "a you or a me."

CLOSURE
Ask students to make inferences about each girl in "maggie and milly and molly and may." Also, ask them to suggest reasons for Cummings' unusual presentation of the poem on the page.

TRANSPARENCIES 1 & 2
Fine Art
Theme: *Self-Image* – invites students to explore artworks depicting people in a process of self-discovery.

For Study and Discussion

Analyzing and Interpreting the Poem

1. The poet tells us that *maggie* "discovered a shell that sang." **a.** What kind of music does a seashell make? **b.** How do you know that *maggie* tends to daydream?

2a. How do you know that the "star" in line 5 is a starfish? (What clues does the poet give you?) **b.** What does *milly*'s discovery tell you about her?

3a. What is the "horrible thing" that races with a sidewise motion? **b.** What does *molly*'s reaction reveal about her?

4a. In what way can a stone be both small and large? Explain the meaning of line 10. **b.** Do you think *may* is imaginative?

5. The poet says in the last line that we always find ourselves in the sea. How does each girl's personality determine what she sees?

6. E. E. Cummings' poetry looks unusual on the page. He experiments with capitalization and punctuation. His purpose, in part, is to make readers approach his poems as original and fresh works. **a.** Can you suggest a reason for *not* capitalizing the names in this poem? **b.** What do you think is the purpose of closing up spaces before parenthetical expressions? **c.** How do these visual devices add a sense of fun?

For Oral Recitation

Preparing a Reading of the Poem

Practice reading Cummings' poem aloud, paying attention to meaning as well as to sound.
1 Where will you pause in your reading? Does
2 Cummings give you any clues in the way he punctuates the poem?

About the Author

E. E. Cummings (1894–1962)

E. E. Cummings, whose full name was Edward Estlin Cummings, was born in Cambridge, Massachusetts, and educated at Harvard University. He went to France during World War I to serve as an ambulance driver, but because of a censor's mistake, he spent three months in a French detention camp. He later wrote about this experience in *The Enormous Room*.

Cummings is known for his highly individual poetic technique, particularly his unusual arrangement of words on the page and his minimal use of capital letters and punctuation. However, the subject matter of his poems is often traditional. Many of his poems are about the beauty and joy of nature.

The Circuit

FRANCISCO JIMÉNEZ°

Chicano literature is literature written by Americans of Mexican descent. A number of Chicano stories, like this one, deal with the hard lives of migrant workers and the hopes and dreams of their children.

It was that time of year again. Ito, the strawberry sharecropper,¹ did not smile. It was natural. The peak of the strawberry season was over and the last few days the workers, most of them braceros,² were not picking as many boxes as they had during the months of June and July.

As the last days of August disappeared, so did the number of braceros. Sunday, only one—the best picker—came to work. I liked him. Sometimes we talked during our half-hour lunch break. That is how I found out he was from Jalisco,³ the same state in Mexico my family was from. That Sunday was the last time I saw him.

When the sun had tired and sunk behind the mountains, Ito signaled us that it was time to

° **Jiménez** (hē-měn′ěz).
1. **sharecropper:** one who farms land belonging to someone else and who pays rent by giving part of his crop to the owner.
2. **braceros** (brä-sâr′ōs): farm laborers.
3. **Jalisco** (hä-lēs′kō): a state in west-central Mexico.

71

MOTIVATIONAL SUMMARY
Panchito likes going to school. To him, it is almost a vacation. His family are migrant farm workers, and he and his father and brother work long, hard hours in the fields. Because his wages are needed to help support the family, Panchito cannot go to school in the fall when the other students begin. He has to wait until the grape-picking season is over in November. But finally the day arrives, and Panchito is eager to get on the school bus and head back to school at last.

PRESENTATION
In "The Circuit," Francisco Jiménez examines the plight of the migrant worker as seen through the eyes of a young boy. Panchito works long hours in the heat seven days a week, picking crops with his father and brother for little pay. Because his

---

4 In California, conditions improved in 1960s due to farm workers union led by Cesar Chavez.

5 Finding Cause and Effect
Why is Panchito sad? Though he works hard here, he does not like moving from place to place.

6 Silence implies this was their last day there; do not want to leave.

7 Painful moving-and-leaving cycle will begin once again.

8 He has earned car with hard labor; car gives family mobility.

9 Necktie is a symbol of importance to Papá—an indication of his poverty and low social status.

10 **Listo:** Spanish for "ready."

11 All possessions, except mattress and pot, fit into four boxes.

12 **Characterization.** Mamá, like Papá, does not complain about her life but maintains sense of pride.

13 This life is hard on Papá, too.

---

go home. "Ya esora,"[4] he yelled in his broken Spanish. Those were the words I waited for **4** twelve hours a day, every day, seven days a **5** week, week after week. And the thought of not hearing them again saddened me.

6 As we drove home Papá did not say a word. With both hands on the wheel, he stared at the dirt road. My older brother, Roberto, was also silent. He leaned his head back and closed his eyes. Once in a while he cleared from his throat the dust that blew in from outside.

Yes, it was that time of year. When I opened the front door to the shack, I stopped. Everything we owned was neatly packed in cardboard boxes. Suddenly I felt even more the weight of hours, days, weeks, and months of work. I sat down on a box. The thought of hav-**7** ing to move to Fresno and knowing what was in store for me there brought tears to my eyes.

That night I could not sleep. I lay in bed thinking about how much I hated this move.

A little before five o'clock in the morning, Papá woke everyone up. A few minutes later, the yelling and screaming of my little brothers and sisters, for whom the move was a great adventure, broke the silence of dawn. Shortly, the barking of the dogs accompanied them.

While we packed the breakfast dishes, Papá went outside to start the "Carcanchita."[5] That was the name Papá gave his old '38 black Plymouth. He bought it in a used-car lot in Santa Rosa in the winter of 1949. Papá was very **8** proud of his little jalopy. He had a right to be proud of it. He spent a lot of time looking at other cars before buying this one. When he finally chose the "Carcanchita," he checked it thoroughly before driving it out of the car lot. He examined every inch of the car. He listened to the motor, tilting his head from side to side like a parrot, trying to detect any noises that spelled car trouble. After being satisfied with the looks and sounds of the car, Papá then insisted on knowing who the original owner was. He never did find out from the car salesman, but he bought the car anyway. Papá figured the original owner must have been an important man because behind the rear seat of the **9** car he found a blue necktie.

Papá parked the car out in front and left the **10** motor running. "Listo," he yelled. Without saying a word, Roberto and I began to carry the **11** boxes out to the car. Roberto carried the two big boxes and I carried the two smaller ones. Papá then threw the mattress on top of the car roof and tied it with ropes to the front and rear bumpers.

Everything was packed except Mamá's pot. It was an old large galvanized[6] pot she had picked up at an army surplus store in Santa **12** María the year I was born. ==The pot had many dents and nicks, and the more dents and nicks it acquired the more Mamá liked it. "Mi olla,"[7] she used to say proudly.==

I held the front door open as Mamá carefully carried out her pot by both handles, making sure not to spill the cooked beans. When she got to the car, Papá reached out to help her with it. Roberto opened the rear car door and Papá gently placed it on the floor behind the front seat. All of us then climbed in. Papá **13** sighed, wiped the sweat off his forehead with his sleeve, and said wearily: "Es todo."[8]

As we drove away, I felt a lump in my throat. I turned around and looked at our little shack for the last time.

At sunset we drove into a labor camp near Fresno. Since Papá did not speak English, Mamá asked the camp foreman if he needed any more workers. "We don't need no more,"

---

4. **Ya esora** (ĕs ô′rä): *es hora* (It's time).
5. **"Carcanchita"** (kär-kän-chē′tä).
6. **galvanized** (găl′və-nīzd′): coated with zinc to resist rust.
7. **Mi olla** (mē ô′yä): My pot.
8. **Es todo** (ĕs tō′thō): That's all.

family must follow the different growing seasons of the various crops, he has no friends, and he can attend school only when he is not needed in the fields. The story's strength lies in Jiménez' ability to show these hardships, rather than simply tell about them, in such a way that readers may feel they have experienced Panchito's hopes and despair.

---

said the foreman, scratching his head. "Check with Sullivan down the road. Can't miss him. He lives in a big white house with a fence around it."

When we got there, Mamá walked up to the **14** house. She went through a white gate, past a row of rose bushes, up the stairs to the front door. She rang the doorbell. The porch light went on and a tall husky man came out. They exchanged a few words. After the man went in, Mamá clasped her hands and hurried back to the car. "We have work! Mr. Sullivan said we can stay there the whole season," she said, gasping and pointing to an old garage near the stables.

15 The garage was worn out by the years. It had no windows. The walls, eaten by termites, strained to support the roof full of holes. The dirt floor, populated by earthworms, looked like a gray road map.

That night, by the light of a kerosene lamp, **16** we unpacked and cleaned our new home. Roberto swept away the loose dirt, leaving the hard ground. Papá plugged the holes in the walls with old newspapers and tin can tops. Mamá fed my little brothers and sisters. Papá and Roberto then brought in the mattress and placed it on the far corner of the garage. "Mamá, you and the little ones sleep on the mattress. Roberto, Panchito, and I will sleep outside under the trees," Papá said.

Early next morning Mr. Sullivan showed us where his crop was, and after breakfast, Papá, Roberto, and I headed for the vineyard to pick.

17 Around nine o'clock the temperature had risen to almost one hundred degrees. I was completely soaked in sweat and my mouth felt as if I had been chewing on a handkerchief. I walked over to the end of the row, picked up the jug of water we had brought, and began drinking. "Don't drink too much; you'll get sick," Roberto shouted. No sooner had he said that than I felt sick to my stomach. I dropped to my knees and let the jug roll off my hands. I remained motionless with my eyes glued on the hot sandy ground. All I could hear was the drone of insects. Slowly I began to recover. I **18** poured water over my face and neck and watched the dirty water run down my arms to the ground.

19 I still felt a little dizzy when we took a break to eat lunch. It was past two o'clock and we sat underneath a large walnut tree that was on the side of the road. While we ate, Papá jotted down the number of boxes we had picked. Roberto drew designs on the ground with a stick. Suddenly I noticed Papá's face turn pale as he looked down the road. "Here comes the school bus," he whispered loudly in alarm. Instinctively, Roberto and I ran and hid in the **20** vineyards. We did not want to get in trouble for not going to school. The neatly dressed boys about my age got off. They carried books **21** under their arms. After they crossed the street, the bus drove away. Roberto and I came out from hiding and joined Papá. "Tienen que tener cuidado,"[9] he warned us.

After lunch we went back to work. The sun kept beating down. The buzzing insects, the wet sweat, and the hot dry dust made the after **22** noon seem to last forever. Finally the mountains around the valley reached out and swallowed the sun. Within an hour it was too dark to continue picking. The vines blanketed the grapes, making it difficult to see the bunches. "Vámonos,"[10] said Papá, signaling to us that it was time to quit work. Papá then took out a pencil and began to figure out how much we had earned our first day. He wrote down numbers, crossed some out, wrote down some **23** more. "Quince,"[11] he murmured.

9. **Tienen que tener cuidado** (tyĕ′nĕn kĕ tĕ-nĕr′ kwē-thä′thō): You have to be careful.
10. **Vámonos** (vä′mä-nōs′): Let's go.
11. **Quince** (kēn′sĕ): Fifteen.

14
Disparity between this nice house and yard to shack family just left and to garage in which they will live.

15
Employer evidently has a very low opinion of farm workers since he expects them to live in these conditions.

16
Use to answer **study question 2, p. 76.**

17
Setting. They must work in this extreme heat all day; Panchito suffers from heat exhaustion.

18
Working conditions prevent proper treatment.

19
Five hours pass before he can stop to rest and recover.

20
Child labor laws as well as compulsory school attendance laws are ignored.

21 Making Inferences
What might be Panchito's attitude toward going to school?
His notice of these boys suggests he would like to be going to school.

22
This long afternoon is but one part of long day; they work after dark.

23
They are paid very little for this hard work—together they earn fifteen dollars (paid by the box).

The Circuit 73

GEOGRAPHY LINK
Encourage students to locate Jalisco on a map. Have them find out about the physical features of the Mexican state and learn about the economy and other features of the narrator's home. Have students discuss why they think the narrator's family moved from Jalisco and stayed in the United States, even though their lives as migrants were difficult.

VISUAL CONNECTIONS
Exploring the Subject
Have students examine this photograph. Make a list of adjectives that could be used to describe the work these men are doing (difficult, boring, tedious, back-breaking, hot, never-ending).

24
Use to answer **study question 2, p. 76.**

25
Another example of physical toll this field work takes on eleven-year-old.

26
Characterization. Panchito does not complain to his family about having to work, but he is grateful for chance to go to school.

27
Often those who cannot attend school but must work instead know its value more than those who are able to attend.

28 Finding Cause and Effect
Why is Panchito relieved when Papá and Roberto leave for work? Feels guilty faced with Roberto's sadness.

29
Panchito is lonely as migrant worker; his family can never stay in one place long enough to make friends.

30
He and his family live on fringe of mainstream society, in subculture that they rarely leave and that is rarely seen by outsiders.

When we arrived home, we took a cold shower underneath a waterhose. We then sat down to eat dinner around some wooden crates that served as a table. Mamá had cooked 24 a special meal for us. We had rice and tortillas with "carne con chile,"[12] my favorite dish.

The next morning I could hardly move. My 25 body ached all over. I felt little control over my arms and legs. This feeling went on every morning for days until my muscles finally got used to the work.

It was Monday, the first week of November. 26 The grape season was over and I could now go to school. I woke up early that morning and lay in bed, looking at the stars and savoring the thought of not going to work and of starting sixth grade for the first time that year. Since I could not sleep, I decided to get up and join Papá and Roberto at breakfast. I sat at the table across from Roberto, but I kept my head down. I did not want to look up and face him.

12. **carne con chile** (kär′nĕ kōn chĕl′ĕ): a dish made of meat, beans, and red peppers.

I knew he was sad. He was not going to school today. He was not going tomorrow, or next week, or next month. He would not go until the cotton season was over, and that was sometime in February. I rubbed my hands together and watched the dry, acid stained skin fall to the floor in little rolls.

When Papá and Roberto left for work, I felt relief. I walked to the top of a small grade next to the shack and watched the "Carcanchita" disappear in the distance in a cloud of dust.

Two hours later, around eight o'clock, I stood by the side of the road waiting for school bus number twenty. When it arrived I climbed in. Everyone was busy either talking or yelling. I sat in an empty seat in the back.

When the bus stopped in front of the school, I felt very nervous. I looked out the bus window and saw boys and girls carrying books under their arms. I put my hands in my pant pockets and walked to the principal's office. When I entered I heard a woman's voice say: "May I help you?" I was startled. I had not

74 REFLECTIONS

MEETING INDIVIDUAL NEEDS

ESL/LEP • List on the chalkboard the following adverbs taken from this page of the story: *finally, enthusiastically, politely, hesitantly, understandingly, gladly, hardly,* and *neatly.* What ending, or suffix, signals that the word is an adverb? (*–ly* ending) What is the function of the adverb? (To describe the verb.) Encourage students to look at the adverbs listed and to determine the adjective form of each one. (*final, enthusiastic, polite, hesitant, understanding, glad, hard, neat*) Which of these requires *–al* before adding the *–ly* ending? (enthusiastic)

heard English for months. For a few seconds I remained speechless. I looked at the lady who waited for an answer. My first instinct was to answer her in Spanish, but I held back. Finally, after struggling for English words, I managed to tell her that I wanted to enroll in the sixth grade. After answering many questions, I was led to the classroom.

Mr. Lema, the sixth-grade teacher, greeted me and assigned me a desk. He then introduced me to the class. I was so nervous and scared at that moment when everyone's eyes **31** were on me that I wished I were with Papá and Roberto picking cotton. After taking roll, Mr. Lema gave the class the assignment for the first hour. "The first thing we have to do this morning is finish reading the story we began yesterday," he said enthusiastically. He walked up to me, handed me an English book, and asked me to read. "We are on page 125," he said politely.

32 When I heard this, I felt my blood rush to my head; I felt dizzy. "Would you like to read?" he asked hesitantly. I opened the book to page 125. My mouth was dry. My eyes began to water. I could not begin. "You can read later," Mr. Lema said understandingly.

For the rest of the reading period I kept get-
33 ting angrier and angrier with myself. I should have read, I thought to myself.

During recess I went into the restroom and opened my English book to page 125. I began to read in a low voice, pretending I was in class. There were many words I did not know. I closed the book and headed back to the classroom.

Mr. Lema was sitting at his desk correcting papers. When I entered he looked up at me **34** and smiled. I felt better. I walked up to him and asked if he could help me with the new words. "Gladly," he said.

35 The rest of the month I spent my lunch hours working on English with Mr. Lema, my best friend at school.

One Friday during lunch hour Mr. Lema asked me to take a walk with him to the music room. "Do you like music?" he asked me as we entered the building.

"Yes, I like corridos,"[13] I answered. He then picked up a trumpet, blew on it and handed it **36** to me. The sound gave me goose bumps. I knew that sound. I had heard it in many corridos. "How would you like to learn how to play it?" he asked. He must have read my face because before I could answer, he added: "I'll teach you how to play it during our lunch hours."

37 That day I could hardly wait to get home to tell Papá and Mamá the great news. As I got off the bus, my little brothers and sisters ran up to meet me. They were yelling and screaming. I thought they were happy to see me, but **38** when I opened the door to our shack, I saw that everything we owned was neatly packed in cardboard boxes.

---

13. **corridos** (kô-rē′*th*ōs): ballads.

31
Strange surroundings are frightening.

32
This time his dizziness is from fear; his family's many moves have left him ill-prepared.

33 Making Inferences
Why do you think he is angry?
Perhaps he wants to prove he can read; he wants to learn.

34
Panchito feels less alienated in these strange surroundings because of Mr. Lema's kindness.

35
Use to answer **study question 3b,** p. 76.

36
Excitement upon hearing trumpet reflects eagerness to learn.

37 Expressing an Opinion
Do you think he will tell his parents about his missed opportunity? Probably not, because he will not want to hurt them.

38
Plot. Story ends abruptly, leaving reader to imagine and share Panchito's response.

The Circuit 75

CLOSURE

Ask students to identify three of the hardships suffered by migrant workers' children (hard work, long hours, no school, poor living conditions, etc.).

EXTENSION AND ENRICHMENT

Ask students to identify things they would miss most if they were uprooted suddenly. What anxieties would they experience? Ask if they can suggest ways the narrator might "break out" of his life.

READING CHECK

1. Strawberry season was ending. They had to move to find more work (p. 71).
2. In garage without windows (p. 73).
3. When grape season is over in November (p. 74).
4. He must wait until cotton season is over in February (p. 74).
5. Working on English with teacher (p. 75).

FOR STUDY AND DISCUSSION

1. Poor living conditions, long hours of hard work, little schooling for children, cannot establish friendships because of moving.
2. Fix and clean up house, make special meals.
3a. He is excited about going to school, spends lunch hour working on English. 3b. Teacher spends extra time helping with English and offers to teach narrator to play trumpet.
4a. His family travels regular path determined by seasonal harvests. 4b. His travels begin again, moving on to next harvest.

LANGUAGE AND VOCABULARY

1. *circuit* **court of appeals:** a legally established district.
circuit **preacher:** a group of churches with one pastor who travels from church to church.
closed *circuit* **telecast:** a broadcast hookup.
lecturer's *circuit*: a group of places in which an entertainer or speaker appears consecutively.
2. Other possible uses: "a line encompassing an area," "a group of theaters with the same management," "an association of leagues or teams."

76

Reading Check

1. At the opening of the story, why is it necessary for the narrator and his family to move?
2. In Fresno where does the narrator's family live?
3. When is the narrator able to start going to school?
4. Why is his brother unable to go to school?
5. How does the narrator spend his lunch hours at school?

For Study and Discussion

Analyzing and Interpreting the Selection

1. The people in this story are migrant workers who move from one region to another in order to harvest crops. What does this story reveal about the hardships of their lives?

2. Despite the difficult lives they lead, how do the father and mother give their children a sense of being a family and having a home?

3a. How does the narrator show that he wants a better life for himself? b. In what ways does his teacher try to help him?

4. A *circuit* is any regular path or journey that someone makes. The person following such a course always returns to the starting point.
a. In what way is the narrator's life a circuit?
b. How does the ending of the story bring him back to the starting point?

76 REFLECTIONS

Language and Vocabulary

Recognizing Special Uses of a Word

The word *circuit* in the title of Jiménez's story refers to the pattern of the characters' lives. They are always breaking up their home to move to some other place where there is work. *Circuit* has several special uses in our language. You have probably heard the word used for the path of electric current. You may also have heard the phrase "circuit breaker" used for a device that interrupts the flow of an electric current.

1. In a college dictionary, find out what the word *circuit* means in each of the following phrases:

circuit court of appeals
circuit preacher
closed circuit telecast
lecturer's circuit

2. What other uses can you add to this list?

About the Author

Francisco Jiménez (1943–)

Like the narrator of his story, Francisco Jiménez was born in Jalisco, a state in west-central Mexico. Educated at the University of Santa Clara, Columbia University, and Harvard University, he is a professor of modern languages and literature at the University of Santa Clara. Jiménez has written and edited books and articles about Chicano literature. He has said: "Because I am bilingual and bicultural, I can move in and out of both American and Mexican cultures with ease; therefore, I have been able to write stories in both languages. I consider that a privilege."

OBJECTIVES
The overall aim is for students to identify the conflicting values discussed in the story. For a complete list of objectives, see the **Teacher's Notes**.

VOCABULARY
The underlined words are in the Glossary. The level of vocabulary should be relatively easy for most seventh-graders.

FOCUS / MOTIVATION
Ask students if they have ever had a pet with which they felt a close personal bond. This story tells about a twelve-year-old boy and a dog he treasures.

Luke Baldwin's Vow

MORLEY CALLAGHAN

This story opens and closes with Luke making a solemn promise. What does he learn about his uncle and what does he find out about himself?

> **TEACHING RESOURCES A**
> Teacher's Notes, p. 137
> Reading Check, p. 140
> Study Guide, p. 141
> Language Skills, p. 143
> Building Vocabulary, p. 145
> Selection Vocabulary Test, p. 147
> Selection Test, p. 148

PREREADING FOCUS
The headnote emphasizes the story's conclusion. You might ask students to think about unexpected lessons that they have learned.

Luke Baldwin's Vow

1
Luke will learn how to deal with people like Henry rather than what Henry teaches him.

2
When Henry becomes unable to work, he will not be discarded — someone will take care of him.

3
Practical man is easily admired; compassionate men are sometimes wrongly considered to be weak.

4
She is dependent, but devoted; does not question his decisions.

5
Characterization. Practicality is established as Henry's central character trait.

6
Possibly Henry's way of showing love for Luke when he tries to teach him his own value system.

7
Henry is expert at practical matters, yet Luke soon learns his values exclude compassion.

That summer when twelve-year-old Luke Baldwin came to live with his Uncle Henry in the house on the stream by the sawmill, he did not forget that he had promised his dying fa-
1 ther he would try to learn things from his uncle; so he used to watch him very carefully.

Uncle Henry, who was the manager of the sawmill, was a big, <u>burly</u> man weighing more than two hundred and thirty pounds, and he had a rough-skinned, brick-colored face. He
2 looked like a powerful man, but his health was not good. He had aches and pains in his back and shoulders which puzzled the doctor. The first thing Luke learned about Uncle Henry
3 was that everybody had great respect for him. The four men he employed in the sawmill were always polite and attentive when he spoke to them. His wife, Luke's Aunt Helen, a kindly,
4 plump, straightforward woman, never argued
5 with him. "You should try and be like your Uncle Henry," she would say to Luke. "He's so wonderfully practical. He takes care of everything in a sensible, easy way."

Luke used to trail around the sawmill after Uncle Henry not only because he liked the fresh clean smell of the newly cut wood and the big piles of sawdust, but because he was impressed by his uncle's precise, firm tone when he spoke to the men.

Sometimes Uncle Henry would stop and explain to Luke something about a piece of lumber. "Always try and learn the essential facts,
6 son," he would say. "If you've got the facts, you know what's useful and what isn't useful, and no one can fool you."

He showed Luke that nothing of value was ever wasted around the mill. Luke used to lis-
7 ten, and wonder if there was another man in the world who knew so well what was needed and what ought to be thrown away. Uncle Henry had known at once that Luke needed a bicycle to ride to his school, which was two miles away in town, and he bought him a good one. He knew that Luke needed good, serviceable clothes. He also knew exactly how much Aunt Helen needed to run the house, the price of everything, and how much a woman should be paid for doing the family washing. In the evenings Luke used to sit in the living room watching his uncle making notations in a black notebook which he always carried in his vest

Luke Baldwin's Vow 77

MOTIVATIONAL SUMMARY

His parents have died, and Luke Baldwin has come to live with his Uncle Henry and Aunt Helen. Uncle Henry is a marvel of practicality, efficient and sensible about everything. Because Luke had promised his father that he would be attentive and would try to learn from Uncle Henry, he tries to understand and appreciate Uncle Henry's teachings. But slowly, he begins to suspect that there might be more important things in life than efficiency and practicality.

PRESENTATION

The conflict between the head and the heart surfaces time and again in literature. This clash of value systems is ably characterized in Morley Callaghan's short story "Luke Baldwin's Vow." Luke's Uncle Henry cannot see beyond mere

8
Luke will learn that good judgment includes wisdom and love.

9 Analyzing
What appears to be missing in Luke's life with Henry and Helen? They take care of Luke's physical needs but do not give him kind of love he needs.

10
Dan gives Luke unconditional love parents gave him.

11
Dan is Luke's best friend; he gives joy to lonely boy and takes Luke's mind off his parents.

12
Dan is still capable of giving and receiving affection.

13
First hint of the callousness resulting in Henry's decision to kill dog.

14
Dan is Luke's confidant.

VISUAL CONNECTIONS
Exploring the Subject
Small rural sawmills, like the one pictured here and the one Uncle Henry owns, are the source of more than half of the lumber produced in the United States. These small mills can be operated by only a few people.

pocket, and he knew that he was assessing the value of the smallest transaction that had taken place during the day.

8 Luke promised himself that when he grew up he, too, would be admired for his good, sound judgment. But, of course, he couldn't always be watching and learning from his Uncle Henry, for too often when he watched him he
9 thought of his own father; then he was lonely. So he began to build in another secret life for himself around the sawmill, and his companion was the eleven-year-old collie, Dan, a dog blind in one eye and with a slight limp in his left hind leg. Dan was a fat, slow-moving old dog. He was very affectionate and his eye was the color of amber. His fur was amber too.
10 When Luke left for school in the morning, the old dog followed him for half a mile down the road, and when he returned in the afternoon, there was Dan waiting at the gate.

Sometimes they would play around the millpond or by the dam, or go down the stream to
11 the lake. Luke was never lonely when the dog was with him. There was an old rowboat that they used as a pirate ship in the stream, and they would be pirates together, with Luke shouting instructions to Captain Dan and with the dog seeming to understand and wagging
12 his tail enthusiastically. Its amber eye was alert, intelligent, and approving. Then they would plunge into the brush on the other side of the stream, pretending they were hunting tigers.
13 Of course, the old dog was no longer much good for hunting; he was too slow and too lazy. Uncle Henry no longer used him for hunting rabbits or anything else.

When they came out of the brush, they would lie together on the cool, grassy bank being affectionate with each other, with Luke talking earnestly, while the collie, as Luke believed, smiled with the good eye. Lying in the
14 grass, Luke would say things to Dan he could not say to his uncle or his aunt. Not that what

material worth and judges everything according to his dollars-and-cents way of thinking. Thus, he can see none of the virtues but only the faults of Luke's beloved dog, Dan, who has become the lonely boy's best friend. In protecting Dan, Luke discovers the fallibility of adults and learns that sometimes disobedience is necessary when authority threatens the good he values.

---

he said was important; it was just stuff about himself that he might have told to his own father or mother if they had been alive. Then they would go back to the house for dinner, and after dinner Dan would follow him down the road to Mr. Kemp's house, where they would ask old Mr. Kemp if they could go with him to round up his four cows. The old man **15** was always glad to see them. He seemed to like watching Luke and the collie running around the cows, pretending they were riding on a vast range in the foothills of the Rockies.

16 Uncle Henry no longer paid much attention to the collie, though once when he tripped over him on the <u>veranda</u> he shook his head and said thoughtfully, "Poor old fellow, he's through. Can't use him for anything. He just eats and sleeps and gets in the way."

One Sunday during Luke's summer holidays, when they had returned from church and had had their lunch, they had all moved out to the veranda where the collie was sleeping. Luke sat down on the steps, his back against the veranda post, Uncle Henry took the rocking chair, and Aunt Helen stretched herself out in the hammock, sighing content- **17** edly. Then Luke, eyeing the collie, tapped the step with the palm of his hand, giving three little taps like a signal, and the old collie, lifting his head, got up stiffly with a slow wagging of the tail as an <u>acknowledgment</u> that the signal had been heard, and began to cross the veranda to Luke. But the dog was sleepy; his bad eye was turned to the rocking chair; in passing his left front paw went under the rocker. With a frantic yelp, the dog went bounding down the steps and hobbled around the corner of the house, where he stopped, hearing Luke coming after him. All he needed was the touch of **18** Luke's hand. Then he began to lick the hand methodically, as if apologizing.

"Luke," Uncle Henry called sharply, "bring that dog here."

When Luke led the collie back to the veranda, Uncle Henry nodded and said, "Thanks, Luke." Then he took out a cigar, lit it, put his big hands on his knees, and began to rock in the chair while he frowned and eyed **19** the dog steadily. Obviously he was making some kind of an important decision about the collie.

20 "What's the matter, Uncle Henry?" Luke asked nervously.

"That dog can't see any more," Uncle Henry said.

"Oh, yes, he can," Luke said quickly. "His bad eye got turned to the chair, that's all, Uncle Henry."

"And his teeth are gone, too," Uncle Henry **21** went on, paying no attention to what Luke had said. Turning to the hammock, he called, "Helen, sit up a minute, will you?"

22 When she got up and stood beside him, he went on, "I was thinking about this old dog the other day, Helen. It's not only that he's about blind, but did you notice that when we drove up after church he didn't even bark?"

"It's a fact he didn't, Henry."

"No, not much good even as a watchdog now."

"Poor old fellow. It's a pity, isn't it?"

"And no good for hunting either. And he eats a lot, I suppose."

"About as much as he ever did, Henry."

"The plain fact is the old dog isn't worth his keep any more. It's time we got rid of him."

"It's always so hard to know how to get rid of a dog, Henry."

23 "I was thinking about it the other day. Some people think it's best to shoot a dog. I haven't had any shells for that shotgun for over a year. Poisoning is a hard death for a dog. Maybe drowning is the easiest and quickest way. Well, I'll speak to one of the mill hands and have him look after it."

Crouching on the ground, his arms around

15
Mr. Kemp appreciates dog and boy; Luke does not show his imaginative side to his practical foster parents.

16
Foreshadowing. Another hint that Henry will decide to kill Dan.

17
Deep rapport between boy and dog; Luke's relationship with adults not as close.

18
Dan draws comfort from Luke just as Luke is comforted by him; Dan is apologetic, not Uncle Henry.

19
Decision stems from his obsessive practicality.

20 Finding Cause and Effect
Why is Luke nervous? He understands his uncle on an intuitive level—knows he is insensitive and fears his power.

21
Henry's disregard of Luke's feelings portrays his misunderstanding of and lack of consideration for boy.

22
Helen simply goes along with Henry's reasoning.

23
Reveals insensitivity to Luke; chooses what he believes to be somewhat humane death, not understanding that killing Dan is in itself cruel.

Luke Baldwin's Vow

TRANSPARENCY 3

Reader Response
Mirror, Mirror – invites students to assess a character's personality traits as if they themselves were the character.

VISUAL CONNECTIONS
Exploring the Subject
Collies, besides being good pets, are working dogs used to herd sheep. Herd dogs were originally selected for size and aggressiveness because of the necessity of protecting the herd from wolves. Nowadays, intelligence is the most valued trait. Collies have the required ability to learn commands and to follow them even when given from a distance.

24
Henry cannot see Dan as valuable in himself but as just "an old dog" that can be easily replaced; he is unthinkingly callous.

25
Dan is alert; he barks now out of concern for Luke.

26
Helen realizes that they upset Luke but provides Henry with lie to explain Dan's absence that is as callous as Henry's words.

27
Characterization. Henry thinks sentiment is shameful weakness.

28
"Sane and sensible" but not sensitive to life and feelings.

29
He will find he can do much more than he thinks to protect Dan.

the old collie's neck, Luke cried out, "Uncle Henry, Dan's a wonderful dog! You don't know how wonderful he is!"

"He's just a very old dog, son," Uncle Henry said calmly. "The time comes when you have to 24 get rid of any old dog. We've got to be practical about it. I'll get you a pup, son. A smart little dog that'll be worth its keep. A pup that will grow up with you."

"I don't want a pup!" Luke cried, turning his 25 face away. Circling around him, the dog began to bark, then flick his long pink tongue at the back of Luke's neck.

Aunt Helen, catching her husband's eye, put 26 her finger on her lips, warning him not to go on talking in front of the boy. "An old dog like that often wanders off into the brush and sort of picks a place to die when the time comes. Isn't that so, Henry?"

"Oh, sure," he agreed quickly. "In fact, when Dan didn't show up yesterday, I was sure that was what had happened." Then he yawned and seemed to forget about the dog.

27 But Luke was frightened, for he knew what his uncle was like. He knew that if his uncle had decided that the dog was useless and that 28 it was sane and sensible to get rid of it, he would be ashamed of himself if he were diverted by any sentimental consideration. Luke 29 knew in his heart that he couldn't move his uncle. All he could do, he thought, was keep the dog away from his uncle, keep him out of

80 REFLECTIONS

READING SKILLS PRACTICE
The underscored paragraph can be used to give students practice in drawing inferences, i.e., drawing logical conclusions. Explain to students that alert readers make inferences about characters by noting the implications of their words and actions and of the narrator's statements about them. While some inferences are straightforward, others require the reader to synthesize information presented in the story. Which of the following can be concluded from the paragraph? **A.** Luke works at the mill. **B.** Luke's uncle gave Sam Carter a cigar in return for Sam's agreeing to do something for him. **C.** Luke's uncle and Sam Carter have been friends for years. **D.** Luke dislikes cigars. (B is a logical conclusion.)

---

the house, feed him when Uncle Henry wasn't around.

▶ Next day at noontime Luke saw his uncle walking from the mill toward the house with old Sam Carter, a mill hand. Sam Carter was a dull, stooped, slow-witted man of sixty with an iron-gray beard, who was wearing blue overalls and a blue shirt. He hardly ever spoke to anybody. Watching from the veranda, Luke no-
30 ticed that his uncle suddenly gave Sam Carter a cigar, which Sam put in his pocket. Luke had never seen his uncle give Sam a cigar or pay much attention to him. ◀

Then, after lunch, Uncle Henry said lazily that he would like Luke to take his bicycle and go into town and get him some cigars.

"I'll take Dan," Luke said.

"Better not, son," Uncle Henry said. "It'll take you all afternoon. I want those cigars. Get going, Luke."

His uncle's tone was so casual that Luke tried to believe they were not merely getting rid of
31 him. Of course he had to do what he was told. He had never dared to refuse to obey an order from his uncle. But when he had taken his bicycle and had ridden down the path that followed the stream to the town road and had got about a quarter of a mile along the road, he
32 found that all he could think of was his uncle handing old Sam Carter the cigar.

Slowing down, sick with worry now, he got off the bike and stood uncertainly on the sunlit
33 road. Sam Carter was a gruff, aloof old man who would have no feeling for a dog. Then suddenly Luke could go no farther without getting some assurance that the collie would not be harmed while he was away. Across the fields he could see the house.

Leaving the bike in the ditch, he started to cross the field, intending to get close enough to the house so Dan could hear him if he whistled
34 softly. He got about fifty yards away from the house and whistled and waited, but there was no sign of the dog, which might be asleep at the front of the house, he knew, or over at the sawmill. With the saws whining, the dog couldn't hear the soft whistle. For a few minutes Luke couldn't make up his mind what to do, then he decided to go back to the road, get on his bike, and go back the way he had come until he got to the place where the river path joined the road. There he could leave his bike, go up the path, then into the tall grass and get close to the front of the house and the sawmill without being seen.

He had followed the river path for about a hundred yards, and when he came to the place where the river began to bend sharply toward the house his heart fluttered and his legs felt
35 paralyzed, for he saw the old rowboat in the one place where the river was deep, and in the rowboat was Sam Carter with the collie.

The bearded man in the blue overalls was smoking the cigar; the dog, with a rope around
36 its neck, sat contentedly beside him, its tongue going out in a friendly lick at the hand holding the rope. It was all like a crazy dream picture to Luke; all wrong because it looked so lazy and friendly, even the curling smoke from Sam Carter's cigar. But as Luke cried out, "Dan! Dan! Come on, boy!" and the dog jumped at
37 the water, he saw that Sam Carter's left hand was hanging deep in the water, holding a foot of rope with a heavy stone at the end. As Luke cried out wildly, "Don't! Please don't!" Carter dropped the stone, for the cry came too late; it was blurred by the screech of the big saws at the mill. But Carter was startled, and he stared stupidly at the riverbank, then he
38 ducked his head and began to row quickly to the bank.

But Luke was watching the collie take what looked like a long, shallow dive, except that the hind legs suddenly kicked up above the surface, then shot down, and while he watched, Luke sobbed and trembled, for it was as if the

---

30
Payment for drowning Dan; attention Henry gives Carter has practical, not friendly motive.

31
Luke now learns that sometimes he must disobey in order to protect what he loves and to follow his own conscience.

32
Luke thinks of the scene because deep down he knows why his uncle gave Carter a cigar.

33
Use to answer **study question 3**, p. 85.

34
Suspense. Tension builds as Luke searches near house.

35
Luke and Dan once played happily in rowboat on river; now boat and river are ominous.

36 Analyzing
Why does the dog lick the man who is going to kill him? Dan has only known kindness from humans; he does not suspect what is about to happen.

37
Tension results from events; Luke does not see stone in time; Carter cannot hear his cry because of noisy saws.

38
Carter acts guiltily; he ducks his head when caught drowning Dan.

▶ Reading Skills Objective: Drawing Logical Conclusions

COOPERATIVE LEARNING

To encourage students to consider other people's values and compare them to their own, you might divide the class into cooperative discussion groups. Ask the groups to think about what makes money important to people. Why do people think they must have more and more money? What is the purpose of saving money? Is it more important to save money for something special or to save money to protect your way of life?

39
Use to answer **study question 2b**, p. 85.

40
Luke's love is tested.

41
"Slinking furtively" suggests feelings of guilt.

42 Drawing Conclusions
Why does Luke wait until Carter leaves? So man will not stop him.

43
Luke can't bring his parents back but can save Dan, even if he endangers his own life.

44
Compare dog's slow ascent with Luke's rapid one.

45
Has foresight to hide in tall grass in case his uncle comes looking for him.

46
Luke has acted very much like man so far, but not type of man Henry is.

47
Consider whether Henry would have acted as well in similar emergency.

48
Luke's words change from hope to faith, then to gratitude and relief.

49
Compare his struggle with Carter's lack of concern; compare rewards: love vs. cigar.

50
Dan's love and gratitude is Luke's reward.

---

39 happy secret part of his life around the sawmill was being torn away from him. But even while 40 he watched, he seemed to be following a plan without knowing it, for he was already fumbling in his pocket for his jackknife, jerking the blade open, pulling off his pants, kicking his shoes off, while he muttered fiercely and prayed that Sam Carter would get out of sight.

It hardly took the mill hand a minute to 41 reach the bank and go slinking furtively around the bend as if he felt that the boy was following him. But Luke hadn't taken his eyes off the exact spot in the water where Dan had 42 disappeared. As soon as the mill hand was out of sight, Luke slid down the bank and took a leap at the water, the sun glistening on his slender body, his eyes wild with eagerness as he ran out to the deep place, then arched his back and dived, swimming under water, his open eyes getting used to the greenish-gray haze of the water, the sandy bottom, and the imbedded rocks.

43 His lungs began to ache, then he saw the shadow of the collie floating at the end of the taut rope, rock-held in the sand. He slashed at the rope with his knife. He couldn't get much strength in his arm because of the resistance of the water. He grabbed the rope with his left hand, hacking with his knife. The collie sud- 44 denly drifted up slowly, like a water-soaked log. Then his own head shot above the surface, and, while he was sucking in the air, he was drawing in the rope, pulling the collie toward him and treading water. In a few strokes he was away from the deep place and his feet touched the bottom.

Hoisting the collie out of the water, he scrambled toward the bank, lurching and stumbling in fright because the collie felt like a dead weight.

He went on up the bank and across the path 45 to the tall grass, where he fell flat, hugging the dog and trying to warm him with his own body. But the collie didn't stir; the good amber eye remained closed. Then suddenly Luke 46 wanted to act like a resourceful, competent man. Getting up on his knees, he stretched the dog out on its belly, drew him between his knees, felt with trembling hands for the soft places on the flanks just above the hipbones, and rocked back and forth, pressing with all his weight, then relaxing the pressure as he straightened up. He hoped that he was work- 47 ing the dog's lungs like a bellows. He had read that men who had been thought drowned had been saved in this way.

48 "Come on, Dan. Come on, old boy," he pleaded softly. As a little water came from the collie's mouth, Luke's heart jumped, and he muttered over and over, "You can't be dead, Dan! You can't, you can't! I won't let you die, 49 Dan!" He rocked back and forth tirelessly, applying the pressure to the flanks. More water dribbled from the mouth. In the collie's body he felt a faint tremor. "Oh, gee, Dan, you're alive," he whispered. "Come on, boy. Keep it up."

With a cough the collie suddenly jerked his head back, the amber eye opened, and there they were looking at each other. Then the collie, thrusting his legs out stiffly, tried to hoist himself up, staggered, tried again, then stood there in a stupor. Then he shook himself like any other wet dog, turned his head, eyed Luke, 50 and the red tongue came out in a weak flick at Luke's cheek.

"Lie down, Dan," Luke said. As the dog lay down beside him, Luke closed his eyes, buried his head in the wet fur, and wondered why all the muscles of his arms and legs began to jerk in a nervous reaction, now that it was all over. "Stay there, Dan," he said softly, and he went back to the path, got his clothes, and came back beside Dan and put them on. "I think we'd better get away from this spot, Dan," he said. "Keep down, boy. Come on." And he crawled

82 REFLECTIONS

on through the tall grass till they were about seventy-five yards from the place where he had undressed. There they lay down together.

In a little while he heard his aunt's voice calling, "Luke. Oh, Luke! Come here, Luke!"

"Quiet, Dan," Luke whispered. A few minutes passed, and then Uncle Henry called, "Luke, Luke!" and he began to come down the
51 path. They could see him standing there, massive and imposing, his hands on his hips as he looked down the path; then he turned and went back to the house.

As he watched the sunlight shine on the back of his uncle's neck, the exultation Luke had felt at knowing the collie was safe beside him turned to bewildered despair, for he knew that even if he should be forgiven for saving the dog when he saw it drowning, the fact was that
52 his uncle had been thwarted.[1] His mind was made up to get rid of Dan, and in a few days' time, in another way, he would get rid of him, as he got rid of anything around the mill that
53 he believed to be useless or a waste of money.

As he lay back and looked up at the hardly moving clouds, he began to grow frightened. He couldn't go back to the house, nor could he take the collie into the woods and hide him and
54 feed him there unless he tied him up. If he didn't tie him up, Dan would wander back to the house.

55 "I guess there's just no place to go, Dan," he whispered sadly. "Even if we start off along the road, somebody is sure to see us."

But Dan was watching a butterfly that was circling crazily above them. Raising himself a little, Luke looked through the grass at the corner of the house, then he turned and looked the other way to the wide blue lake. With a sigh he lay down again, and for hours they lay there together, until there was no sound from the saws in the mill and the sun moved low in the western sky.

56 "Well, we can't stay here any longer, Dan," he said at last. "We'll just have to get as far away as we can. Keep down, old boy," and he began to crawl through the grass, going farther away from the house. When he could no longer be seen, he got up and began to trot across the field toward the gravel road leading to town.

On the road, the collie would turn from time
57 to time as if wondering why Luke shuffled along, dragging his feet wearily, head down. "I'm stumped, that's all, Dan," Luke explained. "I can't seem to think of a place to take you."

When they were passing the Kemp place, they saw the old man sitting on the veranda, and Luke stopped. All he could think of was
58 that Mr. Kemp had liked them both and it had been a pleasure to help him get the cows in the evening. Dan had always been with them. Staring at the figure of the old man on the veranda, he said in a worried tone, "I wish I
59 could be sure of him, Dan. I wish he was a dumb, stupid man who wouldn't know or care whether you were worth anything. . . . Well, come on." He opened the gate bravely, but he felt shy and unimportant.

"Hello, son. What's on your mind?" Mr. Kemp called from the veranda. He was a thin,
60 wiry man in a tan-colored shirt. He had a gray, untidy mustache, his skin was wrinkled and leathery, but his eyes were always friendly and amused.

"Could I speak to you, Mr. Kemp?" Luke asked when they were close to the veranda.

"Sure. Go ahead."

"It's about Dan. He's a great dog, but I guess you know that as well as I do. I was wondering if you could keep him here for me."

"Why should I keep Dan here, son?"

"Well, it's like this," Luke said, fumbling the words awkwardly. "My uncle won't let me keep

---

1. **thwarted** (thwôrt′ĭd): prevented from carrying out his plans.

51
Characterization. Description reflects his impassive, inflexible attitude and Luke's fear of him.

52
Luke has humiliated his uncle by his disobedience; Henry will only try again.

53
Luke has learned that Henry's beliefs are not infallible.

54 Drawing Conclusions
Why could he not leave Dan tied? Too dangerous; he could choke or be at mercy of wild animals or people.

55 Analyzing
How must Luke feel at this moment? Lonely and unloved.

56
Only recourse is to run away.

57
Note Dan is obviously concerned about Luke.

58
Luke likes Mr. Kemp and turns to him for help.

59
Irony. It takes a person who is dumb and stupid (by Henry's standards) to understand true worth.

60
Mr. Kemp's appearance is quite different from Uncle Henry's; joyful eyes not found in Henry.

Luke Baldwin's Vow

61
Kemp's affectionate action comforts Luke and shows compassion.

62
Kemp knows Dan is worth more than his keep to Luke.

63
Kemp wants Luke to continue to respect Henry.

64
Luke pays more attention to Kemp's expressions; they show his sympathy.

65
His smile may be one of joy for Luke or of amusement at Henry.

66
Compromise can be hard; further tests Luke.

67
Characterization. "Wise" contrasts with "important"; Kemp knows people; Henry knows facts.

68
Reacts as if he has seen the dead; assumes Dan dead, not expecting Luke to intervene.

69
Her expression reflects change of heart, realization of how important dog is to Luke.

70 Expressing an Opinion
Why do you think Uncle Henry does not want this confrontation? Answers will vary. One response may be that he knows he has made mistake.

---

him any more . . . says he's too old." His mouth began to tremble, then he blurted out the story.

"I see, I see," Mr. Kemp said slowly, and he got up and came over to the steps and sat down and began to stroke the collie's head. "Of course, Dan's an old dog, son," he said quietly. "And sooner or later you've got to get rid of an old dog. Your uncle knows that. Maybe it's true that Dan isn't worth his keep."

"He doesn't eat much, Mr. Kemp. Just one meal a day."

"I wouldn't want you to think your uncle was cruel and unfeeling, Luke," Mr. Kemp went on. "He's a fine man . . . maybe just a little bit too practical and straightforward."

"I guess that's right," Luke agreed, but he was really waiting and trusting the expression in the old man's eyes.

"Maybe you should make him a practical proposition."

"I—I don't know what you mean."

"Well, I sort of like the way you get the cows for me in the evenings," Mr. Kemp said, smiling to himself. "In fact, I don't think you need me to go along with you at all. Now, supposing I gave you seventy-five cents a week. Would you get the cows for me every night?"

"Sure I would, Mr. Kemp. I like doing it, anyway."

"All right, son. It's a deal. Now I'll tell you what to do. You go back to your uncle, and before he has a chance to open up on you, you say right out that you've come to him with a business proposition. Say it like a man, just like that. Offer to pay him the seventy-five cents a week for the dog's keep."

"But my uncle doesn't need seventy-five cents, Mr. Kemp," Luke said uneasily.

"Of course not," Mr. Kemp agreed. "It's the principle of the thing. Be confident. Remember that he's got nothing against the dog. Go to it, son. Let me know how you do," he added,

with an amused smile. "If I know your uncle at all, I think it'll work."

"I'll try it, Mr. Kemp," Luke said. "Thanks very much." But he didn't have any confidence, for even though he knew that Mr. Kemp was a wise old man who would not deceive him, he couldn't believe that seventy-five cents a week would stop his uncle, who was an important man. "Come on, Dan," he called, and he went slowly and apprehensively[2] back to the house.

When they were going up the path, his aunt cried from the open window, "Henry, Henry, in heaven's name, it's Luke with the dog!"

Ten paces from the veranda, Luke stopped and waited nervously for his uncle to come out. Uncle Henry came out in a rush, but when he saw the collie and Luke standing there, he stopped stiffly, turned pale, and his mouth hung open loosely.

"Luke," he whispered, "that dog had a stone around his neck."

"I fished him out of the stream," Luke said uneasily.

"Oh, oh, I see," Uncle Henry said, and gradually the color came back to his face. "You fished him out, eh?" he asked, still looking at the dog uneasily. "Well, you shouldn't have done that. I told Sam Carter to get rid of the dog, you know."

"Just a minute, Uncle Henry," Luke said, trying not to falter. He gained confidence as Aunt Helen came out and stood beside her husband, for her eyes seemed to be gentle, and he went on bravely, "I want to make you a practical proposition, Uncle Henry."

"A what?" Uncle Henry asked, still feeling insecure, and wishing the boy and the dog weren't confronting him.

"A practical proposition," Luke blurted out quickly. "I know Dan isn't worth his keep to

---

2. **apprehensively** (ăp'rĭ-hĕn'sĭv-lē): fearfully.

WRITING LINK
Ask students to react to this story by writing in their journals. You might ask students to think about a valuable gift they received. What did they like about it? Who gave it to them and why was it given? What made it a valuable gift?

PORTFOLIO ASSESSMENT
Students may want to create a collage to illustrate "Luke Baldwin's Vow." Suggest that students plan their collage and their use of materials before they begin to collect the materials. Collages may be exhibited in the classroom, and students may include in their portfolios photographs of their collages pasted above an evaluation of their experience. Consult with individual students to agree on how their collages will be assessed.

---

you. I guess he isn't worth anything to anybody but me. So I'll pay you seventy-five cents a week for his keep."

"What's this?" Uncle Henry asked, looking bewildered. "Where would you get seventy-five cents a week, Luke?"

"I'm going to get the cows every night for Mr. Kemp."

71 "Oh, for heaven's sake, Henry," Aunt Helen pleaded, looking distressed, "let him keep the dog!" and she fled into the house.

"None of that kind of talk!" Uncle Henry called after her. "We've got to be sensible about this!" But he was shaken himself, and overwhelmed with a distress that destroyed all his confidence. As he sat down slowly in the rocking chair and stroked the side of his big face, 72 he wanted to say weakly, "All right, keep the dog," but he was ashamed of being so weak and sentimental. He stubbornly refused to yield to this emotion; he was trying desperately to turn his emotion into a bit of good, useful 73 common sense, so he could justify his distress. So he rocked and pondered. At last he smiled. "You're a smart little shaver, Luke," he said 74 slowly. "Imagine you working it out like this. I'm tempted to accept your proposition."

"Gee, thanks, Uncle Henry."

"I'm accepting it because I think you'll learn something out of this," he went on ponderously.

"Yes, Uncle Henry."

"You'll learn that useless luxuries cost the smartest men hard-earned money."

75 "I don't mind."

"Well, it's a thing you'll have to learn sometime. I think you'll learn, too, because you certainly seem to have a practical streak in you. It's a streak I like to see in a boy. OK, son," he said, and he smiled with relief and went into the house.

Turning to Dan, Luke whispered softly, "Well, what do you know about that?"

As he sat down on the step with the collie beside him and listened to Uncle Henry talking to his wife, he began to glow with exultation. Then gradually his exultation began to change to a vast wonder that Mr. Kemp should have had such a perfect understanding of Uncle 76 Henry. He began to dream of someday being as wise as old Mr. Kemp and knowing exactly how to handle people. It was possible, too, that he had already learned some of the things about his uncle that his father had wanted him to learn.

Putting his head down on the dog's neck, he vowed to himself fervently that he would always have some money on hand, no matter 77 what became of him, so that he would be able to protect all that was truly valuable from the practical people in the world.

Reading Check

1. Why does Luke live with his Uncle Henry and Aunt Helen?
2. What kind of business is Uncle Henry in?
3. How does Luke become friendly with Mr. Kemp?
4. How does Luke save his dog's life?

For Study and Discussion

Analyzing and Interpreting the Story

1. At the beginning of the story, Luke Baldwin wants to be like his Uncle Henry. Why does Luke admire his uncle?

2a. Why does Uncle Henry believe that Luke's collie is worthless? **b.** What does the dog mean to Luke?

3. When his uncle sends him into town on an errand, Luke becomes worried about Dan.

71
Realizes people more important than arbitrary principle.

72
Conflict. Henry struggles with himself, feeling compassion but still believing it is a fault.

73
Wants to "save face."

74
Luke has learned to understand human nature and to use this to his advantage.

75
Luke knows friend is priceless, not useless luxury.

76
He now values wisdom more than Henry's practicality.

77
Theme. Practicality may destroy precious things.

READING CHECK
1. His parents are dead (p. 77).
2. He manages sawmill (p. 77).
3. Helping him round up his four cows (p. 79).
4. He pulls Dan out of water and pumps water from his lungs (p. 82).

FOR STUDY AND DISCUSSION
1. Sound judgment and practicality.
2a. Too old to hunt or guard.
2b. Luke's best friend, substitute for dead parents.

3. Uncle discussed it; Luke saw Sam receive cigar.
4. Most will agree. Uncle provides for Luke and is moved by Luke's feeling for Dan.
5a. Luke offers 75 cents a week for Dan's keep. 5b. Moved by Luke's devotion but "ashamed."
6. More important values than practicality, but one must deal with practical people on their own terms.
7a. To have money to protect valuables. 7b. Answers will vary.

FOCUS ON READING
1. Practicality.
2. Love and friendship.
3. Clash over Dan's fate.

LANGUAGE AND VOCABULARY
1. *carefully* –adv. –marked with attentive concern.
kindly–adj.–of an agreeable or beneficial nature.
wonderfully–adv.–marvelously.
newly–adv.–lately, recently.
lonely–adj.–without company.
enthusiastically–adv.–marked by strong excitement of feeling.
earnestly–adv.–marked by a sense of seriousness.
thoughtfully–adv.–marked by an absorption in thought.
contentedly–adv.–marked by a feeling of satisfaction.
friendly–adj.–showing kindly interest and goodwill.
fiercely–adv.–marked by violent, hostile temperament.
fervently–adv.–marked by a great intensity of feeling.

Why does he suspect that the collie will come to harm?

4. Mr. Kemp tells Luke that his uncle is not "cruel or unfeeling" but "maybe just a little bit too practical" (page 84). Do you agree with Mr. Kemp's judgment of Uncle Henry? Give evidence from the story to support your answer.

5a. What is the "practical proposition" that Luke offers Uncle Henry? **b.** Why is Uncle Henry upset by the offer?

6. At the end of the story, Uncle Henry accepts Luke's proposition, claiming that it will teach Luke to be practical. Luke does learn an important lesson. How is it different from the lesson Uncle Henry intended to teach him?

7a. A *vow* is a solemn promise. What is Luke's vow? **b.** Is money always the answer to a problem such as the one Luke faced?

Focus on Reading

Drawing Conclusions

Very often, after completing a story, the reader is left with certain thoughts or questions about the meaning of the story—those ideas that reach beyond the individual characters and events. "Luke Baldwin's Vow" tells how a boy manages to save his dog's life by appealing to his uncle's practical nature. The meaning of the story lies in what it tells about *values*, or the things or qualities that are important to people.

1 The story presents the reader with two very different sets of values. What is most impor-
2 tant to Uncle Henry? By contrast, what is most
3 important to Luke? How do these values clash during the course of the story?

Language and Vocabulary

Forming Modifiers with *-ly*

The suffix *-ly* is used to form both adjectives and adverbs. When used to form an adjective, it has the meaning "like" or "characteristic of." When added to the noun *brother*, it forms the word *brotherly*, which means "like a brother."

Used as an adverb-forming suffix, *-ly* means "in the manner of" or "to the extent of." When added to the adjective *nervous*, it forms the adverb *nervously*, which can be defined as "in a nervous manner."

Here is a list of words from the story. Some of the words are adjectives that modify nouns. Other words are adverbs modifying verbs or
1 adjectives. Determine which words are adjectives and which are adverbs. Give the definition of each word.

carefully (page 77)
kindly (page 77)
wonderfully (page 77)
newly (page 77)
lonely (page 78)
enthusiastically (page 78)
earnestly (page 78)
thoughtfully (page 79)
contentedly (page 79)
friendly (page 81)
fiercely (page 82)
fervently (page 85)

CLOSURE
Ask students to explain the differences between Luke's values and his uncle's values. Also, ask them to summarize the outcome of the story.

EXTENSION AND ENRICHMENT
Ask students to examine again the vow Luke makes at the end of story. Perhaps in small groups, have students brainstorm examples of "truly valuable" things they might protect from "the practical people in the world."

Writing About Literature

Supporting a Statement of Theme

Theme is the main idea or the basic meaning of a literary work. Theme is seldom expressed directly and may not be obvious to every reader. Theme is one of those elements that need to be thought about.

"Luke Baldwin's Vow" is a story that makes us think about two different sets of values. What details in the story emphasize Uncle Henry's values? List them in this fashion:

Uncle Henry's Values
Uncle Henry tells Luke to learn useful facts so that no one can fool him (page 77).
Uncle Henry wastes nothing around the mill (page 77).

What details in the story emphasize Luke's values? List them in a similar way:

Luke's Values
Because he is lonely, Luke builds a secret life around the sawmill (page 78).
Luke makes a companion of a collie, Dan (page 78).

Which of these statements comes closest to expressing the theme of this story?

In "Luke Baldwin's Vow," a boy discovers that he can't trust adults and finds it necessary to challenge their authority.

In "Luke Baldwin's Vow," we witness a conflict between two points of view, which is resolved when the main character understands that he must respect other people's values.

In "Luke Baldwin's Vow," we see that there are two kinds of people in the world: those who follow their heads and those who follow their hearts.

Copy the sentence that best expresses the theme of the story. Then write a paragraph in which you cite evidence from the story to support that statement. For assistance in developing your paragraph, see the section called *Writing About Literature* at the back of this textbook.

About the Author

Morley Callaghan (1903–1990)

Morley Callaghan was one of Canada's most distinguished novelists and short-story writers. Born and raised in Toronto, he moved to Paris after the publication of his first novel in 1928. In a famous boxing match in Paris, he defeated his friend and mentor Ernest Hemingway (F. Scott Fitzgerald had accidentally let the fight run three minutes overtime). After Callaghan left Paris, he lived in New York and Pennsylvania, and finally returned to Toronto. In a number of his stories, like "Luke Baldwin's Vow," Callaghan shows a keen understanding of young people and their problems. Some of his well-known stories are "The Snob," "A Cap for Steve," and "All the Years of Her Life."

WRITING ABOUT LITERATURE
Suggested responses:
Uncle Henry's Values
Uncle Henry always seems to know what is needed (p. 77).
Uncle Henry keeps careful notes of each day's transactions (p. 77).
Because Dan is no longer useful, Uncle Henry wants to get rid of him (p. 79).
Uncle Henry would be ashamed if diverted by sentiment (p. 80).
Uncle Henry struck a bargain with Sam Carter to drown Dan (p. 81).
Uncle Henry turns emotion into useful common sense (p. 85).
Luke's Values
It is important to Luke to keep the promise he made to his dying father (p. 77).
Promises himself that he will have sound judgment when he grows up (p. 78).
Luke always obeys his uncle's orders (p. 81).
Luke works desperately and tirelessly to save Dan from drowning (p. 82).
Although he lacks confidence in his success, Luke decides to face Uncle Henry with a practical proposition (p. 84).
Luke vows to always have money to fend off practicality (p. 85).

Students will probably choose the third sentence as the story's **theme.** Your assessment of the paragraphs should be based on how well students support the statements they choose.

ABOUT THE AUTHOR
One critic has called Callaghan the most unjustly ignored writer of English in the world. Another claims that his collection of short stories, *Morley Callaghan's Stories* (1959), deserves a higher place in literature than any one work of his more famous friends, Fitzgerald and Hemingway. Callaghan's stories and his novels, such as *The Loved and the Lost* and *The Many Colored Coat,* have won him many awards.

OBJECTIVES

The overall aim is for students to use evidence and reasoning to state, as a generalization, the **theme** of a story.

PRESENTATION

To initiate a discussion about making generalizations about **theme**, you may want to have volunteers read aloud the information in the text. Then review Gary Soto's story "Seventh Grade" and ask students to respond to the questions on p. 88 and then list reasons to support the generalized statement of **theme**. Next, you might have students work in small groups to determine the **theme** of one of the stories in the activity. Remind students to state their theme in a complete sentence.

MAKING GENERALIZATIONS ABOUT THEME

The ability to make generalizations and understand **themes** in literature fulfills the human need to derive meaning from situations or circumstances, especially those involving conflict. Through the analysis of literary **theme**, students can become more aware about some truths in life; they can learn about others, and they can learn more about themselves.

Answers

Answers may vary.
1. "The Medicine Bag" by Virginia Driving Hawk Sneve—Cultural traditions and one's heritage are important to one's personal identity.
2. "The Fight" by Ruskin Bond—Even people who come from different cultures and who have been conditioned to think they are enemies can find a common ground and become friends.
3. "The Bracelet" by Yoshiko Uchida—We do not need tangible objects in order to remember special people, places, and events.

FOCUS ON Reading and Critical Thinking

MAKING GENERALIZATIONS ABOUT THEME

The **theme** of a story is its main idea or basic meaning. Writers usually do not state the theme of a literary work directly. Readers have to infer or make a reasonable guess about the theme from evidence in the story.

When you make a **generalization** about the theme of a work, you use a broad statement to sum up the work's meaning. The ability to make valid generalizations can help you enjoy literature more. It can also help you sum up the meaning of an experience that you tell about in a personal narrative of your own.

To make valid generalizations, you need to use adequate evidence and sound reasoning. To find the theme of a story, first look for the story's central purpose. Ask, What is the writer trying to show about life or human nature? Then ask questions such as the following:

- *How have the characters changed through the story?* For example, does a character learn a new lesson or undergo a change in attitude? In the story "The Medicine Bag" (page 32), how does Martin change after his grandfather tells him the history of the bag?
- *What major conflicts occur during the story?* Do the conflicts end with characters understanding more about themselves or with my understanding the characters better? Do the characters overcome challenges in the course of the story? How do the boys in "The Fight" (page 56) come to a better understanding of each other?
- *Does the title give a clue to the theme?* What do I learn about a story's message from titles like "The King of Mazy May" or "The Circuit" or "Luke Baldwin's Vow"?

After you determine the theme of a story, state it in a complete sentence as a *generalization* about life or human nature. This means that the statement will apply to many people, not just to the characters in the story. For example, the theme of Gary Soto's story "Seventh Grade" (page 13) might be stated as the following generalization: *One of the most important lessons we can learn is to have confidence in ourselves.*

Using the questions above as guidelines, state, as a generalization, the theme of *one* of the following stories: Virginia Driving Hawk Sneve's "The Medicine Bag" (page 32), Ruskin Bond's "The Fight" (page 56), or Yoshiko Uchida's "The Bracelet" (page 63).

OBJECTIVES

The overall aim is for students to compose a **personal narrative** that relates a true event and explores the meaning of that experience.

PRESENTATION

To set the stage for students' **personal narratives,** you might ask students to bring to class an object, a photograph, or anything else that has value to them. Then plan a show-and-tell day on which students can share briefly the significance of their items. This activity can help students begin to think about events that might be suitable for their narratives.

Students can explore ideas through the memory prompts and then share their lists with the class or a small group. Remind students that a

FOCUS ON Writing

WRITING A PERSONAL NARRATIVE

In a **personal narrative** you tell a true event from your own life and show the meaning of the experience for you. Writing about a personal experience is a good way to explore and express the real "you."

Prewriting

1. Use these guidelines to choose a subject for a personal narrative:

- Choose an experience that you remember well.
- Choose an experience that was important to you.
- Choose an experience that you want to share with others.

You may want to use a chart such as the one below to identify possible topics. What associations do the words at the left prompt in your mind? Feel free to use different memory prompts if you wish.

[See **Focus** assignment on page 18.]

Weekends	_____
Music	_____
Arguments	_____
Family	_____
Sports	_____

2. While you plan your narrative, think about your purpose and audience. Your **purpose** in this kind of writing is to discover your own memories, thoughts, and feelings, as well as to share them with others. Therefore, make notes while you prewrite about the thoughts and feelings you had at the time that you experienced the events.

Your **audience** will probably be your classmates, your teacher, and some trusted adults. Try to make your narrative interesting for them. Remember that most or all of your audience did not share your experience. Think about the background information they may need.

3. Start to gather **details** about the experience you have chosen. You can list these details on a chart like the one below.

Details Chart	
Events _____	Characters _____
Places _____	Thoughts/Feelings _____

[See **Focus** assignment on page 31.]

4. Focus on adding **sensory details** to your chart—details that appeal to sight, hearing, taste, smell, and touch. You can use sensory details to describe events, people, places, or even your own thoughts and feelings. [See **Focus** assignment on page 40.]

HOLT WRITER'S WORKSHOP

This computer program provides help for all types of writing through guided instruction for each step of the writing process. (Program available separately.)

See *Elements of Writing, First Course,* Chapter 4, for more instruction on expressive writing.

WRITING A PERSONAL NARRATIVE

Writing **personal narratives** offers students the opportunity to reflect on the significance and impact of their experiences. Many students will find such writing the most comfortable and inviting of all the forms of writing. **Personal narratives** can enable students to develop writing skills within a nonthreatening context. Narratives can also show students the value of becoming invested in their own writing.

Prewriting

To help students collect vivid details for their **narratives,** you might suggest that they create a chart within a chart. For each category in the chart from the text, they can add a heading for each of the five senses and fill in as many columns as they can. Students might even enjoy working in small groups to develop their charts and to discuss the meaning of their experiences. Group members may be able to provide insights that are not obvious to the individuals who actually had the experiences.

personal narrative can grow out of one of life's big events, or it may come from a seemingly minor event. Wherever the idea comes from, one key element is that the writer shows clearly the impact or meaning of the experience.

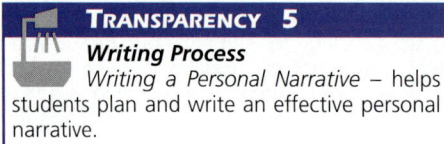

TRANSPARENCY 5
Writing Process
Writing a Personal Narrative – helps students plan and write an effective personal narrative.

Writing
Students might find it easier to write the body of the narrative first, and then add an appropriate introduction and conclusion. Students might benefit from re-examining some of the narratives in this unit for their introductions and conclusions so that they can see the many methods that writers use. At this point, students should not be concerned with grammar, usage, or mechanics. They should concentrate on describing scenes, characters, actions, and their feelings as vividly as possible.

Evaluating and Revising
Students can read their narratives aloud to themselves and to a small group for evaluation.
You may want to model how to use the **Checklist for Evaluation and Revision** with a piece of your own writing or with one from an anonymous writer. Show students how to look for the strengths of others' papers before they deal with the weaknesses and how to offer positive comments. After students have received feedback from their peers, they can decide which suggestions they want to incorporate into their drafts.

5. Arrange your details in **chronological** or **time order.** Plan to use **transitional words and phrases** in your personal narrative. Some useful words include the following: *first, second, then, next, at last,* and *finally.* [See **Focus** assignment on page 62.]

6. Reflect on the **overall meaning** that the experience had for you. Ask yourself these questions:
   ■ What was I like before the experience?
   ■ How did the experience change me?
   ■ What did I learn from the experience about myself and others?

[See **Focus** assignment on page 67.]

Writing

1. Follow an outline like this one to write your narrative.
   I. Introduction
      A. Grab the reader's attention
      B. Give any necessary background
   II. Body
      A. Event 1: Give details about event, people, places; describe your thoughts and feelings
      B. Event 2: Give details about event, people, places; describe your thoughts and feelings
      C. Event 3: Give details about event, people, places; describe your thoughts and feelings
   III. Conclusion
      A. Explain the outcome
      B. Show the meaning of the experience

2. Use **vivid action verbs** to help your readers *see* the action. Also use **dialogue** and **quotations** to bring the characters to life. Finally, you may want to consider telling an **anecdote** in your narrative. [See **Focus** assignments on pages 47 and 53.]

Evaluating and Revising

1. When you have finished a first draft of your narrative, trade papers with a partner. Offer each other some comments and suggestions. Is your narrative clear? Does it read smoothly? Have you told events in chronological order? Have you explained the meaning that the experience had for you?

2. You may find the following checklist helpful as you revise your narrative.

Checklist for Evaluation and Revision
✓ Do I grab the reader's attention in the introduction?
✓ Do I supply any background that may be needed?
✓ Have I told the events in time order?
✓ Does the narrative include vivid details that make people, places, and events seem real?
✓ Do I include details about my own thoughts and feelings?
✓ Are the outcome and meaning of the experience clear?

Here is how one writer revised a paragraph from a personal narrative.

Writer's Model

Just the other day, in fact, my mother had declared the toaster off-limits, after I managed to make a short circuit rather than an English muffin. "Now, class, we are about to learn this morning how easy word processing really is!" said Ms. Scranton, I sat *scrunched* even further down in my seat in front of my *pleasantly user-friendly* glowing screen. I sent up a prayer she wouldn't call on me. Ms. Scranton *Didn't* know that my real name was "Klutz"? Even my family admitted now that I was dangerous around machines.

Proofreading and Publishing

1. Proofread your personal narrative and correct any errors you find in grammar, usage, and mechanics. (Here you may find it helpful to refer to the **Handbook for Revision** on pages 726–767.) Then prepare a final version of your narrative by making a clean copy.

2. Consider some of the following publication methods for your narrative:

- use your narrative to start a scrapbook of memories
- send your narrative to the school magazine or newspaper
- make an anthology of personal narratives with your classmates

Portfolio If your teacher approves, you may wish to make a copy of your work for your writing folder or portfolio.

UNIT 2 ◆ TEACHING GUIDE

THEMES IN LITERATURE
FAMILY ALBUM

OVERVIEW OF THE UNIT

Family relationships, as part of the growing-up process, are the focus of this unit. Some selections are humorous; some are more serious. All feature a young protagonist who—in learning of something shared, unexpected, or valuable in one or more family members—understands both others and himself or herself a little better. A girl's mixed emotions at meeting her grandmother for the first time, two children's amazement at their father's hidden capabilities, a son's realization of the extra efforts taken by his father for his comfort—these are a few of the subjects addressed in this unit.

OBJECTIVES OF THE UNIT

The aims of the unit are for the student:
- To analyze characters
- To identify and explain relevant details
- To demonstrate an ability to use dictionary skills
- To use context clues to determine the meanings of words
- To read parts of a story orally
- To write a description
- To make connections between literature and cultures

CONCEPTS AND SKILLS

The following concepts and skills are treated in this unit:

LANGUAGE AND VOCABULARY SKILLS

Understanding Dialect   98
Adding Different Meanings with *in–*   110
Using Context Clues   121
Finding the Appropriate Meaning   129
Analyzing Words with *–phobia* and *philo–*   137

WRITING OPPORTUNITIES

Focus on Descriptive Writing

Finding a Focus   98
Identifying Your Purpose   111
Using Specific Details   113
Using Sensory Details   121
Using Exact Words   126
Organizing Descriptive Details   130
Using Figures of Speech   138
Writing a Description   139

FOR ORAL READING

Reciting the Story   138

CONNECTIONS

Connecting Cultures   99

TRANSPARENCIES

The following unit support materials with specific correlations to literature selections are available in the **Fine Art and Instructional Transparencies with Teacher's Notes and Blackline Masters** section of your *Audiovisual Resources Binder*.

FINE ART TRANSPARENCIES

Theme: Close Ties
6   *Youth and Old Age,* Norman Rockwell
7   *Two in the Shade,* Sharon Wilson

READER RESPONSE

8   Family Crest
9   Getting Acquainted

LITERARY ELEMENTS

10   Character

WRITING PROCESS

11   Writing a Description

INTRODUCING THE UNIT

You might begin the unit with activities that will introduce the theme of family relationships and motivate students to explore that theme. Possible activities include:

1. Ask students to recall families portrayed in selections previously studied—"The Medicine Bag," "The Cat and the Pain Killer," and "Luke Baldwin's Vow." How are they alike? In what ways are they different? What might be the advantages of living in each household?

2. Ask students to pretend that they are archeologists living in the far distant future who have discovered only limited remains of our civilization. They are particularly interested in what American family life was like in the twentieth century, but they have only videotapes of television commercials and situation comedies to use as resources in their research. Ask each student to write a few notes on how family life is portrayed on television. Students should evaluate the accuracy of this portrayal, supporting their conclusions with examples. Suggest that literature may offer a more accurate view of family life. Ask students to check this hypothesis as they read the stories and poems in this unit.

PLANNING GUIDE

FOR UNIT PLANNING
- Transparencies 6–11: *Audiovisual Resources Binder*
- Portfolio Assessment: *Professional Support Materials*
- Test Generator
- Mastery Tests: *Teaching Resources A*, pp. 258, 261
- Analogy Test: *Teaching Resources A*, p. 264
- Composition Test: *Teaching Resources A*, p. 265

SELECTION (Pupil's Page)	TEACHING RESOURCES A (page numbers shown below)							AV BINDER
	Teacher's Notes	Reading Check	Study Guide	Language Skills	Building Vocabulary	Selection Vocab. Test	Selection Test	Audio-cassette
FAMILY ALBUM Introduction (p. 93)	172							
Merle Hodge from *Crick Crack, Monkey* (p. 94)	173	176	178	181	186	187, 200	189	
Edna St. Vincent Millay *The Courage That My Mother Had* (p. 100)	190		191				240	TAPE 1 SIDE B
Harper Lee *One-Shot Finch* (p. 102)	192	194	195	197	199	200	201	
Robert Hayden *Those Winter Sundays* (p. 112)	203		204			233	240	TAPE 1 SIDE B
Thomas E. Adams *Sled* (p. 114)	205	207	208	210	214	233	216	
Monica Sone from *Nisei Daughter* (p. 122)	218	220	221		223		225	TAPE 1 SIDE B
Gwendolyn Brooks *Home* (p. 127)	227	229	230		232	233	235	
Amy Ling *Grandma Ling* (p. 131)	237		238				240	TAPE 1 SIDE B
James Thurber *The Night the Bed Fell* (p. 133)	242	245	246	248	252	253	254	

PORTFOLIO ASSESSMENT

Suggestions for use of portfolios as support for this unit are described in the **Portfolio Assessment and Professional Support Materials** booklet accompanying this program. Specific suggestions are provided for a variety of student projects that may be suitable for inclusion in a portfolio. In addition, copying masters are provided for guides that may be used for evaluation and assessment of student projects.

FAMILY ALBUM

1. Constructing Family Trees
Ask students to construct their family tree with help from their families. They can write a brief paragraph about each family member. You may want to suggest that the family trees be drawn on a poster, with the paragraphs written or glued beneath the name of each family member.

2. Making a Dictionary
Ask students to make a dictionary of dialect words used by Ma in the excerpt from *Crick Crack, Monkey* by Merle Hodge. Then let them try to write some dialogue using these words from Ma's Caribbean dialect. Some students working in groups may want to then compile a brief, illustrated dictionary of these words.

3. Describing Local Customs
After students have read the excerpt from Monica Sone's *Nisei Daughter*, lead a discussion on the customs of Japanese Americans as they celebrate New Year's. Then redirect the discussion to the students' own ways of celebrating the holiday. For a larger class project, ask students to compile a booklet to help newcomers to this country understand our customs during different holiday periods.

91B

VISUAL CONNECTIONS

About the Artist

Winslow Homer was a self-taught artist who illustrated Civil War battle scenes for *Harper's Weekly*. While working as an illustrator, he began to paint in oils and watercolor, portraying idyllic scenes of country life.

Homer's subsequent stays in France and England influenced him by lightening his color palette and turning his attention to the sea as a subject. On his return to the U.S., he continued to paint seascapes and seafarers, demonstrating increasing artistic strength and technical mastery.

About the Artwork

Winslow Homer was a leading painter of the American School, a group of artists who helped direct American art away from earlier Romanticism to the new Realism, principally promoted by French painters and writers.

American School artists sought to depict an instant in time captured by the artist as he or she saw it.

During the same era, American composers struggled unsuccessfully to find a uniquely expressive style while European composers dominated the music scene.

Exploring the Subject

The Pumpkin Patch captures a moment of time reflecting the theme of family and family relationships. The father has stopped working to be greeted by his wife and child. Ask students to imagine themselves as participants in the scene and explain why the wife has brought her husband a flower. What might the child be saying? What might the husband's reaction be to his wife's and child's greetings?

FAMILY ALBUM

An album is like an anthology because it is a collection of things that go together, such as stamps, photographs, or writings. Imagine what might go into a loose-leaf notebook called Family Album. What kinds of pictures, anecdotes, or souvenirs would you want to collect and preserve in a family album? Choose a snapshot, a postcard, a letter, or another memento you would include. In a line or two, briefly tell the memory that object recalls.

Each selection in this unit might be considered a page or a chapter from a different family album. As you read, let your mind become a camera. Picture the characters and settings. Think of the selections as an album that holds rich memories and fascinating stories about different family relationships.

Detail from *The Pumpkin Patch* (1878) by Winslow Homer (1836–1910). Watercolor (1948.30).

Mead Art Museum, Amherst College. Museum purchase

OBJECTIVES
The overall aim is for students to demonstrate an understanding of the main character's summer visit to her grandmother in the country.

VOCABULARY
The underlined words are in the Glossary. The **Language and Vocabulary** exercise on p. 98 gives students practice in understanding dialect.

FOCUS / MOTIVATION
Ask students if they have ever spent vacation time with an older relative. What do they remember about their visits? Tell students that this story is about a young girl who visits her grandmother in the country.

TEACHING RESOURCES A
Teacher's Notes, p. 173
Reading Check, p. 176
Study Guide, p. 178
Language Skills, p. 181
Building Vocabulary, p. 186
Selection Vocabulary Test, pp. 187, 200
Selection Test, p. 189

PREREADING FOCUS
The headnote explains that Tee, who lives in the city, is visiting her grandmother in the country. Ask students if they have ever spent vacation time in an entirely new environment. What were the pros and cons of spending time in a new place? Were they glad to go home?

Crick Crack, Monkey

1
All grandchildren of family spend part of their vacation at their grandmother's house.

2
Description. Narrator describes grandmother as stern, but tone is one of love and respect.

3
Smoke from fire keeps mosquitoes and sand flies away.

4 Finding Main Ideas
What does ritualized ending of story suggest? Children are actively involved in story, and they enjoy storytelling experience as much as story.

5 Drawing Conclusions
What does Ma's calling to neighbors suggest about her character? That she is friendly and proud of her grandchildren.

94

FROM
Crick Crack, Monkey

MERLE HODGE

The novel Crick Crack, Monkey *is set in the Caribbean islands of Trinidad and Tobago. In the following excerpt, Tee, the main character in the book, is visiting her grandmother, who lives in the country. All the children in the family refer to their grandmother as "Ma." Tee tells what life is like in the country and what she and the other cousins do there during the torrential rains. Note that Ma uses a dialect very different from the speech Tee hears in the city. Listen for the lilting music in her language.*

1 The August holidays had already begun, so that
2 all the multitude was there. Our grandmother was a strong, bony woman who did not smile unnecessarily, her lower jaw set forward at an angle that did not brook[1] opposition or argument. She did not use up too many words at a time either, except when she sat on the step with us teeming around her, when there was a moon, and told us 'nancy-stories.[2] If the night was too dark or if it was raining there was no storytelling—it was inconceivable to her that one should sit inside a house and tell 'nancy-stories. At full moon there was a bonus and then we
3 would light a black-sage fire for the mosquitoes and sand-flies and the smoke smelled like contented drowsiness. And when at the end of the story she said "Crick crack?" our voices clambered over one another in the gleeful haste to chorus back in what ended on an untidy shrieking crescendo:

---
1. **brook:** put up with.
2. **'nancy-stories:** Anancy (or Anansi) is a trickster hero in African and Caribbean folk tales.

4   *Monkey break 'e back*
    On a rotten pommerac![3]

And there was no murmur of protest when she ordered with finality: "That is enough. Find allyu bed."

On most afternoons we descended to the beach in a great band. Ma saluting houses on the way:

5 "Oo-oo Ma-Henrietta!"
"Oo-oo!" a voice would answer from the depths of the house or from somewhere in the backyard.
"Is me an' mih gran's passin'."
"Right, Ma-Josephine!"
Ma brought with her a wooden box and a stick. While we splashed about in the water she sat immobile and straight-backed on her box, her hands resting together on the stick which she held upright in front of her. When someone started to venture too far out she rapped sharply

---
3. **pommerac:** a red fruit resembling a pear.

94 FAMILY ALBUM

MOTIVATIONAL SUMMARY
Tee spends the August holidays with a number of other children at her grandmother's house in the country. Her grandmother, "Ma," fascinates, entertains, and disciplines the children as they enjoy a myriad of adventures. Ma tells them stories by moonlight, takes them to the beach, trudges with them through the lush undergrowth to gather fruit, and marches them to the river after torrential rains.

PRESENTATION
For Tee and the other children, as described in *Crick Crack, Monkey,* summer with Ma in the country is a blend of enchantment and excitement. The narrative is rich with sensory details, such as the smell of smoke from the black-sage

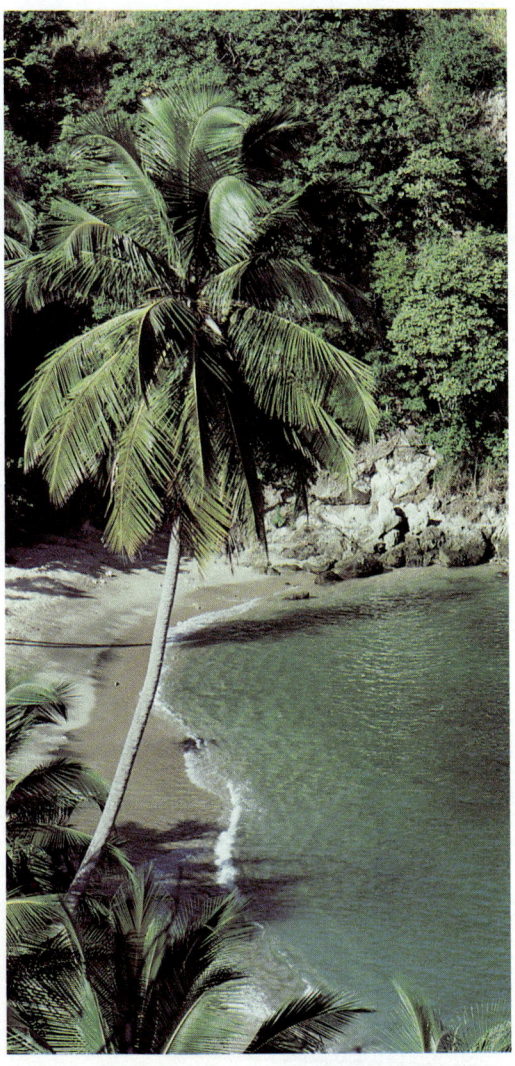

on the box with the stick. And when it was time to go she rapped again: "Awright. Come out that water now!"

Then we walked along the sand, straggled and zig-zagged and played along the sand, to where they drew the nets in, and we "helped" in this
6 latter operation, fastening ourselves like a swarm of bees to the end of the rope and adding as much to the total effort as would a swarm of bees bunched at the end of the thick hauling-rope. Afterwards we swooped down and collected the tiny fishes that they left on the beach, and Ma let us roast these in the fire at home.
7 Ma's land was to us an enchanted country, dipping into valley after valley, hills thickly covered with every conceivable kind of foliage, cool green darknesses, sudden little streams that must surely have been squabbling past in the
8 days when Brar Anancy and Brar Leopard[4] and all the others roamed the earth outsmarting each other. And every now and then we would lose sight of the sea and then it would come into sight again down between trees when you least expected to see it, and always, it seemed, in a
9 different direction; that was frightening too. We went out with Ma to pick fruit, she armed with a cutlass with which she hacked away thick vines and annihilated whole bushes in one swing. We returned with our baskets full of oranges, mangoes, chennettes,[5] Ma bent under a bunch of plantains that was more than half her size.
10 Ma had a spot in the market on Sunday mornings, and she spent a great part of the week stewing cashews, pommes-cythères, cerises,[6] making guava-cheese and guava jelly, sugar-cake, nut-cake, bennay-balls, toolum, shaddock-peel candy, chilibibi.[7]... On these days we hung slyly
11 about the kitchen, if only to feed on the smells; we were never afforded the opportunity of gorg-
12 ing ourselves—we partook of these delicacies when Ma saw fit, and not when we desired. She was full of maxims[8] for our edification, of which the most baffling and maddening was:

---

4. **Brar...Leopard:** animal characters in folk tales, like Brer Rabbit in African American folklore.
5. **chennettes:** tropical fruit.
6. **pommes-cythères:** yellow fruit resembling apples; **cerises:** type of cherries.
7. **bennay-balls:** sesame seeds cooked with sugar; **toolum:** mixture of dried coconut and molasses boiled with water; **shaddock:** type of red grapefruit; **chilibibi:** similar to cornmeal and sweetened with sugar.
8. **maxims** (măk′sĭmz): rules of conduct.

Crick Crack, Monkey 95

6
Simile. Compares children to bees bunched up on a rope. Just as bees would do little to help pull in a hauling-rope, so children do little to help draw in nets.

7
Metaphor. Grandmother's property compared to a place of mystery.

8
Children imagine characters in "'nancy-stories" lived on earth a long time ago.

9
Metaphor. Compares Ma to a soldier going into combat.

10
Ma supports herself by making and selling delicacies.

11
Metaphor. Compares smelling sweet aroma of Ma's cooking to eating.

12 Summarizing
Why are children given only a few delicacies? Ma needs all she can make to sell. She also thinks eating too much is bad for children.

fire, the coolness of the lush foliage, the taste of Ma's delicacies, the cosy darkness inside the house, and the earthy smell of the air after the rain. You may want to have students locate other descriptions that appeal to the senses. In addition, discuss with students the narrator's use of similes and metaphors.

Students will probably be interested in the interactions among the children—the jealousies, the competition, and the camaraderie—and the way Ma handles the group with a blend of authority and kindness.

MEETING INDIVIDUAL NEEDS
ESL/LEP • To help students see more clearly the differences between dialect, for example, Ma's West Indian dialect and standard English, write examples from the text on the chalkboard. Ask the class to supply the corresponding standard forms.

13 Analyzing
Why do children find maxim confusing? They do not understand it because it seems to say that those who ask for something do not care when they do not get it.

14 Making Generalizations
What moral does Ma's saying teach? If children eat everything today, they will not have anything to eat tomorrow except stones of wilderness.

15
Ma's calm reaction is no doubt based on years of raising children and grandchildren.

16
Exaggeration. Emphasizes fear of child caught misbehaving.

17
Some grandchildren live permanently with Ma. These and visiting grandchildren make natural opposing "gangs."

18
These are names visiting grandchildren call the others to tease them.

19
Exaggeration. Narrator overstates case against cousins by calling them "fiends."

VISUAL CONNECTIONS
Relating Expression Skills
Have students use old magazines to create a collage that pictorially describes someone important to them. Have them look for illustrations that relate to this person's hobbies, work, family life, and community spirit. Then have them arrange the pictures in the shape of a silhouette and mount them on a poster board. Ask students to use the poster to explain the character of this person.

96

13
Who ask
don't get
Who don't ask
don't want
Who don't want
don't get
Who don't get
don't care

14 For her one of the cardinal sins of childhood was gluttony: "Stuff yu guts today an' eat the stones of the wilderness tomorrow."...

15 She was equal to all the vagaries[9] of childhood. Nothing took her by surprise—she never rampaged, her initial reaction was always a knowing "Hm." Not that one permitted oneself the maximum of vagaries in Ma's house—her eye was too sharp and her hand too quick. But there were the odd times that somebody thought she wasn't looking. Sometimes there would be a chase, exciting but brief, when the culprit was hauled back panting to face the music in front of us all. Sometimes he was merely set free 16 again, since he was already frightened to death and would certainly never try that one again.

Just as there were enough of us to play Hoop and Rescue and every conceivable game, so there were enough of us for the occasional outbreak of miniature gang-warfare. We sat for 17 hours under the house in two camps proffering hearty insults. The division usually fell between those who were kept by Ma and those of us who didn't really live there. Ma's children were the 18 "bush-monkeys" and "country-bookies" and they in turn made it known to us how deep was their longing for the day when we would all depart so they could have their house and their yard and their land to themselves again. This stung deep, for though we knew beyond doubt that it was equally our house and yard and land 19 yet it was those fiends who lived in the house all

9. **vagaries** (vā′gə-rēz): odd behavior or ideas.

96 FAMILY ALBUM

MEETING INDIVIDUAL NEEDS
Visual Learners • Have students draw or paint one or more of the following scenes vividly described in the story: the grandmother sitting outside on the steps and telling stories to the children; the grandmother and children at the beach; the grandmother in the kitchen preparing food for market; indoor and outdoor scenes of rainy days; or the grandmother and children visiting the river after a rain.

---

year round and played in the yard and went on expeditions into the land with Ma when we were not there. If hostilities lasted till a mealtime, then we placed ourselves on opposite sides of the table and eyed each other with contempt. And if they lasted until night-time, then going to bed was an uncomfortable affair, for it took rather longer to fall asleep when every muscle of your body and every inch of your concentration was taut with the effort of not touching your neighbour. But we the vacation batch always had our revenge when it was time to go home and our big-people had come to fetch us and we were all dressed up for the trip home and being fussed over—Ma's children looked a little envious then....

And there were the days of real rain. We could see it coming, down across the water, a dark ceiling letting down slow grey streamers into the horizon and then it would be pounding the earth like a thousand horses coming at us through the trees. It was frightening and exciting. A sudden greyness had descended upon everything and we had seconds in which to race about the yard like mad-ants helping Ma to place her assortment of barrels and buckets in places where they would catch the water. And all the time the rain pounding nearer, racing to catch us. When the first messenger spray hit us there was pandemonium[10]—we stampeded into the house, some squealing with a contagious excitement. We ran round shutting the windows, pulling out buckets and basins to place under the leaks, still squealing and colliding with each other. As the windows were closed one by one a cosy darkness crept in, and we felt as if our numbers were growing. We all collected into one room. Sometimes we piled onto the big-bed and made a tent of the coverlets, tying them to the four posts of the bed....

Meanwhile Ma bustled about the house—we knew that she was just as excited as we were, barricaded into the darkened house with the rain drumming on the galvanise[11] and surrounding us with heavy purring like a huge mother-cat. Ma seemed to be finding things to do so as not to yield to the temptation to come and crawl under the sheets and play tent with us. Then she came in with a big plate of sugar-cake and guava-cheese, and pretended to be scandalized at the way we were treating the bedclothes.

And when the rain had stopped we dressed up in Grampa's old jackets and went out with Ma to look at the river. This was like a ritual following upon the rain—she had to go and see the river. We walked behind her squelching joyously in the new puddles and mud. The air smelled brown and green, like when the earth was being made. From a long way off the river was calling to us through the trees, in one continuous groan, so that when we finally came to it, wet and splashed from the puddles and from the bushes we had brushed against, it was as though we had been straining along in it the whole time. Ma stopped abruptly and spread out both her arms to stop us, as though it were likely that we would keep on walking right into the fast ochre water. We counted how many trees it had risen past on the bank. If the river came down every week Ma's rapture would be quite as new.

"Eh!" she exclaimed, and then fell back into her trance. Then a little later on "Eh!" shaking her head from side to side, "Well yes, well yes!" We stood around her in an unlikely silence like spattered acolytes[12] in our jumble-sale clothes, in the bright air hanging out crisp and taut to dry, and the river ploughing off with the dirt and everything drenched and bowing and satisfied and resting before the world started up again from the beginning.

---

10. **pandemonium** (păn′də-mō′nē-əm): wild confusion.
11. **galvanise:** a zinc roof.
12. **acolytes** (ăk′ə-līts′): attendants, followers.

---

20 Summarizing
Why is sleeping uncomfortable when a "gang-warfare" is in progress? Cousins sleep together in same bed, and bed partner might belong to rival gang.

21
Even though life at Ma's was fun, children who live with Ma do not have a change of scene to look forward to.

22
Metaphor. Compares dark clouds and heavy rain to a ceiling with streamers of cloth or paper hanging down from it.

23
Simile. Compares noise of rain to sound of large herd of horses.

24
Simile. Compares fast scramble of children to ants running in all directions.

25
Ma catches rainwater to use for drinking, cooking, bathing, and so on.

26 Drawing Conclusions
What do leaks suggest about Ma's standard of living? That she is quite poor.

27
Simile. Compares sound of rain to sound of contented cat.

28 Making Inferences
Why does Ma want to see river after rain? Answers will vary. Some may say to see how high it has gotten in case a flood may be coming.

29
Personification. River has human ability to speak.

Crick Crack, Monkey 97

PORTFOLIO ASSESSMENT

Students may want to compare and contrast Tee's summer vacation to one of their own. Suggest that students not describe their vacations in detail, but rather begin by listing elements of their vacation in one column of a sheet of paper and listing comparative elements of Tee's in another column. From their list, they can develop their comparison in paragraph form. (See *Portfolio Assessment and Professional Support Materials* for additional information on student portfolios.)

READING CHECK
1. August (p. 94).
2. 'Nancy-stories about a trickster hero (p. 94).
3. She raps on the box with the stick when children venture too far out and when it is time to go (pp. 94–95).
4. Gluttony (p. 96).
5. To look at the river (p. 97).

FOR STUDY AND DISCUSSION
1. The varying terrain covered by lush, green foliage offers a refreshing, mysterious, and sometimes frightening playground. Ma seems like a heroic figure in a fairy tale. She hacks a path through the thick vines so the children can gather treasure baskets of delectable fruits.
2. Her storytelling by moonlight and her ritualistic walk to the river after a rainstorm are mysterious; her maxims are baffling.
3. Hear stories by moonlight, light black-sage fires at full moon, parade to the beach and play in the water, "help" with fishing nets and roast little fish they find on the beach, collect various fruits, sample Ma's delicacies, play in the house when it rains, and follow Ma to the river after it rains.
4. Shows her respect and fascination for nature.
5. They have little money but much character, place great value on family, and enjoy life.

LANGUAGE AND VOCABULARY
Definitions will vary. Possible responses include "Monkey break 'e back" means "Monkey breaks his back"; "Find allyu bed" means "All of you go to bed"; "Awright. Come out that water now" means "All right. Come out of that water now."

Reading Check

1. At what time of year does Tee visit her grandmother?
2. What kind of stories does Ma tell the children?
3. Why does Ma bring a wooden box and a stick to the beach?
4. What does Ma consider "one of the cardinal sins of childhood"?
5. Where does Ma take the children after the rains stop?

For Study and Discussion

Analyzing and Interpreting the Selection

1. Tee describes Ma's land as an "enchanted country." Consider both her description of the land and her experiences there. In what ways is it "enchanted" for her?
2. What does Tee find mysterious and baffling about Ma?
3. What adventures do the children enjoy during the holidays?
4. In what way does the final scene reveal Ma's attitude toward nature?
5. What impression do you get of Ma and her family from this excerpt?

Language and Vocabulary

Understanding Dialect

A **dialect** is a special language characteristic of a group of people or region. Tee's grandmother speaks in a Caribbean dialect. For example, she says "Is me an' mih gran's passin'," which in standard English would be "It's me and my grandchildren passing." Dialects within a language vary in pronunciation, sentence structure, and vocabulary. In literature writers use dialect to portray characters realistically and to give readers the flavor of a specific place and time. Find other examples of dialect in *Crick Crack, Monkey*. Read those phrases aloud and use context clues to define what they mean.

Focus on Descriptive Writing

Finding a Focus

In the first paragraph, the details the narrator gives about her grandmother's storytelling at night create a vivid picture. This paragraph is an example of **descriptive writing.**

In a description, you use details to create a picture of a subject. You also use sensory images, exact words, and figures of speech.

When you plan a description, look for a specific focus on your topic. Make a focusing diagram like the one below:

Make a list of familiar people or objects at school or at home. Pick one or two that you might like to describe in an essay. Make a focusing diagram to limit your subject. Save your notes.

98 FAMILY ALBUM

CLOSURE

Ask students to describe Tee's visit to her grandmother. Have them identify words and passages that reveal the way Tee feels about her grandmother and about the visit.

EXTENSION AND ENRICHMENT

Suggest that students write a poem about Tee's grandmother, using some of the narrator's sensory images and descriptive phrases. Or, if students prefer, they might write a poem about their own grandmother or another relative or acquaintance of their choice.

About the Author

Merle Hodge (1944–)

Merle Hodge was born in Trinidad and has spent most of her life living and working in the Caribbean area. Her studies in Trinidad won her a scholarship to attend University College of London, where she earned her undergraduate degree in 1965 and her master's in philosophy in 1967. Her novel *Crick Crack, Monkey* (1970) shows a young girl, Tee, coping with her feelings of isolation in a new school and social setting. Another book dealing with a similar theme is *For the Life of Laetitia* (1993). She lives in Augustine, Trinidad, and is a lecturer in French at the University of the West Indies.

Connecting Cultures

Trickster Heroes

The narrator in *Crick Crack, Monkey* mentions "'nancy-stories." "'Nancy" is a shortened name for Anansi, a trickster hero in West Indian and African folk tales. Anansi was once a man but changed himself into a spider to hide from his enemies. Despite his many character flaws—he is selfish, greedy, and lazy—Anansi is clever. He almost always finds a way to outsmart other animals, avoid hard work, and elude his enemies.

Making Connections: Activities

1. In African American folklore, Brer Rabbit is a famous trickster hero. Anansi and Brer Rabbit share several qualities and have similar adventures. Read some West Indian folk tales about Anansi, such as "Work-let-me-see"; and "Anansi's Old Riding Horse." Two sources for tales are *West Indian Folk-tales* (1966) by Philip Sherlock and *Spiderman Anancy* (1989) by James Berry. Then compare Anansi with Brer Rabbit in Southern folk tales. Which one seems more like a hero? What traits do they share? Why are a rabbit and a spider, two physically weak characters, the heroes of these tales? How might parallel stories have evolved in two separate cultures? Write a short essay comparing and contrasting the two tricksters.

2. Loki, one of the gods in Norse mythology, is also a trickster. Like Anansi, he can change his physical shape in order to fool people. Loki's tricks, however, cause much more damage than do Anansi's. Instead of being considered a hero, Loki is often perceived as a villain by the other gods. Read some of the Norse myths about Loki on pages 636–665 of this book. Then read several folk tales about Anansi. How is each trickster described? Is a trickster valuable to society? Why do you think these two cultures invented stories about troublemaking characters? Make a comparative chart showing the differences and similarities between the Norse trickster and the West Indian one.

FOCUS ON DESCRIPTIVE WRITING

You may want to model the process of choosing and limiting a subject. Brainstorm with the class for possible objects or people to describe, choose one, and then make a focusing diagram on the board to limit the subject.

ABOUT THE AUTHOR

In *Crick Crack, Monkey*, Merle Hodge deals with the cultural ambivalence and the search for identity in the context of one matriarchal household. In presenting the conflict between rural folk culture and urban middle-class society, the book raises a question: Is the West Indian person forced to choose between the two worlds or is there some middle ground?

CONNECTING CULTURES

As an alternative activity, invite students to write short folk tales featuring their own trickster heroes. Encourage students to illustrate their stories. Then compile the stories into a class folk-tale collection.

The Courage That My Mother Had

EDNA ST. VINCENT MILLAY

The courage that my mother had
Went with her, and is with her still:
Rock from New England quarried;°
Now granite in a granite hill.

The golden brooch my mother wore   5
She left behind for me to wear;
I have no thing I treasure more:
Yet, it is something I could spare.

Oh, if instead she'd left to me
The thing she took into the grave!—   10
That courage like a rock, which she
Has no more need of, and I have.

3. **quarried:** dug from a pit.

For Study and Discussion

Analyzing and Interpreting the Poem

1a. In what way is courage like a rock?
b. What does this comparison suggest about the mother's character?

2. Which line suggests that the mother's character was formed by the land where she was born? Explain your answer.

3. The word *granite* appears twice in line 4. What is the granite that is now buried in a "granite hill"?

4. Why does the poet feel that her mother's courage would have been a greater gift than the golden brooch?

About the Author

Edna St. Vincent Millay (1892–1950)

Edna St. Vincent Millay began writing poetry in her childhood. She published "Renascence," a long poem that expressed delight in the world of nature, when she was only nineteen. Her first volume of poetry came out in 1917, the year she graduated from Vassar College. Readers were attracted to the intensity of feeling and highly personal tone in her work. By the 1920s she was recognized as a major American poet. Her volume *The Harp-Weaver and Other Poems* won the Pulitzer Prize in 1923.

CLOSURE
Ask students to make lists of adjectives that could be used to describe the mother and the daughter.

EXTENSION AND ENRICHMENT
Make available a copy of *The Harp-Weaver and Other Poems.* As students sample this volume, let them read favorites aloud to the class or organize an ensemble and perform a choral reading.

Advanced students may wish to write short poems based on a metaphor. One possibility is to choose a trait admired in a parent and express it in terms of comparison with some object of nature.

New England Woman (1895) by Cecilia Beaux. Oil on canvas.

Courtesy of the Pennsylvania Academy of the Fine Arts, Philadelphia. Joseph E. Temple Fund

VISUAL CONNECTIONS
Exploring the Subject
Dressed in turn-of-the-century summer clothes, the woman in this picture has apparently looked up momentarily from reading a letter she holds in her right hand. She has also paused while fanning herself; her fan rests limply in her hand, not immediately ready for use. Judging from the amount of light shining on her from one eye-level source, she seems to be gazing out a window. She looks serene and steadfast, ready to cope with whatever news or trials she must face.

About the Artist
Cecilia Beaux was born in Philadelphia in 1863. She first studied art under the renowned portraitist William Sartain, but later studied in Paris with painters from the famous École des Beaux-Arts, who were noted for their realist portrayals of everyday life. She is best known for her portraits of women and children, particularly the painting reproduced here, and some critics find her work reminiscent of John Singer Sargent's. Among the famous portraits she painted are portrayals of Mrs. Theodore Roosevelt and her daughter.

Ideas for Writing
You may wish to have students write about their impressions of the woman in the painting. What does her posture, facial expression, and dress tell them about her? Who might she be? What do they think was the artist's attitude toward her subject?

The Courage That My Mother Had

OBJECTIVES

The overall aim is for students to explain the changes in the children's attitudes about Atticus and the reasons for those changes. For a complete list of objectives, see the **Teacher's Notes**.

VOCABULARY

The underlined words are in the Glossary. The **Language and Vocabulary** exercise on p. 110 gives students practice in determining the meanings of words that have the prefix *in-*.

FOCUS / MOTIVATION

Explain that "One-Shot Finch" is the chapter from the novel *To Kill a Mockingbird* containing the passage from which the novel takes its title. Suggest that students find an explanation of the title as they read the story.

TEACHING RESOURCES A

Teacher's Notes, p. 192
Reading Check, p. 194
Study Guide, p. 195
Language Skills, p. 197
Building Vocabulary, p. 199
Selection Vocabulary Test, p. 200
Selection Test, p. 201

PREREADING FOCUS

Before beginning the selection, you might ask students to discuss the factors that influence children's views of adults.

One-Shot Finch

1
Children often see adults as being very old; numerical ages seem less "old" as children grow.

2
Atticus' age and late start are misunderstood by children.

3
Atticus reinforces their negative image of him.

4
Highly visible jobs that are easy for children to admire.

5
Foreshadowing. Significant because of test of Atticus' marksmanship that occurs later.

6
Use to answer **study question 1**, p. 109.

7
Atticus defends a black and incurs the wrath of many people; Scout fights to protect Atticus' honor.

8
Characterization. Reflects his peace-loving nature; his caution against killing something innocent reinforces the book's **theme** of equal justice.

One-Shot Finch

HARPER LEE

The selection you are about to read is a chapter from a novel called To Kill a Mockingbird. *"Scout" Finch, the girl who tells the story, and her brother, Jem, think they know all there is to know about their father, Atticus. What do they discover about him that other people have known all along?*

1 Atticus was feeble: he was nearly fifty. When Jem and I asked him why he was so old, he said
2 he got started late, which we felt reflected upon his abilities and manliness. He was much older than the parents of our school contemporaries, and there was nothing Jem or I could say about him when our classmates said, "My father——"

Jem was football-crazy. Atticus was never too tired to play keep-away, but when Jem wanted
3 to tackle him Atticus would say, "I'm too old for that, son."

Our father didn't do anything. He worked in an office, not in a drugstore. Atticus did not
4 drive a dump truck for the county, he was not the sheriff, he did not farm, work in a garage, or do anything that could possibly arouse the admiration of anyone.

5 Besides that, he wore glasses. He was nearly blind in his left eye, and said left eyes were the tribal curse of the Finches. Whenever he wanted to see something well, he turned his head and looked from his right eye.

He did not do the things our schoolmates'
6 fathers did: he never went hunting, he did not play poker or fish or drink or smoke. He sat in the living room and read.

With these attributes, however, he would not remain as inconspicuous as we wished him to: that year, the school buzzed with talk about
7 him defending Tom Robinson,[1] none of which was complimentary. After my bout with Cecil Jacobs,[2] when I committed myself to a policy of cowardice, word got around that Scout Finch wouldn't fight any more, her daddy wouldn't let her. This was not entirely correct: I wouldn't fight publicly for Atticus, but the family was private ground. I would fight anyone from a third cousin upwards tooth and nail. Francis Hancock, for example, knew that.

8 When he gave us our air rifles Atticus wouldn't teach us to shoot. Uncle Jack instructed us in the rudiments thereof; he said Atticus wasn't interested in guns. Atticus said to Jem one day, "I'd rather you shot at tin cans

---

1. **Tom Robinson:** Atticus is a lawyer.
2. **Cecil Jacobs:** a boy who teased Scout about her father's defense of Tom Robinson. Scout fought him.

FAMILY ALBUM

MOTIVATIONAL SUMMARY

Scout Finch thinks her father, Atticus, doesn't show the "manly" qualities that she sees in the fathers of her classmates. He's a lawyer, which Scout doesn't think is very exciting—she wishes he were a dump truck driver or worked in a garage. Scout thinks she knows everything about Atticus, but she is surprised to learn from Miss Maudie, a neighbor, that Atticus is a former checkers champion. Scout begins to wonder if there is more about her father that she doesn't know.

PRESENTATION

Explain that through the eyes of Scout Finch, the young narrator, the reader is treated to a vignette of Southern life in the early 1930s, as well as to a glimpse into the motherless household of Scout, her brother Jem, and their father

Scenes on pages 103 and 106 from a film version of *To Kill a Mockingbird*.

in the backyard, but I know you'll go after birds. Shoot all the bluejays you want, if you 9 can hit 'em, but remember it's a sin to kill a mockingbird."

That was the only time I ever heard Atticus say it was a sin to do something, and I asked Miss Maudie[3] about it.

"Your father's right," she said. "Mockingbirds don't do one thing but make music for us to enjoy. They don't eat up people's gardens, don't nest in corncribs, they don't do one thing but sing their hearts out for us. That's why it's a sin to kill a mockingbird."

"Miss Maudie, this is an old neighborhood, ain't it?"

"Been here longer than the town."

10 "Nome, I mean the folks on our street are old. Jem and me's the only children around here. Mrs. Dubose is close on to a hundred and 11 Miss Rachel's old and so are you and Atticus."

"I don't call fifty very old," said Miss Maudie tartly. "Not being wheeled around yet, am I? Neither's your father. But I must say Providence was kind enough to burn down that old 12 mausoleum of mine, I'm too old to keep it up—maybe you're right, Jean Louise,[4] this is a settled neighborhood. You've never been around young folks much, have you?"

"Yessum, at school."

"I mean young grown-ups. You're lucky, you know. You and Jem have the benefit of your fa-13 ther's age. If your father was thirty you'd find life quite different."

"I sure would. Atticus can't do anything...."

"You'd be surprised," said Miss Maudie. "There's life in him yet."

"What can he do?"

3. **Miss Maudie:** Maudie Atkinson, the family's neighbor.

4. **Jean Louise:** Scout's real name.

9
Emphasizes Atticus' disapproval of needless killing.

10
"Nome" is a Southern pronunciation of "No, ma'am."

11
Again reflects Scout's childish view of age.

12
The phrase "I'm too old" contributes to Scout's notions about age.

13
Atticus has learned the value of peace and compassion, qualities his children will one day be grateful for learning from him.

One-Shot Finch **103**

Atticus. The class should be able to discuss the two **conflicts** in the story. The physical conflict is the threat posed by a mad dog. More important is the children's psychological struggle not to be ashamed of their father.

MEETING INDIVIDUAL NEEDS
ESL/LEP • Like all languages, English has multiple dialects, that is, variations in spelling, grammar, and vocabulary. Ask students to look in this selection for examples of dialect. Then write the standard forms on the chalkboard.

14
Conflict. Scout will not be convinced. Her father's ability to play jew's harp is just further evidence of his difference from other children's fathers.

15
Characterization. Jem respects his father's wishes in not shooting at living things; Scout seems less understanding.

16
Teasing reveals fondness for Miss Maudie.

17
She's teasing; but he does have a playful, devilish side his children don't see.

18
Reflects his belief that gun should only be aimed if intending to shoot.

19 Analyzing
Why does Scout wish her father was "a devil from hell"? Answers may vary. Scout thinks a devil would be awe-inspiring, strong.

20
Added humiliation: father of boy Scout fought to uphold Atticus' honor is good football player.

21
Imitating Atticus' mannerism.

22
"Mobile bus" travels from Maycomb (their town) to Mobile, Alabama.

"Well, he can make somebody's will so airtight can't anybody meddle with it."

"Shoot...."

"Well, did you know he's the best checker player in this town? Why, down at the Landing when we were coming up, Atticus Finch could beat everybody on both sides of the river."

"Good Lord, Miss Maudie, Jem and me beat him all the time."

"It's about time you found out it's because he lets you. Did you know he can play a jew's-harp?"[5]

14 This modest accomplishment served to make me even more ashamed of him.

"Well..." she said.

"Well what, Miss Maudie?"

"Well nothing. Nothing—it seems with all that you'd be proud of him. Can't everybody play a jew's-harp. Now keep out of the way of the carpenters. You'd better go home, I'll be in my azaleas and can't watch you. Plank might hit you."

15 I went to the backyard and found Jem plugging away at a tin can, which seemed stupid with all the bluejays around. I returned to the front yard and busied myself for two hours erecting a complicated breastworks at the side of the porch, consisting of a tire, an orange crate, the laundry hamper, the porch chairs, and a small U.S. flag Jem gave me from a popcorn box.

When Atticus came home to dinner he found me crouched down aiming across the street. "What are you shooting at?"

"Miss Maudie's rear end."

Atticus turned and saw my generous target bending over her bushes. He pushed his hat to the back of his head and crossed the street.

16 "Maudie," he called, "I thought I'd better warn you. You're in considerable peril."

Miss Maudie straightened up and looked 17 toward me. She said, "Atticus, you are a devil from hell."

When Atticus returned he told me to break 18 camp. "Don't you ever let me catch you pointing that gun at anybody again," he said.

19 I wished my father was a devil from hell. I sounded out Calpurnia[6] on the subject. "Mr. Finch? Why, he can do lots of things."

"Like what?" I asked.

Calpurnia scratched her head. "Well, I don't rightly know," she said.

Jem underlined it when he asked Atticus if he was going out for the Methodists and Atticus said he'd break his neck if he did, he was just too old for that sort of thing. The Methodists were trying to pay off their church mortgage, and had challenged the Baptists to a game of touch football. Everybody in town's father was playing, it seemed, except Atticus. Jem said he didn't even want to go, but he was unable to resist football in any form, and he stood gloomily on the sidelines with Atticus 20 and me watching Cecil Jacobs' father make touchdowns for the Baptists.

One Saturday Jem and I decided to go exploring with our air rifles to see if we could find a rabbit or a squirrel. We had gone about five hundred yards beyond the Radley Place when I noticed Jem squinting at something 21 down the street. He had turned his head to one side and was looking out of the corners of his eyes.

"Whatcha looking at?"

"That old dog down yonder," he said.

"That's old Tim Johnson, ain't it?"

"Yeah."

Tim Johnson was the property of Mr. Harry 22 Johnson, who drove the Mobile bus and lived on the southern edge of town. Tim was a liver-colored bird dog, the pet of Maycomb.

"What's he doing?"

---

5. **jew's-harp:** a musical instrument held between the teeth and plucked with a finger.

6. **Calpurnia:** the family's housekeeper. The children's mother is dead.

FAMILY ALBUM

SCIENCE LINK
Have students use encyclopedias and other reference sources to find out more about the mockingbird. Have students record what they learn in their journals or learning logs. Encourage them to include a drawing of the bird as well.

TRANSPARENCIES 6 & 7
Fine Art
Theme: *Close Ties* – invites students to explore artwork showing the relationship between members of families or people of differing generations.

"I don't know, Scout. We better go home."

23 "Aw Jem, it's February."

"I don't care, I'm gonna tell Cal."

We raced home and ran to the kitchen.

"Cal," said Jem, "can you come down the sidewalk a minute?"

"What for, Jem? I can't come down the sidewalk every time you want me."

"There's somethin' wrong with an old dog down yonder."

Calpurnia sighed. "I can't wrap up any dog's foot now. There's some gauze in the bathroom, go get it and do it yourself."

Jem shook his head. "He's sick, Cal. Something's wrong with him."

"What's he doin', trying to catch his tail?"

"No, he's doin' like this."

Jem gulped like a goldfish, hunched his shoulders and twitched his torso. "He's goin' like that, only not like he means to."

"Are you telling me a story, Jem Finch?" Calpurnia's voice hardened.

"No Cal, I swear I'm not."

"Was he runnin'?"

"No, he's just moseyin' along, so slow you can't hardly tell it. He's comin' this way."

Calpurnia rinsed her hands and followed Jem into the yard. "I don't see any dog," she said.

She followed us beyond the Radley Place and looked where Jem pointed. Tim Johnson was not much more than a speck in the distance, but he was closer to us. He walked erratically, as if his right legs were shorter than his 24 left legs. He reminded me of a car stuck in a sand bed.

"He's gone lopsided," said Jem.

Calpurnia stared, then grabbed us by the shoulders and ran us home. She shut the wood door behind us, went to the telephone and shouted, "Gimme Mr. Finch's office!"

"Mr. Finch!" she shouted. "This is Cal. I swear...there's a mad dog down the street a piece—he's comin' this way, yes sir, he's—Mr. Finch, I declare he is—old Tim Johnson, yes sir . . . yessir . . . yes——"

She hung up and shook her head when we tried to ask her what Atticus had said. She rat-
25 tled the telephone hook and said, "Miss Eula May—now ma'am, I'm through talkin' to Mr. Finch, please don't connect me no more—listen, Miss Eula May, can you call Miss Rachel and Miss Stephanie Crawford and whoever's got a phone on this street and tell 'em a mad dog's comin'? Please ma'am!"

Calpurnia listened. "I know it's February, Miss Eula May, but I know a mad dog when I 26 see one. Please ma'am hurry!"

Calpurnia asked Jem, "Radleys got a phone?"

Jem looked in the book and said no. "They won't come out anyway, Cal."

"I don't care, I'm gonna tell 'em."

She ran to the front porch, Jem and I at her heels. "You stay in that house!" she yelled.

Calpurnia's message had been received by 27 the neighborhood. Every wood door within our range of vision was closed tight. We saw no 28 trace of Tim Johnson. We watched Calpurnia running toward the Radley Place, holding her skirt and apron above her knees. She went up to the front steps and banged on the door. She got no answer, and she shouted, "Mr. Nathan, Mr. Arthur, mad dog's comin'! Mad dog's comin'!"

29 "She's supposed to go around in back," I said.

Jem shook his head. "Don't make any difference now," he said.

30 Calpurnia pounded on the door in vain. No one acknowledged her warning; no one seemed to have heard it.

As Calpurnia sprinted to the back porch a black Ford swung into the driveway. Atticus and Mr. Heck Tate got out.

Mr. Heck Tate was the sheriff of Maycomb

23
Old wives' tale that rabies occurs only in summer.

24
Metaphor. Comparison suggests that, like a stuck car, dog exerts much effort but makes little progress.

25
Miss Eula May is the town's sole telephone operator; she knows everyone and hears virtually everything.

26 Drawing Conclusions
Why is it important to warn the neighbors? So they will stay inside to avoid rabid dog; rabies is usually transmitted by biting.

27 Finding Details
What makes you think that the dog is considered dangerous? Neighbors close their doors. While prompt treatment prevents death, rabies shots are very painful.

28
Calpurnia is a brave woman; risks her life to warn neighbors.

29
Servant would be expected to use back door; this is an emergency.

30
Radleys are reclusive and, as Jem said, "won't come out anyway"; Cal cares enough to make sure they will be safe.

One-Shot Finch

SCIENCE LINK

Have students use reference sources to do research on rabies, including information on the description of the disease, its cause, symptoms, treatment, and prevention. Also, encourage students to contact local health departments and veterinarians to ask about the incidence of rabies in wild animals in the local area and about laws and regulations affecting the vaccination of pets and other domestic animals.

31 Making Inferences
Why might Jem and Scout admire Heck Tate? Because of his position of authority and his sharp uniform.

32
Dog's behavior is more predictable in this stage, making him an easier target to shoot.

33
Atticus defers to sheriff by asking for his opinion, but Atticus' prediction, not the sheriff's, is correct.

VISUAL CONNECTIONS
Ideas for Writing
You might ask students to analyze the body language and facial expressions of Scout, Jem, and Calpurnia as they appear in this movie still. Then ask students to make a list of adjectives and adverbs that describe each character.

County. He was as tall as Atticus, but thinner. **31** He was long-nosed, wore boots with shiny metal eyeholes, boot pants and a lumber jacket. His belt had a row of bullets sticking in it. He carried a heavy rifle. When he and Atticus reached the porch, Jem opened the door.

"Stay inside, son," said Atticus. "Where is he, Cal?"

"He oughta be here by now," said Calpurnia, pointing down the street.

"Not runnin', is he?" asked Mr. Tate.

"Naw sir, he's in the twitchin' stage, Mr. Heck." **32**

"Should we go after him, Heck?" asked Atticus. **33**

"We better wait, Mr. Finch. They usually go in a straight line, but you never can tell. He might follow the curve—hope he does or he'll go straight in the Radley backyard. Let's wait a minute."

"Don't think he'll get in the Radley yard," said Atticus. "Fence'll stop him. He'll probably follow the road...."

I thought mad dogs foamed at the mouth, galloped, leaped and lunged at throats, and I **34** thought they did it in August. Had Tim Johnson behaved thus, I would have been less frightened.

Nothing is more deadly than a deserted, waiting street. The trees were still, the mockingbirds were silent, the carpenters at Miss Maudie's house had vanished. I heard Mr. Tate sniff, then blow his nose. I saw him shift his gun to the crook of his arm. I saw Miss Stephanie Crawford's face framed in the glass window of her front door. Miss Maudie appeared and stood beside her. Atticus put his foot on the rung of a chair and rubbed his hand slowly down the side of his thigh.

"There he is," he said softly.

Tim Johnson came into sight, walking dazedly in the inner rim of the curve parallel to the Radley house.

35 "Look at him," whispered Jem. "Mr. Heck said they walked in a straight line. He can't even stay in the road."

36 "He looks more sick than anything," I said.

"Let anything get in front of him and he'll come straight at it."

Mr. Tate put his hand to his forehead and leaned forward. "He's got it all right, Mr. Finch."

37 Tim Johnson was advancing at a snail's pace, but he was not playing or sniffing at foliage: he seemed dedicated to one course and <u>motivated</u> by an invisible force that was inching him toward us. We could see him shiver like a horse shedding flies; his jaw opened and shut; he was <u>alist</u>, but he was being pulled gradually toward us.

"He's lookin' for a place to die," said Jem.

Mr. Tate turned around. "He's far from dead, Jem, he hasn't got started yet."

38 Tim Johnson reached the side street that ran in front of the Radley Place, and what remained of his poor mind made him pause and seem to consider which road he would take. He made a few hesitant steps and stopped in front of the Radley gate; then he tried to turn around, but was having difficulty.

Atticus said, "He's within range, Heck. You better get him now before he goes down the side street—Lord knows who's around the corner. Go inside, Cal."

Calpurnia opened the screen door, latched it behind her, then unlatched it and held onto the hook. She tried to block Jem and me with her body, but we looked out from beneath her arms.

"Take him, Mr. Finch." Mr. Tate handed the **39** rifle to Atticus; Jem and I nearly fainted.

"Don't waste time, Heck," said Atticus. "Go on."

40 "Mr. Finch, this is a one-shot job."

Atticus shook his head <u>vehemently</u>: "Don't just stand there, Heck! He won't wait all day for you——"

"... Mr. Finch, look where he is! Miss and you'll go straight into the Radley house! I can't shoot that well and you know it!"

"I haven't shot a gun in thirty years——"

Mr. Tate almost threw the rifle at Atticus.

41 "I'd feel mighty comfortable if you did now," he said.

In a fog, Jem and I watched our father take the gun and walk out into the middle of the **42** street. He walked quickly, but I thought he moved like an underwater swimmer: time had slowed to a nauseating crawl.

When Atticus raised his glasses Calpurnia murmured, "Sweet Jesus help him," and put her hands to her cheeks.

Atticus pushed his glasses to his forehead;

34
The unexpected often makes people feel vulnerable, not in control.

35
Reflects his respect for Atticus, who predicted dog would follow road.

36
Correct observation; rabid dogs do not act out of malice.

37
Description. Frightening details of his sickness: shivers, spasmodic jaw movements, leaning to one side ("alist"), fixed course.

38
"Poor mind" reflects Scout's sympathy for dog who was once a friend.

39
Children have no knowledge of Atticus' marksmanship.

40
Dog must be killed with one shot; if only wounded, he may still be a danger.

41 Drawing Conclusions
What does Mr. Tate's insistence indicate? Tate's extreme confidence in Atticus' ability.

42
Simile. Tension gives a surreal quality to what the children see.

One-Shot Finch

TRANSPARENCY 10

Literary Elements
Character – helps students identify and analyze ways that an author reveals character.

43
Dog convulses, perhaps prelude to "running stage"; Atticus must act quickly.

44
Tate's comment reflects relief from tension and his admiration of Atticus' skill.

45 Expressing an Opinion
How do you think Atticus feels? Responses will vary. He may feel regret, sadness, relief, surprise at remembered skill.

46
Characterization. Tate's outspoken praise heightens the effect of Atticus' silence; Atticus' silence indicates his modesty, perhaps even embarrassment.

47
Maudie's calling Atticus by his old nickname reveals that he was well known and still remembered for his shooting skill.

48
Rabies caused by virus, carried in mucous membranes. Infection can occur through skin abrasion or mucous membrane of victim coming in contact with contaminated saliva.

49
To run tests on the brain tissue; test used today is direct fluorescent antibody test; at time of the story, Sellar's stain smear test. Most states require test if unvaccinated dog bites someone.

50
Jem's awe is intensified because Atticus is so skilled at something Jem finds difficult to do.

108

---

they slipped down, and he dropped them in the street. In the silence, I heard them crack. Atticus rubbed his eyes and chin; we saw him blink hard.

In front of the Radley gate, Tim Johnson had made up what was left of his mind. He had finally turned himself around, to pursue his original course up our street. He made two steps forward, then stopped and raised his
43 head. We saw his body go rigid.

With movements so swift they seemed simultaneous, Atticus' hand yanked a ball-tipped lever as he brought the gun to his shoulder.

The rifle cracked. Tim Johnson leaped, flopped over and crumpled on the sidewalk in a brown-and-white heap. He didn't know what hit him.

Mr. Tate jumped off the porch and ran to the Radley Place. He stopped in front of the dog, squatted, turned around and tapped his
44 finger on his forehead above his left eye. "You were a little to the right, Mr. Finch," he called.

"Always was," answered Atticus. "If I had my 'druthers I'd take a shotgun."

He stooped and picked up his glasses, ground the broken lenses to powder under his
45 heel, and went to Mr. Tate and stood looking down at Tim Johnson.

Doors opened one by one, and the neighborhood slowly came alive. Miss Maudie walked along the steps with Miss Stephanie Crawford.

Jem was paralyzed. I pinched him to get him moving, but when Atticus saw us coming he called, "Stay where you are."

When Mr. Tate and Atticus returned to the yard, Mr. Tate was smiling. "I'll have Zeebo
46 collect him," he said. "You haven't forgot much, Mr. Finch. They say it never leaves you."

Atticus was silent.

"Atticus?" said Jem.
"Yes?"
"Nothin'."
47 "I saw that, One-Shot Finch!"

Atticus wheeled around and faced Miss Maudie. They looked at one another without saying anything, and Atticus got into the sheriff's car. "Come here," he said to Jem. "Don't you go near that dog, you understand? Don't
48 go near him, he's just as dangerous dead as alive."

"Yes, sir," said Jem. "Atticus——"
"What, son?"
"Nothing."

"What's the matter with you, boy, can't you talk?" said Mr. Tate, grinning at Jem. "Didn't you know your daddy's——"

"Hush, Heck," said Atticus, "let's go back to town."

When they drove away, Jem and I went to Miss Stephanie's front steps. We sat waiting for Zeebo to arrive in the garbage truck.

Jem sat in numb confusion, and Miss Stephanie said, "Uh, uh, uh, who'da thought of a mad dog in February? Maybe he wasn't mad, maybe he was just crazy. I'd hate to see Harry Johnson's face when he gets in from the Mobile run and finds Atticus Finch's shot his dog. Bet he was just full of fleas from somewhere——"

Miss Maudie said Miss Stephanie'd be singing a different tune if Tim Johnson was still coming up the street, that they'd find out soon
49 enough, they'd send his head to Montgomery.

Jem became vaguely articulate: "'d you see him, Scout? 'd you see him just standin' there? . . . 'n' all of a sudden he just relaxed all over, an' it looked like that gun was a
50 part of him . . . an' he did so quick, like . . . I hafta aim for ten minutes 'fore I can hit somethin'. . . ."

Miss Maudie grinned wickedly. "Well now,

108 FAMILY ALBUM

WRITING LINK
Have students rewrite the incident told in the story as an anecdote that an adult Scout might have written years later.

MEDIA LINK
To provide students a broader perspective of the South of the 1930s, access the video *To Kill a Mockingbird* and present short segments that complement the text.

Miss Jean Louise," she said, "still think your father can't do anything? Still ashamed of him?"

"Nome," I said meekly.

"Forgot to tell you the other day that besides playing the jew's-harp, Atticus Finch was the deadest shot in Maycomb County in his time."

"Dead shot . . ." echoed Jem.

"That's what I said, Jem Finch. Guess you'll change *your* tune now. The very idea, didn't you know his nickname was Ol' One-Shot when he was a boy? Why, down at the Landing **51** when he was coming up, if he shot fifteen times and hit fourteen doves he'd complain about wasting ammunition."

52 "He never said anything about that," Jem muttered.

"Never said anything about it, did he?"

"No ma'am."

"Wonder why he never goes huntin' now," I said.

53 "Maybe I can tell you," said Miss Maudie. "If your father's anything, he's civilized in his heart. Marksmanship's a gift of God, a talent—oh, you have to practice to make it perfect, but shootin's different from playing the piano or the like. I think maybe he put his gun down when he realized that God had given him an unfair advantage over most living things. I guess he decided he wouldn't shoot till he had to, and he had to today."

54 "Looks like he'd be proud of it," I said.

55 "People in their right minds never take pride in their talents," said Miss Maudie.

We saw Zeebo drive up. He took a pitchfork from the back of the garbage truck and gingerly lifted Tim Johnson. He pitched the dog onto the truck, then poured something from a gallon jug on and around the spot where Tim fell. "Don't yawl come over here for a while," he called.

When we went home I told Jem we'd really have something to talk about at school on Monday. Jem turned on me.

"Don't say anything about it, Scout," he said.

"What? I certainly am. Ain't everybody's daddy the deadest shot in Maycomb County."

Jem said, "I reckon if he'd wanted us to know it, he'da told us. If he was proud of it, he'da told us."

"Maybe it just slipped his mind," I said.

"Naw, Scout, it's something you wouldn't understand. Atticus is real old, but I wouldn't care if he couldn't do anything—I wouldn't **56** care if he couldn't do a blessed thing."

Jem picked up a rock and threw it jubilantly at the carhouse. Running after it, he called back: "Atticus is a gentleman, just like me!"

Reading Check

1. What is the "tribal curse" of the Finches?
2. According to Miss Maudie, why is it a sin to kill a mockingbird?
3. Who is the first one to spot the mad dog?
4. What happens to Atticus' glasses when he raises them to take aim?
5. Why does Atticus warn Scout and Jem to stay away from the dead dog?

For Study and Discussion

Analyzing and Interpreting the Selection

1. At the opening of the selection, Scout and Jem are disappointed that their father, Atticus, isn't more like their schoolmates' fathers. What are some of the things they wish their father could do?

51
Use to answer **study question 3**, p. 110.

52
Jem may wish he had known; wouldn't have misjudged his father.

53
Characterization. His civilized nature includes his respect for all life and extends to his defense of Tom Robinson.

54
Atticus' sense of morality prevents his feeling pride in killing.

55
A talent, if a gift from God, is something for which he is not responsible; thus, he can't take pride in it.

56 Synthesizing
What has Jem learned? To value true character more than social status or accomplishments.

READING CHECK
1. Weak left eyes (p. 102).
2. They do no harm: they simply make music for people to enjoy (p. 103).
3. Jem (p. 104).
4. They slip off, fall to the street, and the lenses crack (pp. 107–108).
5. Rabid dog is just as dangerous dead as alive (p. 108).

FOR STUDY AND DISCUSSION
1. Hunt, play football and poker, work with hands.

TRANSPARENCY 8

Reader Response
Family Crest – invites students to design a "family crest" symbolizing the relationship between two of the characters in a selection.

2a. They don't know he is a marksman. 2b. Wounded rabid dog might go wild, attack people.
3. As youth, he used no more than one shot hunting birds.
4a. He begins to understand father's reticence. 4b. Father's sense of justice, modesty, gentleness, ability.
5. Dislikes firearms, uses them only when necessary; does not want children to admire casual taking of life.

FOCUS ON READING
1. His unwillingness to hunt or play rough games; comments about killing mockingbird and pointing gun; reluctance to take rifle; not accepting praise after shooting dog.
2. Miss Maudie's explanation of Atticus' modesty; Jem's declaration that Atticus is a gentleman.
3. Stepping out into street and coldly taking aim at dog.
4. Never tells children about checkers ability or his marksmanship; won't allow bragging about dog.

LANGUAGE AND VOCABULARY
1. Suggested answers: *inability:* without; *incomplete:* not; *input:* in; *insane:* not; *intake:* in; *invisible:* not.

110

2a. Why are Scout and Jem surprised when they see Heck Tate, the sheriff, hand his rifle to Atticus? **b.** Why does the sheriff tell Atticus that this is a "one-shot job"?

3. How did Atticus get the nickname "Ol' One-Shot"?

4. After Atticus shoots the mad dog, Scout and Jem see their father in a new light. Scout wants to brag about Atticus' talent, but Jem has a different reaction. **a.** Why does he tell Scout not to mention the shooting? **b.** What has he learned to admire in Atticus?

5. Why do you think Atticus never told his children about his skill as a marksman? Consider what you have learned about his attitude toward guns throughout the selection.

Focus on Reading

Noting Details That Reveal Character

At the opening of the story, you know what Scout and her brother think of their father. They believe that Atticus is "feeble" and has no accomplishments they can be proud of. By the end of the selection, however, you know how wrong they have been. You have been able to form a different opinion of Atticus from what he says and does and from what other characters say about him.

Atticus is not a "feeble" man, as Scout believes at first, but a *gentle* man who dislikes violence. How is this characteristic revealed through Atticus' speech and actions? How is it revealed by what other characters say about him? What does Atticus do that shows that he is brave? How do you learn that Atticus is modest about his accomplishments?

Language and Vocabulary

Adding Different Meanings with *in-*

Scout says that she and her brother wanted Atticus to remain *inconspicuous*. Because they were not proud of Atticus' accomplishments, they did not want him to draw attention to himself.

Conspicuous people attract attention. People who are *inconspicuous* are just the opposite—they do not attract attention. Adding the negative prefix *in-* reverses the meaning of the word *conspicuous*.

See how the addition of *in-* changes the meaning of the following words.

activity	correct	secure
inactivity	incorrect	insecure

In these words, the prefix *in-* means "not" or "without." What pairs can you add to the list?

The prefix *in-* does not always add the meaning "not" or "without" to a word. The prefix *in-* can also mean "in." Decide which meaning the prefix has in each of these words:

inability	input	intake
incomplete	insane	invisible

110   FAMILY ALBUM

CLOSURE
Ask students to explain the children's changes in attitude about Atticus, the importance of the two conflicts in the story, and the title of the novel as it relates to the conflicts.

EXTENSION AND ENRICHMENT
Have students try role-playing the part of Atticus as he is interviewed by reporters for the town newspaper about his beliefs on firearms. Discuss responses in terms of characterization.

Focus on Descriptive Writing

Identifying Your Purpose

Your **purpose** in a description can be either factual or expressive. In a **factual description** you describe something as precisely as you can: for example, by giving its exact size, color, weight, shape, markings, and so on.

In an **expressive description** you use details as well as your own thoughts and feelings to create a mood or overall impression. This is the kind of description that Scout uses to tell about the mad dog in "One-Shot Finch" (see page 107).

Choose two subjects, one for a factual description and one for an expressive description. Each subject should be a person, place, or thing that you know well. Here are some possible subjects:

an aquarium	a vegetable
a tree	a clock
a music store	a baseball

Freewrite for five minutes about each subject, including as many specific details as you can. Save your writing.

About the Author

Harper Lee (1926–)

Harper Lee, whose family is related to Robert E. Lee, was born in Monroeville, Alabama. She attended Huntington College and Oxford University, and studied law at the University of Alabama. In 1961 she received the Pulitzer Prize for her widely acclaimed novel, *To Kill a Mockingbird*. Considered a work of national and social importance, the novel has been translated into ten languages, produced as a film, and adapted for the theater. The plot covers three years in the lives of a young girl named Scout, her older brother, Jem, and their father, Atticus Finch, who live in a small Alabama town during the Depression of the 1930s. The novel is based on Harper Lee's recollections of life in the South. Describing her life as a writer, Lee says that she works slowly, producing one or two pages a day. She believes that studying the law is good training for a writer, because it encourages one to respect and appreciate logical thought.

FOCUS ON DESCRIPTIVE WRITING
Before students freewrite, you may want to share with them examples of descriptive writing and help them to identify the factual and expressive details. When choosing expressive descriptions, look for those that are obvious in their mood or overall impression.

ABOUT THE AUTHOR
Harper Lee originally intended to be a lawyer like her father. However, shortly before she was to have graduated, she quit law school to devote herself to writing. While Lee maintains that her novel is not autobiographical, she believes that a writer must write truthfully and from experience.

One-Shot Finch

Those Winter Sundays

ROBERT HAYDEN

Sundays too my father got up early
and put his clothes on in the blueblack cold,
then with cracked hands that ached
from labor in the weekday weather made
banked fires° blaze. No one ever thanked him.   5

I'd wake and hear the cold splintering, breaking.
When the rooms were warm, he'd call,
and slowly I would rise and dress,
fearing the chronic angers of that house,

Speaking indifferently to him,   10
who had driven out the cold
and polished my good shoes as well.
What did I know, what did I know
of love's austere and lonely offices?

5. **banked fires:** fires kept burning low.

PRESENTATION

Two central images dominate Robert Hayden's "Those Winter Sundays." The image of "banked fires" that "blaze" represents the father's steady, unspoken love for his son. It is set against the "blueblack cold," which suggests the poverty imposed by racial injustice. The father tries to break up the cold of an uncaring world—inside or outside the house—by bringing back the hearth fire. His services on Sundays emphasize his work on the other days as well.

COOPERATIVE LEARNING

Have students work in small groups to compare the father in the poem to the father in "One-Shot Finch." What qualities do they have in common? How are their lives different?

For Study and Discussion

Analyzing and Interpreting the Poem

1. Which lines tell you the father worked hard on weekdays?

2. As a child, the poet feared "the chronic angers" in his house. *Chronic* means "constant" or "recurring." What do you think the phrase "chronic angers" refers to?

3. The word *austere* in line 14 means "requiring sacrifice or self-denial." **a.** Which details in the poem explain why the father's "offices," or duties, could be called "austere"? **b.** Which details explain why they could be called "lonely"?

4. In the last two lines, the poet indicates that as a child he failed to understand his father's expressions of love. What might have happened in the course of time to make him understand and appreciate his father's sacrifices?

Focus On Descriptive Writing

Using Specific Details

The **specific details** in "Those Winter Sundays" help us to see and feel the speaker's house in the early morning. To gather details for your description, use one or more of these methods:

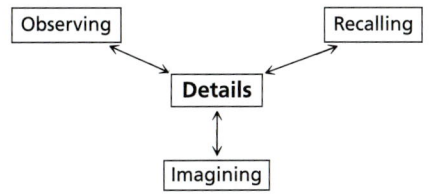

Choose one of the subjects for the assignment on page 111 or focus on another subject for description. Use the three methods above to gather specific details about this subject. Write your details on a chart like the one below. Save your notes.

Details Chart
What I observe: _____
What I recall: _____
What I imagine: _____

About the Author

Robert Hayden (1913–1980)

Robert Hayden, a prizewinning poet and a teacher, grew up in Detroit. One summer when he was in high school, he began reading the works of the poets Edna St. Vincent Millay and Countee Cullen. It was then that he began applying himself seriously to writing poetry, spending hours struggling to get his own thoughts down on paper.

Hayden once said this about his poem "Those Winter Sundays": "It is a sad poem, and one that I had to write.... The last stanza—oh, it's full of regret. Many people have told me this poem expresses their own feelings exactly.... It seems to speak to all people, as I certainly want my poems to do."

FOR STUDY AND DISCUSSION
1. Lines 3–4.
2. Perhaps Father's recurrent anger, also that of other family members, due in part to frustrations caused by poverty.
3a. Father rises early, in the "blueblack cold"; feeding fire each morning; his hands cracked from labor. 3b. No one thanked father; poet's indifference to father; not realizing his love.
4. May have made similar sacrifices for own children.

FOCUS ON DESCRIPTIVE WRITING
You may want to define the three methods and offer some examples. Explain that when students *observe* their subject, they actually sit in front of it and engage all of their senses. When they *recall* details, they shut their eyes and call up a mental picture of their subject, again trying to enlist all of their senses. When they *imagine* their subject, they are free to make up either realistic details or fantastic ones.

ABOUT THE AUTHOR
Robert Hayden was Professor of English at the University of Michigan where he received his M.A. in 1944. He published ten volumes of poetry and won the grand prize for poetry in English at the World Festival of Negro Arts at Dakar, Senegal (1966). His subject matter is diverse: personal feelings, black history, and world events. While many of his poems are complex, some, like "Those Winter Sundays," "The Web," and "The Wheel," are simple and direct.

OBJECTIVES
The overall aim is for students to explain the methods of **characterization** the author uses to make Joey a convincing character. For a complete list of objectives, see the **Teacher's Notes**.

VOCABULARY
The underlined words are in the Glossary. The **Language and Vocabulary** exercise on p. 121 of the textbook gives students practice in using context clues to determine meanings of words.

FOCUS / MOTIVATION
Ask students how and why behavior toward family members, especially siblings, often differs from our behavior toward friends. Introduce "Sled" as the story of a boy who has mixed feelings for his sister.

> **TEACHING RESOURCES A**
> Teacher's Notes, p. 205
> Reading Check, p. 207
> Study Guide, p. 208
> Language Skills, p. 210
> Building Vocabulary, p. 214
> Selection Vocabulary Test, p. 233
> Selection Test, p. 216

PREREADING FOCUS
The headnote focuses on effective **characterization**. You might ask students to discuss elements, based on other stories they have read, that they think make a character believable.

Sled
After students have read the story, the margin annotations may be used to guide discussion and analysis of Joey's character and his relationship with his sister.

1
Conflict. Joey is in conflict with both his mother and his sister; this kitchen scene is a battle for control.

2
Both brother and sister communicate and manipulate without speaking: she knows her smile will anger him, and he knows his untrue apology will allow him to go out.

3
The reader cannot know if she is a liar, although Joey believes it. His mother obviously does not believe him.

4
He has walked into her trap; she now has the upper hand in this power play, and he knows it.

114

Sled

THOMAS E. ADAMS

This short story focuses on the relationship between a brother and sister. As you read, ask yourself how the author makes Joey a convincing character. What makes the change in Joey's attitude toward his sister believable?

All the adventure of the night and snow lay before him: if only he could get out of the house.
1 "You can't go out," his mother said, "until you learn how to act like a gentleman. Now apologize to your sister."
He stared across the table at his sister.
"Go on," his mother said.
His sister was watching her plate. He could
2 detect the trace of a smile at the corners of her mouth.
"I won't! She's laughing at me!" He saw the
3 smile grow more pronounced. "Besides, she *is* a liar!"
His sister did not even bother to look up,
4 and he felt from looking at her that he had said exactly what she had wanted him to say. He grew irritated at his stupidity.
"That settles it," his mother said calmly, without turning from the stove. "No outs for you."
He stared at his hands, his mind in a panic. He could feel the smile on his sister's face. His

114   FAMILY ALBUM

MOTIVATIONAL SUMMARY
Joey is mad at his sister. He disagreed with her at the dinner table, calling her a liar, and now his mother is determined to make him apologize before she'll let him go out to play in the snow with his sled. He figures he'll have to say he's sorry—whether or not he really means it—just so he can escape. His sister points out that his apology doesn't sound very sincere, but his mother lets him go. He plans to take the first opportunity he finds to get even with his sister.

PRESENTATION
This story of sibling relationships is told in the third person. Discuss with students how this **point of view** allows the reader to know more about a character than the first-person point of view used earlier in the unit. Recall the methods of

---

hand fumbled with the fork on his plate. "No," he said meekly, prodding a piece of meat with the fork. "I'll apologize."

His sister looked up at him innocently.

"Well?" said his mother. "Go on."

5 He took a deep breath. "I'm . . ." He met his sister's gaze. "I'm sorry!" But it came out too loudly, he knew.

"He is not," his sister said.

He clenched his teeth and pinched his legs with his fingers. "I am too," he said. It sounded good, he knew; and it was half over. He had 6 control now, and he relaxed a bit and even said further: "I'm sorry I called you a liar."

"That's better," his mother said. "You two should love each other. Not always be fighting."

He paused strategically for a long moment. "Can I go out now?"

"Yes," his mother said.

He rose from the table glaring at his sister with a broad grin, calling her a liar with his eyes.

His hand plucked his jacket from the couch and swirled it around his back. The buttons refused to fit through the holes, so he let them go in despair. He sat down just long enough to pull on his shiny black rubbers. Finally he put 7 on his gloves. Then with four proud strides he arrived at the door and reached for the knob.

"Put your hat on," his mother said without looking at him.

His face toward the door, screwed and tightened with disgust. "Aw, Ma."

"Put it on."

"Aw, Ma, it's not that cold."

"Put it on."

"Honest, Ma, it's not that cold out."

8 "Are you going to put your hat on, or are you going to stay and help with the dishes?"

He sighed. "All right," he said. "I'll put it on."

The door to the kitchen closed on his back and he was alone in the cold gloom of the shed. Pale light streamed through the frosted window and fell against the wall where the sled stood. The dark cold room was silent, and he was free. He moved into the shaft of light and stopped, when from the kitchen he heard the muffled murmur of his mother's voice, as if she were far away. He listened. The murmur9 ing hushed, and he was alone again.

The sled. It was leaning against the wall, its varnished wood glistening in the moonlight. 10 He moved closer to it and saw his shadow block the light, and he heard the cold cracking of the loose linoleum beneath his feet.

11 He picked it up. He felt the smooth wood slippery in his gloved hands. The thin steel runners shone blue in the light as he moved one finger along the polished surface to erase any dust. He shifted the sled in his hands and stood getting the feel of its weight the way he had seen his brother hold a rifle. He gripped the sled tightly, aware of the strength in his 12 arms; and he felt proud to be strong and alone and far away with the sled in the dark cold silent room.

The sled was small and light. But strong. And when he ran with it, he ran very quickly, quicker than anyone, because it was very light and small and not bulky like other sleds. And 13 when he ran with it, he carried it as if it were part of him, as if he carried nothing in his arms. He set the rear end on the floor, now, and let the sled lean against him, his hands on the steering bar. He pushed down on the bar and the thin runners curved gracefully because they were made of shiny blue flexible steel; and with them he could turn sharply in the snow, sharper than anyone. It was the best sled. It was his.

He felt a slight chill in the cold room, and in the moonlight he saw his breath in vapor rising like cigarette smoke before his eyes. His body

---

5 Summarizing
Is Joey's apology sincere? No; he must play by his mother's rules.

6
He manipulates his mother; she believes she has control.

7
Arrogant because of victory.

8
Again Joey manipulates his mother; he puts his hat on only temporarily.

9
Silence and solitude show freedom; no one controls him here.

10
Description. Sensory details add to the aura of secrecy.

11 Finding Details
How do Joey's actions show he loves the sled? By the way he lifts, touches, and holds it.

12
The sled gives him a sense of competence that is lacking in his family life.

13
He feels strong, fast, graceful, and superior when riding the sled.

Sled 115

characterization, and ask students to apply them to Joey's character. The progression of Joey's feelings toward himself and toward his sister is central to the meaning of the story.

SPORTS LINK
Have interested students research the Olympic Winter Games to find out more about the various competitive events that are based on popular winter sports such as sledding, skating, and skiing.

14
He resents her authority intruding into his domain.

15
He disobeys his mother. Outside, her orders carry no force.

16
Imagery. "Cold white silence" and white street contrast with "black branches" and "shadows" to create stark, eerie effect; moment enlarged by comparison of snow heaps to "a string of mountains."

17
Joey is king here; no one can interfere or tell him what to do. This gaze may also be to check the course before sledding.

18
The imperatives "Don't fall, don't fall: now!" are his thoughts as he runs.

19
The phrases "sled whacked in the quiet," "white close to his eyes" give a vivid **description** of what Joey sees and hears.

20 Finding Details
What detail at the end of the ride stresses Joey's solitude?
The only sound is that of "the wind and his breath."

21
This "breakneck speed" suggests an accident to come.

shivered with excitement as he moved hurriedly but noiselessly to the door. He flung it open; and the snow blue and sparkling, and the shadows deep and mysterious, the air silent and cold, all awaited him.

"Joey!" From the kitchen came his mother's voice. He turned toward the kitchen door and refused to answer.

"Joseph!"

14 "What!" His tone was arrogant, and a chill of fear rushed through his mind.

There was a long awful silence.

"Don't you forget to be home by seven o'clock." She hadn't noticed, and his fear was gone.

"All right!" He answered, ashamed of his fear. He stepped across the threshold and
15 closed the door. Then he removed the hat and dropped it in the snow beside the porch.

16 He plodded down the alley, thrilling in the cold white silence—the snow was thick. The gate creaked as he pushed it open, holding and guiding the sled through the portal. The street was white, and shiny were the icy tracks of automobiles in the lamplight above. While between him and the light the black branches of trees ticked softly in the slight wind. In the gutters stood enormous heaps of snow, pale dark in the shadows, stretching away from him like a string of mountains. He moved out of the shadows, between two piles of snow, and into
17 the center of the street, where he stood for a moment gazing down the white road that gradually grew darker until it melted into the gloom at the far end.

Then he started to trot slowly down the street. Slowly, slowly gaining speed without losing balance. Faster he went now, watching the snow glide beneath his shiny black rubbers.
18 Faster and faster, but stiffly, don't slip. Don't fall, don't fall: now! And his body plunged
19 downward, and the sled whacked in the quiet, and the white close to his eyes was flying beneath him as he felt the thrill of gliding alone along a shadowy street, with only the ski-sound of the sled in the packed snow. Then before his eyes the moving snow gradually slowed. And stopped. And he heard only the low sound of
20 the wind and his breath.

Up again and start the trot. He moved to the beating sound of his feet along the ground. His breath came heavily and quickly, and matched the rhythm of his pumping legs, straining to carry the weight of his body without the balance of his arms. He reached a wild dangerous
21 breakneck speed, and his leg muscles swelled

116 FAMILY ALBUM

COOPERATIVE LEARNING
Have students work together in small groups either to create a mural of their favorite things about winter or to draw or paint scenes from the story.

TRANSPARENCY 9
Reader Response
Getting Acquainted – asks students to give an introduction for the character in a social setting.

and ached from the tension, and the fear of falling too early filled his mind: and down he let his body go. The white road rushed to meet him; he was off again, guiding the sled obliquely across the street toward a huge pile of snow near a driveway.

Squinting his eyes into the biting wind, he 22 calculated when he would turn to avoid crashing. The pile, framed against the darkness of the sky, glistened white and shiny. It loomed 23 larger and larger before him. He steered the sled sharply, bending the bar; and the snow flew as the sled churned sideways, and he heard suddenly a cold metallic snap. He and the sled went tumbling over in the hard wet snow. He rolled with it and the steering bar jarred his forehead. Then the dark sky and snow stopped turning, and all he felt was the cold air stinging the bump on his forehead.

The runner had snapped; the sled was broken. He stared at the shiny smooth runner and touched the jagged edge with his fingers. He 24 sat in the middle of the driveway, the sled cradled in his lap, running his fingers up and down the thin runner until he came to the jagged edge where it had broken.

22
He believes he is in control, but he overestimates his mastery of the sled.

23
Plot. Climax occurs when his overconfidence makes him bend the bar too far and the runner snaps.

24 Finding Cause and Effect
What attitude is revealed by the way he holds the sled and by his careful search for the break in the runner? Sorrow.

Sled 117

READING SKILLS PRACTICE
The underlined passage can be used to give students practice in the reading skill of determining the sequence of events. Ask students to read the passage, paying attention to the events that occur. Then ask students to answer the following question.

What happened just before Joey's sister fell off the sled? **A.** She carried the sled awkwardly down the street. **B.** The runner broke. **C.** Joey heard his heart pounding. **D.** He wanted to call to her to stop. (Answer: D)

25
His overconfidence has led him to break the one thing that gives him a sense of competence and freedom.

26
Use to answer **study question 2b**, p. 120.

27
He begins to make his plan.

28
He is about to trick her.

29
Characterization. He is astounded by his ability to perform such a mean and hateful trick.

30
He is careful to hide the break.

31
He knows she will be hurt, but he does not try to stop her.

32
He cannot bring himself to do what he knows to be right.

With his fingers he took the two broken edges and fitted them back into place. They stuck together with only a thin crooked line to indicate the split. But it was like putting a broken cup together. He stared at it, and wished it would be all right and felt like crying.

He got up and walked slowly back down to the street to his house. He sat down between the back bumper of a parked car and a pile of snow. Through his wet eyelids he saw the lamplight shimmering brightly against them. He felt a thickness in his throat, and he swallowed hard to remove it, but it did not go away.

He leaned back, resting his head against the snowpile. Through his wet eyelids he saw the lamplight shimmering brightly against the sky. He closed his eyes and saw again the shiny graceful curve of the runner. But it was broken now. He had bent it too far; too far. With his hand he rubbed his neck, then his eyes, then his neck again. He felt the snow coming wet through his pants. As he shifted to a new position, he heard the creaking of a gate. He turned toward the sound.

His sister was walking away from his house. He watched her move slowly across the street and into the grocery store. Through the plate-glass window he saw her talking with the storekeeper. He stared down at the runner. With his gloves off, he ran his fingers along the cold smooth surface and felt the thin breakline. He got up, brushed the snow off the seat of his pants, and walked to the gate to wait for his sister.

He saw her take a package from the man and come out of the store. She walked carefully on the smooth white, her figure dark in its own shadow as she passed beneath the streetlight, the package in her arm. When she reached the curb on his side, he rested his arms on the nose of the sled and exhaled a deep breath nervously. He pretended to be staring in the opposite direction.

When he heard her feet crunching softly in the snow, he turned: "Hi," he said.

"Hi," she said and she paused for a moment. "Good sledding?"

"Uh-huh," he said. "Just right. Snow's packed nice and hard. Hardly any slush at all." He paused. "I'm just resting a bit now."

She nodded. "I just went for some milk."

His fingers moved slowly down the runner and touched the joined edges.

"Well . . ." she said, about to leave.

His fingers trembled slightly, and he felt his heart begin to beat rapidly: "Do you want to take a flop?" In the still night air he heard with surprise the calm sound of his voice.

Her face came suddenly alive. "Can I? I mean, will you let me? Really?"

"Sure," he said. "Go ahead." And he handed her the sled very carefully. She gave him the package.

▶He put the bag under his arm and watched her move out of the shadows of the trees and into the light. She started to trot slowly, awkwardly, bearing the sled. She passed directly beneath the light and then she slipped and slowed to regain her balance. The sled looked large and heavy in her arms, and seeing her awkwardness, he realized she would be hurt badly in the fall. She was moving away again, out of the reach of the streetlight, and into the gray haze farther down the road.

He moved to the curb, holding the bag tightly under his arm, hearing his heart pounding in his ears. He wanted to stop her, and he opened his mouth as if to call to her; but no sound came. It was too late: her dark figure was already starting the fall, putting the sled beneath her. Whack! And her head dipped with the front end jutting the ground, and the back of the sled and her legs rose like a seesaw and down they came with another muffled sound. The street was quiet, except for a low whimper that filled his ears.◀

MEETING INDIVIDUAL NEEDS
Visual Learners • Students may be interested in doing research on different kinds of sleds and making drawings or diagrams of them. Students may wish to post their drawings on a classroom bulletin board.

---

33 He saw her figure rise slowly and move toward him. He walked out to meet her beneath the light. She held the sled loosely in one hand, the broken runner dangling, reflecting light as she moved.

She sobbed, and looking up he saw bright tears falling down her cheeks and a thin line of blood trickling down her chin. In the corner of her mouth near the red swelling of her lip, a little bubble of spit shone with the blood in the light.

34 He felt that he should say something, but he did not speak.

"I'm . . . I'm sorry," she said, and the bubble broke. "I'm sorry I . . . your sled." She looked down at the sled. "It'll never be the same."

"It'll be all right," he said. He felt that he 35 ought to do something, but he did not move. "I can get it soldered. Don't worry about it." But he saw from her expression that she thought he was only trying to make her feel better.

36 "No," she said, shaking her head emphatically. "No, it won't! It'll always have that weak spot now." She began to cry very hard. "I'm sorry."

37 He made an awkward gesture of forgiveness with his hand. "Don't cry," he said.

She kept crying.

"It wasn't your fault," he said.

"Yes, it was," she said. "Oh, yes, it was."

"No!" he said. "No, it wasn't!" But she didn't seem to hear him, and he felt his words were useless. He sighed wearily with defeat, not 38 knowing what to say next. He saw her glance up at him as if to see whether he were still watching her, then she quickly lowered her gaze and said with despair and anguish: "Oh . . . girls are so stupid!"

There was no sound. She was no longer crying. She was looking at the ground: waiting. His ears heard nothing; they felt only the cold silent air.

"No, they aren't," he said halfheartedly. And he heard her breathing again. He felt he had been forced to say that. In her shining eyes he 39 saw an expression he did not understand. He wished she would go in the house. But seeing the tears on her cheeks and the blood on her 40 chin, he immediately regretted the thought.

41 She wiped her chin with her sleeve, and he winced, feeling rough cloth on an open cut. "Don't do that." His hand moved to his back pocket. "Use my handkerchief."

She waited.

The pocket was empty. "I haven't got one," he said.

Staring directly at him, she patted gingerly the swollen part of her lip with the tips of her fingers.

He moved closer to her. "Let me see," he said. With his hands he grasped her head and tilted it so that the light fell directly on the cut.

"It's not too bad," she said calmly. And as she said it she looked straight into his eyes, and 42 he felt she was perfectly at ease; while standing that close to her, he felt clumsy and out of place.

In his hands her head was small and fragile, and her hair was soft and warm; he felt the rapid pulsing of the vein in her temple: his ears grew hot with shame.

"Maybe I better go inside and wash it off?" she asked.

With his finger he wiped the blood from her chin. "Yes," he said, feeling relieved. "You go inside and wash it off." He took the sled and gave her the package.

He stared at the ground as they walked to the gate in silence. When they reached the curb he became aware that she was watching him.

"You've got a nasty bump on your forehead," she said.

"Yes," he said. "I fell."

"Let me put some snow on it," she said, reaching to the ground.

33
Although he goes to her, he doesn't offer help.

34
She needs his comfort, but he is incapable of giving it.

35
Joe feels guilty, and their relationship is awkward.

36
Characterization. She feels guilty because she knows how important sled is to him. Her sensitivity to his feelings arouses his sensitivity to hers.

37
His efforts to make her feel better are feeble and ineffective; it's too late for him to confess.

38
She thinks his behavior suggests an ulterior motive—she tests his sincerity.

39 Expressing an Opinion
What expression do you think he sees? Responses will vary. Perhaps pain, satisfaction, regret, love.

40
He suddenly realizes her need for his company.

41
Characterization. Joey begins to feel empathy with his sister and makes his first sincere effort to comfort and help her.

42
Sibling rivalry is set aside; makes him feel even worse.

Sled 119

> **TRANSPARENCY 10**
> **Literary Elements**
> *Character* – helps students identify and analyze ways that an author reveals character.

43 Drawing Conclusions
Why can't Joey let his sister repay his kindness? His shame won't let him accept.

44
They have achieved a mutual understanding.

45
His sister is now more important to him than the sled.

46
Characterization. His new humility contrasts vividly with his previous arrogance; he now has genuine concern for his sister.

READING CHECK
1. He called her a liar (p. 114).
2. He steers sled too sharply; bends runner too far (p. 117).
3. When sled overturns, steering bar strikes his forehead (p. 117).
4. Going to grocery store (p. 118).
5. She cuts her lip (p. 119).

FOR STUDY AND DISCUSSION
1a. He feels he is right. Apology would be humiliating. **1b.** So he can go out.
2a. It is light but strong. **2b.** He miscalculated.
3. Answers may vary. Probably for revenge.
4a. Says she's sorry, cries. **4b.** He feels guilty.
5. Offers to put snow on his hurt forehead; reminds him to put hat on; smile together; holds gate open for her; shares her feelings.

120

---

43 He caught her wrist and held it gently. "No," he said.

He saw her about to object: "It's all right. You go inside and take care of your lip." He said it softly, but with his grip and his eyes he told her more firmly.

"All right," she said after a moment, and he released his hold. "But don't forget to put your hat on."

He stared at her.

"I mean, *before* you go back in the house."

44 They both smiled.

"Thanks for reminding me," he said, and he **45** dropped the sled in the snow and hurried to hold the gate open for her.

She hesitated, then smiled proudly as he beckoned her into the alley.

He watched her walk away from him down the dark alley in the gray snow. Her small figure swayed awkwardly as she stepped carefully in the deep snow, so as not to get her feet too wet. Her head was bowed, and her shoulders **46** hunched, and he humbly felt her weakness. And he felt her cold. And he felt the snow running cold down her boots around her ankles. And though she wasn't crying now, he could still hear her low sobbing, and he saw her shining eyes and the tears falling and her trying to stop them and them falling even faster. And he wished he had never gone sledding. He wished that he had never even come out of the house tonight.

The back door closed. He turned and moved about nervously kicking at the ground. At the edge of the curb he dug his hands deep into the cold wet snow. He came up with a handful and absently began shaping and smoothing it. He stopped abruptly and dropped it at his feet.

He did not hear it fall. He was looking up at the dark sky, but he did not see it. He put his cold hands in his back pockets, but he did not feel them. He was wishing that he were some

120 FAMILY ALBUM

---

time a long time away from now and somewhere a long way away from here.

In the corner of his eye something suddenly dimmed. Across the street in the grocery store the light was out: it was seven o'clock.

> **Reading Check**
> 1. Why have Joey and his sister been fighting at the dinner table?
> 2. Why does the runner on Joey's sled snap?
> 3. How does Joey hurt his head?
> 4. Why does Joey's sister come out of the house?
> 5. How is she hurt by her fall?

For Study and Discussion

Analyzing and Interpreting the Story

1. At the opening of the story, Joey does not want to apologize to his sister. **a.** Why not? **b.** Why does he force himself to apologize?

2a. Why does Joey feel that his sled is so special? **b.** After the runner breaks, Joey feels he is to blame. Why?

3. Why do you think Joey offers his sister a ride on the broken sled?

4. Joey's sister, believing she has broken the sled, wants her brother to forgive her. **a.** How does she apologize to Joey? **b.** Why does her behavior make her brother uncomfortable?

5. Early in the story, Joey's mother says, "You two should love each other. Not always be fighting." How do Joey and his sister show that they do care about each other after the accident with the sled? Find passages that support your answer.

CLOSURE
Ask students to explain the methods of **characterization** the author uses to make Joey a convincing character. Then ask how the reader understands the changes in Joey's feelings.

EXTENSION AND ENRICHMENT
Students may interview an older sibling about sibling rivalry and jealousy. They also might write follow-up stories to show whether the relationship between Joey and his sister changes.

Focus on Reading

Inferring Character from Thoughts and Feelings

In addition to learning about Joey from what he says and does, you learn about him from his thoughts and feelings. At the beginning of the story, you can tell that Joey feels humiliated. He has been forced to apologize to his sister, and he sees that she is laughing at him.

1. What passages reveal that the sled makes Joey feel strong and important?
2. When Joey breaks the sled, he feels miserable. What passage reveals his deep hurt?
3. At what point does Joey realize how seriously his sister might be hurt?
4. Where do you learn that Joey feels ashamed of tricking his sister?
5. How do you know that he understands his sister's feelings and sympathizes with her?

Language and Vocabulary

Using Context Clues

While Joey was in the shed, "he heard the muffled *murmur* of his mother's voice, as if she were far away." If you were not familiar with the word *murmur*, you could use clues within the sentence to determine what it means. Other words in the sentence tell you that here the word *murmur* refers to a voice, that it is "muffled," and that it seems "far away." A *murmur* is a sound that is low and unclear.

Use context clues to figure out the meanings of the italicized words in these sentences:

1. The gate creaked as he pushed it open, holding and guiding the sled through the *portal*.
2. Through his wet eyelids he saw the lamplight *shimmering* brightly against the sky.
3. She wiped her chin with her sleeve, and he *winced*, feeling rough cloth on an open cut.

Focus On Descriptive Writing

Using Sensory Details

Sensory details are words and phrases that appeal to the five senses:

sight   sound   smell   taste   touch

In the last paragraph on page 118, for example, Thomas Adams uses details that appeal to sight, sound, and touch to describe the fall of Joey's sister when she rides the broken sled.

Join with a small group of classmates and choose one of the following four subjects for a description. See how many sensory details your group can collect. Write the details on an **observation chart** like the one below. Save your notes.

a pizza   a beach
a zoo   a freight train

Observation Chart

Subject: _____				
Sight	Sound	Touch	Smell	Taste
___	___	___	___	___
___	___	___	___	___
___	___	___	___	___
___	___	___	___	___

About the Author

Thomas E. Adams (1937–)

Thomas E. Adams graduated from La Salle College in Philadelphia and earned his M.A. at the University of Florida. "Sled," his first published story, appeared in the *Sewanee Review* in 1961 and was included in the O. Henry *Prize Stories 1962*. The story was once turned into a play for radio broadcast by The Voice of America.

FOCUS ON READING
Suggested answers:
1. "He gripped the sled tightly . . . far away with the sled . . ." (p. 115). "He pushed down on the bar . . . It was his" (p. 115).
2. Three paragraphs, beginning "With his fingers he took the two broken edges . . ." (p. 118).
3. When he sees that she is unbalanced by the weight of the sled (p. 118).
4. "In his hands her head was small and fragile . . . his ears grew hot with shame" (p. 119).
5. Joey's assuring his sister that it wasn't her fault and that girls aren't stupid (p. 119).

LANGUAGE AND VOCABULARY
1. From the indication that it has to do with a gate and that a sled can be guided through it, students should infer that a *portal* is an entryway.
2. Students should be able to relate *shimmering* (glimmering or shining unsteadily) to the visual image of bright lamplight seen through wet eyelids.
3. From the sensory clue of "feeling rough cloth on an open cut," students will probably be able to figure out that when Joey *winced*, his reaction was to shrink back from or grimace at the sensation.

FOCUS ON DESCRIPTIVE WRITING
Before they choose subjects to describe, you may want to help students create on the chalkboard a sensory word bank. You might start with the following list:
Sight: glossy, bright, hazy
Sound: buzz, shriek, hum
Smell: fresh, musty, spoiled
Touch: wet, smooth, gritty
Taste: bitter, salty, tangy
As students work in groups to complete their observation charts, suggest that they also use thesauruses.

OBJECTIVES
The overall aim is for students to demonstrate an understanding of the New Year's celebration observed by Monica Sone's family in Seattle's Japanese community. For a complete list of objectives, see the **Teacher's Notes**.

VOCABULARY
The underlined words are in the Glossary. In addition, call students' attention to the vocabulary footnotes in their textbooks.

FOCUS / MOTIVATION
Ask students to discuss family celebrations and traditions (not necessarily their own) and why they are important. Tell them they will read about some Japanese New Year's traditions in the selection.

TEACHING RESOURCES A
Teacher's Notes, p. 218
Reading Check, p. 220
Study Guide, p. 221
Building Vocabulary, p. 223
Selection Test, p. 225

AV RESOURCES BINDER
Audiocassette 1, Side B

PREREADING FOCUS
The headnote emphasizes the differences between first- and second-generation Japanese Americans. Students might discuss elements of conflict common to immigrant families.

Nisei Daughter

1 Family time is the pleasure; visiting parents' friends is the agony.

2 Reflects Japanese tradition of sacrificing individual interests for those of the group.

3 Summarizing
What does the act of bathing symbolize? Concepts of ritual purification and of personal cleanliness.

4 Game encourages good memory, appreciation of poetry and Japanese calligraphy.

5 The youngest child is encouraged to learn this game, indicating Japanese tradition is being upheld.

6 Simile. Suggests both activity of the game and the children's behavior.

7 *Hai* means "yes." The children's enthusiasm suggests that they respect and enjoy some aspects of their Japanese heritage.

FROM
Nisei Daughter

MONICA SONE

Monica Sone grew up in Seattle's Japanese community. Her parents were immigrants, known as Issei, *"first generation." She herself was a* Nisei, *the name given to second-generation Japanese Americans. Here she tells how her family celebrated New Year's.*

New Year's, as my family observed it, was a **1** mixture of pleasure and agony. I enjoyed New Year's Eve which we spent together, waiting for midnight. On New Year's Eve, no one argued when Mother marched us into the bathtub, one by one. We understood that something as **2** important as a new year required a special sacrifice on our part. Mother said the bath was a symbolic act, that we must scrub off the old year and greet the new year clean and re- **3** freshed in body and spirit.

The rest of the evening we spent crowded around the table in the living room playing **4** *Karuta*, an ancient Japanese game. It consisted of one hundred old classic poems beautifully brushed upon one hundred cards, about the size of a deck of cards. There was one set of cards on which were written the *shimo no ku*, the second half of the poems. These were laid out on the table before the players. A reader presided over a master set of one hundred cards which contained the *kami no ku*, the first half of the poem as well as the *shimo no ku*. As the reader read from the key cards, the players were to try to pick up the card on the table before anyone else could claim it. The player or the team who picked up the greatest number of cards was the winner. An expert player knew the entire one hundred poems by heart so that when the reader had uttered the first few words, he knew instantly which card was being called out. When several experts competed the game was exciting and stimulating. But in our family only Mother and Father knew the poems, and they slowed their paces to match ours.

Mother was always the reader, chanting out the poems melodically. Sumiko, being the baby of the family, was allowed to stand on a chair at Mother's elbow and get a preview of the card **5** being read. Sumiko would look, jump off the chair, and scurry around the table to find the card while we waited impatiently for Mother to get to the second half of the poem. I howled with indignation, "Mama, make Sumiko stop cheating! It's not fair . . . I'll never find a card as long as she peeks at the *kami no ku*!"

Mother laughed indulgently, "Now, don't get so excited. Sumichan's just a little girl. She has to have some fun, too."

6 The evening progressed noisily as we fluttered about like anxious little moths, eyes riveted on the table. Anyone who found a card **7** would triumphantly shout *"Hai!"* and slam down on it with a force that would have flattened an opponent's fingers. Promptly at mid-

122 FAMILY ALBUM

MOTIVATIONAL SUMMARY

A Japanese-American girl enjoys some aspects of both her national heritages in her family's celebration of the New Year. The festivities include some elements of American as well as Japanese tradition. They play the Japanese poetry game, *Karuta*, as well as sing the New Year's song favored by Americans, "Auld Lang Syne." But then comes their customary New Year's visit to their parents' Japanese friends, the Matsuis; this is the custom that the girl always dreads.

PRESENTATION

For Monica Sone's family, as described in *Nisei Daughter*, New Year's is a curious blend of Japanese and American cultures. This mixture both pleases and annoys the children, who were born in the United States and prefer the relaxed,

---

8 night we stopped. Out in the harbor, hundreds of boats sounded their foghorns to herald the New Year. Automobiles raced by under our windows, their horns blowing raucously. Guns exploded, cowbells clanged, the factory whistle shrilled. Henry swept the cards off the table, leaped into the air in his billowing night-
9 shirt and shouted "Happy New Year, everybody! Happy New Year!" We turned on the radio full blast so we could hear the rest of the city cheer and sing "Auld Lang Syne." Horrified, Father implored us, "Ohhh the guests, the guests. Lower that radio. We'll wake our guests."¹

Then Father and Mother slipped quietly down the hallway to the kitchen to prepare refreshments. Although the black-painted
10 steampipe, running alongside one wall in the room, made energetic knocking noises which meant that it was piping hot, the parlor was
11 chilly. I turned the tiny gas heater higher and Sumiko and I sat in front of it, pulling our voluminous flannel gowns over our knees and cold toes. We sat with our chins resting comfortably on our knees and huddled so close to the heater that our faces began to tighten and glow beet-red. I was floating in half sleep when I heard Mother and Father's voices murmuring gently. "*Sah*, who gets the smallest piece of pie?"

12 "Not me!" Sumiko jumped up defensively. Then she saw Father's eyes smiling.

Father had carried in a pot of hot coffee and fresh, honey-crusted apple pie with its golden juice bubbled through the slits. Mother brought in thick hot chocolate, with plump soft marshmallow floating on top, for us.

It was customary for the Japanese to eat
13 buckwheat noodles on New Year's Eve, but every year whenever Mother wondered aloud whether she should make some, we voted it down. Father said, "No noodles for me either, Mama. A good hot cup of coffee is what will please me most."

Father sliced the pie and as we let the flaky, butter-flavored crust melt in our mouths, we did not envy anyone eating noodles.

The next morning when we were breakfasting on fruit juice, ham and eggs, toast and milk, Mother said, "We really should be eating
14 *ozoni* and *mochi* on New Year's morning."

---

1. **guests:** hotel guests. The family owned the Carrollton Hotel, which was close to the waterfront.

8
The Japanese honor the New Year on January 15; the date of this celebration in the story reflects their Americanization.

9
Also reflects their adaptation to American culture.

10
Steam pipe gives hotel guests heat.

11
Imagery. Sensory details convey cozy warmth and dreamy atmosphere.

12
She fears that because she is the smallest, she will get the smallest piece.

13
The pie, coffee, and hot chocolate replace the noodles, but the structure of the celebration remains the same.

14
Ozoni and *mochi* are traditionally eaten on the Japanese New Year's Day. *Mochi* (rice dumplings) are traditionally offered to the god of water on the first day of the new year; to the farmyard crows on the eleventh to ensure a good harvest.

Americanized atmosphere of their family life to the sometimes complex and exacting Japanese social traditions. It is the restrictive social customs with which the narrator finds fault. The Japanese stress on politeness and self-effacement appears to her American way of thinking to be too forced and too uncomfortable. She honors her parents and many traditions of their homeland, but she clearly enjoys many American customs as well.

GEOGRAPHY LINK
Have students locate on a world map the country of Japan and the city of Seattle. Have them use the scale on the map to estimate the distance between a city in Japan, such as Tokyo, and Seattle.

15
The dumplings are *mochi*. Legend has it that a *mochi* cake used as an archery target turned into a bird and flew away when hit.

16
Born in the U.S., the children are more Americanized than the adults and do not enjoy the formality of traditional Japanese celebration.

17
Use to answer **study question 3a,** p. 126.

18 Finding Details
What two similes are used to show how the children must behave at a Japanese celebration? "Like little Buddhas" and "like meek little ghosts."

19
Formality of this traditional greeting reflects the respect that guests give their hosts, children their elders.

20
Bowing is like a handshake—a form of greeting that shows respect; the deeper the bow, the more respect one shows.

21
Though children are bilingual, they are more comfortable speaking English.

124

We gagged, "Oh, no, not in the morning!"

"Well now, don't turn your nose up like that. It's a perfectly respectable tradition."

15 *Ozoni* was a sort of thick chicken stew with solid chunks of carrots, bamboo sprouts, giant white radishes and taro roots. Into this piping hot mixture, one dipped freshly toasted rice dumplings, puffed into white airy plumpness, in the same way one dunked doughnuts into coffee. But the rice dumpling had an annoying way of sticking to everything like glue . . . to the chopsticks, to the side of the bowl, and on the palate. It was enough to cause a panic when the thick, doughy dumpling fastened itself in the throat and refused to march on down to the stomach.

Father backed us up once more, "*Ozoni* is good, I admit, but I don't like to battle with my food so early in the morning. Let's have some more coffee, Mama."

"Well, having a whimsical family like this certainly saves me a lot of work."

Up to that moment the family was in perfect harmony about whether we would celebrate New Year's in the Japanese or the American way. But a few hours later our peace was shattered when Mother said, "*Sah*, now we must pay our respects to the Matsuis."

"Not again," Henry shuddered.

"Yes again, and I don't want to hear any arguments."

16 "But why must *we* go? Why can't you and Papa go by yourselves this time?"

"We are all going together for the New Year's call," Mother said firmly. "I don't want to hear another word. Put your clothes on."

We sighed loudly as we dressed ourselves. **17** We would have to sit silently like little Buddhas² and listen while our elders dredged up the past and gave it the annual overhaul. Even the prospect of Mrs. Matsui's magnificent holiday feast was dampened by the fact that we knew we would have to eat quietly like meek lit- **18** tle ghosts and politely refuse all second helpings.

"Mama . . . " Henry shouted from his room. "What was that now, that New Year's greeting we have to say to the Matsuis? I've forgotten how it goes. '*Ake-mashite omede toh gozai masu. Konen mo, ahhh, konen mo . . .* ' What comes after that? I can't remember."

Mother said, "*Soh, soh . . .* I want you all to say it properly when we arrive at the Matsui-san's³ home. It goes like this . . . *ake-mashite* **19** *omede toh gozai masu*, which means 'This New Year is indeed a happy occasion.' Then you say *konen mo yoroshiku onegai itashi-masu*. 'I hope that the coming year will find us close friends as ever.' "

As we climbed up Yesler Hill to the Matsuis, we repeated the greeting over and over again. We raised our voices so we could hear ourselves better whenever a chunky bright orange cable car lurched up the hill like a lassoed bronco, inching its way furiously to the top.

The Matsui residence was a large yellow frame house which squatted grandly on an elevated corner lot. At the front door, Father and **20** Mother and Mr. and Mrs. Matsui bowed and murmured, bowed and murmured. Standing behind our parents, we bowed vigorously, too. Then Mrs. Matsui looked at us expectantly and Mother pushed us forward. We bowed again, then started out in unison. "*Ake-mashite omede toh gozai masu.*" A long pause followed. We forgot the rest. Then Henry recalled a fragment, **21** "*Konen mo . . . konen mo . . . ahhh*, something about *onegai shimasu.*"

The adults burst into laughter, bringing the affair to a merciful end.

---

2. **Buddha** (bōō′də, bŏŏd′ə): an Indian philosopher who founded Buddhism, a religion of eastern and central Asia. Statues of Buddha show him meditating.

3. **Matsui-san:** The suffix *san* added to a name is a title of respect.

124 FAMILY ALBUM

MEETING INDIVIDUAL NEEDS
ESL/LEP • At the Matsui home, the children sit on the "davenport." Ask the class to suggest words that are more commonly used to refer to this item of furniture. (sofa, couch)

PORTFOLIO ASSESSMENT
Students may be interested in giving an informative speech about how their families celebrate a particular holiday and what they like or dislike about the celebration. Tape-recorded speeches may be added to student portfolios.

Consult with individual students on how their speeches will be assessed. (See *Portfolio Assessment and Professional Support Materials* for additional information on student portfolios.)

In the living room, we waited patiently while Mrs. Matsui offered the best chairs to Father and Mother who politely refused them. Mrs. 22 Matsui insisted and they declined. When at last we were all seated as Mrs. Matsui wanted—Father and Mother on the overstuffed brown mohair chairs and the four of us primly lined 23 up on the huge davenport, our polished shoes placed neatly together and hands in our laps—she brought in tea and thin, crisp, rice cookies. As she poured the tea, she said, "Perhaps the little folks would rather have 'sodawata' instead?"

Henry and Kenji smirked at each other while Sumiko and I hung our heads, trying not to look eager, but Mother said quickly, "Oh, no, please, Mrs. Matsui, don't trouble yourself. My children love tea." So we sipped scalding tea out of tiny, burning teacups without handles and nibbled at brittle rice wafers.

While the Matsuis and our parents reminisced about the good old days, we thumbed through the worn photograph albums and old Japanese tourist magazines. Finally Mrs. Matsui excused herself and bustled feverishly around the dining room. Then she invited us 24 in. "*Sah*, I have nothing much to offer you, but please eat your fill."

"*Mah, mah*, such a wonderful assortment of *ogochi-soh*," Mother bubbled.

Balding Mr. Matsui snorted deprecatingly. Mrs. Matsui walked around the table with an enormous platter of *osushi*, rice cakes rolled in seaweed. We each took one and nibbled at it daintily, sipping tea. Presently she sailed out of the kitchen bearing a magnificent black and sil- 25 ver lacquered tray loaded with carmine lacquer bowls filled with fragrant *nishime*. In pearly iridescent china bowls, Mrs. Matsui served us hot chocolatey *oshiruko*, a sweetened bean soup dotted with tender white *mochi*, puffed up like oversized marshmallows.

Father and Mother murmured over the superb flavoring of each dish, while Mr. Matsui 26 guffawed politely, "*Nani*, this woman isn't much of a cook at all."

27 I was fascinated with the *yaki-zakana*, barbecued perch, which, its head and tail raised saucily, looked as if it were about to flip out of the oval platter. Surrounding this centerpiece were lacquer boxes of desserts, neatly lined rows of red and green oblong slices of sweet bean cakes, a mound of crushed lima beans, tinted red and green, called *kinton*. There was a vegetable dish called *kimpira* which looked like a mass of brown twigs. It turned out to be burdock,[4] hotly seasoned with red pepper.

Every now and then Mrs. Matsui urged us from the side line, "Please help yourself to more food."

And each time, we were careful to say, "*Arigato*, I have plenty, thank you," although I 28 could have counted the grains of rice I had so far consumed. I felt that a person could starve amidst this feast if he carried politeness too far. Fortunately, Mrs. Matsui ignored our refusals. She replenished our half-empty dishes 29 and kept our teacups filled so that without breaking the illusion that we were all dainty eaters, we finally reached a semiconscious state of satiation.

30 We moved heavily to the parlor to relax. Mrs. Matsui pursued us there with more green, pickled radishes and *kazunoko*, fish eggs, and a bowl of fresh fruit. She brought out 31 fresh tea and *yokan*. To turn down Mrs. Matsui's offer so often was very rude, so we accepted with a wan smile and firmly closed our mouths over the cake and chewed.

When Father and Mother finally came to their senses and decided it was time to go 32 home, we nearly tore the door off its hinges in our rush to get out into the hallway for our wraps.

---

4. **burdock:** a plant that is native to Europe and Asia.

Nisei Daughter **125**

22
Reflects the Japanese emphasis on polite form.

23
Japanese do not wear shoes inside.

24
Mrs. Matsui's comment reflects Japanese modesty.

25
Carmine: crimson-red; **lacquer:** a decorative finish applied on wood using natural varnishes.

26
His—and the Japanese—way of accepting a compliment.

27
Description. Shows that presentation of food is just as important to Japanese as flavor.

28
Narrator uses exaggeration to describe the formalities observed during the meal.

29
"Illusion" is an important part of Japanese ritual.

30
Heavy movement indicates they have eaten heartily, despite the narrator's polite refusal.

31
Yokan: a kind of cake.

32
An exaggeration; such a display of rudeness would insult the Matsuis and shame their parents.

MEETING INDIVIDUAL NEEDS

ESL/LEP • Students may be interested in knowing that "Auld Lang Syne" is a Scottish title that literally means "old long since," or days long past.

CLOSURE

Ask students to discuss details of the New Year's celebration observed by Monica Sone's family in Seattle's Japanese community.

EXTENSION AND ENRICHMENT

Students may write short essays about customs common to a selected holiday, research Japanese manners and customs, prepare Japanese foods, or invite a speaker to give a presentation on Japanese customs.

33 Synthesizing
How does this thought reflect her Americanization? Her parents probably do not find the situation uncomfortable; children living in Japan might enjoy it.

READING CHECK
1. First half of poem with the second half (p. 122).
2. Buckwheat noodles (p. 123).
3. They stuck to everything (p. 124).
4. Thumbed through photograph albums and Japanese tourist magazines (p. 125).

FOR STUDY AND DISCUSSION
1a. Playing *Karuta*, listening to the sounds of ringing in the new year, eating hot apple pie. **1b.** Sister's cheating at card game and visit to Matsuis'.
2. Played traditional Japanese games and ate traditional New Year's dinner with friends; observed American custom of celebrating at midnight, and sang "Auld Lang Syne."
3a. Children were expected to be quiet and polite. **3b.** Scene reveals highly ritualized nature of Japanese customs of hospitality (pp. 124–125). **3c.** Out of respect, children had to sit quietly and listen.
4. Traditional role of Japanese women did not allow them to question the social order.

FOCUS ON DESCRIPTIVE WRITING
Encourage students to use thesauruses and dictionaries of synonyms for this activity. When students have finished rewriting their paragraphs, suggest that they exchange papers to evaluate each other's selection of exact words and to suggest additional synonyms.

I staggered out at last into the frosty night, feeling tight as a drum and emotionally shaken from being too polite for too long. I hoped on our next call our hostess would worry less about **33** being hospitable and more about her guests' comfort, but that was an impudent thought for a Japanese girl.

Reading Check

1. In the game of *Karuta*, what are the players expected to match?
2. What was the customary Japanese food on New Year's Eve?
3. What problem did the children have with rice dumplings?
4. How did the children entertain themselves at the Matsuis' home?

For Study and Discussion

Analyzing and Interpreting the Selection

1. The narrator says that observing New Year's was a mixture of pleasure and agony. **a.** Which activities did she consider pleasurable? **b.** Which did she dislike?

2. In what way did the family observe both Japanese and American customs?

3a. How were the children expected to behave when they visited the Matsuis? **b.** What does this scene reveal about traditional Japanese customs of hospitality? **c.** About the attitude of children toward their elders?

4. At the end of the selection, the narrator tells us that her thought was "impudent." What does this remark reveal about the traditional roles of Japanese women?

Focus On Descriptive Writing

Using Exact Words

Exact words make your description sharp and vivid. Here are some examples of exact words in the first paragraph of the excerpt from Monica Sone's *Nisei Daughter*. Compare the italicized words in Sone's description with those in parentheses.

...a mixture of pleasure and *agony* (*pain*).
...*marched* us into the bathtub (*took*)...
...a special *sacrifice* on our part (*effort*).
...we must *scrub* off the old year (*wash*)...

Read a letter or card that you sent or received recently. Rewrite one paragraph of the message, using precise nouns, verbs, adjectives, and adverbs. Save your writing.

About the Author

Monica Sone (1919–   )

In *Nisei Daughter*, Monica Sone tells about growing up in Seattle's Japanese community, and she describes the intermingling of American and Japanese cultures. After the outbreak of World War II, her family was evacuated to an internment camp. When she left the camp, she went to the Midwest and eventually enrolled at college in Indiana. She now lives in Canton, Ohio.

Home

FROM THE NOVEL *Maud Martha*

GWENDOLYN BROOKS

In this story a family faces a crisis. How does each member of the family react? What are the special things Maud Martha fears losing?

1 What had been wanted was this always, this always to last, the talking softly on this porch, with the snake plant in the jardiniere¹ in the southwest corner, and the obstinate slip from Aunt Eppie's magnificent Michigan fern at the left side of the friendly door. Mama, Maud Martha, and Helen rocked slowly in their rocking chairs, and looked at the late afternoon light on the lawn and at the emphatic iron of the fence and at the poplar tree. These things might soon be theirs no longer. Those shafts and pools of light, the tree, the graceful iron, might soon be viewed possessively by different eyes.

---

1. **jardiniere** (järd′n-îr′): an ornamental pot for plants.

MOTIVATIONAL SUMMARY

Maud Martha is sitting on the porch with her Mama and sister Helen. They are anxious, but trying not to show it. They are waiting for Papa to come home. The family has been having hard times and is behind in the mortgage payments to the bank. Papa has taken his lunch hour to go to the bank and ask for an extension of the loan on their house. If the bank will not allow an extension, the family will lose their home. They sit talking, waiting to see Papa turn the corner with the news.

PRESENTATION

Different people come to terms with disappointment in various ways. In Gwendolyn Brooks' "Home," only Maud Martha honestly faces the sad prospect of leaving her home of fourteen years. Her sister Helen and her Mama mask their

---

4
Point of View. Mama's consoling words about "nice flat" are wishful thinking. Omniscient narrator knows what all three are thinking, that Papa cannot afford the rent.

5
Unusual **figurative language** conveys Maud Martha's efforts to choke back tears.

6
Characterization. Maud Martha is honest about her feelings.

7
Vivid imagery of sky conveys Maud Martha's perception of nature as more beautiful, more real, to her at her home.

8
Helen values material possessions, but she knows that the people make the home.

9
Characterization. Helen hides true feelings. She is trying to be brave (they all are).

10
Mama tries to explain expected loss in an optimistic way.

11
Papa hides his emotions. Long **description** heightens **suspense**.

12 Analyzing
Why is "his gate" changed to "the gate"? Emphasizes uncertainty about ownership.

Papa was to have gone that noon, during his lunch hour, to the office of the Home Owners' Loan. If he had not succeeded in getting another extension, they would be leaving this house in which they had lived for more than fourteen years. There was little hope. The Home Owners' Loan was hard. They sat, making their plans.

4 "We'll be moving into a nice flat[2] somewhere," said Mama. "Somewhere on South Park, or Michigan, or in Washington Park Court." Those flats, as the girls and Mama knew well, were burdens on wages twice the size of Papa's. This was not mentioned now.

"They're much prettier than this old house," said Helen. "I have friends I'd just as soon not bring here. And I have other friends that wouldn't come down this far for anything, unless they were in a taxi."

Yesterday, Maud Martha would have attacked her. Tomorrow she might. Today she said nothing. She merely gazed at a little hopping robin in the tree, her tree, and tried to
5 keep the fronts of her eyes dry.

"Well, I do know," said Mama, turning her hands over and over, "that I've been getting tireder and tireder of doing that firing.[3] From October to April, there's firing to be done."

6 "But lately we've been helping, Harry and I," said Maud Martha. "And sometimes in March and April and in October, and even in November, we could build a little fire in the fireplace. Sometimes the weather was just right for that."

She knew, from the way they looked at her, that this had been a mistake. They did not want to cry.

7 But she felt that the little line of white, sometimes ridged with smoked purple, and all that cream-shot saffron[4] would never drift across

---

2. **flat:** an apartment.
3. **firing:** starting a coal fire.
4. **saffron:** a yellow-orange color.

---

any western sky except that in back of this house. The rain would drum with as sweet a dullness nowhere but here. The birds on South Park were mechanical birds, no better than the poor caught canaries in those "rich" women's sun parlors.

"It's just going to kill Papa!" burst out Maud Martha. "He loves this house! He *lives* for this house!"

"He lives for us," said Helen. "It's us he
8 loves. He wouldn't want the house, except for us."

"And he'll have us," added Mama, "wherever."

9 "You know," Helen sighed, "if you want to know the truth, this is a relief. If this hadn't come up, we would have gone on, just dragged on, hanging out here forever."

10 "It might," allowed Mama, "be an act of God. God may just have reached down and picked up the reins."

"Yes," Maud Martha cracked in, "that's what you always say—that God knows best."

Her mother looked at her quickly, decided the statement was not suspect, looked away.

Helen saw Papa coming. "There's Papa," said Helen.

11 They could not tell a thing from the way Papa was walking. It was that same dear little staccato walk,[5] one shoulder down, then the other, then repeat, and repeat. They watched his progress. He passed the Kennedys', he passed the vacant lot, he passed Mrs. Blakemore's. They wanted to hurl themselves over the fence, into the street, and shake the truth out of his collar. He opened his gate—
12 the gate—and still his stride and face told them nothing.

"Hello," he said.

Mama got up and followed him through the

---

5. **staccato** (stə-kä′tō) **walk:** a walk of short, abrupt steps.

emotions in order to soften the expected loss, but in doing so, they try to deny their love of the home they dread leaving. This hurts Maud Martha, yet Helen does not truly mean any of these harsh words. Mama hides her feelings, too. Although she is less harsh than Helen, she compares their South Side Chicago home unfavorably with some of the more affluent neighborhoods in the city. However, each of these three characters displays courage in her attempt to deal with disappointment.

CLOSURE

Ask students to identify and analyze details that characterize each member of the family. Have them identify words and passages that reveal a change in mood in the last few paragraphs of the story.

---

front door. The girls knew better than to go in too.

19 Presently Mama's head emerged. Her eyes were lamps turned on.

"It's all right," she exclaimed. "He got it. It's all over. Everything is all right."

The door slammed shut. Mama's footsteps hurried away.

20 "I think," said Helen, rocking rapidly, "I think I'll give a party. I haven't given a party since I was eleven. I'd like some of my friends to just casually see that we're homeowners."

Reading Check

1. What news is the family awaiting?
2. What plans does Mama make for moving?
3. What news does Papa bring?
4. Why does Helen plan to give a party?

For Study and Discussion

Analyzing and Interpreting the Selection

1. Why do the members of the family feel they are in danger of losing their home?

2a. What reasons do Mama and Helen give for wanting to move? **b.** Are they telling the truth, or are they trying to prepare themselves for disappointment? Support your answer with passages from the selection.

3. When Mama returns from speaking to Papa, her eyes are described as "lamps turned on." What emotion do you think Mama is feeling?

Focus on Reading

Drawing Conclusions

Gwendolyn Brooks never tells you directly that Maud Martha values the beauties of the natural world. However, you can draw this conclusion from what she tells you about Maud Martha's responses to nature. You are told of the pleasure Maud Martha takes in looking at the late afternoon light on the lawn, in watching a sunset, and in listening to the rain drumming on the roof. You also learn that she feels sorry for "mechanical" birds that are kept in cages.

To understand what an author tells you about characters, you often must read below the surface and draw your own conclusions. Read the following statements about the characters in the story. Do you agree with all of them? Support your answers with passages from the selection.

1 Maud Martha and Helen value different things in life.
2 Their home is in a wealthy neighborhood.
3 Maud Martha is not afraid to be honest about her feelings.
4 Papa has lost his job.

Language and Vocabulary

Finding the Appropriate Meaning

Often the meaning and pronunciation of a word depend on how it is used in a sentence. The word *progress*, for example, may be used as a noun or a verb. Find the word in a dictionary and note the meaning and pronunciation for each part of speech. Look at the word *progress* in this sentence from "Home":

They watched his *progress*.

1 How is *progress* used here? How is it pronounced? Give its meaning.

The word *suspect* may be used as a noun, a

19
Metaphor. Brightness of Mama's eyes reveals her joy.

20
Helen's pride in home revealed. Reverses previous statements.

READING CHECK
1. To hear if Papa has received loan extension (p. 128).
2. She says they will move into a nice flat (p. 128).
3. Extension granted (p. 129).
4. Show friends that they are homeowners (p. 129).

FOR STUDY AND DISCUSSION
1. Bank might foreclose.
2a. Mama says she is tired of starting a coal fire. Helen says flat is prettier than house and in a better neighborhood. 2b. Not telling truth; indicated by reactions when they learn of extension.
3. Joy, exultation.

FOCUS ON READING
Answers will vary.
1. Maud Martha: natural things. Helen: material possessions and social position.
2. Contradicted by Helen's saying move to a better neighborhood and Maud Martha's description of better flats, difficult to afford on wages twice father's.
3. Students will probably agree. She argues with Mama about having to fire stove; says moving will "kill Papa."
4. Goes to bank at lunch hour; Maud Martha mentions Papa's wages.

LANGUAGE AND VOCABULARY
1. *Progress* n. (präg'res); a moving forward.

Home 129

EXTENSION AND ENRICHMENT

Advanced students with a strong interest in words might be asked to examine such poetic phrases as "emphatic iron of the fence." What does the word *emphatic* mean here? Why is it so striking? These students may then list and perhaps illustrate visually other poetic phrases from the story. This activity could provide the first entry for a reader's journal, a log of memorable phrases collected from works read throughout the year.

Other students might imagine what would have happened if Papa had been refused by Home Owners' Loan. Beginning at the point that Mama emerges from her private talk with Papa, several teams might improvise possible concluding scenes.

---

2. *Suspect* adj. (sus'pekt) questionable or suspicious.
suspect n. (sus'pekt) a person who is suspected;
suspect v. (sə spekt') to believe to be guilty;
suspect adj. (sus'pekt) viewed with suspicion.
Used as adjective in sentence.

3. *Excuse* n. (ik-skyōōs') a plea in defense;
excuse v. (ik-skyōōz') to try to free a person of blame.
Perfect n. (pur'fikt) the perfect tense;
perfect v. (per fekt') to bring to completion;
perfect adj. (pur'fikt) complete, without defects.
Record n. (rek'ərd) a written account, a phono-disc;
record v. (ri kôrd') to put in writing, or other form for future use;
record adj. (rek'ərd) establishing a record as the best, largest.

FOCUS ON DESCRIPTIVE WRITING

You may want to list on the chalkboard some transitional words and phrases that are characteristic of each type of order. For spatial order you could list *behind, across, above, beyond, next to, near, on, beside, adjoining,* and *south.* For order of importance you could list *first, last, mainly, more important, then,* and *to begin with.* Ask students to add to the lists.

ABOUT THE AUTHOR

Besides being inducted into the National Women's Hall of Fame (1988), Gwendolyn Brooks has been honored with the American Academy of Arts and Letters Award, two Guggenheim Fellowships, the Frost Medal from the Poetry Society of America, a National Book Award nomination for *In the Mecca,* and the National Endowment for the Arts Lifetime Achievement Award.

---

verb, or an adjective. Find the meaning and pronunciation for each part of speech. How is *suspect* used in this sentence?

> Her mother looked at her quickly, decided the statement was not *suspect,* looked away.

What does the word mean? How is it pronounced?

3 Look up the following words in a dictionary. In how many different ways can each word be used? Give the meaning and pronunciation for each part of speech.

excuse   perfect   record

Focus On Descriptive Writing

Organizing Descriptive Details

A good description is clearly organized and easy to follow. Here are two methods you can use to organize descriptive details:

Spatial Order: Arrange details by location: for example, from top to bottom or bottom to top; from near to far or far to near; from left to right or right to left. This method is often suitable for places and objects. In the first paragraph of "Home," for example, Gwendolyn Brooks uses spatial order to describe the porch (see page 127).

Order of Importance: Arrange details by the importance you want to give them: from least to most important, or vice versa. This method is often useful for describing people and animals.

Write a paragraph in which you describe a favorite person, room, or place. Follow some logical order in your description. Focus on creating a strong overall impression through specific details. Save your writing.

About the Author

Gwendolyn Brooks   (1917–   )

In 1950 Gwendolyn Brooks won the Pulitzer Prize for *Annie Allen,* a collection of poems about a black girl growing up in Chicago. She was the first African American to be awarded the prize. Brooks has received many honorary degrees from universities and colleges across the country. She has been the Poet Laureate of Illinois and the Poetry Consultant to the Library of Congress.

Born in Topeka, Kansas, Brooks has lived in Chicago for much of her life. When asked how she became a writer, she replied: "I always enjoyed reading when I was a child. Pretty soon, I suppose, it occurred to me that it might be wonderful if I could create something, too. I began putting rhymes together when I was seven, so I'm told by my mother. And continued."

The subject of much of Brooks's writing is the African American experience, especially in urban America. Of her novel *Maud Martha* (1953), from which "Home" is taken, she has written: "My one novel is not autobiographical in the usual sense . . . But it is true that much in the 'story' was taken out of my own life, and twisted, highlighted or dulled, dressed up or down. . . . 'Home' is indeed fact-bound. The Home Owners' Loan Corporation was a sickening reality." Her recent books include *The Near-Johannesburg Boy* (1986) and *Winnie* (1988).

Grandma Ling

AMY LING

Terracotta statue with three-color glaze, excavated in 1959 from tomb at Ch'ung Pu near Sian, Shensi, China. Tang Dynasty, early 8th century.

If you dig that hole deep enough,
you'll reach China, they used to tell me,
a child in a backyard in Pennsylvania.
Not strong enough to dig that hole,
I waited twenty years, 5
then sailed back, half way around the world.

In Taiwan I first met Grandma.
Before she came to view, I heard
her slippered feet softly measure
the tatami° floor with even step; 10
the aqua paper-covered door slid open
and there I faced
my five foot height, sturdy legs and feet,
square forehead, high cheeks and wide-set eyes;
my image stood before me, 15
acted on by fifty years.

She smiled, stretched her arms
to take to heart the eldest daughter
of her youngest son a quarter century away.
She spoke a tongue I knew no word of, 20
and I was sad I could not understand,
but I could hug her.

10. **tatami** (tä-tä′mē): straw matting used to cover floors.

point out particular sights and sounds that the poet includes. The last stanza describes a barrier that still exists between the two—one for which physical tenderness can compensate.

TRANSPARENCIES 6 & 7
Fine Art
Theme: *Close Ties* – invites students to explore artwork showing the relationship between members of families or people of differing generations.

TRANSPARENCY 8
Reader Response
Family Crest – invites students to design a "family crest" symbolizing the relationship between two of the characters in a selection.

FOR STUDY AND DISCUSSION
1. Her grandma looks like an older version of herself.
2a. Language barrier. 2b. She feels sad but realizes there are other ways to communicate.
3a. Hug communicates their affection for each other. 3b. How much they mean to each other.

ABOUT THE AUTHOR
Amy Ling has written television scripts, including "Find a Need and Fill It: The Story of Reverend C. C. Hung" (1990) and *The Trampled Spring*, a series for public broadcasting (1990). She is also a contributor of articles, poems, and reviews to periodicals. She sometimes writes under the pseudonym Ariadne Lawrence.

For Study and Discussion

Analyzing and Interpreting the Poem

1. What does the speaker mean when she describes her grandma as her image "acted on by fifty years"?

2. The speaker has overcome certain barriers, such as time and distance, to be with her grandmother. **a.** What other barrier still exists between them? **b.** How does the speaker feel about not being able to overcome this last barrier?

3a. In what way does the "hug" between the speaker and her grandmother represent a form of communication? **b.** What is being "said" by the hug that perhaps may not be adequately conveyed by words?

About the Author

Amy Ling

Amy Ling was born in Beijing, China, and came to the United States when she was six. Although her formal education includes a Ph.D., she has felt compelled to unearth her Chinese American roots in order to complete her education. In school, she remembers, she was rarely assigned a book by a woman and never one by a minority writer. *Between Worlds: Women Writers of Chinese Ancestry* (1990) is the result of ten years of painstaking research. She is also the author of *Chinamerican Reflections* (1984), a collection of her poems and paintings.

Ling has taught English in Taiwan, and literature and writing at Georgetown and Rutgers universities. During the 1989–1990 academic year, she was the Rockefeller Fellow in the Humanities at Queens College, City University of New York.

The Author Comments on Her Poem

"Grandma Ling" is an autobiographical poem. After earning a master's degree in English and American literature from the University of California at Davis, I took a teaching position in the Foreign Language Department of Chengkung University in Tainan, in southern Taiwan. It was my first trip to China since leaving the mainland at age six. At a sugar factory in nearby Da Ling, where she was living with my aunt, I met my father's mother for the first time. The poem describes the mixed emotions of that meeting: the excitement of anticipation, the joy of first sight, my frustration at our inability to communicate, and finally our love. That year in Taiwan brought sharply home to me what it means to be Chinese American and brought me home.

OBJECTIVES
The overall aim is for students to demonstrate an understanding of Thurber's use of absurd events and characters in a family setting to produce a humorous story. For a complete list of objectives, see the **Teacher's Notes**.

VOCABULARY
The underlined words are in the Glossary. Students will appreciate Thurber's lively use of language. The **Language and Vocabulary** exercise on p. 137 of the textbook deals with analyzing words with -*phobia* and *philo*-.

FOCUS / MOTIVATION
If available, a Thurber cartoon or cartoon story would provide a fine introduction, as would a sampling of titles from Thurber collections.

The Night the Bed Fell

JAMES THURBER

Some of the most hilarious stories in American literature are those that James Thurber has told about his family. Here is the story of one memorable night in the Thurber household.

> **TEACHING RESOURCES A**
> Teacher's Notes, p. 242
> Reading Check, p. 245
> Study Guide, p. 246
> Language Skills, p. 248
> Building Vocabulary, p. 252
> Selection Vocabulary Test, p. 253
> Selection Test, p. 254

PREREADING FOCUS
The headnote emphasizes the humorous nature of this story. You might ask students to discuss what they think makes a story humorous. Some of the techniques they might mention are exaggeration, irony, and a sense of the absurd.

I suppose that the high-water mark of my youth in Columbus, Ohio, was the night the bed fell on my father. It makes a better recitation (unless, as some friends of mine have said, one has heard it five or six times) than it does *1* a piece of writing, for it is almost necessary to throw furniture around, shake doors, and bark like a dog, to lend the proper atmosphere and verisimilitude¹ to what is admittedly a some-*2* what incredible tale. Still, it did take place.

It happened, then, that my father had de-*3* cided to sleep in the attic one night, to be away where he could think. My mother opposed the notion strongly because, she said, the old wooden bed up there was unsafe; it was wobbly, and the heavy headboard would crash down on Father's head in case the bed fell, and kill him. There was no dissuading him, however, and at a quarter past ten he closed the attic door behind him and went up the narrow twisting stairs. We later heard ominous creakings as he crawled into bed. Grandfather, who usually slept in the attic bed when he was with us, had disappeared some days before. (On these occasions he was usually gone six or eight days and returned growling and *4* out of temper, with the news that the Federal Union was run by a passel of blockheads and that the Army of the Potomac didn't have a chance.²)

We had visiting us at this time a nervous first cousin of mine named Briggs Beall, who believed that he was likely to cease breathing when he was asleep. It was his feeling that if he were not awakened every hour during the night, he might die of suffocation. He had been accustomed to setting an alarm clock to *5* ring at intervals until morning, but I persuaded him to abandon this. He slept in my room and I told him that I was such a light sleeper that if anybody quit breathing in the same room with me, I would wake instantly. He tested me the first night—which I had suspected he would—by holding his breath after my regular breathing had convinced him I was asleep. I was not asleep, however, and called to

---

1. **verisimilitude** (vĕr′ə-sĭm-ĭl′ə-to͞od′): the appearance of truth.
2. **the Federal . . . chance:** Grandfather, who lives in the past, thinks the Civil War is still going on.

The Night the Bed Fell

1
Foreshadowing. These dramatics foretell the chaos and multiple misunderstandings of this incident.

2 Finding Details
What suggests to the reader that the narrator may be telling a tall tale? His protest of credibility.

3
Father's reclusive eccentricity helps cause some of the night's confusion.

4
A humorous jab at the nation's leaders.

5
Narrator's power of persuasion mirrors his persuasiveness as a teller of an "incredible tale."

The Night the Bed Fell   133

133

MOTIVATIONAL SUMMARY
The Thurber household is filled with eccentric relatives, each with fixed and funny notions. While Grandfather is away and the attic bed where he usually sleeps is vacant, Father decides to sleep away from the whole zany crew for the night. But Grandfather's bed is rickety, and Mother fears that Father may be harmed if the old bed falls on him. When there is a loud crash late at night, each of the relatives assumes that his or her worst fear has finally been realized.

PRESENTATION
At first glance, James Thurber's "The Night the Bed Fell" appears to be quite an excursion of the imagination; it seems these events could never have happened. Yet many of us have family members who possess certain odd traits that—

VISUAL CONNECTIONS
About the Artwork
Some critics have noted a seriousness beneath the whimsical nature of Thurber's drawings. E. B. White, a colleague and collaborator of Thurber's, once retrieved Thurber's discarded sketches, recognizing them as the perfect complement to Thurber's writing.

"He Came to the Conclusion That He Was Suffocating." Drawing by James Thurber of man in bed.

Copyright 1933, 1961 by James Thurber. From *My Life and Hard Times*, Harper & Row

6 Significant detail in light of later events.

7 Illogical assumption that a person dying of suffocation could revive himself with camphor.

8 Characterization. Family members are highly superstitious, irrationally fearful, or paranoid.

9 A not uncommon fear but she carries it to absurd lengths.

10 Fear is pitiable, but its absurdity is humorous.

11 Reflects her disassociation from reality.

12 Archaic language ("Hark!") adds humor.

him. This seemed to allay his fears a little, but
6 he took the precaution of putting a glass of spirits of camphor on a little table at the head of his bed. In case I didn't arouse him until he was almost gone, he said, he would sniff the
7 camphor, a powerful reviver.

Briggs was not the only member of his fam-
8 ily who had his crotchets.³ Old Aunt Melissa Beall (who could whistle like a man, with two fingers in her mouth) suffered under the premonition that she was destined to die on South High Street because she had been born on South High Street and married on South High Street. Then there was Aunt Sarah Shoaf, who never went to bed at night without the fear that a burglar was going to get in and blow chloroform under her door through a tube. To avert
9 this calamity—for she was in greater dread of

3. **crotchets** (krŏch′ĭts): odd or fantastic ideas.

anesthetics than of losing her household goods—she always piled her money, silverware, and other valuables in a neat stack just outside her bedroom, with a note reading
10 "This is all I have. Please take it and do not use your chloroform, as this is all I have." Aunt Gracie Shoaf also had a burglar phobia, but she met it with more fortitude. She was confident that burglars had been getting into her
11 house every night for forty years. The fact that she never missed anything was to her no proof to the contrary. She always claimed that she scared them off before they could take anything, by throwing shoes down the hallway. When she went to bed, she piled, where she could get at them handily, all the shoes there were about her house. Five minutes after she had turned off the light, she would sit up in
12 bed and say "Hark!" Her husband, who had learned to ignore the whole situation as long

134 FAMILY ALBUM

COOPERATIVE LEARNING
Have students work together to plan and present a "Thurber carnival" in which they share favorite Thurber passages and cartoons with the entire class. Suggest that they choose their material from selections that can be found in the school or community libraries, such as *Thurber Carnival, Fables for Our Time, Thurber's Dogs,* and *My Life and Hard Times.*

MEETING INDIVIDUAL NEEDS
ESL/LEP • Thurber uses "sound" words to create a noisy atmosphere of confusion. Pair students with a classmate, having them target the words or word pairs that allow us to "hear" what happens after the army cot collapses.

16
A mild example of his family's peculiarities.

17
Story's name and humor based on misunderstanding.

18
He unknowingly sets off chain reaction.

19
Each character reacts according to what he or she thinks is going on. No one knows what really happened.

20
Briggs doesn't hear the cot crash; the sounds he expects most to hear—cries of distress—awaken him.

21 Expressing an Opinion
In your own experience, have hasty assumptions created problems? Responses will vary.

22
Irony. His attempt to save himself nearly causes the suffocation he dreads.

23
Setting. The house also has its quirks.

---

understanding of what later occurred. In the front room upstairs (just under Father's attic bedroom) were my mother and my brother Herman, who sometimes sang in his sleep, usually "Marching Through Georgia" or "Onward, Christian Soldiers." Briggs Beall and myself were in a room adjoining this one. My brother Roy was in a room across the hall from ours. Our bull terrier, Rex, slept in the hall.

My bed was an army cot, one of those affairs which are made wide enough to sleep on comfortably only by putting up, flat with the middle section, the two sides which ordinarily hang down like the sideboards of a dropleaf table. When these sides are up, it is perilous to roll too far toward the edge, for then the cot is likely to tip completely over, bringing the whole bed down on top of one, with a tremendous banging crash. This, in fact, is precisely what happened about two o'clock in the morning. (It was my mother who, in recalling the scene later, first referred to it as "the night the bed fell on your father.")

Always a deep sleeper, slow to arouse (I had lied to Briggs), I was at first unconscious of what had happened when the iron cot rolled me onto the floor and toppled over on me. It left me still warmly bundled up and unhurt, for the bed rested above me like a canopy. Hence I did not wake up, only reached the edge of consciousness and went back. The racket, however, instantly awakened my mother, in the next room, who came to the immediate conclusion that her worst dread was realized: the big wooden bed upstairs had fallen on Father. She therefore screamed, "Let's go to your poor father!" It was this shout, rather than the noise of my cot falling, that awakened Herman, in the same room with her. He thought that Mother had become, for no apparent reason, hysterical. "You're all right, Mamma!" he shouted, trying to calm her. They exchanged shout for shout for perhaps ten seconds: "Let's go to your poor father!" and "You're all right!" That woke up Briggs. By this time I was conscious of what was going on, in a vague way, but did not yet realize that I was under my bed instead of on it. Briggs, awakening in the midst of loud shouts of fear and apprehension, came to the quick conclusion that he was suffocating and that we were all trying to "bring him out." With a low moan, he grasped the glass of camphor at the head of his bed and instead of sniffing it poured it over himself. The room reeked of camphor. "Ugf, ahfg," choked Briggs, like a drowning man, for he had almost succeeded in stopping his breath under the deluge of pungent spirits. He leaped out of bed and groped toward the open window, but he came up against one that was closed. With his hand, he beat out the glass, and I could hear it crash and tinkle on the alleyway below. It was at this juncture that I, in trying to get up, had the uncanny sensation of feeling my bed above me! Foggy with sleep, I now suspected, in my turn, that the whole uproar was being made in a frantic endeavor to extricate me from what must be an unheard-of and perilous situation. "Get me out of this!" I bawled. "Get me out!" I think I had the nightmarish belief that I was entombed in a mine. "Gugh," gasped Briggs, floundering in his camphor.

By this time my mother, still shouting, pursued by Herman, still shouting, was trying to open the door to the attic, in order to go up and get my father's body out of the wreckage. The door was stuck, however, and wouldn't yield. Her frantic pulls on it only added to the general banging and confusion. Roy and the dog were now up, the one shouting questions, the other barking.

Father, farthest away and soundest sleeper of all, had by this time been awakened by the battering on the attic door. He decided that the house was on fire. "I'm coming, I'm coming!"

136 FAMILY ALBUM

Then, as a whole-class activity, write the students' suggestions on the chalkboard. (banging crash, screamed, shout, moan, crash and tinkle, bawled, shouting, barking, wailed, yelled, weep, howl)

CLOSURE

Ask students to discuss Thurber's use of absurd events, characterization, and personal reflections to produce a humorous story.

EXTENSION AND ENRICHMENT

Small groups of students may choose one part of the story to be performed with the kinds of gestures and sound effects suggested by Thurber in the first paragraph. Students who enjoy this story may be interested in reading other Thurber stories.

---

he wailed in a slow, sleepy voice—it took him many minutes to regain full consciousness. My mother, still believing he was caught under the bed, detected in his "I'm coming!" the mournful, resigned note of one who is preparing to meet his Maker. "He's dying!" she shouted.

"I'm all right!" Briggs yelled to reassure her. 24 "I'm all right!" He still believed that it was his own closeness to death that was worrying Mother. I found at last the light switch in my room, unlocked the door, and Briggs and I joined the others at the attic door. The dog, who never did like Briggs, jumped for him—assuming that he was the culprit in whatever was going on—and Roy had to throw Rex and hold him. We could hear Father crawling out of bed upstairs. Roy pulled the attic door open with a mighty jerk, and Father came down the stairs, sleepy and irritable but safe and sound. My mother began to weep when she saw him. Rex began to howl. "What in the name of heaven is going on here?" asked Father.

The situation was finally put together like a gigantic jigsaw puzzle. Father caught a cold from prowling around in his bare feet, but there were no other bad results. "I'm glad," said Mother, who always looked on the bright side of things, "that your grandfather wasn't here."

Reading Check

1. Why did Thurber's father decide to sleep in the attic?
2. What was Briggs Beall's greatest fear?
3. How did Briggs test Thurber's claim that he was a light sleeper?
4. What was Father's conclusion when he heard the commotion?
5. Why did Rex attack Briggs?

For Study and Discussion

Analyzing and Interpreting the Selection

1. In his opening paragraph Thurber says that the story he is about to tell is a "somewhat incredible tale." After getting to know the members of his family, do you believe that the hilarious events he describes could have taken place? Why or why not?

2. "Crotchets" seem to run in Thurber's family. **a.** Which of the crotchets did you find most amusing? **b.** In what way did Rex, the bull terrier, have his crotchets?

3. During the night, Thurber's cot tipped over and fell on him with a loud crash. How did each member of the household interpret what he or she heard?

4. What do you think might have happened if Grandfather had been there? Why?

Language and Vocabulary

Analyzing Words with -phobia and philo-

Thurber tells us that his Aunt Gracie Shoaf had a "burglar phobia." A *phobia* is an unreasonable fear. It comes from the Greek word *phobos*, meaning "fear." Cousin Briggs also had a phobia, and so did Aunt Melissa Beall.

The word *phobia* can be used alone, as Thurber uses it, or it can be combined with other 1 roots to name particular fears. Look up *hydrophobia* and *claustrophobia* in a dictionary. What specific fears do they name?

The root *philo-* (or *phil-*) comes from the Greek word *philos*, which means "loving." The 2 Greek word *sophia* means "wisdom." What does *philosophy* mean? In Greek the word 3 *adelphos* means "brother." What does the name *Philadelphia* mean?

4 How is *Anglophobia* different from *Anglophilia*? Use a dictionary to find the answer.

24
"Still believed": major element of humor is sustained by keeping track of each character's delusions.

READING CHECK
1. To be where he could think (p. 133).
2. That he would cease breathing when he was asleep (p. 133).
3. By holding his breath (p. 133).
4. That the house was on fire (p. 136).
5. He assumed Briggs was the culprit in whatever was going on (p. 137).

FOR STUDY AND DISCUSSION
1. Responses will vary.
2a. Responses will vary. Examples: Father's decision to sleep in attic; Grandfather's delusions; Briggs' fear of sleep; Aunt Gracie Shoaf's throwing of shoes. **2b.** He "never did like Briggs"; howled at Father.
3. Mother: thought bed fell on Father; Herman: thought Mother hysterical; Briggs: thought he was suffocating; Thurber: thought trapped in mine; Father: thought house on fire.
4. Responses may vary. He might have thought Confederates attacked: obsessed with Civil War.

LANGUAGE AND VOCABULARY
1. *hydrophobia:* fear of water. *claustrophobia:* fear of being trapped in an enclosed space.
2. *philosophy:* love of wisdom or knowledge.
3. *Philadelphia:* brotherly love.
4. *Anglophobia:* hatred of all things English.
Anglophilia: great admiration for the English and their customs and culture.

The Night the Bed Fell 137

PORTFOLIO ASSESSMENT
Groups of students may be interested in acting out Thurber's story as a means of clarifying what happens and where it happens. Suggest to students that in order to be believable, they need to convey their characters' self-absorption. Videotapes and short paragraphs from individual participants describing their experiences may be included in students' portfolios. (See *Portfolio Assessment and Professional Support Materials* for additional information on student portfolios.)

TRANSPARENCY 9
Reader Response
Getting Acquainted – asks students to give an introduction for the character in a social setting.

FOR ORAL READING
Some Thurber selections have been adapted into playscript form in *The Thurber Carnival*. The individual stories are arranged in a series of separate scenes. Students may enjoy presenting one or more of these scenes as oral readings. The dialogue style of plays is usually easier for students to follow in their first experiences with oral readings.

FOCUS ON DESCRIPTIVE WRITING
You may want to caution students about the use of cliches. If students are unfamiliar with the term, explain that cliches are overused, worn-out figures of speech. Give several examples, such as "smart as a whip," "hungry as a horse," and "slow as molasses," and ask students to add to the list. Encourage them to avoid such trite phrases and to strive for fresh, vivid comparisons.

ABOUT THE AUTHOR
Because of his eye injury, Thurber was not eligible for military service during World War I. Instead, he went to Paris as a code clerk. He began his writing career as a newspaper reporter and later became a staff member of and contributor to *The New Yorker.*

"The Secret Life of Walter Mitty" is his best-known short story. *The Thurber Album* (1952) tells of his family and friends. *The Thurber Carnival* (1945) is a collection of his writings and drawings. While Thurber maintained that his work always deals with reality, he also wrote fairy tales for adults. Two of the best known are *The Great Quillow* (1944) and *The 13 Clocks* (1950).

For Oral Reading

Reciting the Story

Thurber claims that the story "makes a better recitation . . . than it does a piece of writing" (page 133). Prepare to read the story aloud. How will you lend it "proper atmosphere?" Rehearse your reading before presenting it to your audience.

Focus On Descriptive Writing

Using Figures of Speech

In a **figure of speech** you compare two very different things. Figures of speech are not meant to be taken literally. For example, when you say that a movie had you "on pins and needles," you don't *really* mean that you were sitting on a sewing kit in the theater! You just mean that the movie was suspenseful. Two figures of speech that you can use in descriptions are similes and metaphors.

In a **simile,** you use the word *like* or *as* to compare two things. For example, Thurber says that Briggs choked from the camphor "like a drowning man" (page 136).

In a **metaphor,** you compare two things directly. For example, the phrase "foggy with sleep" compares sleep to fog or mist (see page 136).

Write a paragraph describing how you feel when you wake up for school in the morning. Use at least one simile and one metaphor in your paragraph. Save your writing.

About the Author

James Thurber (1894–1961)

James Thurber is widely considered to be the finest American humorist since Mark Twain. Despite a childhood accident which resulted in the loss of one eye and the gradual weakening of the other, Thurber had a long and successful writing career. Over a period of thirty years, he contributed hundreds of stories, essays, and articles to *The New Yorker* magazine. Thurber was also a masterful cartoonist.

Thurber used material from his childhood in Columbus, Ohio, to create his most famous collection of stories, *My Life and Hard Times.* "The Night the Bed Fell" is taken from this collection.

OBJECTIVES
The overall aim is for students to write a **description** that uses sensory details, exact words, and figures of speech.

PRESENTATION
To stimulate students' interest in writing **description**, you might bring to class several different fruits for students to describe. Arrange students in groups of four, with each group focusing on a particular fruit. Ask students to freewrite for a few minutes on what they observe, and then have them write freely for a few more minutes about any experiences they might associate with that fruit. Give the groups some time to share their freewriting, and then ask that someone from each group relate to the

FOCUS ON Writing

WRITING A DESCRIPTION

Descriptive writing creates a picture or image of a subject. In a description you use sensory details, exact words, and figures of speech. In this unit you have explored some of the key elements of this kind of writing. Now you will have the chance to write a description of your own.

Prewriting

1. Use these strategies to find a subject and a focus for your paper.
   - Think of a familiar person, place, or thing.
   - Choose a subject that you can observe directly.
   - Focus your subject by limiting it to a topic you can cover in a few paragraphs.

[See **Focus** assignment on page 98.]

2. In a description you may choose to focus on objective facts or on your own impressions and feelings. Decide if the **purpose** of your paper is to write a **factual description** or an **expressive description.**
[See **Focus** assignment on page 111.]

3. Think about your **audience**. How much do they already know about your subject? What might they like to know? How will you get them to see what you describe in the clearest possible way?

4. Use the following techniques to gather factual and sensory details for your description:
   - observing
   - recalling
   - imagining

If you are writing a factual description, list **factual details** on a chart like this one.

Subject of Description: _____
Size: _____ Color: _____
Shape: _____ Weight: _____
Markings: _____
Additional Facts: _____

Sensory details appeal to one of the five senses: sight, sound, taste, touch, and smell. List sensory details on a chart like the one shown here.

Subject of Description: _____			
People	Places	Things	Events
____	____	____	____
____	____	____	____
____	____	____	____

[See **Focus** assignments on pages 113 and 121.]

5. Arrange your details in a logical order. Here are two methods you can use to organize details in a description:
   - **Spatial Order:** Arrange details in the order you see them: top to bottom, near to far, left to right.
   - **Order of Importance:** Put the most important details either first or last.

 HOLT WRITER'S WORKSHOP
This computer program provides help for all types of writing through guided instruction for each step of the writing process. (Program available separately.)

See *Elements of Writing, First Course,* Chapter 5, for more instruction on descriptive writing.

WRITING A DESCRIPTION
When writers use **description**, they often do not record everything that surrounds their subject. Instead, they focus on the aspects of the subject that convey one strong overall impression. Then they supply adequate details that support that single impression. Rather than telling what the impression is, writers *show* their readers through sensory details, specific words, and figurative language.

Prewriting
You may want to give students a few days to find a subject, one that they can spend some time observing directly. Encourage students to take abundant notes as they complete the charts. Students might then benefit from working in small groups to create **metaphors** and **similes** for their descriptions.

You might suggest that a passive **description** may not be as dramatic as one that involves action. Therefore, students may want to put a person in a dynamic situation that will show who that person really is. Remind them that a description of an object might include how that object is used and who uses it and why; and descriptions of places can show the activities that take place there.

Focus on Writing 139

with a little exaggeration and the proper storytelling manner—might become as absurdly funny as the characters in Thurber's family tree. His calm, matter-of-fact tone accentuates the hilarity of the night he describes as well as the comical eccentricities of his relatives. His character is quite persuasive, but he does admit to telling "an incredible tale." The proof of its success lies in its effect on the reader, and no reader can leave this story's cast of characters without a smile.

MEETING INDIVIDUAL NEEDS
Visual Learners • Have students draw one of the characters in the story and include a brief, descriptive caption with each drawing. You might want to display the drawings in the classroom.

---

ago as 1903, would either be sound asleep or pretend to be sound asleep. In either case he would not respond to her tugging and pulling, so that presently she would arise, tiptoe to the door, open it slightly, and heave a shoe down the hall in one direction and its mate down the hall in the other direction. Some nights she 13 threw them all, some nights only a couple of pairs.

14 But I am straying from the remarkable incidents that took place during the night that the bed fell on Father. By midnight we were all in 15 bed. The layout of the rooms and the disposition of their occupants is important to an

13
The number of shoes thrown indicates the intensity of her delusion for a particular night.

14
Plot. Narrator's digression has actually set the stage for events to come.

15 Analyzing
Why is their arrangement important? Mother's proximity to Father and the narrator makes her misjudge the cause of the crash.

VISUAL CONNECTIONS
Ideas for Writing
Thurber maintained that he dealt only with reality in his work. You might ask your students to write a short piece about the nature of reality depicted by the two Thurber drawings included with this selection. How would they describe this reality? What elements do the drawings have in common?

"Some Nights She Threw Them All."
Drawing by James Thurber of woman outside doorway throwing shoe.

Copyright 1933, 1961 by James Thurber. From *My Life and Hard Times*, Harper & Row class what his or her group observed and associated with their fruit.

Now students can put their observations, recollections, and imaginations to work on their own topics. If possible, you might take students on a sensory journey around the school to look for suitable subjects and have them take notes on any vivid scenes they observe.

Students may want at this point to decide how they will publish their descriptions so that they can analyze their **audience** before they begin to write.

Writing
Point out to students that organizing involves two steps—choosing and sequencing. First, they must choose the strongest details that support their main idea. Second, they must order these details into a logical sequence. Therefore, students might need to create a rough outline as a means of organizing their notes so that they can see what pattern evolves.

As students draft their papers, encourage them to write quickly and let their ideas flow. Remind them that they can revise later.

Evaluating and Revising
To evaluate the overall impression of their descriptions, students might read their papers to small groups who listen and draw a picture of what they imagine from the reader's words. The listeners then can share their thoughts, praising the good parts and offering suggestions for weaker parts of the description. Students can also use the **Checklist for Evaluation and Revision** for further feedback.

Students should compare the beginnings of their essays with the endings to make sure there is continuity between the two parts.

Writing

1. Use **exact words**—nouns, verbs, adjectives, and adverbs—to create a sharp, clear image of your subject. Avoid vague, general words like *move, thing, nice,* and *interesting.* [See **Focus** assignment on page 126.]

2. Consider using **figures of speech** for special effects in your description. Figures of speech are imaginative comparisons that are not meant to be taken literally.

 - A **simile** compares two basically unlike things, using the words *like* or *as:* "The scrambled eggs tasted like cardboard."
 - A **metaphor** makes a direct comparison without using *like* or *as.* "The scrambled eggs were cardboard."

[See **Focus** assignment on page 138.]

3. Be sure that all the details you include in your description contribute to a main feeling or impression. Discard any details that do not fit the focus and overall mood of your paper.

4. Use **transitional words and phrases** to show the connections between things and ideas in your paper. Below is a list of useful transitions:

above	first	most important
across	here	over
around	inside	then
before	into	there
behind	last	under
down	mainly	up

Evaluating and Revising

1. Put your first draft aside for a while. Then evaluate it as objectively as you can. Are all your words as exact as you can make them? Do all the details in your description contribute to a main impression?

Here is an example of how one writer revised a paragraph in a description.

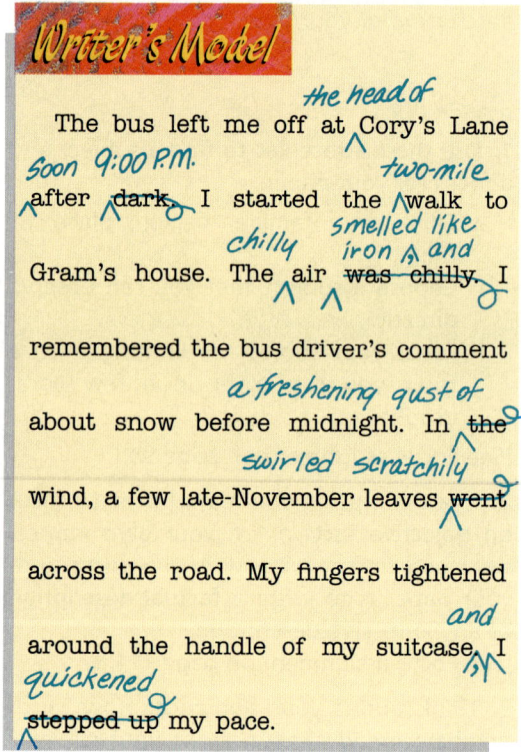

FAMILY ALBUM

> **TRANSPARENCY 11**
> **Writing Process**
> *Writing a Description* – helps students plan and write an effective description.

CLOSURE
Ask students to answer the following questions about their descriptions: What is the best part? The weakest? Why? What is one exceptionally good descriptive detail? Why? Discuss their responses.

2. Use the following checklist to evaluate and revise your writing.

Checklist for Evaluation and Revision

✓ Do I clearly identify my subject?
✓ Do I use sensory and factual details to create a clear picture of my subject?
✓ Do I use exact words and fresh figures of speech?
✓ Do I include my own thoughts and feelings?
✓ Do all my details contribute to a single, main impression?
✓ Have I organized the details in a way that makes sense?

Proofreading and Publishing

1. Proofread your paper to correct errors in grammar, usage, capitalization, and punctuation. (You may find it helpful to refer to the **Handbook for Revision** on pages 726–767.) Then prepare a final version of your paper by making a clean copy.

2. Consider some of the following ways of publishing and sharing your paper:
   - make a classroom display, adding photos, cartoons, or pictures to go with your paper
   - deliver an oral reading of your paper in class
   - send your paper to the school magazine

Portfolio If your teacher approves, you may wish to keep a copy of your work in your writing folder or portfolio.

Proofreading and Publishing
This essay might be a good one for students to proofread specifically for capitalization, punctuation (especially commas), fragments, and run-ons. Students can work in pairs to edit each other's descriptions.

UNIT 3 • TEACHING GUIDE

THEMES IN LITERATURE
THE NATURAL WORLD

OVERVIEW OF THE UNIT

Writers of essays, short stories, and poems in this section demonstrate skill in observing and reporting nature in detail. Their locales range from the Minnesota woods to the South American jungle, from the Mexican desert to the northern Irish coast. While many selections celebrate the beauty of nature, others show its destructive fury. A common element that links these selections is a close observation and effective description of nature. The result is a balanced unit that challenges young people to contemplate the planet earth and to consider their own relationship to the natural surroundings it provides.

In the first selection, "The Wind in the Mountains," Nina Otero describes both the beauty and the destructiveness of nature by detailing her observations of an approaching storm and its aftermath and by contrasting her feelings with those of the native inhabitants of New Mexico.

Similarly, in "Desert Creatures" Edward Abbey reveals his keen powers of observation in his description of the brushy wilderness of the Sonoran Desert and its animal inhabitants, particularly the chulu, a raccoonlike creature, and the javelina, a fierce piglike mammal. His use of sensory details offers vivid imagery that appeals to each of the five senses.

"Last Cover" introduces students to the technique of flashback, which is an interruption of the sequence of a narrative to relate an action that happened at an earlier time. It is through flashback that Paul Annixter provides background of the story about a young boy, his father, and their relationship with a pet fox. Annixter's deft use of the flashback provides a touching, satisfying exploration of this relationship.

Langston Hughes expresses a joyous attitude toward the natural world in "In Time of Silver Rain." The celebration of spring and the wonders that it brings is conveyed through Hughes's use of color imagery and the sound devices of repetition and refrain.

Students will enjoy Henry Wadsworth Longfellow's skillful use of comparisons in "The Wreck of the *Hesperus,*" a ballad that tells a story of a sea captain who, despite the warnings of an old sailor, puts out to sea, taking his beautiful daughter with him. Longfellow's use of similes to depict the ship, the storm, and the sea create vivid mental pictures.

Jim Kjelgaard's "The Tiger's Heart" is an exciting adventure story about a young hunter in a jungle village in tropical America, who is forced to do what no one else in his village has ever done. Kjelgaard's focus on details of background creates mood and builds suspense which leads to a surprising outcome.

The speaker in Robert Frost's "The Runaway" expresses concern for a young colt who has been left out in the snow. Using simple language, straightforward narrative, and vivid figures of speech, Frost's poem both conveys and evokes emotion.

"The Wild Duck's Nest" by Michael McLaverty is a story about a young Irish boy who finds a wild duck's nest with a single egg. His impulsive actions result in feelings of guilt. This experience teaches him to exercise more thought and care in his dealings with nature.

In "Birdfoot's Grampa," Joseph Bruchac illustrates how word choice and image affect the mood of a poem, in this case creating sympathy both for dozens of small toads on a highway and for the old man who carefully tries to carry each one to safety.

Using a Greek myth to focus her theme, Borden Deal, in "Antaeus," shows how a young boy's love for farming and the soil excites a group of his city friends to begin a garden on a rooftop in the middle of a large city. Deal's portrayal of the boys coming to understand the joy of making things grow is a study in gradual and believable characterization.

Throughout this unit, questions encourage students to maintain and develop such previously learned skills as following the order of events and drawing inferences about character. Other exercises provide practice in recognizing unity, locating main ideas, focusing on details of background, understanding comparisons, and identifying and analyzing the use of repetition, refrain, and flashback.

Related vocabulary activities provide practice in determining word origins from prefixes and suffixes, recognizing sensory details, identifying animal names, using the dictionary to find appropriate meaning, forming adverbs from adjectives, using vivid verbs, and determining meaning from context clues.

The composition exercises throughout this unit emphasize informative writing, and the **Focus on Writing** section at the end of the unit uses the writing process to guide students in writing an informative paper.

OBJECTIVES OF THE UNIT

The aims of the unit are for the student:
- To identify and analyze descriptive details
- To identify and analyze the use of simile and flashback
- To determine word meanings by analyzing context, distinguishing among dictionary definitions
- To prepare an oral reading of a poem
- To write an informative paper
- To make connections between literature and science

CONCEPTS AND SKILLS

The following concepts and skills are treated in this unit:

LITERARY ELEMENTS AND READING SKILLS
Following the Order of Events   160
Understanding Similes   168
Focusing on Details of Background   176

PLANNING GUIDE

FOR UNIT PLANNING
- Transparencies 12–16: *Audiovisual Resources Binder*
- Portfolio Assessment: *Professional Support Materials*
- Test Generator
- Mastery Tests: Teaching Resources B, pp. 94, 96, 100
- Analogy Test: Teaching Resources B, p. 102
- Composition Test: Teaching Resources B, p. 103

SELECTION (Pupil's Page)	TEACHING RESOURCES B (page numbers shown below)							AV BINDER
	Teacher's Notes	Reading Check	Study Guide	Language Skills	Building Vocabulary	Selection Vocab. Test	Selection Test	Audio-cassette
THE NATURAL WORLD *Introduction* (p. 143)	1							
Nina Otero *The Wind in the Mountains* (p. 144)	2	4	5		7	19	9	TAPE 1 SIDE B
Edward Abbey *Desert Creatures* (p. 147)	11	13	14	16		19	20	
Paul Annixter *Last Cover* (p. 153)	21	24	25		27	29	30	
Langston Hughes *In Time of Silver Rain* (p. 162)	32		33				74	TAPE 1 SIDE B
Henry Wadsworth Longfellow *The Wreck of the Hesperus* (p. 164)	35		37		39	53	40	TAPE 1 SIDE B
Jim Kjelgaard *The Tiger's Heart* (p. 170)	42	45	46	48	51	53	55	
Robert Frost *The Runaway* (p. 178)	57		58				74	
Michael McLaverty *The Wild Duck's Nest* (p. 180)	59	61	62	64	68	88	70	TAPE 1 SIDE B
Joseph Bruchac *Birdfoot's Grampa* (p. 186)	72		73				74	
Borden Deal *Antaeus* (p. 187)	76	79	80	83	86	88	90	

LANGUAGE AND VOCABULARY SKILLS

Learning Word Origins   146
Recognizing Sensory Details   151
Identifying Animal Names   160
Finding the Appropriate Meaning   177
Forming Adverbs from Adjectives   184
Using Vivid Verbs   184
Using Context Clues   194

WRITING OPPORTUNITIES

Focus on Informative Writing
Choosing a Process to Explain   146
Gathering Details to Explain a Process   152
Organizing Information   161
Exploring Cause and Effect   177
Using Transitional Expressions   185
Preparing an Oral Report   195
Writing an Informative Paper   196

ORAL READING

Preparing a Presentation   169

CONNECTIONS

Literature and Science   161

TRANSPARENCIES

The following unit support materials with specific correlations to literature selections are available in the **Fine Art and Instructional Transparencies with Teacher's Notes and Blackline Masters** section of your *Audiovisual Resources Binder*.

FINE ART TRANSPARENCIES

Theme: Reacting to Our Environment
12 *Mecklenburg Autumn: Early Frost, Cherokee Lands,* Romare Bearden
13 *Approaching Storm Over the St. Johns River,* Hansen Mulford

READER RESPONSE

14 Picture This

LITERARY ELEMENTS

15 Imagery

WRITING PROCESS

16 Writing an Informative Paper

INTRODUCING THE UNIT

To introduce these selections and the theme of humanity's relationship with the natural world, you might display reproductions of well-known paintings that depict natural subjects and have students discuss the artists' visions of nature. Vincent Van Gogh's *Starry Night,* M. C. Escher's *Sky and Water,* Pieter Bruegel's *Hunters in the Snow,* and Winslow Homer's *Huntsman and Dogs* are good for class discussion. Have students note the different techniques that the artists use to convey their vision. You might note that writers also have different ways of portraying nature and our relation to the natural world.

You might also read aloud John Ciardi's "And They Lived Happily Ever After for a While," a poem that protests pollution of the environment. Discuss what seems to be happening to the world of nature in twentieth-century America and what might be done to remedy the situation. Students might express their feelings about this issue in an original poem, in slogans for lapel buttons or bumper stickers, in a poster, or in a letter to the editor of a local newspaper. Relate such concern for the environment to the broader theme of the unit.

As you play key passages of Ferde Grofé's *Grand Canyon Suite,* ask students to make notes on different "moods" of nature. Relate these changing pictures of nature to the multiple views presented by the writers.

Read aloud Nikki Giovanni's "Winter Poem" *(Zero Makes Me Hungry).* What does the speaker in this poem seem to feel for nature? What does she suggest by ending the poem with the statement ". . . I stood perfectly still and was a flower"? Suggest that several of the writers represented in this unit feel the same kinship with nature. As students progress through the unit, ask them to identify selections reflecting this kinship. What different attitudes toward nature are reflected in other selections?

PORTFOLIO ASSESSMENT

Suggestions for use of portfolios as support for this unit are described in the **Portfolio Assessment and Professional Support Materials** booklet accompanying this program. Specific suggestions are provided for a variety of student projects that may be suitable for inclusion in a portfolio. In addition, copying masters are provided for guides that may be used for evaluation and assessment of student projects.

Student Learning Options

THE NATURAL WORLD

1. Changing the Genre
Ask students to write "The Wreck of the *Hesperus*" as a story for a newspaper. The newspaper story should be basically informative, answering these questions: Who? What? Where? When? Why? How? Information could come in the form of comments from sources connected to the wreck.

2. Writing a Letter
Have students select an interesting character from one of the stories in the unit and write a letter to that character. Then ask students to exchange letters, pretend to be the character addressed, and answer the letter.

3. Making a Bulletin Board
After the students have read "Last Cover" by Paul Annixter, ask them to bring pictures or drawings of pets. (Students who do not have a pet can make up a story.) Each student can then write an introduction to the pictured pet, perhaps including a description of the pet and a narrative telling about something the pet has done. Volunteers can design a bulletin board of the pictures and essays.

4. Extending a Story
Have students write an extension of "Antaeus" by Borden Deal, telling what happens to T. J. after the police find him near Nashville.

5. Planting a Garden
Perhaps working with a science teacher, help students plan a class garden, or ask each student to plant seeds in a plastic cup. In either case, the students can write daily observations about the growth of the plants. Ask them to give factual information (such as amount of growth and color), descriptions that include similes, and personal responses.

6. Writing an Animal Book
Ask students to write a booklet on the habits of the animals found in the stories in this unit. Students can work in pairs to research and write about the animal of their choice, although each pair should write about a different animal.

7. Writing a Weather Poem
After reading and discussing "In Time of Silver Rain" by Langston Hughes, have students write a similar poem about another kind of weather, such as snow, thunderstorms, tornadoes, ice, sunshine, or wind.

8. Turning Poetry to Prose
Ask students to write the story of "The Wreck of the *Hesperus*" with action, description, and dialogue.

9. Writing a Radio Show
Divide students into groups and ask each group to choose one of the narrative short stories, such as "The Wild Duck's Nest" or "The Tiger's Heart," to rewrite as a radio play script. Then let each group assign roles and read their script as a radio play. They may even want to include background music when appropriate or a narrator to introduce the production.

VISUAL CONNECTIONS

About the Artist

Trained by his father and his uncle, Kensett became a bank-note engraver. However, in 1840, he, along with artists Asher B. Durand, Thomas P. Rossiter, and John W. Casilear, traveled to Europe to study painting. Kensett's travels and studies developed his interests in landscape painting, the art form for which he is famous. He became a leader of the Hudson River School, a group of nineteenth-century American artists who painted landscapes of the New England area, particularly the Hudson River Valley.

Ideas for Writing

Obviously, we humans interact with the environment around us. In ways less visible, the environment around us affects the way we feel and think. Ask students what kind of feelings a sunset such as the one shown here usually inspires. List student suggestions on the chalkboard; then discuss why the natural environment causes such emotions in people.

Ask students to select one specific outdoor scene and one specific emotion that the person present at the scene is feeling. Then have them write a paragraph describing the person's feelings as he or she reacts to the environment, ascribing to the natural surroundings a sympathy or antipathy toward his or her emotions. (Examples of student titles might be "A Happy Day at the Beach," "Lonely in the Snow," or "The Terrifying Storm.")

Relating Expression Skills

Students might wish to pantomime the scenes which they describe in their paragraphs. Since pantomime is a dramatic communication without the use of words, emphasis is placed on detailed, exaggerated facial expressions, gestures, and movements.

THE NATURAL WORLD

About three thousand years ago, in Biblical times, a poet named David composed sacred songs called *psalms* in praise of God. In these lines from Psalm 8, David celebrates the splendor of the universe. He also tells how humble he feels in the presence of such wonders.

When I consider thy heavens, the work of thy fingers, the moon and the stars, which thou hast ordained;
What is man, that thou art mindful of him?

From earliest times people have responded to the beauty and wonder of the natural world. What aspects of nature has the artist emphasized in the painting shown on these pages? List at least three words or phrases that you could use to describe the mood of *Sunset on the Sea*. Do you think the artist would have agreed with the point of view expressed in Psalm 8?

Sunset on the Sea (1872) by John Frederick Kensett. Oil on canvas.
The Metropolitan Museum of Art, gift of Thomas Kensett, 1874. (74.30)

OBJECTIVES
The overall aim is for students to describe contrasting aspects of nature and the different relationships people have with the natural world. For a complete list of objectives, see the **Teacher's Notes**.

VOCABULARY
The underlined words are in the Glossary. The **Language and Vocabulary** exercise on p. 146 defines *extemporize* and asks students to discuss its Latin origins and to explain the connection between the Latin source and present meaning.

FOCUS / MOTIVATION
You may ask students if they have ever watched and listened to a storm that broke during the night and, if so, how they felt. In this selection, Otero describes her reactions to a storm and its aftermath.

TEACHING RESOURCES B
Teacher's Notes, p. 2
Reading Check, p. 4
Study Guide, p. 5
Building Vocabulary, p. 7
Selection Vocabulary Test, p. 19
Selection Test, p. 9

AV RESOURCES BINDER
Audiocassette 1, Side B

VISUAL CONNECTIONS
Exploring the Subject
Located 60 miles northeast of Albuquerque, at the southern edge of the Sangre de Cristo mountains, Santa Fé suffers extremes of weather. In the winter the mountains are covered with snow, and in the summer the hot, dry climate may be shattered by thunderstorms. Otero shows Santa Fé to be a "region of struggles" where storms may turn arroyos into violent rushes of water, and a shepherd may sleep in the rain and awaken to find lambs have been killed in the night.

PREREADING FOCUS
The headnote refers to an individual's **conflict** with the destructive aspects of nature. Encourage students to discuss experiences in which they felt they were struggling against the forces of nature. (They might suggest flood, snowstorm, tornado, fire, heat wave.)

The Wind in the Mountains

1
Santa Fé is Spanish for "Holy Faith."

2
Theme. Awe of nature's power and beauty.

3
Use to answer **study question 4**, p. 146.

The Wind in the Mountains

NINA OTERO

In this selection the writer refers to the country around Santa Fé as a "region of struggles." What does she mean?

A storm was coming over the country around
1 Santa Fé, the ancient City of the Holy Faith. This southwestern country, explored and settled nearly four hundred years ago by a people who loved nature, worshiped God and feared no evil, is still a region of struggles.

I spent this night on my homestead in a small <u>adobe</u> house in the midst of cedars on
2 the top of a hill. We face the great *Sangre de Cristo*¹ range as we look to the rising sun: a beauty too great for human beings to have had a hand in creating. Cedars and piñones,² twisted, knotted, dwarfed by the wind, were all around me. Arroyos³ were cut in the ground,
3 innocent looking in dry weather, but terrible in storms, for the water rushing through them can fell trees and roll boulders as easily as children roll marbles.

I watched the sun sink gloomily behind a yellow light. The hills looked gray and <u>solemn</u>. At a distance we heard a dog bark, a coyote

---

1. **Sangre de Cristo** (săng'grē də krĭs'tō): a range of the Rocky Mountains extending from central Colorado to northern New Mexico. The name means "Blood of Christ."
2. **piñones** (pĭn-yō'nēz): pine trees.
3. **Arroyos** (ə-roi'ōs): dry gulches formed by running streams.

144 THE NATURAL WORLD

MOTIVATIONAL SUMMARY

A woman living in the mountains near Santa Fé observes that the sunset clouds are threatening, indicating a big storm gathering. Night falls, and she waits anxiously for thunder, lightning, and winds.

PRESENTATION

Santa Fé and the surrounding region of northern New Mexico is culturally diverse. The city was founded c. 1609 by Spanish explorers, who built on the site of ancient Indian ruins. The territory became a part of Mexico in 1821 and a part of the United States in 1846. Pueblo Indians, who came to the area long before the Spanish, built large apartmentlike dwellings called *pueblos*. They still reside in the old pueblos of Taos, Acoma, Laguna, and Jemez.

---

howl. A shepherd was calling to his dog. The shepherd and his dog, taking warning of the coming storm, were herding the sheep to protect them better. Here and there the shepherd picked up a stray lamb and carried it in his arms. He made a fire quickly and soon the fragrance of coffee and burning cedar filled the air. Smoke rose above the trees, a signal in olden times of hospitality, perhaps, or hostility, for the Indians have not always been friendly. Soon the herder laid a sheep pelt, thick with
4 "wool in the grease" and gray with sand, on the most level stretch. He threw his only blanket over his shoulders and lay down on the extemporized bed. A look at the fire, a glance at the sky, the exclamation, "God help us!", and he dropped asleep to the sound of his sheep bleating.

In the only room of my house, a melancholy candle was flickering as if gasping for breath. As the darkness came down like a curtain, I lit the fire to try to make the room more cheerful. I had a feeling of vastness, of solitude, but
5 never of loneliness. Crickets and myriads of other insects were incessantly buzzing. The night was alive with sounds of creatures less fearful than humans, speaking a language I couldn't understand, but could feel with every sense.

In the night the storm broke, wild and dis-
6 mal. The wind hissed like a rattler, and as it struck the branches of the trees, it made a weird sound like a musical instrument out of tune. Trees were bowing as if in obeisance to
7 their Master. An unmuffled candle alone illuminated the small room. It kept vigil through the stormy night.

At dawn, the clouds parted as if a curtain were raised, revealing the outline of the mountains. The hush following the storm was tremendous. Again I heard a voice in the canyon. The shepherd was kindling his fire and rolling up his sheep pelt.

"Ah, me," he said to himself, "we must get out of this wild canyon. Here we must leave four of our little lambs dead. Bad luck! But . . .
8 then . . . here comes the light, the sun, and, after all, *this* is another day."

As the shepherd was extinguishing the camp fire, there appeared on the top of the hill a form with arms stretched to heaven as though
9 offering himself to the sun. The shepherd from his camp and I from my window watched this half-clad figure that seemed to have come from the earth to greet the light. A chant, a hymn—the Indian was offering his prayer to the rising sun. The shepherd, accustomed to his Indian neighbors, went his way slowly, guiding his sheep out of the canyon. The Indian finished his offering of prayer. I, alone, seemed not in complete tune with the instruments of God. I felt a sense of loss that they were closer to nature than I, more understanding of the storm. I had shuddered at the wind as it came through the cracks of my little house; now I had to cover my eyes from the bright rays of the sun, while my neighbors, fearing nothing, welcomed with joy "another day."

Reading Check

1. What makes the arroyos dangerous in bad weather?
2. Where is the narrator during the storm?
3. What does she use for light?
4. What two people does she observe from her window?

4
The grease in wool is lanolin, a natural water repellent and moisturizer.

5
Use to answer **study question 1,** p. 146.

6
Simile. To speaker, storm seems alien and dangerous; and she herself feels out of tune with this wildness.

7 Analyzing
Who is "their Master"? Answers will vary. Earlier passages suggest God.

8
He sounds hopeful rather than sorrowful.

9
Offering is made to divine nature.

READING CHECK
1. In heavy rains, flash floods occur (p. 144).
2. In small hillside adobe house among a clump of cedars (p. 144).
3. A candle (p. 145).
4. A shepherd and an Indian (p. 145).

> **TRANSPARENCIES 12 & 13**
> **Fine Art**
> Theme: *Reacting to Our Environment* – highlights artworks that evoke in the viewer a response about the natural world.

> **TRANSPARENCY 14**
> **Reader Response**
> *Picture This* – prompts students to visualize and sketch details that represent significant ideas in the selection.

CLOSURE
Have students point out passages that illustrate the contrast between the beautiful and the destructive aspects of nature and the contrast between the author's, the shepherd's, and the Indian's response to nature.

FOR STUDY AND DISCUSSION
1. Crickets and other insects.
2a. Gathers his flock together, makes coffee, and prepares his bed. 2b. He says it is bad luck and he is eager to leave the canyon.
3. She feels that the shepherd and Indian are closer to nature than she and that they understand the storm better.
4. The storm is destructive in causing deaths of four lambs. Nature is benevolent in hushed quiet after storm, morning sun, and beauty of mountains.

LANGUAGE AND VOCABULARY
1. A speech made without the speaker having prepared research notes or an outline.
2. Both indicate something done from or at the present time.

FOCUS ON INFORMATIVE WRITING
You may want to discuss with students the importance of considering audience when preparing a **process explanation**. Write the word *beach* on the chalkboard and ask students to volunteer possible topics for the following audiences: seventh-grade students (how to play beach soccer); seashell collectors (how to find rare shells); five-year-olds (how to build a sand castle). Point out how the topic changes to match the audience.

For Study and Discussion

Analyzing and Interpreting the Selection

1. The author says that during the storm she had a feeling of solitude but not of loneliness. What companionship did she have?

2a. How does the shepherd prepare for the storm? b. How does he react to the loss of some of his flock?

3. How is the author affected by both the shepherd and the Indian who prays to the sun?

4. How does this selection show both the benevolent and destructive aspects of nature?

Language and Vocabulary

Learning Word Origins

We are told that the shepherd prepared an "extemporized bed" with a sheep pelt. In other words, he made a makeshift bed out of what was available. To *extemporize* is to do something without preparation or to improvise.

Extemporize is related in meaning to *extemporaneous* (ĕk-stĕm′pə-rā′nē-əs), an adjective meaning "without preparation" or "impromptu." What is an extemporaneous speech?

Both *extemporize* and *extemporaneous* are derived from Latin. The Latin prefix *ex-* means "from" or "out of." The Latin word *tempore* is a form of *tempus*, meaning "time." What connection is there between the Latin source and the present meaning of the words?

Focus on Informative Writing

Choosing a Process to Explain

One important type of **informative writing** is a **process explanation.** In this kind of paper, you explain how to do something or how something works.

Get together with a small group of classmates. Brainstorm with your group to find *two* topics for process papers. One topic should focus on how to do something. The other should focus on how something works. Here are some possibilities:

   how to make pizza   how magnets work
   how to grow roses   how radar works
        how to program a VCR

For each topic, make a chart like the one below. List each step or stage of the process in the correct order. Save your notes.

```
Topic: _____
Audience: _____
Steps/Stages:
   1. _____
   2. _____
   3. _____
   4. _____
```

About the Author

Nina Otero (1882–1965)

Born in Los Lunas, New Mexico, in 1882, Maria "Nina" Otero-Warren was one of the first generation of Hispanic women writers who spoke out to preserve and honor their cultural identity. After pursuing a career in education, Otero-Warren was active in earning women the right to vote. She was nominated to the House of Representatives by the Republican Party in 1922. Her first book, *Old Spain in Our Southwest*, was published in 1936.

Desert Creatures

EDWARD ABBEY

Through his powers of observation and finely tuned senses, Edward Abbey shares with us his experience of the Sonoran Desert in northwest Mexico. As you read, note how carefully he describes the desert creatures and their environment.

1 Into the backlands, the back of beyond, the original and primitive Mexico. For the next three days we would see few human beings and not a motor vehicle of any kind, nor a gas station, nor a telephone pole. The inevitable vultures soaring overhead reminded us, though, that somewhere in this brushy wilderness was life, sentient[1] creation, living meat. Hard to see, of course, during the day, for most desert animals keep themselves concealed in the bush or in burrows under the surface of the ground.

2 But you could see their tracks: birds, lizards,

---

1. **sentient** (sĕn´chĭ-ənt): having sensations and feelings.

MOTIVATIONAL SUMMARY
A man experienced in the ways of the desert describes encounters he has had with some of the interesting creatures of the Sonoran Desert: kangaroo rats, which do not drink water; chulus, which can be tamed as pets; and javelinas, which eat anything. Although the features of these desert animals resemble those of animals with which we are more familiar, each is unique in its adaptation to the harsh desert.

PRESENTATION
After students have read the selection, they should be prepared to discuss Abbey's descriptions of the animal life of the Sonoran Desert. You may ask students to list and comment on the different forms of wildlife discussed. "Desert

4
Ability to identify animals by tracks reflects familiarity with local wildlife.

5
Placing chulu at the end of list suggests its importance and is a preamble to the discussion that soon follows.

6
Abbey moves from the general ("immense variety of mammals") to the specific (habits of kangaroo rat).

7
Use to answer **study question 2b,** page 151.

8
Description. Narrator's ability to observe and describe the chulu reflects his knowledge of wildlife.

9
Comparison to a human adds another facet to already complex **description.**

VISUAL CONNECTIONS
Exploring the Subject
Kangaroo rats are small brown and white rodents (4–6½ inches long) that live in the desert areas of North America. Their long, tufted tails help to balance them as they hop about on their long hind legs. With their short forelegs, they collect vegetation, carrying it in their cheek pouches until they return to their burrows.

148

rodents, now and then a coyote, here and there the handlike footprints of raccoon, the long claws of badger, the prints of ring-tailed cat, the heart-shaped hoof marks of deer and javelina,² the rounded pads of bobcat, the long narrow tracks of the coatimundi,³ or *chulu,* as the Mexicans call it.

I have barely begun to name the immense variety of mammals, large and small, that inhabit this area. There are, for example, dozens of species of little rodents—rock squirrels, pocket gophers, pocket mice, grasshopper mice, cactus mice, kangaroo rats, wood rats, prairie dogs—and a large assortment of skunks, cottontail rabbits, jackrabbits, porcupines, kit foxes and gray foxes.

Some of these animals, especially the rodents and other smaller mammals, may never drink free water in their entire lives. Instead they get by on what moisture they can obtain from plant food and through the internal manufacture of what is called "metabolic water."⁴ Particularly distinguished in this regard is the kangaroo rat, which subsists on a diet of dried seeds, bathes itself in sand, ignores green and succulent plants, and shuns water even when it is available.

But of all these Sonoran beasts surely the most curious is *Nasua narica,* the chulu, or coatimundi. Generally chulus travel in bands of a dozen or more, sometimes as many as two hundred, according to report. But the first one I ever saw was a loner—the older males are often solitary—prowling in a garbage dump near the town of Nogales.⁵ Preoccupied with its search for something to eat, the chulu ignored me, or perhaps did not perceive me, and I had ample opportunity to observe it closely.

It was an old one, a grandfather no doubt, unable to keep up with its band, which would also explain why it had been reduced to scavenging in a dump for survival. It was about four feet long, including the two-foot tail, which in the chulu is held upright, at a right angle to the body. The fur was rusty brown, the tail marked with light and dark rings like that of a raccoon, which the chulu somewhat resembles. But it looked a little like a small bear, too, with long hind legs and shambling gait. In fact it looked like a mixture of several mammals, with the tail of a raccoon, the gait of a bear, the nose of a pig, a face masked like that of a badger, long wolflike canine teeth and the lean slab-sided body of a fox or coyote.

As I watched this chulu, I saw it turn over rocks, tin cans, boards and other junk with its front paws, exhibiting the manual dexterity of a human. It was probably searching for insects,

---

2. **javelina** (hä′və-lē′nə): wild swine resembling small pigs.
3. **coatimundi** (kō-ä′tē mŭn′dē): mammals also called *coati* (kō-ä′tē).
4. **metabolic** (mĕt′ə-bŏl′ĭk) **water:** water produced within the creature's own body.
5. **Nogales** (nō-gäl′əs): in Sonora, in northwest Mexico, adjacent to Nogales, Arizona.

148 THE NATURAL WORLD

Creatures" is primarily expository in that it reflects the author's keen interest in preserving nature. Point out that among Abbey's large repertoire of published works is the novel *The Monkey Wrench Gang*, an underground classic that works with the same nature-related subject as "Desert Creatures." This novel details in a seriocomic manner the escapades of four eccentric characters who attempt, through sabotage, to preserve the natural world from human encroachment.

grubs, arachnids[6] and snakes, as it spent a great deal of time rooting about underneath things with its long and flexible snout. I have learned since that chulus, like coyotes and javelinas, will eat most anything they can find or catch; like us, they are omnivorous.

To see what it would do, I walked toward the chulu, whistled and held out one hand. It looked at me with soft brown eyes, seemingly full of trust, but a snarling grin that exposed long yellow fangs conveyed a different impression. I would not have cared to tangle with this animal bare-handed, but before I got close enough to risk attack it turned tail and scurried as nimbly as a tomcat up the trunk of a big juniper.

My favorite desert animal, I think, after such obvious choices as coyote, vulture, cougar, ring-tailed cat, Gila monster and gopher snake, is the whimsical, cockeyed, half-mad, always eccentric, more or less lovable *Pecari angulatus sonoriensis*, otherwise known as javelina or peccary.[7] A herd of them scampered across the road in front of us as we bounced over the backlands toward the sea. We stopped and watched them go up a hillside and over the crest, the dust flying from their busy hoofs.

What are javelinas? Well, they are piglike animals, but they are not true pigs. They look more like razorback hogs, but they are not true razorbacks either. Someone has likened them to a child's notion of what a pig should look like. They are comical, myopic,[8] vicious and excitable. They have sharp little hoofs, pointed ears, small square bodies and huge heads mounted on massive necks; neck and head appear to take up nearly half the total body volume. The tail is so small as to be ridiculous, but the teeth are sharp. Javelinas are capable (it is said) of inflicting severe—even fatal—damage upon anyone unlucky enough to find himself between a charging javelina and an immovable wall.

I remembered my first encounter with javelinas. I was blundering about in the Sonoran hills, daydreaming as usual, when I gradually became aware of a snorting, snuffling sound ahead, accompanied by the shuffle of many active hoofs. The terrain was brushy, the lilac twilight falling about me, so that I

---

6. **arachnids** (ə-răk′nĭdz): a class of invertebrates having four pairs of legs, such as the spider and the scorpion.

7. **peccary** (pĕk′ə-rē): See footnote 2.
8. **myopic** (mī-ŏp′ĭk, -ō′pĭk): nearsighted.

Desert Creatures **149**

VISUAL CONNECTIONS
Exploring the Subject
Coatimundi (Coati) is a small raccoonlike mammal, distinguished by its long body, dark-ringed tail, and extended, flexible snout. This carnivorous animal of Mexico and Central and South America is a tree-dweller, feeding chiefly on birds, eggs, lizards, and insects. Because of its sociable nature, the coati is frequently tamed as a pet.

10
By noting common traits, narrator stresses animals' kinship with humans. **Omnivorous** means able to eat any type of food.

11 Summarizing
How does the chulu view the extended hand? As a threat rather than as a sign of friendship.

12
List of adjectives adds almost comic touch.

13
As with chulu, narrator compares this unfamiliar animal with a familiar one.

14
Description. Suggests potentially dangerous side of javelina's nature.

15 Finding Details
Which of the javelina's features are described as large and which as small? The head and neck are large; hooves, body, and tail are small.

16
Narrator's inability to see well, his preoccupation, and his "crashing" suggest his similarity to the javelina.

SCIENCE LINK
Have students work individually or in groups to research the four warm deserts of North America: the Sonoran Desert, which Abbey writes about, the Mojave Desert, the Great Basin, and the Chihuahuan Desert. Encourage them to compare the creatures in each of these desert areas and their environments. Have students share the information they find.

VISUAL CONNECTIONS
Exploring the Subject
A peccary is a small, piglike mammal, about three feet long, which lives in the thick brush and forests extending from the southwestern United States to the northern parts of South America. Despite the fierceness and cruelty of these wild, long-legged, tailless animals, hunters track them for their valuable thick hides and porklike flesh. Occassionally, peccaries are captured and virtually domesticated by the Indians of South America.

17
Reflects narrator's ability to empathize with wild animals.

18
Javelinas' fearful escape reinforces earlier implication that javelinas are very dangerous when trapped.

19 Drawing Conclusions
Why do you think the javelinas will have a difficult time regrouping? Dim light and nearsightedness will hinder them.

20
Animals' almost indiscriminate eating suggests adaptability necessary for self-preservation.

could not see much, and besides I was listening primarily to the melancholy chorus of red-spotted toads in the canyon below. I crashed on through the thickets. The nearsighted javelinas did not notice my approach until I almost stumbled over them. At that point the herd exploded in all directions at once, two of them stampeding past me so close on either side that I felt the friction of their bristles. 17 They must have been even more startled than I was. A moment later I stood alone in a now-quiet clearing, among uprooted roots and overturned stones, and sniffed at the curious musky odor in the air. Off in the distance, at 18 sixteen different compass points, I could still hear the panicked scramble, the outraged snorts, squeals and grunts, of the shattered 19 herd of javelinas. It must have taken them hours to get properly reassembled and back to their evening feed.

As with humans and chulus, javelinas will eat anything—snails, locusts, roots, berries, clams, truffles, mushrooms, garlic, bugs, birds, eggs, 20 general assorted garbage. This is reputed to be an indication of intelligence. Living in the Sonoran Desert, however, the javelina special-

150   THE NATURAL WORLD

PORTFOLIO ASSESSMENT
Edward Abbey's description of javelinas begins with the physical, continues with his personal experience, and finishes with the animals' habits of food gathering. Students may want to write a short essay describing one of their favorite wild animals, using Abbey's sequence of topics. Suggest that, if possible, they describe animals that they have been able to observe, such as rodents, birds, snakes, or even insects. Students may want a peer to edit their first draft. Consult with students to agree on how their descriptions will be evaluated. (See *Portfolio Assessment and Professional Support Materials* for additional information on student portfolios.)

---

izes in the consumption of cactus—spines, barbs, hooks, needles, thorns, hair and all; its favorite cactus is the succulent pad of the prickly pear.

The javelina also fancies the barrel cactus—that bloated monster of a vegetable that rises up like an overgrown green fireplug, leaning south over the sunny sides of hills. But the barrel cactus, armored by an intricate network of rosy claws, cannot easily be approached, except for the yellowish fruit on top, which the javelina and other creatures will extricate and consume in due season. The only way a javelina can get at the tender insides of a barrel cactus is from the base, which is sometimes exposed when excessive growth or a storm or a weakened root system causes the plant to keel over. Then the javelina, seizing its chance, drops to its knees and burrows headfirst into 21 the bottom of the now-defenseless plant. I have never actually seen this performance but I have seen barrel cactus fallen over and hollowed out, surrounded by the scuffle marks 22 and scat of the javelina.

Reading Check

1. According to the author, why is it hard to see the desert creatures during the day?
2. Which desert creatures mentioned in the selection "may never drink free water in their entire lives"?
3. The chulu looks "like a mixture of several mammals." Name two and tell how the chulu resembles each one.
4. Though javelinas will eat anything, what is their favorite food?
5. How many days did the trip into the backlands last?

For Study and Discussion

Analyzing and Interpreting the Selection

1a. Although the desert creatures are unseen during the day, what details reveal that they are nearby? **b.** What do these details reveal about Edward Abbey's powers of observation?

2. Abbey describes the chulu as the "most curious" of the Sonoran creatures. **a.** What is so strange about this animal's appearance? **b.** What conclusion does the author come to when he sees a solitary chulu scavenging? **c.** Briefly describe the encounter between the author and the chulu.

3. Abbey states that "as with humans and chulus, javelinas will eat anything," and "this is reputed to be an indication of intelligence." What does he mean?

4. Many forms of wildlife have special features or abilities that help them survive even the harshest conditions. The ability to stay hidden is only one of the survival skills of desert creatures. **a.** What are some other protective means discussed in the selection? **b.** In your opinion, what is a human being's most important asset or ability?

5. At the opening of the selection, Abbey talks about the backlands of Mexico as "the back of beyond." **a.** What does he mean? **b.** In what specific ways are the backlands different from your living environment?

Language and Vocabulary

Recognizing Sensory Details

Abbey's style reveals his sharp powers of observation. Sensory details—those that appeal to our senses—enable us to see the vultures "soaring overhead"; we hear the "shuffle" of the javelina hoofs.

21
Inference. Reflects narrator's ability to draw a conclusion from observed evidence.

22
Scat: droppings.

READING CHECK
1. Most remain in bush or in burrows (p. 147).
2. Rodents and small mammals (p. 148).
3. Has tail of raccoon, gait of bear, nose of pig, face of badger, teeth of wolf, and lean body of fox or coyote (p. 148).
4. Pad of prickly pear cactus (p. 151).
5. Three days (p. 147).

FOR STUDY AND DISCUSSION
1a. Their tracks. **1b.** They are keen.
2a. Looks like mixture of many animals. **2b.** That it is old. **2c.** Abbey watches; then approaches and extends hand. Chulu shows "snarling grin" and runs away.
3. Intelligent animals would know that they must eat to stay alive; therefore, they eat whatever they can find when their favorite food is not available, just as humans do.
4a. Ability to make water inside the body, to find and eat wide variety of foods, to defend itself, and to outdistance attackers.
4b. Responses will vary. Probably our ability to reason.
5a. Area is remote and uninhabited by humans. **5b.** Responses will vary. May include references to climate, vegetation, animal life, and degree of human presence.

Desert Creatures

TRANSPARENCY 15
Literary Elements
Imagery – invites students to examine imagery in nonfiction.

CLOSURE
Ask students to point out how Abbey's use of sensory details in "Desert Creatures" shows his keen power of observation.

EXTENSION AND ENRICHMENT
Students may enjoy seeing a film about desert creatures, reading books about desert wildlife, or writing descriptions about animals from pictures.

LANGUAGE AND VOCABULARY

1. **Smell:** "musky" odor of javelinas. **Taste:** fruit of the prickly pear; a "succulent pad." **Hearing:** "snorting, snuffling" of javelinas. **Touch:** "sharp" hoofs of javelinas, friction of javelina bristles and "prickly" pear. **Sight:** "sharp little hoofs, pointed ears, small square bodies" of javelinas.

FOCUS ON INFORMATIVE WRITING

Discuss with students the importance of using vocabulary that is familiar to their audience. If their process explanations require technical terms, encourage students to define the terms. After students have completed their charts, you might want to have them work in small groups to see if all technical terms are adequately defined.

ABOUT THE AUTHOR

Abbey's experience as a park ranger for the National Park Service from 1956 to 1971 provided material for both his fiction and nonfiction. In his works, he expresses opposition to a society that threatens the preservation of the environment. In novels such as *The Brave Cowboy* (1956) and *Fire on the Mountain* (1962), his protagonists are loners in conflict with the government and industry that destroy the wilderness in the name of progress. Collections of his essays with a similar environmental theme include *Desert Solitaire* (1968), *Appalachian Wilderness* (1970), and *Cactus Country* (1973), all of which insist that the natural surroundings be protected.

---

1 List at least five other examples of sensory details in the selection. Try to find one to illustrate each of the five senses.

Focus on Informative Writing

Gathering Details to Explain a Process

In the last paragraph of "Desert Creatures," Edward Abbey uses clear, specific details to explain how the javelina eats barrel cactus (see page 151).

When you explain a process, you need to give your audience clear, specific information. Usually, your readers need two types of details:

what steps to do
what materials to use

If you are writing about a process with which you are very familiar, you probably have all the information you need. If you need further details, however, look for them in books, articles, or videotapes about the topic.

Make notes for a process explanation on a topic of your choice. Then fill in a chart like the one below to organize your notes. Save your writing.

Topic: How to _____

Steps/Stages	Materials
1. _____	_____
2. _____	_____
3. _____	_____
4. _____	_____

About the Author

Edward Abbey (1927–1989)

A well-known writer with twelve books to his credit, Edward Abbey was a fierce opponent of those who harm the environment. His popular 1976 novel, *The Monkey Wrench Gang*, tells the story of four environmental terrorists determined to stop industrialization in the desert. Abbey's devotion to the wilderness made him a vocal, and often bitter, activist, but as Pulitzer Prize-winning nature writer Edwin Way Teale observed, "the bitter man may be one who cares enough to be bitter and he is often the one who says things that need to be said."

Abbey was educated at the University of New Mexico, and made his home in Wolf Hole, Arizona. In his lifetime he worked as a park ranger and fire lookout for the National Park Service in the Southwest and received a coveted Fulbright fellowship. Abbey was intimate with the desert, the forest, and the Australian outback. In his work and daily life, he expressed deep respect for people who live in harmony with their environments instead of destroying them.

THE NATURAL WORLD

OBJECTIVES
The overall aim is for students to explain the characters' responses to the fox, to nature, and to each other, and to identify the use of **flashbacks** in the story. For a complete list of objectives, see the **Teacher's Notes**.

VOCABULARY
The underlined words are in the Glossary. The **Language and Vocabulary** exercise on p. 160 contains an exercise which gives students practice in identifying animal names.

FOCUS / MOTIVATION
Discuss unusual pets, asking students to share stories about wild animals as pets—perhaps deer, foxes, bears, or cougars. Why do people like to keep young wild animals as pets? What problems occur as the animals mature? Why?

Last Cover

PAUL ANNIXTER

In this story the narrator helps us understand the background of events by using flashbacks. *As you read, note how carefully the passage of time is indicated.*

1 I'm not sure I can tell you what you want to know about my brother; but everything about
2 the pet fox is important, so I'll tell all that from the beginning.

It goes back to a winter afternoon after I'd hunted the woods all day for a sign of our lost pet. I remember the way my mother looked up as I came into the kitchen. Without my speak-
3 ing, she knew what had happened. For six hours I had walked, reading signs, looking for a delicate print in the damp soil or even a hair that might have told of a red fox passing that way—but I had found nothing.

"Did you go up in the foothills?" Mom asked.

I nodded. My face was stiff from held-back tears. My brother, Colin, who was going on twelve, got it all from one look at me and went into a heartbroken, almost silent, crying.

Three weeks before, Bandit, the pet fox Colin and I had raised from a tiny kit, had disappeared, and not even a rumor had been heard of him since.

"He'd have had to go off soon anyway," Mom comforted. "A big, lolloping fellow like
4 him, he's got to live his life same as us. But he may come back. That fox set a lot of store by you boys in spite of his wild ways."

TEACHING RESOURCES B
Teacher's Notes, p. 21
Reading Check, p. 24
Study Guide, p. 25
Building Vocabulary, p. 27
Selection Vocabulary Test, p. 29
Selection Test, p. 30

PREREADING FOCUS
The headnote previews the author's use of **flashback**. Ask students to write a narrative in which they imagine their best friend is moving away. Have them begin the narrative by describing the last minutes with their friend. Students should interrupt the present narrative by remembering a special time they once had with the friend. They should conclude by returning to the present.

Last Cover

1
Suggests a conversation in progress between reader and narrator; personalizes narration.

2
Colin's bond with fox adds insight into boy's nature.

3 Analyzing
What does this silent communication show about the relationship between mother and son? Reflects close relationship, a sympathetic rapport.

4
Foreshadowing. Her prediction comes true.

VISUAL CONNECTIONS
Ideas for Writing
As students examine this photograph, have them speculate on the circumstances that have brought the fox to the lighted door. Ask students to write a brief scenario of these circumstances and of those that the photograph suggests may occur.

Last Cover 153

MOTIVATIONAL SUMMARY
Colin has an unusual degree of artistic talent and an unusual pet—a fox named Bandit. His father disapproves of both. He thinks Colin's art has no practical value and may result in his son's becoming an idle dreamer, and he fears that the fox will inevitably return to the wild, where—having learned not to fear humans—he will become a menace to the henhouses on all the nearby farms. When Bandit runs off and begins stealing chickens, Colin tries to find him before the hunters do.

PRESENTATION
In Paul Annixter's "Last Cover," Colin's special nature and his relationship with his pet fox Bandit are inextricably linked on several levels, and both are a source of tension for the family described. Everything about his pet fox is impor-

---

5
Father's cynicism belittles the special bond between Colin and Bandit.

6 Finding Details
Where does the flashback begin? "From the first, the tame fox . . . ."

7
Conflict. Colin's love for pet conflicts with father's concern for farm.

8
Reflects Stan's respect for Father and his knowledge of the woods.

9
Refers to hibernating animals.

10
Father does not give boys false hope.

11
Implies Colin purges negative emotions through his art.

12
Reflects Stan's concern for Colin.

13
Characterization. Stan underrates himself in his praise of Colin; "tough and strong" doesn't mean ordinary.

---

5 "He set a lot of store by our food, anyway," Father said. He sat in a chair by the kitchen window mending a piece of harness. "We'll be seeing a lot more of that fellow, never fear. That fox learned to pine for table scraps and young chickens. He was getting to be an egg thief, too, and he's not likely to forget that."

"That was only pranking when he was little," Colin said desperately.

6 From the first, the tame fox had made tension in the family. It was Father who said we'd better name him Bandit, after he'd made away with his first young chicken.

7 "Maybe you know," Father said shortly. "But when an animal turns to egg sucking he's usually incurable. He'd better not come pranking around my chicken run again."

It was late February, and I remember the bleak, dead cold that had set in, cold that was a rare thing for our Carolina hills. Flocks of sparrows and snowbirds had appeared to peck hungrily at all that the pigs and chickens didn't eat.

"This one's a killer," Father would say of a morning, looking out at the whitened barn roof. "This one will make the shoats[1] squeal."

A fire snapped all day in our cookstove and another in the stone fireplace in the living room, but still the farmhouse was never warm. The leafless woods were bleak and empty, and I spoke of that to Father when I came back from my search.

"It's always a sad time in the woods when the seven sleepers are under cover," he said.

8 "What sleepers are they?" I asked. Father was full of woods lore.

"Why, all the animals that have got sense 9 enough to hole up and stay hid in weather like this. Let's see, how was it the old rhyme named them?

---

1. **shoats:** young hogs.

Surly bear and sooty bat,
Brown chuck and masked coon,
Chippy-munk and sly skunk,
And all the mouses
'Cept in men's houses.

"And man would have joined them and made it eight, Granther Yeary always said, if he'd had a little more sense."

"I was wondering if the red fox mightn't make it eight," Mom said.

10 Father shook his head. "Late winter's a high time for foxes. Time when they're out deviling, not sleeping."

My chest felt hollow. I wanted to cry like Colin over our lost fox, but at fourteen a boy doesn't cry. Colin had squatted down on the floor and got out his small hammer and nails to start another new frame for a new picture. Maybe then he'd make a drawing for the frame and be 11 able to forget his misery. It had been that way with him since he was five.

I thought of the new dress Mom had brought home a few days before in a heavy cardboard box. That box cover would be fine 12 for Colin to draw on. I spoke of it, and Mom's glance thanked me as she went to get it. She and I worried a lot about Colin. He was small for his age, delicate and blond, his hair much lighter and softer than mine, his eyes deep and wide and blue. He was often sick, and I knew the fear Mom had that he might be predes-13 tined.[2] I'm just ordinary, like Father. I'm the sort of stuff that can take it—tough and strong—but Colin was always sort of special.

Mom lighted the lamp. Colin began cutting his white cardboard carefully, fitting it into his frame. Father's sharp glance turned on him now and again.

"There goes the boy making another frame

---

2. **predestined** (prē-děs'tĭnd): here, fated to die young.

THE NATURAL WORLD

tant in understanding Colin, Colin's art, and his father's attitude toward both. The story's title also reflects this interconnectedness. The "Last Cover" refers to Bandit's last refuge from hunters as well as the box cover on which Colin draws a portrait of the fox hiding in this secret retreat, a drawing which is the "last cover" before his father gives his approval of Colin's art.

---

before there's a picture for it," he said. "It's too much like cutting out a man's suit for a fellow that's, say, twelve years old. Who knows whether he'll grow into it?"

Mom was into him then, quick. "Not a single frame of Colin's has ever gone to waste. The boy has real talent, Sumter, and it's time you realized it."

"Of course he has," Father said. "All kids have 'em. But they get over 'em."

"It isn't the pox[3] we're talking of," Mom sniffed.

14 "In a way it is. Ever since you started talking up Colin's art, I've had an invalid for help around the place."

Father wasn't as hard as he made out, I knew, but he had to hold a balance against all Mom's frothing. For him the thing was the land and all that pertained to it. I was following in Father's footsteps, true to form, but Colin threatened to break the family tradition with his leaning toward art, with Mom "aiding and abetting him," as Father liked to put it. For the past two years she had had dreams of my 15 brother becoming a real artist and going away to the city to study.

It wasn't that Father had no understanding of such things. I could remember, through the years, Colin lying on his stomach in the front room making pencil sketches, and how a good drawing would catch Father's eyes halfway across the room, and how he would sometimes gather up two or three of them to study, frowning and muttering, one hand in his 16 beard, while a great pride rose in Colin, and in me too. Most of Colin's drawings were of the woods and wild things, and there Father was a 17 master critic. He made out to scorn what seemed to him a passive "white-livered" interpretation of nature through brush and pencil instead of rod and rifle.

3. **the pox:** chicken pox.

At supper that night Colin could scarcely eat. Ever since he'd been able to walk, my brother had had a growing love of wild things, but Bandit had been like his very own, a gift of the woods. One afternoon a year and a half before, Father and Laban Small had been running a vixen through the hills with their dogs. With the last of her strength the she-fox had made for her den, not far from our house. The dogs had overtaken her and killed her just before she reached it. When Father and Laban 18 came up, they'd found Colin crouched nearby holding her cub in his arms.

Father had been for killing the cub, which was still too young to shift for itself, but Colin's grief had brought Mom into it. We'd taken the young fox into the kitchen, all of us, except Father, gone a bit silly over the little thing. Colin had held it in his arms and fed it warm milk from a spoon.

"Watch out with all your soft ways," Father had warned, standing in the doorway. "You'll make too much of him. Remember, you can't make a dog out of a fox. Half of that little critter has to love, but the other half is a wild hunter. You boys will mean a whole lot to him 19 while he's kit, but there'll come a day when you won't mean a thing to him and he'll leave you shorn."

For two weeks after that Colin had nursed the cub, weaning it from milk to bits of meat. For a year they were always together. The cub grew fast. It was soon following Colin and me about the barnyard. It turned out to be a patch fox, with a saddle of darker fur across its shoulders.

I haven't the words to tell you what the fox meant to us. It was far more wonderful owning him than owning any dog. There was some- 20 thing rare and secret like the spirit of the woods about him, and back of his calm, straw-gold eyes was the sense of a brain the equal to 21 a man's. The fox became Colin's whole life.

Last Cover **155**

14
Conflict. Father thinks the land is important; Colin and mother value art.

15
Idea is potentially divisive since it calls for break with tradition.

16
Father's opinion is valuable to them since his approval is difficult to earn.

17
Father admires Colin's art but will not admit it; he does not yet realize art requires skills of observation and understanding just as hunting and fishing do.

18
A hunt brings Bandit into their lives; later, he is killed in a hunt.

19
Gruff warning is to protect boys from future pain.

20 Expressing an Opinion
Who else fits this description?
Responses will vary. Colin and, in some ways, Father.

21
The significance of Bandit in understanding Colin.

155

SCIENCE LINK
Have students use encyclopedias and other reference sources to find information about the seven animals named in the rhyme on p. 154 of the story. Then have students use the information to write brief descriptions of each of these animals. Encourage them to include drawings of the animals as well.

VISUAL CONNECTIONS
Exploring the Subject
The red fox is an excellent hunter, with keen hearing, sight, and smell, and a lightning-quick final pounce on its prey. It loves to feast on rabbit, mice, birds, and eggs. The red fox is curious and may react much like a neighborhood dog. Yet, if hunted, the fox is known for its cleverness in avoiding detection. Its weakness is that, for all its speed, the red fox has little endurance.

22 Summarizing
In what way is Colin's knowledge of the woods greater? He goes by instinct; what others have to learn, he just feels.

23
Use to answer **study question 4,** p. 160.

24
Description. Emphasizes Stan's strong memory of the day.

25
Foreshadowing. Scene has enchanted quality; prepares for boys' final meeting with Bandit.

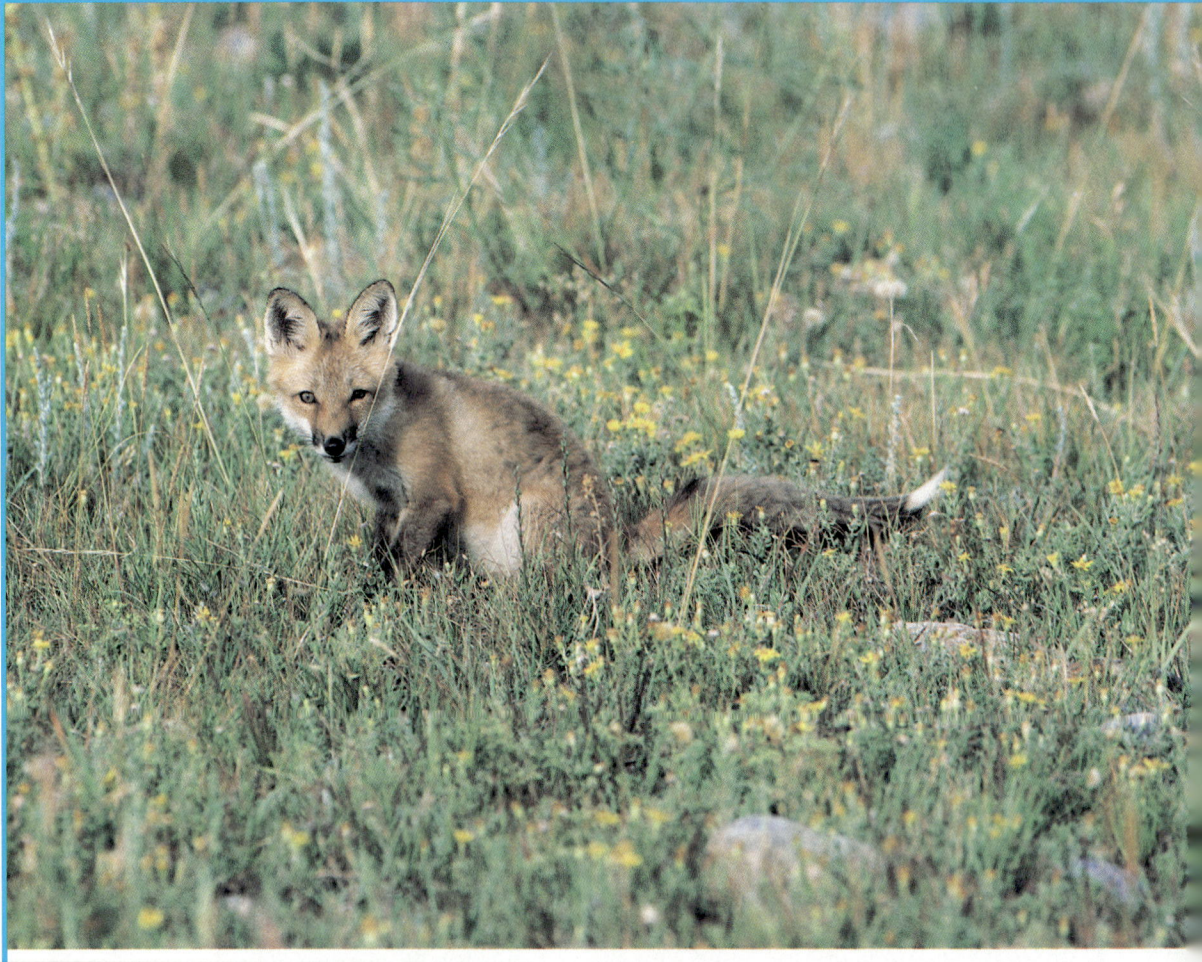

Each day, going and coming from school, Colin and I took long side trips through the woods, looking for Bandit. Wild things' memories were short, we knew; we'd have to find him soon or the old bond would be broken.

Ever since I was ten I'd been allowed to hunt with Father, so I was good at reading signs. 22 But, in a way, Colin knew more about the woods and wild things than Father or me. What came to me from long observation, Colin seemed to know by instinct.

23 It was Colin who felt out, like an Indian, the stretch of woods where Bandit had his den, who found the first slim, small fox-print in the damp earth. And then, on an afternoon in 24 March, we saw him. I remember the day well, the racing clouds, the wind rattling the tops of the pine trees and swaying the Spanish moss. Bandit had just come out of a clump of laurel; in the maze of leaves behind him we caught a glimpse of a slim red vixen, so we knew he had found a mate. She melted from sight like a shadow, but Bandit turned to watch us, his mouth open, his tongue lolling as he smiled his old foxy smile. On his thin chops, I saw a telltale chicken feather.

25 Colin moved silently forward, his movements so quiet and casual he seemed to be standing still. He called Bandit's name, and the fox held his ground, drawn to us with all his senses. For a few moments he let Colin actually put an arm about him. It was then I knew that

156   THE NATURAL WORLD

he loved us still, for all of Father's warnings.
26 He really loved us back, with a fierce, secret love no tame thing ever gave. But the urge of his life just then was toward his new mate. Suddenly, he whirled about and disappeared in the laurels.

Colin looked at me with glowing eyes. "We haven't really lost him, Stan. When he gets through with his spring sparking[4] he may come back. But we've got to show ourselves to him a lot, so he won't forget."

"It's a go," I said.

27 "Promise not to say a word to Father," Colin said, and I agreed. For I knew by the chicken feather that Bandit had been up to no good.

A week later the woods were budding and the thickets were rustling with all manner of wild things scurrying on the love scent. Colin managed to get a glimpse of Bandit every few days. He couldn't get close though, for the spring running was a lot more important to a fox than any human beings were.

Every now and then Colin got out his framed box cover and looked at it, but he never drew anything on it; he never even
28 picked up his pencil. I remember wondering if what Father had said about framing a picture before you had one had spoiled something for him.

I was helping Father with the planting now, but Colin managed to be in the woods every day. By degrees he learned Bandit's range, where he drank and rested and where he was
29 likely to be according to the time of day. One day he told me how he had petted Bandit again, and how they had walked together a long way in the woods. All this time we had kept his secret from Father.

As summer came on, Bandit began to live up to the prediction Father had made. Accus-
30 tomed to human beings he moved without fear about the scattered farms of the region, raiding barns and hen runs that other foxes wouldn't have dared go near. And he taught his wild mate to do the same. Almost every night they got into some poultry house, and by late June Bandit was not only killing chickens and ducks but feeding on eggs and young chicks whenever he got the chance.

Stories of his doings came to us from many sources, for he was still easily recognized by the dark patch on his shoulders. Many a farmer took a shot at him as he fled and some of them set out on his trail with dogs, but they always returned home without even sighting him. Bandit was familiar with all the dogs in

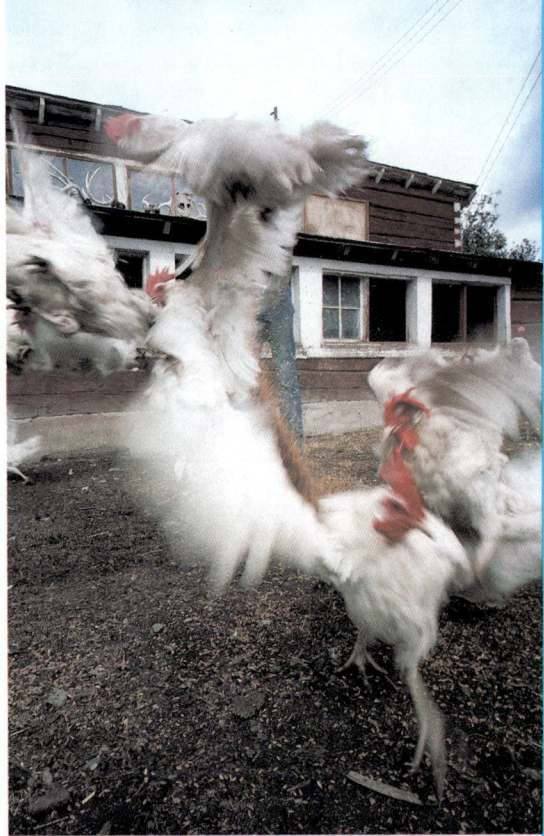

4. **sparking:** courting.

26
Father underestimates the love between the boys and the fox, as he does their understanding and acceptance of Bandit's wildness.

27 Making Inferences
Why do you think Colin does not want Father to know? Responses will vary. Bandit has stolen a chicken; Father would disapprove.

28
If Colin draws to "forget his misery," his looking at (but not drawing on) the cover may show his worry that things may end badly for Bandit.

29
Colin's happiness during this time may also decrease his desire to draw.

30
Bandit's familiarity with humans causes his downfall.

VISUAL CONNECTIONS
Ideas for Writing
Ask students to write a short narrative, in the style of a fairy tale, in which a flock of chickens and a fox try to outwit each other. Students should choose a specific point of view—either the fox's or the chickens'. Have several students read their stories to foster class discussion of the importance of point of view to the whole of a story—i.e., how the story changes depending on who tells it.

TRANSPARENCY 14
Reader Response
Picture This – prompts students to visualize and sketch details that represent significant ideas in the selection.

31
He feels responsible for Bandit's plundering since the fox belongs to his sons.

32
"Ugly" reflects the men's determination; also Stan's perception that this is an ugly business.

33
They are familiar with hunting; fully understand meaning of sound from dogs.

34
Reflects Father's usually hidden concern.

35
Idyllic reminiscing prepares the reader for magical encounter that follows.

36
Stan possesses instincts he thinks only Colin has.

37 Comparing/Contrasting
How is this meeting like the one between the boys that follows? Both reflect mutual understanding, a "oneness" between individuals.

38
Colin's stealth reflects Bandit's still presence.

---

the region, and he knew a hundred tricks to confound them. He got a reputation that year beyond that of any fox our hills had known. His confidence grew, and he gave up wild hunting altogether and lived entirely off the poultry farmers. By late September the hill farmers banded together to hunt him down.

It was Father who brought home that news one night. All time-honored rules of the fox chase were to be broken in this hunt; if the dogs couldn't bring Bandit down, he was to be shot on sight. I was stricken and furious. I remember the misery of Colin's face in the lamplight. Father, who took pride in all the ritual of the hunt, had refused to be a party to such an affair, though in justice he could do nothing but sanction any sort of hunt, for Bandit, as old Sam Wetherwax put it, had been "purely getting in the Lord's hair."

The hunt began next morning, and it was the biggest turnout our hills had known. There were at least twenty mounted men in the party and as many dogs. Father and I were working in the lower field as they passed along the river road. Most of the hunters carried rifles, and they looked ugly.

Twice during the morning I went up to the house to find Colin, but he was nowhere around. As we worked, Father and I could follow the progress of the hunt by the distant hound music on the breeze. We could tell just where the hunters first caught sight of the fox and where Bandit was leading the dogs during the first hour. We knew as well as if we'd seen it how Bandit roused another fox along Turkey Branch and forced it to run for him, and how the dogs swept after it for twenty minutes before they sensed their mistake.

Noon came, and Colin had not come in to eat. After dinner Father didn't go back to the field. He moped about, listening to the hound talk. He didn't like what was on any more than I did, and now and again I caught his smile of satisfaction when we heard the broken, angry notes of the hunting horn, telling that the dogs had lost the trail or had run another fox.

I was restless, and I went up into the hills in midafternoon. I ranged the woods for miles, thinking all the time of Colin. Time lost all meaning for me, and the short day was nearing an end, when I heard the horn talking again, telling that the fox had put over another trick. All day he had deviled the dogs and mocked the hunters. This new trick and the coming night would work to save him. I was wildly glad, as I moved down toward Turkey Branch and stood listening for a time by the deep, shaded pool where for years we boys had gone swimming, sailed boats, and dreamed summer dreams.

Suddenly, out of the corner of my eye, I saw the sharp ears and thin, pointed mask of a fox—in the water almost beneath me. It was Bandit, craftily submerged there, all but his head, resting in the cool water of the pool and the shadow of the two big beeches that spread above it. He must have run forty miles or more since morning. And he must have hidden in this place before. His knowing, crafty mask blended perfectly with the shadows and a mass of drift and branches that had collected by the bank of the pool. He was so still that a pair of thrushes flew up from the spot as I came up, not knowing he was there.

Bandit's bright, harried eyes were looking right at me. But I did not look at him direct. Some woods instinct, swifter than thought, kept me from it. So he and I met as in another world, indirectly, with feeling but without sign or greeting.

Suddenly I saw that Colin was standing almost beside me. Silently as a water snake, he had come out of the bushes and stood there. Our eyes met, and a quick and secret smile

158 THE NATURAL WORLD

MEETING INDIVIDUAL NEEDS
Visual Learners • Have students reread the paragraph at the top of column two on p. 159 and then draw Colin's picture of Bandit hiding in the pool.

MEETING INDIVIDUAL NEEDS
ESL/LEP • The author describes his father as a "born hunter." Ask students, in this context, what part of speech is *born*? (adjective) What does the word *born* mean in this case? (gifted with certain abilities; naturally good at something, as if from birth) Can this adjective also be used in a negative sense? (Yes. For example, "He felt like a born loser.")

---

39 passed between us. It was a rare moment in which I really "met" my brother, when something of his essence flowed into me and I knew all of him. I've never lost it since.

My eyes still turned from the fox, my heart pounding. I moved quietly away, and Colin moved with me. We whistled softly as we went, pretending to busy ourselves along the bank of the stream. There was magic in it, as if by will we wove a web of protection about the fox, a ring-pass-not that none might penetrate. It was so, too, we felt, in the brain of Bandit, and that doubled the charm. To us he was still our little pet that we had carried about in our arms on countless summer afternoons.

Two hundred yards upstream, we stopped beside slim, fresh tracks in the mud where Bandit had entered the branch. The tracks angled upstream. But in the water the wily creature had turned down.

We climbed the far bank to wait, and Colin told me how Bandit's secret had been his secret ever since an afternoon three months before, when he'd watched the fox swim downstream to hide in the deep pool. Today he'd waited on the bank, feeling that Bandit, hard pressed by the dogs, might again seek the pool for sanctuary.

We looked back once as we turned homeward. He still had not moved. We didn't know until later that he was killed that same night by
40 a chance hunter, as he crept out from his hiding place.

That evening Colin worked a long time on his framed box cover that had lain about the house untouched all summer. He kept at it all the next day too. I had never seen him work so hard. I seemed to sense in the air the feeling he
41 was putting into it, how he was *believing* his picture into being. It was evening before he finished it. Without a word he handed it to Father. Mom and I went and looked over his shoulder.

It was a delicate and intricate pencil drawing of the deep branch pool, and there was Bandit's head and watching, fear-filled eyes hiding there amid the leaves and shadows, woven craftily into the maze of twigs and branches, as if by nature's art itself. Hardly a fox there at all, but the place where he was—or should
42 have been. I recognized it instantly, but Mom gave a sort of incredulous sniff.

"I'll declare," she said, "It's mazy as a puzzle. It just looks like a lot of sticks and leaves to me."

Long minutes of study passed before Father's eye picked out the picture's secret, as few men's could have done. I laid that to Father's being a born hunter. That was a picture that
43 might have been done especially for him. In fact, I guess it was.

Finally he turned to Colin with his deep, slow smile. "So that's how Bandit fooled them all," he said. He sat holding the picture with a sort of tenderness for a long time, while we glowed in the warmth of the shared secret.
44 That was Colin's moment. Colin's art stopped being a pox[5] to Father right there. And later, when the time came for Colin to go to art school, it was Father who was his solid backer.

5. **pox:** here, an annoyance.

Reading Check
1. Why is the pet fox named Bandit?
2. What prediction does Father make when Bandit runs away?
3. Why does Father refuse to join the hunt for the fox?
4. What secret does Colin discover?
5. What changes Father's mind about Colin's art?

39
Mood. Stan captures reader's imagination; paints a dreamy picture of moment with Colin and Bandit.

40
"Chance" and understated tone add to effect.

41
Colin's picture coincides with Bandit's death; Colin may have sensed the finality of meeting with Bandit.

42
Colin instinctively knows he can share his feeling about Bandit in a way his father will understand.

43
Picture represents Colin's willingness to confide his secret to his father.

44 Making Generalizations
How has Bandit affected the family's relationship? He has brought family closer together.

READING CHECK
1. Because he steals chickens and eggs (p. 154).
2. Bandit will return for chickens and eggs (p. 154).
3. Rules of traditional hunt are to be broken; fox is to be shot instead of being brought down by dogs (p. 158).
4. Bandit has been hiding in a deep pool (p. 158).
5. Colin's drawing showing how Bandit remained concealed from the hunters (p. 159).

Last Cover

FOR STUDY AND DISCUSSION
1a. Father wants to kill cub to protect chickens. Colin loves and protects cub. **1b.** Father views Bandit as only another fox; Colin fears for Bandit's safety.
2. Fishing and hunting.
3. He correctly predicts Bandit will run away and continue to kill chickens.
4. Finds Bandit's hiding place and knows his habits.
5. Colin's picture of Bandit hiding reveals Colin's knowledge of nature.
6. Provides opportunity for Father to appreciate Colin's love of nature.

FOCUS ON READING
1. "One afternoon a year and a half before..." (p. 155) indicates Bandit ran off about 18 months earlier.
2. "The hunt began next morning"; "Noon came"; "After dinner"; "in midafternoon"; "the coming night"; "That evening."

LANGUAGE AND VOCABULARY
1. *boar:* adult male pig.
buck: adult male deer, goat, rabbit, or antelope.
bull: adult male ox, buffalo, elephant, moose, walrus, or whale.
cow: adult female ox, buffalo, elephant, moose, walrus, or whale; female counterpart of bull.
doe: adult female deer, goat, rabbit, or antelope; female counterpart of buck.
drake: adult male duck.
ewe: adult female sheep.
gander: adult male goose.
gosling: young goose.
kid: young goat or antelope.
mare: adult female horse, mule, or donkey.
pup: young dog, fox, wolf, seal, or whale.
sow: adult female pig or bear.
stag: adult male deer or caribou.
tom: adult male cat or turkey.

For Study and Discussion

Analyzing and Interpreting the Story

1. Both Colin and his father love the woods and wild things, but their responses to the pet fox are different. **a.** How is this difference shown when Colin finds the cub? **b.** When Bandit runs away?

2. Father refers to Colin's drawings as a "passive 'white-livered' interpretation of nature." What does he believe is a more appropriate response to nature?

3. You learn from Stan that Father is full of woods *lore,* or knowledge. How do Father's predictions about Bandit show that this statement is true?

4. How does Colin show that he knows even more about the woods and wild things than his father and his brother know?

5. At the beginning of the story, Father does not take a serious interest in Colin's art. How does he come to respect and appreciate Colin's talent?

6. At first, the pet fox creates tension in the family. How does Bandit's secret finally bring the family closer together?

Focus on Reading

Following the Order of Events

The events in this story cover a period of about six months, from late winter, after Bandit disappears, until September, when he is hunted down and killed. The storyteller carefully notes the passage of time for the reader:

... on an afternoon in March ...
    (page 156, column 1)
A week later ...   (page 157, column 1)
As summer came on ...
    (page 157, column 1)
... by late June ...   (page 157, column 2)
By late September ...   (page 158, column 1)

The storyteller also interrupts the action of his story twice to relate events that have already occurred. These interruptions, which are called **flashbacks,** fill in the background of the story. The first of these flashbacks, which begins on page 154, takes the action back about a year. Stan recalls, "From the first, the tame fox had made tension in the family." We learn how Bandit got his name. We also learn that Father had tried to warn the boys that Bandit would become a chicken thief.

Locate the second flashback, which tells how Bandit was found. How long was Bandit with the family before he ran away?

Reread the passages of the story that relate the events on the day of the hunt (page 158). Identify the words and phrases that specify the time of each action.

Language and Vocabulary

Identifying Animal Names

The word *vixen* is the name of a particular animal—a female fox. The words *cub* and *kit* have a more general meaning. The young of many mammals, such as wolves and foxes, are known as *cubs.* The word *kit* is short for *kitten,* but it may be used for any fur-bearing animal.

See if you can identify each of the animal names in the following list. Tell whether the name refers to the male or female, the adult or young of the species. Tell whether the name is used for one or more species of animals. Use a dictionary to check your answers.

boar	drake	mare
buck	ewe	pup
bull	gander	sow
cow	gosling	stag
doe	kid	tom

160   THE NATURAL WORLD

CLOSURE
Ask students to discuss how the title applies to the relationships in the story and how **flashbacks** contribute to the narrative.

EXTENSION AND ENRICHMENT
Students could collect fox fables and share them with the class. They could select an animal from a zoo and find out as much as possible about its natural habitat and life style.

Focus on Informative Writing

Organizing Information

Since the purpose of informative writing is to share information, you should pay special attention in this kind of paper to the way you organize your details.

In his story "Last Cover," Paul Annixter is careful to make the passage of time and the order of events clear to the reader (see page 160). Likewise, in a process explanation, you will most often find that **chronological** or **time order** is the most helpful way to arrange your details. Discuss the steps or directions for a process in the order that a person should perform them. Be careful to list only the details that will help readers to perform the process.

Locate a recipe from a cookbook or a list of directions from an appliance manual. Get together with a small group of classmates. Take turns reading your recipes or lists aloud. After each reading, discuss whether or not you think the description of the process is clear. If it is not clear, make some notes on how you could organize it better. Save your notes.

About the Author

Paul Annixter (1894–1985)

Paul Annixter, whose real name was Howard Sturtzel, was born in Minneapolis, Minnesota. He began writing stories when he was nineteen. At that time he lived alone in the woods of northern Minnesota, working on a timber claim. During the next thirty-seven years he published more than five hundred short stories. One of his best-known books, *Swiftwater* (1950), is about a boy growing up in the Maine woods. In 1955 he and his wife, Jane Annixter, began collaborating on novels for young people. Among them are the adventure stories *Horns of Plenty* (1960) and *Windigo* (1963).

Literature and Science

Protective Coloration

Like the fox in "Last Cover," many animals conceal themselves from their enemies by *protective coloration*, which allows them to blend into their environment. Think about the natural coloration of animals that are familiar to you. How is a grasshopper protected by its color? a frog? What disguise does a sparrow have? a fawn?

Making Connections

Using a source such as a biology textbook or an encyclopedia, research the various kinds of camouflage that help creatures blend into their backgrounds. Write a paragraph in which you use several examples to show that animals are protected by their coloration. If you wish, concentrate on a particular group—birds, fish, insects, reptiles, cats, and so on. Open your paragraph with a sentence that states the central idea. You may use this sentence if you like: Natural coloration helps animals conceal themselves from their enemies.

FOCUS ON INFORMATIVE WRITING
You could use this assignment as an opportunity to discuss with students the use of props to help organize a process explanation. First, present a list of directions from an appliance manual without showing students the appliance. Then repeat the directions, this time using the appliance and demonstrating the steps. Lead students to see that when developing their own lists of steps for process explanations, props can help with order and accuracy.

ABOUT THE AUTHOR
Inspired by his solitary year and a half on a timber claim in northern Minnesota, Paul Annixter, pseudonym of Howard A. Sturtzel, began writing at age nineteen. Thirty-five years later he had published more than 500 short stories about nature, wildlife, and hunting. His writings include *Wilderness Ways* (1930), *Swiftwater* (1950), and *Devil of the Woods* (1958). In 1955 he and his wife Jane Annixter, also a writer, began collaborating on novels about nature for children. Their works include *The Runner* (1956), *The Phantom Stallion* (1961), and *Wagon Scout* (1965).

LITERATURE AND SCIENCE
You may want to discuss with students the importance of paraphrasing and citing sources of information. Find a source that discusses protective coloration and model for students how to paraphrase the information. Explain to them that if the exact words in the original source are particularly interesting, they may want to quote the author. Model for them how to do so.

Last Cover 161

OBJECTIVES

The overall aim is for students to discuss diction and **imagery** in the poem. For a complete list of objectives, see the **Teacher's Notes**.

PRESENTATION

Langston Hughes eloquently expresses the joy of spring in his poem "In Time of Silver Rain." The images he creates are primarily visual, although the description of the rain as "silver" (metal cool to the touch) and "silken" (fabric cool and sleek on the skin) also appeals to the tactile sense. The poem, which is written with no end-stop punctuation until the end of each stanza, is full of energy and exuberance. The poem quite clearly exalts all of the natural world and humanity's place within it.

TEACHING RESOURCES B
Teacher's Notes, p. 32
Study Guide, p. 33
Selection Test, p. 74

AV RESOURCES BINDER
Audiocassette 1, Side B

PREREADING FOCUS
Have students list words and phrases (both literal and figurative) to describe the rain in the picture. Ask students if any of the words express their attitudes toward rain.

In Time of Silver Rain

1
Connotation. *Silver*—radiant, clear, lustrous, peaceful.

2
"New life" has both physical and spiritual meaning.

3
Plain means both "level land" and "something unadorned." Rain adorns plain land with grasses and flowers.

4 Analyzing
What mood is created by the repetition of this line? A mood of joy, affirming the wonder of life.

5
Imagery. Fanciful image mixes senses of sight, touch, and hearing. Association of butterflies with rainbow suggests color that results from "silver rain."

6
Silken means "glossy, delicate, smooth like silk"; resonates with *silver*.

7
Refrain. Line is repeated three times for emphasis and unity: "In time of silver rain" is spring, which connotes rebirth, as does water (rain).

In Time of Silver Rain

LANGSTON HUGHES

1 In time of silver rain
   The earth
2 Puts forth new life again,
   Green grasses grow
   And flowers lift their heads,   5
3 And over all the plain
   The wonder spreads
4   Of life,
        Of life,
        Of life!   10

   In time of silver rain
5 The butterflies
6 Lift silken wings
   To catch a rainbow cry,
   And trees put forth   15
   New leaves to sing
   In joy beneath the sky
   As down the roadway
   Passing boys and girls
   Go singing, too,   20
7 In time of silver rain
        When spring
        And life
        Are new.

162   THE NATURAL WORLD

MEETING INDIVIDUAL NEEDS
Visual and Kinesthetic Learners • Encourage students to pay close attention to all of the details presented in Hughes's poem and to try to incorporate them in a drawing or painting.

CLOSURE
Ask students to choose and explain other colors that might be used to describe spring rain. Then ask why Langston Hughes might have chosen silver to describe raindrops.

EXTENSION AND ENRICHMENT
Students might enjoy reading other poems about spring. E. E. Cummings' "in Just-" is on p. 439. Students might be asked to write their own poems about spring. Suggest that they try to include a **refrain** in their poems.

For Study and Discussion

Analyzing and Interpreting the Poem

1. In this poem Langston Hughes expresses a joyous attitude toward the natural world. **a.** What does the phrase "silver rain" suggest? **b.** What is the "time of silver rain"?

2. In the second stanza Hughes describes the colorful wings of butterflies in an imaginative way. **a.** What does the word *silken* suggest about the wings? **b.** What is the meaning of line 14?

3. A line or phrase that is repeated at intervals in a poem is called a **refrain**. **a.** What is the refrain in this poem? **b.** What does the poet emphasize by repeating these words? **c.** What other repetition does the poet use? **d.** What is its effect?

About the Author

Langston Hughes (1902–1967)

Langston Hughes was born in Joplin, Missouri. He went to sea in 1922 and worked at a variety of odd jobs around the world before returning to the United States. While he was working in a hotel in Washington, D.C., he came to the attention of the well-known poet Vachel Lindsay. Lindsay read some of Hughes's work at a poetry recital he was giving in the hotel auditorium. The next day newspapers acclaimed Lindsay's discovery of the young poet. *The Weary Blues,* Hughes's first volume of poems, appeared in 1926. Although Hughes is remembered chiefly as a poet, he also wrote short stories, plays, movie scripts, and children's books. In addition, he edited several anthologies of prose and poetry by black writers.

FOR STUDY AND DISCUSSION
1a. Brightness, shininess, happiness. 1b. Spring. 2a. Soft, delicate, luxurious. 2b. Wings reflect colors of rainbow. 3a. "In time of silver rain." 3b. Welcomed light and rain of spring. 3c. "Of life." 3d. Emphasizes joy of spring.

ABOUT THE AUTHOR
Although best known for his poetry, such as *The Weary Blue* (1926), *The Negro Mother* (1931), *Fields of Wonder* (1947), and *Montage of a Dream Deferred* (1951), Hughes also wrote fiction. His novels include *Not Without Laughter* (1930) and *Tambourines to Glory* (1958); collections of his short stories are entitled *The Ways of White Folks* (1934) and *Something in Common* (1963). His most famous prose centers on a Harlem character named Jesse B. Semple (Simple), who appears to be ignorant yet is actually quite astute on a variety of subjects. In 1963, Hughes adapted some of his stories about Semple into a play entitled *Simply Heavenly*. Two autobiographies that detail Hughes' life from his youth to 1938 are *The Big Sea* (1940) and *I Wonder as I Wander* (1956).

OBJECTIVES
The overall aim is for students to demonstrate an understanding of the **similes** and **imagery** in Longfellow's narrative poem. For a complete list of objectives, see the **Teacher's Notes.**

VOCABULARY
The underlined words are in the Glossary. You may want to preteach the nautical terms *schooner, helm, spar, mast, bow,* and *shroud* as well as Longfellow's use of archaic words, such as *ope, spake,* and *hither.*

FOCUS / MOTIVATION
Start a discussion of why people have always feared the sea even as they have found it beneficial and pleasurable. Observe that Longfellow's poem is based on an actual shipwreck.

TEACHING RESOURCES B
Teacher's Notes, p. 35
Study Guide, p. 37
Building Vocabulary, p. 39
Selection Vocabulary Test, p. 53
Selection Test, p. 40

AV RESOURCES BINDER
Audiocassette 1, Side B

VISUAL CONNECTIONS
Ideas for Writing
Longfellow offers a chilling rendition of the wreck of the *Hesperus.* However, Longfellow's version is not historically accurate. Though there is a reef called Norman's Woe, the *Hesperus* was not shipwrecked there. Students might want to research the circumstances surrounding the *Hesperus* disaster, making notes on the causes and the results. Suggest that students compare their findings to Longfellow's ballad.

PREREADING FOCUS
The headnote calls attention to Longfellow's use of vivid comparisons to emphasize the tragedy in this ballad. The **simile,** a comparison between two unlike things using *like* or *as,* is used frequently in this poem. To familiarize students with the use of the simile, ask them to complete the following comparisons:
The salty sea is like _____.
The fearful sailor is as pale as _____.
The cold wind is as strong as _____.
The wooden ship crashed into the rocks like _____.

The Wreck (1939) by Morris Kantor. Oil on linen.
National Museum of American Art, Smithsonian Institution

The Wreck of the *Hesperus*

HENRY WADSWORTH LONGFELLOW

The story told in the following poem is based on an actual shipwreck that occurred more than a hundred years ago. How does Longfellow use vivid comparisons to emphasize the terrible destructiveness of the elements?

164   THE NATURAL WORLD

MOTIVATIONAL SUMMARY
The captain of the schooner *Hesperus* is very confident of his skill. He is so sure that he can handle any danger, even during the stormy winter season, that he has brought his young daughter on board with him. The wind begins to shift, and an old sailor warns that he sees signs of a big storm gathering. He recommends heading for the nearest port, but the captain insists that he can handle even the roughest winds and waves.

PRESENTATION
The cruelty of nature overshadows its gentleness and beauty in Longfellow's dramatic poem "The Wreck of the *Hesperus*." The storm that blindly destroys the ship and all within it is unconcerned that innocence and beauty as well as arrogance

The Wreck of the Hesperus

1 It was the schooner *Hesperus*,
    That sailed the wintry sea;
And the skipper had taken his little daughter,
    To bear him company.

2 Blue were her eyes as the fairy flax,   5
    Her cheeks like the dawn of day,
And her bosom white as the hawthorn buds,
    That ope° in the month of May.

                8. **ope:** open.

The skipper he stood beside the helm,
    His pipe was in his mouth,   10
And he watched how the veering flaw° did blow
3   The smoke now West, now South.

                11. **flaw:** a sudden blast of wind.

Then up and spake an old Sailor,
    Had sailed to the Spanish Main,°
"I pray thee, put into yonder port,   15
    For I fear a hurricane.

                14. **Spanish Main:** parts of the Caribbean Sea once traveled by Spanish ships.

4 "Last night, the moon had a golden ring,
    And tonight no moon we see!"
The skipper, he blew a whiff from his pipe,
    And a scornful laugh laughed he.   20

5 Colder and louder blew the wind,
    A gale from the Northeast,
The snow fell hissing in the brine,
    And the billows frothed like yeast.

Down came the storm, and smote amain°   25
    The vessel in its strength;
She shuddered and paused, like a frighted steed,
    Then leaped her cable's length.

                25. **smote amain:** struck with great force.

"Come hither! come hither! my little daughter,
    And do not tremble so;   30
6 For I can weather the roughest gale
    That ever wind did blow."

1
Allusion. In classical mythology, Hesperus climbed Mt. Atlas to watch the motion of the stars; he was swept away by a whirlwind and became the evening star.

2
Simile. The girl is compared to the gentle aspects of nature.

3
Erratic wind is a forerunner of the gale wind in ll. 21–22.

4
Reference to popular belief which says a ring around the moon means change of weather, often for the worse.

5
Ominous sign of changing weather.

6 Summarizing
What is the skipper's attitude toward the storm? He sees it as a challenge rather than something to be feared; overconfidence causes him to scorn common sense.

The Wreck of the *Hesperus*   **165**

and conceit are doomed by the billowing waves. Perhaps Longfellow is suggesting that humankind is like the people on board the ship. Human beings are tossed about by an unseeing power on whose deaf ears fall such pitiful cries for mercy as the narrator's pleas, "Christ save us all from a death like this." On the other hand, had the arrogant skipper heeded the warnings nature gave him, the tragedy could have been avoided.

GEOGRAPHY LINK
Have students find the northeastern coast of the United States and locate the area around Gloucester, Massachusetts, site of the shipwreck on which the poem is based.

7
He ties her so she will not be swept overboard.

8
Fog bell, guns (l. 41) and the light (l. 45) are warnings from lighthouse that ship is too close to shore.

9
Bells and guns are used when visibility is low due to fog or high waves.

10
Irony. The skipper does not realize his ship is the one in danger.

11
Her ability to see lighthouse light shows ship is very close to shore and will wreck.

12
Lantern is from the lighthouse.

13
Reflects her piety, as does her mistaking lighthouse bells for church bells in l. 37.

14
Simile. Suggests ship's doom; girl's prayers are in vain.

15 Analyzing
What does the word trampling suggest? Destruction.

    He wrapped her warm in his seaman's coat
        Against the stinging blast;
    He cut a rope from a broken spar,   35
7 And bound her to the mast.

    "O father! I hear the church bells ring;
        Oh, say, what may it be?"
8 "'Tis a fog bell on a rock-bound coast!"
    And he steered for the open sea.   40

9 "O father! I hear the sound of guns,
        Oh, say, what may it be?"
10 "Some ship in distress, that cannot live
        In such an angry sea!"

11 "O father! I see a gleaming light;   45
        Oh, say, what may it be?"
    But the father answered never a word,
        A frozen corpse was he.

    Lashed to the helm, and stiff and stark,
        With his face turned to the skies,   50
12 The lantern gleamed through the gleaming snow
        On his fixed and glassy eyes.

    Then the maiden clasped her hands and prayed
        That savèd she might be;
13 And she thought of Christ, who stilled the wave 55
        On the Lake of Galilee.°

    And fast through the midnight dark and drear,
        Through the whistling sleet and snow,
14 Like a sheeted ghost, the vessel swept
        Towards the reef of Norman's Woe.°   60

    And ever the fitful gusts between,
        A sound came from the land;
15 It was the sound of the trampling surf
        On the rocks and the hard sea sand.

55–56. **Christ . . . Galilee:** This story is told in Matthew 8: 23–27.

60. **Norman's Woe:** a chain of rocks near Gloucester, Massachusetts.

166   THE NATURAL WORLD

HISTORY LINK
Encourage students to do research on schooners and other types of sailing vessels and to write a brief paragraph about what they learn. Suggest that they include sketches or diagrams to illustrate the characteristics of each type of vessel.

TRANSPARENCIES 12 & 13
Fine Art
Theme: *Reacting to Our Environment* – highlights artworks that evoke in the viewer a response about the natural world.

VISUAL CONNECTIONS
Ideas for Writing
The ship seems fragile and defenseless against the waves that threaten to engulf it. This picture may serve as a springboard for student writing on other manifestations of nature's power—tornadoes, hurricanes, thunderstorms, etc.

The breakers were right beneath her bows,   65
  She drifted a dreary wreck,
And a whooping billow swept the crew
  Like icicles from her deck.

She struck where the white and fleecy waves
16   Looked soft as carded° wool,   70   70. **carded:** combed.
  But the cruel rocks, they gored her side
    Like the horns of an angry bull.

17 Her rattling shrouds,° all sheathed in ice,   73. **shrouds:** ropes hanging from the mast.
  With the masts went by the board;
18 Like a vessel of glass, she stove° and sank;   75   75. **stove:** smashed.
  Ho! ho! the breakers roared!

16
Deceptive beauty of shore contrasts with cruelty of the rocks.

17
Shroud also refers to a garment worn by the dead.

18 Analyzing
What does "glass" suggest?
Ship is iced over, ship is fragile.

The Wreck of the *Hesperus*   **167**

COOPERATIVE LEARNING
Have students work in small groups to create storyboards (a pictorial outline of key scenes used in planning a movie) that they might use if they were making a movie of the poem. Suggest that they begin by dividing a large sheet of paper into six parts or frames and by then sketching major scenes in chronological order within the frames. Each sketch should show whether the scene is to be a long shot, a medium shot, or a close-up. Encourage groups to share their completed storyboards and explain the scenes and camera angles they chose.

19
Imagery. Dawn should bring light and joy; here it breaks over a "black" beach and a scene of great sorrow.

20
Description. Reflects sea instead of land.

21
Plea recalls girl's unanswered prayers.

FOR STUDY AND DISCUSSION
1a. Wind changes directions, sailor warns of ringed moon. **1b.** Confident of his seamanship.
2. To keep her from being swept overboard.
3a. Fog bell. **3b.** Steers for open sea.
4a. Skipper thinks distress call from another ship; really a warning to his ship. **4b.** From lighthouse—ship very near shore.
5a. Skipper freezes to death; crew swept overboard. **5b.** Freezes to death.
6. Lines 25–28 and ll. 61–76.

LITERARY ELEMENTS
1. The ship rocks erratically in the storm.
2. Compared to bull's horns in ll. 71–72.
3. Storm is violent like bull.
4. Lines 5–8 use happy, delicate images of nature. Lines 81–84 use coarse, grotesque images of sea.
5. Powerful waves began to surge.
6. The ice-covered ship drifted toward destruction.
7. A powerful wave sent helpless sailors into sea.
8. Ship struck rocks disguised by seemingly gentle sea.
9. The fragile ship sank.

---

19 At daybreak, on the black sea beach,
    A fisherman stood aghast,
To see the form of a maiden fair,
    Lashed close to a drifting mast.   80

20 The salt sea was frozen on her breast,
    The salt tears in her eyes;
And he saw her hair, like the brown seaweed,
    On the billows fall and rise.

Such was the wreck of the *Hesperus*,   85
    In the midnight and the snow!
21 Christ save us all from a death like this,
    On the reef of Norman's Woe!

For Study and Discussion

Analyzing and Interpreting the Poem

1a. What signs are there of the approaching storm? **b.** Why is the skipper confident that he can ride out the storm?

2. Why does the skipper bind his daughter to the mast?

3a. What is the first warning from the people on land? **b.** How does the skipper react to this warning?

4. Two other warnings are sent to the ship. **a.** What do you think is the meaning of the guns in line 41? **b.** The gleaming light in line 45?

5a. What is the fate of the skipper and his crew? **b.** Of the skipper's daughter?

6. In which lines does Longfellow emphasize the strength and cruelty of the storm?

Literary Elements

Understanding Similes

Longfellow gives this description of the ship's movement when the storm strikes:

    She shuddered and paused, like a frighted steed,
    Then leaped her cable's length.

The ship is compared here to a frightened horse that trembles, then springs from the ground. What can you picture happening to the ship?

Longfellow is here using a special kind of comparison known as a **simile**. A simile is a comparison between two unlike things which uses a word such as *like* or *as* to express the comparison.

In which lines does the poet compare the rocks to the horns of a bull? How does this simile emphasize the violence of the storm?

How do the similes in lines 5–8 stress the girl's delicate beauty? Compare this picture with the one in lines 81–84.

Tell in your own words what the similes in the following lines suggest to you.

168   THE NATURAL WORLD

5 And the billows frothed like yeast.
                                                (line 24)
6 Like a sheeted ghost, the vessel swept
       Towards the reef of Norman's Woe.
                                             (lines 59–60)
7 And a whooping billow swept the crew
       Like icicles from her deck.
                                             (lines 67–68)
8 She struck where the white and fleecy waves
       Looked soft as carded wool,
                                             (lines 69–70)
9 Like a vessel of glass, she stove and sank;
                                                (line 75)

For Oral Reading

Preparing a Presentation

Imagine that you are to deliver Longfellow's poem in a public reading. How will you prepare your presentation so that it is dramatic and effective? How should the lines in each stanza be spoken? Where, for example, should you pause? Where should you raise or lower your voice? How will you indicate the change of speakers by your tone? Practice with a classmate and then, if you wish, tape your reading and listen to it before your performance.

About the Author

Henry Wadsworth Longfellow (1807–1882)

For many years, Longfellow was one of the best-loved and most widely read of all American poets. He was one of a group of New England poets who became known as the "Fireside Poets." Their poetry had a large family audience. The members of a family would gather together, often before the fireside, and read poems aloud.

For a number of years, Longfellow combined a literary career with teaching. He was a professor of modern languages at Bowdoin College and later at Harvard University. Eventually he was able to leave teaching and devote himself to writing poetry full time. "The Wreck of the *Hesperus*" is one of his best-known poems.

The Wreck of the *Hesperus* 169

OBJECTIVES
The overall aim is for students to analyze the author's use of specific details of **setting** and to demonstrate an understanding of the main character's actions. For a complete list of objectives, see the **Teacher's Notes**.

Teaching Resources B
Teacher's Notes, p. 42
Reading Check, p. 45
Study Guide, p. 46
Language Skills, p. 48
Building Vocabulary, p. 51
Selection Vocabulary Test, p. 53
Selection Test, p. 55

VISUAL CONNECTIONS
Ideas for Writing
Ask students to examine this photograph and to imagine that they are on an expedition in the heart of a jungle in tropical America. Have them write a brief description in which they describe their surroundings by appealing to each of the five senses. What is the weather like, and how do they try to keep comfortable? How would they describe the odor of the lush vegetation and the damp atmosphere? What sounds do they hear in the daytime and late at night? What sights do they see: plants, animals, people, activities? What kinds of food do they eat, and what do they drink?

PREREADING FOCUS
Ask students to brainstorm ideas that might answer the two questions posed in the headnote. You may wish to lead their discussion by asking the questions in **Ideas for Writing** above.

The Tiger's Heart

1
Setting. Evidently, this is a primitive peasant village with no electricity and nothing to protect or to distract the people from the fears of the night.

2
Animals and humans alike are potential victims; their silence suggests a desire for invisibility.

VOCABULARY
The underlined words are in the Glossary. The **Language and Vocabulary** exercise on p. 177 deals with finding the appropriate meanings of words to match specific contexts.

FOCUS / MOTIVATION
Begin by reading aloud the first two paragraphs of the story and asking students to share their mental pictures of the **setting**. You might also have students discuss impressions created by the word *tiger*.

The Tiger's Heart

JIM KJELGAARD°

This story takes you to a jungle in tropical America. How is the natural world depicted? What do you think the title refers to?

1 The approaching jungle night was, in itself, a threat. As it deepened, an eerie silence enveloped the thatched village. People were silent. *2* Tethered cattle stood quietly. Roosting chickens did not stir and wise goats made no noise. Thus it had been for countless centuries and thus it would continue to be. The brown-skinned inhabitants of the village knew the jungle. They had trodden its dim paths, forded its sulky rivers, borne its steaming heat, and were intimately acquainted with its deer, tapir,[1] crocodiles, screaming green parrots and countless other creatures.

° **Kjelgaard** (kĕl′gärd).

1. **tapir** (tā′pər): large jungle animals related to the rhinoceros.

MOTIVATIONAL SUMMARY
All the villagers in Pepe Garcia's village are afraid when a jaguar raids their village and steals a goat. A jaguar is ferocious, much too dangerous to hunt with machetes—which are the only weapons the other villagers own. Only Pepe owns a rifle, and only he is bold enough to go into the jungle to hunt the marauding tiger, which will surely come for more livestock if not killed. Pepe waits patiently and contentedly for the goat's owner to come hire him to kill the jaguar.

PRESENTATION
The phrase "tiger's heart" suggests a kind of courage based on the instinct for survival and the need for self-preservation. Pepe Garcia, in Jim Kjelgaard's "The Tiger's Heart," is a man obsessed with retaining his power and hero status

---

That was the daytime jungle they could see, feel and hear, but at night everything became different. When darkness came, the jungle was alive with strange and horrible things which no man had ever seen and no man could describe. **3** They were shadows that had no substance and one was unaware of them until they struck and killed. Then, with morning, they changed themselves back into the shape of familiar things. Because it was a time of the unknown, night had to be a time of fear.

Except, Pepe Garcia[2] reflected, to the man who owned a rifle. As the night closed in, Pepe reached out to fondle his rifle and make sure that it was close beside him. As long as it was, **4** he was king.

That was only just, for the rifle had cost him dearly. With eleven others from his village, Pepe had gone to help chop a right of way for the new road. They used machetes,[3] the indispensable long knife of all jungle dwellers, and they had worked hard. Unlike the rest, Pepe **5** had saved every peso[4] he didn't have to spend for immediate living expenses. With his savings, and after some haggling, he had bought his muzzle-loading rifle, a supply of powder, lead, and a mold in which he could fashion bullets for his rifle.

Eighty pesos the rifle had cost him. But it was worth the price. Though the jungle at night was fear itself, no man with a rifle had to fear. The others, who had only machetes with which to guard themselves from the terrors **6** that came in the darkness, were willing to pay well for protection. Pepe went peacefully to sleep.

He did not know what awakened him, only that something was about. He listened intently, but there was no change in the jungle's monotonous night sounds. Still, something was not as it should be.

7 Then he heard it. At the far end of the village, near Juan Aria's[5] hut, a goat bleated uneasily. Silence followed. The goat bleated again, louder and more fearful. There was a pattering rush of small hoofs, a frightened bleat cut short, again silence.

8 Pepe, who did not need to people the night with fantastic creatures because he owned a rifle, interpreted correctly what he had heard. A tiger, a jaguar,[6] had come in the night, leaped the thorn fence with which the village was surrounded, and made off with one of Juan Aria's goats.

Pepe went peacefully back to sleep. With **9** morning, certainly, Juan Aria would come to him.

He did not awaken until the sun was up. Then he emerged from his hut, breakfasted on a papaya he had gathered the day before, and **10** awaited his expected visitor. They must always come to him; it ill befitted a man with a rifle to seek out anyone at all.

Presently Pepe saw two men, Juan Aria and his brother, coming up one of the paths that wound through the village. Others stared curiously, but nobody else came because their **11** flocks had not been raided. They had no wish to pay, or to help pay, a hunter.

Pepe waited until the two were near, then said, "*Buenos días.*"[7]

"*Buenos días,*" They replied.

12 They sat down in the sun, looking at nothing in particular, not afraid any more, because the day was never a time of fear. By daylight, only now and again did a tiger come to raid a flock of goats, or kill a burro or a cow.

---

2. **Pepe Garcia** (pā′pä gär-sē′ä).
3. **machetes** (mə-shĕt′ēz).
4. **peso** (pā′sō): a monetary unit in several Latin American countries.
5. **Juan Aria** (hwän ä-rē′ä).
6. **jaguar** (jăg′wär′): a large cat of tropical America, similar to the leopard. The word *tiger* is often used for several animals of the cat family; here, for the jaguar.
7. **Buenos días** (bwā′nōs dē′äs): Spanish for "Good day."

3
Predatory jungle animals.

4
Rifle makes him superior to other villagers; he depends on it for power.

5
Pepe's sacrifice to get gun hints at his later decision to lie about tiger, to give up respect for power.

6 Summarizing
How does Pepe make his living? Guarding villagers' property.

7
Suspense. Tension built by alternating silence and bleats.

8
Rifle frees him from superstition; allows him to face jungle unafraid.

9
Pepe shows no compassion for Juan Aria.

10
Characterization. Reflects his self-importance and condescension.

11
Pepe's attitude isn't unique; evidently, no one wants to help a neighbor.

12
Setting. Tiger rules night and humanity rules day.

in his village. His rifle gives him this power and position by making him appear more capable and less afraid of the terrors of the night. The villagers never see through the mystique of the rifle to the ordinary man because Pepe will not let them. The tiger and Pepe have much in common. Both are "jungle born." Both depend on the fear of others to sustain power and livelihood; their courage results from their own fear. Both will fight when backed into a corner, and both are proud and arrogant.

13
Pepe plays on Aria's superstition and weakness.

14
This belief maintains Pepe's lofty status.

15
Implies Aria can afford Pepe's fee so long as it is not as high as tiger's toll.

16 Drawing Conclusions
What does this statement show about the villagers' view of Pepe? They look up to him, feeling incapable of protecting themselves.

VISUAL CONNECTIONS
Exploring the Subject
The jaguar is the largest South American cat, found as far north as the southwestern United States. It resembles a leopard but is slightly larger (four to six feet in length) and has a shorter tail. The jaguar is light yellow to reddish in color, with large, dark, circular spots. Its prey consists of goats, mice, deer, monkeys, turtles, fish, and peccaries (small, piglike mammals). The jaguar is incredibly strong, capable of killing and dragging large animals dozens of miles.

After a suitable lapse of time, Juan Aria said, "I brought my goats into the village last night, thinking they would be safe."

"And were they not?"

"They were not. Something came and killed one, a fine white-and-black nanny, my favorite. When the thing left, the goat went too. Never again shall I see her alive."

"What killed your goat?" Pepe inquired.

"A devil, but this morning I saw only the tracks of a tiger."

"Did you hear it come?"

"I heard it."

13 "Then why did you not defend your flock?"

Juan Aria gestured with eloquent hands. "To 14 attack a devil, or a tiger, with nothing but a machete would be madness."

"That is true," Pepe agreed. "Let us hope that the next time it is hungry, this devil, or tiger, will not come back for another goat."

"But it will!"

Pepe relaxed, for Juan Aria's admission greatly improved Pepe's bargaining position. And it was true that, having had a taste of easy game, the tiger would come again. Only death would end his forays, and since he knew where to find Juan Aria's goats, he would continue to attack them.

15 Pepe said, "That is bad, for a man may lose many goats to a tiger."

"Unless a hunter kills him," Juan Aria said.

"Unless a hunter kills him," Pepe agreed.

"That is why I have come to you, Pepe," Juan Aria said. A troubled frown overspread his face. "I hope you will follow and kill this tiger, 16 for you are the only man who can do so."

"It would give me pleasure to kill him, but I cannot work for nothing."

"Nor do I expect you to. Even a tiger will not eat an entire goat, and you are sure to find what is left of my favorite nanny. Whatever the

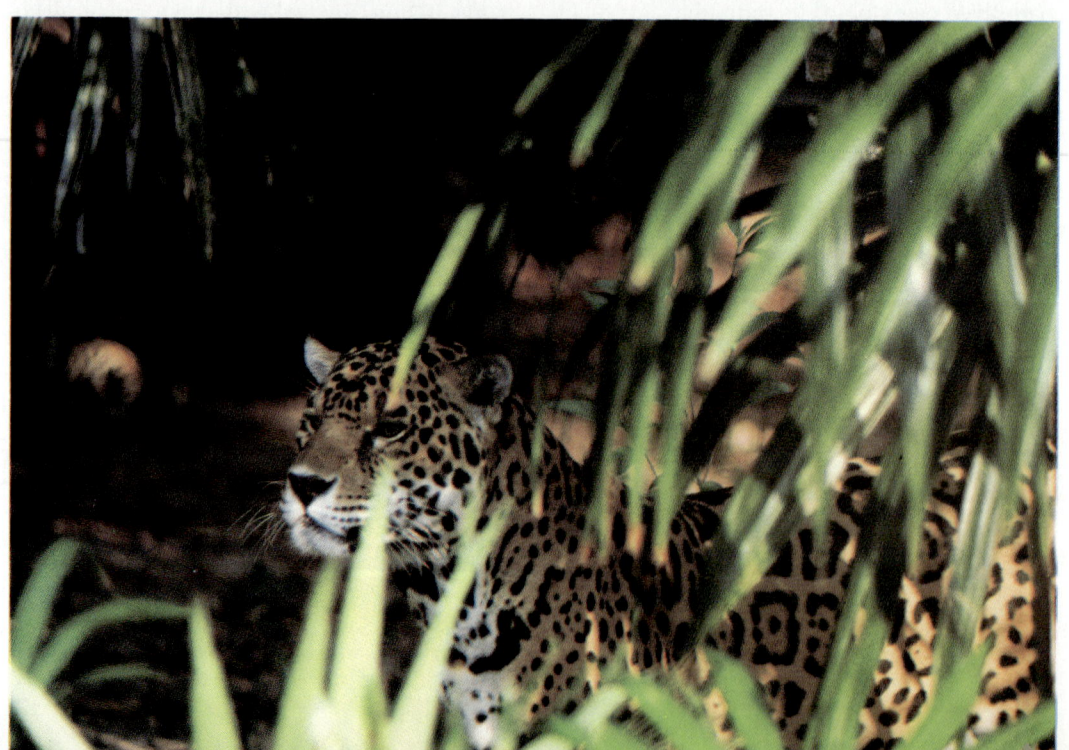

READING SKILLS PRACTICE
The underlined passage can be used to give students practice in the reading skill of using context to understand word meaning. In the passage marked, the meaning of the word *indifference* can be inferred from the context of the paragraph in which it appears. Ask students to choose the most accurate synonym for *indifference* in this passage. **A.** Sameness; **B.** Excitement; **C.** Disinterest; **D.** Happiness. (Answer: **C.** In this context, the man became alert after he stopped (shed) his indifference, so *indifference* means the quality of not being alert or not being interested. The one-word synonym is *disinterest*.)

---

tiger has not eaten, you may have for your pay."

17 Pepe bristled. "You are saying that I should put myself and my rifle to work for carrion left by a tiger?"

"No, no!" Juan Aria protested. "In addition I will give you one live goat!"

"Three goats."

"I am a poor man!" the other wailed. "You would bankrupt me!"

18 "No man with twenty-nine goats is poor, though he may be if a tiger raids his flock a sufficient number of times," Pepe said.

"I will give you one goat and two kids."

"Two goats and one kid."

"You drive a hard bargain," Juan Aria said,
19 "but I cannot deny you now. Kill the tiger."

Affecting an air of nonchalance, as befitted the owner of a firearm, Pepe took his rifle from the fine blanket upon which it lay when he was not carrying it. He looked to his powder horn and bullet pouch, strapped his machete on, and sauntered toward Juan Aria's hut. A half-dozen worshipful children followed.

"Begone!" Pepe ordered.

They fell behind, but continued to follow until Pepe came to that place where Juan Aria's flock had passed the night. He glanced at the dust, and saw the tiger's great paw marks imprinted there. It was a huge cat, lame in the right front paw, or it might have been injured in battle with another tiger.

Expertly, Pepe located the place where it had gone back over the thorn fence. Though the tiger had carried the sixty-pound goat in its jaws, only a couple of thorns were disturbed at the place where it had leaped.

Though he did not look around, Pepe was aware of the villagers watching him and he knew that their glances would be very respectful. Most of the men went into the jungle from time to time to work with their machetes, but none would work where tigers were known to be. Not one would dare take a tiger's trail. Only Pepe dared and, because he did, he must be revered.

Still affecting nonchalance, Pepe sauntered through the gate. Behind him, he heard the village's collective sigh of mingled relief and admiration. A raiding tiger was a very real and
20 terrible threat, and goats and cattle were not easily come by. The man with a rifle, the man able to protect them, must necessarily be a hero.

▶ Once in the jungle, and out of the villagers' sight, Pepe underwent a transformation.
21 He shed his air of indifference and became as alert as the little doe that showed him only her white tail. A rifle might be a symbol of power, but unless a man was also a hunter, a
22 rifle did him no good. Impressing the villagers was one thing; hunting a tiger was quite another. ◀

23 Pepe knew the great cats were dappled death incarnate. They could move with incredible swiftness and were strong enough to kill an ox. They feared nothing.

Jungle-born, Pepe slipped along as softly as a jungle shadow. His machete slipped a little,
24 and he shifted it to a place where his legs would not be bumped. From time to time he glanced at the ground before him.

To trained eyes, there was a distinct trail. It consisted of an occasional drop of blood from the dead goat, a bent or broken plant, a few hairs where the tiger had squeezed between trees, paw prints in soft places. Within the first quarter-mile Pepe knew many things about this tiger.

25 He was not an ordinary beast, or he would have gone only far enough from the village so his nostrils could not be assailed by its unwelcome scents and eaten what he wanted there, then covered the remainder of the goat with sticks and leaves. He was not old, for his was not the lagging gait of an old cat, and the ease

▶ Reading Skills Objective: Using Context to Understand Word Meaning

---

17 Characterization. Pepe's arrogance works for him in bargain.

18 Aria will lose more goats—either to tiger or Pepe.

19 Aria's demand suggests he thinks Pepe will kill the tiger by some kind of magic in the rifle.

20 Confirms Pepe's high fee, yet underscores his own risk.

21 Pepe's indifference is pretense; he knows danger.

22 Prepares reader for Pepe's ability to kill tiger.

23 Analyzing
What does "dappled death incarnate" refer to? Possible answers: tiger's spots, embodiment of destruction, great power.

24 Alerts reader to machete's presence.

25 Makes Pepe's killing him more impressive.

The Tiger's Heart

Science Link

Have students research various wild cats of North and South America. Encourage them to discover the characteristics of these large cats and to record what they learn in their journals or learning logs.

26 Increases odds against Pepe, thus making his victory more remarkable.

27 Intellect tells him not to fear; he has rifle.

28 Plot. Climax, or turning point, of story.

29 Pepe's self-assurance momentarily turns to self-doubt.

30 Tiger attacks to protect prey.

31 Pepe's observations occur instantly.

32 Tiger acts out of instinct for survival, not malice.

33 Analyzing
How do you think Pepe knows this? He is "jungle-born" and has studied this tiger.

34 Slashing tiger will only anger it further.

35 Backward step entices tiger to attack.

---

with which he had leaped the thorn fence with a goat in his jaws was evidence of his strength.

Pepe stopped to look to the loading and priming of his rifle. There seemed to be nothing amiss, and there had better not be. When he saw the tiger, he must shoot straight and true. Warned by some super jungle sense, Pepe slowed his pace. A moment later he found his game.

He came upon it suddenly in a grove of scattered palms. Because he had not expected it 26 there, Pepe did not see it until it was nearer than safety allowed.

The tiger crouched at the base of a palm whose fronds waved at least fifty feet above the roots. Both the beast's front paws were on what remained of the dead goat. It did not snarl or grimace, or even twitch its tail. But there was a lethal quality about the great cat and an extreme tension. The tiger was bursting with raw anger that seemed to swell and grow.

Pepe stopped in his tracks and cold fear 27 crept up his spine. But he did not give way to fear. With deliberate, studied slowness he brought the rifle to his shoulder and took aim. He had only one bullet and there would be no time to reload, but even a tiger could not withstand the smash of that enormous leaden ball right between the eyes. Pepe steadied the rifle.

His finger tightened slowly on the trigger, for he must not let nervousness spoil his aim. When the hammer fell, Pepe's brain and body became momentarily numb.

28 There was no satisfying roar and no puff of black powder smoke wafting away from the muzzle. Instead there was only a sudden hiss, as though cold water had spilled on a hot stone, and the metallic click of the falling ham- 29 mer. Pepe himself had loaded the rifle, but he could not have done so correctly. Only the powder in the priming pan flashed.

It was the spark needed to explode the anger in the tiger's lithe and deadly body. He emitted a coughing snarl and launched his charge. 30 Lord of the jungle, he would crush this puny man who dared interfere with him.

Pepe jerked back to reality, but he took time to think of his rifle, leaning it lovingly against a tree and in the same motion jerking his machete from its sheath.

It was now a hopeless fight, to be decided in the tiger's favor, because not within the memory of the village's oldest inhabitant had any man ever killed a tiger with a machete. But it was as well to fight hopelessly, as to turn and run, for if he did that he would surely be killed. No tiger that attacked anything was ever known to turn aside.

31 Machete in hand, Pepe studied the onrushing cat. He had read the tracks correctly, for from pad to joint the tiger's right front foot was swollen to almost twice the size of the other. It must have stepped on a poisonous thorn or been bitten by a snake.

Even with such a handicap, a tiger was more than a match for a man armed only with a machete—but Pepe watched the right front paw carefully. If he had any advantage, it lay 32 there. Then the tiger, a terrible, pitiless engine of destruction, flung himself at Pepe. Pepe had 33 known from the first that the tiger's initial strike would be exactly this one, and he was ready for it. He swerved, bending his body outward as the great cat brushed past him. With all the strength in his powerful right arm, he swung the machete. He stopped his downward stroke just short of the tiger's silken back, 34 for he knew suddenly that there was just one way to end this fight.

The tiger whirled, and hot spittle from his mouth splashed on the back of Pepe's left hand. Holding the machete before him, like a 35 sword, he took a swift backward step. The tiger sprang, launching himself from the ground as

174 THE NATURAL WORLD

though his rear legs were made of powerful steel springs, and coming straight up. His flailing left paw flashed at Pepe. It hooked in his shirt, ripping it away from the arm as though it were paper, and burning talons sank into the flesh. Red blood welled out.

Pepe did not try again to slash with the machete, but thrust, as he would have thrust with a knife or sword. The machete's point met the tiger's throat, and Pepe put all his strength and weight behind it. The blade explored its way into living flesh, and the tiger gasped. Blood bubbled over the machete.

With a convulsive effort, the tiger pulled himself away. But blood was rushing from his throat now and he shook his head, then stumbled and fell. He pulled himself erect, looked with glazing eyes at Pepe and dragged himself toward him. There was a throttled snarl. The tiger slumped to the ground. The tip of his tail twitched and was still.

Pepe stared, scarcely seeing the blood that flowed from his lacerated arm. He had done the impossible, he had killed a tiger with a machete. Pepe brushed a hand across his eyes and took a trembling forward step.

He picked up his rifle and looked again to the priming. There seemed to be nothing wrong. Repriming, Pepe clasped the rifle with his elbow and seized the machete's hilt. Bracing one foot against the tiger's head, he drew the machete out.

Then he held his rifle so close to the machete wound that the muzzle caressed silken fur. He pulled the trigger. The wound gaped wider and smoke-blackened fur fringed it. All traces of the machete wound were obliterated. Pepe knew a second's anguished regret, then steeled himself, for this was the way it must be.

Everybody had a machete. In his village, the man who owned a rifle must remain supreme.

> **TRANSPARENCY 15**
> **Literary Elements**
> *Imagery* – invites students to examine imagery in nonfiction.

READING CHECK
1. As a laborer, clearing land for a new road (p. 171).
2. Tiger will return for other goats (p. 172).
3. Some of his flock (pp. 172–173).
4. He did not load it correctly (p. 174)
5. Pepe reprimes his rifle and fires into the wound (p. 175).

FOR STUDY AND DISCUSSION
1. They imagine jungle "alive with strange and horrible things."
2a. By protecting villagers' property with rifle. 2b. Frightens them so they will pay him.
3. Bargains for higher price.
4. He drops pretense and is alert.
5a. He knows to look for drops of blood, hair, etc. 5b. Does not run; uses knowledge to his advantage.
6. To retain stature and business as only one who can kill a tiger.
7. Responses will vary. Refers to Pepe's courage.

FOCUS ON READING
1. "Tethered cattle," quiet chickens and goats in village; "dim paths," "sulky rivers," "streaming heat"; deer, tapir, crocodiles, and "screaming green parrots" in jungle.
2. To convey villagers' fear and ignorance of jungle at night.
3. Emphasizes jungle's mystery.

Reading Check

1. How did Pepe earn the money for his rifle?
2. How does Juan Aria know that the tiger will come again?
3. What does he offer Pepe in place of money?
4. Why does Pepe's rifle fail to fire?
5. How does Pepe destroy all traces of the machete wound?

For Study and Discussion

Analyzing and Interpreting the Story

1. The opening paragraphs of the story contrast daytime and nighttime in the jungle. How is the imagination of the villagers affected by the darkness?

2a. How does Pepe earn a living? **b.** How does Pepe take advantage of the villagers' fears?

3. How does Pepe show that he is a shrewd businessman when Juan Aria comes to seek his help?

4. To the people of the village, Pepe acts like a man without fear or concern. How does Pepe's attitude change when he enters the jungle?

5. Pepe knows that unless a man is a hunter, a rifle does him no good. **a.** How does Pepe's experience as a hunter help him to follow the jaguar's trail? **b.** How does he show that he is a great hunter when his rifle proves to be useless?

6. You are told that no one in the village had ever killed a tiger with a machete. Instead of boasting about his amazing deed, Pepe chooses to keep the truth from the villagers. Why?

7. The word *heart* is sometimes used as a synonym for *courage*. To be *stouthearted* or *lionhearted* is to be very brave. What do you think the title of the story means?

Focus on Reading

Focusing on Details of Background

A writer generally attempts to catch the reader's attention at the beginning of a story. Notice how Kjelgaard arouses interest with the opening sentence of "The Tiger's Heart":

> The approaching jungle night was, in itself, a threat.

This sentence draws you into the world of the story—the jungle—and promises you excitement and danger. Notice how the first two paragraphs carry out both purposes of the opening sentence in developing the physical background of the story. What details in the first paragraph give you a vivid picture of the village life of jungle dwellers? Compare this description with the description in the second paragraph. Why does the author deliberately choose less specific details in the second paragraph? What characteristic of the jungle does he wish to emphasize there?

The writer of a short story seeks to create a world the reader can believe in. One way to get the reader to believe in the characters and events of a story is to present them against a lifelike background. Look back at the story and find additional details that give you a realistic picture of village life.

176 THE NATURAL WORLD

Language and Vocabulary

Finding the Appropriate Meaning

A dictionary often gives more than one meaning for a word. To determine which of the definitions is appropriate for a particular word, you must decide how the word is being used. You must decide which meaning best fits the context. For example, the word *air* may be used as a noun, an adjective, or a verb. As a noun, it has several different meanings. It may mean the mixture of gases that surrounds the earth. It may also mean a song or tune. It may also mean a person's outward appearance or manner.

1. Which meaning does *air* have in this sentence?

   He shed his *air* of indifference and became as alert as the little doe that showed him only her white tail.

2. Use a dictionary to find the appropriate meaning of the italicized word in each of these sentences.

   Pepe stopped to look at the loading and *priming* of his rifle.

   Pepe had known from the first that the tiger's *initial* strike would be exactly this one, and he was ready for it.

   Bracing one foot against the tiger's head, he drew the machete out.

Focus on Informative Writing

Exploring Cause and Effect

A **cause-and-effect** paper is a type of informative writing in which you answer the question *Why does that happen?* (cause) or *What is the result?* (effect).

When you explore causes and effects, you will often find that a single event or situation has more than one cause. Similarly, a single event can lead to more than one effect. Study the diagram below.

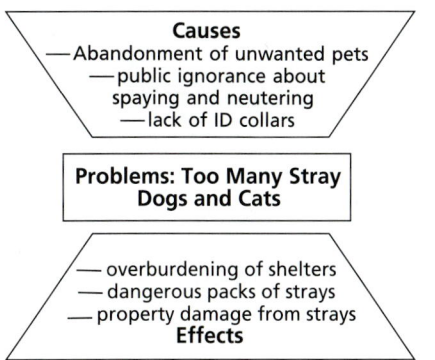

```
           Causes
   —Abandonment of unwanted pets
     —public ignorance about
      spaying and neutering
      —lack of ID collars

   Problems: Too Many Stray
          Dogs and Cats

   —overburdening of shelters
   —dangerous packs of strays
   —property damage from strays
           Effects
```

Make some notes for a cause-and-effect essay on a topic that interests you. To find a topic, ask yourself questions like these:

I wonder why . . .

What would be the result(s) if . . . ?

Save your notes.

About the Author

Jim Kjelgaard   (1910–1959)

Jim Kjelgaard was born in New York City but grew up in the Pennsylvania mountains. He worked at several different jobs before turning to writing. His first book, *Forest Patrol*, which appeared in 1941, was based on his own experiences and those of his brother, a forest ranger. Kjelgaard is well known for his stories about dogs. Three of his books are about Irish setters: *Big Red, Irish Red,* and *Outlaw Red.* In addition to stories about dogs and other animals, Kjelgaard wrote two books about the American frontier—*Rebel Siege* and *Buckskin Brigade.*

The Tiger's Heart   **177**

OBJECTIVES
The overall aim is for students to interpret details of the colt's behavior and to express the **theme** of the poem. For a complete list of objectives, see the **Teacher's Notes**.

Teaching Resources B
Teacher's Notes, p. 57
Study Guide, p. 58
Selection Test, p. 74

PREREADING FOCUS
In reference to the headnote, have students speculate on what the title suggests about the setting, characters, and emotions in the poem.

The Runaway

1
Implies first snowfall of the winter; evidently, colt was born previous spring and has never seen snow.

2
One meaning of **bolt** is "to run away."

3
"Miniature" refers to horse's small size; "thunder," to sound of his hooves; "thunder" also has link to "bolt."

4
Simile. Makes colt seem small and vulnerable; suggests onlookers' sympathy.

5
"Breaking" horse is training him to be ridden; thus, "isn't winter-broken" suggests horse unaccustomed to winter weather.

6 Drawing Conclusions
What does climbing on the wall suggest the colt desires? He wants to escape, as if running away will free him from his fear.

7
Showing the whites of his eyes, holding his tail high, and trembling (ll. 16–18) reflect fear.

8
Theme. Suggested rather than stated directly—stems from speaker's concern for the colt.

PRESENTATION
After reading the poem aloud to your students, ask them to characterize the unidentified onlookers in the poem. What kind of people would stop by a pasture to watch the colt and express concern for his well-being? Ask students if the onlooker is implying in the last three lines that someone has acted irresponsibly in caring for the colt? What is the attitude expressed by the speaker in the poem?

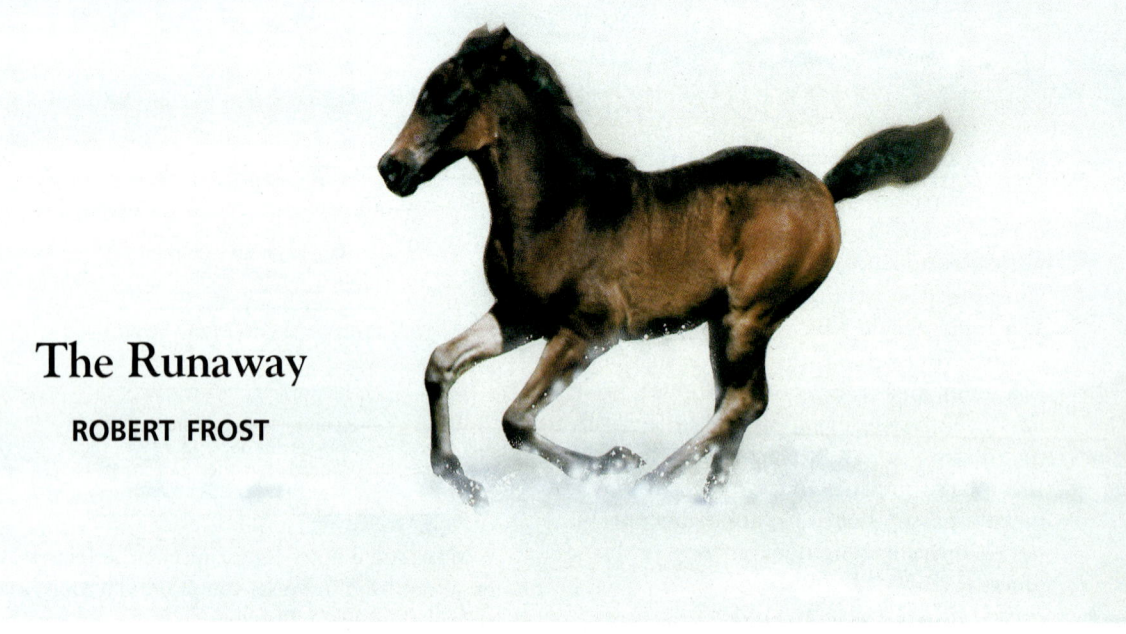

The Runaway
ROBERT FROST

The horse in this poem is one of an American breed of light horses that originated in Vermont. As you read, take into account the setting, the onlookers, and the emotion of the speaker.

1 Once when the snow of the year was beginning to fall,
   We stopped by a mountain pasture to say, "Whose colt?"
   A little Morgan had one forefoot on the wall,
   The other curled at his breast. He dipped his head
2 And snorted at us. And then he had to bolt.   5
3 We heard the miniature thunder where he fled,
4 And we saw him, or thought we saw him, dim and gray,
   Like a shadow against the curtain of falling flakes.
   "I think the little fellow's afraid of the snow.
5 He isn't winter-broken. It isn't play   10
   With the little fellow at all. He's running away.
   I doubt if even his mother could tell him, 'Sakes,
   It's only weather.' He'd think she didn't know!
   Where is his mother? He can't be out alone."
   And now he comes again with clatter of stone,   15
6 And mounts the wall again with whited eyes
   And all his tail that isn't hair up straight.
7 He shudders his coat as if to throw off flies.
8 "Whoever it is that leaves him out so late,
   When other creatures have gone to stall and bin,   20
   Ought to be told to come and take him in."

178 THE NATURAL WORLD

CLOSURE
Ask students to restate the **theme** of the poem and explain how it relates to the emotion of the speaker.

EXTENSION AND ENRICHMENT
Students might like to write an explanation for the colt's being left outside in the snow, or they might compose monologues expressing the colt's thoughts and feelings during his first snowfall.

For Study and Discussion

Analyzing and Interpreting the Poem

1. In the poem we are told that some people stop by a mountain pasture to watch a colt. **a.** What does the colt do when he sees them? **b.** The phrase "miniature thunder" in line 6 is a **figure of speech**, an imaginative way of drawing a comparison between two unlike things. What do you think the phrase refers to?

2. One of the onlookers believes that the colt is afraid of the snow because he isn't "winter-broken." What does the speaker mean by this expression?

3. What details in lines 15–18 confirm the onlooker's belief that the colt is afraid?

4. Many readers think that Frost uses this incident of the colt to express his deep concern for nature's creatures. Other readers believe that the poem also touches on the issue of responsibility. What is your interpretation of the poem?

About the Author

Robert Frost (1874–1963)

Although he was born in the West (San Francisco) and named after a Southerner (Robert E. Lee), Robert Frost has become known as a New England poet. After his father died, his mother brought the family to Lawrence, Massachusetts. There Frost wrote poems while working as a mill hand, a schoolteacher, a baseball coach, a newspaper reporter, and a cobbler.

From 1900 to 1912, while raising chickens on a small farm in Derry, New Hampshire, Frost wrote some of his best-known poems. However, magazine editors rejected them. He had no greater success at farming. In 1912 Frost decided to end his isolation and frustration. He sold the farm and sailed for England with his wife and four children. There he made friends with other struggling poets who were interested in his work. He put together two major collections, *A Boy's Will* (1913) and *North of Boston* (1914). These books brought Frost to the attention of influential critics, including Ezra Pound, who helped Frost build a reputation in America.

By the time he returned to this country in 1915, Frost was already a famous poet. He settled once again on a farm, this time on a hill near Franconia, New Hampshire. For the rest of his life, he was America's unofficial poet laureate. He received many honors, including four Pulitzer Prizes. In 1961 he was asked to participate in the inauguration of John F. Kennedy. At the ceremony, he recited one of his poems, "The Gift Outright."

FOR STUDY AND DISCUSSION
1a. He dips his head, snorts, and runs away. **1b.** The sound of the colt's hooves as he flees.
2. The colt doesn't accept snow.
3. The "clatter of stone," the "whited eyes," "all his tail that isn't hair up straight," and the shudder.
4. Answers will vary. Poem conveys deep concern for colt's fright. However, final three lines convey a reproach to "whoever" has shirked responsibility by not bringing the colt in for the night.

ABOUT THE AUTHOR
Frost once said that a poem should "begin in delight and end in wisdom." Most readers will find that Frost's poetry does just that. Students might enjoy reading "The Death of the Hired Man," "Mending Wall," "The Road Not Taken," "Birches," and "Stopping by Woods on a Snowy Evening."

The Runaway

OBJECTIVES
The overall aim is for students to analyze the main character's actions and feelings and to identify the effective use of adverbs and vivid verbs. For a complete list of objectives, see the **Teacher's Notes**.

> **TEACHING RESOURCES B**
> Teacher's Notes, p. 59
> Reading Check, p. 61
> Study Guide, p. 62
> Language Skills, p. 64
> Building Vocabulary, p. 68
> Selection Vocabulary Test, p. 88
> Selection Test, p. 70
>
> **AV RESOURCES BINDER**
> Audiocassette 1, Side B

VISUAL CONNECTIONS
Exploring the Subject
Rathlin Island, five miles long and three miles wide, is noted for producing grain, fish, and kelp. It is best known, however, as setting for the famous tale of the spider and the web. According to legend, Robert the Bruce (1274–1329), struggling to free Scotland from England, was hiding in the ruins of a castle on the island. Above his bed, a spider on a slender thread failed six times to swing from one beam to another, just as Bruce had lost six battles to the English. On the seventh try the spider succeeded and Bruce, heartened, went on to victory at the Battle of Bannockburn (1314). He became king of an independent Scotland in 1328.

PREREADING FOCUS
Ask students to describe what their emotional responses might be if they were to see the following: an injured bird, a colorful sunset, a forest fire, a field of daisies, a polluted stream. What do their reactions tell them about their relationship with the natural world?

The Wild Duck's Nest
1
The hoofprints in the path clue the reader to the cow's presence by the lake.

2
This burst of energy, like Colm's jaunty walk and his "exultant whoop," reflects his exuberance.

VOCABULARY
The underlined words are in the Glossary. The **Language and Vocabulary** exercises on p. 184 give students practice in forming adverbs and using vivid verbs.

FOCUS / MOTIVATION
You might ask your students whether they have ever inadvertently done something to threaten or harm a wild creature, perhaps a bird. What kind of feelings resulted from such an experience?

The Wild Duck's Nest

MICHAEL McLAVERTY

As you read this story, note how the main character responds to nature and how nature itself seems to mirror his shifting moods.

The sun was setting, spilling gold light on the low western hills of Rathlin Island.[1] A small
1 boy walked <u>jauntily</u> along a hoof-printed path that wriggled between the folds of these hills and opened out into a craterlike valley on the clifftop. Presently he stopped as if remember-
2 ing something, then suddenly he left the path, and began running up one of the hills. When

1. **Rathlin Island:** an island a few miles off the northern coast of Ireland.

180 THE NATURAL WORLD

MOTIVATIONAL SUMMARY

Colm—a young Irish lad—is thrilled to see a wild duck land on the lake. When Colm sees that she is heading into the reeds, he realizes that she must have a nest there. By searching carefully, he finds the nest. It contains one beautiful egg, and without thinking, Colm picks it up to examine it more closely. Then he realizes that if the duck smells his human scent on the egg and the nest, she may abandon them.

PRESENTATION

Sometimes good intentions do not excuse thoughtless behavior, as Colm discovers in Michael McLaverty's short story "The Wild Duck's Nest." The boy's curiosity and his desire to protect the duck's nest do not justify disturbing the

he reached the top he was out of breath and stood watching streaks of light radiating from golden-edged clouds, the scene reminding him of a picture he had seen of the Transfiguration.[2] A short distance below him was the cow standing at the edge of a reedy lake. Colm[3] ran down to meet her waving his stick in the air, and the wind rumbling in his ears made him give an exultant whoop which splashed upon the hills in a shower of echoed sound. A flock of gulls lying on the short grass near the lake rose up languidly, drifting like blown snowflakes over the rim of the cliff.

2. **the Transfiguration:** an event in the life of Jesus Christ, told in Matthew 17:1–8. A painting of this event would probably show a mountaintop with a shining cloud overhead.
3. **Colm** (kŭl′əm).

The lake faced west and was fed by a stream, the drainings of the semicircling hills. One side was open to the winds from the sea and in winter a little outlet trickled over the cliffs making a black vein in their gray sides. The boy lifted stones and began throwing them into the lake, weaving web after web on its calm surface. Then he skimmed the water with flat stones, some of them jumping the surface and coming to rest on the other side. He was delighted with himself and after listening to his echoing shouts of delight he ran to fetch his cow. Gently he tapped her on the side and reluctantly she went towards the brown-mudded path that led out of the valley. The boy was about to throw a final stone into the lake when a bird flew low over his head, its neck astrain, and its orange-colored legs clear in the soft light. It was a wild duck. It circled the lake twice, thrice, coming lower each time and then with a nervous flapping of wings it skidded along the surface, its legs breaking the water into a series of silvery arcs. Its wings closed, it lit silently, gave a slight shiver, and began pecking indifferently at the water.

Colm with dilated eyes eagerly watched it making for the farther end of the lake. It meandered between tall bulrushes,[4] its body black and solid as stone against the graying water. Then as if it had sunk it was gone. The boy ran stealthily along the bank looking away from the lake, pretending indifference. When he came opposite to where he had last seen the bird he stopped and peered through the sighing reeds whose shadows streaked the water in a maze of black strokes. In front of him was a soddy islet guarded by the spears of sedge[5] and separated from the bank by a narrow channel of water. The water wasn't too deep—he could wade across with care.

4. **bulrushes** (bool′rush′ĭz): grasslike plants.
5. **sedge:** a grasslike plant with pointed leaves.

3
Use to answer **study question 1,** p. 184.

4
Description. This shower of joyful sound both suggests and contrasts with the falling rain the next day.

5
These "webs" of concentric circles are comparable to the "silvery arcs" the duck makes when it lands on the water.

6
Characterization. Colm's gentle treatment of his cow reflects his love for animals and nature.

7
The duck's indifference is a ruse, intended to mislead any observer.

8
The spears guarding the islet and the moat-like channel suggest a fortress into which Colm intrudes.

The Wild Duck's Nest **181**

duck and jeopardizing the hatching of the egg. Colm learns to respect another living being's needs and learns that his seemingly innocent curiosity threatens the duck and egg he so admires.

MEETING INDIVIDUAL NEEDS
ESL/LEP • Several different bodies of water are mentioned on p. 181. Ask students to identify and define these, grouping them from largest to smallest. (sea, lake, stream, outlet) Which of these may be considered synonyms? (stream, outlet)

GEOGRAPHY LINK
Have students find Ireland on a world map and then locate the rural northern coast of the island where the story takes place. Suggest to students that they also look up Ireland in an encyclopedia to get an overview of the country and its people.

9
Personification. Winking makes bubbles seem alive, and perhaps aware of something Colm does not know.

10
Description. The egg's beauty overwhelms him; suggests importance he attaches to this meeting with nature.

11
Realizes he is an intruder; he should not interfere with nature.

12
Feels he has broken a law of nature; fears his scent on egg will cause duck to abandon nest.

13
Use to answer **study question 4,** p. 184.

14
The chill night reflects his dismal state of mind.

15 Finding Cause and Effect
Why do you think Paddy spoils the discovery? His jealousy prompts him to exacerbate Colm's fear.

16
The weather's influence on his state of mind is further evidence of the profound effect nature has on him.

17
Imagery. His fearful mind imagines the worst: the nest wet and empty, the egg cold.

18
Fidgeting with cover also suggests his agitation.

Rolling up his short trousers he began to wade, his arms outstretched, and his legs brown and stunted in the mountain water. As he drew near the islet, his feet sank in the cold 9 mud and bubbles winked up at him. He went more carefully and nervously. Then one trouser leg fell and dipped into the water; the boy dropped his hands to roll it up, he unbalanced, made a splashing sound, and the bird arose with a squawk and whirred away over the cliffs. For a moment the boy stood frightened. Then he clambered onto the wet-soaked sod of land, which was spattered with sea gulls' feathers and bits of wind-blown rushes.

Into each hummock[6] he looked, pulling back the long grass. At last he came on the nest, facing seawards. Two flat rocks dimpled the face of the water and between them was a neck of land matted with coarse grass containing the nest. It was untidily built of dried rushes, straw and feathers, and in it lay one solitary egg. Colm was delighted. He looked 10 around and saw no one. The nest was his. He lifted the egg, smooth and green as the sky, with a faint tinge of yellow like the reflected light from a buttercup; and then he felt he had 11 done wrong. He put it back. He knew he shouldn't have touched it and he wondered would the bird forsake the nest. A vague sadness stole over him and he felt in his heart he 12 had sinned. Carefully smoothing out his foot- 13 prints he hurriedly left the islet and ran after his cow. The sun had now set and the cold 14 shiver of evening enveloped him, chilling his body and saddening his mind.

In the morning he was up and away to school. He took the grass rut that edged the road, for it was softer on the bare feet. His house was the last on the western headland and after a mile or so he was joined by Paddy McFall; both boys dressed in similar hand-

6. **hummock** (hŭm'ək): a small mound of earth.

knitted blue jerseys and gray trousers carried homemade schoolbags. Colm was full of the nest and as soon as he joined his companion he said eagerly: "Paddy, I've a nest—a wild duck's with one egg."

"And how do you know it's a wild duck's?" asked Paddy, slightly jealous.

"Sure I saw her with my own two eyes, her brown speckled back with a crow's patch on it, and her yellow legs—"

"Where is it?" interrupted Paddy in a challenging tone.

"I'm not going to tell you, for you'd rob it!"

"Aach! I suppose it's a tame duck's you have or maybe an old gull's."

Colm put out his tongue at him. "A lot you know!" he said; "for a gull's egg has spots and this one is greenish-white, for I had it in my hand."

And then the words he didn't want to hear 15 rushed from Paddy in a mocking chant. "You had it in your hand! . . . She'll forsake it! She'll forsake it! She'll forsake it!" he said, skipping along the road before him.

Colm felt as if he would choke or cry with vexation.

His mind told him that Paddy was right, but somehow he couldn't give in to it and he replied: "She'll not forsake it! She'll not! I know she'll not!"

But in school his faith wavered. Through the 16 windows he could see moving sheets of rain—rain that dribbled down the panes filling his mind with thoughts of the lake creased and 17 chilled by wind; the nest sodden and black with wetness; and the egg cold as a cave stone. He shivered from the thoughts and fidgeted 18 with the inkwell cover, sliding it backwards and forwards mechanically. The mischievous look had gone from his eyes and the school day dragged on interminably. But at last they were out in the rain, Colm rushing home as fast as he could.

182 THE NATURAL WORLD

MEETING INDIVIDUAL NEEDS
ESL/LEP • In describing the duck's nest on p. 182, the author uses the adverb *untidily*. In this case, there are three parts: *un + tidi + ly*. Ask the class what the prefix *un–* indicates. (not) What adjective forms the root of this word? (*Tidy*, meaning neat, in order. The *y* has been changed to *i*.) What is the significance of the *–ly* ending? (The *–ly* suffix makes the word an adverb, telling us *how* the nest was built.) Write the following adjectives on the chalkboard: *happy, lucky, kind, selfish,* and *usual*. Can students change them to adverbs in the negative sense?

VISUAL CONNECTIONS
Exploring the Subject
Ducks build nests in a variety of places, depending on species. Some dig burrows into the ground, some build nests in trees, and others, as in this story, build nests in dense grasses near water. A few species never build their own nests, and even those that do often lay some of their eggs in another duck's nest until their own is complete.

Ducks pluck from their chests special feathers called "nest-down" feathers with which they line the bottom and rim of the nest. If the nest is in a hole so that no protection is needed, the nest-down is white in color. If the nest is in the open, the down is dark, and when parents leave the nest, they cover the eggs with this down for camouflage. It is true that in some cases birds will abandon their eggs if they have been handled by humans.

He was no time at all at his dinner of potatoes and salted fish until he was out in the valley now smoky with drifts of slanting rain. Opposite the islet he entered the water. The wind was blowing into his face, rustling noisily the rushes heavy with the dust of rain. A moss cheeper,[7] swaying on a reed like a mouse, filled 19 the air with light cries of loneliness.

20   The boy reached the islet, his heart thumping with excitement, wondering did the bird forsake. He went slowly, quietly, onto the strip of land that led to the nest. He rose on his toes, looking over the ledge to see if he could see her. And then every muscle tautened. She was on, her shoulders hunched up, and her bill lying on her breast as if she were asleep. Colm's heart hammered wildly in his ears. She hadn't forsaken. He was about to turn stealthily away. Something happened. The bird moved, her neck straightened, twitching nervously from side to side. The boy's head swam with lightness. He stood transfixed. The wild duck, with a panicky flapping, rose heavily, and flew off 21 towards the sea. . . . A guilty silence enveloped the boy. . . . He turned to go away, hesitated, and glanced back at the bare nest; it'd be no harm to have a look. Timidly he approached it, standing straight, and gazing over the edge. There in the nest lay two eggs. He drew in his breath with delight, splashed quickly from the 22 island, and ran off whistling in the rain.

7. **moss cheeper:** a songbird.

19
The moss cheeper's lonely cries reflect Colm's expectation that he will find nest abandoned.

20
Suspense. Anticipation of nest's abandonment causes anxiety within Colm and reader.

21 Summarizing
Why does Colm feel guilty? He has again disturbed the nest.

22
His joy transcends the dreary weather.

MEETING INDIVIDUAL NEEDS
Visual and Kinesthetic Learners • Encourage students to make drawings or paintings of the wild duck's nest. Display students' work on a classroom bulletin board.

WRITING LINK
Encourage interested students to write an imaginary epilogue to the story, telling what happened to the two eggs. Did they hatch safely? If so, did Colm ever see the ducklings?

READING CHECK
1. To fetch the cow (p. 181).
2. Colm tries to roll up his trouser leg and makes a splash that frightens the bird (p. 182).
3. He says that Paddy would rob it (p. 182).
4. To find out if bird has forsaken nest (p. 123).

FOR STUDY AND DISCUSSION
1. His "watching streaks of light radiating from golden edged clouds"; his running down to the cows, "waving his stick in the air"; and his "exultant whoop" as he runs.
2. Stealthily follows bird and searches each hummock.
3a. He is attracted to the egg's beauty. 3b. He feels that the duck might forsake the nest and egg.
4. He puts back the egg and carefully smooths out his footprints.
5a. To be sure that the duck has not forsaken nest. 5b. Duck has laid a second egg, and he now knows the nest has not been forsaken.
6. Responses will vary. Colm no longer feels the nest is his. He realizes the nest belongs to the wild duck.
7. Responses will vary. Colm learns to exercise more thought and care in his dealings with nature.

LANGUAGE AND VOCABULARY
1. **Gentle** becomes *gently*.
2. Some of the adverbs and adjectives are as follows:
jauntily: *jaunty*.
presently: *present*.
suddenly: *sudden*.
languidly: *languid*.
gently: *gentle*.
reluctantly: *reluctant*.
silently: *silent*.
indifferently: *indifferent*.
stealthily: *stealthy*.
carefully: *careful*.
nervously: *nervous*.
untidily: *untidy*.
hurriedly: *hurried*.

184

Reading Check

1. At the opening of the story, why does Colm come to the valley?
2. How does he cause the bird to leave its nest?
3. Why does Colm refuse to tell Paddy where the wild duck has built its nest?
4. Why does Colm return to the nest?

For Study and Discussion

Analyzing and Interpreting the Story

1. At the opening of the story, you learn that Colm enjoys the beauty of the countryside. What details in the first paragraph show his delight in nature?

2. How do Colm's actions show that he suspects the wild duck has built a nest on the islet?

3. Colm does not wish to rob the nest. **a.** Why, then, does he lift the egg? **b.** Why does he feel that he has sinned?

4. What steps does Colm take to protect the nest from further harm?

5a. Why does Colm return to the wild duck's nest? **b.** How is he relieved by what he finds?

6. When Colm first finds the nest, he feels that it is his. Do you think he still feels this way at the end of the story? Explain your answer.

7. Sometimes human beings destroy nature through thoughtlessness or carelessness. What do you think Colm learns from his experience with the wild duck's nest?

Language and Vocabulary

Forming Adverbs from Adjectives

Michael McLaverty uses a great many adverbs as modifiers of verbs. In the first paragraph of the story, you are told that Colm "walked *jauntily*." The gulls, disturbed by his shouting, "rose up *languidly*."

Many adverbs in our language are formed by adding the suffix *-ly* to an adjective. When you add *-ly* to the adjective *languid*, you form the adverb *languidly*. The adverb *jauntily* is formed from the adjective *jaunty*. Notice that the *y* in *jaunty* changes to *i* when *-ly* is added.

1 What happens when you change the adjective *gentle* to an adverb?

2 How many adverbs ending in *-ly* can you locate in the story? List them and give the adjectives from which they are formed.

Using Vivid Verbs

In the first paragraph of the story, the author says that a path "wriggled" between the hills. *Wriggled* is an effective verb because it makes the reader think of the path weaving in and out like a snake.

There are other good descriptive verbs in **3** the story. Explain why each of the following italicized verbs is a good choice.

Then he *skimmed* the water with flat stones . . . .
. . . his feet sank in the cold mud and bubbles *winked* up at him.
And then every muscle *tautened*.
Colm's heart *hammered* wildly in his ears.

Using vivid verbs will make your own writing more lively and interesting. **4** Think of an effective verb to substitute for each of the italicized verbs in these sentences.

The stealthy cat *moved* across the lawn toward the unsuspecting birds.
The surprised winner of the contest *went* to the stage when her name was called.
The hungry lion *ate* its prey.

184 THE NATURAL WORLD

TRANSPARENCY 15
Literary Elements
Imagery – invites students to examine imagery in nonfiction.

CLOSURE
Ask students to discuss the ways in which McLaverty uses language to create a sense of place and to involve the reader in Colm's experience.

EXTENSION AND ENRICHMENT
Ask students to discuss the relative merits of city and country life and to present their conclusions in a pair of contrasting real-estate advertisements.

Focus on Informative Writing

Using Transitional Expressions

Transitional expressions help to clarify the relationship of events and ideas in your writing. In "The Wild Duck's Nest," for example, notice the transitions that Michael McLaverty uses in the first paragraph on page 182: *began, as, then, for a moment*. These words and phrases help to show the connections of events in chronological or time order.

The chart below lists transitions you may find useful for two different kinds of informative papers.

Process Paper	Cause-and-Effect Paper
after, before, finally, first, next, often, second, then, until, when	as a result, because consequently, for, since, so that, therefore

Find a magazine article on a topic that interests you. Read the article carefully, and make a list of all the transitional words and phrases the writer uses. Share your list with a small group of classmates. Save your notes.

About the Author

Michael McLaverty (1904–1992)

Michael McLaverty was born in Monaghan, Ireland. In 1935 he earned his degree at The Queen's University of Belfast, Northern Ireland. He published his first novel, *Call My Brother Back*, four years later. Other novels by McLaverty include *Truth in the Night* (1957) and *The Brightening Day* (1965). For many years McLaverty served as the Headmaster of St. Thomas's Secondary School in Belfast. "The Wild Duck's Nest" is from his third collection, *The Game Cock and Other Stories* (1947).

mechanically: *mechanical.*
interminably: *interminable.*
noisily: *noisy.*
slowly: *slow.*
quietly: *quiet.*
wildly: *wild.*
3. They are good choices because they appeal to the senses. **Skimmed, winked:** precise visual appeal. **Tautened, hammered:** kinesthetic appeal.
4. **moved:** *slinked, sneaked, crept, edged.*
went: *staggered, raced.*
ate: *devoured, engulfed, tore at.*

FOCUS ON INFORMATIVE WRITING
After students have completed their lists, you may want to have them identify any cause-and-effect relationships in their articles. Suggest that they use their lists of **transitions** as clues. Although their articles probably will be examples of informative writing, discuss with students that cause-and-effect relationships can also be found in creative, expressive, and persuasive writing.

ABOUT THE AUTHOR
McLaverty was an Irish regional writer, best known for his short stories about the people of eastern Ulster. His *Collected Short Stories* (1978) includes stories similar to "The Wild Duck's Nest." McLaverty extends his love for the inner peacefulness of nature in his novels, which frequently contrast rural and urban life. His first novel, *Call Back My Brother* (1939), is his best known. This novel covers four years in the life of Colm McNeill, a teenager who moves from the poor but idyllic setting of Rathlin island to attend school in Belfast, a city of turmoil and oppression.

Birdfoot's Grampa

JOSEPH BRUCHAC

What information in the title of this poem gives you insight into the characters?

The old man
must have stopped our car
two dozen times to climb out
and gather into his hands
the small toads blinded   5
by our lights and leaping,
live drops of rain.

The rain was falling,
a mist about his white hair
and I kept saying   10
you can't save them all
accept it, get back in
we've got places to go.

But, leathery hands full
of wet brown life,   15
knee deep in the summer
roadside grass,
he just smiled and said
they have places to go to
too.   20

For Study and Discussion

Analyzing and Interpreting the Poem

1. This poem tells about someone who stops a car during a heavy rainfall in order to save some creatures that would otherwise be run over. **a.** How does the poet create sympathy for the animals? **b.** What is the "wet brown life" referred to in line 15?

2a. Contrast the speaker's attitude toward the events with the older man's. **b.** How does the old man show a deep reverence for the natural world?

About the Author

Joseph Bruchac (1942–   )

Joseph Bruchac (brōō'shăk) has contributed poetry to more than four hundred periodicals and has won a number of awards and honors for his work. He has said, "My writing is informed by several key sources. One of these is nature, another is Native American experience (I'm part Indian)....I like to work outside, in the earth mother's soil, with my hands."

OBJECTIVES	VOCABULARY	FOCUS / MOTIVATION
The overall aim for students is to explain how the writer conveys the significance of the bond between people and the natural world. For a complete list of objectives, see the **Teacher's Notes**.	The underlined words are in the Glossary. The **Language and Vocabulary** exercise on p. 194 provides students with practice in defining unfamiliar words by using clues supplied by the context.	Ask students why they think city dwellers place so much importance upon maintaining the natural landscape in city parks or growing indoor and outdoor plants and flowers. Why do people seem to need such contact with nature?

Antaeus°

BORDEN DEAL

In a story told by the ancient Greeks, Antaeus was a giant whose strength came from the earth. As long as he remained in contact with the earth, no one could defeat him in combat. To find out how he was overcome, see "The Adventures of Hercules" on page 622. In this story you will read about a modern Antaeus.

1 This was during the wartime, when lots of people were coming North for jobs in factories and war industries, when people moved around a lot more than they do now, and sometimes kids were thrown into new groups and new lives that were completely different from anything they had ever known before. I remember this one kid, T. J. his name was, from somewhere down South, whose family moved into our building during that time. They'd come North with everything they owned piled into the back seat of an old-model sedan that you wouldn't expect could make the trip, with T. J. and his three younger sisters riding shakily on top of the load of junk.

Our building was just like all the others there, with families crowded into a few rooms, and I guess there were twenty-five or thirty kids about my age in that one building. Of course, there were a few of us who formed a gang and ran together all the time after school, and I was the one who brought T. J. in and started the whole thing.

The building right next door to us was a factory where they made walking dolls. It was a low building with a flat, tarred roof that had a parapet¹ all around it about head-high, and we'd found out a long time before that no one, not even the watchman, paid any attention to the roof because it was higher than any of the other buildings around. So my gang used the roof as a headquarters. We could get up there by crossing over to the fire escape from our own roof on a plank and then going on up. It was a secret place for us, where nobody else could go without our permission.

I remember the day I first took T. J. up there to meet the gang. He was a stocky, robust kid with a shock of white hair, nothing sissy about him except his voice; he talked in this slow, gentle voice like you never heard before. He talked different from any of us and you noticed it right away. But I liked him anyway, so I told him to come on up.

We climbed up over the parapet and dropped down on the roof. The rest of the gang were already there.

"Hi," I said. I jerked my thumb at T. J. "He just moved into the building yesterday."

He just stood there, not scared or anything, just looking, like the first time you see somebody you're not sure you're going to like.

° **Antaeus** (ăn-tē′əs).

1. **parapet** (păr′ə-pĭt): a low protective wall.

TEACHING RESOURCES B
Teacher's Notes, p. 76
Reading Check, p. 79
Study Guide, p. 80
Language Skills, p. 83
Building Vocabulary, p. 86
Selection Vocabulary Test, p. 88
Selection Test, p. 90

PREREADING FOCUS
The headnote suggests a comparison between Antaeus of Greek mythology and the central character in this story. Ask students to predict characteristics of this modern Antaeus. Have them speculate on the character's age, physical features, background, likes, dislikes, weaknesses, and strengths.

Antaeus

1
Setting. Refers to World War II, when the demand for defense plant workers was high.

2
T. J., too, finds it difficult to adjust to his new life, no matter how hard he tries.

3 Analyzing
What does use of "junk" to describe T.J.'s family's belongings suggest? That family owns little of value.

4
Prepares the reader for T. J.'s influence on the group and his plan that forms the nucleus of the story.

5
Irony. Boys use roof without permission and will be forced to leave; gang is in control as long as adults aren't involved.

6
Indicates narrator has never traveled to different parts of country and has never met anyone from South before.

Antaeus 187

MOTIVATIONAL SUMMARY

A group of city boys has a secret haven on the roof of a factory. The boys are not sure what to make of T. J.—a slow-talking, deep-feeling country boy—who joins the group and suggests that the roof would make a fine place to make a garden. The city boys have never seen a real garden and can't imagine why T. J. finds growing things so fascinating, but the idea of a project of their own appeals to them. One of their first challenges, though, is how to get a lot of dirt onto the roof.

PRESENTATION

Two major forces are at work in Borden Deal's "Antaeus," and the story's **climax** results from the conflict between the two. T. J.'s struggle to maintain his bond with the land teaches the city boys the virtues of tenderness and nurturing

---

7
T. J.'s identification with county rather than town reflects rural way of life.

8
To T. J., Marion County is whole world, thus his expectation that boys know about it and know where it is.

9
Characterization. His self-assurance defeats their attempts at childish teasing.

---

7 "Hi," Blackie said. "Where are you from?"
"Marion County," T. J. said.
We laughed. "Marion County?" I said. "Where's that?"
He looked at me for a moment like I was a **8** stranger, too. "It's in Alabama," he said, like I ought to know where it was.
"What's your name?" Charley said.
"T. J.," he said, looking back at him. He had pale blue eyes that looked washed-out, but he looked directly at Charley, waiting for his reaction. He'll be all right, I thought. No sissy in him, except that voice. Who ever talked like that?
"T. J.," Blackie said. "That's just initials. What's your real name? Nobody in the world has just initials."
"I do," he said. "And they're T. J. That's all the name I got."
9 His voice was resolute with the knowledge of his rightness, and for a moment no one had anything to say. T. J. looked around at the rooftop and down at the black tar under his feet. "Down yonder where I come from," he said, "we played out in the woods. Don't you-all have no woods around here?"
"Naw," Blackie said. "There's the park a few blocks over, but it's full of kids and cops and old women. You can't do a thing."
T. J. kept looking at the tar under his feet.

VISUAL CONNECTIONS
Exploring the Subject
Most of the other stories in this unit have settings involving lush expanses of nature. For the boys in "Antaeus," in a city of tall buildings and asphalt streets, the natural world seems a long-ago dream. Ask students to discuss ways in which people try to bring the natural world into city life: window boxes, potted plants, roof gardens, parks, zoos, etc.

For contrast, ask students to discuss advantages that a large city might have over a natural setting as found, for example, in "The Wild Duck's Nest": large libraries, vast array of theaters, concerts, fancy restaurants, shops, specialized health care, etc.

care, qualities not encouraged by the adults these children encounter in their lives. In fact, much of these boys' play involves secrecy and building a world apart from adults. The adult world is almost synonymous with city life; it is grimly painted in this story as impersonal, prison-like, and destructive of joy and hope. It ultimately crushes T. J. and his link with the earth, leaving him as stripped of his identity as the "anonymous earth" thrown on the concrete.

"You mean you ain't got no fields to raise nothing in?—no watermelons or nothing?"

10 "Naw," I said scornfully. "What do you want to grow something for? The folks can buy everything they need at the store."

11 He looked at me again with that strange, unknowing look. "In Marion County," he said, "I had my own acre of cotton and my own acre of corn. It was mine to plant and make ever' year."

He sounded like it was something to be proud of, and in some obscure way it made the 12 rest of us angry. Blackie said, "Who'd want to have their own acre of cotton and corn? That's just work. What can you do with an acre of cotton and corn?"

T. J. looked at him. "Well, you get part of the bale offen your acre," he said seriously. "And I fed my acre of corn to my calf."

We didn't really know what he was talking about, so we were more puzzled than angry; otherwise, I guess, we'd have chased him off the roof and wouldn't let him be part of our 13 gang. But he was strange and different, and we were all attracted by his stolid sense of rightness and belonging, maybe by the strange softness of his voice contrasting our own tones of speech into harshness.

He moved his foot against the black tar. "We could make our own field right here," he said softly, thoughtfully. "Come spring we could raise us what we want to—watermelons and garden truck² and no telling what all."

"You'd have to be a good farmer to make these tar roofs grow any watermelons," I said. We all laughed.

But T. J. looked serious. "We could haul us some dirt up here," he said. "And spread it out even and water it, and before you know it, we'd have us a crop in here." He looked at us intently. "Wouldn't that be fun?"

2. **truck:** here, vegetables grown to be sold.

"They wouldn't let us," Blackie said quickly.

14 "I thought you said this was you-all's roof," T. J. said to me. "That you-all could do anything you wanted to up here."

15 "They've never bothered us," I said. I felt the idea beginning to catch fire in me. It was a big idea, and it took a while for it to sink in; but the more I thought about it, the better I liked it. "Say," I said to the gang. "He might have something there. Just make us a regular roof garden, with flowers and grass and trees and 16 everything. And all ours, too," I said. "We wouldn't let anybody up here except the ones we wanted to."

"It'd take a while to grow trees," T. J. said quickly, but we weren't paying any attention to him. They were all talking about it suddenly, all excited with the idea after I'd put it in a way they could catch hold of it. Only rich people had roof gardens, we knew, and the idea of our own private domain excited them.

"We could bring it up in sacks and boxes," 17 Blackie said. "We'd have to do it while the folks weren't paying any attention to us, for we'd have to come up the roof of our building and then cross over with it."

"Where could we get the dirt?" somebody said worriedly.

"Out of those vacant lots over close to school," Blackie said. "Nobody'd notice if we scraped it up."

I slapped T. J. on the shoulder. "Man, you had a wonderful idea," I said, and everybody grinned at him, remembering that he had 18 started it. "Our own private roof garden."

He grinned back. "It'll be ourn," he said. "All ourn." Then he looked thoughtful again. "Maybe I can lay my hands on some cotton seed, too. You think we could raise us some cotton?"

We'd started big projects before at one time or

10
The narrator views farming as a means to an end—food—not as a fulfilling experience.

11
T. J. can't comprehend way of life not based on farming.

12
They feel inferior, that T. J. looks down on them, since he had something they lack.

13
Characterization. T. J. knows his purpose in life is connected to the land.

14
T. J. takes their claim seriously, not realizing it's only a part of their play.

15
Narrator suggests adult silence means consent.

16
Irony. Adults who own it will carry out these words.

17
Blackie's fear of the adult world shows alienation from parents.

18 Making Inferences
Why do you think the city boys emphasize the concept of privacy? They have never had their own space.

Antaeus 189

MEETING INDIVIDUAL NEEDS

ESL/LEP • To help students see more clearly the differences between T.J.'s dialect and standard English, write examples from the selection on the chalkboard. Ask the class to supply the corresponding standard forms.

19 Summarizing
What keeps this plan alive?
T. J.'s persistence; this is not a game to him but a cause.

20
His methods of encouragement reflect his shrewdness; he needs the boys' help and knows he must convince them to help.

21
Dirt is dirt to the city boys; T. J. understands that growing soil must be fertile.

22
Ironic since the owners do care—and disapprove.

23
New Testament language, "signs and wonders," suggests miracle of life T. J. demonstrates to boys.

24
T. J. opens a new world to the city boys that adds meaning to their lives.

25
T. J. hungers for the nurturing process.

26
Allusion. Antaeus' mother was Gaea, the earth; he had invincible strength as long as he touched her.

190

---

another, like any gang of kids, but they'd always petered out for lack of organization and direction. But this one didn't; somehow or **19** other T. J. kept it going all through the winter months. He kept talking about the watermelons and the cotton we'd raise, come spring, and when even that wouldn't work, he'd switch around to my idea of flowers and grass and trees, though he was always honest enough to add that it'd take a while to get any trees started. He always had it on his mind and he'd mention it in school, getting them lined up to carry dirt that afternoon, saying in a casual way that he reckoned a few more weeks ought to see the job through.

Our little area of private earth grew slowly. **20** T. J. was smart enough to start in one corner of the building, heaping up the carried earth two or three feet thick so that we had an immediate result to look at, to contemplate with awe. Some of the evenings T. J. alone was carrying earth up to the building, the rest of the gang distracted by other enterprises or interests, but T. J. kept plugging along on his own, and eventually we'd all come back to him again and then our own little acre would grow more rapidly.

He was careful about the kind of dirt he'd let us carry up there, and more than once he dumped a sandy load over the parapet into the areaway below because it wasn't good enough. He found out the kinds of earth in all the vacant lots for blocks around. He'd pick it up and feel it and smell it, frozen though it was some- **21** times, and then he'd say it was good growing soil or it wasn't worth anything, and we'd have to go on somewhere else.

Thinking about it now, I don't see how he kept us at it. It was hard work, lugging paper sacks and boxes of dirt all the way up the stairs of our own building, keeping out of the way of the grown-ups so they wouldn't catch on to what we were doing. They probably wouldn't **22** have cared, for they didn't pay much attention to us, but we wanted to keep it secret anyway. Then we had to go through the trapdoor to our roof, teeter over a plank to the fire escape, then climb two or three stories to the parapet and drop down onto the roof. All that for a small pile of earth that sometimes didn't seem worth the effort. But T. J. kept the vision bright within us, his words shrewd and calculated toward the fulfillment of his dream; and he worked harder than any of us. He seemed driven toward a goal that we couldn't see, a particular point in time that would be defi- **23** nitely marked by signs and wonders that only he could see.

The laborious earth just lay there during the cold months, inert and lifeless, the clods lumpy and cold under our feet when we walked over it. But one day it rained, and afterward there was a softness in the air, and the earth was live and giving again with moisture and warmth.

That evening T. J. smelled the air, his nostrils dilating with the odor of the earth under his feet. "It's spring," he said, and there was a gladness rising in his voice that filled us all with the same feeling. "It's mighty late for it, but it's spring. I'd just about decided it wasn't never gonna get here at all."

We were all sniffing at the air, too, trying to smell it the way that T. J. did, and I can still remember the sweet odor of the earth under our **24** feet. It was the first time in my life that spring and spring earth had meant anything to me. I looked at T. J. then, knowing in a faint way the **25** hunger within him through the toilsome winter months, knowing the dream that lay behind **26** his plan. He was a new Antaeus, preparing his own bed of strength.

"Planting time," he said. "We'll have to find us some seed."

"What do we do?" Blackie said. "How do we do it?"

190 THE NATURAL WORLD

"First we'll have to break up the clods," T. J. said. "That won't be hard to do. Then we plant the seeds, and after a while they come up. Then you got you a crop." He frowned. "But you ain't got it raised yet. You got to tend it and hoe it and take care of it, and all the time it's growing and growing, while you're awake and while you're asleep. Then you lay it by when it's growed and let it ripen, and then you got you a crop."

"There's those wholesale seed houses over on Sixth," I said. "We could probably swipe some grass seed over there."

T. J. looked at the earth. "You-all seem mighty set on raising some grass," he said. "I ain't never put no effort into that. I spent all my life trying not to raise grass."

"But it's pretty," Blackie said. "We could play on it and take sunbaths on it. Like having our own lawn. Lots of people got lawns."

"Well," T. J. said. He looked at the rest of us, hesitant for the first time. He kept on looking at us for a moment. "I did have it in mind to raise some corn and vegetables. But we'll plant grass."

He was smart. He knew where to give in. And I don't suppose it made any difference to him, really. He just wanted to grow something, even if it was grass.

"Of course," he said, "I do think we ought to plant a row of watermelons. They'd be mighty nice to eat while we was a-laying on that grass."

We all laughed. "All right," I said. "We'll plant us a row of watermelons."

Things went very quickly then. Perhaps half the roof was covered with the earth, the half that wasn't broken by ventilators, and we swiped pocketfuls of grass seed from the open bins in the wholesale seed house, mingling among the buyers on Saturdays and during the school lunch hour. T. J. showed us how to prepare the earth, breaking up the clods and smoothing it and sowing the grass seed. It looked rich and black now with moisture, receiving of the seed, and it seemed that the grass sprang up overnight, pale green in the early spring.

We couldn't keep from looking at it, unable to believe that we had created this delicate growth. We looked at T. J. with understanding now, knowing the fulfillment of the plan he had carried along within his mind. We had worked without full understanding of the task, but he had known all the time.

We found that we couldn't walk or play on the delicate blades, as we had expected to, but we didn't mind. It was enough just to look at it, to realize that it was the work of our own hands, and each evening the whole gang was there, trying to measure the growth that had been achieved that day.

One time a foot was placed on the plot of ground, one time only, Blackie stepping onto it with sudden bravado. Then he looked at the crushed blades and there was shame in his face. He did not do it again. This was his grass, too, and not to be desecrated.³ No one said anything, for it was not necessary.

T. J. had reserved a small section for watermelons, and he was still trying to find some seed for it. The wholesale house didn't have any watermelon seeds, and we didn't know where we could lay our hands on them. T. J. shaped the earth into mounds, ready to receive them, three mounds lying in a straight line along the edge of the grass plot.

We had just about decided that we'd have to buy the seeds if we were to get them. It was a violation of our principles, but we were anxious to get the watermelons started. Somewhere or other, T. J. got his hands on a seed catalog and brought it one evening to our roof garden.

3. **desecrated** (dĕs′ə-krāt′ĭd): treated with disrespect.

27
City boys want to create what they have never possessed; T. J. wants what he has lost.

28
Willingness to give in reflects their good nature and T. J.'s persuasiveness.

29 Summarizing
How do the boys react to the new growth? They are awestruck by delicate plants that represent life and growth.

30
Reflects boys' fascination with magic of life.

31
This plot of grass has become sacred to the boys.

32
This contrasts interestingly with boys' skepticism when T. J. first suggests growing watermelons.

33
One effect of this inverted code of ethics is to subvert order of adult world.

COOPERATIVE LEARNING
Have interested students work together to create a mural that illustrates the boys' garden on the roof of the factory.

34
Intrusion shatters boys' joyful, private world and suggests destruction to come.

35
T. J. accepted boys' claim that roof is theirs; he doesn't understand seriousness of matter.

36
Setting. Plot of grass is an oasis, a refuge from the impersonal world of the city.

37
Conflict. Adult authority clashes with boys' values; threatens their haven and their freedom.

38
T. J. seemingly expects adults to be supportive and to set few limits.

39
"Junk" reflects man's inability to see beauty of grass.

40 Analyzing
In what sense does the earth belong to the boys? They brought it up to the rooftop themselves and planted it; to T. J., bond between people and the land they tend is sacred.

41
Confirms narrator's idea that adults usually ignore children unless punishing them.

42
Their refusal to acknowledge his claim is insult according to T. J.'s values.

192

"We can order them now," he said, showing us the catalog. "Look!"

We all crowded around, looking at the fat, green watermelons pictured in full color on the pages. Some of them were split open, showing the red, tempting meat, making our mouths water.

"Now we got to scrape up some seed money." T. J. said, looking at us. "I got a quarter. How much you-all got?"

We made up a couple of dollars among us and T. J. nodded his head. "That'll be more than enough. Now we got to decide what kind to get. I think them Kleckley Sweets. What do you-all think?"

He was going into esoteric matters[4] beyond our reach. We hadn't even known there were different kinds of melons. So we just nodded our heads and agreed that yes, we thought the Kleckley Sweets too.

"I'll order them tonight," T. J. said. "We ought to have them in a few days."

"What are you boys doing up here?" an adult voice said behind us.

34 It startled us, for no one had ever come up here before in all the time we had been using the roof of the factory. We jerked around and saw three men standing near the trap door at the other end of the roof. They weren't policemen or night watchmen, but three men in plump business suits, looking at us. They walked toward us.

"What are you boys doing up here?" the one in the middle said again.

We stood still, guilt heavy among us, levied[5] by the tone of voice, and looked at the three strangers.

The men stared at the grass flourishing behind us. "What's this?" the man said. "How did this get up here?"

---
4. **esoteric** (ĕs′ə-tĕr′ĭk) **matters:** special knowledge.
5. **levied** (lĕv′ēd): imposed or placed upon. The man's tone of voice makes the boys feel guilty.

35 "Sure is growing good, ain't it?" T. J. said conversationally. "We planted it."

The men kept looking at the grass as if they 36 didn't believe it. It was a thick carpet over the earth now, a patch of deep greenness startling in the sterile industrial surroundings.

"Yes, sir," T. J. said proudly. "We toted that earth up here and planted that grass." He fluttered the seed catalog. "And we're just fixing to plant us some watermelon."

The man looked at him then, his eyes 37 strange and faraway. "What do you mean, putting this on the roof of my building?" he said. "Do you want to go to jail?"

T. J. looked shaken. The rest of us were silent, frightened by the authority of his voice. We had grown up aware of adult authority, of policemen and night watchmen and teachers, and this man sounded like all the others. But it 38 was a new thing to T. J.

"Well, you wasn't using the roof," T. J. said. He paused a moment and added shrewdly, "So we just thought to pretty it up a little bit."

"And sag it so I'd have to rebuild it," the man said sharply. He started turning away, saying to another man beside him, "See that all 39 that junk is shoveled off by tomorrow."

"Yes, sir," the man said.

T. J. started forward. "You can't do that," he said. "We toted it up here, and it's our earth. We planted it and raised it and toted it up here."

The man stared at him coldly. "But it's my building," he said. "It's to be shoveled off tomorrow."

40 "It's our earth," T. J. said desperately. "You ain't got no right!"

41 The men walked on without listening and descended clumsily through the trapdoor. T. J. stood looking after them, his body tense with anger, until they had disappeared. They 42 wouldn't even argue with him, wouldn't let him defend his earth-rights.

He turned to us. "We won't let 'em do it," he

192 THE NATURAL WORLD

said fiercely. "We'll stay up here all day tomorrow and the day after that, and we won't let 'em do it."

We just looked at him. We knew there was no stopping it.

He saw it in our faces, and his face wavered for a moment before he gripped it into determination. "They ain't got no right," he said. "It's our earth. It's our land. Can't nobody touch a man's own land."

We kept looking at him, listening to the words but knowing that it was no use. The adult world had descended on us even in our richest dream, and we knew there was no calculating the adult world, no fighting it, no winning against it.

We started moving slowly toward the parapet and the fire escape, avoiding a last look at the green beauty of the earth that T. J. had planted for us, had planted deeply in our minds as well as in our experience. We filed slowly over the edge and down the steps to the plank, T. J. coming last, and all of us could feel the weight of his grief behind us.

"Wait a minute," he said suddenly, his voice harsh with the effort of calling.

We stopped and turned, held by the tone of his voice, and looked up at him standing above us on the fire escape.

"We can't stop them?" he said, looking down at us, his face strange in the dusky light. "There ain't no way to stop 'em?"

"No," Blackie said with finality. "They own the building."

We stood still for a moment, looking up at T. J., caught into inaction by the decision working in his face. He stared back at us, and his face was pale and mean in the poor light, with a bald nakedness in his skin like cripples have sometimes.

"They ain't gonna touch my earth," he said fiercely. "They ain't gonna lay a hand on it! Come on."

He turned around and started up the fire escape again, almost running against the effort of climbing. We followed more slowly, not knowing what he intended. By the time we reached him, he had seized a board and thrust it into the soil, scooping it up and flinging it over the parapet into the areaway below. He straightened and looked at us.

"They can't touch it." he said. "I won't let 'em lay a dirty hand on it!"

We saw it then. He stooped to his labor again and we followed, the gusts of his anger moving in frenzied labor among us as we scattered along the edge of earth, scooping it and throwing it over the parapet, destroying with anger the growth we had nurtured with such tender care. The soil carried so laboriously upward to the light and the sun cascaded swiftly into the dark areaway, the green blades of grass crumpled and twisted in the falling.

It took less time than you would think; the task of destruction is infinitely easier than that of creation. We stopped at the end, leaving only a scattering of loose soil, and when it was finally over, a stillness stood among the group and over the factory building. We looked down at the bare sterility of black tar, felt the harsh texture of it under the soles of our shoes, and the anger had gone out of us, leaving only a sore aching in our minds like overstretched muscles.

T. J. stood for a moment, his breathing slowing from anger and effort, caught into the same contemplation of destruction as all of us. He stooped slowly, finally, and picked up a lonely blade of grass left trampled under our feet and put it between his teeth, tasting it, sucking the greenness out of it into his mouth. Then he started walking toward the fire escape, moving before any of us were ready to move, and disappeared over the edge.

We followed him, but he was already halfway down to the ground, going on past the board

WRITING LINK
Have students retell the events of the story from T. J.'s **point of view**. Remind them to include what they imagine are his thoughts and feelings.

PORTFOLIO ASSESSMENT
Suggest that students take time to review and assess their portfolios. Students may find that their reflections lead them to make different choices for their portfolios. Allow students to revise or replace selections as needed. Ask that they write a self-evaluation of their portfolios that includes statements about what they learned by completing their projects. (See *Portfolio Assessment and Professional Support Materials* for additional information about student portfolios.)

51
Force of hatred strips earth of identity, just as it does T. J.

52
Destruction of T. J.'s small connection to the land drives him to escape.

53
Suggests boys never again seek to escape confines of adult world.

READING CHECK
1. The roof of a factory building (p. 187).
2. Watermelons, corn, and cotton (p. 189).
3. From vacant lots (p. 189).
4. He wants to go back home to the South where he can be in touch with the land (p. 194).

FOR STUDY AND DISCUSSION
1. Excited by novelty of project and thought of having something of their own.
2. After it rains and they can smell "the sweet odor of the earth." Students should cite the paragraph on p. 190 beginning, "We were all sniffing at the air too. . . ."
3a. Man who owns building discovers garden and plans to destroy it. 3b. T. J. remembers the South as a place where he lived close to the earth and knew the joy of growing crops.
4. Joyful experience of living close to soil and working to grow things.
5. Answers will vary. Students might cite spiritual strength or strength of character.

LANGUAGE AND VOCABULARY
1. *inert:* "just lay there," "lifeless," "lumpy and cold."
2. *cascaded:* "swiftly," "falling."

---

where we crossed over, climbing down into the areaway. We saw the last section swing down with his weight, and then he stood on the concrete below us, looking at the small pile of *51* anonymous earth scattered by our throwing. Then he walked across the place where we *52* could see him and disappeared toward the street without glancing back, without looking up to see us watching him.

They did not find him for two weeks.

Then the Nashville police caught him just outside the Nashville freight yards. He was walking along the railroad track, still heading south, still heading home.

As for us, who had no remembered home to call us, none of us ever again climbed the *53* escapeway to the roof.

Reading Check

1. What do the boys in the narrator's gang use as their headquarters?
2. What does T. J. want the boys to raise?
3. Where do the boys get the soil for their garden?
4. Why does T. J. run away?

For Study and Discussion

Analyzing and Interpreting the Story

1. The boys in the narrator's gang are city boys accustomed to living without trees or grass of their own. Why do they become so excited at the idea of a roof garden?

2. The boys work at the garden without fully understanding what it means to T. J. At what point do they begin to experience the wonder of making things grow? Find the passage that gives the answer.

3. In the ancient story, Antaeus' bond with the earth was broken when he was held in midair and strangled. **a.** How is T. J.'s bond with the earth broken? **b.** In what way is his return to the South an attempt to renew that bond?

4. The narrator says that he avoided "a last look at the green beauty of the earth that T. J. had planted for us, had planted deeply in our minds as well as in our experience." What gift has T. J. given the boys that will last even though the garden is gone?

5. Like the character Antaeus in the Greek story, T. J. seems to gain strength from contact with the earth. Antaeus' strength was physical. How would you describe the kind of strength T. J. draws from the earth?

Language and Vocabulary

Using Context Clues

You can often get the meaning of an unfamiliar word by using clues supplied by the context.

> The laborious earth just lay there during the cold months, *inert* and lifeless, the clods lumpy and cold under our feet when we walked over it.

The word *inert* means "not moving; inactive." *1* What clues in the sentence help give you this meaning?

2 What context clues help you get the meaning of the word *cascaded* in this sentence?

> The soil carried so laboriously upward to the light and the sun *cascaded* swiftly into the dark areaway, the green blades of grass crumpled and twisted in the falling.

The verb *cascade* means "to fall swiftly from a height, like a waterfall."

Write sentences of your own using the words *inert* and *cascade*.

3 Use context clues to determine the meaning

194 THE NATURAL WORLD

CLOSURE

Have students select and discuss passages that illustrate the bonds between T. J. and the city boys, and the city boys and the soil.

EXTENSION AND ENRICHMENT

Students who are interested in mythology might clip magazine or newspaper advertisements that allude to some myth—for example, in brand names.

Students might wish to report on projects in which they have tried to grow things—perhaps a vegetable garden, a terrarium, or flowers.

Another possibility is to invite students to extend the story by telling what might have happened to T. J. after he was caught in Nashville.

---

of each of these words. Check your answers in the glossary.

domain	(page 189, column 2)
contemplate	(page 190, column 1)
distracted	(page 190, column 1)

Focus on Informative Writing

Preparing an Oral Report

In "Antaeus" T. J. shows the boys how to plant a garden on the factory roof. First he helps the boys find good growing soil in vacant lots. Then he shows them how to prepare the earth for planting by breaking up the clods, smoothing the soil, and sowing the grass seed.

Choose one of the topics below, or select your own topic. Write notes for an oral report in which you will explain to your classmates how to perform a process. Be sure to include all the materials that will be needed. If you must use any technical words, be sure to explain what they mean. Save your notes.

How to paint a room
How to mow a lawn
How to make a kite
How to bathe a dog
How to prepare for a storm

About the Author

Borden Deal (1922–1985)

Borden Deal was born on a cotton farm in Mississippi. Before devoting himself full time to writing, he had a variety of jobs. He worked as a firefighter for the Civilian Conservation Corps, a roustabout for a circus and a showboat, an auditor, a finance collector, and a writer for a radio station. He produced several novels and more than one hundred short stories. His work has been adapted for the stage, the movies, and television, and has been translated into many languages.

---

3. *Domain:* refers to roof garden described as "private." Students should infer "land that is privately owned."

Contemplate: occurs in sentence "T. J. was smart enough to start in one corner. . . ." Since the boys are looking at result with "awe," students should infer "to look at intently and thoughtfully."

Distracted: occurs in sentence "Some of the evenings T. J. alone was carrying. . . ." Since other boys kept from working on project by "other enterprises or interests," students should infer "diverted from or drawn in another direction."

FOCUS ON INFORMATIVE WRITING

Suggest that students work in pairs to ensure they are not omitting any necessary steps in the writing process. If possible, pair students who are somewhat unfamiliar with each other's activity. As one partner explains the steps, the other partner can attempt the activity. Partners also can check each other for inclusion of necessary materials and explanation of technical terms.

ABOUT THE AUTHOR

Deal's own family's struggles as farmers during the Great Depression provided ample material for his fiction. A major **theme** of Deal's works is a person's spiritual attachment to the earth, as is seen in "Antaeus." His novels that treat this theme, particularly his first two novels, *Walk Through the Valley* (1956) and *Dunbar's Cove* (1958), show a strong sense of place and time: the American South in the 1930s.

OBJECTIVES
The overall aim is for students to write an **informative** paper to show a **process** or to explain **cause and effect**.

PRESENTATION
To introduce **informative writing,** you might explain to students that nearly any subject they encounter in their daily lives, especially in their reading, can become the basis for an **informative essay.** Tell them to ask questions such as What is? Why does? How can? or How does? about everything they see, hear, and read. Then you might send students out with a journal or writing notebook to look for suitable topics for a **process** or **cause-and-effect** paper. Once students have decided on a topic and a purpose,

HOLT WRITER'S WORKSHOP

This computer program provides help for all types of writing through guided instruction for each step of the writing process. (Program available separately.)

See *Elements of Writing, First Course,* Chapter 7, for more instruction on informative writing.

WRITING AN INFORMATIVE PAPER

An **informative** paper often incorporates both **description** and **narration.** Since students already have experience with these strategies, using them in an **informative** context is a valuable experience. Tell students that relying on their knowledge and intuition will lend authenticity and interest to their papers.

Prewriting

When students come to class with their topics and purposes, you might want to have each student give you a purpose statement, such as "I am going to write a paper explaining how to construct a kite," or "I am going to write a paper explaining the causes and effects of air pollution." This procedure will enable you to see how many students are writing each kind of paper so that you can group them for other activities. It will also help students by engaging the entire class in talking and thinking about topics and approaches to the writing task.

You might want to encourage students to create a graphic aid to help them collect and record information for their papers. The chart in the text will work for a **cause-and-effect** paper. For a **process** paper, students might create a chart on which they list the steps in the left column and then describe the materials or other pertinent notes in the right column.

196

FOCUS ON Writing

WRITING AN INFORMATIVE PAPER

*I*n **informative writing** your purpose is to share information. In a **process paper,** you show how to do something or how something works. In a **cause-and-effect explanation,** you explore the reasons and/or the results of an event or situation.

Prewriting

1. To find a topic for an expository paper, ask yourself questions like the ones below:
   - What do I like to do?
   - What do I do well?
   - I wonder why . . .

[See **Focus** assignments on pages 146 and 177.]

2. List the steps or stages of a process carefully. Remember to arrange them in the exact order in which they happen.

For a cause-and-effect paper, you may want to fill out a chart like the one below. Remember that a single event may have more than one cause and may lead to more than one effect.

Causes
Event/Problem/Situation
Effects

3. For a "how-to" paper, write one sentence stating the reason your audience should learn the process. For example: "If you follow five simple steps, food shopping can be fun and economical." For a cause-and-effect paper, write a one-sentence statement of your main idea. For example: "There are three important causes for the town board's recent decision to close our neighborhood park."

Writing

1. Follow an **outline** when you write your first draft. Below are two sample outlines that you will find helpful.

Process Paper
   I. Introduction
      A. Grab reader's attention
      B. State reason for learning process
   II. Body
      A. List necessary materials
      B. Explain each step
   III. Conclusion
      Summarize value of process

Cause-and-Effect Explanation
   I. Introduction
      A. Grab reader's attention
      B. State main idea
   II. Body
      Discuss causes/effects in a logical order
   III. Conclusion
      Sum up main points and add comment

2. Help your readers to understand the connections of ideas in your paper by using **transitions.** [See **Focus** assignment on page 185.]

you might want them to determine how they want to publish their papers. They might want to write their papers with their classmates as the audience. If so, you can devote a few days to an Information Fair, during which students can share their ideas with the class.

CLOSURE
Have students identify differences and similarities between **process** papers and **cause-and-effect** papers. Write students' responses on the chalkboard and discuss them.

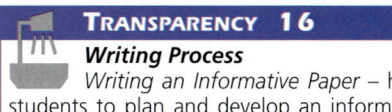

TRANSPARENCY 16

Writing Process
Writing an Informative Paper – helps students to plan and develop an informative essay.

Evaluating and Revising

1. After you have written your first draft, look it over for places that need editing and revision. Pay special attention to using specific, exact adjectives and nouns.

Here is one writer's revision of a paragraph in a process paper.

Writer's Model

The beavers start to build their *lodge* ~~house~~ by using *waterlogged* wood *to*. ~~They~~ make an artificial island in a pond or lake. Their long teeth are perfect tools for *chisel-like* felling trees *in*. *waterside* After a tree falls, the beavers trim *the side branches* ~~it~~ from the main stem, cut all the pieces of wood into *convenient* lengths, and swim to the *lodge* location to put the wood in place. ~~Then they use fresh~~ *Finally,* ~~wood to build the lodge higher.~~ They use mud to plaster the outside walls.

2. Use the following checklist when you revise your paper:

Checklist for Evaluation and Revision

✓ Does the introduction catch the reader's interest?
✓ Do I state the reason for learning the process? Do I state my main idea in a cause-and-effect paper?
✓ Do I list any necessary materials?
✓ Do I discuss the stages in a process or the causes and effects of an event in a logical order?
✓ Do I end my paper with a strong conclusion?

Proofreading and Publishing

1. Proofread your paper and correct any errors you find in grammar, usage, and mechanics. (Here you may find it helpful to refer to the **Handbook for Revision** on pages 726–767.) Then prepare a final version of your paper by making a clean copy.

2. Consider some of the following publication methods for your paper:

- join with classmates and stage a class "how-to" day
- send your essay to a hobby magazine
- illustrate your paper with charts, diagrams, or other visual aids, and then post it on the class bulletin board

Portfolio If your teacher approves, you may wish to keep a copy of your work in your writing folder or portfolio.

Writing
You might want to brainstorm with students some methods they can use to grab their reader's attention. Some suggestions might include asking a question, using an interesting statement or fact, or telling an anecdote. Students might experiment with several strategies after they have written the bodies of their essays and then choose the one that is most suitable.

Evaluating and Revising
To help students evaluate their papers, you might recommend that students go back and make an outline of their essays so that they can look for gaps or inconsistencies in their organization. You might also pair students, directing them to outline each other's papers.

In small groups students can work to identify dull or imprecise words in one another's essays. Using a thesaurus or a dictionary, students should try to replace these words with words that will make their descriptions come alive.

Proofreading and Publishing
You might work with students to create an editing sheet that includes some of the common errors that students continue to make in their writing. Students can then work in small groups to identify and correct these mistakes in each other's essays.

Focus on Writing 197

198

PART II

FORMS OF LITERATURE

Unit Four
SHORT STORIES
201

Unit Five
DRAMA
307

Unit Six
NONFICTION
381

Unit Seven
POETRY
429

Unit Eight
THE NOVEL
501

FORMS OF LITERATURE

The first unit in this section provides a natural introduction to the study of genre. The stories in the unit are ones that seventh-graders will easily relate to and enjoy. Students will learn to recognize the basic elements of fiction and relate these elements to the stories they read.

Although students might not be as familiar with the reading of drama as a literary form, they will certainly have watched many presentations of plays and scripts on television. Students will enjoy opportunities to present their own versions of scenes from one or more of the plays in the Drama unit and, perhaps, even write original scripts for class presentation. The selections in the Nonfiction unit offer quality, high-interest reading. Questions and exercises that follow each selection develop a wide range of reading skills to help students become critical readers of the barrage of factual reading material that they face daily as students and will face later as adults. In the Poetry unit, students will explore the language of poetry and respond to the sometimes poignant, sometimes humorous selections in the unit. They will discover that poetry is a form of expression that speaks to *them*, just as it has spoken to both the young and the old of times past and present.

Pacific Crossing, the novel featured in the final unit of this section, contains the theme of self-reliance. Students will easily relate to young Lincoln's trials and frustrations as he faces and overcomes the challenges of living in a foreign country.

UNIT 4 ◆ TEACHING GUIDE

FORMS OF LITERATURE
SHORT STORIES

OVERVIEW OF THE UNIT

The focus of this unit is the short story. This provides a starting point for emphasizing and encouraging appreciation of major story elements such as plot, conflict, foreshadowing, point of view, characterization, setting, theme, and irony.

Each of the selections provides a memorable reading experience, and each is particularly suited for highlighting one or more of the important elements or techniques used by the author in crafting the short story.

Gardner's "The Dinner Party" illustrates the importance of plot. At the home of a colonial official in India, a British colonel asserts that men, partly because of their superior nervous control, react more bravely and efficiently than do women. A young girl opposes his stereotypical view of female timidity. Unknown to them, a cobra is in the room. One of the sexes will prove superior, at least in this crisis, in Gardner's tightly plotted tale.

Beachcroft's "The Erne from the Coast" gives an example of effective use of conflict. When an eagle carries off a lamb while Harry Thorburn is guarding the flock, the young man must deal with three conflicts: with his father, who does not believe Harry's account of what happened; with the eagle, which will return again to attack the sheep; and with himself, since he must overcome his feelings of shame and inadequacy.

Dahl's "The Landlady" provides a study of suspense and foreshadowing. When Billy decides to spend the night at a boarding house run by an eccentric lady, Dahl offers sufficient clues to warn the reader that Billy is in great danger. Yet he also creates suspense by keeping the reader uncertain whether Billy will escape or not.

Methods of characterization are emphasized in Kipling's "Rikki-tikki-tavi." The main character is a mongoose, yet he takes on all the qualities of a person. Using direct characterization, Kipling describes what the mongoose and the other animals in the story are like. Using indirect characterization, Kipling shows what the animals are like through their thoughts, their words, their actions, and the reactions of other characters to them.

Hemingway's "A Day's Wait" features the use of point of view, showing the effects to be gained with skillful use of first person. A young boy is unaware of the difference between measurements in Celsius and measurements in Fahrenheit, and so thinks he is dying of an abnormally high temperature. The narrator, the boy's father, cannot understand why his son is taking his illness so seriously. The reader also is curious because the story is told only from the father's viewpoint—what he sees, what he hears, what he thinks. Because of this restricted viewpoint, the reader shares the father's surprise and relief when the boy confesses his fears.

The effective use of setting is illustrated in Irving's "Rip Van Winkle." The famous story of a man who falls asleep for twenty years is made more believable by Irving's insistence on sharp detail and precise description. Rip's everyday world is described in realistic detail, even down to the houses built of yellow bricks from Holland. The troubles at the Winkle farm, which include fences falling and cows in the cabbage, are vividly described. Even the Catskill Mountains seem alive and magical as Irving envelops them with weather, sky, and setting sun.

Wuorio's "You Can't Take It with You" helps students understand theme and irony. Everyone tells rich Uncle Basil that "he can't take it with him," but when Basil dies, his relatives are suddenly not so sure. With a careful ordering of events, Wuorio uses irony and surprise to illustrate her comic theme.

In "Zlateh the Goat," Isaac Bashevis Singer offers a story that has the simplicity and universal appeal of a folk tale. The story's theme emerges from the communication between Aaron and the goat as they finally find shelter together during a snowstorm.

Finally, Dickens' "A Christmas Carol" allows for a reiteration of all these elements, plus an illustration of the literary technique of onomatopoeia. Several **For Study and Discussion** exercises provide an in-depth study of character, plot, setting, point of view, and theme in Dickens' story.

Writing activities throughout the unit and a special section at the end guide students in applying what they have learned to write an original short story.

OBJECTIVES OF THE UNIT

The aims of the unit are for the student:
- To demonstrate an understanding of the plot, setting, and characters of a short story
- To identify the conflict and the climax of a short story
- To recognize the use of foreshadowing in a short story
- To demonstrate an understanding of the use of direct and indirect characterization
- To identify the narrator and point of view in a short story
- To demonstrate recognition of character types
- To identify examples of irony used in a short story
- To demonstrate an understanding of the theme of a short story
- To write essays analyzing the setting, plot, theme, and characterization in various short stories
- To write an original short story
- To make connections between literature and cultures and the arts

PLANNING GUIDE

FOR UNIT PLANNING
- Transparencies 17–23: *Audiovisual Resources Binder*
- Portfolio Assessment: *Professional Support Materials*
- Test Generator
- Mastery Tests: Teaching Resources B, pp. 227, 230, 234
- Analogy Test: Teaching Resources B, p. 236
- Composition Test: Teaching Resources B, p. 237

SELECTION (Pupil's Page)	TEACHING RESOURCES B (page numbers shown below)							AV BINDER
	Teacher's Notes	Reading Check	Study Guide	Language Skills	Building Vocabulary	Selection Vocab. Test	Selection Test	Audio-cassette
SHORT STORIES Introduction (p. 201)	105							
Close Reading of a Short Story Mona Gardner *The Dinner Party* (p. 202)	106							
T. O. Beachcroft *The Erne from the Coast* (p. 208)	107	110	111	114	117	132	118	
Roald Dahl *The Landlady* (p. 220)	120	123	124	127	131	132	133	
Rudyard Kipling *Rikki-tikki-tavi* (p. 229)	135	137	138	142	145	157	146	
Ernest Hemingway *A Day's Wait* (p. 242)	148	150	151	153	156	157	158	
Washington Irving *Rip Van Winkle* (p. 247)	159	162	163	165	168	171, 172	173	TAPE 2 SIDES A & B
Eva-Lis Wuorio *You Can't Take It with You* (p. 264)	175	178	179	182	185		187	
Isaac Bashevis Singer *Zlateh the Goat* (p. 270)	189	191	192	194			198	
Charles Dickens *A Christmas Carol* (p. 276)	200		204	207	210, 212, 217	218, 220	222	TAPE 2 SIDE B

199B

CONCEPTS AND SKILLS

The following concepts and skills are treated in this unit:

CLOSE READING OF A SHORT STORY

Guidelines for Close Reading 203
One Reader's Response 204
Looking at Yourself as a Reader 207

LITERARY ELEMENTS/TERMS AND TECHNIQUES

Understanding Conflict and Plot 218
Understanding Suspense and Foreshadowing 227
Understanding Methods of Characterization 240
Understanding the Narrator's Point of View 245
Focusing on Setting 260
Understanding Character Types 261
Recognizing Irony 268
Interpreting Theme 274
Understanding Point of View 275
Recognizing Onomatopoeia 300

LANGUAGE AND VOCABULARY SKILLS

Understanding Dialect 218
Prefixes Used in Measurement 246
Recognizing Shades of Meaning 262
Determining Exact Meanings 268
Recognizing Analogies 301

WRITING OPPORTUNITIES

Writing About Literature

Showing How Conflict is Developed and Resolved 219
Analyzing Methods of Characterization 240
Explaining the Function of Setting 262
Discussing Stock Characters 269

Creative Writing

Writing About Characters in Action 240

Focus on Writing a Short Story

Finding a Story Idea 219
Building a Plot 228
Creating Characters 241
Exploring Point of View 246
Listing Details of Setting 262
Experimenting with Irony 269
Exploring a Theme 275
Making a Story Map 301
Writing a Short Story 304

CONNECTIONS

Connecting Cultures 241
Literature and the Arts 263, 302

FOCUS ON READING AND CRITICAL THINKING

Evaluating Short Stories 303

TRANSPARENCIES

The following unit support materials with specific correlations to literature selections are available in the **Fine Art and Instructional Transparencies with Teacher's Notes and Blackline Masters** section of your *Audiovisual Resources Binder*.

FINE ART TRANSPARENCIES

Theme: Building Blocks

17 *Steaming Streets,* George Bellows
18 *Navaho Woman Weaver,* Andrew Tsinajinnie

READER RESPONSE

19 First Response
20 Tug-of-War

LITERARY ELEMENTS

21 Evaluating Short Stories
22 Story Map

WRITING PROCESS

23 Writing a Short Story

INTRODUCING THE UNIT

You might begin the unit with activities designed to concentrate student attention on the short story as a genre:

1. Encourage students to go beyond the readings in the anthology by assembling a classroom library of short-story collections borrowed from the school library, personally-owned paperbacks, and textbooks containing short stories. Include magazines noted for good fiction.

2. Post a bibliography of recommended stories. This is even more effective if selections are cross-referenced: "If you enjoyed _____ be sure to try _____."

3. Try to reserve one day a week for independent reading to be continued at home. Have students record on 3" x 5" cards the titles and authors of stories read as well as a rating. A suggested rating system is to rank from ★ ("Okay, but I don't recommend it") to ★★★★ ("The greatest—don't miss it!"). From these cards, compile and post a weekly list of three- and four-star stories.

Since **Reflections, Family Album,** and **The Natural World** contain a number of short stories, students might use the selections they have already read for a number of activities to help generate interest in this unit:

1. Ask each student to scan the table of contents for the first three units and to pick a favorite selection. (If the class runs true to form, short stories will dominate the list.) Ask students to explain their choices and to account for the popularity of short stories. They may also wish to mention all-time favorites not included in the anthology. You may want to link this discussion to the introductory comments on p. 202 in the pupil's textbook.

2. Provide recent newspapers and let each student clip a front-page story of special interest and then highlight or underline the first sentence, which usually tells what, who, where, when, and perhaps why or how. Ask students to look at the opening of one of the short stories in the anthology. Do writers of fiction usually give away as much as reporters do in their first sentences? Why not? Ask each student to write the first paragraph of a short story that could be based on events in the news story they have chosen. Post clippings and story openers in pairs on the bulletin board, or suggest that students use techniques gleaned from the short-story unit to finish their stories. As a culminating activity for the unit, stories may be compiled in a class mini-anthology and shared with other classes.

3. Capitalize upon popular television programs by asking students to list favorite situation comedies, adventure shows—any series with a story line—and to describe the kinds of conflict in each. Make chalkboard notes. Note that many of these conflicts are unpleasant, if not downright dangerous, for those involved. Why do we like to watch other people as they struggle? Would there really be any story to watch if there were no conflict? Observe that fiction also allows readers to participate vicariously in the conflicts of others. Then use the kinds of conflict noted earlier to spark a brief preview of selections in the unit.

PORTFOLIO ASSESSMENT

Suggestions for use of portfolios as support for this unit are described in the *Portfolio Assessment and Professional Support Materials* booklet accompanying this program. Specific suggestions are provided for a variety of student projects that may be suitable for inclusion in a portfolio. In addition, copying masters are provided for guides that may be used for evaluation and assessment of student projects.

Student Learning Options

SHORT STORIES

1. Changing the Point of View
Have students rewrite "A Day's Wait" by Ernest Hemingway from the boy's point of view.

2. Looking into the Future
After reading and discussing "Rip Van Winkle," ask students what they think life will be like twenty years from today. Then ask students to write their own "Rip Van Winkle" story. Ask them to think about how the world might be better or worse.

3. Publishing a Newspaper
After brainstorming about different kinds of stories in newspapers, assign each short story in this unit to a small group of students. Instruct them to write a story for a class newspaper, based on the short story. Possible types of stories include a news story, a feature story, a business advice column (by Uncle Basil in "You Can't Take It With You"), or an editorial. As an extension of this activity, you might type the final drafts in column widths and paste them up in newspaper format, complete with headlines and pictures, to display in the classroom.

4. Celebrating Heroes
Because young people can perform heroic acts, as in "The Erne from the Coast," brainstorm with the class to think of brave deeds of young people they know, have heard of, or have read about. Then guide the students to create a bulletin board entitled Young Heroes—with illustrated stories of what those young people accomplished. Each student could write about a different hero, or students could work in small groups.

5. Marking Settings of Short Stories
Most of these short stories were set in countries outside our own. Using a globe or a map, have students locate the place where each short story occurred.

6. Illustrating New Vocabulary Words
Ask students to find three to five new words in each story of the unit, draw an illustration of each word's meaning, and write the definition below the illustration. You might want to put these illustrations on the wall. You could even have a Vocabulary Time each day when two to three students each present a new word and help the other students remember it. Students may want to present new words in song lyrics, in poems, by acting out scenarios, or in other creative ways.

199D

VISUAL CONNECTIONS

About the Artist

James Jebusa Shannon was born in 1862 in Mount Auburn, New York. As a young man, he studied art in England, where he found great success as a portraitist. Typical of his work is the use of decorative, vividly colorful patterns and elaborately costumed figures in the realistic depiction of his subject. By 1905, his portraits were much in demand. Shortly after the turn of the century, he came to New York to complete a number of commissions, painting portraits of Mrs. Rockefeller, Mrs. Sears, and Mrs. Mellon, among others. He returned to England in 1909, becoming a member of the Royal Academy. In recognition of his work, he was knighted in 1922.

About the Artwork

Jungle Tales shows the artist's favorite subjects: his wife and his daughter Kitty (profile). The title of the painting is believed to refer to the book they are enjoying: Kipling's *The Jungle Book,* which gained enormous popularity in England after its publication in 1894. The painting was first exhibited in Paris in 1900, where it was purchased by G. McCulloch, a collector from London, who apparently changed the painting's title. When it was next shown at the Royal Academy in London, it was listed under the name *Fairy Tales.*

SHORT STORIES

Do you have a favorite story that you enjoy reading or listening to over and over again even though you know how it turns out? "A Christmas Carol" is that kind of story. Some people read it or listen to it being read every year at Christmastime.

Look at the painting on these pages. How much can you tell about the figures in the painting from details the artist has provided? Has the reader reached the best part of the story? Are the listeners eager to hear more?

Imagine yourself telling a story about the people in this painting. Create the dialogue for one of the following episodes:

1. The reader is tired and wishes to stop, but the listeners urge her to finish the story.
2. The reader has come to a part of the story that the girls don't understand and they interrupt to ask questions.
3. The reader turns to the end of the story and finds the last page missing from the book.

Jungle Tales (Contes de la Jungle) (1895) by James Jebusa Shannon (1862–1923). Oil on canvas.
The Metropolitan Museum of Art, Arthur Hoppock Hearn Fund, 1913 (13.143.1).

TEACHING RESOURCES B
Teacher's Notes, p. 105

SHORT STORIES
Short stories are popular with young people. They offer the same attractions as full-length books—exciting plots, interesting characters, and new and different settings—but with the added advantage that most short fiction can be read in one sitting.

A deeper understanding of the major elements and techniques of the short story is the focus of this unit. Some selections are short, some are longer, but all offer especially effective illustrations of the use of the elements of fiction.

Throughout the unit, students answer questions related to analysis and interpretation of the various selections. The **Literary Elements** features throughout the unit help students analyze conflict, plot, suspense, foreshadowing, characterization, point of view, setting, character types, irony, and use of onomatopoeia.

Close Reading OF A SHORT STORY

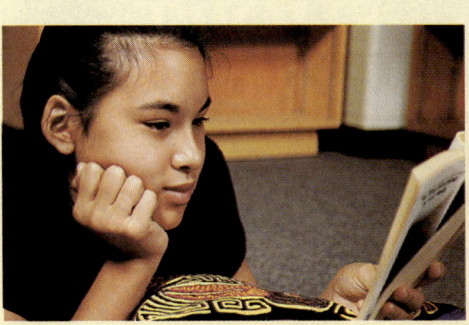

You may have heard the story of Scheherazade (shə-hĕr′ə-zä′də), the narrator of tales in the Arabian Nights Entertainment. She is sentenced to death by the sultan, her husband, but each night she tells such a fascinating story that her execution is postponed for another day. After a thousand and one nights of tales, the sultan pardons her and the couple live happily ever after.

A good story has the power to captivate an audience. It keeps you reading because you want to know what happens to the characters. You become interested in them as if they were real people.

When you examine the stories in this unit closely, you will find that they are made up of similar elements. For example, each story has a main character. In "The Erne from the Coast," the main character is a boy of your own age. In "Rikki-tikki-tavi," the central character is an animal. You will find that each story has a plot, or sequence of events. "Zlateh the Goat" has a relatively simple plot. "A Christmas Carol" has a more complicated plot, with many threads to the action. Each story has a location in place and time called the setting. One of the stories in this unit is set in the Catskill Mountains in New York State in the late 1700s. Another story takes place in nineteenth-century India. Every story is told from a particular point of view. In "A Day's Wait," the narrator is an observer who knows what each character thinks and feels. In addition to entertaining readers, a short story generally reveals some idea about life or interpretation of experience. This element is called the theme of the story. Sometimes the theme is stated directly. Sometimes it is not stated, but may be inferred from the characters and events in the story.

In this unit you will be introduced to these and other basic elements in short stories. The better you understand how these elements work together, the better you will understand and appreciate the storyteller's art. Read actively, asking questions as you read and noting your own reactions to characters and events. The following guidelines can help you become a more skillful reader.

202 SHORT STORIES

short story. **Looking at Yourself as a Reader,** following the story, comments on the similarities and differences to be expected in students' responses.

GEOGRAPHY LINK
Have students locate India on a world map and then use the encyclopedia to find out more about the country and its people. Tell students to pay particular attention to the period when the British ruled. Both this story and Kipling's "Rikki-tikki-tavi" are set during this period.

Guidelines for Close Reading

1. Read for both enjoyment and understanding. An imaginative work of fiction can yield pleasure and can also provide you with insight into yourself and others. Keep both objects in mind as you read.
2. Actively question the author's purpose and method. Ask yourself what importance there might be to details that the author gives you.
3. Question unfamiliar words and references. If you cannot get the meaning from context clues, check in a dictionary or other reference work.
4. Draw inferences about the characters and events. Some information may be provided directly, but most often information about characters will be revealed indirectly through the reactions of other characters.
5. Make predictions as you read. Anticipate what is coming. Become aware of your own responses to characters and actions.
6. Relate what happens in the story to your own life and experiences. Probe for the central idea or underlying meaning of the story. Try to state this theme in your own words.

Here is a brief story that has been read carefully by one reader. The notes in the margin show how this reader has responded to the story. If
4 you wish, cover up the printed notes as you read and make notes of your own on a separate sheet of paper. You may compare your responses with the printed comments after you have completed your reading.

GUIDELINES FOR CLOSE READING
1. Students may need to be reminded that analysis of literature should enhance, not preclude, enjoyment.
2. Discuss with students various questions they might ask about purpose and method. For example, "Does the author simply want to entertain, or is the author trying to make a specific point?" "Do the conversation and descriptive details in the story help to bring the main character to life?"
3. **Language and Vocabulary** exercises throughout the text give students practice in use of context clues.
4. Students may need practice in identifying and analyzing **direct characterization** (in which author explicitly reveals character) and **indirect characterization** (in which author describes actions from which reader draws inference about character).
5. Explain to students that when they make predictions, they look for clues left by the writer. They can also look for clues in illustrations.
6. Remind students that although the **theme** of a story is sometimes stated directly, more often it must be inferred from the characters and events in the story.

4
Explain to students that the questions they ask about the literature and the conclusions they draw might differ greatly from the responses of their classmates or from those of the reader in the textbook. There are no right or wrong answers.

©Thomas Ives/The Stock Market

203

The Dinner Party

MONA GARDNER

1   The country is India. A colonial official[1] and his wife are giving a large dinner party. They are seated with their guests—army officers and government attachés[2] and their wives, and a visiting American naturalist[3]—in their spacious dining room, which has a bare marble floor, open rafters and wide glass doors opening onto a veranda.

2   A spirited discussion springs up between a young girl who insists that women have outgrown the jumping-on-a-chair-at-the-sight-of-a-mouse era and a colonel who says that they haven't.

3   "A woman's unfailing reaction in any crisis," the colonel says, "is to scream. And while a man may feel like it, he has that ounce more of nerve control than a woman has. And that last ounce is what counts."

4   The American does not join in the argument but watches the other guests. As he looks, he sees a strange expression come

5   over the face of the hostess. She is staring straight ahead, her muscles contracting slightly. With a slight gesture she summons the native boy standing behind her chair and whispers to him. The boy's eyes widen: he quickly leaves the room.

6   Of the guests, none except the American notices this or sees the boy place a bowl of milk on the veranda just outside the open doors.

7   The American comes to with a start. In India, milk in a bowl means only one thing—bait for a snake. He realizes there must be a cobra in the room. He looks up at the rafters—the likeliest place—but they are bare. Three corners of the room are empty, and in the fourth the servants are waiting to serve the next course. There is only one place left—under the table.

8   His first impulse is to jump back and warn the others, but he knows the commotion would frighten the cobra into striking.

9   He speaks quickly, the tone of his voice so arresting that it

---

1. **colonial official:** When this story was published, in 1942, India was still a British colony.
2. **attachés** (ăt′ə-shāz′, ă-tă′shāz): individuals on the diplomatic staff of an ambassador or a minister to another country.
3. **naturalist:** someone who is a trained observer of animals and plants.

Close Reading
OF A SELECTION

ONE READER'S RESPONSE

I've seen movies that take place in this kind of setting.

I wonder how the author is going to use this conflict in the story.

What can this expression mean? Why does she look tense?

The boy must be frightened or surprised.

Why does he place a bowl of milk outside the house?

He's a naturalist so he's a trained observer.

Now this story is getting exciting. Is there a snake under the table?

---

1   In addition to **setting,** first paragraph gives details indicating main characters enjoy wealth and privilege.

2   Second paragraph introduces central issue: whether women have developed self-control.

3   Repetition and elaboration emphasize issue; colonel insists men have better control of nerves than women.

4   **Characterization.** American is set apart (spotlighted) by non-involvement in **debate;** suggests he may be wiser or less compelled to "prove a point" than colonel.

5   Hostess highlighted here: her actions show something is wrong.

6   The earlier description of the American as a naturalist suits his talents of close observance of details.

7   Not only is naturalist a good observer, but he knows animal life; realizes what the milk is for.

8   Here is an example of a man's exhibiting good self-control.

9   The American thinks fast; he not only keeps himself still, he finds a way to "freeze" others so cobra will not be provoked.

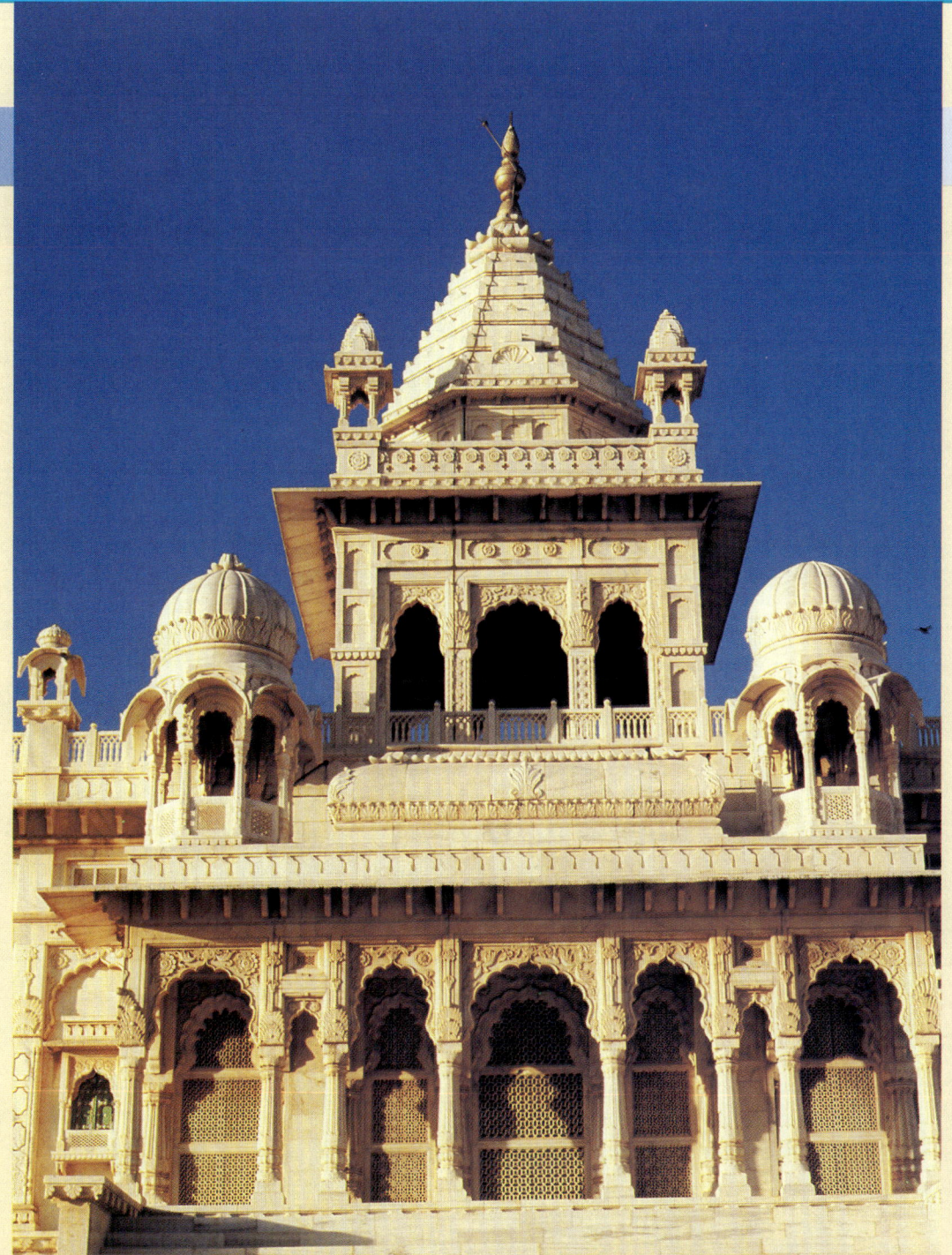

Jodhpur, Rajasthan, India.

VISUAL CONNECTIONS
Exploring the Subject
This building, Jaswant Thada, is a mausoleum built for Maharajah Singh II in 1899. Mausoleums are large monuments that entomb one or more people. Like the one pictured here, they are sometimes large, imposing buildings that become cultural markers for later generations.

Ideas for Writing
Students might write a letter to a friend describing this mausoleum that they have toured during a trip to India. Included in the letter should be their personal reaction to the size and beauty of the structure.

Relating Expression Skills
Although mausoleums are built as tombs, they are more importantly monuments honoring a particular person. Have students work individually or with a group to design a monument honoring someone they admire. The students could draw their design on paper or build the monument out of craft materials.

VISUAL CONNECTIONS

About the Artwork
Mosaic is a process by which pictures or designs are made with small pieces of glass, tile, or colored stone set in mortar or cement. The Romans first developed mosaic pavements. Many Christian churches of Italy and the Byzantine Empire used mosaic to adorn walls throughout the Middle Ages. It has also been used as inlays for furniture and small objects in the Aztec art of Mexico.

Relating Expression Skills
Students might wish to create their own mosaic of a peacock or other colorful bird. Have them cut construction paper into small, random shapes. Then have them arrange the pieces in the form of a bird on a sheet of black or gray construction paper. Tell them to glue the pieces down and then coat the whole picture with school glue to preserve the color and to give their mosaic a finished appearance. Display the artwork around the classroom.

Mosaic peacock, Jaipur, India.

Portfolio Assessment

Students may be interested in producing a portfolio of drawings related to the stories in this unit. Suggest that they mount their drawings and include on a facing page a paragraph or two identifying the title and author, summarizing the story, and describing the incident that inspired the drawing. Some students may want to display their portfolios in the classroom. (See Portfolio Assessment and Professional Support Materials.)

CLOSURE

Ask students to briefly identify the main elements of the story: **characters, plot, setting, point of view,** and **theme.**

---

sobers everyone.

"I want to know just what control everyone at this table has. I will count to three hundred—that's five minutes—and not one of you is to move a muscle. Those who move will forfeit[4] fifty rupees.[5] Ready!"

The twenty people sit like stone images while he counts. He is saying, "…two hundred and eighty…" when, out of the corner of his eye, he sees the cobra emerge and make for the bowl

10 of milk. Screams ring out as he jumps to slam the veranda doors safely shut.

11 "You were right, Colonel!" the host exclaims. "A man has just shown us an example of perfect control."

"Just a minute," the American says, turning to his hostess.

12 "Mrs. Wynnes, how did you know that cobra was in the room?"

A faint smile lights up the woman's face as she replies:

13 "Because it was crawling across my foot."

4. **forfeit** (fôr′fĭt): give up, as a penalty.
5. **rupees** (roo-pēz′, roo′pēz): The rupee is the basic monetary unit of India, like the dollar in the United States.

He's clever. He invents a game to keep people from moving.

Will the cobra strike?

Now I understand why I needed a clear picture of the scene.

How did she know?

Wow! This is a great ending.

10
The screams show American is right: others might have panicked if they were told about cobra.

11
Irony. Host sees incident as example of male superiority (vs. apparently female "screams"). He does not realize his wife has best self-control of all.

12
Only the naturalist's earlier observation leads to this question.

13
Reversal: the issue is resolved in a surprising manner; not only has woman exhibited greater self-control; but if naturalist had not noticed and asked, no one would have known.

Looking at Yourself as a Reader

If you have made your own notes on "The Dinner Party," compare them with the printed comments that appear alongside the story. Meet with several classmates and compare your responses with theirs. Are there important similarities and differences in all these reactions?

Here are several statements about "The Dinner Party." Which do you think comes closest to stating the main point of the story?

1. This story shows that the colonel is unfairly prejudiced against women.
2. The story reveals that in a crisis anybody can keep a cool head and act logically.
3. The events of the story show that both women and men can show remarkable courage and self-control.

LOOKING AT YOURSELF AS A READER

Students might feel more comfortable about sharing their personal responses to the story if you share yours also. Discuss with students the importance of accepting differing opinions. Encourage a friendly classroom environment that is conducive to sharing.

Most students will probably choose the third statement as the main point of the story. Whichever statement they choose, ask students to support their choices with examples from the story.

Close Reading of a Short Story

OBJECTIVES	VOCABULARY	FOCUS / MOTIVATION
The overall aim is for students to identify internal and external **conflict** in the story. For a complete list of objectives, see the **Teacher's Notes**.	The underlined words are in the Glossary. The **Language and Vocabulary** section on p. 218 gives students practice in understanding dialect words through context clues and sound similarities.	Explain to the class that sometimes people are faced with emotional as well as physical dangers. In this story, a boy's fear of adult disapproval is stronger than his fear of physical danger.

> **TEACHING RESOURCES B**
> Teacher's Notes, p. 107
> Reading Check, p. 110
> Study Guide, p. 111
> Language Skills, p. 114
> Building Vocabulary, p. 117
> Selection Vocabulary Test, p. 132
> Selection Test, p. 118

PREREADING FOCUS
The headnote emphasizes the literary elements of **plot, conflict,** and **climax.** You may want to discuss these terms with students to be sure they understand each of them.

The Erne from the Coast

1
Thorburn's manner suggests he calls a dog rather than a boy.

2
Details showing how Mr. Thorburn has worked hard for his prosperity: "red-faced, powerful" and "well-fleshed."

3
Example of sarcasm. It is a bad time of year for old Michael to leave the farm.

4
Michael is Thorburn's shepherd.

5
Thorburn's harsh reply shows he feels Harry isn't "measuring up."

6
Setting. Rural and isolated, in the rugged hills of northern England.

The Erne from the Coast

T. O. BEACHCROFT

The term plot *refers to the sequence of incidents or actions in a story—whatever the characters do or whatever happens to them. The most important element in a plot is* conflict. *In this story, note how the action builds toward an exciting* climax.

I

"Where's Harry?" Mr. Thorburn came out of the back of the farmhouse. He stood in the 1 middle of the well-kept farmyard. "Here, Harry!" he shouted. "Hi, Harry!"

He stood leaning on a stick and holding a letter in his hand as he looked round the farmyard.

2 Mr. Thorburn was a red-faced, powerful man; he wore knee breeches and black leather gaiters.[1] His face and well-fleshed body told you at a glance that Thorburn's Farm had not done too badly during the twenty years of his married life.

Harry, a fair-haired boy, came running across the yard.

"Harry," said the farmer to his son, "here's a letter come for old Michael. It will be about this visit he's to pay to his sick brother.

---
1. **gaiters:** coverings worn over shoes, and sometimes, as here, the calves of the legs.

3 Nice time of year for this to happen, I must say. You'd better take the letter to him at once."

"Where to?" said Harry.

4 "He's up on the hill, of course," said the farmer. "In his hut, or with the sheep some-
5 where. Your own brains could have told you that. Can't you ever use them? Go on, now."

"Right," said Harry. He turned to go.

"Don't take all day," said his father.

Mr. Thorburn stood looking after his son. He leaned heavily on the thorn stick which he always carried. Harry went through the gate in the low gray wall which ran round one side of 6 the yard, where there were no buildings. Directly he left the farmyard, he began to climb. Thorburn's Farm was at the end of a valley. Green fields lay in front of it, and a wide road sloped gently down to the village a mile away; behind, the hill soared up, and high on the ridge of the hill was Michael's hut, three miles off, and climbing all the way.

208 SHORT STORIES

MOTIVATIONAL SUMMARY

Harry feels like he can't do anything right, at least to suit his father. Running a successful sheep farm has required Harry's father to be capable and clever: the very qualities he despairs of finding in his son. Stung by his father's constant criticism, Harry himself fears he will never measure up. But when Old Michael, the most experienced shepherd, must be absent, Harry ends up taking his place. This, Harry thinks, may be his chance to prove himself to his father.

PRESENTATION

"The Erne from the Coast" is a story of great internal, as well as external, conflict that must be seen in the context of its setting. Survival on the mountainous coast of 1920s England was a struggle for the people who lived there. Al-

VISUAL CONNECTIONS
Exploring the Subject
Shown in the picture is a sheep farm in the same type of hilly terrain in which the story is set. Enclosures such as the circular pen in the foreground may be used for isolating newborn lambs and their mothers to allow bonding or to hold richer food for young lambs (with a narrow grate in the opening to prevent entry of grown sheep).

7
"Slip of a boy" implies youth, lightness, smallness.

8
Characterization. Shows Harry's overeagerness to please his father, also his youthful and ill-planned exuberance.

9
"Coltish" refers to a young horse; implies unbridled youth.

10 Finding Details
What details help give a sense of an almost primitive rural setting? The baker's cart and stone walls.

11
Repeated emphasis on earth tones: especially gray (boulders) and brown (like bracken, earth).

12
The time stresses the isolation of hut from farm.

13
"Lambing season" is spring, the time of year lambs are born.

Harry was thirteen, very yellow-haired and
7 blue-eyed. He was a slip of a boy. It seemed unlikely that he could ever grow into such a stolid, heavy man as his father. Mr. Thorburn was every pound of fourteen stone,[2] as the men on the farm could have told you the day he broke his leg and they had to carry him back to the farmhouse on a hurdle.[3]
8 Harry started off far too fast, taking the lower slopes almost at a run. His body was
9 loose in its movements, and coltish, and by the time the real work began he was already tiring. However, the April day was fresh and rainy, and the cold of it kept him going. Gray gusts and showers swept over the hillside, and between them, with changing light, came faint gleams of sunshine, so that the shadows of the clouds raced along the hill beside him. Presently he cleared the gorse and heather[4] and came out on to the open hillside, which was bare except for short, tussocky grass.[5] His home began to look far-off beneath him. He could see his mother walking down towards
10 the village with one of the dogs, and the baker's cart coming up from the village towards
11 her. The fields were brown and green round the farmhouse, and the buildings were gray, with low stone walls.
12 He stopped several times to look back on the small distant farm. It took him well over an hour to reach the small hut where Michael lived by day and slept during most nights
13 throughout the lambing season. He was not in his hut, but after a few minutes' search Harry found him. Michael was sitting without movement, watching the sheep and talking to his gray-and-white dog. He had a sack across his

---

2. **stone:** a unit of weight used in Great Britain, equal to 14 pounds (about 6 kilograms).
3. **hurdle:** here, a movable framework of twigs, used to enclose sheep.
4. **gorse and heather** (hĕ*th*′ər): low-growing shrubs found in the highlands of Great Britain.
5. **tussocky** (tŭs′ək-ē) **grass:** grass growing in clumps.

The Erne from the Coast 209

though Mr. Thorburn is a prosperous man, he most likely had to work very hard to achieve this security and must continue to struggle, as his concerns for his farm reveal. The initiation rite that Harry experiences reflects the severity of this life; killing may be seen as an appropriate means of proving manhood in this place, where physical prowess might be necessary for survival. In the end, Harry wins the love and respect he deserved from his father all along.

VISUAL CONNECTIONS
Exploring the Subject
A newborn lamb is soft, cuddly, and almost totally helpless. It must depend on its mother for nourishment and protection until it can walk steadily.

14
Simile. Comparison of Michael to a rock underscores his close connection to the earth.

15
Michael's country ways include his accent and dispensing with chitchat like saying "hello."

16
Michael's solemn look at letter makes reader think he can read.

17
Michael is wise but cannot read.

18
Vivid description relies on natural, rustic **imagery.**

19
Echoing Michael's comment shows Harry's admiration.

20
Michael's earlier prediction that sun would come out shows knowledge of nature.

21
Harry considers reading a simple and basic skill.

22
Conflict. Harry realizes that his father finds him exasperating; undermines his own self-esteem.

23
"Tortoise-shell" refers to cat's markings, resembling circular lines on turtle's back.

14 shoulders, which made him look rather like a rock with gray lichen on it. He looked up at Harry without moving.
15 "It's a hildy wildy day," he said, "but there'll be a glent of sunsheen yet."
16 Harry handed Michael the letter. Michael looked at it, and opened it very slowly, and spread the crackling paper out on his knee with brown hands. Harry watched him for some minutes as he studied the letter in silence.
    "Letter'll be aboot my brother," said Michael at length. "I'm to goa and see him." He handed
17 the letter to Harry. "Read it, Harry," he said. Harry read the letter to him twice.
    "Tell thy dad," said Michael, "I'll be doon at farm i' the morn. Happen[6] I'll be away three days. And tell him new lamb was born last neet, but it's sickly."
    They looked at the small white bundle that lay on the grass beside its mother, hardly moving.
    "'T'll pick up," said Michael. He slowly stood and looked round at the distance.
    Michael had rather long hair; it was between gray and white in color, and it blew in the
18 wind. It was about the hue of an old sheep's skull that has lain out on the bare mountain. Michael's clothes and face and hair made Harry feel that he had slowly faded out on the hillside. He was all the color of rain on the stones and last year's bracken.[7]
    "It'll make a change," said Michael, "going off and sleeping in a bed."
    "Goodbye," said Harry. "You'll be down at the farm tomorrow, then?"
    "Aw reet," said Michael.
19 "Aw reet," said Harry.
    Harry went slowly back to the farm. The

---

6. **Happen:** perhaps.
7. **bracken:** coarse ferns. "Last year's bracken" would be dried out and therefore brownish in color.

rain had cleared off, and the evening was sunny, with a watery light, by the time he was
20 home. Michael had been right. Harry gave his father the message, and told him about the lamb.
21 "It's a funny thing," said Harry, "that old Michael can't even read."
    "Don't you be so smart." said Mr. Thorburn. "Michael knows a thing or two you don't. You don't want to go muckering about with[8] an old fellow like Michael—best shepherd I've ever known."
22 Harry went away feeling somewhat abashed. Lately it seemed his father was always down on him, telling him he showed no sign of sense; telling him he ought to grow up a bit; telling him he was more like seven than thirteen.
    He went to the kitchen. This was a big stone-floored room with a huge plain table, where the whole household and several of the farm hands could sit down to dinner or tea at the same time. His mother and his aunt from the village were still lingering over their teacups, but there was no one else in the room except a
23 small tortoise-shell cat, which was pacing

---

8. **muckering about with:** getting in the way of; hindering.

MEETING INDIVIDUAL NEEDS
ESL/LEP • On p. 209, Harry is portrayed as "a slip of a boy." Explain the meaning of this idiom as "a young, slim person." Ask students to name other ways *slip* may be used as a noun.
   a *slip* of paper (small piece)
   a white *slip* (petticoat)
   a *slip* of the tongue (error; mistake)

---

round them asking for milk in a loud voice. The yellow evening light filled the room. His mother gave him tea and ham and bread and butter, and he ate it in silence, playing with the cat as he did so.

II

Next morning at nine o'clock there was a loud rap with a stick at the kitchen door, and there by the pump, with the hens running round his legs, stood Michael.

"Good morning, Mrs. Thorburn," he said. "Is Measter about?"

"Come on in with you," said Mrs. Thorburn, "and have a good hot cup o' tea. Have you eaten this morning?"

24 Michael clanked into the kitchen, his hobnails striking the flags,[9] and he sat down at one end of the table.

"Aye," he said, "I've eaten, Missus. I had a good thoom-bit[10] when I rose up, but a cup of tea would be welcome."

As he drank the tea, Mr. Thorburn came in, bringing Harry with him. Michael, thought Harry, always looked rather strange when he 25 was down in the village or in the farmhouse; rather as a pile of bracken or an armful of leaves would look if it were emptied out onto the parlor floor.

Michael talked to Mr. Thorburn about the sheep; about the new lamb; about young Bob, his nephew, who was coming over from another farm to look after the sheep while he was away.

"Tell en to watch new lamb." said Michael; "it's creachy.[11] I've put en in my little hut, and owd sheep is looking roun' t' doorway."

After his cup of tea Michael shook hands all round. Then he set off down to the village, 26 where he was going to fall in with a lift.

Soon after he had gone, Bob arrived at the farm. He was a tall young man with a freckled face and red hair, big-boned and very gentle in his voice and movements. He listened to all Mr. Thorburn's instructions and then set out for the shepherd's hut.

However, it seemed that Mr. Thorburn's 27 luck with his shepherds was dead out. For the next evening, just as it was turning dark, Bob walked into the farmhouse kitchen. His face was tense with pain, and he was nursing his left arm with his right hand. Harry saw the ugly distorted shape and swelling at the wrist. Bob had fallen and broken the wrist earlier in the day, and by evening the pain had driven him back.

28 "I'm sorry, Mr. Thorburn," he kept on saying. "I'm a big fule."

The sheep had to be left for that night. Next morning it was again a cold, windy day, and 29 clouds the color of gunmetal raced over the hill. The sun broke through fitfully, filling the valley with a steel-blue light in which the green 30 grass looked vivid. Mr. Thorburn decided to send Harry out to the shepherd's hut for the day and night.

"Happen old Michael will be back sometime tomorrow," he said. "You can look to the sheep, Harry, and see to that sick lamb for us. 31 It's a good chance to make yourself useful."

Harry nodded.

"You can feed the lamb. Bob said it didn't seem to suck enough, and you can let me know if anything else happens. And you can keep an eye on the other lambs and see they don't get 32 over the edges. There's no need to fold them at night; just let the dog round them up and see the flock is near the hut."

"There's blankets and everything in the hut, Harry," said Mrs. Thorburn, "and a spirit 33 lamp to make tea. You can't come to harm."

---

9. **flags:** here, flagstones, which are used in paving.
10. **thoom-bit:** a piece of meat eaten on bread.
11. **creachy:** sick.

24
Hobnails: nails put on shoe soles to give traction when climbing.

25 Making Generalizations
Where does Michael seem to belong? Out in the fields, where he blends with his surroundings.

26
"Fall in with a lift" means "to get a ride."

27
"Dead out" means "gone, lost."

28
Accident does not make him a fool; remark shows men here feel need to be strong at all times.

29
Imagery. "Gunmetal" and "steel-blue" suggest cold harshness of wild landscape.

30
Use to answer **study question 2,** p. 218.

31
Thorburn's suggestion shows that he doesn't often consider Harry to be useful.

32
Fold means "to place in a pen."

33
Irony. Harm will come.

The Erne from the Coast

MEETING INDIVIDUAL NEEDS
ESL/LEP • Beachcroft makes use of coastal dialect from 1920s England. Much of the dialogue can be understood from context. However, to aid in comprehension, list the following words on the chalkboard and ask the class to supply standard spellings.
p. 210:
glent of sunsheen—glint of sunshine
aboot—about
goa—go
doon—down

Aw reet—All right
p. 211:
Measter—Mister
en—him
fule—fool

34
Harry tries to emulate Michael.

35
At first sight, Harry sees bird only as an amazing natural event.

36
This is not an American eagle. Story takes place before eagles of any kind were endangered species.

37
Tassie immediately recognizes bird as enemy.

38
Tassie is intimidated; dog knows it's no match for bird.

39
Bird kills lamb only for survival; emphasizes hard, "natural" order of rural life.

40
Conflict. External conflict here is between Harry and a natural force.

41
Dog's chasing eagle shows dog's bravery and loyalty.

42 Finding Details
What details suggest how Harry feels at this point? He walks slowly; landscape is bare; dog is subdued.

43
Dog's actions mirror Harry's.

212

Harry set off up the hill and began to climb. Out on the hilltop it was very lonely, and the wind was loud and gusty, with sudden snatches of rain. The sheep kept near the wooden hut most of the time; it was built in the lee[12] of the ridge, and the best shelter was to be found near it. Harry looked after the sick lamb and brewed himself tea. He had Tassie, the gray and white sheep dog, for company. Time did **34** not hang heavy. When evening came he rounded up the sheep and counted them, and, true to advice that Michael had given him, he slept in his boots as a true shepherd does, warmly wrapped up in the rugs.

He was awakened as soon as it was light by the dog barking. He went out in the gray dawn light and found a rustle and agitation among the sheep. Tassie ran to him and back towards the sheep. The sheep were starting up alert, and showed a tendency to scatter. Harry looked round, wondering what the trouble was. Then he saw. A bird was hovering over the flock, and it was this that had attracted the sheep's attention. But what bird was it? It hovered like a hawk, soaring on outstretched wings; yet it was much too big for a hawk. As the bird came nearer Harry was astonished at its size. Once or twice it approached and then went soaring and floating away again. It was larger than any bird he had ever seen before—
35 brownish in color, with a gray head and a hawk's beak.

Suddenly the bird began to drop as a hawk drops. A knot of sheep dashed apart. Tassie rushed towards the bird, his head down and his tail streaming out behind him. Harry fol-
36 lowed. This must be an eagle, he thought. He saw it, looking larger still now it was on the ground, standing with outstretched wings over a lamb.

37 Tassie attacked, snarling in rage. The eagle rose at him. It struck at him with its feet and a flurry of beating wings. The dog was thrown back. He retreated slowly, snarling savagely as he went, his tail between his legs. He was **38** frightened now, and uncertain what to do.

The eagle turned back to the lamb, took it in **39** its talons again, and began to rise. It could not move quickly near the ground, and Harry **40** came up with it. At once the eagle put the lamb on a rock and turned on him. He saw its talons driving towards his face, claws and spurs of steel—a stroke could tear your eyes out. He put up his arms in fear, and he felt the rush of wings round his face. With his arm above his head he sank on one knee.

When he looked up again, the eagle was back on the lamb. It began to fly with long slow wingbeats. At first it scarcely rose, and flew with the lamb almost on the ground.

Harry ran, throwing a stone. He shouted. **41** Tassie gave chase, snapping at the eagle as it went. But the eagle was working towards a chasm, a sheer drop in the hillside where no one could follow it. In another moment it was floating in the air, clear and away. Then it rose higher, and headed towards the coast, which was a few miles away over the hill.

Harry stood and watched it till it was out of sight. When it was gone, he turned and walked slowly back to the hut. There was not a sound to be heard now except the sudden rushes of wind. The hillside was bare and coverless ex-**42** cept for the scattered black rocks. Tassie walked beside him. The dog was very subdued **43** and hardly glanced to right or left.

It took some time to round the sheep up, or to find, at least, where the various parts of the flock had scattered themselves. The sick lamb and its mother had been enclosed all this time in a fold near the hut. The ewe[13] was still terrified.

---

12. **in the lee:** on the protected side.

13. **ewe** (yo͞o): a female sheep.

212 SHORT STORIES

An hour later Harry set off down the mountainside to the farm. Tassie looked after him doubtfully. He ran several times after him, but Harry sent him back to the hut.

It was the middle of the morning when Harry came back to the farmyard again. His father was standing in the middle of the yard, leaning on his stick, and giving advice to one of his cowmen. He broke off when he saw Harry come in through the gate and walk towards him across the farmyard.

"Well," he said, "anything wrong, Harry? I thought you were going to stay till Michael came back."

"We've lost a lamb," said Harry, breathlessly. "It's been carried off by an eagle. It must have been an eagle."

"An eagle?" said Mr. Thorburn. He gave a laugh which mocked Harry. "Why didn't you stop it?"

"I tried," said Harry. "But I . . ."

Mr. Thorburn was in a bad mood. He had sold some heifers[14] the day before at a disappointing price. He had had that morning a letter from the builders about repairs to some of the farm buildings, and there was work to be done which he could hardly afford. He was worried about Michael's absence. He felt as if the world were bearing down on him and he had too many burdens to support.

He suddenly shouted at Harry, and his red face turned darker red.

"That's a lie!" he said. "There's been no eagle here in my lifetime. What's happened? Go on—tell me."

Harry stood before him. He looked at his father, but said nothing.

"You've lost that lamb," said Thorburn. "Let it fall down a hole or something. Any child from the village could have watched those sheep for a day. Then you're frightened and come back here and lie to me."

Harry still said nothing.

"Come here," said Thorburn suddenly. He caught him by the arm and turned him round. "I'll teach you not to lie to me," he said. He raised his stick and hit Harry as hard as he could; then again and again.

"It's true," began Harry, and then cried out with pain at the blows.

At the third or fourth blow he wrenched himself away. Thorburn let him go. Harry walked away as fast as he could, through the gate and out of the yard without looking round.

"Next time it will be a real beating," his father shouted after him. "Bring the eagle back, and then I'll believe you."

III

As soon as Harry was through the gate, he turned behind one of the barns where he was out of sight from the yard. He stood trembling and clenching his fists. He found there were tears on his face, and he forced himself not to cry. The blows hurt, yet they did not hurt very seriously. He would never have cried for that. But it had been done in front of another man. The other man had looked on, and he and his father had been laughing as he had almost run away. Harry clenched his fists; even now they were still talking about him.

He began to walk and then run up the hillside toward the hut. When he reached it, he was exhausted. He flung himself on the mattress and punched it again and again and clenched his teeth.

The day passed and nobody came from the farm. He began to feel better, and presently a new idea struck him, and with it a new hope. He prayed now that old Michael would not return today; that he would be able to spend an-

---

14. **heifers** (hĕf′ərz): young cows.

SOCIAL STUDIES LINK
Have students find out about sheep dogs like Tassie and other types of working dogs. Encourage them to learn about how the dogs work, where they are used today, and so on. Have students share their information with the class.

52
Use to answer **study question 5a**, p. 218.

53 Analyzing
Why does Harry think he must kill the eagle? Harry thinks only of his father's challenge.

54
Mrs. Thorburn evidently does not believe Harry either.

55
Irony. Great harm will occur: to Tassie, another lamb, the eagle, and Harry.

56
Conflict. Harry's internal conflict lies in his self-criticism; he is obsessed with father's disappointment in him.

57
Use to answer **study question 5b**, p. 218.

58
Bird's second appearance differs from first. Harry now sees it as powerful enemy.

59
Appropriate epitaph for Tassie.

---

52 other night alone in the hut; and that the eagle would come back next morning and attack the sheep again, and give him one more chance.

Harry went out and scanned the gray sky, and then knelt down on the grass and prayed for the eagle to come. Tassie, the gray and white sheep dog, looked at him questioningly. Soon it was getting dark, and he walked about the hill and rounded up the sheep. He counted the flock, and all was well. Then he looked round for a weapon. There was no gun in the hut, but he found a thick stave[15] tipped with metal, part of some broken tool that had been thrown aside. He poised the stave in his hand and swung it; it was just a good weight to hit 53 with. He would have to go straight at the eagle without hesitation and break its skull. After thinking about this for some time, he made himself tea, and ate some bread and butter and cold meat.

Down at the farm Mr. Thorburn in the evening told his wife what had happened. He was 54 quite sure there had been no eagle. Mrs. Thorburn did not say much, but she said it was an extraordinary thing for Harry to have said. She told her husband that he ought not to have beaten the boy, but should have found out what the trouble really was.

55 "But I dare say there is no great harm done," she ended, philosophically.

Harry spent a restless night. He slept and lay awake by turns, but, sleeping or waking, he was tortured by the same old images. He saw all the events of the day before. He saw how the eagle had first appeared above him; how it had attacked; how it had driven off Tassie and then him. He remembered his fear, and he planned again just how he could attack the eagle when it came back. Then he thought of himself going down towards the farm, and he saw again the scene with his father.

15. **stave:** a stick of wood.

56 All night long he saw these pictures and other scenes from his life. In every one of them he had made some mistake; he had made himself look ridiculous, and grown men had laughed at him. He had failed in strength or in common sense; he was always disappointing himself and his father. He was too young for 57 his age. He was still a baby.

So the night passed. Early in the morning he heard Tassie barking.

He jumped up, fully clothed, and ran outside the hut. The cold air made him shiver; but he saw at once that his prayer had been answered. There was the eagle, above him, and already dropping down towards the sheep. It floated, poised on huge wings. The flock stood nervously huddled. Suddenly, as before, the attacker plunged towards them. They scattered, running in every direction. The eagle followed and swooped on one weakly running lamb. At once it tried to rise again, but its heavy wingbeats took it along the earth. Near the ground it seemed cumbersome and awkward. Tassie was after it like a flash; Harry seized his weapon, the stave tipped with iron, and followed. When Tassie caught up with the eagle it turned and faced him, standing over the lamb.

Harry, as he ran, could see blood staining the white wool of the lamb's body; the eagle's wings were half spread out over it and moving 58 slowly. The huge bird was grayish-brown with a white head and tail. The beak was yellow and the legs yellow and scaly.

It lowered its head, and with a fierce movement threatened Tassie; then, as the dog approached, it began to rock and stamp from foot to foot in a menacing dance; then it opened its beak and gave its fierce, yelping cry. Tassie hung back, his ears flattened against his head, snarling, creeping by inches towards the 59 eagle; he was frightened, but he was brave. Then he ran in to attack.

214 SHORT STORIES

The eagle left the lamb. With a lunging spring it aimed heavily at Tassie. It just cleared the ground and beat about Tassie with its wings, hovering over him. Tassie flattened out his body to the earth and turned his head upwards with snapping jaws. But the eagle was over him and on him, its talons plunged into his side, and a piercing scream rang out. The eagle struck deliberately at the dog's skull three times; the beak's point hammered on his head, striking downwards and sideways. Tassie lay limp on the ground, and, where his head had been, a red mixture of blood and brains flowed on the grass. When Harry took his eyes away from the blood, the eagle was standing on the lamb again.

Harry approached the eagle slowly, step by step. He gripped his stick firmly as he came. The eagle put its head down. It rocked on its feet as if preparing to leap. Behind the terrific beak, sharp as metal, was a shallow head, flat and broad as a snake's, glaring with light yellow un-animal eyes. The head and neck made weaving movements towards him.

At a pace or two from the eagle Harry stood still. In a second he would make a rush. He could break the eagle's skull, he told himself, with one good blow; then he could avenge Tassie and stand up to his father.

But he waited too long. The eagle tried to rise, and with its heavy sweeping beats was beginning to gain speed along the ground. Harry ran, stumbling over the uneven ground, among boulders and outcroppings of rock, trying to strike at the eagle as he went. But as soon as the eagle was in the air it was no longer heavy and clumsy. There was a sudden rush of wings and buffeting about his head as the eagle turned to drive him off. For a second he saw the talons sharp as metal, backed by the metal strength of the legs, striking at his face. He put up his arm. At once it was seared with a red-hot pain, and he could see the blood rush out.

He stepped back, and back again. The eagle, after this one fierce swoop at him, went round in a wide, low circle and returned to the lamb. Harry saw that his coat sleeve was in ribbons, and that blood was running off the ends of his fingers and falling to the ground.

He stood panting; the wind blew across the empty high ground. The sheep had vanished from sight. Tassie lay dead nearby, and he was utterly alone on the hills. There was nobody to watch what he did. The eagle might hurt him, but it could not jeer at him. He attacked it again, but already the eagle with its heavy wingbeats had cleared the ground; this time it took the lamb with it. Harry saw that it meant to fly, as it had flown yesterday, to an edge; and then out into the free air over the chasm, and over the valley far below.

Harry gave chase, stumbling over the broken ground and between the boulders—striking at the eagle as he went, trying to beat it down before it could escape. The eagle was hampered by his attack; and suddenly it swooped onto a projection of rock and turned again to drive him off. Harry was now in a bad position. The eagle stood on a rock at the height of his own shoulders, with the lamb beside it. It struck at his chest with its talons, beating its wings as it did so. Harry felt clothes and flesh being torn; buffeting blows began about his head, but he kept close to the eagle and struck at it again. He did not want simply to frighten it away, but to kill it. The eagle fought at first simply to drive Harry off; then, as he continued to attack, it became ferocious.

Harry saw his only chance was to keep close to the eagle and beat it down; but already it was at the height of his face. It struck at him from above, driving its steel claws at him, beating its wings about him. He was dazed by the buffeting which went on and on all round him; then with an agonizing stab he felt the claws seize and pierce his shoulder and neck. He

The Erne from the Coast

VISUAL CONNECTIONS
Exploring the Subject
An erne in full attack is an awe-inspiring sight. The bird can be described as a large, white-tailed European eagle *(Haliaetus albicilla)*. It usually flies low over the ocean or over rivers and streams that empty into larger bodies of water and snatches up trout, salmon, or other big fish. The erne is related to the bald eagle (the American symbol, called *Haliaetus leucocephalus* for its white-feathered head and neck) and shares with it characteristics such as a large, high-arched beak and bare lower legs. Ernes usually rely on fish for food and have special small spikes on their toepads to help them in grasping slippery prey. In some cases, though, these birds or prey will hunt small animals, which may include young domesticated animals such as lambs. Eagles are strong, but not fast. They prefer live prey, which they surprise and overwhelm by swift, savage attacks and carry off in their strong, sharp talons.

67
Harry now fights for sight and for life, not just pride.

68
Plot. Climax occurs as Harry realizes he has won battle.

69
Harry's triumph, like earlier humiliation, is witnessed by father and another adult.

struck upwards desperately and blindly. As the eagle drove its beak at his head, his stick just turned the blow aside. The beak struck a glancing blow off the stick and tore away his eyebrow.

Harry found that something was blinding him, and he felt a new sickening fear that already one of his eyes was gone. The outspread beating wings and weight of the eagle dragged **67** him about, and he nearly lost his footing. He had forgotten, now, that he was proving anything to his father; he was fighting for his eyes. Three times he fended off the hammer stroke of the beak, and at these close quarters the blows of his club found their mark. He caught the eagle's head each time, and the bird was half stunned.

Harry, reeling and staggering, felt the grip of the claws gradually loosen, and almost unbelievably the body of his enemy sagged, half fluttering to the ground. With a sudden spurt of new strength, Harry attacked and rained blows on the bird's skull. The eagle struggled, and he followed, beating it down among the **68** rocks. At last the eagle's movements stopped. He saw its skull was broken and that it lay dead.

He stood for many minutes panting and unmoving, filled with a tremendous excitement; then he sat on a boulder. The fight had taken him near a steep edge a long way from the body of Tassie.

His wounds began to ache and burn. The sky and the horizon spun round him, but he forced himself to be firm and collected. After a while he stooped down and hoisted the eagle onto his shoulder. The wings dropped loosely down in front and behind. He set off towards the farm.

IV

When he reached his home, the low gray walls, the plowed fields, and the green pasture fields were swimming before his eyes in a dizzy pattern. It was still the early part of the morning, but there was plenty of life in the farmyard, as usual. Some cows were being driven out. One of the carthorses was standing harnessed to a **69** heavy wagon. Harry's father was talking to the carter and looking at the horse's leg.

When they saw Harry come towards them, they waited, unmoving. They could hardly see

WRITING LINK
Encourage interested students to think of Harry as a father or grandfather sitting by his fireplace many years later and telling his children or grandchildren about the events in the story. Have students write Harry's monologue or a dialogue between Harry and one of the children.

---

at first who or what it was. Harry came up and dropped the bird at his father's feet. His coat was gone. His shirt hung in bloodstained rags about him; one arm was caked in blood; his right eyebrow hung in a loose flap, with the blood still oozing stickily down his cheek.

"Harry!" said Thorburn, catching him by the arm as he reeled.

He led the boy into the kitchen. There they gave him a glass of brandy and sponged him with warm water. There was a deep long wound in his left forearm. His chest was crisscrossed with cuts. The flesh was torn away from his neck where the talons had sunk in.

Presently the doctor came. Harry's wounds began to hurt like fire, but he talked excitedly. **70** He was happier than he had ever been in his life. Everybody on the farm came in to see him and to see the eagle's body.

All day his father hung about him, looking into the kitchen every half-hour. He said very little but asked Harry several times how he felt. **71** "Are you aw reet?" he kept saying. Once he took a cup of tea from his wife and carried it across the kitchen in order to give it to Harry with his own hands.

Later in the day old Michael came back, and Harry told him the whole story. Michael turned the bird over. He said it was an erne, a white-tailed sea eagle from the coast. He measured the wingspan, and it was seven and a half feet. Michael had seen two or three when he was a boy—always near the coast—but this one, he said, was easily the largest.

72 Three days later Mr. Thorburn took Harry, still stiff and bandaged, down to the village **73** inn. There he set him before a blazing fire all the evening, and in the presence of men from every cottage and farm Thorburn praised his son. He bought him a glass of beer and made Harry tell the story of his fight to everyone.

As he told it, Thorburn sat by him, hearing the story himself each time, making certain that Harry missed nothing about his struggle. Afterwards every man drank Harry's health, and clapped Thorburn on the back and told him he ought to be proud of his son.

Later, in the silent darkness, they walked back to the farm again, and neither of them **74** could find anything to say. Harry wondered if his father might not refer to the beating and apologize. Thorburn moved round the house, raking out fires and locking up. Then he picked up the lamp and, holding it above his head, led the way upstairs.

"Good night, Harry," said his father at last, as he took him to his bedroom door. "Are you aw reet?"

His father held the lamp up and looked into Harry's face. As the lamplight fell on it, he nodded. He said nothing more.

75 "Aye," said Harry, as he turned into his bedroom door, "I'm aw reet."

Reading Check

1. At what time of year does the story take place?
2. How is Michael employed by Mr. Thorburn?
3. Why does Michael have to leave?
4. Why is Bob unable to look after the flock?
5. Why does Mr. Thorburn beat Harry?
6. Who or what is Tassie?
7. What is unusual about the eagle in this story?
8. Where does Harry's battle with the eagle take place?
9. What weapon does Harry use against the bird?
10. Why is Harry happy at the end of the story?

The Erne from the Coast 217

---

70 Finding Cause and Effect *Why is Harry happy?* He is now the center of attention, particularly his father's; he has earned his father's respect.

71 Use to answer **study question 6,** page 218.

72 Harry's triumph is costly, however. Tassie was killed and Harry wounded in killing eagle.

73 Harry gains acceptance and respect from father and village men.

74 Thorburn is unable to apologize directly.

75 Harry demonstrates his newfound confidence, indicating that his **internal conflict** over self-worth is resolved.

READING CHECK
1. Spring (April) (p. 209).
2. Tends sheep (p. 208).
3. His brother is sick (p. 208).
4. His wrist is broken (p. 211).
5. Thinks Harry is lying; angry about lost lamb (p. 213).
6. The sheepdog (p. 212).
7. Not usually seen in area; very large one (p. 212).
8. On steep edge of hill (p. 215).
9. Stave (stick) (p. 214).
10. Earned father's respect and developed sense of self-worth (p. 217).

FOR STUDY AND DISCUSSION

1. Fights eagle alone; has courage and strength of man; "aw reet" at end shows new confidence.
2. Michael has to visit sick brother; Bob breaks wrist.
3. Father accuses Harry of not using brains; father criticizes Harry for remark about Michael's not being able to read; says for Harry to make himself useful by watching sheep (implies that he usually isn't); father accuses Harry of lying about eagle to hide loss of lamb and beats him.
4. His pride is injured; he was beaten in front of another man.
5a. Wants to conquer own doubts; prove himself. 5b. Sees his own failures.
6. Shows concern about Harry's wounds; takes Harry to inn and boasts of his courage.
7. Victory over erne; raises his self-esteem and gains father's approval.

LITERARY ELEMENTS

1. Father thinks Harry doesn't use brains, is useless, and lied about eagle to excuse loss of lamb.
2. Other **external conflict** is with erne.
3. **Climax:** killing of eagle.
4. Solves **internal conflicts** by building self-confidence; solves **external conflicts** by earning father's respect.

LANGUAGE AND VOCABULARY

1. *Hildy-wildy:* "windy, cloudy, threatening rain." *Glent of sunsheen:* "glint of sunshine." *Fule:* "fool." *Aw reet:* "all right."

218

For Study and Discussion

Analyzing and Interpreting the Story

1. Some characters are the same at the end of a story as they are at the beginning. Other characters change as a result of the experiences they undergo. At the beginning of this story, Harry has no confidence in himself. How do you know at the end of the story that he has changed?

2. Taking care of the sheep is not Harry's responsibility. How does he come to assume that job?

3. From Harry's point of view, "his father was always down on him, telling him he showed no sign of sense; telling him he ought to grow up a bit; telling him he was more like seven than thirteen" (page 210). Find three incidents in the story that confirm Harry's judgment.

4. After Mr. Thorburn beats Harry, you learn that "the blows hurt, yet they did not hurt very seriously. He would never have cried for that." Why, then, are there tears on Harry's face?

5a. Why does Harry pray for the eagle to return? b. What does Harry find out about himself during the restless night he spends on the mountain?

6. When Harry and his father return from the village inn, Harry wonders if his father will apologize for beating him. Has Mr. Thorburn already apologized in some way? Explain.

7. Harry wins two victories in this story. What are they?

Literary Elements

Understanding Conflict and Plot

Conflict

In most stories the characters are involved in some sort of problem or struggle called a conflict. Sometimes the characters are involved in more than one conflict.

A conflict with a person, with an animal, or with some force of nature is known as an **external conflict.** What is Harry's conflict with his father? What other external conflict is there in "The Erne from the Coast"?

In addition to these external conflicts, Harry has to overcome his feelings of shame and inadequacy. He also has to struggle against panic when he fights the eagle. Struggles within a character are known as **internal conflicts.**

Plot

The sequence of incidents or actions that make up a story is known as the **plot.** Once the conflict or conflicts of a story have been established, the reader wants to know how things will turn out. The author chooses events that develop the conflict to a peak, or **climax,** and that provide an ending, or **resolution,** to the conflict.

One way to recognize the climax of a story is to look for the moment of most intense, exciting action. Which event is the climax in "The Erne from the Coast"? How does it solve Harry's internal and external conflicts?

Language and Vocabulary

Understanding Dialect

Writers use regional expressions to make the backgrounds and characters of their stories seem authentic. A number of the expressions in Beachcroft's story belong to the **dialect**—the regional variety of English—spoken in the sheep country of Great Britain. The words *thoom-bit* and *creachy* have been defined for you in footnotes. What do you think *hildy-wildy, glent of sunsheen, fule,* and *aw reet* mean?

218 SHORT STORIES

CLOSURE

Ask students to identify the internal and the external **conflicts** that Harry faces in this story. How does he resolve each of these?

EXTENSION AND ENRICHMENT

Remind students that most people have experiences that change them. Tell the class that these events need not be as dramatic as battling an eagle. For a young child, something as simple as walking to school alone for the first time can dramatically increase self-confidence. Ask students to discuss events and achievements that have been significant to them.

Writing About Literature

▶ **Showing How Conflict is Developed and Resolved**

You have seen that there is more than one conflict in "The Erne from the Coast." Choose one of Harry's conflicts: the conflict with his father, the conflict with the eagle, or his inner conflict. Show how this conflict develops in the story and how it is resolved. Cite specific evidence from the story to support your statements. Plan your essay before writing, and include a *thesis statement,* such as this one:

> Harry's relationship with his father worsens progressively until Harry's courage and determination change his father's attitude.

Focus on Writing a Short Story

Finding a Story Idea

At the end of "The Erne from the Coast," Thorburn has his son Harry tell everyone at the inn the true story of the fight with the eagle. Similarly, you can use your own experiences as the basis for a short story. You might get a good idea for a story, for example, from a daydream or a nightmare you had. A story idea might occur to you as you look at a magazine or a photograph album.

Another good way to find an idea for a short story is to play a "What if?" game. Imagine changes or new things such as the following:

What if I stowed away on a ship?
What if I shrank to one percent of my size?
What if I had a time machine?
What if I were trapped inside a computer?

Brainstorm with a partner or a small group of classmates and jot down some notes about ideas for short stories. Save your notes.

About the Author

T. O. Beachcroft (1902–1988)

T. O. Beachcroft was born in Clifton, England, and educated at Oxford University. In the 1920s, while he was working for the British Broadcasting Corporation (BBC) in London, several of his short stories were accepted for publication by literary magazines. This success later prompted him to collect the stories in a book called *A Young Man in a Hurry, and Other Stories* (1934). Over the next fifty years he wrote ten more books, including two studies on the art of the short story.

In *The Modest Art: A Survey of the Short Story in English* (1968), Beachcroft said that a short story often takes very little time to read. "Yet in those few minutes it may enter into the reader's mind, in a way which will never be forgotten. Plainly it must go deep to do this. It is not a trick. It is an encounter between two people—a passage of truth from one mind to another."

WRITING ABOUT LITERATURE

Students without extensive writing experience may need to be reminded that a *thesis statement* expresses a viewpoint that is supported through explanation and example.

FOCUS ON WRITING A SHORT STORY

As students work with partners or in small groups, suggest that they play a word association game to help them find short story ideas. Have one student in the group suggest a noun, such as *apple*. Then have the other members of the group offer "What if?" questions about an apple, such as "What if everything I ate tasted like an apple?" Each student in the group should suggest at least one noun.

ABOUT THE AUTHOR

Thomas Owen Beachcroft's short stories have been praised as being especially representative of the English short story. Several of his short stories have been included in well-respected anthologies such as *Introduction to Modern English and American Literature,* edited by Somerset Maugham, and a number of editions of the British *Best Stories of the Year.* Other works of his that have been published include poems and literary criticism.

▶ Before students begin this writing assignment, you may want to refer them to the **Writing About Literature** section on p. 688.

OBJECTIVES

The overall aim is for students to explain **foreshadowing** and how it is used to create **suspense**. For a complete list of objectives, see the **Teacher's Notes**.

VOCABULARY

The underlined words are in the Glossary. In addition, call students' attention to the vocabulary footnotes in their textbooks.

FOCUS / MOTIVATION

Discuss how a young person might feel as he or she arrives in a strange town to look for an apartment and begin a new job. In what ways would this situation be exciting? Threatening? How might it make a person vulnerable?

TEACHING RESOURCES B
Teacher's Notes, p. 120
Reading Check, p. 123
Study Guide, p. 124
Language Skills, p. 127
Building Vocabulary, p. 131
Selection Vocabulary Test, p. 132
Selection Test, p. 133

PREREADING FOCUS

The headnote emphasizes the literary elements of **suspense** and **foreshadowing**. You may want to discuss with the class ways in which stories, or movies and television shows, build suspense. Ask them to identify specific instances of foreshadowing in these stories or video presentations.

The Landlady

1
Imagery. "Deadly" and "blade" help create threatening atmosphere of the story.

2
Characterization. Billy's youth, the newness of his clothes, and his simple idealizing show he is beginning his career and is probably not very experienced.

3
Neglected houses warn of trouble inside.

4
Here *façade* refers to a housefront. Can also indicate pretense, a mask.

The Landlady

ROALD DAHL°

Uncertainty about what will happen next in a story is known as **suspense**. *To build up suspense, a writer will drop hints about what is to come. This use of clues is called* **foreshadowing**. *Watch for clues as you read Dahl's story.*

Billy Weaver had traveled down from London on the slow afternoon train, with a change at Reading on the way, and by the time he got to Bath it was about nine o'clock in the evening and the moon was coming up out of a clear starry sky over the houses opposite the station **1** entrance. But the air was deadly cold and the wind was like a flat blade of ice on his cheeks.

"Excuse me," he said, "but is there a fairly cheap hotel not too far away from here?"

"Try The Bell and Dragon," the porter answered, pointing down the road. "They might take you in. It's about a quarter of a mile along on the other side."

Billy thanked him and picked up his suitcase and set out to walk the quarter-mile to The Bell and Dragon. He had never been to Bath before. He didn't know anyone who lived there. But Mr. Greenslade at the Head Office in London had told him it was a splendid town. "Find your own lodgings," he had said, "and then go along and report to the Branch Manager as soon as you've got yourself settled."

2 Billy was seventeen years old. He was wearing a new navy-blue overcoat, a new brown trilby hat,[1] and a new brown suit, and he was feeling fine. He walked briskly down the street. He was trying to do everything briskly these days. Briskness, he had decided, was *the* one common characteristic of all successful businessmen. The big shots up at Head Office were absolutely fantastically brisk all the time. They were amazing.

There were no shops on this wide street that he was walking along, only a line of tall houses on each side, all of them identical. They had porches and pillars and four or five steps going up to their front doors, and it was obvious that once upon a time they had been very swanky **3** residences. But now, even in the darkness, he could see that the paint was peeling from the woodwork on their doors and windows, and **4** that the handsome white façades were cracked and blotchy from neglect.

Suddenly, in a downstairs window that was

° **Roald Dahl** (rō̄′äl däl).

1. **trilby hat:** a soft felt hat.

MOTIVATIONAL SUMMARY

Billy Weaver is an eager but not very experienced young man who has come to the city of Bath to begin a new job. His first requirement is to find a place to live. Billy thinks perhaps he might take rooms at a friendly pub. But he also wants to be very careful with his money, saving for the future. Then he sees a cozy-looking boardinghouse. The landlady is a little odd, but she greets him with a warm welcome; Billy thinks this may be the place for him.

PRESENTATION

As Alfred Hitchcock once noted, **suspense** depends upon the audience's awareness of danger before the story's characters even suspect it. In Roald Dahl's "The Landlady," the reader knows something is out of the ordinary from Billy

A view of Bath, England.

VISUAL CONNECTIONS
Exploring the Subject
The city of Bath is ancient and takes its name from its natural hot springs. According to legend, these were discovered in 863 B.C. by Bladud, the father of King Lear. Bladud's soaking in the steamy waters cured him of disease, and Bath gained a reputation as a health spa. The Romans built a huge marble spa, which was maintained for over 400 years until the town was destroyed by invading Saxons in 577 A.D. In 1702, Queen Anne visited the site and Bath's reputation as a fashionable health spa was reborn. (The fact that one usually goes to Bath for one's health was certainly known to the author of this story; it adds to the irony of Billy Weaver's fate.)

This picture shows a working-class district of Bath, with many row houses. These are houses, which, to save money, were built so that they share common side walls.

brilliantly illuminated by a streetlamp not six yards away, Billy caught sight of a printed notice propped up against the glass in one of the upper panes. It said BED AND BREAKFAST. There was a vase of yellow chrysanthemums, tall and beautiful, standing just underneath the notice.

5   He stopped walking. He moved a bit closer. Green curtains (some sort of velvety material) were hanging down on either side of the win-
6 dow. The chrysanthemums looked wonderful beside them. He went right up and peered through the glass into the room, and the first thing he saw was a bright fire burning in the
7 hearth. On the carpet in front of the fire, a pretty little dachshund was curled up asleep with its nose tucked into its belly. The room it-

self, so far as he could see in the half-darkness, was filled with pleasant furniture. There was a baby-grand piano and a big sofa and several plump armchairs; and in one corner he spot-
8 ted a large parrot in a cage. Animals were usually a good sign in a place like this, Billy told himself; and all in all, it looked to him as though it would be a pretty decent house to stay in. Certainly it would be more comfortable than The Bell and Dragon.

On the other hand, a pub² would be more congenial than a boardinghouse. There would be beer and darts in the evenings, and lots of people to talk to, and it would probably be a good bit cheaper, too. He had stayed a couple

2. **pub:** tavern or inn.

5
Short sentences emphasize the way Billy is drawn to window.

6
Use to answer **study question 2a,** p. 227.

7
Healthy-looking pets in household normally indicate kindness and compassion of person caring for them.

8
Irony. These animals are a sign, but one of danger.

Weaver's first notice of an unusual bed-and-breakfast sign. Billy is an unworldly and inexperienced youth, easily taken in by appearances. He does not suspect the strange sign, or other warnings. He suspects something is not right when he recognizes two previous guests' names in the register, but he overlooks danger signals all around him that the reader sees and understands. The reader watches as Billy's chances of escaping the landlady's "little nest" grow slimmer.

TRANSPARENCIES 17 & 18
Fine Art
Theme: *Building Blocks* — invites students to explore artworks that show how individual elements contribute to the whole.

9
The sign is mesmerizing. Words are like eyes, suggesting that someone or something hidden inside the house is watching and controlling him.

10
Landlady's quick actions show she may indeed have been watching Billy.

11
Polite phrase is more like a command; Billy obeys.

12
She seems to have expected him.

13
The trap becomes even more enticing.

14 Summarizing
What is Billy's first impression of the woman? She seems like a mother.

of nights in a pub once before and he had liked it. He had never stayed in any boardinghouses, and, to be perfectly honest, he was a tiny bit frightened of them. The name itself conjured up images of watery cabbage, rapacious[3] landladies, and a powerful smell of kippers[4] in the living room.

After dithering about[5] like this in the cold for two or three minutes, Billy decided that he would walk on and take a look at The Bell and Dragon before making up his mind. He turned to go.

And now a queer thing happened to him. **9** He was in the act of stepping back and turning away from the window when all at once his eye was caught and held in the most peculiar manner by the small notice that was there. BED AND BREAKFAST, it said. BED AND BREAKFAST, BED AND BREAKFAST, BED AND BREAKFAST. Each word was like a large black eye staring at him through the glass, holding him, compelling him, forcing him to stay where he was and not to walk away from that house, and the next thing he knew, he was actually moving across from the window to the front door of the house, climbing the steps that led up to it, and reaching for the bell.

He pressed the bell. Far away in a back room **10** he heard it ringing, and then *at once*—it must have been at once because he hadn't even had time to take his finger from the bell-button—the door swung open and a woman was standing there.

Normally you ring the bell and you have at least a half-minute's wait before the door opens. But this dame was like a jack-in-the-box. He pressed the bell—and out she popped! It made him jump.

She was about forty-five or fifty years old, and the moment she saw him, she gave him a warm welcoming smile.

"*Please* come in," she said pleasantly. She **11** stepped aside, holding the door wide open, and Billy found himself automatically starting forward. The compulsion or, more accurately, the desire to follow after her into that house was extraordinarily strong.

"I saw the notice in the window," he said, holding himself back.

"Yes, I know."

"I was wondering about a room."

"It's *all* ready for you, my dear," she said. **12** She had a round pink face and very gentle blue eyes.

"I was on my way to The Bell and Dragon." Billy told her. "But the notice in your window just happened to catch my eye."

"My dear boy," she said, "why don't you come in out of the cold?"

"How much do you charge?"

"Five and sixpence[6] a night, including breakfast."

It was fantastically cheap. It was less than **13** half of what he had been willing to pay.

"If that is too much," she added, "then perhaps I can reduce it just a tiny bit. Do you desire an egg for breakfast? Eggs are expensive at the moment. It would be sixpence less without the egg."

"Five and sixpence is fine," he answered. "I should like very much to stay here."

"I knew you would. Do come in." **14**

She seemed terribly nice. She looked exactly like the mother of one's best school friend welcoming one into the house to stay for the Christmas holidays. Billy took off his hat, and stepped over the threshold.

"Just hang it there," she said, "and let me help you with your coat."

---

3. **rapacious** (rə-pā′shəs): greedy; also, living on prey.
4. **kippers:** dried or smoked fish, regularly eaten for breakfast in Great Britain.
5. **dithering about:** hesitating.

6. **Five and sixpence:** about seventy-five cents at the time of the story.

MEETING INDIVIDUAL NEEDS
Visual Learners • Have students paint or draw the scene Billy sees through the window of the boarding house. Tell them to reread the description of the scene on p. 221 and then include as many of the author's details as they can.

---

15 There were no other hats or coats in the hall. There were no umbrellas, no walking sticks—nothing.

"We have it *all* to ourselves," she said, smiling at him over her shoulder as she led the way upstairs. "You see, it isn't very often I have the pleasure of taking a visitor into my little nest."

The old girl is slightly dotty, Billy told him-
16 self. But at five and sixpence a night, who gives a hang about that? "I should've thought you'd be simply swamped with applicants," he said politely.

"Oh, I am, my dear, I am, of course I am. But the trouble is that I'm inclined to be just a teeny-weeny bit choosy and particular—if you see what I mean."

"Ah, yes."

"But I'm always ready. Everything is always ready day and night in this house just on the off chance that an acceptable young gentleman will come along. And it is such a pleasure, my dear, such a very great pleasure when now and again I open the door and I see someone
17 standing there who is just *exactly* right." She was halfway up the stairs, and she paused with one hand on the stair rail, turning her head
18 and smiling down at him with pale lips. "Like you," she added, and her blue eyes traveled slowly all the way down the length of Bill's body, to his feet, and then up again.

On the second-floor landing she said to him, "This floor is mine."

They climbed up another flight. "And this one is *all* yours," she said. "Here's your room. I do hope you'll like it." She took him into a small but charming front bedroom, switching on the light as she went in.

"The morning sun comes right in the window, Mr. Perkins. It *is* Mr. Perkins, isn't it?"

"No," he said. "It's Weaver."

"Mr. Weaver. How nice. I've put a water bottle between the sheets to air them out, Mr. Weaver. It's such a comfort to have a hot water bottle in a strange bed with clean sheets, don't you agree? And you may light the gas fire at any time if you feel chilly."

"Thank you," Billy said. "Thank you ever so much." He noticed that the bedspread had been taken off the bed, and that the bedclothes had been neatly turned back on one side, all ready for someone to get in.

"I'm so glad you appeared," she said, looking earnestly into his face. "I was beginning to get worried."

"That's all right," Billy answered brightly.
19 "You mustn't worry about me." He put his suitcase on the chair and started to open it.

"And what about supper, my dear? Did you manage to get anything to eat before you came here?"

"I'm not a bit hungry, thank you," he said. "I think I'll just go to bed as soon as possible because tomorrow I've got to get up rather early and report to the office."

"Very well, then. I'll leave you now so that you can unpack. But before you go to bed, would you be kind enough to pop into the sitting room on the ground floor and sign the
20 book? Everyone has to do that because it's the law of the land, and we don't want to go breaking any laws at *this* stage in the proceedings, do we?" She gave him a little wave of the hand and went quickly out of the room and closed the door.

Now, the fact that his landlady appeared to be slightly off her rocker didn't worry Billy in
21 the least. After all, she not only was harmless—there was no question about that—but she was also quite obviously a kind and generous soul.
22 He guessed that she had probably lost a son in the war, or something like that, and had never gotten over it.

So a few minutes later, after unpacking his suitcase and washing his hands, he trotted downstairs to the ground floor and entered the

The Landlady 223

15
Foreshadowing. Hint that there is something wrong.

16
Desire for cheap room helps blind him to danger.

17
"Acceptable" and the "right" gentleman for *what* is not yet clear.

18
Her words and behavior should warn Billy that something is wrong.

19
Use to answer **study question 3b**, p. 227.

20
Foreshadowing. Hint that at some point a law will be broken.

21 Analyzing
Why does Billy think the landlady is harmless? He is still taken in by appearances, and a slight mental disorder seems a reasonable explanation of her strangeness.

22
Use to answer **study question 4a**, p. 227.

23
Billy should find it strange that the dog has not moved.

24
"Bit of all right" means good. His thoughts are ironic in light of what will soon happen.

25
Suspense. Created by Billy's inability to remember exactly where he has seen these names.

26
She holds tray away from her as if to avoid breathing the rising steam.

27
Tension builds as reader can guess why names are familiar but Billy cannot.

28
Foreshadowing. Another hint at Billy's fate. Resemblance to previous houseguests suggests he is in line for the same fate.

29
Irony. There is quite a lot "extraordinary about all this," but Billy doesn't add up the right details.

---

living room. His landlady wasn't there, but the fire was glowing in the hearth, and the little dachshund was still sleeping soundly in front of it. The room was wonderfully warm and cozy. I'm a lucky fellow, he thought, rubbing his hands. This is a bit of all right.

He found the guest book lying open on the piano, so he took out his pen and wrote down his name and address. There were only two other entries above his on the page, and, as one always does with guest books, he started to read them. One was a Christopher Mulholland from Cardiff. The other was Gregory W. Temple from Bristol.

That's funny, he thought suddenly. Christopher Mulholland. It rings a bell.

Now where on earth had he heard that rather unusual name before?

Was it a boy at school? No. Was it one of his sister's numerous young men, perhaps, or a friend of his father's? No, no, it wasn't any of those. He glanced down again at the book.

Christopher Mulholland
                      231 Cathedral Road, Cardiff
Gregory W. Temple
                      27 Sycamore Drive, Bristol

As a matter of fact, now he came to think of it, he wasn't at all sure that the second name didn't have almost as much of a familiar ring about it as the first.

"Gregory Temple?" he said aloud, searching his memory. "Christopher Mulholland? . . ."

"Such charming boys," a voice behind him answered, and he turned and saw his landlady sailing into the room with a large silver tea tray in her hands. She was holding it well out in front of her, and rather high up, as though the tray were a pair of reins on a frisky horse.

"They sound somehow familiar," he said.

"They do? How interesting."

"I'm almost positive I've heard those names before somewhere. Isn't that odd? Maybe it was in the newspapers. They weren't famous in any way, were they? I mean famous cricketers[7] or footballers or something like that?"

"Famous," she said, setting the tea tray down on the low table in front of the sofa. "Oh no, I don't think they were famous. But they were incredibly handsome, both of them, I can promise you that. They were tall and young and handsome, my dear, just exactly like you."

Once more, Billy glanced down at the book. "Look here," he said, noticing the dates. "This last entry is over two years old."

"It is?"

"Yes, indeed. And Christopher Mulholland's is nearly a year before that—more than *three years* ago."

"Dear me," she said, shaking her head and heaving a dainty little sigh. "I would never have thought it. How time does fly away from us all, doesn't it, Mr. Wilkins?"

"It's Weaver," Billy said. "W-e-a-v-e-r."

"Oh, of course it is!" she cried, sitting down on the sofa. "How silly of me. I do apologize. In one ear and out the other, that's me, Mr. Weaver."

"You know something?" Billy said. "Something that's really quite extraordinary about all this?"

"No, dear, I don't."

"Well, you see, both of these names—Mulholland and Temple—I not only seem to remember each one of them separately, so to speak, but somehow or other, in some peculiar way, they both appear to be sort of connected together as well. As though they were both famous for the same sort of thing, if you see what I mean—like . . . well . . . like Dempsey and

---

7. **cricketers:** Cricket is a popular national sport in Great Britain. It is played on a large field with bats, a ball, and wickets.

COOPERATIVE LEARNING
While they work in groups, have students make lists of words that describe Billy's personality (possible words: young, naive, trusting, inexperienced, innocent, frugal). Have them discuss how these characteristics get Billy in trouble.

TRANSPARENCY 21
Literary Elements
Evaluating Short Stories — helps students apply critical thinking skills to analyze a short story.

Tunney,[8] for example, or Churchill and Roosevelt."

30 "How amusing," she said. "But come over here now, dear, and sit down beside me on the sofa and I'll give you a nice cup of tea and a ginger biscuit before you go to bed."

"You really shouldn't bother," Billy said. "I didn't mean you to do anything like that." He stood by the piano, watching her as she fussed about with the cups and saucers. He noticed that she had small, white, quickly moving hands, and red fingernails.

"I'm almost positive it was in the newspapers I saw them," Billy said. "I'll think of it in a second. I'm sure I will."

There is nothing more tantalizing than a thing like this that lingers just outside the borders of one's memory. He hated to give up.

"Now wait a minute," he said. "Wait just a minute. Mulholland . . . Christopher Mulholland . . . wasn't *that* the name of the Eton schoolboy who was on a walking tour through the West Country, and then all of a sudden . . ."

"Milk?" she said. "And sugar?"

"Yes, please. And then all of a sudden . . ."

31 "Eton schoolboy?" she said. "Oh no, my dear, that can't possibly be right because *my* Mr. Mulholland was certainly not an Eton schoolboy when he came to me. He was a Cambridge undergraduate. Come over here now and sit next to me and warm yourself in front of this lovely fire. Come on. Your tea's all ready for you." She patted the empty place beside her on the sofa, and she sat there smiling at Billy and waiting for him to come over.

He crossed the room slowly, and sat down on the edge of the sofa. She placed his teacup on the table in front of him.

8. **Dempsey and Tunney:** Jack Dempsey and Gene Tunney, heavyweight boxing champions. Tunney defeated Dempsey in a fight for the world title in 1926, and again in 1927.

"*There* we are," she said. "How nice and cozy this is, isn't it?"

Billy started sipping his tea. She did the same. For half a minute or so, neither of them spoke. But Billy knew that she was looking at him. Her body was half turned toward him, and he could feel her eyes resting on his face, watching him over the rim of her teacup. Now 32 and again, he caught a whiff of a peculiar smell that seemed to emanate directly from her person. It was not in the least unpleasant, and it reminded him—well, he wasn't quite sure what it reminded him of. Pickled walnuts? New leather? Or was it the corridors of a hospital?

At length, she said, "Mr. Mulholland was a great one for his tea. Never in my life have I seen anyone drink as much tea as dear, sweet Mr. Mulholland."

"I suppose he left fairly recently," Billy said. He was still puzzling his head about the two names. He was positive now that he had seen them in the newspapers—in the headlines.

"Left?" she said, arching her brows. "But my dear boy, he never left. He's still here. Mr. Temple is also here. They're on the fourth 33 floor, both of them together."

Billy set his cup down slowly on the table and stared at his landlady. She smiled back at him, and then she put out one of her white hands and patted him comfortingly on the knee. "How old are you, my dear?" she asked.

"Seventeen."

"Seventeen!" she cried. "Oh, it's the perfect 34 age! Mr. Mulholland was also seventeen. But I think he was a trifle shorter than you are; in fact I'm sure he was, and his teeth weren't *quite* so white. You have the most beautiful teeth, Mr. Weaver, did you know that?"

"They're not as good as they look," Billy said. "They've got simply masses of fillings in them at the back."

"Mr. Temple, of course, was a little older," she said, ignoring his remark. "He was actually

---

30
She may find it amusing to watch him struggle to remember information that might save him.

31
She changes subject; she does not want him to realize why name is familiar.

32
He probably smells formaldehyde, a preservative used in taxidermy.

33 Finding Details
Why should Billy suspect something is wrong here? She had said that they were alone in the house.

34
He doesn't seem to notice that she's now talking of former guests in past tense.

The Landlady 225

35 Drawing Conclusions
How could she know his skin was perfect? She could not know this unless she had seen it.

36
Parrot is stuffed; the reader can suspect Billy's fate.

37
He tastes something unusual in the tea but does not guess it is poison.

38
Inference. Billy's fate will be same as two previous victims'.

READING CHECK
1. Head Office recommended it (p. 220).
2. Briskness (p. 220).
3. It will be comfortable (p. 221).
4. They are stuffed (p. 226).
5. Names in newspapers; both have disappeared (p. 225).

---

twenty-eight. And yet I never would have guessed it if he hadn't told me, never in my whole life. There wasn't a *blemish* on his body."

"A what?" Billy said.

"His skin was *just* like a baby's."

There was a pause. Billy picked up his teacup and took another sip of his tea, then he set it down again gently in its saucer. He waited for her to say something else, but she seemed to have lapsed into another of her silences. He sat there staring straight ahead of him into the far corner of the room, biting his lower lip.

36 "That parrot," he said at last. "You know something? It had me completely fooled when I first saw it through the window. I could have sworn it was alive."

"Alas, no longer."

"It's most terribly clever the way it's been done," he said. "It doesn't look in the least bit dead. Who did it?"

"I did."

"*You* did?"

"Of course," she said. "And have you met my little Basil as well?" She nodded toward the dachshund curled up so comfortably in front of the fire. Billy looked at it. And suddenly, he realized that this animal had all the time been just as silent and motionless as the parrot. He put out a hand and touched it gently on the top of its back. The back was hard and cold, and when he pushed the hair to one side with his fingers, he could see the skin underneath, grayish-black and dry and perfectly preserved.

"Good gracious me," he said. "How absolutely fascinating." He turned away from the dog and stared with deep admiration at the little woman beside him on the sofa. "It must be most awfully difficult to do a thing like that."

"Not in the least," she said. "I stuff *all* my little pets myself when they pass away. Will you have another cup of tea?"

"No, thank you," Billy said. The tea tasted **37** faintly of bitter almonds, and he didn't much care for it.

"You did sign the book, didn't you?"

"Oh, yes."

"That's good. Because later on, if I happen to forget what you were called, then I could always come down here and look it up. I still do that almost every day with Mr. Mulholland and Mr. . . . Mr. . . . ."

"Temple," Billy said. "Gregory Temple. Excuse my asking, but haven't there been *any* other guests here except them in the last two or three years?"

Holding her teacup high in one hand, inclining her head slightly to the left, she looked up at him out of the corners of her eyes and gave him another gentle little smile.

38 "No, my dear," she said. "Only you."

Reading Check
1. Why has Billy Weaver come to Bath?
2. What is the quality Billy Weaver believes is common to all successful businessmen?
3. What does Billy think will be the advantage of staying at a boardinghouse?
4. What does Billy discover about the animals in the living room?
5. Why do the names in the guest book sound familiar to Billy?

PORTFOLIO ASSESSMENT

Some students may be interested in writing a sequel to "The Landlady" in which they tell what happens to Billy Weaver and to the landlady. Will the landlady poison Billy slowly, or is she innocent of the implications in the story? Does Billy live through the night? Will he visit Christopher Mulholland and Gregory Temple on the fourth floor? Consult with students in the planning stages of their sequel to agree on how their papers will be assessed. (See *Portfolio Assessment and Professional Support Materials*, for additional information on student portfolios.)

For Study and Discussion

Analyzing and Interpreting the Story

1. What you learn about Billy Weaver at the beginning of the story helps explain why he later chooses to stay at the landlady's house. When you first meet Billy, he is looking for a fairly cheap hotel. How does his desire for a bargain drive him into a trap?

2. Billy is obviously impressed by appearances. **a.** What details of the landlady's house first attract him? **b.** Which of these details are not what they appear to be?

3. Billy overlooks dangers that are quite obvious to the reader. What he finds in the landlady's house does not arouse his suspicions. **a.** What clues does Billy ignore? **b.** What explanation does he give for the landlady's odd behavior?

4. The landlady tells Billy, "I was beginning to get worried." **a.** How does Billy interpret this remark? **b.** Considering the number of entries in her guest book, what do you think she was worried about?

5. Potassium cyanide, which is extremely poisonous, is known for its faint, bitter-almond taste. This is what Billy tastes in the landlady's tea. Find as many clues as you can that indicate what Billy's fate is to be.

6. Billy is shown to be quite observant throughout the story. Why does he fail to recognize the danger he is in?

7. Roald Dahl has been called "a master of the macabre and fantastic," and his tales are known for their skillful surprise endings. His stories belong to a tradition of escape literature that is written primarily for entertainment. Such stories may contain no particular moral or lesson or greatly increase our understanding of human nature. The characters (the landlady, for example) may be convincing in the story but would never be mistaken for real human beings. What other stories have you read that you would put in the category of escape literature?

Literary Elements

Understanding Suspense and Foreshadowing

When you read "The Landlady," you find yourself responding to danger signals that Billy Weaver fails to recognize. You can see clearly what is going to happen, but you have no way of warning Billy. You read on, eager to see whether he will connect the clues and act in time to save himself.

This uncertainty about what is going to happen next in a story is known as **suspense.** Roald Dahl creates suspense by placing Billy in danger and keeping you uncertain about whether he will escape or not.

Early in the story, Dahl creates suspense by presenting you with a mystery. When Billy sees the sign in the landlady's window, something strange happens to him.

> Each word was like a large black eye staring at him through the glass, holding him, compelling him, forcing him to stay where he was and not to walk away from that house, and the next thing he knew, he was actually moving across from the window to the front door of the house, climbing the steps that led up to it, and reaching for the bell.

What is this magnetic force that attracts Billy? What will happen when Billy presses the doorbell? Who will be waiting there behind the door? These are the questions that the reader wants answered.

To build up suspense, a writer will drop hints about what is going to come later in the story. This practice is called **foreshadowing.** All the information about Billy's fate is supplied in hints. Dahl never tells what the landlady plans to do to Billy. But we can guess.

FOR STUDY AND DISCUSSION

1. He is so pleased at "bargain" rates that he is not suspicious.
2a. Sign, vase of flowers, fire, piano, sofa, armchairs, animals.
2b. Animals are stuffed.
3a. No hats, coats, umbrellas, or walking-sticks in hall; bed is made as if he were expected; names in guest book familiar; dates in guest book; peculiar smell; landlady says other two guests have left; parrot and dog are stuffed—landlady says she stuffed them; bitter taste of tea.
3b. Thinks her "dotty" but harmless; thinks she might have lost a son in the war; still shocked.
4a. He thinks she was worried about him for some reason.
4b. No guests for two years; that she wouldn't find another.
5. He will be added to stuffed pet collection. Clues: peculiar smell from landlady (of formaldehyde preservative); the other two guests have never left (they are on fourth floor); landlady uses past tense; knowledge of unblemished skin on one guest; she stuffed pets.
6. He is only seventeen, inexperienced, too easily impressed by appearances, too excited by cheapness of rates to notice oddities.
7. Responses will vary.

The Landlady 227

CLOSURE

Ask students to choose from the story three examples of things the landlady says or does that **foreshadow** her intentions for Billy Weaver. In what ways do these details add **suspense** to the story?

EXTENSION AND ENRICHMENT

Have students develop a brief opening to a short story in which they deliberately use foreshadowing to create suspense. Students may enjoy completing this assignment in groups, one completing another's stories.

FOCUS ON WRITING A SHORT STORY

You may want to model the process of building a **plot** by recreating the chart on the chalkboard and working with students to fill in the blocks. As the exercise suggests, choose an event that could be the high point of a story, and then have students suggest a **conflict**, background, and outcome.

ABOUT THE AUTHOR

Roald Dahl has had a successful and varied career as a writer. His adult fiction has earned him two Edgar Allan Poe awards from the Mystery Writers of America. In 1979, a number of his stories were adapted as a television series entitled "Tales of the Unexpected." His children's stories have also met with success. One favorite, *Charlie and the Chocolate Factory*, became the popular film *Willy Wonka and the Chocolate Factory*. Dahl wrote the screenplay for *Chitty Chitty Bang Bang* and for the James Bond movie *You Only Live Twice*.

Focus on Writing a Short Story

Building a Plot

A good short story always includes a **conflict** or struggle. In Roald Dahl's story, the conflict is between Billy Weaver and the landlady. The plot of a short story develops the conflict so that it leads to a **high point** or **climax**. This is the point of greatest tension or excitement. In Dahl's story the climax occurs at the end, when the landlady tells Billy that he is the only other guest besides Mulholland and Temple.

The climax is the turning point of a story because it settles the conflict one way or the other. In most stories, the **outcome** shows how the conflict is settled and what happens when it is. In "The Landlady," Roald Dahl leaves the outcome to the reader's imagination.

Choose an event that could be the high point or climax of a story plot: for example, the opening night of a play or an argument with a family member. Experiment with building a plot around this event by filling out a chart like the one below. Save your notes.

Background	
Conflict	Climax
	Outcome

About the Author

Roald Dahl (1916–1990)

Roald Dahl grew up in Llandaff, South Wales. At sixteen he left school to join an exploratory expedition to Newfoundland. When World War II broke out in 1939, he volunteered for the Royal Air Force as a fighter pilot. Although he was seriously wounded when he crash-landed in the Libyan desert, Dahl continued to fly until 1942, when he was sent to Washington, D.C., as an assistant to the British ambassador. He later recounted these adventures in his autobiography, *Going Solo* (1986).

Dahl's writing career began when the novelist C. S. Forester asked him to write an account of his most exciting flying experience. He went on to publish nine collections of short stories and nineteen children's books, in addition to many television plays and screenplays. Among his well-known children's books are *James and the Giant Peach* (1961), *Charlie and the Chocolate Factory* (1964), and *Danny the Champion of the World* (1975). One critic noted his ability "to steer an unwavering course along the hairline where the gruesome and the comic meet and mingle." "The Landlady" is a good example of the bizarre element in Dahl's work.

OBJECTIVES
The overall aim is for students to analyze how Kipling uses **direct** and **indirect characterization** and explores the **conflict** between good and evil. For a complete list of objectives, see the **Teacher's Notes**.

VOCABULARY
The underlined words are in the Glossary. The **Connecting Cultures** feature on p. 241 gives students the opportunity to investigate some words that have come to the English language from India.

FOCUS / MOTIVATION
Invite students to recall animals in stories, poems, or movies that talk and behave like humans. Tell students that Rikki-tikki-tavi, the mongoose who is the leading character in this story, is just such an animal.

> **TEACHING RESOURCES B**
> Teacher's Notes, p. 135
> Reading Check, p. 137
> Study Guide, p. 138
> Language Skills, p. 142
> Building Vocabulary, p. 145
> Selection Vocabulary Test, p. 157
> Selection Test, p. 146

Rikki-tikki-tavi

RUDYARD KIPLING

Characters in a short story are revealed in several ways. Writers may tell us about characters by describing them directly. Most often, however, writers prefer to show us what characters are like, through their thoughts, their words, their actions, and the reactions of other characters in the story. As you read this story, note how Kipling uses both direct and indirect methods of characterization.

This is the story of the great war that Rikki-tikki-tavi fought single-handed, through the bathrooms of the big bungalow in Segowlee cantonment.¹ Darzee, the tailorbird, helped him, and Chuchundra,² the muskrat, who never comes out into the middle of the floor, but always creeps round by the wall, gave him advice; but Rikki-tikki did the real fighting.

He was a mongoose, rather like a little cat in

---
1. **Segowlee** (sē-gou′lē) **cantonment:** a British army post in Segowlee, India.
2. **Chuchundra** (chōō-chŭn′drə).

PREREADING FOCUS
The headnote defines and explains the use of **direct** and **indirect characterization**. You may want to review these methods with the class by asking them to write three sentences demonstrating characterization of each type.

Rikki-tikki-tavi

1
Suggests story's epic nature, Rikki-tikki-tavi's heroic status, and narrator's familiarity with events.

2
Bungalow: one-storied house with thatched roof, often with wide veranda.

3
Cantonment: originally meant just an army post, but later often included homes of merchants, civil servants, and other non-military personnel.

4
Tailorbirds are small, sparrow-like; native to Asia and Africa; named for nest-building habits: "stitch" leaves together to form holder for nest.

VISUAL CONNECTIONS
Exploring the Subject
The gray mongoose of India (*Herpestes edwardsi*) is a fierce creature. It has a pointed nose like a ferret, small ears, and a long furry tail. It is a predator, and eats birds, small animals, eggs, and reptiles.

229

MOTIVATIONAL SUMMARY

A mongoose, Rikki-tikki-tavi, becomes the pet of a British family living in India. Rikki-tikki is very curious about nature and he explores his new home, meeting the other animals who live in the garden and identifying new friends—like Darzee and his wife, the tailorbirds. But not everyone is a friend. Two cobras also live in the garden, and cobras are a mongoose's natural enemies. They, too, recognize the mongoose as a threat. Soon, they start plotting to get rid of him.

PRESENTATION

Rudyard Kipling's "Rikki-tikki-tavi" applies the broad **theme** of good against evil to a cast of humanized animal characters. Cobras are predators: they are potentially life-threatening to human beings and have little value to humans.

---

5 Finding Details
Which of Rikki-tikki's characteristics gives him his name? His war cry.

6 Point of View. Story is told from third-person omniscient point of view, but details are often presented as Rikki-tikki sees them.

7 Point of View. Omniscient point of view: narrator adds information Rikki-tikki does not know.

8 In addition to curiosity, mongoose's other major characteristic is enmity to snakes, particularly cobras.

9 Motto characterizes typical mongoose: very active, energetic, and curious.

10 Summarizing
What is Rikki-tikki's first motive for staying? Curiosity.

11 Foreshadowing. Rikki-tikki's battle with cobras and protection of Teddy are foreshadowed.

---

his fur and his tail, but quite like a weasel in his head and his habits. His eyes and the end of his restless nose were pink; he could scratch himself anywhere he pleased with any leg, front or back, that he chose to use; he could fluff up his tail till it looked like a bottlebrush, and his war cry, as he scuttled through the long grass was:

5 "*Rikk-tikk-tikki-tikki-tchk!*"

One day, a high summer flood washed him out of the burrow where he lived with his father and mother, and carried him, kicking and clucking, down a roadside ditch. He found a little wisp of grass floating there, and clung to
6 it till he lost his senses. When he revived, he was lying in the hot sun on the middle of a garden path, very draggled indeed, and a small boy was saying: "Here's a dead mongoose. Let's have a funeral."

"No," said his mother; "let's take him in and dry him. Perhaps he isn't really dead."

They took him into the house, and a big man picked him up between his finger and thumb and said he was not dead but half choked; so they wrapped him in cotton wool and warmed him over a little fire, and he opened his eyes and sneezed.

7 "Now," said the big man (he was an Englishman who had just moved into the bungalow); "don't frighten him, and we'll see what he'll do."

It is the hardest thing in the world to frighten a mongoose, because he is eaten up
8 from nose to tail with curiosity. The motto of
9 all the mongoose family is "Run and find out"; and Rikki-tikki was a true mongoose. He looked at the cotton wool, decided that it was not good to eat, ran all round the table, sat up and put his fur in order, scratched himself, and jumped on the small boy's shoulder.

"Don't be frightened, Teddy," said his father. "That's his way of making friends."

"Ouch! He's tickling under my chin," said Teddy.

Rikki-tikki looked down between the boy's collar and neck, snuffed at his ear, and climbed down to the floor, where he sat rubbing his nose.

"Good gracious," said Teddy's mother, "and that's a wild creature! I suppose he's so tame because we've been kind to him."

"All mongooses are like that," said her husband. "If Teddy doesn't pick him up by the tail, or try to put him in a cage, he'll run in and out of the house all day long. Let's give him something to eat."

They gave him a little piece of raw meat. Rikki-tikki liked it immensely, and when it was finished he went out into the veranda and sat in the sunshine and fluffed up his fur to make it dry to the roots. Then he felt better.

"There are more things to find out about in this house," he said to himself, "than all my family could find out in all their lives. I shall
10 certainly stay and find out."

He spent all that day roaming over the house. He nearly drowned himself in the bathtubs; put his nose into the ink on a writing table, and burned it on the end of the big man's cigar, for he climbed up in the big man's lap to see how writing was done. At nightfall he ran into Teddy's nursery to watch how kerosene lamps were lighted, and when Teddy went to bed Rikki-tikki climbed up too; but he was a restless companion, because he had to get up and attend to every noise all through the night and find out what made it. Teddy's mother and father came in, the last thing, to look at their boy, and Rikki-tikki was awake on the pillow. "I don't like that," said Teddy's mother; "he may bite the child."

"He'll do no such thing," said the father.
11 "Teddy's safer with that little beast than if he had a bloodhound to watch him. If a snake came into the nursery now——"

But Teddy's mother wouldn't think of anything so awful.

Early in the morning Rikki-tikki came to early breakfast in the veranda, riding on Teddy's shoulder, and they gave him banana and some boiled egg; and he sat on all their laps one after the other, because every well-brought-up mongoose always hopes to be a house mongoose someday and have rooms to run about in; and Rikki-tikki's mother (she used to live in the general's house at Segowlee) had carefully told Rikki what to do if ever he came across Englishmen.

Then Rikki-tikki went out into the garden to see what was to be seen. It was a large garden, only half cultivated, with bushes, as big as summer houses, of roses, lime and orange trees, clumps of bamboos, and thickets of high grass. Rikki-tikki licked his lips. "This is a splendid hunting ground," he said, and his tail grew bottle-brushy at the thought of it, and he scuttled up and down the garden, snuffling here and there till he heard very sorrowful voices in a thornbush. It was Darzee, the tailorbird, and his wife. They had made a beautiful nest by pulling two big leaves together and stitching them up the edges with fibers, and had filled the hollow with cotton and downy fluff. The nest swayed to and fro, as they sat on the rim and cried.

"What is the matter?" asked Rikki-tikki.

"We are very miserable," said Darzee. "One of our babies fell out of the nest yesterday and Nag[3] ate him."

"H'm!" said Rikki-tikki; "that is very sad—but I am a stranger here. Who is Nag?"

Darzee and his wife only cowered down in the nest without answering, for from the thick grass at the foot of the bush came a low hiss—a horrid cold sound that made Rikki-tikki jump back two clear feet. Then inch by inch out of the grass rose up the head and spread hood of Nag, the big black cobra, and he was five feet long from tongue to tail. When he had lifted one third of himself clear of the ground, he stayed balancing to and fro exactly as a dandelion tuft balances in the wind, and he looked at Rikki-tikki with the wicked snake's eyes that never change their expression, whatever the snake may be thinking of.

"Who is Nag?" he said. "*I* am Nag. The great god Brahm[4] put his mark upon all our people,

---

3. **Nag** (näg).

4. **Brahm** (bräm): in the Hindu religion, the creator of the universe; usually known as *Brahma*.

ART LINK

Have students illustrate one or more scenes from the story which feature Teddy and Rikki together. Encourage them to provide captions or quotations from the story.

---

17 Nag is watching for Nagaina, his mate, hoping she will kill Rikki-tikki.

18 A full-grown mongoose is the only animal that will seek out and fight cobras.

19 Mongooses also destroy cobras' eggs and any baby snakes in nest.

20 Point of View. Kipling as narrator interprets and explains action for readers.

21 A fight between a cobra and a mongoose is a marvel: both are very fast, but mongoose must be faster. Mongoose bite may not be fatal, but one glancing snake bite can kill mongoose.

232

---

when the first cobra spread his hood to keep the sun off Brahm as he slept. Look, and be afraid!"

He spread out his hood more than ever, and Rikki-tikki saw the spectacle mark on the back of it that looks exactly like the eye part of a hook-and-eye fastening. He was afraid for the minute; but it is impossible for a mongoose to stay frightened for any length of time, and though Rikki-tikki had never met a live cobra before, his mother had fed him on dead ones, and he knew that all a grown mongoose's business in life was to fight and eat snakes. Nag knew that too and, at the bottom of his cold heart, he was afraid.

"Well," said Rikki-tikki, and his tail began to fluff up again, "marks or no marks, do you think it is right for you to eat fledglings out of a nest?"

17 Nag was thinking to himself, and watching the least little movement in the grass behind
18 Rikki-tikki. He knew that mongooses in the garden meant death sooner or later for him and his family; but he wanted to get Rikki-tikki off his guard. So he dropped his head a little, and put it on one side.

19 "Let us talk," he said. "You eat eggs. Why should not I eat birds?"

"Behind you! Look behind you!" sang Darzee.

Rikki-tikki knew better than to waste time in staring. He jumped up in the air as high as he could go, and just under him whizzed by the head of Nagaina,[5] Nag's wicked wife. She had crept up behind him as he was talking, to make an end of him; and he heard her savage hiss as the stroke missed. He came down almost across her back, and if he had been an old mongoose he would have known that then was the time to break her back with one bite; but he was afraid of the terrible lashing return stroke of the cobra. He bit, indeed, but did not bite long enough, and he jumped clear of the whisking tail, leaving Nagaina torn and angry.

"Wicked, wicked Darzee!" said Nag, lashing up as high as he could reach toward the nest in the thornbush; but Darzee had built it out of reach of snakes, and it only swayed to and fro.

Rikki-tikki felt his eyes growing red and hot (when a mongoose's eyes grow red, he is angry), and he sat back on his tail and hind legs like a little kangaroo, and looked all around him, and chattered with rage. But Nag and Nagaina had disappeared into the grass. When a snake misses its stroke, it never says anything or gives any sign of what it means to do next. Rikki-tikki did not care to follow them, for he did not feel sure that he could manage two snakes at once. So he trotted off to the gravel
20 path near the house, and sat down to think. It was a serious matter for him. If you read the old books of natural history, you will find they say that when the mongoose fights the snake and happens to get bitten, he runs off and eats some herb that cures him. That is not true.
21 The victory is only a matter of quickness of eye and quickness of foot—snake's blow against the mongoose's jump—and as no eye can follow the motion of a snake's head when it strikes, this makes things much more wonderful than any magic herb. Rikki-tikki knew he was a young mongoose, and it made him all the more pleased to think that he had managed to escape a blow from behind. It gave him confidence in himself, and when Teddy came running down the path, Rikki-tikki was ready to be petted. But just as Teddy was stooping, something wriggled a little in the dust, and a tiny voice said: "Be careful. I am Death!" It was Karait,[6] the dusty brown snakeling that lies for choice on the dusty earth; and his bite is as dangerous as the cobra's. But he is so small that

---

5. **Nagaina** (nə-gī′nə).

6. **Karait** (kə-rīt′).

232 SHORT STORIES

VISUAL CONNECTIONS
Exploring the Subject
Pictured here is the result of a battle between a mongoose and a cobra. Although the snake's body is coiled around the mongoose, this type of snake cannot crush its enemies with its coils. The violence of its last-ditch fight is only a sign of how desperately the snake has tried to free itself from the mongoose's hold. The mongoose is biting the cobra at the base of the snake's neck, where its sharp teeth and powerful jaws will sever the spinal cord. To be cautious, the mongoose will continue its relentless grip until the snake has completely finished its death struggle.

22
A mongoose in battle fights balanced on hind legs; makes harder target to hit plus gives energetic push in spring to attack.

23
A mongoose has a long, thin, agile body; in battle, often leaps and flips like an acrobat.

24
The human and animal worlds are separate. The family does not name Rikki-tikki, nor do they know his "animal" name.

25 Making Inferences
Why does the father beat the dead snake? Perhaps to make sure it is dead; also expresses his fear.

26
Characterization. Rikki-tikki does not see himself as heroic since his killing of the snake was as instinctive and fun as playing in dust might be for Teddy.

---

nobody thinks of him, and so he does the more harm to people.

22 Rikki-tikki's eyes grew red again, and he danced up to Karait with the peculiar rocking, swaying motion that he had inherited from his family. It looks very funny, but it is so perfectly balanced a gait that you can fly off from it at any angle you please; and in dealing with snakes this is an advantage. If Rikki-tikki had only known, he was doing a much more dangerous thing than fighting Nag, for Karait is so small, and can turn so quickly, that unless Rikki bit him close to the back of the head, he would get the return stroke in his eye or his lip. But Rikki did not know: his eyes were all red, and he rocked back and forth, looking for a good place to hold. Karait struck out, Rikki jumped sideways and tried to run in, but the wicked little dusty gray head lashed within a fraction of his shoulder, and he had to jump
23 over the body, and the head followed his heels close.

Teddy shouted to the house: "Oh, look here!
24 Our mongoose is killing a snake"; and Rikki-tikki heard a scream from Teddy's mother. His father ran out with a stick, but by the time he came up, Karait had lunged out once too far, and Rikki-tikki had sprung, jumped on the snake's back, dropped his head far between his forelegs, bitten as high up the back as he could get hold, and rolled away. That bite paralyzed Karait, and Rikki-tikki was just going to eat him up from the tail, after the custom of his family at dinner, when he remembered that a full meal makes a slow mongoose, and if he wanted all his strength and quickness ready, he must keep himself thin. He went away for a dust bath under the castor-oil bushes, while
25 Teddy's father beat the dead Karait. "What is the use of that?" thought Rikki-tikki; "I have settled it all"; and then Teddy's mother picked him up from the dust and hugged him, crying that he had saved Teddy from death, and Teddy's father said that he was a providence, and Teddy looked on with big scared eyes.
26 Rikki-tikki was rather amused at all the fuss, which, of course, he did not understand. Teddy's mother might just as well have petted Teddy for playing in the dust. Rikki was thoroughly enjoying himself.

That night, at dinner, walking to and fro among the wineglasses on the table, he might have stuffed himself three times over with nice things; but he remembered Nag and Nagaina,

Rikki-tikki-tavi

TRANSPARENCY 20

Reader Response
Tug-of-War – allows students an opportunity to explore conflicts faced by one of the characters in a selection.

27
Rikki-tikki knows he must kill the cobras. His awareness of inevitable fight overrides desire for human attention.

28
Characterization. Comment characterizes Rikki-tikki indirectly by revealing his high opinion of himself and low view of Chuchundra.

29
Suspense. Chuchundra's speech builds tension, suggesting evil is nearby though unseen.

30 Making Inferences
Why do you think the snakes say the "big man" killed Karait? Perhaps got false report from others; perhaps do not want to admit Rikki-tikki's capability of harming them.

31
Rikki-tikki learns of the eggs, which are about to hatch.

---

and though it was very pleasant to be patted and petted by Teddy's mother, and to sit on Teddy's shoulder, his eyes would get red from time to time, and he would go off into his long **27** war cry of "*Rikk-tikk-tikki-tikki-tchk!*"

Teddy carried him off to bed, and insisted on Rikki-tikki's sleeping under his chin. Rikki-tikki was too well bred to bite or scratch, but as soon as Teddy was asleep he went off for his nightly walk round the house, and in the dark he ran up against Chuchundra, the muskrat, creeping round by the wall. Chuchundra is a brokenhearted little beast. He whimpers and cheeps all the night, trying to make up his mind to run into the middle of the room; but he never gets there.

"Don't kill me," said Chuchundra, almost weeping. "Rikki-tikki, don't kill me!"

28 "Do you think a snake-killer kills muskrats?" said Rikki-tikki scornfully.

"Those who kill snakes get killed by snakes," said Chuchundra, more sorrowfully than ever. "And how am I to be sure that Nag won't mistake me for you some dark night?"

"There's not the least danger," said Rikki-tikki; "but Nag is in the garden, and I know you don't go there."

"My cousin Chua, the rat, told me——" said Chuchundra, and then he stopped.

"Told you what?"

29 "H'sh! Nag is everywhere, Rikki-tikki. You should have talked to Chua in the garden."

"I didn't—so you must tell me. Quick, Chuchundra, or I'll bite you!"

Chuchundra sat down and cried till the tears rolled off his whiskers. "I am a very poor man," he sobbed. "I never had spirit enough to run out into the middle of the room. H'sh! I mustn't tell you anything. Can't you *hear*, Rikki-tikki?"

Rikki-tikki listened. The house was as still as still, but he thought he could just catch the faintest *scratch-scratch* in the world—a noise as faint as that of a wasp walking on a windowpane—the dry scratch of a snake's scales on brickwork.

"That's Nag or Nagaina," he said to himself; "and he is crawling into the bathroom sluice. You're right, Chuchundra; I should have talked to Chua."

He stole off to Teddy's bathroom, but there was nothing there, and then to Teddy's mother's bathroom. At the bottom of the smooth plaster wall there was a brick pulled out to make a sluice for the bath water, and as Rikki-tikki stole in by the masonry curb where the bath is put, he heard Nag and Nagaina whispering together outside in the moonlight.

"When the house is emptied of people," said Nagaina to her husband, "*he* will have to go away, and then the garden will be our own again. Go in quietly, and remember that the **30** big man who killed Karait is the first one to bite. Then come out and tell me, and we will hunt for Rikki-tikki together."

"But are you sure that there is anything to be gained by killing the people?" said Nag.

"Everything. When there were no people in the bungalow, did we have any mongoose in the garden? So long as the bungalow is empty, we are king and queen of the garden; and re- **31** member that as soon as our eggs in the melon bed hatch (as they may tomorrow), our children will need room and quiet."

"I had not thought of that," said Nag. "I will go, but there is no need that we should hunt for Rikki-tikki afterward. I will kill the big man and his wife, and the child if I can, and come away quietly. Then the bungalow will be empty, and Rikki-tikki will go."

Rikki-tikki tingled all over with rage and hatred at this, and then Nag's head came through the sluice, and his five feet of cold body followed it. Angry as he was, Rikki-tikki was very frightened as he saw the size of the big cobra. Nag coiled himself up, raised his head, and

234 SHORT STORIES

SCIENCE LINK
Have students research the mongoose, especially its appearance and habits. Then have them compare their findings with Kipling's fictitious Rikki-tikki-tavi to see how accurately the author describes the mongoose. Encourage students to write a brief paragraph about this comparison.

---

looked into the bathroom in the dark, and Rikki could see his eyes glitter.

32 "Now, if I kill him here, Nagaina will know; and if I fight him on the open floor, the odds are in his favor. What am I to do?" said Rikki-tikki-tavi.

Nag waved to and fro, and then Rikki-tikki heard him drinking from the biggest water jar that was used to fill the bath. "That is good," said the snake. "Now, when Karait was killed, the big man had a stick. He may have that stick still, but when he comes in to bathe in the morning he will not have a stick. I shall wait here till he comes. Nagaina—do you hear me? I shall wait here in the cool till daytime."

There was no answer from outside, so Rikki-
33 tikki knew Nagaina had gone away. Nag coiled himself down, coil by coil, round the bulge at the bottom of the water jar, and Rikki-tikki stayed still as death. After an hour he began to move, muscle by muscle, towards the jar. Nag was asleep, and Rikki-tikki looked at his big back, wondering which would be the best place for a good hold. "If I don't break his back at the first jump," said Rikki, "he can still fight; and if he fights—O Rikki!" He looked at the thickness of the neck below the hood, but that was too much for him; and a bite near the tail would only make Nag savage.

"It must be the head," he said at last; "the head above the hood; and when I am once
34 there, I must not let go."

Then he jumped. The head was lying a little clear of the water jar, under the curve of it; and, as his teeth met, Rikki braced his back against the bulge of the red earthenware to hold down the head. This gave him just one second's purchase,[7] and he made the most of it. Then he was battered to and fro as a rat is shaken by a dog—to and fro on the floor, up and down, and round in great circles, but his eyes were red and he held on as the body cartwhipped over the floor, upsetting the tin dipper and the soap dish and the fleshbrush, and banged against the tin side of the bath. As he held he closed his jaws tighter and tighter, for he made sure[8] he would be banged to death, and, for the honor of his family, he preferred to be found with his teeth locked. He was dizzy, aching, and felt shaken to pieces when something went off like a thunderclap just behind him; a hot wind knocked him senseless and red fire singed his fur. The big man had been wakened by the noise, and had fired both barrels of a shotgun into Nag just behind the hood.

Rikki-tikki held on with his eyes shut, for now he was quite sure he was dead; but the head did not move, and the big man picked him up and said: "It's the mongoose again, Alice; the little chap has saved *our* lives now." Then Teddy's mother came in with a very white face, and saw what was left of Nag, and Rikki-tikki dragged himself to Teddy's bedroom and spent half the rest of the night shaking himself tenderly to find out whether he really was broken into forty pieces, as he fancied.

When morning came he was very stiff, but well pleased with his doings. "Now I have Nagaina to settle with, and she will be worse
35 than five Nags, and there's no knowing when the eggs she spoke of will hatch. Goodness! I must go and see Darzee," he said.

Without waiting for breakfast, Rikki-tikki ran to the thornbush where Darzee was singing a song of triumph at the top of his voice. The news of Nag's death was all over the garden, for the sweeper had thrown the body on the rubbish heap.

36 "Oh, you stupid tuft of feathers!" said Rikki-tikki angrily. "Is this the time to sing?"

---

7. **purchase:** here, advantage.
8. **made sure:** here, felt sure.

---

32 Rikki-tikki is clever not to be too hasty; the cobra is bigger and he must find an advantageous time to attack.

33 **Suspense.** Nag's decision to wait gives Rikki-tikki time to look for an opportunity to attack.

34 Rikki-tikki realizes he may only get one good chance.

35 Drawing Conclusions
Why will Nagaina be worse than Nag? She is more clever than Nag, she will be angered by Nag's death, and she will protect her eggs fiercely.

36 Finding Cause and Effect
Why is Rikki-tikki angry with Darzee? He does not think Darzee should be singing, under the circumstances: the war still rages; Nagaina is still alive, and the eggs will hatch soon.

37
Darzee's praise should come when the war is over, not at the end of one battle. Rikki-tikki is still in great danger.

38
Characterization. Darzee is characterized indirectly as silly. He is about to get upset at the idea of Rikki-tikki's eating eggs—even snakes' eggs.

39
Narrator's jibe: sometimes humans are all talk, no action.

40 Expressing an Opinion
Do you think animals are capable of this type of vengeance? Answers will vary. Students may use their own observation of animals.

41
Ironic that Nagaina plans revenge by destroying the human child; it will be her progeny that perish.

---

37 "Nag is dead—is dead—is dead!" sang Darzee. "The valiant Rikki-tikki caught him by the head and held fast. The big man brought the bang-stick, and Nag fell in two pieces! He will never eat my babies again."

"All that's true enough; but where's Nagaina?" said Rikki-tikki, looking carefully round him.

"Nagaina came to the bathroom sluice and called for Nag," Darzee went on; "and Nag came out on the end of a stick—the sweeper picked him up on the end of a stick and threw him upon the rubbish heap. Let us sing about the great, the red-eyed Rikki-tikki!" And Darzee filled his throat and sang.

"If I could get up to your nest, I'd roll your babies out!" said Rikki-tikki. "You don't know when to do the right thing at the right time. You're safe enough in your nest there, but it's war for me down here. Stop singing a minute, Darzee."

"For the great, beautiful Rikki-tikki's sake I will stop," said Darzee. "What is it, O Killer of the terrible Nag?"

"Where is Nagaina, for the third time?"

"On the rubbish heap by the stables, mourning for Nag. Great is Rikki-tikki with the white teeth."

"Bother[9] my white teeth! Have you ever heard where she keeps her eggs?"

"In the melon bed, on the end nearest the wall, where the sun strikes nearly all day. She hid them there weeks ago."

"And you never thought it worthwhile to tell me? The end nearest the wall, you said?"

38 "Rikki-tikki, you are not going to eat her eggs?"

"Not eat exactly; no. Darzee, if you have a grain of sense you will fly off to the stables and pretend that your wing is broken, and let Nagaina chase you away to this bush! I must get to the melon bed, and if I went there now she'd see me."

Darzee was a featherbrained little fellow who could never hold more than one idea at a time in his head; and just because he knew that Nagaina's children were born in eggs like his own, he didn't think at first that it was fair to kill them. But his wife was a sensible bird, and she knew that cobra's eggs meant young cobras later on; so she flew off from the nest, and left **39** Darzee to keep the babies warm, and continue his song about the death of Nag. Darzee was very like a man in some ways.

She fluttered in front of Nagaina by the rubbish heap and cried out, "Oh, my wing is broken! The boy in the house threw a stone at me and broke it." Then she fluttered more desperately than ever.

Nagaina lifted up her head and hissed, "You warned Rikki-tikki when I would have killed him. Indeed and truly, you've chosen a bad place to be lame in." And she moved toward Darzee's wife, slipping along over the dust.

"The boy broke it with a stone!" shrieked Darzee's wife.

40 "Well! It may be some consolation to you when you're dead to know that I shall settle accounts with the boy. My husband lies on the rubbish heap this morning, but before night **41** the boy in the house will lie very still. What is the use of running away? I am sure to catch you. Little fool, look at me!"

Darzee's wife knew better than to do *that,* for a bird who looks at a snake's eyes gets so frightened that she cannot move. Darzee's wife fluttered on, piping sorrowfully, and never leaving the ground, and Nagaina quickened her pace.

Rikki-tikki heard them going up the path from the stables, and he raced for the end of the melon patch near the wall. There, in the warm litter about the melons, very cunningly hidden, he found twenty-five eggs, about the

---

9. **Bother:** here, never mind.

size of a bantam's eggs,[10] but with whitish skins instead of shells.

"I was not a day too soon," he said; for he could see the baby cobras curled up inside the skin, and he knew that the minute they were hatched they could each kill a man or a mongoose. He bit off the tops of the eggs as fast as he could, taking care to crush the young cobras, and turned over the litter from time to time to see whether he had missed any. At last there were only three eggs left, and Rikki-tikki began to chuckle to himself, when he heard Darzee's wife screaming:

"Rikki-tikki, I led Nagaina toward the house, and she has gone into the veranda, and—oh, come quickly—she means killing!"

Rikki-tikki smashed two eggs, and tumbled backward down the melon bed with the third egg in his mouth, and scuttled to the veranda as hard as he could put foot to the ground. Teddy and his mother and father were there at early breakfast; but Rikki-tikki saw that they were not eating anything. They sat stone-still, and their faces were white. Nagaina was coiled up on the matting by Teddy's chair, within easy striking distance of Teddy's bare leg, and she was swaying to and fro, singing a song of triumph.

"Son of the big man that killed Nag," she hissed, "stay still. I am not ready yet. Wait a little. Keep very still, all you three! If you move I strike, and if you do not move I strike. Oh, foolish people, who killed my Nag!"

Teddy's eyes were fixed on his father, and all his father could do was to whisper, "Sit still, Teddy. You mustn't move. Teddy, keep still."

Then Rikki-tikki came up and cried: "Turn round, Nagaina; turn and fight!"

"All in good time," said she, without moving her eyes. "I will settle my account with *you* presently. Look at your friends, Rikki-tikki. They are still and white. They are afraid. They dare not move, and if you come a step nearer I strike."

"Look at your eggs," said Rikki-tikki, "in the melon bed near the wall. Go and look, Nagaina."

The big snake turned half round and saw the egg on the veranda. "Ah-h! Give it to me," she said.

Rikki-tikki put his paws one on each side of the egg, and his eyes were blood-red. "What price for a snake's egg? For a young cobra? For a young king cobra? For the last—the very last of the brood? The ants are eating all the others down by the melon bed."

Nagaina spun clear round, forgetting everything for the sake of the one egg; and Rikki-tikki saw Teddy's father shoot out a big hand, catch Teddy by the shoulder, and drag him across the little table with the teacups, safe and out of reach of Nagaina.

"Tricked! Tricked! Tricked! *Rikk-tck-tck!*" chuckled Rikki-tikki. "The boy is safe, and it was I—I—I that caught Nag by the hood last night in the bathroom." Then he began to jump up and down, all four feet together, his head close to the floor. "He threw me to and fro, but he could not shake me off. He was dead before the big man blew him in two. I did it! *Rikki-tikki-tck-tck!* Come then, Nagaina. Come and fight with me. You shall not be a widow long."

Nagaina saw that she had lost her chance of killing Teddy, and the egg lay between Rikki-tikki's paws. "Give me the egg, Rikki-tikki. Give me the last of my eggs, and I will go away and never come back," she said, lowering her hood.

"Yes, you will go away, and you will never come back; for you will go to the rubbish heap with Nag. Fight, widow! The big man has gone for his gun! Fight!"

---

10. **bantam's eggs:** small eggs. A bantam is a small chicken.

---

42 Eggs near hatching: Rikki-tikki must bite each baby cobra to be sure it is dead.

43 Making Inferences
Why does he not smash the last egg? Perhaps he foresees need for way of distracting and bargaining with Nagaina.

44 Nagaina is in control until Rikki-tikki arrives.

45 Her focus on Teddy wavers as her maternal instinct is roused.

46 He goads her into missing her chance to strike at Teddy.

47 Rikki-tikki is not gloating, just trying to lure Nagaina away.

48 Analyzing
Can Nagaina be trusted to keep her word? Not unless her character radically changes.

49
Nagaina has not forgotten; her sparring with Rikki-tikki was apparently calculated to bring her close to the egg.

50
Evidently, her underground lair is close by; the bird tries to prevent her from entering it.

51
Characterization. Whether bravery or foolishness, his action shows the intensity of the pursuit and his persistent nature.

52
Darzee is again too quick with his news.

53
Plot. Rikki-tikki's fight with Nagaina and its outcome constitute the **climax** of the story.

Rikki-tikki was bounding all round Nagaina, keeping just out of reach of her stroke, his little eyes like hot coals. Nagaina gathered herself together, and flung out at him. Rikki-tikki jumped up and backwards. Again and again and again she struck, and each time her head came with a whack on the matting of the veranda and she gathered herself together like a watchspring. Then Rikki-tikki danced in a circle to get behind her, and Nagaina spun round to keep her head to his head, so that the rustle of her tail on the matting sounded like dry leaves blown along by the wind.

49 He had forgotten the egg. It still lay on the veranda, and Nagaina came nearer and nearer to it, till at last, while Rikki-tikki was drawing breath, she caught it in her mouth, turned to the veranda steps, and flew like an arrow down the path, with Rikki-tikki behind her. When the cobra runs for her life, she goes like a whiplash flicked across a horse's neck. Rikki-tikki knew that he must catch her, or all the trouble would begin again. She headed straight for the long grass by the thornbush, and as he was running Rikki-tikki heard Darzee still singing his foolish little song of tri-**50** umph. But Darzee's wife was wiser. She flew off her nest as Nagaina came along, and flapped her wings about Nagaina's head. If Darzee had helped they might have turned her; but Nagaina only lowered her hood and went on. Still, the instant's delay brought Rikki-tikki up to her, and as she plunged into the rathole where she and Nag used to live, his little white teeth were clenched on her tail, and **51** he went down with her—and very few mongooses, however wise and old they may be, care to follow a cobra into its hole. It was dark in the hole; and Rikki-tikki never knew when it might open out and give Nagaina room to turn and strike at him. He held on savagely, and stuck out his feet to act as brakes on the dark slope of the hot, moist earth. Then the grass by the **52** mouth of the hole stopped waving, and Darzee said: "It is all over with Rikki-tikki! We must sing his death song. Valiant Rikki-tikki is dead! For Nagaina will surely kill him underground."

So he sang a very mournful song that he made up all on the spur of the minute, and just as he got to the most touching part the grass quivered again, and Rikki-tikki, covered with dirt, dragged himself out of the hole leg by leg, licking his whiskers. Darzee stopped with a little shout. Rikki-tikki shook some of the dust **53** out of his fur and sneezed. "It is all over," he said. "The widow will never come out again." And the red ants that live between the grass stems heard him, and began to troop down one after another to see if he had spoken the truth.

Rikki-tikki curled himself up in the grass and slept where he was—slept and slept till it was late in the afternoon, for he had done a hard day's work.

"Now," he said, when he awoke, "I will go back to the house. Tell the Coppersmith, Darzee, and he will tell the garden that Nagaina is dead."

The Coppersmith is a bird who makes a noise exactly like the beating of a little hammer on a copper pot; and the reason he is always making it is because he is the town crier to every Indian garden, and tells all the news to everybody who cares to listen. As Rikki-tikki went up the path, he heard his "attention" notes like a tiny dinner gong; and then the steady "*Ding-dong-tock!* Nag is dead—*dong!* Nagaina is dead! *Ding-dong-tock!*" That set all the birds in the garden singing, and the frogs croaking, for Nag and Nagaina used to eat frogs as well as little birds.

When Rikki got to the house, Teddy and Teddy's mother (she looked very white still, for she had been fainting) and Teddy's father came out and almost cried over him; and that night he ate all that was given him till he could eat no more, and went to bed on Teddy's shoulder, where Teddy's mother saw him when she came to look late at night.

"He saved our lives and Teddy's life," she said to her husband. "Just think, he saved all our lives!"

Rikki-tikki woke up with a jump, for the mongooses are light sleepers.

54 "Oh, it's you," said he. "What are you bothering for? All the cobras are dead; and if they weren't, I'm here."

Rikki-tikki had a right to be proud of himself; but he did not grow too proud, and he kept that garden as a mongoose should keep it, with tooth and jump and spring and bite, till never a cobra dared show its head inside the walls.

Reading Check

1. According to the author, why is it difficult to frighten a mongoose?
2. What is the motto of Rikki-tikki's family?
3. Why is Nag afraid of Rikki-tikki?
4. Who are Rikki-tikki's allies in the war against the cobras?
5. What happens to Rikki-tikki's eyes when he gets angry?
6. Why does Rikki-tikki refrain from eating Karait?
7. Who warns Rikki-tikki that the cobras may come into the house?
8. Why do the cobras want to kill the people in the house?
9. What does Rikki-tikki consider a greater danger than Nag and Nagaina?
10. Where does Rikki-tikki find the cobra's eggs?

For Study and Discussion

Analyzing and Interpreting the Story

1. The major characters in the story are animals that have been given human motives. Identify the major characters in the story that represent the forces of good and those that represent the forces of evil.

2. What conflict, or struggle, does Rikki-tikki face?

3. Kipling says that his story is about "the great war that Rikki-tikki-tavi fought single-handed. . . ." **a.** Identify at least five "battles" in this war. **b.** At what points in the war does Darzee's wife assist Rikki-tikki?

4. Match each character in the left-hand column with one or more of the adjectives in the right-hand column. You may use each adjective as often as you like, but be sure to use each adjective at least once. Support your answers with passages from the story.

Darzee	cold
	cunning
	curious
	featherbrained
Darzee's wife	intelligent
	proud
	quick-witted
	resourceful
Rikki-tikki	sensible
	stupid
	valiant
	wicked
Nagaina	wise

5. Writers frequently treat animals in stories as if they could think, talk, and feel as people do. **a.** Why do you suppose they write about animals in this way? **b.** What other selections have you read in which animals have been given human characteristics?

54
Theme. Battle between good and evil has resolved itself in a victory for the forces of good. Evil has been routed from the garden.

READING CHECK
1. Mongooses are curious (p. 230).
2. "Run and find out" (p. 230).
3. Mongoose fights and kills snakes (p. 232).
4. Tailorbirds and muskrat (p. 229).
5. They turn red (p. 232).
6. Doesn't want to grow fat and slow (p. 233).
7. Muskrat (p. 234).
8. Think mongoose will leave if people gone (p. 234).
9. Eggs soon to hatch (p. 236).
10. In melon patch (p. 236).

FOR STUDY AND DISCUSSION
1. Good: Rikki-tikki, Darzee and wife. Evil: Nag and Nagaina.
2. **External conflict** with cobras.
3a. Nagaina almost bites him; kills Karait; kills Nag; kills all baby cobras but one; fights Nagaina on veranda; kills Nagaina in hole.
3b. Gets Nagaina to pursue her; tells Rikki-tikki Nagaina heading for house; delays Nagaina in fleeing.
4. Darzee: featherbrained, stupid; Darzee's wife: intelligent, sensible, wise, valiant; Rikki-tikki: curious, intelligent, proud, quick-witted, resourceful, sensible, valiant, wise; Nagaina: cold, cunning, intelligent, valiant, wicked.
5a. Animals as characters are simpler, more easily defined.
5b. Answers will vary. Perhaps *Alice in Wonderland, Wind in the Willows, Black Beauty*.
6. Responses will vary.

PORTFOLIO ASSESSMENT
Students who enjoyed reading "Rikki-tikki-tavi" may also enjoy reading and reacting to more of Kipling's short stories, his novels, or his poetry. See *About the Author* on p. 241 for a partial list of additional writings. Student reactions may take the form of dramatic readings of poetry or evaluations of some short stories or a novel. Oral presentations may be videotaped for inclusion in student portfolios. (See *Portfolio Assessment and Professional Support Materials.*)

LITERARY ELEMENTS

1. Chuchundra says: "Rikki-tikki, don't kill me! . . . I am a very poor man. I never had spirit enough to run out into the middle of the room." Chuchundra nearly weeps from fear; is so frightened he can't finish sentences.
2. Rikki-tikki thinks Chuchundra is a coward, and weak. He is scornful of the muskrat.
3. Yes. Confirms Kipling's description and adds dimension of Rikki-tikki the fighter's disdain for muskrat.
4. Direct characterization: Rikki-tikki has fur like a cat's, head like a weasel's, tail that grows bushy when he fights, eyes grow red when angry, he is brave and curious.
5. Indirect characterization: Rikki-tikki shows curiosity in exploring house and garden, pride in escaping being struck by Nagaina, bravery in killing Karait, vanity in saying he has taken care of the snake (to Teddy's father), wisdom in keeping weight down so he can fight well, arrogance in scorn of Chuchundra's weakness, cleverness in plan to ambush Nag in the bathroom, bravery and determination in fighting Nag, intelligence in seeking news of Nag and knowing his work is not done, impatience at Darzee's stupidity, cleverness in foiling Nagaina's plan to bite Teddy, pride in bragging that he caught Nag by the hood, and bravery in following Nagaina into her hole.

CREATIVE WRITING
Students may need to be reminded that when writing action narratives, they should describe events in the order they occur, use action verbs to convey a sense of motion and excitement, and include sensory details that appeal to the reader's imagination.

6. Choose passages of description, conversation, or exciting events that you find appealing. Prepare to read them aloud in class.

Literary Elements

Understanding Methods of Characterization

The way in which writers let you know what the individuals in a story are like is called **characterization.** When writers *tell* you what characters are like through description, they are using **direct characterization.** For instance, Kipling tells us: "Chuchundra is a broken-hearted little beast. He whimpers and cheeps all the night, trying to make up his mind to run into the middle of the room, but he never gets there."

Writers may also *show* you what characters are like through their thoughts, their speech, their actions, and the reactions of other characters to them. This kind of characterization is called **indirect characterization.** What does Chuchundra say and do (page 234) that confirms Kipling's description of him? What is Rikki-tikki's opinion of Chuchundra? Does his opinion add anything to Kipling's statement?

Show how Kipling develops Rikki-tikki's character through direct and indirect characterization. Be sure to answer the following questions:

Direct Characterization

What does the author tell you about the character?

Indirect Characterization

What does the character think, say, and do? What do others think and say about the character? How do they treat the character?

Writing About Literature

Analyzing Methods of Characterization

You have seen that Kipling develops Rikki-tikki's character through direct and indirect characterization. Choose a character in another story you have read, such as Victor in "Seventh Grade" (page 13) or Harry Thorburn in "The Erne from the Coast" (page 208). Write an essay in which you analyze the author's methods of characterization.

Prewriting Suggestions: Use two columns, one for *direct characterization* and one for *indirect characterization.* As you reread the story, list details in the appropriate categories. You can then edit your lists to select the best details for your essay. For additional help, see *Writing About Literature.*

Creative Writing

Writing About Characters in Action

Rikki-tikki's last fight with Nagaina occurs "offstage," so to speak. Kipling does not describe the battle. He leaves it to the reader's imagination.

Using your knowledge of the characters of Rikki-tikki and Nagaina, write your version of the missing battle. Remember that Nagaina is almost a match for Rikki-tikki and that she is fighting to save her very last egg.

You might open with these sentences taken from the story:

> It was dark in the hole; and Rikki-tikki never knew when it might open out and give Nagaina room to turn and strike at him. He held on savagely, and stuck out his feet to act as brakes on the dark slope of the hot, moist earth.

Focus on Writing a Short Story

Creating Characters

In "Rikki-tikki-tavi," Rudyard Kipling uses vivid, specific **details** to help you "see" the main characters. When you create characters for your own stories, use details to help bring each figure to life. Fill out a chart like the one below:

Character Chart
Name: _____ Age: _____
Appearance: _____
Clothing: _____
Movements: _____
Way of Speaking: _____
Personality Traits: _____

Look over the notes for the writing assignment on page 228, or choose another story idea. Create at least two characters for your story by filling out a character chart for each one. Save your notes.

About the Author

Rudyard Kipling (1865–1936)

When Rudyard Kipling wrote "Rikki-tikki-tavi," he drew on his memories of India, where he was born. Kipling was six when his parents sent him to school in England. He returned to India in 1882 and became a journalist. He soon began to write sketches, short stories, and light verse.

In 1886 his first book, a collection of poems called *Departmental Ditties,* appeared. Between 1887 and 1889 he produced six volumes of short stories. When he returned to England in 1889, he was already considered one of the great writers of his day.

Kipling's short stories, novels, and poems have delighted readers of all ages. Some of his best-known works of fiction are *The Light That Failed, The Jungle Books, Captains Courageous,* and *Kim.* Among his most popular poems are "If," "The Ballad of East and West," and "Danny Deever." Several of Kipling's works have been made into movies. In 1907 he became the first English writer to win the Nobel Prize for literature.

Connecting Cultures

Words of Indian Origin

There are various languages spoken in India, including Bengali, Hindi, Hindustani, and Urdu, among others. When Rudyard Kipling wrote "Rikki-tikki-tavi," India was part of the British Empire. Many words of Indian origin found their way into the English language. The word *bungalow,* for example, is an *Anglo-Indian* word; it is an English word borrowed from an Indian language. The origin of bungalow is the Hindi word *bāṅglā,* which means "thatched house."

Making Connections: Activities

The origin and development of a word is known as its **etymology** (ĕt′ə-mŏl′ə-jē). Many dictionaries show the various changes a word has undergone in form and meaning since its earliest known use. The etymology of a word is often shown in brackets at the beginning of a dictionary entry. Trace the origin and development of each of these words in a college or an unabridged dictionary.

bandanna	jungle	pariah
curry	mango	shampoo
dungaree	pajamas	veranda

A Day's Wait

ERNEST HEMINGWAY

Sometimes the narrator of a story is a character who appears in the story. At other times, the narrator tells the story as an outside observer who plays no role in the events. The point of view *from which a writer chooses to have a story told affects your impression of the characters and events. In reading this story, ask yourself why Hemingway has chosen the father as narrator.*

1   He came into the room to shut the windows while we were still in bed, and I saw he looked ill. He was shivering, his face was white, and he walked slowly as though it ached to move.

2   "What's the matter, Schatz?"[1]

"I've got a headache."

"You better go back to bed."

"No, I'm all right."

"You go to bed. I'll see you when I'm dressed."

3   But when I came downstairs he was dressed, sitting by the fire, looking a very sick and miserable boy of nine years. When I put my hand on his forehead I knew he had a fever.

"You go up to bed," I said, "you're sick."

"I'm all right," he said.

When the doctor came he took the boy's temperature.

"What is it?" I asked him.

4   "One hundred and two."

Downstairs, the doctor left three different medicines in different colored capsules with instructions for giving them. One was to bring down the fever, another a purgative, the third to overcome an acid condition. The germs of influenza can only exist in an acid condition, he

5   explained. He seemed to know all about influenza and said there was nothing to worry about if the fever did not go above one hundred and four degrees. This was a light epidemic of flu and there was no danger if you avoided pneumonia.

Back in the room I wrote the boy's temperature down and made a note of the time to give the various capsules.

"Do you want me to read to you?"

6   "All right. If you want to," said the boy. His face was very white and there were dark areas under his eyes. He lay still in the bed and seemed very detached from what was going on.

I read aloud from Howard Pyle's *Book of Pirates;* but I could see he was not following what I was reading.

---

1. **Schatz:** a nickname taken from a German term of affection.

MOTIVATIONAL SUMMARY

A father is concerned when his son becomes ill, and he calls a doctor to examine the boy. The doctor takes the boy's temperature, which is one hundred and two degrees, and then pulls the father aside for a consultation. He tells the father privately that the boy has the flu, nothing to worry about unless his temperature climbs. A little later, the boy seems to be getting worse and begins to say things that don't make sense to his father. What is it that the boy is so worried about?

PRESENTATION

The **point of view** of a story determines what and how much the reader sees and knows. In the case of "A Day's Wait," the story is told through the eyes of only one of the characters, the father. Since the father cannot know the other charac-

---

"How do you feel, Schatz?" I asked him.

"Just the same, so far," he said.

I sat at the foot of the bed and read to myself while I waited for it to be time to give another capsule. It would have been natural for him to go to sleep, but when I looked up he was looking at the foot of the bed, looking very strangely.

"Why don't you try to go to sleep? I'll wake you up for the medicine."

7 "I'd rather stay awake."

8 After a while he said to me, "You don't have to stay in here with me, Papa, if it bothers you."

"It doesn't bother me."

"No, I mean you don't have to stay if it's going to bother you."

9 I thought perhaps he was a little lightheaded and after giving him the prescribed capsules at eleven o'clock I went out for a while.

It was a bright, cold day, the ground covered with a sleet that had frozen so that it seemed as if all the bare trees, the bushes, the cut brush and all the grass and the bare ground had been varnished with ice. I took the young Irish setter for a little walk up the road and along a frozen creek, but it was difficult to stand or walk on the glassy surface, and the red dog slipped and slithered and I fell twice, hard, once dropping my gun and having it slide away over the ice.

10 We flushed a covey of quail under a high clay bank with overhanging brush and I killed two as they went out of sight over the top of the bank. Some of the covey lit in trees, but most of them scattered into brush piles and it was necessary to jump on the ice-coated mounds of

11 brush several times before they would flush. Coming out while you were poised unsteadily on the icy, springy brush they made difficult shooting, and I killed two, missed five, and

---

7

Characterization. He wants to meet head-on whatever is coming.

8

Father apparently thinks boy means wasting time, sitting around the sickroom.

9

Use to answer **study question 2, p. 244.**

10

Covey means "a flock."

11

"Flushing" the quail refers to frightening them out of their hiding places.

VISUAL CONNECTIONS

Ideas for Writing

Ask students to imagine that they are parents of the little boy in the picture. The boy is ill, with a condition that could be serious if left untreated but can be cured with one simple treatment. Unfortunately, the treatment is very unpleasant, and the boy is frightened and refuses to allow the doctor to treat him. What might a parent say to convince the child to agree to something that is necessary for his own long-term good but is not pleasant in the short run? Students could write a paragraph as if it were the parent's explanation to the child, or they might act out the scene in which the insistent parents and the reluctant child discuss the issue.

243

ters' thoughts, as an omniscient narrator can, he cannot reveal certain information to the reader.

In this story, the father's limited point of view is necessary for there to be a story at all. If he had known initially how terrified his son was and why, the father would have immediately reassured him. The misunderstanding and the limited viewpoint allow the story's **conflict** to develop.

> **TRANSPARENCY 19**
> **Reader Response**
> *First Response* – asks students to assess their overall reaction to a story and support their opinions with specific details.

12
Father's attempt at reassurance is ironic in view of son's fear.

13
He has accepted what he thinks is coming but can't keep from thinking about it.

14
Plot. Expansion of father's awareness of son's fear leads to **climax** of story.

15
Boy has attended school in France, where degrees are measured in centigrade (Celsius), not Fahrenheit.

16
Kilometers are a metric measurement and are shorter than miles.

READING CHECK
1. He has the flu (p. 242).
2. If temperature rises above 104, boy may be in danger (p. 242).
3. He believes his disease is fatal; doesn't want others to catch it (p. 244).
4. He sees boy isn't listening (pp. 242, 244).

FOR STUDY AND DISCUSSION
1. French boys said a temperature above 44 degrees was fatal; boy didn't know they meant Celsius, not Fahrenheit.
2. Thinks son is just uncomfortable due to flu, "lightheaded" from medication.

244

---

started back pleased to have found a covey close to the house and happy there were so many left to find on another day.

At the house they said the boy had refused to let anyone come into the room.

"You can't come in," he said. "You mustn't get what I have."

I went up to him and found him in exactly the position I had left him, white-faced, but with the tops of his cheeks flushed by the fever, staring still, as he had stared, at the foot of the bed.

I took his temperature.

"What is it?"

12 "Something like a hundred," I said. It was one hundred and two and four tenths.

"It was a hundred and two," he said.

"Who said so?"

"The doctor."

"Your temperature is all right," I said. "It's nothing to worry about."

"I don't worry," he said, "but I can't keep
13 from thinking."

"Don't think," I said. "Just take it easy."

"I'm taking it easy," he said and looked straight ahead. He was evidently holding tight on to himself about something.

"Take this with water."

"Do you think it will do any good?"

"Of course it will."

I sat down and opened the *Pirate* book and commenced to read, but I could see he was not following, so I stopped.

"About what time do you think I'm going to die?" he asked.

"What?"

"About how long will it be before I die?"

14 "You aren't going to die. What's the matter with you?"

"Oh, yes, I am. I heard him say a hundred and two."

"People don't die with a fever of one hundred and two. That's a silly way to talk."

"I know they do. At school in France the boys told me you can't live with forty-four de-
15 grees. I've got a hundred and two."

He had been waiting to die all day, ever since nine o'clock in the morning.

"You poor Schatz," I said. "Poor old Schatz. It's like miles and kilometers. You aren't going to die. That's a different thermometer. On that thermometer thirty-seven is normal. On this kind it's ninety-eight."

"Are you sure?"

16 "Absolutely," I said. "It's like miles and kilometers. You know, like how many kilometers we make when we do seventy miles in the car?"

"Oh," he said.

But his gaze at the foot of the bed relaxed slowly. The hold over himself relaxed too, finally, and the next day it was very slack and he cried very easily at little things that were of no importance.

Reading Check
1. What is the doctor's diagnosis of the boy's illness?
2. Why does the father keep a record of the boy's temperature?
3. Why does the boy refuse to let anyone come into his room?
4. Why does the father stop reading aloud?

For Study and Discussion

Analyzing and Interpreting the Story

1. The boy in the story assumes that he is going to die before the day is over. What mistake leads him to this conclusion?

2. The father in the story doesn't realize what is going on in his son's mind. What does he assume is troubling the boy?

244 SHORT STORIES

MEETING INDIVIDUAL NEEDS
ESL/LEP • While waiting for his son's fever to break, the author hunts a covey of quail. The word *covey* describes a group of quail. Write the following expressions on the chalkboard and have students work together to fill in the appropriate "group" words:

a _____ of sheep (flock)
a _____ of ants (colony)
a _____ of lions (pride)
a _____ of fish (school)
a _____ of geese (flock; gaggle)
a _____ of cattle (herd)

Ernest Hemingway with his son.

3a. How does the boy show courage in facing what he believes to be his own death? **b.** How does he show concern for his father?

4. People often hold back their emotions when they face a crisis. How does the boy finally show the strain he has been under?

Literary Elements

Understanding the Narrator's Point of View

The person telling this story—the **narrator**—is a character in the story. You see the other characters and events from his point of view. Everything you learn in the story is what the narrator tells you—what he sees, what he hears, what he thinks. What you learn about the boy in the story is what the narrator reveals through direct observation. You have only his impressions of what is happening.

In real life you perceive events the way the narrator in this story does. You cannot read the minds of other people any more than the father in this story can read his son's thoughts.

"A Day's Wait" is an example of a story written from a **first-person point of view.** The term **first person** refers to the form of the pronoun. The narrator is the "I" telling the story.

What the author is able to show through this point of view is how the characters in the story fail to communicate. They talk without making themselves clear to each other. Here, for example, the father and son do not realize that they are talking about different things:

> After a while he said to me, "You don't have to stay here with me, Papa, if it bothers you."
> "It doesn't bother me."
> "No, I mean you don't have to stay if it's going to bother you."
> I thought perhaps he was a little lightheaded and after giving him the prescribed capsules at eleven o'clock I went out for a while.

1 What does the boy think is going to bother his
2 father? How does the father interpret the boy's words?
3 Find another passage in the story that shows a similar misunderstanding between father and son.

VISUAL CONNECTIONS
Exploring the Subject
According to some biographers, Hemingway was a fond father to his young sons. He was said to be so tender towards them that he rarely punished them and sometimes spoiled them. One incident revealed in Hemingway's *Letters* involved his son Jack, who had spit at the maid for frightening his brothers with a big live crab. The angry maid demanded that Hemingway spank Jack for his insolence. Hemingway took Jack into the next room, closed the door, and slapped his own leg, pretending to beat Jack, who contributed to the play-acting by wailing for mercy.

3a. Won't talk of his fear of dying; won't let anyone in, thinking they'd get fatally ill. **3b.** Tells father he doesn't have to stay if it bothers him.
4. He relaxes; next day he cries easily at little things.

LITERARY ELEMENTS
1. The boy thinks he is going to die. He has misunderstood and believes that he has a fatal illness. He thinks that he cannot live very much longer and that his death will upset his father. This is the reason that he suggests that the father can leave if *it* (his death) will bother him.
2. The father, thinking that the son is talking about his being ill with the flu, doesn't understand that he is talking about his own death. He thinks that his son is mildly delirious, not making sense because of his fever or because of the medication he is taking.
3. The passage on p. 242, which begins "I read aloud . . ." and ends on p. 243 " . . . to give another capsule," is another example of misunderstanding.

A Day's Wait 245

TRANSPARENCY 21
Literary Elements
Evaluating Short Stories – helps students apply critical thinking skills to analyze a short story.

CLOSURE
The author chose to tell this story from the father's **point of view** rather than the boy's. Ask students to write a brief explanation of how the choice of point of view creates the story's impact.

EXTENSION AND ENRICHMENT
Hemingway's definition of courage was "grace under pressure." Other definitions of courage include "doing what is right even when you are afraid to do it." Ask students to write their own definitions of courage.

FOCUS ON WRITING A SHORT STORY
You may want to discuss the two kinds of **third-person point of view**. In **third-person limited** the narrator is outside the story but enters the mind of one character. In **third-person omniscient** the narrator is outside of the story and can enter any character's mind. Find examples of both and help students to recognize the difference. Then encourage students to experiment with third person omniscient when writing the second version of their paragraphs.

ABOUT THE AUTHOR
Ernest Hemingway was named for his maternal grandfather, Ernest Hall, who fought and was wounded in the Civil War. The young Hemingway was raised on tales of military glory and professed that his favorite fiction included Tolstoy's battle scenes in *War and Peace*, Kipling's tales of British foot soldiers in colonial India, and Jack London's adventure tales. Hemingway wanted to go off to war in 1917 when World War I broke out in Europe, but his family convinced him to take a job as a journalist for the *Kansas City Star*. Determined to enlist but rejected by the army for defective vision, he later volunteered as an ambulance driver. When a shell exploded near his ambulance, he was seriously injured but carried to an aid station by an Italian soldier even more seriously injured than he. The first American wounded in the war, he was later cited by the Italian government for bravery.

LITERATURE AND MATH
1. *Kilogram* = 1000 grams.
Kiloliter = 1000 liters.
2. *Millimeter* = 1/1000th of a meter.
Milligram = 1/1000th of a gram; *milliliter* = 1/1000th of a liter.
3. *Decameter* = 10 meters; *decagram* = 10 grams.
Decigram = 1/10th of a gram; *deciliter* = 1/10th of a liter.
Hectometer = 100 meters; *centimeter* = 1/100th of a meter.

Focus on Writing a Short Story

Exploring Point of View

The **point of view** in a story is the angle from which the events are told. When you write a story, you can choose between first-person point of view and third-person point of view.

Write a paragraph for a story about a contest or disagreement in which you were involved. Use first-person point of view (with pronouns like *I*, *me*, and *my*) in your paragraph. Then write another version of the same events, using third-person point of view (with pronouns like *she*, *he*, *they*, *them*). Get together with a classmate and trade papers. Which version of each other's writing do you prefer and why? Save your writing.

About the Author

Ernest Hemingway (1899–1961)

Ernest Hemingway, who once defined courage as "grace under pressure," admired people who could face their own suffering bravely. The events in "A Day's Wait" are based on an actual incident in Hemingway's life when one of his sons was ill.

Hemingway perfected a simple, spare style that has influenced many other writers. He won the Pulitzer Prize in 1953 for his novel *The Old Man and the Sea*, which has become a favorite with young readers. In 1954 he was awarded the Nobel Prize for literature.

Literature and Mathematics

Prefixes Used in Measurement

The boy in the story confuses two systems of measurement. He assumes that the doctor is using the Celsius scale of temperature. On this scale, a normal temperature is 37 degrees. The boy doesn't realize that the doctor is using a Fahrenheit thermometer, on which the normal reading is 98.6 degrees.

In order to clear up the boy's confusion, the father uses the example of miles and kilometers, which are two different units of distance. As you probably know, a kilometer is a unit of measurement in the metric system. The *meter* is the basic unit of measurement for length or distance.

Making Connections: Activities

1. A kilometer is one thousand meters, which is equal to 0.6214 miles. The prefix *kilo-* comes from a Greek word meaning "a thousand." What is the word for a thousand grams? A thousand liters?

2. The prefix *milli-* comes from a Latin word meaning "thousand." When it is used in units of measurement, it means "one thousandth." What is the word for a thousandth of a meter? Of a gram? Of a liter?

3. Here are other prefixes used in the metric system and their meanings:

deca- (*or* deka-)	ten
deci-	one tenth
hecto-	one hundred
centi-	one hundredth

What is the meaning of *decameter*? Of *decagram*? Of *decigram*? Of *deciliter*? What is the difference between a *hectometer* and a *centimeter*?

Rip Van Winkle

WASHINGTON IRVING

"Rip Van Winkle" is among the best-known stories in world literature. In the nineteenth century, Joseph Jefferson turned Irving's story into a play, which had a long and successful run on the stage. One of the story's most celebrated aspects is Irving's use of setting to create mood. You may enjoy reading Irving's descriptive passages aloud.

1 Whoever has made a voyage up the Hudson must remember the Catskill Mountains. They are a branch of the great Appalachian family,[1] and are seen away to the west of the river, swelling up to a noble height, and lording it over the surrounding country. Every change of season, every change of weather, indeed, every hour of the day, produces some change in the magical hues and shapes of these mountains, and they are regarded by all the good wives, far and near, as perfect barometers. When the weather is fair and settled, they are clothed in blue and purple, and print their bold outlines on the clear evening sky; but, sometimes, when the rest of the landscape is cloudless, they will gather a hood of gray vapors about their summits, which, in the last rays of the setting sun, will glow and light up like a crown of glory.

At the foot of these fairy mountains, the voy-

Illustrations for the 1848 edition of *Rip Van Winkle* by Felix O. C. Darley (1822–1888).

---

1. **Appalachian** (ăp′ə-lā′chē-ən) **family:** a chain of mountains that extends from Quebec in eastern Canada to northern Alabama.

MOTIVATIONAL SUMMARY

Rip Van Winkle is well-liked by everyone except his wife. Dame Van Winkle nags Rip constantly to try to make him do this or that chore, but her scolding tongue makes the easygoing Rip long for escape. One day, Rip sets off for a day's hunting in the mountains. He meets an odd little man, whom Rip decides to help with his cask of ale. Rip thinks this is a pleasant way to postpone his much-dreaded return home, but the postponement is far longer than he expects.

PRESENTATION

A famous tall tale, Washington Irving's "Rip Van Winkle" carries the reader into a magical landscape where the impossible may happen, if the reader is willing to believe it. This escape into fantasy benefits greatly from Irving's beguiling

---

3
Setting. This idyllic village setting helps create calm, peaceful **mood.**

4
Latticed means "crisscrossed with woven strips of wood"; *gable* is a triangular wooden roof-brace.

5
Pre-Revolutionary War era.

6 Summarizing
Why is Rip popular in the village? He is friendly, good-natured, kind, meek.

VISUAL CONNECTIONS
Exploring the Subject
Rip Van Winkle likes making toys for children. He has whittled a tiny sailboat (clue: woodshavings under his bench) which he is testing in a washtub as two of the children watch and two others romp and climb on him. There are some clues that Rip needs to do chores instead of play: a broken window pane, vines growing on the roof. The illustration also contains a number of tools in places where they would not ordinarily be. Perhaps Rip set them out for a purpose but was then distracted, or perhaps Dame Van Winkle set them out as reminders and Rip ignored them. The tools include a ladder leaning against the house, a rake and pitchfork in the doorway, a saddle on the doorpost, and a frayed horse collar on the wall. Rip also has his rifle tucked under his arm, as if he were on his way out to hunt when he decided to make a sailboat for the children instead.

---

3 ager may have seen the light smoke curling up from a village, whose shingle roofs gleam among the trees, just where the blue tints of the upland melt away into the fresh green of the nearer landscape. It is a little village, of great antiquity, having been founded by some of the Dutch colonists, in the early times of the province. There were some of the houses of the original settlers standing within a few years,[2] built of small yellow bricks brought 4 from Holland, having latticed windows and gable fronts, surmounted with weathercocks.

2. **within a few years:** until a few years ago. This story was written around 1820.

In that same village, and in one of these very houses, which was sadly timeworn and weather-beaten, there lived many years since, 5 while the country was yet a province of Great Britain, a simple, good-natured fellow, of the name of Rip Van Winkle. He was a descendant of the Van Winkles who figured so gallantly in the chivalrous days of Peter Stuyvesant.[3] He inherited, however, but little of the martial char- 6 acter of his ancestors. I have observed that he was a simple, good-natured man; he was,

3. **Peter Stuyvesant** (stī′və-sənt): the last governor (1646–1664) of the Dutch colony of New Netherland, which was renamed New York after the British took control of it in 1664.

248 SHORT STORIES

descriptions of the Catskill Mountains of New York. Irving's protagonist, Rip Van Winkle, longs to escape many things: work, responsibility for his children, and especially his nagging wife. He does not realize it at the time, but the little men he meets in the woods and the enchanted drink they give him will allow him the escape he desires; however, it costs him many things that others would not willingly give up.

moreover, a kind neighbor, and an obedient, henpecked husband. Indeed, to the latter circumstance might be owing that meekness of spirit which gained him such universal popularity; for those men are most apt to be conciliating[4] abroad who are under the discipline of shrews at home. Their tempers, doubtless, are rendered pliant in the fiery furnace of domestic trouble, which is worth all the sermons in the world for teaching the virtues of patience and long-suffering. A quarrelsome wife may, therefore, in some respects, be considered a tolerable blessing; and if so, Rip Van Winkle was thrice blessed.

Certain it is, that he was a great favorite among all the good wives of the village, who took his part in all family squabbles, and never failed, whenever they talked those matters over in their evening gossipings, to lay all the blame on Dame Van Winkle. The children of the village, too, would shout with joy whenever he approached. He assisted at their sports, made their playthings, taught them to fly kites and shoot marbles, and told them long stories of ghosts, witches, and Indians. Whenever he went dodging about the village, he was surrounded by a troop of them, hanging on his coat skirts, clambering on his back, and playing a thousand tricks on him with impunity,[5] and not a dog would bark at him throughout the neighborhood.

The great error in Rip's character was an insuperable dislike of all kinds of profitable labor. It could not be from the want of perseverance; for he would sit on a wet rock, with a rod as long and heavy as a Tartar's lance,[6] and fish all day without a murmur, even though he should not be encouraged by a single nibble. He would carry a fowling piece[7] on his shoulder for hours together, trudging through woods and swamps, and up hill and down dale, to shoot a few squirrels or wild pigeons. He would never refuse to assist a neighbor even in the roughest toil, and was a foremost man at all country frolics for husking Indian corn, or building stone fences. The women of the village, too, used to employ him to run their errands, and to do such little odd jobs as their less obliging husbands would not do for them. In a word, Rip was ready to attend to anybody's business but his own; but as to doing family duty, and keeping his farm in order, he found it impossible.

In fact, he declared it was of no use to work on his farm; it was the most pestilent[8] little piece of ground in the whole country; everything about it went wrong, and would go wrong, in spite of him. His fences were continually falling to pieces; his cow would either go astray or get among the cabbages; weeds were sure to grow quicker in his fields than anywhere else; the rain always made a point of setting in just as he had some outdoor work to do; so that his estate had dwindled away under his management, acre by acre, until there was little more left than a mere patch of Indian corn and potatoes, and was the worst-conditioned farm in the neighborhood.

His children, too, were as ragged and wild as if they belonged to nobody. His son Rip promised to inherit the habits, with the old clothes, of his father. He was generally seen trooping like a colt at his mother's heels, equipped in a pair of his father's castoff galligaskins,[9] which he had to hold up with one hand, as a fine lady does her train in bad weather.

---

4. **conciliating:** friendly; easygoing.
5. **with impunity** (ĭm-pyōō'nə-tē): without fear of punishment.
6. **Tartar's** (tär'tərz) **lance:** The Tartars were Mongolian tribes that invaded Europe in the thirteenth century. The Tartar warriors used lances, or long, heavy spears.
7. **fowling piece:** a light gun, used most often for shooting birds.
8. **pestilent:** here, troublesome.
9. **galligaskins** (găl'ĭ-găs'kĭnz): loose, wide breeches.

7
Dame Van Winkle is three times as quarrelsome as the average quarrelsome wife.

8
Dame Van Winkle does not actually appear very often in the story, yet a negative view of her is established early.

9
Foreshadowing. Stories of ghosts and witches and children's "tricks" foreshadow trick played by ghosts in mountains.

10
Characterization. Rip enjoys fishing, hunting, and helping his neighbors rather than doing his own work.

11 Finding Details
What excuses does Rip make for not working on his farm?
"Pestilent" farm, falling fences, straying cows, growing weeds, inopportune weather.

12
Young Rip will follow in father's idle footsteps.

13
A *train* is a long, trailing part of a lady's skirt.

MEETING INDIVIDUAL NEEDS

ESL/LEP • Rip uses the following archaic words in conversation with his dog Wolf: *thou, thy,* and *thee*—forms which may be unfamiliar to students. Explain that *thy* is used in place of *your* to indicate possession. *Thee* substitutes for *you* as a direct or indirect object or as an object of the preposition. *Thou* is used in place of *you* as the subject of a sentence.

14
Based on the narrator's description of Rip, her criticism is apparently justified.

15 Drawing Conclusions
Why does his response provoke his wife? Among other things, it shows Rip's complacency and preference for doing nothing.

16
Humorous exaggeration: the only "side" of the house for a henpecked husband is the "outside."

17
Detailed list humorously depicts Wolf's "hangdog" manner.

18
Humor based on aphorism; translates individual (Rip's) experience to universal application.

19
Newspapers are not easy to find, so the "sages" debate old news.

VISUAL CONNECTIONS
Relating Expression Skills
The story refers to Derrick Van Bummel, the schoolmaster, as being the person who usually reads the news to the other members of the "club of the sages." Van Bummel is described as being "dapper," meaning neat or well-dressed. Ask students to identify at least three "dapper" aspects of the newspaper-reader's attire. Students might use the illustration on p. 247 for contrast. (Answers may include the following: fancy buckles on his shoes, a walking stick, a tidy cap to restrain his hair, a vest, and a prim, high collar.)

Rip Van Winkle, however, was one of those happy mortals, of foolish, well-oiled dispositions, who take the world easy, eat white bread or brown, whichever can be got with least thought or trouble, and would rather starve on a penny than work for a pound.¹⁰ If left to himself, he would have whistled life away in perfect contentment; but his wife kept continually dinning in his ears about his idleness, his carelessness, and the ruin he was bringing on his family. Morning, noon, and night, her tongue was incessantly going, and everything he said or did was sure to produce a torrent of household eloquence. Rip had but one way of replying to all lectures of the kind, and that, by frequent use, had grown into a habit. He shrugged his shoulders, shook his head, cast up his eyes, but said nothing. This, however, always provoked a fresh volley from his wife; so that he would take to the outside of the house—the only side which, in truth, belongs to a henpecked husband.

Rip's sole domestic adherent¹¹ was his dog Wolf, who was as much henpecked as his master; for Dame Van Winkle regarded them as companions in idleness, and even looked upon Wolf with an evil eye, as the cause of his master's going so often astray. True it is, in all points of spirit befitting an honorable dog, he was as courageous an animal as ever scoured the woods—but what courage can withstand the terrors of a woman's tongue? The moment Wolf entered the house his crest fell, his tail drooped to the ground, or curled between his legs, he sneaked about with a gallows air, casting many a sidelong glance at Dame Van Winkle, and at the least flourish of a broomstick or ladle, he would fly to the door, yelping.

Times grew worse and worse with Rip Van Winkle as years of matrimony rolled on; a tart temper never mellows with age, and a sharp tongue is the only edged tool that grows keener with constant use. For a long while he used to console himself, when driven from home, by frequenting a kind of perpetual club of the sages, philosophers, and other idle personages of the village, which held its sessions on a bench before a small inn, designated by a portrait of His Majesty George the Third. Here they used to sit in the shade through a long, lazy summer's day, talking listlessly over village gossip, or telling endless sleepy stories about nothing. But it would have been worth any statesman's money to have heard the profound discussions that sometimes took place, when by chance an old newspaper fell into their hands from some passing traveler. How

---

10. **pound:** the basic unit of British money, used in the colonies.
11. **adherent** (ăd-hîr′ənt): follower or supporter.

250 SHORT STORIES

READING SKILLS PRACTICE
The underlined passage can be used to give students practice in the reading skill of identifying specific details. Ask students to read the passage and choose the correct response to the question "Who is the terrible shrew?"

A. Nicholas Vedder. (Incorrect detail. Vedder is the inn's landlord and the "august personage.") **B.** Rip's wife. (Correct.) **C.** A small mammal. (Incorrect. *Shrew* is used here with a different meaning.) **D.** The "august personage." (Incorrect detail. The "august personage" is Nicholas Vedder.)

---

solemnly they would listen to the contents, as drawled out by Derrick Van Bummel, the schoolmaster, a dapper, learned little man, who was not to be daunted by the most gigantic word in the dictionary; and how sagely they would deliberate upon public events some months after they had taken place.

20 The opinions of this club were completely controlled by Nicholas Vedder, a patriarch[12] of the village, and landlord of the inn, at the door of which he took his seat from morning till night, just moving sufficiently to avoid the sun and keep in the shade of a large tree; so that the neighbors could tell the hour by his movements as accurately as by a sundial. It is true he 21 was rarely heard to speak, but smoked his pipe incessantly. His adherents, however, perfectly understood him, and knew how to gather his opinions. When anything that was read or related displeased him, he was observed to smoke his pipe <u>vehemently</u>, and to send forth short, frequent, and angry puffs; but when pleased, he would inhale the smoke slowly and <u>tranquilly</u>, and emit it in light and <u>placid</u> clouds; and sometimes, taking the pipe from his mouth, and letting the fragrant vapor curl about his nose, would gravely nod his head in token of perfect <u>approbation</u>.

▶From even this stronghold the unlucky Rip was at length routed by his wife, who would suddenly break in upon the tranquillity of the assemblage and call the members all to naught; nor was that august[13] personage, Nicholas Vedder himself, sacred from the daring tongue of this terrible shrew, who charged him outright with encouraging her husband in habits of idleness.◀

22 Poor Rip was at last reduced almost to despair; and his only alternative, to escape from the labor of the farm and clamor of his wife, was to take gun in hand and stroll away into the woods. Here he would sometimes seat himself at the foot of a tree, and share the contents of his wallet[14] with Wolf, with whom he sympathized as a fellow sufferer in persecution.
23 "Poor Wolf," he would say, "thy mistress leads thee a dog's life of it; but never mind, my lad, whilst I live thou shalt never want a friend to stand by thee!" Wolf would wag his tail, look wistfully in his master's face, and if dogs can feel pity, I believe he returned the <u>sentiment</u> with all his heart.

24 In a long ramble of the kind on a fine autumnal day, Rip had unconsciously scrambled to one of the highest parts of the Catskill Mountains. He was after his favorite sport of squirrel shooting, and the still solitudes[15] had echoed and reechoed with the reports of his gun. Panting and fatigued, he threw himself, late in the afternoon, on a green <u>knoll</u>, covered with mountain herbage, that crowned the brow 25 of a <u>precipice</u>. From an opening between the trees he could overlook all the lower country for many a mile of rich woodland. He saw at a distance the lordly Hudson, far, far below him, moving on its silent but majestic course, with the reflection of a purple cloud, or the sail of a lagging bark,[16] here and there sleeping on its glassy bosom, and at last losing itself in the blue highlands.

On the other side he looked down into a deep mountain glen, wild, lonely, and shagged, the bottom filled with fragments from the overhanging cliffs, and scarcely lighted by the reflected rays of the setting sun. 26 For some time Rip lay musing on this scene. Evening was gradually advancing. The mountains began to throw their long blue shadows

---

12. **patriarch** (pā′trē-ärk′): a man who is head of a family or a tribe; here, an old man of great dignity and authority.
13. **august** (ô-gŭst′): deserving respect.
14. **wallet**: here, a bag for carrying provisions.
15. **solitudes**: deserted places.
16. **bark**: boat.

---

20 Characterization. Vedder is so lazy that he sits all day every day, moving his seat only to avoid the sun.

21 Finding Details
How does Vedder reveal his opinions? By the way he smokes his pipe.

22 His efforts to escape his wife drive him to the ill-fated meeting in the woods.

23 Rip unintentionally breaks this promise later; Wolf is left friendless while Rip sleeps.

24 It is autumn, when many animals prepare to hibernate for the winter; foreshadows Rip's long sleep.

25 Mood. Stillness and dreamlike quality in description of distant scene; contrasts with Rip's henpecked life in town.

26 Dark, wild glen contrasts with the rich woodland described in preceding paragraph; sets **mood** for strange events that follow.

▶Reading Skills Objective: Identifying Specific Details

MEETING INDIVIDUAL NEEDS
ESL/LEP • Irving often uses compound words in describing his characters, including the following adjectives:

henpecked husband (p. 249)

foremost man (p. 249)
weather-beaten countenance (p.253)
statuelike gaze (p. 253)
lackluster countenances (p. 253)
self-important man (p. 257)

Write these on the chalkboard, encouraging students to use the context of the sentence to guess at their meanings.

27
Darkness in the forest is less frightening than his wife.

28 Analyzing
How do you know Rip is not dreaming? Wolf's behavior proves Rip is not dreaming; he senses danger.

29
Characterization. Despite his fear, Rip helps the stranger.

30
"Antique" (old-fashioned) dress is as odd to Rip as his own attire is upon his return to the village.

31
Setting. Dramatic landscape sets scene and **mood,** foreshadowing events to follow. "Rolling" relates to the later-discovered source of the sound.

32
Ninepins is a bowling game.

---

over the valleys. He saw that it would be dark before he could reach the village, and he 27 heaved a heavy sigh when he thought of encountering the terrors of Dame Van Winkle.

As he was about to descend, he heard a voice from a distance, hallooing, "Rip Van Winkle! Rip Van Winkle!" He looked round, but could see nothing but a crow winging its solitary flight across the mountain. He thought his fancy[17] must have deceived him, and turned again to descend, when he heard the same cry ring through the still evening air: "Rip Van Winkle! Rip Van Winkle!" At the same time 28 Wolf bristled up his back, and giving a low growl, skulked to his master's side, looking fearfully down into the glen. Rip now felt a vague apprehension[18] stealing over him; he looked anxiously in the same direction, and perceived a strange figure slowly toiling up the rocks, and bending under the weight of something he carried on his back. He was surprised to see any human being in this lonely and un- 29 frequented place, but supposing it to be someone of the neighborhood in need of his assistance, he hastened down to yield it.

On nearer approach he was still more surprised at the singularity of the stranger's appearance. He was a short, square-built old fellow, with thick, bushy hair and a grizzled 30 beard. His dress was of the antique Dutch fashion—a cloth jerkin[19] strapped round the waist—several pairs of breeches, the outer one of ample volume, decorated with rows of buttons down the sides, and bunches at the knees. He bore on his shoulder a stout keg, that seemed full of liquor, and made signs for Rip to approach and assist him with the load. Though rather shy and distrustful of this new acquaintance, Rip complied with his usual

readiness; and mutually relieving one another, they clambered up a narrow gully, apparently the dry bed of a mountain torrent. As they as- 31 cended, Rip every now and then heard long rolling peals, like distant thunder, that seemed to issue out of a deep ravine, or rather cleft, between lofty rocks, toward which their rugged path conducted. He paused for an instant, but supposing it to be the muttering of one of those transient thundershowers which often take place in mountain heights, he proceeded. Passing through the ravine, they came to a hollow, like a small amphitheater,[20] surrounded by perpendicular precipices, over the brinks of which trees shot their branches, so that you only caught glimpses of the azure sky and the bright evening cloud. During the whole time Rip and his companion had labored on in silence; for though Rip marveled greatly what could be the object of carrying a keg of liquor up this wild mountain, yet there was something strange and incomprehensible about the unknown, that inspired awe and checked familiarity.

On entering the amphitheater, new objects of wonder presented themselves. On a level spot in the center was a company of odd- 32 looking personages playing at ninepins. They were dressed in a quaint, outlandish fashion; some wore short doublets,[21] others jerkins, with long knives in their belts, and most of them had enormous breeches, of style similar to that of the guide's. Their visages,[22] too, were peculiar. One had a large head, broad face, and small, piggish eyes. The face of another seemed to consist entirely of nose, and was surmounted by a white sugar-loaf hat,[23] set off with a little red cock's tail. They all had

---

17. **fancy:** imagination.
18. **apprehension** (ăp′rĭ-hĕn′shən): fear.
19. **jerkin:** a short, fitted jacket.

20. **amphitheater** (ăm′fə-thē′ə-tər): here, a level area surrounded by mountain slopes.
21. **doublets:** close-fitting, elaborate jackets.
22. **visages** (vĭz′ĭj-əz): faces.
23. **sugar-loaf hat:** a cone-shaped hat.

GEOGRAPHY LINK

As you read and discuss this story, you might want to bring to class a map of New York or the northeastern United States so that you can point out the Hudson River and the Catskill Mountains. You might want to use a topographical map of the region to show the Appalachian mountain range and its relationship to the Catskills.

TRANSPARENCIES 17 & 18
Fine Art
Theme: *Building Blocks* — invites students to explore artworks that show how individual elements contribute to the whole.

---

beards, of various shapes and colors. There was one who seemed to be the commander. He was a stout old gentleman, with a weather-beaten <u>countenance</u>; he wore a laced doublet, broad belt and hanger,[24] high-crowned hat and feather, red stockings, and high-heeled 33 shoes, with roses in them. The whole group reminded Rip of the figures in an old Flemish[25] painting, in the parlor of the village parson, which had been brought over from Holland at the time of the settlement.

What seemed particularly odd to Rip was that, though these folks were evidently amus-
34 ing themselves, yet they maintained the gravest faces, the most mysterious silence, and were the most melancholy party of pleasure he had

ever witnessed. Nothing interrupted the stillness of the scene but the noise of the balls, which, whenever they were rolled, echoed along the mountains like rumbling peals of thunder.

As Rip and his companion approached them, they suddenly stopped their play, and stared at him with such fixed, statuelike gaze, 35 and such strange, lackluster countenances, that his heart turned within him, and his knees smote together. His companion now emptied the contents of the keg into large flagons,[26] and made signs to him to wait upon the company. He obeyed with fear and trembling; they quaffed[27] the liquor in profound silence, and then returned to their game.

By degrees Rip's awe and apprehension sub-

24. **hanger:** here, a short sword.
25. **Flemish:** referring to Flanders, a former country in northwest Europe that included part of modern-day France, all of Belgium, and the southern portion of the Netherlands, or Holland.

26. **flagons** (flăg′ənz): containers with handles and spouts.
27. **quaffed** (kwäft): drank deeply.

33
Foreshadowing. A clue to their identity: as ghosts, their dress has not changed.

34
Play on "gravest": the men are from beyond the grave; their demeanor reflects this.

35
Lackluster means "dim" and refers to their ghostliness, contributing to Rip's "fear and trembling."

VISUAL CONNECTIONS
Exploring the Subject
As the sun sets over the Catskills, Rip pours ale for the strange men who have been playing ninepins in the mountain ravine. Rip is apparently unnerved by the experience: the ale he is pouring is missing the cup. All of the men are wearing wide Dutch pantaloons, popular in a much earlier era than Rip's. They are also wearing jerkins: jackets that are fitted closer to the chest and worn belted. The "commander" is more richly attired than his followers, wearing a belted jerkin with lace on it ("laced"), a long-feathered cap, a filagreed short sword, and fancy rose decorations on his shoes.

36 "Naturally a thirsty soul" suggests that Rip has always enjoyed liquor.

37 Waking on the knoll implies he may have fallen asleep there and dreamed everything.

38 Irony. He has slept many years there.

39 Characterization. Rip blames the flagon for his difficulties, much as he previously blamed the elements for his farming problems.

40 Summarizing
What does Rip think has happened to his gun? That the strange men have stolen it.

41 Another clue that things are not what they seem.

---

sided. He even ventured, when no eye was fixed upon him, to taste the beverage, which he found had much of the flavor of excellent 36 Holland gin. He was naturally a thirsty soul, and was soon tempted to repeat the draft.[28] One taste provoked another; and he repeated his visits to the flagon so often that at length his senses were overpowered, his eyes swam in his head, his head gradually declined, and he fell into a deep sleep.

37 On waking, he found himself on the green knoll whence he had first seen the old man of the glen. He rubbed his eyes—it was a bright sunny morning. The birds were hopping and twittering among the bushes, and the eagle was wheeling aloft, and breasting the pure moun-
38 tain breeze. "Surely," thought Rip, "I have not slept here all night." He recalled the occurrences before he fell asleep. The strange man with a keg of liquor—the mountain ravine—the wild retreat among the rocks—the woebegone party at ninepins—the flagon—
39 "Oh! that flagon! that wicked flagon!" thought Rip—"what excuse shall I make to Dame Van Winkle?"

He looked round for his gun, but in place of the clean, well-oiled fowling piece, he found an old firelock lying by him, the barrel incrusted with rust, the lock falling off, and the stock worm-eaten. He now suspected that the grave roisters[29] of the mountain had put a trick upon him, and, having dosed him with liquor, had
40 robbed him of his gun. Wolf, too, had disappeared, but he might have strayed away after a squirrel or partridge. He whistled after him and shouted his name, but all in vain; the echoes repeated his whistle and shout, but no dog was to be seen.

He determined to revisit the scene of the last evening's gambol,[30] and if he met with any of the party, to demand his dog and gun. As he rose to walk, he found himself stiff in the joints. "These mountain beds do not agree with me," thought Rip, "and if this frolic should lay me up with a fit of the rheumatism, I shall have a blessed time with Dame Van Winkle." With some difficulty he got down into the glen. He found the gully up which he and his companion had ascended the preceding evening; but to his astonishment a mountain stream was now foaming down it, leaping from rock to rock, and filling the glen with babbling murmurs. He, however, made shift to scramble up its sides, working his toilsome way through thickets of birch, sassafras, and witch hazel, and sometimes tripped up or entangled by the wild grapevines that twisted their coils or tendrils from tree to tree, and spread a kind of network in his path.

At length he reached to where the ravine had opened through the cliffs to the amphitheater; but no traces of such opening remained. The rocks presented a high wall over which the torrent came tumbling in a sheet of feathery foam, and fell into a broad, deep basin, black from the shadows of the surrounding forest. Here, then, poor Rip was brought to a stand. He again called and whistled after his dog; he was only answered by the cawing of a flock of idle crows, who seemed to look down and scoff at the poor man's perplexities. What was to be done? The morning was passing away, and Rip felt famished for want of his breakfast. He grieved to give up his dog and gun; he dreaded to meet his wife; but it would not do to starve among the mountains. He shook his head, shouldered the rusty firelock, and, with a heart full of trouble and anxiety, turned his steps homeward.

As he approached the village, he met a num-
41 ber of people, but none whom he knew, which somewhat surprised him, for he had thought himself acquainted with everyone in the coun-

---
28. **draft:** here, a drink.
29. **roisters:** merrymakers; also called *roisterers*.
30. **gambol:** frolic.

try round. Their dress, too, was of a different fashion from that to which he was accustomed. They all stared at him with equal marks of surprise, and whenever they cast their eyes upon him, invariably stroked their chins. The recurrence of this gesture induced Rip to do the same, when, to his astonishment, he found his beard had grown a foot long!

He had now entered the outskirts of the village. A troop of strange children ran at his heels, hooting after him, and pointing at his gray beard. The dogs, too, not one of which he recognized for an old acquaintance, barked at him as he passed. The very village was altered; it was larger and more populous. There were rows of houses which he had never seen before, and those which had been his familiar haunts had disappeared. Strange names were over the doors—strange faces at the windows—everything was strange. His mind now misgave him; he began to doubt whether both he and the world around him were not bewitched. Surely this was his native village, which he had left but the day before. There stood the Catskill Mountains—there ran the silver Hudson at a distance—there was every hill and dale precisely as it had always been—Rip was sorely perplexed. "That flagon last night," thought he, "has addled[31] my poor head sadly!"

31. **addled:** confused.

It was with some difficulty that he found the way to his own house, which he approached with silent awe, expecting every moment to hear the shrill voice of Dame Van Winkle. He found the house gone to decay—the roof fallen in, the windows shattered, and the doors off the hinges. A half-starved dog that looked like Wolf was skulking about it. Rip called him by name, but the cur snarled, showed his teeth, and passed on. This was an unkind cut indeed. "My very dog," sighed poor Rip, "has forgotten me!"

42 Expressing an Opinion
Does it seem likely that Rip would not have noticed his long beard earlier? Answers will vary. Most readers will note that Rip is slow to pick up on the clues about what has happened to him.

43
Suspense. The clues don't yet reveal the cause of the confusion; the first-time reader of this should be as perplexed as Rip.

44
Due to Rip's neglect of his household, its "overnight" destruction may not tell him how much time has passed.

VISUAL CONNECTIONS
Exploring the Subject
Rip Van Winkle has returned to his village, but he has not yet realized the length of his absence or its effect on him. Shown here is his shock that a dog he thinks is his own Wolf snarls at him (the dog is apparently one of Wolf's descendants). Rip is described in the story as being unaware of how he has changed, although it seems that he should have noticed. His hair and beard have turned white and grown long, his gun is rusty, his shoes have lost the toes, and his clothes have decayed into rags.

MEETING INDIVIDUAL NEEDS
Visual Learners • Students can follow closely the changes taking place in this story if they make a time line of some of the events that occurred in American history during Rip's sleep. You might suggest that students consult a history textbook or a reference source, which lists major events in the United States between the American Revolution and Independence.

45
Irony. He is so frightened by the changes that he even calls out for his wife.

46
The "Union" refers to the newly formed United States; the flag is an early "stars and stripes" American flag.

47
King George III's portrait and George Washington's are humorously similar: red-faced with white periwigs; only clothing details are different.

48 Summarizing
How has the atmosphere of the village changed? Village is now busy and up-to-date on the news. Villagers are a "new" people: Americans now.

49
The new men at the tavern are similar to Rip's old friends in their interest in political discussion.

50
Rip's strange actions and odd appearance arouse suspicion; though won, the war is still uppermost in people's minds.

He entered the house, which, to tell the truth, Dame Van Winkle had always kept in neat order. It was empty, forlorn, and apparently abandoned. **45** This desolateness overcame all his fears—he called loudly for his wife and children—the lonely chambers rang for a moment with his voice, and then all again was silence.

He now hurried forth, and hastened to his old resort, the village inn—but it too was gone. A large, rickety wooden building stood in its place, with great gaping windows, some of them broken and mended with old hats and petticoats, and over the door was painted, **46** "The Union Hotel, by Jonathan Doolittle." Instead of the great tree that used to shelter the quiet little Dutch inn of yore, there now was reared a tall naked pole, with something on the top that looked like a red nightcap,³² and from it was fluttering a flag, on which was a singular assemblage of stars and stripes—all this was strange and incomprehensible. He recognized **47** on the sign, however, the ruby face of King George, under which he had smoked so many a peaceful pipe; but even this was singularly changed. The red coat was changed for one of blue and buff, a sword was held in the hand instead of a scepter, the head was decorated with a cocked hat, and underneath was painted in large characters, GENERAL WASHINGTON.

There was, as usual, a crowd of folk about the door, but none that Rip recollected. The very character of the people seemed changed. There was a busy, bustling tone about it, instead of the accustomed tranquillity. He looked in vain for the sage Nicholas Vedder, with his broad face, double chin, and fair long pipe, uttering clouds of tobacco smoke instead of idle speeches; or Van Bummel, the schoolmaster, doling forth the contents of an ancient newspaper. In place of these, a lean, bilious-looking³³ fellow, with his pockets full of handbills, was talking vehemently about rights of citizens—elections—members of Congress—liberty—Bunker's Hill—heroes of **48** seventy-six—and other words, which were a perfect Babylonish jargon³⁴ to the bewildered Van Winkle.

The appearance of Rip, with his long, grizzled beard, his rusty fowling piece, his uncouth dress, and an army of women and children at his heels, soon attracted the attention of the **49** tavern politicians. They crowded round him, eyeing him from head to foot with great curiosity. The orator bustled up to him, and drawing him partly aside, inquired "on which side he voted?" Rip stared in vacant stupidity. Another short but busy little fellow pulled him by the arm, and, rising on tiptoe, inquired in his ear, "whether he was Federal or Democrat?"³⁵ Rip was equally at a loss to comprehend the question, when a knowing, self-important old gentleman, in a sharp cocked hat, made his way through the crowd, putting them to the right and left with his elbows as he passed, and planting himself before Van Winkle, with one arm akimbo,³⁶ the other resting on his cane, his keen eyes and sharp hat penetrating, as it were, into his very soul, demanded in an aus- **50** tere tone, "what brought him to the election with a gun on his shoulder, and a mob at his heels; and whether he meant to breed a riot in the village?"

---

32. **red nightcap:** Rip's interpretation of the liberty cap, a symbol of freedom.
33. **bilious** (bĭl′yəs) **-looking:** having a bad-tempered look.
34. **Babylonish** (băb′ə-lŏn′ĭsh) **jargon:** unintelligible language. According to Genesis 11:1–9, the people of Babel, or Babylon, tried to build a tower that would reach to heaven. They were forced to stop their work when God caused them to speak different languages.
35. **Federal or Democrat:** a member of the Federalist Party or the Democratic-Republican Party. These were the two political parties in the early years of United States history.
36. **akimbo:** holding the hand on the hip with the elbow outward.

51 "Alas! gentlemen," cried Rip, somewhat dismayed, "I am a poor quiet man, a native of the place, and a loyal subject of the King, God bless him!"

Here a general shout burst from the bystanders—"A Tory![37] a Tory! a spy! a refugee! hustle him! away with him!" It was with great difficulty that the self-important man in the cocked hat restored order; and demanded again of the unknown culprit, what he came there for, and whom he was seeking. The poor man humbly assured him that he meant no harm, but merely came there in search of some of his neighbors, who used to keep about the tavern.

"Well—who are they?—name them."

Rip bethought himself a moment, and inquired, "Where's Nicholas Vedder?"

52 There was a silence for a little while, when an old man replied, in a thin, piping voice, "Nicholas Vedder! why, he is dead and gone these eighteen years! There was a wooden tombstone in the churchyard that used to tell all about him, but that's rotten and gone too."

"Where's Brom Dutcher?"

"Oh, he went off to the army in the beginning of the war; some say he was killed at the storming of Stony Point[38]—others say he was drowned in a squall at the foot of Antony's Nose.[39] I don't know—he never came back again."

"Where's Van Bummel, the schoolmaster?"

"He went off to the wars too, was a great militia general, and is now in Congress."

Rip's heart died away at hearing of these sad changes in his home and friends, and finding himself thus alone in the world. Every answer puzzled him, too, by treating of such enormous lapses of time, and of matters which he could not understand: war—Congress—Stony Point; he had no courage to ask after any more friends, but cried out in despair, "Does nobody here know Rip Van Winkle?"

53 "Oh, Rip Van Winkle!" exclaimed two or three; "oh, to be sure! that's Rip Van Winkle yonder, leaning against the tree."

Rip looked, and beheld a precise copy of himself, as he went up the mountain; apparently as lazy, and certainly as ragged. The poor fellow was now completely bewildered. He doubted his own identity, and whether he was himself or another man. In the midst of his bewilderment, the man in the cocked hat demanded who he was, and what was his name.

"God knows," exclaimed he, at his wit's end; "I'm not myself—I'm somebody else—that's me yonder—no—that's somebody else got into my shoes—I was myself last night, but I fell asleep on the mountain, and they've changed my gun, and everything's changed, and I'm changed, and I can't tell what's my name, or who I am!"

54 The bystanders began now to look at each other, nod, wink significantly, and tap their fingers against their foreheads. There was a whisper, also, about securing the gun, and keeping the old fellow from doing mischief, at the very suggestion of which the self-important man in the cocked hat retired

55 quickly. At this critical moment a fresh, comely[40] woman pressed through the throng to get a peep at the gray-bearded man. She had a chubby child in her arms, which, frightened at his looks, began to cry. "Hush, Rip," cried she, "hush, you little fool; the old man

---

37. **Tory:** someone who sided with the British cause during the American Revolution.
38. **Stony Point:** a town on the Hudson River where American Revolutionary troops under General Anthony Wayne won an important battle against the British in July 1779.
39. **Antony's Nose:** a mountain on the Hudson River. It was called *Antonies Neus* by the Dutch, and changed to *Anthony's Nose* by the British.
40. **comely** (kŭm′lē): beautiful.

51
Irony. Exactly the wrong words to say.

52
The only person who remembers Vedder is an old man, a hint at how long Rip has been gone.

53 Making Inferences
Who do you think this "precise copy" of Rip is? Rip's son, also named Rip, who even when young "promised to inherit the habits, with the old clothes, of his father" (p. 249).

54
They think he is crazy.

55 Analyzing
Why is this moment "critical"? One response might be that they will lock him up before he can learn what has happened to his family and to himself.

won't hurt you." The name of the child, the air of the mother, the tone of her voice, all awakened a train of recollections in his mind. "What is your name, my good woman?" asked he.

"Judith Gardenier."

"And your father's name?"

"Ah, poor man, Rip Van Winkle was his name, but it's twenty years since he went away from home with his gun, and never has been heard of since—his dog came home without him; but whether he shot himself, or was carried away by the Indians, nobody can tell. I was then but a little girl."

Rip had but one question more to ask; but he put it with a faltering voice: "Where's your mother?"

"Oh, she too had died but a short time since; she broke a blood vessel in a fit of passion at a New England peddler."

There was a drop of comfort, at least, in this intelligence.[41] The honest man could contain himself no longer. He caught his daughter and her child in his arms. "I am your father!" cried he—"Young Rip Van Winkle once—old Rip Van Winkle now!—Does nobody know poor Rip Van Winkle?"

All stood amazed, until an old woman, tottering out from among the crowd, put her hand to her brow, and peering under it in his face for a moment, exclaimed, "Sure enough! it is Rip Van Winkle—it is himself! Welcome home again, old neighbor. Why, where have you been these twenty long years?"

Rip's story was soon told, for the whole twenty years had been to him as but one night. The neighbors stared when they heard it; some were seen to wink at each other, and put their tongues in their cheeks; and the self-important man in the cocked hat, who, when the alarm was over, had returned to the field, screwed down the corners of his mouth, and shook his head—upon which there was a general shaking of the head throughout the assemblage.

It was determined, however, to take the opinion of old Peter Vanderdonk, who was seen slowly advancing up the road. He was a descendant of the historian of that name, who wrote one of the earliest accounts of the province. Peter was the most ancient inhabitant of the village, and well versed in all the wonderful events and traditions of the neighborhood. He recollected Rip at once, and corroborated his story in the most satisfactory manner. He assured the company that it was a fact, handed down from his ancestor the historian, that the Catskill Mountains had always been haunted by strange beings. That it was affirmed that the great Henry Hudson, the first discoverer of the river and country,[42] kept a kind of vigil there every twenty years, with his crew of the *Half-Moon;* being permitted in this way to revisit the scenes of his enterprise and keep a guardian eye upon the river and the great city called by his name. That his father had once seen them in their old Dutch dresses playing at ninepins in a hollow of the mountain; and that he himself had heard, one summer afternoon, the sound of their balls, like distant peals of thunder.

To make a long story short, the company broke up, and returned to the more important concerns of the election. Rip's daughter took him home to live with her; she had a snug, well-furnished house, and a stout, cheery farmer for a husband, whom Rip recollected for one of the urchins that used to climb upon his back. As to Rip's son and heir, who was the ditto of himself, seen leaning against the tree, he was employed to work on the farm; but showed an hereditary disposition to attend to anything else but his business.

---

41. **intelligence:** here, a piece of news.

42. **country:** here, the Catskill area.

MEETING INDIVIDUAL NEEDS
ESL/LEP • When Rip returns after twenty years, he finds many people who were once his "cronies." Explain that *cronies* is a slang expression derived from the Greek word for time, *chronos,* and means friends. *Cronies* are friends that one has made over a long period of time. Other English words such as *chronic* (lasting a long time; recurring) and *chronological* (arranged in the order of occurrence over time) also come from *chronos*. Use these words in context so that students fully understand their meanings.

VISUAL CONNECTIONS
Exploring the Subject
Rip sits on a bench at the inn, apparently telling stories of "the old times before the war." The artist has included a number of details as points of comparison with the Rip of twenty years before (which, to Rip, seems like yesterday), as shown in the illustration on p. 248. The little girl in the past (p. 248) is recalled by the woman in the present day: the similarity of their positions and their duplicate posture suggest the idea that this might be the same little girl, now grown up and with a little girl of her own. Another duplication is the placement of the Catskill Mountains at the upper left-hand corner of each picture: a reminder of the place where Rip's adventure with the strange men took place. Also duplicated is the position of Wolf in the earlier illustration and the similar dog (Wolf's descendant?) in this drawing. The artist seems to be suggesting that although surface details may change, people's lives follow patterns that are very similar.

Rip now resumed his old walks and habits; he soon found many of his former cronies, though all rather the worse for the wear and tear of time; and preferred making friends among the rising generation, with whom he soon grew into great favor.

Having nothing to do at home, and being arrived at that happy age when a man can be idle with impunity, he took his place once more on the bench at the inn door, and was reverenced as one of the patriarchs of the village, and a 61 chronicle of the old times "before the war." It was some time before he could get into the regular track of gossip, or could be made to comprehend the strange events that had taken place during his sleep. How that there had been a Revolutionary War—that the country had thrown off the yoke of old England—and that, instead of being a subject of His Majesty George the Third, he was now a free citizen of the United States. Rip, in fact, was no politician; the changes of states and empires made but little impression on him; but there was one species of despotism under which he had long 62 groaned, and that was—petticoat government. Happily that was at an end; he had got his neck out of the yoke of matrimony, and could go in and out whenever he pleased, without dreading the tyranny of Dame Van Winkle. When-63 ever her name was mentioned, however, he shook his head, shrugged his shoulders, and cast up his eyes; which might pass either for an expression of resignation to his fate, or joy at his deliverance.

61
His memory of "old times" is clear since to him it all happened just yesterday.

62
Comparison might be made between country's new freedom and Rip's new freedom.

63
Same expression Rip used when nagged by wife.

COOPERATIVE LEARNING

Have students project twenty years into the future and think about what they might expect if they were to fall asleep for twenty years. Divide the class into groups to make forecasts about the next twenty years. You could either give students a list of areas of change to consider or ask them to categorize the ideas they come up with. Groups might use their lists to write an awakening scenario for a modern-day Rip Van Winkle, or you could use the best ideas that each group contributes to write a class story.

64
Human nature to polish and revise an experience to make a good story.

65
Figurative Language. Means they would like to be able to escape their troubles as he did.

READING CHECK
1. The Dutch (p. 248).
2. His dog Wolf (p. 250).
3. Men who meet at inn to talk (p. 250).
4. A keg of liquor (p. 252).
5. Noise of balls used in ninepins game (p. 253).
6. To serve the liquor (p. 253).
7. Been stolen (p. 254).
8. It has fallen into decay (p. 255).
9. Died of burst blood vessel (p. 258).
10. Old woman in crowd (p. 258).

FOR STUDY AND DISCUSSION
1. Foreshadowing; makes Catskills sound haunted.
2a. Fishing, hiking, helping neighbors, running errands, husking corn, church socials, amusing children. 2b. Helping stranger carry keg, serving liquor.
3a. Rip is happy-go-lucky; she is shrewish and impatient. 3b. Between demands of home life and desire for freedom from responsibility. 3c. Village represents responsibility; mountains represent escape.
4a. All are strangers; more, busier people; house in decay; dog snarls at him; inn is Union Hotel; flag with stars and stripes; George Washington on sign; sages replaced by political talkers. 4b. Rip, like U.S., has thrown off a tyrannous yoke.
5. His weaknesses are familiar; he has enviable gift for enjoying life, making friends.

260

He used to tell his story to every stranger that arrived at Mr. Doolittle's hotel. He was observed, at first, to vary on some points every time he told it, which was, doubtless, owing to *64* his having so recently awaked. It at last settled down precisely to the tale I have related, and not a man, woman, or child in the neighborhood but knew it by heart. Some always pretended to doubt the reality of it, and insisted that Rip had been out of his head, and that this was one point on which he always remained flighty. The old Dutch inhabitants, however, almost universally gave it full credit. Even to this day they never hear a thunderstorm of a summer afternoon about the Catskills but they say Henry Hudson and his crew are at their game of ninepins; and it is a common wish of all henpecked husbands in the neighborhood, when life hangs heavy on their hands, that they *65* might have a quieting draft out of Rip Van Winkle's flagon.

Reading Check
1. Who were the original colonists of Rip's village?
2. Who is Rip's only follower?
3. What is the "club of the sages"?
4. What is the stranger in the glen carrying?
5. What is the "thunder" Rip hears?
6. Why is Rip asked to follow the stranger?
7. When Rip wakes up, what does he assume has happened to his gun?
8. What does Rip find when he returns to his home?
9. What has happened to Dame Van Winkle?
10. Who finally recognizes Rip Van Winkle?

260 SHORT STORIES

For Study and Discussion

Analyzing and Interpreting the Selection

1. Although this story is about Rip Van Winkle, Washington Irving doesn't introduce Rip until the third paragraph of the story. In the first two paragraphs, Irving describes the **setting** of the story—the place and the time of the action. How do the phrases "magical hues and shapes" and "fairy mountains" prepare you for the strange events to come?

2. Rip is described as having a "dislike of all kinds of profitable labor." **a.** What kinds of "unprofitable labor" does he enjoy? **b.** What "unprofitable labor" does he find in the mountains?

3a. What contrast is there between Rip's temperament and that of Dame Van Winkle? **b.** How would you describe Rip's conflict? **c.** How is this conflict related to the two places where the action occurs, the village and the mountains?

4. "Rip Van Winkle" opens during the colonial period of American history. By the end of the story, you learn that the colonies have "thrown off the yoke of old England" and become free. **a.** What changes does Rip find in the village when he returns? **b.** In what way is Rip's "history" like the history of his country?

5. The story "Rip Van Winkle" has appealed to generations of readers who have recognized in Rip's experience the fulfillment of their own wishes. Why do you think readers can put themselves in Rip's place so easily?

Literary Elements

Focusing on Setting

Some readers become impatient with descriptions of setting. They are eager to get on with the action and may wonder why the writer interrupts the story with passages describing the physical surroundings.

The setting of "Rip Van Winkle" brings Rip's conflict into sharp focus for the reader. The world of Rip's everyday existence is drawn in realistic detail. Irving describes the houses "built of small yellow bricks brought from Holland," which have "latticed windows and gable fronts, surmounted with weathercocks." He also gives you a detailed and comic picture of Rip's domestic troubles. In this passage he tells you how everything on Rip's farm would go wrong: "His fences were continually falling to pieces; his cow would either go astray or get among the cabbages; weeds were sure to grow quicker in his fields than anywhere else. . . ."

Find the passage that shows you why Rip was a great favorite with the children in the village. **1** What kinds of "unprofitable labor" did Rip perform for the children?

When Irving describes the Catskill Mountains, he dwells on their unreal, magical quality:

> Every change of season, every change of weather, indeed, every hour of the day, produces some change in the magical hues and shapes of these mountains. . . . When the weather is fair and settled, they are clothed in blue and purple, and print their bold outlines on the clear evening sky; but, sometimes, when the rest of the landscape is cloudless, they will gather a hood of gray vapors about their summits, which, in the last rays of the setting sun, will glow and light up like a crown of glory.

The description suggests what the mountains represent for Rip—an escape from the real world and all its problems.

Find the passage on page 251 in which Irving describes evening falling on the mountains. **2** Which words give you an eerie feeling about the mountains? Henry Hudson and his crew are also part of the setting. **3** Which words does Irving use to make the men seem as strange and unusual as the mountains?

Understanding Character Types

Dame Van Winkle's situation is hardly comical. She has a shiftless husband who allows his farm to fall to pieces, who spends more time away from his family than with them, and who leaves his children ill-fed and ill-clothed. Yet Irving treats Dame Van Winkle as a comic character who provides a great deal of humor in the story.

You can laugh at Dame Van Winkle because Irving shows her in only one light. Whenever you see Dame Van Winkle in the story, she is scolding or nagging Rip, his dog Wolf, or his cronies in the village. If you were allowed to see Dame Van Winkle laughing with her children or crying in despair over her hardships, your reaction to her would probably be very different. However, Irving does not show these other qualities in Dame Van Winkle. She is represented only as a *shrew*, a bad-tempered, quarrelsome woman.

You have seen that a writer can use the element of surprise—the contrast between the expected and the unexpected—to produce humor. A writer can also use **exaggeration** for humorous effects. Irving makes Dame Van Winkle laughable by exaggerating one side of her character.

> Morning, noon, and night, her tongue was incessantly going, and everything he said or did was sure to produce a torrent of household eloquence.

The word *torrent* generally refers to a heavy rain. **4** What does Irving mean by the phrase "a torrent of household eloquence"? Find other examples in the story where Dame Van Winkle's bad temper is humorously exaggerated.

Irving also enjoys treating the conflict between Rip and his wife as a series of battles. By shrugging his shoulders, Rip "always provoked **5** a fresh *volley* from his wife." What is a *volley*?

Dame Van Winkle is described as invading the "club of the sages": "From even this strong-

LITERARY ELEMENTS
Focusing on Setting

1. Rip was a favorite with children because he "assisted at their sports, made their playthings, taught them to fly kites and shoot marbles, and told them long stories of ghosts, witches, and Indians." (p. 249).

2. Eerie words used to describe mountains include *wild*, *lonely*, and *shagged*, which stress that the glen is not visited by many people, and *long blue shadows*, which makes the setting seem unreal.

3. Words that emphasize the unusual nature of the men include *odd-looking*, *quaint*, *outlandish*, *mysterious*, and *melancholy*.

Understanding Character Types

4. The *torrent* is a **metaphor** for Dame Van Winkle's scolding. Other passages showing her temper include her attack on Nicholas Vedder (p. 251), her scolding of Rip's dog (p. 251), and her quarrel with the New England peddler (p. 258).

5. A *volley* is a discharge of objects such as arrows, bullets, or stones. Here, it is Dame Van Winkle's harsh words.

Rip Van Winkle

LANGUAGE AND VOCABULARY

1. In the story, the word *strange* appears in these places: "a strange figure slowly toiling up the rocks" (p. 252); "something strange and incomprehensible about the unknown" (p. 252); "such strange lackluster countenances" (p. 253); "The strange man with a keg of liquor" (p. 254); "A troop of strange children" (p. 255); "Strange names were over the doors—strange faces at the windows" (p. 255); "all this was strange and incomprehensible" (p. 256); "the Catskill Mountains had always been haunted by strange beings" (p. 258); "the strange events that had taken place during his sleep" (p. 259).

2. Shades of meaning of words closely related to *strange*:
quaint = strange + old-fashioned.
outlandish = strange + odd, fantastic (even stronger than odd).
peculiar = strange + puzzling.

3. Words in the passage that have the same feeling as *lonely* are *forlorn, abandoned,* and *desolateness*. **Forlorn** means "without hope, deprived, or miserable." **Abandoned** means "given up entirely, deserted out of necessity, or yielded completely." **Desolateness** means "wretchedness."

WRITING ABOUT LITERATURE

You may want to encourage students to reread in its entirety the story they select, concentrating on setting rather than action. Then request that as they write, students concentrate on including specific examples to show the role of setting in the story selected.

262

---

hold the unlucky Rip was at length *routed* by his wife" (page 251). The word *routed* calls up the image of an army being driven from a fortress in complete disorder and bewilderment. When you realize that this invader uses no weapon but her tongue, the comparison becomes laughable. Rip has as great a fear of his wife's harsh words as a soldier might have of his enemy's firearms.

Irving, of course, is not suggesting that all wives are shrewish any more than he is saying that all husbands are lazy. Irving is showing the reader that there are some qualities in people that provoke laughter if they are carried to excess.

Dame Van Winkle is not presented as a fully rounded individual. She is a **character type**—someone who fits a pattern and who can be recognized by certain typical characteristics. In the case of a shrew, the typical characteristics are nagging and scolding.

Language and Vocabulary

Recognizing Shades of Meaning

1 Throughout the story Irving stresses the strangeness of Rip's experience. The word *strange* is used on ten separate occasions to describe something unfamiliar. See if you can locate each instance.

Irving also uses words that are closely related in meaning to *strange*:

> On a level spot in the center was a company of *odd*-looking personages playing at ninepins. They were dressed in a *quaint, outlandish* fashion.... Their visages, too, were *peculiar.*

The word *odd* has the general meaning "strange," but also carries an additional meaning of being "out of the ordinary":

> odd = strange + out of the ordinary

In a dictionary find the words *quaint, outland-*
2 *ish,* and *peculiar.* What shade of meaning does

262 SHORT STORIES

---

each word have in addition to the meaning of "strange"?

The word *lonely* also appears several times in the story, along with synonyms. Look at the passage where Rip returns to his deserted
3 house (page 256). What words in this passage have the meaning of "lonely"? What additional meaning does each of the words have?

Writing About Literature

▶ **Explaining the Function of Setting**

Consider the importance of setting in one of the other stories you have read. For example, think about the element of setting in "The Wild Duck's Nest" (page 180). How is the setting in that story a key to the character's thoughts and feelings? How does the change in setting reflect the change in the way Colm feels?

Think about the setting in "Antaeus" (page 187). How is it essential to the plot?

Write a short essay in which you explain the role of setting in one of these stories or another story of your choice.

Focus on Writing a Short Story

Listing Details of Setting

Setting is the time and place of the action in a short story. The setting of a story can give information about the characters and the conflict, as in "Rip Van Winkle." The setting can also create a mood. The details that Irving uses to describe the mountains, for example, help to create a mood of mystery.

Create a setting for a short story of your own. Your setting could be realistic: for example, a soccer field on an autumn afternoon. The setting could be completely imaginary or fantastic: for example, a planet in another galaxy. Collect

▶ Before students begin this writing assignment, you may want to refer them to the **Writing About Literature** section on p. 688.

details for your setting by filling out a chart like the one below:

```
              Setting Chart
Place: _____
Time: _____
Weather: _____
Time of Year/Time of Day: _____
Objects: _____
Sights/Sounds/Smells: _____
_____
_____
```

About the Author

Washington Irving (1783–1859)

Washington Irving said, "When I first wrote the legend of Rip Van Winkle, my thoughts had been for some time turned toward giving a color of romance and tradition to interesting points of our national scenery." Irving borrowed the idea for his story from an Old German folk tale, but he set it in the Hudson River country of New York. In this way, he glorified an American place as no writer before him had done. Today he is remembered as America's first major literary figure.

As a boy, Irving was adventurous and restless. When he was fourteen, he planned to run away to sea. He prepared for this adventure by eating salt pork and sleeping on the hard floor of his room. He liked to spend his time wandering around New York. "I knew every spot," he said, "where a murder or robbery had been committed, or a ghost seen." He had a lively imagination, and although he studied law, he was quickly drawn to a literary career.

From 1807 to 1808, he contributed humorous essays to *Salmagundi,* a periodical he had helped to create. In 1809 he published the first of his two great books, a comic history of New York with a long title, now known simply as *Knickerbocker's History of New York.* Irving's masterpiece, *The Sketch Book,* appeared ten years later. It was a collection of over thirty pieces, including his two most famous stories, "Rip Van Winkle" and "The Legend of Sleepy Hollow." In his later years, Irving spent a great deal of time in Europe searching for more old tales and anecdotes. After he returned to America, he built himself a remarkable house in Tarrytown, New York, which he called "Sunnyside." There he spent his remaining days writing a five-volume biography of George Washington.

Literature and the Arts

Illustrated Editions

The story of Rip Van Winkle has appealed to the imagination of several artists. The illustrations that appear in this anthology are by Felix O. C. Darley and were done for an 1848 edition of Irving's story. Other illustrators of the story are John Quidor and N. C. Wyeth.

Making Connections: Activities

Look for early illustrated editions of "Rip Van Winkle" in your school or local library. If possible, bring the books to class and show the illustrations. Compare the interpretations of different artists. How well does each one capture the character of Rip? How effective are the illustrations of setting? What details from the story do you recognize in the illustrations? Prepare an oral or written report evaluating the work of these illustrators.

You Can't Take It with You

EVA-LIS WUORIO°

Sometimes in a short story characters' actions bring about an unexpected result. Such a situation, in which things turn out to be different from what characters expect, is called an ironic situation.

What is ironic about the outcome of this story? Is the ending satisfying?

There was no denying two facts. Uncle Basil was rich. Uncle Basil was a miser.

The family were unanimous about that. They had used up all the words as their temper and their need of ready money dictated. Gentle Aunt Clotilda, who wanted a new string of pearls because the one she had was getting old, had merely called him Scrooge[1] Basil. Percival, having again smashed his Aston Martin[2] for which he had not paid, had declared Uncle Basil a skinflint, a miser, tightwad, churl, and usurer with colorful adjectives added. The rest had used up all the other words in the dictionary.

"He doesn't have to be so parsimonious,[3] that's true, with all he has," said Percival's mother. "But you shouldn't use rude words, Percival. They might get back to him."

"He can't take it with him," said Percival's sister Letitia, combing her golden hair. "I need a new fur but he said, 'Why? it's summer.' Well! He's mingy,[4] that's what he is."

° **Eva-Lis Wuorio** (ā′vă-lēs wôr′ē-ō).
1. **Scrooge:** the most famous miser in literature. See Dickens' "A Christmas Carol," page 276.
2. **Aston Martin:** a very expensive sports car.
3. **parsimonious** (pär′sə-mō′nē-əs): stingy.
4. **mingy** (mĭn′jē): mean and stingy.

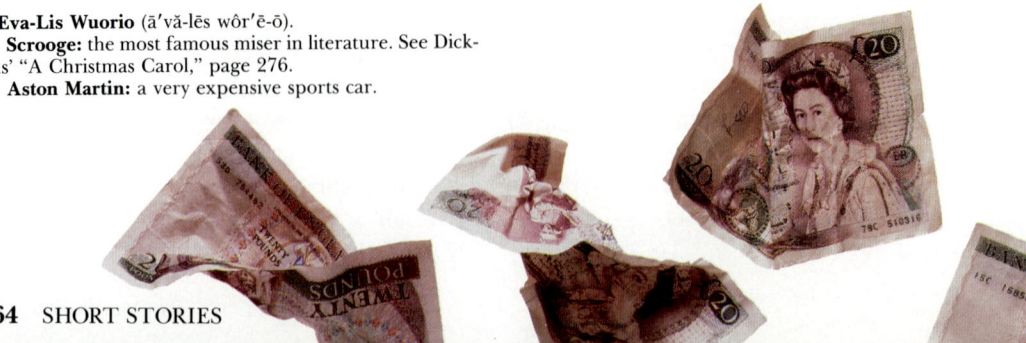

MOTIVATIONAL SUMMARY
Uncle Basil's family thinks he's stingy. He has made a fortune, but he won't give them the kind of cash they want to buy the luxuries they crave. Because he's hard of hearing, they whisper behind his back that they should all be patient, that he can't take his money with him when he dies, and they'll get their hands on his fortune after he's gone. But Uncle Basil hears more than they think. He starts to plan for a way that he *can* take his fortune with him.

PRESENTATION
An author sometimes uses humor to explore a **theme** or to teach a lesson. In her lighthearted story "You Can't Take It with You," Eva-Lis Wuorio does just this. She assembles a cast of one-dimensional, stereotyped characters and

3 "He can't take it with him" was a phrase the family used so often it began to slip out in front of Uncle Basil as well.

"You can't take it with you, Uncle Basil," they said. "Why don't you buy a sensible house out in the country, and we could all come and visit you? Horses. A swimming pool. The lot. Think what fun you'd have, and you can certainly afford it. You can't take it with you, you know."

Uncle Basil had heard all the words they called him because he wasn't as deaf as he made out. He knew he was a mingy, stingy, penny-pinching screw, scrimp, scraper, pinchfist, hoarder, and curmudgeon⁵ (just to start with). There were other words, less gentle, he'd also heard himself called. He didn't *4* mind. What <u>galled</u> him was the oft repeated warning, "You can't take it with you." After all, it was all his.

5. **curmudgeon** (kər-mŭj′ən): ill-tempered, disagreeable person.

He'd gone to the Transvaal⁶ when there was still gold to be found if one knew where to look. He'd found it. They said he'd come back too old to enjoy his fortune. What did they know? He enjoyed simply having a fortune. He *5* enjoyed also saying no to them all. They were like circus animals, he often thought, behind the bars of their thousand demands of something for nothing.

Only once had he said yes. That was when his sister asked him to take on Verner, her somewhat slow-witted eldest son. "He'll do as your secretary," his sister Maud had said. Verner didn't do at all as a secretary, but since all

6. **Transvaal** (trăns-väl′, tränz-): a province of the Republic of South Africa, formerly known as South African Republic.

3
Second use of expression referring to uselessness of money after death.

4
Truth does not anger him; nagging does.

5
Simile. Basil compares his relatives to circus animals, trapped in cage of greed.

VISUAL CONNECTIONS
Exploring the Subject
Shown here is the money that Uncle Basil's relatives don't think he can take with him when he dies. Modern English pounds are slightly larger than American dollars. Each note is printed in several different colors of ink to discourage forgery. The front of these twenty-pound notes shows Queen Elizabeth II and a stylized, colorful design of St. George (patron saint of England) slaying the dragon. On the reverse is William Shakespeare and a stylized inset of the balcony scene from *Romeo and Juliet.* A feature common to several modern European currencies is specially designed paper that discourages counterfeiting. With this special paper, an Italian lira, a French franc, or an English pound note (such as the twenty-pound notes shown) will—when held up to ordinary light—show a telltale "ghost" in the white-looking area of the note. (On English currency, it's the Queen's portrait.) These embedded designs are extremely difficult to duplicate, and counterfeit notes can be easily detected by ordinary people, without having to rely on special equipment.

You Can't Take It with You

wittily tells a story of hypocrisy, greed, and poetic justice. In these respects, as well as in the improbability of the story's events, this short story resembles a fable, though one with an ironic twist to its implicit moral. Indeed, Uncle Basil teaches his family how ill-advised is their greedy meddling by proving their words wrong. He can, and does, take his money with him.

6 Basil's unpretentiousness contrasts with family's greed for luxuries.

7 Unlike the rest of family, Verner is polite, willing to work, and simple in his pursuits; thus an ideal companion for Basil.

8 Irony. Verner's obliviousness to Basil's money is ironic in light of fact that he will be one of a few to receive any.

9 Making Inferences
What might Basil's family think about his buying an inexpensive coffin? Probably that he is just being miserly.

10 Foreshadowing. This line provides a hint as to how Basil will "take it with him."

11 The family thinks this means that one person will inherit all the money.

12 Drawing Conclusions
Why had the family not bothered him? They each wanted the money and so none of them dared bother him for fear of not being the one chosen to inherit the money.

---

he wanted to be happy was to be told what to do, Uncle Basil let him stick around as an all-around handyman.

6 Uncle Basil lived neatly in a house very much too small for his money, the family said, in an unfashionable suburb. It was precisely like the house where he had been born. Verner looked after the small garden, fetched the papers from the corner tobacconist, and filed his 7 nails when he had time. He had nice nails. He never said to Uncle Basil, "You can't take it with you," because it didn't occur to him.

Uncle Basil also used Verner to run messages to his man of affairs, the bank, and such, since he didn't believe either in the mails or the 8 telephone. Verner got used to carrying thick envelopes back and forth without ever bothering to question what was in them. Uncle Basil's lawyers, accountants, and bank managers also got used to his somewhat unorthodox[7] business methods. He did have a fortune, and he kept making money with his investments. Rich men have always been allowed their foibles.

Another foible of Uncle Basil's was that, while he still was in excellent health he had Verner drive him out to an old-fashioned carpenter shop where he had himself measured for a coffin. He wanted it roomy, he said.

The master carpenter was a dour countryman of the same generation as Uncle Basil, and he accepted the order matter-of-factly. They consulted about woods and prices, and 9 settled on a medium-price, unlined coffin. A lined one would have cost double.

10 "I'll line it myself," Uncle Basil said. "Or Verner can. There's plenty of time. I don't intend to pop off tomorrow. It would give the family too much satisfaction. I like enjoying my fortune."

---

7. **unorthodox** (ŭn′ôr′thə-dŏks′): not customary or traditional.

Then one morning, while in good humor and sound mind, he sent Verner for his lawyer. The family got to hear about this and there were in-fights, out-fights, and general quarreling while they tried to find out to whom Uncle Basil had decided to leave his money. To put them out of their misery, he said, he'd tell them the truth. He didn't like scattering money 11 about. He liked it in a lump sum. Quit bothering him about it.

That happened a good decade before the morning his housekeeper, taking him his tea, found him peacefully asleep forever. It had 12 been a good decade for him. The family hadn't dared to worry him, and his investments had risen steadily.

Only Percival, always pressed for money, had threatened to put arsenic in his tea but when the usual proceedings were gone through Uncle Basil was found to have died a natural death. "A happy death," said the family. "He hadn't suffered."

They began to remember loudly how nice they'd been to him and argued about who had been the nicest. It was true too. They had been attentive, the way families tend to be to rich and stubborn elderly relatives. They didn't know he'd heard all they'd said out of his hearing, as well as the flattering drivel they'd spread like soft butter on hot toast in his hearing. Everyone, recalling his own efforts to be thoroughly nice, was certain that he and only he would be the heir to the Lump Sum.

They rushed to consult the lawyer. He said that he had been instructed by Uncle Basil in sane and precise terms. The cremation was to take place immediately after the death, and they would find the coffin ready in the garden shed. Verner would know where it was.

"Nothing else?"

"Well," said the lawyer in the way lawyers have, "he left instructions for a funeral repast to be sent in from Fortnum and Mason.[8] Everything of the best. Goose and turkey, venison and beef, oysters and lobsters, and wines of good vintage plus plenty of whiskey. He liked to think of a good send-off, curmudgeon though he was, he'd said."

The family was a little shaken by the use of the word "curmudgeon." How did Uncle Basil know about that? But they were relieved to hear that the lawyer also had an envelope, the contents of which he did not know, to read to them at the feast after the cremation.

They all bought expensive black clothes, since black was the color of that season anyway, and whoever inherited would share the wealth. That was only fair.

Only Verner said that couldn't they buy Uncle Basil a smarter coffin? The one in the garden shed was pretty tatty, since the roof leaked. But the family hardly listened to him. After all, it would only be burned, so what did it matter?

So, duly and with proper sorrow, Uncle Basil was cremated.

The family returned to the little house as the housekeeper was leaving. Uncle Basil had given her a generous amount of cash, telling her how to place it so as to have a fair income for life. In gratitude she'd spread out the Fortnum and Mason goodies, but she wasn't prepared to stay to do the dishes.

They were a little surprised, but not dismayed, to hear from Verner that the house was now in his name. Uncle Basil had also given him a small sum of cash and told him how to invest it. The family taxed[9] him about it, but the amount was so nominal they were relieved to know Verner would be off their hands. Verner himself, though mildly missing the old man because he was used to him, was quite content with his lot. He wasn't used to much, so he didn't need much.

The storm broke when the lawyer finally opened the envelope.

There was only one line in Uncle Basil's scrawl.

"I did take it with me."

Of course there was a great to-do. What about the fortune? The millions and millions!

Yes, said the men of affairs, the accountants, and even the bank managers, who finally admitted, yes, there had been a very considerable fortune. Uncle Basil, however, had drawn large sums in cash, steadily and regularly, over the past decade. What had he done with it? That the men of affairs, the accountants, and the bank managers did not know. After all, it had been Uncle Basil's money, ergo,[10] his affair.

Not a trace of the vast fortune ever came to light.

No one thought to ask Verner, and it didn't occur to Verner to volunteer that for quite a long time he had been lining the coffin, at Uncle Basil's behest, with thick envelopes he brought back from the banks. First he'd done a thick layer of these envelopes all around the sides and bottom of the coffin. Then, as Uncle Basil wanted, he'd tacked on blue sailcloth.

He might not be so bright in his head but he was smart with his hands.

He'd done a neat job.

---

10. **ergo** (ûr′gō, âr′-): therefore.

---

8. **Fortnum and Mason:** a well-known store that supplies food for parties.
9. **taxed:** expressed disapproval of; criticized.

PORTFOLIO ASSESSMENT
Groups of students may want to write, produce, and videotape a television commercial advertising an upcoming production of "You Can't Take It with You." Suggest that commercials include answers to the questions "who?," "what?," "when?," "where?," and "why?" in addition to interviews with actors playing main characters or excerpts from the production. Require each group member to assess his or her experience in the project. (See *Portfolio Assessment and Professional Support Materials*.)

READING CHECK
1. He found gold in the Transvaal (p. 265).
2. Vernon is all-around handyman (p. 266).
3. He is to be cremated in coffin; funeral meal ordered for family (pp. 266, 267).
4. "I did take it with me" (p. 267).
5. Thick envelopes filled with money (p. 267).

FOR STUDY AND DISCUSSION
1. Lines coffin with money; it is burned when he is cremated.
2. They are too cheap to buy Uncle Basil a better coffin.
3. Neither was after his money.
4a. Basil thinks family is greedy.
4b. He has Vernon bring envelopes from bank; orders roomy coffin without lining; will's declaration, "I did take it with me."

LANGUAGE AND VOCABULARY
1. Other words for stingy person: *Scrooge, usurer, stingy, screw, scraper, pinchfist, hoarder,* and *curmudgeon.*
2. *Parsimonious* and *penny-pinching* are less negative than *mingy* and *stingy; hoarder* less negative than its synonyms; *curmudgeon* is archaic; *Scrooge* is gentler than *skinflint, miser, tightwad,* and *pinchfist.*

Reading Check
1. How did Uncle Basil make his fortune?
2. How does Uncle Basil employ Verner?
3. What instructions does Uncle Basil leave for his funeral?
4. What is Uncle Basil's last message to his family?
5. What did Verner use to line Uncle Basil's coffin?

For Study and Discussion

Analyzing and Interpreting the Story

1. How does Uncle Basil manage to take his vast fortune with him when he dies?

2. How do the greed and selfishness of his family assist Uncle Basil in carrying out his plan?

3. Although Uncle Basil is a miser, he provides well for Verner and for his housekeeper. Why does he treat these two people with consideration?

4. You often enjoy a humorous situation more if you know that it is coming. **a.** How do you know that Uncle Basil has some surprises in store for his family? **b.** How are you, the reader, prepared for the ending? Find clues that the author supplies throughout the story.

Literary Elements

Recognizing Irony

Throughout the story Uncle Basil's relatives keep reminding him that he can't take his fortune with him when he dies. They expect, of course, that he will leave his money to them. Uncle Basil turns the tables on them so that they don't get a penny. Such a reversal of expectations is **ironic.**

There are other ironic situations in the story. Verner wishes to replace the tatty coffin in the garden shed with a nicer coffin. Because of their greed, the relatives refuse. They don't want to spend any money; ironically, they allow all the money to be destroyed.

An ironic ending is satisfying when it grows out of the events in the story. Think about Uncle Basil's attitude toward money. Think about his attitude toward his family. Consider also his strange business dealings. Are you prepared for the ending?

Language and Vocabulary

Determining Exact Meanings

There are a number of words used in this story to describe a stingy person. Among the nouns are *miser, skinflint, tightwad,* and *churl.* The adjectives include *mingy, penny-pinching,* and *parsimonious.* What other words used in the story can you add to these lists? Which words are slang?

Check the meanings of these words in a college or unabridged dictionary. How many of the words are exact synonyms? What differences are there in shades of meaning?

CLOSURE

Irony is the difference between what is expected to happen and what really does happen. Ask students to describe at least three ironic situations in this story.

EXTENSION AND ENRICHMENT

Discuss Uncle Basil's decision. Did he do the right thing? Did his relatives need the money? Did he have the right to do what he pleased with his own money? What other choices did he have?

Writing About Literature

Discussing Stock Characters

In humorous stories, like "Rip Van Winkle" (page 247) and "You Can't Take It with You," comic characters are frequently **stock characters,** or types, rather than individuals. The characters in Wuorio's story are not intended to be three-dimensional. Uncle Basil is a miser; Letitia is a gold digger; Verner is the slow-witted but good-hearted lackey.

Discuss the stock figures in some of the stories you have read. Who are the stock characters in Westerns? In detective stories?

Focus on Writing a Short Story

Experimenting with Irony

As you have seen in "You Can't Take It with You," **irony** depends on a contrast. Study the chart below:

Verbal Irony	Situational Irony
What is said	What we expect
What is meant	What happens

Life is full of ironies, because things often don't turn out the way we expect. Jot down some notes on how you might work an ironic situation into a short story of your own. Then get together with a small group of classmates to exchange ideas about irony in storytelling. Save your notes.

About the Author

Eva-Lis Wuorio (1918–)

Eva-Lis Wuorio was born in Finland. At the age of eleven, she emigrated to Canada. She began her writing career working for newspapers in Toronto. Among her books are two novels about World War II: *Code Polonaise*, set in Poland, and *To Fight in Silence*, about the Dutch underground. She has also written a number of children's books. In 1962 *The Island of Fish in the Trees* was chosen by *The New York Times* as one of the Best Illustrated Children's Books of the Year. "You Can't Take It with You" is from a collection of tales called *Escape If You Can*.

WRITING ABOUT LITERATURE

Some students may not be familiar with the term *stock character*. They may need to be informed that stock characters are those who are not fully developed. Stock characters are often almost cartoonlike stereotypes whose characteristics are easily recognized. Examples from the textbook include the nagging wife and shiftless husband in "Rip Van Winkle." Westerns often have the outlaw with a "heart of gold" and evil ranchers or bankers. Detective stories often have the beautiful victim or client and the tough, relentless detective.

FOCUS ON WRITING A SHORT STORY

Small groups of students could work together to generate ironic situations for stories. Have each student in the group offer his or her story idea, and ask the other group members to suggest possible ironic situations. You may want to have each group share its best suggestion with the rest of the class.

ABOUT THE AUTHOR

Eva-Lis Wuorio's birthplace is a small harbor town on the Gulf of Finland. She has written that when she was very young, the most exciting event of the year was the breaking up of the ice-jam in the harbor. She always looked forward to the arrival of the first ship and, accompanied by all the other children of the village, would rush to the dock when it approached. One year, when the ship was being unloaded, a crate of blood oranges broke and the sailors, who didn't speak Finnish, gave them to the children. Wuorio describes this incident as the time she became a storyteller, making up a tale of the islands where the unusual blood oranges grew.

OBJECTIVES
The overall aim is for students to explain the role of nature in the story and to demonstrate an understanding of the story's theme. For a complete list of objectives, see the **Teacher's Notes.**

VOCABULARY
The word *exude(d)* is defined in the Glossary. Students will find the style and vocabulary of this story simple, much like that of a folk tale or fable.

FOCUS / MOTIVATION
How do pets express hunger, anger, a desire to play, contentment, or other feelings? Do they seem to understand human language? "Zlateh the Goat" is the story of a rare bond between a boy and an animal.

TEACHING RESOURCES B
Teacher's Notes, p. 189
Reading Check, p. 191
Study Guide, p. 192
Language Skills, p. 194
Selection Test, p. 198

PREREADING FOCUS
The headnote defines **theme.** The concept is one that many students find elusive. You may want to review and discuss with students the examples and explanation given about theme in the **Literary Terms and Techniques** (p. 725).

Zlateh the Goat

1
Use of "village" and "peasants" emphasizes story's focus on a poor country family.

2
A *furrier* is one who makes or sells fur goods.

3
To celebrate Hanukkah (the Festival of Lights), special candles are required. The potato pancakes the family will eat are called *latkes.*

4
The family's distress indicates that Zlateh is almost a pet.

5
Though sensing something is wrong, Zlateh is obedient.

270

Zlateh the Goat

ISAAC BASHEVIS SINGER

In addition to offering entertainment, a short story often expresses some idea about human nature or interpretation of experience that gives us insight into ourselves and others. This underlying meaning is known as the theme *of the story. As you read, ask yourself what meaning Singer attributes to the events in his story.*

1   At Hanukkah[1] time the road from the village to the town is usually covered with snow, but this year the winter had been a mild one. Hanukkah had almost come, yet little snow had fallen. The sun shone most of the time. The peasants complained that because of the dry weather there would be a poor harvest of winter grain. New grass sprouted, and the peasants sent their cattle out to pasture.

2   For Reuven the furrier it was a bad year, and after long hesitation he decided to sell Zlateh the goat. She was old and gave little milk. Feyvel the town butcher had offered eight gulden[2] for her. Such a sum would buy Hanukkah candles, potatoes and oil for pancakes, gifts for the children, and other holiday necessaries for the house. Reuven told his oldest boy, Aaron, to take the goat to town.

   Aaron understood what taking the goat to Feyvel meant, but he had to obey his father.

4   Leah, his mother, wiped the tears from her eyes when she heard the news. Aaron's younger sisters, Anna and Miriam, cried loudly. Aaron put on his quilted jacket and a cap with earmuffs, bound a rope around Zlateh's neck, and took along two slices of bread with cheese to eat on the road. Aaron was supposed to deliver the goat by evening, spend the night at the butcher's, and return the next day with the money.

   While the family said goodbye to the goat, and Aaron placed the rope around her neck, Zlateh stood as patiently and good-naturedly as ever. She licked Reuven's hand. She shook her small white beard. Zlateh trusted human beings. She knew that they always fed her and never did her any harm.

   When Aaron brought her out on the road to town, she seemed somewhat astonished. She'd never been led in that direction before. She 5 looked back at him questioningly, as if to say, "Where are you taking me?" But after a while she seemed to come to the conclusion that a goat shouldn't ask questions. Still, the road was different. They passed new fields, pastures, and huts with thatched roofs. Here and there a

---
1. **Hanukkah** (ĸнä′nŏŏ-kə): a Jewish holiday, usually in December, celebrated for eight days.
2. **gulden** (gŏŏl′dən): coins used in several European countries; also called *guilders.*

270   SHORT STORIES

MOTIVATIONAL SUMMARY

Zlateh the goat is almost a family pet. However, Reuven the furrier and his family want to buy some candles and other holiday necessities for Hanukkah, so Reuven orders his son Aaron to take the goat into town and sell her to the butcher. But while Aaron and Zlateh are on their way into town, a terrible blizzard begins. The two travelers are in great danger of freezing, and Aaron tries to find shelter from the awful storm. How can he save himself and Zlateh from freezing?

PRESENTATION

Like "The Erne from the Coast," an earlier selection in this unit, Isaac Bashevis Singer's "Zlateh the Goat" is set in a rural environment where life revolves around nature. In the earlier story, an animal is the boy's enemy, while in Singer's

Illustration by Maurice Sendak. © 1987.

From *Zlateh the Goat and Other Stories* by Isaac Bashevis Singer

VISUAL CONNECTIONS
About the Artist
Maurice Sendak has had a very successful career as an illustrator and as a writer. He has written seventeen children's books, all of them self-illustrated. The most famous—and controversial—of these is *Where the Wild Things Are*. Three times he has won the Notable Book Award from the American Library Association. He has also been awarded the Caldecott Medal, won the New York Times Best Illustrated Children's Book Award, has been named to the Horn Book honor list, and awarded the Hans Christian Andersen Medal. In addition to his own works, he has illustrated more than sixty books, including the collection of Isaac Bashevis Singer's short stories, *Zlateh the Goat and Other Stories*, which won the American Library Association Notable Book award and was named to the Horn Book honor list.

dog barked and came running after them, but Aaron chased it away with his stick.

6   The sun was shining when Aaron left the village. Suddenly the weather changed. A large black cloud with a bluish center appeared in the east and spread itself rapidly over the sky. A cold wind blew in with it. The crows flew low, croaking. At first it looked as if it would rain, but instead it began to hail as in summer. It was early in the day, but it became dark as dusk. After a while the hail turned to snow.

In his twelve years Aaron had seen all kinds of weather, but he had never experienced a snow like this one. It was so dense it shut out the light of the day. In a short time their path was completely covered. The wind became as cold as ice. The road to town was narrow and winding. Aaron no longer knew where he was. He could not see through the snow. The cold soon penetrated his quilted jacket.

At first Zlateh didn't seem to mind the change in weather. She too was twelve years old and knew what winter meant. But when her legs sank deeper and deeper into the snow, she began to turn her head and look at Aaron 7 in wonderment. Her mild eyes seemed to ask, "Why are we out in such a storm?" Aaron hoped that a peasant would come along with his cart, but no one passed by.

The snow grew thicker, falling to the ground in large, whirling flakes. Beneath it Aaron's boots touched the softness of a plowed field. He realized that he was no longer on the road. He had gone astray. He could no longer figure out which was east or west, which way

6

Imagery. Sensory details of storm: "large black cloud," "bluish center," "cold wind," "hail," "dark as dusk," "snow."

7 Comparing/Contrasting
What do Aaron and Zlateh have in common? Both are twelve years old, and both wonder at such a storm.

Zlateh the Goat   **271**

story, an animal is the friend who saves the boy from a natural force that threatens them both. The humans in this story learn a valuable lesson: that love is priceless and far more important than material goods.

> **TRANSPARENCY 20**
> **Reader Response**
> *Tug-of-War* – allows students an opportunity to explore conflicts faced by one of the characters in a selection.

was the village, the town. The wind whistled, howled, whirled the snow about in eddies. It looked as if white imps were playing tag on the fields. A white dust rose above the ground. Zlateh stopped. She could walk no longer. Stubbornly she anchored her cleft hooves in the earth and bleated as if pleading to be taken home. Icicles hung from her white beard, and her horns were glazed with frost.

Aaron did not want to admit the danger, but he knew just the same that if they did not find shelter they would freeze to death. This was no ordinary storm. It was a mighty blizzard. The 8 snowfall had reached his knees. His hands were numb, and he could no longer feel his toes. He choked when he breathed. His nose felt like wood, and he rubbed it with snow. Zlateh's bleating began to sound like crying. Those humans in whom she had so much con- 9 fidence had dragged her into a trap. Aaron began to pray to God for himself and for the innocent animal.

10 Suddenly he made out the shape of a hill. He wondered what it could be. Who had piled snow into such a huge heap? He moved toward it, dragging Zlateh after him. When he came near it, he realized that it was a large haystack which the snow had blanketed.

11 Aaron realized immediately that they were saved. With great effort he dug his way through the snow. He was a village boy and knew what to do. When he reached the hay, he hollowed out a nest for himself and the goat. No matter how cold it may be outside, in the hay it is always warm. And hay was food for Zlateh. The moment she smelled it she became contented and began to eat. Outside the snow continued to fall. It quickly covered the passageway Aaron had dug. But a boy and an animal need to breathe, and there was hardly any air in their hideout. Aaron bored a kind of a window through the hay and snow and carefully kept the passage clear.

Zlateh, having eaten her fill, sat down on her hind legs and seemed to have regained her confidence in man. Aaron ate his two slices of bread and cheese, but after the difficult journey he was still hungry. He looked at Zlateh 12 and noticed her udders were full. He lay down next to her, placing himself so that when he milked her he could squirt the milk into his mouth. It was rich and sweet. Zlateh was not accustomed to being milked that way, but she did not resist. On the contrary, she seemed eager to reward Aaron for bringing her to a shelter whose very walls, floor, and ceiling were made of food.

Through the window Aaron could catch a glimpse of the chaos outside. The wind carried before it whole drifts of snow. It was completely dark, and he did not know whether night had already come or whether it was the darkness of the storm. Thank God that in the hay it was not cold. The dried hay, grass, and field flowers exuded the warmth of the summer sun. Zlateh ate frequently; she nibbled from above, below, from the left and right. Her body gave forth an animal warmth, and 13 Aaron cuddled up to her. He had always loved Zlateh, but now she was like a sister. He was alone, cut off from his family, and wanted to talk. He began to talk to Zlateh. "Zlateh, what do you think about what has happened to us?" he asked.

"Maaaa," Zlateh answered.

"If we hadn't found this stack of hay, we would both be frozen stiff by now," Aaron said.

"Maaaa," was the goat's reply.

"If the snow keeps on falling like this, we may have to stay here for days," Aaron explained.

"Maaaa," Zlateh bleated.

"What does 'Maaaa' mean?" Aaron asked. "You'd better speak up clearly."

"Maaaa. Maaaa," Zlateh tried.

---

8 Finding Details
What details show that Aaron is in danger of freezing?
Numbness in hands and toes, nose feels wooden, choking when breathing.

9 Aaron feels responsible for Zlateh and includes her in his prayer for safety.

10 Immediate reply to his prayer.

11 He knows the hay will trap their body heat and shield them from the wind.

12 Evidence of Aaron's resourcefulness and Zlateh's willingness to provide food.

13 A natural bonding results from affection and shared experience.

272 SHORT STORIES

JOURNAL WRITING LINK

Students may have lost a favorite pet or prized possession through no fault of their own. Ask students if they have had such an experience. Could the loss have been prevented? How?

Ask students to write about the experience in their journals or notebooks. Did they try to locate the pet or look for the possession? What good came out of that experience?

TRANSPARENCY 22

Literary Elements
Story Map – explores the building blocks of fiction: characters, plot, setting, conflict, point of view, and theme.

"Well, let it be 'Maaaa' then," Aaron said patiently. "You can't speak, but I know you understand. I need you and you need me. Isn't that right?"

"Maaaa."

Aaron became sleepy. He made a pillow out of some hay, leaned his head on it, and dozed off. Zlateh too fell asleep.

When Aaron opened his eyes, he didn't know whether it was morning or night. The snow had blocked up his window. He tried to clear it, but when he had bored through to the length of his arm, he still hadn't reached the outside. Luckily he had his stick with him and was able to break through to the open air. It was still dark outside. The snow continued to fall and the wind wailed, first with one voice and then with many. Sometimes it had the sound of devilish laughter. Zlateh too awoke, and when Aaron greeted her, she answered, "Maaaa." Yes, Zlateh's language consisted of only one word, but it meant many things. Now she was saying, "We must accept all that God gives us—heat, cold, hunger, satisfaction, light, and darkness."

Aaron had awakened hungry. He had eaten up his food, but Zlateh had plenty of milk.

For three days Aaron and Zlateh stayed in the haystack. Aaron had always loved Zlateh, but in these three days he loved her more and more. She fed him with her milk and helped him keep warm. She comforted him with her patience. He told her many stories, and she always cocked her ears and listened. When he patted her, she licked his hand and his face. Then she said, "Maaaa," and he knew it meant, I love you too.

The snow fell for three days, though after the first day it was not as thick and the wind quieted down. Sometimes Aaron felt that there could never have been a summer, that the snow had always fallen, ever since he could remember. He, Aaron, never had a father or mother or sisters. He was a snow child, born of the snow, and so was Zlateh. It was so quiet in the hay that his ears rang in the stillness. Aaron and Zlateh slept all night and a good part of the day. As for Aaron's dreams, they were all about warm weather. He dreamed of green fields, trees covered with blossoms, clear brooks, and singing birds. By the third night the snow had stopped, but Aaron did not dare to find his way home in the darkness. The sky became clear and the moon shone, casting silvery nets on the snow. Aaron dug his way out and looked at the world. It was all white, quiet, dreaming dreams of heavenly splendor. The stars were large and close. The moon swam in the sky as in a sea.

On the morning of the fourth day Aaron heard the ringing of sleigh bells. The haystack was not far from the road. The peasant who drove the sleigh pointed out the way to him—not to the town and Feyvel the butcher, but home to the village. Aaron had decided in the haystack that he would never part with Zlateh.

Aaron's family and their neighbors had searched for the boy and the goat but had found no trace of them during the storm. They feared they were lost. Aaron's mother and sisters cried for him; his father remained silent and gloomy. Suddenly one of the neighbors came running to their house with the news that Aaron and Zlateh were coming up the road.

There was great joy in the family. Aaron told them how he had found the stack of hay and how Zlateh had fed him with her milk. Aaron's sisters kissed and hugged Zlateh and gave her a special treat of chopped carrots and potato peels, which Zlateh gobbled up hungrily.

Nobody ever again thought of selling Zlateh, and now that the cold weather had finally set in, the villagers needed the services of Reuven

14 Language is unnecessary to show affection.

15 **Theme.** Story's meaning emerges from the communication between Aaron and Zlateh. The opposites that life holds are part of God's plan.

16 **Mood.** Details showing magical quality of night scene: "silvery nets," "dreaming dreams of heavenly splendor," "moon swam in the sky as in a sea."

17 Reuven's decision sent the two into the storm.

18 Storm brings good to Zlateh and to Reuven's business.

Zlateh the Goat   273

the furrier once more. When Hanukkah came, Aaron's mother was able to fry pancakes every evening, and Zlateh got her portion too. Even though Zlateh had her own pen, she often came to the kitchen, knocking on the door with her horns to indicate that she was ready to visit, and she was always admitted. In the evening Aaron, Miriam, and Anna played dreidel.[3] Zlateh sat near the stove watching the children and the flickering of the Hanukkah candles.

Once in a while Aaron would ask her, "Zlateh, do you remember the three days we spent together?"

And Zlateh would scratch her neck with a horn, shake her white bearded head and come out with the single sound which expressed all her thoughts, and all her love.

[3]. **dreidel** (drā′dəl): a game played with a four-sided top; also, the top itself.

Reading Check

1. What kind of work does Reuven do?
2. What does Aaron dream about during the storm?
3. How does Aaron know that the haystack is not far from the road?
4. How does the family celebrate Hanukkah?

For Study and Discussion

Analyzing and Interpreting the Story

1. Nature plays an important role in this story. How does nature bring misery and then happiness to Reuven's family?

2. Why does Reuven decide to sell Zlateh?

3. Just when it seems that Aaron and Zlateh will perish in the storm, Aaron finds the haystack. How does the storm, which threatens their lives, become the means of saving Zlateh?

4. During the three days that Aaron and Zlateh spend in the haystack, they become completely dependent upon each other. What decision does Aaron come to?

5. When Aaron is alone with Zlateh, he begins to acquire wisdom about the meaning of his experience. **a.** What do you think he learns? **b.** What evidence in the story supports your opinion?

Literary Elements

Interpreting Theme

You have seen that a short story is made up of several basic elements. Often, the elements in a short story work together to express a central meaning or idea called the **theme.** Sometimes the theme of a story is stated directly. Sometimes the theme must be inferred from the other elements in a story.

The theme of "Zlateh the Goat" might be stated in this way: The hardships of life often serve to bind us more closely to those we love. Let us see how this statement grows out of the specific events in the story.

The characters in the story are faced with circumstances they cannot control. Reuven is forced through necessity to sell Zlateh. Both Zlateh and Aaron seem headed for tragedy through no fault of their own. They are saved quite unexpectedly when Aaron comes across a haystack. The storm turns out to be a godsend, for the family's circumstances are reversed by the change in weather. The events of the story suggest that the fate of all living creatures is beyond their understanding or control.

However, while the characters have no power to control their circumstances, they are

---

READING CHECK
1. He is a furrier (p. 270).
2. Warm weather (green fields, blossoming trees, brooks, birds) (p. 273).
3. He hears sleigh bells (p. 273).
4. They eat pancakes, light candles; children play dreidel (p. 274).

FOR STUDY AND DISCUSSION
1. Because of storm, Aaron and Zlateh are lost, believed dead. Storm and cold bring Reuven (a furrier) business.
2. She is old, gives little milk; he wants Hanukkah necessaries.
3. If not lost in storm, Zlateh would have been sold to butcher. Instead, because of storm, both are saved.
4. He will never part with Zlateh.
5a. Answers will vary. He decides he should have faith.
5b. Students may cite statement which begins "We must accept all that God gives us—" (p. 273).

CLOSURE

One message of this story is that "love is more important than money." Ask students to explain how this message is expressed in "Zlateh the Goat," using specific examples to support their explanations.

EXTENSION AND ENRICHMENT

Students may be interested in researching how different animals communicate with humans. Or students may wish to discuss their own pets and the place these animals have in their family.

---

not helpless, for they are sustained by love and trust. This idea becomes clear in the central episode of the story. When Aaron and Zlateh are cut off from the rest of the world, Aaron grows to love Zlateh more and more, and he determines that he will never part with her. When he returns to the village, there is no more talk of selling Zlateh, for the family has learned how much Zlateh means to all of them. We see that the bonds of this family have been strengthened by their ordeal.

1 Have you a different interpretation of the story? How would you express the theme?

Understanding Point of View

You have seen that a story may be told from the point of view of one of its characters. In "A Day's Wait" (page 242), the narrator is the boy's father. The story is written from a **first-person point of view.**

The narrator in "Zlateh the Goat" stands outside the action as an observer. This narrator tells us not only what the characters say and do, but also what they think and feel. Because the narrator is all-knowing, we refer to this point of view as **omniscient** (ŏm-nĭsh′ənt).

Find passages in the story where you are allowed to share characters' thoughts and feel-
2 ings. How does the omniscient point of view bring you closer to the characters?

Stories with the omniscient point of view are always written in the third person. Sometimes a writer using the third person will purposely limit the point of view to what one particular character sees, hears, and thinks. "The Landlady" is written in the third person, but the author has chosen to reveal only what Billy knows and feels. This point of view is called **limited third-person point of view.**

Find the passage on page 225 that tells you
3 what Billy is thinking as he sips his tea. Do you know what the landlady is thinking in this passage? If the author had revealed the landlady's thoughts during this scene, would the end of the story have been a surprise?

Focus on Writing a Short Story

Exploring a Theme

Choose a **theme** for a short story. Here are some ideas:

Don't bite the hand that feeds you.
Humor is the best medicine.
Honesty is the best policy.

Make some notes about a plot, a setting, and some characters that you might use to develop the theme into a story. Save your notes.

About the Author

Isaac Bashevis Singer (1904–1991)

Isaac Bashevis Singer is well known for his stories of Jewish life in eastern Europe. He was born in Radzymin, Poland, and was educated in Warsaw, the nation's capital. In 1935 he moved to New York City, where he worked for the *Jewish Daily Forward* for the next fifty-six years. Singer wrote only in Yiddish. He published more than fifty novels, short story collections, children's books, and plays. In 1978 he was awarded the Nobel Prize for literature.

When interviewed about the subjects of his stories, he said: "I prefer to write about the world which I knew, which I know, best. This is Bilgoray, Lublin, the Jews of Kreshev. This is enough for me. I can get from these people art.... I write about the things where I grew up, and where I feel completely at home."

LITERARY ELEMENTS

Interpreting Theme

1. Students may suggest different interpretations, perhaps involving the special relationship that can form between people and animals. Be sure that students state this theme clearly and show how it grows from specific events in the story. They can use the interpretation given in this exercise as an example.

Understanding Point of View

2. Students will be able to select passages throughout the story that demonstrate omniscient point of view. For example, paragraph that begins "For three days Aaron and Zlateh . . ." (p. 273) reveals thoughts and feelings of Aaron and Zlateh. Enabling the reader to share in these thoughts and feelings increases involvement with the characters.

3. In "The Landlady," the woman's thoughts are unknown to the reader; thus the reader is kept in suspense regarding her intentions.

ABOUT THE AUTHOR

Isaac Bashevis Singer has written more than twenty books, many of them in the style of folk tales. His stories have appealed to readers of all ages and many cultures. Several of his stories have been adapted for presentation on television, and others into films—including the film *Yentl* starring Barbra Streisand.

Zlateh the Goat

OBJECTIVES
The overall aim is for students to discuss **characterization, plot, theme,** and **setting** in the story. For a complete list of objectives, see the Teacher's Notes.

VOCABULARY
The underlined words are in the Glossary. The **Language and Vocabulary** exercise on p. 301 gives students practice in recognizing analogies and completing missing terms from analogies.

FOCUS / MOTIVATION
Ask students to think about how a person's life might be changed if he or she could see the future. In what ways could such knowledge be harmful or beneficial? "A Christmas Carol" is the story of a beneficial change.

TEACHING RESOURCES B
Teacher's Notes, p. 200
Study Guide, p. 204
Language Skills, p. 207
Building Vocabulary, pp. 210, 212, 217
Selection Vocabulary Test, pp. 218, 220
Selection Test, p. 222

AV RESOURCES BINDER
Audiocassette 2, Side B

PREREADING FOCUS
The headnote points out the various literary elements that are highlighted in this classic story: **characterization, plot, setting,** and **theme.** Each of these has been the particular focus in one of the selections in this unit, but you may want to use this story as a summary and review of these terms and their application.

**A Christmas Carol
Stave One**

1
Foreshadowing. Finality of this and other statements about Marley's death suggests the supernatural aspect of his later appearance.

2 Drawing Conclusions
Analyzing
What type of man has only one friend and mourner? What must this say about Scrooge? Answers will vary.

3
He and Marley evidently shared the same world view; thus Scrooge's description also applies to Marley.

A Christmas Carol

CHARLES DICKENS

Dickens' story has all the elements of a great classic: memorable characters, an intriguing plot, setting that evokes mood, a superb style, and a wonderful, compassionate theme. The tale is ageless, and despite the many adaptations for film, television, and the stage, one never tires of the story.

Dickens wanted to be an actor, and he enjoyed reading his works to the public. Many generations have discovered the pleasure of listening to "A Christmas Carol" read aloud. Share this pleasure with your classmates.

Stave[1] One:
Marley's Ghost

1 Marley was dead, to begin with. There is no doubt whatever about that. The register of his burial was signed by the clergyman, the clerk, the undertaker, and the chief mourner. Scrooge signed it. And Scrooge's name was good upon 'Change[2] for anything he chose to put his hand to.

Old Marley was as dead as a doornail.

Scrooge knew he was dead? Of course he did. How could it be otherwise? Scrooge and he were partners for I don't know how many years. Scrooge was his sole executor, his sole administrator, his sole assign, his sole resid-

2 uary legatee,[3] his sole friend, his sole mourner.

Scrooge never painted out old Marley's name, however. There it yet stood, years afterward, above the door—SCROOGE AND MARLEY. The firm was known as SCROOGE AND MARLEY. Sometimes people new to the business called

3 Scrooge "Scrooge," and sometimes "Marley." He answered to both names. It was all the same to him.

Oh! But he was a tightfisted hand at the grindstone, was Scrooge! A squeezing, wrenching, grasping, scraping, clutching, <u>covetous</u> old sinner! External heat and cold had little influence on him. No warmth could

---

1. **Stave:** a stanza of a poem or song; here, a section of Dickens' "carol."
2. **'Change:** the Exchange, the place where merchants, brokers, and bankers conduct their business.
3. **executor** (ĕg-zĕk′yə-tər); **administrator; assign; residuary legatee** (rĭ-zĭj′ōō-ĕr′ē lĕg′ə-tē′): legal terms used in a will. Marley had left everything he owned to Scrooge, who handled all the business arrangements after Marley's death.

276 SHORT STORIES

MOTIVATIONAL SUMMARY
Ebenezer Scrooge hates Christmas. Among other annoyances of the season, he resents paying a day's wages for his employee Bob Cratchit's only day off. Heading to his stingy rooms, all alone on Christmas Eve, Scrooge is startled when he reaches for his doorknocker: it briefly changes into the face of his old partner, Jacob Marley. Surely, Scrooge thinks, he's seeing things: Marley's been dead exactly seven years, and there are no such things as ghosts. Or are there?

PRESENTATION
Ebenezer Scrooge is perhaps the best remembered of Charles Dickens' characters. His name is a part of most English speakers' vocabularies. To call a person a "Scrooge" is to conjure up all the images of coldhearted parsimony that Dickens

---

4 warm, no cold could chill him. No wind that blew was bitterer than he, no falling snow was more intent upon its purpose, no pelting rain less open to entreaty. Foul weather didn't know where to have him. The heaviest rain and snow and hail and sleet could boast of the advantage over him in only one respect—they often "came down"[4] handsomely, and Scrooge never did.

Nobody ever stopped him in the street to say, with gladsome looks, "My dear Scrooge, how are you? When will you come to see me?" No beggars implored him to bestow a trifle, no children asked him what it was o'clock, no man or woman ever once in all his life inquired the way to such and such a place of Scrooge. Even the blind men's dogs appeared to know him, and when they saw him coming on, would tug their owners into doorways and up courts, and then would wag their tails as though they said, "No eyes at all is better than an evil eye, dark master!"

But what did Scrooge care! It was the very thing he liked. To edge his way along the crowded paths of life, warning all human sympathy to keep its distance, was what the knowing ones call "nuts" to Scrooge.

Once upon a time—of all the good days in the year, upon a Christmas Eve—old Scrooge sat busy in his countinghouse. It was cold, bleak, biting, foggy weather; and the city clocks had only just gone three, but it was quite dark already.

The door of Scrooge's countinghouse was open, that he might keep his eye upon his
5 clerk, who, in a dismal little cell beyond, a sort of tank, was copying letters. Scrooge had a very small fire, but the clerk's fire was so very much
6 smaller that it looked like one coal. But he couldn't replenish it, for Scrooge kept the coalbox in his own room, and so surely as the clerk came in with the shovel, the master predicted that it would be necessary for them to part. Wherefore the clerk put on his white comforter[5] and tried to warm himself at the candle; in which effort, not being a man of a strong imagination, he failed.

"A Merry Christmas, Uncle! God save you!" cried a cheerful voice. It was the voice of Scrooge's nephew, who came upon him so quickly that this was the first intimation Scrooge had of his approach.

"Bah!" said Scrooge. "Humbug!"

"Christmas a humbug, Uncle! You don't mean that, I am sure?"

7 "I do. Out upon merry Christmas! What's Christmastime to you but a time for paying bills without money; a time for finding yourself a year older, and not an hour richer; a time for balancing your books and having every item in 'em through a round dozen of months presented dead against you? If I had my will, every idiot who goes about with 'Merry Christmas' on his lips should be boiled with his own pudding and buried with a stake of holly through his heart. He should!"

"Uncle!"

"Nephew, keep Christmas in your own way, and let me keep it in mine."

"Keep it! But you don't keep it."

"Let me leave it alone, then. Much good may it do you! Much good it has ever done you!"

8 "There are many things from which I might have derived good, by which I have not profited, I dare say, Christmas among the rest. But I am sure I have always thought of Christmastime, when it has come round—apart from the veneration due to its sacred origin, if anything belonging to it *can* be apart from that—as a good time; a kind, forgiving, charitable, pleasant time; the only time I know of, in the long calendar of the year, when men and women

---

4. **"came down"**: slang for "made a gift or donation."
5. **comforter**: a long scarf.

4
Characterization. The narrator characterizes Scrooge directly, comparing him with the unpleasant qualities of nature; he is even worse than they are.

5
Connotation. "Cell" and "tank" suggest confinement, prison.

6
Scrooge threatens to fire him if he uses more than his meager allotment of coal.

7
Scrooge's observations dwell solely on the negative aspects of the season; he refuses to see any good in it.

8
Theme. Scrooge's nephew makes a distinction between things that have done him "good" and things by which he has "profited." (Scrooge thinks the only good *is* profit.)

uses to describe the cynical old miser. The compassion and warmth of the reborn Scrooge have been lost in the vernacular usage of his name, perhaps because Dickens' characterization of Scrooge before the Christmas Eve visit of the spirits is especially vivid. Scrooge, however, is neither a stock character nor a flat character, no matter what his name has come to mean. His conversion from crotchety miser to warm humanitarian is the heart of the story. Other characters are also memorable. Most readers never forget Cratchit, the clerk, or his crippled son, Tiny Tim.

"A Christmas Carol" is a sentimental and didactic work, but, because of Dickens' rich language, gentle humor, subtle wordplay, and eye for detail, the story is a literary classic rather than a sermon. The modern reader can learn a great

---

9 Scrooge means this as a dismissal.

10 Foreshadowing. Significant: this night is the anniversary of Marley's death.

11 Tone suggests a memorized speech repeated to potential donors.

12 Refers to debtors' prisons; those jailed for nonpayment of debts were released when debts were paid.

13 In this prison system, debtors could not work to pay their debts while in jail.

14 Making Generalizations *What does this remark reveal about Scrooge?* His extreme callousness.

15 Unlike Scrooge, the clerk is eager to go home to celebrate the holiday.

---

seem by one consent to open their shut-up hearts freely and to think of people below them as if they really were fellow travelers to the grave, and not another race of creatures bound on other journeys. And therefore, Uncle, though it has never put a scrap of gold or silver in my pocket, I believe that it *has* done me good, and *will* do me good; and I say, God bless it!"

The clerk in the tank involuntarily applauded.

"Let me hear another sound from *you*," said Scrooge, "and you'll keep your Christmas by losing your situation! You're quite a powerful speaker, sir," he added, turning to his nephew. "I wonder you don't go into Parliament."

"Don't be angry, Uncle. Come! Dine with us tomorrow."

9 "Good afternoon."

"I want nothing from you; I ask nothing of you; why cannot we be friends?"

"Good afternoon."

"I am sorry, with all my heart, to find you so resolute. We have never had any quarrel to which I have been a party. But I have made the trial in homage to Christmas, and I'll keep my Christmas humor to the last. So a Merry Christmas, Uncle!"

"Good afternoon!"

"And a Happy New Year!"

"Good afternoon!"

His nephew left the room without an angry word, notwithstanding. The clerk, in letting Scrooge's nephew out, had let two other people in. They were portly gentlemen, pleasant to behold, and now stood, with their hats off, in Scrooge's office. They had books and papers in their hands, and bowed to him.

"Scrooge and Marley's, I believe," said one of the gentlemen, referring to his list. "Have I the pleasure of addressing Mr. Scrooge or Mr. Marley?"

"Mr. Marley has been dead these seven 10 years. He died seven years ago this very night."

11 "At this festive season of the year, Mr. Scrooge," said the gentleman, taking up a pen, "it is more than usually desirable that we should make some slight provision for the poor and destitute, who suffer greatly at the present time. Many thousands are in want of common necessaries; hundreds of thousands are in want of common comforts, sir."

12 "Are there no prisons?"

"Plenty of prisons. But under the impression that they scarcely furnish Christian cheer of mind or body to the unoffending multitude, a few of us are endeavoring to raise a fund to buy the poor some meat and drink, and means of warmth. We choose this time, because it is a time, of all others, when want is keenly felt, and abundance rejoices. What shall I put you down for?"

"Nothing!"

"You wish to be anonymous?"

"I wish to be left alone. Since you ask me what I wish, gentlemen, that is my answer. I don't make merry myself at Christmas, and I 13 can't afford to make idle people merry. I help to support the prisons and workhouses—they cost enough—and those who are badly off must go there."

"Many can't go there; and many would rather die."

14 "If they would rather die, they had better do it, and decrease the surplus population."

At length the hour of shutting up the countinghouse arrived. With an ill will Scrooge, dismounting from his stool, tacitly[6] admitted the 15 fact to the expectant clerk in the tank, who instantly snuffed his candle out and put on his hat.

"You want all day tomorrow, I suppose?"

---

6. **tacitly** (tăs'ĭt-lē): without speaking.

278 SHORT STORIES

deal about life in 1840s London and, at the same time, enjoy a compelling story and entertaining characters.

MEETING INDIVIDUAL NEEDS
ESL/LEP • The character of Scrooge is often associated with the expression "Bah! Humbug!" (Scrooge's memorable response to the Christmas celebration) You may want to explain that *humbug!* is a slang expression that originated in the eighteenth century, meaning "nonsense".

"If quite convenient, sir."

"It's not convenient, and it's not fair. If I was to stop half a crown for it, you'd think yourself mightily ill-used, I'll be bound?"

"Yes, sir."

"And yet you don't think *me* ill-used when I pay a day's wages for no work."

"It's only once a year, sir."

16 "A poor excuse for picking a man's pocket every twenty-fifth of December! But I suppose you must have the whole day. Be here all the earlier *next* morning."

The clerk promised that he would, and Scrooge walked out with a growl. The office was closed in a twinkling, and the clerk, with the long ends of his white comforter dangling below his waist (for he boasted no greatcoat), went down a slide, at the end of a lane of boys, twenty times, in honor of its being Christmas Eve, and then ran home as hard as he could pelt, to play at blindman's buff.

17 Scrooge took his melancholy dinner in his usual melancholy tavern; and having read all the newspapers and beguiled[7] the rest of the evening with his banker's book, went home to bed. He lived in chambers which had once belonged to his deceased partner. They were a gloomy suite of rooms in a lowering[8] pile of a building up a yard. The building was old enough now, and dreary enough, for nobody lived in it but Scrooge, the other rooms being all let out as offices.

18 Now it is a fact that there was nothing at all particular about the knocker on the door of his house, except that it was very large; also, that Scrooge had seen it, night and morning, during his whole residence in that place; also, that Scrooge had as little of what is called fancy[9] about him as any man in the city of London.

And yet Scrooge, having his key in the lock of the door, saw in the knocker, without its undergoing any intermediate process of change, not a knocker, but Marley's face.

Marley's face, with a dismal light about it, like a bad lobster in a dark cellar. It was not angry or ferocious, but it looked at Scrooge as Marley used to look—ghostly spectacles turned up upon its ghostly forehead.

As Scrooge looked fixedly at this phenomenon, it was a knocker again. He said, "Pooh, pooh!" and closed the door with a bang.

19

The sound resounded through the house like thunder. Every room above, and every cask in the wine merchant's cellars below, appeared to have a separate peal of echoes of its own. Scrooge was not a man to be frightened by echoes. He fastened the door and walked across the hall and up the stairs. Slowly, too, trimming his candle as he went.

20

Up Scrooge went, not caring a button for its being very dark. Darkness is cheap, and Scrooge liked it. But before he shut his heavy door, he walked through his rooms to see that all was right. He had just enough recollection of the face to desire to do that.

Sitting room, bedroom, lumber room,[10] all as they should be. Nobody under the table, nobody under the sofa; a small fire in the grate; spoon and basin ready; and the little saucepan of gruel (Scrooge had a cold in his head) upon the hob.[11] Nobody under the bed; nobody in the closet; nobody in his dressing gown, which was hanging up in a suspicious attitude against the wall. Lumber room as usual. Old fireguards, old shoes, two fish baskets, washing stand on three legs, and a poker.

Quite satisfied, he closed his door and locked himself in; double-locked himself in, which

---

7. **beguiled** (bĭ-gīld′): spent or whiled away.
8. **lowering** (lou′ər-ĭng): dark and threatening.
9. **fancy**: imagination.
10. **lumber room**: storeroom.
11. **hob**: a small shelf at the back or side of a fireplace, used to keep a kettle or a saucepan warm.

A Christmas Carol 279

16
Scrooge grudgingly gives Cratchit a paid Christmas holiday, his one day a year off.

17
Contrast Cratchit's joy despite poverty to Scrooge's gloom despite wealth.

18
Foreshadowing. Emphasis on the knocker's ordinariness and Scrooge's lack of imagination sets stage for supernatural events; transformation foreshadows arrival of Marley's ghost.

19
His scoff is intended for reassurance.

20
Characterization. Scrooge is not superstitious, making future encounters with supernatural more credible.

MEETING INDIVIDUAL NEEDS

ESL/LEP • You may want to contrast the use of the expression *let out* in the following sentences from the story:

". . . the other rooms being all **let out** as offices." (rented out) (p. 279)

". . . the slow potatoes, bubbling up, knocked loudly at the saucepan lid to be **let out** and peeled." (released) (p. 286)

VISUAL CONNECTIONS
Exploring the Subject
Scrooge, in his nightcap and slippers, sits by his meager fire. Determined not to admit that he sees Marley's ghost, Scrooge merely looks sour, while the flame on his candle reacts with a humorously horrified expression. Marley wears, on his head, a bandage around the jaws. In the Victorian era, this was often done to keep the deceased person's jaws from gaping open. From Marley's chains hang his ledger books and a collection of keys, which presumably open lockboxes that store money.

About the Artist
John Leech was a popular illustrator in early nineteenth-century England, principally known for his caricatures in *Punch* magazine and *The Illustrated London News*.

21 Bells announce the ghost's arrival.

22 Suspense. "Deep down below" suggests depths of hell; description of slow approach builds tension.

23 Drawing Conclusions
Why do you think Scrooge never thought of Marley as a cruel person? Scrooge is like Marley.

24 His disbelief explains his bold manner.

25 The "much" Marley wants is the complete transformation of Scrooge's character.

280

---

was not his custom. Thus secured against surprise, he took off his cravat,[12] put on his dressing gown and slippers and his nightcap, and sat down before the very low fire to take his gruel.

As he threw his head back in the chair, his glance happened to rest upon a bell, a disused bell, that hung in the room and communicated, for some purpose now forgotten, with a chamber in the highest story of the building. It was with great astonishment, and with a strange inexplicable dread, that, as he looked, **21** he saw this bell begin to swing. Soon it rang out loudly, and so did every bell in the house.

22 This was succeeded by a clanking noise, deep down below, as if some person were dragging a heavy chain over the casks in the wine merchant's cellar.

Then he heard the noise much louder on the floors below; then coming up the stairs; then coming straight toward his door.

It came on through the heavy door, and a specter passed into the room before his eyes. And upon its coming in, the dying flame leaped up, as though it cried, "I know him! Marley's ghost!"

The same face, the very same. Marley in his pigtail, usual waistcoat, tights, and boots. His body was transparent; so that Scrooge, observing him, and looking through his waistcoat, could see the two buttons on his coat behind.

Scrooge had often heard it said that Marley **23** had no bowels,[13] but he had never believed it until now.

No, nor did he believe it even now. Though he looked the phantom through and through and saw it standing before him—though he felt the chilling influence of its death-cold eyes and

---

[12] **cravat** (krə-văt'): a necktie, or a scarf resembling a necktie.
[13] **bowels:** the intestines, which used to be regarded as the source of pity and mercy. When people said Marley had no bowels, they meant that he was cruel.

280 SHORT STORIES

Marley's Ghost.
Illustrations by John Leech are from the 1846 edition of *A Christmas Carol*.

noticed the very texture of the folded kerchief bound about its head and chin—he was still incredulous.

"How now!" said Scrooge, caustic and cold **24** as ever. "What do you want with me?"

"Much!"—Marley's voice, no doubt about it. **25**

"Who are you?"

"Ask me who I *was*."

"Who *were* you then?"

"In life I was your partner, Jacob Marley."

"Can you—can you sit down?"

"I can."

"Do it, then."

Scrooge asked the question because he didn't know whether a ghost so transparent might find himself in a condition to take a chair, and felt that, in the event of its being im-

READING SKILLS PRACTICE
The underlined passage can be used to give students practice in the reading skill of using context to understand word meaning. In the passage marked, the meaning of the word *countinghouse* can be inferred from the context of the paragraph in which it appears. Ask students to choose the most accurate synonym for *countinghouse* in this passage. **A.** Library; **B.** Place where account books are kept and business transacted; **C.** Office of weights and measures; **D.** Freight office. (Answer: **B.** In this context, money-changing hole is a clue to the meaning of *countinghouse* because it emphasizes the monetary nature of the transactions, which also implies bookkeeping or accounting.)

---

possible, it might involve the necessity of an embarrassing explanation. But the ghost sat down on the opposite side of the fireplace, as if he were quite used to it.

"You don't believe in me."

"I don't."

"What evidence would you have of my reality beyond that of your senses?"

"I don't know."

"Why do you doubt your senses?"

26 "Because a little thing affects them. A slight disorder of the stomach makes them cheats. You may be an undigested bit of beef, a blot of mustard, a crumb of cheese, a fragment of an underdone potato. There's more of gravy than of grave about you, whatever you are!"

Scrooge was not much in the habit of cracking jokes, nor did he feel in his heart by any means waggish then. The truth is that he tried to be smart, as a means of distracting his own attention and keeping down his horror.

But how much greater was his horror when, the phantom taking off the bandage round its head, as if it were too warm to wear indoors, its lower jaw dropped down upon its breast!

"Mercy! Dreadful apparition, why do you trouble me? Why do spirits walk the earth, and why do they come to me?"

27 ▶ "It is required of every man that the spirit within him should walk abroad among his fellowmen and travel far and wide; and if that spirit goes not forth in life, it is condemned to do so after death. I cannot tell you all I would. A very little more is permitted to me. I cannot rest, I cannot stay, I cannot linger anywhere. My spirit never walked beyond our countinghouse—mark me!—in life my spirit never roved beyond the narrow limits of our money-changing hole; and weary journeys lie before me!" ◀

"Seven years dead. And traveling all the time? You travel fast?"

"On the wings of the wind."

"You might have got over a great quantity of ground in seven years."

28 "O blind man, blind man! not to know that ages of incessant labor by immortal creatures for this earth must pass into eternity before the good of which it is susceptible is all developed.¹⁴ Not to know that any Christian spirit working kindly in its little sphere, whatever it may be, will find its mortal life too short for its vast means of usefulness. Not to know that no space of regret can make amends for one life's opportunities misused! Yet I was like this man; I once was like this man!"

"But you were always a good man of business, Jacob," faltered Scrooge, who now began to apply this to himself.

29 "Business!" cried the ghost, wringing its hands again. "Mankind was my business. The common welfare was my business; charity, mercy, forbearance, benevolence, were all my business. The dealings of my trade were but a drop of water in the comprehensive ocean of my business!"

Scrooge was very much dismayed to hear the specter going on at this rate, and began to quake exceedingly.

"Hear me! My time is nearly gone."

"I will. But don't be hard upon me! Don't be flowery, Jacob! Pray!"

"I am here tonight to warn you that you have yet a chance and hope of escaping my fate. A chance and hope of my procuring,¹⁵ Ebenezer."

"You were always a good friend to me," said Scrooge. "Thank'ee!"

"You will be haunted by three spirits."

31 "Is that the chance and hope you mentioned, Jacob? I—I think I'd rather not."

"Without their visits, you cannot hope to

---

14. **ages . . . developed:** In other words, heavenly spirits must work for countless years before the goodness that is possible in the world can come into being.
15. **of my procuring:** that I got for you.

26
Characterization. Though probably frightened, Scrooge retains wit; tries to attribute ghost to indigestion.

27 Expressing an Opinion
Why do you think the spirit must travel among his fellow men? One response may be that a person living in selfish isolation cannot learn love.

28
Theme. Marley states theme of story: purpose of life is to do good for humanity, and we have only short time to do so.

29 Analyzing
Why does Marley's description of wasted life begin to frighten Scrooge? Scrooge is just like him.

30
"Business," as used ironically by Marley, means concern, not money-making.

31
Humor: when Marley says the "chance" he's gotten for Scrooge includes visits by three spirits, Scrooge says he'd "rather not."

▶Reading Skills Objective: Using Context to Understand Word Meaning.   A Christmas Carol

PORTFOLIO ASSESSMENT
A reading journal is a record containing summaries, questions, words, and phrases that are important to the reader, as well as other responses to literature. Students may want to keep a reading journal as they study "A Christmas Carol" in order to clarify the literary elements in the story. Suggest that students' reading journals may contain personal artwork and may be included in student portfolios. (See *Portfolio Assessment and Professional Support Materials* for additional information.)

32
He tries to dismiss the vision as unreal but cannot.

Stave Two

1
Setting. Blackness of night and ominous toll of clock create eerie, expectant **mood.**

2
Youth and age combined; receding effect reflects memory's diminishing grasp on the past.

3
Spirit's oddest attribute is light shining from crown of head, perhaps representing memory.

4 Summarizing
What prevents Scrooge from falling when he and the spirit go out the window? Spirit lays its hand over his heart; suggests that he will be upheld spiritually as well as physically.

---

shun the path I tread. Expect the first tomorrow night, when the bell tolls one. Expect the second on the next night at the same hour. The third, upon the next night, when the last stroke of twelve has ceased to vibrate. Look to see me no more; and look that, for your own sake, you remember what has passed between us!"

It walked backward from him; and at every step it took, the window raised itself a little, so that, when the apparition reached it, it was wide open.

Scrooge closed the window, and examined the door by which the ghost had entered. It was double-locked, as he had locked it with his own hands, and the bolts were undisturbed. **32** Scrooge tried to say, "Humbug!" but stopped at the first syllable. And being, from the emotion he had undergone, or the fatigues of the day, or his glimpse of the invisible world, or the dull[16] conversation of the ghost, or the lateness of the hour, much in need of repose, he went straight to bed, without undressing, and fell asleep on the instant.

Stave Two:
The First of the Three Spirits

1 When Scrooge awoke, it was so dark that, looking out of bed, he could scarcely distinguish the transparent window from the opaque walls of his chamber, until suddenly the church clock tolled a deep, dull, hollow, melancholy ONE.

Light flashed up in the room upon the instant, and the curtains of his bed were drawn **2** aside by a strange figure—like a child; yet not so like a child as like an old man, viewed through some supernatural medium, which gave him the appearance of having receded from the view and being diminished to a child's proportions. Its hair, which hung about

16. **dull:** here, gloomy.

its neck and down its back, was white as if with age; and yet the face had not a wrinkle in it, and the tenderest bloom was on the skin. It held a branch of fresh green holly in its hand; and, in singular contradiction of that wintry emblem, had its dress trimmed with summer **3** flowers. But the strangest thing about it was that from the crown of its head there sprang a bright, clear jet of light by which all this was visible; and which was doubtless the occasion of its using, in its duller moments, a great extinguisher for a cap, which it now held under its arm.

"Are you the spirit, sir, whose coming was foretold to me?"

"I am!"

"Who and what are you?"

"I am the Ghost of Christmas Past."

"Long past?"

"No. Your past. The things that you will see with me are shadows of the things that have been; they will have no consciousness of us."

Scrooge then made bold to inquire what business brought him there.

"Your welfare. Rise and walk with me!"

It would have been in vain for Scrooge to plead that the weather and the hour were not adapted to pedestrian purposes; that bed was warm, and the thermometer a long way below freezing; that he was clad but lightly in his slippers, dressing gown, and nightcap; and that he had a cold upon him at that time. The grasp, though gentle as a woman's hand, was not to be resisted. He rose; but finding that the spirit made toward the window, clasped its robe in supplication.

"I am a mortal, and liable to fall."

"Bear but a touch of my hand *there*," said the spirit, laying it upon his heart, "and you shall **4** be upheld in more than this!"

As the words were spoken, they passed through the wall and stood in the busy thoroughfares of a city. It was made plain enough by the dressing of the shops that here, too, it was Christmastime. The ghost stopped at a certain warehouse door and asked Scrooge if he knew it.

"Know it! I was apprenticed here!"

They went in. At sight of an old gentleman in a Welsh wig, sitting behind such a high desk that, if he had been two inches taller, he must have knocked his head against the ceiling, Scrooge cried in great excitement: "Why, it's old Fezziwig! Bless his heart, it's Fezziwig, alive again!"

Old Fezziwig laid down his pen and looked up at the clock, which pointed to the hour of seven. He rubbed his hands; adjusted his capacious waistcoat; laughed all over himself, from his shoes to his organ of benevolence;[17] and called out in a comfortable, oily, rich, fat, jovial voice: "Yo ho, there! Ebenezer! Dick!"

A living and moving picture of Scrooge's former self, a young man, came briskly in, accompanied by his fellow apprentice.

"Dick Wilkins, to be sure!" said Scrooge to the ghost. "My old fellow 'prentice, bless me, yes. There he is. He was very much attached to me, was Dick. Poor Dick! Dear, dear!"

"Yo ho, my boys!" said Fezziwig. "No more work tonight. Christmas Eve, Dick. Christmas, Ebenezer! Let's have the shutters up, before a man can say 'Jack Robinson'! Clear away, my lads, and let's have lots of room here!"

Clear away! There was nothing they wouldn't have cleared away, or couldn't have cleared away, with old Fezziwig looking on. It was done in a minute. Every movable was packed off, as if it were dismissed from public life forevermore; the floor was swept and watered, the lamps were trimmed, fuel was heaped upon the fire; and the warehouse was as snug and warm and dry and bright a ballroom as you would desire to see on a winter night.

In came a fiddler with a music book, and went up to the lofty desk, and made an orchestra of it, and tuned like fifty stomachaches. In came Mrs. Fezziwig, one vast substantial smile. In came the three Miss Fezziwigs, beaming and lovable. In came the six young followers whose hearts they broke. In came all the young men and women employed in the business. In came the housemaid, with her cousin, the baker. In came the cook, with her brother's particular friend, the milkman. In they all came one after another; some shyly, some boldly, some gracefully, some awkwardly, some pushing, some pulling; in they all came, anyhow and everyhow. Away they all went, twenty couples at once; hands half round and back again the other way; down the middle and up again;

Mr. Fezziwig's Ball.

---

17. **organ of benevolence** (bə-nĕv′ə-ləns): the part of the head where the forehead meets the crown.

A Christmas Carol 283

TRANSPARENCY 20

Reader Response
Tug-of-War – allows students an opportunity to explore conflicts faced by one of the characters in a selection.

---

11 Fezziwig provides well for his guests.

12 Fezziwig's dancing reflects his joy in life.

13 The spirit's comment is an echo of Scrooge's miserly, money-conscious self.

14 Scrooge argues that Fezziwig has the power to make his employees happy or miserable; he chooses to make them happy.

15 Drawing Conclusions
Why does Scrooge wish to see his clerk? He is beginning to regret his harsh treatment of his own employee.

---

round and round in various stages of affectionate grouping; old top couple always turning up in the wrong place; new top couple starting off again, as soon as they got there; all top couples at last, and not a bottom one to help them. When this result was brought about, old Fezziwig, clapping his hands to stop the dance, cried out, "Well done"; and the fiddler plunged his hot face into a pot of porter[18] especially provided for that purpose.

11 There were more dances, and there were forfeits[19] and more dances, and there was cake, and there was negus,[20] and there was a great piece of cold roast, and there was a great piece of cold boiled,[21] and there were mince pies, and plenty of beer. But the great effect of the evening came after the roast and boiled, when the fiddler struck up "Sir Roger de **12** Coverley."[22] Then old Fezziwig stood out to dance with Mrs. Fezziwig. Top couple, too; with a good stiff piece of work cut out for them; three- or four-and-twenty pairs of partners; people who were not to be trifled with; people who *would* dance, and had no notion of walking.

But if they had been twice as many—four times—old Fezziwig would have been a match for them, and so would Mrs. Fezziwig. As to *her*, she was worthy to be his partner in every sense of the term. A positive light appeared to issue from Fezziwig's calves. They shone in every part of the dance. You couldn't have predicted, at any given time, what would become of 'em next. And when old Fezziwig and Mrs. Fezziwig had gone all through the dance—advance and retire, turn your partner, bow and curtsy, corkscrew, thread the needle, and back again to your place—Fezziwig "cut"—cut so deftly, that he appeared to wink with his legs.

When the clock struck eleven this domestic ball broke up. Mr. and Mrs. Fezziwig took their stations, one on either side of the door, and, shaking hands with every person individually as he or she went out, wished him or her a Merry Christmas. When everybody had retired but the two 'prentices, they did the same to them; and thus the cheerful voices died away, and the lads were left to their beds, which were under a counter in the back shop.

13 "A small matter," said the ghost, "to make these silly folks so full of gratitude. He has spent but a few pounds of your mortal money—three or four perhaps. Is that so much that he deserves this praise?"

"It isn't that," said Scrooge, heated by the remark, and speaking unconsciously like his for- **14** mer, not his latter, self—"it isn't that, Spirit. He has the power to render us happy or unhappy; to make our service light or burdensome; a pleasure or a toil. Say that his power lies in words and looks; in things so slight and insignificant that it is impossible to add and count 'em up: what then? The happiness he gives is quite as great as if it cost a fortune."

He felt the spirit's glance, and stopped.

"What is the matter?"

"Nothing particular."

"Something, I think?"

15 "No, no. I should like to be able to say a word or two to my clerk just now. That's all."

"My time grows short," observed the spirit. "Quick!"

This was not addressed to Scrooge, or to anyone whom he could see, but it produced an immediate effect. For again he saw himself. He was older now; a man in the prime of life.

He was not alone, but sat by the side of a fair

---

18. **porter:** dark brown beer.
19. **forfeits** (fôr′fĭts): a game in which the players must forfeit, or give up, something if they lose.
20. **negus** (nē′gəs): punch.
21. **boiled:** boiled beef.
22. **"Sir Roger de Coverley":** a square-dance tune.

SHORT STORIES

young girl in a black dress, in whose eyes there were tears.

"It matters little," she said softly to Scrooge's former self. "To you very little. Another idol has displaced me; and if it can comfort you in time to come, as I would have tried to do, I have no just cause to grieve."

"What idol has displaced you?"

"A golden one. You fear the world too much. I have seen your nobler aspirations fall off one by one, until the master passion, gain, engrosses you. Have I not?"

"What then? Even if I have grown so much wiser, what then? I am not changed toward you. Have I ever sought release from our engagement?"

"In words, no. Never."

"In what, then?"

"In a changed nature; in an altered spirit; in another atmosphere of life; another hope as its great end. If you were free today, tomorrow, yesterday, can even I believe that you would choose a dowerless[23] girl; or, choosing her, do I not know that your repentance and regret would surely follow? I do; and I release you. With a full heart, for the love of him you once were."

"Spirit! remove me from this place."

"I told you these were shadows of the things that have been," said the ghost. "That they are what they are, do not blame me!"

"Remove me!" Scrooge exclaimed. "I cannot bear it! Leave me! Take me back! Haunt me no longer!"

As he struggled with the spirit, he was conscious of being exhausted and overcome by an irresistible drowsiness; and, further, of being in his own bedroom. He had barely time to reel to bed before he sank into a heavy sleep.

---

23. **dowerless** (dou′ər-lĭs): without a dowry, the money and property that a woman formerly brought to her husband at marriage.

Stave Three: The Second of the Three Spirits

Scrooge awoke in his own bedroom. There was no doubt about that. But it and his own adjoining sitting room, into which he shuffled in his slippers, attracted by a great light there, had undergone a surprising transformation. The walls and ceiling were so hung with living green that it looked a perfect grove. The leaves of holly, mistletoe, and ivy reflected back the light, as if so many little mirrors had been scattered there; and such a mighty blaze went roaring up the chimney, as that petrifaction[24] of a hearth had never known in Scrooge's time, or Marley's, or for many and many a winter season gone. Heaped upon the floor, to form a kind of throne, were turkeys, geese, game, brawn,[25] great joints of meat, suckling pigs, long wreaths of sausages, mince pies, plum puddings, barrels of oysters, red-hot chestnuts, cherry-cheeked apples, juicy oranges, luscious pears, immense twelfth-cakes,[26] and great bowls of punch. In easy state upon this couch there sat a giant glorious to see, who bore a glowing torch, in shape not unlike Plenty's horn, and who raised it high to shed its light on Scrooge, as he came peeping round the door.

"Come in—come in! and know me better, man! I am the Ghost of Christmas Present. Look upon me! You have never seen the like of me before?"

"Never."

"Have never walked forth with the younger members of my family; meaning (for I am very young) my elder brothers born in these later years?" pursued the phantom.

---

24. **petrifaction** (pĕt′rə-făk′shən): something petrified, or turning to stone. The hearth, or fireplace, is cold and hard because it has never known a generous fire.
25. **brawn:** boar meat.
26. **twelfth-cakes:** fruitcakes made for Epiphany, or Twelfth Day, a holiday that occurs on January 6, twelve days after Christmas.

---

16 Summarizing
What choice does the girl remind Scrooge of? He has chosen money over love.

17
She cannot bring a dowry to marriage, and she knows the money-loving Scrooge would be unhappy married to a poor woman.

18
The scene upsets Scrooge, revealing his regret for the love he lost. He has no one to blame but himself, the spirit tells him.

Stave Three

1
Description. Rich bounty foreshadows what Scrooge will learn from second spirit. The catalog of plentiful foods is common in Victorian writing.

2
Allusion. "Plenty's horn" is the cornucopia (horn of plenty), symbol of abundance. Refers to horn of goat that nursed infant Zeus in Greek mythology and whose horn he later made magically filled to overflowing.

MEETING INDIVIDUAL NEEDS

ESL/LEP • Dickens' use of language, some of which is archaic, may require explanation. Here are some examples:

aught—anything (p. 286)
hob—ledge at the back of a fireplace (p. 287)
made fast—locked (p. 291)
shan't—shall not (p. 296)
beheld—saw (p. 296)
Thankee—Thank you (p. 297)

VISUAL CONNECTIONS
Exploring the Subject
Scrooge's third visitor—the first was Jacob Marley and the second was the Ghost of Christmas Past—is the Ghost of Christmas Present. When he arrives, Scrooge's rooms are filled with good things to eat and drink, fare that the tightfisted Scrooge has never had there before. The normally bare walls of Scrooge's rooms are decorated with greenery, and his tiny fire blazes up with unaccustomed warmth and cheerful light. The spirit himself seems to be the epitome of one who understands enjoyment: he is richly and comfortably dressed, is stout as if he enjoys partaking of food and drink, and wears a crown of greenery in honor of the season.

3
The ghost's "brothers" are all the Christmas celebrations that have come before. Scrooge has not met them because he has never truly celebrated Christmas.

4   Making Generalizations
What lesson do you think Scrooge learned the night before? Answers will vary. That an employer can make work happy or miserable, that his greed cost him love.

5
A "Christian name" is a person's first name; comes from custom of giving name to child when he/she is christened.

6   Finding Details
What signs of poverty show in their dress? "Twice-turned gown," cheap ribbons, and a hand-me-down shirt collar.

Scrooge's Third Visitor.

3   "I don't think I have; I am afraid I have not. Have you had many brothers, Spirit?"

"More than eighteen hundred."²⁷

"A tremendous family to provide for! Spirit, conduct me where you will. I went forth last
4   night on <u>compulsion</u>, and I learned a lesson which is working now. Tonight, if you have aught to teach me, let me profit by it."

"Touch my robe!"

Scrooge did as he was told, and held it fast.

The room and its contents all vanished instantly, and they stood in the city streets upon a snowy Christmas morning.

27. **More . . . hundred:** Since this story was written in 1843, the Ghost of Christmas Present would have more than eighteen hundred brothers.

Scrooge and the ghost passed on, invisible, straight to Scrooge's clerk's; and on the threshold of the door the spirit smiled, and stopped to bless Bob Cratchit's dwelling with the sprinklings of his torch. Think of that! Bob had but fifteen "bob"²⁸ a week himself; he pocketed on
5   Saturdays but fifteen copies of his Christian name; and yet the Ghost of Christmas Present blessed his four-roomed house!

Then up rose Mrs. Cratchit, Cratchit's wife,
6   dressed out but poorly in a twice-turned²⁹ gown, but brave in ribbons, which are cheap and make a goodly show for sixpence; and she laid the cloth, assisted by Belinda Cratchit, second of her daughters, also brave in ribbons; while Master Peter Cratchit plunged a fork into the saucepan of potatoes, and, getting the corners of his monstrous shirt collar (Bob's private property, conferred upon his son and heir in honor of the day) into his mouth, rejoiced to find himself so gallantly attired, and yearned to show his linen in the fashionable parks. And now two smaller Cratchits, boy and girl, came tearing in, screaming that outside the baker's³⁰ they had smelled the goose and known it for their own; and basking in luxurious thoughts of sage and onion, these young Cratchits danced about the table, and exalted Master Peter Cratchit to the skies, while he (not proud, although his collar nearly choked him) blew the fire until the slow potatoes, bubbling up, knocked loudly at the saucepan lid to be let out and peeled.

"What has ever got your precious father then?" said Mrs. Cratchit. "And your brother Tiny Tim! And Martha warn't as late last Christmas Day by half an hour!"

28. **"bob":** slang for "shilling" (or "shillings"), a former British coin worth one twentieth of a pound.
29. **twice-turned:** remade twice so that worn parts would not show.
30. **the baker's:** In the days when people of small means had fireplaces but no ovens, they would rent space in the local baker's oven to roast poultry or large pieces of meat.

Cultural Diversity

For Christmas dinner, the Cratchit family enjoys a goose, mashed potatoes, applesauce, pudding in brandy, apples, oranges, and roasted chestnuts. Ask students to discuss preparations for special dinners they have had. What types of food are prepared? Where is dinner served? Is the meal just for family, or are other guests invited? Do the students help in preparing the meal? If so, what task do they usually perform?

"Here's Martha, Mother!" said a girl, appearing as she spoke.

"Here's Martha, Mother!" cried the two young Cratchits. "Hurrah! There's *such* a goose, Martha!"

"Why, bless your heart alive, my dear, how late you are!" said Mrs. Cratchit, kissing her a dozen times, and taking off her shawl and bonnet for her.

7 "We'd a deal of work to finish up last night," replied the girl, "and had to clear away this morning, Mother!"

"Well! Never mind so long as you are come," said Mrs. Cratchit. "Sit ye down before the fire, my dear, and have a warm, Lord bless ye!"

"No, no! There's Father coming," cried the two young Cratchits, who were everywhere at once. "Hide, Martha, hide!"

So Martha hid herself, and in came little Bob, the father, with at least three feet of comforter, exclusive of the fringe, hanging down **8** before him; and his threadbare clothes darned up and brushed, to look seasonable; and Tiny Tim upon his shoulder. Alas for Tiny Tim, he bore a little crutch and had his limbs supported by an iron frame!

"Why, where's our Martha?" cried Bob Cratchit, looking round.

"Not coming," said Mrs. Cratchit.

"Not coming!" said Bob, with a sudden declension³¹ in his high spirits; for he had been **9** Tim's blood horse all the way from church, and had come home rampant³²—"not coming upon Christmas Day!"

Martha didn't like to see him disappointed, if it were only in joke; so she came out prematurely from behind the closet door, and ran into his arms, while the two young Cratchits hustled Tiny Tim, and bore him off into the **10** washhouse, that he might hear the pudding singing in the copper.

"And how did little Tim behave?" asked Mrs. Cratchit, when she had rallied Bob on his credulity,³³ and Bob had hugged his daughter to his heart's content.

"As good as gold," said Bob, "and better. Somehow he gets thoughtful, sitting by himself so much, and thinks the strangest things you ever heard. He told me, coming home, that he hoped the people saw him in the church be- **11** cause he was a cripple, and it might be pleasant to them to remember, upon Christmas Day, who made lame beggars walk and blind men see."

Bob's voice was <u>tremulous</u> when he told **12** them this, and trembled more when he said that Tiny Tim was growing strong and hearty.

His active little crutch was heard upon the floor, and back came Tiny Tim before another word was spoken, escorted by his brother and sister to his stool beside the fire; and while Bob, turning up his cuffs—as if, poor fellow, they were capable of being made more shabby—<u>compounded</u> some hot mixture in a jug with gin and lemons, and stirred it round and round, and put it on the hob to simmer, Master Peter and the two ubiquitous³⁴ young Cratchits went to fetch the goose, with which they soon returned in high procession.

13 Mrs. Cratchit made the gravy (ready beforehand in a little saucepan) hissing hot; Master Peter mashed the potatoes with incredible vigor; Miss Belinda sweetened up the applesauce; Martha dusted the hot plates; Bob took Tiny Tim beside him in a tiny corner at the table; the two young Cratchits set chairs for everybody, not forgetting themselves, and,

---

31. **declension:** sinking or falling off.
32. **rampant:** rearing up like a horse; here, high-spirited.
33. **rallied Bob on his credulity** (krə-dōō′lə-tē): teased Bob for being so easily fooled by their joke.
34. **ubiquitous** (yōō-bik′wə-təs): being everywhere at the same time.

---

7 Drawing Conclusions
What can you tell about Martha's employer? Since she had to work on Christmas Eve and Christmas morning, her employer must be as hard-hearted as Scrooge.

8 The Cratchits attempt to make their worn-out clothes look as nice as possible.

9 A "blood horse" is a thoroughbred.

10 "Pudding singing" refers to sound of steam escaping while it cooks; the "copper" is a kettle.

11 Allusion. Reference to Jesus' miraculous healing of the lame and blind.

12 Evidently, Tiny Tim is not growing strong; Bob tries not to face this fact.

13 Each family member helps joyously with the feast and is clearly eager for it, perhaps indicating meagerness of everyday meals.

A Christmas Carol 287

mounting guard upon their posts, crammed spoons into their mouths, lest they should shriek for goose before their turn came to be helped. At last the dishes were set on, and grace was said. It was succeeded by a breathless pause, as Mrs. Cratchit, looking slowly all along the carving knife, prepared to plunge it in the breast; but when she did, and when the long-expected gush of stuffing issued forth, one murmur of delight arose all around the board, and even Tiny Tim, excited by the two young Cratchits, beat on the table with the handle of his knife, and feebly cried; "Hurrah!"

There never was such a goose. Bob said he didn't believe there ever was such a goose cooked. Its tenderness and flavor, size and cheapness, were the themes of universal admiration. Eked out by applesauce and mashed potatoes, it was a sufficient dinner for the whole family; indeed, as Mrs. Cratchit said with great delight (surveying one small atom of a bone upon the dish), they hadn't ate[35] it all at last! Yet everyone had had enough, and the youngest Cratchits in particular were steeped in sage and onion to the eyebrows! But now, the plates being changed by Miss Belinda, Mrs. Cratchit left the room alone—too nervous to bear witnesses—to take the pudding up and bring it in.

Suppose it should not be done enough! Suppose it should break in turning out! Suppose somebody should have got over the wall of the backyard and stolen it while they were merry with the goose—a supposition at which the two young Cratchits became livid![36] All sorts of horrors were supposed.

Hallo! A great deal of steam! The pudding was out of the copper. A smell like a washing day! That was the cloth.[37] A smell like an eating house and a pastry cook's next door to each other, with a laundress' next door to that! That was the pudding! In half a minute Mrs. Cratchit entered—flushed but smiling proudly—with the pudding, like a speckled cannonball, so hard and firm, blazing in half of half a quartern[38] of ignited brandy and bedight[39] with Christmas holly stuck into the top.

Oh, a wonderful pudding! Bob Cratchit said, and calmly too, that he regarded it as the greatest success achieved by Mrs. Cratchit since their marriage. Mrs. Cratchit said that now the weight was off her mind, she would confess she had had her doubts about the quantity of flour. Everybody had something to say about it, but nobody said or thought it was at all a small pudding for a large family. Any Cratchit would have blushed to hint at such a thing.

At last the dinner was all done, the cloth was cleared, the hearth swept, and the fire made up. The compound in the jug being tasted, and considered perfect, apples and oranges were put upon the table, and a shovelful of chestnuts on the fire.

Then all the Cratchit family drew round the hearth, in what Bob Cratchit called a circle, and at Bob Cratchit's elbow stood the family display of glass—two tumblers, and a custard cup without a handle.

These held the hot stuff from the jug, however, as well as golden goblets would have done; and Bob served it out with beaming looks, while the chestnuts on the fire spluttered and crackled noisily. Then Bob proposed:

"A Merry Christmas to us all, my dears. God bless us!"

14
Cratchits' "sufficient dinner" is not a big feast; sharp contrast with cornucopia displayed earlier by ghost.

15
The meal is barely enough; only one tiny bone is left over.

16
Simile. Comparison of pudding to blazing cannonball emphasizes its magnificence in eyes of family.

17
Inference. The pudding *is* too small for the large family.

18
The "compound" (mixture) is the warm gin and lemon drink that Bob Cratchit left to simmer earlier.

19
The family owns only three glasses and must drink in turns.

20
This toast and Tiny Tim's response are among the most famous passages in literature.

---

35. **ate** (ĕt): an alternate form of *eaten*, used in Great Britain.
36. **livid:** pale.
37. **cloth:** The pudding was wrapped in cloth and then boiled.
38. **quartern:** one fourth of a pint.
39. **bedight** (bĭ-dīt'): decorated.

MEETING INDIVIDUAL NEEDS
Visual Learners • Divide the class into five groups. Assign each group a part (stave) of the story to draw in comic strip form. Then in sequence, have each group present its comic strip to the class.

Which all the family reechoed.

"God bless us every one!" said Tiny Tim, the last of all.

He sat very close to his father's side, upon his little stool. Bob held his withered little hand in his, as if he loved the child and wished to keep him by his side, and dreaded that he might be taken from him.

Scrooge raised his head speedily, on hearing his own name.

21 "Mr. Scrooge!" said Bob; "I'll give you Mr. Scrooge, the Founder of the Feast!"

"The Founder of the Feast indeed!" cried Mrs. Cratchit, reddening. "I wish I had him here. I'd give him a piece of my mind to feast upon, and I hope he'd have a good appetite for it."

"My dear," said Bob, "the children! Christmas Day."

22 "It should be Christmas Day, I am sure," said she, "on which one drinks the health of such an odious, stingy, hard, unfeeling man as Mr. Scrooge. You know he is, Robert! Nobody knows it better than you do, poor fellow!"

"My dear," was Bob's mild answer, "Christmas Day."

"I'll drink his health for your sake and the day's," said Mrs. Cratchit, "not for his. Long life to him! A Merry Christmas and a Happy
23 New Year! He'll be very merry and very happy, I have no doubt!"

The children drank the toast after her. It was the first of their proceedings which had no heartiness in it. Tiny Tim drank it last of all, but he didn't care twopence for it. Scrooge was the ogre of the family. The mention of his name cast a dark shadow on the party, which was not dispelled for full five minutes.

After it had passed away, they were ten times merrier than before from the mere relief of Scrooge the Baleful[40] being done with. Bob

40. **Baleful:** wretched.

24 Cratchit told them how he had a situation in his eye for Master Peter, which would bring him, if obtained, full five and sixpence weekly.
25 The two young Cratchits laughed tremendously at the idea of Peter's being a man of business; and Peter himself looked thoughtfully at the fire from between his collars, as if he were deliberating what particular investments he should favor when he came into the receipt of that bewildering income. Martha, who was a poor apprentice at a milliner's, then told them what kind of work she had to do, and how many hours she worked at a stretch, and how she meant to lie abed tomorrow morning for a good long rest—tomorrow being a holiday she passed at home. Also how she had seen a countess and a lord some days before, and how the lord "was much about as tall as Peter"; at which Peter pulled up his collars so high that you couldn't have seen his head if you had been there. All this time the chestnuts and the jug went round and round; and by and by they had a song about a lost child traveling in the snow from Tiny Tim, who had a plaintive little voice, and sang it very well indeed.

26 There was nothing of high mark in this. They were not a handsome family; they were not well dressed; their shoes were far from being waterproof; their clothes were scanty; and Peter might have known, and very likely did, the inside of a pawnbroker's. But they were happy, grateful, pleased with one another, and contented with the time; and when they faded, and looked happier yet in the bright sprinklings of the spirit's torch at parting, Scrooge had his eye upon them, and especially on Tiny Tim, until the last.

It was a great surprise to Scrooge, as this scene vanished, to hear a hearty laugh. It was a much greater surprise to Scrooge to recognize it as his own nephew's, and to find himself in a bright, dry, gleaming room, with the spirit

---

21 Analyzing
What does this toast reveal about Cratchit? He is compassionate and forgiving.

22
Mrs. Cratchit is less forgiving than her husband; she must stretch his meager earnings for the entire family.

23
Sarcasm: she is sure Scrooge will not be happy.

24
A *situation* is a job.

25
Peter is very young, but his working is necessary to help the family financially.

26
Theme. Scrooge sees that although Cratchits are poor, they are happy.

A Christmas Carol 289

TRANSPARENCY 22
Literary Elements
Story Map – explores the building blocks of fiction: characters, plot, setting, conflict, point of view, and theme.

27 Scrooge's name brings anger and sadness to the Cratchits; it elicits derision from his nephew's family and guests.

28 Description of Scrooge's niece suggests the joy of married life Scrooge has missed.

29 Summarizing
What does Scrooge's nephew realize about Scrooge? The one Scrooge hurts most is himself.

30 Parallel to Cratchits: they, too, are having Christmas dinner, ready for dessert; they, too, are forgiving Scrooge.

31 Like Cratchits, they share musical entertainments and games.

32 *Blindman's buff:* game in which blindfolded player tries to catch and identify another player. Topper and the girl he likes may remind Scrooge of his younger self and fiancée.

---

standing smiling by his side and looking at that same nephew.

It is a fair, even-handed, noble adjustment of things, that while there is infection in disease and sorrow, there is nothing in the world so irresistibly contagious as laughter and good humor. When Scrooge's nephew laughed, Scrooge's niece by marriage laughed as heartily as he. And their assembled friends, being not a bit behindhand, laughed out lustily.

27 "He said that Christmas was a humbug, as I live!" cried Scrooge's nephew. "He believed it, too!"

"More shame for him, Fred!" said Scrooge's niece, indignantly. Bless those women! they never do anything by halves. They are always in earnest.

28 She was very pretty; exceedingly pretty. With a dimpled, surprised-looking, capital face; a ripe little mouth that seemed made to be kissed—as no doubt it was; all kinds of good little dots about her chin that melted into one another when she laughed; and the sunniest pair of eyes you ever saw in any little creature's head. Altogether she was what you would have called provoking, but satisfactory, too. Oh, perfectly satisfactory.

"He's a comical old fellow," said Scrooge's nephew, "that's the truth, and not so pleasant as he might be. However, his offenses carry their own punishment, and I have nothing to **29** say against him. Who suffers by his ill whims? Himself, always. Here he takes it into his head to dislike us, and he won't come and dine with us. What's the consequence? He don't lose much of a dinner."

30 "Indeed, I think he loses a very good dinner," interrupted Scrooge's niece. Everybody else said the same, and they must be allowed to have been competent judges, because they had just had dinner; and, with the dessert upon the table, were clustered round the fire, by lamplight.

"Well, I am very glad to hear it," said Scrooge's nephew, "because I haven't any great faith in these young housekeepers. What do *you* say, Topper?"

Topper clearly had his eye on one of Scrooge's niece's sisters, for he answered that a bachelor was a wretched outcast, who had no right to express an opinion on the subject. Whereat Scrooge's niece's sister—the plump one with the lace tucker,[41] not the one with the roses—blushed.

31 After tea they had some music. For they were a musical family and knew what they were about when they sang a glee or catch,[42] I can assure you—especially Topper, who could growl away in the bass like a good one, and never swell the large veins in his forehead, or get red in the face over it.

But they didn't devote the whole evening to music. After a while they played at forfeits; for it is good to be children sometimes, and never better than at Christmas, when its mighty Founder was a child himself. There was first a **32** game at blindman's buff though. And I no more believe Topper was really blinded than I believe he had eyes in his boots. Because the way in which he went after that plump sister in the lace tucker was an outrage on the credulity of human nature. Knocking down the fire irons, tumbling over the chairs, bumping up against the piano, smothering himself among the curtains; wherever she went, there went he! He always knew where the plump sister was. He wouldn't catch anybody else. If you had fallen up against him, as some of them did, and stood there, he would have made a feint[43] of endeavoring to seize you, which would have been an affront to your under-

---

41. **tucker:** a covering for the neck and shoulders, something like a large collar.
42. **glee; catch:** songs for three or more voices, unaccompanied by instruments.
43. **feint** (fānt): pretense.

SHORT STORIES

standing, and would instantly have sidled off in the direction of the plump sister.

33 "Here is a new game," said Scrooge. "One half-hour, Spirit, only one!"

34 It was a game called Yes and No, where Scrooge's nephew had to think of something, and the rest must find out what; he only answering to their questions Yes or No, as the case was. The fire of questioning to which he was exposed <u>elicited</u> from him that he was 35 thinking of an animal, a live animal, rather a disagreeable animal, a savage animal, an animal that growled and grunted sometimes, and talked sometimes, and lived in London, and walked about the streets, and wasn't made a show of, and wasn't led by anybody, and didn't live in a <u>menagerie,</u> and was never killed in a market, and was not a horse, or an ass, or a cow, or a bull, or a tiger, or a dog, or a pig, or a cat, or a bear. At every new question put to him, this nephew burst into a fresh roar of laughter, and was so inexpressibly tickled, that he was obliged to get up off the sofa and stamp. At last the plump sister cried out: "I have found it out! I know what it is, Fred! I know what it is!"

"What is it?" cried Fred.

"It's your Uncle Scro-o-o-oge!"

Which it certainly was. Admiration was the universal sentiment, though some objected that the reply to "Is it a bear?" ought to have been "Yes."

Uncle Scrooge had <u>imperceptibly</u> become so gay and light of heart, that he would have drunk to the unconscious company in an <u>inaudible</u> speech. But the whole scene passed off in the breath of the last word spoken by his nephew; and he and the spirit were again upon their travels.

Much they saw, and far they went, and many homes they visited, but always with a happy 36 end. The spirit stood beside sickbeds, and they were cheerful; on foreign lands, and they were close at home; by struggling men, and they were patient in their greater hope; by poverty, and it was rich. In almshouse, hospital, and jail, in misery's every refuge, where vain man in his little brief authority had not made fast the door and barred the spirit out, he left his blessing, and taught Scrooge his precepts.⁴⁴ Suddenly, as they stood together in an open place, the bell struck twelve.

Scrooge looked about him for the ghost, and saw it no more. As the last stroke ceased to vibrate, he remembered the prediction of old Jacob Marley, and, lifting up his eyes, beheld a solemn phantom, draped and hooded, coming like a mist along the ground toward him.

Stave Four: The Last of the Spirits

The phantom slowly, gravely, silently approached. When it came near him, Scrooge bent down upon his knee; for in the air through which this spirit moved it seemed to scatter gloom and mystery.

It was <u>shrouded</u> in a deep black garment, which concealed its head, its face, its form, and left nothing of it visible save one outstretched hand. He knew no more, for the spirit neither spoke nor moved.

"I am in the presence of the Ghost of Christmas Yet to Come? Ghost of the Future! I fear 1 you more than any specter I have seen. But as I know your purpose is to do me good, and as I hope to live to be another man from what I was, I am prepared to bear you company, and do it with a thankful heart. Will you not speak to me?"

It gave him no reply. The hand was pointed straight before them.

"Lead on! Lead on! The night is waning fast, 2 and it is precious time to me, I know. Lead on, Spirit!"

44. **precepts** (prē′sĕpts′): rules of living.

A Christmas Carol 291

3 Two fellow-merchants are discussing Scrooge's death; he doesn't realize it yet.

4 Irony. Scrooge sees brisk business and assumes he's seeing the future after he has reformed, rather than after his death.

5 Rag-and-bone shop: sells all sorts of disgusting and stolen merchandise.

6 "What odds" means "what's the difference."

7 These three—cleaning woman, laundress, and undertaker's assistant—performed a service for the dead man; each used the opportunity to steal.

8 Justifies her theft by saying the "old screw" (miser) wasn't "natural" (had no human nature); died alone; no one will miss him or his belongings.

They scarcely seemed to enter the city; for the city rather seemed to spring up about them. But there they were in the heart of it; on 'Change, among the merchants.

The spirit stopped beside one little knot of businessmen. Observing that the hand was pointed to them, Scrooge advanced to listen to their talk.

"No," said a great fat man with a monstrous chin. "I don't know much about it either way. I **3** only know he's dead."

"When did he die?" inquired another.

"Last night, I believe."

"Why, what was the matter with him? I thought he'd never die."

"Goodness knows," said the first, with a yawn.

"What has he done with his money?" asked a red-faced gentleman.

"I haven't heard," said the man with the large chin. "Company, perhaps. He hasn't left it to me. That's all I know. Bye-bye."

Scrooge was at first inclined to be surprised that the spirit should attach importance to conversation apparently so trivial, but feeling assured that it must have some hidden purpose, he set himself to consider what it was likely to be. It could scarcely be supposed to have any bearing on the death of Jacob, his old partner, for that was past, and this ghost's province was the future.

He looked about in that very place for his own image; but another man stood in his accustomed corner, and though the clock pointed to his usual time of day for being there, he saw no likeness of himself among the multitudes that poured in through the porch. **4** It gave him little surprise, however; for he had been revolving in his mind a change of life, and he thought and hoped he saw his newborn resolutions carried out in this.

5 They left this busy scene and went into an obscure part of the town to a low shop where iron, old rags, bottles, bones, and greasy offal[45] were bought. A gray-haired rascal, of great age, sat smoking his pipe. Scrooge and the phantom came into the presence of this man just as a woman with a heavy bundle slunk into the shop. But she had scarcely entered, when another woman, similarly laden, came in too; and she was closely followed by a man in faded black. After a short period of blank astonishment, in which the old man with the pipe had joined them, they all three burst into a laugh.

"Let the charwoman[46] alone to be the first!" cried she who had entered first. "Let the laundress alone to be the second; and let the undertaker's man alone to be the third. Look here, old Joe, here's a chance! If we haven't all three met here without meaning it!"

"You couldn't have met in a better place. You were made free of it long ago, you know; and the other two ain't strangers. What have you got to sell? What have you got to sell?"

"Half a minute's patience, Joe, and you shall see."

6 "What odds then! What odds, Mrs. Dilber?" said the woman. "Every person has a right to take care of themselves. *He* always did! Who's the worse for the loss of a few things like these? **7** Not a dead man, I suppose."

Mrs. Dilber, whose manner was remarkable for general propitiation,[47] said, "No, indeed, ma'am."

8 "If he wanted to keep 'em after he was dead, a wicked old screw, why wasn't he natural in his lifetime? If he had been, he'd have had somebody to look after him when he was struck with death, instead of lying gasping out his last there, alone by himself."

---

45. **offal** (ôf′əl): the waste parts of an animal that has been butchered for meat.
46. **charwoman:** a woman employed to clean a house or an office.
47. **propitiation** (prō-pĭsh′ē-ā′shən): ability to keep the peace.

ART LINK
Have students find a favorite line or section of the story to use on a greeting card. Then have each student design a holiday card, using the line from the story for the front or inside of the card. You might have students design an appropriate logo and brand name for the back of the card. You could display the cards for your classes and have students select their favorites.

"It's the truest word that ever was spoke, it's a judgment on him."

"I wish it was a little heavier judgment, and it should have been, you may depend upon it, if I could have laid my hands on anything **9** else. Open that bundle, old Joe, and let me know the value of it. Speak out plain. I'm not afraid to be the first, nor afraid for them to see it."

Joe went down on his knees for the greater convenience of opening the bundle, and dragged out a large and heavy roll of some dark stuff.

"What do you call this? Bed curtains!"

"Ah! Bed curtains! Don't drop that oil upon the blankets, now."

"*His* blankets?"

"Whose else's do you think? He isn't likely to take cold without 'em, I dare say. Ah! You may look through that shirt till your eyes ache; but you won't find a hole in it, nor a threadbare place. It's the best he had, and a fine one too. They'd have wasted it by dressing him up in it, if it hadn't been for me."

Scrooge listened to this dialogue in horror.

10 "Spirit! I see, I see. The case of this unhappy man might be my own. My life tends that way, now. Merciful Heaven, what is this?"

The scene had changed, and now he almost touched a bare, uncurtained bed. A pale light, rising in the outer air, fell straight upon this bed; and on it, unwatched, unwept, uncared for, was the body of this plundered unknown man.

11 "Spirit, let me see some tenderness connected with a death, or this dark chamber, Spirit, will be forever present to me."

The ghost conducted him to poor Bob Cratchit's house—the dwelling he had visited before—and found the mother and the children seated round the fire.

Quiet. Very quiet. The noisy little Cratchits were as still as statues in one corner and sat looking up at Peter, who had a book before him. The mother and her daughters were engaged in needlework. But surely they were very quiet!

12 "'And he took a child, and set him in the midst of them.'"[48]

Where had Scrooge heard those words? He had not dreamed them. The boy must have read them out, as he and the spirit crossed the threshold. Why did he not go on?

The mother laid her work upon the table and put her hand up to her face. "The color **13** hurts my eyes," she said.

The color? Ah, poor Tiny Tim!

"They're better now again. It makes them weak by candlelight; and I wouldn't show weak eyes to your father when he comes home, for the world. It must be near his time."

"Past it rather," Peter answered, shutting up his book. "But I think he has walked a little **14** slower than he used, these few last evenings, Mother."

"I have known him walk with—I have known him walk with Tiny Tim upon his shoulder, very fast indeed."

"And so have I," cried Peter. "Often."

"And so have I," exclaimed another. So had all.

"But he was very light to carry, and his father loved him so, that it was no trouble—no trouble. And there is your father at the door!"

She hurried out to meet him; and little Bob in his comforter—he had need of it, poor fellow—came in. His tea was ready for him on the hob, and they all tried who should help him to it most. Then the two young Cratchits got upon his knees and laid, each child, a little cheek against his face, as if they said, "Don't mind it, Father. Don't be grieved!"

Bob was very cheerful with them, and spoke

---

48. **"And he . . . them"**: a quotation from Mark 9:36.

9
She wants Joe to estimate value of stolen goods.

10
Irony. He feels pity for the dead man (not realizing it's himself).

11
Setting. Bleak aspect of room underscores loneliness of death.

12
Allusion. Verse quoted refers to the scene in which Jesus "suffers the little children" to be with him; family is reading this to console themselves that Tiny Tim is now in heaven.

13
The mother blames the thread color for "hurting" her eyes, rather than admit she is crying. Family tries to shield father from their grief.

14
Bob Cratchit is much slower coming home now; he has lost his joy since Tim's death.

A Christmas Carol 293

15 The mother and girls embroider for the funeral, which Bob implies will be on Sunday.

16 He has visited the cemetery where Tim will be buried.

17 If he had been less close to Tiny Tim, he might be able to control his grief.

18 Scrooge begins to suspect the identity of the wretched dead man he was shown.

19 Scrooge wants assurance that his grim future is not unchangeable.

20 **Plot.** Scrooge's vow to change is **climax** of story.

VISUAL CONNECTIONS
Exploring the Subject
The Ghost of Christmas Yet to Come points to the grave of the man Scrooge has seen earlier, unmourned and lonely. To his horror, Scrooge has discovered that the man was himself and that the name on the weed-choked grave is his own. Scrooge is almost overwhelmed by his terror, but he finally realizes that nothing in the future is decided yet. He then resolves to change his life so that the horror he has seen will never come to pass.

---

pleasantly to all the family. He looked at the work upon the table, and praised the industry and speed of Mrs. Cratchit and the girls. They would be done long before Sunday, he said.

"Sunday! You went today, then, Robert?"

"Yes, my dear," returned Bob. "I wish you could have gone. It would have done you good to see how green a place it is. But you'll see it often. I promised him that I would walk there on a Sunday. My little, little child! My little child!"

He broke down all at once. He couldn't help it. If he could have helped it, he and his child would have been farther apart, perhaps, than they were.

"Specter," said Scrooge, "something informs

The Last of the Spirits.

me that our parting moment is at hand. I know it, but I know not how. Tell me what man that was, with the covered face, whom we saw lying dead?"

The Ghost of Christmas Yet to Come conveyed him to a dismal, wretched, ruinous churchyard.

The spirit stood among the graves, and pointed down to one.

"Before I draw nearer to that stone to which you point, answer me one question. Are these the shadows of the things that will be, or are they shadows of the things that may be only?"

Still the ghost pointed downward to the grave by which it stood.

"Men's courses will foreshadow certain ends, to which, if **persevered** in, they must lead. But if the courses be departed from, the ends will change. Say it is thus with what you show me!"

The spirit was immovable as ever.

Scrooge crept toward it, trembling as he went; and following the finger, read upon the stone of the neglected grave his own name—EBENEZER SCROOGE.

"Am *I* that man who lay upon the bed? No, Spirit! Oh no, no! Spirit! hear me! I am not the man I was. I will not be the man I must have been but for this intercourse. Why show me this, if I am past all hope? Assure me that I yet may change these shadows you have shown me by an altered life."

For the first time the kind hand faltered.

"I will honor Christmas in my heart, and try to keep it all the year. I will live in the Past, the Present, and the Future. The spirits of all three shall strive within me. I will not shut out the lessons that they teach. Oh, tell me I may sponge away the writing on this stone!"

Holding up his hands in one last prayer to have his fate reversed, he saw an alteration in the phantom's hood and dress. It shrunk, collapsed, and dwindled down into a bedpost.

Stave Five: The End of It

Yes! and the bedpost was his own. The bed was his own, the room was his own. Best and happiest of all, the time before him was his own, to make amends in!

"I will live in the Past, the Present, and the Future!" Scrooge repeated, as he scrambled out of bed. "The spirits of all three shall strive within me. Oh, Jacob Marley! Heaven and the Christmastime be praised for this! I say it on my knees, old Jacob, on my knees!"

He was so fluttered and so glowing with his good intentions that his broken voice would scarcely answer to his call. He had been sobbing violently in his conflict with the spirit, and his face was wet with tears.

"They are not torn down," cried Scrooge, folding one of his bed curtains in his arms; "they are not torn down, rings and all. They are here; I am here; the shadows of the things that would have been may be dispelled. They will be. I know they will!"

His hands were busy with his garments all this time; turning them inside out, putting them on upside down, tearing them, mislaying them, making them parties to every kind of extravagance.

"I don't know what to do!" cried Scrooge, laughing and crying in the same breath, and making a perfect Laocoon[49] of himself with his stockings. "I am as light as a feather; I am as happy as an angel; I am as merry as a schoolboy; I am as giddy as a drunken man. A Merry Christmas to everybody! A Happy New Year to all the world. Hallo here! Whoop! Hallo!"

He had frisked into the sitting room, and was now standing there perfectly winded.

"There's the saucepan that the gruel was in!" cried Scrooge, starting off again and frisking round the fireplace. "There's the door by which the ghost of Jacob Marley entered! There's the corner where the Ghost of Christmas Present sat! There's the window where I saw the wandering spirits! It's all right; it's all true; it all happened. Ha, ha, ha!"

Really, for a man who had been out of practice for so many years, it was a splendid laugh, a most illustrious laugh. The father of a long, long line of brilliant laughs!

"I don't know what day of the month it is!" said Scrooge. "I don't know how long I've been among the spirits. I don't know anything. I'm quite a baby. Never mind. I don't care. I'd rather be a baby. Hallo! Whoop! Hallo here!"

He was checked in his transports,[50] by the churches' ringing out the lustiest peals he had ever heard. Clash, clang, hammer, ding, dong, bell. Bell, dong, ding, hammer, clang, clash! Oh, glorious, glorious!

Running to the window, he opened it and put out his head. No fog, no mist; clear, bright, jovial, stirring cold; cold, piping for the blood to dance to; golden sunlight; heavenly sky; sweet fresh air; merry bells. Oh, glorious. Glorious!

"What's today?" cried Scrooge, calling downward to a boy in Sunday clothes, who perhaps had loitered in to look about him.

"Eh?" returned the boy, with all his might of wonder.

"What's today, my fine fellow?" said Scrooge.

"Today!" replied the boy. "Why, CHRISTMAS DAY."

"It's Christmas Day!" said Scrooge to himself. "I haven't missed it. The spirits have done it all in one night. They can do anything they like. Of course they can. Of course they can. Hallo, my fine fellow?"

---

49. **Laocoon** (lā-ŏk'ō-ŏn'): a character in a Greek myth who was strangled by sea serpents.

50. **transports:** feelings of great joy.

A Christmas Carol 295

8
Signs of the new Scrooge: buying the turkey and giving the boy money.

9
Indicates the turkey's great size.

10
Characterization. The old Scrooge would not have cared about turkey's being heavy to carry, nor have hired a cab.

11
Indicates that nothing can dampen his joy.

12 Summarizing
How do others respond to Scrooge's new manner? With friendly greetings.

"Hallo!" returned the boy.

"Do you know the poulterer's,[51] in the next street but one, at the corner?" Scrooge inquired.

"I should hope I did," replied the lad.

"An intelligent boy!" said Scrooge. "A remarkable boy! Do you know whether they've sold the prize turkey that was hanging up there? Not the little prize turkey; the big one?"

"What, the one as big as me?" returned the boy.

"What a delightful boy!" said Scrooge. "It's a pleasure to talk to him. Yes, my buck!"

"It's hanging there now," replied the boy.

"Is it?" said Scrooge. "Go buy it."

"Walk-ER!"[52] exclaimed the boy.

8 "No, no," said Scrooge, "I am in earnest. Go and buy it, and tell 'em to bring it here, that I may give them the direction where to take it. Come back with the man, and I'll give you a shilling. Come back with him in less than five minutes, and I'll give you half a crown!"[53]

The boy was off like a shot. He must have had a steady hand at a trigger who could have got a shot off half so fast.

"I'll send it to Bob Cratchit's!" whispered Scrooge, rubbing his hands, and splitting with a laugh. "He shan't know who sends it. It's twice the size of Tiny Tim. No one ever made such a joke as sending it to Bob's will be!"

The hand in which he wrote the address was not a steady one, but write it he did, somehow, and went downstairs to open the street door, ready for the coming of the poulterer's man. As he stood there, waiting his arrival, the knocker caught his eye.

"I shall love it as long as I live!" cried Scrooge, patting it with his hand. "I scarcely ever looked at it before. What an honest expression it has in its face! It's a wonderful knocker! Here's the turkey. Hallo! Whoop! How are you? Merry Christmas!"

9 It *was* a turkey! He could never have stood upon his legs, that bird. He would have snapped 'em off short in a minute, like sticks of sealing wax.

"Why, it's impossible to carry that to Camden Town," said Scrooge. "You must have a cab."

10 The chuckle with which he said this, and the chuckle with which he paid for the turkey, and the chuckle with which he paid for the cab, and the chuckle with which he recompensed the boy were only to be exceeded by the chuckle with which he sat down, breathless, in his chair again, and chuckled till he cried.

Shaving was not an easy task, for his hand continued to shake very much; and shaving requires attention, even when you don't **11** dance while you are at it. But if he had cut the end of his nose off, he would have put a piece of sticking plaster over it, and been quite satisfied.

He dressed himself "all in his best," and at last got out into the streets. The people were by this time pouring forth, as he had seen them with the Ghost of Christmas Present; and walking with his hands behind him, Scrooge re- **12** garded everyone with a delighted smile. He looked so irresistibly pleasant, in a word, that three or four good-humored fellows said, "Good morning, sir! A Merry Christmas to you!" And Scrooge said often, afterward, that of all the blithe[54] sounds he had ever heard, those were the blithest in his ears.

He had not gone far, when coming on toward him he beheld the portly gentleman who had walked into his countinghouse the day before and said, "Scrooge and Marley's, I

---

51. **poulterer's:** shop where poultry is sold.
52. **Walk-ER!:** a slang word used to express disbelief, equivalent to "You're kidding!"
53. **half a crown:** a coin equal to one eighth of a pound.
54. **blithe** (blīth): cheerful.

13 believe?" It sent a pang across his heart to think how this old gentleman would look upon him when they met; but he knew what path lay straight before him, and he took it.

"My dear sir," said Scrooge, quickening his pace, and taking the old gentleman by both his hands. "How do you do? I hope you succeeded yesterday. It was very kind of you. A Merry Christmas to you, sir!"

14 "Mr. Scrooge?"

"Yes," said Scrooge. "That is my name, and I fear it may not be pleasant to you. Allow me to ask your pardon. And will you have the goodness——" Here Scrooge whispered in his ear.

15 "Lord bless me!" cried the gentleman, as if his breath were gone. "My dear Mr. Scrooge, are you serious?"

"If you please," said Mr. Scrooge. "Not a far-
16 thing[55] less. A great many back payments are included in it, I assure you. Will you do me that favor?"

"My dear sir," said the other, shaking hands with him, "I don't know what to say to such munifi——"[56]

"Don't say anything, please," retorted Scrooge. "Come and see me. Will you come and see me?"

"I will!" cried the old gentleman. And it was clear he meant to do it.

"Thankee," said Scrooge. "I am much obliged to you. I thank you fifty times. Bless you!"

He went to church, and walked about the streets, and watched the people hurrying to and fro, and patted children on the head, and questioned beggars, and looked down into the kitchens of houses, and up to the windows; and found that everything could yield him pleasure. He had never dreamed that any walk—that anything—could give him so much happiness. In the afternoon, he turned his steps toward his nephew's house.

17 He passed the door a dozen times before he had the courage to go up and knock. But he made a dash, and did it.

"Is your master at home, my dear?" said Scrooge to the girl. Nice girl! Very.

"Yes, sir."

"Where is he, my love?" said Scrooge.

"He's in the dining room, sir, along with mistress. I'll show you upstairs, if you please."

"Thankee. He knows me," said Scrooge, with his hand already on the dining-room lock. "I'll go in here, my dear."

He turned it gently, and sidled his face in round the door. They were looking at the table (which was spread out in great array); for these young housekeepers are always nervous on such points, and like to see that everything is right.

"Fred!" said Scrooge.

Dear heart alive, how his niece by marriage started! Scrooge had forgotten, for the moment, about her sitting in the corner with the footstool, or he wouldn't have done it, on any account.

18 "Why, bless my soul!" cried Fred. "Who's that?"

"It is I. Your Uncle Scrooge. I have come to dinner. Will you let me in, Fred?"

19 Let him in! It is a mercy he didn't shake his arm off. He was at home in five minutes. Nothing could be heartier. His niece looked just the same. So did Topper when *he* came. So did the plump sister when *she* came. So did everyone when *they* came. Wonderful party, wonderful games, wonderful unanimity,[57] wonderful happiness!

---

55. **farthing** (fär′*th*ĭng): a former British coin worth one quarter of a penny.
56. **munificence** (myoō-nĭf′ə-səns): great generosity. Scrooge prevents the gentleman from finishing the word.
57. **unanimity** (yoō′-nə-nĭ′mĭ-tē): agreement.

---

13 Facing the man he treated rudely is a harder task than sending an anonymous gift.

14 Scrooge's manner is so changed that the man isn't sure it's Scrooge.

15 Drawing Conclusions
What can be inferred from the gentleman's response to Scrooge? Scrooge has donated a large sum of money.

16 Scrooge owes "back payments" on debt to humankind.

17 Must swallow his pride.

18 Irony. Fred knows old Scrooge but not new one.

19 Welcome is warm and genuine.

A Christmas Carol 297

COOPERATIVE LEARNING
Divide the class into groups of five or six to discuss the lessons that Scrooge has learned in this story. Ask them to talk about the things that Scrooge would like to change in his life as he is visited by each of the spirits. Ask students what really changes in his life as a result of each thing he learns. Encourage students to form a conclusion about the lessons Scrooge learns about life.

VISUAL CONNECTIONS
Exploring the Subject
True to his intention, Scrooge has become a new man. Many of the changes in his rooms are those that also occurred with the arrival of the Ghost of Christmas Present (see illustration on p. 286). This suggests that Scrooge has truly learned to celebrate the Christmas spirit. His rooms are decorated with greenery, his fire blazes with warmth and a cheery tea kettle, and he and Bob Cratchit are apparently sharing the bowl of smoking bishop that Scrooge mentioned when he surprised his employee that morning with his amazing and happy transformation of character.

20 Drawing Conclusions
Why does Scrooge want to catch Bob Cratchit coming late? He is being playful—wants to surprise Bob with his transformation.

21
Difficult for Scrooge even to pretend old self.

22
What does Bob's thought indicate? He thinks Scrooge has gone mad.

23
Plot. Change in Scrooge's personality has carried plot to its resolution.

---

20 But he was early at the office next morning. Oh, he was early there. If he could only be there first, and catch Bob Cratchit coming late! That was the thing he had set his heart upon.

And he did it; yes, he did! The clock struck nine. No Bob. A quarter past. No Bob. He was full eighteen minutes and a half behind his time. Scrooge sat with his door wide open, that he might see him come into the tank.

His hat was off before he opened the door; his comforter too. He was on his stool in a jiffy, driving away with his pen as if he were trying to overtake nine o'clock.

21 "Hallo!" growled Scrooge, in his accustomed voice as near as he could feign it. "What do you mean by coming here at this time of day?"

"I am very sorry, sir," said Bob. "I *am* behind my time."

"You are?" repeated Scrooge. "Yes, I think you are. Step this way, sir, if you please."

"It's only once a year, sir," pleaded Bob, appearing from the tank. "It shall not be repeated. I was making rather merry yesterday, sir."

"Now, I'll tell you what, my friend," said Scrooge, "I am not going to stand this sort of thing any longer. And therefore," he continued, leaping from his stool, and giving Bob such a dig in the waistcoat that he staggered back into the tank again, "and therefore I am about to raise your salary!"

22 Bob trembled, and got a little nearer to the ruler. He had a momentary idea of knocking Scrooge down with it, holding him, and calling to the people in the court for help and a strait waistcoat.[58]

"A Merry Christmas, Bob!" said Scrooge, with an earnestness that could not be mistaken, as he clapped him on the back. "A merrier Christmas, Bob, my good fellow, than I have

---

58. **strait waistcoat:** a straitjacket.

Scrooge and Bob Cratchit.

given you for many a year! I'll raise your salary, and endeavor to assist your struggling family, and we will discuss your affairs this very afternoon, over a Christmas bowl of smoking bishop,[59] Bob! Make up the fires, and buy another coal scuttle before you dot another *i*, Bob Cratchit!"

23 Scrooge was better than his word. He did it all, and infinitely more; and to Tiny Tim, who did *not* die, he was a second father. He became as good a friend, as good a master, and as good a man, as the good old city knew, or any other good old city, town, or borough, in the good old world. Some people laughed to see the alteration in him, but he let them laugh, and little heeded them; for he was wise enough to know that nothing ever happened on this globe, for good, at which some people did not have their fill of laughter in the outset; and

---

59. **bishop:** a hot drink made of spiced port wine.

PORTFOLIO ASSESSMENT
Some students might want to watch the movie version of "A Christmas Carol" with the purpose of comparing it to the version in the textbook. Suggest that they examine the elements that combine to make the movie version more sentimental than the written story. Some may want to write their comparison while others may want to present it orally to the class. (See *Portfolio Assessment and Professional Support Materials* for additional information on student portfolios.)

---

knowing that such as these would be blind anyway, he thought it quite as well that they should wrinkle up their eyes in grins, as have the malady in less attractive forms. His own heart laughed, and that was quite enough for him.

24

He had no further intercourse with spirits, but lived upon the total-abstinence principle,[60] ever afterward; and it was always said of him that he knew how to keep Christmas well, if any man alive possessed the knowledge. May that be truly said of us, and all of us! And so, as Tiny Tim observed, God Bless Us, Every One!

60. **total-abstinence** (ăb′stə-nəns) **principle:** the giving up of "spirits" completely, usually alcoholic "spirits," but here ghostly "spirits."

Reading Check

1. Who was Jacob Marley?
2. Why do the two gentlemen visit Scrooge in his countinghouse on Christmas Eve?
3. What is the first supernatural event?
4. Why does Marley's spirit visit Scrooge?
5. What two scenes from his past does Scrooge relive?
6. What toast does Bob Cratchit make on Christmas Day?
7. What vow does Scrooge make to the last spirit?
8. What is Scrooge's first charitable act?
9. Why does Scrooge hesitate before visiting his nephew?
10. How does Scrooge help Bob Cratchit?

For Study and Discussion

Analyzing and Interpreting the Story

Character

1. "A Christmas Carol" contains many sequences with supernatural characters and events. Yet it is Ebenezer Scrooge, the human being, who is the center of attention. It is his transformation, or change, that forms the central action of the story. How is Scrooge different at the end of the story?

2. At the beginning of the story, the author must convince you that Scrooge is a hard-hearted miser. He does this through direct and indirect characterization. He *tells* you that Scrooge is a "tightfisted hand at the grindstone"—in other words, a stingy person. Locate other passages that *tell* you how miserly Scrooge is. You learn that in his countinghouse, Scrooge keeps the coalbox in his own room, and that his clerk tries to warm himself at his candle. This scene *shows* you how stingy Scrooge is. Point out other passages that *show* Scrooge's miserliness. (For a review of direct and indirect characterization, see page 240.)

3. During the visit of each Christmas spirit, Scrooge learns something about himself that helps him to change. At the end of Stave Two, for example, Scrooge realizes that he lost his fiancée through his own greed and stupidity. **a.** What does Scrooge learn about himself by the end of Stave Three? **b.** By the end of Stave Four?

4. At the beginning of the story, Scrooge is described as a "squeezing, wrenching, grasping, scraping, clutching, covetous old sinner!" What words would you use to describe him at the end of the story?

Plot

5. The plot of a story turns upon a conflict, or struggle, of some kind. What is the conflict in

---

24
Theme. Scrooge's kind heart has made him happier than money ever did.

READING CHECK
1. Scrooge's business partner (p. 276).
2. They want a contribution for the poor (p. 278).
3. Door knocker turns into Marley's face (p. 279).
4. To prepare him for the three spirits and to save him (p. 281).
5. Christmas Eve at the Fezziwigs' and his fiancée's breaking their engagement (pp. 283, 285).
6. He wishes everyone a merry Christmas, with God's blessing; toasts Scrooge (pp. 288, 289).
7. To honor Christmas in his heart; to keep it all year (p. 294).
8. Sends prize turkey to Cratchit's home (p. 296).
9. Has to find courage (p. 297).
10. Raises Cratchit's salary; becomes second father to Tiny Tim (p. 298).

FOR STUDY AND DISCUSSION
1. Scrooge becomes generous, good-natured.
2. Direct: ". . . covetous old sinner" (p. 276); ". . . 'came down' handsomely, and Scrooge never did" (p. 277); "Darkness is cheap, and Scrooge liked it" (p. 279). Indirect: refusing to give to the poor; begrudging Bob Cratchit a day's wages on Christmas; spending evening after dinner looking at bank book.
3a. Learns he casts a pall on lives of others. **3b.** If he does not change, he will die a wretched and dismal man.
4. Answers will vary. Merry, goodhearted, kind, generous, warm, pleasant, playful.
5. Conflicts: Scrooge vs. others and society at large. Conflict of values: love of money vs. human sympathy.

6a. Marley's face appearing on door knocker; Marley's return as ghost. 6b. If he were imaginative, reader could assume he imagined ghosts.
7. Seeing his tombstone.
8a. Dark and gloomy, like Scrooge; reflect miserliness with small fire. 8b. Fire blazes up, making rooms festive; floor is heaped with foods. 8c. It is turned into ballroom with dancing and merriment. 8d. There is joy, good will, feasting.
9. Answers will vary. Before: has "ill will" on shutting office; satisfied as he locks himself in; is astonished and filled with dread at ringing bell; remains unbelieving looking at Marley's ghost. After: hears bells and thinks "glorious"; can't believe a simple walk could cause such happiness; imagines surprising Bob Cratchit coming in late.
10. Throughout the story. Examples: Stave One, in paragraph 5; Stave Two, on Fezziwig and dancing; Stave Three, on Cratchits, Topper, and game; Stave Four, on Bob Cratchit; Stave Five, on Scrooge.
11a. Responsibility. 11b. Has become a philanthropist and second father to Tiny Tim. 11c. Welfare of others.
12. Scrooge changes destiny by altering character; implies people can control their fates.

LITERARY ELEMENTS
1. *S* sound in tightfisted, grindstone, Scrooge, squeezing, grasping, scraping, covetous, sinner.

300

this story? (For a review of conflict, see page 218.)

6. The first thing the author tells you is that Marley is dead. **a.** What later events are being foreshadowed? **b.** You are also told that Scrooge is a man of no "fancy," or imagination (page 279). Why is it important to emphasize this fact about Scrooge?

7. Which scene in the story forms the climax, the point at which Scrooge makes a decision to change?

Setting
8. An important part of the action of the story is set in Scrooge's rooms. **a.** In what way are the rooms a reflection of Scrooge's character? **b.** How is this setting transformed, or changed, by the appearance of the Ghost of Christmas Present? **c.** How is the spirit of Christmas reflected in Fezziwig's warehouse? **d.** In the homes of Bob Cratchit and of Scrooge's nephew?

Point of View
9. Dickens has chosen an omniscient point of view for the story. Find passages that reveal Scrooge's innermost thoughts and feelings before and after his transformation.

10. Although the narrator doesn't appear in the story, he makes his opinions of the characters and events known to us. For example, on page 290, when he describes the game of blindman's buff at Fred's home, he says, "And I no more believe Topper was really blinded than I believe he had eyes in his boots." Where else does the narrator comment on the characters and actions in his own person?

Theme
11. Marley's ghost tells Scrooge, "Mankind was my business . . . charity, mercy, forbearance, benevolence, were all my business" (page 281). **a.** What does the word *business* mean in

300 SHORT STORIES

Marley's statement? **b.** How do you know by the end of the story that Scrooge has made mankind *his* business? **c.** What does the story suggest is everyone's business?

12. Scrooge asks the Ghost of Christmas Yet to Come if the visions he has seen are shadows of what will be or what may be (page 294). What does the conclusion of "A Christmas Carol" imply about the ability of people to determine their own futures?

Literary Elements

Recognizing Onomatopoeia

Many words in English imitate sounds. For example, when you say the word *buzz*, you hear the sound of buzzing at the end of the word. When you say *plop*, you hear the sound that is made by an object when it strikes water. The technical name for this use of words is **onomatopoeia** (ŏn′ə-măt′ə-pē′ə).

In "A Christmas Carol" there is a "clanking" of chains before Marley's ghost enters; Mrs. Cratchit makes the gravy "hissing" hot; and you are told that the chestnuts "crackled" in the fire. The words *clank*, *hiss*, and *crackle* imitate the sounds made by dragging chains, steaming gravy, and roasting chestnuts, respectively. When Dickens uses these words, he helps you experience vividly what he is describing.

Writers may also use the sounds of words to suggest something about character. Read aloud these lines describing Scrooge:

> Oh! But he was a tightfisted hand at the grindstone, was Scrooge! A squeezing, wrenching, grasping, scraping, clutching, covetous old sinner!

Many sounds in the passage are harsh sounds. The sound **s** suggests hissing. How often is the sound **s** repeated? Can you find repeated **r** sounds that give you the impression of some-

Language and Vocabulary

Recognizing Analogies

You are familiar with vocabulary questions that ask you to identify synonyms or antonyms. These questions usually involve a pair of words. Some other vocabulary questions, called **analogies,** involve two pairs of words. You must first decide what relationship exists between the words in the first pair. The same relationship applies to the second pair.

An analogy question has a special format and uses special symbols. This is one type of analogy question:

little : small :: strong : _____
 a. tiny **b.** great **c.** powerful **d.** large

The two dots (:) stand for "is to"; the four dots (::) stand for "as." The example, therefore, reads "Little *is to* small *as* strong *is to* _____." Since the first two words, *little* and *small*, are synonyms, the correct answer is *c*. The word that is a synonym for *strong* is *powerful*.

Here are some questions involving synonym and antonym relationships. Before you complete the analogies, check the meanings of words in your glossary or in a dictionary.

1. covetous : greedy :: destitute : _____
   a. hateful
   b. sad
   c. determined
   d. poor
2. melancholy : cheerful :: trivial : _____
   a. significant
   b. motionless
   c. unimportant
   d. cautious
3. apparition : phantom :: aspiration : _____
   a. scorn
   b. ambition
   c. self-control
   d. good will
4. inexplicable : clear :: inaudible : _____
   a. deceitful
   b. low
   c. deafening
   d. noticeable

Focus on Writing a Short Story

Making a Story Map

A **story map** shows all the important elements of a short story. Here is a sample story map:

Story Map

Title: _____
Point of View: _____
Setting
   Time: _____
   Place: _____
Characters
   1: _____
   2: _____
   3: _____
Plot
   Background: _____
   Conflict: _____
      Event 1: _____
      Event 2: _____
      Event 3: _____
   Climax: _____
   Outcome: _____

Make a story map for a short story of your own. Develop one of the story ideas explored during this unit, or choose a new idea. Share your work with a small group of classmates. Offer each other suggestions on how to improve your stories. Save your writing.

CLOSURE

Ask students to give three examples each of direct and indirect **characterization** of Scrooge. Ask them to write a brief description of the **setting** of "A Christmas Carol" and then to state and explain its **theme**.

EXTENSION AND ENRICHMENT

Ask students to write a character sketch of Ebenezer Scrooge before his transformation and another describing his character after his Christmas Eve experience.

ABOUT THE AUTHOR

Well known to many modern readers, "A Christmas Carol" has had an interesting history. Dickens' original version was roughly twice as long, and appeared in serial installments during most of 1843. One of Dickens' purposes in writing the story was to encourage the celebration of the Christmas holiday which, during the Victorian early industrial era, had almost ceased to be observed as a public holiday: few businesses closed; most people worked. Publication of the full-length book was greeted with interest, and when Dickens prepared to make his second tour of the United States in 1867, he abridged the story for presentation in his public readings. The story and the tour were popular, and the shorter version of "A Christmas Carol" (used in this textbook) is by far the better known. Some scholars credit Dickens, and this story, for the almost single-handed preservation of Christmas as a holiday in England.

LITERATURE AND THE ARTS

For students who are unfamiliar with reader's theater, you may want to explain how this form of oral interpretation differs from a play. In a play, the actors generally speak directly to each other and ignore the audience. In reader's theater the actors direct their reading to the audience.

For this activity, allow students adequate time to practice before they present their reading to the class. If students are interested and the opportunity arises, encourage them to perform for other classes or groups.

About the Author

Charles Dickens (1812–1870)

Charles Dickens spent the happiest years of his childhood in Chatham, a dockyard town near London. He was a keen observer of the city life around him. He roamed the area, observing the great black prisons that jutted out over the Medway River and the gray, square ruins of Rochester Castle. He saw the inhumane conditions existing in the local hospitals, prisons, and poorhouses.

Dickens was an avid reader. He spent many free hours reading the works of Shakespeare and *The Arabian Nights,* and rummaging through old novels piled up in the attic of his home. Dickens' schooling was cut short when his father fell deeply into debt. At the age of twelve, he was forced to take a job in a warehouse, where he worked twelve hours a day, pasting labels on bottles. This experience was shattering, and it aroused in Dickens a fierce determination to fight poverty and social injustice—an ideal he expressed passionately in many of his books.

Dickens' literary career began in 1836, when he published *Sketches by Boz,* a collection of short, fictional pieces based on his observations of London life. Shortly afterward, he was asked to write a comic narrative to accompany a set of engravings by a well-known artist. The result was *The Pickwick Papers,* which brought him instant fame. In such classics as *Oliver Twist* (1837–1838), *David Copperfield* (1850), and *Great Expectations* (1861), he created some of the most vivid characters and memorable situations in English literature.

Dickens also acted in amateur plays and gave readings from his works in England and in America. The version of "A Christmas Carol" that appears in this book was prepared by Dickens for his public readings.

Literature and the Arts

Adaptations of "A Christmas Carol"

Two months after Dickens completed "A Christmas Carol," no fewer than eight theater productions of the story were running in London. Since then, "A Christmas Carol" has been adapted in almost every way imaginable. Works based on the story include operas, musicals, radio plays, sound recordings, ballets, mime, puppet and marionette shows—even a piano suite. Eight silent films and more than a dozen sound-film adaptations have been made.

Making Connections: Activities

With a group of other students, create and perform a reader's theater production of "A Christmas Carol," following these guidelines:

Using the story as a guide, create a script and assign dialogue parts. Eliminate dialogue not essential to the plot, and write transitions where necessary.

Assign dialogue parts to group members. You will probably want to assign a narrator to read some of the story's descriptive passages.

Readers do not have to memorize the script, but they should read expressively and remember that their voices help to create the characters.

Readers might want to use minimal costumes or props (hats, scarves, glasses), especially if they are reading more than one role.

Start the reading with a brief introduction including the title, author, and a description to set the scene.

OBJECTIVES
The overall aim is for students to develop skills in critical thinking by using specific criteria for evaluation of a short story.

PRESENTATION
You might begin this section by defining the word *evaluate* (to find the value of; estimate the worth or importance of). Then explain that the word *judge*, which is used as a synonym, should not carry a negative connotation. Literally, the word means "to make up one's mind about; form an opinion; to think, suppose, and draw conclusions." Therefore, it is only through extensive evaluation that we can make a good judgment about a piece of literature.

FOCUS ON Reading and Critical Thinking

EVALUATING SHORT STORIES

This unit has introduced you to certain basic elements of short stories. Below are some standards you can use to *evaluate*, or judge, the quality of any short story you read. Use a separate sheet of paper to answer the questions marked with the symbol ■.

Plot

1. *Is the main conflict of the story well developed?* Even a story with an unexpected ending, such as Eva-Lis Wuorio's "You Can't Take It with You," should end with a believable solution to the conflict.

2. *Are the elements of suspense and foreshadowing handled skillfully?*

- How does the story "Rikki-tikki-tavi" (page 229) show skillful use of these plot elements?

Character

3. *Are the characters believable and consistent in their actions? Are their actions well motivated? Are you sufficiently prepared for any change in a character's actions or thoughts?*

4. *Are the characters presented effectively? Does the author reveal characters directly or indirectly? Are the characters clearly individualized or are they types?*

- How do these criteria apply to all the characters in "A Christmas Carol" (page 276)?

Setting

5. *What role does the setting play? Does it have an important connection to the plot? Does it help to create atmosphere?*

- What is the importance of setting in "The Landlady" (page 220) and in "Zlateh the Goat" (page 270)?

Point of View

6. *What point of view is used and what is its purpose?*

- How does the narrator in "Rip Van Winkle" (page 247) control your reactions to Rip and to Dame Van Winkle?

Irony

7. *How is irony used and how does it affect the story?*

- How is the situation in "The Landlady" (page 220) ironic? Why is this irony essential to the story?

Theme

8. *Does the story offer some insight into human experience?*

- How would you state the theme or message of "The Erne from the Coast" (page 208)? Test your statement by seeing if it includes all the important aspects of the story.

Answers
Answers may vary.
1. The **conflict** in "You Can't Take It with You" is developed well and has a surprising but satisfactory ending as Uncle Basil outwits his relatives even in death.
2. Early in "Rikki-tikki-tavi," **foreshadowing** occurs when the father says, "If a snake came into the nursery now. . . ." **Repetition** of the word *death* creates **suspense** along with some of the events which prolong Rikki-tikki-tavi's battle with the cobras.
3. The **characters** in "A Christmas Carol" are presented as distinct individuals. Dickens explains in great detail why and how Scrooge has become a cynical old miser, and his change of heart is entirely plausible.
4. Dickens uses direct and indirect **characterization** to present his characters.
5. The **setting** of "The Landlady" reinforces the main idea that appearances can be deceiving by adding the mysterious **mood** and underscoring the irony of events. In "Zlateh the Goat" the weather conditions are essential to the conflicts in the story.
6. In "Rip Van Winkle" the narrator uses **first-person point of view** (but rarely uses the word *I*). He controls the reader's reactions to Dame Van Winkle by presenting her in exaggerated terms. She becomes a character type—the bad-tempered, quarrelsome woman. Rip is more of a three-dimensional character—lazy but likable.
7. Billy thinks he has found a homelike place to stay, complete with a mother figure, when in reality he has walked into a dangerous situation controlled by a deranged woman. The **irony** provides the story with its surprise ending.
8. The **theme** might be stated as follows: By confronting problems with courage, perseverance, and pride, people gain both self-respect and the respect of others.

OBJECTIVES
The overall aim is for students to write a **short story** that uses the important elements of the genre.

PRESENTATION
To stimulate interest in stories, ask students to tell which story in this unit is their favorite and why. A few volunteers might write titles and reasons for liking the story on the chalkboard for discussion.

Be sure to give students plenty of time for thorough prewriting, especially time to share their ideas with and to receive feedback from their classmates. The drafting step will probably involve independent work, but you might want to confer with students when they need help.

HOLT WRITER'S WORKSHOP

This computer program provides help for all types of writing through guided instruction for each step of the writing process. (Program available separately.)

See *Elements of Writing, First Course,* Chapter 6, for more instruction on creative writing.

WRITING A SHORT STORY
Where do stories begin? Some stories begin in the author's mind as a **setting** with a particular **atmosphere**. Other stories begin with a **plot**, while still others might begin with a **character** who has a problem to solve. Some writers start with a **theme** around which they develop a story. Usually, any one of these elements will lead the writer to the others. Regardless of where stories begin, writers use their own experiences to relate **character, settings,** and **conflicts** to **plot;** and all of these are tied together to produce **theme.**

Prewriting
Help students brainstorm story ideas by asking each student to complete at least two "What if?" questions. Then have volunteers write their ideas on the chalkboard to produce a long list from which students can see the variety of possibilities. Students may find something in the list that triggers a story idea.

Encourage students to develop an outline, a chart, or a story map to help them organize their prewriting notes. Before students begin writing, they might share their notes in small groups to make sure they have used the necessary literary elements and created sufficient details to give substance to their stories.

FOCUS ON *Writing*

WRITING A SHORT STORY

A good **short story** entertains the reader, presents lifelike characters and a specific setting, and solves a conflict or problem. Now that you have seen some of the important elements of short stories, you will have the chance to write a story of your own.

Prewriting

1. To find a story idea, ask yourself some "What if?" questions like the following:

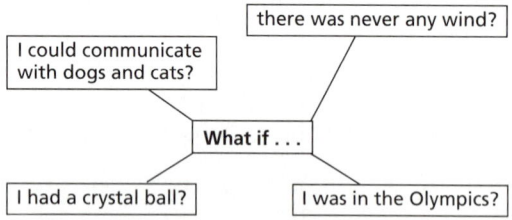

[See **Focus** assignment on page 219.]

2. Develop the **plot** of your story by making some notes on:

- background
- conflict
- climax
- outcome

Focus on the main **conflict,** and plan to introduce it early in order to hook the reader's interest. You can choose these kinds of conflicts:

- a person versus another person (external conflict)
- a person versus a force of nature (external conflict)
- a struggle within a character's mind (internal conflict)

Also decide what the **high point** or **climax** of your story will be—the point where the conflict is settled one way or the other. [See **Focus** assignment on page 228.]

3. A short story usually has at least two **characters.** Fill out a character chart like the one below for each character you create:

Name: _____ Age: ____
Physical Appearance: _____
Way of Moving and Speaking: _____
Personality Traits: _____

[See **Focus** assignment on page 241.]

4. Make a list of descriptive details for the **setting** of your story—the time and place of the events. Focus especially on **sensory details.** [See **Focus** assignment on page 262.]

5. Decide on the **point of view,** or angle, from which you will tell the story. [See **Focus** assignment on page 246.]

Writing

1. Use **chronological** or **time order** to tell the events of your story in the order they happened. **Transitional words and phrases** can help your readers understand the connections of events and ideas.

2. Use **dialogue** to reveal the characters' actions, emotions, and personality. Use fragments, contractions, and slang if informal English suits the character. Also remember to use **vivid verbs** and **sensory details.**

304 SHORT STORIES

Evaluating and Revising

1. Put your first draft aside for a while. Then read your story as a critic or as a reader who wants to be entertained.

Here is one writer's revision of a passage from a short story.

Writer's Model

After Peter regained consciousness,
                    eagerly
he looked around, trying to identify
         Overhead
his surroundings. ~~There~~ was a tangled
web of yellow, red, and black cables.
      one
Each ~~cable was~~ the thickness of his
waist. One entire wall glowed with a
   amber
soft light. On the floor, spaced at regu-
                         metal
lar intervals, were large boxes with
dozens of
switches on them. Suddenly, he heard
       loud electronic
a series of ten tones. "A modem!" he
exclaimed
~~said~~. His whereabouts were no longer
                              gigantic
a mystery. He was trapped inside a ~~big~~

P.C.

2. You may find the following checklist helpful as you revise your short story.

Checklist for Evaluation and Revision

- ✓ Does the beginning catch the reader's interest?
- ✓ Do I present a strong conflict early in the story?
- ✓ Are the characters lifelike and believable?
- ✓ Do I describe the setting clearly?
- ✓ Does the plot have a clear high point and a satisfying outcome?

Proofreading and Publishing

1. Proofread your short story and correct any errors you find in grammar, usage, and mechanics. (Here you may find it helpful to refer to the **Handbook for Revision** on pages 726–767.) Then prepare a final version of your story by making a clean copy.

2. Consider some of the following publication methods for your story:

- make your story the basis for a series of giant comic-book murals and use them to decorate your classroom
- submit your story to the school magazine
- organize a story theater for younger students

Portfolio If your teacher approves, you may wish to keep a copy of your work in your writing folder or portfolio.

Focus on Writing **305**

UNIT 5 ♦ TEACHING GUIDE

FORMS OF LITERATURE
DRAMA

OVERVIEW OF THE UNIT

Most young people have spent many hours watching television and attending movies. Thus, even those who have never seen actors bring a play to life on stage will find drama a familiar form.

However, watching a play is very different from reading one. Students must understand that a script is not a play any more than a recipe is a chocolate cake; both are directions for creating something. Once they grasp this distinction, students must develop the interpretive skills necessary to create an imaginary performance complete with characters, costumes, lighting, sets, props, and other theatrical trappings. This unit is directed toward the development of such skills.

The drama unit features five short plays. *The Mazarin Stone* is a dramatization of a Sherlock Holmes story. As you will see in the example given in "Introducing the Unit," the difference between the story and the drama is immense. This drama contains very little added action, yet the playwrights have done a remarkable job of revealing the intricate thought processes, the second-guessing and outsmarting which mark Sherlock Holmes's every interaction as effective drama. Too often on television and in modern films, students are exposed to conflict only as armed combat between rivals fighting for some material possession. Holmes prefers to use his wits against his opponent(s) in a struggle for justice. A thorough comparison of the two types of conflict, physical and intellectual, will heighten students' appreciation of drama of the mind.

In *A Sunny Morning*, characterization is the prime force behind the drama. As students learn about the elderly pair of main characters, who they are and, more importantly, who they have been to each other, they are drawn to continue reading by their fascination with the information being revealed. The use of asides in dramatic writing will be new to most because it is not found in television or movies. Students will need to watch closely as this technique is used to advance character development and thereby advance the play itself.

Theme and irony are the key elements of *The Governess*, as might be expected in a Neil Simon play. Students will have seen instances of irony in previous units. Thus, they should be prepared for the more difficult task of understanding the slow building of an ironic situation solely through characterization. In this instance, characters are developed in nothing more than a simple dialogue between a superior and her employee; yet the climax is as rich and delicate as in any lengthy novel. Students will have much to discuss and dispute regarding the play's ending.

In *When the Rattlesnake Sounds*, Alice Childress dramatizes an episode from the life of Harriet Tubman, famous leader of the Underground Railroad. The play's three characters come together for a common purpose but find they are faced with conflicts both within themselves and with one another. Characterization is strengthened by effective use of dialect.

Finally, James Ene Henshaw's play *The Jewels of the Shrine* includes a character who acts as a trickster figure, spinning intrigue that propels the action of the play and motivates its characters. Like the selections in Unit 2, this play focuses on relationships among family members and will give students a glimpse into another culture's beliefs and values regarding the family.

In learning to imagine a play in performance, students analyze stage directions and dialogue. After working with conflict as the basis for plot, they analyze sound effects and the use of music to heighten mood. A final exercise based on levels of formality in dialogue yields increased understanding of language as it sharpens reading comprehension. Since drama requires special interpretive skills, questions and activities throughout the unit focus on these. The unit ends with a **Focus on Reading and Critical Thinking** section, **Drawing Inferences,** and a **Focus on Writing** section in which students synthesize and apply newly acquired skills to write an original dramatic scene.

OBJECTIVES OF THE UNIT

The aims of the unit are for the student:
- To demonstrate an understanding of the elements of a play: plot, characterization, mood, setting, theme, stage directions, sound effects, and dialogue
- To predict probable outcome in plays
- To assemble a director's notebook
- To write an analysis of a character in a play
- To write a dramatic scene
- To make connections between literature and cultures

CONCEPTS AND SKILLS

The following concepts and skills are treated in this unit:

CLOSE READING OF A PLAY

Guidelines for Close Reading   308
One Reader's Response   309
Looking at Yourself as a Reader   317

LITERARY ELEMENTS/TERMS AND TECHNIQUES

Understanding Plot   333

LANGUAGE AND VOCABULARY SKILLS

Recognizing Cockney Speech   334

PLANNING GUIDE

FOR UNIT PLANNING
- Transparencies 24–29: *Audiovisual Resources Binder*
- Portfolio Assessment: *Professional Support Materials*
- Test Generator
- Mastery Tests: Teaching Resources C, pp. 70, 73, 78
- Analogy Test: Teaching Resources C, p. 82
- Composition Test: Teaching Resources C, p. 84

SELECTION (Pupil's Page)	TEACHING RESOURCES C (page numbers shown below)							AV BINDER
	Teacher's Notes	Reading Check	Study Guide	Language Skills	Building Vocabulary	Selection Vocab. Test	Selection Test	Audio-cassette
DRAMA Introduction (p. 307)	1							
Close Reading of a Play Milton Geiger *In the Fog* (p. 308)	2							
Michael and Molly Hardwick *The Mazarin Stone* (p. 318)	3	6	7	11	14		15	
Serafín and Joaquín Quintero *A Sunny Morning* (p. 335)	18		20	22	25		26	
Neil Simon *The Governess* (p. 343)	28	31	32		34		37	
Alice Childress *When the Rattlesnake Sounds* (p. 347)	39	41	43	46			49	
James Ene Henshaw *The Jewels of the Shrine* (p. 357)	51	54	56	59	62	64	66	

WRITING OPPORTUNITIES

Writing About Literature
Analyzing Character 342

Focus on Writing a Scene
Using Improvisation to Explore a Scene 334
Creating Dialogue 355
Visualizing a Scene for Stage Directions 371
Writing a Scene 377

FOR DRAMATIZATION
Assembling a Director's Notebook 355

CONNECTIONS
Connecting Cultures 372

FOCUS ON READING AND CRITICAL THINKING
Imagining a Play in Performance 333
Drawing Inferences 376

TRANSPARENCIES

The following unit support materials with specific correlations to literature selections are available in the **Fine Art and Instructional Transparencies with Teacher's Notes and Blackline Masters** section of your *Audiovisual Resources Binder*.

FINE ART TRANSPARENCIES
Theme: Literature Out Loud
24 *An Iron Cauldron and the Moon at Night,* Taiso Yoshitoshi
25 *Étude pour un Grand Orchestre,* Raoul Dufy

READER RESPONSE
26 An Interview with a Character
27 Certificate of Merit

LITERARY ELEMENTS
28 Conflict

WRITING PROCESS
29 Writing a Scene

INTRODUCING THE UNIT

You will want to launch this unit with an activity that instructs as well as motivates. Here are several approaches that should arouse interest in drama and build readiness for the first selection:

1. Copy and distribute the following two versions of the same scene:

> **Holmes.** That boy is a problem, Watson. How far am I justified in letting him be in danger?
> **Watson.** Danger of what, Holmes?
> **Holmes.** Of sudden death.
> **Watson.** Holmes!

> As the door clicked shut, Sherlock Holmes stared in the direction the boy had disappeared. He puffed distractedly on his pipe before turning troubled eyes to his old friend and speaking. "That boy is a problem, Watson. How far am I justified in letting him be in danger?"
> The room seemed very quiet as Watson considered the question. When he spoke he tried to keep his voice casual.
> "Danger of what, Holmes?"
> "Of sudden death," Holmes answered flatly.
> Watson jumped from his chair and grasped the master detective's arm. "Holmes!" he shouted.

Allow five or ten minutes for students to study the two versions and list major differences. Compile and discuss differences. Be sure to discuss amount of detail, dialogue form, and point of view. Use this discussion to lead into the introductory comments at the beginning of the drama unit on p. 307 in the textbook.

2. Show a scene from a television show or motion picture with the sound off. Ask students to infer as much as possible about characters, situations, and conflict. Compare inferences. Discuss such clues as facial expression, costumes, and set. Explain that all of these details must be imagined by the reader of a dramatic script, which will include only the dialogue with general description of setting and broad directions to actors. Discuss the role of sound in television productions. Ask the students about their reactions to laugh tracks, background music, and naturalistic background sound. Relate this discussion to the introductory comments on p. 307 in the textbook.

3. Allow ten minutes for students to write their own dramatic versions of the following scene. (To help with form, you may wish to put a short sample dialogue on the board.)

> Thirteen-year-old Robin Moore was baby-sitting for her next-door neighbor when her best friend came to the door to say that she had unexpectedly been given tickets to a concert and wanted Robin to go. While Robin was talking, three-year-old Timmy spilled his ice cream on the living-room rug. When Robin ran to wipe up the mess, her friend became angry and left, slamming the door behind her.

Divide the class into groups of four or five; ask each group to share scripts, choose a favorite, and act it out for the class. Discuss dramatic presentations and identify methods used by actors to bring the scene alive. Explain that readers of plays must use their imaginations to supply such details. Direct attention to the introductory paragraph on p. 307 in the textbook.

4. Assign several group pantomimes. Here are some suggestions you might offer students to help them get started:
   a. Pretend that you are watching a movie. Without using words, react to it as either a comedy, a horror show, or a love story. As specifically as possible, make your reactions suggest what is happening on the screen.
   b. Pretend that you are walking down the hall at school and witness a confrontation of some kind. Without using words, demonstrate what is happening.
   c. Pretend that you are a spectator at a sports event. Without words, show what kind of game you are watching and what is happening in the game.

After each student has participated in a group pantomime, discuss the various nonverbal techniques used to convey impressions to the audience. Ask how nonverbal elements like movement, gesture, and facial expression help to create characters. Why are visual elements such as costume and setting also important in drama? Explain that such details must be visualized by a person reading a play. Relate this point to the introductory comments on p. 307 in the textbook.

You may wish to discuss with students the role of the audience. Point out that performers need a responsive audience if they are to do their best work. Interaction with the audience teaches a performer the art of timing—particularly with comedic roles. The relationship between audience and actor is in large part responsible for the fact that each live performance is unique. You may point out that this is one of the essential differences between theater and motion pictures.

Most students will enjoy the enrichment activities suggested for this unit. Although you will want to encourage students to read additional plays, extension activities should not be limited to reading. Watch for outstanding dramatic specials on network television and encourage evening viewings. If your community has a professional or college theater, try to arrange a class field trip to an appropriate performance. If a field trip is not feasible, invite groups of actors to visit your school and present selected scenes. In the absence of professional or college groups, high-school drama departments often welcome such invitations. Still another possibility is to rent a feature-length motion picture. Whatever the activity, the goal is a shared experience of a dramatic performance.

During the course of this unit, you might also wish to experiment with reader's theater. This is a minimalist theater which demands much of the mind and little of the eye, making it perfect for classroom use. Students are challenged by the simplicity of the style: not only do they not need makeup and costumes and sets, but they are prohibited from using these to create atmosphere.

Cast, or have a student director (or a committee of students) cast each other according to suitability of voice to character. Girls need not always play women, and boys need not always read male roles. Casting could be done with eyes closed.

The only props used in strict reader's-theater style dramas are music stands (to hold scripts) and stools, preferably stools which allow students' feet to touch the ground but which swivel, allowing them to turn to face the audience when they should enter and turn away when the play calls for them to leave. If a particular hand-held prop is frequently used by a character, you and the students can decide whether to allow the student who has the role to keep the prop in hand or to require that the prop be pantomimed.

If music stands and stools are not available, students may hold the texts in their hands and be seated on their own desk chairs which have been brought up to the "stage" you create in the classroom. If chairs are used rather than stools, turn the chairs sideways to allow students room to swing around to the audience and back the other way.

Long before students present a play to the class, they must practice reading their parts, with special attention to timing. Timing can mean how quickly or how slowly they respond to another character's words. Sometimes a long pause is called for by the text—you will be able to tell when a pause makes sense. During these pauses, facial expression is crucial to hold the audience's interest and keep the play's continuity. Facial expression and small gestures are an important part of reader's theater, but no gesture should overpower the actor's voice or that of another actor.

You may be surprised at how readily students respond as both performers and audience, and how much more they get out of plays through performing them in reader's-theater style than through simply reading them.

PORTFOLIO ASSESSMENT

Suggestions for use of portfolios as support for this unit are described in the *Portfolio Assessment and Professional Support Materials* booklet accompanying this program. Specific suggestions are provided for a variety of student projects that may be suitable for inclusion in a portfolio. In addition, copying masters are provided for guides that may be used for evaluation and assessment of student projects.

Student Learning Options

DRAMA

1. Constructing Models for Sets
Allowing the students to work in groups, ask them to design and construct miniature sets for each play read. Assign one set (or play) to each group of students. Encourage the students to read the play carefully for clues as to how the set should look. The sets could be constructed in shoe boxes or in other small boxes.

2. Designing Costumes for the Plays
To help students visualize the plays in this unit, have them select a character from any of the five plays. Ask them to design a costume for this character, noting carefully either the writer's comments or the character's comments in the play about the clothing.

3. Producing a Radio Play
Ask groups of students to produce some of the plays as radio productions—sounds only. (If some students have to read more than one part, they should change their voices to make the characters sound different.) After each group has chosen a play to produce, it should assign roles and perhaps devise sound effects required to make the radio show seem realistic. After the groups have practiced, arrange for them to record their production to be played for the entire class.

4. Spelling New Words
Make a list of new vocabulary words indicated in the plays the students read. Call out the words orally, asking the students to spell them as accurately as they can. Then spell each word for the students, asking them to circle any incorrect letters in the words on their papers. In this way, they can identify any problems with the word spellings.

5. Creating "Asides"
After the students read *A Sunny Morning* by Serafín and Joaquín Quintero, noticing the many "asides" in the play, ask them to bring several pictures of people from magazines or newspapers (or you can provide the pictures) and to create "asides" these people might say. The "asides" can be either humorous comments or statements the person would not want others to hear.

6. Tracing the Underground Railroad
Have students make maps of the Underground Railroad and then indicate the routes referred to in *When the Rattlesnake Sounds* by Alice Childress. The students might also wish to do some research and then indicate on the map the places that were part of Harriet Tubman's life story.

7. Helping the Elderly
After students read *The Jewels of the Shrine* by James Ene Henshaw, brainstorm with them a list of ways they can make the lives of their family members better or more pleasant. Ask students to make the list specific to their own families, and then have them choose two or three ideas on the list to carry out. Students may then write a brief report on the results on their journals.

8. Making Programs
Ask students in small groups to design programs for the plays they read. As an example, you can show them a program for a real dramatic production you have attended. Ask them to cast real people, famous or not, in the program and to include illustrations.

305D

VISUAL CONNECTIONS

Exploring the Subject
Ask students to study the artist's rendering of a theater in which plays are performed. Ask students whether they have seen live performances of plays. Volunteers might describe plays they have seen. Ask them to consider the differences between the theater pictured here and a movie theater. Do actors seem more remote on a screen than in a live stage performance? How is the control of the lighting different in a theater for live performances from that in a movie theater? What are some possible differences in types of scenery used?

About the Artist
Today, Adolf Von Menzel is best known for his impressionist paintings of everyday life. However, he considered his paintings celebrating Prussian nationalism (done for members of the Prussian establishment) to be his best work. By the time the picture reproduced here was painted, the plays of Schiller and Goethe had revived German theater, which became a vital part of the cultural life of the German states.

Ideas for Writing
Von Menzel has used impressionist technique to convey visually the excitement of an evening at the theater. Ask students to write a paragraph recreating this scene, using words instead of paint.

DRAMA

Have you ever played a part in a school play or written material for other actors and actresses to perform? Have you helped create scenery and props for a production or worked the lights at an actual performance? What was the highlight of your experience? Was it hard work as well as fun? What three words or phrases could you use to describe your thoughts and feelings on the day or evening of the opening performance?

The word *drama* comes from a Greek word meaning "to do" or "to act." Some form of drama has existed from earliest times. Fortunately, you can enjoy drama even if you can't attend a theater. When you read a play, you can rely on your imagination to create the performance. You can visualize the setting and costumes; you can imagine the shifting tones of voice in which the performers would deliver their lines.

In this unit you will have opportunity to use your imagination to interpret different roles as they would be interpreted for you by players on a stage.

Theatre du Gymnase in Paris (1856) by Adolph Von Menzel. Oil on canvas.
Nationalgalerie Staatliche Museen Preussischer Kulturbesitz, Berlin

FOCUS / MOTIVATION

Ask students whether they have ever been to a play or have read one. Explain that in reading a play, they will receive clues, through stage direction and scene description, which they can use to imagine an actual performance.

PRESENTATION

An important aspect of **suspense** is the verisimilitude with which the story is presented. The reader must feel that what is happening to the protagonist could also happen to him or her. Stories like those from the familiar television series *The Twilight Zone* rely particularly on **setting** and **mood** to establish a feeling of suspense, mystery, or the supernatural. By using stage directions, sound effects, and **dialogue**, the author of *In the Fog* sets an eerie scene, introduces strange characters, and keeps the

TEACHING RESOURCES C

Teacher's Notes, p. 2

GUIDELINES FOR CLOSE READING

1. Encourage students to try to visualize the play's **setting**. The **setting** often affects the **mood** of the play.
2. Stage directions offer clues to **characterization**. To understand a character's personality, students should consider what motivates the character and how the character deals with **conflict**.
3. Explain to students that when they make predictions, they look for clues left by the writer. Every event and **description** has been included for a particular reason. Tell students to be ready to change their predictions with each new clue or turn of events.
4. Urge students to note the various elements that contribute to **mood**, such as the **setting**, the **characters**, and the **dialogue**.
5. Encourage students to listen to their inner voices and to respond without worrying about what others might think. The questions they ask and the conclusions they draw might differ greatly from the responses of their classmates or from those of the reader in the textbook.

Close Reading OF A PLAY

There is a great difference between seeing a play performed in a theater or on a screen and reading that play in class or at home. When you watch a performance, you are seeing the results of other people's imaginative efforts. For many weeks or months before a play is produced, there is careful planning. Sets must be created; costumes must be designed and fitted; actors and actresses must study and rehearse their parts. If you have ever seen a live performance, you know that the theater darkens, and that when the curtain rises, only the stage area is lit. You become involved in the play and think of the stage as a new world.

When you read a play, your imagination takes over. You picture what the characters look like and how they sound. You infer their gestures and facial expressions from their words. You cooperate with the playwright in making the story come alive.

Guidelines for Close Reading

1. Note any information that reveals the setting or the situation. Sometimes this information is given in stage directions. Sometimes background information is provided during the opening scenes of the play.
2. Look for clues that tell you what the characters are doing or how their lines are spoken. A pause, for example, can indicate hesitation, deep reflection, surprise, as well as other reactions. As you read, you must interpret clues to characters' thoughts and feelings that are implied rather than directly stated in dialogue.
3. Try to predict the action that will develop out of each scene. A play, like a short story, depends upon a sequence of cause-and-effect events.
4. Be aware of the mood of the play and shifts in tone. Ask yourself how these shifts affect your response to the characters and to the play as a whole.
5. Note your own reactions to the characters, language, and events of the play. State the theme or the underlying idea of the play in your own words.

reader's interest by giving the least information possible to hold that interest. The title itself reveals an intention to create a mood of uncertainty and suspense.

Here is a one-act play by Milton Geiger, called *In the Fog*. The comments in the margin alongside the play represent one reader's responses. You may wish to cover up these notes and take notes of your own on a separate sheet of paper. After you have read the play, you may wish to compare both sets of responses.

In the Fog
MILTON GEIGER

ONE READER'S RESPONSE

CLOSE READING OF A PLAY

1
Setting. Minimal props listed in first stage direction provide reader with a sense of desolation and emptiness.

1 Sets: *A signpost on Pennsylvania Route 30. A rock or stump in the fog. A gas station pump.*
   Night. At first we can only see fog drifting across a dark scene devoid of[1] detail. Then, out of the fog, there emerges toward us a white roadside signpost with a number of white painted signboards pointing to right and to left. The marker is a Pennsylvania State Route—marked characteristically "PENNA-30." Now, a light as from a far headlight sweeps the signs.
2 *An automobile approaches. The car pulls up close. We hear the car door open and slam, and a man's footsteps approaching on the concrete. Now the signs are lit up again by a more localized, smaller source of*
3 *light. The light grows stronger as the man, offstage, approaches. The* Doctor *enters, holding a flashlight before him. He scrutinizes[2] the road*
4 *marker. He flashes his light up at the arrows. We see the legends on the markers. Pointing off right there are markers that read: York, Columbia, Lancaster; pointing left the signs read: Fayetteville, McConnellsburg, Pennsylvania Turnpike.*
5 *The* Doctor's *face is perplexed and annoyed as he turns his flashlight on a folded road map. He is a bit lost in the fog. Then his flashlight fails him. It goes out!*
6 **Doctor.** Darn! (*He fumbles with the flashlight in the gloom. Then a voice is raised to him from off-stage.*)
7 **Eben** (*offstage, strangely*). Turn around, mister....

1. **devoid** (dĭ-void′) **of:** without.
2. **scrutinizes** (skrōōt′n-īz′əz): examines carefully.

This is eerie—fog and darkness on a lonely road.

What does this sign mean?

2 Making Generalizations
Since this scene involves a moving automobile, for which medium was it most likely developed? Probably television, although it could be adapted for stage by not showing automobile.

3 Analyzing
What is the effect of the lights and sounds so far? Suspense; creates eerie mood and makes audience wonder what will happen.

4
Legends here are names of towns or brief descriptions accompanying directional arrows.

It's so dark he needs a flashlight to see the sign. I guess he's lost.

5 Drawing Conclusions
What does the Doctor's expression suggest about his situation? He is lost.

I suppose he didn't find what he was looking for.

6
Doctor's exclamation suggests total exasperation. Stage direction shows that character's action reflects his exclamation.

This is scary. Is the second person a robber?

7
Suspense. Description of Eben's voice adds to suspense; order to turn around evokes anticipation of trouble.

Close Reading of a Play

TRANSPARENCY 28
Literary Elements
Conflict – invites students to explore aspects of internal and external conflict.

Close Reading OF A PLAY

8 Analyzing
What effect does the rifle have on the mood of the scene? Adds possibility of real danger to vague feeling of suspense.

9 Characterization. Stage direction provides **tone** of **dialogue**. Clue to Doctor's temperament and courage.

10 They avoid Doctor's questions, arousing more suspicion.

11 Dialect. Eben and Zeke's archaic dialect indicates they are from a remote region or time.

12 Strangers add to mystery by not answering question directly.

13 Making Inferences
From the description of the Doctor's expression, what do you suppose he is thinking? Perhaps he is wondering whether he should run for his car or go with the men.

14 Men's voices and words indicate they are tired and, perhaps, sad.

15 Suspense. Sudden revelation of men's terrifying appearance is dramatic; increases tension.

Who are these characters? Are they hunters?

These characters don't speak the way people speak today. Their language seems old-fashioned.

Who can the third man be?

They look like they've been in an accident or in a fight.

[*The* Doctor *turns sharply to stare offstage.*]

Zeke (*offstage*). You don't have to be afraid, mister....

The Doctor *sees two men slowly approaching out of the fog. One carries a lantern below his knees. The other holds a heavy rifle. Their features are utterly indistinct as they approach, and the rifleman holds up*
8 *his gun with quiet threat.*]

Eben. You don't have to be afraid.
9 **Doctor** (*more indignant than afraid*). So you say! Who are you, man?
Eben. We don't aim to hurt you none.
Doctor. That's reassuring. I'd like to know just what you mean by this? This gun business! Who *are* you?
Zeke (*mildly*). What's your trade, mister?
Doctor. I...I'm a doctor. Why?
10 **Zeke** (*to* Eben). Doctor.
Eben (*nods; then to* Doctor). Yer the man we want.
11 **Zeke.** Ye'll do proper, we're thinkin'.
Eben. So ye'd better come along, mister.
Zeke. Aye.
Doctor. Why? Has—anyone been hurt?
12 **Eben.** It's for you to say if he's been hurt nigh to the finish.
Zeke. So we're askin' ye to come along, doctor.

13 [*The* Doctor *looks from one to another in indecision and puzzlement.*]

Eben. In the name o' mercy.
Zeke. Aye.
Doctor. I want you to understand—I'm not afraid of your gun! I'll go to your man all right. Naturally, I'm a doctor. But I demand to know who you are.
Zeke (*patiently*). Why not? Raise yer lantern, Eben...
14 **Eben** (*tiredly*). Aye.

15 [Eben *lifts his lantern. Its light falls on their faces now, and we see that they are terrifying. Matted beards, clotted with blood; crude head bandages, crusty with dirt and dry blood. Their hair, stringy and disheveled. Their faces are lean and hollow-cheeked; their eyes sunken and*

310 DRAMA

VISUAL CONNECTIONS

Ideas for Writing
Tell students to use this photograph as the inspiration for a stage set. In a short paragraph, ask them to describe the set design as a playwright would at the beginning of a scene in a dramatic script.

Relating Expression Skills
With the help of the school librarian, have students look up information about landscape photographers. (Ansel Adams is one example.) Encourage them to share pictures of landscapes that they find unusual and appealing. They might also research techniques that photographers use for "shooting" landscapes.

16 Synthesizing
What kind of music do you think would accompany this scene in a television production? Perhaps burst of shrill music.

17
Again, vague answer does not provide useful information.

18
Characterization. Doctor's words further indicate his courage and straightforward manner.

19
Moonshiners characteristically operate in remote areas to escape detection.

20
Laws that moonshiners ignore concern quality control and taxation.

21
Zeke's words may indicate that he does not like moonshiners or violence either.

22
Doctor assumes wounded person is another of their type.

23
Prodding with rifle reinforces idea that Doctor is being forced.

Close Reading OF A PLAY

They never seem to answer questions directly. How come?

The doctor thinks they're making and selling whiskey unlawfully.

They don't deny it.

Why are they sad?

What do they regret?

16 *tragic. The Doctor is shocked for a moment—then bursts out—]*

Doctor. Good heavens!—
Zeke. That's Eben; I'm Zeke.
Doctor. What's happened? Has there been an accident or...what?
17 **Zeke.** Mischief's happened, stranger.
Eben. Mischief enough.
Doctor (*looks at rifle at his chest*). There's been gunplay—hasn't there?
Zeke (*mildly ironic*). Yer tellin' us there's been gunplay!
18 **Doctor.** And I'm telling you that I'm not at all frightened! It's my duty to report this, and report it I will!
Zeke. Aye, mister. You do that.
Doctor. You're arrogant about it now! You don't think you'll be caught and dealt with. But people are losing patience with you
19 men....You...you moonshiners![3] Running wild...a law unto
20 yourselves...shooting up the countryside!
Zeke. Hear that, Eben? Moonshiners.
Eben. Mischief's happened, mister, we'll warrant[4] that....
Doctor. And I don't like it!
21 **Zeke.** Can't say we like it better'n you do, mister....
Eben (*strangely sad and remote*). What must be, must.
Zeke. There's no changin' or goin' back, and all 'at's left is the wishin' things were different.
Eben. Aye.
22 **Doctor.** And while we talk, your wounded man lies bleeding, I suppose—worthless though he may be. Well? I'll have to get my instrument bag, you know. It's in the car.

[*Eben and Zeke part to let Doctor pass between them. The Doctor reenters, carrying his medical bag.*]

Doctor. I'm ready. Lead the way.

[*Eben lifts his lantern a bit and goes first. Zeke prods the Doctor ever
23 so gently and apologetically, but firmly with the rifle muzzle. The Doctor leaves. Zeke strides off slowly after them.*]

3. **moonshiners:** people who distill liquor illegally.
4. **warrant** (wôr′ənt, wŏr′): declare positively.

24 [*A wounded man is lying against a section of stone fence. He, too, is bearded, though very young, and his shirt is dark with blood. He breathes but never stirs otherwise.* Eben *enters, followed by the* Doctor *and* Zeke.]

Zeke. Ain't stirred a mite since we left 'im.
Doctor. Let's have that lantern here! (*The* Doctor *tears the man's*
25 *shirt for better access to the wound. Softly*) Dreadful! Dreadful...!
Zeke's voice (*off scene*). Reckon it's bad in the chest like that, hey?
Doctor (*taking pulse*). His pulse is positively racing...! How long has he been this way?
26 **Zeke.** A long time, mister. A long time....
Doctor (*to* Eben). You! Hand me my bag.

[Eben *puts down lantern and hands bag to* Doctor. *The* Doctor *opens bag and takes out a couple of retractors.*[5] Zeke *holds lantern close now.*]

27 **Doctor.** Lend me a hand with these retractors. (*He works on the man.*) All right...when I tell you to draw back on the retractors—draw back.
Eben. Aye.
Zeke. How is 'e, mister?
Doctor (*preoccupied*). More retraction. Pull them a bit more. Hold it....
Eben. Bad, ain't he?
Doctor. Bad enough. The bullet didn't touch any lung tissue
28 far as I can see right now. There's some pneumothorax[6] though. All I can do now is plug the wound. There's some cotton and gauze wadding in my bag. Find it....

[Zeke *probes about silently in the bag and comes up with a small dark box of gauze.*]

29 **Doctor.** That's it. (*Works a moment in silence*) I've never seen anything quite like it.

---

5. **retractors** (rĭ-trăk′tərz): surgical instruments for holding back the flesh at the edge of a wound.
6. **pneumothorax** (nōō′mō-thôr′ăks, nyōō′): air or gas in the chest cavity.

This is suspenseful. Who is the injured person? What will happen to the doctor?

They never give a straight answer.

Why does the doctor find the wound unusual?

24
Setting. Still outside, yet away from highway. Stone fence suggests rural area.

25
Characterization. Doctor probably does not treat many gunshot wounds, but voice inflection indicates he is calm.

26
Foreshadowing. Hint as to mysterious men's identities.

27
Doctor proceeds confidently.

28
Doctor's technical jargon tells the men very little, just as they have told him very little.

29
Foreshadowing. Doctor does not know how true these words will be.

30 Finding Details
Eben refers to the Doctor as "young." What else do we know about the Doctor? He is confident, capable, and courageous.

31
Eben's manner emphasizes idea that Doctor is no longer needed.

32 Making Inferences
Why might men hesitate to take injured man to a hospital? Answers may vary. Men might be criminals who fear apprehension; they might have superstitious fear of hospitals; they might not care what happens to the injured man.

33
Eben's question suggests his limited knowledge and experience; sees bleeding as main danger.

34
Zeke dismisses Doctor casually; indication of lack of concern for wounded man.

35
Setting. The men come and go with the fog.

36
Tone of voice indicates regret.

37
Suspense. Suggests that the men have committed serious crimes, yet there is no indication of what or why.

Close Reading
OF A PLAY

I wonder why they won't allow him to be moved.

Is the fog significant?

30 Eben. Yer young, doctor. Lot's o' things you've never seen.
Doctor. Adhesive tape!

[Zeke *finds a roll of three-inch tape and hands it to the* Doctor, *who tears off long strips and slaps them on the dressing and pats and smooths them to man's chest.* Eben *replaces equipment in* Doctor's *bag* **31** *and closes it with a hint of the finality to come. A preview of dismissal, so to speak.*]

Doctor (*at length*). There. So much for that. Now then—(*Takes man's shoulders*) give me a hand here.
Zeke (*quiet suspicion*). What fer?
Doctor. We've got to move this man.
Zeke. What fer?
Doctor (*stands; indignantly*). We've got to get him to a hospital for treatment; a thorough cleansing of the wound; irrigation.[7] I've done all I can for him here.
32 Zeke. I reckon he'll be all right 'thout no hospital.
Doctor. Do you realize how badly this man's hurt!
33 Eben. He won't bleed to death, will he?
Doctor. I don't think so—not with that plug and pressure dressing. But bleeding isn't the only danger we've got to—
Zeke (*interrupts*). All right, then. Much obliged to you.
Doctor. This man's dangerously hurt!
34 Zeke. Reckon he'll pull through now, thanks to you.
Doctor. I'm glad you feel that way about it! But I'm going to report this to the Pennsylvania State Police at the first telephone I reach!
Zeke. We ain't stoppin' ye, mister.
35 Eben. Fog is liftin', Zeke. Better be done with this, I say.
36 Zeke (*nods, sadly*). Aye. Ye can go now, mister...and thanks. (*Continues*) We never meant a mite o' harm, I can tell ye. If we killed, it was no wish of ours.
37 Eben. What's done is done. Aye.
Zeke. Ye can go now, stranger....

[Eben *hands* Zeke *the* Doctor's *bag.* Zeke *hands it gently to the* Doctor.]

7. **irrigation:** here, flushing out a wound with water or other fluid.

DRAMA

Doctor. Very well. You haven't heard the last of this, though!
Zeke. That's the truth, mister. We've killed, aye; and we've been hurt for it....
38 **Eben.** Hurt bad.

[*The* Doctor's *face is puckered with doubt and strange apprehension.*]

39 **Zeke.** We're not alone, mister. We ain't the only ones. (*Sighs*) Ye can go now, doctor...and our thanks to ye....

40 [*The* Doctor *leaves the other two, still gazing at them in strange enchantment and wonder and a touch of indignation.*]

41 **Eben's voice.** Thanks mister....
Zeke's voice. In the name o'mercy...We thank you....
Eben. In the name o' mercy.
Zeke. Thanks, mister....
Eben. In the name o' kindness....

[*The two men stand with their wounded comrade at their feet—like a group statue in the park. The fog thickens across the scene. Far off the long, sad wail of a locomotive whimpers in the dark.*
42 *The scene now shifts to a young* Attendant *standing in front of a gasoline pump taking a reading and recording it in a book as he prepares to close up. He turns as he hears the car approach on the gravel drive.*
The Doctor *enters.*]

Attendant (*pleasantly*). Good evening, sir. (*Nods off at car*) Care to pull 'er up to this pump, sir? Closing up.
43 **Doctor** (*impatiently*). No. Where's your telephone, please? I've just been held up!
Attendant. Pay station inside, sir....
Doctor. Thank you! (*The* Doctor *starts to go past the* Attendant.)
Attendant. Excuse me, sir....
Doctor (*stops*). Eh, what is it, what is it?
44 **Attendant.** Uh...what sort of looking fellows were they?
Doctor. Oh—two big fellows with a rifle; faces and heads bandaged and smeared with dirt and blood. Friend of theirs with a gaping hole in his chest. I'm a doctor, so they forced me to

What does he mean?

I guess the doctor got away.

38 Comments about retribution for killing add to mystery.

39 Analyzing
What do Zeke's comments about not being the "only ones" suggest? Perhaps trying to excuse actions somewhat.

40 Perhaps he wonders why they allowed him to go free, knowing that he intends to go to the police.

41 Characterization. Here, Zeke and Eben appear truly thankful and nonviolent.

42 Setting. Shift in scene also changes **mood**; new character is introduced.

43 Voice inflection ("impatiently") indicates Doctor's anger.

44 Drawing Conclusions
What does attendant's hesitation in asking question indicate? That he already suspects what answer will be.

MEETING INDIVIDUAL NEEDS
Kinesthetic Learners • To familiarize students with the basic parts of a theater, you might want to have them make three-dimensional models of a typical theater.

Students could use shoe boxes or packing boxes and cut out, label, and glue tagboard or plastic foam parts in place to represent the areas of a theater. You could give them a list to locate and label on their models, including these parts of a theater: auditorium and front of house; gallery, box, and/or balcony seats; orchestra pit; stage; apron stage and proscenium; and wings areas.

45
Attendant's suspicions are confirmed by Doctor's description of men.

46
Doctor's exclamation shows surprise that the men are known but have not been apprehended.

47
Attendant seems to offer even further confirmation of his suspicions.

Close Reading OF A PLAY

The attendant must know who those men are. He doesn't seem surprised.

attend him. Why?
45 **Attendant.** *Those* fellers, huh?
46 **Doctor.** Then you know about them!
Attendant. I guess so.
Doctor. They're armed and they're desperate!
47 **Attendant.** That was about two or three miles back, would you say?
Doctor (*fumbling in pocket*). Just about—I don't seem to have the change. I wonder if you'd spare me change for a quarter…?

PORTFOLIO ASSESSMENT
Students may be interested in presenting dramatic readings of parts of some of the plays in this unit. Suggest that small groups who present the readings use appropriate expression and emotion. Provide lecterns or music stands on which to rest the scripts so that students' arms are free for gesturing. Require students to write a short paragraph of self-assessment in which they describe what they learned from their participation in the readings. (See *Portfolio Assessment and Professional Support Materials*.)

CLOSURE
Review with students the **Guidelines for Reading a Play.** Ask them to name the setting, stage direction, clues to the outcome of the play, and the mood of *In the Fog*.

Attendant (*makes change from metal coin canister at his belt*). Certainly, sir....
Doctor. What town was that back there, now?
Attendant (*dumps coins in other's hand*). There you are, sir.
Doctor (*impatient*). Yes, thank you. I say—what town was that back there, so I can tell the police?
48 **Attendant.** That was...Gettysburg, mister....
Doctor. Gettysburg...?
Attendant. Gettysburg and Gettysburg battlefield.... (*Looks off*)
49 When it's light and the fog's gone, you can see the gravestones. Meade's men...Pickett's men, Robert E. Lee's.[8]...

50 [*The* Doctor *is looking off with the* Attendant; *now he turns his head slowly to stare at the other man.*]

51 **Attendant** (*continues*). On nights like this—well—you're not the first those men've stopped...or the last. (*Nods off*) Fill 'er up, mister?
52 **Doctor.** Yes, fill 'er up....

8. **Meade's men...Lee's:** The Battle of Gettysburg was a turning point in the Civil War. On July 1–3, 1863, the Confederacy's forces, under Robert E. Lee, met the Union forces, under George Gordon Meade. The climax of the battle came when 15,000 Confederate soldiers, led by George Pickett, charged Cemetery Ridge and were repelled. The North suffered about 23,000 casualties; the South about 20,000.

> I get it. Those men must have been soldiers in the Civil War. They're still haunting the place where they fought and died.

48
Inference. *Gettysburg* provides the clue the Doctor needs to begin to understand what has happened.

49
Mention of gravestones is further indication of what has happened.

50
Plot. Doctor's realization that he has seen ghosts from the Civil War is the play's **climax.**

51
Attendant is very familiar with tales of incidents such as the one described by the Doctor.

52
Plot. Doctor's reply marks **resolution** of play; indicates he has accepted incident as supernatural event.

Looking at Yourself as a Reader

Were all your questions answered in the last scene of the play or did you still have questions about the three strangers? Do you now understand the significance of the signpost and the place names that appear early in the play?

If you took your own notes as you were reading, compare your responses with those in the margins alongside the selection. Do you have any points of agreement with these printed responses? Do you disagree with any of them?

Imagine a sequel to this play or another drama based on a similar idea. Meet with several classmates to try out ideas and plan a script.

LOOKING AT YOURSELF AS A READER
Remind students that any reasonable answer that they can justify will be right when they respond personally to the literature. The unique experiences that each student brings to the reading will help to shape his or her responses.

Close Reading of a Play

OBJECTIVES
The overall aim is for students to demonstrate an understanding of **conflict** as a battle of wits rather than a battle of physical elements. For a complete list of objectives, see the **Teacher's Notes**.

VOCABULARY
The underlined words are in the Glossary. The **Language and Vocabulary** exercise on p. 334 will introduce students to one characteristic of cockney dialect.

FOCUS / MOTIVATION
Ask students who have read stories or seen movies about Sherlock Holmes to describe him and his associate, Dr. Watson. How does each look? dress? move? speak? What images do names and occupations of other characters suggest?

TEACHING RESOURCES C
Teacher's Notes, p. 3
Reading Check, p. 6
Study Guide, p. 7
Language Skills, p. 11
Building Vocabulary, p. 14
Selection Test, p. 15

PREREADING FOCUS
The headnote emphasizes **conflict** as a plot element. Students might discuss the ways an intellectual conflict might be more suitable for a stage production than physical contact.

The Mazarin Stone

1
Attendant here is one who accompanies as companion or, in this case, servant.

2
Address has become famous as Holmes's.

3 Making Inferences
What does the presence of the dummy representing Holmes imply? That it will be used in trick to help catch a criminal.

4
Parasol suggests a woman's presence.

5
Characterization. Holmes, often preoccupied with solving crimes, needs help with personal affairs; can afford both page boy and housekeeper.

The Mazarin Stone

MICHAEL AND MOLLY HARDWICK

Adapted from a story by Sir Arthur Conan Doyle

Conflict, as you have seen, is not always physical. The conflict in this play is a battle of wits between Sherlock Holmes and the criminals who have stolen the great yellow Mazarin Stone. As you read, observe how Holmes uses his intelligence to outwit his opponents.

Characters

Sherlock Holmes
Dr. Watson, Holmes's friend and associate
1 Billy, Holmes's attendant
Count Negretto Sylvius, a big-game hunter and adventurer
Sam Merton, a boxer
Lord Cantlemere, a nobleman of high standing and political influence
Police Sergeant
Constables[1]

The play takes place in London around the beginning of the twentieth century.

2 Setting: *The parlor of 221B Baker Street. For this play, whose entire action takes place here, a curtain at the back of the stage must be capable of being drawn aside to reveal an* alcove, *backed by a window with blinds drawn. Seated beside this window, in pro-*
3 *file to it and to the audience, is a dummy representing Sherlock Holmes. It is wearing an old dressing gown, and sits in a large, high-backed chair. If the window blind were not down, it would appear to occupants of the houses opposite that Holmes himself is seated there. When the play begins, the chair and its occupant are concealed from the audience by the alcove curtain.*

Two doorways are necessary: one for characters arriving and departing—"parlor door"—and one leading off into Holmes's bedroom—"bedroom door." As the course of the action will reveal, an offstage route is necessary between the "bedroom" and the alcove.

4 *The lamp is lit. A* parasol *stands against a chair.*
5 *Billy, the page boy, is holding up* Holmes's ulster,[2] *brushing it vigorously.*

There is a tap at the parlor door. It opens, and Watson's head peers round.

Billy. Dr. Watson, sir! Come in, sir!

[*Watson enters, closing the door.*]

---

1. **Constables** (kŏn′stə-bəlz): in England, policemen.

2. **ulster:** a long, loose overcoat made of heavy material, usually worn with a belt.

318 DRAMA

MOTIVATIONAL SUMMARY

A devious criminal has stolen one of the Crown jewels, a diamond called the Mazarin Stone. After brilliant detective work, Sherlock Holmes has identified the thief. However, the thief has learned of Holmes's inquiries, and he visits Holmes's house, intending to murder the great detective. Undaunted, Holmes sees the thief's presence as his opportunity to trick the criminal mastermind into revealing the whereabouts of the stolen diamond.

PRESENTATION

Sherlock Holmes is a private detective renowned for his ability to solve cases by using his powers of deduction. Students who have never read a Sherlock Holmes story might be told of Holmes's extreme dedication to fighting criminals, solving

---

6 **Watson.** Well, Billy, my boy! Keeping the moths at bay?
Billy. That's it, sir.

7 [*He folds the coat and puts it down on a chair, as Watson lays aside his hat and stick. Watson glances round the room.*]

8 **Watson.** It doesn't seem to have changed much, Billy.
Billy. Not much, sir.
Watson. You don't change, either. I hope the **9** same can be said of *him*?
Billy. I think he's in bed and asleep.
10 **Watson** (*laughs*). At seven o'clock of a lovely summer's evening. He *hasn't* changed, then! I suppose it means a case?
Billy. Yes, sir. He's very hard at it just now. Fair frightens me.
Watson. What does?
Billy. His health, Dr. Watson. He gets paler, and thinner, and he never eats nothing. I heard Mrs. Hudson asking him when he would take his dinner. "Seven thirty," he told her—
11 "the day after tomorrow!"
Watson (*sighs*). Yes, Billy, I know how it is.
Billy (*confidentially*). I can tell you one thing, sir—he's following somebody.

[*Watson, amused, copies Billy's manner and leans towards him conspiratorially.*]

Watson. Really?
12 **Billy.** One disguise after another. Yesterday he was a workman, looking for a job. Today he was an old woman. Fairly took me in, he did—and I ought to know his ways by now. (*He picks up the parasol briefly.*) Part of the old girl's outfit.
Watson (*laughs*). What's it all about, Billy?
Billy (*glancing round cautiously*). I don't mind telling you, sir—but it shouldn't go no farther.... (*Watson gives his head a meaningful shake and places a finger to his lips.*) It's this case of the Crown diamond.³
Watson. What—the hundred-thousand-pound burglary?
Billy. Yes, sir. They must get it back. Why, we've had the Prime Minister and Home Secretary⁴ both sat in this very room!
Watson. You don't say!
Billy. Mr. Holmes was very nice to them. Promised he would do all he could. Then there's Lord Cantlemere.
Watson (*dismally*). Oh!
Billy. Ah, you know what that means, Dr. Wat-
13 son! He's a stiff 'un, and no mistake. Now, I can get along with the Prime Minister—and I've nothing against the Home Secretary.... But I can't *stand* His Lordship! (*Watson laughs*
14 *heartily.*) Mr. Holmes can't, neither, sir! You can tell, Lord Cantlemere don't believe in Mr. Holmes. He was against employing him, and he'd rather he failed.
Watson. And Mr. Holmes knows it?
Billy. Mr. Holmes *always* knows what there is to know.
Watson (*hastily*). Oh, quite, quite! Well, Billy, we'll just hope that he won't fail, and then
15 Lord Cantlemere will be confounded. But I'd better be getting home to my wife. (*He moves towards his hat and stick, but catches sight of the curtain.*) I say, Billy! Bit early to have the curtains drawn and the lamp lit, isn't it?
Billy. Well—there's something funny behind there.
Watson. Something *funny*?
Billy. You can see it, sir. (*Billy draws the curtain, revealing the dummy.*)
Watson. Bless my soul!
Billy. Yes, sir.

---

3. **Crown diamond:** a diamond belonging to the monarchy.
4. **Home Secretary:** a British Cabinet minister in charge of keeping internal law and order, with authority over the London police.

6
Comment refers to brushing Holmes's wool coat.

7
Watson, an older gentleman, carries a cane for fashion rather than from need.

8
Although Watson has assisted with many cases, he evidently has not been around lately.

9 Analyzing
To whom does "him" refer here? Holmes.

10
Inference. Holmes has irregular sleeping pattern when involved in a case.

11
Shows deep involvement in case and reason for Billy's concern.

12
Foreshadowing. Holmes is a master of disguise.

13
"Stiff 'un": Someone difficult to deal with; unpleasant.

14
Characterization. Use of double negative "can't, neither" implies little formal education.

15
Confounded means "proved wrong."

The Mazarin Stone

difficult cases, and using his amazing intellect and unusual disguises and tricks to catch criminals.

Ask students to keep their own visual images of characters and stage setting and time period firmly in mind so that the play becomes a mental movie as it is read.

Assign roles to skillful readers for a carefully prepared readers' theater rendition of *The Mazarin Stone*. Break the presentation into two parts, the first ending just before Holmes says, "Don't break it, Count Sylvius" (p. 324). At this point, encourage questions about the first part of the play and conjectures about the ways in which Holmes will outwit the Count. After the final reading, check the accuracy of the earlier conjectures.

16
Holmes has gone to great lengths to set trap or play trick.

17
Suspense. Suggests that someone is watching Holmes's window.

18
Watson has spent a good deal of time at 221B Baker Street.

19 Summarizing
What seems to be Holmes's attitude toward danger? Nonchalance towards danger or, perhaps, genuine acceptance of the possibility.

20
Holmes's behavior is extreme, yet many people avoid eating full meals before anything requiring deep thought.

21
Holmes always displays humor in times of stress, often parodying sentimental behavior. In reality, he takes very dim view of Scotland Yard.

22
Characterization. Watson dying to be included in case but shy about taking initiative with Holmes.

23
Holmes often teases Watson with a straight face.

24
Holmes hopes that Sylvius will lead him to the diamond.

---

16 Watson (*examining the figure*). A perfect replica of Sherlock Holmes! Dressing gown and all!

[*Billy turns the chair so that the dummy chances to finish up with its back to the parlor door.*]

Billy. We put it at different angles every now and then, like this, so's it'll look more lifelike.
17 Mind, I wouldn't dare touch it if the blind wasn't drawn. When it's up you can see this from right across the way.
Watson. We used something of the sort once before, you know.
Billy. Before my time, sir.
Watson. Er—yes.

[*Unseen by either of them the bedroom door opens and* Holmes *appears in his dressing gown.*]

Billy. There's folk who watch us from over yonder, sir. You may catch a peep of them now. (*He is about to pull back a corner of the blind to enable* Watson *to look out.*)
Holmes (*sharply*). That will do, Billy!

[*Billy and* Watson *spin round.*]

Watson. Holmes!
Holmes (*severely*). You were in danger of your life, then, my boy. I can't do without you just yet.
Billy. (*humbly*). Yes, sir.
Holmes. That will be all for now.
Billy. Very good, sir. (*He exits by the parlor door.*)
Holmes. That boy is a problem, Watson. How far am I justified in letting him be in danger?
Watson. Danger of what, Holmes?
Holmes. Of sudden death.
Watson. Holmes!
Holmes. But it's good to see you in your old
18 quarters once again, my dear Watson!
Watson (*concerned*). Holmes—this talk of sudden death. What are you expecting?

19 Holmes (*simply*). To be murdered.
Watson. Oh, come now! You're joking!
Holmes. Even my limited sense of humor could evolve a better joke than that, Watson. (*Brightening*) But we may be comfortable in the meantime, mayn't we? Let me see you once more in the customary chair.
Watson. Pleasure, Holmes! But why not eat?
20 Holmes. Because the faculties[5] become refined when you starve them. Surely, as a doctor, you must admit that what your digestion gains in the way of blood supply is so much lost to the brain? *I* am a brain, Watson. The rest of me is mere appendix. Therefore, it's the brain I must consider.
Watson. But—this danger . . . ?
Holmes. Ah, yes. Just in case it should come off, it would be as well for you to know the
21 name of the murderer. You can give it to Scotland Yard, with my love and a parting blessing.
Watson. Holmes!
Holmes. His name is Sylvius—Count Negretto Sylvius, No. 136 Moorside Gardens, London N.W. Got it?
22 Watson. Yes. (*Hesitantly*) Er—Holmes . . . I've got nothing to do for a day or two. Count me in.
23 Holmes (*sadly shaking his head*). Your morals don't improve, Watson.
Watson. My *morals*?
Holmes. You've added fibbing to your other vices. You bear every sign of the busy medical man, with calls on him every hour.
Watson. Not such important ones. But—can't you have this fellow arrested?
Holmes. Yes, Watson, I could. That's what worries him so.
Watson. Then why don't you?
24 Holmes. Because I don't know where the diamond is.

---

5. **faculties** (făk′əl-tēz): natural abilities.

SOCIAL STUDIES LINK
Students may not understand what the loss of a jewel like the Mazarin Stone might represent, since a wealthy monarch would not feel the loss of one stone. To relate the disappearance of the jewel to a similar loss they might understand, you could ask students if anyone has visited the White House, a presidential library, a state house, or a museum such as the Smithsonian. What items of historical value were on view? Were there donations from citizens and gifts from other countries? Could the items be replaced or were they often one of a kind? Explain that a jewel lost from the crown jewels might represent to the British people a historical loss, as well as a financial one.

Scenes on pages 321, 323, 330, and 332 are from early films based on Sherlock Holmes stories. Basil Rathbone (*shown at right*) played Sherlock Holmes; Nigel Bruce played Dr. Watson.

VISUAL CONNECTIONS
Ideas for Writing
Pictured here are the famous Sherlock Holmes and the devoted Dr. Watson, portrayed, as they were in many films, by Basil Rathbone (on the right) and Nigel Bruce. After reading the play, students might write character sketches of one or both of the fictional heroes.

Watson. Ah! Billy was telling me—the missing Crown jewel!

25 **Holmes.** The great yellow Mazarin Stone. I've cast my net and I have my fish. But I have *not* got the stone. Yes, I could make the world a better place by laying *them* by the heels; but it's the stone I want.

Watson. And is Count Sylvius one of your fish?

26 **Holmes.** Yes—and he's a *shark*. He bites. The other is Sam Merton, the boxer. Not a bad fellow, Sam, but the Count has used him. Sam's just a great, big, silly, bull-headed gudgeon;[6] but he's flopping about in my net, all the same.

Watson. Where is Count Sylvius now?

27 **Holmes.** I've been at his elbow all morning.

28
29 (*He gets up.*) You've seen me as an old lady, Watson?

6. **gudgeon** (gŭj′ən): a small fish that is easily caught and used for bait; here, a person who is easily tricked or used.

25
Conflict. Reveals that he has caught the thieves, but it is the stone that he wants.

26 Analyzing
What does Holmes imply about Sylvius by calling him a "shark"? That he is very dangerous, ruthless.

27
Metaphor. Merton presented as less dangerous character than Sylvius, yet indications are that he, too, will pay for crime.

28
"At his elbow": close to him.

29
Use to answer **study question 1**, p. 332.

The Mazarin Stone

Watson (*chuckling*). Oh, yes indeed!

[Holmes *assumes the posture and walk of an old lady.*]

Holmes (*in a cracked old voice*). I was never more convincing, Doctor. Never! (Watson *laughs as* Holmes *straightens up. Normal voice*) He actually picked up my parasol for me once. (Holmes *picks up the parasol and gesticulates with it.*)

Watson. He didn't!

[Holmes *makes an elaborate bow, holding out the parasol in both hands.*]

Holmes (*mimicking* Sylvius). By your leave, madam. (Holmes *resumes his normal voice and manner and lays the parasol aside.*) He's half Italian, you know. Full of the Southern[7] graces when he's in the mood. But he's a devil incarnate[8] in the other mood. Life is full of whimsical happenings, Watson.

Watson (*with a snort*). Whimsical! It might have been tragedy!

Holmes. Well, perhaps it might. Anyway, I followed him to old Straubenzee's workshop in the Minories.[9] Straubenzee made the air gun—a very pretty bit of work, as I understand. I fancy it's in the opposite window at present, ready to put a bullet through this dummy's beautiful head whenever I choose to raise that blind.

[*Knock at parlor door, which opens.* Billy *enters, carrying a salver.*[10]]

Billy. Mr. Holmes, sir . . .

---

7. **Southern:** The reference is to southern Europe. The Count is from Italy.
8. **devil incarnate** (ĭn-kär′nĭt): a devil in human form.
9. **Minories:** a street in London, once famous for its gun makers.
10. **salver:** a small tray.

Holmes. What is it, Billy?

Billy. There's a gentleman to see you, sir.

[Holmes *takes the visiting card from the salver and looks at it.*]

Holmes. Thank you. (*He replaces the card.*) The man himself, Watson!

Watson. Sylvius!

Holmes (*nods*). I'd hardly expected this. Grasp the nettle,[11] eh! A man of nerve, Watson. But possibly you've heard of his reputation as a big-game shooter? It'd be a triumphant ending to his excellent sporting record if he added me to his bag.

Watson. Send for the police, Holmes!

Holmes. I probably shall—but not just yet. Would you just glance carefully out of the window and see if anyone is hanging about in the street?

Watson. Certainly. (*He goes to the window and peeps cautiously round the corner of the blind.*) Yes—there's a rough-looking fellow near the door.

Holmes. That will be Sam Merton—the faithful but rather fatuous[12] Sam. Billy, where is Count Sylvius?

Billy. In the waiting room, sir.

Holmes. Show him up when I ring.

Billy. Yes, sir.

Holmes. If I'm not in the room, show him in all the same.

Billy. Very good, Mr. Holmes. (*He leaves by the parlor door.*)

Watson. Look here, Holmes, this is simply ridiculous. This is a desperate man who sticks at nothing, you'd have me believe. He may have come to murder you.

---

11. **Grasp the nettle:** a proverbial expression meaning "Act boldly to gain an advantage over someone." A nettle is a plant with delicate thorns. If the plant is touched gently, the thorns sting. If it is grasped firmly, they feel soft.
12. **fatuous** (făch′ōō-əs): foolish.

Meeting Individual Needs

Visual Learners • If you have students read parts for a reader's-theater presentation of this Holmes mystery, you might want to have another group of students make a list of the characters in the play to display for the class as the students read. They could emphasize the melodramatic elements of the play with decorative lettering and scrollwork appropriate for a period mystery. Or students might make placards to display in front of the readers as they present the mystery.

TRANSPARENCIES 24 & 25

Fine Art
Theme: *Literature Out Loud* – features artwork that shows how interpretation is essential to the meaning of a dramatic performance.

Holmes. I shouldn't be surprised.
Watson. Then I insist on staying with you!
Holmes. You'd be horribly in the way.
37 **Watson.** In *his* way!
38 **Holmes.** No, my dear fellow—in mine.

[Watson *sits down stubbornly*.]

Watson. Be that as it may, I can't possibly leave you.

39 **Holmes.** Yes you can, Watson. And you will—for you've never failed to play the game. I'm sure you'll play it to the end. (*He crosses to his desk and begins to scribble a note.*) This man has come for his own purpose, but he may stay for mine. I want you to take a cab to Scotland Yard and give this note to Youghal, of the C.I.D.[13] Come back with the police.

13. **C.I.D.:** Criminal Investigation Department, a division of the London Police.

37
Watson believes that his presence will keep Sylvius from killing Holmes.

38
Holmes is straightforward with Watson.

39
Plot. "The game" is Holmes's plan; Watson has faithfully helped with Holmes's plans in past. The plan continues to unfold as Holmes sends Watson for police.

VISUAL CONNECTIONS
Exploring the Subject
In this characteristic pose, Holmes is in deep thought and smoking a pipe, while Watson shows his concern for Holmes and his anticipation of the plan Holmes will devise.

323

READING SKILLS PRACTICE
The underlined passage can be used to give students practice in the reading skill of drawing logical conclusions. Ask students to read the passage and choose the answer that can be best concluded from the selection. **A.** Holmes has been tracking Sylvius with dogs. ("Creatures" is used figuratively.) **B.** Sylvius has decided to retaliate by tracking Holmes with dogs. (Contradicted in the passage.) **C.** Sylvius believes Holmes has hired people to follow him. (Correct.) **D.** Sylvius is annoyed with Holmes, but still wishes to join his game. (Contradicted in the passage; "game" is used figuratively.)

40
Plot. Holmes intends to observe Sylvius without Sylvius' knowledge; behavior might offer clues about intentions.

41
Characterization. Holmes fond of joking at tense moment. Funny contrast between exalted language ("noble head") and slang term ("forty winks").

42 Summarizing
What do we know about Holmes's plan? Only that he plans to trick Sylvius into revealing location of diamond and that he has sent Watson for police.

43
This action would eliminate any doubts about Sylvius' intentions; yet Holmes remains calm.

44
Conflict. Moment of tension as adversaries confront each other.

45
"Sit on it": keep it.

46 Analyzing
Whom does Sylvius mean when he refers to Holmes's "creatures"? Spies; in reality Holmes disguised as workman and old woman.

47
Holmes says Sylvius is wrong; means that it was not "his creatures," but Holmes himself.

324

Watson (*rising*). I'll do that with joy!
Holmes (*handing* Watson *the note*). Before you get back I may just have time to find out where the stone is. Now, I'll just ring for Billy to show him up, and I think we'll go out through the bedroom. (Holmes *presses a bell, while* Watson *gathers his things.* Holmes *ushers him towards the bedroom door.*) This second exit is exceedingly
40 useful, you know. I rather want to see my shark without his seeing me.

[Watson *halts.*]

Watson. The dummy! Shouldn't the curtain be drawn over it again?
Holmes. No, no. We'll leave it as it is. (*He moves*
41 *swiftly to the dummy.*) Perhaps just a touch to this noble head . . . (*He adjusts the head to bow upon the breast*) as though somewhere in the middle of forty winks. (*He ensures that the dummy has its back to the parlor door.*) There! Now, come along.
Watson. I hope you know what you're doing, that's all!

[*They exit by the bedroom door, closing it behind them. A slight pause, then the parlor door opens.* Billy *enters and* Count Sylvius *walks in past him.*]

Billy. If you'll just wait, sir.

42 [Sylvius *ignores him.* Billy *withdraws, closing the door behind him.* Sylvius *looks round the room for a moment, then notices the dummy. He grips his stick more firmly and creeps a cautious pace or two towards it. Satisfied that the figure is dozing, he steps forward and raises his stick to strike.* Holmes *enters*
43 *silently from the bedroom.*]

Holmes. Don't break it, Count Sylvius!

[Sylvius *whirls round, his stick still upraised, a look of disbelief on his face.*]

324 DRAMA

Sylvius. What!
Holmes. It's a pretty little thing. (Sylvius *lowers the stick and walks round to look at the dummy in astonishment.*) Tavernier, the French modeler, made it. He's as good at waxworks as your friend Straubenzee is at air guns. (Holmes *turns the chair to face the window. The dummy is now completely hidden from the audience.*)
Sylvius. Air guns? What do you mean, sir?
Holmes. Put your stick on the side table, before you're tempted to do any other form of damage.

44 [*There is a momentary hesitation, in which we think* Sylvius *might spring at* Holmes. *But* Holmes *stands still, looking at him hard, one hand in his pocket, in which we sense him to have a revolver.* Sylvius *relaxes and obeys.*]

Sylvius. Very well.
Holmes. Thank you. Would you care to put your revolver out, also? (*At the mention of "revolver"* Sylvius' *hand flies to his hip pocket. He does not draw, but stands poised defiantly. Blandly*) Oh,
45 very well, if you prefer to sit on it. (Holmes *moves to a chair and sits.*) Your visit is really most opportune, Count Sylvius. I wanted badly to have a few minutes' chat with you.

[Sylvius *stumps over to a chair opposite* Holmes.]

▶ **Sylvius.** I, too, wished to have some words with you, Holmes! That is why I am here. Because you have gone out of your way to annoy
46 me. Because you have put your creatures on my track!
47 **Holmes.** Oh, I assure you no!
Sylvius. I have had them followed! Two can play at that game, Holmes! ◀
Holmes. It's a small point, Count Sylvius, but perhaps you would kindly give me my prefix[14]

14. **prefix:** here, a title, such as *Dr., Mr.,* or *Mrs.,* before a person's name.

▶ Reading Skills Objective: Drawing Logical Conclusions

MEETING INDIVIDUAL NEEDS
Visual Learners • To generate student interest in the era in which Doyle wrote his famous detective stories and in the historical setting for this drama, you might suggest that students find an illustrated copy of the Holmes stories in a modern edition with the original Sidney Paget drawings, reprinted from the *Strand Magazine*. Have them analyze the drawings so that they can report to the class on the costumes and hairstyles, poses or stances and activities of the characters, architectural features, furniture and decorative items, modes of transportation, and anything else that could lend authenticity to a performance of the play.

---

when you address me? You can understand that, with my routine of work, I should find myself on familiar terms with half the rogues' 48 gallery,[15] and you'll agree that exceptions are invidious.[16]

Sylvius (*sneering*). Well, *Mr.* Holmes, then.
Holmes. That's better. But I assure you that you're mistaken about my alleged agents.
49 **Sylvius** (*laughs contemptuously*). Other people can observe as well as you! Yesterday there was an old sporting man. Today it was an elderly woman. They kept me in view all day.
50 **Holmes.** Really, sir, you compliment me! Old Baron Dowson said the night before he was hanged that in my case what the law had gained the stage had lost.
Sylvius. It . . . It was you?
Holmes. You can see in the corner the parasol which you so politely handed to me in the Minories before you began to suspect.
Sylvius. If I had known that, you might never have . . .
Holmes. . . . have seen this humble abode again? I was well aware of that. But, as it happens, you did *not* know, so here we are!
Sylvius. So it was not your agents, but your play-acting, busybodying self! You admit that you dogged me. Why?
51 **Holmes.** Come now, Count: you used to shoot lions in Algeria.
Sylvius. What about it?
Holmes. Why did you?
Sylvius. The sport—the excitement—the danger.
52 **Holmes.** And, no doubt, to free the country from a pest?
Sylvius. Exactly.
Holmes. My reasons in a nutshell!

15. **rogues' gallery:** photographs of criminals kept in police files for purposes of identification.
16. **invidious** (ĭn-vĭd′ē-əs): unfair; offensive. Holmes isn't on familiar terms with criminals and says (jokingly) that it wouldn't be fair to make an exception in the Count's case.

[*Sylvius springs to his feet in fury and reaches in-* 53 *stinctively towards his revolver pocket.*]

Sylvius. For that, I will . . . !
Holmes. Sit down, sir, sit down! (*He gives Sylvius a steely stare. Sylvius hesitates for a moment, then obeys.*) I had another, more practical reason for following your movements. I want that yellow diamond.

[*Sylvius begins to relax and chuckle. He stretches his legs and makes himself comfortable.*]

Sylvius. Upon my word—*Mr.* Holmes!
Holmes. You know that I was after you for that. The real reason why you're here tonight is to find out how much I know and how far my removal is absolutely essential. Well, I should say that from *your* point of view it *is* absolutely essential. You see, I know all about the diamond—save only one thing, which you are about to tell me.
Sylvius. Indeed? Pray, what is this missing fact?
Holmes. Where the Crown diamond now is.
Sylvius. And how should I be able to tell you that?
Holmes. You can, and you will.
Sylvius. You astonish me!
Holmes. You can't bluff me, Count Sylvius. You are absolute plate glass. I can see to the 54 very back of your mind.
Sylvius. Oh! Then, of course, you can see where the diamond is.
55 **Holmes** (*delighted*). Then you *do* know!
Sylvius. No!
Holmes. You've admitted it.
Sylvius. I admit nothing!

[*Holmes gets up and goes to a drawer, which he opens.*]

The Mazarin Stone   **325**

48
Holmes plays a kind of psychological game with Sylvius, letting him know that *he* knows Sylvius.

49
Irony. Sylvius' "proof" of his sharp-wittedness proves the opposite.

50
Characterization. Holmes's contradictions often delivered indirectly, as elegant allusions that require deduction to be understood. Often contain sly references to fate of other opponents.

51
Holmes compares reasons for play-acting and following Sylvius to reasons that Sylvius enjoyed big-game hunting.

52
Holmes loves to trick opponent into insulting himself.

53
Holmes has infuriated Sylvius, no doubt part of plan.

54
Use to answer **study question 2, p. 332.**

55 Summarizing
Is it important that Sylvius admitted that he knows where the diamond is? No; Holmes was already certain that Sylvius knew.

MEETING INDIVIDUAL NEEDS
ESL/LEP • The author uses several idiomatic expressions that may require explanation:
"... somewhere in the middle of **forty winks**." (a short sleep; nap) (p. 324)
"You are **absolute plate glass**." (absolutely transparent, i.e., I can see exactly what you are thinking.) (p. 325)
"... the other fellow has **all the trumps** ..." (every advantage) (p. 326)
"If I may put it **in a nutshell** ..." (in a few words) (p. 327)
"*Deuce take you,* Holmes!" (May the devil take you!) (p. 329)

56
Conflict. Battle of wits escalates as Holmes reveals evidence against Sylvius.

57
Holmes has prepared complete case against Sylvius; explains earlier claim that Holmes has caught his "fish."

58
Plot. Holmes has added false accusation to get Sylvius to admit indirectly to other crimes.

59
Holmes wants to play out his hand one step at a time, making sure he has Sylvius where he wants him.

60
Use to answer **study question 3,** p. 332.

61
Holmes appears to have airtight case against Sylvius, but knows thief will not give up stone if he is arrested.

62
Holmes is baiting his hook. Bait must be big for shark to take it.

63 Drawing Conclusions
Would Holmes give up the search for the stone? No. This is more bait.

326

Holmes. Now, Count, if you'll be reasonable we can do business.
Sylvius. And *you* talk about bluff!

[Holmes *takes a notebook from the drawer.*]

Holmes. Do you know what I keep in this book?
Sylvius. No, sir. I do not.
Holmes. I keep *you* in it.
Sylvius. Me?
56 **Holmes.** You are all here—every action of your vile and dangerous life.
Sylvius. There are limits to my patience, Holmes!
Holmes (*waving the book at* Sylvius). Yes, it's all here: the real facts about the death of old Mrs. Harold, who left you the Blymer estate to gamble away. (Holmes *taunts* Sylvius *with the book,* Sylvius *making a grab for it whenever it approaches, but always missing.*)
Sylvius. You're dreaming!
Holmes. And the complete life history of Miss
57 Minnie Warrender.
Sylvius. You'll make nothing of that!
Holmes. There's plenty more, Count: the robbery in the train-de-luxe to the Riviera[17] on February 13, 1892; the forged check in the same year on the Credit Lyonnais.[18]
Sylvius. No! There you *are* mistaken!
58 **Holmes.** Then I *am* right on the others! (*He throws the book into the drawer, which he closes, resuming his seat.*) Now, Count, you're a card player. You know that when the other fellow has all the trumps it saves time to throw in your hand.
Sylvius. Just what has all this talk to do with the jewel?
59 **Holmes.** Gently, Count! Restrain that eager mind! Let me get to the points in my own hum-

---
17. **Riviera** (rĭv′ē-âr′ə): a resort area along the Mediterranean Sea.
18. **Credit Lyonnais** (krĕ′dē lē′ō-nā′): a French bank.

326 DRAMA

---

drum fashion. (*Gesturing towards the closed drawer*) I have all that against you. But, above all, I have a clear case against you and your fighting bully in the theft of the Crown diamond.
Sylvius. Indeed?
Holmes (*enumerating the points on his fingers*). I
60 have the cabman who took you to Whitehall,[19] and the cabman who brought you away. I have the commissionaire[20] who saw you near the case. I have Ikey Sanders, who refused to cut the stone up for you. Ikey has talked, Count, and the game is up!
Sylvius. I don't believe you!
Holmes. That's the hand I play from. I put it all on the table. Only one card is missing. It's the King of Diamonds. I don't know where the
61 stone is. (*He presses the bell.*)
Sylvius. And you never will! Why are you ringing that bell? (*He gets to his feet suspiciously.*)
Holmes. Be reasonable, Count! Consider the situation. You are going to be locked up for twenty years. So is Sam Merton. What good are you going to get out of your diamond? None in
62 the world. But if you hand it over—well, I'm prepared to compound a felony.[21] We don't want you or Sam. We want the stone. Give that up, Count Sylvius, and so far as I'm concerned you can go free. But if you make another slip in the future . . . ! Well, it'll be the last.
Sylvius. And if I refuse?
63 **Holmes** (*sighs*). Then I'm afraid it must be you, and not the stone.

[*Knock at parlor door.* Billy *enters.*]

Billy. Did you ring, sir?

---
19. **Whitehall:** a London street where many government departments are located.
20. **commissionaire** (kə-mĭsh′ə-nâr′): in England, a doorman.
21. **compound a felony:** to add to a crime by not telling the police.

Holmes. Yes, Billy. You will see a large and ugly gentleman outside the front door. Ask him to come up.
Billy. Yes, sir. (*He is about to go, but hesitates.*) What if he won't, sir?
Holmes. Oh, no violence, Billy! Don't be rough with him! If you tell him that Count Sylvius wants him he will come.
64 Billy. Very good, sir. (*He exits with a grin, closing the door.*)
Holmes. I think it would be as well to have your friend Sam at this conference. After all, his interests should be represented.

[Sylvius *resumes his seat.*]

Sylvius. Just what do you intend to do now?
Holmes. I was remarking to my friend, Dr. Watson, a short while ago that I had a shark and a gudgeon in my net. Now I'm drawing in the net, and up they come together.
65 Sylvius. You won't die in your bed, Holmes!
Holmes. I've often had that same idea. But does it matter very much? After all, Count, your own exit is more likely to be perpendicular than horizontal. (*Sylvius' hand jerks towards his gun pocket. Holmes waves an admonishing finger.*) It's no use, my friend. Even if I gave you time to draw it, you know perfectly well you daren't use it. Nasty, noisy things, revolvers. Better stick to air guns. (*Knock at parlor door. Billy shows in Sam Merton coldly and withdraws without speaking. Merton glares about him, tensed for action.*) Good day, Mr. Merton. Rather dull in the street, isn't it?
Merton. What's up, Count?
Holmes. If I may put it in a nutshell, Mr. Merton, I should say the *game* was up.
66 Merton. 'Ere! Is this cove[22] trying to be funny? I'm not in the funny mood meself.

22. **cove:** slang for "fellow."

Holmes. I think I can promise you'll feel even less humorous as the evening advances.

[Merton *lumbers aggressively towards* Holmes, *but is halted by a gesture from* Sylvius.]

Sylvius. That will do, Sam!
Holmes. Thank you, Count. (*Holmes gets to his feet.*) Now, look here—I'm a busy man and I
67 can't waste time. I'm going into that bedroom to try over the *Hoffmann* "Barcarolle"[23] on my violin. You can explain to your friend how the matter lies, without the restraint of my presence. (*Holmes goes to the bedroom door.*) In five minutes I shall return for your final answer. You quite grasp the alternative, don't you? Shall we take you, or shall we have the stone?

[Holmes *exits, closing the bedroom door behind him.* Sylvius *jumps up and paces about thoughtfully.*]

Merton. 'Offmann who? What's the chap on
68 about?
Sylvius. Shut up, Sam! Let me think!

[*Sounds of violin strings being plucked and tuned in the bedroom.*]

69 Merton. If it's trouble, why didn't you plug 'im?
Sylvius. You're a fool, Sam! Anyone but you could have seen he was holding a revolver in his dressing-gown pocket.
Merton. Aw! (*The violin begins to play the "Barcarolle" from* The Tales of Hoffmann. *It is expertly played. Having established it, diminish somewhat*
70 *under following dialogue. Disgustedly*) Cor!
Sylvius. Ikey Sanders has split[24] on us.

23. **"Barcarolle"** (bär′kə-rōl′): a famous piece of music in *The Tales of Hoffmann*, an opera by Jacques Offenbach.
24. **split:** slang for "informed on one's partners."

64 Drawing Conclusions
Why does Billy grin as he closes the door? Has no intention of getting "rough" with big boxer Merton; catches Holmes's humor.

65
Conflict. Sylvius' statement is veiled threat of murder.

66
'Ere: here. Cockney dialect leaves off *h* sounds at beginning of words.

67
Plot. No doubt another part of Holmes's plan.

68
"On about": talking about.

69
Merton sees simple solution—"plugging" (killing) Holmes.

70
"Cor!": slang word emphasizes Merton's disgust at turn of events.

71
Merton means he'll kill Ikey even if he must hang for the crime.

72
Foreshadowing. Sylvius hears something but dismisses it as street noise; this will be important to later action.

73
Merton admits that if physical violence will not work, he is no help.

74
Use to answer **study question 5a,** p. 332.

75 Analyzing
How strong does Sylvius' counterplan seem to be? Sylvius' counterplan is not nearly as precise and well-developed as Holmes's plan.

76
Plot. This episode is the play's **climax.** "Street noise" was Holmes taking dummy's place.

77
Use to answer **study question 5b,** p. 333.

78
Holmes seems to take great pride in explaining to Sylvius (and audience) how he tricked him.

Merton. Split, 'as 'e? I'll do 'im a thick 'un for
71 that, if I swing for it!
Sylvius. How do you think that will help us? We've got to make up our minds what to do.
Merton. (*lowering his voice*). 'Arf a mo',[25] Count! That's a leary cove[26] in there. D'you suppose 'e's listening?
Sylvius. How can he listen and play that thing?
Merton. Aw, that's right!
Sylvius. Now *you* listen! He can lag[27] us over this stone, but he's offered to let us slip if we only tell him where it is.
Merton. Wot! Give up a 'undred thousand quid![28]
Sylvius. It's one or the other. He knows too much.
Merton. Well . . . listen! 'E's alone in there. Let's do 'im! Then we've nothing to fear of.
Sylvius. He's armed and ready. If we shot him we could hardly get away in a place like this. Besides, it's likely enough the police know he's on to something. Listen! (*They listen. The violin*
72 *plays steadily on.*) It was just a noise in the street, I think.
Merton. Look, guv'nor—you've got the brains.
73 If slugging's no use, then it's up to you.
Sylvius. I've fooled better men than Holmes. The stone's here, in my secret pocket. I take no
74 chances leaving it about. It can be out of England tonight and cut into four pieces in Amsterdam before Sunday. One of us must slip round to Lime Street with the stone and tell Van Seddar to get off by the next boat.
Merton. But the false bottom ain't ready yet. Van Seddar don't expect to go till next week!
75 **Sylvius.** He must go now, and chance it. As to Holmes, we can fool him. We'll promise him

---

25. **'Arf a mo':** Merton's pronunciation of "Half a mo'," an expression meaning "Wait a moment."
26. **leary cove:** slang for "clever fellow."
27. **lag:** slang for "arrest."
28. **quid** (kwĭd): slang for "pound" (or "pounds"), the basic unit of British money.

---

the stone, then put him on the wrong track; and by the time he finds out we'll be in Holland, too.
Merton. Now you're talking, Count!
Sylvius. You go now and see the Dutchman, Sam. Here . . . (Sylvius *pulls* Sam *aside.*) Just in case, come out of line with that keyhole.

76 [Sylvius *reaches into his secret pocket and produces a large yellow gem. The "dummy" in the chair near the window begins to move cautiously, and we see that during the preceding dialogue* Holmes *has contrived to seat himself in its place. Unobserved by* Sylvius *or* Merton *he sidles towards them. He has a revolver in his hand.*]

Merton. I don't know 'ow you dare carry it about!
Sylvius. Where could I keep it safer? If we could take it out of Whitehall, someone else could easily take it from my lodgings.

[Holmes *sneaks quickly forward and plucks the stone from* Sylvius' *hand.*]

77 **Holmes.** Or out of your hand! (Sylvius *and* Merton *are too flabbergasted to react. They stare speechlessly at* Holmes, *and then at the chair.*) Thank you, Count. It will be safe with me.
Merton. There was a blooming waxworks in that chair!

[*He jerks the chair round; it is empty.* Holmes *moves carefully back to a position from where he can cover them both.*]

Holmes. Your surprise is very natural, Mr. Merton. You are not aware, of course, that a second door from my bedroom leads behind
78 that curtain. I fancied you must have heard me, Count, as I slipped into the dummy's chair, but luck and a passing cab were on my side. They enabled me to listen to your racy

conversation, which would have been painfully constrained had you been aware of my presence.

[Sylvius *lurches towards* Holmes, *who raises the revolver slightly.*]

79 **Sylvius.** Deuce take you, Holmes!
Holmes. No violence, gentlemen! Consider the furniture! (*They stand still.*) It must be very clear to you that the position is an impossible one. The police are waiting below.
Merton. Guv'nor? Shall I . . . ?
Sylvius (*resignedly*). No, Sam. I give you best, Holmes. I believe you are the devil himself.
Holmes. Not *far* from him, at any rate.

[Merton *suddenly points to the bedroom door.*]

80 **Merton.** 'Ere! That blooming fiddle! It's playing itself!
Holmes. Oh, let it play. These modern gramophones[29] are a remarkable invention!
Merton. Aw!

81 [*Men's voices approaching the parlor door. It opens suddenly.* Watson *hastens in.*]

Watson. This way, officers!

[*A Police Sergeant and two Constables hurry after him and seize* Sylvius *and* Merton.]

Sergeant. Come on, Sam! We've been waiting to get hold of you!
Merton. Gar!
82 **Sylvius.** Take your hands off me, my man!
Constable. Not blooming likely![30]

[*They are led away, struggling. At the door,* Merton *stops, looks back into the room, then at* Holmes.]

29. **gramophones:** phonographs.
30. **Not blooming likely:** slang for "not very likely."

Merton. Waxworks! Grammerphones! Garrr! (*He is led off as* Billy *enters.*)
83 **Billy** (*with distaste*). Lord Cantlemere is here, sir.

[Holmes *goes to the bedroom door.*]

Holmes. Show His Lordship up, Billy, while I
84 turn off the—er—"grammerphone."
Billy. Very good, sir.

[Holmes *and* Billy *exit by the bedroom and parlor doors respectively, leaving both of them open.* Watson *lays down his hat and stick. The music ceases abruptly and* Holmes *returns, shutting the bedroom door.* Billy *reenters the parlor door.*]

Billy. Lord Cantlemere, sir. (*He steps aside to let* Cantlemere *enter, then goes out, closing the door.*)
Cantlemere. What on earth's going on here, Holmes? Constables and fellahs all over the place!
Holmes. How do you do, Lord Cantlemere? May I introduce my friend and colleague, Dr. Watson?
Watson. How d'you do, my lord?
Cantlemere (*brusquely*). D'yer do?
Holmes. Watson, pray help me with His Lordship's overcoat. (Holmes *takes hold of the coat, preparing to take it off.*)
Cantlemere. No, thank you. I will not take it off.

85 [Holmes *pawing the coat.*]

Holmes. Oh, but my friend Dr. Watson would assure you that it is most unhealthy to retain a coat indoors, even at this time of the year.
Cantlemere (*releasing himself*). I am quite comfortable as I am, sir! I have no need to stay. I have simply looked in to know how your self-appointed task is progressing.

79
"Deuce": the devil.

80
Merton still has not figured out Holmes's scheme.

81
Plot. This scene marks the plot's **resolution.** Holmes's plan has worked out to the minute, as Watson arrives with police.

82
Sylvius tries to salvage last shred of dignity, but policeman is unimpressed.

83 **Finding Cause and Effect**
Why does Billy announce Lord Cantlemere "with distaste"? Cantlemere did not like Holmes or want his services.

84
Holmes mimics Merton by mispronouncing *gramophone*.

85
Foreshadowing. Holmes acts suspiciously here by paying undue attention to Cantlemere's coat. Introduces **climax** of second **conflict**—between Holmes and Cantlemere.

The Mazarin Stone

TRANSPARENCY 27

Reader Response
Certificate of Merit – invites students to identify and explain a trait they admire in a fictional character.

VISUAL CONNECTIONS
Exploring the Subject
Sherlock Holmes and Lord Cantlemere both have expressions of smug satisfaction. Students might speculate on why Cantlemere would take satisfaction in what he assumes is Holmes's failure, remembering that Cantlemere is the House Secretary and has power over the offical police who often resent Holmes's "unofficial" superiority.

86
Holmes has another plan; continues to play "game" with Cantlemere.

87
Conflict. Cantlemere has been opposed to Holmes's methods and is now indulging in some self-satisfaction of his own.

88
Skillful actor Holmes draws Cantlemere into his trap by playing dumb.

89
Words reflect an "I told you so" attitude, yet Cantlemere is sincere in offer to help.

330

[Holmes *assumes a troubled air*.]

86 Holmes. It's difficult—very difficult.

87 Cantlemere (*with gleeful malice*). Ha! I feared you'd find it so! Every man finds his limitations, Holmes—but at least it cures us of the weakness of self-satisfaction.

Holmes. Yes, sir. I admit I have been much perplexed.

Cantlemere. No doubt!

Holmes. Especially upon one point. Perhaps
88 you could help me?

[Cantlemere *takes a chair*. Holmes *sits opposite him*, Watson *standing behind his chair*.]

89 Cantlemere. You apply for my advice rather late in the day. I thought you had your own self-sufficient methods. Still, I am ready to help you.

330 DRAMA

Holmes. Your Lordship is most obliging. You see, we can no doubt frame a case against the actual thieves.
Cantlemere. When you've caught them.
Holmes. Exactly. But the question is, how shall we proceed against the receiver?
Cantlemere. Receiver? Isn't this rather premature?
Holmes. It's as well to have our plans ready. Now, what would you regard as final evidence against the receiver?
Cantlemere. The actual possession of the stone, of course.
Holmes. You'd arrest him on that?
Cantlemere. Undoubtedly.
Holmes (slyly). In that case, my dear sir, I shall be under the painful necessity of advising your arrest!

[Cantlemere leaps to his feet.]

Cantlemere. Holmes! In fifty years of official life I cannot recall such a liberty being taken! I am a busy man, engaged upon important affairs, and I have neither time nor taste for foolish jokes. (Holmes slowly rises.) I may tell you frankly, sir, that I have never been a believer in your powers. I have always been of the opinion that the matter was far safer in the hands of the regular police force. Your conduct confirms all my conclusions. (He moves stiffly towards the parlor door.) I have the honor, sir, to wish you good evening!
Holmes. One moment, sir! (Cantlemere turns to face him inquiringly.) Actually to go off with the Mazarin Stone would be an even more serious offense than to be found in temporary possession of it!
Cantlemere. Sir, this is intolerable!
Holmes. Put your hand in the right-hand pocket of your overcoat.
Cantlemere. What? What do you mean?
Holmes. Come, come! Do what I ask!

[Cantlemere splutters with fury, but feels in his pocket.]

Cantlemere. I'll make an end to this charade,[31] and you'll wish you'd never begun it! I . . . I . . . (His fury suddenly abates, giving way to surprise, then astonishment, as he slowly withdraws from his pocket the Mazarin Stone and holds it up.)
Watson. Great heavens!
Holmes. Too bad of me, Lord Cantlemere. My old friend here will tell you that I have an impish habit of practical joking. Also that I can never resist a dramatic situation. I took the liberty—the very great liberty, I confess—of putting the stone into your pocket at the beginning of our interview.
Cantlemere. I . . . I'm bewildered! This is the Mazarin Stone! (Holmes bows slightly.) Hol . . . Mr. Holmes, we are greatly your debtors. Your sense of humor may, as you admit, be somewhat perverted, and its exhibition untimely—remarkably untimely! (Watson stifles a grin.) But at least I withdraw any reflection I have made upon your professional powers.
Holmes. Thank you, Lord Cantlemere. I hope your pleasure in reporting this successful result in the exalted circle to which you return will be some small atonement for my joke. I will supply the full particulars in a written report.

[Cantlemere bows and goes to the parlor door. Watson hastens to open it for him.]

Cantlemere. Once more, good evening. (He nods to Watson.) And to you, sir, good evening.
Watson.} Good evening.
Holmes.

[Cantlemere exits. Watson gives him a rigid mili-

---

31. **charade** (shə-rād'): game; pretense.

---

90 **Receiver** here refers to one who receives stolen property and thereby violates law.

91 Holmes is setting up Cantlemere to incriminate himself.

92 Drawing Conclusions
What is Holmes trying to accomplish through this game? He wants to make Cantlemere look foolish and cure him of "weakness of self-satisfaction."

93 Becomes clear that as Holmes pawed Cantlemere's coat he was "planting" diamond in pocket.

94 Use of "Mr." reveals new respect Cantlemere has for Holmes.

95 **Conflict. Resolution** of conflict between Cantlemere and Holmes occurs with Cantlemere's apology.

MEETING INDIVIDUAL NEEDS
Visual and Kinesthetic Learners • If you can find a film version of this story at a video store, you might allow students to follow up their reading of the play with a screening of the movie.

Ask students to examine the planning that went into the sets and costumes. What kinds of props are used and how does the lighting contribute to the drama?

Ask students to analyze the movements of the actors on the movie set. You might even ask them to turn off the sound and study the actions. How do students feel about the way the stage is set or organized? Does the camera come in close or is it set farther from the actors to give the audience a better feel for the **setting**?

96
Mrs. Hudson is Holmes's housekeeper.

READING CHECK
1. A parasol (p. 319).
2. Lord Cantlemere (p. 319).
3. To keep wits sharp (p. 320).
4. Wants to find diamond (p. 320).
5. To take note to Yard and bring back police (p. 323).
6. Details of Sylvius' crimes (p. 326).
7. To withhold information from police (p. 326).
8. Sam Merton (p. 321).
9. In a secret pocket (p. 328).
10. Puts it in Cantlemere's coat pocket; lets him announce its recovery (p. 331).

FOR STUDY AND DISCUSSION
1. Dresses as workman and old woman; old-woman disguise deceives both Billy and Sylvius.
2. Tells Sylvius he can read his mind; response reveals Sylvius knows diamond's location.
3. Cabmen who drove Sylvius to and from Whitehall; commissionaire who saw him near diamond case; Ikey Sanders, who refused to cut stone.
4. Confront Sylvius and Merton, trick them into revealing stone's location; eavesdrop on conversation by taking dummy's place while gramophone is playing.
5a. Plans to get accomplice to take stone to Amsterdam, to promise Holmes diamond while misleading him, to escape to Holland. 5b. Holmes seizes diamond when Sylvius takes it from his pocket; covers criminals with revolver until police come.
6a. To embarrass Cantlemere for his low opinion of Holmes. 6b. Holmes's skill in recovering diamond and planting it in Cantlemere's pocket.

---

tary salute behind his retreating back, then closes the door.]

Watson. Well, Holmes.
Holmes. He's an excellent and loyal person, but rather of the old regime.³² (*He goes to Watson and claps him on the shoulder.*) And now, my dear Watson, pray touch the bell, and Mrs. **96** Hudson shall lay dinner for two—as of old!

[*Final curtain.*]

32. **old regime** (rə-zhēm′): the old order of things, now out of date.

Reading Check

1. What prop has Holmes used in his disguise as an old woman?
2. Which nobleman opposed putting Holmes on the case?
3. Why is Holmes going without food?
4. Why hasn't Holmes had Sylvius arrested?
5. What instruction does Holmes give Watson?
6. What information is contained in Holmes's notebook?
7. What does Holmes offer Sylvius in exchange for the diamond?
8. Who is Sylvius' accomplice?
9. Where has Sylvius hidden the diamond?
10. What does Holmes do with the Crown diamond?

For Study and Discussion

Analyzing and Interpreting the Play

1. One of Holmes's well-known talents is "play-acting." How does he show that he is skillful at disguise?

2. Holmes is expert at tricking criminals into telling him what he wants to know. How does he trick the Count into admitting that he knows where the diamond is?

3. Holmes is sure that the Count has stolen the diamond. What evidence has he used in building his case?

4. Describe Holmes's plan for recovering the diamond. What part do the dummy and the gramophone play in this plan?

5. The Count claims that he has fooled better men than Holmes. **a.** How does he plan to

CLOSURE

Ask students to describe the major **conflict** in *The Mazarin Stone* and to identify the conflict as either physical or mental. Then ask them to describe minor conflicts in the play and identify them as physical or mental.

EXTENSION AND ENRICHMENT

Several students might improvise a scene not included in the play—for example, Dr. Watson's visit to Scotland Yard, Billy's streetcorner conversation with Sam Merton, the ride of the captive criminals and the policemen to the police station, or the dinner Sherlock Holmes and Dr. Watson are about to have at the end of the play.

Other students might write narrative versions of brief scenes and compare them with the dramatic version.

---

get away with the diamond? **b.** How does Holmes prevent his escape?

6a. Why does Holmes play a practical joke on Lord Cantlemere? **b.** How does Lord Cantlemere become convinced that Holmes is a "brain"?

Focus on Reading

Imagining a Play in Performance

In reading a play, you let your imagination do the work that would be done for you in a theater by actors, costumes, scenery, lighting, and sound effects. You imagine how the characters would be dressed, how they would speak their lines, what facial expressions they would use, and what movements they would make.

A playwright often gives players instructions for acting. These are called **stage directions**. Stage directions appear in italics within parentheses or brackets. A stage direction may tell the actor how a line should be spoken.

> **Watson** (*dismally*). Oh!
> **Holmes** (*sharply*). That will do, Billy!
> **Billy** (*humbly*). Yes, sir.

A stage direction may call for a specific action or movement.

> **Holmes** (*sadly shaking his head*). Your morals don't improve, Watson.
> [Holmes *makes an elaborate bow, holding out the parasol in both hands.*]

Stage directions may tell an actor what kind of facial expression to use.

> [Sylvius *whirls round, his stick still upraised, a look of disbelief on his face.*]

Most of the time, directions for acting are built into the dialogue of the play. As you read the speeches of the characters, you must imagine what they feel and think as well as what they do with their voices, their expressions, and their gestures.

Here is some dialogue from the play. Decide
1 how the actors would speak these lines. <u>How would they move? What facial expressions would they use?</u>

> **Watson.** Look here, Holmes, this is simply ridiculous. This is a desperate man who sticks at nothing, you'd have me believe. He may have *come* to murder you. (page 322)
>
> **Sylvius.** I, too, wished to have some words with you, Holmes! That is why I am here. Because you have gone out of your way to annoy me. Because you have put your creatures on my track! (page 324)
>
> **Holmes.** Oh, no violence, Billy! Don't be rough with him! If you tell him that Count Sylvius wants him he will come. (page 327)
>
> **Cantlemere.** I'll make an end to this charade, and you'll wish you'd never begun it! I . . . I . . . (page 331)

Literary Elements

Understanding Plot

In a play, as in a short story, the **plot**, or sequence of events, follows a certain pattern. The action generally develops out of one or more conflicts or problems. At the opening of *The Mazarin Stone*, we learn that a diamond has been stolen and that Holmes has been called in on the case. Holmes's problem is to get the criminals to assist him in recovering the stone. The central conflict of the play is not physical—it is a battle of wits between Sherlock Holmes and the thieves. That battle is won and the conflict resolved when Holmes takes the diamond from the thieves and has them arrested.

1 <u>What is Holmes's conflict with Lord</u>
2 <u>Cantlemere? How is it resolved?</u>

FOCUS ON READING

1. Students might have an assortment of suggestions. Here are some possibilities:

Watson (*a grave look on his face, his voice full of concern*). Look here, Holmes . . . [*He pauses a moment, then looks* Holmes *in the eye.*] He may have come to murder you.

Sylvius (*his voice shrill with anger*). I, too, have wished to have some words with you . . . [*As he speaks, he advances menacingly toward* Holmes, *who calmly stands his ground.*]

Holmes (*a thin, mocking smile on his face*). Oh, no violence . . .

Cantlemere (*his face red, his voice choked with rage*). I'll make an end to this charade, and you'll wish you'd never begun it! [*As he speaks, he slowly raises his right hand, almost as if to strike* Holmes.]

LITERARY ELEMENTS

1. **Conflict** with Cantlemere arises out of Cantlemere's low opinion of Holmes's **character** and abilities and the nobleman's opposition to employing the detective.

2. **Conflict** is resolved through Holmes's recovery of diamond and success in planting it on Cantlemere.

LANGUAGE AND VOCABULARY

1. 'ere for here; 'Offmann for Hoffmann; 'e for he; 'undred for hundred; and 'ow for how (pp. 327–328).

FOCUS ON WRITING A SCENE

If tape recorders are available, you might suggest that students record their **improvisations**. With the recordings to refer to, students can accurately write down the **dialogue** they use. Suggest that students also add to their notes stage directions about how the lines are spoken.

ABOUT THE AUTHOR

The Holmes stories were in part inspired by Edgar Allan Poe's work, and Sherlock Holmes was based on one of Doyle's medical school professors, Dr. Joseph Bell. Dr. Bell impressed students with his ability not only to diagnose disease but also to deduce occupation and other personal details from an individual's appearance. Doyle continued his medical studies even after he began writing the successful Holmes stories. He eventually gave up his medical practice when, after becoming qualified as an eye surgeon, he failed to attract many patients. His interest in detection carried over into real life. He obtained pardons for two wrongfully convicted men by proving that it would have been impossible for them to have committed the crimes for which they were convicted.

Language and Vocabulary

Recognizing Cockney Speech

In drama characters are distinguished not only by their actions and words but by their manner of speech. Sam Merton, Sylvius' accomplice, speaks a London dialect known as *cockney*. Originally the word referred to someone born close to the church of Saint Mary-le-Bow in the East End of London. One characteristic of the cockney dialect is loss of the letter *h* at the beginning of words: *'im* for *him*. Find examples of this characteristic in Merton's speeches.

Focus on Writing a Scene

Using Improvisation to Explore a Scene

Scenes are the building blocks of plays. At the heart of a good scene is a dramatic situation that involves a conflict or problem.

You can use **improvising** to explore a dramatic situation. When you improvise, you act without a script. You do not plan what you will say or do. You make up the actions and words as you go along, responding to what other actors say and do.

Get together with one or more partners and improvise one of the following situations. Notice that each situation contains a conflict. Decide in advance who will play each role in the situation. Then relax and use your imagination.

1. You have not practiced your music. You try to distract the teacher so that the hour will be up before you have to play.
2. You would like to go to the beach, but your friends would like to go to the mountains. You try to persuade your friends to go to the beach.
3. You are at a sale counter. Two other people want to buy the article you've chosen.
4. You are trapped in an elevator with several other people. You do not agree with them about what is to be done.

After the improvisation, work as a group to jot down as much of the dialogue as you can. These notes can serve as the framework for a dramatic scene. Save your writing.

About The Author

Sir Arthur Conan Doyle (1859-1930)

Sir Arthur Conan Doyle began writing detective fiction while he was practicing medicine. His greatest creation was Sherlock Holmes, one of the most famous characters in all English fiction. Holmes first appeared in *A Study in Scarlet*, published in 1887. He became a great success with readers. The demand for new books about Holmes meant that Doyle had to spend more and more time creating new adventures for his popular hero. Tiring of his creation or perhaps running out of ideas, Doyle had Holmes killed off in *The Memoirs of Sherlock Holmes*. However, Sherlock Holmes's fans had become so numerous and their appetite for new stories so strong that Doyle was persuaded to bring him back. He explained that Holmes had merely disappeared, not died.

OBJECTIVES

The overall aim is for students to analyze **characterization** in *A Sunny Morning* and demonstrate an understanding of dynamic characters. For a complete list of objectives, see the **Teacher's Notes.**

VOCABULARY

The underlined words are in the Glossary. Students will be introduced to a number of Spanish words in the play. Studying the footnoted words as they read will increase their understanding of the play.

FOCUS / MOTIVATION

It is sometimes difficult for students this age to really believe that older people were once young and in love. Ask volunteers to share with the class stories they have heard about the ways in which their grandparents met and fell in love.

A Sunny Morning

SERAFÍN AND JOAQUÍN QUINTERO

TEACHING RESOURCES C
Teacher's Notes, p. 18
Study Guide, p. 20
Language Skills, p. 22
Building Vocabulary, p. 25
Selection Test, p. 26

In stories some characters remain the same while other characters undergo some kind of change. In drama, also, characters may be static or dynamic. As you read this comedy, ask yourself how the characters change and how the dramatists make that change believable.

PREREADING FOCUS

The headnote emphasizes **characterization.** You might discuss with students how the dramatist might make a character's change believable. Reasons students might mention are occurrence of external events that prompt a change by increasing an understanding of self and others. Stress that such change must usually be conveyed in drama through dialogue alone.

A Sunny Morning

Characters

Doña (dō'nyä)[1] Laura
Petra
Don Gonzalo
Juanito (hwä-nē'tō)

Scene: *A sunny morning in a retired corner of a park in Madrid. Autumn. A bench at right.*

Doña Laura, *a handsome, white-haired old lady of about seventy, refined in appearance, her bright eyes and entire manner giving evidence that despite her age her mental faculties are* unimpaired, *enters leaning upon the arm of her maid,* Petra. *In her free hand she carries a parasol, which serves also as a cane.*

Doña Laura. I am so glad to be here. I feared
1 my seat would be occupied. What a beautiful morning!
Petra. The sun is hot.
2 **Doña Laura.** Yes, you are only twenty. (*She sits down on the bench.*) Oh, I feel more tired today
3 than usual. (*Noticing* Petra, *who seems impatient*) Go, if you wish to chat with your guard.

Petra. He is not mine, señora;[2] he belongs to the park.
4 **Doña Laura.** He belongs more to you than he does to the park. Go find him, but remain within calling distance.
Petra. I see him over there waiting for me.
Doña Laura. Do not remain more than ten minutes.
Petra. Very well, señora. (*Walks toward the right*)
Doña Laura. Wait a moment.
Petra. What does the señora wish?
Doña Laura. Give me the bread crumbs.
Petra. I don't know what is the matter with me.
Doña Laura (*smiling*). I do. Your head is where your heart is—with the guard.
Petra. Here, señora. (*She hands* Doña Laura *a small bag. Exit* Petra *by the right.*)
Doña Laura. Adiós.[3] (*Glances toward trees at the right*) Here they come! They know just when to expect me. (*She rises, walks toward the right, and throws three handfuls of bread crumbs.*) These are
5 for the spryest, these for the gluttons, and these for the little ones which are the most per-

---

1. **Doña:** a Spanish title of courtesy used with a woman's given name. The title *Don* is used with a man's given name.
2. **señora** (sān-yōr'ä): a title for a married woman, like *Mrs.* or *madam* in English.
3. **Adiós** (äd'ē-ōs'): Spanish for "goodbye."

1
Laura's reference to "my seat" indicates she visits park often.

2
Laura indicates that their different reactions to weather are due to contrast in ages.

3
Characterization. Laura reveals herself as perceptive and kind.

4
During visits to park, Petra has fallen in love with park guard.

5
Laura apparently enjoys feeding birds and does it often.

A Sunny Morning 335

MOTIVATIONAL SUMMARY

On a sunny morning in Madrid, the elderly Doña Laura goes to sit on her favorite park bench. A short time later, the elderly Don Gonzalo arrives, but is disappointed to see that his favorite park bench is occupied by men deep in conversation and not ready to leave. Annoyed, Don Gonzalo is forced to share Doña Laura's bench. Off to a bad start, they begin to talk, and are surprised to discover they have much more in common than their park bench.

PRESENTATION

This one-act **comedy** takes place in a park in Madrid on a sunny autumn morning. Two elderly people are forced to share a bench. Their conversation leads to the realization that they were once lovers who had lost track of each other.

---

6 Analyzing
Why does Doña Laura call one of the pigeons a philosopher?
It appears to have the human characteristic of preferring to be alone to think.

7
Don Gonzalo is same age as Laura but not as healthy; gout is disease which causes arthritic discomfort.

8
Characterization. Gonzalo's attitude suggests he is accustomed to being pampered and to having his own way.

9
Gonzalo angers Laura when he scares away the birds; his failure to see situation indicates he is self-centered.

10
Characterization. Gonzalo demonstrates his selfishness and rudeness.

11
Gonzalo is cornered so he falls back on diversionary tactic: rule of etiquette. Customary in Spain that people be formally introduced before they speak.

12
Comic touch in Gonzalo's complete disregard of what has gone before.

13
Characterization. Gonzalo is very formal; has rules down pat.

---

sistent. (*Laughs. She returns to her seat and watches, with a pleased expression, the pigeons feeding.*) There, that big one is always first! I know him by his big head. Now one, now another, now two, now three—That little fellow is the least timid. I believe he would eat from my hand. That one takes his piece and flies up to

6 that branch alone. He is a philosopher. But where do they all come from? It seems as if the news had spread. Ha, ha! Don't quarrel. There is enough for all. I'll bring more tomorrow.

[*Enter* Don Gonzalo *and* Juanito *from the left cen-*
7 *ter.* Don Gonzalo *is an old gentleman of seventy, gouty and impatient. He leans upon* Juanito's *arm and drags his feet somewhat as he walks.*]

Don Gonzalo. Idling their time away! They should be saying Mass.

Juanito. You can sit here, señor.⁴ There is only a lady.

[Doña Laura *turns her head and listens.*]

Don Gonzalo. I won't, Juanito. I want a bench to myself.

Juanito. But there is none.

Don Gonzalo. That one over there is mine.

Juanito. There are three priests sitting there.

8 Don Gonzalo. Rout them out. Have they gone?

Juanito. No, indeed. They are talking.

Don Gonzalo. Just as if they were glued to the seat. No hope of their leaving. Come this way,
Juanito. (*They walk toward the birds, right.*)

9 Doña Laura (*indignantly*). Look out!

Don Gonzalo. Are you speaking to me, señora?

Doña Laura. Yes, to you.

Don Gonzalo. What do you wish?

---

4. **señor** (sän′yōr′): a Spanish title of courtesy, like *Mr.* or *sir* in English.

Doña Laura. You have scared away the birds who were feeding on my crumbs.

10 Don Gonzalo. What do I care about the birds?

Doña Laura. But I do.

Don Gonzalo. This is a public park.

Doña Laura. Then why do you complain that the priests have taken your bench?

Don Gonzalo. Señora, we have not met. I can-
11 not imagine why you take the liberty of addressing me. Come, Juanito. (*Both go out right.*)

Doña Laura. What an ill-natured old man! (*Looking toward the right*) I am glad. He lost that bench, too. Serves him right for scaring the birds. He is furious. Yes, yes; find a seat if you can. Poor man! he is wiping the perspiration from his face. Here he comes. A carriage would not raise more dust than his feet.

[*Enter* Don Gonzalo *and* Juanito *by the right and walk toward the left.*]

Don Gonzalo. Have the priests gone yet, Juanito?

Juanito. No, indeed, señor. They are still there.

Don Gonzalo. The authorities should place more benches here for these sunny mornings. Well, I suppose I must resign myself and sit on the bench with the old lady. (*Muttering to himself, he sits at the extreme end of* Doña Laura's *bench and looks at her indignantly. Touches his hat*
12 *as he greets her.*) Good morning.

Doña Laura. What, you here again?

Don Gonzalo. I repeat that we have not met.

Doña Laura. I was responding to your salute.⁵

13 Don Gonzalo. "Good morning" should be answered by "good morning," and that is all you should have said.

---

5. **salute:** here, a greeting.

You may want to begin by emphasizing to students that *A Sunny Morning* is a comedy and alerting them to the play's **irony**. The selection is very brief and can be easily dramatized in one class period. The setting is simple and the characters few, making this an excellent vehicle for students to practice designing sets and creating costumes. Students might also practice make-up design, attempting to create realistic images of Doña Laura and Don Gonzalo.

---

14 Doña Laura. You should have asked permission to sit on this bench, which is mine.
Don Gonzalo. The benches here are public property.
Doña Laura. Why, you said the one the priests have was yours.
Don Gonzalo. Very well, very well. I have noth-
15 ing more to say. (*Between his teeth*) She ought to be at home knitting and counting her beads.[6]
Doña Laura. Don't grumble anymore. I'm not going to leave just to please you.
Don Gonzalo (*brushing the dust from his shoes with his handkerchief*). If the ground were sprinkled a little it would be an improvement.
Doña Laura. Do you use your handkerchief as a shoebrush?
Don Gonzalo. Why not?
16 Doña Laura. Do you use a shoebrush as a handkerchief?
Don Gonzalo. What right have you to criticize my actions?
Doña Laura. A neighbor's right.
Don Gonzalo. Juanito, my book. I do not care to listen to nonsense.
17 Doña Laura. You are very polite.
Don Gonzalo. Pardon me, señora, but never interfere with what does not concern you.
Doña Laura. I generally say what I think.
Don Gonzalo. And more to the same effect.
18 Give me the book, Juanito.
Juanito. Here, señor.

[*Juanito takes a book from his pocket, hands it to Don Gonzalo, then exits by right. Don Gonzalo, casting indignant glances at Doña Laura, puts on an enormous pair of glasses, takes from his pocket a reading glass, adjusts both to suit him, and opens his book.*]

Doña Laura. I thought you were taking out a telescope.

---

6. **counting her beads:** praying with a rosary.

Don Gonzalo. Was that you?
Doña Laura. Your sight must be keen.
Don Gonzalo. Keener than yours is.
Doña Laura. Yes, evidently.
19 Don Gonzalo. Ask the hares and partridges.
Doña Laura. Ah! Do you hunt?
Don Gonzalo. I did, and even now—
Doña Laura. Oh, yes, of course!
Don Gonzalo. Yes, señora. Every Sunday I take my gun and dog, you understand, and go to
20 one of my estates near Aravaca and **kill time**.
Doña Laura. Yes, kill time. That is all you kill.
Don Gonzalo. Do you think so? I could show you a wild boar's head in my study—
Doña Laura. Yes, and I could show you a tiger's skin in my **boudoir**. What does that prove?
Don Gonzalo. Very well, señora, please allow me to read. Enough conversation.
Doña Laura. Well, you **subside**, then.
Don Gonzalo. But first I shall take a pinch of
21 snuff.[7] (*Takes out snuffbox*) Will you have some? (*Offers box to* Doña Laura)
Doña Laura. If it is good.
Don Gonzalo. It is of the finest. You will like it.
Doña Laura (*taking pinch of snuff*). It clears my head.
Don Gonzalo. And mine.
Doña Laura. Do you sneeze?
Don Gonzalo. Yes, señora, three times.
Doña Laura. And so do I. What a coincidence!

[*After taking the snuff, they await the sneezes, both anxiously, and sneeze alternately three times each.*]

Don Gonzalo. There, I feel better.
22 Doña Laura. So do I. (*Aside*) The snuff has made peace between us.

---

7. **snuff** (snŭf): finely ground tobacco, inhaled through the nostrils.

14
Laura shows that two can play Gonzalo's game.

15
Outwitted so wants to put opponent in her (stereotypical) place.

16
Characterization. Laura shows herself to be feisty, quick-witted, and provocative.

17 Making Inferences
Considering the conversation so far, do you think Doña Laura really means this statement? No; she is being sarcastic.

18
Gonzalo prefers not to match wits with Laura since he loses every time.

19 Analyzing
What does Gonzalo mean by "ask the hares and partridges"? Indicates he is—or was—sharp-eyed hunter.

20
Characterization. Substitution of "time" for prey shows that Gonzalo can joke, ironically, at his own expense.

21
Plot. Conflict between "friendly enemies" is being resolved.

22
An *aside* is stage direction for comment made by characters to themselves; audience hears but supposedly other characters do not.

A Sunny Morning

SOCIAL STUDIES LINK
Post a map of Spain in the classroom and have students locate Madrid, Seville, Valencia, and Andalusia before you begin your study of the play. You could also have students research Spanish social customs.

---

23 Characterization. Gonzalo has chosen to read love poems, suggesting he is a romantic.

24 Foreshadowing. These lines describe what will happen in the climax of the play.

25 Suspense. Her familiarity with lines that attract him indicates that something momentous is about to happen for them.

26 Characterization. Gonzalo tries to impress Laura by telling her he has known great Spanish poets.

27 Now Laura's insults are light-hearted teases rather than sarcastic barbs.

28 Plot. Realization that he knew her shocks Laura.

Don Gonzalo. You will excuse me if I read aloud?
Doña Laura. Read as loud as you please; you will not disturb me.
23 Don Gonzalo (*reading*). "All love is sad, but sad as it is, it is the best thing that we know." That is from Campoamor.[8]
Doña Laura. Ah!
Don Gonzalo (*reading*). "The daughters of the mothers I once loved kiss me now as they would a graven image."[9] Those lines, I take it, are in a humorous vein.
Doña Laura (*laughing*). I take them so, too.
Don Gonzalo. There are some beautiful poems in this book. Here. "Twenty years pass. He returns."
Doña Laura. You cannot imagine how it affects me to see you reading with all those glasses.
Don Gonzalo. Can you read without any?
Doña Laura. Certainly.
Don Gonzalo. At your age? You're jesting.
Doña Laura. Pass me the book, then. (*Takes book; reads aloud*)
24 "Twenty years pass. He returns.
And each, beholding the other, exclaims—
Can it be that this is he?
Heavens, is it she?"

[*Doña Laura returns the book to Don Gonzalo.*]

Don Gonzalo. Indeed, I envy you your wonderful eyesight.
25 Doña Laura (*aside*). I know every word by heart.
Don Gonzalo. I am very fond of good verses, very fond. I even composed some in my youth.
Doña Laura. Good ones?
Don Gonzalo. Of all kinds. I was a great friend **26** of Espronceda, Zorrilla, Bécquer,[10] and others. I first met Zorrilla in America.
Doña Laura. Why, have you been in America?
Don Gonzalo. Several times. The first time I went I was only six years old.
27 Doña Laura. You must have gone with Columbus in one of his caravels!
Don Gonzalo (*laughing*). Not quite as bad as that. I am old, I admit, but I did not know Ferdinand and Isabella. (*They both laugh.*) I was also a great friend of Campoamor. I met him in Valencia. I am a native of that city.
Doña Laura. You are?
Don Gonzalo. I was brought up there and there I spent my early youth. Have you ever visited that city?
Doña Laura. Yes, señor. Not far from Valencia there was a villa that, if still there, should retain memories of me. I spent several seasons there. It was many, many years ago. It was near the sea, hidden away among lemon and orange trees. They called it—let me see, what did they call it—Maricela.
Don Gonzalo (*startled*). Maricela?
Doña Laura. Maricela. Is the name familiar to you?
Don Gonzalo. Yes, very familiar. If my memory serves me right, for we forget as we grow old, there lived in that villa the most beautiful woman I have ever seen, and I assure you I have seen many. Let me see—what was her name? Laura—Laura—Laura Llorente.
28 Doña Laura (*startled*). Laura Llorente?
Don Gonzalo. Yes.

---

8. **Campoamor:** Ramon de Campoamor (rä-mōn′ dā käm′ pō-ä-môr′), once a popular Spanish poet, known for his humorous short poems (1817–1901).
9. **graven image:** an idol carved in stone or wood. In other words, he is treated with respect rather than affection.
10. **Espronceda . . . Bécquer:** José de Espronceda (hō-sā′ dā ās′prōn-thā′thä), a Spanish romantic poet (1808–1842), known as the Spanish Byron; José Zorrilla y Moral (hō-sā′ thô-rē′lyä ē mō-räl′), a Spanish poet and dramatist (1817–1893); Gustavo Adolfo Bécquer (gōō-stä′vō ä-dôl′fō bā′kĕr), a Spanish poet and writer known for his romantic tales (1836–1870).

338 DRAMA

Detail from *The Balcony* (1869) by Édouard Manet (1832–1883). Oil on canvas.
The Louvre, Paris

[*They look at each other intently.*]

Doña Laura (*recovering herself*). Nothing. You reminded me of my best friend.
Don Gonzalo. How strange!
Doña Laura. It is strange. She was called "The Silver Maiden."
Don Gonzalo. Precisely, "The Silver Maiden." By that name she was known in that locality. I seem to see her as if she were before me now, at that window with the red roses. Do you remember that window?
Doña Laura. Yes, I remember. It was the window of her room.
Don Gonzalo. She spent many hours there. I mean in my day.
Doña Laura (*sighing*). And in mine, too.
Don Gonzalo. She was ideal. Fair as a lily, jet-black hair and black eyes, with an uncommonly sweet expression. She seemed to cast a radiance wherever she was. Her figure was beautiful, perfect. "What forms of sovereign[11] beauty God models in human clay!" She was a dream.
Doña Laura (*aside*). If you but knew that dream was now by your side, you would realize what dreams come to. (*Aloud*) She was very unfortunate and had a sad love affair.
Don Gonzalo. Very sad.

[*They look at each other.*]

Doña Laura. Did you hear of it?
Don Gonzalo. Yes.

11. **sovereign** (sŏv′ər-ən): supreme.

A Sunny Morning 339

COOPERATIVE LEARNING
The use of asides by the characters in this play is vital to the audience's understanding. You might have students in small groups consider ways asides are used in movies and television and discuss ways to adapt and use an aside on the screen. For example, a character might walk to the front of the camera or away from the other characters and talk directly to the audience. The sound of a character's voice might be heard, but the character might not appear to be speaking. In a comedy, a bubble might appear above a character's head with lines of dialogue directed to the audience. The groups can then share and demonstrate their ideas for the class.

33
Plot. Gonzalo also lies about his identity; former lovers play out parts as best friend and cousin of the lovers.

34
Use to answer **study question 2, p. 342.**

35
Both well remember details of sad love affair.

36
Plot. This is the moment of realization for Gonzalo.

37 Drawing Conclusions
Laura decides to keep up the charade. Why? Perhaps she feels his memories would be ruined by reality of who she is now.

38
Irony. Both believe they have fooled the other.

39
Gonzalo makes up romantic story about cousin's death to explain why he never returned to Laura.

40
Gonzalo is pleased with dramatic story of his death.

41
Gonzalo suspects that Laura soon recovered from the loss and did not miss him.

42
Not to be outdone, Laura invents her own tragic story.

Doña Laura. The ways of Providence are strange. (*Aside*) Gonzalo!
Don Gonzalo. The gallant lover, in the same affair—
Doña Laura. Ah, the duel?
33 Don Gonzalo. Precisely, the duel. The gallant lover was—my cousin, of whom I was very fond.
Doña Laura. Oh, yes, a cousin? My friend told me in one of her letters the story of that affair, **34** which was truly romantic. He, your cousin, passed by on horseback every morning down the rose path under her window, and tossed up to her balcony a bouquet of flowers which she caught.
Don Gonzalo. And later in the afternoon the gallant horseman would return by the same path, and catch the bouquet of flowers she would toss him. Am I right?
Doña Laura. Yes. They wanted to marry her to a merchant whom she would not have.
Don Gonzalo. And one night, when my cousin waited under her window to hear her sing, this other person presented himself unexpectedly.
35 Doña Laura. And insulted your cousin.
Don Gonzalo. There was a quarrel.
Doña Laura. And later a duel.
Don Gonzalo. Yes, at sunrise, on the beach, and the merchant was badly wounded. My cousin had to conceal himself for a few days and later to fly.
Doña Laura. You seem to know the story well.
Don Gonzalo. And so do you.
Doña Laura. I have explained that a friend repeated it to me.
Don Gonzalo. As my cousin did to me. (*Aside*) **36** This is Laura!
37 Doña Laura (*aside*). Why tell him? He does not suspect.
38 Don Gonzalo (*aside*). She is entirely innocent.
Doña Laura. And was it you, by any chance, who advised your cousin to forget Laura?
Don Gonzalo. Why, my cousin never forgot her!
Doña Laura. How do you account, then, for his conduct?
Don Gonzalo. I will tell you. The young man took refuge in my house, fearful of the consequences of a duel with a person highly regarded in that locality. From my home he went to Seville, then came to Madrid. He wrote Laura many letters, some of them in verse. But undoubtedly they were intercepted by her parents, for she never answered at all. Gonzalo then, in despair, believing his love lost to him forever, joined the army, went to Africa, and **39** there, in a trench, met a glorious death, grasping the flag of Spain and whispering the name of his beloved Laura—
Doña Laura (*aside*). What an atrocious lie!
Don Gonzalo (*aside*). I could not have killed **40** myself more gloriously.
Doña Laura. You must have been prostrated[12] by the calamity.
Don Gonzalo. Yes, indeed, señora. As if he were my brother. I presume, though, on the contrary, that Laura in a short time was chas-**41** ing butterflies in her garden, indifferent to regret.
Doña Laura. No, señor, no!
Don Gonzalo. It is woman's way.
42 Doña Laura. Even if it were woman's way, "The Silver Maiden" was not of that disposition. My friend awaited news for days, months, a year, and no letter came. One afternoon, just at sunset, as the first stars were appearing, she was seen to leave the house, and with quickening steps wend her way toward the beach, the beach where her beloved had risked his life. She wrote his name on the sand, then sat down upon a rock, her gaze fixed upon the horizon. The waves murmured their eternal threnody[13] and slowly crept up to the rock where the

---
12. **prostrated** (prŏs′trā′təd): overcome.
13. **threnody** (thrĕn′ə-dē): lament.

maiden sat. The tide rose with a boom and swept her out to sea.

Don Gonzalo. Good heavens!

Doña Laura. The fishermen of that shore, who often tell the story, affirm that it was a long time before the waves washed away that name written on the sand. (*Aside*) You will not get ahead of me in decorating my own funeral.

Don Gonzalo (*aside*). She lies worse than I do.

Doña Laura. Poor Laura!

Don Gonzalo. Poor Gonzalo!

Doña Laura (*aside*). I will not tell him that I married two years later.

Don Gonzalo (*aside*). In three months I ran off to Paris with a ballet dancer.

Doña Laura. Fate is curious. Here are you and I, complete strangers, met by chance, discussing the romance of old friends of long ago! We have been conversing as if we were old friends.

Don Gonzalo. Yes, it is curious, considering the ill-natured prelude to our conversation.

Doña Laura. You scared away the birds.

Don Gonzalo. I was unreasonable, perhaps.

Doña Laura. Yes, that was evident. (*Sweetly*) Are you coming again tomorrow?

Don Gonzalo. Most certainly, if it is a sunny morning. And not only will I not scare away the birds, but I will bring a few crumbs.

Doña Laura. Thank you very much. Birds are grateful and repay attention. I wonder where my maid is? Petra! (*Signals for her maid*)

Don Gonzalo (*aside, looking at* Laura, *whose back is turned*). No, no, I will not reveal myself. I am grotesque[14] now. Better that she recall the gallant horseman who passed daily beneath her window tossing flowers.

Doña Laura. Here she comes.

Don Gonzalo. That Juanito! He plays havoc with the nursemaids. (*Looks to the right and signals with his hand*)

14. **grotesque** (grō-tĕsk′): ugly in appearance.

Doña Laura (*aside, looking at* Gonzalo, *whose back is turned*). No, I am too sadly changed. It is better he should remember me as the black-eyed girl tossing flowers as he passed among the roses in the garden.

[Juanito *enters by the right,* Petra *by the left. She has a bunch of violets in her hand.*]

Doña Laura. Well, Petra! At last!

Don Gonzalo. Juanito, you are late.

Petra (*to* Doña Laura). The guard gave me these violets for you, señora.

Doña Laura. How very nice! Thank him for me. They are fragrant. (*As she takes the violets from her maid a few loose ones fall to the ground.*)

Don Gonzalo. My dear lady, this has been a great honor and a great pleasure.

Doña Laura. It has also been a pleasure to me.

Don Gonzalo. Goodbye until tomorrow.

Doña Laura. Until tomorrow.

Don Gonzalo. If it is sunny.

Doña Laura. A sunny morning. Will you go to your bench?

Don Gonzalo. No, I will come to this—if you do not object?

Doña Laura. This bench is at your disposal.

Don Gonzalo. And I will surely bring the crumbs.

Doña Laura. Tomorrow, then?

Don Gonzalo. Tomorrow!

[Laura *walks away toward the right, supported by her maid.* Gonzalo, *before leaving with* Juanito, *trembling and with a great effort, stoops to pick up the violets* Laura *dropped. Just then* Laura *turns her head and surprises him picking up the flowers.*]

Juanito. What are you doing, señor?

Don Gonzalo. Juanito, wait—

Doña Laura (*aside*). Yes, it is he!

Don Gonzalo (*aside*). It is she, and no mistake.

---

43 Laura adds epic quality to story with detail about name staying in sand.

44 Plot. Neither of them believes other's story, but each continues to play the game.

45 Both admit in asides that they soon found new loves.

46 Characterization. Gonzalo is now apologetic about beginning of their meeting; attitude has changed considerably.

47 Characterization. Laura is no longer sarcastic; "sweetly," perhaps coyly, asks if he will come again.

48 Characterization. Has dropped all arrogance now and laments his lost charms.

49 Analyzing
What is ironic about their decisions to keep their identities secret? Both already know other's identity.

50 Plans to share a bench tomorrow indicate interest on both sides.

51 Use to answer **study question 6b,** p. 342.

52 Finding Cause and Effect
Why does Gonzalo pick up the flowers Laura has dropped? Wants memento of their reunion. Recall that he used to catch flowers which she threw from window.

[Doña Laura *and* Don Gonzalo *wave farewell.*]

Doña Laura. "Can it be that this is he?"
Don Gonzalo. "Heavens, is it she?"

[*They smile once more, as if she were again at the window and he below in the rose garden, and then disappear upon the arms of their servants.*]

[*Curtain.*]

Reading Check

1. Why is Don Gonzalo forced to share a bench with Doña Laura?
2. How does Don Gonzalo make peace with Doña Laura?
3. Why is Doña Laura able to read Don Gonzalo's book without glasses?
4. What was the name of Don Gonzalo's great love?
5. What was the outcome of the duel Don Gonzalo fought?

For Study and Discussion

Analyzing and Interpreting the Play

1. The plot of this play depends on a coincidence. Two elderly people, who once were lovers but who no longer recognize each other, chance to meet in a park one sunny morning. In the course of casual conversation, they reveal who they are and what their relationship was in the past. Why do you think Doña Laura and Don Gonzalo wish to keep their identities a secret from each other?

2. Don Gonzalo is reading a book of love poems, which Doña Laura claims to know by heart. How is this interest in romance reflected in the portraits they paint of each other as youthful lovers?

3. Both Doña Laura and Don Gonzalo got over their love affair rather painlessly. Why, then, do they want each other to believe that they suffered and died for their love?

4. When they first meet in the park, Doña Laura and Don Gonzalo take an immediate dislike to each other. Given their past relationship as lovers, why is this conflict amusing?

5. The reunion of lovers is often handled as a touching, emotional scene. In this play, however, the reunion is light and comical. How do the characters of Don Gonzalo and Doña Laura contribute to the lighthearted mood of the play?

6a. What change does Don Gonzalo undergo after he meets Doña Laura? b. What does the ending of the play imply about their future relationship?

Writing About Literature

▶ **Analyzing Character**

Write a short essay telling how one of the characters changes in the course of the play. State your *thesis* at the opening of your essay in this fashion: *When we first meet him, Don Gonzalo is a cranky, peevish old man who seems to live only for his memories, but after he recognizes Doña Laura, he becomes interested again in life and in romance.*

About the Authors

Serafín Alvárez Quintero   (1871–1938)
Joaquín Alvárez Quintero   (1873–1944)

The Quintero brothers had their first play produced when they were still teenagers. They collaborated on more than fifty plays, most of which are set in Andalusia, Spain. Some of their best-known plays are *Lady from Alfaqueque*, *One Hundred Years Ago*, and *Fortunato*.

OBJECTIVES
The overall aim is for students to observe the lessons that the characters in *The Governess* teach one another and to identify the "lesson" that Neil Simon teaches the audience.

VOCABULARY
The underlined words are in the Glossary. You may want to review with students the term *irony*, perhaps discussing both situational and verbal irony and relating the terms to the play.

FOCUS / MOTIVATION
Request that students think about what it would be like to care for young children as a full-time job. What might their duties be? What would their rights be? How would they insist on these rights?

> **TEACHING RESOURCES C**
> Teacher's Notes, p. 28
> Reading Check, p. 31
> Study Guide, p. 32
> Building Vocabulary, p. 34
> Selection Test, p. 37

The Governess

NEIL SIMON

Based on a Short Story by Anton Chekhov°

A theme is the basic meaning of a literary work. It is an idea about life or an interpretation of experience. What is the theme of this play?

PREREADING FOCUS
The headnote emphasizes **theme** as a literary element. Ask students how theme might be expressed in a play, since the author cannot speak directly. (It might be expressed by a character or left to interpretation of audience.)

The Governess

1 Mistress is mother of children Julia teaches.

2 Characterization. Julia's entrance reveals immediately that she is obedient and polite.

3 Body language ("head down") shows submissive role.

4 Most children of wealthy families in late 1800s were taught French.

5 Drawing Conclusions
What does the Mistress imply when she says, "Well, why not?" Gives herself credit for her children's intelligence.

6 Inference. "Surprised" indicates that misunderstanding is honest on Julia's side.

7 Analyzing
Why does the audience immediately believe Julia rather than the Mistress? Mistress is aggressive; audience favors underdog.

8 Making Inferences
Why does Julia accept what Mistress says? Perhaps needs job badly; feels powerless.

---

1 Mistress. Julia! (*Calls again*) Julia!

2 [*A young governess,* Julia, *comes rushing in. She stops before the desk and curtsies.*]

3 Julia (*head down*). Yes, madame?
Mistress. Look at me, child. Pick your head up. I like to see your eyes when I speak to you.
Julia (*lifts her head up*). Yes, madame. (*But her head has a habit of slowly drifting down again.*)
Mistress. And how are the children coming
4 along with their French lessons?
Julia. They're very bright children, madame.
Mistress. Eyes up . . . They're bright, you say.
5 Well, why not? And mathematics? They're doing well in mathematics, I assume?
Julia. Yes, madame. Especially Vanya.
Mistress. Certainly. I knew it. I excelled in mathematics. He gets that from his mother, wouldn't you say?
Julia. Yes, madame.
Mistress. Head up . . . (*She lifts head up.*) That's it. Don't be afraid to look people in the eyes,

my dear. If you think of yourself as inferior, that's exactly how people will treat you.
Julia. Yes, ma'am.
Mistress. A quiet girl, aren't you? . . . Now then, let's settle our accounts. I imagine you must need money although you never ask me for it yourself. Let's see now, we agreed on thirty rubles¹ a month, did we not?
6 Julia (*surprised*). Forty, ma'am.
Mistress. No, no, thirty. I made a note of it. (*Points to the book*) I always pay my governesses thirty . . . Who told you forty?
7 Julia. You did, ma'am. I spoke to no one else concerning money . . .
Mistress. Impossible. Maybe you *thought* you heard forty when I said thirty. If you kept your head up, that would never happen. Look at me again and I'll say it clearly. *Thirty rubles a month.*
8 Julia. If you say so, ma'am.
Mistress. Settled. Thirty a month it is . . . Now then, you've been here two months exactly.
Julia. Two months and five days.
Mistress. No, no. Exactly two months. I made

°**Chekhov** (chĕk´ôf´): a major Russian dramatist and short-story writer (1860–1904).

1. **rubles** (rōō´bəlz): The ruble is the Russian unit of money, like the dollar in the United States.

The Governess 343

MOTIVATIONAL SUMMARY
In a wealthy household in turn-of-the-century Russia, the Mistress of the house calls Julia, the governess, for a settling of accounts. However, it soon becomes clear that Julia is held accountable for a great number of things, and every one of them results in deductions from her already meager wages. The Mistress becomes annoyed at Julia's meek manner and urges her to look her in the eye and speak up. Will Julia tell her employer what she really thinks?

PRESENTATION
Explain that girls not much older than today's high-school students used to be hired as governesses to live with well-to-do families to care for and to educate the family's children. This one-act play involves a conversation between a young

---

9 Characterization. Likes to offer herself as role model.

10 Expressing an Opinion
Julia must be viewed here as either forgetful, a liar, or a victim. Which do you think she is? Probably a victim.

11 Making Inferences
Do you think Julia really remembers? Probably not; going along to please Mistress.

12 Appears that Julia has won a minor but satisfying point.

13 Characterization. Julia is asked to decide a fair settlement, but backs down again.

14 Mistress deducts full day's pay because Julia stopped working early; obviously Julia is being cheated.

15 Irony. Mistress is obviously not "used to taking losses."

16 Mistress appears to be greedy tyrant, using dominant position to take advantage of subordinate.

17 Irony. Even if Julia's salary was "good money" at first, it is not now.

---

9 a note of it. You should keep books the way I do so there wouldn't be these discrepancies.[2] So—we have two months at thirty rubles a month . . . comes to sixty rubles. Correct?
Julia (*curtsies*). Yes, ma'am. Thank you, ma'am.
Mistress. Subtract nine Sundays . . . We did agree to subtract Sundays, didn't we?
10 **Julia.** No, ma'am.
Mistress. Eyes! Eyes! . . . Certainly we did. I've always subtracted Sundays. I didn't bother making a note of it because I always do it. Don't you recall when I said we will subtract Sundays?
Julia. No, ma'am.
Mistress. Think.
Julia (*thinks*). No, ma'am.
Mistress. You weren't thinking. Your eyes were wandering. Look straight at my face and look hard . . . Do you remember now?
11 **Julia** (*softly*). Yes, ma'am.
Mistress. I didn't hear you, Julia.
Julia (*louder*). Yes, ma'am.
Mistress. Good. I was sure you'd remember. . . . Plus three holidays. Correct?
Julia. Two, ma'am. Christmas and New Year's.
Mistress. And your birthday. That's three.
Julia. I worked on my birthday, ma'am.
Mistress. You did? There was no need to. My governesses never worked on their birthdays . . .
Julia. But I did work, ma'am.
Mistress. But that's not the question, Julia. We're discussing financial matters now. I will, 12 however, only count two holidays if you insist . . . Do you insist?
Julia. I did work, ma'am.
Mistress. Then you *do* insist.
Julia. No, ma'am.
Mistress. Very well. That's three holidays;

2. **discrepancies** (dĭs-krĕp′ən-sēz): disagreements.

---

therefore we take off twelve rubles. Now then, four days little Kolya was sick, and there were no lessons.
Julia. But I gave lessons to Vanya.
Mistress. True. But I engaged you to teach two children, not one. Shall I pay you in full for doing only half the work?
13 **Julia.** No, ma'am.
Mistress. So we'll deduct it . . . Now, three days you had a toothache and my husband gave you permission not to work after lunch. Correct?
Julia. After four. I worked until four.
Mistress (*looks in the book*). I have here: "Did not work after lunch." We have lunch at one and are finished at two, not at four, correct?
Julia. Yes, ma'am. But I——
Mistress. That's another seven rubles . . . Seven and twelve is nineteen . . . Subtract . . . 14 that leaves . . . forty-one rubles . . . Correct?
Julia. Yes, ma'am. Thank you, ma'am.
Mistress. Now then, on January fourth you broke a teacup and saucer, is that true?
Julia. Just the saucer, ma'am.
Mistress. What good is a teacup without a saucer, eh? . . . That's two rubles. The saucer was an heirloom. It cost much more, but let it go. 15 I'm used to taking losses.
Julia. Thank you, ma'am.
Mistress. Now then, January ninth, Kolya climbed a tree and tore his jacket.
Julia. I forbad him to do so, ma'am.
16 **Mistress.** But he didn't listen, did he? . . . Ten rubles . . . January fourteenth, Vanya's shoes were stolen . . .
Julia. By the maid, ma'am. You discharged her yourself.
17 **Mistress.** But you get paid good money to watch everything. I explained that in our first meeting. Perhaps you weren't listening. Were you listening that day, Julia, or was your head in the clouds?
Julia. Yes, ma'am.
Mistress. Yes, your head was in the clouds?

344 DRAMA

governess, Julia, and her mistress. The setting is a room in what is probably a fine home in Russia around 1900.

Students will find this play easy to read and understand. It is brief and can be dramatized in one class period. Students may be challenged by considering the play's dramatic **irony**. Remind them that the mistress is attempting to teach Julia a lesson. Is it possible that Julia may have taught her mistress a lesson?

TRANSPARENCY 28
Literary Elements
Conflict – invites students to explore aspects of internal and external conflict.

Julia. No, ma'am. I was listening.
Mistress. Good girl. So that means another five rubles off. (*Looks in the book*) . . . Ah yes . . . the sixteenth of January I gave you ten rubles.
Julia. You didn't.
Mistress. But I made a note of it. Why would I make a note of it if I didn't give it to you?
Julia. I don't know, ma'am.
Mistress. That's not a satisfactory answer, Julia . . . Why would I make a note of giving you ten rubles if I did not in fact give it to you, eh? . . . No answer? . . . Then I must have given it to you, mustn't I?
Julia. Yes, ma'am. If you say so, ma'am.
Mistress. Well, certainly I say so. That's the point of this little talk. To clear these matters up . . . Take twenty-seven from forty-one, that leaves . . . fourteen, correct?
18 Julia. Yes, ma'am. (*She turns away, softly crying.*)
Mistress. What's this? Tears? Are you crying? Has something made you unhappy, Julia? Please tell me. It pains me to see you like this. I'm so sensitive to tears. What is it?
Julia. Only once since I've been here have I ever been given any money and that was by your husband. On my birthday he gave me three rubles.
Mistress. Really? There's no note of it in my book. I'll put it down now. (*She writes in the book.*) Three rubles. Thank you for telling me. Sometimes I'm a little lax with my accounts . . .
19 Always shortchanging myself. So then, we take three more from fourteen . . . leaves eleven . . . Do you wish to check my figures?
Julia. There's no need to, ma'am.
Mistress. Then we're all settled. Here's your salary for two months, dear. Eleven rubles. (*She puts the pile of coins on the desk.*) Count it.
20 Julia. It's not necessary, ma'am.
Mistress. Come, come. Let's keep the records straight. Count it.

Julia (*reluctantly counts it*). One, two, three, four, five, six, seven, eight, nine, ten . . . ? There's only ten, ma'am.
Mistress. Are you sure? Possibly you dropped one . . . Look on the floor; see if there's a coin there.
Julia. I didn't drop any, ma'am. I'm quite sure.
Mistress. Well, it's not here on my desk and I *know* I gave you eleven rubles. Look on the floor.
21 Julia. It's all right, ma'am. Ten rubles will be fine.
Mistress. Well, keep the ten for now. And if we don't find it on the floor later, we'll discuss it again next month.
22 Julia. Yes, ma'am. Thank you, ma'am. You're very kind, ma'am. (*She curtsies and then starts to leave.*)
Mistress. Julia! (*Julia stops, turns.*) Come back here. (*She crosses back to the desk and curtsies again.*) Why did you thank me?
Julia. For the money, ma'am.
23 Mistress. For the money? . . . But don't you realize what I've done? I've cheated you . . . *Robbed* you! I have no such notes in my book. I made up whatever came into my mind. Instead of the eighty rubles which I owe you, I gave you only ten. I have actually stolen from you and still you thank me . . . Why?
Julia. In the other places that I've worked, they
24 didn't give me anything at all.
Mistress. Then they cheated you even worse than I did . . . I was playing a little joke on you.
25 A cruel lesson just to teach you. You're much too trusting, and in this world that's very dangerous . . . I'm going to give you the entire eighty rubles. (*Hands her an envelope*) It's all ready for you. The rest is in this envelope. Here, take it.
Julia. As you wish, ma'am. (*She curtsies and starts to go again.*)
Mistress. Julia! (*Julia stops.*) Is it possible to be so spineless? Why don't you protest? Why don't

---

18 Drawing Conclusions
What do you think Julia must be feeling at this point? Probably utter helplessness and frustration.

19 Analyzing
What makes the Mistress' claim to be "always shortchanging myself" ironic? She is shortchanging Julia, not herself.

20 Drawing Conclusions
Why does Julia say it is "not necessary" to recount money and "no need" to check figures? Powerless to change anything even if she finds mistake.

21
Characterization. Julia has given up completely; will not insist she is owed one ruble.

22
Irony. Julia's assertion that Mistress is "very kind" is ironic in light of the way she has been treated.

23
Plot. Revelation of the truth is the play's **turning point**. Audience is relieved as Mistress admits that she has cheated Julia.

24
Julia feels she is doing well to get ten rubles.

25 Summarizing
What lesson is the Mistress trying to teach Julia? To be more assertive and less trusting of others.

The Governess 345

CLOSURE
Ask students what lessons they think the characters teach each other in the play.

TRANSPARENCY 26
Reader Response
An Interview with a Character — invites students to participate in a creative dialogue with a character.

EXTENSION AND ENRICHMENT
Have students recreate the scene between the Mistress and Julia in pantomime. Upon completion of the pantomime, initiate a discussion of the importance of facial expressions, movements, and gestures in the stage play.

26
Mistress asks important questions that readers want answered.

27
Theme. Smile suggests that "simpleton" role is pose adopted for self-protection in a world that demands poses for survival.

READING CHECK
1. To pay her (p. 343).
2. Two, Vanya and Kolya (p. 344).
3. French and mathematics (p. 343).
4. Eighty rubles (p. 345).

FOR STUDY AND DISCUSSION
1. When Mistress admits that she has cheated Julia.
2a. To be more assertive and less trusting. 2b. Most will agree that she is not.
3. Answers will vary. Most will agree that Julia has armored herself against shocks by attitude of polite resignation; keeps real opinions to herself.
4. Julia's "trace of a smile" and Mistress' look of "bafflement" inidcate that he is sympathetic toward Julia.
5. People form defenses under mistreatment and will stick to them even in times of relief.

ABOUT THE AUTHOR
Neil Simon is known for his comic plays, and, as a result, some do not consider him a serious writer. However, Simon has said that one of his goals is to show people the absurdity in their lives, and humor is a way of doing so. He uses humor in serious ways; it may function as a defense, a weapon, an escape; it may reveal truth.

346

---

26 you speak up? Why don't you cry out against this cruel and unjust treatment? Is it really possible to be so guileless,³ so innocent, such a—pardon me for being so blunt—such a simpleton?

27 **Julia** (*the faintest trace of a smile on her lips*). Yes, ma'am . . . it's possible.

[*She curtsies again and runs off. The* Mistress *looks after her a moment, a look of complete bafflement on her face. The lights fade.*]

---

3. **guileless** (gīl′lĭs): simple; without deceit.

Reading Check

1. Why has the Mistress summoned Julia?
2. How many children does Julia take care of?
3. What subjects does the Mistress inquire about during the interview?
4. How much money does the Mistress actually give Julia?

For Study and Discussion

Analyzing and Interpreting the Play

1. The **turning point** of a play occurs when there is a decisive change or turn in the action. What is the turning point in *The Governess*?

2a. What is the "lesson" Julia's mistress wishes to teach her? **b.** Do you think she is successful?

3. This play is based on a short story called "A Nincompoop." A *nincompoop* is a person who is easily deceived. Do you believe Julia gives in so easily because she is stupid, or do you think there is another explanation for her meekness?

4. What do you think is the author's attitude toward Julia? Is he critical? sympathetic?

5. What insight into human nature does this play give?

About the Author

Neil Simon (1927–   )

Neil Simon was born in New York City. He is known for his comedies and his portrayal of American family life. He has written and adapted more than fifty plays and screenplays. In an interview for *Life,* he described his first taste of comedy and his goal as a playwright: "When I was a kid, I climbed up on a stone ledge to watch an outdoor movie of Charlie Chaplin. I laughed so hard I fell off, cut my head open and was taken to the doctor, bleeding and laughing.... My idea of the ultimate achievement in a comedy is to make a whole audience fall onto the floor, writhing and laughing so hard that some of them pass out."

Among Simon's well-known comedies are *Barefoot in the Park* (1962), *The Odd Couple* (1965), *Brighton Beach Memoirs* (1982), and *Biloxi Blues* (1984). His many honors include an Emmy award, two Tony awards, and three Writers Guild awards. In 1983 he was elected into the Theater Hall of Fame. Simon used his experience as a scriptwriter for *Laughter on the 23rd Floor* (1993), which is about a group of television comedy writers in the 1950s.

346 DRAMA

OBJECTIVES
The overall aim is for students to demonstrate an understanding of how realistic **dialogue** advances the **plot** and brings the **characters** to life. For a complete list of objectives, see the **Teacher's Notes**.

VOCABULARY
The underlined words are in the Glossary. In addition, call students' attention to the vocabulary footnotes in their textbooks.

FOCUS / MOTIVATION
Ask students if they have ever been afraid of something and ashamed to admit their fear. Explain that one of the play's characters experiences this difficult combination of emotions.

When the Rattlesnake Sounds

ALICE CHILDRESS

Harriet Tubman was the most famous leader of the Underground Railroad, a system that helped enslaved people escape to freedom during the mid-1800s. She has often been compared to Moses, the Biblical leader of the Israelites, because she helped more than three hundred fugitive slaves reach safety and freedom. In this play, Alice Childress re-creates the language that might have been spoken by people who were poor and had little or no schooling. As you read, look for the lines that explain the title of the play.

Characters

Harriet Tubman, *an experienced leader who knows how to handle people with firmness...and love. Actually she was a little woman, five feet tall, but for the purposes of a play the qualities of leadership and compassion are more important than actual appearance. She is in her early forties.*

Lennie, *a strong, determined, no-nonsense kind of young woman. She is used to hard work and is perhaps physically stronger than Harriet, but does not have the tact to handle leadership. She is about twenty-five years old.*

Celia, *a very attractive young woman who has certainly been more sheltered than the other two. Celia is also a dedicated person...but she sees the freedom struggle in romantic terms...and has the tendency to get fed up when the going is grubby and ordinary.*

1 Time: *Very close to the end of legal slavery.*
2 Place: *Cape May, New Jersey.*
Scene: *A hotel laundry room.*

There is a pile of loose laundry on the floor waiting to be done...much with flounces and lace to suggest the summer clothing of ladies in the 1860s. There are three washtubs filled with water and laundry; in each tub is a washboard. Harriet, Lennie, *and* Celia *are washing clothes. The women are dressed in calico dresses and aprons.* Harriet *and* Lennie *work vigorously, absorbed in the task.* Celia *is slowing up and finally stops.*

3 **Celia** (*cautiously watching* Harriet *and* Lennie). Lord, I'm tired. (*Others keep working.*) Seem like we workin way past our dinnertime, don't it? Harriet? Lennie?

TEACHING RESOURCES C
Teacher's Notes, p. 39
Reading Check, p. 41
Study Guide, p. 43
Language Skills, p. 46
Selection Test, p. 49

PREREADING FOCUS
The headnote emphasizes that the play is based on actual events. Ask students to predict from the title what they think the play will be about.

When the Rattlesnake Sounds

1
President Lincoln signed Emancipation Proclamation in 1863 in middle of Civil War. War ended in 1865, and 13th Amendment, which made slavery illegal, was passed same year.

2
New Jersey ended slavery in 1804, so characters, though African American, are not slaves. They work in hotel laundry to earn their livings.

3 Analyzing
Why does Celia watch other women cautiously? She wants to see their reaction to her announcement that she is tired.

When the Rattlesnake Sounds

MOTIVATIONAL SUMMARY
Three women are vigorously washing clothes in the washtubs of a hotel laundry room. The women have agreed to wash and iron clothes to raise money to help slaves escape from the South. Celia, one of the younger women, expresses doubt and fear about their undertaking, so Harriet describes her fearful flight from slavery to freedom and her desire to make freedom possible to all slaves.

PRESENTATION
You may want to explain to students that the Thirteenth Amendment to the Constitution (1865) was the final act in freeing slaves. Some slaves had been freed earlier by state legislatures. New Jersey had ended slavery, so the

4
Dinner, main meal of day, was served around noon. Evening meal was light and was called supper.

5
Exaggeration. Celia says she was so tired night before that even her bones were tired.

6 Finding Cause and Effect
Why does singing make work go faster? Singing takes people's minds off work.

7
Conflict. Lennie wants to annoy Celia.

8 Analyzing
What does Celia's unwillingness to sing suggest about her attitude? That she is not as caught up in work as other women are.

9 Drawing Conclusions
Is Celia sincere in her question? No. She knows as well as others do why they work so hard.

10
Women apparently earn twenty-five cents per bundle.

VISUAL CONNECTIONS
Exploring the Subject
Harriet Tubman was born into slavery in 1820. Despite scant education and the threat of betrayal by her husband, Tubman escaped to the North in 1848. During the next ten years, she helped over three hundred other slaves find freedom through the Underground Railroad. During the Civil War she served in the Union Army in various capacities. In her later years she founded a home for the aged and the poor with the twenty-dollar-a-month pension she received from the government. She died in 1913.

4 **Lennie.** Not much past dinner. It feels like about one o'clock.
Harriet. We're gonna stop an eat by 'n by. We'll put out five bundles of wash today. Yesterday was only four.
5 **Celia.** *Only* four? When I went to bed last night, I cried, I was so bone-weary. Only? How can four bundles of wash be *only*?
6 **Harriet.** Just a while longer, Celia. Let's sing. When you singin, the work goes fast. You pick a song, Lennie.
7 **Lennie** (*decides to pick one that will annoy* Celia). Wadin in the water, wadin in the water (children). Wadin in the water, God gonna trouble the water.

[Harriet *joins her in singing.*]

8 **Celia** (*drying her hands on her apron*). I want my dinner now. I'm hungry.
Lennie. We all hungry, Celia. Can't you hold out a little more?
Celia. If we *all* hungry, why don't we *all* eat? We been up since seven this mornin...workin. For what? Why?
Lennie. You know why! We got to finish five bundles.
9 **Celia** (*to the heavens above*). Five bundles for what?
10 **Lennie.** For a dollar and a quarter, that's what! (*Grumbling*) I'm tellin you...some people.

Harriet Tubman, shown far left, with some of the fugitive slaves she helped to free.

348 DRAMA

characters in the play are not slaves. Harriet, however, had escaped from slavery and knew its hardships and fears.

Through the dialogue and actions of the three women, much can be learned about their personalities. Have students locate passages that support Harriet's generosity, wisdom, and dedication to her cause. Discuss with students the changes that Lennie and Celia undergo in the course of the play. If *When the Rattlesnake Sounds* is read aloud, you will probably want to assign parts in advance to give readers an opportunity to practice the language and the emotional delivery of some of the lines.

Harriet (*sensing trouble, she stops washing*). Celia is right, Lennie. It's not good to kill yourself workin.

Lennie (*in anger*). She knows why we're doin it, Harriet. Some people...I'm tellin you.

Harriet (*firmly*). Let's have our dinner Lennie.

Lennie (*her eyes on* Celia). Did you fix it again, Harriet? We suppose to take turns. I take a turn, you take a turn, then...

11 **Harriet** (*hastily cutting her off*). I got some nice corn bread and some side meat. The coffee should be ready. (*Handing out paper parcels to the girls*) We need to rest awhile. Here, Celia, and that's yours, Lennie. (*Going back to her tub*) I'll just wash out these few more pieces before my water turns cold.

Lennie. I ain't restin unless you rest too. Not like some people I know.

Celia. She keep sayin *some people*. Wonder who she means?

12 **Harriet** (*with a sigh*). I'll stop too.

Celia (*looking at the pile of unwashed clothes as she unwraps her lunch*). White folks love white clothes and they love to sit in the grass too...and I'm sick of scrubbin grass stains.

Harriet. Well, we need the money.

Celia (*puts down her lunch and snatches up a*
13 *flouncy white dress*). Look at all the money *they* got. This cost every bit of twelve dollars. (*Imitating the hotel guests*) Spendin the summer in a big hotel, ridin round in carriages. (*Drops her airy act and goes back to anger*) If just one of em give us what she spend in a week...we wouldn't have to work two months in no hotel laundry.

14 **Lennie.** I got a life-size picture of them givin you that much money. They ain't gonna give you nothin, so you better be glad you got the chance to *earn* some.

Celia. Scrubbin! Ain't that a damn somethin to
15 be glad about? Excuse me, Harriet, I meant to say dern or drat.

Harriet. Celia got somethin on her mind, and she need to talk, so let her talk, Lennie. But no dammin, dernin, or drattin either. All here got more manners than to cuss.

Lennie (*as she looks at* Harriet's *food*). Is that your dinner? You ain't got no meat on your bread, Harriet.

Harriet. I don't too much like meat.

Lennie. I know who do. Some people.

Celia (*bursting out at* Harriet). Stop sayin that! You do too like meat! Stop makin out like you don't. You goin without so you can save another
16 nickel. Yall drivin me outta my head. Maybe I'm just not suited for this kinda thing.

Lennie. But I am, huh?

17 **Harriet** (*quietly and seriously*). You tired of this bargain we made? You sorry about it and don't know how to quit?

Lennie (*flaring with anger*). She promised and she got to stick by it! Your father is a *deacon of the*
18 *church*...and if you don't keep your word, you gonna bring disgrace down on him and *every member* of your family.

Harriet. Lennie, don't be so brash. Mother and father is one thing...child is another. Each one stands upon his own deeds. She don't have to stay. Celia, you can go if you want.

Celia. I don't really want to get out of it. But I want *some* of my money for myself. I'm tired of sleepin three in a room. I want to spend a little of the money...just a little, Harriet. Buy a few treats.

Lennie. She's jealous of them rich white ladies...cause they got silk parasols to match they dresses. I heard her say it. "Wish I had me a silk parasol."

Harriet. We eatin and sleepin. We spend for that and nothin more...that was the bargain.

19 **Celia** (*to* Lennie). I could own a silk parasol *and* carry it...without actin like a field hand.

Harriet. I been a field hand, children. Harness to a plow like a workhorse.

Celia. Scuse me, I'm sorry.

When the Rattlesnake Sounds

---

11 Drawing Conclusions
Why does Harriet cut Lennie off? She sees where Lennie's comments are headed and wants to prevent a major argument.

12 Finding Cause and Effect
Why does Harriet agree to stop working? She realizes an argument is about to start between other women, and she stops to prevent it.

13
Celia resents fact that hotel guests seem to have a great deal of money.

14
Irony. Lennie means she cannot imagine guests giving Celia money. Statement is ironic because it means opposite of what it says literally.

15 Analyzing
Why does Celia apologize to Harriet for her language and not to both women? As oldest, Harriet serves as a kind of mother to other women. Celia has greater respect for her than for Lennie.

16
Exaggeration. Celia implies she is being driven insane, but she is really only annoyed.

17
Inference. Harriet has inferred from Celia's comments that she is deeply dissatisfied with bargain they made. She states her concern in form of question.

18
A *deacon* is a leader of church. Because of this, he and his family are prominent members themselves.

19 Analyzing
What does Celia imply about her breeding and social standing? That Lennie is beneath her and would act like a field hand if she had a parasol.

MEETING INDIVIDUAL NEEDS
ESL/LEP • You may want to emphasize that the Underground Railroad was not an actual railroad under or above the ground. Explain that the term *underground* in this case means "secret" or "hidden." The term *railroad* simply implies movement (of people) from one location to another.

---

20 Lennie taunts Celia because Celia has apparently lost some of her commitment to cause of abolition of slavery.

21 Tone. Celia becomes serious and sad.

22 Removal of aprons and beginning of music indicate a transition in play. Director might also call for change in lighting to mark transition even further.

23 Flashback. Following scene is a reenactment of events that took place before Harriet moved to New Jersey.

24 People in church show their approval of Harriet and of what she is saying by responding aloud during her speech.

25 Harriet describes her experiences in helping escaped slaves from South get to North on Underground Railroad.

26 Metaphor. Compares work of leading people to freedom in North to a farmer plowing field to plant crop.

27 Allusion. Joan of Arc was burned at stake for her beliefs. The gesture Celia refers to suggests she is willing to suffer and die for her beliefs about freedom.

28 End of music and putting on of aprons marks end of flashback and return to present time of play.

---

20 **Lennie** (*really sarcastic*). Celia, that don't sound nothin like them big speeches you used to make in church meetin. (*Mocking* Celia) "I'll die for my freedom!"...Had everybody whoopin and hollerin every time you open your mouth, whole church stompin and shoutin amen.

21 **Celia** (*sadly*). I remember how it was.

22 [*The women remove their aprons and* Harriet *takes her place center stage. Church music in from offstage tape or recording of "The Old Ship of Zion," or any of the African Methodist Episcopal Zion songs. Harriet Tubman was a member of that church. She addresses the audience as though they are the congregation.*]

23 **Harriet** (*music and humming are in low as she speaks*). God bless you, brothers and sisters, bless you, children.

24 **Offstage Voices plus Lennie and Celia.** Amen...Amen...Bless God.
Harriet. I thank the good Lord for the support of the African Methodist Episcopal Zion Church in the freedom struggle. There is comfort and good fellowship here.
Church Voices. Yes, Lord. Amen.

25 **Harriet.** Not like hidin in the bitter cold, with the huntin dogs followin you down with no restin place in sight. We had to give the little babies paregoric¹ so they wouldn't cry and let the paddy-rollers² know where to find us. We crossed some lonely roads and rivers...the dark of the night around us, the clouds cuttin off the sight of the North Star.³ But everything was all right cause where I go...God goes...and I carry a gun...two guns...a hand pistol and a shoulder rifle...just in case the Lord tell me I got to use it!

---

1. **paregoric** (păr′ə-gôr′ĭk): a medicine to soothe pain.
2. **paddy-rollers:** patrollers; slave catchers.
3. **North Star:** Polaris, the North Star, pointed the way to freedom.

Church Voices. Amen! Speak! Praise the holy name! Amen!
Harriet. I thank the Father for the help and assistance of the Society of Friends and the abolitionists,⁴ and all well-wishers.
Church Voices. Amen, Amen, Amen.

26 **Harriet.** But as I put my hand to the plow to do the work of Freedom, so I also put *my money* into the work. I have none now, so I will spend my summer washin and ironin so that when the fall come I have *some of my own* to put...to buy food, medicine, paregoric for the babies, and ammunition for the pistol....Lord grant I never use it. Any ladies here want to go with me to wash clothes and give the money to free our slave brethren?⁵
Lennie (*stands by* Harriet's *side*). If you would have me, Mrs. Tubman, it would be the greatest honor, a great honor indeed.
Harriet. Thank you, my daughter.

27 **Celia** (*stands up and throws her arms out in a Joan of Arc gesture*). I'll die for my freedom! Take me, Sister! I'm ready to fight the good fight. Hallelujah!
Church Voices (Celia *has set the church to rocking*). Glory! Glory! Hallelujah! Fight the good fight! Amen!

28 [*Music fades out as women don their aprons again.*]

Celia. I remember how it was, Lennie, and the promise I made. But how much can we get like this? Maybe if *everybody* worked and gave their money to the Underground, it would mean somethin. This way I just can't see it, but I believe in freedom and I understand.
Harriet. Ain't no such thing as only "understandin." Understandin mean action. You have

---

4. **Society of Friends:** Quakers, who helped runaway slaves; **abolitionists** (ăb′ə-lĭsh′ən-ĭsts): those who wished to put an end to, or abolish, slavery.
5. **brethren** (brĕth′rən): brothers.

PORTFOLIO ASSESSMENT
Rock opera is a popular form of drama among young adults. Some students may be interested in converting *When the Rattlesnake Sounds* into a rock opera, complete with rock or rap music, and performing it for the class. Suggest that they disregard sets and costumes, and perform on a bare stage. Other students may want to organize stage crews and a filming crew to photograph and videotape the production. Consult with students about their participation in the production and mutually agree on how it will be assessed. Written paragraphs describing their participation may be included in student portfolios along with production photographs. (See *Portfolio Assessment and Professional Support Materials,* especially the section entitled **Suggestions for Portfolio Projects.**)

Seale Graphics/The Image Bank

to look after what *Celia* does... and if *nobody*
29 *else* do nothin, you got to. Freedom is just a baby, and you its mother. You don't stop lovin and carin for it just cause others don't care.
Celia. Maybe it's easy to talk like that when you
30 Moses. It's easy to kill yourself for somethin when thousands of people be cheerin you on. Lennie and Celia don't mean nothin to nobody. We could die here and nobody would know or care.
Lennie. Don't you talk for me! Ain't nothin
31 greater to me than to be able to say... "I, Lennie Brown, scrubbed clothes side by side with Moses." If you lookin for praise, you don't belong here.

Harriet. Children, let us keep peace. We act like we hate each other worse than we hate the slave owner.
Celia. I know what I sound like.... (*falls at Harriet's feet and holds out her hands*). Oh, Harriet, my hands are skinned sore.
32 **Lennie.** Do, Jesus, look at Celia's hands.
Harriet (*turns Celia's head and searches for the*
33 *truth*). But it ain't your hands that's really botherin you. It ain't food, it ain't sleepin three in a room, and it ain't about silk parasols. What's botherin you, Celia?
34 **Celia.** I'm so shame for feelin the way I do. Lord knows I'm shame.
Harriet. Tell it. Speak your shame.

When the Rattlesnake Sounds **351**

29
Metaphor. Compares freedom to baby. Both need to be loved, taken care of, and guarded.

30
Harriet Tubman was called Moses by people familiar with her work for Underground Railroad. In Bible, Moses leads Israelites out of slavery in Egypt; Tubman leads African Americans out of slavery in South.

31
Irony. Lennie scolds Celia for wanting praise, but she looks forward to telling people about working with Harriet Tubman so people will praise her.

32
Irony. Lennie's tone is sarcastic, a bitter form of irony.

33 Making Inferences
How does Harriet know something deeper is bothering Celia? Answers will vary. Her age and experience give her insight into young woman.

34 Summarizing
Why does Celia feel ashamed? She feels that she has gone back on her promise to help slaves escape.

MEETING INDIVIDUAL NEEDS

ESL/LEP • You may want to alert students to the following variations in spelling:

1. Deletion of final *–g* on *–ing* forms
   workin / singin / mornin

2. Deletion of initial *–a*
   cross —across
   fraid —afraid
   bout —about

3. Substitution of *–a* for *of*, *have*, and *to*
   outta —out of
   kinda —kind of
   musta —must have

4. Other variations
   scuse —excuse
   em —them
   ceptin —except

35
Harriet Tubman was well known for her work helping slaves escape. Some slave holders had offered a reward for her capture.

36 Analyzing
Why does Celia want to hide her fear? She thinks others will consider her weak and her character flawed.

37
Metaphor. Compares Celia to a rabbit, which Lennie believes to be a timid animal.

38
Harriet refers to her fear when she escaped slavery all by herself.

39
Simile. Compares light of sun to shine of gold, meaning she considered sunlight very valuable.

40 Making Generalizations
What does Harriet mean by the reference to her heart being with them? She had strong emotional attachments to people she left behind.

41
Lennie indicates she does not believe Harriet is serious, especially in her last sentence.

42
By "free labor" Harriet means that dresses had not been made by slaves.

43
Simile. Compares look of goodness on Captain Brown's face to a burning light that can light up darkness.

---

35 **Celia.** I'm *scared*. If these people in this hotel knew who you was. Forty thousand dollars' reward out for you!
Lennie (*dashes to the door to see if anyone is around to listen*). Hush your fool mouth! Moses got the charm. Slave holder will never catch Moses.
36 **Celia.** I'm so shame. All those other things just lies. I ain't so terrible tired. I'm just scared and shame cause I'm afraid. Me talkin so big. Sure, I'd work all summer and give the money to the Underground. It did sound so good in the meetin where it was all warm and friendly. Now I'm scared of gettin into trouble. I never been no slave. And I'm scared of nothin round me but white folks.
37 **Lennie.** We ain't got no room for no rabbity, timid kinda women in this work.
Harriet. Oh, yes, Lennie, we got room for the timid and the brave. Poor little Celia. Child, you lookin at a woman who's been plenty afraid. When the rattlesnake sounds a warnin . . . it's time to be scared. Ain't that natural? When I
38 run away was nobody to cheer me on . . . don't you think I was scared?
Lennie. But you got to freedom.
Harriet (*the feeling of a "meeting" begins*). Oh, but when I found I'd crossed that line! There was
39 such a glory over everything. The sun came shinin like gold through the trees.
Lennie (*feels she is at church meeting*). You felt like you was in heaven! You was free!
Harriet. But there was no one to welcome me in the land of freedom. I was a stranger in a strange land. My home, after all, was down in the old cabin quarters with the ones I knew and loved . . . my slave mother and father, brothers, sisters and friends. Aunt Day . . . she used to be midwife, tend the sick, bury the dead. Two field hands I knew, they used to ease some the work off the women who was expectin. There I was
40 standin on free land, with my heart back down there with them. What good is freedom without your people?

41 **Lennie.** Go on, Harriet!
Harriet. And so to this solemn resolution I come: As I was free . . . *they* would be free also.
Lennie. Praise God, that's Harriet Tubman!
Harriet. Sometimes I was scared in the icy river. Chilled to the bone and just might drown.
Lennie. But you got cross.
Harriet. I was scared in the dark and the swamp . . . but I come to the light. Most times I was full of hatred for the white folks.
Lennie. And you came to the Friends.
Harriet. And I came to John Brown.[6] (*Offstage music . . . soft violin . . . sound of voices ad-libbing[7] at a reception*). There was this big, fine affair, A reception. Abolitionist reception. The ladies
42 were all dressed in lovely gowns, made by free labor. I was in my best too . . . but that wasn't too much better than what I'm standin in. They had pretty cakes and a punch bowl . . . the grandest party. Violin music . . . what you call elegant. There was a goodly crowd, and I was way on the other side of the room, away from the main door where the people would enter. Everybody called him Captain Brown . . . Captain.

[*Harriet moves to the far side of the stage and turns toward the opposite door to illustrate the distance between her and Captain Brown.*]

Harriet. The whisper started way down the hall and came through the room . . . "It's Captain Brown. He's here. Captain Brown is about
43 to enter." Then he came in the door. He was a fine, stern-lookin gentleman . . . goodness glowed from his face like a burnin light. The room got quiet. He looked all around until he saw me. Mind now, we had never met. The ladies and gentlemen were all tryin to meet

---

6. **John Brown:** an abolitionist who led a raid at Harpers Ferry and was hanged for treason in 1859.
7. **ad-libbing:** improvising freely.

MEETING INDIVIDUAL NEEDS
Auditory Learners • Students may more fully appreciate the play's conversational **tone** and the characters' revealing emotions if students hear the language. You might want to choose some of your more expressive readers to prepare a presentation for the class. Be sure to include offstage voices and appropriate spiritual music for the reading.

Autobiography: Water/Ancestors/Middle Passage/ Family Ghosts (1988) by Howardena Pindell (1943–). Mixed media on canvas.

Wadsworth Atheneum, Hartford. The Ella Gallup Sumner and Mary Catlin Sumner Collection. ©Wadsworth Atheneum

VISUAL CONNECTIONS

About the Artist
Howardena Pindell (1943–) is a contemporary African American artist educated at Boston and Yale universities. Pindell worked at the Museum of Modern Art in New York City as a curator, while at the same time gaining national recognition for her work. In 1980, she left her position at the Museum of Modern Art to devote more time to her art career. Pindell's work is included in over thirty museums around the world.

About the Artwork
Autobiography: Water/Ancestors/ Middle Passage/Family Ghosts was created with mixed media. "Mixed media" is an art term that indicates that more than one medium was used in creating a piece. An artist may mix watercolor with pencil, collage with oil paint, pastel with marker, or any other combination. The artist's careful use of various media often results in striking and unusual works.

When the Rattlesnake Sounds 353

HISTORY LINK

Students who are interested in learning about the life of Harriet Tubman and her work with the Underground Railroad might prepare background information about Tubman, which could be presented to the class before the drama is read. If several students are doing research, you might have them combine their efforts and plan a choral reading, with each student giving information about a different segment of Harriet Tubman's life.

44 Metaphor. By calling Harriet Tubman "General," Brown implies that she is superior to him in rescuing slaves.

45 Metaphor. Harriet compares sights and sounds of battle to a storm and bodies of dead soldiers to a horrible crop.

46 Metaphor. Compares African American baby born in freedom to a monument honoring Celia's work.

47 Making Inferences
Why does Celia cry? Answers will vary. Perhaps she is ashamed of being afraid. Perhaps she realizes importance of her work and is overcome by realization.

48 Tone. Lennie becomes warmer and friendlier toward Celia, perhaps because she realizes for first time how scared Celia is.

49 Lennie wants Celia to know that everything is all right between them.

READING CHECK
1. Cape May, New Jersey (p. 347).
2. To spend the summer washing and ironing clothes to earn money (p. 350).
3. To buy food, medicine, and ammunition for the Underground Railroad (p. 350).
4. Moses (p. 351).
5. She is afraid of getting into trouble with the white folks for helping the slaves escape, and she is ashamed of her fear (p. 352).

---

him.... Oh, it was Captain, Captain, Captain. He held up his hand. There was silence, then
44 he said... "The first I see is General Tubman. The second is General Tubman. The third is General Tubman." He crossed the room and bowed to me... and I shook his hand.
Lennie. And he died for us, didn't he?
Harriet. Celia, he was a brave man, but I believe he must have been scared sometimes. But he did what he had to do.
Celia. I guess he was just brave. Some folks braver than others.
Harriet. I was with hundreds of brave black
45 men on battleground. I was there, Celia. We saw the lightning and that was the guns, then we heard the thunder and that was the big guns, then we heard the rain falling.... And that was the drops of blood. And when we came to get the crops, it was dead men we reaped.
Lennie. Fightin for us to be free. I guess they musta been scared sometimes.
Harriet. Give me your hand, Celia. Look, see the skin broken across the knuckles. Counta you some man or woman gonna have warm socks and boots to help em get to freedom. See the cuts the lye soap put in your skin. Counta you some little baby is gonna be born on free soil. It won't matter to him that you was afraid, won't matter that he did not know your name.
46 Won't nothin count ceptin he's free. A livin
47 monument to Celia's work. (*Celia cries.*) You go to the room and rest. Maybe you might want to stay here after you think about it.
48 **Lennie.** Sure, Celia... think bout it. We can manage. And if you want to go home, we won't hold it against you. I ought not to have said what I did. Sometimes I get scared myself... but it makes me act evil *and* brave, you know?
Celia. I don't want to go home. Guess there's worse things than fear. I'm glad to know I don't have to be shame about it.
Harriet. That's right. If you was home doin nothin, what would you have to be fraid bout? That's when a woman oughta feel shame, shame to her very soul.
Celia (*gathers up clothes, places them in tub, starts working.* Harriet *goes to her tub.*) If we sing, the work goes faster.
49 **Lennie** (*goes to her tub*). Your time to pick a song, Celia.

[*Celia starts scrubbing. They all work for a few moments. Celia has decided on a song. She sings out.*]

Celia.
Oh Lord, I don't feel no ways tired
Children, Oh, Glory Hallelujah
For I hope to shout *Glory* when this world is all on fire
Oh, Glory, Hallelujah

[*The others join her on the second round.*]

Oh, Lord, I don't feel no ways tired....

[*Curtain.*]

Reading Check
1. Where does the play take place?
2. What is the "bargain" the women have made?
3. What do they plan to do with the money that they earn?
4. By what other name is Harriet Tubman known?
5. What is Celia's real fear?

TRANSPARENCY 26

Reader Response
An Interview with a Character – invites students to participate in a creative dialogue with a character.

For Study and Discussion

Analyzing and Interpreting the Play

1a. How does Harriet prevent an argument between Lennie and Celia? **b.** Why would an argument endanger their plans?

2. During the course of the play, the author uses flashbacks to reveal action that happened at an earlier time. Locate these flashbacks. What information in these sequences helps you understand the background of the play?

3. What does Harriet mean by "Freedom is just a baby, and you its mother"?

4. At the end of the play, the women have renewed their sense of purpose. How does Harriet help them to overcome their fear?

5. Although this play is fictional, it is based on actual events in the life of Harriet Tubman. Do you feel that you have a better understanding of her courage and her achievement?

6. What does the title mean? Find evidence in the play to support your answer.

Focus on Writing a Scene

Creating Dialogue

Dialogue is talk or conversation between two or more characters. In a play, dialogue is the writer's main tool for carrying the plot forward and revealing character.

When you create dialogue for a dramatic scene, you will find these guidelines helpful:

1. Be sure your dialogue sounds natural and colloquial—the way people speak in real life. Say the characters' speeches out loud to test their realism and liveliness.
2. Be sure the dialogue suits the personality of the speaker.
3. Be sure the dialogue moves the plot along.

Review the notes for the assignment on page 334, or choose another dramatic situation for a scene. Use the guidelines above to create or revise each speaker's dialogue. When you have finished, exchange papers with a classmate. Offer each other suggestions on the dialogue in your dramatic scenes. Save your writing.

For Dramatization

Assembling a Director's Notebook

Suppose you were asked to direct Alice Childress' play. You would have to make many decisions. Read through the play again and jot down what you might need under the following headings:

Sets. What furniture would you need? Would you use any painted cloths, or backdrops, across the back of the stage?

Costumes. Some costumes are specified in the stage directions. Others are not and might have to be researched. How would John Brown be dressed and what would he look like?

Props. Some props are mentioned in the stage directions. Make a list of all the props you would need.

Lighting. Would lights of different colors help set the mood? How would you light the flashback sequences?

Sound. How would you provide the music called for in the play? What other sound effects might you use?

When the Rattlesnake Sounds

FOR STUDY AND DISCUSSION

1a. One time she agrees to stop washing clothes and eat an early lunch. Several other times she uses calming words to keep the peace. **b.** Their cause is a secret so an overheard discussion could endanger them.
2. The first relates the church meeting where the women volunteer to wash and iron clothes to earn money for the Underground Railroad; the second relates Harriet's arrival to freedom, her presence at the abolitionist reception, and her meeting with Captain Brown.
3. That freedom cannot grow and prosper without dedicated people who care.
4. By convincing them that fear is a natural emotion, and reminding them that their fear will help the freedom cause.
5. Responses will vary, but most students will probably agree that they do have a better understanding.
6. Fear is a natural reaction to dangerous situations. For example, when a rattlesnake sounds, you are aware of the danger. Many of the people associated with the Underground Railroad—the escaping slaves as well as those who helped them escape—had cause for fear, but their fear did not disable them; instead, it made them fight harder.

FOCUS ON WRITING A SCENE

You may want to encourage students to jot down some background information about the scenes for which they are creating **dialogue**. Have them include a list of **characters** with descriptions, the time of the play, and a **description** of the place. Having this information readily available will help partners to evaluate whether the dialogue suits the personality of the speaker, sounds natural, and moves the plot along.

CLOSURE
Ask students to explain how the use of realistic **dialogue** helps to advance the play's **plot** and to bring the **characters** to life.

EXTENSION AND ENRICHMENT
Suggest that students research the Underground Railroad to learn more about its history. Have them delve further into the life of Harriet Tubman and the importance of such people as Levi Coffin, a Cincinnati Quaker; Lucretia Mott, an abolitionist and feminist; and Lydia Child, a reformer and abolitionist who founded the first monthly magazine for children in the United States.

FOR DRAMATIZATION
Suggested answers:
1. *Sets.* Other than washtubs, no furniture necessary. Laundry room could have small table, and podium could be used for church scene. Because scenes change quickly in flashback, no time to change sets; therefore, dark backdrop would be appropriate.
2. *Costumes.* Students may answer that John Brown is dressed in typical attire of the period: long-sleeve shirt, vest, jacket, large-brimmed hat, dark trousers.
3. *Props.* Loose laundry, washtubs filled with laundry and water, washboards, paper parcels of lunch, flouncy white dress.
4. *Lighting.* Different-colored lights suggest different moods. The church scene might have blue muted lighting with spotlights on the speakers. The abolitionist reception might have multicolored lights to give festive air.
5. *Sound.* Tape recording of "The Old Ship of Zion," tape recording of soft violin music; several people humming "The Old Ship of Zion," church voices, reception voices, tinkling glasses at reception.

ABOUT THE AUTHOR
Alice Childress has won numerous awards and honors for her works, including the Obie Award for best original Off-Broadway play for *Trouble in the Mind* (1956); Virgin Islands film festival award for best screenplay for *A Hero Ain't Nothin' but a Sandwich* (1977); Filmmakers Hall of Fame (1977); and "Alice Childress Week" officially observed in Charleston, S.C. and Columbia, S.C. to celebrate opening of *Sea Island Song* (1977).

About the Author

Alice Childress (1916–1994)

Alice Childress was born in Charleston. She was raised by her grandmother, who encouraged her to keep a record of her thoughts. Before she became a writer, Childress worked at a variety of jobs in New York City. For a time she was an actress with the American Negro Theater. Her first major success as a writer came with her 1955 play, *Trouble in Mind,* which gave black actors an alternative to the stereotypical roles they were usually given.

Childress is known for her honest portrayal of her race, and her plays, novels, and screenplays have often been controversial. Her novel about teenage heroin addiction, *A Hero Ain't Nothin' but a Sandwich* (1973), received several awards and was adapted for the screen. In collaboration with her husband, Nathan Woodard, she wrote musicals, including *Young Martin Luther King.* At the time of her death Childress was working on a novel about her great-grandmothers, one of whom had been a slave.

Underground Railroad (1982), a quilt made by an interracial group of senior citizens from Oberlin, Ohio. The episodes in the quilt tell the story of the Underground Railroad and how Oberlin helped fugitive slaves.

OBJECTIVES
The overall aim is for students to analyze a **plot** involving a series of related events that allow **conflict** to develop and to be resolved. For a complete list of objectives, see the **Teacher's Notes.**

VOCABULARY
The underlined words are in the Glossary. In addition, call students' attention to the vocabulary footnotes in their textbooks.

FOCUS / MOTIVATION
Ask students to think of characters in books or movies whose greed brings about their downfall. Tell students that the disrespectful grandsons in this play fall prey to their desire for treasure.

The Jewels of the Shrine
A Play in One Act

JAMES ENE HENSHAW

Many folk tales involve characters who are tricksters. They use their wits to outsmart other characters who may be bigger and stronger. In Norse myths, for example, Loki, the god of fire, likes to play tricks on others (see page 641). Trickster heroes are often animal characters: Coyote in Native American tales, Anansi in African folklore, Brer Rabbit in the African American oral tradition.
Who is the trickster in this play from Nigeria?

> **TEACHING RESOURCES C**
> Teacher's Notes, p. 51
> Reading Check, p. 54
> Study Guide, p. 56
> Language Skills, p. 59
> Building Vocabulary, p. 62
> Selection Vocabulary Test, p. 64
> Selection Test, p. 66

PREREADING FOCUS
The headnote points out that many folk tales contain tricksters. Ask students to share trickster tales that they are familiar with.

The Jewels of the Shrine

1
Setting. All action happens in one place, avoiding scenery change.

2 Drawing Conclusions
What does presence of hoes suggest about family? That they work as farmers.

Characters

Okorie (ō-kŏ-rē-ĕ), an old man
Arob (ă-rŏb) ⎱
Ojima (ō-jē-mə) ⎰ Okorie's grandsons
Bassi (bä-sē), a woman
A Stranger

Setting: *An imaginary village close to a town*
1 *in Nigeria. All the scenes of this play take place in Okorie's mud-walled house. The time is the present.*

Scene 1

The hall in Okorie's *house. There are three doors. One leads directly into* Okorie's *room. The two others are on either side of the hall. Of these, one leads to his grandsons' apartment, while the other acts as a general exit.*
  The chief items of furniture consist of a wide bamboo bed—on which is spread a mat—a wooden chair,
2 *a low table, and a few odds and ends, including three hoes.*

Okorie, *an old man of about eighty years of age,*
3 *with scanty grey hair and dressed in the way his village folk do, is sitting at the edge of the bed. He holds*
4 *a stout, rough walking-stick and a horn filled with palm wine.*
  On the wooden chair near the bed sits a Stranger, *a man of about forty-five years of age. He too occasionally sips wine from a calabash¹ cup. It is evening. The room is rather dark, and a cloth-in-oil lantern hangs from a hook on the wall.*

5 **Okorie.** Believe me, Stranger, in my days things were different. It was a happy thing to become an old man, because young people were taught to respect elderly men.

6 **Stranger** (*sipping his wine*). Here in the village you should be happier. In the town where I come from, a boy of ten riding a hired bicycle will knock down a man of fifty years without any feeling of pity.

7 **Okorie.** Bicycle. That is why I have not been to

---
1. **calabash** (kăl′ə-băsh′): a fruit with a hard shell that is often used as a dish or a cup.

3
Description. Description of Okorie as being dressed in traditional way emphasizes his old age and commitment to old ways.

4 Making Inferences
Why does Okorie use a horn for his wine? Animal horns are durable and readily available.

5 Analyzing
What does use of "Stranger," instead of name, suggest about this person? Stranger takes on mysterious importance.

6
Stranger tries to make Okorie happier about his situation by comparing life in village, where older people are still respected, to life in town, where there is no respect for older people at all.

7
First part of play, until Stranger's exit, is **exposition,** in which basic situation of play is outlined.

The Jewels of the Shrine **357**

MOTIVATIONAL SUMMARY
Okorie, an old man, confides in a stranger that he fears his grandsons will disgrace him by not giving him a proper burial. After the conversation, Okorie appears revived and shares a secret with his housekeeper about hidden jewels on his farm. The promise of wealth prompts the grandsons to treat Okorie with kindness and to give him a decent burial. But how will their insincerity be repaid?

PRESENTATION
In this one-act play, an old man with the help of a stranger tricks his greedy, disrespectful grandsons. The conversation in the first scene between Okorie and the stranger provides background information and mysteriously light-

An arm ornament with ivory and copper studs in the form of a lion. Benin City, Nigeria.

8 Irony. When Okorie is dead, he will not know whether he is or is not disgraced.

9 Bassi is a servant, not a relative, even though she addresses Okorie as "Grandfather" out of respect.

10 Okorie is transformed after Stranger's visit.

11 Description. Physical appearance of Okorie gives clue to how he felt about his life before Stranger's visit.

12 Finding Cause and Effect
What did Stranger say to bring about transformation of Okorie? Answers will vary. Perhaps Stranger helped Okorie see that he is better off with his grandsons than he thought he was.

13 By saying Stranger was God, Okorie suggests his new mood is result of a miracle.

town for ten years. Town people seem to enjoy rushing about doing nothing. It kills them.
Stranger. You are lucky that you have your grandchildren to help you. Many people in town have no one to help them.
Okorie. Look at me, Stranger, and tell me if these shabby clothes and this dirty beard show that I have good grandchildren. Believe me, Stranger, in my younger days things were different. Old men were happy. When they died they were buried with honour. But in my case,
8 Stranger, my old age has been unhappy. And my only fear now is that when I die my grandsons will not accord me the honour due to my age. It will be a disgrace to me.
Stranger. I will now go on my way, Okorie. May God help you.
Okorie. I need help, Stranger, for although I have two grandsons I am lonely and unhappy because they do not love or care for me. They tell me that I am from an older world. Farewell, Stranger. If you call again and I am alive, I will welcome you back. (*Exit* Stranger.)

9 [Bassi, *a beautiful woman, of about thirty years, enters.*]

Bassi. Who was that man, Grandfather?
Okorie. He was a stranger.
Bassi. I do not trust strangers. They may appear honest when the lights are on. But as soon as there is darkness, they creep back as thieves.

[Okorie *smiles and drinks his wine.*]

Bassi (*pointing to him*). What has happened,
10 Grandfather? When I left you this afternoon, you were old, your mind was worried, and your
11 eyes were swollen. Where now are the care, the sorrow, the tears in your eyes? You never smiled before, but now——
12 **Okorie.** The stranger has brought happiness back into my life. He has given me hope again.
Bassi. But don't they preach in town that it is only God who gives hope? Every other thing gives despair.
13 **Okorie.** Perhaps that stranger was God. Don't the preachers say that God moves like a stranger?
Bassi. God moves in strange ways.
Okorie. Yes, I believe it, because since that stranger came, I have felt younger again. You

358 DRAMA

ens the mood of the old man. Students will not recognize the importance of this conversation until Okorie's scheme comes to light later in the play. Because the **plot** has several twists, you may want to discuss the sequence of events after students have finished reading each scene.

know, woman, when I worshipped at our forefathers' shrine I was happy. I knew what it was all about. It was my life. Then the preachers came, and I abandoned the beliefs of our fathers. The old ways did not leave me; the new ways did not wholly accept me. I was therefore unhappy. **14** But soon I felt the wings of God carrying me high. And with my loving and helpful son, I thought that my old age would be as happy as that of my father before me. **15** But death played me a trick. My son died and I was left to the mercy of his two sons. Once more unhappiness gripped my life. With all their education my grandsons lacked one thing—respect for age. But today the stranger who came here has once more brought happiness to me. Let me tell you this——

Bassi. It is enough, Grandfather. Long talks make you tired. Come, your food is now ready.

Okorie (*happily*). Woman, I cannot eat. When happiness fills your heart, you cannot eat.

[*Two voices are heard outside, laughing and swearing.*]

Bassi. Your grandchildren are coming back.

16 Okorie. Don't call them my grandchildren. I am alone in this world.

[*Door flings open. Two young men, about eighteen and twenty, enter the room. They are in shirt and trousers.*]

Arob. By our forefathers, Grandfather, you are still awake!

Bassi. Why should he not keep awake if he likes?

17 Arob. But Grandfather usually goes to bed before the earliest chicken thinks of it.

Ojima. Our good grandfather might be thinking **18** of his youthful days when all young men were fond of farming and all young women loved the kitchen.

Bassi. Shame on both of you for talking to an old man like that. When you grow old, your own children will laugh and jeer at you. Come, Grandfather, and take your food.

[Okorie *stands up with difficulty and limps with the aid of his stick through the exit followed by* Bassi, *who casts a reproachful look on the two men before she leaves.*]

Arob. I wonder what Grandfather and the woman were talking about.

19 Ojima. It must be the usual thing. We are bad boys. We have no regard for the memory of our father, and so on.

Arob. Our father left his responsibility to us. **20** Nature had arranged that he should bury Grandfather before thinking of himself.

Ojima. But would Grandfather listen to Nature **21** when it comes to the matter of death? Everybody in his generation, including all his **22** wives, have died. But Grandfather has made a bet with death. And it seems that he will win.

Okorie (*calling from offstage*). Bassi! Bassi! Where is that woman?

Ojima. The old man is coming. Let us hide ourselves. (*Both rush under the bed.*)

Okorie (*comes in, limping on his stick as usual*). Bassi, where are you? Haven't I told that girl never . . .

Bassi (*entering*). Don't shout so. It's not good for you.

Okorie. Where are the two people?

Bassi. You mean your grandsons?

Okorie. My, my, well, call them what you like.

Bassi. They are not here. They must have gone into their room.

Okorie. Bassi, I have a secret for you. (*He narrows his eyes.*) A big secret. (*His hands tremble.*) Can you keep a secret?

Bassi. Of course I can.

14 Metaphor. Compares "emotional high" of his religion to being carried high on wings.

15 Personification. Death has human ability of playing tricks on people.

16 Expressing an Opinion
Why does Okorie say he has no grandchildren? Answers will vary. Perhaps he means he does not have grandchildren who behave toward him as he thinks they should.

17 Personification. Chickens think like human beings.

18 Ojima implies that times have changed to point that many young people are no longer interested in traditional occupations.

19 Drawing Conclusions
What does Ojima's comment suggest about previous conversations with their grandfather? That their shortcomings and neglect of their grandfather are familiar topics of conversation.

20 Personification. Nature has human ability to arrange events. Fathers usually die before their sons, but in Okorie's case reverse is true.

21 Ojima implies his grandfather is stubborn and resists laws of nature.

22 Personification. Death has human ability to bet.

The Jewels of the Shrine

23 Making Inferences
Why does Okorie rub his forehead? Answers will vary. Perhaps to help him remember what he was talking about.

24
Bassi shows great patience and real concern for old man.

25 Making Inferences
Who might Okorie hear? Answers will vary. It probably is not grandsons, because talk would give them away. Okorie might think he hears voice of Stranger, but he might also sense grandsons' presence.

26
Irony. Bassi refuses to look under bed because she thinks it is absurd for anyone to be there. In fact, grandsons are hiding there.

27
Once again Bassi shows her great patience and compassion for Okorie.

28
Personification. Death once again has human qualities.

29 Summarizing
Did Stranger really give Okorie this information? Answers will vary. Stranger did not say anything about jewels in audience's hearing, but he could have said something before play started.

30
Irony. Bassi refers to Okorie as "young" to make him feel better about his old age.

31
This is probably response from Bassi Okorie is hoping for.

360

---

23 Okorie (*rubbing his forehead*). You can, what can you? What did I say?
Bassi (*holding him and leading him to sit on the bed*). You are excited. You know that whenever you are excited you begin to forget things.
Okorie. That is not my fault. It is old age. Well, but what was I saying?
Bassi. You asked me if I could keep a secret.
Okorie. Yes, yes, a great secret. You know, Bassi, I have been an unhappy man.
Bassi. I have heard it all before.
Okorie. Listen, woman. My dear son died and left me to the mercy of his two sons. They are the worst grandsons in the land. They have sold all that their father left. They do not care for me. Now when I die what will they do to me? Don't you think that they will abandon me in disgrace? An old man has a right to be properly cared for. And when he dies he has a right to a good burial. But my grandchildren do not think of these things.
24 Bassi. See how you tremble, Grandfather! I have told you not to think of such things.
25 Okorie. Why should I not? But sh! . . . I hear a voice.
Bassi. It's only your ears deceiving you, Grandfather.
Okorie. It is not my ears, woman. I know when old age hums in my ears and tired nerves ring bells in my head, but I know also when I hear a human voice.
Bassi. Go on, Grandfather, there is no one.
Okorie. Now, listen. You saw the stranger that came here. He gave me hope. But wait, look around, Bassi. Make sure that no one is listening to us.
Bassi. No one, Grandfather.
Okorie. Open the door and look.
Bassi (*opens the exit door*). No one.
Okorie. Look into that corner.
Bassi (*looks*). There is no one.
26 Okorie. Look under the bed.
Bassi (*irritably*). I won't, Grandfather. There is no need, I have told you that there is nobody in the house.
Okorie (*pitiably*). I have forgotten what I was talking about.
27 Bassi (*calmly*). You have a secret from the stranger.
Okorie. Yes, the stranger told me something. Have you ever heard of the "Jewels of the Shrine"?
Bassi. Real jewels?
Okorie. Yes. Among the beads which my father got from the early white men were real jewels. When war broke out, and a great fever invaded all our lands, my father made a sacrifice in the village Shrine. He promised that if this village were spared he would offer his costly jewels to **28** the Shrine. Death roamed through all the other villages, but not one person in this village died of the fever. My father kept his promise. In a big ceremony, the jewels were placed on our Shrine. But it was not for long. Some said they **29** were stolen. But the stranger who came here knew where they were. He said that they were buried somewhere near the big oak-tree in our farm. I must go out and dig for them. They can be sold for fifty pounds[2] these days.
Bassi. But, Grandfather, it will kill you to go out in this cold and darkness. You must get someone to do it for you. You cannot lift a hoe.
Okorie (*infuriated*). So, you believe I am too old to lift a hoe. You, you, oh, I . . .
30 Bassi (*coaxing him*). There now, young man, no
31 temper. If you wish, I myself will dig up the whole farm for you.
Okorie. Every bit of it?
Bassi. Yes.
Okorie. And hand over to me all that you will find?
Bassi. Yes.

2. **pounds:** Until 1960, Nigeria was a colony and protectorate of Britain. The basic monetary unit in Nigeria today is the *naira* (nī′rə).

360 DRAMA

> **READING SKILLS PRACTICE**
> The underlined passage may be used to give students practice in the reading skill of identifying the main idea. Ask students to read the passage and choose the answer that not only is accurate but also encompasses the most important details. **A.** The harvest is over. (True, but this is not the main point of the passage.) **B.** Something besides digging crops is drawing the grandsons to the farm because they avoided the digging during harvest time. (Correct.) **C.** The grandsons had important business to attend to in town during harvest. (Not supported in the passage.) **D.** The boys helped with the digging of crops during harvest time, so they will not go to the farm now. (Contradicted in the passage.)

Okorie. And you will not tell my grandsons?
Bassi. No, Grandfather, I will not.
Okorie. Swear, woman, swear by our Fathers' Shrine.
Bassi. I swear.

32 **Okorie** (*relaxing*). Now life is becoming worthwhile. Tell no one about it, woman. Begin digging tomorrow morning. Dig inch by inch until you bring out the jewels of our Forefathers' Shrine.
Bassi. I am tired, Grandfather, I must sleep now. Good night.
Okorie (*with feeling*). Good night. God and our
33 Fathers' Spirits keep you. When dangerous bats alight on the roofs of wicked men, let them not trouble you in your sleep. When far-seeing owls hoot the menace of future days, let their
34 evil prophecies keep off your path. (*Bassi leaves.*)

Okorie (*standing up and trembling, moves to a corner and brings out a small hoe; and struggling with his senile joints he tries to imitate a young man dig-*
35 *ging*). Oh, who said I was old? After all, I am only eighty years. And I feel younger than most young men. Let me see how I can dig. (*He tries to dig again.*) Ah! I feel aches all over my hip. Maybe the soil here is too hard. (*He listens.*) How I keep on thinking that I hear people whispering in this room! I must rest now. (*Carrying the hoe with him, he goes into his room.* Arob and Ojima *crawl out from under the bed.*)

36 **Arob** (*stretching his hip*). My hip, oh my hip!
Ojima. My legs!
Arob. So there is a treasure in our farm; we must waste no time. We must begin digging soon.
Ojima. Soon? We must begin tonight; now. The old man has taken one hoe. (*Pointing to the corner*) There are two over there. (*They fetch two hoes from among the heap of things in a corner of the*
37 *room.*) If we can only get the jewels we can go and live in town and let the old man manage as he can. Let's move now.

[*As they are about to go out, each holding a hoe,* Okorie *comes out with his own hoe. For a moment the three stare at each other in silence and surprise.*]

38 **Arob.** Now, Grandfather, where are you going with a hoe at this time of night?
Ojima (*impudently*). Yes, Grandfather, what is the idea?
39 **Okorie.** I should ask you; this is my house. Why are you creeping about like thieves?
Arob. All right, Grandfather, we are going back to bed.
Okorie. What are you doing with hoes? You were never fond of farming.
Ojima. We intend to go to the farm early in the morning.
▶ **Okorie.** But the harvest is over. When everybody in the village was digging out the crops, you were going around the town with your hands in your pockets. Now you say you are going to the farm. ◀
Ojima. Digging is good for the health, Grandfather.
Okorie (*re-entering his room*). Good night.
Arob and **Ojima.** Good night, Grandfather.

[*They return to their room. After a short time* Arob *and* Ojima *come out, each holding a hoe, and tip-toe out through the exit. Then, gently,* Okorie *too comes out on his toes, and placing his hoe on the shoulder, warily leaves the hall.*]

[*Curtain.*]

▶ Reading Skills Objective: Drawing Logical Conclusions

The Jewels of the Shrine **361**

32
Bassi's agreeing to help him find jewels gives Okorie new hope for his future.

33
Symbol. Bats and owls represent evil.

34
Bassi lives with her own family and returns to their house for night.

35
Exaggeration. Okorie exaggerates his strength and vigor by saying he feels younger than most men.

36
Boys make fun of their grandfather by imitating his mannerisms and his complaints about his pain.

37 Drawing Conclusions
What do Ojima's comments suggest about Okorie's opinion of boys? That Okorie is correct in thinking they will neglect him.

38 Analyzing
Is this what you would expect boys to say? No. This is kind of question Okorie would ask them.

39
Irony. Audience knows boys plan to steal jewels if they find them. This question is an example of **dramatic irony.**

TRANSPARENCY 26
Reader Response
An Interview with a Character – invites students to participate in a creative dialogue with a character.

---

40 Drawing Conclusions
Why does Okorie ask Bassi where she is going? He apparently does not remember he told her to go to farm.

41
Inference. Okorie did not see them, but he inferred this when he saw them with hoes night before.

42
Symbol. Okorie's rubbing of his forehead symbolizes his inability to remember details.

43
Simile. Okorie compares Stranger's face to brightness of sun and to what he imagines face of God looks like.

44
Bassi seems genuinely concerned about Okorie's health.

45
Despite his age and feebleness, Okorie is still clever when it comes to dealing with his grandsons.

46 Summarizing
Why does Okorie take delight in imagining his grandsons working all night? Because he knows how much they hate hard work.

47 Expressing an Opinion
Do grandsons really wish their grandfather poverty and disgrace? Answers will vary. Grandsons probably do not wish bad things for their grandfather. They just do not want to be bothered with taking care of him.

48
Okorie may have known grandsons were hiding under bed. If he did, some of what he told Bassi may have been for their benefit.

Scene 2

The same, the following morning.

Bassi (*knocking at* Okorie's *door. She is holding a* 40 *hoe*). Grandfather, wake up. I am going to the farm.
Okorie (*opening the door*). Good morning. Where are you going so early in the morning?
Bassi. I am going to dig up the farm. You remember the treasure, don't you?
Okorie. Do you expect to find a treasure while you sleep at night? You should have dug at night, woman. Treasures are never found in the day.
Bassi. But you told me to dig in the morning, Father.
41 **Okorie.** My grandsons were in this room somewhere. They heard what I told you about the Jewels of the Shrine.
Bassi. They could not have heard us. I looked everywhere. The stranger must have told them.
42 **Okorie** (*rubbing his forehead*). What stranger?
Bassi. The stranger who told you about the treasure in the farm.
Okorie. So it was a stranger who told me! Oh yes, a stranger! (*He begins to dream.*) Ah, I 43 remember him now. He was a great man. His face shone like the sun. It was like the face of God.
Bassi. You are dreaming, Grandfather. Wake up! I must go to the farm quickly.
Okorie. Yes, woman, I remember the jewels in the farm. But you are too late.
Bassi (*excitedly*). Late? Have your grandsons discovered the treasure?
Okorie. They have not, but I have discovered it myself.
Bassi (*amazed*). You?

[Okorie *nods his head with a smile on his face.*]

Bassi. Do you mean to say that you are now a rich man?
Okorie. By our Fathers' Shrine, I am.
44 **Bassi.** So you went and worked at night. You should not have done it, even to forestall[3] your grandchildren.
Okorie. My grandsons would never have found it.
Bassi. But you said that they heard us talking of the treasure.
Okorie. You see, I suspected that my grandsons 45 were in this room. So I told you that the treasure was in the farm but in actual fact it was in the little garden behind this house, where the village Shrine used to be. My grandsons travelled half a mile last night to the farm for nothing.
Bassi. Then I am glad I did not waste my time.
46 **Okorie** (*with delight*). How my grandsons must have toiled in the night! (*He is overcome with laughter.*) My grandsons, they thought I would 47 die in disgrace, a pauper, unheard of. No, not now. (*Then boldly*) But those wicked children must change, or when I die I shall not leave a penny for them.
Bassi. Oh, Grandfather, to think you are a rich man!
Okorie. I shall send you to buy me new clothes. My grandsons will not know me again. Ha—ha—ha—ha! (Okorie *and* Bassi *leave.*)

48 [Arob *and* Ojima *crawl out from under the bed, where for a second time they have hidden. They look rough, their feet dirty with sand and leaves. Each comes out with his hoe.*]

Arob. So the old man fooled us.
Ojima. Well, he is now a rich man, and we must treat him with care.
Arob. We have no choice. He says that unless we

---

3. **forestall:** prevent or hinder by taking precautions.

362 DRAMA

change, he will not leave a penny to us.

[*A knock at the door.*]

Arob and Ojima. Come in.
Okorie (*comes in, and seeing them so rough and dirty, bursts out laughing. The others look surprised*). Look how dirty you are, with hoes and all. "Gentlemen" like you should not touch hoes. You should wear white gloves and live in towns. But see, you look like two pigs. Ha—ha—ha—ha! oh what grandsons! How stupid they look! Ha—ha—ha! (*Arob and Ojima are dumbfounded.*[4]) I saw both of you a short while ago under the bed. I hope you now know that I have got the Jewels of the Shrine.
Arob. We, too, have something to tell you, Grandfather.
Okorie. Yes, yes, "gentlemen." Come, tell me. (*He begins to move away.*) You must hurry up. I am going to town to buy myself some new clothes and a pair of shoes.
Arob. New clothes?
Ojima. And shoes?
Okorie. Yes, Grandsons, it is never too late to wear new clothes.
Arob. Let us go and buy them for you. It is too hard for you to——
Okorie. If God does not think that I am yet old enough to be in the grave, I do not think I am too old to go to the market in town. I need some clothes and a comb to comb my beard. I am happy, Grandchildren, very happy.

[*Arob and Ojima are dumbfounded.*]

Okorie. Now, "gentlemen," why don't you get drunk and shout at me as before? (*Growing bolder*) Why not laugh at me as if I were nobody? You young puppies, I am now somebody, somebody. What is somebody? (*Rubbing his forehead as usual.*)
Arob (*to Ojima*). He has forgotten again.
Okorie. Who has forgotten what?
Ojima. You have forgotten nothing. You are a good man, Grandfather, and we like you.
Okorie (*shouting excitedly*). Bassi! Bassi! Bassi! Where is that silly woman? Bassi, come and hear this. My grandchildren like me, I am now a good man. Ha—ha—ha—ha! (*He limps into his room.*)

[*Arob and Ojima look at each other. It is obvious to them that the old man has all the cards now.*]

Arob. What has come over the old man?
Ojima. Have you not heard that when people have money, it scratches them on the brain? That is what has happened to our grandfather now.
Arob. He does not believe that we like him. How can we convince him?
Ojima. You know what he likes most; someone to scratch his back. When he comes out, you will scratch his back, and I will use his big fan to fan at him.
Arob. Great idea. (*Okorie coughs from the room.*) He is coming now.
Okorie (*comes in*). I am so tired.
Arob. You said you were going to the market, Grandfather.
Okorie. You do well to remind me. I have sent Bassi to buy the things I want.
Ojima. Grandfather, you look really tired. Lie down here. (*Okorie lies down and uncovers his back.*) Grandfather, from now on, I shall give you all your breakfast and your midday meals.
Arob (*jealously*). By our Forefathers' Shrine, Grandfather, I shall take care of your dinner and supply you with wine and clothing.
Okorie. God bless you, little sons. That is how it should have been all the time. An old man has

---

4. **dumbfounded:** amazed; astonished.

The Jewels of the Shrine 363

Cultural Diversity

Okorie is upset that his grandsons have no respect for age. When Okorie was young, the old people in his village were treated with honor and respect. However, that cultural tradition has changed. Invite students to discuss the status of older people in their own cultures. Are older people valued and treated with respect? If not, why not? In students' opinions, what are the special gifts that only older people can give us?

59
Grandsons pretend they enjoy taking care of their grandfather.

60
Irony. Less money Okorie spends on himself, more boys will inherit when he dies. They pretend, though, that they want to take care of Okorie out of generosity.

61
Arob says how he really feels about his grandfather when he thinks he is asleep.

62
Okorie proves himself to be more clever than his grandsons.

63 Making Inferences
Why does Okorie want grandsons to help? He may really need help getting dressed, but he may also just want to see their reactions to new clothes.

64 Analyzing
What does Okorie's greeting suggest? That he was expecting Stranger.

65
Metaphor. Compares Okorie's still being alive to someone holding on to a lifeline or some other type of lifesaving device.

---

a right to live comfortably in his last days.

Ojima. Grandfather, it is a very long time since we scratched your back.

59 Arob. Yes, it is a long time. We have not done it since we were infants. We want to do it now. It will remind us of our younger days when it was a pleasure to scratch your back.

Okorie. Scratch my back? Ha—ha—ha—ha. Oh go on, go on; by our Fathers' Shrine you are now good men. I wonder what has happened to you.

Ojima. It's you, Grandfather. You are such a nice man. As a younger man you must have looked very well. But in your old age you look simply wonderful.

Arob. That is right, Grandfather, and let us tell **60** you again. Do not waste a penny of yours any more. We will keep you happy and satisfied to the last hour of your life.

[*Okorie appears pleased. Arob now begins to pick at, and scratch, Okorie's back. Ojima kneels near the bed and begins to fan the old man. After a while, a slow snore is heard. Then, as Arob warms up to his task, Okorie jumps up.*]

Okorie. Oh, that one hurts. Gently, children, gently. (*He relaxes and soon begins to snore again. Ojima and Arob gradually stand up.*)

61 Arob. The old fogy⁵ is asleep.

Ojima. That was clever of us. I am sure he believes us now.

62 [*They leave. Okorie opens an eye and peeps at them. Then he smiles and closes it again.*

Bassi enters, bringing some new clothes, a pair of shoes, a comb and brush, a tin of face powder, etc. She pushes Okorie.]

Bassi. Wake up, Grandfather.

---
5. **fogy** (fō′gē): someone whose habits and ideas are considered old-fashioned.

Okorie (*opening his eyes*). Who told you that I was asleep? Oh! you have brought the things. It is so long since I had a change of clothes. Go on, woman, and call those grandsons of mine. **63** They must help me to put on my new clothes and shoes.

[*Bassi leaves. Okorie begins to comb his hair and beard, which have not been touched for a long time. Bassi re-enters with Arob and Ojima. Helped by his grandsons and Bassi, Okorie puts on his new clothes and shoes. He then sits on the bed and poses majestically like a Chief.*]

[*Curtain.*]

Scene 3

The same, a few months later. Okorie is lying on the bed. He is well dressed and looks happy, but it is easily seen that he is nearing his end. There is a knock at the door. Okorie turns and looks at the door, but cannot speak loudly. Another knock; the door opens and the Stranger enters.

64 Okorie. Welcome back, Stranger. You have come in time. Sit down. I will tell you of my Will.

[*Door opens slowly. Bassi walks in.*]

Bassi (*to Stranger*). How is he?

65 Stranger. Just holding on.

Bassi. Did he say anything?

Stranger. He says that he wants to tell me about his Will. Call his grandsons. (*Bassi leaves.*)

Okorie. Stranger.

Stranger. Yes, Grandfather.

Okorie. Do you remember what I told you about my fears in life?

COOPERATIVE LEARNING
Divide the class into small discussion groups and ask each group to consider the following topic: Are older people treated less respectfully now than they were in the past? Allow each group time to talk about the subject and to pick a spokesperson from the group. Then, hold a panel discussion with the spokesperson for each group joining the panel. Allow each panel member time to present ideas from his or her group. To close, ask a few students to review the ideas and come to a consensus about the topic.

VISUAL CONNECTIONS

About The Artwork
When an Oba assumes power in Benin, one of his first responsibilities is to create an ancestral shrine. This altar, used as a point of contact with his ancestors, is dedicated to the Oba's father, from whom the Oba's powers come. The altars are adorned with sculptured heads of earlier kings. Portrayal of the head in Benin art honors the role of the head in controlling the body and a person's achievements. These sculptures are not actual portraits, but rather generalized representations.

Exploring the Subject
The Oba rules the Kingdom of Benin. He is said to be a descendant of an Oni of Ife, ruler of Ife. Ife is the ancient center of the Yoruba people, which they associate with the beginning of the world. This kinship provides the basis of the Oba's spiritual powers and adds strength to his temporal responsibilities. The first Oba, Eweka I, is thought to have come to power around 1300.

Bronze head of Oba (Benin king) from an ancestral shrine.

The Jewels of the Shrine

Stranger. You were afraid your last days would be miserable, and that you would not have a decent burial.

Okorie. Now, Stranger, all that is past. Don't you see how happy I am? I have been very well cared for since I saw you last. My grandchildren have done everything for me, and I am sure they will bury me with great ceremony and rejoicing. I want you to be here when I am making my Will. Bend to my ears, I will whisper something to you. (Stranger *bends for a moment.* Okorie *whispers. Then he says aloud*) Is that clear, Stranger?

Stranger. It is clear.
Okorie. Will you remember?
Stranger. I will.
Okorie. Do you promise?
Stranger. I promise.
Okorie (*relaxing on his pillow*). There now. My end will be more cheerful than I ever expected.

[*A knock.*]

Stranger. Come in.

[Arob, Ojima, *and* Bassi *enter. The two men appear as sad as possible. They are surprised to meet the* Stranger, *and stare at him for a moment.*]

Okorie (*with effort*). This man may be a stranger to you, but not to me. He is my friend. Arob, look how sad you are! Ojima, how tight your lips are with sorrow! Barely a short while ago, you would not have cared whether I lived or died.
Arob. Don't speak like that, Grandfather.
Okorie. Why should I not? Remember, these are my last words on earth.
Ojima. You torture us, Grandfather.
Okorie. Since my son, your father, died, you have tortured me. But now you have changed, and it is good to forgive you both.
Stranger. You wanted to make a Will.

Okorie. Will? Yes, Will. Where is Bassi? Has that woman run away already?
Bassi (*standing above the bed*). No, Grandfather, I am here.
Okorie. Now there is my family complete.
Stranger. The Will, Grandfather, the Will.
Okorie. Oh, the Will; the Will is made.
Arob. Made? Where is it?
Okorie. It is written out on paper.
Arob and Ojima (*together*). Written? What?
Okorie (*coolly*). Yes, someone wrote it for me soon after I had discovered the treasure.
Arob. Where is it, Grandfather?
Ojima. Are you going to show us, Grandfather?
Okorie. Yes, I will. Why not? But not now, not until I am dead.
Arob and Ojima. What?
Okorie. Listen here. The Will is in a small box buried somewhere. The box also contains all my wealth. These are my wishes. Make my burial the best you can. Spend as much as is required, for you will be compensated.[6] Do not forget that I am the oldest man in this village. An old man has a right to be decently buried. Remember, it was only after I had discovered the Jewels of the Shrine that you began to take good care of me. You should, by carrying out all my last wishes, atone for all those years when you left me poor, destitute, and miserable.

(*To the* Stranger, *in broken phrases*) Two weeks after my death, Stranger, you will come and unearth the box of my treasure. Open it in the presence of my grandsons. Read out the division of the property and share it among them. Bassi, you have nothing. You have a good husband and a family. No reward or treasure is greater than a good marriage and a happy home. Stranger, I have told you where the box containing the Will is buried. That is all. May God——

---

6. **compensated** (kŏm′pən-sāt′əd): repaid.

Arob and Ojima (*rushing to him*). Grandfather, Grandfather——
Stranger. Leave him in peace.

[*Bassi, giving out a scream, rushes from the room.*]

Stranger. I must go now. Don't forget his Will. Unless you bury him with great honour, you may not touch his property. (*He leaves.*)

[*Curtain.*]

Scene 4

All in this scene are dressed in black. Arob, Ojima, and Bassi are sitting around the table. There is one extra chair. The bed is still there, but the mat is taken off, leaving it bare. The hoe with which Grandfather dug out the treasure is lying on the bed as a sort of memorial.

Arob. Thank God, today is here at last. When I get my own share, I will go and live in town.
Ojima. If only that foolish stranger would turn up! Why a stranger should come into this house and——
Bassi. Remember, he was your grandfather's friend.
Ojima. At last, poor Grandfather is gone. I wonder if he knew that we only played up just to get something from his Will.
Arob. Well, it didn't matter to him. He believed us, and that is why he has left his property to us. A few months ago, he would rather have thrown it all into the sea.
Ojima. Who could have thought, considering the way we treated him, that the old man had such a kindly heart!

[*There is a knock. All stand. Stranger enters from Grandfather's room. He is grim, dressed in black, and carries a small wooden box under his arm.*]

Arob. Stranger, how did you come out from Grandfather's room?
Stranger. Let us not waste time on questions. This box was buried in the floor of your grandfather's room. (*He places the box on the table; Arob and Ojima crowd together. Sternly*) Give me room, please. Your grandfather always wanted you to crowd around him. But no one would, until he was about to die. Step back, please. (*Both* Arob *and* Ojima *step back.* Ojima *accidentally steps on* Arob.)
Arob (*to* Ojima). Don't you step on me!
Ojima (*querulously*[7]). Don't you shout at me!

[*Stranger looks at both.*]

Arob. When I sat day and night watching Grandfather in his illness, you were away in town, dancing and getting drunk. Now you want to be the first to grab at everything.
Ojima. You liar! It was I who took care of him.
Arob. You only took care of him when you knew that he had come to some wealth.
Bassi. Why can't both of you——
Arob (*very sharply*). Keep out of this, woman. That pretender (*pointing to* Ojima) wants to bring trouble today.
Ojima. I, a pretender? What of you, who began to scratch the old man's back simply to get his money?
Arob. How dare you insult me like that! (*He throws out a blow.* Ojima *parries.*[8] *They fight and roll on the floor. The* Stranger *looks on.*)
Bassi. Stranger, stop them.
Stranger (*calmly looking at them*). Don't interfere, woman. The mills of God,[9] the preachers tell us, grind slowly.
Bassi. I don't know anything about the mills of

---

7. **querulously** (kwĕr′ə-ləs-lē): in a complaining voice.
8. **parries** (păr′ēz): resists or fends off a blow.
9. **mills of God:** millstones used for grinding grain. This metaphor refers to divine vengeance.

74
Bassi screams and rushes from room out of grief at Okorie's death.

75
Arob expresses his relief that whole matter of Okorie's death and burial are almost over.

76
Okorie got what he wanted, so it hardly matters that boys were kind to him just to be rewarded. He could have died without revealing anything about treasure.

77 Expressing an Opinion
Why do characters stand when they hear knock? Answers will vary. Some may say they stand as a nervous reaction. Others may say they stand out of respect.

78
Irony. It is ironic that boys did not want to be close to their grandfather, but they do want to be close to his treasure.

79
Conflict. Grandsons are tense as they wait to get treasure, and they get angry easily.

80
Calling Ojima "pretender" shows that Arob does not believe his brother was sincere in helping their grandfather.

81
Conflict. Grandsons are in conflict over which one did more for their grandfather before he died.

82 Analyzing
Is Bassi's concern about their killing themselves justified? No. Even though boys are angry, saying they will kill themselves is an exaggeration.

83
Even though boys are angry, they are more interested in treasure than in fighting.

84
Stranger tires of grandsons' bickering and refocuses discussion back on topic.

85
Suspense. Everyone present is eager to find out what is in box.

86 Drawing Conclusions
Why do grandsons make noises when they hear news? They are shocked at what they learn.

87
Metaphor. Okorie once again compares grandsons to puppies, perhaps because of the boys' immature and irresponsible natures.

88 Drawing Conclusions
Why did Okorie not punish boys before he died? He wanted to make sure he was well treated to end. If he had punished boys before, they might have abandoned him.

89 Analyzing
Is Ojima's question justified? No. Okorie could sell his property to anyone he wanted, any time he wanted.

368

God. Stop them, or they will kill themselves.

Stranger (*clapping his hands*). Are you ready to proceed with your grandfather's Will, or **83** should I wait till you are ready? (*They stop fighting and stand up, panting.*) Before I open this box, I want to know if all your grandfather's wishes have been kept. Was he buried with honour?

Arob. Yes, the greatest burial any old man has had in this village.

Ojima. You may well answer, but I spent more money than you did.

Arob. No, you did not. I called the drummers and the dancers.

Ojima. I arranged for the shooting of guns.

Arob. I paid for the wine for the visitors and the mourners.

Ojima. I——

84 Stranger. Please, brothers, wait. I ask you again, was the old man respectably buried?

Bassi. I can swear to that. His grandsons have sold practically all they have in order to give him a grand burial.

Stranger. That is good. I shall now open the **85** box. (*There is silence. He opens the box and brings out a piece of paper.*)

Arob (*in alarm*). Where are the jewels, the money, the treasure?

Stranger. Sh!——Listen. This is the Will. Perhaps it will tell us where to find everything. Listen to this.

Arob. But you cannot read. Give it to me.

Ojima. Give it to me.

Stranger. I can read. I am a school-teacher.

Arob. Did you write this Will for Grandfather?

Stranger. Questions are useless at this time. I did not.

Arob. Stop talking, man. Read it.

Stranger (*reading*). Now, my grandsons; now that I have been respectably and honourably buried, as all grandsons should do to their grandfathers, I can tell you a few things.

First of all, I have discovered no treasure at all. There was never anything like the "Jewels **86** of the Shrine." (*Arob makes a sound as if something had caught him in the throat. Ojima sneezes violently.*) There was no treasure hidden in the farm or anywhere else. I have had nothing in life, so I can only leave you nothing. The house which you now live in was my own. But I sold it some months ago and got a little money for what I needed. That money was my "Jewels of the Shrine." The house belongs now to the stranger who is reading this Will to you. He shall take possession of this house two days after the Will has been read. Hurry up, there- **87** fore, and pack out of this house. You young puppies, do you think I never knew that you had no love for me, and that you were only playing up in order to get the money which you believed I had acquired?

When I was a child, one of my first duties was to respect people who were older than myself. But you have thrown away our traditional love **88** and respect for the elderly person. I shall make you pay for it. Shame on you, young men, who believe that because you can read and write, you need not respect old age as your forefathers did! Shame on healthy young men like you, who leave the land to go to waste because they will not dirty their hands with work!

Ojima (*furiously*). Stop it, Stranger, stop it, or I will kill you! I am undone. I have not got a penny left. I have used all I had to feed him and to bury him. But now I have not even got a **89** roof to stay under. You confounded[10] Stranger, how dare you buy this house?

Stranger. Do you insult me in my own house?

Arob (*miserably*). The old cheat! He cheated us to the last. To think that I scratched his back only to be treated like this! We are now poorer than he had ever been.

Ojima. It is a pity. It is a pity.

---

10. **confounded:** cursed.

DRAMA

A bronze hip pendant showing an Oba (Benin king), which was part of the Oba's regalia or finery. Benin City, Nigeria, 17th century.

VISUAL CONNECTIONS

Exploring the Subject
Benin is located in the southern portion of the African nation of Nigeria. The kingdom itself lies in a tropical rain forest north of the Niger River Delta. The arts of Benin reflect its historical and spiritual roots. Although the western world only became aware of its art in the late nineteenth century, Benin's strong cultural heritage has flourished for over five hundred years. The kingdom is still in existence. Its capital is known as Benin City.

About the Artwork
Hip ornaments were worn for palace ceremonies by the Obas, chiefs, and title holders in Benin. The Oba often wore a series of ornaments hanging from the waist. These ornaments were fashioned to resemble a variety of things, including the human head, the leopard, and the ram.

> **TRANSPARENCY 28**
> **Literary Elements**
> Conflict – invites students to explore aspects of internal and external conflict.

VISUAL CONNECTIONS

About the Artwork

These plaques, hung on pillars in the buildings and courtyards of the Palace of the Kings, record the people and events of the court. The largest figure portrayed on the plaques is usually the most important. The details of the figures' costumes reveal their status and position within the court. Scholars believe these plaques were created only in the sixteenth and seventeenth centuries.

Exploring the Subject

The representation of the mudfish king is a powerful and symbolic image in Benin art. Its portrayal is thought to have its origin in Oba Ohen, son of Olokun, the god of the Sea. Oba Ohen, whose legs were paralyzed, ruled in the early fifteenth century, and attempted to hide this disability from his people. He was killed for his deception; thus the representation of the mudfish king serves as a reminder to the Oba not to abuse the respect of the people. In addition, the mudfish reflects the Oba's divine nature, as a ruler able to span the realms of both the land and the sea and as a leader in contact with the spirit world. The mudfish symbolizes many other important concepts in Benin culture.

Ideas for Writing

Have students research the symbolism of the mudfish in Benin culture. In particular, ask them to point out how the mudfish represents the power of the Oba.

British Museum, London

A bronze plaque from the palace of the Obas (Benin kings), depicting an Oba with mud-fish legs. According to legend, this Oba was a descendant of the Sea god, Olokun. Benin City, Nigeria, early 17th century.

PORTFOLIO ASSESSMENT A model of a setting often brings a story or play into focus on a realistic level. Henshaw's description of the setting in *The Jewels of the Shrine* is somewhat vague, leaving much to the imagination of the producers. Students may be interested in researching mud-walled housing in Nigeria and constructing a realistic replica of Okorie's village house. Suggest that students use as many natural components as possible to construct the home. They may even want to place models of Okorie and other **characters** in the rooms of the house. Consult with students to agree on how their models will be assessed. (See *Portfolio Assessment and Professional Support Materials,* especially the section entitled **Suggestions for Portfolio Projects.**)

Stranger. What is a pity?

Ojima. It is a pity we cannot dig him up again.

[*Suddenly a hoarse, unearthly laugh is heard from somewhere. Everybody looks in a different direction. They listen. And then again——*]

90 **Voice.** Ha—ha—ha—ha!

[*They all look up.*]

Voice. Ha—ha—ha—ha!

[*The voice is unmistakably Grandfather* Okorie's *voice. Seized with terror, everybody except* Bassi *runs in confusion out of the room, stumbling over the table, box, and everything. As they run away, the voice continues.*]

Ha—ha—ha—ha!

[Bassi, *though frightened, boldly stands her ground. She is very curious to know whether someone has been playing them a trick.*]

Voice (*louder*). Ha—ha—ha—ha!

[Bassi *too is terrorized and runs in alarm off the stage.*]

Voice (*continues*). Ha—ha—ha—ha!!!

[*Curtain.*]

Reading Check

1. What does Okorie believe his grandsons lack?
2. What secret does Okorie reveal to Bassi?
3. How do Okorie's grandsons learn about the treasure?
4. When the will is read, what do the grandsons discover?
5. Who does the Stranger turn out to be?

For Study and Discussion

Analyzing and Interpreting the Play

1. According to Okorie, how has the world changed during his lifetime?
2. How does Okorie trick his grandsons into treating him kindly and giving him a proper burial?
3. Bassi says that she does not trust strangers. Why is the mistrust of strangers ironic in light of what happens in the play?
4. In Scene 2 Okorie says to his grandsons, "by our Father's Shrine you are now good men." In what way is this a statement with a double meaning?

Focus on Writing a Scene

Visualizing a Scene for Stage Directions

The **stage directions** in a play give the director and the actors much important information about feelings, tones of voice, movements, gestures, props, and scene design.

Notice, for example, all the details that James Ene Henshaw gives in the stage directions for the last few moments of dialogue and action in *The Jewels of the Shrine* (see page 371). These

---

90 Expressing an Opinion
Whose voice do they hear?
Answers will vary. Some may say it is Okorie's from beyond grave. Others may say that someone hired by Okorie is playing trick on them.

READING CHECK
1. Respect for age (p. 359).
2. Jewels are buried in his farm (p. 360).
3. They hide under the bed and listen as he speaks to Bassi (p. 361).
4. No treasure exists, and Okorie has sold the farm, leaving grandsons homeless (p. 368).
5. Buyer of house (p. 368).

FOR STUDY AND DISCUSSION
1. Young people no longer respect age. In his younger days, old men were happy and were buried with honor.
2. He tells them that he has found the treasure and is now a rich man. To get a proper burial, he tells the Stranger to unearth and open the box with his will and treasure and to divide it between his grandsons only if they give him a decent burial.
3. With the Stranger's help, Okorie lives the last months of his life in comfort and receives the proper burial that he so much desires.
4. They now are acting as he always hoped they would but only because they think he has found the Jewels of the Shrine.

FOCUS ON WRITING A SCENE
You may want to explain to students that the tone of the speaker's voice and his or her gestures, movements, and facial expressions must suit the personality of the character. All of these details must combine with what the **character** says to move the **plot** along.

CLOSURE
Have students identify the sequence of events in the play. Then ask them to identify the **conflict** and its **resolution**.

EXTENSION AND ENRICHMENT
As the ending of the play is somewhat ambiguous, suggest that students revise it. They might write a continuation of Scene 4 in which the voice is explained. Perhaps the ghost of Okorie appears or someone else explains the final trick.

Some students might choose to rewrite some of the existing scene rather than continue it as written. Perhaps they will have the Stranger or Bassi be a part of the final trick. Ask students to share their revised scenes.

ABOUT THE AUTHOR
For James Ene Henshaw, writing plays offers a welcome diversion from medical practice. From his medical profession he draws ideas about human behavior and attitudes. In addition to plays, he has written "Matron's Darling," a short story which appeared in the *Eastern Nigerian Medical Journal*. He has also contributed articles to medical journals in Africa and England.

CONNECTING CULTURES
You may want to gather a collection of folk stories and make them available to students in the classroom. Try to include tales from various cultures. After students have completed their comic strips, encourage them to compile their creations into a class book that can be displayed in the library.

---

directions are vitally important for the effect of the play's surprise ending.

To write stage directions for a dramatic scene, you will find it helpful to **visualize the scene,** moment by moment, in your mind's eye. Review the dialogue you have created in this unit for a dramatic scene, or write dialogue for a new scene. Then imagine that the scene is being played on stage. For each speech in your scene, consider the following points:

the tone of the speaker's voice
gestures or movements during the speech
the speaker's facial expression
any sounds or events occurring on stage

Using these hints for visualizing the scene, add stage directions to your play script. Save your writing.

About the Author

James Ene Henshaw (1924–   )

James Ene Henshaw, who is a physician as well as a writer, was born in Nigeria. His works for the theater include *This Is Our Chance: Plays from West Africa* (1957); *Children of the Goddess and Other Plays* (1964); and *Medicine For Love* (1964). *The Jewels of the Shrine* was performed at the Nigerian Festival of the Arts in 1953.

In his plays Henshaw hopes to maintain a basic, honest communication with young Africans. The audience, he says, should feel as if the events in the play could have happened to them that day. Henshaw, who has great faith in traditional values, has said: "These good traditions, such as the respect for the older person…and the obligatory sharing of the other person's burdens, should not merely make the young African distinct, but should continue to be the earth he walks on, and the air he breathes."

Connecting Cultures

The Trickster in Folk Tales

Folk literature contains many characters who trick their friends and neighbors. Almost every culture has an animal trickster. It is often a wolf, fox, rabbit, coyote, or raven. In many Hopi folk tales, the coyote outsmarts unwary humans. In African American folklore, Brer Rabbit gets the better of other characters who are bigger and stronger. African folk tales have three tricksters who play a prominent role: Anansi, the spider; Zomo, the rabbit; and Ijapa, the tortoise. Anansi is most famous for getting others to do his work for him. Anansi also appears in Caribbean folk tales as a character named Nancy.

Making Connections: Activities

Find a folk tale about a trickster in an anthology of folk stories. Create a comic strip based on the story. Use both illustrations and dialogue "balloons" in your comic strip.

A scene from an off-Broadway production of *Really Rosie*.

A scene from a production of *Beauty and the Beast*.

Frog Dancers from Bali, Indonesia.

Japanese puppet and handlers.

Traditional Italian puppets.

A richly costumed princess, a character in a Beijing opera.

Legong Dancers from Bali, Indonesia.

A scene from *The Mikado*, a Gilbert and Sullivan operetta.

The Jewels of the Shrine

OBJECTIVES
The overall aim is for students to demonstrate an ability to draw inferences about characters in plays.

PRESENTATION
Begin this activity by defining the word *inference* (conclusions based on evidence that is only hinted at, or implied). Then explain that people make inferences all the time, not only from what they read, but from what they see and hear. Ask students to work first on each question independently and then discuss their responses in small groups. A group leader can share the group's inferences with the class.

DRAWING INFERENCES
When we read, as when we listen, we can deepen our appreciation of what is being said by looking for implications and making **inferences**. Remind students not to confuse these two terms. (The writer or speaker "implies," and the reader or listener "infers.") Drawing the appropriate **inference** and thus understanding the writer's implication can provide insight and pleasure.

Answers
Answers may vary.
1. Celia changes from a complaining, scared woman to one who understands that even her small contribution to the Underground can help others. Celia overcomes some of her shame at feeling afraid of getting in trouble. The words of the song Celia chooses indicate that she no longer will complain of being "tired," and that she is ready to "shout *Glory*" when all the world is free.
2. We might infer that Okorie's grandchildren are selfish, have little respect for Okorie, and do not visit him often. The stage directions say the young men are swearing. Okorie says, "I am alone . . .," and Arob says, ". . . you are still awake!" implying that they had hoped their grandfather would be asleep so they would not have to see him.

FOCUS ON Reading and Critical Thinking

DRAWING INFERENCES

Some playwrights present actions and situations directly, leaving little for the audience to guess about. Plays are usually more interesting, however, when the audience has to draw **inferences**, or conclusions, about aspects of the plot, the characters, or the setting.

For example, at the beginning of *The Mazarin Stone*, the stage directions call attention to the dummy of Sherlock Holmes beside the window (see page 318). Early in the play, the dialogue between Watson and Billy stresses the fact that Holmes is a master of disguise (see page 319). Did you draw any inferences at this point about how the dummy might turn out to be important in the plot of the play?

Reread the passages below. Then use a separate sheet of paper to answer the questions marked with the symbol (■) after each passage.

1. Celia (*gathers up clothes, places them in tub, starts working. Harriet goes to her tub.*) If we sing, the work goes faster.

Lennie (*goes to her tub*). Your turn to pick a song, Celia.

[*Celia starts scrubbing. They all work for a few moments. Celia has decided on a song. She sings out.*]

Celia.
Oh, Lord, I don't feel no ways tired
Children, Oh, Glory Hallelujah
For I hope to shout *Glory* when this world is all on fire . . .

—Alice Childress, *When the Rattlesnake Sounds*
(page 354)

■ What inference can you draw from this passage about how Celia has changed during the play? What inner struggle has she resolved? What clues in the passage support your conclusion?

2. [*Two voices are heard outside, laughing and swearing.*]

Bassi. Your grandchildren are coming back.
Okorie. Don't call them my grandchildren. I am alone in this world.

[*Door flings open. Two young men, about eighteen and twenty, enter the room. They are in shirt and trousers.*]

Arob. By our forefathers, Grandfather, you are still awake!

—James Ene Henshaw, *The Jewels of the Shrine*
(page 359)

■ What inference does this passage suggest about the relationship of Okorie and his grandsons? What clues in the dialogue and the stage directions support your inference?

FOCUS ON Writing

WRITING A SCENE

A *drama* is a story acted out, usually on a stage, by actors and actresses who take the parts of specific characters. The principal difference between a dramatic scene and a short story is that in drama the author's main tool for moving the plot forward is dialogue, rather than narration or description. Now that you have seen some of the key elements of drama, you will have the chance to write a dramatic scene of your own.

Prewriting

1. Although dramas and short stories have different formats, they have many elements in common. Like a good short story, a dramatic scene depends on **conflict,** or struggle. Get together with a small group of classmates, and brainstorm to fill in a chart like the one below. Some sample ideas on the chart have been filled in for you.

Idea Chart for a Dramatic Scene	
Characters	**Conflict**
Mother Daughter	Why can't I have money to go to the rock concert?
Columbus First Mate	Why don't we turn back to Spain?
_____	_____
_____	_____
_____	_____
_____	_____

2. Use **improvising** to explore one of the dramatic conflicts you have listed on your chart. Join with a group of partners. Decide in advance who will play each role in the dramatic situation. Then relax and make up your lines as you go. If you wish, appoint one member of the group to take notes. See if your improvisation leads to a high point and a resolution for the conflict. [See **Focus** assignment on page 334.]

3. Write an **outline** for your scene. Be sure your outline covers the elements listed on the diagram below:

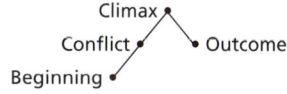

4. Make notes about the **setting** of your dramatic scene—the specific time and place of the action. Decide if the setting has an important relationship to the conflict, or if it can play a role in creating atmosphere or mood in your scene.

Writing

1. Set the stage by using **stage directions** to describe the scenery, lighting, and characters that the audience will see at the beginning of your scene. As a model, you can use the stage directions at the beginning of *A Sunny Morning* (see page 335).

2. Follow your outline and write the **dialogue** for your scene. Remember to observe the conventions for identifying speakers and punctuating dialogue in drama. Here is an example from *The Mazarin Stone* (page 319):

Watson (*laughs*). What's it all about, Billy?
Billy (*glancing round cautiously*). I don't mind telling you, sir—but it shouldn't go no farther. . . .

3. Use these guidelines when you write dialogue:

- Be sure that the dialogue carries the plot forward.
- Be sure that the speeches sound natural—the way people speak in real life. Say your dialogue out loud to test it for realism and naturalness.
- Check to see that the dialogue suits the character of the speaker. Notice, for example, that Billy the attendant uses a double negative ("shouldn't go no farther") in the passage above from *The Mazarin Stone*. This kind of informal English, however, would not be suitable for some of the other characters, such as Dr. Watson or Sherlock Holmes.

[See **Focus** assignment on page 355.]

4. Add **stage directions** to your play script to indicate information about the characters' feelings or emotions, tones of voice, movements, and gestures. Stage directions can also refer to props and important elements of scene design, as well as to any sounds or events occurring on stage during your scene. When you write your stage directions, imagine that you are the director as well as the playwright. **Visualize** your scene being played on stage, moment by moment and speech by speech. How does each of your characters look? How do the characters move? How do they react to the speeches of others? [See **Focus** assignment on page 371.]

5. Give your scene a title that hooks the reader's interest and sums up the action.

Evaluating and Revising

1. When you have finished a first draft of your scene, join with your group. Organize a reading of each member's scene. Offer each other suggestions on how to improve dialogue and stage directions.

Here is one writer's revision of part of a dramatic scene.

Writer's Model

(In the waiting room of the ^Vet^ clinic.)

MRS. MAKRIS (taking her daughter's hand). We all love Lightning, honey, but we just don't have the money ^for that surgery^.

NIKKI. ^But^ Mom! Dr. Turetsky said ^Lightning will^ he'd go blind if one of his cataracts isn't removed!

MRS. MAKRIS. We can still keep him, ^Nikki^. That ^dog^ animal has nothing else wrong with him.

(Nikki is silent for a moment, deep in concentration. Then she ^bursts^ speaks out.)

NIKKI. What if I could pay half of

CLOSURE
Have students answer the following questions about their scenes: What is the strongest element (**conflict, character, setting, stage directions, dialogue**)? What is the weakest? Why? Which part of the writing process was the most difficult? Why?

> the eight hundred ~~dollars~~ *bucks*, Mom? I know I could make four hundred this *by baby-sitting* summer! I'll use every cent of it for Lightning's *vs eye operation*!
>
> MRS. MAKRIS (hesitating, then realizing how much Nikki loves Lightning. *honey, With your help,* She smiles.) I'll talk to Dad, I think we can work something out.

2. You may find the following checklist helpful as you revise your scene:

Checklist for Evaluation and Revision

✓ Do I clearly identify the scene and the characters?
✓ Do I establish a strong conflict early in the scene?
✓ Does the scene contain a climax and a resolution?
✓ Does my dialogue sound natural? Is it appropriate to each character? Does it move the plot forward?
✓ Do I use stage directions to give important information?
✓ Have I used the correct format?

Proofreading and Publishing

1. Proofread your scene and correct any errors you find in grammar, usage, and mechanics. (Here you may find it helpful to refer to the **Handbook for Revision** on pages 726–767.) Then prepare a final version of your scene by making a clean copy.

2. Consider some of the following ways to share your scene:

- join with classmates and take turns giving informal readings of your scenes
- organize a group of classmates to present a full staging of your scene, complete with scenery, costumes, and props

Portfolio If your teacher approves, you may wish to keep a copy of your work in your writing folder or portfolio.

Proofreading and Publishing
Remind students as they proofread their scenes that they should use standard grammar and usage unless they are trying to establish **character** through nonstandard language patterns. Also, students should be aware that punctuation is important to the correct interpretation of the lines of **dialogue**.

UNIT 6 ♦ TEACHING GUIDE

FORMS OF LITERATURE
NONFICTION

OVERVIEW OF THE UNIT

All the selections in this unit should appeal to seventh-graders' natural interest in real people and actual events.

Questions and exercises written for these selections develop a wide range of reading skills. After each selection, questions engage students in the kind of close reading so basic to all schoolwork—for example, identifying details that support a general statement, drawing inferences, analyzing cause and effect. Exercises provide concentrated practice in understanding inverted sentence order and finding humor in the unexpected.

Besides introducing many new words and thus providing sustained opportunity for vocabulary growth, the unit contains an exercise on forming words with the suffix *–logy* and another on tracing word histories.

Selections in the unit provide excellent models of the writer's craft. Opportunities for teaching about organization and style abound. The major composition assignments in the unit involve students in writing biographical reports. **Focus on Reading and Critical Thinking** rounds out the unit with a discussion of understanding cause and effect.

OBJECTIVES OF THE UNIT

The aims of the unit are for students:
- To demonstrate an understanding of the elements of exposition, description, and narration in nonfiction writing
- To understand cause and effect in nonfiction writing
- To identify examples of cause-and-effect relationships within a nonfiction selection
- To use a dictionary for vocabulary development
- To write a biographical report

CONCEPTS AND SKILLS

The following concepts and skills are treated in this unit:

CLOSE READING OF AN ESSAY
Guidelines for Close Reading 382
One Reader's Response 383
Looking at Yourself as a Reader 385

LITERARY ELEMENTS/TERMS AND TECHNIQUES
Recognizing Allusions 396

LANGUAGE AND VOCABULARY
Analyzing Words with the Same Combining Form 392
Forming Words with *–logy* 403
Using Context Clues 412
Recognizing Ranch Terms 423

WRITING OPPORTUNITIES

Writing About Literature
Describing the Narrator 413

Focus on Biographical Report
Choosing a Subject 392   Using Anecdotes 413
Gathering Details 396   Organizing a Report 423
Identifying a Main Idea 403   Writing a Biographical Report 425

FOCUS ON READING AND CRITICAL THINKING
Understanding Cause and Effect 424

TRANSPARENCIES

The following unit support materials with specific correlations to literature selections are available in the **Fine Art and Instructional Transparencies with Teacher's Notes and Blackline Masters** section of your *Audiovisual Resources Binder*.

FINE ART TRANSPARENCIES
Theme: Real People, Actual Events
30 *The Totonac Civilization,* Diego Rivera
31 *Head of a Woman,* Anonymous

READER RESPONSE
32 Compare and Contrast Characteristics

LITERARY ELEMENTS
33 Evaluating Nonfiction

WRITING PROCESS
34 Writing a Biographical Report

INTRODUCING THE UNIT

To generate interest in nonfiction as a literary genre, you may wish to use one of these activities:

A day or two before the unit is to be introduced, ask each student to keep a twenty-four hour reading log listing by title *all* material read and specifying the amount of time spent on each item. Using entries selected from various students' logs, demonstrate how each entry can be classified as fiction, poetry, drama, or nonfiction. Then have students categorize all entries on their own logs and figure the percentage of total reading time spent on each category.

In most cases, the percentage of time spent on nonfiction will be quite high. Ask why. On the board, list sample entries illustrating different kinds of nonfiction—for example, chapters from textbooks, encyclopedia entries, newspaper articles, essays of different kinds, biographies and autobiographies, and so on. Why are these kinds of nonfiction so important? What are some of the

379A

PLANNING GUIDE

For Unit Planning
- Transparencies 30–34: *Audiovisual Resources Binder*
- Portfolio Assessment: *Professional Support Materials*
- Test Generator
- Mastery Tests: Teaching Resources C, pp. 152, 154, 156
- Analogy Test: Teaching Resources C, p. 158
- Composition Test: Teaching Resources C, p. 159

SELECTION (Pupil's Page)	Teacher's Notes	Reading Check	Study Guide	Language Skills	Building Vocabulary	Selection Vocab. Test	Selection Test	AV Binder Audio-cassette
NONFICTION Introduction (p. 381)	86							
Close Reading of an Essay Barry Holstun Lopez from *River Notes* (p. 382)	87							
Jane Goodall from *In the Shadow of Man* (p. 386)	88	90	91	94	98		100	
Julia Alvarez *Names/Nombres* (p. 393)	102	104	106		109	111	112	
Marjorie Kinnan Rawlings *Rattlesnake Hunt* (p. 398)	113	115	116	119	121	123	124	
Ved Mehta from *Sound-Shadows of the New World* (p. 404)	126		129	131	134		136	
J. Frank Dobie *When I Was a Boy on the Ranch* (p. 414)	138		140	143	146		148	

reasons for reading each kind? Use this discussion to lead into the introductory section on p. 381.

Initiate the unit by providing newspapers and magazines and giving students time to browse through them. Ask each student to find at least one article of interest. As students share highlights of their browsing, list articles on the chalkboard by type—for example, news story, feature or human-interest story, book or movie review. Use these examples to introduce nonfiction as a literary type. Ask students to add other forms of factual literature to the list. Relate this activity to the introductory comments on p. 381.

Another approach is to schedule a visit to the school library. Have the librarian point out the different kinds of nonfiction and the location of each. Allow time for browsing and checkout so that students may begin reading nonfiction beyond that in the anthology.

PORTFOLIO ASSESSMENT

Suggestions for use of portfolios as support for this unit are described in the **Portfolio Assessment and Professional Support Materials** booklet accompanying this program. Specific suggestions are provided for a variety of student projects that may be suitable for inclusion in a portfolio. In addition, copying masters are provided for guides that may be used for evaluation and assessment of student projects.

Student Learning Options

NONFICTION

1. Using the Scientific Method
Ask students to select an animal they can observe every day for a week. Then divide the class into groups according to the animal chosen. (If there are more than five students in a group, make two smaller groups.) Possible subjects include a chicken, a cat, a dog, a bird, a horse, a squirrel, a gerbil, or a frog. Ask students to observe the habits of the selected animal for at least thirty minutes each day and to take notes on the animal's habits. Then have groups combine their observations and generalize about the habits of the animal, writing a scientific report similar to the excerpt from Jane Goodall's *In the Shadow of Man.*

2. Learning Meanings of Names
Ask students to look up the meanings of their own names. Guide them in finding resource materials.

VISUAL CONNECTIONS

About the Artwork
Guy Carleton Wiggins is known for his scenes of New York City. He used impressionist technique but little color. The gritty reality of this painting also shows the influence of the "Ashcan School," which was grounded in the realist tradition. One artist, expressing the views of the new group, said that the city was the proper subject for art and that the artists should paint the city as they saw it—even its imperfections.

Exploring the Subject
By the beginning of the twentieth century, the widespread use of photography and photoengraving made it possible to reproduce images of real people, events, and even art, and brought a new kind of realism to artists and the public.

At the same time, the blues—which deals with unromanticized experience—and ragtime were popular and truly American forms of musical expression. For the first time popular American music influenced serious European and American composers.

Muckrakers, both journalists and novelists, portrayed the unpleasant realities of American life and helped to bring about an age of reform.

Ideas for Writing
The painting shows the changed character of the American city, which by the turn of the century had become a manufacturing center, not just a population and commercial center. Students might write a description of the city as pictured here. They might also write about the artist's impression of the city as opposed to their own impressions of cities. Has the nature of cities changed?

NONFICTION

Nonfiction deals with facts, but, like other forms of literature, it appeals to the imagination. In nonfiction, real people are the characters, and real life is the setting. There are many kinds of nonfiction. Newspaper and magazine articles, biographies and autobiographies, serious and humorous essays, interviews, memoirs, diaries, speeches, letters, and scientific articles all fall into this broad category of literature.

Imagine yourself as a visitor to the scene shown in this painting. What can you tell about the different buildings? Give your impressions in the form of a diary entry or an informal letter. Compare your responses with those of others in the class.

Evaluate your work. What details have others seen that you missed? Are you able to look at the painting more carefully now that you have written about it and listened to others' responses?

Metropolitan Tower (1912) by Guy C. Wiggins. Oil on canvas.
The Metropolitan Museum of Art, George A. Hearn Fund

FOCUS / MOTIVATION
Have students write three specific details about a storm, perhaps describing rain, winds, or lightning. Then have them write a simile for each of their details. Example: *strong* wind; wind as *strong as a rushing bull*.

PRESENTATION
This excerpt from Barry Holstun Lopez' *River Notes* illustrates the **informal essay**. Lopez uses vivid **imagery** to convey his own personal impressions of an event to the reader. The essay is, in fact, so informal and so personal that the reader clearly "hears" the writer's "voice" as he tells about a storm that, if not a tornado, at least had the power of one.

TEACHING RESOURCES C
Teacher's Notes, p. 87

GUIDELINES FOR CLOSE READING
1. In the following selection from *River Notes*, the author is chiefly interested in explaining his own experiences and communicating his impressions to the reader.
2. An objective, scientific essay would not include the many impressionistic comparisons that Lopez draws, such as the image of fallen trees and beached whales.
3. Lopez uses more than a half-dozen **similes** to create striking images of the storm.
4. Call students' attention to **One Reader's Response.** Remind students that their responses may differ greatly from this reader.
5. The first sentence from *River Notes* states the **thesis**. The rest of the essay consists of "proof" that the thesis assertion is valid.

382

Close Reading OF AN ESSAY

*T*he essay is one kind of nonfiction. It is a literary form that can be adapted to many different purposes. An essay can be informative or instructive; it can be entertaining; it can be persuasive. Essays are generally divided into two types: *informal* and *formal*. The informal essay is light, personal, and often humorous. The formal essay is serious and impersonal. As you read an essay, pay close attention to style—the way the writer uses language. Note your responses to the author's ideas and language.

Guidelines for Close Reading

1. Determine the purpose of the essay. Ask yourself if the author's chief object is to inform, to explain, to persuade, or to achieve some combination of these objectives.

2. Determine the tone of the essay. A formal essay is serious in tone and generally objective. An informal essay is told from a personal point of view.

3. Note the author's style and types of writing. Writers of essays use descriptive writing in order to create images and communicate sensory impressions; narrative writing to relate a series of events; informative writing to present facts or to present a process; and persuasive writing to influence the reader's ideas.

4. Clarify your responses as you read. What impression do you have of the writer? Do you agree or disagree with the writer's ideas?

5. Determine the main idea of the essay. The main idea may not be stated directly, but may be implied. Try to state this idea in your own words.

The following selection is from *River Notes*, a collection of brief meditations about a mountain river, in which naturalist Barry Holstun Lopez discovers and conveys the beauty of the wilderness. In this entry he captures the awesome, destructive power of a storm. As you read, note how he combines specific details with imaginative comparisons.

382 NONFICTION

MEETING INDIVIDUAL NEEDS
Visual Learners • Students might benefit from periodically reviewing the **Guidelines for Close Reading** during their study of this unit. You might point out the important words for them to remember and make an outline or visual presentation that would organize the information, as they discuss and write about the selections in this section. You might want to use the words *why*, for the author's purpose in writing, and *how*, for the style or methods the author employs, so that analysis is simple for students to grasp.

The notes alongside the essay represent one reader's responses. If you wish, cover these notes and write your own comments on a separate sheet of paper as you read. Then at a later point compare your own responses with the printed comments.

FROM
River Notes
BARRY HOLSTUN LOPEZ

1 A storm came this year, against which all other storms were to
2 be measured, on a Saturday in October, a balmy afternoon.
   Men in the woods cutting firewood for winter, and children
3 outside with melancholy thoughts lodged somewhere in the
   memory of summer. It built as it came up the valley as did every
4 fall storm, but the steel-gray thunderheads,[1] the first sign of it
5 anyone saw, were higher, much higher, too high. In the still-

1. **thunderheads:** dense clouds that appear before a thunderstorm.

ONE READER'S RESPONSE

This must have been a powerful storm if it became the measure of others.

This storm was a total surprise.

CLOSE READING OF AN ESSAY

1
With initial focus on a storm, author makes promise to reader that essay will be about the storm.

2
Setting. People are going about normal routines in wooded community on fall day.

3
"Melancholy" implies children are wistfully thinking of summer and sadly realizing that winter is coming.

4
Suspense. Author builds suspense with image of "steel-gray thunderheads."

5
Uses repetition to emphasize that clouds were unusually high.

383

6
Comparison emphasizes impending danger and sudden shock of storm.

7
Simile. Comparison of wind to cutting scythe, to piranha, and to force of water through hole in a dike suggests destructive power.

8
Simile. Comparison of limbs to mortar shells evokes image of war zone as the storm snaps the trees.

9 Finding Details
Which details in the remainder of the paragraph create sound images? "Broken-china explosion," "yawing screech" of pickup, "rivet popping and twang" of wires.

©1991 Scott McKiernan/Black Star

These comparisons give me an idea of how terrifying and destructive the storm was.

It takes incredible strength to snap a tree.

He makes the trees sound almost human by using the word screaming.

6 ness before it hit, men looked at each other as though a fast and wiry man had pulled a knife in a bar. They felt the trees falling before they heard the wind, and they dropped tools and scram-
7 bled to get out. The wind came up suddenly and like a scythe, like piranha[2] after them, like seawater through a breach in a dike. The first blow bent trees half to the ground, the second
8 caught them and snapped them like kindling, sending limbs raining down and twenty-foot splinters hurtling through the air like mortar shells to stick quivering in the ground. Bawling cattle running the fences, a loose lawnmower bumping across a lawn, a stray dog lunging for a child racing by. The big trees went down screaming, ripping open holes in the wind that were
9 filled with the broken-china explosion of a house and the yawing screech of a pickup rubbed across asphalt, the rivet popping and twang of phone and electric wires.

2. **piranha** (pĭ-rän′yə, -răn′yə): carnivorous fish with very sharp teeth.

CLOSURE
Ask students to describe, either orally or in writing, a storm they have experienced. They should concentrate on specific details, especially as conveyed through striking comparisons.

---

10   It was over in three or four minutes. The eerie, sucking silence it left behind seemed palpably³ evil, something that would get into the standing timber, like insects, a memory.
   No one was killed. Roads were cut off, a bridge buckled. No power. A few had to walk in from places far off in the steep wooded country, arriving home later than they'd ever been up.
11   Some said it pulled the community together, others how they hated living in the trees with no light. No warning. The next day it rained and the woods smelled like ashes. It was four or five days before they got the roads opened and the phones
12   working, electricity back. Three sent down to the hospital in
13   Holterville. Among the dead, Cawley Besson's dog. And two deer, butchered and passed quietly in parts among neighbors.

14   Of the trees that fell into the river, a number came up like beached whales among willows at the tip of an island.

3. **palpably** (păl′pə-blē): distinctly, as of something that can be touched or felt.

It was lucky that no people were killed.

I've read about hurricanes that do this kind of damage.

The image of the whale makes me feel sorry for the trees that were destroyed.

10
After the many sound images, the sudden silence seems evil, something to be remembered a long time.

11
Suggests some people will have positive attitude in face of adversity; others, negative.

12
Author's frequent use of sentence fragments creates conversational style appropriate in informal essay.

13
This first mention of a name brings reader to deeper involvement; evokes sympathy for Cawley Besson and his dog.

14
Simile. "Liked beached whales" evokes image of trees as giants that are out of their element.

Looking at Yourself as a Reader

Think about your response to the essay. Did you enjoy reading it? Did you learn something from it? Would you be interested in reading other essays of this kind? If so, what sources could you consult to get more information?

If you wrote your own responses while you were reading the essay, compare your notes with the printed notes. Did you have similar reactions or not? Did the printed responses clarify any of your own reactions to the essay?

Which of these statements do you think best expresses the central idea of the essay? If you don't agree with any of the choices, state your own idea in a sentence or two.

1. Lopez feels that trees always suffer the most in a storm.
2. The struggle against a powerful storm is like a war.
3. Despite our experience with natural disasters, we are still at the mercy of nature's awesome and brutal power.
4. A powerful storm is terrifying in its sounds.
5. According to Lopez, there is never any warning when a destructive storm is on the way.

LOOKING AT YOURSELF AS A READER
You may want to discuss with students that their responses to the essay might help them to understand why they liked or disliked the essay. Students who liked the essay might be interested in reading *River Notes* in its entirety.

As students compare their notes with the printed notes, discuss the value of varied responses. Students' reactions to the essay might differ greatly from the printed notes or from the responses of their classmates. Remind students that there are no right or wrong responses.

Most students will probably choose the third statement as the central idea of the essay. If they choose another or state the main idea in their own words, ask them to support their choices with examples from the essay.

Close Reading of an Essay

FROM
In the Shadow of Man

JANE GOODALL

In 1960, when she was twenty-six years old, Jane Goodall traveled to Gombe National Park in Tanzania, Africa, to study chimpanzees in their natural habitat. In the following chapter, called "First Observations," she discusses her methods of observation and the discoveries she made. As you read, compare her descriptions with the photographs of the chimpanzees she studied.

As the weeks went by the chimpanzees became less and less afraid. Quite often when I was on one of my food-collecting expeditions I came across chimpanzees unexpectedly, and after a time I found that some of them would tolerate my presence provided they were in fairly thick forest and I sat still and did not try to move closer than sixty to eighty yards. And so, during my second month of watching from the Peak,[1] when I saw a group settle down to feed I sometimes moved closer and was thus able to make more detailed observations.

It was at this time that I began to recognize a number of different individuals. As soon as I was sure of knowing a chimpanzee if I saw it again, I named it. Some scientists feel that animals should be labeled by numbers—that to name them is anthropomorphic[2]—but I have always been interested in the *differences* between individuals, and a name is not only more individual than a number but also far easier to remember. Most names were simply those which, for some reason or other, seemed to suit the individuals to whom I attached them. A few chimps were named because some facial expression or mannerism reminded me of human acquaintances.

The easiest individual to recognize was old Mr. McGregor. The crown of his head, his neck, and his shoulders were almost entirely devoid of hair, but a slight frill remained around his head rather like a monk's tonsure.[3] He was an old male—perhaps between thirty and forty years of age (chimpanzees in captivity can live more than fifty years). During the early months of my acquaintance with him, Mr. McGregor was somewhat belligerent. If I accidentally came across him at close quarters he would threaten me with an upward and backward jerk of his head and a shaking of branches before climbing down and vanishing from my sight. He reminded me, for some reason, of Beatrix Potter's old gardener in *The Tale of Peter Rabbit*.

---

1. **Peak:** a vantage point in the Gombe Stream Chimpanzee Reserve, just east of Lake Tanganyika in Tanzania.
2. **anthropomorphic** (ăn′thrə-pə-môr′fĭk): giving the characteristics of human beings to nonhuman things.
3. **tonsure** (tŏn′shər): the part of the head that is shaved.

MOTIVATIONAL SUMMARY

Jane Goodall is studying chimpanzees in their natural habitat in Africa. As the weeks progress and the chimpanzees become more accustomed to her unobtrusive presence, she is able to move closer for more detailed observations. She begins to recognize certain individuals and gives them names. Before the end of her trial period in the field, she makes two exciting discoveries—findings that overturn former scientific beliefs.

PRESENTATION

Jane Goodall's book *In the Shadow of Man* is based on her ten years of research in Africa. Before students read the selection, you may want to have them predict the kinds of observation methods they think she might use. In addition,

Fifi, Faustino, and Flossy.

5   Ancient Flo with her deformed, bulbous nose and ragged ears was equally easy to recognize. Her youngest offspring at that time were two-year-old Fifi, who still rode everywhere on her mother's back, and her juvenile son, Figan, who was always to be seen wandering around with his mother and little sister. He was then about seven years old; it was approximately a year before he would attain puberty. Flo often traveled with another old mother, Olly. Olly's long face was also distinctive; the fluff of hair on the back of her head—though no other feature—reminded me of my aunt, Olwen. Olly, like Flo, was accompanied by two children, a daughter younger than Fifi, and an adolescent son about a year older than Figan.

Then there was William, who, I am certain, must have been Olly's blood brother. I never saw any special signs of friendship between them, but their faces were amazingly alike. They both had long upper lips that wobbled when they suddenly turned their heads. William had the added distinction of several thin, deeply etched scar marks running down his upper lip from his nose.

Two of the other chimpanzees I knew well by sight at that time were David Graybeard and Goliath. Like David and Goliath in the Bible, these two individuals were closely associated in my mind because they were very often together. Goliath, even in those days of his prime, was not a giant, but he had a splendid physique and the springy movements of an athlete. He probably weighed about one hundred pounds. David Graybeard was less afraid of me from the start than were any of the other chimps. I was always pleased when I picked out his handsome face and well-marked silvery beard in a chimpanzee group, for with David to calm the others, I had a better chance of approaching to observe them more closely.

Before the end of my trial period in the field I made two really exciting discoveries—discoveries that made the previous months of frustra-

5 Metaphor. Compares Flo's nose to light bulb because of shape of nose.

6 Author estimates age based on size and other physical characteristics, but she cannot be certain how old animals are.

7 Making Inferences *Would Aunt Olwen be flattered by having a chimpanzee named for her?* Probably not, especially if she knew reason.

8 Description. Author describes details of appearance that helped her recognize chimpanzees as individuals.

9 Allusion. Refers to Biblical story of boy David who killed giant Goliath (I Samuel 17:23–54).

10 Drawing Conclusions *What might have happened when author approached if David had been afraid of her?* He might have run away, causing others to do the same.

11 Suspense. Author creates suspense by telling readers big discoveries are coming up.

tion well worth while. And for both of them I had David Graybeard to thank.

One day I arrived on the Peak and found a small group of chimps just below me in the upper branches of a thick tree. As I watched I saw that one of them was holding a pink-looking object from which he was from time to time pulling pieces with his teeth. There was a female and a youngster and they were both reaching out toward the male, their hands actually touching his mouth. Presently the female picked up a piece of the pink thing and put it to her mouth: it was at this moment that I realized the chimps were eating meat.

After each bite of meat the male picked off some leaves with his lips and chewed them with the flesh. Often, when he had chewed for several minutes on this leafy wad, he spat out the remains into the waiting hands of the female. Suddenly he dropped a small piece of meat, and like a flash the youngster swung after it to the ground. Even as he reached to pick it up the undergrowth exploded and an adult bushpig charged toward him. Screaming, the juvenile leaped back into the tree. The pig remained in the open, snorting and moving backward and forward. Soon I made out the shapes of three small striped piglets. Obviously the chimps were eating a baby pig. The size was right and later, when I realized that the male was David Graybeard, I moved closer and saw that he was indeed eating piglet.

For three hours I watched the chimps feeding. David occasionally let the female bite pieces from the carcass and once he actually detached a small piece of flesh and placed it in her outstretched hand. When he finally climbed down there was still meat left on the carcass; he carried it away in one hand, followed by the others. Of course I was not sure, then, that David Graybeard had caught the pig for himself, but even so, it was tremendously exciting to know

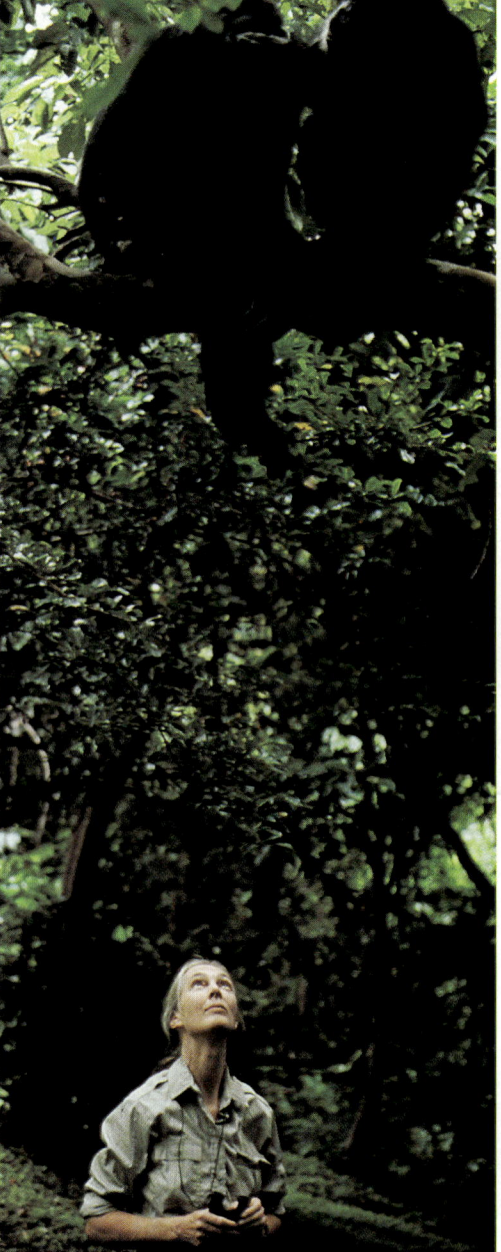

Jane Goodall observing Evert and Goblin grooming.

details.
A. The chimpanzees' diet consists entirely of fruit and vegetables. (Information in passage contradicts this.) **B.** The discovery that chimpanzees eat meat disproves previous beliefs about their diet. (Correct.) **C.** Chimpanzees prefer eating meat when it is available. (This may be true but is unsupported by this selection.) **D.** Scientists believed that chimpanzees might supplement their diet with insects or small rodents. (This is too narrow. It does not encompass all the important details.)

that these chimpanzees actually ate meat. Previously scientists had believed that although these apes might occasionally supplement their diet with a few insects or small rodents and the like they were primarily vegetarians and fruit eaters. No one had suspected that they might hunt larger mammals.

16 It was within two weeks of this observation that I saw something that excited me even more. By then it was October and the short
17 rains had begun. The blackened slopes were softened by feathery new grass shoots and in some places the ground was carpeted by a variety of flowers. The Chimpanzees' Spring, I called it. I had had a frustrating morning, tramping up and down three valleys with never
18 a sign or sound of a chimpanzee. Hauling myself up the steep slope of Mlinda Valley I headed for the Peak, not only weary but soaking wet from crawling through dense undergrowth. Suddenly I stopped, for I saw a slight movement in the long grass about sixty yards away. Quickly focusing my binoculars I saw that it was a single chimpanzee, and just then he turned in my direction. I recognized David Graybeard.

Cautiously I moved around so that I could see what he was doing. He was squatting beside the red earth mound of a termite nest, and as I watched I saw him carefully push a long grass
19 stem down into a hole in the mound. After a moment he withdrew it and picked something from the end with his mouth. I was too far away to make out what he was eating, but it was obvious that he was actually using a grass stem as a tool.

20 I knew that on two occasions casual observers in West Africa had seen chimpanzees using objects as tools: one had broken open palm-nut kernels by using a rock as a hammer, and a group of chimps had been observed pushing sticks into an underground bees' nest and lick-

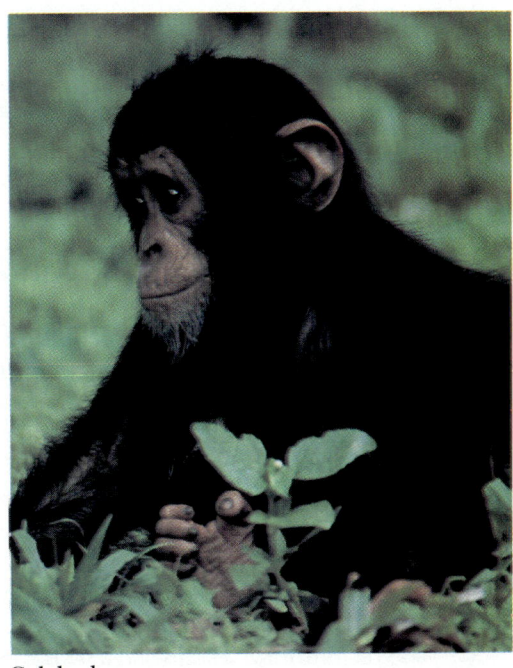
Galahad.

ing off the honey. Somehow I had never dreamed of seeing anything so exciting myself.
21 For an hour David feasted at the termite mound and then he wandered slowly away. When I was sure he had gone I went over to examine the mound. I found a few crushed insects strewn about, and a swarm of worker termites sealing the entrances of the nest passages into which David had obviously been pok-
22 ing his stems. I picked up one of his discarded tools and carefully pushed it into a hole myself. Immediately I felt the pull of several termites as they seized the grass, and when I pulled it out there were a number of worker termites and a few soldiers, with big red heads, clinging on with their mandibles.[4] There they remained, sticking out at right angles to the stem with their legs waving in the air.

4. **mandibles** (măn′də-bəlz): biting jaws.

16
Author's discoveries excite her because they mean her work is worthwhile.

17
Metaphor. New grass shoots compared to feather because of their softness and lightness. Flowers compared to carpet because they cover ground.

18
Metaphor. Compares climbing slope of valley to hauling a load.

19
Termites crawl onto grass stem, and David eats them.

20 Analyzing
Why does author use "casual" to describe observers? To distinguish them from scientists.

21
Exaggeration. Author uses "feasted" to describe David's meal to emphasize that it lasted long time.

22 Finding Cause and Effect
Why does author repeat David's routine? To make sure he had been doing what she thought he was doing.

▶ Reading Skills Objective: Identifying the Main Idea

Before I left I trampled down some of the tall dry grass and constructed a rough hide—just a few palm fronds leaned up against the low branch of a tree and tied together at the top. I planned to wait there the next day. But it was another week before I was able to watch a chimpanzee "fishing" for termites again. Twice chimps arrived, but each time they saw me and moved off immediately. Once a swarm of fertile winged termites—the princes and princesses, as they are called—flew off on their nuptial flight, their huge white wings fluttering frantically as they carried the insects higher and higher. Later I realized that it is at this time of year, during the short rains, when the worker termites extend the passages of the nest to the surface, preparing for these emigrations. Several such swarms emerge between October and January. It is principally during these months that the chimpanzees feed on termites.

On the eighth day of my watch David Graybeard arrived again, together with Goliath, and the pair worked there for two hours. I could see much better: I observed how they scratched open the sealed-over passage entrances with a thumb or forefinger. I watched how they bit the ends off their tools when they became bent, or used the other end, or discarded them in favor of new ones. Goliath once moved at least fifteen yards from the heap to select a firm-looking piece of vine, and both males often picked three or four stems while they were collecting tools, and put the spares beside them on the ground until they wanted them.

Most exciting of all, on several occasions they picked small leafy twigs and prepared them for use by stripping off the leaves. This was the first recorded example of a wild animal not merely *using* an object as a tool, but actually modifying an object and thus showing the crude beginnings of tool*making*.

Frodo and Freud.

PORTFOLIO ASSESSMENT
If possible, have students access an online service to find published scientific research about an animal species, common or endangered. Retrieved data may be used to write an essay about the experience of researching online and a summary of the data received. Suggest that students evaluate their experience, telling whether or not they would like to do research using online services more often and why. (See *Portfolio Assessment and Professional Support Materials* for additional information.)

Reading Check

1. What was the vantage point Goodall used to observe chimpanzees?
2. How long did it take her to begin recognizing different chimpanzees?
3. What was Goodall's reason for giving the animals names rather than numbers?
4. What made Mr. McGregor easy to recognize?
5. Which of the chimpanzees seemed less afraid of Goodall than the others?

For Study and Discussion

Analyzing and Interpreting the Selection

1. In this excerpt from her book, Jane Goodall shares with readers her early experiences observing chimpanzees. To judge from her success, what characteristics are necessary for someone who wishes to study animals in their natural habitat?
2. How would you describe Goodall's attitude toward the animals she observed?
3. Why was she excited to discover that chimpanzees eat meat?
4. According to Goodall, "casual observers" had seen chimpanzees using objects as tools. What is the significance of her finding that chimpanzees are able to modify the tools they use?
5. Jane Goodall's work with chimpanzees was the first of its kind. What effect do you think her studies may have had on future studies of animal behavior?

Focus on Reading

Finding the Main Idea of a Paragraph

The word *paragraph* comes from two Greek words: *para*, meaning "beside," and *graphein*, meaning "to write." Centuries ago, when books were copied by hand, scribes did not divide a manuscript into paragraphs as we do today. Instead they wrote a certain mark beside the place where a new idea began. This mark was called a paragraph.

Today, of course, we use the word *paragraph* to refer to a series of sentences that develop a single idea or topic. We indicate the beginning of a paragraph by indenting the first sentence in the series.

Sometimes a writer will state the main idea or topic of a paragraph in a sentence called the **topic sentence.** The topic sentence is usually placed at the beginning of the paragraph.

Look at this paragraph from *In the Shadow*
1 *of Man.* Which sentence states the main idea of the paragraph?

> The easiest individual to recognize was old Mr. McGregor. The crown of his head, his neck, and his shoulders were almost entirely devoid of hair, but a slight frill remained around his head rather like a monk's tonsure. He was an old male—perhaps between thirty and forty years of age (chimpanzees in captivity can live more than fifty years). During the early months of my acquaintance with him, Mr. McGregor was somewhat belligerent. If I accidentally came across him at close quarters he would threaten me with an upward and backward jerk of his head and a shaking of branches before climbing down and vanishing from my sight. He reminded me, for some reason, of Beatrix Potter's old gardener in *The Tale of Peter Rabbit.*

2 What details does Goodall give in the para-
3 graph? How do these details support the main idea?

READING CHECK
1. The Peak in the Gombe Stream Chimpanzee Reserve (p. 386).
2. A little over a month (p. 386).
3. Name is more individual and easier to remember (p. 386).
4. Little hair on crown of head, neck, and shoulders, but a frill of hair around his head; was an old male with belligerent mannerisms (p. 387).
5. David Graybeard (p. 387).

FOR STUDY AND DISCUSSION
1. Responses will vary. Possibilities include patience, perseverance, curiosity, ability to deal with frustration and physical discomfort, respect for the animals, attention to detail.
2. She respected their space, rejoiced in their accomplishments, and genuinely seemed to care for them.
3. They had been considered primarily vegetarians and fruit eaters. No one had suspected that they might hunt larger mammals.
4. Chimpanzees show the crude beginnings of making tools, which requires more intelligence than using tools.
5. Answers will vary. Perhaps researchers began to set up camp for longer periods of time, in order to observe animals in their natural habitat.

FOCUS ON READING
1. The first sentence states the main idea.
2. Details include absence of hair on head, neck, and shoulders, frill of hair around head, age between thirty and forty years, belligerent mannerisms of backward jerk of head and shaking of branches before climbing down to disappear.
3. The details, describing Mr. McGregor's unique characteristics, explain how easy it was to identify him.

In the Shadow of Man

Language and Vocabulary

Analyzing Words with the Same Combining Form

Jane Goodall says that some scientists consider the naming of animals *anthropomorphic*. The word *anthropomorphic* is made up of two **combining forms.** The combining form *anthropo-* means "human beings." The combining form *-morph* means "having a certain form." The word *anthropomorphic* literally means "of human form." It is generally used when human characteristics are attributed to nonhuman things or creatures.

1. Look up the meaning of the following words in a college or an unabridged dictionary. Tell how the original meaning of the combining form survives in each case.

   anthropology   metamorphosis
   anthropocentric   isomorphic
   anthropogenic   pseudomorph

Focus on Biographical Report

Choosing a Subject

A biography is the life story of a person written by someone else. A **biographical report** is a shorter form of biography. In this kind of expository writing, you share information about a real person's life, personality, and accomplishments.

When you choose a subject for a biographical report, ask yourself these questions:

1. What is interesting and special about the person? Why should my readers be interested in him or her?
2. What are the person's achievements?
3. Can I get the information I need about the person?

Assume that you are considering Jane Goodall as the subject for a biographical report. Using information from the selection and from **About the Author,** jot down some notes to answer the three questions listed in this exercise. Save your notes.

About the Author

Jane Goodall (1934–   )

"My interest in animals was not just a passing phase, but was rooted deep," says Jane Goodall. As a child in England, Goodall closely observed nature and recorded her observations. While she made frequent visits to the London zoo, she longed to travel to Africa and observe animals in the wild. In 1960, when she was just twenty-six years old, Goodall was chosen to conduct a research project to study chimpanzees in the Gombe Stream Reserve in Tanzania, Africa. Since then, she has contributed to scientific books and magazines, appeared on television specials, and written several books. In 1977 she established the Jane Goodall Institute for Wildlife Research, Education, and Conservation in Tucson, Arizona. Goodall's discoveries about chimpanzee behavior in the wild have overturned former scientific beliefs. Her two most famous observations are discussed in the excerpt from *In the Shadow of Man* (1971) included in this anthology.

Names/Nombres

JULIA ALVAREZ

Cultures around the world differ in their customs of choosing names for families and individuals. In the United States, most people have a surname (the common family name) and a given name. In addition, some people have a middle name and some have a nickname. Many authors have a pen name. What other kinds of names are common in our society?

In this essay, Julia Alvarez explains how she adjusted to the naming customs of her new country. As you read, ask yourself why she gives her essay a title in two languages.

When we arrived in New York City, our names changed almost immediately. At Immigration, the officer asked my father, *Mister Elbures,* if he had anything to declare. My father shook his head, "No," and we were waved through. I was too afraid we wouldn't be let in if I corrected the man's pronunciation, but I said our name to myself, opening my mouth wide for the organ blast of the *a,* trilling my tongue for the drumroll of the *r, All-vah-rrr-es!* How could anyone get *Elbures* out of that orchestra of sound?

At the hotel my mother was *Missus Alburest,* and I was *little girl,* as in, "Hey, little girl, stop riding the elevator up and down. It's *not* a toy."

When we moved into our new apartment building, the super called my father *Mister Alberase,* and the neighbors who became mother's friends pronounced her name *Jew-lee-ah* instead of *Hoo-lee-ah.* I, her namesake, was known as *Hoo-lee-tah* at home. But at school, I was *Judy* or *Judith,* and once an English teacher mistook me for *Juliet.*

It took awhile to get used to my new names.

I wondered if I shouldn't correct my teachers and new friends. But my mother argued that it didn't matter. "You know what your friend Shakespeare said, 'A rose by any other name would smell as sweet.'"[1] My family had gotten into the habit of calling any famous author "my friend" because I had begun to write poems and stories in English class.

By the time I was in high school, I was a popular kid, and it showed in my name. Friends called me *Jules* or *Hey Jude,* and once a group of troublemaking friends my mother forbade me to hang out with called me *Alcatraz.* I was *Hoo-lee-tah* only to Mami and Papi and uncles and aunts who came over to eat *sancocho*[2] on Sunday afternoons—old world folk whom I would just as soon go back to where they came from and leave me to pursue whatever mischief I wanted to in America. JUDY ALCATRAZ: the name on the

---

1. **A rose...as sweet:** a quotation from *Romeo and Juliet* (II, 2, 43–44). Juliet means that names are not important. Changing a rose's name would not affect its beauty.
2. ***sancocho*** (sän-kō'chō): a stew.

MOTIVATIONAL SUMMARY
Upon arriving in New York City from the Dominican Republic, Julia notices immediately the way native New Yorkers mispronounce her family's names. At first, she desires to be recognized by her Dominican name, but the desire fades as she grows older. As she attempts to blend in with her American friends, she compares the customs of her new country with those of her Dominican heritage.

PRESENTATION
Julia Alvarez' essay resembles a short story in that its main character faces and resolves conflict. The focus of the narrative, a struggle between two cultures, is one with which students might be familiar—either from stories or movies

7
Metaphor. Compares women's voices to soft cooing sounds made by birds.

8 Drawing Conclusions
Why was mother embarrassed? Her daughter's Spanish name emphasizes mother's difference from American women.

9
Irony. Mami is self-conscious about her daughter's not having "American" name, but American woman thinks Spanish names are pretty.

10
Metaphor. Compares her sister's name to physical burden she has to carry around.

11 Drawing Conclusions
Why was it thought important to pronounce Third World names correctly? Answers will vary. Perhaps as sign of respect for other cultures.

394

Wanted Poster would read. Who would ever trace her to me?

My older sister had the hardest time getting an American name for herself because *Mauricia* did not translate into English. Ironically, although she had the most foreign-sounding name, she and I were the Americans in the family. We had been born in New York City when our parents had first tried immigration and then gone back "home," too homesick to stay. My mother often told the story of how she had almost changed my sister's name in the hospital.

7 After the delivery, Mami and some other new mothers were cooing over their new baby sons and daughters and exchanging names and
8 weights and delivery stories. My mother was embarrassed among the Sallys and Janes and Georges and Johns to reveal the rich, noisy name of *Mauricia*, so when her turn came to brag, she gave her baby's name as *Maureen*.
9 "Why'd ya give her an Irish name with so many pretty Spanish names to choose from?" one of the women asked.

My mother blushed and admitted her baby's real name to the group. Her mother-in-law had recently died, she apologized, and her husband had insisted that the first daughter be named after his mother, *Mauran*. My mother thought it the ugliest name she had ever heard, and she talked my father into what she believed was an improvement, a combination of *Mauran* and her own mother's name, *Felicia*.

"Her name is *Mao-ree-shee-ah*," my mother said to the group of women.

"Why that's a beautiful name," the new mothers cried. "*Moor-ee-sha, Moor-ee-sha,*" they cooed into the pink blanket. *Moor-ee-sha* it was when we returned to the States eleven years later. Sometimes, American tongues found even that mispronunciation tough to say and called her *Maria* or *Marsha* or *Maudy* from her nickname

394 NONFICTION

Pepita of Santa Fe (1917) by Robert Henri (1865–1929). Oil painting.
Los Angeles County Museum of Art, Mr. and Mrs. William Preston Harrison Collection

10 *Maury.* I pitied her. What an awful name to have to transport across borders!

My little sister, Ana, had the easiest time of all. She was plain *Anne*—that is, only her name was plain, for she turned out to be the pale, blond "American beauty" in the family. The only Hispanic thing about her was the affectionate nicknames her boyfriends sometimes gave her. *Anita,* or as one goofy guy used to sing to her to the tune of the banana advertisement,[3] *Anita Banana.*

11 Later, during her college years in the late '60s, there was a push to pronounce Third World names correctly. I remember calling her long distance at her group house and a roommate answering.

---
3. **banana advertisement:** an advertisement for Chiquita bananas.

or from personal experience. Julia vacillates between pride for her Dominican heritage and shame for being different from her friends. The tone of her informal essay is personal and humorous.

MEETING INDIVIDUAL NEEDS
You might ask students if anyone has been given a nickname or a shortened form of their own name that they do not like. How do they react to it? Do they try to keep people from using it?

To demonstrate the significance of names, you might have students select different names to use for a day. Have them pick names they might have given to themselves. Ask them to report on how the new name affected them during the day.

---

12 "Can I speak to Ana?" I asked, pronouncing her name the American way.

"Ana?" The man's voice hesitated. "Oh! you must mean *Ah-nah!*"

Our first few years in the States, though, ethnicity was not yet "in." Those were the blond, blue-eyed, bobby sock years of junior high and high school before the '60s ushered in peasant 13 blouses, hoop earrings, sarapes.[4] My initial desire to be known by my correct Dominican name faded. I just wanted to be Judy and merge with the Sallys and Janes in my class. But inevitably, my accent and coloring gave me away. "So where are you from, Judy?"

"New York," I told my classmates. After all, I had been born blocks away at Columbia Presbyterian Hospital.

"I mean, *originally.*"

"From the Caribbean," I answered vaguely, for if I specified, no one was quite sure on what continent our island was located.

"Really? I've been to Bermuda. We went last April for spring vacation. I got the worst sunburn! So, are you from Portoriko?"[5]

"No," I sighed. "From the Dominican Republic."

"Where's that?"

15 "South of Bermuda."

They were just being curious, I knew, but I burned with shame whenever they singled me out as a "foreigner," a rare, exotic friend.

16 "Say your name in Spanish, oh please say it!" I had made mouths drop one day by rattling off my full name, which according to Dominican custom, included my middle names, Mother's and Father's surnames for four generations back.

17 "Julia Altagracia María Teresa Álvarez Tavares Perello Espaillat Julia Pérez Rochet González," I pronounced it slowly, a name as chaotic with sounds as a Middle Eastern bazaar or market day in a South American village.

My Dominican heritage was never more apparent than when my extended family attended school occasions. For my graduation, they all came, the whole lot of aunts and uncles and the many little cousins who snuck in without tickets. They sat in the first row in order to better understand the Americans' fast-spoken English. But how could they listen when they were constantly speaking among themselves in florid-sounding phrases, rococo[6] consonants, rich, rhyming vowels?

Introducing them to my friends was a further trial to me. These relatives had such complicated names and there were so many of them, and their relationships to myself were so convoluted. There was my Tía[7] Josefina, who was not really an aunt but a much older cousin. And her daughter, Aida Margarita, who was adopted, *una hija de crianza.*[8] My uncle of affection, Tío José, brought my *madrina*[9] Tía Amelia and her *comadre*[10] Tía Pilar. My friends rarely had more than a "Mom and Dad" to introduce.

After the commencement ceremony my family waited outside in the parking lot while my friends and I signed yearbooks with nicknames which recalled our high school good times: 18 "Beans" and "Pepperoni" and "Alcatraz." We hugged and cried and promised to keep in touch.

Our goodbyes went on too long. I heard my father's voice calling out across the parking lot, "*Hoo-lee-tah! Vamonos!*"[11]

Back home, my *tíos* and *tías* and *primas*,[12]

---

4. **sarapes** (sə-rä′pēz): woolen cloaks or ponchos.
5. **Portoriko:** Puerto Rico.
6. **rococo** (rə-kō′kō): here, elaborate; showy.
7. **Tía** (tē′ä): aunt. The word for uncle is **Tío** (tē′ō).
8. **una hija de crianza** (o͞o-nä ē′hä thä krē-än′sä).
9. **madrina** (mä-thrē′nä): godmother.
10. **comadre** (kō-mä′thrä): close friend.
11. **Vamonos** (bä′mō-nōs): Let's leave.
12. **primas** (prē′mäs): female cousins.

12
Irony. Julia pronounces her sister's name "American" way because she assumes roommates do. Ironically, roommate corrects her.

13
The longer she lives in the United States, the more American Julia becomes.

14
Friend's pronunciation of Puerto Rico emphasizes her lack of knowledge of Spanish.

15
Irony. Bermuda is not in Caribbean; it is in Atlantic Ocean, about 640 miles east of North Carolina. Dominican Republic is about 1,000 miles south of Bermuda.

16
Julia seems to enjoy teasing her friends by saying her full name.

17
Simile. Compares pronunciation of her full name to noise of crowded marketplace.

18 Analyzing
What purpose do nicknames serve for friends? They help create sense of closeness among friends.

Names/Nombres

MEETING INDIVIDUAL NEEDS
Visual Learners • Ask students to make a collage about their name and its meaning. Have them use visual representations for their name (and associated nicknames) and its personal connotations. Is their name in a song title? Is their name in the dictionary? Is their name the same as someone else's in the family, a famous person's, or a comic-book character's? Does the name automatically bring to mind associations? Have students collect pictures from magazines and paste them together with a photograph of themselves on a collage. Have them label their collection, "What's in a name?"

19
By using American spelling, family seems to acknowledge Julia's status as American.

READING CHECK
1. Dominican Republic (p. 395).
2. New York City (p. 394).
3. Friends call her *Jules, Hey Jude,* and *Judy Alcatraz* (p. 393).
4. That her name would be well known throughout the United States (p. 395).

FOR STUDY AND DISCUSSION
1a. Officer at immigration says *Elbures;* building super says *Alberase;* friends call Julia *Alcatraz.*
1b. She becomes *Judy, Judith,* or *Juliet.*
2. Julia is her mother's namesake; Mauricia named for father's mother; Julia's full name, according to Dominican custom, includes Mother's and Father's surnames for four generations back.
3. She laughs about not knowing which name she will go by if she becomes famous.
4. She includes both the United States and the Dominican Republic languages because the essay focuses on adjusting to the naming customs of a different country.

LITERARY ELEMENTS
1. *The Sun also Rises* is from the Old Testament, Eccl.1:5.
Death Be Not Proud comes from sonnet X of John Donne's *Holy Sonnets.*
The Fire Next Time is taken from a slave song recreated from the Bible.
Leave Her to Heaven comes from Shakespeare's *Hamlet.*

396

Mami and Papi, and *mis hermanas*[13] had a party for me with *sancocho* and a store-bought *pudín,*[14] **19** inscribed with *Happy Graduation, Julie.* There were many gifts—that was a plus to a large family! I got several wallets and a suitcase with my initials and a graduation charm from my godmother and money from my uncles. The biggest gift was a portable typewriter from my parents for writing my stories and poems.

Someday, the family predicted, my name would be well-known throughout the United States. I laughed to myself, wondering which one I would go by.

13. *mis hermanas* (mēs âr-mä′näs): my sisters.
14. *pudín* (pōō-thēn′): pudding.

Reading Check
1. Where had Julia's family lived before coming to New York?
2. Where were Julia and Mauricia born?
3. What was Julia's nickname in high school?
4. What prediction did Julia's family make at her graduation party?

For Study and Discussion

Analyzing and Interpreting the Essay

1. Julia Alvarez says that their names changed when her family arrived in New York. **a.** How was the family name changed? **b.** How was Julia's given name changed?
2. How does Alvarez' essay show that names in her family are an important part of her heritage?
3. The author says that as a child she found it hard to get used to all her new names. How does the last paragraph reveal a different attitude toward having been known by so many different names?
4. Why do you think Julia Alvarez gives her essay a title in two languages?

Literary Elements

Recognizing Allusions

An **allusion** is a reference to a work of literature or art, or to some well-known person, place, or event. Julia's mother refers to a famous line in Shakespeare's *Romeo and Juliet* in order to make the point that one should not place too much importance on names. People sometimes say that someone has the patience of Job, alluding to the Biblical character whose faith in God survived repeated calamities. Some allusions are obvious and easy to recognize. Other allusions may need to be inferred from context.

Each of the following titles is an allusion to a **1** well-known work of literature. Using a dictionary, a book of quotations, or other reference work, identify the source of each one.

The Sun also Rises
Death Be Not Proud
The Fire Next Time
Leave Her to Heaven

Focus on Biographical Report

Gathering Details

The details that Julia Alvarez gives about her family in "Names/Nombres" come from her own memories. When you gather details for a biographical report, however, you will usually need to consult **sources** about your subject.

If your subject is a celebrity, past or present, you will often be able to use magazine articles or books about the person. When you take notes from these sources, keep a list of references to identify the works you consult, as well

396 NONFICTION

CLOSURE
Ask students to identify how the author changes in her attitude toward names. Ask what they think causes the change.

EXTENSION AND ENRICHMENT
According to Dominican custom, Julia's full name includes her mother's and father's surnames for four generations back. Ask students to find out the history behind their own names. Were they named after certain relatives or famous people? Do their names have special meanings? Inquiry into their names may even pique students' interest to research family trees.

---

as the page numbers where the information is located.

If you are writing about a family member or a friend, hold an **interview** with the person, as well as with others who know him or her. Keep notes on the questions and answers in your interviews.

Choose a subject for a biographical report: for example, a famous person from history, a current celebrity, or a friend or family member whom you admire. As you gather details about your subject, fill out a chart like the one below. Save your notes.

Details Chart

Job/Profession: _____
Education: _____
Date and Place of Birth: _____
_____
Achievements/Special Awards: _____
_____
Family: _____
_____
Opinions/Outlook on Life: _____
_____
Statements/Quotations: _____
_____

About the Author

Julia Alvarez (1950–)

Julia Alvarez left the Dominican Republic for the United States when she was ten. After earning degrees in literature and writing, she taught poetry for twelve years in schools across the country. Her first book of poetry, *Homecoming*, appeared in 1986. It was followed by *The Housekeeping Book* (1984) and *Daughters of Invention* (1990). *How the Garcia Girls Lost Their Accents* (1991), a collection of interrelated stories, was honored as an ALA Notable Book of the Year.

The Author Comments on Her Work

The day I sat down to write this story, I was thinking about all the little things that changed when we came to this country. I didn't want to write about the BIG THINGS: how we left behind a whole other country that was an island, how we left behind year-round warm weather, how we left behind Spanish as the language everyone used. Those were too big and important. I always write about the little things that make up the big important events in my life.

I thought about how when we landed in New York, the air smelled like a ham sandwich. Don't ask me why, it just did. My skin felt different, dry from always wearing too many clothes (to keep warm) and lonely because lots of aunts and uncles weren't around to hug me and hold me. Everyone looked different, dressed up, covered up, in a hurry, talking funny. I didn't know what they were saying, even when they were calling me by my own name.

Then it hit me. That was another little change. My name didn't sound like my name. It didn't really call to the person inside me. And so I tried to remember little moments when I realized that my name, along with everything else, was changing.

Now, people can mispronounce my name or call me something Englishfied, and I don't even blink. I know they're talking to the person inside me. But when it first happened, it was strange. I realized in writing this story that part of becoming American was when the person inside me could answer to those American names without feeling funny. She had learned that she also existed in English!

FOCUS ON BIOGRAPHICAL REPORT
You may want to use this opportunity to discuss effective interviewing procedures. Before the interview, students should make lists of the questions they want to ask. To avoid *yes* and *no* answers, they might ask questions that begin with *who, what, when, where,* and *how.* Suggest that students make appointments and be on time for their interviews.

ABOUT THE AUTHOR
Julia Alvarez has won the American Academy of Poetry Prize. Much of her poetry deals with domestic subjects such as dusting and making beds. Another common theme in her works is the exploration of her lost Caribbean heritage.

OBJECTIVES
The overall aim is for students to explain the cause-and-effect relationship between the author's new knowledge of rattlesnakes and the decrease in her fear of them. For a complete list of objectives, see the **Teacher's Notes.**

VOCABULARY
The underlined words are in the Glossary. Before reading the selection, students might work the **Language and Vocabulary** exercise on p. 403 for practice using the dictionary to find meanings of the roots of words.

FOCUS / MOTIVATION
Ask students to decide whether or not the word *rattlesnake* carries with it a negative feeling. If they agree that it does, have them give reasons.

> **TEACHING RESOURCES C**
> Teacher's Notes, p. 113
> Reading Check, p. 115
> Study Guide, p. 116
> Language Skills, p. 119
> Building Vocabulary, p. 121
> Selection Vocabulary Test, p. 123
> Selection Test, p. 124

PREREADING FOCUS
The headnote emphasizes that Rawlings' narrative is structured like a short story. Ask students to define **climax** and to discuss how this could function in nonfiction.

Rattlesnake Hunt

1 Analyzing
Why do people hunt rattlesnakes? For skin; for edible meat; for population reduction; for a zoo; for sport; for study.

2
Setting. Big Prairie area of Florida. Seminole Indians live in villages in Everglades; still live and dress much like their ancestors.

3 Drawing Conclusions
Why does this seem particularly dangerous? Rattlers would be fleeing fire and be agitated.

4
Use to answer **study question 1,** p. 402.

5
Conventional snake hunter might use a stick with a Y-shaped end that goes around the snake's neck.

6
Use to answer **study question 2,** p. 402.

7
Conflict. Author struggles with her fear and revulsion.

398

Rattlesnake Hunt

MARJORIE KINNAN RAWLINGS

This selection is from Cross Creek, *a collection of remembrances. Like a short story, this narrative has a conflict that builds to a climax and then is resolved. As you read, note how Rawlings makes you aware of the changes in her attitude.*

Ross Allen, a young Florida herpetologist,[1] invited me to join him on a hunt in the upper Everglades[2]—for rattlesnakes.

The hunting ground was Big Prairie, south of Arcadia and west of the northern tip of Lake Okeechobee. Big Prairie is a desolate cattle country, half marsh, half pasture, with islands of palm trees and cypresses and oaks. At that time of year the cattlemen and Indians were burning the country, on the theory that the young fresh wire grass that springs up from the roots after a fire is the best cattle forage.

Ross planned to hunt his rattlers in the forefront of the fires. They lived in winter, he said, in gopher holes, coming out in the midday warmth to forage, and would move ahead of the flames and be easily taken. We joined forces with a big fellow named Will, his snake-hunting companion of the territory, and set out in early morning, after a long rough drive over deep-rutted roads into the open wilds.

I hope never in my life to be so frightened as I was in those first few hours. I kept on Ross's footsteps, I moved when he moved, sometimes jolting into him when I thought he might leave me behind. He does not use the forked stick of conventional snake hunting, but a steel prong, shaped like an L, at the end of a long stout stick. He hunted casually, calling my attention to the varying vegetation, to hawks overhead, to a pair of the rare whooping cranes that flapped over us. In midmorning he stopped short, dropped his stick, and brought up a five-foot rattlesnake draped limply over the steel L. It seemed to me that I should drop in my tracks.

"They're not active at this season," he said quietly. "A snake takes on the temperature of its surroundings. They can't stand too much heat for that reason, and when the weather is cool, as now, they're sluggish."

The sun was bright overhead, the sky a translucent blue, and it seemed to me that it was warm enough for any snake to do as it willed. The sweat poured down my back. Ross dropped the rattler in a crocus sack[3] and Will carried it. By noon, he had caught four. I felt faint and ill. We stopped by a pond and went

---
1. **herpetologist** (hûr′pə-tŏl′ə-jĭst): a person who studies reptiles and amphibians.
2. **Everglades:** a large area of swampland in southern Florida.
3. **crocus sack:** a sack made of coarse material, such as burlap.

398 NONFICTION

MOTIVATIONAL SUMMARY
A woman remembers when she was invited to go on a hunt for rattlesnakes in the Big Prairie area of Florida. She is afraid of snakes, but she agrees to go because she is curious and interested in this activity. At first, she is terrified to move, never getting more than a foot or two away from her experienced guide who, to her amazement, does not seem to be frightened or to be continuously vigilant in watching for the poisonous rattlers. And there are a lot of rattlers.

PRESENTATION
Point out that people often fear things that they do not understand. Ask students to imagine that they are a bit nervous about participating in one of the rattlesnake roundups held annually in West Texas. Here is a true-false quiz to see how

VISUAL CONNECTIONS
Ideas for Writing
Students might write a brief narrative in which they are walking through the brush in the photograph when they come upon a huge rattlesnake. Students should make the story seem real by using specific details that appeal to the senses and by including factual information about the snakes.

8
Her imagination is running wild. Some people—the author too, seemingly—have an overly developed fear of snakes.

9 Making Inferences
Why would Ross expect the hunting to be better in the afternoon? As sun warms earth, more rattlers come out of hiding.

10 Analyzing
What do you suspect the author's attitude might be when she says "The hunting was much better"? Slight sarcasm; hunting was better for Ross, but she would have preferred to see fewer snakes.

11
Tension is building. After fearful imagining, Rawlings now sees real snakes.

swimming. The region was flat, the horizon limitless, and as I came out of the cool blue **8** water I expected to find myself surrounded by a ring of rattlers. There were only Ross and Will, opening the lunch basket. I could not eat. Ross never touches liquor and it seemed to me that I would give my hope of salvation for a <u>dram</u> of whiskey. Will went back and drove his **9** truck closer, for Ross expected the hunting to be better in the afternoon. The hunting was **10** much better. When we went back to the truck to deposit two more rattlers in the wire **11** cage, there was a rattlesnake lying under the truck.

Ross said, "Whenever I leave my car or truck with snakes already in it, other rattlers always appear. I don't know whether this is because they scent or sense the presence of other

Rattlesnake Hunt

snakes, or whether in this arid area they come to the car for shade in the heat of the day."

12 The problem was scientific, but I had no interest.

That night Ross and Will and I camped out in the vast spaces of the Everglades prairies. We got water from an abandoned well and cooked supper under buttonwood bushes by a flowing stream. The campfire blazed cheerfully under the stars and a new moon lifted in the sky. Will told tall tales of the cattlemen and 13 the Indians and we were at peace.

Ross said, "We couldn't have a better night for catching water snakes."

After the rattlers, water snakes seemed innocuous[4] enough. We worked along the edge of the stream and here Ross did not use his L-shaped steel. He reached under rocks and along the edge of the water and brought out harmless reptiles with his hands. I had said nothing to him of my fears, but he understood them. He brought a small dark snake from under a willow root.

"Wouldn't you like to hold it?" he asked. "People think snakes are cold and clammy, but they aren't. Take it in your hands. You'll see that it is warm."

14 Again, because I was ashamed, I took the
15 snake in my hands. It was not cold, it was not clammy, and it lay trustingly in my hands, a thing that lived and breathed and had mortality[5] like the rest of us. I felt an upsurgence of spirit.

The next day was magnificent. The air was crystal, the sky was aquamarine, and the far horizon of palms and oaks lay against the sky. I felt a new boldness and followed Ross bravely. He was making the rounds of the gopher holes. The rattlers came out in the midmorning warmth and were never far away. He

4. **innocuous** (ĭ-nŏk′yoō-əs): harmless.
5. **had mortality** (môr-tăl′ĭ-tē): like all living things, would someday die.

could tell by their trails whether one had come out or was still in the hole. Sometimes the two men dug the snake out. At times it was down so long and winding a tunnel that the digging was hopeless. Then they blocked the entrance and went on to other holes. In an hour or so they made the original rounds, unblocking the holes. The rattler in every case came out hurriedly, as though anything was preferable to being shut in. All the time Ross talked to me, telling me the scientific facts he had discovered about the habits of the rattlers.

16 "They pay no attention to a man standing perfectly still," he said, and proved it by letting Will unblock a hole while he stood at the entrance as the snake came out. It was exciting to watch the snake crawl slowly beside and past the man's legs. When it was at a safe distance he walked within its range of vision, which he had proved to be no higher than a man's knee, and the snake whirled and drew back in an attitude[6] of fighting defense. The rattler strikes only for paralyzing and killing its food, and for defense.

"It is a slow and heavy snake," Ross said. "It lies in wait on a small game trail and strikes the rat or rabbit passing by. It waits a few minutes, then follows along the trail, coming to the small animal, now dead or dying. It noses it from all sides, making sure that it is its own kill, and that it is dead and ready for swallowing."

A rattler will lie quietly without revealing itself if a man passes by and it thinks it is not seen. It slips away without fighting if given the chance. Only Ross's sharp eyes sometimes picked out the gray and yellow diamond pattern, camouflaged among the grasses. In the 17 cool of the morning, chilled by the January air, the snakes showed no fight. They could be looped up limply over the steel L and dropped

6. **attitude:** here, a position of the body.

400 NONFICTION

SCIENCE LINK
You might ask students to look back at the story to see how the writer ensures her safety when exploring nature. As they discuss these techniques, you might write them on the chalkboard with the title "Facing Fears in the Environment."

Students might include practices such as these: "went with an expert," "gained knowledge about her prey's habits and traits," "took proper equipment," "took safety measures," and "had enough people around to handle an emergency."

in a sack or up into the wire cage on the back of Will's truck. As the sun mounted in the sky and warmed the moist Everglades earth, the snakes were warmed too, and Ross warned that it was 18 time to go more cautiously. Yet having learned that it was we who were the aggressors;[7] that immobility meant complete safety; that the snakes, for all their lightning flash in striking, were inaccurate in their aim, with limited vision; having watched again and again the liquid grace of movement, the beauty of pattern, suddenly I understood that I was drinking in freely the magnificent sweep of the horizon, with no fear of what might be at the moment under my feet. I went off hunting by myself, and though I found no snakes, I should have 19 known what to do.

The sun was dropping low in the west.

7. **aggressors** (ə-grĕs′ərz): those who attack first.

Masses of white cloud hung above the flat marshy plain and seemed to be tangled in the tops of distant palms and cypresses. The sky turned orange, then saffron. I walked leisurely back toward the truck. In the distance I could see Ross and Will making their way in too. The season was more advanced than at the Creek, two hundred miles to the north, and I noticed that spring flowers were blooming among the lumpy hummocks. I leaned over to pick a 20 white violet. There was a rattlesnake under the violet.

If this had happened the week before, if it had happened the day before, I think I should have lain down and died on top of the rattlesnake, with no need of being struck and poisoned. The snake did not coil, but lifted its head and whirred its rattles lightly. I stepped 21 back slowly and put the violet in a buttonhole. I reached forward and laid the steel L across

18
Use to answer **study question 4,** p. 402.

19
Knowing what to do does not always mean a person can perform a difficult task under pressure.

20
Plot. In the **climax** of this story, Rawlings comes face to face with a rattlesnake and with her own fears.

21
Use to answer **study question 5a,** p. 402.

VISUAL CONNECTIONS
Exploring the Subject
Rattlesnakes have a keen sense of smell. They cannot hear, but they are extremely sensitive to ground vibrations and can feel the approach of a person even at quite a distance. Usually, rattlesnakes will rattle to dissuade possible intruders, and the rattle can be heard up to 200 feet away. However, rattlesnakes may strike without warning.

PORTFOLIO ASSESSMENT
Students may want to write about one of their fears or a fear they have overcome. Suggest that they first define the fear, next tell how it affects their lives, and finally describe how they overcame it or would like to overcome it. Students may want to illustrate the final drafts of their essays. Consult with students individually to agree on how their essays will be assessed. (See *Portfolio Assessment and Professional Support Materials* for additional information on student portfolios.)

TRANSPARENCY 32
Reader Response
Compare and Contrast Characteristics – invites students to compare qualities of characters from different selections in the unit.

22
Ross is giving Rawlings a chance to test her new confidence.

23
She has not yet gathered the courage to pick up a rattler with her hands.

24
Snake is captured. Rawlings has, to great extent, conquered fear and resolved her conflict.

READING CHECK
1. Believed that wire grass that grows after a fire makes best cattle food (p. 398).
2. In gopher holes (p. 398).
3. Are cold-blooded; take on temperature of environment and become sluggish when cold (p. 398).
4. Water snakes (p. 400).
5. Have limited vision (p. 401).

FOR STUDY AND DISCUSSION
1. Follows closely behind Ross.
2. Accustomed to handling snakes; knows they are not active in winter season and are unlikely to strike.
3a. That snakes are warm to touch, not clammy, and that snakes are living creatures, not monsters. 3b. Feels "upsurgence of spirit"; her extreme fear is dispelled and she gains insight into kinship of all living things.
4. Magnificent day cheers her; has overcome some of her fears and has learned that rattlesnakes are sluggish at this time of year.
5a. Steps back slowly, and calmly puts violet in buttonhole. 5b. Partly successful. Manages to pick up snake and carry to truck but is unable to lift it into cage. Unable to overcome fear of picking up snake by hand.
6. Elated and victorious; she has conquered a "great fear."

402

---

the snake's neck, just back of the blunt head. I called to Ross: "I've got one."

He strolled toward me.

"Well, pick it up," he said.

I released it and slipped the L under the middle of the thick body.

22 "Go put it in the box."

He went ahead of me and lifted the top of the wire cage. I made the truck with the rattler, but when I reached up the six feet to drop it in the cage, it slipped off the stick and dropped on Ross's feet. It made no effort to strike.

"Pick it up again," he said. "If you'll pin it down lightly and reach just back of its head with your hand, as you've seen me do, you can drop it in more easily."

I pinned it and leaned over.

23 "I'm awfully sorry," I said, "but you're pushing me a little too fast."

He grinned. I lifted it on the stick and again as I had it at head height, it slipped off, down Ross's boots and on top of his feet. He stood as still as a stump. I dropped the snake on his feet for the third time. It seemed to me that the most patient of rattlers might in time resent being hauled up and down, and for all the man's quiet certainty that in standing motionless there was no danger, would strike at whatever was nearest, and that would be Ross.

I said, "I'm just not man enough to keep this up any longer," and he laughed and reached down with his smooth quickness and lifted the snake back of the head and dropped it in the cage. It slid in among its mates and settled in a corner. The hunt was over and we drove back over the uneven trail to Will's village and left him and went on to Arcadia and home. Our catch for the two days was thirty-two rattlers.

24 I said to Ross, "I believe that tomorrow I could have picked up that snake."

Back at the Creek, I felt a new lightness. I had done battle with a great fear, and the victory was mine.

402 NONFICTION

Reading Check
1. Why were cattlemen and Indians burning the land in Big Prairie?
2. Where do the rattlesnakes live during the winter?
3. Why are the rattlesnakes sluggish?
4. What kinds of snakes does Ross catch at night?
5. Why are rattlesnakes often inaccurate in aim?

For Study and Discussion

Analyzing and Interpreting the Selection

1. During the first day of the rattlesnake hunt, how does the author show her terror?

2. Ross Allen is a herpetologist—an expert on reptiles and amphibians. At the start of the hunt, he calmly picks up a five-foot rattlesnake with a steel prong. Why is he able to hunt so "casually"?

3. At first, the author thinks snakes are cold and clammy. **a.** What does she discover when she holds a small, dark snake in her own hands? **b.** How does this new knowledge affect her?

4. Why is she less frightened on the second day of the hunt?

5. The author's new-found courage is put to a test when she encounters a rattlesnake on her own. **a.** What small gesture indicates that she is no longer afraid (see page 401)? **b.** How successful is she in catching the snake?

6. At the end of the selection, the author indicates that she has gained control over her fear. How does she now feel?

Language and Vocabulary

Forming Words with -logy

In "Rattlesnake Hunt," Ross Allen is described as a *herptologist*, someone who specializes in *herpetology*. The word *herpetology* has two parts. The first part, *herpeto-*, comes from a Greek word meaning "reptile." The second part, *-logy*, also comes from Greek and means "the science or study of something." *Herpetology* is the science or study of reptiles.

1. *Geo-* is a root meaning "of the earth." What is *geology*? *Biology*? *Zoology*? Check your answers in a dictionary.

Look up the following roots in a dictionary.

2. What does each one mean?

    anthropo-   ethno-   theo-

3. What word is formed by adding *-logy* to each root? Tell what each word means.

Focus on Biographical Report

Identifying a Main Idea

To focus your material in a biographical report, you need to develop a **main idea.** Writers often state the main idea of a report or essay in the introduction. In "Rattlesnake Hunt," however, Marjorie Kinnan Rawlings states her main idea at the end of the essay: "I had done battle with a great fear, and the victory was mine" (page 402). All the details in Rawlings' essay contribute to this idea.

Review your notes for the writing assignment on page 392 or make some notes on a new subject for a biographical report. Use your notes to develop a specific main idea. State this idea as clearly as you can in one or two sentences. Save your writing.

About the Author

Marjorie Kinnan Rawlings (1896–1953)

Marjorie Kinnan Rawlings grew up on a farm in Maryland. She attended the University of Wisconsin, where she was active in theater productions and literary magazines. In 1919 she married Charles Rawlings, a journalist. The next ten years involved a great deal of moving and traveling, and during that time, she worked as a newspaper reporter. She disliked this kind of work, however, and began to devote time to writing fiction.

OBJECTIVES
The overall aim is for students to analyze Ved Mehta's character and feelings in the excerpt from *Sound-Shadows of the New World*. For a complete list of objectives, see the **Teacher's Notes**.

VOCABULARY
The underlined words are in the Glossary. The **Language and Vocabulary** exercise on pp. 412–413 will give students practice in using context clues to determine word meanings.

FOCUS / MOTIVATION
Ask the class to list what fears they would have if they were to lose their sight. Then have them consider how they might begin to overcome each of those fears.

TEACHING RESOURCES C
Teacher's Notes, p. 126
Study Guide, p. 129
Language Skills, p. 131
Building Vocabulary, p. 134
Selection Test, p. 136

PREREADING FOCUS
The headnote emphasizes that this selection is from the autobiography of a blind person. You might ask students to discuss how this knowledge prepares the reader for the writer's point of view. What kinds of sensory details will the writer most likely use?

Sound-Shadows of the New World

1
"Social adjustment" refers to adapting to new environment. It includes interacting and communicating with other people.

2
Miss Harper uses common southern expression "y'all" to mean "you all."

3
Use to answer **study question 1a**, p. 412.

4 Synthesizing
What kinds of sounds might a room have? Movement, echoes, heating/air conditioning noises.

5
Ved seems keenly aware of location of objects in gym.

6
With the sudden perception of new sounds, students have questions about their environment.

FROM
Sound-Shadows of the New World

VED MEHTA

Ved Mehta has been blind since the age of four. When he was fifteen, he left his native India to enroll in the Arkansas School for the Blind, in Little Rock, Arkansas. In these excerpts from his autobiographical narrative, Sound-Shadows of the New World, *he describes a mobility program that trained blind boys and girls to sense objects by using "facial vision."*

1 At the start of one social-adjustment period, Miss Harper took us into the gymnasium and lined us up at the edge of the floor, saying, "Mr. Woolly has just come back from San Francisco, where he attended a conference of the American Association of Workers for the Blind. At the conference, he heard rehabilitation workers complain that youngsters are coming out of residential schools for the blind without mobility—without the skills to get around by themselves out on the streets. If they can't get to regular jobs, then there's no hope of their ever leading a life outside the sheltered workshops for the blind. We've therefore decided to go all out for our mobility program and help you youngsters develop **2** your facial vision. As y'all know, facial vision is **3** a term for the ability many of you totally blind boys and girls have to sense objects through echoes and changes in air pressure around the **4** ear." She added, "I'm sure the gym sounds very different to you boys and girls from the way it usually does."

But the gymnasium always sounds different, I thought. It sounds different with mats on the floor when we are doing calisthenics,[1] without mats when we are getting it ready for a party, and with people dancing on the wooden floor during a party. At any of those times, though, it sounds full near the floor and hollow near the ceiling. Now, however, I, along with others, suddenly realized it was the other way around. The sound-shadows were floating like airy, **5** ghostlike shapes around and above our heads.

"What is it?"
"What are they?"
6 "What's happening?"

1. **calisthenics** (kăl'əs-thĕn'ĭks): exercises for physical fitness.

404 NONFICTION

MOTIVATIONAL SUMMARY
Ved Mehta is blind. He attends a training school in Arkansas where he hopes to learn the skills that will enable him to get along in a world built for the sighted. At his school, he practices the skill of "facial vision," learning to sense the "sound-shadows" created by obstacles. Finally, on the day he is ready to attempt a trip into town, he decides to trust his ability to sense "sound-shadows." He leaves his white cane in the gutter and heads for town.

PRESENTATION
The headnote established the setting as a school for the blind in Arkansas. The author is at least fifteen years old. The term "sound-shadows" will no doubt be new to everyone. Students might speculate about possible meanings of the

7 "Mr. Tyson strung up some cotton-pickin' mannequins² to show us what'll happen if we don't do well in mobility?" Oather asked Miss Harper.

Miss Harper laughed, and then explained
8 that suspended on tracks from the ceiling were lightweight fiberboard panels of various sizes. The panels, which she could raise or lower by means of ropes and pulleys, formed a movable obstacle course. "The purpose of the obstacle
9 course is to help y'all develop your facial vision," she said. "As y'all walk through it, we'll see how easily you're able to spot panels, big or

2. **mannequins** (măn'ĭ-kĭns): life-size dummies such as those used by window dressers.

7
"Cotton-pickin' " is a colloquialism associated with speakers from the South.

8
Use to answer **study question 1b, p. 412.**

9 Synthesizing
How would development of "facial vision" help the students in the world outside the school? Help them detect objects and people in order to avoid collisions.

405

term before reading the story. The selection has two parts. The first describes how Mehta's teachers tried to train him and his classmates to use "facial vision." This part introduces many characters. You might read this part to the class, stopping to discuss each new character as he or she is introduced. The second part, which chronicles a trip into town, can be assigned for independent reading.

10
Characterization. Dialogue and statement by author quickly show one aspect of Lois' personality.

11
Example emphasizes reasons new challenge could be frightening to blind person.

12 Analyzing
What technique has the author used to give us information about blindness? Gives information through dialogue.

13
Different perspective regarding use of Seeing Eye dogs; evidently, school encouraged greater independence.

14
Characterization. Ved uses imagination to create exciting, challenging event out of obstacle course.

small, and avoid running into them. Some of y'all may not do well at first, but the more you do it the better you should get at it."

Everyone talked at once.

10 "How am I going to keep from bumping into those things and getting all bruised up?" Lois Woodward asked. She was known for fretting about such matters, as if the smallest bruise could disfigure her.

"We've got plenty of obstacles around the school—why do they have to go and invent some more?" Oather asked. He went on to answer his own question. "I guess these panels 11 are better than glass doors." When Oather was about nine, he had run into the door of the boys' solarium. His arm had gone right through its glass pane, and had never completely recovered from the injury. But this hadn't stopped him from tearing around the school like a racing car.

"I thought that people good in facial vision went blind when they were really little, and grew up having it," Treadway said. "I didn't think you could teach it later on."

"I'm not going to mention any names, but there are people standing right here who went blind when they were little who crash around 12 like a bird in a cage," Oather said. He himself was a perfect example of what Treadway was talking about, but, as usual, he was playing the devil's advocate.³

"Well, maybe their mothers didn't let them run around when they were little, so they weren't able to develop facial vision and coordination," Miss Harper said. She added that she didn't know for certain whether people were born with facial vision or could acquire it with training, but that the obstacle course was a good experiment and we should all cooperate.

"Miss Harper, why do we need classes in fa-

3. **devil's advocate:** someone who deliberately takes the opposite side or wrong side of an argument.

cial vision when we can get ourselves Seeing Eye dogs?" a boy I'll call Branch Hill asked, as if he had just woken up. The boys referred to Branch as another Dumb Joe Wright, but, unlike Joe, Branch was totally blind.

13 Many of us jumped on Branch, because we thought that Seeing Eye dogs were really for blind people who didn't want to help themselves and wanted people to feel sorry for them.

"Even if you somehow get a Seeing Eye dog, you won't regret having good facial vision," Miss Harper said.

There was some more discussion in this vein, and then Miss Harper said, "Y'all are getting het up⁴ about some little old panels that will just swing away if you bump into them. Yet when you get to traveling around town you're going to meet up with all kinds of real, dangerous obstacles, like lampposts and mailboxes, ladders and scaffolding. Everywhere, you'll come across parking meters and fire hydrants, and manholes left uncovered. You'll have to learn to navigate around them, so you might as well get started here, right now, and try to train your facial vision."

14 I imagined the gymnasium with its obstacle course as a forest that one had to find one's way through with the perceptiveness⁵ of a dog, the cunning of a fox, the fearlessness of a tiger. I felt excited, and hoped that Miss Harper would call on me to walk through it first. But she called on Bruton.

Bruton, who was known for his prowess on the wrestling mat, sounded uncharacteristically timorous going through the obstacle course.

"No hands out in front of you, please," Miss Harper said to him. "Keep your arms at your sides. . . . You're doing fine. . . . Don't stop."

4. **het up:** slang for "excited" or "angry."
5. **perceptiveness** (pər-sĕp′tĭv-nəs): awareness; sensitivity.

406 NONFICTION

MEETING INDIVIDUAL NEEDS
Auditory Learners • To help students gain more awareness of environmental sounds, ask them to close their eyes for three minutes and try to remember the sounds they hear. After three minutes, you could ask them to keep their eyes closed as different students describe the sounds. What subtleties of sound are they able to pick up? Can they distinguish sounds outside the room? Can anyone determine the exact place that a sound is coming from? Can they tell if the sound is high or low, to the right or left of the classroom, or if it is full or hollow? Ask students to imagine using these clues as sound-shadows that would direct their own movements.

Treadway and Vernelle, perhaps becoming restive at having nothing to do, started working out the harmony for "Button Up Your Overcoat."

"Please tell them to be quiet," Bruton said to Miss Harper, from the middle of the floor. "Their singing is interfering with my facial vision."

Miss Harper shushed Treadway and Vernelle but then said to Bruton that in the gymnasium he had only a little singing to contend with, while on the street there might be wind or jackhammers. He had to learn to put up with all kinds of noises.

Bruton bumped his head against a panel, cursed, and returned to the edge of the floor. However much Miss Harper coaxed him, he wouldn't go back out. "I'm resting now," he said.

Miss Harper called on Branch next. He went around the floor bumping into panel after panel, as if the purpose of the exercise were to score hits. People called out to him that he was doing really fine—that that was the only way to go at those blooming panels. He seemed to take their goading good-naturedly, and kept on going.

Finally, I myself was in the midst of the obstacle course. I got so caught up in the spirit of the moment, felt so happy and self-confident, that I imagined that my whole childhood of running around in Indian *gullis*[6] and compounds,[7] of flying kites and riding my bicycle, of living in different places and having to adjust constantly to new surroundings had been a preparation only for this obstacle course. Here was a big panel, which I was sure I could have detected even with a pneumatic drill hammering in my ear. Here was a small panel just above my eyebrow, which I was able to deftly avoid, although I didn't notice it until I was almost upon it. There, just ahead, was a panel at chin level. I easily went around it, tilting my head a little bit. As I weaved my way through the obstacle course, going now one way, now another, Miss Harper noiselessly pulled up panels so high that the gymnasium felt open, like a field, and dropped them down so close together that it felt like a thicket. Some of the panels that suddenly appeared in front of my face were even harder to detect than the slim lampposts at home, which would materialize out of nowhere when I was walking with an inattentive sighted companion, and bruise me, as if they had a will of their own. Then I would imagine that the gods were punishing me for my misdeeds, such as pinching Usha, my little sister. I now decided that if I got through the obstacle course without brushing against a single panel I would best the gods.

I skirted panels, ducked under them, sprinted past them. I put my hands in my pockets and whistled under my breath. Just ahead was a panel that hung down to my chest. I easily walked around it, but then I slipped on the short incline that framed the floor and fell. In the game of mobility, one concentrates on the signals from the region of the face only to be tripped up by things around the feet, I thought. Perhaps there is no way of besting the gods after all.

"You fell because you got overconfident," Miss Harper said primly after she had rushed over to me and I had assured her that I wasn't hurt.

In subsequent social-adjustment periods, we were made to go through the obstacle course again and again. Although the avowed purpose of the exercise was to improve our facial vision, no one ever seemed to do better or worse than before. Years later, Mr. Woolly told me, "In your time, it was the vogue to try to teach and develop facial vision. That's why we

---

6. ***gullis*** (gŭl′ēz): back lanes.
7. **compound:** an enclosed area, usually encircled by a high wall.

---

15 Miss Harper seems practical; does not "shelter" her students.

16 Making Inferences
How might Bruton's lack of success affect others? Bruton is known for his strength, yet he quits. Could frighten others.

17 Branch seems to have no facial vision; he was one who wanted Seeing Eye dog.

18 Ved uses exaggeration to create humorous image.

19 Personification. Inanimate objects seem to take on human quality of aggression to Ved.

20 Characterization. Ved's active imagination reveals him to be motivated, confident person.

21 Author creates exciting scene with use of vivid verbs.

TRANSPARENCY 33
Literary Elements
Evaluating Nonfiction – provides a structure for analyzing nonfiction using a questioning strategy.

22
Emphasizes how ideas and theories are revised.

23
Ved is apparently first to try skills in "real" world.

24
Travel for blind person is much more an intellectual activity than for sighted person.

25 Drawing Conclusions
Why does Mr. Hartman tell Ved not to think American towns are "orderly and simple"? Does not want him to be overly confident.

26
Mr. Hartman states purpose and scope of training program.

27
Ved is self-motivated; not satisfied with vague knowledge but wants to know as much as possible.

28
Allusion. Refers to Biblical story of idolatrous and covetous Jezebel—wife of King of Israel, ninth century B.C.

---

spent endless hours making every blind youngster walk through that obstacle course over and over. It was a long time before we learned that either people have facial vision or they don't— or, at least, that there is no scientific evidence **22** that the skill can be taught. In fact, we're not sure anymore what facial vision is, or even if there *is* such a thing. The only thing we are sure of is that some blind people have an extra sensitivity—some kind of combination of all the senses they've got—that somehow enables them to detect the presence of obstacles."

23 On Saturday morning, Mr. Hartman walked out with me onto the school's front drive to send me off downtown. "As you must know from your trips with partially sighted boys, the trolley goes along West Markham Street all the way to downtown and turns onto Main Street," he said. "Main Street runs north and south, while the numbered streets, which intersect it, run east and west. Now, if you're walking south on Main Street from West Markham, the numbers of the cross streets will be going up. You can count the blocks, and you'll always know what cross street you're at." As Mr. Hartman talked, I imagined Little Rock as a checkerboard set up for the game of mobility. In that **24** game, I would use feet in place of fingers to make my moves, playing against people, cars, and obstacles.

"It seems that American towns are orderly and simple—that's a blind person's dream," I said, recalling how streets at home twisted and turned and snaked in such a way that it was hard for me ever to know exactly where I was.

25 "Don't go getting any such notion in your head," Mr. Hartman said. "Wait till you start moving around just here in Little Rock by yourself, boy. There are all kinds of exceptions. What should be called First Street is just the stretch of West Markham Street that runs through downtown. If a blind individual didn't know that, he could spend hours going in circles looking for First Street."

I still thought that American towns sounded relatively orderly and simple compared with those at home, but I didn't press the point. Instead, I asked, "How high up do the numbered streets go?"

"They go up to at least Ninth Street—you'll never need to go beyond that."

"And what are the names of the streets on either side of Main Street?"

"To the west is Louisiana Street. To the west of that, there are two other streets—I've forgotten their names, but you won't need to fool with either of them. We visually handicapped people only need to worry about where we can **26** buy what we need, and where we live and work."

I said I wondered what the names and numbers of the streets were between the school and downtown.

"I don't know," Mr. Hartman said. "I've always gone downtown on the trolley." He added vaguely, "There must be houses and things there."

I decided that I would have to think of the area between the school and downtown as a **27** mysterious trolley run until such time as I could somehow come up with the information for myself.

"You'll know when a trolley's coming because the power lines it runs on bang and rattle **28** like Jezebel's teeth," Mr. Hartman was saying. "The trolley will stay on West Markham until the second right-hand turn, which is onto Main Street, and you, boy, get off at the stop right after that turn."

Mr. Hartman gave me three tokens—one for going downtown, one for coming back, and an extra one for any emergency. He also gave me a couple of dollars and told me to go into the Rexall drugstore on the southeast corner of Main and Fifth and buy for him and his wife a

408 NONFICTION

READING SKILLS PRACTICE
The underlined passage can be used to give students practice in the reading skill of drawing logical conclusions. Ask students to read the passage and choose the statement that can be most logically concluded from the paragraph.

A. He tried to break the cane so that he could cross West Markham. (Not supported by the passage.) **B.** Crossing to Stifft's Station didn't count because he had his cane with him. (Contradicted by the passage.) **C.** He felt that it was easier to cross the street by himself than with sighted attendants. (Not supported by the passage.) **D.** He flung his cane in the gutter because he wanted to be independent. (Correct.)

---

black Ace pocket comb, two sixty-watt light bulbs, a pair of brown shoelaces, and a packet of bobby pins. "You spend the morning going around the town and getting acquainted with it," he said. "I'll meet you at one o'clock at the restaurant in Pfeifer's department store. I'll buy you a milkshake." He added jokingly, "That is, if you're still alive."

"Will you be following me—watching me?"

"Boy, this is no piddling trip to Stifft's Station,[8] with me ready to rush to your side if you land yourself in trouble. The only way you're ever going to learn to do things by yourself is to do them. Sink or swim—"

"I know—that's your philosophy."

Finally, I was on my way, thinking that it was typical of Mr. Hartman to test me by loading me up with so much last-minute information and instruction. I stepped along the front drive smartly, swinging and tapping my cane in front of my feet and feeling like a soldier going out on a dangerous mission. But as I approached the gate the *tap-tap* of the cane made me feel shy and self-conscious. "Tap-tap, here comes a blind boy from the blind school—look out!" the cane seemed to shout.

I stopped at the school gate to reflect on why I disliked the cane so much. I had always disapproved of the boys who wore dark glasses inside the school building, as if to hide their blind eyes from visitors, because it seemed to me that they were denying their blindness. But there was all the difference in the world between covering up the fact of blindness with dark glasses and not wanting to advertise it with a cane. I conceded that a cane might be useful to blind people less adept than I was, but I felt that in my case it could be only an impediment to my acceptance as just another normal person on the street or on the trolley.

After all, the point of mobility was to win that acceptance.

I stood there holding my cane. It seemed to extend from my hand like an embarrassing appendage that, do what I might, could not be quieted, hidden, laid to rest—a symbol of all that was awkward and adolescent in my blindness. I whacked the cane on the ground, thinking that it was weighing down my hopes of being as independent as the sighted.

▶I held the cane poised just above the ground, in the grip of an idea. After listening to make sure that no one was around, I caught up the cane by both ends, put my foot in the middle, and tried to break it. But it would yield only to spring back. I flung it in the gutter by the side of the drive, making a mental note of the spot, so I could pick it up later if anyone asked for it, and hurried across West Markham. I got across it so easily that I couldn't imagine why I had ever needed sighted attendants, why I had waited until that day to strike out on my own for downtown. (Somehow, the crossing to Stifft's Station earlier that week didn't seem to count now, because Mr. Hartman had been tailing me.)◀

The sun was out in its full April glory. The air around my face was fresh, the sidewalk underfoot was smooth. I felt like bursting out in song.

I was at the trolley stop, but it was so pleasant that I decided to continue walking and explore the route. To my right, there was no steady sound-shadow of a wall or a fence to guide me along the sidewalk; there was just empty, undifferentiated[9] space. To my left, there was a steady stream of cars going both ways at about forty miles an hour, with an occasional large vehicle whose passing sounded like the roar of an airplane and temporarily

---

8. **Stifft's Station:** the place where Ved had gone on an earlier trip.

9. **undifferentiated** (ŭn-dĭf′ə-rĕn′shē-āt′əd): without any differences or distinctions.

▶Reading Skills Objective: Drawing Logical Conclusions

Sound-Shadows of the New World 409

---

29 Drawing Conclusions
What might be the purpose of this rather harsh joke? To make Ved cautious.

30
Mr. Hartman's lecture seems harsh, but he has probably successfully used the method on other students.

31
"Smartly" creates image of confident step.

32
Characterization. Ved's strong ego makes him feel self-conscious about his handicap.

33
Use to answer **study question 3a,** p. 412.

34
Ved states his goal; he has high expectations for himself.

35
Flinging cane in gutter is a dramatic act of independence and determination.

36
"Sound-shadow" refers to echoes from wall or fence.

37
Ved's active imagination again provides thoughts that make him happy.

38
Feeling of well-being can be shattered in an instant. Assailed by doubts about having thrown cane away.

39 Analyzing
Why does Ved feel that people on the trolley are staring at him? Feels guilty because he has broken "rules."

40
Being "confined" would be another obstacle in Ved's quest for independence.

41
Story skips over Ved's wait for next trolley and his ride downtown.

42 Finding Cause and Effect
Ved begins to realize that he can sense the existence of a store as he passes it. How can he know? Detects sound-shadows of doorways, smells of different shops.

---

paralyzed my facial vision. But my facial vision—or whatever it is that enables the blind to perceive obstacles—soon got more or less adjusted to the noise of the traffic echoing in that undifferentiated space. Happily, I imagined that I was by the sea listening to the waves breaking at high tide.

The sidewalk suddenly ended in an abrupt drop. It's a manhole, I thought. My cane, my cane! But the drop turned out to be a high curb that had not been preceded by the usual signal of a footworn depression. I regained my balance, and although I had no idea whether I was in an alleyway or had come to the end of the sidewalk, I stepped along, if a little shakily. Soon the sidewalk resumed.

There was the clanging vibration of the trolley wires overhead and, almost a block behind, a smooth rumble with a slight whistle in it, reminiscent of the sound effects in the outer-space radio program "Dimension X." It was the trolley. A sighted teacher may be in the trolley, I thought guiltily. They may be checking up on me. It's childish to think that I can leave the school authorities behind like my cane.

The trolley was getting closer. I felt that eyes were staring out at me, burning a hole in the back of my neck. I ran for the trolley stop, which I supposed must be just ahead, and narrowly avoided signs and posts that appeared as suddenly as the panels in the gymnasium.

The trolley passed me. I was at an intersection. I could hear the "Dimension X" rumble and whistle of the trolley on the other side of the intersection, and the light was against me.

I remembered that trolleys came at intervals of twenty minutes or more, and I put my arms out in front of me, held my breath, and stepped off the curb. I recalled in a flash what Mamaji used to say when I was riding my bicycle in the compound with my hands off the handlebars: "You'll kill yourself." I used to reply smugly, "Death only comes once." But now, with cars honking all around me, I had a vision of something much worse than death—losing a limb and being confined to a wheelchair for life. I said a quick prayer.

Somehow, I was across—and in one piece. I kept on running, and gaining on the trolley, its "Dimension X" rumble and whistle ever louder in my ear. A few feet ahead, I finally sensed the trolley stop. I heard the whoosh and clatter of the trolley door opening and the clicking of the coin box inside. I made a dash for the door but crashed into the bench at the stop, which I sensed too late to avoid. I missed the trolley. . . .

I was finally downtown: in a metropolis, as I thought of it, with Main Street, with M. M. Cohn's and Pfeifer's department stores, with McLellan's and Woolworth's dime stores, with the Rexall drugstore and the Lido restaurant—all the landmarks we heard advertised on the radio. I got off at the first downtown stop, at West Markham and Main. I had more than half an hour at my disposal before I was supposed to meet Mr. Hartman, so I started slowly walking up to the Rexall drugstore, trying at once to get a sense of downtown and to practice my mobility. I had walked Main Street with friends repeatedly, but I felt I was noticing some things for the first time, like the fact that there were so many shops in a block. Also, I had previously imagined that I would have difficulty telling the intersections, but I found that they almost announced themselves, being preceded by an interruption in the sound-shadows of the buildings, by a sense of openness, by an increase in the noise of the cross-street traffic, and by the footworn depression at the curb. How different walking downtown is from walking in quiet Stifft's Station, I thought. Here, there is so much traffic, and so many people are rushing in and out of

43 doorways or barreling along the street, hardly looking where they're going. No obstacle course could have prepared me for this. But what an excellent place to test my senses to the limit. I must make a mental note of the shops I'm passing, so that I can come back and explore further. 44 What's this? It's a whiff of a clean paper smell—I must be passing a stationer's. Now I'm walking through a dull roasted aroma—this must be a nut shop. Here is a strong odor of leather and polish, but it's hard to tell if it's being given off by a shoeshop or a leather-goods store. Now, here is a store that's unmistakable—this peanutty exhaust could only be pumped out of a dime store.

I was at Fifth and Main, just across from the Rexall drugstore. The light was in my favor, but I didn't know how long it had been that way. Deciding to play it safe for a change, I waited.

"You have the light," a man said, nudging me.

"I know."

"Why don't you walk, then? Do you need a hand?"

45 "I would rather wait."

The man crossed the street, exclaiming in annoyance, "I won't help *your* kind again!"

I didn't like leaving him with a bad impression of the blind. Yet I wondered what choice I had had. There had been no quick way to explain to him the logic behind my waiting—one explanation would have necessarily involved another. Anyway, I had to concentrate on getting around, not on educating strangers, say what Miss Harper might about each of us 46 being an emissary to the country of the sighted. The only way to avoid frustrating encounters with the sighted was to act as if I had some sight, I concluded—not for the first time.

The traffic stopped on Main Street and started on Fifth. I quickly crossed over.

I listened for the sweep and brush of the revolving door to locate the Rexall drugstore, and, when there was a pause in its turning, 47 made a dash for it.

Inside, in the front, a clerk was busy with a woman customer at the cash register. I stood a little to one side, breathing in the smell of rubbing alcohol, soap, and cough medicine, my heart beating to the screech and click of his machine. The register drawer sprang open. The woman got her change, gathered up some packages, and left.

I stepped up to the register and asked the clerk where the light bulbs were kept.

"Just look around."

I stayed put, and he looked up. "Oh. Straight to the back—the second counter to the right." He thinks I have some sight, I thought. I'm doing well.

48 By quietly asking sales assistants, by surreptitiously[10] touching things on the shelves, by listening to other customers, I was able to find everything Mr. Hartman had told me to buy, and to leave the shop in good order.

I was hot, and looked forward to my reward of a cold milkshake. Pfeifer's, which was barely a block up, was easy to locate—it had by far the busiest entrance on the block. I followed people in through a double set of swinging doors. Toward the back, through the ringing of festive bells, I heard an elevator door open, and walked to it briskly.

"The restaurant floor, please," I said, stepping in and surrendering myself to a waking dream: A champion wrestler had me now in a jackknife maneuver, now in a half-nelson lock; he tried to pin me, but I managed to keep one shoulder off the mat. No, it wasn't a wrestler at all but Mary Ann Lambert, and we were on our first date, walking hand in hand. The cane 49 stuck out from my other hand like a symbol of

10. **surreptitiously** (sûr′əp-tĭsh′əs-lē): secretly or stealthily.

43
Irony. Ved imagines that people are not looking where they are going—ironic because Ved cannot look where he is going.

44
Imagery. Ved's sense of smell is so keen that he detects stationery store, nut shop, shoeshop, and dime store.

45 Drawing Conclusions
Why does Ved refuse help? He needs to be independent.

46
Teacher has referred to "country of the sighted" as if it were foreign country that blind person visits.

47
Ved's facial vision is highly effective here, as it helps him through revolving door.

48
Through intelligence and determination, Ved is successful on his own.

49
Ved's dream reveals anger and determination; his goal in life is to be like everyone else.

Sound-Shadows of the New World

> **TRANSPARENCY 32**
> **Reader Response**
> *Compare and Contrast Characteristics* – invites students to compare qualities of characters from different selections in the unit.

50 Summarizing
What had happened to Ved's body without his realizing it?
Had become tense.

51
Answer somewhat evasive; did have some trouble, yet "found everything, all right."

READING CHECK
1. To begin training in "facial vision" (p. 404).
2. Became overconfident (p. 407).
3. Flings it in gutter (p. 409).
4. Crashes into bench at the stop (p. 410).
5. Has busiest entrance on block (p. 411).

FOR STUDY AND DISCUSSION
1a. "Ability . . . to sense objects through echoes and changes in air pressure around the ear." **1b.** Panels of various sizes that can be raised or lowered. **1c.** Easily maneuvers around panels.
2. Perhaps closest that sighted people can come to defining "sound-shadow" is to call it a sound wave.
3a. Regards cane as advertisement of blindness that will prevent people from accepting him as normal person. **3b.** Refuses help of man at crosswalk; does not ask sales clerk to get required items.
4. Touch: senses "footworn depressions" at curbs. Smell: odor of paper, roasted nuts, leather and polish. Hearing: hears location of intersections, whether traffic is stopped, when to enter revolving door, location of cash register and elevator door.

412

---

painful effort—like a miserable deformity. I had to get rid of it for good—be like everyone else.

"You're doing fine," a voice said.

I jumped. It took me a second to realize that it was Mr. Hartman at my elbow, and that he must have been in the elevator the whole time.

The elevator door opened, and we got out. I fell in step with Mr. Hartman, the back of my hand barely touching the sleeve of his shirt. All **50** of a sudden, every muscle in my body relaxed, and I feared that I was going to slump to the floor.

We sat down at a table in the restaurant.

"You get everything? You have any trouble?"

51 "I found everything, all right."

Reading Check

1. Why are Ved and his classmates taken to the gymnasium?
2. What causes Ved to fall while he is going through the obstacle course?
3. What does Ved do with his cane before starting off for downtown Little Rock?
4. What causes Ved to miss the trolley?
5. How does Ved know when he has reached Pfeifer's?

For Study and Discussion

Analyzing and Interpreting the Selection

1a. How does Miss Harper define "facial vision"? **b.** What does the obstacle course consist of? **c.** How does Ved demonstrate that he has an extra sensitivity that enables him to detect obstacles?

2. Throughout the selection Ved uses the phrase "sound-shadows." He is able to tell the intersections because they are "preceded by an interruption in the sound-shadows of the buildings." What does he mean?

3. Ved says that his goal is "acceptance as just another normal person on the street or on the trolley." **a.** Why does he feel that carrying a cane will be an impediment to him? **b.** How does he show his need for independence when he is downtown?

4. How does Ved use his senses of smell, touch, and hearing to familiarize himself with his surroundings?

Language and Vocabulary

Using Context Clues

You have seen that you can often work out the meaning of an unfamiliar word by looking at
1 the context in which it appears. What context clues help you determine the meaning of *timorous* in this sentence?

> Bruton, who was known for his prowess on the wrestling mat, sounded uncharacteristically *timorous* going through the obstacle course.

Did you get the meaning "afraid" or "full of
2 fear"? What clues were supplied by the words *prowess*, *wrestling*, and *uncharacteristically*?

3 Use context clues to figure out the meanings of the italicized words in these sentences from the selection. Check your answers in the glossary or in a dictionary.

412 NONFICTION

CLOSURE

Ask students to identify and explain examples of Ved's feelings and aspects of his character that are revealed in the excerpt from *Sound-Shadows of the New World*.

EXTENSION AND ENRICHMENT

Some students might enjoy reading all of *Sound-Shadows of the New World* and reporting to the class other important events in Mehta's life. Or, should you want to stress that Mehta's narrative is an autobiography, you may ask that students read another autobiography of their choice and summarize a formative event in the subject's life. Students might write of an experience that they feel changed their own lives.

Treadway and Vernelle, perhaps becoming *restive* at having nothing to do, started working out the harmony for "Button Up Your Overcoat."

Some of the panels that suddenly appeared in front of my face were even harder to detect than the slim lampposts at home, which would *materialize* out of nowhere when I was walking with an inattentive sighted companion, and bruise me, as if they had a will of their own.

Anyway, I had to concentrate on getting around, not on educating strangers, say what Miss Harper might about each of us being an *emissary* to the country of the sighted.

Writing About Literature

▶ **Describing the Narrator**

What is your impression of Ved Mehta from the account he gives of himself in this selection? What adjectives would you use to describe him: independent? rebellious? determined? daring? imaginative? In a paragraph give a brief description of his character, citing evidence from the selection.

Focus on Biographical Report

Using Anecdotes

An **anecdote** is a very short story with a simple, usually amusing point. You may find anecdotes useful in a biographical report, especially if they show important character traits of your subject.

Skim recent issues of magazines to find some brief stories about celebrities you like. Then make some notes on these anecdotes. Do they reveal anything about the subject's personality? Could you use them in a biographical report about the subject? Save your notes.

About the Author

Ved Mehta (1934–   )

Ved Mehta was born in Lahore, India, and became a United States citizen in 1975. An illness at the age of four left him totally blind. To save him from a life of begging or caning chairs, Mehta's father sent him to the Dadar School for the Blind in Bombay when he was five years old. At fifteen Mehta journeyed to the United States, where he studied at the Arkansas School for the Blind and learned to use "sound-shadows" to get around by himself. Later he attended Pomona College in California, Balliol College in Oxford, England, and Harvard University.

Mehta has written a series of autobiographical books about his life in India and his experiences in the United States, including *Vedi* (1982), *The Ledge Between the Streams* (1984), and *Stolen Light* (1989). *Vedi* is his only book that completely ignores the visual sense, relying on the other senses to convey the experience of blindness. Other books contain rich visual imagery, which has led reviewers to call Mehta the blind man who can see better than we can.

LANGUAGE AND VOCABULARY

1. *Prowess, wrestling,* and *uncharacteristically* establish that the way Bruton feels as he goes through obstacle course is opposite of way he acts and feels when he wrestles.
2. *Prowess* tells us Bruton is brave and skillful; *wrestling* reinforces idea of bravery and adds that of physical strength. When we read the word *uncharacteristically,* we know that in this new situation, Bruton is not brave, skillful, or strong.
3. *Restive:* context clue is provided in words *at having nothing to do.* Since people often become restless when they have nothing to do, and because both *restive* and *restless* have the same root word, students should arrive at the correct meaning: "restless." *Materialize:* Context clues are words *appeared out of nowhere,* and those at end of sentence which tell us that the objects are real and tangible—*and bruise me, as if they had a will of their own. Materialize* here means "appear in three dimensions." *Emissary:* Clues in this sentence are *educating strangers* and *country of the sighted.* Here, *emissary* means "a person sent on a specific mission."

WRITING ABOUT LITERATURE

Students will probably agree that Ved Mehta may be described by some or all of the adjectives listed in the textbook. They may cite his coming to a foreign country at a young age and his journey into the city without his cane as examples of his independence, determination, and daring. His rebelliousness and imagination are evidenced by his refusal to use the cane and his being able to find items in the drugstore. Some students may suggest that the narrator is prideful and vain; they could cite the pride he takes in navigating the obstacle course and his efforts to disguise his handicap.

▶ Before students begin this writing assignment, you may want to refer them to the **Writing About Literature** section on p. 688.

Sound-Shadows of the New World   413

OBJECTIVES
The overall aim is for students to identify Dobie's purpose and to show how the children's play prepared them to be ranchers. For a complete list of objectives, see the **Teacher's Notes**.

VOCABULARY
The underlined words are in the Glossary. The **Language and Vocabulary** exercise on p. 423 will give students practice recognizing terms of a specialized occupation and lifestyle.

FOCUS / MOTIVATION
Ask students to describe some of the "pretend" games they played as children. Ask them if they might have learned valuable skills in their play. Ask them to keep this in mind as they read.

> **TEACHING RESOURCES C**
> Teacher's Notes, p. 138
> Study Guide, p. 140
> Language Skills, p. 143
> Building Vocabulary, p. 146
> Selection Test, p. 148

PREREADING FOCUS
The headnote emphasizes that this selection tells about childhood memories. You might ask students to discuss how important they think **setting** will be to this autobiography.

When I Was a Boy on the Ranch

1
Setting. Established as ranch in southwest Texas.

2 Analyzing
What does the author's choice of verbs (outrun, drowned out, and dimmed) tell us about his feelings about the past? In noting that much of the past has been left behind, he expresses a nostalgia for it.

3
Author introduces reader to regional name, distinguishing it from name more widely used.

4
Author finds comfort in fact that, even in midst of progress, some things stay the same.

5
Statement of author's purpose.

6
Use to answer **study question 2a**, p. 422.

7 Finding Cause and Effect
What factors other than that they "liked ranching" make it logical that the children would play that game? Had more knowledge of ranching than any other occupation; ranching a way of life, not just occupation.

414

When I Was a Boy on the Ranch

BY J. FRANK DOBIE

In this autobiographical essay, J. Frank Dobie tells about his boyhood on a Texas ranch. Note that Dobie uses a leisurely plan for his essay, letting his memory carry him from one pleasant pastime to another. How does he provide transitions between these individual memories?

There were six of us children and our ranch
1 was down in the brush country of Texas between the Nueces River[1] and the Rio Grande. The automobiles have outrun the horses since then; radios have drowned out many a cricket's voice and many a coyote's wailing cry; in many a ranch yard the lights of Delco plants[2] have
2 dimmed the glowing points of the fireflies—
3 "lightning bugs," we called them. But the ranch of our childhood is still a ranch. And south of it clear to the Mexican border, and northwest of it into the Rocky Mountains and on up beyond the line where Montana joins Canada, there are millions and millions of acres of other ranches on which boys and girls live.
4 Despite automobiles these boys and girls still ride horses. Despite radios they still listen in the evening to crickets and frogs, and sometimes in the night to the wailing cries of coyotes. As for electric lights on the ranches, they light such small spaces that the fireflies in the grass and the stars in the sky never notice them. The country is still country. For all the changes brought by invention, ranches are still ranches.
5 So if I tell how we children lived on our ranch, I'll also be telling how children still live on other ranches scattered all over the western half of the United States.

We liked ranching so much that our best
6 game used to be "playing ranch." There were fine live oak trees between the yard fence and the pens about the stables and barns, and it was in the shade of these trees, especially during
7 the summer, that we built our "ranches."

To build a pasture we drove little stakes close together in the ground until a plot about as big as a kitchenette was enclosed; sometimes the pasture was made by setting up "posts" of stakes in the ground and then stretching cords, in imitation of barbed wire, from one corner of

---

1. **Nueces** (nōō-ā'səs, nyōō-) **River:** in southwestern Texas.
2. **Delco plants:** private electrical systems used on farms and ranches.

414   NONFICTION

MOTIVATIONAL SUMMARY
J. Frank Dobie remembers his growing-up years on a ranch in southwest Texas. With a little imagination, the ranch children could invent games. Some of their favorites mimicked adult activity. For example, they often liked to "play ranch," building miniature fences, farm buildings, and houses and using snail shells, thread spools, and oak balls for the livestock. In addition, the range was filled with real animals, both wild and domestic, to interest and amuse them.

PRESENTATION
J. Frank Dobie is noted for his clear yet lively style, and students should have little difficulty reading this selection independently. In "When I Was a Boy on the Ranch," Dobie describes a typical childhood in the West. Beginning with "playing

VISUAL CONNECTIONS
Exploring the Subject
If your students live on a ranch or are familiar with such a life style, ask them to write about favorite games and pastimes. If students know little about ranch life, ask them to write about how they think they would entertain themselves on a ranch. Though Dobie writes about pleasant memories, students might write about hard work or even danger involved in running a ranch.

8
Corrals are wooden (sometimes metal) enclosures used for confining livestock.

9
Pickets are pointed wooden pales used to make fences.

10
Fences are important on ranches both to contain livestock and maintain boundaries.

11
Even now, memory of stocking the play ranch with livestock seems to spark pleasant feeling for author.

12
"High-grade" cattle were purebred; "common" cattle were mixed breeds.

the "pasture" to the other. Each ranch had several pastures, and of course each ranch had 8 headquarters, where houses and corrals were built. The houses were generally of boards; the 9 corrals were of pickets laid between pairs of upright posts.
10 Fencing in the pastures was never so much fun as getting them stocked. It took work to fence in land and improve it with dirt tanks, which never would hold water very long. It took patience to construct corral gates that would open and shut and to make a house that would not fall down when a turkey stepped on 11 it or a pup ran against it. But stocking this land with cattle and horses and goats was nothing but fun.
12 We had two kinds of cattle—high-grade cattle and common "stuff." The horn tips of real

When I Was a Boy on the Ranch 415

ranch," he winds his way to his favorite pets, games, and animals of the Texas brush country.

Before students read this selection, point out on a map the area of the Dobie ranch—between the Nueces River and the Rio Grande River, reviewing with the class the climate of this area—hot summers and mild winters. Tell the class that J. Frank Dobie, in his essay, shares with us what it was like to grow up on a ranch in southwest Texas.

---

13 Drawing Conclusions
Why would a rancher raise goats? For meat and milk.

14
Sheep and cattle ranchers were often at odds, sometimes prompting range wars.

15
Brands: each owner has unique design cast in metal, heated and burned on livestock to mark them permanently.

16
Fannie is author's sister; Elrich and Lee are brothers.

17
This branding exercise was perhaps play activity that was most like later work.

18 Making Inferences
Why would the children not often trade goats? Probably because adults rarely traded goats.

19
Bluing: preparation, often of indigo, used to counteract yellowing when laundering white clothes.

---

cattle—which were clipped off at branding time—became our purebred animals. Sometimes we had hundreds of them. Our "common Mexican cattle" were represented by oak balls.

But we prized our horses far more than our cattle. Horses consisted of sewing-thread spools; most of our clothes were made on the ranch, and those clothes took an astonishing amount of thread. Moreover, when we went visiting we had our eyes open for discarded spools, but visits of any kind were rare and those that brought spools were rarer. A spool has a long "side" that can be branded and it has a long "back" that can be saddled. I can't think of any better kind of play-horse than a spool.

The ranches in our part of the country had
13 herds of white Mexican goats. White-shelled snails were abundant in our neighborhood, and these shells became our goats. A live snail would not stay in a pasture, for he can climb straight up and carry his shell with him, so our goats were always empty shells. There were no sheep in the country; we had never heard any-
14 thing particularly good connected with sheepmen; and so we had no sheep—just cattle, horses, and goats.
15 Each of us had a brand. Mine was ⟦NEv⟧, which an uncle of ⟦♡⟧ mine named
16 Neville used. Fannie's was ⟦X⟧, Elrich's was an *E*; Lee's brand was *L*. The two younger children were too small to build ranches and brand herds by themselves; consequently if Henry and Martha got into the game, they got in as "hired help." Our branding irons were short pieces of bailing wire, with a crook at one end. This kind of branding iron is called a "running iron." When we had occasion to
17 brand, we built a fire close to ranch headquarters, heated the "running irons," and burned our brands on the spool-horses, the common oak-ball cattle, and the fine horn cattle.

Like real ranchmen, we bought and sold stock. When a trade was made, the cattle or
18 horses—we seldom traded goats—had to be gathered up, driven to the shipping pens, loaded on the railroad cars, transported, and delivered. Then after they were delivered they had to be branded with the brand of the new owner. (A great many of the "common cattle" were decayed on the inside and when they were branded collapsed into nothing!) We had to sell cheap for the very simple reason that dollars were scarce and cattle were plentiful.

The dollars we had, however, were extraordinarily good dollars of sound coinage and pure metal. The ranch kitchen used a considerable amount of canned goods, particularly canned tomatoes, salmon, and sardines, along with some peaches and corn. We held the empty can in a fire with tongs until the solder started to run, and then caught the solder in an old spoon, pouring it into a round wooden box
19 that had once held bluing. The diameter of this round bluing box was—and still is—about that of a silver dollar. The dollars we coined were sometimes thicker than a silver dollar and they were always heavier, but in buying cattle they were worth just as much.

We had another source of metal for our dollars. In the fall of the year hunters would be on the ranch, either camped out or staying with us at the house. They usually shot up a good many boxes of shells practicing on trees. After the shooting was over, we children gouged out the lead bullets lodged in the trees and melted them into dollars.

I spoke of shipping cattle. The train was a string of empty sardine cans coupled to each other with wire hooks. Motive power was the chief problem. We tried hitching horned frogs and green lizards to it, but neither pulled with any strength. A horned frog would sometimes pull an empty wagon made of a cardboard matchbox. Old Joe, the best dog we ever had, would pull the train pretty well if he went in a straight line, but when he didn't, he caused several bad wrecks that overturned cars and spilled cattle out. If a delivery of cattle had to be made promptly, the simplest and surest way to make the engine pull the train was to tie a string to it and pull it yourself.

20 Of course there were *real* horses and *real* cattle to interest us. Children brought up on a ranch usually learn to ride only a little later than they learn to walk. Old Stray, Dandy, and Baldy were the horses on our ranch that could
21 be trusted with the youngest children. Old Stray was a common Mexican pony that some Mexican had ridden down and turned loose on our ranch. When we first saw him he was as thin as a stick-horse. Nobody claimed him, so after a while we used him. He seemed to appreciate having plenty of grass to eat but he had no intention of ever exerting himself again. In short, he was not only gentle but "pokey." If a child fell off him, he would stop and graze until the child got up again. Baldy was an enormous horse, and by the time a boy was big enough to scramble upon his back without help from a man or a friendly fence, that boy was nearly ready for "long pants."

22 Dandy was a black horse of thoroughbred trotting stock. He alone of all the horses was entitled to corn the year around. The other

When I Was a Boy on the Ranch 417

MEETING INDIVIDUAL NEEDS
ESL/LEP • On the ranch, Dobie encountered many wild creatures. Have students make a list of these animals. How many can students find? Their lists should include the following creatures: *fireflies, crickets, jackdaws, frogs, scissortails, coyotes, wrens, horned frogs, hawks, lizards, bob-whites, coons (raccoons), doves, chickens, snakes, wild turkeys, deer, ground squirrels,* and *jack-rabbits.*

23
The phrase "drove him" means used him to pull wagon or cart.

24
Anecdote. Essay contains many anecdotes. This one gives example of Dandy's intelligence.

25
Horses often live into their twenties; some much longer.

26
Anecdote. Buck displays intelligence by stopping when Dobie falls off.

27
Emphasizes bond between Dobie and his horse.

28
Use to answer **study question 2c**, p. 422.

29
Use to answer **study question 3a**, p. 422.

418

23 horses lived mostly on grass. We rode Dandy sometimes as well as drove him, but he had too much life in him for mere beginners. He was
24 as kind and intelligent as he was lively. One time when my brother Elrich was very small he toddled into Dandy's stall while Dandy was eating. The flies were bothering Dandy and he was switching his tail and stamping his feet. He knew that the little boy was in danger. He put a hind foot against the child and shoved him out of the stall. He did not kick him—just shoved him.

By the time I was eight years old I had several horses to ride. There was Maudie, a little Spanish mare, that would kick up when I punched her in the shoulder with my finger or pointed my hand down toward her flank or tail. Later there was Buck, a horse raised on the ranch. He was a bay with a white face and stocking feet. I kept him as long as he lived and
25 he died on the ranch where he was born. He could be turned loose in camp and would not
26 stray off. Once when I was running to head some wild steers and Buck gave a quick dodge, the saddle, which was loosely girted, turned, throwing me to the ground and nearly breaking my hip. Buck could "turn on a dime" and stop as quickly as one can snap a finger. On this occasion he stopped so suddenly that he did not drag me a foot, though I was still in the saddle when my hip struck the ground. He was the best cowhorse I ever rode. Often when we were alone I talked to him. By the time I was twelve years old and a regular ranch hand, I was sometimes on him from daylight until long after dark. More than once I went to sleep riding him. I loved him and he loved me. I think
27 of Buck oftener now than I think of many people who have been my friends.

As range cows do not give as much milk as dairy cows, we usually had a pen full of them to milk, especially in the summertime. Each cow had her calf, and the calves were allowed part of the milk. A Mexican man usually did the milking, but it was the privilege of us boys
28 to bring in the calves from the calf pasture each evening and then to ride them.

Now, riding calves is about as much fun as a
29 ranch boy can possibly have. The calf is roped around the neck, and a half hitch, called a "bosal," is put around its nose. Then, using the rope as a bridle, the boy mounts. Until the calf is gentled, it will "pitch like a bay steer." One

418 NONFICTION

calf that I remember particularly was a black heifer with a white face. She became very gentle and we named her Pet. I trained Pet so well that I could mount her and guide her all over the calf pasture. Usually, no matter how well "broke" to riding, a calf won't go where you want it to go. It won't go anywhere. Saddles don't fit calves or grown cattle and, although it was sometimes fun to saddle yearlings, what actual riding we did was bareback. As we grew older we caught range cattle coming into the big pen to water and rode the calves and yearlings.

Each of us children had a few head of cattle to call our own. They were for the most part dogies or of dogie origin. A "dogie" is a motherless calf. When one was found on the range, it would be brought in and some cow with a calf of like age would be tied at night and morning and forced to let the motherless calf

READING SKILLS PRACTICE

The underlined passage can be used to give students practice in the reading skill of distinguishing between fact and opinion. Have students read the passage and answer the question "Which of the following statements is an opinion presented in the selection?" **A.** The game called "tournament" was easy for boys of all ages. (Contradicted opinion. Narrator says the game required skill.) **B.** The tournament pole was sharp and dangerous. (Irrelevant opinion. Statement includes information not found in the passage.) **C.** The narrator's horse Buck had a marvelously smooth running style for the game. (Correct. Expresses narrator's belief or judgment.) **D.** Metal rings were attached to arms of wood on three posts 100 yards apart. (Fact. This statement is not an opinion.)

---

33 A "muley cow" is a cow that does not have horns.

34 Materially: here, "financially."

35 Use to answer **study question 3b**, p. 422.

36 Summarizing *How were the boys punished for missing school?* By being "switched."

37 Use to answer **study question 3b**, p. 422.

38 Coon: shortened form of "raccoon."

---

33 share her milk. We had one old muley cow that was so kind to dogies that the dogie always fared better than her own offspring. She would moo to it and lick its hair and otherwise mother it.

Pet was originally a dogie. When she grew up and had calves of her own, we milked her. If she was a good "saddle horse," a red-roan calf that she had was a better one. Pet had so many calves and those calves grew up and had so many calves of their own that the little stock 34 of cattle coming from her helped materially to put me through college one year.

We went to a country school, which was on our own ranch, where the children of five or six other ranch families attended. Most of them rode to school horseback. One of our games was "cats and dogs." This we boys—for girls did not join in it—played at noon recess. 35 The "cats" would set out in the brush afoot. About three minutes later the "dogs," mounted on horses and yelling like Apache Indians, would take after them. The brush had thorns and the idea of the "cat" was to get into brush so thick that the "dog" could not follow him, or to crawl into a thicket where he could not be seen. Sometimes the chase would last until long after the bell had sounded. I remember one great chase that kept us out until three o'clock. An hour later eight or nine boys were alone with the teacher and a pile of 36 huajilla³ switches.

▶Another game on horseback that the older 37 boys played was "tournament." Three posts are erected in a line a hundred yards apart. Each post has an arm of wood about a yard long. Hanging from this arm is a metal ring about two inches in diameter. It is held by a spring clasp so that it can be easily disengaged. The runner takes a sharpened pole—the "tournament pole"—in his right hand and, holding it level, with the point out in front of him, runs lickety-split down the line of rings trying to spear them. The game requires skill. Buck was a wonderfully smooth-running horse, and he and I together hooked plenty of rings. ◀

My sisters and girl cousins joined us in playing Indian and in making houses. Our ranch was built on a dry arroyo, or creek, named Long Hollow. Just below the house this creek had bluffs about forty feet high. For years we children worked periodically at digging caves back into the bluffs. Here we played Indian. If the soil had not been so gravelly and consequently inclined to cave in, we might have made dwelling places as ample as some of the ancient cliff dwellings. As it was, we got the caves big enough for us to hide in. When Long Hollow ran water after a rain, we made water wheels of sticks and cornstalks and watched them turn.

The house of our own construction that we enjoyed most was in a tree. It was a live oak 38 called "the Coon Tree," from the fact that a coon hungry for chickens had once been found in it. Climbing up into this tree was an enormous mustang grapevine. This grapevine afforded us a kind of ladder to the limbs of the Coon Tree. We took planks up to these limbs and nailed them so that we had a solid floor.

In our country we did not have many fruits, but around the ranch house were prolific pomegranate bushes. No matter how dry the season, these pomegranates always bore fruit. In the summertime we would pick pomegranates,[4] borrow some sugar, spoons, and glasses from the kitchen, and, with a jug of water, gather on the platform in the Coon Tree for a picnic. We had a rope with which to pull up the jug and a bucket containing the other articles.

---

3. **huajilla** (wä-hēl′yä): a shrub.

4. **pomegranate** (pŏm′grăn′ĭt, pŭm′-): fruit with a juicy red pulp containing many seeds.

▶Reading Skills Objective: Distinguishing Between Fact and Opinion

The point of the picnic was to make "pomegranateade" out of sugar, the fruit seeds, and water.

39 Sometimes we took books and read in the Coon Tree. *Beautiful Joe* and *Black Beauty* were favorites. Our real house had matting on the floor, and when this matting was discarded and we covered the platform in the Coon Tree with it, we felt that we had reached the height of luxury. I don't understand why none of us ever fell out of the Coon Tree.

40 I have spoken of our life with horses and calves. There were other animals to interest us, as there always are in the country. The trees about the ranch were inhabited each spring and summer by hundreds of jackdaws, a kind of blackbird. They built their nests in the trees so flimsily that disaster to the newly hatched birds was inevitable. Before they could fly or even walk, young birds would fall out of the trees and sprawl helpless on the ground, a ready prey for cats, turkeys, and other ene-
41 mies. The distressed cries of the parent jackdaws were at times almost deafening, but these parents could do nothing toward getting their young back into the nests. We used to pick up the young birds and put them in straw-filled wooden nail-kegs, which we placed on the roofs of a shed and smokehouse under the Coon Tree. I have seen three or four parent
42 jackdaws feeding their young at the same time in one of these kegs. Sometimes each keg held as many as eight young birds.

Scissortails built their hanging nests in the very tops of the higher trees, but their young never fell out. We never tired of watching the scissortails fly, especially if they were chasing a hawk, darting at his head and driving him away. The wrens nested in tool boxes in the stable, in coils of rope, even in the leather toe-fenders—called *tapaderos*[5]—covering the stirrups of saddles. When we found these nests, we made it our duty to warn our father and the
43 Mexican laborers not to disturb them. One time a saddle had to go unused for weeks until a wren that had built in the *tapadero* of one stirrup had brought off her brood.

Under Mother's direction we raised chick-
44 ens, turkeys, and guineas. The guineas were good "watchdogs," alarming, with their wild

---

5. *tapaderos* (tăp′ə-där′ōz).

39
Author's life is almost like storybook itself: full, active, and adventurous.

40
The children, curious about things around them, learned about nature by observing it.

41 Summarizing
Why did the parent birds caw?
To warn babies of danger.

42
Parents' feeding of babies refutes common belief that parent bird will abandon babies that have been touched by humans.

43 Making Generalizations
What does this episode reveal about the author's attitude toward nature? Loves and respects living creatures.

44
Guineas are domestic fowl, originally from Africa; most common species is dark gray with white spots.

TRANSPARENCY 33
Literary Elements
Evaluating Nonfiction – provides a structure for analyzing nonfiction using a questioning strategy.

---

45 Drawing Conclusions
Why would Dobie remember seeing a deer kill a rattlesnake? Probably uncharacteristic of deer, as they are not aggressive animals.

46
Looking back, Dobie feels a little guilty about disturbing wild animals.

READING CHECK
1. Empty thread spools (p. 416).
2. Coins made of metal from empty tin cans and lead bullets (p. 416).
3. Motherless calf (p. 419).
4. "Cats and dogs" and "tournament" (p. 420).
5. Picnics and a place to read (pp. 420–421).

FOR STUDY AND DISCUSSION
1a. To tell how children on ranches live. **1b.** Third paragraph.
2a. Building and filling pastures, houses, corrals; branding, trading, shipping stock. **2b.** Shifts from discussion of imaginary horses and cattle to that of real ones. **2c.** Helped herd calves.
3a. Roping it, putting hitch around its nose. **3b.** For "cats and dogs," had to ride well, hide in thorny brush; for "tournament," had to ride fast horse, aim pole at rings, and hook them.
4. Rescuing jackdaws, putting baby doves back in nests, watching animals; mother taught them to raise fowl.
5. Involved learning about ranch duties and practicing on "pretend" objects; pastimes often imitated skills needed in real ranching.

422

---

cries, everything and everybody within hearing distance when a hawk was approaching. Hawks, chicken snakes, and coyotes were constant enemies of the barnyard. We boys sometimes set traps for the coyotes. I remember seeing my mother, before I was old enough to handle a gun, shoot one with a rifle very near the house.

The evening call of the bob-white brought—as it yet brings—a wonderful peace. In the early mornings of certain times of the year we could hear wild turkeys "yelping" out in the brush back of the field. Once a large flock of them grazed up to the schoolhouse, but the teacher would not let us out to chase them. Although deer were plentiful, and some other children in the country had a pet fawn, we never had one. Once while riding in the pas-
45 ture I halted a long time to watch a doe kill a rattlesnake.

I can honestly say that we did not enjoy "tormenting" animals and that we did not rob birds' nests. But when we snared lizards with a horsehair looped on the end of a pole; when we poured buckets of water down the holes of ground squirrels to make them come out; and when we hitched horned toads to matchboxes,
46 we no doubt did torment those animals, though we seldom injured them. I have since killed noble buck deer, mountain lions, wild boars, and other game, but no memory of hunting is so pleasant as that of rescuing little jackdaws, of restoring a tiny dove fallen from its nest, and of watching, without molesting them, baby jack-rabbits in their cotton-lined nest against the cowpen fence—memories all of a ranch boy.

Ranch girls and boys always find so many ways to play and so many creatures of nature to interest them that the days are never long enough. And no life can be long enough for a ranch-bred boy or girl to forget the full times of childhood.

Reading Check
1. When the children were "playing ranch," what did they use for horses?
2. What did the children use for money when they bought and sold their stock?
3. What is a "dogie"?
4. What games were played on horseback?
5. What did the children use the tree house for?

For Study and Discussion

Analyzing and Interpreting the Essay

1a. What is Dobie's purpose? **b.** Where does he state it?

2a. What kinds of activities were included in "playing ranch"? **b.** How does Dobie make a transition from the game of playing ranch to the pleasures of actual ranch life? **c.** What responsibilities did children have in helping to run the ranch?

3a. What was involved in riding calves? **b.** What skills were needed for the games of "cats and dogs" and "tournament"?

4. Dobie has particularly fond memories of animals on the ranch. How did the children learn to care for birds and other wild creatures?

5. Dobie describes the different activities and interests of children growing up on a ranch. In what way might their play be considered schooling or preparation for their future lives as ranchers?

422 NONFICTION

CLOSURE
Ask students to identify the author's purpose in "When I Was a Boy on the Ranch" and to explain how play helped prepare Dobie and his friends for careers as ranchers.

EXTENSION AND ENRICHMENT
Students who like this essay by Dobie should be encouraged to read a tale from Dobie's *The Longhorns* and retell the story to the class. Another excellent book that describes a boy's childhood is *The Least One* by Borden Deal.

For writing practice, have students write an essay that describes some of their childhood games, improvised toys, or perhaps a fond memory from their childhood.

Language and Vocabulary

Recognizing Ranch Terms

Dobie uses a number of words that have special meaning to someone living and working on a ranch. When he talks about riding calves, he says that before it "is gentled," a calf will "pitch like a bay steer." The word *gentle* is used here as a verb with the special meaning of "to tame or train an animal"—usually a horse. **1** What do you suppose the expression "pitch like a bay steer" means?

2 Make a list of other ranch terms and expressions used in the selection and tell what they mean.

Focus on Biographical Report

Organizing a Report

Biographical reports usually follow **chronological** or **time order.** When you use this method, you tell events in the order in which they happen. You can also help your readers follow your report by using **transitional words and phrases.** For example, notice how J. Frank Dobie uses these transitions to show time order in the paragraph that describes Buck (see page 418): *by the time, when, later, once, on this occasion, often, sometimes, more than once, now.*

Write an outline like the one shown on this page for a biographical report of three paragraphs. Look through recent issues of magazines to get some ideas for the subject and the details of your report. Save your notes.

I. Introduction
   A. Attention grabber: _____
   B. Statement of main idea: _____
II. Body
   Facts/Anecdotes: _____
   _____
   _____
   _____
   _____
III. Conclusion
   A. Restatement of main idea: _____
   B. Summary of person's importance: _____

About the Author

J. Frank Dobie (1888–1964)

James Frank Dobie was born on a ranch in Live Oak County, Texas, in the brush country close to the Mexican border. He began writing in college and after receiving a master's degree from Columbia University, he taught at the University of Texas. He left teaching to manage a ranch for his uncle. While he was working on the ranch, he grew interested in the folklore and traditions of the Southwest. When he returned to teaching, he began writing books and editing publications of the Texas Folklore Society. His works include *A Vaquero of the Brush Country; Coronado's Children,* tales of buried treasure and lost mines in the Southwest; and *The Longhorns,* a collection of tales about longhorn steers.

LANGUAGE AND VOCABULARY

1. To "pitch like a bay steer" means "to rear and plunge vigorously."

2. Below is a list of ranch terms with suggested definitions:
Barbed wire: wire for fences, having sharp barbs or points of metal.
Corral: pen for livestock.
Stocking the land: to furnish land with horses, cattle, etc.
Purebred cattle: cattle of known parentage belonging to recognized breed.
Common cattle: cattle of mixed breeds.
To brand: to mark with hot iron.
Brand: mark of identification.
Bailing wire: wire used to bind hay.
Running iron: improvised branding iron.
Half hitch: type of knot.
Heifer: young cow that has not yet had calf.
Broke: tamed; trained.
Yearlings: animals which are one year old.
Bareback: without a saddle.
Dogie: motherless calf.
Roan: reddish-brown horse with spots of gray or white.
Thoroughbred trotting stock: breed of racehorse.
Flank: fleshy side between ribs and hip of animal.
Bay: reddish-brown horse.
Stocking feet: white feet.
Steers: young castrated male cattle.
Girted: strapped; girt strap is part of saddle that goes under horse's stomach.
"Turn on a dime": turn quickly.
Cowhorse: horse used for herding cattle.
Toefenders: pieces of leather that cover side of stirrup.
Cowpen: Enclosure for cows.

OBJECTIVES
The overall aim is for students to demonstrate an understanding of cause-and-effect relationships.

PRESENTATION
To reinforce the concept of cause and effect, you might begin this section by defining cause and then effect. Discuss some effects that students deal with on a daily basis and ask them to identify the causes. For example, what might be the causes of some school rules? What are the possible effects on the students and school if rules are broken? Then have students read and analyze the passage independently. After students have finished, read each question aloud, and ask volunteers to respond.

UNDERSTANDING CAUSE AND EFFECT
Human beings inherently like to know why things happen and what the consequences of certain events might be. Therefore, writers often use cause and effect to provide the answers. To be effective, this kind of discussion depends on clear reasoning and thorough examination of all possible causes or effects.

Answers
1. While taking care of some friends' dog, Thomas began to observe the dog's curious habits.
2. Misha could jump most fences.
3. Thomas and Misha violated the dog leash law. Thomas received complaints from people in surrounding communities and from these, she established the dog's home range.

FOCUS ON Reading and Critical Thinking

UNDERSTANDING CAUSE AND EFFECT

*W*riters often develop ideas by explaining causes and effects. A *cause* is a reason that something happens; an *effect* is a result of something that happens. In the following passage from *The Hidden Life of Dogs,* Elizabeth Marshall Thomas discusses how she began to observe dogs. Read the passage carefully, and then answer the questions that follow.

I began observing dogs by accident. While friends spent six months in Europe, I took care of their husky, Misha. An agreeable two-year-old Siberian with long, thin legs and short, thick hair, Misha could jump most fences and travel freely. He jumped our fence the day I took him in. A law requiring that dogs be leashed was in effect in our home city of Cambridge, Massachusetts, and also in most of the surrounding communities. As Misha violated the law I would receive complaints about him, and with the help of these complaints, some from more than six miles distant, I soon was able to establish that he had developed a home range of approximately 130 square miles. This proved to be merely a preliminary home range, which later he expanded considerably. . . . What was Misha doing?

Obviously, something unusual. Here was a dog who, despite his youth, could navigate flawlessly, finding his way to and from all corners of the city by day and by night. Here was a dog who could evade dangerous traffic and escape the dog officers and the dognappers. . . . Misha always came back from his journeys feeling fine, ready for a light meal and a rest before going out again. How did he do it?

For a while I looked for the answer in journals and books, availing myself of the fine libraries at Harvard and reading everything I could about dogs to see if somewhere the light of science had penetrated this corner of dark. But I found nothing. Despite a vast array of publications on dogs, virtually nobody, neither scientist nor layman, had ever bothered to ask what dogs do when left to themselves.

Understanding Cause and Effect

1. What caused the author to begin observing dogs?

2. What was the cause of Misha being able to travel freely?

3. What effects did these journeys lead to?

424 NONFICTION

OBJECTIVES

The overall aim is for students to write a **biographical report** in which they present information about a person's life, character traits, and achievements.

PRESENTATION

Ask students to name the people in the world today who interest them most—from sports and entertainment personalities to world leaders. Then ask students how they know about these people. Much of what they know will probably come from articles and interviews presented in the media. Now explain how they will have the chance to learn more about an accomplished person of their choice.

You may want to incorporate a research or library unit with this writing project so that stu-

HOLT WRITER'S WORKSHOP

This computer program provides help for all types of writing through guided instruction for each step of the writing process. (Program available separately.)

See *Elements for Writing, First Course,* Chapter 10, for more instruction on writing a report.

WRITING A BIOGRAPHICAL REPORT

A **biographical report** is a form of informative writing based on research and the synthesis of ideas from several sources. Report writing is one of the most common kinds of writing done in many disciplines; therefore, students will benefit from using the writing process to understand the nature and structure of a report.

Prewriting

Encourage students to choose a person who fits the criteria listed in the text, but not to choose someone about whom they already know a great deal. Instead, they should make a list of at least three people about whom they want to know more and rank them in order of preference. Then, if they consult their sources and discover that they cannot find enough information on their first choice, they can go to their second or third choice.

Students can collect their information in chart form, or they might want to use note cards on which they use the same categories as the headings on the chart and record information according to important dates. When students get ready to write their drafts, they can arrange their note cards accordingly. Students might want to add **anecdotes** as another category.

FOCUS ON Writing

WRITING A BIOGRAPHICAL REPORT

*I*n a **biographical report,** you present information about a person's life, character traits, and achievements. In this unit you have studied some of the important elements of a report. Now you will have the chance to write a biographical report on a subject of your choice.

Details Chart for a Biographical Report
Date and Place of Birth: _____
Education: _____
Job/Profession: _____
Achievements/Special Awards: _____
Family: _____
Opinions/Outlook on Life: _____
Statements/Quotations: _____
_____

Prewriting

1. Use these guidelines when you select a subject for a biographical report. Choose a person

   - who will interest your audience
   - with one or more special achievements
   - about whom you can get the information you need

You can brainstorm for subjects by looking at newspapers and magazines, listening to news reports on radio and TV, skimming family albums, or talking about celebrities with a group of classmates. [See **Focus** assignment on page 392.]

2. Start to gather **details** about your subject. Here are some of the **sources** of information you can use:

   - books
   - interviews
   - encyclopedias
   - photo essays
   - newspaper articles
   - photograph albums
   - magazine articles
   - letters

You should try to consult at least three different sources about your subject. As you gather details, you may find it helpful to fill out a chart like the one on this page.

Keep a record of the sources you consult. For each source, write the title, the author, the date and place of publication, and the page number where you found the information. If your teacher wants you to make a **Works Cited** list, your record of sources will be useful later. [See **Focus** assignment on page 396.]

3. Develop a **main idea** to focus your report. State this idea as clearly as you can in one or two sentences. Stating a main idea will help you evaluate and organize your details. For example, here is the way you might state the main idea for a report on Hatshepsut, the ancient Egyptian queen: *Queen Hatshepsut was a remarkable ruler, not only because she was Egypt's only woman pharaoh, but also because of her trade and building programs.* [See **Focus** assignment on page 403.]

4. Think about how you might use **anecdotes,** or very short stories, in your report. Good anecdotes usually have a humorous point, and they reveal an important character trait about your subject. [See **Focus** assignment on page 413.]

Focus on Writing **425**

Writing

You may want to work closely with students during this stage to make sure they understand the importance of differentiating between their ideas and words and the ideas and words they have borrowed. You can use several approaches here based on your curriculum and students' skill level: You can teach students how to document borrowed sources; you can discuss the importance of giving credit to their sources and have students do a simple bibliography or list works consulted; or if you do not want students to use documentation form, you might have them include a page at the end of their report on which they acknowledge everything and everyone who helped them with their papers.

Evaluating and Revising

Students might use colored markers to evaluate organization and supporting details of their reports. They should underline their main idea, and then highlight each transition word or phrase in one color, each fact in another color, and any anecdotes in a fourth color. Then students can work in small groups and use the **Checklist for Evaluation and Revision** for additional suggestions to improve their reports.

Writing

1. Use **chronological** or **time order** when you write your report. Remember also to use **transitional words and phrases** to make the connections of events and ideas clear. Here are some helpful transitions:

after	first, second, third	then
before	next	until
finally	often	when

[See **Focus** assignment on page 423.]

2. You may wish to follow an **outline** such as the one below as you write your first draft:

  I. Introduction
     A. Attention grabber
     B. Statement of main idea
 II. Body: Facts/Anecdotes in chronological order
III. Conclusion
     A. Restatement of main idea
     B. Summary of person's importance

Evaluating and Revising

1. After you finish your first draft, get together with a partner and trade papers. Read each other's report. Then share ideas about how to improve each other's work. Take some notes about how to make your report clearer and more interesting.

Here is one writer's revision of a paragraph in a biographical report.

Writer's Model

Queen Hatshepsut's husband, ^the pharaoh Thutmosis II, had a son ^by another wife. When the pharaoh died ^in 1503 B.C., this son was still too young to ~~have~~ ^succeed to the throne. Hatshepsut ^thus became the first woman to rule ancient Egypt—although pictures and carvings show her dressed as a man. She held power for ~~a while~~ ^twenty-one years before she turned over the kingdom to ~~the boy~~ ^her stepson, Thutmosis III.

426 NONFICTION

TRANSPARENCY 34
Writing Process
Writing a Biographical Report – helps students to plan and write an effective biographical report.

CLOSURE
Have students tell what happens at each stage of the writing process for a **biographical report**.

2. You may find the following checklist helpful as you revise your report.

Checklist for Evaluation and Revision
- ✓ Does my opening grab the reader's attention?
- ✓ Do I clearly identify the subject of my report?
- ✓ Do I state my main idea in the introduction?
- ✓ Do I present enough important information about my subject?
- ✓ Do I arrange my information in chronological order?
- ✓ Have I checked my facts for accuracy? Have I made a record for the source of each item?
- ✓ Do I end with a strong conclusion?

Proofreading and Publishing

1. Proofread your report and correct any errors you find in grammar, usage, and mechanics. (Here you may find it helpful to refer to the **Handbook for Revision** on pages 726–767.) Then prepare a final version of your report by making a clean copy.

2. Consider some of the following publication methods for your report:
   - deliver your report orally to the class
   - illustrate your report with photographs and drawings, and then post it on the class bulletin board
   - submit your report to the school newspaper or magazine
   - join with other students to compile a biographical anthology

Portfolio If your teacher approves, you may wish to keep a copy of your work in your writing folder or portfolio.

Proofreading and Publishing
You may want to provide students with a focus for their proofreading. Students can work in small groups and edit for subject-verb agreement, pronoun usage, and proper punctuation and capitalization for source titles, documentation, and bibliographical entries.

Focus on Writing   427

Unit 7 ♦ Teaching Guide

Forms of Literature
POETRY

OVERVIEW OF THE UNIT

The overriding purpose of this unit is to stimulate active response to poetry, to help students connect with language at its most intense. Individually, poems have been chosen for intrinsic appeal; together, they illustrate the range and diversity of this oldest literary genre.

The unit consists of three sections: *Language and Meaning, Sound and Meaning,* and *Types of Poetry.* The introduction encourages students to read poems closely. It provides a sample poem, "May Day" by Sara Teasdale, and **Guidelines for Close Reading.** You may want to refer to these guidelines frequently as you teach the unit.

The first section, *Language and Meaning,* examines speaker, diction, imagery, figurative language, and theme. Poems such as E. E. Cummings' "in Just-" and Robert Frost's "Stopping by Woods on a Snowy Evening" provide eloquent and provocative examples of these poetic elements. The section titled *Sound and Meaning,* which includes classics like Edgar Allan Poe's "Annabel Lee," demonstrates the poetic power of repetition, rhyme, onomatopoeia, and rhythm. To illustrate the dramatic impact of sound, this section also features "The Highwayman" by Alfred Noyes.

The final section, *Types of Poetry,* introduces students to four kinds of poems: narrative, lyric, dramatic, and comic. Examples of both folk ballads and literary ballads are included. This section ends with limericks and other comic verse.

Each section offers opportunities for oral and written expression. The questions in **For Study and Discussion** sharpen comprehension and heighten recognition of poetic devices. Activities throughout the unit engage students in the process of writing their own poems. Also included are opportunities for other types of creative writing, writing about literature, and oral reading.

OBJECTIVES OF THE UNIT

The aims of the unit are for the student:
- To identify the speakers in poems
- To relate a poet's diction to mood and meaning in a poem
- To demonstrate an understanding of the use of imagery in poetry
- To identify and analyze themes in poems
- To demonstrate an understanding of the characteristics of different forms of poetry
- To identify and analyze the use of sound devices in poetry
- To analyze and interpret literal and figurative word meanings in poetry
- To write poems and brief analyses and interpretations of poems

CONCEPTS AND SKILLS

The following concepts and skills are treated in this unit:

Close Reading of a Poem
Guidelines for Close Reading   430
Looking at Yourself as a Reader   432

Literary Elements/Terms and Techniques
Understanding the Role of Diction   438
Understanding the Purpose of Poetic License   440
Understanding the Purpose of Inversion   442
Understanding the Role of Dialect   444
Understanding Figurative Language   451
Understanding Repetition in Poetry   463
Understanding the Refrain   465
Understanding How Sounds Convey Feeling   466
Understanding How Sound Imitates Action   472
Responding to Rhythm   473
Recognizing Personification   489
Understanding Haiku   492

Language and Vocabulary Skills
Recognizing Denotative and Connotative Meanings   487

Writing Opportunities
Writing About Literature
Paraphrasing a Poem   442
Interpreting a Poem   459
Analyzing Ballad Characteristics   477

Creative Writing
Assuming Another Identity   435
Composing a Haiku   492
Writing a Limerick   496

Focus on Writing a Poem
Choosing a Subject   436
Experimenting with Imagery   442
Listing Sensory Details   449
Using Figurative Language   454
Experimenting with Sound Effects   463
Writing a Poem   498

For Oral Reading
Avoiding Singsong   463
Presenting a Choral Reading   473

427A

PLANNING GUIDE

FOR UNIT PLANNING
- Transparencies 35–40: *Audiovisual Resources Binder*
- Portfolio Assessment: *Professional Support Materials*
- Test Generator
- Mastery Tests: Teaching Resources D, pp. 142, 146, 149
- Analogy Test: Teaching Resources D, p. 151
- Composition Test: Teaching Resources D, p. 152

SELECTION (Pupil's Page)	TEACHING RESOURCES D (page numbers shown below)							AV BINDER
	Teacher's Notes	Reading Check	Study Guide	Language Skills	Building Vocabulary	Selection Vocab. Test	Selection Test	Audio-cassette
POETRY *Introduction* (p. 429)	1							
Robert Graves *The Caterpillar* (p. 433)	2		4				24	
Sara Henderson Hay *One of the Seven Has Somewhat to Say* (p. 435)	2		4	7			24	
Carl Sandburg *Fog* (p. 437)	9		11				54	
Lucille Clifton *The 1st* (p. 438)	9		11				24	TAPE 3 SIDE A
E. E. Cummings *in Just-* (p. 439)	9		11				24	TAPE 3 SIDE A
Randall Jarrell *The Chipmunk's Day* (p. 441)	14		15				24	
James Whitcomb Riley *When the Frost is on the Punkin* (p. 443)	17		19		22		24	
John Masefield *Trade Winds* (p. 447)	26		28				54	
May Sarton *A Parrot* (p. 448)	26		28		37		54	
May Swenson *Living Tenderly* (p. 450)	31		33				54	
Robert P. Tristram Coffin *The Spider* (p. 452)	31		33		37		54	
Robert Frost *Stopping by Woods on a Snowy Evening* (p. 455)	39		40				54	TAPE 3 SIDE A
Walter de la Mare *The Listeners* (p. 457)	42		44		47	68	54	TAPE 3 SIDE A
Edgar Allan Poe *Annabel Lee* (p. 460)	49		51				54	TAPE 3 SIDE A
Vachel Lindsay *The Broncho That Would Not Be Broken* (p. 464)	56		59	63	66	68	69	
William Shakespeare *Full Fathom Five* (p. 466)	72		73		75	85		TAPE 3 SIDE A

427B

SELECTION (Pupil's Page)	TEACHING RESOURCES D (page numbers shown below)							AV BINDER
	Teacher's Notes	Reading Check	Study Guide	Language Skills	Building Vocabulary	Selection Vocab. Test	Selection Test	Audio-cassette
Alfred Noyes *The Highwayman* (p. 468)	77		79		83	85	86	TAPE 3 SIDE A
Anonymous *The Golden Vanity* (p. 475)	89		91		93	111	95	TAPE 3 SIDE A
Robert Browning *The Pied Piper of Hamelin* (p. 478)	97		99	102		111	106	
Henry Wadsworth Longfellow *Snowflakes* (p. 488)	108		113		109	111	122	
James Stephens *Little Things* (p. 490)	112		113		116		122	
Emily Dickinson *I'm Nobody* (p. 490)	118		120				122	
Bashō, Chosu, Chiyo *Haiku* (p. 491)	118		120				122	
Lewis Carroll *Father William* (p. 493)	124		126	128	132		138	
Edward Lear *The Bearded Man* (p. 496)	134		136				138	
Carolyn Wells *A Tutor* (p. 496)	134		136				138	
Ogden Nash *The Lama* (p. 496)	134		136				138	

FOCUS ON READING AND CRITICAL THINKING
Relating Sound to Meaning 497

TRANSPARENCIES
The following unit support materials with specific correlations to literature selections are available in the **Fine Art and Instructional Transparencies with Teacher's Notes and Blackline Masters** section of your *Audiovisual Resources Binder*.

FINE ART TRANSPARENCIES
Theme: Special Language, Special Meaning
35 *Flower Power*, Gary Greene
36 *Zapatos Calientes (Hot Shoes)*, Michael Jacques

READER RESPONSE
37 Charting a Response to Poetry
38 Jewels in the Crown

LITERARY ELEMENTS
39 Sound Effects in Poetry

WRITING PROCESS
40 Writing a Poem

INTRODUCING THE UNIT
Begin by having the students explore the world of emotions. Ask them to suggest abstract "feeling" nouns, such as joy, sadness, grief, and anger. Mention that poems often use words to evoke feelings. You may want to have students begin this unit by writing their own "pyramid" poems similar to the following. Poems should begin with one "feeling" noun. Example:
                Joy
           A quiet room
      Where I can be me
And no one makes my mind mind

You may wish to allow time for students to share their poems either with the rest of the class or in small groups.

You might then have students select a favorite popular song. Write its lyrics on the board, and play a recorded version. Ask what makes the song so enjoyable that it can be listened to repeatedly. In what ways are the lyrics like a poem? Apart from the music, are the words appealing? Do they have any musical qualities of their own? Use the discussion to lead into the introductory comments (p. 429).

PORTFOLIO ASSESSMENT

Suggestions for use of portfolios as support for this unit are described in the **Portfolio Assessment and Professional Support Materials** booklet accompanying this program. Specific suggestions are provided for a variety of student projects that may be suitable for inclusion in a portfolio. In addition, copying masters are provided for guides that may be used for evaluation and assessment of student projects.

Student Learning Options

POETRY

1. Color-Coding to Analyze Poems
After modeling with one poem, ask students to use colored pens or pencils to analyze poems of their choice. First, instruct the students to place a red diagonal mark (virgule) at the end of each sentence or complete thought. Then ask them to underline each simile or metaphor in blue, each sensory image in yellow, and each connotative word in green. Last, ask them to underline the main idea of the poem or to write it in their own words if it is implied. You can also ask them to paraphrase the poem. In this way, each student will read the poem several times, adding meaning each time.

2. Using a Fairy Tale to Write a Poem
Divide the class into groups, asking each group to write a poem based on a fairy tale, as Sara Henderson Hay has done in "One of the Seven Has Somewhat to Say" on p. 435. You might begin by brainstorming with the whole class about possible fairy tales to draw from.

3. Drawing Pictures
Ask each student to draw a picture brought to mind by one or more of the poems read. The students can then show their pictures to the class and explain them. Encourage them to display their pictures around the room.

4. Making a Dictionary
To help them understand the poem, ask students to work with a partner to make a small dictionary of dialect words in James Whitcomb Riley's poem "When the Frost Is on the Punkin" on p. 443. They can start with the word "punkin." Have students include illustrations when appropriate.

5. Reading Orally
Organize an oral reading program, asking each student to choose at least twenty to thirty lines of poetry to read aloud to the rest of the class. They should determine who the speaker is and how that speaker would talk.

6. Writing a Riddle Poem
After reading and discussing May Swenson's "Living Tenderly" on p. 450, divide the class into groups and ask the groups to write a riddle poem to read to the rest of the class, who can then guess what or who the poem is about. You can also let them read their poems to another class and let that class try to guess the subject of each poem.

7. Telling the Stories of Poems
First, read to the students several narrative poems, such as "The Highwayman," "The Broncho That Would Not Be Broken," "The Listeners," "The Golden Vanity," and "The Pied Piper of Hamelin." Then, after dividing the class into small groups, ask each group to select a different narrative poem and retell it as they might relate a story to a friend. Each group should divide the story into parts so that each student tells part of the story.

VISUAL CONNECTIONS

Exploring the Subject

Like Roesen and other artists of the nineteenth century, composers, such as Franz Liszt (1811–1886), Frederic Chopin (1810–1849), Richard Wagner (1813–1883), and Giuseppe Verdi (1813–1901), sought a greater freedom of artistic expression, which they found in the creation of the symphonic poem. This type of musical composition is arranged for a full symphony orchestra, and its purpose is to interpret poetic or descriptive themes musically. Using innovative combinations of instruments, symphonic poems evoke distinct emotions and moods, just as poems and paintings do.

About the Artwork

Still-life painting is the depiction of inanimate objects, emphasizing the qualities of form, composition, color, and texture. Severin Roesen, like other nineteenth-century still-life painters, illustrated flowers and fruit with realistic detail. The dusky backdrop in this painting intensifies the vivid colors of the flowers and fruit. The painting's relaxed composition projects a natural harmony among the subjects. The emotional response evoked is one of serenity.

With techniques similar to those of artists, poets, too, elicit diverse emotional reactions. Their precise word choice and arrangement, striking images, figurative language, and various sound devices combine to depict the form, composition, color, and texture of a poem that convey its meaning, mood, and emotion.

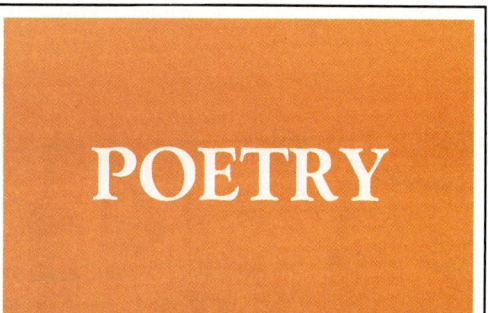

POETRY

Poets use words very carefully. Each word is so important that changing a single word can create a different mood or effect.

Examine the still life on these pages. Working with other students, identify as many of the flowers and fruits as you can. Make a list of the objects in the painting. Imagine that you were "painting" this still life of flowers and fruit in words rather than in pigment. What words could you use to describe the colors in the painting? the feel of the objects? the scent of the flowers and the fruit?

Try writing several lines of poetry about the painting. Use rhyme if you like. Exchange your verses with other students and look closely at the words that have been chosen. You may wish to work on your poem again after you have completed this unit.

Still Life: Flowers and Fruit (c. 1850) by Severin Roesen. Oil on canvas.
The Metropolitan Museum of Art, Purchase, Charles Allen Munn Bequest; Fosburgh Fund, Inc. Gift; Mr. and Mrs. J. William Middendorf II Gift; and Henry G. Keasbey Bequest, 1967 (67.111)

FOCUS / MOTIVATION
Ask students why people enjoy solving mysteries, riddles. Point out that close reading of poetry is similar to solving puzzles. Close reading is necessary; it yields the reward of better understanding of a poem.

PRESENTATION
Explain that the class will read a poem and then read an explication of the poem. Ask students to close their eyes and think of spring. Have them suggest images that come to mind when they think of this season. Write their ideas on the board. Read "May Day" aloud to them. Discuss the images in the poem as they correspond to students' list.

Remind students that by following the guidelines they will gain greater insight into the meaning of the poem.

CLOSE READING OF A POEM

1
Poets select words for connotative as well as denotative meanings.

2
Figurative language and **imagery** stimulate imagination and convey meaning.

3
Rhyme scheme of first stanza of "May Day" is *abcb*.

4
Poets often invert words to emphasize ideas or to maintain patterns of rhythm and rhyme.

GUIDELINES FOR CLOSE READING

1. Commas indicate only a slight pause, whereas other punctuation calls for longer breaks. With poems such as "in Just-," "The Spider," and "Fog," in which there is little punctuation at ends of lines, remind students not to pause until they have read a complete thought.
2. Effective diction conveys emotional meaning in "The 1st," captures the movements of the chipmunk in "The Chipmunk's Day," depicts dialect of a particular group of people in "When the Frost Is on the Punkin," contributes to characterization in "The Pied Piper of Hamelin," and reveals poet's tone in "I'm Nobody."
3. You may encourage such active reading by allowing time and creating an atmosphere in which students are comfortable with asking questions and discussing with others the inferences they have made.

430

Close Reading OF A POEM

*P*oetry is older than any other kind of literature. Poetry developed long before prose; as a matter of fact, there was poetry long before there was a written language of any kind. In early times poems were memorized and passed down from generation to generation by word of mouth. We know that poems were often sung. Ancient Greek poets sang to the accompaniment of a lyre, a stringed instrument something like a small harp. Our word lyric shows this connection between poetry and music.

1   Poetry has a special language and structure. Poets rely on the suggestive power of language and choose words for their emotional effect as
2   well as for their literal meaning. Through images and figures of speech poets appeal to the mind and to the senses. Poets also make use of pat-
3   terns of sound, such as rhyme and rhythm; special forms, such as haiku; and unusual arrangements of words on a page.

In order to express themselves in effective and imaginative ways,
4   poets take liberties with language. They do not always use complete sentences or complete thoughts. They may reverse the normal order of words. They may choose not to use conventional punctuation.

Guidelines for Close Reading

1. Read the poem several times and aloud at least once. Look for complete thoughts instead of reading line for line. Follow the author's clues for phrasing. Commas, semicolons, periods, and other marks of punctuation tell you where to pause.
2. Respond to the effect of the poet's language. A word in a poem often has special connotations, or associations. Be aware of suggested meanings as well as the literal meanings of words. Look up any words or references you don't recognize.
3. Ask questions as you read. Don't become discouraged if you aren't able to understand every phrase or line immediately. Try to find clues to meaning in the context of a specific phrase or line.
4. Listen for the sound effects or music of the poem, including rhythm and patterns of repetition.

430 POETRY

COOPERATIVE LEARNING
Have students work together in pairs or small groups to discuss what spring is like where they live and then have them make lists of specific things—such as the maple leaves and pear trees in Teasdale's poem—that signify the arrival of this season. Encourage students to write group poems using the items from their lists. Display the completed poems on a classroom bulletin board.

5. Write a paraphrase of any lines that need clarification or simplification. A paraphrase (see page 442) helps a reader understand imagery and figurative language. A paraphrase also puts any inverted constructions into normal word order.
6. Using your responses, arrive at the central idea or meaning of the poem. Try to state this central idea, or theme, in one or two sentences. Test your statement by rereading the poem and asking if your statement covers all the important elements in the poem.

Read the following poem several times. Then write one or two sentences telling what you think the poem is saying. Compare your responses with those of your classmates.

May Day

SARA TEASDALE

A delicate fabric of bird song
    Floats in the air,
The smell of wet wild earth
    Is everywhere.

Red small leaves of the maple   5
    Are clenched like a hand,
Like girls at their first communion°
    The pear trees stand.

Oh I must pass nothing by
    Without loving it much,   10
The raindrop try with my lips,
    The grass at my touch;

For how can I be sure
    I shall see again
The world on the first of May   15
    Shining after the rain?

7. **first communion** (kə-myoon′yən): Girls traditionally wear white for this religious ceremony.

Close Reading of a Poem **431**

---

4. Sound devices are used effectively in "Annabel Lee," "The Broncho That Would Not Be Broken," "Full Fathom Five," "The Highwayman," "The Golden Vanity," and "Little Things."
5. A **paraphrase** is a prose summary that utilizes simple, straightforward language. To clarify meaning, a paraphrase of "The Caterpillar," "One of the Seven Has Somewhat to Say," and "The Chipmunk's Day" may be helpful.
6. **Theme** is specific focus of "Stopping by Woods on a Snowy Evening" and "The Listeners."

1
May Day is a celebration of beginning of spring.

2
Metaphor. Bird song is compared to delicate piece of cloth.

3
Imagery. Earth smells fresh after a spring rain.

4
Simile. Line conveys image of beauty and innocence.

5
Imagery. Appeals to sense of taste.

6
Imagery. Appeals to sense of touch; poet lovingly touches grass.

7 Summarizing
Why does the poet want to sense so fully the wonders of May Day? Worries that she may not have another opportunity to experience wonders of spring.

PORTFOLIO ASSESSMENT
Students may be interested in writing and collecting paraphrases of the poems in this unit and poems they read independently. Suggest that they collect their paraphrases in a computer database that can be alphabetically sorted by author and title. Some students may want to illustrate their final printout. Consult with them to agree on how their paraphrase collections will be assessed. (See *Portfolio Assessment and Professional Support Materials* for additional information on student portfolios.)

CLOSURE
Ask students to explain briefly the six guidelines for reading a poem.

LOOKING AT YOURSELF AS A READER
Most students will probably choose the second statement as the central meaning of the poem. Whichever statement they choose, ask students to support their choices with examples from the poem.

Looking at Yourself as a Reader

Which of these statements best expresses the central meaning of the poem? Examine your response carefully. Does your answer account for all the important elements in the poem?

1. The speaker expresses pleasure in the natural beauty of the season.
2. The speaker feels that it is important to experience nature's beauty fully because there is no certainty that such a perfect day will ever return.
3. The speaker enjoys the earth best in its wild or natural state.
4. The pear trees in bloom are like girls at their first communion.

Language and Meaning

THE SPEAKER

Who is the speaker in a poem? Is the speaker always the poet? Emily Dickinson assured someone once that he must not think that; she spoke of a "supposed person" as her speaker. Of course, the poet does write the poems, but he or she may be wearing a disguise. The voice may be that of some other person or thing. As you read "The Caterpillar" and "One of the Seven Has Somewhat to Say," ask yourself whose voice is speaking. Then read each poem aloud just the way that speaker would want to be heard.

The Caterpillar

ROBERT GRAVES

Under this loop of honeysuckle,
A creeping, colored caterpillar,
I gnaw the fresh green hawthorn spray,
I nibble it leaf by leaf away.

Down beneath grow dandelions,
Daisies, old-man's-looking-glasses;
Rooks° flap croaking across the lane.
I eat and swallow and eat again.

Here come raindrops helter-skelter;
I munch and nibble unregarding:
Hawthorn leaves are juicy and firm.
I'll mind my business: I'm a good worm.

When I'm old, tired, melancholy,
I'll build a leaf-green mausoleum°
Close by, here on this lovely spray,
And die and dream the ages away.

7. **rooks:** birds resembling crows.

14. **mausoleum** (mô′sə-lē′əm, mô′zə-): tomb.

The Caterpillar   433

Some say worms win resurrection,°
With white wings beating flitter-flutter,
But wings or a sound sleep, why should
    I care?
Either way I'll miss my share.

Under this loop of honeysuckle,
A hungry, hairy caterpillar,
I crawl on my high and swinging seat,
And eat, eat, eat—as one ought to eat.

17. **resurrection** (rĕz′ə-rĕk′shən): rebirth.

20

For Study and Discussion

Analyzing and Interpreting the Poem

1a. Who is speaking in the poem? **b.** What is the "business" (line 12) that needs minding? **c.** Which words in the poem refer to eating?

2. What different things does the speaker ignore?

3. A caterpillar turns into a butterfly or moth. Where does the speaker refer to this change?

4a. What does the poem tell you about the habits of caterpillars? **b.** Judging from your own experiences, are these habits described accurately?

5. Is the tone of this poem serious or humorous? Explain.

One of the Seven Has Somewhat to Say

SARA HENDERSON HAY

As you read, determine the identity of the speaker, and then figure out to whom he is speaking.

Remember how it was before she came—?
The picks and shovels dropped beside the door,
The sink piled high, the meals any old time,
Our jackets where we'd flung them on the floor?
The mud tracked in, the clutter on the shelves,   5
None of us shaved, or more than halfway clean . . .
Just seven old bachelors, living by ourselves?
Those were the days, if you know what I mean.

She scrubs, she sweeps, she even dusts the ceilings;
She's made us build a tool shed for our stuff.   10
Dinner's at eight, the table setting's formal.
And if I weren't afraid I'd hurt her feelings
I'd move, until we get her married off,
And things can gradually slip back to normal.

For Study and Discussion

Analyzing and Interpreting the Poem

1a. At what point did you guess the identity of the speaker?   **b.** What clues led you to your conclusion?

2a. According to the speaker, how have things changed since "she" arrived?   **b.** How does he feel about the old life and the new?

3. What is the speaker's attitude toward the young woman?

Creative Writing

Assuming Another Identity

Use your imagination to pretend that you are someone else—a teacher, a television personality, a figure in the news, even an animal. Decide what the "new you" might feel angry or indignant about. Write a poem in which your "speaker" makes clear his or her views.

CLOSURE

Ask students to identify the speaker in "The Caterpillar" and "One of the Seven Has Somewhat to Say." Have them justify their identification by referring to specific clues in the poem.

EXTENSION AND ENRICHMENT

Have small groups write dialogues in which the dwarfs in "Snow White and the Seven Dwarfs" disagree about how their lives have changed since Snow White has come to live with them. The groups might present their dialogues to the class.

FOCUS ON WRITING A POEM

To help students get ideas for poems, you could have several poetry collections on hand. Encourage students to leaf through the books to see the wide range of subjects that are covered by the poems.

ABOUT THE AUTHORS

Robert Graves

Robert Graves first began publishing poetry while still a soldier in World War I. For a brief time he was a literature professor in Egypt, but he spent World War II in England. Primarily a poet, he also wrote a great deal of prose, including his autobiography. Many readers not familiar with Graves as a poet have either read or seen the television production of *I, Claudius,* his historical novel about Roman Emperor Claudius (10 B.C. to A.D. 54). Graves won many honors for his work and was a professor of poetry at Oxford from 1961 to 1966.

Sara Henderson Hay

Sara Henderson Hay has published six books of poetry; the most recent is *A Footing on This Earth: New and Selected Poems.* Her poetry attends to the details that make daily life meaningful and explores such subjects as nature, children, animals, and human communication.

Focus on Writing a Poem

Choosing a Subject

To find a subject for a poem of your own, start by thinking about people and things you know best. For example, a family member might make a good subject for a poem. You could also choose a familiar object, event, or experience. Here are some examples of subjects you might consider:

running a race	an orange
an ice storm	a glass
a squirrel	a mailbox

Remember that almost anything can be a subject for a poem. You may find it easier, in fact, to write something new and fresh about an unexpected subject (a potato, for example) than about a "poetic" topic (such as a snowfall or a sunset).

Make a list of four possible subjects for a poem. Then exchange lists with a partner. Give each other comments on the subjects you've chosen. Save your notes.

About the Authors

Robert Graves (1895–1985)

Robert Graves was born in Wimbledon, England. He was wounded in France during World War I. After the war, he studied at Oxford University. A well-known contemporary writer, he wrote critical essays, mythological studies, and historical novels in addition to poetry. He also translated books from other languages into English.

Sara Henderson Hay (1906–1987)

Sara Henderson Hay was born in Pittsburgh, Pennsylvania. She attended Brenau College and Columbia University. Her poems were published in many journals, including *Atlantic Monthly, The New Yorker,* and *The Saturday Review.* Among Hay's six collections of poetry, her most popular books are *Field of Honor* (1933); *The Delicate Balance* (1951), which was awarded the Edna St. Vincent Millay Memorial Award from the Poetry Society of America; and *The Stone and the Shell* (1959). Remarking on her writing, one critic said: "What is memorable to her is...the daily event; the small communications between people or animals which make for a kind of wholeness."

DICTION

Diction refers to a writer's choice of words or manner of expression. Poets choose words carefully for precise effects, to arouse particular moods or sensations. They depend on the rich associations, or *connotations,* of words as well as on their literal, or *denotative,* meanings.

The diction of a poem may be formal or informal. In "One of the Seven Has Somewhat to Say" (page 435), the speaker refers to "our stuff" in line 10. The word *stuff* is an informal word for "belongings."

Sometimes poets take freedom with language, making up new words, running words together, or using unusual word order. In the hands of a poet like E. E. Cummings (page 439), this *poetic license* results in striking effects.

Poets will also change the normal order of words in a sentence. This technique, called *inversion,* is used most often when the poet wishes to give emphasis to a word or an idea.

Fog

CARL SANDBURG

In this poem, fog is compared to a cat. Note how effectively Sandburg uses simple, familiar words.

The fog comes
on little cat feet.

It sits looking
over harbor and city
on silent haunches
and then moves on.

The 1st

LUCILLE CLIFTON

The words in this poem are extremely simple, yet charged with emotional feeling. What is the effect of the repetition in the last two lines?

What I remember about that day
is boxes stacked across the walk
and couch springs curling through the air
and drawers and tables balanced on the curb
and us, hollering,
leaping up and around
happy to have a playground;

nothing about the emptied rooms
nothing about the emptied family

For Study and Discussion

Analyzing and Interpreting the Poem

1. The first of the month is generally the day when rent is due. What details in the poem tell you what is happening to the family?

2a. What words does the speaker use to describe herself and the other children in lines 5–7? **b.** How do the words in the last two lines change the emotional feeling of the poem?

3a. What do you think the phrase "emptied family" means? **b.** How is the connotation of "emptied rooms" different from "emptied family"?

4. Why do you suppose the speaker repeats the words *nothing* and *emptied* in the last two lines?

Literary Elements

Understanding the Role of Diction

Precise, clear diction helps the reader understand exactly what is happening in a poem. In Clifton's poem the couch springs are *curling* upward. We can see the coils that have come through the worn padding. The children are *hollering*—shouting in play, unaware of what is happening to the family. The furniture is *balanced* on the curb.

Effective diction is one of the elements through which a poet reveals emotional meaning. What phrase conveys the family's feeling of loss as they leave their home?

438 POETRY

in Just-

E. E. CUMMINGS

Cummings wants his readers to approach his poems as original and fresh works. What kinds of poetic license does he use here?

in Just-
spring   when the world is mud-
luscious the little
lame balloonman

whistles   far   and wee

and eddieandbill come
running from marbles and
piracies and it's
spring

when the world is puddle-wonderful

the queer
old balloonman whistles
far   and   wee
and bettyandisbel come dancing

from hop-scotch and jump-rope and

it's
spring
and
    the

      goat-footed°

balloonMan   whistles
far
and
wee

20. **goat-footed:** Pan, a god of woods and fields in Greek mythology, was represented with the legs of a goat.

MEETING INDIVIDUAL NEEDS
Kinesthetic Learners • Have students clip and arrange words and phrases from newspapers and magazines to make poems. Tell them to try to give new or unusual meanings to the words and phrases by the way they combine and arrange them. Have students paste their poems on paper and display them in the classroom.

TRANSPARENCY 37
Reader Response
Charting a Response to Poetry — prompts students to respond to a poem.

VISUAL CONNECTIONS
Relating Expression Skills
As an exercise in nonverbal communication, ask students to stand and relax their bodies. Next, ask them to imagine they are balloons being slowly filled with air. Then, tell students that air is slowly escaping, returning them to shapelessness.

FOR STUDY AND DISCUSSION
1a. First days of spring. **1b.** To child, mud and puddles are fun to play in. **1c.** Marbles, pirates, hopscotch, jumprope.
2. *We,* suggesting all share children's excitement.
3a. Separated even more. **3b.** On separate lines. **3c.** Whistle becoming more faint.
4. Suggests he is re-creating an ancient rite of spring.
5. Lines 6–9 and 15 suggest eager, breathless, uneven movement of children at play.

LITERARY ELEMENTS
1. *Mud-luscious* and *puddle-wonderful* connote fun-loving and positive attitude children have toward playing in mud and puddles; *muddy* and *wet* imply annoyance and unpleasantness.
2. Cool, oozy texture.
3. Splashy fun.
4. The very first joyous days after winter.
5. Arrangement of lines suggests skipping, running, jumping of children.
6. "Balloonman" becomes "balloonMan" when he is associated with Greek god.
7. Answers will vary. Convey freedom and spirit of new season.

440

For Study and Discussion

Analyzing and Interpreting the Poem

1a. When is "Just-spring"? **b.** From the point of view of a young child, why might the world be "mud-luscious" and "puddle-wonderful" at this time? **c.** What games do the children in the poem play?

2. The word *wee,* meaning "very small or little," is often used in children's stories. It also sounds like *whee,* a word used by children when they are excited or happy. What other word might be intended?

3. The sound of the balloonman's whistle is first heard in line 5. Notice the space between the words *whistles, far,* and *and wee.* **a.** What happens to the space between these words in lines 12–13? **b.** In lines 21–24? **c.** What do you think is happening to the sound of the whistle?

4. The balloonman is described as "goat-footed." As explained in the note to line 20, Pan was believed to have the legs of a goat. He was fond of music and dancing, and was thought to be the inventor of the shepherd's pipes. Why do you think the balloonman is associated with Pan?

5. How is the movement of the lines across the page like the movement of the children in the poem?

Literary Elements

Understanding the Purpose of Poetic License

In his poem Cummings wishes the reader to experience spring as it is experienced by children who are filled with wonder and happiness. Note the hyphenated words *mud-luscious* and *puddle-wonderful.* Why are these words more effective than the words *muddy* and *wet*? To a child, what makes mud *luscious*? What makes a puddle *wonderful*?

Cummings also runs together the names *eddieandbill* and *bettyandisbel,* and he does not capitalize the names, perhaps to suggest that the individual names are not important—the names of other children could easily be substituted. In the phrase *Just-spring,* Cummings capitalizes the word *Just.* What does he wish to emphasize about the season?

When you look at the poem, the lines have an irregular pattern, and the eye is forced to skip across spaces. How does this arrangement capture the spirit of the children and their movement?

What other examples of poetic license have you found in Cummings' poem? Can you explain the purpose for these elements?

440 POETRY

The Chipmunk's Day

RANDALL JARRELL°

Sometimes the most familiar things take on new significance as the result of a poet's fresh observations. How does the poet's language capture the movements of the chipmunk?

In and out the bushes, up the ivy,
Into the hole
By the old oak stump, the chipmunk flashes.
Up the pole

To the feeder full of seeds he dashes, 5
Stuffs his cheeks,
The chickadee and titmouse scold him.
Down he streaks.

Red as the leaves the wind blows off the maple,
Red as a fox, 10
Striped like a skunk, the chipmunk whistles
Past the love seat, past the mailbox,

Down the path,
Home to his warm hole stuffed with sweet
Things to eat. 15
Neat and slight and shining, his front feet

Curled at his breast, he sits there while the sun
Stripes the red west
With its last light: the chipmunk
Dives to his rest. 20

° **Jarrell** (jə-rĕl′).

COOPERATIVE LEARNING
Have students work together to collect and illustrate animal poems for a bulletin-board zoo. They may also want to include selected nursery rhymes about animals that they have rewritten by inverting key sentences—and adjusting rhymes accordingly—in the style of Jarrell's poem.

TRANSPARENCIES 35 & 36
Fine Art
Theme: *Special Language, Special Meaning* – features artwork in which the artist attempts to express an opinion about a specific idea.

FOR STUDY AND DISCUSSION
1. Verbs "flashes," "dashes," "streaks," "whistles," "dives" emphasize rapid, darting movements.
2. Since readers pause after commas, short phrases suggest chipmunk's rapid movements with pauses and changes of direction in between.

LITERARY ELEMENTS
1. Emphasis shifts to the trip up the hill.
2. The chipmunk flashes in and out of the bushes, up the ivy, into the hole by the old oak stump.
3. Chipmunk's quick movements and changes of direction.
4. Inversion in ll. 4–5 emphasizes chipmunk's destination as he goes up pole to feeder.

WRITING ABOUT LITERATURE
You might clarify for students that a paraphrase is not a summary, but a restatement. The following is a sample paraphrase of the poem:

The chipmunk runs up a pole to a feeder full of seeds, where he stuffs his cheeks, while the chickadee and titmouse scold him. The chipmunk is as red as the leaves blowing off the maple trees; he is as red as a fox and striped like a skunk. The chipmunk runs quickly past the love seat and the mailbox, down the path to his home. His warm hole is full of food. Small and shining, he sits there with his front feet curled at his breast. With its last light, the sun seems to paint stripes in the red western sky. The chipmunk dives into his home to rest.

442

For Study and Discussion

Analyzing and Interpreting the Poem

1. List the verbs that describe the chipmunk's movements. What kind of movement is emphasized?

2. The first sentence of the poem is interrupted three times by commas. Read these lines aloud. How do the lines suggest the chipmunk's movements?

Literary Elements

Understanding the Purpose of Inversion

Most sentences in the English language follow a pattern in which the subject comes before the predicate. Consider the effect of varying this pattern in a line from a familiar nursery rhyme.

> Jack and Jill went up the hill
> Up the hill went Jack and Jill

1 What change in emphasis occurs when the order of words is shifted?

A reversal of the normal arrangement of words in a sentence is called **inversion**. Inverting word order calls attention to the word or phrase that has been shifted. A poet can give a word or phrase special importance by placing it at the beginning or at the end of a line.

2 What would be the normal order of the words in the following lines?

> In and out the bushes, up the ivy,
> Into the hole
> By the old oak stump, the chipmunk flashes.

3 What does the poet emphasize by inversion in these lines?

4 Locate another example of inversion in the poem and tell what its purpose is.

442 POETRY

Writing About Literature

▶ **Paraphrasing a Poem**

A **paraphrase** is a summary of a literary work. When you paraphrase a poem, you restate its language and ideas in your own words. A paraphrase is helpful in clarifying what a poem means.

The first three lines of Jarrell's poem might be paraphrased in this way:

> The chipmunk moves swiftly in and out of the bushes, up the ivy vine, and into the hole near the stump of the old oak tree.

Paraphrase the rest of the poem. Check to see that your paraphrase includes all the details in the poem.

Focus on Writing a Poem

Experimenting with Imagery

Imagery is language that appeals to any one or any combination of the five senses: sight, sound, smell, taste, and touch. Images are important in poetry because they can reveal meaning powerfully and vividly.

Choose *two* of the subjects identified for the assignment on page 436 or select a different pair of subjects. For each subject, make an image chart like the one below. Fill in a specific image for as many senses as you can. Save your notes.

Image Chart		
Subject	Sense	Image
_____	sight	_____
	sound	_____
	smell	_____
	taste	_____
	touch	_____

▶ Before students begin this writing assignment, you may wish to refer them to the **Writing About Literature** section on p. 688.

VOCABULARY
The word *souse* is in the Glossary. The **Teacher's Notes** provides an activity that examines the pronunciation and spelling of words in **dialect**.

PRESENTATION
Students might recognize words such as "kyouck" and "hallylooyer" as representations of the sounds of turkeys and roosters. "Fodder" refers to animal food for which the term *hay* is used in some regions, *straw* in others.

Bring to class a comic strip in which characters speak in a dialect, or ask students to give examples of dialect used in popular television shows. How does dialect contribute to characterization? Relate discussion to the headnote. Ask students to watch for unusual vocabulary,

TEACHING RESOURCES D
Teacher's Notes, p. 17
Study Guide, p. 19
Building Vocabulary, p. 22
Selection Test, p. 24

When the Frost Is on the Punkin

JAMES WHITCOMB RILEY

Dialect is a form of speech belonging to a particular region or to a particular group of people. A dialect may be distinguished by characteristics of vocabulary, grammar, and pronunciation.

This poem is written in a dialect that was spoken in rural Indiana many years ago. If you read the poem out loud, you will have no problem understanding words like russel *and* medder.

When the frost is on the punkin and the fodder's in the shock,°
And you hear the kyouck and gobble of the struttin' turkey cock,
And the clackin' of the guineys,° and the cluckin' of the hens,
And the rooster's hallylooyer as he tiptoes on the fence;
O, it's then's the time a feller is a-feelin' at his best, 5
With the risin' sun to greet him from a night of peaceful rest,
As he leaves the house, bareheaded, and goes out to feed the stock,
When the frost is on the punkin and the fodder's in the shock.

They's something kindo' harty-like about the atmusfere
When the heat of summer's over and the coolin' fall is here— 10
Of course we miss the flowers, and the blossoms on the trees,
And the mumble of the hummin'birds and buzzin' of the bees;
But the air's so appetizin'; and the landscape through the haze
Of a crisp and sunny morning of the airly autumn days
Is a pictur' that no painter has the colorin' to mock— 15
When the frost is on the punkin and the fodder's in the shock.

The husky, rusty russel of the tossels of the corn,
And the raspin' of the tangled leaves, as golden as the morn;
The stubble in the furries—kindo' lonesome-like, but still
A-preachin' sermuns to us of the barns they growed to fill; 20
The strawstack in the medder, and the reaper in the shed;
The hosses in theyr stalls below—the clover overhead!—
O, it sets my hart a-clickin' like the tickin' of a clock,
When the frost is on the punkin and the fodder's in the shock!

1. **shock:** a pile of stalks and leaves set in a field to dry.

3. **guineys** (gĭn'ēz): guinea fowls.

When the Frost Is on the Punkin

1 Finding Main Ideas
When is the frost on the "punkin"? Autumn (October–November) when nighttime temperature dips below freezing.

2
Refrain. Opening line recurs throughout poem, emphasizing time of the year.

3
Speaker associates early-morning autumn sounds with his good feelings.

4
Use to answer **study question 3,** p. 444.

5 Drawing Conclusions
Why would a painter not be able to capture this beauty? Scene is too beautiful to be represented artificially.

6
Onomatopoeia. "Russel" and "raspin'" imitate sound of wind in tossels and leaves.

7 Analyzing
Why were the "furries" (furrows) lonesome? Were bare of crops.

8
Use to answer **study question 4a,** p. 444.

When the Frost Is on the Punkin 443

grammar, and spelling as they read. Since phonetic spelling makes this poem appear more difficult than it is, oral reading is especially important. After hearing the poem read aloud, volunteers might try reading one stanza each with the rest of the class joining in on the refrain.

MEETING INDIVIDUAL NEEDS
ESL/LEP • Because of the dialect in the poem, students may have difficulty in determining from context the meaning of some words. As a whole-class activity, have students target words that are spelled in dialect form. Emphasize that these spellings reflect how the words are actually pronounced in the poem. Write these forms on the chalkboard and have students provide standard spellings.

9
Use to answer **study question 5,** p. 444.

10
Dialect. Here and throughout the poem, poet uses phonetic spellings and surprising word choices representing actual speech patterns rather than grammatically correct patterns.

9 Then your apples all is gethered, and the ones a feller keeps 25
Is poured around the celler floor in red and yeller heaps;
And your cider makin's over, and your wimmern folks is
   through
With theyr mince and apple butter, and theyr souse and
   sausage, too!
I don't know how to tell it—but ef sich a thing could be
10 As the Angels wantin' boardin', and they'd call around on *me*— 30
I'd want to 'commodate 'em—all the whole indurin' flock—
When the frost is on the punkin and the fodder's in the shock!

FOR STUDY AND DISCUSSION
1. Indiana farmer.
2. Kyouck, gobble, clackin', cluckin', hallylooyer.
3. Cool air, sight of landscape.
4a. Stubble on farmland after reaping; barns full of crops; stacks of straw; reaper in barn; "fodder in the shock." 4b. Corn tassels. 4c. Furrows.
5. Gathering apples; storing them; making cider, mince, apple butter; making souse and sausage.
6. Beauty of season; has rich harvest; has done necessary labor and provided for winter.

LITERARY ELEMENTS
1. The sense of an old farmer speaking to us straight from his heart about a particular place and time he loves.

For Study and Discussion

Analyzing and Interpreting the Poem

1. Who is the speaker in this poem?

2. This poem tells what life was like on an Indiana farm during early autumn many years ago. In the first stanza the speaker notes the sounds he hears early in the morning. Which words imitate the sounds of farm animals?

3. In the second stanza the speaker describes the "atmusfere" of early fall. What characteristics of the morning does he enjoy?

4. Autumn is the time when crops are harvested. **a.** What details in the third stanza tell you that the harvesting is over? **b.** What are the "tossels" in line 17? **c.** The "furries" in line 19?

5. What tasks of the autumn season are described in the last stanza?

6. Why do you think autumn fills the speaker with such a sense of well-being?

Literary Elements

Understanding the Role of Dialect

The use of dialect in literature is a way of giving authenticity to a region and its people. If you have read "The Erne from the Coast" (page 208), you may remember that the characters use a dialect spoken in the sheep country of Great Britain. They say *aboot* for "about" and *aw reet* for "all right." In *The Mazarin Stone* (page 318), Sam Merton speaks a variety of English called *cockney*, which is associated with the East End of London. One characteristic of this dialect is the dropping of the letter *h*: 'ere for "here."

James Whitcomb Riley makes use of dialect to give us the flavor of a particular place and
1 time. What would be lost if you substituted standard speech for the dialect?

About the Authors

Carl Sandburg (1878–1967)

Carl Sandburg was born in Galesburg, Illinois. He left school at thirteen and helped support his family by working at odd jobs. After serving in the Spanish-American War, he decided to enroll in college. In 1914 his poem "Chicago," a vibrant picture of this Midwestern city, was published in *Poetry* magazine and won the Levinson Prize. His volume *Chicago Poems*, which came out in 1916, received wide acclaim. Five more volumes of poetry followed. Sandburg spent fifteen years writing a six-volume biography of Abraham Lincoln, his boyhood hero. He also wrote tales and lyrics for children and edited a collection of folk songs called *The American Songbag*. Sandburg was awarded the Pulitzer Prize for both poetry and history.

Lucille Clifton (1936–)

Lucille Clifton was born in Depew, New York, and attended Howard University. Among the many honors she has received are National Endowment for the Arts awards, the Coretta Scott King Award, and the position of Poet Laureate of Maryland. Her first collection of poetry, *Good Times*, from which "The 1st" is taken, came out in 1969. Recent collections are *Next* (1987), *Quilting* (1991), and *The Book of Light* (1993). She has also written novels, short stories, children's fiction, and a memoir of her family called *Generations* (1976). Her innate sense of the rhythms and music of the spoken African American language gives her work freshness and power. Clifton once claimed that the duty of the artist was to "tell the truth."

E. E. Cummings (1894–1962)

For a biography of Cummings, see page 70.

Randall Jarrell (1914–1965)

Randall Jarrell was born in Nashville, Tennessee. He enjoyed a distinguished career as a poet, teacher, and literary critic. He served as Consultant in Poetry at the Library of Congress. In 1961 he won the National Book Award for poetry. In addition to poetry, he wrote a novel and two volumes of essays. "The Chipmunk's Day" is from *The Bat Poet*, a story about a bat that writes poems.

James Whitcomb Riley (1849–1916)

James Whitcomb Riley, known as "the Hoosier poet," worked for some years as a sign painter, an actor, and a small-town journalist. Then he went to work for the *Indianapolis Daily Journal*, which regularly published his poems. Riley had a keen eye for the local scene and characters, and sometimes made use of the Hoosier (Indiana country) dialect. One of his best-known poems is "Little Orphant Annie."

OBJECTIVES

The overall aim is for students to analyze the use of **imagery** in "Trade Winds" and "A Parrot." For a complete list of objectives, see the **Teacher's Notes**.

FOCUS / MOTIVATION

Write on the board *flower, popcorn, bell, fireworks, rock*. Ask students to describe these by creating images that appeal to each of the senses.

PREREADING FOCUS

The headnote emphasizes that **imagery** is an element through which the poet conveys meaning by appealing to the senses. Images not only convey meaning and appeal to the imagination but also evoke emotion. A description of a lamb grazing in a field may arouse in the reader feelings of contentment and peace. Images of mob riots or armed highwaymen may arouse feelings of fear and insecurity.

IMAGERY

Imagery is language that appeals to the senses. Imagery in poetry is most often visual, but it can appeal to any of the other senses—hearing, smell, taste, and touch. Riley's poem "When the Frost Is on the Punkin" (page 443) appeals to all the senses. Riley uses visual imagery when he describes the apples "poured around the celler floor in red and yeller heaps." The "gobble" of the turkcy cock and the "buzzin" of the bees appeal to the sense of hearing. The reference to "mince and apple butter, and theyr souse and sausage" appeals to the sense of taste. "The stubble in the furries" appeals to the sense of touch.

Imagery is one of the elements through which a poet reveals meaning. As you read "Trade Winds" and "A Parrot," note how the poets select images that appeal to your imagination and that also convey meaning.

Trade Winds

JOHN MASEFIELD

In the colonial period, Spanish merchant ships traveled in the Caribbean Sea, which became known as the Spanish Main. The Trade Winds, which blow toward the equator from the east, are still very important to navigators.

In the harbor, in the island, in the Spanish Seas,
Are the tiny white houses and the orange trees,
And daylong, nightlong, the cool and pleasant breeze
    Of the steady Trade Winds blowing.

There is the red wine, the nutty Spanish ale,
The shuffle of the dancers, the old salt's° tale,   5
The squeaking fiddle, and the soughing° in the sail
    Of the steady Trade Winds blowing.

And o' nights there's fireflies and the yellow moon,
And in the ghostly palm trees the sleepy tune
Of the quiet voice calling me, the long low croon°   10
    Of the steady Trade Winds blowing.

6. **old salt:** an experienced sailor.
7. **soughing** (sŭf′əng, sou′əng): soft rustling.
11. **croon:** soft singing.

For Study and Discussion

Analyzing and Interpreting the Poem

1a. What is the setting of the poem? **b.** What impression do you receive of the setting from the imagery in the poem?
2a. Who is the speaker in the poem? **b.** What clues are there to his identity?
3a. What are the pleasures that the speaker enjoys on land? **b.** What is the "voice" that calls to him in line 11?
4. Repetition of a word or a line in a poem is usually done for emphasis. What is the effect of repeating the same line at the end of each stanza?

A Parrot

MAY SARTON

My parrot is emerald green,
His tail feathers, marine.°
He bears an orange half-moon
Over his ivory beak.
He must be believed to be seen,   5
This bird from a Rousseau° wood.
When the urge is on him to speak,
He becomes too true to be good.

He uses his beak like a hook
To lift himself up with or break   10
Open a sunflower seed,
And his eye, in a bold white ring,
Has a lapidary° look.
What a most astonishing bird,
Whose voice when he chooses to sing   15
Must be believed to be heard.

That stuttered staccato scream
Must be believed not to seem
The shriek of a witch in the room.
But he murmurs some muffled words   20
(Like someone who talks through a
   dream)
When he sits in the window and sees
The to-and-fro wings of wild birds
In the leafless improbable trees.

2. **marine:** here, a blue-green color. 6. **Rousseau** (rōō-sō′): Henri Rousseau (1844–1910), a French painter known for the vivid colors of his canvases. 13. **lapidary** (lăp′ə-dĕr′ē): precious stone.

For Study and Discussion

Analyzing and Interpreting the Poem

1. The poet uses chiefly color imagery in the first two stanzas to describe the parrot. Why does the bird seem to be something out of a painting?

2. Why does the speaker call the parrot "a most astonishing bird"?

3a. What kinds of sounds does the bird make? **b.** How does he react to the sight of wild birds? **c.** Why would the trees outdoors seem *improbable* to him?

4. We usually say that something must be seen to be believed, or that something is too good to be true. **a.** How has the poet changed these expressions? **b.** Can you suggest a reason for these changes?

Focus on Writing a Poem

Listing Sensory Details

Sensory details appeal to one of the five senses: sight, sound, smell, taste, and touch. Most of the details May Sarton uses in "A Parrot" appeal to sight and sound. Notice, however, that the details about the parrot's beak in lines 9–11 appeal vividly to the sense of touch.

Choose a plant or animal you have seen at the botanical garden, a pet shop, or the zoo. List as many sensory details as you can about your subject. Make sure that the items on your list involve all five senses at least once. Then exchange papers with a classmate. See if you can add any items to each other's lists. Save your notes.

About the Authors

John Masefield (1878–1967)

The Granger Collection, New York

John Masefield was born in Ledbury, England. When he was fourteen, he ran away to sea. After two years, he landed in New York City with only five dollars to his name. He worked at various jobs, all the while reading as many books as he could buy at secondhand bookshops. His first volume of poems, *Salt-Water Ballads*, told of the ships and seamen he had known. One of his most famous novels is *Jim Davis*. In 1930 Masefield became poet laureate of England.

May Sarton (1912–)

May Sarton was born in Belgium and emigrated to the United States with her family when she was four years old. She is well-known as a poet, novelist, and nonfiction writer. She once said of her writing, "I'm a lyric poet and music is not fashionable in poetry, but I think it's one of the essentials. Like rock-and-roll, it hits below the belt." She has received many honors, including the Human Dignity Award in 1984 and the American Book Award in 1985. Her collections of poetry include *Collected Poems* (1974), *Letters from Maine* (1984), and *The Silence Now* (1988). Her thoughts at the age of eighty have recently appeared in *Encore: A Journal of the Eightieth Year* (1993).

About the Authors **449**

FIGURATIVE LANGUAGE

Figurative language is language that is not intended to be understood in a strict literal sense. Many everyday expressions are figurative. When you ask someone "to lend a hand," you are speaking figuratively. You are asking for that person's help. When used imaginatively, figurative language adds a dimension of meaning to speech or writing.

The term *figure of speech* is often used for a specific kind of figurative language. Two common figures of speech are *simile* and *metaphor*. A simile uses a word such as *like* or *as* to express some kind of likeness between two different things. In "May Day" (page 431), Teasdale says that the small leaves of the maple are "clenched *like* a hand." A metaphor draws a comparison between two unlike things by identifying them. Had Teasdale written "The leaves of the maple are clenched hands," she would have used a metaphor.

As you read the following poems, identify the figures of speech and note how they appeal to your imagination.

Living Tenderly

MAY SWENSON

This is a riddle poem. In order to guess the identity of the speaker, you must correctly interpret the figurative language.

My body a rounded stone
with a pattern of smooth seams.
My head a short snake,
retractive,° projective.°
My legs come out of their sleeves   5
or shrink within,
and so does my chin.
My eyelids are quick clamps.

My back is my roof.
I am always at home.   10
I travel where my house walks.
It is a smooth stone.
It floats within the lake,
or rests in the dust.
My flesh lives tenderly   15
inside its bone.

---

4. **retractive** (rĭ-trăk′tĭv): capable of drawing back. **projective** (prə-jĕk′tĭv): capable of moving forward.

a riddle. To identify its speaker, they must again explain the figurative language of the poem.

JOURNAL WRITING LINK
Have students collect and record in their journals **similes** and **metaphors** used in magazine advertisements, radio and television commercials, and on billboards. Ask them to describe briefly why each one is fresh or trite. Encourage students to write their own similes or metaphors for each of the examples they find.

For Study and Discussion

Analyzing and Interpreting the Poem

1a. What does the poem describe? **b.** What details in the poem give you the answer?

2a. What does the "pattern of smooth seams" refer to? **b.** What are the "sleeves" referred to in line 5?

3a. Describe the way a clamp works. **b.** Why do you think the eyelids are called "quick clamps"?

4. State in your own words what the last two lines of the poem mean.

Literary Elements

Understanding Figurative Language

Look again at the opening lines of the poem:

> My body a rounded stone
> with a pattern of smooth seams.

In these lines a body is identified with a stone. In reality, that is not possible: a body cannot be a stone. But the poet is not speaking **literally**—that is, in terms of reality. She is speaking **figuratively**—that is, in terms of poetic imagination. The poet means to suggest that there is some similarity between two different things.

To speak of a body as if it were a stone suggests something about the shape and feel of that body. What do the lines suggest to you?

In the opening lines the poet is using a kind of figurative language called **metaphor**. A metaphor draws a comparison between two things that are basically different. Explain the metaphors in line 3 and in line 8.

In addition to metaphor, poets use a figurative device called **simile**. Like metaphor, a simile draws a comparison between two unlike things. However, a simile uses a word such as *like, as,* or *than* to express the comparison. Explain the simile in these lines:

> And green and blue his sharp eyes twinkled,
> Like a candle flame where salt is sprinkled . . .

4 What two things are compared in this simile?

> My heart is like an apple tree
> Whose boughs are bent with thickset fruit.

5 Identify the metaphors and similes in the following lines. Explain each comparison.

> Deep in the sun-scorched growths the dragonfly
> Hangs like a blue thread, loosened from the sky.

> The lightning is a yellow fork
> From tables in the sky. . . .

> The day is done, and the darkness
>   Falls from the wings of night,
> As a feather is wafted downward
>   From an eagle in his flight.

FOR STUDY AND DISCUSSION
1a. Turtle. **1b.** "Stone" body; "retractive, projective" head; legs emerging from "sleeves"; "roof" (back of shell); "I travel where my house walks"; last two lines.
2a. Indentations on turtle's shell. **2b.** Folds of skin.
3a. Has stationary bottom and a top that screws down to grip object. **3b.** Eyelids close like tops of clamps moving down quickly.
4. Answers will vary. Answers should refer to soft flesh of turtle within hard shell.

LITERARY ELEMENTS
1. Responses may vary. Suggests old, very hard object.
2. Metaphor in l. 3 compares darting movement of turtle's head with movement of snake. Metaphor in l. 8 compares movement of eyelids to movement of clamps.
3. Twinkling of eyes is compared to flickering of candle.
4. Heart is compared to weighted apple tree boughs.
5. Flickering appearance of dragonfly is compared to wisp of blue thread, from fabric of sky; suggests mysterious, marvelous appearance of insect.

Next, appearance of lightning is compared to gigantic fork fallen from huge table in sky.

Final passage contains metaphor ("the wings of night") and simile ("darkness / Falls . . . / As a feather is wafted"); both compare nightfall to something that might fall from wings of bird in flight; suggests mysterious nature of universe.

Living Tenderly

The Spider

ROBERT P. TRISTRAM COFFIN

What is the speaker's attitude toward the spider? How is that attitude revealed in the metaphors of the poem?

With six small diamonds for his eyes
He walks upon the Summer skies,
Drawing from his silken blouse
The lacework of his dwelling house.

He lays his staircase as he goes   5
Under his eight thoughtful toes
And grows with the concentric° flower
Of his shadowless, thin bower.°

His back legs are a pair of hands,
They can spindle out the strands   10
Of a thread that is so small
It stops the sunlight not at all.

He spins himself to threads of dew
Which will harden soon into
Lines that cut like slender knives   15
Across the insects' airy lives.

He makes no motion but is right,
He spreads out his appetite
Into a network, twist on twist,
This little ancient scientist.   20

He does not know he is unkind,
He has a jewel for a mind
And logic deadly as dry bone,
This small son of Euclid's° own.

7. **concentric** (kən-sĕn′trĭk): having circles, one within another, with a common center.
8. **bower:** here, dwelling place.

24. **Euclid** (yōō′klĭd): Greek mathematician of third century B.C., who wrote a basic work in geometry.

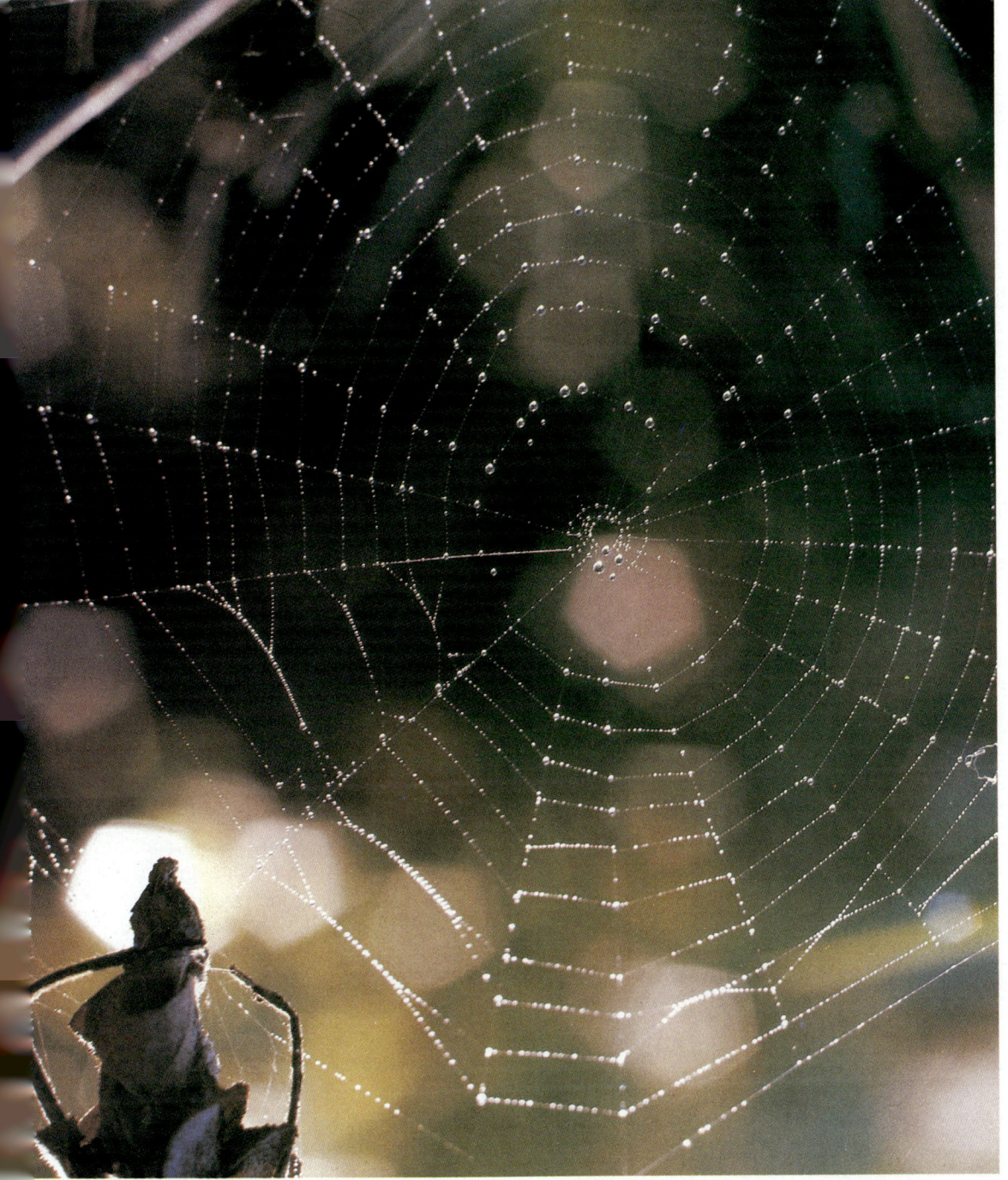

VISUAL CONNECTIONS
Relating Expression Skills
This photograph may interest students in close study of other phenomena of nature. For example, they might observe ants, birds, cats, a storm, or a sunset. They might make notes for an oral description of what they studied, including in their descriptions appropriate figures of speech such as similes and metaphors.

The Spider

CLOSURE
Ask students to define **metaphor** and **simile** and give examples of each from "Living Tenderly" and "The Spider."

EXTENSION AND ENRICHMENT
Have students collect memorable metaphors and similes from other poems. Or ask each student to write a simile each about a freeway, the ocean, and thunder and then to rewrite those similes as metaphors.

FOR STUDY AND DISCUSSION
1a. "Silken blouse" is tip of spider's abdomen; silk is forced through many tiny holes from spinning organs there. "Lacework" is silk that spider manufactures. "Dwelling house" is web itself. **1b.** "Staircase" is pattern of web.
2. It is invisible to insects who are trapped by its "lines that cut like slender knives."
3. Spider, like scientist, is careful and methodical in what he does. Spider is compared to Euclid; web's design suggests work of geometrician.
4a. In awe of spider's skill and precision. **4b.** Contrives deadly, invisible web that will provide him with food.

ABOUT THE AUTHORS
May Swenson
May Swenson's creative use of sound devices and figurative language, as seen in "Living Tenderly," can be found in her collection entitled *Poems to Solve* (1966) and *More Poems to Solve* (1971). These riddle poems will appeal especially to young students.

Robert Coffin
Robert Coffin made his Maine surroundings the subject of many of his poems. He was a prolific poet, publishing many works including *Ballads of Square-Toed Americans*, *There Will Be Bread and Love*, *Poems for a Son with Wings*, and *Apples By the Ocean*. In 1935, he won a Pulitzer Prize for his collection *Strange Holiness*. He also wrote novels, an autobiography, essays, and a biography of a Maine family living on board a sailing ship.

454

For Study and Discussion

Analyzing and Interpreting the Poem

1. Although the word *web* is not used, it is clear that the poem is figuratively describing the spider spinning a web. **a.** What are the "silken blouse," the "lacework," and the "dwelling house" referred to in the first stanza? **b.** What is the "staircase" in line 5?

2. We are told that the web is so delicate that the thread "stops the sunlight not at all." How are we also reminded of the deadly nature of the web?

3. In the final lines, the spider is compared to a scientist and to a mathematician. What is the basis for these comparisons?

4a. What is the speaker's attitude toward the spider? **b.** What is the spider's logic and why is it deadly?

Focus on Writing a Poem

Using Figurative Language

Figurative language is language that is not intended to be interpreted in a strict, literal sense. Poets use figures of speech to appeal to our imagination in fresh, unexpected ways.

The chart below shows three of the most common figures of speech. You may want to use one or more of these in your own poems.

Figures of Speech	
Simile: uses *like* or *as* to compare two different things	The desert was like an oven.
Metaphor: compares two different things directly	The desert was an oven.
Personification: gives human qualities to something nonhuman	We felt the hot breath of the desert.

Choose a familiar subject: for example, a flower, a pet, a road, or a pretzel. Create a chart like the one on this page by making up three figures of speech to describe your subject. Save your notes.

About the Authors

May Swenson (1919–1989)

May Swenson was born in Logan, Utah, and graduated from Utah State University. After moving to New York in the 1930s, she worked as a stenographer, an editor, and a translator. Her first collection of poems, *Another Animal*, was published in 1954. She went on to publish eight more books of poetry, and was known for her sense of humor, playfulness, and careful observation of ordinary experiences. Discussing Swenson's *Poems to Solve* (1966), the poet Richard Howard stated: "Swenson intended these poems to be solvable riddles as well as poems, a means of using language to make an object more clearly known instead of more hazy."

Robert P. Tristram Coffin (1892–1955)

Robert Peter Tristram Coffin was a Maine author who graduated from Bowdoin College. He was a Rhodes scholar at Oxford University and became a professor of English at Wells College in New York. Besides his many volumes of poetry, he wrote essays, biographies, and novels. His poetry often focuses on the hearty outdoors life and on closely observed wonders of nature.

454 POETRY

OBJECTIVES
The overall aim is for students to demonstrate an understanding of the **theme** of "Stopping by Woods on a Snowy Evening" and "The Listeners." For a complete list of objectives, see the **Teacher's Notes.**

FOCUS / MOTIVATION
Play a word-association game with the words *snow, dark,* and *sleep.* After exchanging and discussing responses, ask students to put lists aside for later use (associations may be useful for **study question 4**).

PRESENTATION
Divide the students into small groups. Allow them to work on an oral interpretation of this poem. Remind them that tone of voice, gesture, and pace all contribute to interpretation. Have each group read the poem before the class. Then

THE IDEAS IN A POEM

All the elements you have studied thus far are ways for the poet to communicate meaning. Some poems yield their meaning at a single reading. More complex poems can be read on several levels and interpreted in more than one way.

Like other forms of literature, a poem often has an underlying idea, or *theme,* that offers a point of view about life or gives some insight into human experience. As you read, learn to explore poetry for these deeper meanings.

Stopping by Woods on a Snowy Evening

ROBERT FROST

This poem tells the story of a man who stops to watch snow falling in the woods. Most readers of the poem think that Frost is using a simple, everyday experience to reveal some deep truth or understanding about life.

1 Whose woods these are I think I know.
His house is in the village, though;
He will not see me stopping here
To watch his woods fill up with snow.

My little horse must think it queer
2 To stop without a farmhouse near
Between the woods and frozen lake
The darkest evening of the year.

3 He gives his harness bells a shake
To ask if there is some mistake.   10
The only other sound's the sweep
Of easy wind and downy flake.

4 The woods are lovely, dark, and deep,
5 But I have promises to keep,
And miles to go before I sleep,   15
And miles to go before I sleep.

TEACHING RESOURCES D
Teacher's Notes, p. 39
Study Guide, p. 40
Selection Test, p. 54

AV RESOURCES BINDER
Audiocassette 3, Side A

PREREADING FOCUS
One of the joys of reading poetry is the adventure of unfolding the meaning in a poem. Explain that because poems are so rich in **figurative language,** we must look below the surface meanings of words. A poem has a **theme** when it comments on or gives insight into the meaning of life.

Stopping by Woods on a Snowy Evening

1 Analyzing
Who is the speaker in the poem? A person out for a ride on a winter's night.

2
Setting. Isolated, rural place.

3 Making Inferences
The horse seems to be in a hurry. Could his hurry have a deeper meaning? Perhaps fast pace of daily lives; horse is not used to stopping for speaker to enjoy scenery.

4
Mood. "Dark" and "deep" usually suggest something frightening, yet here, combined with "lovely," suggest the appeal of the mysterious.

5 Making Inferences
What might be the speaker's "promises"? Answers may include speaker's responsibilities and obligations.

Stopping by Woods on a Snowy Evening

discuss the different effects of each group's interpretation.

Ask students to define **theme,** and then have them read the introductory passage. Tell them that a work of literature may have more than one main idea. As students read the poems in this section, alert them to the poems' meanings.

> **TRANSPARENCY 38**
> **Reader Response**
> *Jewels in the Crown* – invites students to explore specific words or images that make a strong impression.

VISUAL CONNECTIONS
Ideas for Writing
Many people see snow as a treacherous and dangerous element of nature. Others, however, regard it as serene and beautiful. Ask each student to imagine that he or she is alone in the snow scene depicted here. Then have students describe what their actions, thoughts, and feelings might be in this situation. Encourage students to create images that appeal to all five senses.

FOR STUDY AND DISCUSSION
1a. To enjoy loveliness of woods filling up with snow. **1b.** Speaker's horse reacts as if event were unusual.
2a. Woods at evening, filling up with snow, near a frozen lake. **2b.** Suggests that time is Dec. 21, night of winter solstice; or suggests that speaker's sense of darkness is greater than ever before.
3a. Must hurry on to tend to affairs and fulfill obligations. **3b.** Answers will vary. Perhaps practical affairs or emotional ties.
4. Answers will vary. Students' interpretations should be based on details in poem. Should account for following: distance of woods from village; "darkest evening of the year"; what horse represents; "promises" speaker must keep.

456

For Study and Discussion

Analyzing and Interpreting the Poem

1a. Why has the speaker stopped? **b.** How do you know that it is unusual for the speaker to stop in these woods?

2a. Describe the scene that you see in the poem. **b.** What does the phrase "the darkest evening of the year" tell you?

3a. Why can't the speaker linger to look at the woods? **b.** What do you think his "promises" are?

4. This poem has been interpreted in a number of ways. Some readers believe that the woods in Frost's poem represent an escape from the world and its pressures. Others believe that the poem is about the obligations that keep people from enjoying the beauty of the world. Still others suggest that the word *sleep* in the last two lines of the poem is a reference to death. Do you agree with any of these interpretations? Give reasons for your answer.

456 POETRY

The Listeners
WALTER DE LA MARE

This poem contains many mysterious elements. What explanation can you offer for its strange events?

"Is there anybody there?" said the Traveler,
   Knocking on the moonlit door;
And his horse in the silence champed the grasses
   Of the forest's ferny floor;
And a bird flew up out of the turret,   5
   Above the Traveler's head:
And he smote upon the door again a second time;
   "Is there anybody there?" he said.
But no one descended to the Traveler;
   No head from the leaf-fringed sill   10

PORTFOLIO ASSESSMENT
Students may want to write a prologue to "The Listeners" in which they tell the event that precipitates the Traveler's visit. Has he come as a messenger? Is he looking for a lost relative or lover? Why does de la Mare describe him as lonely? Some students may want to write their prologue in the form of a letter to the Traveler from the listeners. Encourage students to use their imaginations to create a plausible scenario. (See *Portfolio Assessment and Professional Support Materials*.)

TRANSPARENCY 38
Reader Response
Jewels in the Crown – invites students to explore specific words or images that make a strong impression.

3
Phantom means "ghostly."

4
"Lone house" and "quiet moonlight" contribute to eerie **mood**.

5
Suggests listeners are dead.

6
Imagery. Strong visual image of phantoms crowding together in the moonlight on the staircase, listening to the Traveler call.

7
Traveler senses presence of listeners.

8
Traveler evidently returned to fulfill promise.

9
"The one man left awake" may mean that others are ghosts.

10
Only silence when Traveler is gone.

>   Leaned over and looked into his gray eyes,
>   Where he stood perplexed and still.
> 3 But only a host of phantom listeners
> 4   That dwelt in the lone house then
>   Stood listening in the quiet of the moonlight
> 5   To that voice from the world of men:
> 6 Stood thronging the faint moonbeams on the dark stair
>   That goes down to the empty hall,
>   Hearkening in an air stirred and shaken
>   By the lonely Traveler's call.
> 7 And he felt in his heart their strangeness,
>   Their stillness answering his cry,
>   While his horse moved, cropping the dark turf,
>   'Neath the starred and leafy sky;
>   For he suddenly smote on the door, even
>   Louder, and lifted his head—
> 8 "Tell them I came, and no one answered,
>   That I kept my word," he said.
>   Never the least stir made the listeners,
>   Though every word he spake
>   Fell echoing through the shadowiness of the still house
> 9   From the one man left awake:
>   Aye, they heard his foot upon the stirrup,
>   And the sound of iron on stone,
> 10 And how the silence surged softly backward,
>   When the plunging hoofs were gone.

458   POETRY

CLOSURE

Ask students to discuss the meaning of both "Stopping by Woods on a Snowy Evening" and "The Listeners." Encourage students to support their discussion with words or lines from the poems.

EXTENSION AND ENRICHMENT

Some students might collect folders of poems about one of the four seasons and illustrate their interpretations of the poems.

Others might transpose "The Listeners" into comic-strip format. How many lines of the poem are depicted in each frame? How do visual representations of both the Traveler and the "phantom listeners" differ? How do other details vary? Are all comic strips consistent with images in the poem?

For Study and Discussion

Analyzing and Interpreting the Poem

1. "The Listeners" tells of a man who knocks three times at the door of a house in a forest and, receiving no answer, mounts his horse and gallops away. **a.** Who do you think the Traveler is? **b.** Who do you think the listeners are?

2. Words like *phantom* in line 13 and *shadowiness* in line 31 add mystery to the poem. What other words can you find that contribute to the poem's eerie effect?

3. Why do you think the Traveler has come to the house? (What meaning do you see in lines 27–28?)

4. The Traveler is the central figure in the poem. Yet the poem is called "The Listeners." Why do you think the poet chose this title?

Writing About Literature

▶ **Interpreting a Poem**

In a short essay give your interpretation of "Stopping by Woods on a Snowy Evening" or "The Listeners." Support your interpretation with evidence from the poem. For assistance in planning and writing your paper, see the section called *Writing About Literature* at the back of this textbook.

▶ Before students begin this writing assignment, you may want to refer them to the **Writing About Literature** section on p. 688.

About the Authors

Robert Frost (1874–1963)

For a biography of the author, see page 179.

Walter de la Mare (1873–1956)

Walter de la Mare, who created magical worlds in his poems and stories, spent nearly twenty years as a bookkeeper in the London office of an oil company. In 1908 he received a grant that enabled him to become a full-time writer. Over a period of forty years he published many collections of enchanting poems and tales. "The Listeners" is famous for its beautiful music and its eerie mystery. According to one account, de la Mare got the idea for the poem from a class reunion. On the day that he and his former classmates were to meet at a school, no one but de la Mare appeared. The empty rooms and corridors of the building inspired him to write the poem.

FOR STUDY AND DISCUSSION

1a. Could be anyone on the journey through life. **1b.** Departed friends and relatives; may be ghosts or Traveler's memories of friends.
2. "Moonlit," "perplexed," "lone," "faint," "strangeness," "stillness," "dark," "silence."
3. Responses will vary. Encourage students to bring own meanings to poem. Traveler has returned to house to fulfill agreement to reunite with someone.
4. Enhances mystery by emphasizing those who are present to listen to Traveler, who may be phantoms that he cannot see or hear, but whose presence he can feel.

WRITING ABOUT LITERATURE

You might consider reading "Responding to Poetry" by Robert W. Blake and Anna Lunn in the *English Journal* (NCTE, February 1986). This article may give you some additional ideas of what to require in student responses to this assignment. Encourage your students to create their personal interpretation based on a close reading of the poem.

ABOUT THE AUTHOR
Walter de la Mare
Walter de la Mare began his literary career in 1902 with a volume of poetry for children entitled *Songs of Childhood*. However, it was *The Listeners and Other Poems* in 1912 that won him critical acclaim. These poems are representative of de la Mare's use of fairy tale and legend qualities that create an atmosphere of magical enchantment.

OBJECTIVES

The overall aim is for students to analyze the use of **repetition** and **rhyme** in poems by Edgar Allan Poe, Vachel Lindsay, and William Shakespeare. For a complete list of objectives, see the **Teacher's Notes.**

FOCUS / MOTIVATION

Before poetry was written, it was memorized and passed down orally from generation to generation. Ask students to speculate on why the devices of repetition and rhyme are helpful in memorizing poems.

PRESENTATION

Ask students to recall familiar songs on the enduring theme of lost love. What kind of music is expected in a song about love lost through death? Suggest that students listen to learn how "Annabel Lee" achieves a similar musical effect

TEACHING RESOURCES D
Teacher's Notes, p. 49
Study Guide, p. 51
Selection Test, p. 54

AV RESOURCES BINDER
Audiocassette 3, Side A

PREREADING FOCUS

Since the art of composing poetry started before people were able to write down their words, **repetition** and **rhyme** served as memory aids as poems were passed down from generation to generation. Repetition and rhyme also add to the enjoyment of a poem because we are often able to predict what will follow because of a pattern of rhyme or because a phrase has already appeared in the poem.

The headnote emphasizes that repetition and rhyme are devices that not only please the reader's ear but also convey meaning and emphasis.

Annabel Lee

1
Setting. Poe sets poem in fairy-tale time and place, lending magical feeling to poem.

2
Speaker notes strength of their love; "no other thought" implies Annabel Lee's complete devotion.

460

Sound and Meaning

REPETITION AND RHYME

You have seen that poets carefully select and arrange words to appeal to your senses, your imagination, and your emotions. To convey meaning, poets also use devices of sound. One of the most important devices at the poet's disposal is *repetition*. Repetition may occur in the form of *rhyme*, in which similar sounds are repeated within or at the end of lines. Repetition may also occur with a single letter or group of letters, as in this line from "A Parrot" (page 448): "That *s*tuttered *s*taccato *s*cream." This kind of repetition is called *alliteration* (ə-lĭt′ə-rā′shən). The poet may also choose to repeat a word, a phrase, or an entire line. The term for this kind of repetition is *refrain*. In John Masefield's poem "Trade Winds" (page 447), the refrain appears at the end of each stanza.

While repetition is one of the elements that give us pleasure in reading and listening to poetry, it is also a way of emphasizing and communicating meaning.

Annabel Lee

EDGAR ALLAN POE

Poe claimed that in his poetry he chose each sound to produce a desired effect. Read this poem aloud, noting particularly his use of repetition and rhyme. Then ask yourself how these sounds help reinforce the speaker's feelings.

1   It was many and many a year ago,
        In a kingdom by the sea,
    That a maiden there lived whom you may know
        By the name of Annabel Lee;
2   And this maiden she lived with no other thought   5
        Than to love and be loved by me.

460 POETRY

*I was a child and *she* was a child,
    In this kingdom by the sea,
But we loved with a love that was more than love—
    I and my Annabel Lee—
With a love that the wingèd seraphs° of Heaven
    Coveted° her and me.

And this was the reason that, long ago,
    In this kingdom by the sea,
A wind blew out of a cloud, chilling
    My beautiful Annabel Lee;
So that her highborn kinsmen came
    And bore her away from me,
To shut her up in a sepulcher°
    In this kingdom by the sea.

The angels, not half so happy in Heaven,
    Went envying her and me:
Yes!—that was the reason (as all men know,
    In this kingdom by the sea)
That the wind came out of the cloud by night,
    Chilling and killing my Annabel Lee.

But our love it was stronger by far than the love
    Of those who were older than we—
    Of many far wiser than we—
And neither the angels in Heaven above,
    Nor the demons down under the sea,
Can ever dissever° my soul from the soul
    Of the beautiful Annabel Lee:

For the moon never beams, without bringing me dreams
    Of the beautiful Annabel Lee;
And the stars never rise, but I feel the bright eyes
    Of the beautiful Annabel Lee:
And so, all the nighttide,° I lie down by the side
Of my darling—my darling—my life and my bride,
    In the sepulcher there by the sea—
    In her tomb by the sounding sea.

11. **seraphs** (sĕr'əfs): angels.
12. **Coveted** (kŭv'ĭ-tĭd): envied.

19. **sepulcher** (sĕp'əl-kər): a tomb or burial place.

32. **dissever** (dĭ-sĕv'ər): separate.

38. **nighttide:** nighttime.

Annabel Lee **461**

COOPERATIVE LEARNING

Have students work together in small groups to analyze Poe's use of **alliteration** in the poem. Have each group select one of its members or take turns line by line to read aloud the first stanza of the poem. Ask the groups to look and listen for repeated consonant sounds (such as the *m* and *l* in this stanza). Have groups repeat the process for the last two stanzas of the poem. Encourage students to report to the class how Poe's use of alliteration contributes to the **mood** and the meaning of the poem.

TRANSPARENCIES 35 & 36
Fine Art
Theme: *Special Language, Special Meaning* – features artwork in which the artist attempts to express an opinion about a specific idea.

VISUAL CONNECTIONS
Ideas for Writing
A refrain, like a chorus in music, is a form of repetition that occurs at regular intervals in a poem, usually at the end of each stanza. Have students look closely at this watercolor. Ask them to discuss what it suggests about time, place, and mood, or about the woman's movements, thoughts, and feelings. From their discussion of the watercolor, students might write a four-line refrain that could be appropriately inserted at the end of each stanza of ''Annabel Lee.''

Annabel Lee (1911) by W. L. Taylor. Watercolor.

TRANSPARENCY 37
Reader Response
Charting a Response to Poetry – prompts students to respond to a poem.

For Study and Discussion

Analyzing and Interpreting the Poem

1. What do you learn about Annabel Lee in the first three stanzas of the poem?

2a. Whom does the speaker blame for Annabel Lee's death? **b.** What reason does he give in lines 11–12 and lines 21–22?

3a. Why does the speaker believe that his soul and the soul of Annabel Lee cannot be separated? **b.** How is he continually reminded of her?

4a. Which sounds are repeated with frequency? **b.** How do these sounds reinforce the overall mood and meaning of the poem?

Literary Elements

Understanding Repetition in Poetry

In "Annabel Lee" Poe repeats certain words, sounds, and phrases. The name Annabel Lee
1 appears at least once in every stanza. What other words and phrases are repeated several
2 times? What ideas and feelings are emphasized by these repetitions?
3 Rhyme is a form of repetition. What words are repeatedly linked together through rhyme?

Sometimes words within a single line are rhymed. This kind of rhyme is called **internal rhyme**. Look at line 26:

Chilling and *killing* my Annabel Lee.

4 How many times does Poe use internal rhyme in the last stanza?

For Oral Reading

Avoiding Singsong

In reading poetry aloud, people sometimes enjoy the sounds so much that they ignore the meaning of individual lines. Unfortunately, they may read in a monotonous pattern called *singsong*.

One way to avoid singsong is to read a poem naturally. Do not stress rhyme by overstressing accented syllables, by raising your voice, or by pausing mechanically at the end of each line. Follow the punctuation and meaning of the poem.

In "Annabel Lee," how would you read lines 3–4 in the first stanza? Lines 9–10 in the second stanza? Lines 23–25 in the fourth stanza? Practice reading the poem aloud, paying close attention to meaning as well as sound.

Focus on Writing a Poem

Experimenting with Sound Effects

Reading "Annabel Lee" aloud shows you how important **sound effects** can be in a poem. Here are some sound effects that you can use in your own poems:

repetition	rhyme
alliteration	refrain

Choose *two* of these devices and experiment with them. Write a few lines of prose or poetry in which you use each sound effect. For example, you might create a sentence with alliteration like the following: "The *w*inter *w*ind *w*ailed *w*ildly with a *w*hine." Save your writing.

FOR STUDY AND DISCUSSION

1. Lived many years ago in "kingdom by the sea"; she and speaker loved each other; she died; her "highborn kinsmen" took her away.
2a. Angels. 2b. Angels envied his and Annabel Lee's love.
3a. Their love is too strong; spiritual love has joined their souls forever. 3b. Moon brings dreams of her; stars remind him of her bright eyes.
4a. Answers will vary. Some repeated sounds are *m, l, ing, s,* long *e*. 4b. Answers will vary. Hypnotic, mournful mood reinforces supernatural, eerie thought of two lovers still communing even though one is dead.

LITERARY ELEMENTS

1. These words occur more than twice in poem: "love, sea, kingdom."
2. Repetition of "love" suggests constancy of love between speaker and Annabel Lee, repetition of "sea" suggests both constancy and death; "a kingdom by the sea" suggests containment, as does "sepulcher there by the sea"; speaker's wish to lie down with Annabel Lee "in her tomb by the sounding sea" suggests he wants to die so that he will be reunited with her; repetition of "love" and "sea" suggests themes of love and death are linked.
3. "Annabel Lee," "sea," "me," "we."
4. Three instances of internal rhyme: "beams / dreams," "rise / eyes," "nighttide / side."

Annabel Lee   463

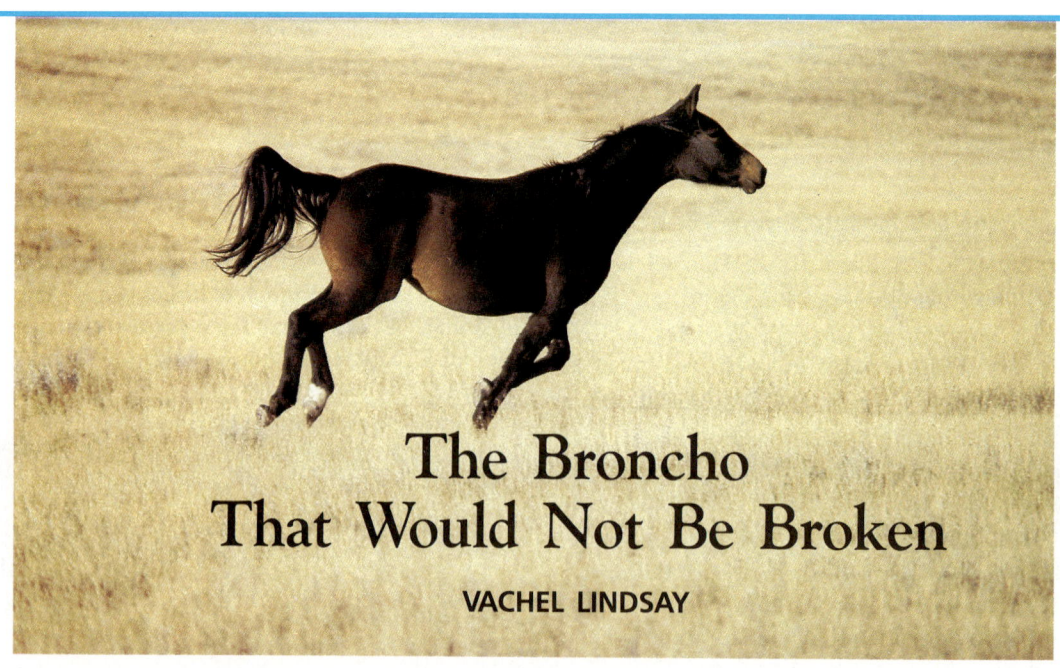

The Broncho That Would Not Be Broken

VACHEL LINDSAY

In this poem, note the refrain at the end of each stanza. What other patterns of repetition can you find? How do they reinforce the meaning of the poem?

A little colt—broncho, loaned to the farm
To be broken in time without fury or harm,
Yet black crows flew past you, shouting alarm,
Calling "Beware," with lugubrious° singing. . . .
The butterflies there in the bush were romancing, 5
The smell of the grass caught your soul in a trance,
So why be a-fearing the spurs and the traces,
O broncho that would not be broken of dancing?

You were born with the pride of the lords great and olden
Who dance, through the ages, in corridors golden. 10
In all the wide farmplace the person most human.
You spoke out so plainly with squealing and capering,
With whinnying, snorting, contorting, and prancing,
As you dodged your pursuers, looking askance,
With Greek-footed figures, and Parthenon° paces, 15
O broncho that would not be broken of dancing.

The grasshoppers cheered. "Keep whirling," they said.
The insolent sparrows called from the shed,
"If men will not laugh, make them wish they were dead."
But arch° were your thoughts, all malice displacing. 20

4. **lugubrious** (lōō-gōō′brē-əs): sad.

15. **Parthenon** (pär′thə-nän′): an ancient Greek temple decorated with sculptures of lively horses.

20. **arch:** sly.

464 POETRY

7 Though the horse-killers came, with snakewhips advancing.
 You bantered and cantered away your last chance.
8 And they scourged you with hell in their speech and their faces,
 O broncho that would not be broken of dancing.

9 "Nobody cares for you," rattled the crows,   25
 As you dragged the whole reaper, next day, down the rows.
 The three mules held back, yet you danced on your toes.
 You pulled like a racer, and kept the mules chasing.
 You tangled the harness with bright eyes side-glancing,
 While the drunk driver bled you—a pole for a lance— 30
 And the giant mules bit at you—keeping their places.
 O broncho that would not be broken of dancing.

 In that last afternoon your boyish heart broke.
 The hot wind came down like a sledge-hammer stroke.
10 The blood-sucking flies to a rare feast awoke.   35
 And they searched out your wounds, your death warrant tracing.
11 And the merciful men, their religion enhancing,
 Stopped the red reaper to give you a chance.
 Then you died on the prairie, and scorned all disgraces,
 O broncho that would not be broken of dancing.   40

For Study and Discussion

Analyzing and Interpreting the Poem

1. What does the word *dancing* tell you about the broncho's natural grace and spirit?

2. What words in the poem describe the broncho's playfulness?

3. How do the men try to subdue the colt and break its spirit?

4. Other animals witness what is happening to the broncho. **a.** Which of them are in sympathy with the colt? **b.** In what way are the "broken" creatures cruel to the colt?

5. By dying, the broncho "scorned all disgraces." What disgraces would he have endured had he continued to live?

6. Explain in your own words what this poem is saying about "breaking," or destroying, nature's creatures.

Literary Elements

Understanding the Refrain

A phrase or line that is repeated regularly in a poem is called a **refrain**. A refrain usually occurs at the end of a stanza. A line that is repeated often in a poem can be easily learned and remembered. In folk songs and ballads, you will often find refrains at the end of each stanza, where an audience is expected to join in the singing.

1 What is the refrain in Lindsay's poem? How
2 does it foreshadow the broncho's fate?

The Broncho That Would Not Be Broken 465

PRESENTATION

To dramatize the importance of sound effects in poetry, recall such nursery rhymes as "Mary, Mary, Quite Contrary" or read aloud a Dr. Seuss passage illustrating **alliteration** and other devices utilizing repetition of sound. Or list on the board such clichés as "the more the merrier," "helter-skelter," and "short and sweet." Without using technical terms, guide students to identify different patterns of repeated sounds. Ask students why these musical devices have such wide appeal. Present "Full Fathom Five" as a poem that makes subtle but powerful use of sound effects.

Be sure to discuss the headnote with students before they read the poem. To ensure that students hear the musical quality of the poem, you may wish to read it aloud.

TEACHING RESOURCES D
Teacher's Notes, p. 72
Study Guide, p. 73
Building Vocabulary, p. 75
Selection Vocabulary Test, p. 85

AV RESOURCES BINDER
Audiocassette 3, Side A

Full Fathom Five

1
Alliteration. Sounds of *f* and *th*. Long *i* sound is also repeated.

2
These things would normally deteriorate in the sea.

3
Onomatopoeia. "Ding-dong" and rhyming words imitate sound of bell.

4
Alliteration. Sounds of *h* and *d*.

FOR STUDY AND DISCUSSION
1a. Bones have become coral; eyes, pearls. **1b.** Rather than decomposing, parts of body have become precious objects.
2. Answers will vary. One of awe and mystery.

LITERARY ELEMENTS
1. The *ur* sound in "pearls" and "were"; the *th* in "those" and "that"; the related *th* sound in "nothing" and "doth"; the *z* sound in "pearls" and "eyes"; the *a* sound in "fade" and "sea-change." Note that long vowels in "eyes," "fade," and "sea-change" and repetition of consonant sounds give these lines quality of an incantation, as if a magic spell were being intoned.
2. Alliteration occurs in "hark/hear" and "ding/dong."

Full Fathom Five
WILLIAM SHAKESPEARE

This song is sung by Ariel, an airy spirit in The Tempest, *one of Shakespeare's plays. Prince Ferdinand believes that his father has been drowned in a shipwreck. The song tells him of a magical transformation that has taken place. Read the poem aloud. What mood is evoked by the music of its sounds?*

1 Full fathom° five thy father lies:
   Of his bones are coral made;
   Those are pearls that were his eyes;
   Nothing of him that doth fade
2 But doth suffer° a sea-change
   Into something rich and strange.
3 Sea nymphs° hourly ring his knell:°
         Ding-dong.
4 Hark! now I hear them—ding-dong, bell.

1. **fathom** (făth′əm): a depth of 6 feet (about 2 meters).
5. **suffer:** undergo. 7. **Sea nymphs** (nĭmfs): goddesses once thought to inhabit the sea. **knell** (nĕl): the tolling of a death bell.

For Study and Discussion

Analyzing and Interpreting the Poem

1a. According to the song, what change has the sea made in Ferdinand's father? **b.** Why is this change "rich and strange"?

2. How would you describe the mood of this poem?

Literary Elements

Understanding How Sounds Convey Feeling

You have seen that a poet makes music by repeating key words and lines and by using rhyme. A poet also makes music by repeating the sounds of certain consonants and vowels.

Look again at the opening line of Shakespeare's poem: "Full *f*athom *f*ive thy *f*ather lies." Shakespeare uses several words that begin with the same consonant sound: **f**. He also repeats sounds in the middle of words. The sound **th** is repeated in *fathom*, *thy*, and *father*. This technique is known as **alliteration** (ə-lĭt′ə-rā′shən).

The sounds **f** and **th** are gentle sounds. They do not explode the way the sound **p** does in this line: "Peter Piper picked a peck of pickled peppers." The long vowel sound in *five*, *thy*, and *lies* helps slow up the movement of the line and thereby contributes to the mood of the poem.

1 What sounds are repeated in lines 3–5? Can
2 you find another example of alliteration in the poem?

466 POETRY

About the Authors

Edgar Allan Poe (1809–1849)

Edgar Allan Poe was born in Boston to a family of traveling actors. After his mother died, he was taken into the home of a wealthy Virginia merchant named John Allan. Although Poe took Allan as his middle name, his relations with his guardian were always strained. In 1826 he entered the University of Virginia but had to leave within a year because of his heavy gambling debts. He then enlisted in the army and served two years. John Allan helped him secure an appointment to West Point, but Poe got himself dismissed for misconduct. At this point he turned to writing and editing in order to earn a living. In 1836 he married his young cousin Virginia, but this marriage ended tragically in 1847, when Virginia died of tuberculosis. Poe died in poverty at the age of forty.

Despite his personal difficulties, Poe produced a remarkable body of short stories, poems, and essays. His short-story masterpieces include "The Tell-Tale Heart," "The Cask of Amontillado," "The Pit and the Pendulum," and "The Fall of the House of Usher"—strange tales of terror and fantasy. Among his most beautiful and melodic poems are "Eldorado," "The Raven," and "The Bells."

Vachel Lindsay (1879–1931)

Vachel Lindsay was born in Springfield, Illinois. As a young man, he took long, solitary walking tours throughout America. Called the "vagabond poet," he hoped to convert people to a doctrine of life's beauty and social reform. He became famous with the publication of his poems "General William Booth Enters into Heaven" (1913) and "The Congo" (1914). Like many of Lindsay's poems, these lend themselves to being chanted or sung, which is how the poet himself delivered them before large and enthusiastic audiences.

William Shakespeare (1564–1616)

William Shakespeare is generally considered the greatest dramatist—some believe the greatest writer—in the English language. He was born in Stratford-on-Avon in England. As a young man, he journeyed to London, where he joined an acting company. He wrote thirty-seven plays—comedies, tragedies, romances, and historical dramas. In addition to plays, he wrote some of the most magnificent sonnets in our language. Today he is probably the world's most widely read and performed playwright.

OBJECTIVES The overall aim is for students to demonstrate an understanding of the use of **onomatopoeia** and **rhythm** in Alfred Noyes's "The Highwayman." For a complete list of objectives, see the **Teacher's Notes**.	**VOCABULARY** The underlined words are in the Glossary. Before students read the poem, you may want to familiarize them with these words and those numbered beside the lines of the poem.	**FOCUS / MOTIVATION** Start a discussion of famous outlaws, such as Robin Hood, who have been transformed into heroes. Include current motion picture and television characters.

TEACHING RESOURCES D
Teacher's Notes, p. 77
Study Guide, p. 79
Building Vocabulary, p. 83
Selection Vocabulary Test, p. 85
Selection Test, p. 86

AV RESOURCES BINDER
Audiocassette 3, Side A

PREREADING FOCUS
The headnote emphasizes that **rhythm** not only gives poetry a musical quality but can also be used to reflect the action in a poem. The popularity of "The Highwayman" is largely due to the drama created by the poem's sound devices, **rhythm**, and visual **imagery**.

ONOMATOPOEIA AND RHYTHM

In "The Wreck of the *Hesperus*" (page 164), Longfellow describes the snow falling into the sea by saying that the "snow fell hissing in the brine." The word *hissing* to some degree imitates the actual sound made. Longfellow is making use of *onomatopoeia* (ŏn′ə-măt′ə-pē′ə), a technique that is commonly used by poets.

Rhythm is the pattern of stressed and unstressed sounds in a line of poetry. Rhythm contributes to the musical quality of a poem. It can also be used to imitate action and to give emphasis to key words and ideas.

The Highwayman

ALFRED NOYES

Historically, the highwayman was an outlaw who held up travelers on public roads. In literature, he often appears as a handsome, bold, and romantic figure. This poem is well known for its exciting story and captivating sound. As you read the poem aloud, see if you can hear the rhythm of horses' hoofs.

The Highwayman

1
Imagery. Images appealing to both sight and physical sensation create an atmosphere of mystery and suspense.

2
Repetition. Creates exciting action.

3
Use to answer **study questions 2a** and **2b**, p. 472.

Part 1

1 The wind was a <u>torrent</u> of darkness among the gusty trees,
  The moon was a ghostly galleon° tossed upon cloudy seas,
  The road was a ribbon of moonlight over the purple <u>moor</u>,
2 And the highwayman came riding—
    Riding—riding—   5
  The highwayman came riding, up to the old inn door.

3 He'd a French cocked hat on his forehead, a bunch of lace
      at his chin,
  A coat of the claret° velvet, and breeches of brown doe skin;
  They fitted with never a wrinkle: his boots were up to the
      thigh!
  And he rode with a jeweled twinkle,   10
    His pistol butts a-twinkle,
  His rapier hilt° a-twinkle, under the jeweled sky.

2. **galleon** (găl′ē-ən): a large sailing ship.

8. **claret** (klăr′ət): deep red, like claret wine.

12. **rapier** (rā′pē-ər) **hilt:** the handle of a light sword.

468 POETRY

PRESENTATION
Read the headnote to introduce poem. Then offer the following summary of the first thirty lines to arouse students' interest: The highwayman rides up to the window of his beloved Bess, the landlord's daughter. When he taps on her shutters with his whip and then whistles, Bess appears. He informs her that he is after a "prize," some gold, and then he will come back to her. She is to look for him "by moonlight." Little does he know that his words are being overheard by the ostler, Tim.

This poem lends itself to dramatic interpretation. After students have listened to your reading, encourage them to follow in their books as each stanza of the poem is read aloud a second time by student volunteers.

---

4 Over the cobbles he clattered and clashed in the dark innyard
And he tapped with his whip on the shutters, but all was locked and barred;
He whistled a tune to the window, and who should be waiting there   15
5 But the landlord's black-eyed daughter,
   Bess, the landlord's daughter,
Plaiting° a dark red love knot into her long black hair.

And dark in the dark old innyard a stable wicket creaked
6 Where Tim the ostler° listened; his face was white and peaked;   20
His eyes were hollows of madness, his hair like moldy hay,
But he loved the landlord's daughter,
   The landlord's red-lipped daughter,
Dumb as a dog he listened, and he heard the robber say—

7 "One kiss, my bonny sweetheart, I'm after a prize tonight,   25
But I shall be back with the yellow gold before the morning light;
Yet, if they press me sharply, and harry° me through the day,
8 Then look for me by moonlight,
   Watch for me by moonlight,
9 I'll come to thee by moonlight, though hell should bar the way."   30

10 He rose upright in the stirrups; he scarce could reach her hand,
But she loosened her hair i' the casement!° His face burned like a brand
As the black cascade of perfume came tumbling over his breast;
And he kissed its waves in the moonlight,
   (Oh, sweet black waves in the moonlight!)   35
Then he tugged at his rein in the moonlight, and galloped away to the west.

Part 2

11 He did not come in the dawning; he did not come at noon;
And out o' the tawny sunset, before the rise o' the moon,
When the road was a gypsy's ribbon, looping the purple moor,
A redcoat troop came marching—   40
   Marching—marching—
12 King George's men came marching, up to the old inn door.

18. **Plaiting:** braiding.

20. **ostler** (ŏs′lər): stableman; also called *hostler* (hŏs′lər).

27. **harry:** attack repeatedly.

32. **casement:** a window that opens outward on hinges.

4
Onomatopoeia. "Clattered" and "clashed" suggest sounds of hoofs on cobbles.

5
Use to answer **study questions 2a** and **2b,** p. 472.

6
Foreshadowing. Tim's eavesdropping suggests that he is going to make trouble for the lovers.

7 Drawing Conclusions
What is the meaning of "after a prize"? Highwayman plans to rob someone.

8
Use to answer **study question 4a,** p. 472.

9
Prophetic, in view of the tragedy that occurs.

10
The **rhythm** in each stanza is steady, echoing the sound of the highwayman's horse's hoofs and symbolizing the fateful, tragic progression of events in the poem.

11 Drawing Conclusions
Of what significance is the failure of the highwayman to arrive during the day? Indicates there is trouble.

12
Setting. Eighteenth-century England.

WRITING LINK
Have students imagine the diary account that Tim the ostler might have made in which he tells the story from his point of view and explains his role in it. Tell students to write this account in their journals. As an alternative or additional activity, students may wish to write an account of the events in the poem as they might have appeared in the local newspaper.

They said no word to the landlord, they drank his ale instead,
But they gagged his daughter and bound her to the foot of
    her narrow bed;
Two of them knelt at her casement, with muskets at their side!   45
13 There was death at every window;
    And hell at one dark window;
For Bess could see, through her casement, the road that *he*
    would ride.

They had tied her up to attention, with many a sniggering jest;
They had bound a musket beside her, with the barrel
    beneath her breast!   50
14 "Now keep good watch!" and they kissed her. She heard the
    dead man say—
Look for me by moonlight;
    Watch for me by moonlight;
I'll come to thee by moonlight, though hell should bar the way!

15 She twisted her hands behind her; but all the knots held good!   55
She writhed her hands till her fingers were wet with sweat
    or blood!
They stretched and strained in the darkness, and the hours
    crawled by like years,
Till, now, on the stroke of midnight,
    Cold, on the stroke of midnight,
16 The tip of one finger touched it! The trigger at least was hers!   60

The tip of one finger touched it; she strove no more for the
    rest!
Up, she stood to attention, with the barrel beneath her breast,
She would not risk their hearing; she would not strive
    again;
17 For the road lay bare in the moonlight;
    Blank and bare in the moonlight;   65
And the blood in her veins in the moonlight throbbed to
    her love's refrain.

---

13 Foreshadowing. A tragedy is about to occur.

14 Making Inferences *The soldiers know that she is waiting for the highwayman. How could they have known his plans?* Tim, the jealous stableman, told them.

15 Description. Suggests painful determination.

16 Drawing Conclusions *What do you think Bess is trying to do?* Preparing to fire gun at herself to warn the highwayman, rather than let the redcoats kill him.

17 Repetition. Narrative intensifies as it approaches the climax.

HISTORY LINK
The poem refers to the soldiers as "redcoats," a term the American colonists used for British soldiers before and during the American Revolution. Have students use an encyclopedia or other reference source to learn more about the Colonial Period in American history. Encourage students to find out about life during these periods, including how people traveled and what the inns in which they stayed were like.

TRANSPARENCY 39
Literary Elements
Sound Effects in Poetry – explores a variety of sound effects used in poetry, such as rhyme, rhythm, refrain, alliteration, and onomatopoeia.

---

18 *Tlot-tlot; tlot-tlot!* Had they heard it? The horse hoofs ringing
    clear;
Tlot-tlot, tlot-tlot, in the distance? Were they deaf that they
    did not hear?
Down the ribbon of moonlight, over the brow of the hill,
The highwayman came riding,   70
    Riding, riding!
19 The redcoats looked to their priming! She stood up, straight
    and still!

Tlot-tlot, in the frosty silence! *Tlot-tlot*, in the echoing night!
Nearer he came and nearer! Her face was like a light!
Her eyes grew wide for a moment; she drew one last deep
    breath,   75
Then her finger moved in the moonlight,
    Her musket shattered the moonlight,
20 Shattered her breast in the moonlight and warned him—
    with her death.

He turned; he spurred to the westward; he did not know
    who stood
Bowed, with her head o'er the musket, drenched with her
    own red blood!   80
Not till the dawn he heard it, his face grew gray to hear
How Bess, the landlord's daughter,
    The landlord's black-eyed daughter,
Had watched for her love in the moonlight, and died in the
    darkness there.

21 Back, he spurred like a madman, shrieking a curse to the sky,   85
With the white road smoking behind him, and his rapier
    brandished high!
Blood-red were his spurs i' the golden noon; wine-red his
    velvet coat,
When they shot him down on the highway,
    Down like a dog on the highway,
22 And he lay in his blood on the highway, with a bunch of
    lace at his throat.   90

18
Onomatopoeia. Conveys sound of horse's hoofs.

19
What are the redcoats' intentions? They are going to kill the highwayman.

20
Plot. Climax occurs as Bess sacrifices herself to warn her lover.

21 Summarizing
What is the highwayman's response when he hears the news? In his rage, he rides down open road toward redcoats.

22
"Lace at his throat" is striking contrast to "shot . . ./Down like a dog."

The Highwayman 471

Portfolio Assessment

Groups of students may be interested in organizing and presenting a choral reading of "The Highwayman" in which they read much as a chorus would sing. Suggest that groups assign appropriate lines to different types of voices, rehearse, and then present their reading to the class. Readings may be audiotaped or videotaped. Suggest they include a paragraph in their portfolios to describe their experience. (See *Portfolio Assessment and Professional Support Materials*.)

FOR STUDY AND DISCUSSION

1. Begins at night; soldiers come at twilight next day; highwayman returns during night. At dawn, discovers that Bess shot herself, returns by noon. Reference to innyard and "stable wicket" suggests country inn as scene. Redcoats are British soldiers; reference to King George and description of clothing establish time as eighteenth century.
2a. The highwayman and Bess.
2b. Highwayman wears French hat, lace at chin, velvet coat, doeskin breeches, boots; carries pistols and rapier. Bess has black eyes, long black hair. 2c. Tim is secretly in love with Bess and is jealous of highwayman. He overhears highwayman tell Bess that he will return. It may be inferred that Tim betrays highwayman to soldiers.
3. Gives soldiers clear view of highwayman.
4a. Lines 28–30 are repeated as ll. 52–54. 4b. Repetition creates suspense; readers know highwayman will return and ride into trap.
5. Transform love story into legend; highwayman and Bess become immortal lovers, who play out scene of happy return over and over again.

LITERARY ELEMENTS
Understanding How Sound Imitates Action
1. *Gusty, tapped, creaked, sniggering, tlot-tlot, shrieking, clatters, clangs.*
2. "When the Frost Is on the Punkin": *mumble*—sound of hummingbirds; *buzzin'*—sound of bees. "Trade Winds": *squeaking*—flapping noise of sail. "The Broncho That Would Not Be Broken": *squealing, whinnying, snorting*—sounds colt makes. "Full Fathom Five": *ding-dong*—sound of bell.

And still of a winter's night, they say, when the wind is in the trees,
When the moon is a ghostly galleon tossed upon cloudy seas,
When the road is a ribbon of moonlight over the purple moor,
A highwayman comes riding—
   Riding—riding—   95
A highwayman comes riding, up to the old inn door.

Over the cobbles he clatters and clangs in the dark innyard;
And he taps with his whip on the shutters, but all is locked and barred;
He whistles a tune to the window, and who should be waiting there
But the landlord's black-eyed daughter,   100
   Bess, the landlord's daughter,
Plaiting a dark red love knot into her long black hair.

For Study and Discussion

Analyzing and Interpreting the Poem

1. This poem tells a story. Where and when does the story take place? Find details in the poem that help you to establish the time and place. (What do lines 40–42 tell you?)
2a. Who are the major characters in the story?
b. What details in the poem tell you what they look like? c. What role does Tim the ostler play in the story?
3. There are many references to moonlight in the poem. The meeting of lovers by moonlight is traditional in stories of romance. Why is moonlight also important to the action of the story?
4a. Which lines in the fifth stanza are echoed in the second part of the poem? b. Why do you think the poet wants you to recall these lines?
5. How do the last two stanzas add to the mystery and romance of the poem?

Literary Elements

Understanding How Sound Imitates Action

In poetry words are often chosen because their sounds seem to imitate the action they describe. In line 13 of Noyes's poem, we read

> Over the cobbles he clattered and clashed in the dark innyard

The words *clattered* and *clashed* suggest the actual sounds of hoofs on the cobbles. We call this effect **onomatopoeia** (ŏn′ə-măt′ə-pē′ə).
1 What other examples of onomatopoeia can you find in the poem?
2 Find examples of onomatopoeia in the following poems and tell what each sound suggests:

"When the Frost Is on the Punkin" page 443, stanza 2
"Trade Winds" page 447, stanza 2
"The Broncho That Would Not Be Broken" page 464, stanza 2
"Full Fathom Five" page 466

CLOSURE
Ask students to define **onomatopoeia** and **rhythm**, to give examples of the terms from Noyes's "The Highwayman," and to explain what the examples add to the poem.

EXTENSION AND ENRICHMENT
Because of vivid visual imagery in this poem, the class might work together on a butcher-paper mural depicting major scenes in the story.

Since "The Highwayman" also contains abundant auditory images, several students might rewrite the story as a radio script, complete with sound effects. If possible, make a tape recording to be played for the class.

Several students might like to work together to compose an updated version of "The Highwayman," featuring contemporary characters.

Responding to Rhythm

Rhythm refers to the pattern of stressed and unstressed sounds in a line of poetry. Rhythm contributes to the musical quality of a poem. Rhythm can also be used to imitate the action being described in the poem.

Reread the first two lines of "The Highwayman" and listen to the way your voice rises and falls on the syllables of the words:

> The **wind** was a **tor**rent of **dark**ness a**mong** the **gus**ty **trees**,
> The **moon** was a **ghost**ly **gall**eon **tossed** upon **cloud**y **seas**,

The syllables in boldface are those that are stressed when the lines are read aloud. The other syllables are unstressed.

Using your finger, tap out the rhythm of lines 3–6. What pattern do you get?

Below are lines 3–6. The stressed syllables are marked (´); the unstressed syllables (˘). Is this the pattern you tapped out?

> The road was a ribbon of moonlight over the purple moor,
> And the highwayman came riding—
> Riding—riding—
> The highwayman came riding, up to the old inn door.

Do you hear the rhythm of horses' hoofs? Reread the poem, listening carefully to its rhythm.

For Oral Reading

Presenting a Choral Reading

"The Highwayman" lends itself well to choral presentation. In the choral reading of a poem, speaking voices are used much as singing voices are used in a chorus. Some lines are assigned to individuals as solo parts; some lines are assigned to small groups of voices; some are assigned to all voices.

Choral reading takes a good deal of preparation and practice. You must decide which lines are best for solo voices and which are best for many voices. You must interpret how lines are to be read. You must determine when the voices should be raised or lowered and when the pace of reading should be stepped up or slowed down.

When you have decided how you wish to read the poem, choose a chorus leader. The chorus leader acts as a conductor who signals when different members of the chorus are to speak. If there is a tape recorder available, record your practice sessions. Listen to the tapes and suggest ways to improve the performance of the group.

About the Author

Alfred Noyes (1880–1958)

The Granger Collection, New York

Alfred Noyes drew material for some of his best-known poems from England's real and legendary past. He wrote "The Highwayman" at night while he was visiting Bagshot Heath, a lonely moor in England that outlaws had roamed two centuries before. Besides poetry, Noyes wrote plays, literary criticism, and an autobiography called *Two Worlds from Memory*. The first of his worlds was England, and the second was America. Noyes taught English literature at Princeton University from 1914 to 1923.

Responding to Rhythm
Some students might have difficulty with this concept. You may wish to divide class into groups to identify the pattern of stressed and unstressed syllables as you read the passage aloud. Have groups compare patterns.

FOR ORAL READING
You may want to show students a transparency of the poem with the following markings to indicate how the lines should be interpreted:
Pause = //
Soft voice = ↓
Loud voice = ↑
Fast pace = shade passage
Emphasis = underscore words

ABOUT THE AUTHOR
Two volumes of poetry, *Forty Singing Seaman* (1907) and *Drake* (1908), show his patriotism and love for the sea. His *Collected Poems* (1950) contains some of his best-known poems, similar to "The Highwayman."

OBJECTIVES
The overall aim is for students to identify narrative techniques in "The Golden Vanity" and "The Pied Piper of Hamelin." For a complete list of objectives, see the **Teacher's Notes**.

VOCABULARY
The underlined words are in the Glossary. Students should note that the repetition of words advances the story in the poem.

FOCUS / MOTIVATION
Ask students to recall the narrative poems "The Highwayman" and "The Broncho That Would Not Be Broken." Have them list on the board some of the characteristics these poems have in common (tell story, contain repetition, etc.).

PREREADING FOCUS
The headnote emphasizes that narrative poetry contains the elements that short stories do: action, setting, characters, and a story line. **Ballads** are one type of narrative poem. Characteristics of ballads include the following: story revolves around an extraordinary event; story concerns one incident; storyteller does not make judgments about the characters or events; the language is plain; and repetition is used as musical device (an aid to memory when ballads were passed down orally) and for dramatic effect.

Types of Poetry

NARRATIVE POETRY

A *narrative* poem tells a story, and like a short story, it has characters, a setting, and action. You have already read some well-known stories in verse: "The Wreck of the *Hesperus*" (page 164), "The Listeners" (page 457), "Annabel Lee" (page 460), and "The Highwayman" (page 468).

One special kind of narrative poem with a long history is the *ballad*. The original ballads, called *folk ballads*, have no known authors. They were not written down; they were passed down by word of mouth from one generation to another.

One of the most popular subjects in English ballads is the legendary Robin Hood, who appears in about forty ballads. Some ballads celebrate historical events and battles. Many ballads tell tragic love stories and tales of jealousy, betrayal, and revenge.

A great many of the old ballads were brought to America by early colonists. In addition to these imported ballads, which underwent change, Americans have composed original ballads, such as "Casey Jones" and "John Henry."

One of the poems included here is an old folk ballad. The other poem, by Robert Browning, is based on an old German legend about an unusual musician.

MOTIVATIONAL SUMMARY
A cabin boy on the British ship *Golden Vanity* volunteers to sink single-handedly a threatening Spanish vessel. The boy is promised silver, gold, and the captain's daughter in marriage if he succeeds.

PRESENTATION
List characteristics of a ballad on the board. Ask students to identify them as you read the ballad orally. Encourage students to join in oral readings, especially in the refrains.

The Golden Vanity

A great many ballads have come down to us in more than one version. This is an American version of an English sea ballad about a ship called the **Golden Vanity.** *In older texts it is known as the* **Sweet Trinity,** *which supposedly was the name of Sir Walter Raleigh's flagship.*

'Twas all on board a ship down in a southern sea,
And she goes by the name of the *Golden Vanity*;
I'm afraid that she'll be taken by this Spanish crew,
   As she sails along the Lowlands,
   As she sails along the Lowlands low.   5

Then up speaks our saucy cabin boy, without fear or joy,
Saying, "What will you give me, if I will her destroy?"
"I'll give you gold and silver, my daughter fine and gay,
   If you'll destroy her in the Lowlands,
   If you'll sink her in the Lowlands low."   10

The boy filled his chest and so boldly leaped in,
The boy filled his chest and then began to swim;
He swam alongside of the bold Spanish ship,
   And he sank her in the Lowlands,
   And he sank her in the Lowlands low.   15

Some were playing cards and some were playing dice,
And some were in their hammocks sleeping very nice;
He bored two holes into her side, he let the water in,
   And he sank her in the Lowlands,
   And he sank her in the Lowlands low.   20

The boy then swam back unto our good ship's side,
And being much exhausted, bitterly he cried;
"Captain, take me in, for I'm going with the tide,
   And I'm sinking in the Lowlands,
   And I'm sinking in the Lowlands low."   25

"I will not take you in," our captain then replied,
"I'll shoot you and I'll stab you and I'll sink you in the tide,
   And I'll sink you in the Lowlands,
   And I'll sink you in the Lowlands low."

TEACHING RESOURCES D
Teacher's Notes, p. 89
Study Guide, p. 91
Building Vocabulary, p. 93
Selection Vocabulary Test, p. 111
Selection Test, p. 95

AV RESOURCES BINDER
Audiocassette 3, Side A

The Golden Vanity

1
Ballad. This kind of poetry usually provides little exposition.

2
Speaker fears an imminent act of piracy.

3
Refrain. Enhances musical quality of poem's rhythm.

4
Plot. Unfolds as captain promises rich reward for sinking Spanish ship.

5
Refrain. Changes throughout to advance story.

6
Speaker succinctly recounts boy's extraordinary feat.

7 Analyzing
What is the pattern of rhyme in the poem? First two lines of each stanza rhyme, except in stanza 8.

8
Stanza. This stanza is only four lines long, perhaps to indicate **turning point** of narrative.

9
Speaker relates captain's words of betrayal objectively.

The boy then swam around next the larboard° side,
And being more exhausted, bitterly he cried,
"Messmates, take me in, for I'm going with the tide,
   And I'm sinking in the Lowlands,
   And I'm sinking in the Lowlands low." 30

They hove the boy a rope and they hoisted him on deck, 35
They laid him on the quarter deck, the boy here soon died;
They sewed him up in a canvas sack, they hove him in the tide,
   And they buried him in the Lowlands,
   So they buried him in the Lowlands low.

30. **larboard** (lär′bərd): the port side, the left-hand side of the ship.

> **TRANSPARENCY 38**
> **Reader Response**
> *Jewels in the Crown* – invites students to explore specific words or images that make a strong impression.

Portuguese carracks. Detail from a fifteenth-century painting.
National Maritime Museum, Greenwich

▶ Before students begin this writing assignment, you may want to refer them to the **Writing About Literature** section on p. 688.

For Study and Discussion

Analyzing and Interpreting the Poem

1. The cabin boy is described as *saucy* in line 6. How does he show that he is high-spirited and bold?

2a. What does the word *her* in line 7 refer to?
b. How do you know?

3. No explanation is given for the captain's treachery. What do you suppose is his reason for betraying the cabin boy?

4. How do you know that the narrator is an eyewitness to the events recounted in the poem?

5. A **folk ballad**, also known as a **popular ballad**, was passed from generation to generation by word of mouth. What devices in the poem show that it was meant to be sung?

6. **Repetition** is a characteristic of folk ballads. A word, phrase, line, or group of lines repeated regularly in a poem is called a **refrain**. Sometimes the refrain is repeated exactly the same way, and sometimes it is varied slightly.
a. What is the refrain in "The Golden Vanity"?
b. How do the variations advance the story?

Writing About Literature

▶ **Analyzing Ballad Characteristics**

Show how any *three* of the following characteristics of ballads are revealed in "The Golden Vanity":

1. The story concerns something out of the ordinary.
2. The poem deals with one incident.
3. The storyteller does not offer an opinion of the events or judge the characters.
4. The language is plain.
5. Repetition is used as a musical device and for dramatic effect.

FOR STUDY AND DISCUSSION
1. Offers to destroy Spanish ship; speaks "without fear or joy." Leaps boldly into sea.
2a. Spanish ship. 2b. Lines 9–10 also refer to Spanish ship as *her.*
3. Possibly regrets his rash promises; possibly jealous.
4. Refers to himself as one of crew; in ll. 6, 21, and 26, he uses possessive *our.*
5. Last two lines in each stanza form **refrain**. Regular meter lends itself to singing.
6a. Last two lines in each stanza. Most often "And . . . the Lowlands,/ . . . the Lowlands low." 6b. Refrain reflects poem's shift in focus from description of Spanish ship to English captain, sinking of ship, sinking of cabin boy, and burial at sea.

WRITING ABOUT LITERATURE
Suggest that students make notes of details or examples that illustrate three of these characteristics and then write an essay with a well-developed body paragraph for each characteristic.

The Golden Vanity 477

The Pied Piper of Hamelin

ROBERT BROWNING

Browning wrote this poem for the son of a friend. He is the Willy who is addressed in the last stanza of the poem. Browning intended to amuse the boy during an illness and to "give him a subject for illustrative drawings."

I

Hamelin Town's in Brunswick,°
    By famous Hanover city;
The river Weser,° deep and wide,
Washes its wall on the southern side;
A pleasanter spot you never spied; 5
    But, when begins my ditty,
    Almost five hundred years ago,
To see the townsfolk suffer so
    From vermin, was a pity.

II

Rats! 10
They fought the dogs and killed the cats,
    And bit the babies in the cradles,
And ate the cheeses out of the vats,
    And licked the soup from the cooks' own ladles,
Split open the kegs of salted sprats,° 15
Made nests inside men's Sunday hats,
And even spoiled the women's chats
    By drowning their speaking
    With shrieking and squeaking
In fifty different sharps and flats. 20

III

At last the people in a body
    To the Town Hall came flocking:
"'Tis clear," cried they, "our Mayor's a noddy;°
    And as for our Corporation°—shocking

---

1. **Brunswick:** a former German state.
3. **Weser** (vāˈzər, wēˈ-).
15. **sprats:** fish, like herring.
23. **noddy:** fool.
24. **Corporation:** governing body.

6 To think we buy gowns lined with ermine
For dolts that can't or won't determine
What's best to rid us of our vermin!
You hope, because you're old and obese,° 25
To find in the furry civic robe ease?
Rouse up, Sirs! Give your brains a racking
To find the remedy we're lacking, 30
7 Or, sure as fate, we'll send you packing!"
At this the Mayor and Corporation
Quaked with a mighty consternation.

IV

An hour they sat in council;
At length the Mayor broke silence: 35
"For a guilder° I'd my ermine gown sell,
I wish I were a mile hence!
8 It's easy to bid one rack one's brain—
I'm sure my poor head aches again, 40
I've scratched it so, and all in vain.
Oh for a trap, a trap, a trap!"
9 Just as he said this, what should hap
At the chamber door but a gentle tap?
"Bless us," cried the Mayor, "what's that?" 45
(With the Corporation as he sat,
Looking little though wondrous fat;
Nor brighter was his eye, nor moister
Than a too-long-opened oyster,
Save when at noon his paunch grew mutinous 50
For a plate of turtle green and glutinous)°
"Only a scraping of shoes on the mat?
Anything like the sound of a rat
Makes my heart go pit-a-pat!"

V

"Come in!"—the Mayor cried, looking bigger: 55
10 And in did come the strangest figure!
His queer long coat from heel to head
Was half of yellow and half of red,
And he himself was tall and thin,
With sharp blue eyes, each like a pin, 60
And light loose hair, yet swarthy skin,
No tuft on cheek nor beard on chin,
But lips where smiles went out and in;

28. **obese** (ō-bēs'): extremely fat.

37. **guilder** (gĭl'dər): silver or gold coin.

51. **glutinous** (glōōt'n-əs): gluey, thick.

The Pied Piper of Hamelin 479

GEOGRAPHY LINK
Have students locate on a world map the continent of Europe, the country of Germany, and the city of Hanover. Then have them find the European country of Romania and its region known as Transylvania (referred to on p. 486).

11
Foreshadowing. The Piper is able to charm "all creatures," and he *mainly* uses his ability on creatures that harm people—but not always.

12 Summarizing
With what does the Piper charm "all creatures"? With his instrument, the pipe.

13
Use to answer **study question 4b,** p. 486.

14
Mayor implies job is worth fifty times what Piper asks.

There was no guessing his kith and kin:
And nobody could enough admire   65
The tall man and his quaint attire.
Quoth one: "It's as my great-grandsire,
Starting up at the Trump of Doom's tone,°
Had walked this way from his painted tombstone!"

68. **Trump of Doom:** the trumpet of doomsday, the end of the world.

VI

He advanced to the council table: 70
11 And, "Please your honors," said he, "I'm able,
By means of a secret charm, to draw
   All creatures living beneath the sun,
   That creep or swim or fly or run,
After me so as you never saw!   75
And I chiefly use my charm
On creatures that do people harm,
The mole and toad and newt and viper;
And people call me the Pied Piper."
(And here they noticed round his neck   80
   A scarf of red and yellow stripe,
To match with his coat of the selfsame check;
12 And at the scarf's end hung a pipe;
And his fingers, they noticed, were ever straying
As if impatient to be playing   85
Upon this pipe, as low it dangled
Over his vesture so old-fangled.)
"Yet," said he, "poor piper as I am,
13 In Tartary° I freed the Cham,°
   Last June, from his huge swarms of gnats;   90
I eased in Asia the Nizam°
   Of a monstrous brood of vampire bats:
And as for what your brain bewilders,
   If I can rid your town of rats
Will you give me a thousand guilders?"   95
14 "One? fifty thousand!"—was the exclamation
Of the astonished Mayor and Corporation.

89. **Tartary** (tär′tə-rē): a region in Asia and eastern Europe. **Cham** (kăm): khan (archaic).

91. **Nizam** (nĭ-säm′, -zăm′, nī-): title of the ruler of Hyderabad (hī′dər-ə-băd′, bäd′), a former state in India.

VII

Into the street the Piper stepped,
   Smiling first a little smile,
As if he knew what magic slept   100
   In his quiet pipe the while;
Then, like a musical adept,°

102. **adept** (ə-dĕpt′): expert.

MEETING INDIVIDUAL NEEDS
ESL/LEP • The poem contains vocabulary that may be unfamiliar, including numerous archaic words. Write on the chalkboard these terms from pp. 480–481 and invite the class to use context clues to guess at their meanings.

(p. 480)
kith and kin—relatives
Quoth—Said
the selfsame—exactly the same
vesture—clothing
old-fangled—old-fashioned

(p. 481)
ere—before
staved—punctured or smashed
methought—it seemed to me

To blow the pipe his lips he wrinkled,
15 And green and blue his sharp eyes twinkled,
Like a candle flame where salt is sprinkled; 105
16 And ere three shrill notes the pipe uttered,
You heard as if an army muttered;
And the muttering grew to a grumbling;
And the grumbling grew to a mighty rumbling;
17 And out of the houses the rats came tumbling. 110
Great rats, small rats, lean rats, brawny rats,
Brown rats, black rats, gray rats, tawny rats,
Grave old plodders, gay young friskers,
  Fathers, mothers, uncles, cousins,
Cocking tails and pricking whiskers, 115
  Families by tens and dozens,
Brothers, sisters, husbands, wives—
Followed the Piper for their lives.
From street to street he piped advancing,
And step for step they followed dancing, 120
Until they came to the river Weser,
  Wherein all plunged and perished!
18 —Save one who, stout as Julius Caesar,
Swam across and lived to carry
  (As he, the manuscript he cherished°) 125
To Rat-land home his commentary:
19 Which was, "At the first shrill notes of the pipe,
I heard a sound as of scraping tripe,
And putting apples, wondrous ripe,
Into a cider press's gripe: 130
And a moving away of pickle-tub boards,
And a leaving ajar of conserve cupboards,
And a drawing the corks of train-oil° flasks,
And a breaking the hoops of butter casks:
And it seemed as if a voice 135
  (Sweeter far than by harp or by psaltery°
Is breathed) called out, 'Oh rats, rejoice!
  The world is grown to one vast drysaltery!°
So munch on, crunch on, take your nuncheon,°
Breakfast, supper, dinner, luncheon!' 140
And just as a bulky sugar-puncheon,°
All ready staved, like a great sun shone
Glorious scarce an inch before me,
20 Just as methought it said, 'Come, bore me!'
—I found the Weser rolling o'er me." 145

125. Once, when his ship was captured, Julius Caesar swam to shore, carrying his journals.

133. **train-oil:** fish oil.

136. **psaltery** (sôl′tə-rē): an ancient stringed instrument.

138. **drysaltery:** a store selling salted foods.
139. **nuncheon:** snack.

141. **sugar-puncheon:** sugar cask.

15
Simile. The Piper's eyes twinkle mischievously like a flame.

16
With confidence, Piper begins playing pipe.

17
Rats begin to follow Piper through streets to river.

18
Allusion. Julius Caesar was powerful Roman dictator and general (100–44 B.C.).

19
Simile. The way the Piper's music sounds to the rats is described in a series of comparisons, all relating to foods.

20 Summarizing
What happened to the rat who was describing effect of pipe's sounds? Instead of receiving the promised food, finds himself in river.

The Pied Piper of Hamelin

21
Town rejoices and proceeds to destroy rats' nests and blocked holes.

22
Piper asks for his money.

23
Characterization. Greedy Mayor and Corporation would rather buy wine with money than pay the Piper.

24
Conflict. Mayor doesn't intend to honor agreement.

25 Summarizing
How does Mayor try to justify breach of agreement? By claiming to have been joking; by claiming losses make thrift necessary.

26
Piper is angry; he refuses to take less than a thousand guilders.

27
Piper threatens to use secret charm in a different way.

VIII
You should have heard the Hamelin people
Ringing the bells till they rocked the steeple.
21 "Go," cried the Mayor, "and get long poles,
Poke out the nests and block up the holes!
Consult with carpenters and builders,   150
And leave in our town not even a trace
Of the rats!"—when suddenly, up the face
Of the Piper perked in the marketplace,
22 With a "First, if you please, my thousand guilders!"

IX
A thousand guilders! The Mayor looked blue;   155
So did the Corporation too.
23 For council dinners made rare havoc
With Claret, Moselle, Vin-de-Grave, Hock;°
And half the money would replenish
Their cellar's biggest butt° with Rhenish.°   160
To pay this sum to a wandering fellow
With a gipsy coat of red and yellow!
"Beside," quoth the Mayor with a knowing wink,
"Our business was done at the river's brink;
24 We saw with our eyes the vermin sink,   165
And what's dead can't come to life, I think.
So, friend, we're not the folks to shrink
From the duty of giving you something for drink,
And a matter of money to put in your poke;
25 But as for the guilders, what we spoke   170
Of them, as you very well know, was in joke.
Beside, our losses have made us thrifty.
A thousand guilders! Come, take fifty!"

X
The Piper's face fell, and he cried,
"No trifling! I can't wait, beside!   175
I've promised to visit by dinnertime
Bagdad, and accept the prime
Of the Head Cook's pottage,° all he's rich in,
For having left, in the Caliph's° kitchen,
Of a nest of scorpions no survivor: 180
With him I proved no bargain-driver,
26 With you, don't think I'll bate° a stiver!°
And folks who put me in a passion
27 May find me pipe after another fashion."

158. **Claret, Moselle** (mō-zĕl′), **Vin-de-Grave** (văN-də-gräv′), **Hock:** wines.
160. **butt:** cask. **Rhenish** (rĕn′ĭsh): Rhine wine.

178. **pottage** (pŏt′ĭj): thick soup.
179. **Caliph** (kā′lĭf, kăl′ĭf): ruler in a Moslem country.
182. **bate:** subtract. **stiver** (stī′vər): one-twentieth of a guilder.

XI

"How?" cried the Mayor, "d'ye think I brook 185
Being worse treated than a Cook?
Insulted by a lazy ribald
28 With idle pipe and vesture piebald?
You threaten us, fellow? Do your worst,
29 Blow your pipe there till you burst!" 190

XII

Once more he stepped into the street,
   And to his lips again
     Laid his long pipe of smooth straight cane;
30 And ere he blew three notes (such sweet
   Soft notes as yet musician's cunning 195
     Never gave the enraptured air)
31 There was a rustling that seemed like a bustling
Of merry crowds justling at pitching and hustling;
Small feet were pattering, wooden shoes clattering,
Little hands clapping and little tongues chattering, 200
And, like fowls in a farm-yard when barley is scattering,
Out came the children running.
All the little boys and girls,
With rosy cheeks and flaxen curls,
And sparkling eyes and teeth like pearls, 205
Tripping and skipping, ran merrily after
32 The wonderful music with shouting and laughter.

XIII

The Mayor was dumb, and the Council stood
As if they were changed into blocks of wood,
33 Unable to move a step, or cry 210
To the children merrily skipping by,
—Could only follow with the eye
That joyous crowd at the Piper's back.
34 But how the Mayor was on the rack,°
And the wretched Council's bosoms beat, 215
As the Piper turned from the High Street
To where the Weser rolled its waters
Right in the way of their sons and daughters!
However, he turned from South to West,
And to Koppelberg Hill his steps addressed, 220
And after him the children pressed;
Great was the joy in every breast.

214. **on the rack:** a metaphor for "suffering." The rack was an instrument of torture.

28
Piebald means "of different colors."

29
Mayor sees no basis in Piper's threat.

30
Piper again plays three magical notes.

31
Description. The children's response to the music is immediate; **onomatopoetic** words help illustrate the children's movement.

32 Making Inferences
What do you think the Piper plans to do with the children? Perhaps he plans to lead children away to get revenge on town.

33
Mayor and Council appear spellbound by Piper.

34
Mayor and Council suffer in their helplessness as the happy children follow Piper out of town.

WRITING LINK
Have students write a letter as Willy, the boy for whom the poem was written, to Robert Browning, thanking him for the poem and telling him why they liked it, and perhaps including some illustrative drawings. As an alternative or additional activity, students may wish to write stories about what happened to the band of children who were deposited in Transylvania.

TRANSPARENCIES 35 & 36
Fine Art
Theme: *Special Language, Special Meaning* – features artwork in which the artist attempts to express an opinion about a specific idea.

VISUAL CONNECTIONS
Ideas for Writing
The happy, innocent children have no thoughts of the dangers that lie ahead. They simply follow the wonderful promises of the Pied Piper's music. The picture might serve as a starter for student journal entries about the dangers of following the legendary Pied Piper—following a promise that seems too good to be true without asking where it is leading.

35
Mayor again underestimates Piper as he predicts that Piper cannot cross the mountain.

36
Plot. This is the **climax** to which all action has led: the Piper has actually taken the townspeople's children away. As if by magic, the mountain opens and all the children, except one, go in.

37
One lame child not lost to Piper tells of wonderful promise of the Piper's music.

35 "He never can cross that mighty top!
 He's forced to let the piping drop,
 And we shall see our children stop!"
 When, lo, as they reached the mountainside, 225
36 A wondrous portal opened wide,
 As if a cavern was suddenly hollowed;
 And the Piper advanced and the children followed,
 And when all were in to the very last, 230
 The door in the mountainside shut fast.
 Did I say, all? No! One was lame,
  And could not dance the whole of the way;
 And in after years, if you would blame
  His sadness, he was used to say,— 235
37 "It's dull in our town since my playmates left!
 I can't forget that I'm bereft

484 POETRY

Of all the pleasant sights they see,
Which the Piper also promised me.
38 For he led us, he said, to a joyous land,
Joining the town and just at hand,
Where waters gushed and fruit trees grew,
And flowers put forth a fairer hue,
And everything was strange and new;
The sparrows were brighter than peacocks here,
And their dogs outran our fallow deer,°
And honeybees had lost their stings,
And horses were born with eagles' wings;
And just as I became assured
My lame foot would be speedily cured,
The music stopped and I stood still,
And found myself outside the hill,
Left alone against my will,
To go now limping as before,
And never hear of that country more!"

246. fallow deer: small, pale-colored deer.

XIV

Alas, alas for Hamelin!
   There came into many a burgher's° pate°
39   A text which says, that heaven's gate
    Opes to the rich at as easy rate
  As the needle's eye takes a camel in!°
40 The Mayor sent East, West, North and South,
To offer the Piper, by word of mouth,
   Wherever it was men's lot to find him,
Silver and gold to his heart's content,
If he'd only return the way he went,
   And bring the children behind him.
But when they saw 'twas a lost endeavor,
41 And Piper and dancers were gone forever,
They made a decree that lawyers never
   Should think their records dated duly
If, after the day of the month and year,
These words did not as well appear,
"And so long after what happened here
42   On the Twenty-second of July,
Thirteen hundred and seventy-six":
And the better in memory to fix
The place of the children's last retreat,
43 They called it, the Pied Piper's Street—

257. burgher (bûr′gər): town-dweller. **pate** (pāt): head.

260. This text is from the Bible (Matthew 19:24): "It is easier for a camel to go through the eye of a needle, than for a rich man to enter into the kingdom of God."

MEETING INDIVIDUAL NEEDS

ESL/LEP • Guide students in defining *subterraneous* (l. 295). Ask students to determine the root word (*terra,* meaning earth). Explain that *sub–* is a prefix, meaning under. When these two parts are put together, the word means "under the earth; underground." The *–ous* ending signals that the word is what part of speech? (adjective) Can students think of any other words that might have *terra* as their root? (territory, terrestrial)

CLOSURE

Ask students to identify characteristics of the narrative poems, "The Golden Vanity" and "The Pied Piper of Hamelin." Also, ask students to suggest reasons for the poems' longevity and popularity.

44
Story is written on post near mountain and on church window so the world will know.

45
Optimistic tale of people who rose out of underground prison lends hope that they were the children of Hamelin.

46
Theme. To pay one's debts is lesson recommended to Willy.

Where anyone playing on pipe or tabor°
Was sure for the future to lose his labor. 280
Nor suffered they hostelry° or tavern
  To shock with mirth a street so solemn;
But opposite the place of the cavern
44 They wrote the story on a column,
And on the great church window painted 285
The same, to make the world acquainted
How their children were stolen away,
And there it stands to this very day.
And I must not omit to say
45 That in Transylvania there's a tribe 290
Of alien people who ascribe
The outlandish ways and dress
On which their neighbors lay such stress,
To their fathers and mothers having risen
Out of some subterraneous prison 295
Into which they were trepanned°
Long time ago in a mighty band
Out of Hamelin town in Brunswick land,
But how or why, they don't understand.

XV

46 So, Willy, let me and you be wipers 300
Of scores out with all men—especially pipers!
And, whether they pipe us free from rats or from mice,
If we've promised them aught, let us keep our promise!

279. **tabor** (tā′bər): small drum.

281. **hostelry** (hŏs′təl-rē): inn.

296. **trepanned** (trĭ-pănd′): trapped.

FOR STUDY AND DISCUSSION

1. Rats fight dogs, kill cats, bite babies, eat cheeses out of vats, lick soup from cook's ladles, split open kegs, make nests inside men's hats, drown out women's conversations.
2a. Appear to be fat, old, dull, and cowardly. **2b.** Answers will vary. Characteristics produce negative feelings in reader.
3a. Wears half yellow, half red coat; is tall and thin with sharp blue eyes, light hair, and swarthy skin. **3b.** Astonishes Mayor and Corporation.
4a. That his secret charm draws all creatures after him. **4b.** Freed Cham from huge swarms of gnats; Nizam of vampire bats. **4c.** Mayor and Corporation are to pay him one thousand guilders to rid Hamelin of rats.
5. Descriptions of different kinds of rats and their relationships to each other.
6. Promise of all wonderful things that rats like to eat.
7a. Yes; they seem greedy and selfish. **7b.** Lures children to follow him; they disappear into mountain.

For Study and Discussion

Analyzing and Interpreting the Poem

1. At the opening of the poem, Hamelin is overrun by rats. What are the ways in which the townsfolk suffer?

2a. What characteristics of the Mayor and the Corporation are stressed in lines 23–54? **b.** How do these characteristics affect your reaction to the town officials?

3a. Describe the Pied Piper's appearance. **b.** What impression does he make?

4a. What claims does the Pied Piper make for his abilities? **b.** What evidence does he offer for his successes? **c.** What agreement is reached?

5. Read aloud the description in Part VII, of how the Piper charms the rats into following him. What parts of the description are particularly vivid and amusing?

6. One rat survives to bring the news to "Ratland." According to him, what is the charm in the Piper's music?

7. The Mayor and the Corporation refuse to live up to their agreement with the Piper. **a.** Is this behavior consistent with their characters? **b.** What is the Piper's revenge for their treachery?

486 POETRY

EXTENSION AND ENRICHMENT
Ask the school librarian or media specialist to help you assemble a collection of books containing ballads. Each student might want to read a ballad, make notes on it, and then present it to the rest of the class.

Encourage students to write their own ballads.

Remind students of the definition of *imagery* (a description that appeals to any one or any combination of the five senses). Have them re-read the poems to find passages they think are good examples of imagery.

Some students might enjoy drawing or painting pictures of the boy or the captain in "The Golden Vanity" or the Pied Piper or Mayor in "The Pied Piper of Hamelin." Some might sketch a series of pictures illustrating the plot of either poem.

---

8. One child, who is lame, never reaches the door in the mountainside. What does he reveal about the Piper's music?

9. How do the people of Hanover commemorate the tragedy?

10. What conclusion to the legend is suggested in lines 289–299?

11. The poem ends with four lines of advice to Willy, the little boy for whom Browning wrote the poem. **a.** What is the advice? **b.** How does it apply to the legend of Hamelin?

12. The events in this poem are actually found in the town records of Hamelin. The disaster is said to have occurred in 1284. **a.** What is Browning's attitude toward this disaster? **b.** Is your judgment of the events the same?

Language and Vocabulary

Recognizing Denotative and Connotative Meanings

You have seen that poets rely on the denotative and connotative meanings of words. Look at the meanings of the word *ermine* in line 25:

Word	Denotation	Connotation
ermine	soft, white fur from a kind of weasel	rich and splendid fur, often worn by royalty

1. Using this chart as a model, find the denotative and connotative meanings of the following words in the poem:

vermin (line 9)
quaint (line 66)
flaxen (line 204)

About the Author

Robert Browning (1812–1889)

As a young man, Robert Browning read most of the books in his father's huge library, traveled in Europe, and wrote poetry. Almost from the first, his poetry showed a keen understanding of human nature and a mastery of difficult poetic forms. In 1846, Browning eloped with Elizabeth Barrett, a well-known poet whose father had virtually imprisoned her at home. During their life together, she was the better known writer, but after her death, his reputation grew steadily. With the publication of a long poem, *The Ring and the Book*, he became recognized as one of the major poets of his day.

---

8. Promises wonderful land where miracles happen: honey bees had lost stings, horses born with eagles' wings, everything more beautiful.

9. Lawyers date records from day children disappeared; street renamed for Piper, and no one there is allowed to play pipe or drum or be merry; story is written on column and on church window.

10. Children come out of mountain, settle in Transylvania, and have children of their own. No one understands exactly how they got there.

11a. To pay all debts he has, especially to pipers. 11b. Had Mayor and Corporation honored their contract with Piper, he would not have stolen their children.

12a. Seems to be light-hearted, yet sees valuable lesson in story. 12b. Some will agree that story teaches important lesson.

LANGUAGE AND VOCABULARY

1. Suggested answers with denotation followed by connotation:

vermin: small insects or animals that are annoying or destructive; repulsive, offensive people.

quaint: agreeably curious or old-fashioned; odd, peculiar.

flaxen: made of or resembling pale yellow flax fiber; light, golden color associated with hair of young, innocent children.

ABOUT THE AUTHOR
Early in his career, Browning began writing plays in verse. However, with "The Pied Piper of Hamelin," he is regarded as a master of dramatic poetry.

OBJECTIVES
The overall aim is for students to identify characteristics of lyric poetry in "Snowflakes," "Little Things," "I'm Nobody," and Japanese haiku. For a complete list of objectives, see the **Teacher's Notes**.

VOCABULARY
The underlined words are in the Glossary. Students should notice the concrete, specific nouns used to create visual images, and also the vivid action verbs, especially in the haiku.

FOCUS / MOTIVATION
Have students bring to class the lyrics of some of their favorite songs. Discuss and compare the lyrics. Ask them why they are appealing. Lead them to the definition of a lyric given on this page.

TEACHING RESOURCES D
Teacher's Notes, p. 108
Study Guide, p. 113
Building Vocabulary, p. 109
Selection Vocabulary Test, p. 111
Selection Test, p. 122

PREREADING FOCUS
Lyric is derived from Greek and Latin word *lyra*, which became *lyre*, a harplike instrument used by the Greeks. Hence, early poems meant to be accompanied by music were called **lyrics**. Now, the word *lyric* is applied to many kinds of short poems.

The headnote emphasizes that lyric poems are brief, intense, and expressive. They generally deal with personal feelings and thoughts.

Snowflakes

1
Personification. "Bosom" and "her garments" personify sky as a woman.

2
Alliteration. Repetition of *s* and *and* creates gentle image of falling snow.

3
"Divine expression" may be poetry that reveals speaker's imaginative ideas ("cloudy fancies").

4 **Finding Details**
In this analogy, what does the speaker compare his "confession" to? Sky's release of snow.

5
"Poem of the air" is falling snow.

6
Snowflakes are the sky's "secret of despair."

488

LYRIC POETRY

A *lyric* poem is the form used for the expression of personal thoughts and feelings. Most lyrics tend to be brief. "Full Fathom Five" (page 466) is a pure lyric, intended to be sung. A lyric poem generally leaves the reader with a single, intense impression.

Snowflakes

HENRY WADSWORTH LONGFELLOW

In this poem Longfellow is drawing an analogy, *or comparison, between certain natural events and certain human feelings. What similarity does he find?*

1 Out of the bosom of the Air,
   Out of the cloud-folds of her garments shaken,
Over the woodlands brown and bare,
   Over the harvest-fields forsaken,
2   Silent and soft and slow   5
   Descends the snow.

   Even as our cloudy fancies take
3   Suddenly shape in some divine expression,
4 Even as the troubled heart doth make
   In the white countenance confession,   10
     The troubled sky reveals
     The grief it feels.

5 This is the poem of the air,
   Slowly in silent syllables recorded;
6 This is the secret of despair,   15
   Long in its cloudy bosom hoarded,
     Now whispered and revealed
     To wood and field.

488 POETRY

PRESENTATION
Tell students that an analogy is a comparison of two things to show their similarities and to make a point. In "Snowflakes," the gloomy clouds produce the beauty of snow just as the poet produces a poem out of his dark despair.

SCIENCE LINK
Have interested students do some research on the seven separate types of snow crystals and make drawings of them in their journals. Have them label each drawing and, if they wish, include descriptive information.

For Study and Discussion

Analyzing and Interpreting the Poem

1. Although the title of this poem is "Snowflakes," it is clear that the poet is speaking about some deep, personal grief that has been held in check and that suddenly has found release. Longfellow sees a relationship between the "troubled heart" and the "troubled sky." What do they have in common?

2. The "divine expression" in line 8 might refer to poetry, in which the poet's "cloudy fancies," or gloomy ideas, are revealed. What is the "poem of the air" (line 13)?

3. What eventually happens to the "secret of despair"?

4. Consider the connotative meanings of the words *bare, forsaken, troubled, grief, despair*. How do they contribute to the mood of the poem?

Literary Elements

Recognizing Personification

In poetry, an animal, an object, or an idea is often given personality, or described as if it were human. Longfellow talks about the air as if it were a woman shaking snow out of her garments, the clouds. This is a figure of speech **1** known as **personification**. How does Longfellow personify the sky in lines 11–12?

VISUAL CONNECTIONS
Exploring the Subject
Snowflakes are airborne ice crystals formed around a central ice fragment or a particle of dirt, dust, or chemical material. No matter how large or small the flakes, the characteristic six-sided shape can be seen under a microscope. This outer shape is the result of the internal arrangement of oxygen atoms in water vapor which, in freezing into a solid, form themselves into an open hexagonally symmetrical lattice. There are seven separate types of snow crystals. The one shown in the center of this photograph is a two-dimensional *stellar* shape, notable for its lacy "arms." Other forms include rodlike *columns, needles,* and three-dimensional *spatial dendrites*.

Ideas for Writing
Have students look at this particular snowflake, imagining that it is real and they can touch it. Ask them to do a three- or four-minute focused freewriting describing the snowflake and their feelings about snow.

FOR STUDY AND DISCUSSION
1. Both seem to need to be unburdened, to feel release of heavy sadness and grief.
2. Softly falling snow.
3. Is "whispered and revealed."
4. Words connote extreme loneliness and sadness.

LITERARY ELEMENTS
1. Suggested answer: Longfellow personifies sky by giving it human ability to be troubled and to experience grief.

Little Things

JAMES STEPHENS

How does the repetition of the word little *add to the effectiveness of this poem?*

1   Little things, that run, and quail,
    And die, in silence and despair!

    Little things, that fight, and fail,
    And fall, on sea, and earth, and air!

    All trapped and frightened little things,
    The mouse, the coney°, hear our prayer!   5

2   As we forgive those done to us,
    —The lamb, the linnet, and the hare—

    Forgive us all our trespasses,
    Little creatures, everywhere!   10

6. **coney** (kō'nē): rabbit.

For Study and Discussion

Analyzing and Interpreting the Poem

1. How does the poet create sympathy for the creatures in this poem?

2a. What is a trespass? **b.** What special meaning does the word have in this poem?

3. What single, intense impression does this poem make?

I'm Nobody

EMILY DICKINSON

What is the speaker's attitude toward fame?

    I'm nobody! Who are you?
    Are you nobody, too?
    Then there's a pair of us—don't tell!
1   They'd banish us, you know.

    How dreary to be somebody!
2   How public, like a frog
    To tell your name the livelong day
    To an admiring bog!

For Study and Discussion

Analyzing and Interpreting the Poem

1. What does the speaker mean by the words *nobody* and *somebody*?

2a. Why does the speaker enjoy anonymity? **b.** What is her attitude toward those who have achieved reputation or renown?

3a. To whom is she talking? **b.** Might she be speaking directly to the reader?

4. The tone of Emily Dickinson's poetry is often described as playful and witty. Does this poem share those characteristics?

Haiku

A haiku (hī′kōō) is a three-line poem, of Japanese origin, containing seventeen syllables. There are five syllables in the first line, seven syllables in the second line, and five syllables in the third line. Such a poem must communicate meaning through very few words. The subject matter of a haiku is usually drawn from nature.

> The lightning flashes!
> And slashing through the darkness,
> A night-heron's screech.
>
> *Matsuo Bashō*

> Broken and broken
> again on the sea, the moon
> so easily mends.
>
> *Chosu*

> I must go begging
> for water . . . morning glories
> have captured my well.
>
> *Chiyo*

Flowers and Birds by Seshu Toyo.

For Study and Discussion

Analyzing and Interpreting the Poems

1a. What images do you see and hear in the first haiku? **b.** What words suggest pain or violence?

2. The second haiku uses the word *broken* in an unusual way. We speak of breaking an object such as a dish. In what way is the moon "broken" repeatedly on the sea?

3. What image is suggested by the word *captured* in the third haiku?

CLOSURE
Ask students to identify characteristics of **lyric** poetry as represented in Longfellow's "Snowflakes," Stephens' "Little Things," Dickinson's "I'm Nobody," and the haiku.

EXTENSION AND ENRICHMENT
Remind students that a **lyric** poem generally leaves the reader with a single, intense impression of a personal thought or feeling. They might look through their journals to find ideas for writing their own lyrics. They might share them with either a small group or with the rest of the class. Some students might make a decorative frame for their lyrics or illustrate them in some other way. Others might play background music of their choice as they read their lyrics aloud.

LITERARY ELEMENTS
1. First haiku: contrasts between darkness and lightning and between darkness and heron's screech, which slashes through air like lightning. Second haiku: implied contrast between real moon and its image, which seems to break and mend easily. Third haiku: implied contrast between peaceful look of morning glories and their assault on well.

ABOUT THE AUTHORS
James Stephens
Stephens is renowned for his fairy tales set in the slums of Dublin, Ireland, and for his sensitive poems about animals. *The Crock of Gold* established his literary reputation in 1912.

Emily Dickinson
Dickinson's poems are renowned for their apparent simplicity. In an era when many popular poets wrote long, flowery, sentimental verse, she composed brief poems that focused only on one or two vivid images. Many see similarities between Dickinson's poetic style and Oriental verse forms, such as Japanese haiku. Each is compact and deceptively simple.

Literary Elements
Understanding Haiku
Harry Behn, who has translated Japanese haiku, believes that the best haiku are as "natural as breathing." He writes that a haiku "is made by speaking of something natural and simple suggesting spring, summer, autumn, or winter. There is no rhyme. Everything mentioned is just what it is, wonderful, here, but still beyond."

Haiku often use contrasts that catch the reader by surprise. **1** What examples of this kind of contrast can you find in the poems on page 491?

Creative Writing
Composing a Haiku
Writing a haiku can be challenging and fun. You might start by recalling one striking or memorable image that made a special impression on you. This image, along with your feelings about it, should be compressed into no more than seventeen syllables, in three lines. The lines should have five, seven, and five syllables, respectively.

For example, if a beautiful red sun going down slowly behind the water at a beach made an impression on you, you might come up with a haiku similar to this:

A bright flaming ball,	5 syllables
Nestling down on the water	7 syllables
That swallows it whole.	5 syllables

Write at least one haiku, selecting your words carefully to appeal to your reader's senses and imagination. You may work in a little surprise in the third line. If you wish, illustrate your haiku and then read it aloud to a small group of students or to the rest of the class.

About the Authors
Henry Wadsworth Longfellow (1807–1882)
For a biography of the author, see page 169.

James Stephens (1882–1950)

James Stephens did not have a formal education, but he was deeply interested in reading, art, and folk music. A fascinating storyteller, Stephens enjoyed entertaining others with Irish stories, legends, and poetry. He is known for his novels and poems.

Emily Dickinson (1830–1886)

The Granger Collection, New York

Emily Dickinson was born into one of the leading families of Amherst, Massachusetts. She attended Mount Holyoke Female Seminary, the first women's college. Gradually, she became a recluse, dressing all in white and rarely seeing visitors. While some people think she was disappointed in love, others believe she deliberately secluded herself to write the almost two thousand poems she kept neatly stitched together in her bureau. She allowed only eight or nine poems to be published during her lifetime. Today she is considered one of the greatest American poets.

OBJECTIVES
The overall aim is for students to recognize the contrast between the speakers' attitudes in Lewis Carroll's "Father William." For a complete list of objectives, see the **Teacher's Notes.**

VOCABULARY
Students might select words that they feel add to the humor of the poem because the terms are unusual or have a comical sound or rhythm.

FOCUS / MOTIVATION
Draw the students into a discussion of whether or not they have teased adult family members about being old-fashioned or out of step with the times. How did the adults respond to their comments?

TEACHING RESOURCES D
Teacher's Notes, p. 124
Study Guide, p. 126
Language Skills, p. 128
Building Vocabulary, p. 132
Selection Test, p. 138

PREREADING FOCUS
An important part of dramatic poetry is the fictional situation in which the characters are placed. In dramatic poetry, readers know that the poet is not the speaker, but that created characters speak from their own points of view. The headnote emphasizes that dramatic poems contain dialogues or monologues spoken by characters in the poems.

DRAMATIC POETRY

Dramatic poems present characters who speak to other characters or to some unidentified listener. Most dramatic poems contain dialogue. Others, like the *dramatic monologue,* contain a single speech by one character.

Father William

LEWIS CARROLL

This poem is a parody, *or humorous imitation, of a poem by Robert Southey called "The Old Man's Comforts." Carroll's poem is a father and son dialogue, with some delightful surprises.*

1 "You are old, Father William," the young man said,
  "And your hair has become very white;
And yet you incessantly stand on your head—
  Do you think, at your age, it is right?"

2 "In my youth," Father William replied to his son, 5
  "I feared it might injure the brain;
3 But now that I'm perfectly sure I have none,
  Why, I do it again and again."

Illustrations by John Tenniel.

Father William

1
Characterization. First line introduces contrasting characters, old Father William and his young son.

2
The change of speakers is indicated by the start of a new stanza.

3
Father William's clever answer establishes humorous tone.

VISUAL CONNECTIONS
About the Artist
Sir John Tenniel (1820–1914), an English illustrator and painter, is renowned for his illustrations of Lewis Carroll's *Alice's Adventures in Wonderland* and *Through the Looking-Glass,* and *Aesop's Fables.* His paintings include *St. Cecilia,* a fresco, and *Pygmalion,* a watercolor.

PRESENTATION
Explain that "Father William" is a **dramatic** poem, that is, one in which the characters converse with each other. You may wish to allow the students time to read the poem silently. Then ask for volunteers for reading the parts aloud. Remind students to read with expression, as if they were performing in a play.

4
Dialogue. Conversation continues throughout poem, the youth's questions alternating with his father's replies.

5
Father implies that son is less agile than he.

6
The son marvels at Father's eating habits.

7
Father implies that his current abilities with his mouth are a result of much practice in his youth.

8 Analyzing
What is the poem's rhyme pattern so far? First and third lines in each stanza rhyme; second and fourth lines in each stanza rhyme (abab).

4   "You are old," said the youth, "as I mentioned before,
     And have grown most uncommonly fat;   10
  Yet you turned a back somersault in at the door—
     Pray, what is the reason of that?"

  "In my youth," said the sage, as he shook his gray locks,
     "I kept all my limbs very supple
  By the use of this ointment—one shilling the box—   15
5   Allow me to sell you a couple."

  "You are old," said the youth, "and your jaws are too weak
     For anything tougher than suet;
  Yet you finished the goose, with the bones and the beak;
6   Pray, how did you manage to do it?"   20

7   "In my youth," said his father, "I took to the law,
     And argued each case with my wife;
  And the muscular strength which it gave to my jaw,
8   Has lasted the rest of my life."

CLOSURE
Ask students to compare "Father William" to other stories that they have read such as "A Day's Wait" on p. 242, which features a relationship between a father and a son.

EXTENSION AND ENRICHMENT
Interested students might enjoy reading excerpts from Lewis Carroll's *Alice's Adventures in Wonderland*. They might write "Who Am I?" poems or short sketches from the point of view of one of the characters.

The class might like to prepare a Lewis Carroll bulletin board, illustrating his varied interests (writing, mathematics, teaching, photography, etc.) and his creations, some of the most memorable characters in literature (Alice, Mad Hatter, Cheshire cat, etc.).

"You are old," said the youth; "one would hardly suppose 25
  That your eye was as steady as ever;
Yet you balanced an eel on the end of your nose—
9   What made you so awfully clever?"

"I've answered three questions, and that is enough,"
  Said his father; "don't give yourself airs! 30
Do you think I can listen all day to such stuff?
10 Be off, or I'll kick you downstairs!"

For Study and Discussion

Analyzing and Interpreting the Poem

1. The son in the poem asks his father a number of questions. **a.** What are they? **b.** How does the father respond to each question?

2. How does the father's attitude toward growing older differ from the son's attitude?

3. What do you think is the most humorous aspect of this poem?

About the Author

Lewis Carroll (1832–1898)

Lewis Carroll was the pen name of Charles Lutwidge Dodgson, who was a professor of mathematics at Oxford University in England. *Alice's Adventures in Wonderland* (1865) and *Through the Looking-Glass* (1871), his two most famous books, were written to entertain the children of friends. Carroll's books are great fun, but they are also subtle and complex works that have fascinated readers for more than a hundred years.

9 Summarizing
What seems to be the son's attitude about getting older? Age should keep one from doing the things of youth.

10
Father's surprising response indicates that son's patronizing questions do not warrant answers.

FOR STUDY AND DISCUSSION
1a. Whether father should stand on his head, why he turned a somersault, how he managed to eat with weak jaws, and how he balanced an eel on his nose. **1b.** That he is no longer afraid to stand on his head because he is sure that he has no brain to injure; that he has always kept his limbs supple by using ointment; that his jaws became muscular through arguing with his wife; that he has heard enough questions and if the son does not leave him alone, he will kick him down the stairs.
2. Father hasn't allowed age to make any difference: he's as quick-witted, agile, and absurd as ever. Son assumed a superiority over his old father and deserves his comeuppance.
3. Responses will vary. Father says he is perfectly sure that he has no brain; son says the father eats a goose, beak and bones included; father balances an eel on his nose.

ABOUT THE AUTHOR
Carroll is famous not only for his novels but also for his fanciful verse, especially *The Hunting of the Snark* and "Jabberwocky." Students might read from his collections titled *Phantasmagoria and Other Poems* (1869) and *Rhyme? and Reason?* (1883).

COMIC VERSE

Some poets, like Edward Lear and Ogden Nash, have specialized in writing humorous poetry. One kind of comic verse that is extremely popular is the *limerick*.

The Bearded Man

EDWARD LEAR

A limerick is a humorous poem of five lines with a characteristic rhythm and rhyme pattern. See if you can determine this pattern as you read.

There was an old man with a beard,
Who said, "It is just as I feared!
   Two owls and a hen,
   Four larks and a wren
Have *all* built their nests in my beard!"

The Lama

OGDEN NASH

Nash's poetry is known for its comic rhymes and unusual spellings. Find examples in this poem of both devices.

The one-l lama,
He's a priest.
The two-l llama,
He's a beast.
And I will bet
A silk pyjama
There isn't any
Three-l lllama.

A Tutor

CAROLYN WELLS

A tutor who tooted the flute
Tried to tutor two tooters to toot.
   Said the two to the tutor,
   "Is it harder to toot, or
To tutor two tooters to toot?"

Creative Writing

Writing a Limerick

Limericks have a definite form. Which lines rhyme? Which lines are shorter than the others? The rhymes are often funny and unexpected. What comic rhymes can you find in the limericks on these pages?

Write a limerick of your own. Here are two lines you might use to begin:"

   There once was a student named Wayne,
   Whose homework was lost on a train. . . .

OBJECTIVES
The overall aim is for students to analyze the **sound devices** in poetry.

PRESENTATION
To begin this section, you may want to review sound devices by asking students to explain each term listed below or by finding examples in the poems from this unit. Then you or a volunteer can read aloud the poem for analysis. Students should work in small groups to do the activities. Then the groups can share their responses with the class.

FOCUS ON Reading and Critical Thinking

RELATING SOUND TO MEANING

You have learned during this unit that the sounds of a poem's words can be closely related to its meaning. Sound devices in poetry include rhyme, repetition, alliteration, refrain, rhythm, and onomatopoeia.

Read aloud the poem below. Then join with a small group of classmates for the activity that follows.

My Father's Song

Wanting to say things,
I miss my father tonight.
His voice, the slight catch,
the depth from his thin chest,
the tremble of emotion   5
in something he has just said
to his son, his song:

We planted corn one Spring at Acu—
we planted several times
but this one particular time   10
I remember the soft damp sand
in my hand.

My father had stopped at one point
to show me an overturned furrow;
the plowshare had unearthed   15
the burrow nest of a mouse
in the soft moist sand.

Very gently, he scooped tiny pink animals
into the palm of his hand
and told me to touch them.   20
We took them to the edge
of the field and put them in the shade
of a sand moist clod.

I remember the very softness
of cool and warm sand and tiny alive mice   25
and my father saying things.
—Simon J. Ortiz

Relating Sound to Meaning

1. Working in small groups, use a sheet of paper to list the sound devices that are used in this poem. List one or more specific examples from the poem for each sound device.

2. How do you think the speaker feels about his father? Discuss with your group what you think is the speaker's mood.

RELATING SOUND TO MEANING
Poetry allows writers to use language in powerful and unusual ways. Poets choose words for their sounds as well as for their meaning. Just like a musical composer who carefully arranges each note to create melodious tones and rhythms, the poet selects words to achieve special sounds and effects to help create the meaning of the poem.

Answers
1. ll. 11 and 12 rhyme. The words *we* and *remember* are repeated. Repetition of *t*'s, *p*'s, and *s*'s provides alliteration.
2. Answers may vary. Students may answer that the speaker seems to have a very loving memory of his father with whom he shares a respect for nature.

OBJECTIVES
The overall aim is for students to write a poem that captures a personal thought or feeling.

PRESENTATION
You might ask students to bring their favorite poems to read aloud to the class. Suggest that students consider the form and elements of their favorite poems as models for the poem they will be writing.

Students will benefit from using several prewriting strategies to help them find suitable subjects and develop their ideas. They can use brainstorming, clustering, listing, and freewriting. When students begin the drafting stage, you might want to make them aware of the recursive

HOLT WRITER'S WORKSHOP

This computer program provides help for all types of writing through guided instruction for each step of the writing process. (Program available separately.)

See *Elements of Writing, First Course,* Chapter 6, for more instruction on creative writing.

WRITING A POEM
A poem is a form of imaginative writing that is more tightly structured than a story. To create its special effect, a poet uses words to convey meaning, to paint pictures, and to produce a kind of music. A poem can begin with an **image** and expand to include an experience; it can begin with an emotion or mood, or a setting that leads to that emotion or mood. Poets can explore the outside world, or they can turn inward to probe their minds and hearts.

Prewriting
Recommend to students that they choose at least three subjects that are suitable for poems and then use a variety of prewriting strategies to collect details for each subject. If one subject does not work out, then they have others to use.

To complete their image charts, students might create a layered pattern. First they create words and phrases associated with their subject by sensory **image**. Then students create a second list of more words and phrases for each image they have just created. Encourage students to think of words and phrases based on sound and meaning. Recommend that students listen for sound patterns by speaking words aloud as they work. Finally, remind students to collect more details than they think they will use in their poems.

FOCUS ON Writing

WRITING A POEM

Poets offer readers new ways of seeing the world. In this unit, you have studied some of the important elements of poetry. Now you will have the chance to capture a thought or feeling of your own by writing a short poem.

Prewriting

1. Find a subject for your poem by brainstorming about people, objects, and events that you know well. Talk over possible subjects with a small group of classmates. Remember that almost anything can be a good subject for a poem. To jump-start your imagination, think about your associations with the following:

- an onion
- a school bus
- iced tea
- rain

[See **Focus** assignment on page 436.]

2. After you have chosen a subject, explore it further by listing some **sensory details.** Make an **image chart** like the one below.

Sense	Image
Sight	_____
Sound	_____
Smell	_____
Taste	_____
Touch	_____

[See **Focus** assignments on pages 442 and 449.]

3. Try out some phrases in which you use **figures of speech** and **sound effects.** Here are some of the devices you can use to make your language more interesting:

Figures of Speech
- **simile:** uses *like* or *as* to compare two different things
- **metaphor:** compares two different things directly
- **personification:** gives human qualities to something nonhuman

Sound Effects
- repetition
- alliteration
- refrain
- rhythm
- rhyme
- onomatopoeia

[See **Focus** assignments on pages 454 and 463.]

4. Use one of the following methods to organize the details for your poem. If you wish, make an **outline** of your poem in note form.

- chronological order
- spatial order
- order of the senses

Writing

1. Write a first draft of your poem. Focus on making each word as precise and vivid as you can. You do not need to use rhyme or regular rhythm, although you can use both these devices for special effects.

2. Make sure that all the details in your poem contribute to a single, overall impression or main effect.

3. Make up some of your own new words if you wish. Be sure, however, that your readers can guess the meaning of your new words from the context.

nature of writing and tell them that when they get stuck, they can always go back to any of the prewriting strategies to get images flowing again.

Develop with the class a holistic scoring guide so that students will know at the outset the expectations for this writing project.

CLOSURE
Have students list the elements of poetry they have included and explain why they have used those devices.

TRANSPARENCY 40
Writing Process
Writing a Poem – helps students to plan and write a creative poem.

---

4. Give your poem a title that describes the subject or refers to your overall meaning.

Evaluating and Revising

1. After you have written a first draft, try to evaluate it as objectively as possible. Add, cut, reorder, or replace words. Trade papers with a partner, and offer each other suggestions.

   Here is one writer's revision of a short poem.

Writer's Model

The Cabin

Old, overgrown cabin,

Set back from the railroad tracks in
weeds,
the grass,

With the oil stains on the floor,
   sticky with dust
And the cobwebs in the corners,
What tales can you tell?
I could tell stories about you.
   palace
Whose house were you last winter,
   drove all creatures in?
When cold made everyone go inside?

2. You may find the following checklist helpful as you revise your poem.

Checklist for Evaluation and Revision

✓ Is there a single main impression in the poem?
✓ Do I use vivid descriptions and sensory details?
✓ Do the figures of speech create fresh and lively images?
✓ Do I use sound effects that help to convey my meaning?
✓ Are all the words as exact as I can make them?

Proofreading and Publishing

1. Proofread your poem and correct any errors you find in grammar, usage, and mechanics. (Here you may find it helpful to refer to the **Handbook for Revision** on pages 726–767.) Then prepare a final version of your poem by making a clean copy.

2. Consider some of the following publication methods for your poem:
   - submit your poem to the school literary magazine
   - read your poem aloud in a poetry forum
   - illustrate your poem and post it on the class bulletin board

Portfolio If your teacher approves, you may wish to keep a copy of your work in your writing folder or portfolio.

Writing
To help students get started, you might suggest that they draft their poems quickly without worrying about form—just let the ideas and images flow. Then they can experiment with form by moving lines and whole sections around and playing with line lengths. In their first drafts, they may not even want to make final decisions on word choices.

Evaluating and Revising
The Checklist for Evaluation and Revision will be beneficial to students as they work in groups to get feedback on the overall impact of their poems. You might have students do their revision in stages: they might work first to enhance meaning and tone; second, to improve poetic devices and polish word choices; third, to give their poem a relevant and thought-provoking title.

Proofreading and Publishing
Students should proofread their poems for spelling, punctuation, and grammatical correctness. Make sure students are aware that a reader must understand any intentional rule violation. Encourage students to analyze the capitalization and the punctuation to see if these elements contribute to or detract from the total effect of their poems.

Focus on Writing **499**

UNIT 8 ◆ TEACHING GUIDE

THE NOVEL

OVERVIEW OF THE UNIT

For some students, this unit may be their first contact with a novel. Although they may have read and studied short stories, they will discover that the novel is different in that it features more fully developed characters and more elaborate and detailed events than those found in short stories. To enhance students' appreciation of the novel and the opportunity it provides for sustained reading, the **Introduction** includes suggestions about how students can become more aware of themselves as readers and how the right environment can help them to read well. It also provides **Guidelines for Close Reading,** which can help students understand how the novel achieves its effects.

Pacific Crossing, the selection in this unit, offers an intimate look at the daily life and culture of Japanese people from the point of view of a Mexican American teenager who spends part of a summer with a Japanese family in a farming village near Tokyo. Like Lincoln, the main character, students will discover fundamental similarities between Americans and Japanese, despite cultural differences.

The novel is divided into two parts, and each part is followed by exercises and activities. These will help students understand the novel and can assist them in exploring aspects of Japanese culture mentioned in the story.

OBJECTIVES OF THE UNIT

The aims of the unit are for the student:
- To identify and describe settings and the customs associated with them
- To analyze the development of the main character
- To analyze aspects of the novel's plot
- To analyze the point of view of the novel
- To identify and analyze aspects of the English language
- To write analytical essays about aspects of the novel
- To write a sequel to the novel
- To write personal and business letters
- To make connections between literature and cultures

CONCEPTS AND SKILLS

The following concepts and skills are treated in this unit:

LITERARY ELEMENTS/TERMS AND TECHNIQUES
Understanding the Novel   529, 561

LANGUAGE AND VOCABULARY
Recognizing Idioms   562
Identifying Different Levels of Language   562

WRITING OPPORTUNITIES
Writing About Literature
Analyzing Character   530
Focus on Writing a Letter
Writing a Personal Letter   530
Writing a Business Letter   562
Writing a Letter   567

CONNECTIONS
Connecting Cultures   530–531
Connecting Cultures   564–565

FOCUS ON READING AND CRITICAL THINKING
Using Analysis and Synthesis   566

TRANSPARENCIES

The following unit support materials with specific correlations to literature selections are available in the **Fine Art and Instructional Transparencies with Teacher's Notes and Blackline Masters** section of your *Audiovisual Resources Binder.*

FINE ART TRANSPARENCIES
Theme: More of the "Good Stuff"
41 *Mary Lou Williams: The Piano Lesson,* Romare Bearden
42 *Aged Tutor and Young Students,* Harrison Begay

READER RESPONSE
43 Add Up the Ratings

LITERARY ELEMENTS
44 Analyzing and Evaluating a Novel

WRITING PROCESS
45 Writing a Letter

INTRODUCING THE UNIT

One meaning of the word novel is "new or different." This definition seems appropriate for *Pacific Crossing* because it introduces readers to a country and a culture that may very well be new to them. Through the eyes of fourteen-year-old Lincoln Mendoza of San Francisco, California, students meet a middle-class Japanese family and learn much about how they live. One of the most important lessons of this novel is that people in Japan and in America have enormously more in common than the differences their cultures suggest. The reason, of course, is that human nature is the same everywhere, and Gary Soto, the author of *Pacific Crossing,* makes this point clear.

Because Japanese culture is central to the novel, the exercises and activities at the end of each part of the novel offer opportunities for

PLANNING GUIDE

FOR UNIT PLANNING
- Transparencies 41–45: *Audiovisual Resources Binder*
- Portfolio Assessment: *Professional Support Materials*
- Test Generator
- Mastery Test: Teaching Resources D, p. 189
- Analogy Test: Teaching Resources D, p. 191
- Composition Test: Teaching Resources D, p. 192

SELECTION (Pupil's Page)	TEACHING RESOURCES D (page numbers shown below)							AV BINDER
	Teacher's Notes	Reading Check	Study Guide	Language Skills	Building Vocabulary	Selection Vocab. Test	Selection Test	Audio-cassette
THE NOVEL Gary Soto *Pacific Crossing*, Chapters 1–8 (p. 503)	154	158	160	163	166	168	169	
Pacific Crossing, Chapters 9–16 (p. 532)	171	175	176	179	182	184	185	

students to explore aspects of Japanese life. Some of the exercises focus on aspects of culture mentioned in the novel, while others explore areas that Lincoln could have become aware of but that do not figure in the story. It may be helpful to establish in the classroom a temporary shelf of books, magazines, objects, and videotapes related to Japan for students to browse through and use for research as they read and discuss the novel.

Pacific Crossing is relatively short, but it features well-developed characters and a complex plot. In fact, the main character undergoes considerable growth in his awareness of Japanese culture and in his appreciation of his mother and his home. Although *Pacific Crossing* can be classified as a travel story in that it deals with a trip to a foreign country, it is also a coming-of-age novel in that Lincoln leaves San Francisco as a naive boy and returns an experienced and responsible young man. This theme is likely to appeal to seventh-grade students because it represents the kind of transformation they are going through as they enter adolescence.

Students may be familiar with concepts associated with plot, setting, character, point of view, and theme from their study of short stories and other literary works. These concepts are reinforced and extended in the **Literary Elements** exercises at the end of each section. **Language and Vocabulary** activities are at the end of each part of the novel, and they focus on aspects of language that are relevant to the novel.

PORTFOLIO ASSESSMENT
Suggestions for use of portfolios as support for this unit are described in the **Portfolio Assessment and Professional Support Materials** booklet accompanying this program. Specific suggestions are provided for a variety of student projects that may be suitable for inclusion in a portfolio. In addition, copying masters are provided for guides that may be used for evaluation and assessment of student projects.

Student Learning Options

1. Making a Map
Have students make a map showing the islands of Japan, the principal cities, the town of Atami, mountains, rivers, and other significant geographical features.

2. Cooking Japanese Food
Some students may be interested in cooking traditional Japanese food and letting the class sample it. Students will have to do research to obtain recipes from Japanese or international cookbooks, and they can share these recipes with the class.

3. Meeting Japanese Americans
Invite people of Japanese ancestry to discuss aspects of Japanese culture with the class. You can ask your guests to bring any objects or works of art that illustrate distinctive Japanese style.

4. Planning a Trip
Have small groups of students use travel guides and other resources to plan a two-week trip to Japan. Students should produce an itinerary that includes visits to primary cultural and tourist attractions.

5. Gathering Information About Japan
Ask students to write to the Japanese embassy and to the Japanese consulate in the largest city near you, requesting free brochures, maps, posters, and other items about Japan. When these arrive, put them on display in the classroom, school library, or some other prominent place where students can see them. When the unit is over, ask your school librarian if these items would be useful for the library's vertical file.

VISUAL CONNECTIONS

Exploring the Subject

Mount Fuji, or Fujiyama, is 12,388 feet (3,776 meters) high. It is located about sixty miles west of Tokyo, on the Japanese island of Honshu. Fuji's slopes are long and symmetrical, and clouds often hide its peak, which contains an inactive volcano crater. The Japanese have considered the mountain sacred since ancient times. Every year, more than fifty thousand Japanese make a pilgrimage to its summit.

Ideas for Writing

Ask students if they would want to climb Mount Fuji. Suggest that mountain climbers experience the full force of nature. Although they have the opportunity to see the beauty of nature, they also have to endure harsh conditions and danger. Ask students to locate books and magazines containing mountain climbers' firsthand accounts of their experiences. Then ask students to write brief paragraphs on interesting aspects of mountain climbing.

THE NOVEL

Mount Fuji, the highest peak in Japan.

THE NOVEL

Pacific Crossing offers students an opportunity to learn about a Mexican American teenager who spends a summer in Japan with a Japanese family. In addition to the insights students will gain about growing up and becoming self-reliant, they will also gain valuable knowledge about Japanese and Mexican American culture.

Students are probably already familiar with basic concepts of **plot, setting, character, point of view,** and **theme** from their study of short stories and other literary forms. These concepts are reinforced and developed further in this unit as they are applied to the longer literary form of the novel.

The unit provides opportunities for students to develop language and vocabulary skills with foreign words incorporated into English and with idiomatic expressions. Writing assignments focus on literary analysis, creative writing, and letter-writing skills. Features on aspects of Japanese culture extend students' knowledge of life in Japan.

INTRODUCTION TO THE NOVEL

1
As an exchange student, Lincoln lives with a Japanese family and is treated like another son.

2
Sometimes writers only imply the reasons behind a character's actions. Readers then have to infer the character's motives.

3
Often it is helpful to try to visualize an actor or friend who could play the part of a character in a movie version of a novel.

GUIDELINES FOR CLOSE READING

1. It is often helpful for students to jot down questions they have or details they notice so that they can use these notes later in class discussions and in writing assignments.
2. In this novel the primary **setting** is a small farm in Japan. Lincoln, a city dweller from the United States, has to adjust to farm life as well as life in a new country.
3. As Lincoln settles into Japanese family life, he adjusts quickly.
4. The main **conflict** centers on adjusting to an unfamiliar culture. Episodes reveal how Lincoln adjusts.
5. The **third-person point of view** allows the narrator to give an objective picture of what happens.
6. The **theme** is the author's implied statement about life that applies to everybody, not just to the characters in the novel.

In this unit you will read Gary Soto's novel *Pacific Crossing*, the story of
1 Lincoln Mendoza, an American teenager who travels to Japan as an exchange student. For Lincoln the summer holds many adventures and, at the same time, the opportunity to learn a great deal not only about another culture but also about himself.

As you read this novel, try to learn something about yourself as a reader. Where do you like to do your reading? Do you need absolute
2 silence to concentrate? When you are reading, do you try to guess what will happen next in the story? Do you question why characters act
3 as they do? Do you find yourself imagining what the characters and the setting look like? Do you become one of the characters? At the end of the novel, do you continue to think about the characters and their story?

Here are some suggestions to guide you in your reading.

Guidelines for Close Reading

1. Read actively, asking questions as you read. Try to predict how some incident or event will turn out, based on information about characters. Remember that plot and character are often interrelated because how a character acts and responds to events generates the plot. Try to determine the author's purpose as you work through the novel.

2. Become aware of information that establishes the setting. The language of characters, for example, can help set the time and place. Consider whether the setting of the novel is important and if the story might develop differently in any other setting.

3. Look for clues that reveal what characters are like: key speeches, important actions, and descriptive details. Discover how characters develop and change as the novel progresses. Determine how minor characters contribute to the story.

4. Determine what forms the major action of the novel. The conflicts and motivations of the main character often drive the action of the story. As you read, consider how individual episodes are connected to the main plot.

5. Note the point of view of the novel. Seek to understand the author's reason in selecting this point of view.

6. Consider how all the elements of the novel contribute to its theme. Pay attention to important scenes, to the title, and to what the main character learns. Try to clarify your own understanding of the author's underlying idea.

OBJECTIVES
The overall aim is for students to demonstrate an understanding of the elements of **plot, character, setting, point of view,** and **theme** in a novel. For a complete list of objectives, see the **Teacher's Notes.**

VOCABULARY
The underlined words are in the Glossary. The **Language and Vocabulary** exercise at the end of Part I will give students practice in recognizing words from languages other than English.

FOCUS / MOTIVATION
Ask if any students have ever visited a foreign country. What aspects of everyday life were hard to adjust to? If no one has visited a foreign country, ask students to consider what adjustments they might have to make.

Pacific Crossing

GARY SOTO

> **TEACHING RESOURCES D**
> Teacher's Notes, p. 154
> Reading Check, p. 158
> Study Guide, p. 160
> Language Skills, p. 163
> Building Vocabulary, p. 166
> Selection Vocabulary Test, p. 168
> Selection Test, p. 169

PREREADING FOCUS
Before students begin reading *Pacific Crossing*, discuss the **Guidelines for Close Reading** with them. Ask them to consider how they would feel if they and a classmate were on their way to a foreign country where they did not speak the language and where they knew no one.

Pacific Crossing Chapter 1

1
Lincoln has been asleep, so he is a little disoriented when he is abruptly awakened.

2
Metaphor. Describes loudspeaker voice by saying it has metallic quality, like tin.

3 Making Inferences
Why does Lincoln try to wake up Tony? Answers will vary. Perhaps he is bored and wants company. Perhaps he is embarrassed by his friend's drooling.

4
Simile. Emphasizes that ice cubes have shrunk a great deal by comparing them to aspirin tablets.

5
Plane is flying west into setting sun.

6
Airline provides magazine specially written and produced for its passengers. This is called "in-flight" magazine.

1

Lincoln Mendoza was startled awake by a strong jolt and the sound of his plastic cup of 7Up sliding across the fold-down tray in front
1 of him. For a second he didn't know where he was. He felt groggy. Another jolt, and he remembered he was thirty-seven thousand feet above the earth, on his way to Japan with his lifelong friend, his blood, his *carnal*,[1] his neighbor from the *barrio*,[2] his number-one man on the basketball floor at Franklin Junior High—Tony Contreras. They were both on a jumbo jet for the first time.

"Please be sure your seatbelts are securely
2 fastened," a tinny voice said over the loudspeaker. The instructions were repeated in Japanese—or so Lincoln assumed, because the Japanese passengers began to fumble with their seatbelts.

Lincoln nudged Tony. Tony's eyes were half-open, and a ribbon of drool was starting to flow from the corner of his mouth. He sighed and shifted away from Lincoln and up against the shoulder of the woman next to him.
3 "Wake up, man. We're almost there," Lincoln said. "You're drooling."

---
1. *carnal* (kär-näl'): close friend; a "blood brother."
2. *barrio* (bä′ryō): neighborhood, a word often used for Mexican American communities in the United States.

"No," Tony muttered. "The game ain't started yet."

"What game?" Lincoln asked, chuckling.

Tony was dreaming, gripping a crushed napkin. His knee jerked, like Lincoln's dog Flaco's legs jerked when he traveled through his doggish dreams.

Lincoln let Tony sleep. He drained the soda
4 in his cup, the ice cubes now as small as aspirins. He finished Tony's soda as well and turned to look out the window. The Pacific
5 Ocean was silver in the glare of the late-afternoon sun. In the distance, an island lay in a bluish haze.

When the stewardess came down the aisle, Lincoln asked her when they would arrive. She smiled, and said it would be another hour. She took the boys' cups.

Lincoln sighed and threw his head back into his seat. He had read two books, three battered
6 issues of *Sports Illustrated,* and the in-flight magazine, though it was mostly in Japanese. He had played cards and won $1.50 from Tony, all in nickels and dimes. He had started a crossword puzzle but given up because it had to do with biology terms, which reminded him of school. He had eaten three times and watched a movie that was funny but not so funny that he laughed out loud. And in the boredom of the eight-hour flight he had even listened to the classical-music station on his earphones. Lin-

Pacific Crossing **503**

MOTIVATIONAL SUMMARY

Lincoln Mendoza, a fourteen-year-old Mexican American boy from San Francisco, and his best friend Tony are chosen to participate in a six-week student exchange program with a Japanese family. Lincoln has been interested in the Japanese martial art called *shorinji kempō* for some time, but he knows little about Japanese culture. Lincoln is excited about his trip. In a matter of a day or two he feels right at home with Mitsuo and the rest of the Ono family.

PRESENTATION

Pacific Crossing by Gary Soto combines the fun and adventure of foreign travel with the exploits of two fourteen-year-old boys, one Japanese and one American, as they get to know each other through a series of episodes. Although

---

Chapter 2

1
Plot. Story goes back to earlier time to tell readers what led up to trip to Japan.

2
Tony's and Lincoln's families apparently visit one another at Christmas each year, and they tell story of baby teeth as means of reminiscing.

3
Exaggeration. Narrator overstates what happened in order to emphasize mother's excitement.

4
Simile. Compares jacket to limp flag to emphasize that jacket is of no use to Lincoln.

5
Police took magician away because people are giving magician money to perform.

504

---

coln had never known that sitting down could be so tiring.

He looked out the window. The island was now farther away. The sunlight on the silver water was blinding. Lincoln lowered the shade, tilted his head, and went back to sleep.

2

1 Before the end of his seventh-grade year, Lincoln and his mother had moved from Sycamore, a suburb that blazed with the boredom of television and weekend barbecues with his mother's yuppie[1] friends. He had left Columbus Junior High and returned to Franklin in San Francisco. He liked that. He had been reunited with Tony, his friend from childhood, the friend who had kicked Lincoln's baby teeth out—or so the story went, a story that 2 was rehashed by the families every Christmas.

Lincoln and his mother settled in Noe Valley near the Mission District, where Lincoln had spent his first twelve years. They were in the city, but away from the rumbles, break-ins, graffitied walls, loud barroom music, *cholos*[2] in wino shoes, *veteranos*[3] with tattooed arms and pinkish scars, and the scuttling litter of Mission and Twenty-fourth. They settled in a two-bedroom apartment off Dolores Street. His mother was happy because there was a small backyard where she could work the earth into neat rows 3 of petunias, daffodils, and tulips. And she almost jumped up and down with excitement when a single tomato plant took root and reached pathetically skyward for its circle of sunshine.

Before they moved back Lincoln had grown moody. He loathed the suburbs. He had even given up doing his homework. Instead, he played his Hammer cassettes with the volume boosted so high that the walls of his house shook and neighbors complained. He had gotten into fights at school, some he'd won and others—particularly the one against Meathead Bukowski—he'd lost.

Lincoln had become the boyfriend of a girl named Monica, but her father didn't like him. Her mother wasn't too happy with him either, especially after his bike ran over a row of her flowers. He tried to make the flowers stand back up, but they were goners.

He felt bad after he and Monica had broken up. He had cut lawns and washed cars to buy her a Raiders' jacket. When he gave it to her, wrapped in Christmas paper even though it wasn't Christmas, she cried and hugged him. He was amazed how hot tears were when one slid from her cheek and landed on his forearm. But her parents had made her give the jacket back, and now she was gone. The jacket was 4 hanging in Lincoln's closet, limp as a flag with no wind.

After Lincoln and his mom moved back to San Francisco in January, he began to study *shorinji kempō*,[4] a Japanese martial art, at the Soto Zen Center. He had discovered the center one Saturday after he and Tony, *barrio* brothers in red sneakers, got on the wrong bus and ended up in Japantown. They kicked around for a while, looking at the vases, lacquer boxes, and pearls in store windows. They bought a box of popcorn and watched girls. They stood among a small cluster of onlookers watching a second-rate magician yank scarves from his 5 sleeve. They watched the cops haul the magician away—a public nuisance because he was pulling down bucks from the crowd.

---

1. **yuppie** (yŭp′ē): a word coined in the 1980s for Y(oung) U(rban) P(rofessional); that is, a young person who lived in a city, worked hard, and believed his or her career to be more important than other concerns.
2. **cholos** (chō′lōs): gang members.
3. **veteranos** (bĕ-tĕ-rä′nōs): war veterans.

4. **shorinji kempō** (shō-rēn-jē kĕm-pō). In Japanese, all syllables receive approximately the same stress.

504 THE NOVEL

Lincoln teaches his Japanese friend Mitsuo Ono about American culture, Lincoln is really a student. His major lesson is that Japanese and Mexican American teenagers are far more alike than they are different.

You might want to start by asking students to write on a piece of paper the first thing that comes to mind when they think of Japan. Through class discussion, encourage students to create a comprehensive list of Japanese associations. The list might include electronic equipment, types of food, martial arts, traditional clothing, and art. You might want to have students read the first chapter in class in order to clarify with them any misunderstandings they may have. After students have read the remaining chapters, you may want to discuss the events of the **plot** to make sure everyone has an

While walking up Pine Street, they heard grunting sounds. They looked up and saw a 6 blood red sign: two combatants and the words *Shorinji Kempō*. They followed the grunts and yells down a hallway and were surprised to come to a room full of people working out in white uniforms.

The *sensei*,[5] a large, barrel-chested Japanese 7 man whose face shone with sweat, welcomed them by pointing to a row of folding chairs along the wall. Their hands squeezed into fists, Lincoln and Tony sat and watched, excited by the kicks, punches, and obviously painful pins and throws. The next week they were taking classes.

Tony quit after two months, but Lincoln stayed, advancing to *sankyu*[6]—brown belt—in six months. *Shorinji kempō* didn't have lots of col-
8 ored belts. A student went from white to brown, with no rainbow stops in between. The school didn't go to tournaments, believing that martial art was to be used in a wicked chance meeting in the streets, not as a game for spectators.

Back with his friends at Franklin Junior High, Lincoln improved his grades from C's to 9 A's. He turned down the volume of his stereo and did the dishes whenever his mother asked. He was happy. His dog, Flaco, was happy. His mother was happy and even thinking of marrying her boyfriend, Roy, a guy with bum knees but a good heart.

One day at school while Lincoln was in metal

6 Analyzing
Why does narrator call sign "blood red"? Since sign is for martial arts studio, "blood red" suggests blood might flow in fights in studio.

7
Sweat on man's face reflects light and makes his face appear to shine.

8
Metaphor. Compares many colors of belts of some martial arts disciplines to rainbow.

9 Drawing Conclusions
What does turning down volume imply about Lincoln's attitude? He is no longer eager to tune out his mother and rest of world. His attitude is improving.

5. *sensei* (sĕn-sā): teacher.

6. *sankyu* (sän-kyōō).

Pacific Crossing

accurate idea of what is taking place in the story. Sometimes having students write brief summaries of the chapters helps motivate them to keep up with reading assignments, and the summaries can be helpful in working on the exercises at the end of Part I.

PORTFOLIO ASSESSMENT
Some students might enjoy writing a letter from Tony's or Lincoln's point of view to thank Mr. Ayala for the opportunity to participate in the student-exchange program and to tell him what they intend to do to bring honor to their school. Students may want to design their own stationery for their final drafts. (See *Portfolio Assessment and Professional Support Materials* for additional information on student portfolios.)

10 Summarizing
Why is Mr. Ayala proud of his scar? It is a sign of his toughness.

11 Apparently Lincoln only associated principal with being in trouble.

12 Metaphor. Compares being in trouble at school to loss of favor with God through sin.

13 Metaphor. Compares open top of garbage can to mouth that consumes garbage as though it were food.

14 "Five o'clock shadow" refers to dark beard stubble. If a man shaves early in morning, by five o'clock in afternoon beard will have grown enough to create illusion of shadow on man's face.

15 Lincoln shows he does not know much about Japan, even though he has studied a Japanese martial art for some time.

16 Metaphor. Compares falling white cherry blossoms to tiny parachutes floating from sky.

17 Making Generalizations
What does Mr. Ayala mean by "goodwill gesture"? Trip is intended to create better understanding and respect, and thereby goodwill, between Japanese and American people.

18 Tony's answer shows he knows no more about Japan than Lincoln does.

---

shop welding two pieces of pipe together, the teacher, Mr. Parish, his mouth full of half-chomped sandwich, called, "Mendoza. Mr. Ayala wants to see you."

Mr. Ayala was the principal, an ex-cop who had worked the Haight-Ashbury during San Francisco's hippie days.[7] He was tough, and proud of the ridged knife scar on his forearm. Few boys talked back to him, but when one did, Mr. Ayala would push him against the wall, a huge hand around the boy's skinny neck, and hiss, "Wise guy, huh?"

Lincoln was baffled by the summons. He dipped the pipe into a trough of gray water, sending up a cloud of metallic steam that stung his nose. He took off his apron and washed his hands, wondering what he had done wrong.

As he walked across the lawn to Principal Ayala's office, he searched his mind for a clue to his fall from grace. He was certain his record was clean. Then he stopped in his tracks as he recalled that yesterday at break he and Tony had gotten an armful of empty milk cartons and hurled them one by one at the mouth of a garbage can. They had joked and played; and when the bell sounded, the milk cartons were left on the ground, oozing white dribbles of milk. What was the big deal? Lincoln thought. But, feeling guilty, he gathered pieces of litter—gum wrappers, Popsicle sticks, paper cups, and crushed milk cartons—as he made his way to the office.

But the smiling, pencil-tapping Mr. Ayala sat Lincoln down and told him that he wasn't in trouble.

"What do you think of Japan?" the principal asked. It was still morning, but his face showed the traces of a five o'clock shadow. His tie was loose, and the cuffs of his shirt were rolled up. His scar was pink in the morning light.

"It's far away," Lincoln responded doubtfully. "They make good cars."

"Wise guy, huh?" Mr. Ayala said, smirking. He explained that a school district in Japan was looking for exchange students for the summer. The student would not have to go to school; he would just stay with a family. The principal had thought of Lincoln because he knew he was taking "some kind of karate."[8]

Lincoln was curious. His mind formed an image of a dojo[9] and a *sensei* sitting in meditation before a bowl of incense. He pictured snowcapped mountains and cherry blossoms parachuting from black branches. He pictured himself as a boy warrior in a white *gi*[10] stained with the blood of enemies.

"You mean I could go to Japan? Me?" Lincoln asked.

"Yes, you. You'll be an exchange student. You know, a goodwill gesture," Mr. Ayala remarked. He bent a paper clip.

Just then Tony walked into the office looking guilty and smelling of hair oil. Tony seemed to be about to confess to doing something wrong when Lincoln whispered, "*Cállate*.[11] You ain't in trouble."

The principal laughed. "You think you're busted, huh, Tony?" Mr. Ayala said as he pointed Tony to a chair. "And what do *you* think of Japan?"

Tony rubbed his chin. "They make good cars, I guess." His eyes were shining. "Am I right?"

"Another wise guy, huh?" Mr. Ayala said, smiling so the lines on his face deepened. He told Tony about the student-exchange program.

---

7. **Haight-Ashbury...hippie days:** San Francisco became a center for the youth protest movement in the 1960s. Hippies, sometimes called "flower children," lived together in small groups, often in substandard conditions, and many of them used illicit drugs. In 1967 about 75,000 hippies converged on Haight-Ashbury, a neighborhood in San Francisco.

8. **karate** (kə-rä′tē): a Japanese art of self-defense. The opponents use sharp blows and kicks.
9. **dojo** (dō-jō): a school for martial arts.
10. **gi** (gē): a martial-arts uniform.
11. **Cállate** (kä′yä-tā): Shut up!

506 THE NOVEL

MEETING INDIVIDUAL NEEDS

ESL/LEP • Before leaving for Japan, Lincoln and Tony "kicked around" Japantown and watched a magician "pulling down bucks" from the crowd (p. 504). Ask the class to guess at the meaning of these colloquial expressions, basing their guesses on sentence context. (*to kick around*—to move from place to place; *to pull down bucks*—to elicit money)

He said that he was nominating them because they had shown an interest in Japan by taking martial arts.

19 "Your grades are crummy," Mr. Ayala said as he opened the folder that held Tony's school records. "But it could do you good to see another country. I want you to make us proud. ¿*Entiendes?*"[12]

Lincoln and Tony nodded.

"I'll talk with your parents," Mr. Ayala said. He threw the paper clip at the wastebasket. He missed by a foot, easy. "There will be costs involved. Six hundred dollars for airfare."

"Six hundred?" they both said.

"Don't worry. The PTA will pay for half. You 20 two better go cut some lawns."

Lincoln and Tony left the office bewildered. They had seldom been invited anywhere, and now they were being invited to Japan.

"But I quit *kempō*," Tony said.

"He doesn't know that. Don't say anything."

21 Lincoln punched Tony in the arm and returned to metal shop, wondering how he and Tony were going to get the money for airfare when sometimes it was difficult to get bus fare. That was the only drawback. Too bad it was such a big one. Maybe his mother would give 22 him some of her savings. He would have to treat her nice for the rest of the century, if not longer.

That night Lincoln told his mother about the student-exchange program. "But it's going to cost us at least three hundred for airfare," he added.

Lincoln's mother was happy for her son. When she was his age, fourteen, she had wanted to go to France as an exchange student, but her family hadn't had the money to send her.

"Money grows on trees," she said, eyes twinkling. "You're going, *mi'jo.*"[13]

12. *¿Entiendes?* (ĕn-tyĕn'dĕs): Do you understand?
13. *mi'jo* (mē'hō): my son (shortened form of *mi hijo*).

Lincoln knew what that meant. In her bedroom his mother had hung the key to their safe on the limb of a ficus plant. When the time came, she would snatch that key off the limb and open the safe.

23 At Tony's house, the family's savings were kept in the refrigerator, smashed in the back of the freezer compartment between a package of frozen peas and a one-eyed salmon that Tony's uncle had caught in Alaska.

Both boys would go to Japan with wads of spending money, because both mothers knew 24 how to save and save, even on rainy days.

25 The jet dipped, and its engines rumbled as its speed slowed. Lincoln woke to see Tony looking at him.

"You got *moco*[14] in your eyes," Tony told him, rubbing his own eyes.

Lincoln wiped his eyes and yawned with a hand over his mouth.

"What time is it?" Lincoln asked. "I feel lousy."

"I don't know, bro'. Seems like we were born on this jet. Is Japan near the moon?"

The Fasten Seatbelts sign lit up and the stewardess came down the aisle, speaking in Japanese, then English, collecting empty cups and glasses.

"She forgot us Spanish-speaking *gente*," Tony quipped. "*Señorita, mi amigo es muy feo y un tonto también.*"[15]

The woman smiled, her eyes crinkling into triangles. "*No, chavalo, su amigo es lindo y listo.*"[16]

Lincoln and Tony looked at each other, big-eyed with surprise.

"Fresh! She knows Spanish!" they said. They

14. *moco* (mō'kō): mucus.
15. "*Señorita, mi amigo...también*" (sĕ-nyo-rē'tä mē ä-mē'gō ĕs moo'ē fā'ō ē ōōn tôn'tō täm-byĕn'): "Miss, my friend is very ugly and foolish too."
16. "*No, chavalo...listo*" (nō chä-bä'lō soo ä-mē'gō ĕs lēn'dō ē lēs'tō): "No, young man, your friend is handsome and smart."

Pacific Crossing 507

---

19 Making Inferences
Why does Mr. Ayala mention Tony's grades? Probably to suggest that most people would expect honor student to be chosen for exchange program.

20
Few jobs other than mowing lawns are available for students at Lincoln and Tony's age.

21 Finding Cause and Effect
Why does Lincoln punch Tony? As sign of affection and excitement.

22
Exaggeration. Emphasizes Lincoln will have to be nice to his mother for a long time if she gives him money for airfare.

23 Drawing Conclusions
Why does family keep money in freezer? Burglars would not think to look for it there.

24
Ordinarily people save "for a rainy day," meaning for when times are hard. Lincoln's and Tony's mothers save *on* rainy days, meaning they have figured out how to save money even when times are hard.

25
Plot. Story returns to present, indicating background information is finished.

MEETING INDIVIDUAL NEEDS

ESL/LEP • The author uses the image of *scuttling litter* on p. 504. Explain that *to scuttle* means "to run or move quickly," as a crab scuttling across the ocean floor. *Litter* is another word for "bits or pieces of trash." Encourage students to think about the image the author is trying to convey to the reader. Write student suggestions on the chalkboard.

26
Metaphor. Lights from city compared to flower to suggest their beauty in darkness of night.

27 Making Inferences
Why does Lincoln tell Tony to shut up? Answers will vary. Perhaps he is embarrassed by what Tony is saying. Perhaps he does not want to attract unnecessary attention.

28
Tony shows he is a little nervous and scared about being in Japan by suggesting there are better things he could be doing.

29
Classes were probably designed to teach students what to expect and how to react in unfamiliar culture.

30 Analyzing
What does being on their own imply? That Lincoln and Tony will not have anyone to rely on for advice or support. They will have to learn to solve problems and to get along without benefit of other Americans to help them.

31 Analyzing
What is significant about fact both families live on small farms? Lincoln and Tony are both city boys. Living on farm, even a small one, is big change for them.

---

26 laughed and looked out the window, where a flower of lights from Tokyo glowed against the night sky. Soon they could distinguish buildings, and large freighters docked in the harbor. The jet slowly descended through wispy clouds. They could make out houses, hills, factories, a bridge, and a river of lights—cars on a freeway. They could see a train and, as they dropped lower, a Japanese sign advertising Coca-Cola.

As the jet landed, the passengers sighed, and some clapped. It had been a long journey—almost nine hours of stale air, cramped seats, and magazines read and reread.

They went through customs, and the white-gloved officers searched handbags and carry-ons. Passports were brought out. Tony joked about being caught and frisked by *la migra*.[17]

27 He kept joking until Lincoln told him to shut up.

"Can't you think of anything else to say?" Lincoln scolded.

"Yeah, what am I doing here? I don't take
28 martial arts. You're the dude. I coulda been workin' at my uncle Rudy's restaurant and makin' money instead of spendin' it."

"Who wants to work? You got your whole life to do that."

"Yeah, you're right," Tony agreed.

They went through customs without a hitch. As they walked up a ramp to meet their host families, Lincoln hoped that he and Tony would see each other soon

29 Back in California, they had taken a week of orientation classes with other young people going to Japan through the same exchange pro-
30 gram. Now they were on their own. They were the only students staying in Atami,[18] a small farming village three hours outside Tokyo. Lincoln was with the Ono family, and Tony would

---

17. *la migra* (lä mē'grä): immigration authorities.
18. **Atami** (ä-tä-mē).

---

31 be with the Inaba[19] family. Both lived on tiny one-acre farms. Lincoln knew that his sponsor worked for the railroad, that his wife took care of their small farm, and that they had a son

19. **Ono** (ō-nō); **Inaba** (ē-nä-bä).

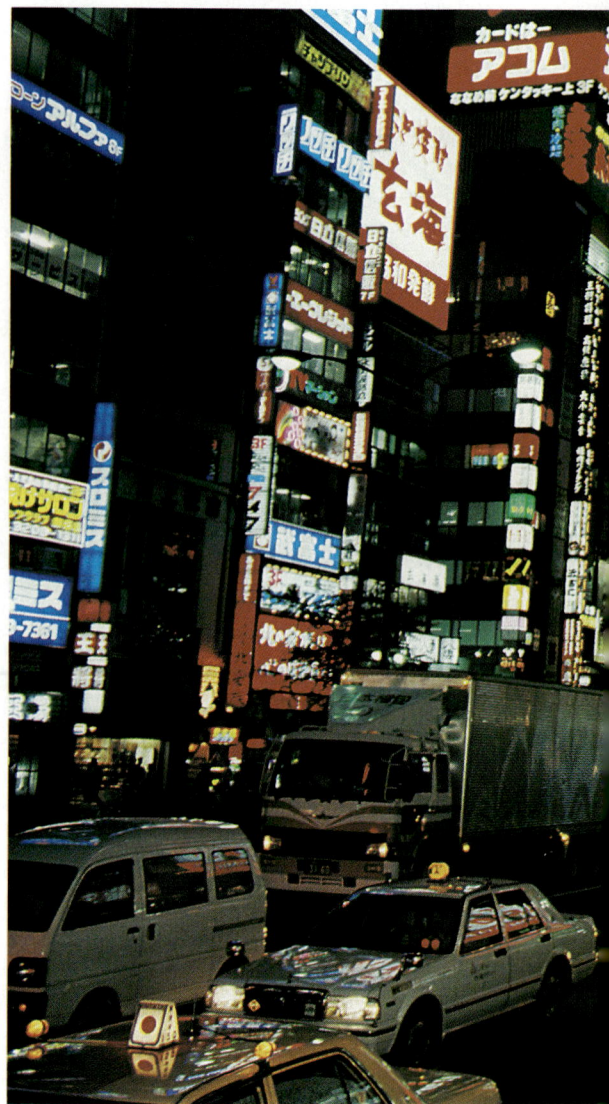

Shinjuku area at night.

MEETING INDIVIDUAL NEEDS

ESL/LEP • Both Lincoln's and Tony's mothers know how to save money, "even on rainy days." Explain to students that this expression (on p. 507) does not literally mean that it is raining on these days; instead, *rainy days* refers to times of difficulty or need. Often used in the singular form, *a rainy day* may refer to a time in the future, as in "She's saving her money for a rainy day."

---

32 near his age. He looked forward to his days in Japan. He wanted to study *kempō*,[20] and to learn to speak some Japanese. He had six weeks to do it.

20. **kempō** (kĕm-pō): a martial art.

33 "This is weird," Lincoln heard Tony say as he
34 was swallowed up by a cluster of people. The whole Inaba family—father, mother, and son—smiled, bowed over and over, and welcomed Tony with little gifts wrapped in beautifully designed paper.

32
Figurative Language. Narrator uses "days" to stand for whole time boys will be in Japan.

33
Tony is surprised by his reception by Inaba family.

34
Metaphor. Compares people gathering around Tony to giant animal swallowing him.

Pacific Crossing 509

Meeting Individual Needs

ESL/LEP • Explain that in English some nouns, like *shoulder,* can also be used as verbs. On p. 510, Soto describes Lincoln "shouldering his flight bag." Other nouns denoting the arms and upper body can be used as verbs as well. How many of these can the class name? (back, hand, elbow, finger) Can students use these verbs in sentences? Here are some examples:

He carefully *backed* the car into his driveway.
The mailman *handed* me two letters.
They *elbowed* their way through the crowd.
She *fingered* every piece of fruit before finally selecting one.

Chapter 3

1
Metaphor. Compares years of providing for family to long trip.

2 Expressing an Opinion
How does Lincoln feel about way Tony is acting? Answers will vary. Possibilities include embarrassment and amusement.

3
Metaphor. Compares lights on radio tower to stalk of red flowers.

4
Fact that Tokyo resembles San Francisco suggests that Japan and America, and people of each country, may be more alike than different.

5
Suggests advertising uses universal language of its own.

6 Drawing Conclusions
What do Mr. Ono's responses suggest about his experience with America? That he may have visited America at some point in past.

7
Simile. Mr. Ono compares size of America to size of sky to emphasize that America is enormous compared to Japan.

8
Lincoln thinks of mother's car because automobiles are what he and Tony associate with Japan.

3

Mr. Ono bowed and asked, "Mr. Lincoln Mendoza?"

Lincoln stood before a small man with watery eyes. His dignified face was lined and dark. It **1** bespoke the long haul of providing for a family. Lincoln bowed a little more deeply than his sponsor. "Yes, I'm Lincoln Mendoza. Thank you for having me."

"Good," Mr. Ono remarked. He pumped Lincoln's outstretched hand, and Lincoln could feel the power of a working man's grip.

Shouldering his flight bag, Lincoln turned and saw Tony giving a *raza*-style handshake[1] to Mr. Inaba. Tony was laughing, and his sponsor was smiling and asking to see the handshake again.

"¡*Órale, Papi!*"[2] Tony screamed. "You got it down!"

2 Nine thousand miles from home, thought Lincoln, and Tony's acting like a regular *vato*.[3] Lincoln called, "See ya in town," and Tony, playing up the homeboy image, raised a clenched fist and shouted, "¡*Viva la Raza!*"[4]

Lincoln hurried alongside Mr. Ono. They walked briskly, sliding between the rush of travelers racing to catch their flights.

They gathered the luggage, and only in the car did Mr. Ono say in near-perfect English, "My family is waiting at home." Lincoln's head jerked as the car shifted into second, then third, rumbling from a bad muffler.

Lincoln watched Tokyo unfold from the freeway. The evening skyline was bright with neon and skyscrapers. Street-long oil tankers lay docked in the harbor, where the moonlight failed to shimmer on the dark water. A tall **3** radio antenna stood on a hill, a stalk of red lights blinking slowly. Lincoln thought Tokyo **4** resembled San Francisco, where houses stood against the backdrop of the Bay.

The billboards on the side of the freeway advertised in *kanji*,[5] Japanese writing, with now and then an English word like "shampoo" or "luxury." He couldn't understand the *kanji* but **5** could easily understand that they were announcing cars, cigarettes, beer, and liquor—the same products as in the United States.

The drivers were just as crazy as in San Francisco, but the honking cars seemed quieter, less obnoxious. The traffic was stop-and-go until they reached a four-lane highway that would take them out of the city.

"Tokyo's like America," Lincoln said, smiling and trying to make conversation. "You know, we even have our own Cherry Blossom Festival. In San Francisco."

"Yes," Mr. Ono said, braking so hard that Lincoln had to hold on to the dashboard. "Yes, **6** yes." A car was stalled in the left lane. Mr. Ono wiggled his steering wheel as he maneuvered dangerously into the next lane.

"I'm from San Francisco," Lincoln continued. "We're right on a bay like Tokyo."

"Yes, but America is very large," Mr. Ono said as he swerved back into the left lane, his **7** eyes looking in the mirror. "It is big as the sky." A car honked at them, but Mr. Ono ignored it.

Big as the sky, Lincoln thought. He didn't know how to respond. He turned his attention to the harbor and its huge freighters weighed **8** down with exports. Lincoln thought of his mother's car, a Maxima made in Japan, and how it was closing in on a hundred thousand miles without a breakdown. It was dented on one side, and the back window was cracked

---

1. **raza-style handshake:** Mr. Soto says, "A *raza* handshake starts out like a normal handshake, but after a series of prescribed moves on the part of both handshakers' hands, it ends with a fist tap."
2. **Órale, Papi** (ô′rä-lā pä′pē): All right, Dad.
3. **vato** (bä′tō): dude.
4. **Viva la Raza** (bē′bä lä rä′sä): Hurray for the Mexican people.

5. **kanji** (kän-jē): Chinese characters used in Japanese writing.

COOPERATIVE LEARNING
Have students work in small groups to research the climate, geography, and geology of Japan's four main islands: Honshu, Hokkaido, Kyushu, and Shikoku. Ask interested students to report on typhoons and other severe weather events that often affect Japan. Students may also want to research evidence of the geologic instability of the region, including volcanic activity and earthquakes.

---

from when Tony accidentally slammed it with a bat.

The muggy air made Lincoln feel lousy. Sweat blotched his underarms and pasted his shirt to his skin. It was July, one of the hottest times in Tokyo, and the cement and asphalt still blazed from the punishing daytime sun. Lincoln looked at a Coca-Cola sign and ran his tongue over his lips, thirsting for one precious swallow.

9 Mr. Ono noticed; he reached into the backseat and pulled a bottle from a bag. "*Ramune*.[6] It's good. Can you say?"

Lincoln took the bottle and turned it over. "*Ramune*," he said under his breath.

Mr. Ono opened the bottle by pushing down **10** on the top, dislodging a marble stopper. Lincoln took a long, serious swallow, which cleared his throat and made him feel good. He looked at the characters on the label but couldn't figure out if the drink was soda or juice.

"What is it again?"

"*Ramune*. It's good for you, Lincoln-kun."[7]

Lincoln shrugged his shoulders, drank until the bottle was empty, and placed the bottle in the backseat. "That was good." He beamed. "Thanks."

11 Soon the city gave way to a patchwork of small farms rippling with stalks of rice lit by the July moonlight. As the car picked up speed, the fender rattled. Lincoln had noticed when they got in the car that the fender was old and buckled. He had seen that Mr. Ono was dressed plainly and that his hands were as rough as the hands of Lincoln's uncle Ray, a radiator man. He had imagined that everyone in Japan was doing well, living off the riches of high-tech computers and first-rate cars. But he had been wrong.

In the dark, Lincoln could just make out the features of Mr. Ono puffing on a cigarette, the red glow of the ash brightening his face. He looked like a worker, stubble on his chin, eyes sagging from fatigue. He looked Mexican, dark and tough skinned from years of work. Lincoln pulled down the car's visor and looked at himself in the mirror. His skin was unblemished, **12** his eyes bright, and his hair black and shiny as a polished shoe.

The hum of the car's engine lulled Lincoln into a drowsy stupor. He was tired from the long flight, as well as from the night before, when he hadn't been able to sleep from anticipation of the trip. He had turned over and over restlessly, his mind loaded with an image of Japan: a dojo swept clean and a faint aura of incense in the air. Now he was in Japan, and **13** Japan looked more like San Francisco than like the calendars his mom got from Sumitomo Bank. To Lincoln, Tokyo was disappointingly modern.

Lincoln had started wondering about Japan after he had begun taking *kempō*, and he had become interested in the history and culture after he and his mother had gone to a festival of Japanese movies. His favorite movie was *Yojimbo*, about a blind swordsman who slashed evil from a small village. But Tokyo was nothing like the movie. Not one woman was wearing a kimono; not one man was walking in *geta*,[8] wooden sandals.

Lincoln fell asleep. When he woke, the car was pulling into a driveway. A cat's eyes were lit by the headlights. The sky was no longer filled **14** with the harsh, blistering light of the city. It was **15** black, stars pulsating above. Crickets chattered in the grasses. A dog barked in the distance. A radio was playing classical music. They had driven nearly 150 miles, and Tokyo was gone.

---

6. *Ramune* (rä-mōō-nĕ).
7. **Lincoln-kun:** Kun (kōōn) is an informal ending used for male personal names.
8. *geta* (gā-tä).

---

9 Drawing Conclusions
What does Mr. Ono's response suggest about his awareness of Lincoln? That he is sensitive to boy's needs, as any good host would be.

10 Drawing Conclusions
What does detail about marble stopper suggest about what will happen to bottle when it is empty? That it will be recycled and perhaps reused many times before it is discarded.

11
Metaphor. Compares fields of rice to small lakes reflecting moonlight.

12
Simile. Compares Lincoln's hair to well-shined leather shoe.

13
Lincoln's ideas about what Japan is like are based on advertising and on his imagination. Reality of Japan is quite different.

14
In city, street lights and light from signs illuminate sky and make it almost impossible to see stars. In country, stars are visible.

15
Personification. Noise crickets make compared to sound of people talking.

Pacific Crossing

Cultural Diversity

In modern Japan, as Lincoln discovers when he first arrives in Tokyo, most people dress like people in the United States. On special occasions, like weddings and New Year's Day, however, many wear a traditional kimono. Many cultures have traditional costumes. Have students present a report to the class that shows illustrations or photographs of the traditional wear of several cultures. Have them describe on what occasions these costumes are worn. Possible reference sources are *Folk Costumes of the World* by Robert Harrold and Phyllida Legg and *Folk and Festival Costume of the World* by R. Turner Wilcox.

---

16 Summarizing
What does narrator mean by "western-style house"? House is like type found in Western Hemisphere. It is not built in traditional Japanese style.

17 Simile. Moon compared to a nickel coin, which is also silver-colored and round.

18 Making Inferences
Why does Lincoln not repeat his statement? Answers will vary. Maybe Lincoln feels Mrs. Ono might be offended by being compared to his mother.

19 Metaphor. Heavy luggage makes Lincoln walk like a duck, whose walk is called a waddle.

20 Lincoln probably learned of the Japanese custom of removing shoes in house during orientation session or from his teacher of kempō.

21 Drawing Conclusions
Why are mother and son surprised? They are surprised Lincoln knows name of drink.

22 Simile. Compares Lincoln's head to heavy boulder to emphasize how tired he is.

23 Mitsuo shows he knows something about American baseball.

24 Exaggeration. Exaggerates size of yawn to emphasize that yawn is big and, probably, long.

Lincoln ran a moist hand over his face, stretched, and yawned. He felt dirty, his shirt was stiff with dried sweat, and his mouth was sour from not having brushed his teeth since breakfast, many time zones ago, when he'd been in California. He opened the car door and lowered a leg stiffly to the ground. He was **16** "home," and home was a small western-style house on a tiny farm. He could smell the vegetables in the field. He could smell the faint **17** stinks of chickens and compost. The moon hung, silver and round as a nickel, between two trees.

Lincoln got out of the car slowly, trying his best to show his happiness to the Onos and their son, Mitsuo.[9]

"Welcome, Lincoln," Mrs. Ono said, bowing. "You must be tired."

Lincoln bowed and said, "Yes, I'm tired. Thank you for having me."

Mrs. Ono seemed taller than her husband. She reminded Lincoln of his own mother, big-boned and dark, with a smile that made him smile back. She was dressed in jeans and a plaid blouse, and her hair was pinned back into a bun.

Lincoln couldn't help himself; he blurted out, "You look like my mom."

"My English is not so good," the mother said as she helped with the luggage. "Please say again."

18 "Oh, I mean, thank you for having me," Lincoln said, and he bit his tongue. He shouldered his backpack and took the luggage from Mrs. **19** Ono. "I can do it." Lincoln waddled under the heaviness of the luggage as he followed the Onos into the house.

Only when the family stared at Lincoln's **20** shoes[10] did he realize that he should take them off. He banged his head with the heel of his palm and said, "Oops, sorry." They smiled, and Mrs. Ono handed him a pair of slippers.

"Would you like something to drink?" Mitsuo asked. Mitsuo was as tall as Lincoln. But while Lincoln's hair was long, almost straggly, Mitsuo's hair was cropped to almost nothing. He was strong. When he took the luggage from Lincoln, his biceps tightened into globes of veined muscle. His T-shirt was stretched over his chest, showing two plates of muscle and flesh.

"*Ramune*, please," Lincoln said.

21 The mother and son looked at each other, surprised. Mitsuo went to the kitchen for four *ramune* and they settled in the living room. They looked at each other, smiling and drinking. Lincoln's arms felt limp, his head **22** heavy as a boulder, and his eyes small from lack of sleep.

In careful English Mitsuo asked, "Do you play baseball?"

"No, basketball. But I like baseball. I played Little League for two years."

"Basketball is not so popular here. Baseball is our game. I play the outfield."

While Lincoln nursed his drink, the heaviness of sleep settled on him. He rubbed his eyes, yawned, and sat up straight, trying to keep awake. His host family seemed ready for Lincoln to tell them something about himself. "Baseball. I, ah . . ." Lincoln couldn't concentrate; his mind kept sliding into fatigue. "Sports, ah—I like movies . . ."

23 "Do you like the San Francisco Giants? We have the Tokyo Giants."

"Yes, plenty of times," Lincoln responded, thinking he had been asked if he had seen the Giants play at Candlestick Park. He drained his drink and watched his host family talk, their **24** mouths moving as they asked questions. Lincoln opened his mouth into a yawn as wide as a hat. He fell asleep on the couch, an empty bottle of *ramune* in his hands.

---

9. **Mitsuo** (mēt-sōō-ō).
10. **shoes:** It is customary in Japanese homes to remove one's shoes upon entering anyone's home.

TRANSPARENCIES 41 & 42
Fine Art
Theme: *More of the "Good Stuff"* – invites students to explore artworks depicting someone sharing, exchanging, or appreciating the culture of others.

4

Lincoln woke to the buzz of a fly circling above him. He slowly opened his eyes, stared at the ceiling, and muttered to himself, "I'm in Japan."

He rolled out of his *futon*¹ and tried to get up but sat back down, feeling dizzy and lethargic. He lay back with a sigh, and after a few minutes of staring at the hypnotic figure eights of the circling fly, he fell asleep again. When he woke a second time, Mitsuo was standing over him, pounding his fist into a baseball glove. The room was hot, sunlight slanting in from an open window. Two flies were circling the air where there had been only one.

"Lincoln-kun, are you awake?"

Lincoln propped himself up on his elbows, blinking sleep from his eyes. "Yeah. I was tired from the flight. What time is it?"

"Lunchtime. Do you like *rāmen*?² *Haha* is in the field. *Chichi* is working at the station."

"Who?"

"'*Haha*' is 'Mother,' and '*Chichi*' is 'Father,'" Mitsuo explained. He placed his glove in the closet and pulled back the curtain so that sunlight flooded the room. "Come on, let's eat."

Lincoln rose, washed quickly in the bathroom, and joined Mitsuo in the kitchen. They ate in silence, watching each other and smiling now and then. Lincoln liked Mitsuo. "You are good with *hashi*," Mitsuo complimented.

"You mean chopsticks?"

"Yes, 'chopsticks.' Very funny word. We have spoons if you need one."

Lincoln sucked in a cheekful of noodles. He wanted to tell Mitsuo that he ate mostly using a tortilla, but how, on the first day, could he explain that he was both Mexican and American? He drained the broth of his *rāmen*. Maybe later I'll tell them about Mexican food, he thought as he wiped his mouth with a paper napkin.

Mitsuo got up and said, "I have to get back to work. You rest."

"No, I'll help," Lincoln said, taking his bowl to the sink.

"You are our guest."

"No, please. I want to help."

Mitsuo thought for a moment. "OK, but let me get you something." He left and returned with a long-sleeved work shirt.

"Here." Mitsuo handed Lincoln the shirt. "The flies will bite if you don't wear a shirt. And use this hat."

Lincoln put on the hat and looked at himself reflected in the kitchen window. He liked what he saw. "My mom would be proud. She used to work in the fields."

"Your mother is a farmer?" Mitsuo asked, lacing up his boots. "Here, wear Father's boots."

"No, but she used to pick grapes when she was little. Now she works in an office." Lincoln picked up the boots, whose tips were curled, and stuffed his feet into them.

The two of them joined Mrs. Ono, who was knee-deep in eggplant leaves. The family would harvest in a month, but now, in early July, the eggplant fruits poked through the green growth, still swelling like balloons. The vegetables needed to be weeded, irrigated, and examined for worms.

"*Nasu*," Mitsuo said and pointed to the eggplant.

"*Nasu*," Lincoln repeated.

Lincoln knew nothing about work, though he used to wash his uncle's BMW for money and cut a few lawns. Most of his relatives had once worked in the fields chopping cotton, cutting grapes, and picking oranges, cantaloupes, and almonds on the west side of the San Joaquin Valley. But field work—even in a one-acre patch of eggplant, his least favorite vegetable, and

---
1. *futon* (foo′tän′): a thin mattress placed on the floor, used as a bed.
2. *rāmen* (rä-män): Japanese noodles served in a broth.

Pacific Crossing 513

Chapter 4

1
Lincoln is still exhausted from his long trip, even after a night's sleep.

2 Drawing Conclusions
What does baseball glove suggest about Mitsuo? That baseball is his passion and that he thinks about it much of time.

3
Mitsuo teaches Lincoln Japanese words informally. Learning Japanese is one of Lincoln's goals for his trip.

4 Drawing Conclusions
Why do boys eat in silence? They do not know one another yet and are a little shy.

5 Making Inferences
Why does Lincoln insist on helping Mitsuo with his work? Answers will vary. Perhaps he wants to get to know Mitsuo better. Perhaps he fears being bored staying in house.

6
Even though it is hot, Mitsuo gives Lincoln a long-sleeved shirt because he knows flies are worse than heat.

7
Simile. Compares eggplant fruit to balloons, which sometimes have egg shape of eggplants.

8
Mitsuo continues his informal instruction in Japanese.

READING SKILLS PRACTICE
To help students practice the reading skill of drawing conclusions, ask students to read the underlined passage and to choose the response that correctly answers the question. How does Mrs. Ono feel when Lincoln says he is part of the family? **A.** She is embarrassed to have Lincoln as a family member. (Incorrect; unsupported.) **B.** Mrs. Ono is pleased to hear that Lincoln feels at home. (Correct.) **C.** Mrs. Ono is eager to get on with her work in the house. (Incorrect; irrelevant.) **D.** Mrs. Ono wants to make sure Lincoln does the work in the field correctly. (Incorrect; unsupported.)

9
Exaggeration. Narrator uses "staggered" to emphasize Lincoln has trouble walking in Mr. Ono's large boots.

10
Metaphor. Compares streak of sweat to ribbon to suggest streak is straight and reflects light like shiny ribbon.

11
Lincoln risks embarrassing family because he does not know Japanese customs regarding guests, but he recovers quickly by saying he is part of family.

12 Making Inferences
Why does Mrs. Ono laugh? Answers will vary. Perhaps she is delighted that Lincoln wants to be family member. Perhaps she laughs at idea of resting because she knows she has more work to do inside.

13 Analyzing
Why is Lincoln exhausted after working only a few hours? Perhaps he is still tired from his trip. Perhaps he is not used to work, so only a little tires him out.

14
Sights and sounds in Japanese village very similar to sights and sounds in American town.

15
Simile. Compares Lincoln's stretching to cat's stretching.

16
Personification. Compares homesickness to shadow and gives it human ability to touch.

514

---

three rows of tomato plants—was something new to Lincoln. He felt proud as he staggered about in oversized boots, a hat shading his eyes from the sun.

Mrs. Ono looked up. "Good morning, Lincoln-kun." She looked skyward. "No, good afternoon."

"I was so sleepy," Lincoln said. And even now, though it was midday, he felt groggy from the flight. "I'm sorry I woke up late."

"It was a long trip," Mrs. Ono said. Her face was hidden in the shadow of her hat; mud clung to her boots. "Did you eat?"

"*Rāmen.*"

"Do you like *rāmen?*"

"Of course," Lincoln said good-naturedly as he took the hoe from her. He saw a ribbon of sweat roll down her cheek, and flakes of dirt on her brow. "You rest. Mitsuo and I will finish up."

▶ "Lincoln-kun would like to help," Mitsuo said.

Mrs. Ono turned to Lincoln. "But you are our guest."

"I want to help, though."

"But if you are a guest, you cannot work. This would be embarrassing for us."

"I'm part of the family," Lincoln countered. "You rest and Mitsuo and I will take over."

Mrs. Ono's face softened with tenderness. She laughed and wiped the sweat from her face. "I have work inside. And dinner to prepare." She left the field, undoing her hat and wiping her neck with a bandanna.

Mitsuo took up a hoe and said, "Like this." He walked between the narrow rows, parting the leaves and gently whacking at the weeds. Lincoln followed, and they hoed in silence, the hot sun riding on their backs. ◀

Lincoln's lower back sparked with pain as he leaned his hoe against the shed. The sun hovered in the west, slipping behind the tiled roofs

▶ Reading Skills Objective: Drawing Conclusions

514 THE NOVEL

---

of the neighbors' houses. He had worked for only three hours, but he was exhausted. A cat on the fence watched Lincoln as he sat down and started to unlace his muddy boots. When the cat meowed, Lincoln hissed at him.

"You have to work every day?" Lincoln asked.

"Every day," Mitsuo answered as he unlaced his own mud-caked boots and took off his shirt. "We must."

His first full day in Japan, and the only things he had seen were the purple snouts of eggplant. Lincoln laughed to himself as he drank a bottle of icy *ramune*, his Adam's apple rising and falling with each swallow. He and Mitsuo sat on the *engawa*,[3] the wooden porch that faced the backyard, and eyed the field, each quiet in his own thoughts. The air was heavy, moist, and scented with earth. Over the nearby roofs, Lincoln spied the tallest buildings of Atami. Far away, a car with a bad muffler roared. A neighbor was yelling at a barking dog, and two kids were playing with plastic swords in the street. Lincoln, finishing his drink, was too exhausted to be curious about where he was. He lay back and fell asleep for a few minutes, the bottle in his hand, and woke only when he heard Mitsuo's voice.

"Are you tired?"

"A little bit." Lincoln stretched like a cat.

As he lay there, his hands behind his head, Lincoln thought about home. He wasn't homesick yet, but he knew it would come, an overwhelming shadow of sadness that would touch him when he least expected it. Once he had visited his aunt in the Imperial Valley[4] of California, and after three days he was weeping into his pillow, longing for home. He was only eight then. Now he was fourteen and a lot wiser.

---

3. *engawa* (ĕn-gä-wä)
4. **Imperial Valley:** an agricultural region in southeastern California. Formerly it was a desert, but because of irrigation, it has become fertile and produces much of the nation's fruits and vegetables.

Still, he knew that he'd get homesick. For now, he was just hot and sticky. And hungry.

"You know, it's probably lunchtime in San Francisco." Lincoln's stomach grumbled, and he wished he could throw his jaw around a cheeseburger.

"What's San Francisco like?"

"It's like Tokyo. But not hot. I thought I was going to die on the way from the airport."

"We hear California has many crazy persons. Is it true?"

"Some. There are some crazy dudes who walk the street."

"Do you have a gun?" Mitsuo asked, rolling
17 the empty bottle of *ramune* over his chest. Its coolness raised a herd of chills on his skin.

Lincoln rose on his elbows and looked at Mitsuo, bewildered. "A gun? I don't even have a car."

"We hear all Americans carry guns."

18 Lincoln laughed, then stopped. He remembered a *vato loco*[5] from his old street getting shot, all because he hadn't paid a two-dollar bet on a football game. He didn't die, but his knee was shattered. "Yeah, some dudes trip out with guns. But most people are cool."

"Cool? What is 'cool'?"

"It means OK—you know, nice."

"Cool," Mitsuo said, reflecting on the word.

"Where did you learn English?" Lincoln asked.

"School. It's required. America is number
19 one, and Japan is number two, so we must learn your language."

"No, it's the other way around," Lincoln countered as he peeled off his shirt. "You people have got it together. I like your cars."

"Cars are nothing," Mitsuo argued.
20 "Hammer is number one!"

Lincoln laughed. He spread his legs into a V and began to stretch, fingers to toes. Mitsuo had told him that *kempō* practice would begin that evening, and Lincoln wanted to be <u>limber</u>.

The boys were silent for a long time. Two huge crows bickered on a telephone wire, and from the house came the sound of a knife chopping on a wooden block. Then Mitsuo sat up, rolling the bottle across the porch. "Let's go."

"Where?" asked Lincoln, rising slowly and putting on his T-shirt.

"You'll see."

Mitsuo handed Lincoln a pair of *geta*, wooden slippers. "Wear these."

Lincoln turned them over, then slipped them on. He took a few careful steps. Wearing them was like walking on stilts. "They're fresh."

"'Fresh'?" asked Mitsuo, putting on a clean shirt that had been hanging on the rail of the porch. "You like them, you mean?"

"They're real cool."

21 "Fresh," Mitsuo muttered as they left the porch, the *karakoro*[6] sound of the *geta* ringing on the stone walk that led to the gate. They waved to Mrs. Ono, who was at the kitchen window. She shouted that they should come home in time for dinner.

5

Lincoln and Mitsuo walked briskly between the one-acre fields; almost all of them were thick
1 with the green growth of vegetables. The fields soon gave way to homes and small businesses—bars, restaurants, a cyclery,[1] a fish market, appliance stores. The dirt road gave way to
2 cement sidewalks. The street was crowded with men returning home, ties loosened and white shirts limp from long hours of work.

Atami was a growing farm town. For cen-

---

6. **karakoro** (kä-rä-kō-rō): clickety-clackety; the rhythmic knocking of wooden clogs against stone.

1. **cyclery** (sī′kəl-rē): a place where bicycles are made, sold, and repaired.

5. **vato loco** (bä′tō lō′kō): crazy guy.

17
Metaphor. Compares skin bumps to herd of cattle or other animals.

18
Lincoln laughs because he is surprised at Mitsuo's misunderstanding of America.

19 Analyzing
What does being "number two" have to do with learning English? Mitsuo thinks Japanese need to learn English to communicate with American business people in order to compete economically.

20
Mitsuo is familiar with American rap music and admires singer Hammer.

21 Analyzing
Why is Mitsuo interested in learning American slang? It is one way he can sound more natural speaking English.

Chapter 5
1
Boys can quickly walk from countryside to town. This shows small scale of area Mitsuo lives in.

2 Drawing Conclusions
What time of day is it? Late afternoon when people are getting off work.

Pacific Crossing

3 Imagery. Rattling sound of bicycle appeals to sense of hearing.

4 Drawing Conclusions
What does Lincoln's question suggest about his reaction to bathhouse? Lincoln is surprised at idea of taking bath in public.

5 Simile. Compares heat of water to heat of molten rock from volcano.

6 Mr. Ono jokes about temperature of water to tease Lincoln.

7 Allusion. "Poker-faced" refers to face that shows no emotion, in order to conceal value of poker hand.

---

turies, its farms had pushed up to the mountains. Apples and pears grew on the foothills. Today Atami's main street was choked with cars 3 and gleaming with tall glass buildings. Bicycles came rattling down the narrow streets and pushed pedestrians against the walls.

Lincoln followed Mitsuo into a building where the air was moist and thick with the sound of rain. A husky man sat at a counter. His glasses were fogged up, and a newspaper was spread in front of him. He looked up, wiped his glasses, and muttered in Japanese to Mitsuo, who produced some yen.²

"What is this place?" Lincoln asked.

"A *sentō*.³ It's a public bathhouse."

4 "We're going to take a bath?"

Lincoln trailed after Mitsuo, who was already pulling off his shirt. They entered a small steamy room where men were soaping themselves and rinsing from buckets.

"Here goes," Lincoln said and pulled off his shirt. He was a bit embarrassed when he saw three men sitting in what looked like a shallow swimming pool.

The boys put their clothes in a wicker basket. The *geta* went along the wall.

"I show you," Mitsuo said. "Sit down."

Lincoln sat down on a small wood-slat stool. Mitsuo started to soap and scrub his back in large, swirling circles.

"This is weird. I feel like I'm in a car wash," Lincoln muttered. He had heard about public baths, but he still found it shocking to be in one.

After Mitsuo rinsed him off, Lincoln soaped and scrubbed Mitsuo, who laughed and groaned, "Scrub harder, harder."

They climbed into the tiled tub, Mitsuo nearly jumping in and Lincoln stepping in one leg at a time.

---

2. **yen:** The yen is the basic monetary unit of Japan, like the dollar in the United States.
3. *sentō* (sĕn-tō′).

---

5 "Man, it's hot as lava," Lincoln hissed.

Through the puffs of steam, Lincoln caught sight of a naked Mr. Ono, who was saying hello to a friend. Mr. Ono called to Mitsuo, and Mitsuo climbed out of the bath to scrub his father's back. Then both of them joined Lincoln in the tub. He was now red as a crab, his forehead beaded with sweat.

"Lincoln-kun," the father said, "how are you? You look hot."

"I am."

"Good," Mr. Ono said as he threw a handful 6 of water on his face. "The tub is cold. They should turn up the heat."

Lincoln laughed. Mr. Ono was a comedian, like Lincoln's uncle Slic Ric, who was a member of the Chicano comedy act Culture Clash. It was all jokes from that *vato,* and from Mr. Ono 7 it was poker-faced humor, even after a hard day at the railroad. Lincoln had always thought of Japanese people as reserved and serious. Now he was having second thoughts.

Mitsuo and Lincoln started to climb out of

A Japanese bathhouse.

> **PORTFOLIO ASSESSMENT**
> Some students may be interested in interviewing a person from Japan or researching a specific area of Japanese culture in the library. Suggest that students present the results of their interviews or library research to the rest of the class in informative speeches. Speeches may be audiotaped or videotaped for inclusion in students' portfolios. (See *Portfolio Assessment and Professional Support Materials* for additional information on student portfolios.)

---

the bath. Their bodies were pink from the hot water.

8   His father waved them off and turned to talk with a man at the other end of the tub.

Lincoln and Mitsuo dressed and left the *sentō* refreshed. They bought Coca-Colas and looked at magazines at a newsstand. Lincoln didn't understand the *kanji*, but was satisfied to look at a comic book of samurai[4] warriors on horseback. Lincoln thumbed through the pages. At the end, some of the warriors were killed, their heads stuck on lances and paraded around a
9   defeated city. Lincoln swallowed and thought, *That must hurt.*

"Do you know *pachinko*?"[5] Mitsuo asked as he returned his magazine to the rack.

"No," Lincoln answered.

"I'll show you." Mitsuo pulled on Lincoln's arm. They hurriedly crossed the street, which
10 was jammed by a car accident. Two men were standing by their cars, each shouting and seeming to blame the other.

They walked three short blocks and stood looking through a storefront window at what Lincoln thought at first were video games. These were machines for *pachinko,* a kind of upright pinball game. The place reminded Lincoln of his uncle Trino's bar, La Noche de Guadalajara.[6] His uncle used to shove a handful of quarters into Lincoln's shirt pocket and let him play the games, even though he was underage and everyone around him was drinking beer.

Lincoln suggested that they go in and play a game.

"We can't. It's for adults. You have to be at least sixteen," Mitsuo said.

---

4. **samurai** (săm′ə-rī′): professional warriors belonging to the feudal military aristocracy of Japan.
5. **pachinko** (pä-chĭn′kō).
6. **La Noche de Guadalajara** (lä nō′chä *thä* gwä-*thä*-lä-hä′rä): "Guadalajara Night." Guadalajara is the name of a city in Mexico and a province in Spain.

Lincoln took a closer peek. Rows of players, mostly men, hunkered over the machines. The chrome balls fell noisily from one level to the next.

"Aw, man," Lincoln whined. "I wish I could play just one game."

11 Mitsuo thought a moment, then said, "Let's try."

"Really? You don't think we'll get in trouble?" When Mitsuo shook his head, Lincoln said, "OK, but you lead the way."

They started up the steps, their heads down, trying to look tough. Smoke laced the air. Loud music blared from speakers in the ceiling. They found an open machine and started playing, but within a few minutes they were collared and thrown out.

12 "Don't try again," the man warned. He was small but thick as a refrigerator. He looked dangerous.

The boys shrugged. Lincoln rubbed his scraped elbow.

"The man is not cool," Mitsuo muttered. Through his cupped hands, he yelled back through the doorway, "You are not cool!"

"Give it to him, the fat slob," Lincoln growled. "I was just starting to like the game."

13 The man started toward them, but Lincoln and Mitsuo were too fast.

After the *pachinko* parlor, they kicked around the town, looking in shop windows and following two girls who were eyeing them and giggling. But Lincoln and Mitsuo left the girls alone. They bought bags of pumpkin seeds and walked around eating the seeds, shells and all.

"Our town is small," Mitsuo said. "You will see your friends soon. We have only twenty thousand people in this town."

14 Lincoln thought of Tony. He was probably either complaining about the field work or teaching his host family to play poker. Tony had learned poker from his older brother, who was

---

8 Bathhouse allows Mr. Ono chance to visit with friends.

9 **Understatement.** Narrator understates pain in a kind of reverse exaggeration.

10 Detail of car accident and way men react emphasizes similarity of Japan to United States: people are same about some things, at least.

11 Making Generalizations *What does Mitsuo's willingness to try getting in suggest about his character?* He is adventurous and full of mischief.

12 **Simile.** Compares man's shape to refrigerator to emphasize his strength and toughness.

13 Analyzing *Does man understand what Mitsuo is saying?* Answers will vary. Probably not; he reacts to boy's body language and tone of voice.

14 Lincoln has been too busy to think about Tony very much.

Pacific Crossing 517

15 Making Inferences
How do you think Tony's brother means to help Chicanos? Tony's brother wants to work against prejudice and hardships some Mexican Americans face.

16
Lincoln knows from his own experience that talking about something you do not do well can be painful, so he respects Mitsuo's defeat in judo.

17
Exaggeration. Exaggerates size of key to emphasize that it is large.

18
Simile. Compares Lincoln's sudden realization about dojo to rapidly evaporating rain.

19 Finding Cause and Effect
Why is Lincoln disappointed? Answers will vary. Lincoln is discovering that Japan is different in some ways from ways he imagined it would be.

Chapter Six

1
Mr. and Mrs. Ono have told visitor about Lincoln.

---

15 a *Mechista*[7] in college, a guy ready to better the world for Chicanos.

Mitsuo pointed to a wooden building with slat windows. "I took judo[8] there but quit." A wind chime banged in the breeze.

"You took judo?" Lincoln asked, excited. "That's bad."

"No, judo is good."

"No, I mean bad. In California, if you like something a lot, then it's bad."

Mitsuo gave Lincoln another strange look. He said, "In Japan, everyone takes judo or *kempō*. I didn't like judo. For me, it was not 'bad.' Baseball is 'bad.'" Mitsuo then pointed to a round man walking down the street. "He's Takahashi-*sensei*. He's OK, but his assistant is mean. He was mean to me because I lost a match at a tournament."

"You went to tournaments? Sounds fun."

"I went to a few, but I wasn't very good."

"Sure you were."

"No, really."

16 Lincoln let the subject drop because he knew how sensitive he was when a defeat came up in conversation. He recalled the basketball games back home. Except for basketball at school, he had to work hard at everything, even spelling.

17 They watched the *sensei* open the dojo with a key as large as a can opener. He entered, his shoes in his hand. The door closed behind him, and a light went on.

"I'll show you the *kempō* dojo," Mitsuo said.

"All right!" Lincoln cried.

They hurried through an alley and down three blocks, their mouths full of pumpkin seeds. When Mitsuo stopped, Lincoln nearly bumped into him.

"There," Mitsuo said, pointing.

---

7. **Mechista** (mĕ-chēs′tä): a member of a political group known as MECA.
8. **judo** (jōō′dō): a martial art used as much for physical training and discipline as for fighting.

"Where?" Lincoln asked, confused. He was facing a cement driveway with a border of wild grass.

"There."

"Where?"

"There, Lincoln-kun!"

"You mean this *driveway?*"

"Yes, they practice there and on the lawn. I think they practice at the university in winter."

18 Lincoln's image of a cleanly swept dojo
19 evaporated like rain on a hot sidewalk. He was disappointed. He had come to Japan expecting to practice on tatami[9] mats in a templelike dojo.

"They practice on concrete," he whispered.

6

When Mitsuo and Lincoln returned home, Mitsuo's father and mother were sitting with a woman on the *engawa*. The woman sat erect, her face composed. All three were drinking iced tea, Mrs. Ono cooling herself with a fan that showed a picture of a baseball team.

Mitsuo gave the woman a short bow and greeted her in Japanese. Lincoln bowed, too.

"Lincoln-kun, this is Mrs. Oyama," the father said. He raised his glass, sipped, and put it down by his feet. "You and Mitsuo worked hard. The field looks tidy."

After a moment of silence, Mrs. Oyama
1 asked, "So, Lincoln, you practice *shorinji kempō?*" Her face was turned away, as if she were asking Mr. Ono.

"Yes," Lincoln answered, his back straight.

"You must be very good. You're so young and strong," Mrs. Oyama said, a smile starting at the corner of her mouth. She was still looking in the direction of Mr. Ono.

"Well, I guess so," Lincoln said, flattered,

---

9. **tatami** (tä-tä′mē): mats made of rice straw, used in floor coverings.

ART LINK

This story offers glimpses into two rich cultures: Japanese and Mexican American. Invite some students to research and create a traditional Japanese craft, such as origami, calligraphy, or flower arranging. Encourage other students to research and create traditional Mexican crafts, such as paper flower decorations, weavings, and papier-mâché piñatas. Designate an area in the classroom to display students' work.

---

tightening his fist so that a rope of muscle showed in his forearm. He tried to hold back a smile. "I'm *sankyu* rank."

2 "*Sankyu*. Very good for your age," Mrs. Oyama said, an eyebrow lifted. She turned to Mrs. Ono and said, "Such a strong boy."

"Oh yes, he worked so hard in the garden today," Mrs. Ono said, fanning the cool air in Lincoln's direction.

3 He sat straight up, his chest puffed out a little. "Well, I am pretty good. That's what Nakano-*sensei* says. I'll be a black belt when I'm fifteen."

"I'm impressed." Mrs. Oyama beamed, pressing her hands together. "I'm so happy to hear that in America we have dedicated youth."

The telephone rang in the living room.
4 Mitsuo jumped to his feet. Lincoln started to follow, but the adults told him to stay.

"Mitsuo will answer it," Mr. Ono told Lincoln. He lit a cigarette, a wafer of smoke hanging in the air, and asked, "Lincoln-kun, what does your mother do?"

"She's sort of an artist. She has her own company." Lincoln bit his lower lip as he tried to think of what she actually did for a living. "She's a commercial artist. She does work for computer firms."

Mr. Ono shook his head, sighing, "Ah yes."

"And your father?" Mrs. Ono asked.

5 Lincoln had known this was coming. He had known ever since he'd boarded the jet to come to Japan that he would be asked this question.

"He's a police officer," Lincoln said, not adding that he hadn't seen his father in six years.
6 His parents had been divorced since Lincoln was seven, a hurt that had never healed.

The adults looked at each other, nodding their heads. They sipped tea and stirred the air with newspaper shaped into fans.

7 Mrs. Oyama rose. "I will see you tomorrow, if not sooner," she said to Lincoln and Mitsuo, who had returned from the living room. She bowed to Mr. and Mrs. Ono, thanked them for the tea, and walked down the path to the street.

While they ate fish for dinner, the Ono family helped Lincoln practice some Japanese phrases. He wanted to learn so that when he returned home he could talk in Japanese to his *kempō* instructor. So Mrs. Ono taught him some phrases. "How are you doing? Nice day. Let's eat." Her eyes shone when Lincoln said, "*Ima Atami ni sun'de imasu.*[1] I am now living in Atami."

"You are a strong, smart boy," she said.

On the *engawa* after dinner, Mr. Ono said to Mitsuo, "Take Lincoln to the dojo." Mr. Ono was enjoying a small cup of sake with an evening cigarette. "You are not too tired, are you, Lincoln-kun? It is almost eight o'clock."

"No, not at all," Lincoln said as he left the room to get his *gi*. He felt good. He was ready to practice, even in a driveway.

Mr. Ono spoke to Mitsuo in Japanese, and Mitsuo turned away, almost laughing.

"What is *Chichi* joking about?" Lincoln asked, smiling as well.

8 "He is glad you are here," Mitsuo said as he slipped on his *geta*. "I'll take you to *kempō*."

They walked four blocks in silence, and when they arrived at the driveway, Mitsuo turned
9 away, a smile starting on his face. "I will see you in one hour. Have fun."

Puzzled at Mitsuo's smile, Lincoln watched him hurry away, *geta* ringing on the stone walk. Lincoln shrugged his shoulders as he entered the driveway with a fistful of yen, his monthly dues. On his way down the driveway, Lincoln stopped to *gasshō*[2]—salute—to three black belts who were stretching on the lawn, sweat already

---

1. "*Ima Atami ni sun'de imasu*" (ē-mä ä-tä-mē nē so͞on-dē e-mäs).
2. *gasshō* (gä-shō).

---

2 Drawing Conclusions
What does Mrs. Oyama's response suggest about her knowledge of *kempō*? She is knowledgeable about sport.

3
Lincoln is proud of his achievements in *kempō*.

4
Exaggeration. "Jumped" emphasizes that Mitsuo gets up quickly.

5 Analyzing
Why is Lincoln nervous about question about his father? Answers will vary. Perhaps he is embarrassed his parents are divorced. Perhaps he is angry and hurt by divorce.

6
Metaphor. Compares Lincoln's feelings about parents' divorce to physical injury.

7
Foreshadowing. Mrs. Oyama's saying "if not sooner" suggests she may be more than friend who has stopped by for glass of tea.

8 Making Inferences
Is Mitsuo telling truth about what his father said? Answers will vary. Perhaps he is, but Mitsuo's attitude suggests a joke may be in making.

9
Mitsuo's smile reinforces idea he will play joke on Lincoln.

Pacific Crossing

10 Pointing suggests men know who Lincoln is and expect him.

11 Expressing an Opinion
Why does Lincoln wish he were on plane? Answers will vary. Perhaps he is homesick. More probably, he is nervous about being in strange place without Mitsuo.

12 Lincoln goes to back of line in hope of not being recognized.

13 Exaggeration. Overstates Lincoln's facial expression to emphasize his concern about his previous bragging about his skill.

14 Exaggeration. Emphasizes how uncomfortable Lincoln feels.

15 Drawing Conclusions
Why do smiles make Lincoln feel better? Answers will vary. Perhaps smiles make him feel accepted and welcome.

16 Competition from older people brings out Lincoln's best efforts.

17 Onomatopoeia. "Snapped" imitates sound of punches and kicks.

18 Drawing Conclusions
Why is Lincoln reluctant to let others know of his pain? He does not want to appear soft to strangers.

19 Simile. Compares pain in arm to pain Lincoln imagines a chicken would feel if its leg were pulled off.

---

soaking into the backs of their *gis*. They rose to
10 their feet, saluted to Lincoln, and pointed to the side of the building. Lincoln went around and saw two others changing, a father and son. He changed there as well, folding his clothes neatly and placing his *geta* along the wall. He took off his watch, which glowed in the dark: 8:10.

Everyone was speaking in Japanese. No one paid Lincoln any attention as he joined the others on the lawn. He looked skyward at a plane **11** cutting across the sky, and at that moment he wished he were on that plane.

A light lit the yard, reflecting off a small kidney-shaped pond, set among reeds and bamboo. Lincoln went and looked at the pond. He saw the reflection of his face in the murky water, rippling from long-legged water bugs.

He rejoined the others on the lawn and began stretching and practicing punches and kicks. His chest rose and fell, and his breathing became shallow. In the warm summer air, sweat was already starting to run from his body.

The *sensei* came out of the house, hands raised in a *gasshō*. She smiled and welcomed everyone as they formed two lines.

Lincoln's mouth fell open. It was Mrs. Oyama, whom he had met just before dinner—
12 Oyama-*sensei*! He found a place at the back of
13 the line, his face twisted with worry. Only an hour ago he had been bragging that he was *sankyu* rank, that he was as strong as any kid in the world.

After a formal salute to the spirit of *kempō*, some meditation, and warm-ups, the group finally started basic exercises. Only after basics did Oyama-*sensei* point to Lincoln, and everyone looked in his direction.

14 Lincoln forced a toothy smile. He hated life at that moment. He wished that he were on that plane, going back home to San Francisco. He promised himself this would be the last time he bragged.

"Lincoln, please," Oyama-*sensei* called, her outstretched hand gesturing for him to come up to the front. "Please tell us about yourself."

I'm a loudmouthed braggart, Lincoln thought; that's what I could tell you about myself.

Sweat streamed down his face, more from embarrassment than from the workout. He walked to the front, where he gave a *gasshō* and told his fellow practitioners—all eight of them—that he was from San Francisco and that he was staying with the Ono family for the sum-
15 mer. When they smiled at him, he felt a little better.

They practiced *juhō*[3]—grabs and pinning techniques—and *embu*[4]—planned attacks. He
16 tried his best. He didn't want these adult black belts to think he was sorry, just because he was from America and a fourteen-year-old brown
17 belt. His punches and kicks snapped against his *gi*. His arm locks were executed quickly, but not with the ease of the adults'.

Lincoln had never worked out on grass before. In San Francisco, he had practiced on linoleum. He liked the way the grass tickled the bottoms of his feet. He also liked having the grass to cushion his falls; he fell a lot when he practiced with the advanced belts. He was thrown and twisted into painful holds, his face pressed harshly against the grass. He got up
18 quickly when they let go, and he didn't let on
19 that his arm felt like a drumstick being torn from the body of a chicken.

When class ended at 9:30, Oyama-*sensei* called him aside. "Lincoln-kun, you are a good boy. Strong."

"I'm not that strong," he said, this time not wanting to brag about himself. He was still

---

3. *juhō* (jōō-hō).
4. *embu* (ĕm-bōō).

warm from the workout, and his chest was rising and falling. Grass clung to his *gi* and his tousled hair.

"You are very good. In six weeks, if you practice hard, we will see about a promotion." One side of her face was hidden in the dark; the other side glowed in the porch light. Her eyes gave away nothing.

Lincoln started to walk away, but she called him back. "Lincoln-kun, you must shave your hair."

"My hair?" he asked, touching the hair around his ears.

"Yes, it must be gone."

Lincoln changed from his *gi* to his street clothes and was greeted by Mitsuo, who was waiting in the driveway.

"How come you didn't tell me?" Lincoln asked. "She's the *sensei*, and you didn't tell me. That was cold."

"Sorry, Lincoln, but Father wanted to make a joke. He likes you." Mitsuo thought for a moment, then asked, "What is 'cold'?"

"'Cold' is, is—I don't know how to explain it. But that was a 'cold' shot," Lincoln said as the two of them walked down the street, their *geta* ringing in unison. "Yeah, your dad is a wise guy."

"Yes, he is sometimes very wise," Mitsuo agreed.

Lincoln stopped in his tracks and was about to explain "wise guy" and the Three Stooges,[5] but he was too tired. It had been a long day in Japan.

The stores were closed. A few cars passed in the street, silent as cats. Only a small neon light glowed in a bar window. They tiptoed over and looked inside, where men sat playing *go*, an ancient board game similar to checkers, or talking in dark corners.

"Just like California," Lincoln said.

"Really?"

"Yeah. People get off work and get ripped—some people, at least."

"My father used to come here, but he doesn't anymore. He likes it better at home."

Lincoln wanted to tell Mitsuo about his father—about his lack of a father—but didn't know how. In the United States, it was not uncommon to come from a broken home. But in Japan families all seemed to be intact—father, mother, children, all walking down the street together. In the *sentō*, fathers scrubbed their children, and, in turn, the children scrubbed their fathers with all their might. It wasn't Lincoln's fault that his parents' marriage hadn't worked out. Still, at times he felt lonely and embarrassed.

They walked home. Lincoln showered and then went out to the *engawa* to join Mitsuo, who was relacing his baseball mitt after having taken out some of the padding.

"This is my favorite mitt," Mitsuo said proudly. "My grandfather gave it to me."

"Nice." The night was quiet. A cat strode the thin rail of a bamboo fence, his tail waving in the moonlight. The neighbors were watching television. The vegetable garden rustled in the breeze. Lincoln felt tired but happy. He was already feeling at home.

---

5. **Three Stooges:** Larry, Moe, and Curly, who were popular in movies and television shows for their slapstick routines. One of them would refer to the others as "wise guys" before hitting them or inflicting other injuries, while sound effects exaggerated the noise of blows.

7

The next day, Lincoln and Mitsuo worked in the field again, this time hauling buckets of water to irrigate the rows. They worked hard, shirtless. Flies nibbled at their backs, and Lincoln and Mitsuo complained and cursed their luck. But secretly they felt good.

---

20 Lincoln is out of breath from his workout.

21 Metaphor. Compares comment to something without heat of emotion. In other words, Lincoln thinks joke showed a lack of feeling for him.

22 Mitsuo takes Lincoln's comment literally.

23 Simile. Compares cars to cats that noiselessly stalk prey.

24 Finding Cause and Effect
Why do boys tiptoe? They do not want to make noise that would call attention to themselves.

25 Lincoln feels his secret about his father is a kind of barrier between him and Mitsuo.

26 Making Inferences
Why does Lincoln focus on bathing as symbol of parent-child relations in Japan? Answers will vary. Perhaps because bathhouses and way people scrub one another seems so odd to Lincoln.

Chapter 7

1 Setting. Chapter opening sets time and place.

2 Farm plot is small enough to water crop by hand.

3 Making Inferences
Why do Lincoln and Mitsuo feel good working in field? Answers will vary. Perhaps they enjoy using their muscles. Perhaps sun feels good.

4
Mitsuo seems to know a lot about American culture, including American food.

5
Exaggeration. Overstates trickle of tea to suggest it seems like a lot of liquid to Lincoln.

6 Analyzing
Why is Mitsuo confused? Even though he knows about America, his knowledge is limited.

7
Lincoln understands what this means, showing he has some knowledge of Japanese culture.

8 Drawing Conclusions
What does Lincoln imply by saying his legs are skinny? He implies descendants of Aztec warriors should have large, muscular legs. Since he does not, he is not descended from Aztec warriors.

9
Mitsuo again shows he is adventurous.

10
Personification. Poles given human ability to jump.

11
Metaphor. Compares shape of perspiration stains to shape of half moon.

12 Making Inferences
Why is Mitsuo curious about Mississippi River? Answers will vary. He has probably heard or read about it.

At lunch, they sat on the *engawa* eating *nigirimeshi*[1]—rice balls—and drinking a pitcher of iced tea.

"They're good," Lincoln said as he chomped into the rice balls.

4 "But wouldn't you rather have a hamburger?" Mitsuo asked.

Lincoln shook his head. "You know what I'd like to have? A burrito."[2]

"A burrito?"

Lincoln cleared his throat. "A tortilla with *frijoles*."[3]

Mitsuo tilted his head curiously and asked, "What is 'tortilla'? And that other word—'free-holies'?"

Lincoln licked his lips and drank long and
5 hard from his glass. A stream of tea ran down his chest and pooled in his belly button. He laughed as he wiped his belly. "It's this way, Mitsuo. I'm from California, but I'm Mexican-American, and that's Mexican-American food."

"Mexican and American," Mitsuo said slowly,
6 reflecting on the words. "Are you from two countries?"

"Sort of. Just like you. If you came to the United States, you would be Japanese-American."

"Ah, I understand. Then you are from Mexico."

"No. From California."

"Then your mother is from Mexico?"

"No. She's from California, too."

"Then it must be your father?"

"No, not him either. It's my grandparents."

Mitsuo looked at Lincoln and said, "Family history is very complicated. My father says we're from a samurai line."

7 "Really?" Lincoln asked, his interest piqued.

"He says so, but I doubt it. Our family has been farmers for centuries. I don't think we have samurai blood. My father is always making things up."

"I can relate. My mom says that we're de-
8 scendants of Aztec warriors. But look at my legs—skinny!" He gripped his thighs with both hands.

After lunch, the two boys left with fishing
9 poles and tackle. Just outside town, they hopped a ride on the back of a produce truck, and three dusty miles later they jumped off when the truck slowed at a railroad crossing. Only now aware that they had ridden his truck, the driver cursed and shook a fist at them.

10 Lincoln and Mitsuo ran away, their poles jumping about on their shoulders. They walked another mile, the sun beating down on their heads, and entered waist-high brush where a shallow river flowed over small rocks. They
11 threw themselves on the bank, moons of sweat under each arm.

"Man, it's hot," Lincoln grumbled. "Is it always like this?"

"In the summer," Mitsuo said, opening the tackle box.

They dipped their faces in the water but didn't drink. They flicked off their *geta* and let their feet cool in the water. They felt calm. A wind had picked up, rustling some low-lying brush where two sparrows bickered.

12 "Is the Mississippi River very big?" Mitsuo asked, splicing a worm on his hook.

"Very big. But I've never seen it." Lincoln recalled classroom spelling bees when the word had stumped the boys' team. The girls had laughed at the boys who either put in one too many *p*'s or not enough *s*'s. Lincoln figured that the word "Mississippi" should be banned from the English language.

"One day I'd like to go to America."

"Yeah. You and I could hang out together. You could stay with us."

---

1. *nigirimeshi* (nē-gē-rē-mā-zhē).
2. *burrito* (bŏŏ-rē′tō): a Mexican dish consisting of a flour tortilla filled with beans, meat, or cheese.
3. *frijoles* (frē-hō′lĕs): pinto beans.

522 THE NOVEL

WRITING LINK
Encourage students to write a haiku, a poetry form developed in Japan, in reaction to a particular passage in the story. A haiku is a seventeen-syllable poem, usually written in three lines. Students may learn more about haiku on pp. 491–492 and in the **Literary Terms and Techniques** section on p. 714.

Mitsuo smiled. " 'Hang out,' " he murmured.
13 "Nice words." He stared at a ripple on the water.

"You'd like it. We can get my mom to take us to Great America.⁴ The roller coaster is tough."

Lincoln stared at the water. His mind drifted to Oyama-*sensei*. She must have a sense of humor, he thought. Or why would she visit the Onos and not let on that she's a *kempō* master?
14 Lincoln smiled to himself. When his line went taut, he was ready and rose to his feet. He reeled the line in and found the hook snagged with nothing but slimy grass.

They fished until two old men arrived and told them to go away, that it was *their* fishing spot. The men sat down with tired sighs and brought out a lunch and bottles of beer, which they rolled into the river to cool. Lincoln wanted to argue with them, but Mitsuo touched his arm and begged, "Let's not. We didn't catch anything anyhow."

15 One of the old men cast, and almost immediately a fish came up, its back shimmering in the sunlight. The old man grinned at Lincoln, showing his black teeth as if to say, We're the fishermen.

From the river the boys returned to the main highway, where they got a ride in the back of a truck loaded with chickens on the way to restaurants in Atami.

"It's sad," Lincoln said. "They're gonna have their throats cut."

The chickens blinked their small eyes at Lincoln and Mitsuo, and fluttered their wings occasionally. Only when the truck dipped into a pothole did the chickens cluck. Only when the truck braked did they panic and beat their wings against the wooden sides of the crates.

When the truck pulled into town, the boys jumped off and waved to the driver, who waved
16 back. Lincoln couldn't help himself—he waved to the chickens. One of them seemed to raise a wing in salute—*adios, amigo*.⁵

They had started up the street and were skipping over puddles where the merchants had washed the storefronts when Lincoln heard, "Hey, Linc, it's your *carnal*." Lincoln stopped in his tracks and slowly turned around. It was Tony, in a blue-and-white *yukata*,⁶ a long robe, and *geta* on his feet. His hair was shaved so he looked like a monk.

"Tony!" Lincoln screamed. They ran to each other and shook hands *raza*-style. Lincoln raked his hand over Tony's hair and fingered the robe. "Yeah, check this out. You look like a skinny Yojimbo. How'd you get the haircut? I gotta get mine cut for *kempō*."

"¡*Pues sí!*⁷ *Haha* did it. And check out *mis sandalias*,⁸ my shoes, wise guy." Tony wiggled his big toes and danced so that the wooden sandals sounded against the sidewalk.

Lincoln introduced Tony to Mitsuo, who
17 bowed. Tony bowed and then shook hands *raza*-style. Mitsuo smiled and asked, "Please, shake hands again." They shook hands slowly, over and over, until Mitsuo pulled his hand away and muttered, "Interesting."

"Where you guys coming from?" Tony asked
18 as they walked down the street together. "You look like Tom Sawyer and Huck Finn."⁹

"We went fishing."

"Fishing? Where's the river? I don't see one." Always the joker, Tony shaded his eyes and looked skyward, then up and down the street. "There's a river in town?"

19 They crossed the street and moved into the shadows that hugged the storefronts. It was not much cooler there; it might even have been hot-

---

4. **Great America:** an amusement park.
5. ***adios, amigo*** (ä-thyōs ä-mē-gō): Goodbye, my friend.
6. ***yukata*** (yōō-kä-tä).
7. ***Pues sí*** (pwĕs sē′): Well, yes.
8. ***mis sandalias*** (mē sän-däl′yäs): my sandals.
9. **Tom Sawyer and Huck Finn:** two characters from novels by Mark Twain. They grow up along the banks of the Mississippi River and often go fishing together.

---

13 Mitsuo again shows his interest in American slang.

14 Summarizing
Why does Lincoln smile? He realizes joke is amusing, even if it is at his expense.

15 Irony. Old men say it is their fishing spot and prove it by catching fish where Lincoln and Mitsuo had no luck.

16 Expressing an Opinion
Why is Lincoln so interested in chickens? Answers will vary. Perhaps he feels sorry for them, or perhaps they interest him because, growing up in city, he has never been around them before.

17 Tony, like Lincoln, is getting used to Japanese customs, such as bowing.

18 Irony. Mitsuo earlier asked Lincoln about Mississippi River. Tony now says they look like two literary characters who grew up on Mississippi.

19 Personification. Shadow given human ability to hug.

Pacific Crossing

ter among the hordes of shoppers. As they passed the *sentō*, Lincoln asked Tony, "You been here yet?"

20 "Aw, man, three times a day," Tony said. "*Hace mucho calor*[10] in this *barrio*. I thought Japan was near the North Pole. How come it's so hot?"

"It just is," Mitsuo answered, shrugging.

The three of them stopped for bottles of Coca-Cola, which they drank while thumbing through comic books. Lincoln and Tony enjoyed the futuristic drawings.

Mitsuo asked Tony to come to his house for dinner, but Tony declined. "Thank you, but my folks expect me." Turning to Lincoln, he said, "Check this out, homes." He straightened his robe and stood straight up. "I'm an artist."

"What do you mean?"

"I mean, I'm an artist, a regular Picasso.[11] My family makes statues of these holy dudes, and I'm helping them out."

"Dudes?"

21 "You know—saints or something."

Mitsuo said, "Buddhas."[12]

"Yeah, that's the guy, and some other *vatos*."

"Lighten up, Tony. It's not cool to call them *vatos*. If they're saints."

Tony thought for a moment. "I guess you're right. Anyways, I gotta go. See ya."

As Tony started to walk away, Lincoln pulled him aside, whispering, "You know what would 22 be nice—if we could cook our *familias* Mexican food."

Tony snapped his fingers. "Good idea. I tried to explain *frijoles* and enchiladas to them, but they didn't get it."

"But we don't have any beans, or flour for tortillas."

---

10. **Hace mucho calor** (ä′sā mōō′chō kä-lōr′): It's very hot.
11. **Picasso** (pĭ-kä′sō): Pablo Picasso (1881–1973), a famous Spanish artist.
12. **Buddhas** (bōō′dəz): representations of Gautama Buddha, who founded Buddhism, a religion of eastern and central Asia.

"That's what you think." Tony grinned.

"You brought some?" Lincoln asked, eyebrows lifted.

"Sho 'nuff. Five-pound bag. You thought I was going to be in Japan six whole weeks and not grub on *frijoles*?"

Lincoln punched him in the arm. "You're my main man, Tony."

"How 'bout we meet at the *sentō* tomorrow. Four?"

"Sounds good."

"Catch you later."

23 Lincoln turned to Mitsuo, who had been watching them conspire.

Lincoln and Mitsuo started home, their fishing poles over their shoulders. It was not until they got to the gate of the farm that Mitsuo asked, "Are you mad at Tony?"

Lincoln furrowed his brow. "Mad?"

"Yes. You hit him in the arm."

"No way," Lincoln said, closing the gate 24 behind him. "It's something you do." Lincoln thought for a moment, then said, "It's sorta like a bow. It means you like the person." Lincoln punched Mitsuo in the arm softly.

Mitsuo reflected on the punch, then said, "I like it."

8

After dinner, the family sat on the *engawa*, 1 catching the evening wind and eating ice cream. Mrs. Ono fanned herself with a magazine, cheeks flushed, strands of hair out of place. Mr. Ono, glasses on, read the newspaper, 2 his empty bowl at his feet. He reported, "There was a fire in San Francisco, Lincoln-kun."

Lincoln looked over his shoulder, scraping the bottom of his bowl with his spoon. "Where?"

Mr. Ono pointed a thick finger at the story. "It says it was at an oil repository. Hunters Point."

---

20 Exaggeration. Tony overstates his visits to *sentō* to indicate he knows place.

21 Tony does not seem to have good grasp of some aspects of Japanese culture.

22 Analyzing *What does Tony's use of Spanish word for "families" imply about how he feels toward them?* Use of Spanish implies he feels toward them as he does toward his own family in America.

23 Drawing Conclusions *Why do Tony and Lincoln step aside from Mitsuo for their talk?* They want the Mexican dinner to be a surprise that only they work on.

24 Mitsuo and Lincoln exchange information about their cultures as ideas come up in conversation.

Chapter 8

1 Metaphor. Compares breeze to an object that can be caught, like an animal or a ball.

2 Report of fire suggests Japanese interested in every aspect of American life.

3   Repository? Lincoln thought. What's that?

"Do you know Hunters Point?" asked Mr. Ono as he took off his glasses and wiped sweat from his brow.

"I've never been there. But I know it's near Candlestick Park."

4   Mr. Ono grunted and said, "San Francisco must be very, very big," and returned to reading his newspaper.

5   Lincoln turned to Mrs. Ono. "Will you please cut my hair? For *kempō*."

She looked at his long and straggly hair and asked Mitsuo in Japanese for the scissors. Mitsuo scurried into the house and came out with a wooden box.

"*Dōzo*.[1] Please come," she said to Lincoln, rising.

In the yard, in the glow of the porch light, Lincoln sat with a dishcloth wrapped around his shoulders.

"You'll look different," Mitsuo commented, eating a juicy peach. He licked his fingers and wiped his hands on his pants. "You'll look like me." He raked his hand over his shaved head.

6

7   Mrs. Ono worked quickly, the cold scissors snaking around Lincoln's ears. Then she ran a clipperlike scissor over the top of his head. The hair piled onto the towel, and some strands drifted to the ground, where the cat batted at them.

8   Lincoln's long locks were gone. In their place were bristles that tickled his palm.

Lincoln rose from the chair and brushed the hair off his shoulders.

"I am not finished," Mrs. Ono said. She spoke to Mitsuo in Japanese, and he went inside.

Lincoln's eyes grew big when Mitsuo returned with a smooth, foot-long stick.

9   "What's that?" It looked like some sort of doctor's tool and reminded Lincoln of every injection he had had at Kaiser Hospital.

"A *mimikaki*.[2] An ear pick. It will not hurt,"

Mrs. Ono said, prodding him up to the *engawa*. She sat down and patted her lap. "Put your head here."

10 "My head!" Lincoln felt embarrassed; no one had ever cleaned his ears. He looked at Mitsuo for help, but Mitsuo was eating another peach and holding back a sticky smile. "It's painless," he said. "Easy."

11 Lincoln narrowed his eyes in distrust. When he was five he had stuck a match inside his ear, and the match snapped off. He didn't tell his mother for three days, not until he had lost most of his hearing in that ear and went around yelling "Huh?" whenever his mother spoke to him. Even the doctor had had a difficult time getting the match out.

"It feels good. I'll show you." Mitsuo snuggled his head onto his mother's lap and closed his eyes as she probed his right ear. Now and then she pulled out a clot of wax and wiped it onto a paper towel.

After both ears were cleaned, Mitsuo jumped to his feet. "See?" He cupped a hand around his ear. "I can hear better."

Knowing that he had no choice, Lincoln laid his head in Mrs. Ono's lap. He winced as the ear pick probed in slow circles. But as Mitsuo had said, it felt good. He almost fell asleep.

Mrs. Ono laughed and wiped the *mimikaki* on the towel. "Lots of lumps," she said.

Lincoln laughed to hide his embarrassment. He promised himself that he would clean his ears more carefully from that day on.

That night at *kempō*, he felt strong. Dressed in his *gi*, he stretched between two black belts on the lawn. He did fifty push-ups and a hundred sit-ups, and he jumped to his feet, breathing hard. He ran his hand over his head. Smooth was his favorite feeling.

They practiced throws during the intense

---

1. *Dōzo* (dō-zō): Please.
2. *mimikaki* (mē-mē-kä-kē).

---

3 Irony. Lincoln wonders about meaning of English word used by Mr. Ono, whose native language is Japanese.

4 Making Inferences
Why does Mr. Ono arrive at this conclusion? Answers will vary. Perhaps he thinks native of San Francisco would have been to every part of city if it were small.

5 Analyzing
Why is Lincoln so willing to have his hair cut short? His interest in *kempō* is stronger than his attachment to his hair. Also, very short hair is popular in Japan, and Lincoln may feel pressure to fit in.

6 Mitsuo is only mildly encouraging of Lincoln getting his hair cut.

7 Metaphor. Compares movement of scissors to wiggly movement of snake.

8 Alliteration. Narrator uses repeated *l* sound to add interest and variety to passage.

9 Lincoln is anxious because he does not know what to expect.

10 Making Inferences
Why does Lincoln feel embarrassed? Answers will vary. Perhaps he feels he is too old to have someone clean his ears for him.

11 Lincoln's embarrassment is replaced by feeling of distrust because of his previous unpleasant experience with matchstick in his ear.

12 Simile. Compares way Lincoln lands to way cat lands.

13 Expressing an Opinion
Why does Lincoln feel so confident of his skills? Answers will vary. Perhaps studying *kempō* in Japan has given him more confidence.

14 Lincoln is impressed by Oyama-*sensei*'s skill.

15 Imagery. Narrator uses words that appeal to senses of hearing ("ring") and vision ("flashing").

16 Analyzing
Why is Mitsuo proud of his uncle's skill in making swords? Because uncle has achieved high degree of success in ancient craft important to martial arts.

17 Apprentice uses traditional metalworking techniques to make sword.

18 Drawing Conclusions
Why does uncle apologize? He would like to be able to entertain Mitsuo and his friend, and he tells them he is sorry he cannot.

19 Lincoln's respect for Japanese culture grows as he experiences more of it.

---

12 workout. Lincoln was tossed repeatedly, coming down each time like a cat. He had seen his *sensei* in San Francisco come down on both feet,
13 his hands up and ready to fight. Now *he* was doing it, and he felt like he could take on the world—or at least his neighborhood back in San Francisco.

Oyama-*sensei* had been studying Lincoln's technique from a distance. She stepped in between Lincoln and another brown belt, both of whom were breathing hard.

"Like this," she explained, gripping Lincoln's *gi* as she pivoted her hip onto his. She pulled Lincoln off balance and tossed him into the air. He came down halfway across the yard, on his knees, with one hand in the pond and the other in the mud. He shook the mud off his hands
14 and, looking up, said, "Wow!"

"Sorry, Lincoln-kun," Oyama-*sensei* said. "Are you OK?"

Lincoln shrugged it off. "I'm fine."

That night he hobbled home, a spark of pain in his back.

The next day, after Lincoln and Mitsuo had worked only a few hours in the field, Mitsuo's mother said, "Go and have a drink." She pressed yen into their hands.

The boys hurried into town for a soda. In a far corner of the ice-cream parlor, two old men sat under an overhead fan playing *go*. Lincoln and Mitsuo drank their sodas quickly, ordered seconds, and watched the men, neither of whom seemed to notice the boys. The men sat quietly, and thoughtfully rubbed their whiskered chins as they considered the next strategy.

Lincoln and Mitsuo were wandering around town again when Mitsuo said, "Let me show you something very interesting." He led Lincoln
15 down a narrow alley filled with smoke. The ring of iron on iron sounded in the air, and flames could be seen flashing in a work shed.

"My uncle is a master sword maker," Mitsuo
16 said, a hint of pride in his voice.

Lincoln's curiosity grew as he peeked inside the shed and saw a young man turning a length of metal over an open fire.

"Is that your uncle?" Lincoln asked.

"No, that's an apprentice." Mitsuo spoke to the young man in Japanese. The apprentice pointed to another room and returned to work.

For a few minutes Lincoln and Mitsuo
17 watched the apprentice roll the crude sword over the fire, then dip it into water mixed with ash. A gray cloud puffed up and drifted toward the darkened ceiling.

The uncle appeared from the other room, tying his hair back with a *hachimaki*,[3] a headband. His skin was dark, his arms splotched from burns, and his clothes black with soot. His eyeglasses were flecked with ash.

"Mitsuo-kun, what brings you here?" he asked in Japanese.

Mitsuo bowed deeply to his uncle and introduced Lincoln, who bowed in turn and said, "*Ohayō gozaimasu.*"[4]

18 "*Ohayō*," the uncle greeted them. He apologized that he didn't have anything for them to drink. He offered them a stick of gum, and they accepted politely with bows of thanks, though each of them already had a pack of gum.

"We were just passing," Mitsuo said. "Lincoln is staying with us for the summer. He's from California."

"Ah, so. California." He beamed, turning to Lincoln. Mitsuo translated for his uncle, who said that his best customers were from California.

19 Lincoln smiled but didn't say anything. He was in awe of the master swordsmith. He was in awe of Japan. He had already met two honest-to-goodness masters—first in *kempō* and now in sword making.

---

3. *hachimaki* (hä-chē-mä-kē).
4. *Ohayō gozaimasu* (ō-hä-yō gō-zī-mäs): Good morning.

The court sword of Kazadachi, Japan, crafted with elaborate enamel and gilt work. Eighteenth century.

Werner Forman/Art Resource, NY

Mitsuo's uncle talked, hands pressed together, and Mitsuo translated, "Uncle asks if there are millionaires on every street in California. That's what he hears."

"Not on my street," Lincoln replied. He thought of his old neighborhood in the Mission District, where junky cars often sat on blocks and litter scuttled freely when the wind picked up. If there were a millionaire, it would probably be the liquor-store owner, who did a brisk business at five when the workers got off from the warehouse near Valencia Street.

Lincoln and Mitsuo stayed awhile. They watched the length of metal as it was heated over the fire. The apprentice rolled it through the flames, pounded it over an anvil, and heated it again until it glowed neon orange.

"It's bad," Lincoln said in praise.

"Yes, very, very bad," Mitsuo repeated.

From the sword foundry, Lincoln and Mitsuo returned home. While they played catch in the yard, Mitsuo lamented the fact that he hadn't made the summer baseball league.

"That's a drag," Lincoln said as he picked up an easy grounder and sidearmed it to Mitsuo.

"A 'drag'?" Mitsuo asked. "What do you mean?"

Lincoln explained, and after much thought, Mitsuo remarked, "Very American."

"Americans talk in slang. There is Mexican slang, black slang, Asian slang, yuppie slang."

Mitsuo sighed and said, "I'll never learn English. It is too difficult."

"You will. When you come to see me in San Francisco, you'll be rattlin' your lips like the rest of us."

When it was close to four, Lincoln told Mitsuo that he had to meet Tony.

"I'll come," Mitsuo said, tossing his glove onto the porch and scaring the cat.

20
Mitsuo's uncle probably deals mainly with rich Americans who can afford custom-made swords, so he thinks many Americans are rich.

21
Irony. Lincoln lives on street that seems poor and uncared for.

22 Summarizing
Why does Mitsuo fear he will not learn English? Mitsuo already speaks English very well, but he is becoming more aware that there is more to language than he learns in school.

23
Metaphor. Lincoln compares speaking English well to rattling noise made by lips moving effortlessly.

Pacific Crossing **527**

COOPERATIVE LEARNING

Have students work in small groups to think about places in their community where they would want to take an exchange student. Then have each group create a brochure describing their community in detail. Students may wish to include a map; descriptions of landmarks and buildings; historical facts; information on amusement parks, theaters, libraries; and a directory of important telephone numbers. One or more groups may wish to plan and record on audiotape a guided walking tour of the community. Have groups share their completed work.

24
Mitsuo seems satisfied with Lincoln's explanation for why Mitsuo cannot go with him to meet Tony.

25 Summarizing
Why does Lincoln feel bad about leaving Mitsuo? Mitsuo has been kind to Lincoln, and Lincoln does not want to hurt his feelings.

26 Summarizing
How do Lincoln and Tony know what man wants? They can tell by his tone of voice and other nonverbal clues.

27
Exaggeration. Emphasizes Lincoln has watched his mother often.

28
Lincoln realizes they may have trouble finding ingredients for Mexican meal.

29
Figurative Language. Tony means green color of money, but not necessarily green in general, is his favorite color.

"No," Lincoln said. He and Tony were going to plan the party for their host families and it had to be a surprise.

Mitsuo looked hurt; Lincoln tried to explain that they were meeting to plan something special. "It's a surprise," Lincoln said. "You'll see."

"A surprise?"

"Yes. A surprise."

24 "Don't get lost." Mitsuo walked Lincoln to the gate. He pointed down the street and told him three times to take a left and go right at the first signal. Lincoln turned around when he was halfway down the street and saw Mitsuo at the gate, pointing right.

That *vato* is all right, Lincoln said to him-
25 self. He felt bad leaving Mitsuo at home. I should have invited him, he told himself. As punishment, he punched a wall and hurt his hand.

Lincoln found Tony already undressed. An old man was scrubbing his back, muttering something in Japanese.

"Hey, Linc," Tony greeted him.

"Who's the guy?" Lincoln asked.

"I don't know. He just started scrubbing my back."

Lincoln undressed as he watched Tony trade places and scrub the man's back. The man scolded in Japanese, and although neither Lincoln nor Tony could understand the words,
26 both knew that the man wanted to be scrubbed hard. Lincoln grabbed a washcloth and helped Tony rub the man's back. When they finished, the man stood up, bowed, and got into the pool, sighing loudly.

Lincoln and Tony planned the party as they sat in the tub.

"How 'bout Friday?" Tony asked.

"Sounds good. Do you know how to make tortillas?"

"No. I thought you did."

27 "Not really. But I've watched my mom a million times." Lincoln fanned his face. "Man, you could kill someone with this water."

"Tell you what, Linc. I brought the beans. Why don't I give them to you and let you cook them?"

"You brought the beans?"

"Yeah." Tony pointed to his backpack, which was in the wicker basket.

"Fair enough, if you make the tortillas." Lincoln rose from the water and toweled off.
28 "See if you can find some avocados. I'll look for chilies and tomatoes, and make some salsa. Let's meet here again tomorrow."

They dressed and started home, stopping to drink Cokes and thumb through comic books at a newsstand.

Lincoln said, "Let me try some Japanese on you." He thought deeply and then said, "*Anata no tan 'joobi wa itsu desu ka?*"[5]

"Whatta you say?" Tony asked.

"I think, 'What day is your birthday?' or 'What is your favorite color?' I forget which. Mitsuo was trying to teach me."

29 "Today's my birthday," Tony cracked, "and money's my favorite color. ¿*Entiendes?*"

Lincoln punched his friend in the arm and headed home.

---
5. "***Anata...desu ka?***" (ä-nä-tä nō tänjō-bē wä ē'tsoō děs kä): "When is your birthday?"

Reading Check

1. Why are Lincoln and Tony chosen for the student-exchange program?
2. What is *shorinji kempo*?
3. How does Lincoln's mother react when he tells her about the student-exchange program to Japan?
4. Where is the Ono family home?
5. What mistake does Lincoln make when he first walks into the Onos' home?
6. What is Mitsuo's favorite sport?
7. What does Lincoln do to help the family?
8. Why is Lincoln embarrassed when he meets Oyama-sensei at the *shorinji kempo dojo*?
9. What do Lincoln and Tony plan to do for their host families?
10. Why does Lincoln think he has hurt Mitsuo's feelings?

For Study and Discussion

Analyzing and Interpreting the Novel

1. What is your impression of Lincoln? Consider his conversations with friends, his thoughts and feelings, and his past problems.

2. Why is Lincoln happy to be back in San Francisco?

3. How does Lincoln prove that he is different from Tony when he decides to continue studying the martial arts?

4. When Mr. Ayala, the school principal, calls Lincoln and Tony into his office, he asks them what they think of Japan. **a.** What do their answers reveal? **b.** Would you expect their impressions to change after their visit to Japan?

5. Why is Lincoln disappointed when he first arrives in Japan? **b.** What things about Japan and the people he meets pleasantly surprise him?

6. Locate two places in the novel where Japanese characters express their ideas about Americans. How does Lincoln try to correct their views?

7. In what ways are Lincoln and Mitsuo similar and in what ways are they different?

Literary Elements

Understanding the Novel

Setting

1. Setting is the time and place of a story. Describe the two settings of *Pacific Crossing*.

Character

2. In order for characters to be believable, they must act consistently. **a.** How is Lincoln's behavior consistent with that of an average teenager? **b.** How are his actions consistent with what you know about his personality?

Plot

3. Plot requires conflict of some kind, such as conflict with the environment, one's self, or other people. To help the reader understand the major conflicts of the story, the author provides necessary background information. **a.** What important information do you learn about Lincoln in the first two chapters? **b.** What possible conflicts are revealed?

Point of View

4. *Pacific Crossing* is written from the third-person point of view. An **omniscient** narrator knows what all the characters are thinking and feeling. A **limited third-person** narrator generally reveals the unspoken thoughts and feelings of one character. Does the narrator of *Pacific Crossing* have an omniscient or a limited point of view? How do you know?

READING CHECK

1. They have shown an interest in Japan by taking martial arts (p. 507).
2. Japanese martial art (p. 504).
3. She is happy for her son (p. 507).
4. Atami, a small farming village three hours outside Tokyo (p. 508).
5. He forgets to take off his shoes (p. 512).
6. Baseball (p. 512).
7. He helps in field (p. 513).
8. He had bragged about his *kempō* skill to her before he knew she was *sensei* (p. 520).
9. Cook Mexican food (p. 524).
10. He leaves Mitsuo at home when he meets Tony to plan a Mexican dinner (p. 528).

FOR STUDY AND DISCUSSION

1. Most students will like Lincoln. He is tough and street-wise but also sensitive, friendly, and enthusiastic.
2. Suburbs were boring; Lincoln missed Tony. Mother likes garden.
3. *Kempō* is important to Lincoln. Lincoln can stay with something that is difficult.
4a. All they know about Japan is that the Japanese make good cars. **b.** Yes. Boys will have many impressions of Japan.
5a. Mr. Ono is formal; Tokyo looks American and is modern; it is hot and muggy. **b.** People are not reserved and serious; many places like U.S. places.
6. Tells Mitsuo only some have guns. Explains ethnic groups. Sets uncle straight about millionaires on every street.
7. Mitsuo is a farm boy, likes baseball, and lives with both parents. Lincoln is a city boy, likes basketball, and lives with his mother. Boys are similar in having good sense of humor, liking to have fun, and being adventurous.

> **TRANSPARENCY 43**
> **Reader Response**
> *Add Up the Ratings* – asks students to evaluate and tally their responses to various aspects of a novel.

LITERARY ELEMENTS
1. Contemporary, passenger cabin of jumbo jet; contemporary, small farm and town in Japan. Some students may state San Francisco as one setting even though a flashback.
2a. Does what average teenager does: sports, hanging out with friends, uses slang. 2b. He is friendly and easy going, and his actions fit these traits.
3a. He does not know much about Japan, lives in city, likes martial arts. b. Clash of cultures and lifestyles, and problems with martial artists.
4. Limited. Lincoln is only character whose thoughts we know.

WRITING ABOUT LITERATURE
After they have chosen a pair of characters, encourage students to make a chart with a column for each character for listing aspects of relationships. Have them draw lines connecting aspects that are similar. Essays should contain specific examples from novel to support ideas.

FOCUS ON WRITING A LETTER
Besides following the correct form for a personal letter, students should focus on an event that occurs in the story and use concrete details to help create a mental picture of what they write about.

CONNECTING CULTURES
Games from Around the World
You might want to consider sponsoring a contest for the best student-made game. Appoint a committee to serve as judges for the contest and have each contestant explain his or her game to the class. You can keep the games in the classroom for students to look at when time permits.

530

Writing About Literature

Analyzing Character

One way to understand a character is by analyzing his or her relationship to others. Write a short essay in which you analyze Lincoln's relationship with two characters who play similar roles in his life, for example, his friendships with Tony and Mitsuo or his relationship with his mother and Mrs. Ono.

Focus on Writing a Letter

Writing a Personal Letter

In a **personal letter,** you share your ideas, feelings, and experiences. Personal letters may also include thank-you notes and letters of invitation or regret. When you write a personal letter, you should use an informal, friendly style and tone.

Study the form of a personal letter in the outline below.

Your Address
Today's Date

Dear _____,

_____
_____
_____
_____
_____
_____

Sincerely,

Keep your purpose and audience in mind when you write a personal letter. Remember to write about things that interest you and the person you're writing to.

Imagine that you are Lincoln. Write a letter to your mother about one of the experiences you've had after reaching Japan. Use Lincoln's point of view in your letter and remember to include thoughts and feelings, as well as events. Save your writing.

530 THE NOVEL

Connecting Cultures

Games from Around the World

Some games commonly played in the United States, such as chess and dominoes, originated in other countries. Chess is said to have come from India.

Many cultures play the same games or slightly different versions. *Pachinko*, which is a kind of pinball machine, is one of the many games Japanese enjoy. Japanese also play *mah-jong*, which came from China, and is played not only in this country but also in other parts of the world. Western chess has its Japanese counterpart in *shogi*. Another popular Japanese game is *go*. In *go* a player maneuvers black and white stones on a simple grid that serves as a playing board in order to gain more territory than his or her opponent. Many people are already familiar with *go* in countries outside of Asia.

Making Connections: Activities

With other students form a game club in which members meet to learn about and play games from other countries. Have one member be responsible each week for finding a game. Sometimes it may be possible to borrow a game from a friend. Some games may also be constructed from everyday objects. *Go*, for example, consists of a grid, one set of black stones, and one set of white stones. At the library find books that discuss various games, rules, and strategies. Also keep in mind that many games played in the United States have come from other countries. Try games that you have never played before.

CLOSURE
Ask students to review orally the main events of the novel thus far. You can make a time line on the chalkboard to assist them in remembering events. This may be especially helpful in having students understand that Chapter 2 is a **flashback**.

EXTENSION AND ENRICHMENT
Some of your students may be knowledgeable about one or more of the martial arts. Ask such students to provide a demonstration and an explanation for the class. If you do not have any resident martial artists, you might want to consider inviting a practitioner of martial arts to class to discuss the purposes, ranks, and other aspects of the sport. Your students might be particularly interested in learning whether the martial arts are portrayed accurately in movies and television shows.

The game of *shogi* is played with 40 pieces on a board of 81 squares.

International Exchange
Japanese culture is a mix of both traditional and Western ways. For example, while people mainly eat traditional foods like *nigirimeshi*—rice balls—and noodles, many also go to the local burger shop for a meal once in a while. Japanese also love the traditional American pastime of baseball. Like Japan, the United States enjoys the foods, pastimes, and arts of other countries. Many people eat sushi, celebrate the first cherry blossoms of the season, and are skillful at crafts like origami—the Japanese art of folding paper into shapes such as flowers and birds.

Making Connections: Activities
1. With a group of students learn about the crafts of other cultures. Choose a craft such as origami and, with your teacher's permission, designate an area in the classroom to display your work. Puppet-making, a craft shared by many cultures, is another possibility. Each student might make a puppet of a different culture. Many books available at your local library will provide directions for making these objects.

2. Having a pen pal is a good way to learn about another culture. Locate a pen pal in another country by contacting student-exchange organizations, other youth groups, and language clubs, or by asking your teacher for information. Many students in other countries like Japan study English and would enjoy the opportunity to communicate by letter with an American student. Also consider choosing a pen pal whose native language you are studying. In this way you will have the opportunity to learn more about another culture, practice writing a foreign language, and discuss common interests such as baseball.

CONNECTING CULTURES
International Exchange
1. Craft catalogs that feature imports from other cultures are widely available in the United States. Ask students to bring some of these catalogs to put on display in the classroom. If you know someone who practices a craft from another culture, you might consider inviting that person to talk to the class about his or her craft.
2. Letter writing offers students a chance to practice practical writing skills. You might want to consider sponsoring a pen pal club at your school. Meetings could be devoted to sharing letters students send and receive.

Pacific Crossing

OBJECTIVES
The overall aim is for students to explain how **plot, character, setting,** and **point of view** advance and develop the novel's theme. For a complete list of objectives, see the **Teacher's Notes.**

VOCABULARY
The underlined words are in the Glossary. The **Language and Vocabulary** exercises at the end of Part II will give students practice in recognizing idioms and identifying different levels of language.

FOCUS / MOTIVATION
Ask volunteers to describe what homesickness feels like. Then ask them how they might feel if they had to say goodbye to a close friend in order to go home after a long trip. Would they feel sad, glad, or both?

> **TEACHING RESOURCES D**
> Teacher's Notes, p. 171
> Reading Check, p. 175
> Study Guide, p. 176
> Language Skills, p. 179
> Building Vocabulary, p. 182
> Selection Vocabulary Test, p. 184
> Selection Test, p. 185

Chapter 9

1
Mitsuo is disappointed that he and Lincoln have to change their plans.

2
Exaggeration. Emphasizes that weeds are tall and that garden needs attention.

3
Lincoln tries to have positive attitude about work.

4 Analyzing
Is Mitsuo serious? No, he is joking, but he wants to make point that their work will be hard.

5
Exaggeration. Compares weeds to falling trees to emphasize their size.

6
Metaphor. Sweat stains on shirts resemble lines on map.

7 Drawing Conclusions
Why does Mitsuo doubt old woman is relative? He resents having to do work, which he would have done more cheerfully for relative.

8
Lincoln seems to be aware of one significant difference between American and Japanese agriculture, even though he lives in city.

9
Simile. Narrator compares speed and sound of flies to speed and sound of jet airplanes.

532

9

The next morning, after breakfast, Mrs. Ono asked Lincoln and Mitsuo to work in a neighbor's field. The neighbor was too old to tend the crop of green beans herself; her husband, a distant relative of Mrs. Ono's, had passed away the spring before. When Mitsuo protested that he and Lincoln had planned to play baseball that morning, Mrs. Ono scolded him.

"She is old. You must help her."

"Why us?" Mitsuo pleaded. His baseball mitt hung from the end of his arm.

"Because you must."

"Doesn't she have relatives?"

"We are her relatives. Now, please, do not argue. Someday when you are old, you will see."

So the boys shouldered their hoes and walked to the neighbor's garden. The weeds were as tall as car antennas, and gnats swarmed around the fruit the peach tree had dropped.

Lincoln and Mitsuo looked at each other.

"This is going to be a lot of work," Lincoln said, rolling up his shirt sleeves. He tried to convince himself that it would make him stronger for *kempō*. Whacking at the weeds would pump blood to his arms and legs.

"We may die before the day is over," Mitsuo said as he unbuttoned his shirt and let it hang open. He shaded his eyes with his hand and looked toward the blazing sun.

Mrs. Nakayama, a wizened[1] woman with only a few teeth and a face puckered with wrinkles, came out to the back porch and greeted them. Mitsuo and Lincoln each gave a short, polite bow.

Bowing in return, she thanked them for coming—and then told them to get to work. She sat in the shade of the porch and banged her cane, scaring up a puff of dust.

1. **wizened** (wĭz′ənd): withered.

532 THE NOVEL

Without a word, Lincoln and Mitsuo started hoeing fiercely, the weeds falling like timber as they advanced up the first row. Maps of sweat spread on the backs of their shirts. Sweat dripped from the end of Lincoln's nose. Sweat rolled into his ears. He saw a large bead of sweat hanging on the end of Mitsuo's nose as well. It dropped on a leaf, like rain, and another bead formed.

Mitsuo looked at the woman, whose cat lay sleeping in her lap. "My mother says she's a relative of ours, but I doubt it."

Lincoln wiped his face with his shirt sleeve and blinked away a crust of dirt from his eyelashes. He thought about the neighbor in San Francisco for whom he had mowed the lawn for three quarters and a bagful of crushed aluminum cans. That woman was so cheap she couldn't even offer Lincoln a smile.

He stood up, leaning on his hoe to give himself a rest. "You know, Mitsuo, the farms in California are sometimes a thousand acres —or even bigger."

Mitsuo squinted a doubtful eye at Lincoln. "Really?"

"Yeah. I know they're small here, but whenever we drive through the San Joaquin Valley, the farms go on for miles. But they don't belong to everybody, just to big growers."

"I would like to see this," Mitsuo said.

"You will. When you come and visit us."

The sun moved slowly overhead. Flies buzzed past their ears like fighter jets. Some of the gnats left the rotting peaches and hovered around their faces.

"This is gross," Lincoln said. He smacked his neck and three bloody gnats lay squashed in his palm. He washed his hand in a puddle of muddy water.

Mitsuo cursed in Japanese and apologized. "See what I mean," he said. "We just work and never play."

"Yeah." Lincoln grunted as he raised a

MOTIVATIONAL SUMMARY
After a few weeks with the Onos, Lincoln feels like part of the family. He and Mitsuo are the best of friends, but Lincoln misses his mother, his dog, and his customary diet. Lincoln and Tony prepare Mexican food for their families, and then Lincoln, Mitsuo, and Mr. Ono go on a camping trip to the mountains. While on the trip, Mr. Ono is bitten by a poisonous spider, and it is up to Lincoln and Mitsuo to save his life. But the adventure does not end there, for the boys later spend a hectic day in Tokyo.

PRESENTATION
The events in Part II of the novel happen fast and are somewhat more exciting than the events in the first part. You might want to encourage students to see each event as a glimpse into Lincoln's developing character and as a step

---

bucket of water onto his shoulder. "Maybe we should sneak away."

"Sneak away! My father would kill me, and you too. We must respect our elders. We have to stay."

Lincoln *staggered* to the row and splashed the water among the green beans. "How come she don't have a garden hose?" he asked.

10 "She works the old way."

11 "But she's not doing the work. We are!"

Three hours later they finally finished working. Mitsuo poured a bucket of cold water over Lincoln, and Lincoln poured one over Mitsuo.

The old neighbor climbed down the steps to inspect their work. She pointed to weeds they had missed.

"We can't please her," Lincoln hissed as he plucked the last weeds.

Mitsuo said, "Let's go."

"Yeah, let's blow this place."

"What is the meaning of 'blow this place'?"

"It means 'let's leave'—*adios!*"

The old neighbor called them back and shook a paper bag at them.

"*¡Ay, caramba!*² What does the *vieja*³ want now?" Lincoln asked. "Do we have to take out her garbage?"

They turned and walked back. Mitsuo bowed and accepted the bag. Only when they were down the street and happy to be free did they
12 open it. They found bruised peaches, which gave off a strong fruity odor and a *horde* of gnats that rose from the bag like smoke.

Mitsuo splattered the peaches, one by one, against a wall.

"Rotten luck, rotten peaches," Lincoln said. "Hey, that's pretty good. I'm doin' rap."

Back home, they joined the cat and fell asleep on the porch. They woke when Mr. Ono came home, nudged Mitsuo in the rib with his foot, and said, "Let us eat."

They staggered to the bathroom and scrubbed their faces and arms before joining Mitsuo's father and mother at the table. A letter lay next to Lincoln's placemat.

"A letter from my mom!" Lincoln smiled.

Mr. Ono, his cheek fat with rice, said, "Let us hear, Lincoln-kun."

"Yes, please," Mrs. Ono said as she poured tea for her husband.

Lincoln tore open the letter. He was occasionally homesick, especially at night, when he would lie in bed and think about his mother. He missed her. He missed his own bedroom and the familiar streets of San Francisco. And he was anxious to hear if his dog, Flaco, was OK. Before he'd left for Japan, Flaco had gotten into a fight with an alley cat who had dug her claws into Flaco's nose. Lincoln began to read silently:

Dear *Mi'jo,*

13 I miss you very much. I hope you and Tony are behaving and not goofing around. I don't want your host family to think you're a low-class *chango.*⁴ Do you hear me? I miss you very much, but how come you didn't tell me where you left the key to the back door? Nothing is really happening around here,
14 except that that stupid Maxima is in the shop, and it's going to cost nearly a thousand dollars to fix. It's a piece of junk after all. And your crazy dog brought a dead sparrow into the house. I could've killed him. His nose is better....

Lincoln swallowed a mouthful of rice and won-
15 dered how he could share this letter. He didn't want the Onos to think that his mother was

2. *Ay, caramba* (ī kä-räm′bä): Oh, wow.
3. *vieja* (byä′hä): old woman.
4. *chango* (chän′gō): pest.

---

10 **Analyzing**
What does Mitsuo mean by working "the old way"? Neighbor uses traditional farming methods, not modern ones that save labor.

11
Lincoln is aware of irony in neighbor's belief in traditional farming methods.

12 **Drawing Conclusions**
Why does old lady give boys rotten peaches? She intends peaches as a thank-you gift. Rotten peaches may be all she has to give them.

13
Tone. Tone of letter is same as tone Lincoln's mother would use in talking to him.

14
Irony. Lincoln and Tony have great respect for Japanese cars, but these cars, too, have problems that need expensive repairs.

15 **Making Generalizations**
What does Lincoln's concern about letter show about his awareness of Japanese culture? He realizes Onos would not understand his mother's tone and would think less of her.

in his coming of age.

As the novel concludes, Lincoln's emotions run high. On one hand, he is homesick for his mother, his dog, and his home in America. On the other hand, he has grown to love Mitsuo as a brother and Mr. and Mrs. Ono as parents. He is reluctant to leave them. Help students understand Lincoln's emotions by pointing out the mixed feelings he has as he prepares to leave Japan.

The questions in the **For Study and Discussion** exercise will help students clarify their reactions to the characters and events of the novel, and the questions in the **Literary Elements** exercise will help students focus on aspects of the novel that work together to create its effect.

16
Lincoln's decision to change letter for Onos proves to be correct one.

17 Finding Cause and Effect
Why does Mr. Ono tell this story? Probably because letter from Lincoln's mother brings it to mind.

18
Women had to take places of men who were away fighting.

19
Mrs. Ono and Mitsuo do not want to look Lincoln in the eye.

20
Simile. Compares drops of water from faucet to person crying.

21 Analyzing
Why is simile about tears appropriate at this point in novel? Mr. Ono's story about his grandmother is sad.

---

mean or anything. So he read aloud his own version:

"My dearest Lincoln,
 I miss you very much. I am lonely and in need of your excellent help. It seems that I damaged the Maxima when I braked too hard. Now the brakes are stuck. I know that you could fix them if you were here. You have a mechanical mind. You are as smart as any boy in all of San Francisco, and maybe the whole West. I miss you very much. You are my only son, and sweet Tony is like a son, too. I know you two boys are bringing Mexican pride to Japan."

Lincoln read a few more made-up sentences, then folded the letter and placed it in his shirt pocket next to his heart.

16 "Nice mother," Mrs. Ono said, her eyes shining with affection. "One day we would like to meet her."

"You will," Lincoln said. "When you come to San Francisco."

Mr. Ono put down his chopsticks and said reflectively, "A thoughtful mother." With his
17 hands resting in his lap he began to tell a story about his grandmother, who used to write weekly letters to her son, Mr. Ono's father.

Mr. Ono explained that the war[5] had just broken out. His grandparents and their family were living in Hiroshima.[6] For more than four generations they had been carpenters, but the war changed that. The men were sent to fight,
18 and women, even mothers, were forced to work in factories. Seeing that a large city in wartime was no place for children, his grandparents had decided to move their children—including Mr. Ono's father—to the countryside, where they

---
5. **war:** The United States entered World War II in December 1941.
6. **Hiroshima** (hĭr′ə-shē′mə, hĭ-rō′shĭ-mə): The city was destroyed in 1945 by the first atomic bomb.

---

would wait out the war on an uncle's farm.

"Was this World War Two?" Lincoln asked.

"Yes. It was long ago. It was a terrible time for our country. The world. I was not born then, not until after the war. But I know my parents and grandparents had very little to eat, almost nothing. Not like this." He tapped his bowl of rice with his chopstick. Lincoln and Mitsuo stopped eating to listen. "My father told me that he received a letter from his mother every week. She was still living in the city. She was working in a tire factory. It was very sad for my father."

Mr. Ono said the letters were like poetry. "She would write my father little songs, which he and his brothers sang. Clapped and sang. Sometimes she would slip a piece of gum into the letters. He liked that. All the brothers had to share it, but still, a little sweetness went a long way." He took a sip of tea and continued, "My great uncle—Uncle Kaz—was a fine man. He grew apples, and my father helped him as much as he could. Poor Father, he missed his mother. He was eleven years old then."

"He must have been happy to see her when the war was over," Lincoln said. He took a sip of his tea, which was now cold.

Mr. Ono's face darkened. Mitsuo and Mrs. Ono grew quiet, and Lincoln put down his cup.

"He did not see her. The letters stopped. Everything stopped," Mr. Ono said. "She worked three years in the tire factory, and then—"

19 Mother and son looked down at their food. They knew this story.

20 The house was so quiet Lincoln could hear
21 the kitchen faucet dripping like tears. The wooden floor creaked. The neighbor's dog barked. Lincoln studied his hands, which were rough from work and *kempō*.

Mr. Ono said softly, "Lincoln-kun, it is not your fault, but your country dropped the atomic bomb on Hiroshima."

THE NOVEL

HISTORY LINK
Lincoln is deeply disturbed when he learns that Mr. Ono's grandparents were living in Hiroshima during World War II. Encourage students to learn about what happened in Hiroshima and what happened to the people living there during and after the war. Extend this activity by inviting students to read *Sadako and the Thousand Paper Cranes* (Eleanor Coerr, New York: Dell Publishing, 1977), a moving book based on the true life story of Sadako Sasaki, a young girl living in Hiroshima during World War II.

The "Peace Dome" in Hiroshima Peace Park, an area that was at the center of the bomb blast on August 6, 1945.

Lincoln felt awful. In his mind, he saw a flash of silvery light fill the sky and a mushroom cloud unfold. **He saw families crying and tongues of flames wagging from charred buildings.**

Before Lincoln could say anything, Mr. Ono smiled at him and said, "That is why you are here. You are an American boy. As an exchange student, you share yourself with us." He lifted his chopsticks and clicked them together as he raised his bowl. "Let us eat. No food should be wasted."

The family took up their bowls, filled them with new, hot rice, and ate. After dinner Lincoln volunteered to wash the dishes. He scrubbed the pots with vigor, mad at himself for ever thinking that war movies were fun.

After the dishes were done, Lincoln left for *kempō*, his *gi* over his shoulder. He was disturbed that Mr. Ono had grown up without knowing his grandmother, and that she had died so terribly. Lincoln felt the need to work out hard, to feel real pain. That night he was thrown into the air more than a dozen times, sometimes coming down on his feet like a cat. More often than not, he came down on his back. The wind was knocked out of him each time, and twice he felt his bones crack. He wished he could hurt even more, but the cushion of spongy grass saved him from any serious injury.

Before he left, Oyama-*sensei* called him aside. "Lincoln-kun," she said quietly. "Please come and see me tomorrow. At twelve."

"OK," Lincoln said. He wondered why but held his tongue. He *gasshō*-ed, saluted, and raced home under the star-flecked sky. **He thought that Oyama-*sensei* might want to teach him a new technique, one that would fend off even the baddest of bad dudes.**

22
Metaphor. Compares fire to human tongues because of shape of flames and their quick flickering movement.

23 Drawing Conclusions
Why does Lincoln volunteer to wash dishes? Answers will vary. He may feel need to make up for atomic bomb in some small way.

24
Lincoln wants to share pain of Mr. Ono and his grandmother.

25 Making Inferences
Why does Oyama want to see Lincoln? Answers will vary. Perhaps she has noticed he is not fighting back and protecting himself as he should.

26
Exaggeration. Lincoln overstates what he might be capable of accomplishing in area of *kempō*.

Pacific Crossing

TRANSPARENCY 44

Literary Elements
Analyzing and Evaluating a Novel — invites students to assess how various elements of fiction contribute to the reader's experience of a novel.

Chapter 10

1
Word Choice. Narrator uses *collapsed* and *exhausted* to reinforce fact that push-ups take a lot of energy.

2 Drawing Conclusions
What does Mitsuo's smile suggest? That he intends to skip numbers in his counting and not do as many push-ups as he agreed to do.

3
Lincoln makes a joke about eating Japanese food.

4
Mrs. Mendoza apparently does not know much about diet of most Japanese.

5
Metaphor. Compares Mrs. Mendoza's voice to object breaking apart to show she is emotional.

6
Lump in Lincoln's throat is his emotional reaction to saying goodbye to his mother on telephone.

7 Analyzing
What does "born yesterday" mean? That Lincoln might be naive and unable to spot a trick.

8
Irony. This statement becomes ironic in light of what Oyama really wants to see Lincoln about.

10

"Ninety-seven, ninety-eight, ninety-nine, one hundred." Lincoln grunted as he finished a set
1 of a hundred push-ups, and collapsed so exhausted that his arms twitched. He was still tired from yesterday's hard *kempō* workout. His face pressed to the porch, he saw an ant stagger past, carrying a grain of rice. He remembered reading somewhere that for their size ants were about the strongest creatures on earth. Lincoln blew at the ant and sent it sailing.

"OK, my turn," Mitsuo said. He readied for his last set of push-ups and started counting. "*Ichi, ni, san, shi…*"¹

Mrs. Ono called from the house. "Lincoln-kun," she said. "It is your mother on the telephone."

Lincoln grinned and jumped to his feet. He wagged a playfully threatening finger at Mitsuo. "You better play fair. Don't slack off."

2 "I promise," Mitsuo grunted, holding back a mischievous smile.

Lincoln took the call in the living room. "Hi, Mom. How's everything?"

"Hi, *mi'jo*," said the crackling voice on the other end. "Fine. Roy and I just got back from dinner and a movie."

"It's night there?"

"Yes, it's really late."

"That's funny. It's morning over here," Lincoln said. "What did you have for dinner?"

"Japanese food. In honor of you."

3 "That's funny, so did we."

Mrs. Mendoza asked Lincoln if he was eating enough vegetables, getting enough meat, and
4 drinking enough milk.

"Lots," he lied. He had eaten more vegetables in one week in Japan than he did in one year in California, and so much spinach that he felt like Popeye. But he had eaten almost no meat and had drunk only a few swallows of milk. The Onos, like most Japanese families, preferred seafood and tea to meat and milk.

"How's Flaco?" Lincoln asked.

"*Está bien*,"² she answered. "He got in another fight with that cat, but I think he won this time. He had some cat fur between his teeth."

"The stud," Lincoln crowed. "Give him a dog biscuit for me."

5 By the time they said good-bye, his mother's voice was cracking.

"Drink all your milk," his mother sobbed. "I'll see you in a few weeks. I miss you. *Adios.*"

6 As Lincoln hung up, he felt a lump in his throat. He missed his mother, and he missed Flaco, his best friend on shaggy fours.

Outside, he found Mitsuo in push-up position, counting, "a thousand three, a thousand four, a thousand five…"

"You liar," Lincoln growled, and pushed Mitsuo over with his foot.

"Really," Mitsuo pleaded, laughing. "I did a thousand. Look at all this sweat."

Lincoln looked at the small puddles and thought for a moment that maybe, just maybe, Mitsuo had actually done a thousand push-ups. Then Lincoln spied the garden hose lying
7 nearby. "You think I was born yesterday?" Lincoln scowled, pointing to the hose. "Let's go. Oyama-*sensei* wants to talk to me."

"About what?"

Lincoln shrugged, his shoulders sore from
8 the push-ups. "I don't know," he said. "Maybe she's gonna teach me a death blow or something."

When they arrived, Oyama was on her porch, sipping tea. She worked at home as a translator of medical dictionaries. Her languages were French and English, and she knew some Spanish.

---

1. *Ichi…shi* (ē-chē nē sän shē): One, two, three, four.

2. *Está bien* (ĕs-tä′ byĕn): It's OK.

536 THE NOVEL

Lincoln and Mitsuo bowed deeply, then climbed the steps and gave a second slight bow. Oyama gestured for them to join her. They plopped down, folding their legs underneath them. Lincoln looked around the yard. The grass was wild along the fence, and there was a green pond in the middle of the yard. A rusty bicycle leaned against a tree.

"Lincoln-kun, I need your help," Oyama began solemnly, rattling a sheaf of papers at Lincoln. "These are poems by a Japanese poet that I am translating into English. I would like you to read them carefully and suggest changes. My English is good, but yours, I feel, is better."

"Poems?" Lincoln asked. "I don't know how to spell good."

"They have nothing to do with spelling. Now please, take them home and read them carefully. If you think my language is wrong, please circle." She handed him the papers.

Lincoln and Mitsuo stared at the poems and read the start of one:

> Overcast for days, and the gull circles
> This place of sleep. The shadows gobble
> The birds. I'm fifty-seven,
> My sled of years riding on my back.

"Sounds all right to me," Lincoln said. "Except 'gobble.' That sounds weird. It reminds me of Thanksgiving."

"Good, Lincoln-kun. This is exactly what I'm looking for." Oyama beamed. "Please read the poems, and if the words are wrong, please tell me."

Oyama rose, her empty teacup in her hand, and Lincoln and Mitsuo scrambled to their feet. "I will see you tonight," she said. She bowed and went inside.

The boys gathered the poems and went to get a soda. They took their drinks to a small park not too far from a shrine where passersby were bowing, lighting incense, and praying.

"Do you believe in God?" Lincoln asked.

"Yes. I believe if we make a mistake, God corrects us," Mitsuo said. He finished his drink and spun the bottle.

"I'm Catholic," Lincoln said. "When we make mistakes, we say confession."

"What's 'confession'?"

Lincoln took a swallow of his soda and answered, "It's when you go into a box in church and tell the priest what you did wrong. This way Jesus Christ forgives our sins, and we can start over."

"Box?"

"Well, not exactly a box. It's sort of like a closet. You're supposed to say your sins in private."

Mitsuo searched Lincoln's face and then asked, "Have you sinned?"

"Not really. I stole some things—gum and

Sculpture of Buddha at a sacred site near Mitaki dera (temple) in Hiroshima, Japan.

READING SKILLS PRACTICE
The underlined passage can be used to give students practice in the reading skill of determining the sequence of events. Ask students to read the passage, paying attention to the events that occur. Then ask students to identify which of the events listed answers the following question. What does Lincoln say just before he tells about eating with tortillas, not forks, spoons, or chopsticks? **A.** He describes enchiladas and tacos. **B.** He says that nothing is better than scraping a small "rip" of tortilla across a puddle of chicken *mole.* **C.** He tells of tortillas made of corn and flour and wrapped in a dish towel. **D.** He praises the fiery salsa of his *tío* Junior and the tamales on Christmas Day at his *tía* Linda's house. (Correct)

13
Exaggeration. Describes spanking as lashing to emphasize that it was more serious than other spankings he had gotten.

14 Analyzing
Does it seem like four hours have passed since Lincoln's 12 o'clock meeting with Oyama? No; not enough has happened to take up four hours. Author speeds up time because an hour-by-hour record of what boys do is not important to story.

Chapter 11

1 Expressing an Opinion
Is Mr. Ono serious about knowing smell and taste of *frijoles*? Answers will vary. Probably not. He is probably only pretending to recognize them as a joke.

2
Mrs. Ono acknowledges her guests before she drinks.

3 Summarizing
What does Mrs. Ono mean when she says her husband is not very adventurous? He does not like to try new foods.

4
Simile. Mr. Ono thinks a snake's movements make it look slippery. By saying he feels slippery as a snake, he means he sometimes tricks people.

5
Irony. American boys bring together Japanese families who have heard of one another but who have apparently never met.

538

---

pumpkin seeds, and one time this." He tapped his soda bottle. "And once I took some glow-in-the-dark shoelaces from Woolworth—
13 Woolworth is a store. I got caught. Mom lashed me good. Even my dog, Flaco, cried with me."

"We're Buddhist," Mitsuo said. "Almost all Japanese are Buddhist, but not many go to temple."

"What is Buddhist?" Lincoln asked.

"It's hard to explain. We worship Buddha. He's like your Jesus Christ."

Lincoln suddenly remembered that he had to meet Tony at the *sentō* at four so they could
14 finish planning the Mexican dinner. He was already ten minutes late.

"Mitsuo, I got to tell you. Tony and I are planning a party for our families."

"A party?"

"Yeah, with Mexican food."

"Mexican food? How is food from Mexico?"

▶ As they hurried up the street, Lincoln described enchiladas and tacos, piping-hot *frijoles* in a black pan, and steaming rice. He told of tortillas made of corn and flour, and wrapped in dish towels. He praised the fiery salsa of his *tío*[3] Junior, and tamales on Christmas Day at his *tía*[3] Linda's. And he told about eating with tortillas, not forks or spoons or chopsticks, and said there was nothing better than scraping a small rip of tortilla across a puddle of chicken *mole*.[4]

"Sounds good," Mitsuo remarked.

"It is. *Es muy rico.*"[5]

At the *sentō*, Tony was neck deep in hot water. He whistled at Lincoln and Mitsuo. Soon their three heads bobbed on the surface of the water.

They talked food that afternoon, their mouths watering for a pile of cheese-laced *frijoles*.

---

3. *tío* (tē′ō) . . . *tía* (tē′ä): uncle; aunt.
4. *mole* (mō′lā): a spicy sauce.
5. *Es muy rico* (ĕs moō′ē rē-kō): It's delicious.

▶ Reading Skills Objective: Determining Sequence of Events

538 THE NOVEL

11

Mr. Ono raised his dinner plate to his face and studied the puddle of steaming *frijoles* curiously. His nostrils sniffed its aroma. "I know this smell," he said as he raked a chopstick across the plate and sucked on the end. He closed his eyes and smiled as the steam rose from the dish.

"I know this taste," he concluded, opening his eyes and nodding his head in approval.

"How can you know?" Mrs. Ono said.
1 "I just *know*," he answered.

Mrs. Ono looked at their guests, the Inabas,
2 and raised her glass of beer in salute to them. They, in turn, saluted the Onos. She took a tiny, birdlike sip and said, "My husband thinks that he likes foreign food. He just likes noodles
3 and fish. He is not very adventurous."

"I like all kinds of food," Mr. Ono argued.

"Noodles and fish," Mrs. Ono countered playfully.

"No, I am an international eater. Don't you recall the time I tried snake when I was in Thailand? I tried it, but I felt guilty because
4 sometimes I feel slippery as a snake. How could I eat my own kind?" He laughed at his joke and took a drink of his beer, smacking his lips.

Mrs. Ono rolled her eyes and got up to check on the boys in the kitchen. For the past three hours, Lincoln and Tony had been preparing the food. They'd cooked the beans and smashed them into *frijoles;* they'd chopped chilies, onions, and tomatoes for salsa; they'd squeezed dough and rolled it into odd-shaped tortillas; they'd cooked ground beef. Now they brought the rest of the food to the table and joined their families.

"We are honored that you invited us," Mr. Inaba said to the Onos, smiling so that the gold
5 crowns on his teeth showed. "We have heard so much about your family."

MATH LINK
Challenge students who enjoy working with numbers to plan a budget for a one-month trip to Japan, traveling from the United States. Remind students to include transportation costs to, from, and within Japan (airfare, trains, taxis), housing costs, and food. They may also wish to contact a local travel agency to get current information on airfare and hotel costs.

"We have heard about your family as well," Mrs. Ono said.

Mrs. Inaba looked at Tony. "Tony-kun is a hard-working boy."

Tony raised his hands and showed them his **6** dime-sized blisters. Along with the Inabas' son, Toshi, he had worked their patch of cabbages and radishes into healthy vegetables they would later sell on the roadside.

"He also taught our son valuable American words."

"Such as?" Mr. Ono asked, trying some more *frijoles*.

Mr. Inaba thought and then said, "*Órale, ése*."[1] He turned to Tony, who was headed back to the kitchen to fry more tortillas, and yelled, ¡*Órale, ése!*

"*Simón que sí, Papi*,"[2] Tony called back as he turned over one of his homemade tortillas. The tortilla puffed up like a blimp. Tony stabbed it **7** with a fork and the hot air sighed out.

"Lincoln is nice boy, too," Mrs. Ono volunteered. "He is practicing *kempō*."

"*Kempō*?" Mr. Inaba looked at Lincoln, sizing him up, and asked, "Who is your teacher?"

"Oyama-*sensei*," Lincoln said. "She's bad."

"'Bad'?" repeated Mr. Inaba. "But I thought she was an excellent teacher."

"'Bad' means good," Mrs. Ono said. "It is an **8** American expression. Very valuable word."

Tony returned from the kitchen with a dish towel of warm tortillas. "Here, try another before they get cold."

Lincoln took the dish towel from Tony and offered the stack of tortillas to Mr. Inaba, who was sampling his *frijoles*. When Mr. Inaba bit into a tortilla, it crackled like a Dorito. He grunted and commented, "Interesting food."

Lincoln looked at Tony, and Tony looked **9** back. Lincoln muttered, "We messed up. These tortillas are hard as rocks."

"Harder," Tony whispered back. "And the avocados ain't any good either. Five bucks **10** apiece, man, and they're mostly black as the soul of my cousin Pete. And the dude's in jail."

"No wonder you two are so strong," Mrs. Inaba said, attempting a compliment. "The food is so hard." Even the *frijoles* were undercooked, so they had to mash them with their teeth before they could swallow. They washed them down with tea or beer. The salsa was more like ketchup than the fiery sauce that Lincoln's and Tony's mothers concocted every Saturday morning. But the families tried it all, smiled between bites, drank their beer and tea, and made small talk about the weather, the traffic, and the new emperor.

After dinner the four boys went to Mitsuo's room, where they played Nintendo and ate *nigirimeshi*, rice balls, because they were still hungry. Tony and Lincoln punched each other in the arm.

"We messed up," Tony said, a grain of rice clinging to his chin.

"You've got rice on your face," Lincoln said. He turned to the Japanese boys. "Mexican food *really* is good. If we knew how to cook, you'd die in paradise. My mom makes the best enchiladas."[3]

"We believe you," said Toshi. "If we had to make Japanese food, we would make it terrible also."

"I'm sure you guys could do better," Tony said.

"No, we would starve," Mitsuo said. Toshi **11** nodded in agreement.

Mitsuo suggested that they go and get ice-

---

1. *Órale, ése* (Ô'rä-lā ě'sā): All right, dude.
2. *Simón que sí, Papi* (sē-mōn' kā sē pä'pē): Of course, Dad.
3. **enchiladas** (ĕn'chə-lä'dəz): rolled tortillas stuffed with meat or cheese and covered with sauce.

Pacific Crossing **539**

6
Tony, like Lincoln, is treated as any child of his family would be treated. He helps with work that has to be done.

7
Word Choice. Compares sound of air leaving tortilla to sound made by person sighing.

8 Analyzing
Why does Mrs. Ono say "bad" is a valuable word? Because it can have two opposite meanings and, therefore, can be used more than a word with only one meaning.

9
Lincoln implies tortillas are supposed to be soft, not hard and crunchy.

10
Simile. By comparing the black avocados to his cousin's soul, Tony implies cousin has done bad deeds.

11
When it comes to cooking, Japanese boys are no different from American boys in their lack of skill.

Side notes (left margin)

12 Making Inferences
Why do boys leave through window? Answers will vary. Perhaps it is a shortcut. Perhaps they do not want their parents to know they are leaving.

13
Simile. Compares shape of moon to curved blade of a sickle.

Chapter 12

1
Exaggeration. Narrator overstates Lincoln's fear to emphasize he is unsure of his skills.

2 Expressing an Opinion
Do Mr. Ono and boys look forward to same things on camping trip? Answers will vary. Probably not; boys are probably looking forward to adventure.

3
Simile. Compares Lincoln's body to ice of Popsicle to emphasize how cold he feared it would be.

4
While perhaps not impossible, it seems unlikely these things would happen to someone camping.

5 Analyzing
What does Mr. Ono really mean? Their laughter is annoying him.

6
Metaphor. Lincoln compares his upset stomach to having an imaginary frog jumping around inside him.

7
Fasting, or eating and drinking very little, seems to be linked to religious nature of pilgrimage.

cream cones. They left through the window, stepping carefully over the garden for fear that they would trample a tomato. Then they would really be in trouble.

When they saw that they had been gone nearly an hour, they raced home, knots of hunger twisting in their stomachs. And they arrived just in time: the adults were frying a fish that was nearly as large as a guitar. A new pot of rice was steaming. The tea was simmering, and icy bottles of *ramune* were waiting. Then, at a quarter to ten, with the moon hanging like a sickle in the sky, the fiesta really began.

12

Mr. Ono packed the car with borrowed camping gear. He had a week of vacation, and he planned to spend a few days in the forest with Lincoln and Mitsuo. They would bike up a path where Buddhist worshipers went to pray at shrines and pay homage to dead ancestors. Mrs. Ono would stay home, enjoying a vacation from the three of them and their incessant need for food.

Lincoln was free to go because he had returned the poems to Oyama-*sensei*, marked up with changes. He had been glad to get them out of the way. His own writing was terrible, and the thought of helping someone write poems scared him to death. As parting advice, Oyama-*sensei* had told him to practice *kempō* while he was away because soon after he returned he would have to take his second *kyu*[1] test.

"It is good to get away," Mr. Ono said as he stuffed the backpacks and feather-light tent into the trunk of the car. "Tall trees. Silence. Peace."

Lincoln enjoyed camping. Once he had spent four days in Yosemite[2] hiking in the snow with two uncles. He had thought he would freeze stiff as a root-beer Popsicle, but actually he had been hot most of the time, because hiking in the snow was tiring. His mother frowned at the idea of camping. She liked to sleep in a bed, not on the ground. She was scared that a raccoon might bite her while she slept, or that a spider might climb into her ear and hatch eggs that would make their way into a gray fold in her brain.

Mr. Ono and the boys drove for three hours, until they came to a mountain. Then the car began to climb and the air thinned. When they rolled down the windows, the air rushed into their lungs so Lincoln and Mitsuo had difficulty breathing. When they took a corner, their chewing gum flew from their mouths. At this they laughed so hard that Mr. Ono growled and told them to shut up because they were disturbing nature.

When they arrived at the foot of the trail, Mitsuo and Lincoln were nearly carsick. The last six miles had been twists and turns. At five thousand feet, the towns had given way to acres of trees.

"I got a frog in my stomach," Lincoln groaned.

"A frog?" Mitsuo asked.

"I feel like I'm going to throw up my breakfast."

"I suggest that you do not," Mr. Ono said, heaving the backpacks onto the ground. "From now on we eat once a day. Only *nigirimeshi*."

"Only rice balls?" Lincoln asked, leaning against the car.

"Rice and tea. We are here on a pilgrimage."

The path started out wide as a city street but soon narrowed into a trail of pine needles and dank earth. They walked single file, silent.

---

1. *kyu* (kē-ōō): class or grade to achieve a particular rank.

2. **Yosemite** (yō-sĕm′ĭ-tē): a national park in California.

Lincoln's nausea had left him, and now he was hungry. He thought, Rice and tea. Rice and tea. The pine needles crunched under the soles of his shoes; with each crunch he pictured a bowl of Shredded Wheat, his least-favorite cereal. Right now it didn't sound so bad.

After an hour they rested on a fallen tree that was green with moss. A shred of blue sky showed between the tall pines. In the distance, they could hear a river rushing over rocks.

"This feels good," Mr. Ono said as he peeled off his gloves.

8 High branches of trees form a canopy that lets in little light.

Sacred turtles on temple grounds.

Cultural Diversity

Lincoln comes from a Roman Catholic background, whereas the Onos are Buddhists. During Lincoln's visit to a Buddhist shrine, Mr. Ono points to *Jizō*, protector of children. Lincoln remembers that a Catholic saint also protects children, but he has forgotten the saint's name. The boy blames himself for not paying more attention in catechism. Explain that the Catholic Church teaches the principles of its religion through a series of questions and answers called catechism.

---

9 Exaggeration. Lincoln means he could eat a lot. Mitsuo does not understand figure of speech.

10 Drawing Conclusions *Why does Mr. Ono think it is lucky few people are around?* Answers will vary. Perhaps he thinks crowds would distract him from his religious practice.

11 Mitsuo and Lincoln appear not to know much about their religions.

12 Symbol. Statue's belly, where womb is located in women, symbolizes a safe place for unborn babies. Thus, *Jizō* is protector of children.

13 Summarizing *What does Lincoln mean by "I'm hurting"?* He has been hiking for a long time and is sore from effort.

14 Lincoln is stiff from sleeping on hard ground in sleeping bag.

Mitsuo whispered to Lincoln, "Are you hungry?"

Lincoln licked his lips and pressed the heel of 9 his palm into his cavernous stomach. "I could eat a horse."

"A horse?" Mitsuo asked. "Do Americans eat horses?"

"It's an expression, Mitsuo. But I *could* eat a small pig. Between slices of bread." The boys laughed at the image of a whole pig laid out between huge slices of bread.

"On a pilgrimage, we go hungry," Mr. Ono said. "In a little while you will see a shrine and maybe a priest praying. Maybe other people like us."

They were four miles into the forest and hadn't seen any other hikers.

"Where is everyone?" Lincoln asked.

"It's the wrong season," Mitsuo said. "Most 10 come in October, not July. We are lucky that few people are around. Usually it is crowded."

"I wouldn't mind seeing some people. What if something happened to us?"

"Yeah, we could starve. I don't know why my father is not letting us eat."

After a few swallows of water from their canteens, they started again. Lincoln's backpack felt as heavy as his cousins used to when he would give them piggyback rides around the front yard. Although the late-afternoon air was chilly, he was sweating.

They soon came upon a shrine, where a stone statue wore a woven hat and sat under a wooden shelter. A stalk of incense sent up a feathery, sweet-smelling smoke that the wind broke apart.

"This is the *Jizō*.³ He watches over children," Mr. Ono said to Lincoln. "He protects you, and you, too, Mitsuo."

Hands pressed together in prayer, he bowed toward the shrine. Mitsuo and Lincoln bowed with their eyes closed.

11 "There's a Catholic saint who protects children, but I forgot his name," Lincoln said. You should have paid more attention in catechism, he scolded himself. And what if I need to call on this saint? How would I ask? Please, Saint What's-Your-Name—help me!

"*Jizō* means 'womb,'" Mr. Ono said, touching 12 the statue's belly. "He gives you comfort. We will see him many times on our trip."

They took a few swallows of water and continued their trek. It was nearly dark. They walked three more miles, then pitched a tent among the ferns.

"Feels good," Mitsuo said, unlacing his boots.

13 Lincoln cracked the knuckles of his toes. "I'm hurting."

"Could you eat a horse?" Mitsuo asked.

"If I had enough mustard, I could eat it alive."

But there were no horses to eat for dinner. They each ate two rice balls, washing them down with cold tea. After this Mr. Ono whittled a stick, and Lincoln and Mitsuo talked awhile, mostly about baseball and girls, arguing whether girls were more beautiful with long or short hair. Then they climbed into their sleeping bags. Lincoln felt sticky but good. His stomach growled, but he didn't care. This was the fifth time he had gone camping, and the first in a foreign country. Now if only he could dream in Japanese.

14 Lincoln woke in the morning stiff as a twig. He was hurting from the long walk and the hard earth, earth that had looked so soft when they pitched the tent. He stretched and let out a sleepy yawn. One of his socks had worked its way off his foot. He plunged a groping hand to the end of the sleeping bag and fetched it. He then nudged Mitsuo and said, "Get up, man."

Mitsuo let out a small moan but didn't stir.

---

3. *Jizō* (jē-zō): in the Buddhist religion, the saint who protects children.

THE NOVEL

Lincoln pulled back the flap of the tent and crawled out. Mr. Ono, unshaven, was rubbing his hands over a small fire. He said, "*Ohayō!*⁴ Good morning, Lincoln-kun."

"*Ohayō*," Lincoln said as he pulled himself to his feet. He did a few squats to get the blood going, then joined Mr. Ono for tea.

"Smell the trees," Mr. Ono said. He stretched, sucked in some fresh air, and let it out in a long sigh. "Hm—my arm has some pain. Right here." He touched his shoulder.

Lincoln splashed water from a metal pot onto his sleepy face. "Maybe you slept wrong," he said, shuddering from the cold. "I slept on my shoe." He rubbed his back where the shoe had poked him all night.

"No, this is different." Mr. Ono peeled off his jacket and shirt, and probed his arm. When he saw two red, swollen points, he looked serious.

"So this is it," he said calmly. "They look like spider bites." He pinched the bites until a clear pus ran like tears.

"It's ugly," Lincoln said, now fully awake. He had awakened hungry, but now his hunger collapsed to nothing. "Does it hurt?"

"No. What spider can hurt an old man like me?"

Mitsuo surfaced from the tent and asked, "What's going on?"

"A spider bit your dad," Lincoln said.

"It is nothing," Mr. Ono said. He handed cups of steaming tea to the boys and shrugged back into his shirt.

"Let me see," Mitsuo asked.

"It is nothing. I get hurt at work all the time. Now hurry up and let us get ready to go." He buttoned his shirt and slipped his jacket back on.

Lincoln had been bitten countless times. Once by a parrot, twice by a dog, six times by a cat, and every summer for fourteen years by a zillion blood-sucking mosquitoes. And once he had been bitten by a baby cousin. Luckily, the baby was toothless; it only took a tickle under her chin to relax her jaws.

To get his blood going, Lincoln practiced prearranged *kempō* forms. Mitsuo followed along, laughing because he couldn't do them right.

"You're not helping," Lincoln scolded. "Be serious. I'm going to test in two weeks."

After their breakfast of rice balls and tea, they broke camp and continued on their journey. They walked in a line between the shadows of the tall trees, with Lincoln last. The ferns unfolded like large green waves, and moss gripped the speckled rocks. Salamanders squirmed in the loose peat, and hordes of dragonflies hovered in the air.

Mitsuo turned and asked, "Are your forests like this in America?"

"I've only been to Yosemite. It's pretty nice, except for all the campers," Lincoln said. "Doesn't anyone ever visit this forest?"

Mr. Ono responded, "If they want to pray."

Lincoln thought about this. He liked camping, but walking for five hours wearing a backpack to pray was not what he had expected.

As they rounded a corner, an owl-like bird blinked at Lincoln, then snapped at a dragonfly and caught it.

"Did you see that bird?" Lincoln asked. "He's looking at us."

Mitsuo turned and gazed at the bird. "No, he's looking at you."

And so it seemed to Lincoln. His grandmother always said that birds were a warning, and Lincoln wondered about this bird's message. The bird stared at Lincoln, unblinking.

Lincoln thought of the spider bites. He squeezed his arm hard, but he didn't feel any pain. Still, he wondered whether he had also been bitten and if a stream of poison were flooding his veins and arteries.

---

4. *Ohayō* (ō-hä-yō).

Pacific Crossing **543**

TRANSPARENCIES 41 & 42
Fine Art
Theme: *More of the "Good Stuff"* – invites students to explore artworks depicting someone sharing, exchanging, or appreciating the culture of others.

23 Drawing Conclusions
Why do boys whisper? They are concerned about Mr. Ono but do not want him to know it.

24 Description. Monk's unusual appearance gives him look of person unconcerned about the ordinary and completely devoted to religion.

25 Even though monk apparently does not speak English, he can tell by Lincoln's expression and tone of voice that he is impressed.

26 Making Inferences
Why does Mitsuo want monk to look at bites? Answers will vary. Perhaps he thinks monk knows something about medicine. Perhaps he wants opinion of another adult who is more objective than his father is.

27 Finding Cause and Effect
Why does monk tell Mitsuo about seriousness of his father's condition, rather than Mr. Ono himself? He thinks Mitsuo may be able to convince his father of need to get medical attention.

28 Mr. Ono apologizes because he thinks boys will be disappointed at having to go home early.

29 Symbol. Incense symbolizes monk's prayers and best wishes.

30 Making Inferences
Would walk back to car be as strenuous as walk to shrine? Probably not, because they are walking downhill.

"You OK?" Mitsuo asked.

"Yeah. I'm wondering if I got bit, too."

"You would know it," Mitsuo said. "In our country, spider bites are serious. They can kill you." He looked at his father and whispered, "He looks sick, doesn't he?"

Lincoln searched Mr. Ono's face. It was shiny with sweat, but was it sweat from the walk or 23 from poison working in his system? "We'll watch him," Lincoln whispered.

In the quiet of the forest, Lincoln had plenty of time to think of home. He wondered whether it was day or night there. Was his mother at home, watching television with Roy? He wondered what Flaco was doing. Was he in another fight? Was he in trouble for running through the flower bed? Was he missing the late-night handouts Lincoln would give him from the refrigerator? As much as Lincoln had enjoyed his first four weeks in Japan, he was becoming homesick.

Just before noon, they reached another shrine. A monk was raking leaves with a straw broom. He greeted them in Japanese, and the three of them bowed. Incense made the place smoky and mysterious.

"Cold day," Mr. Ono said, after offering a short prayer at the shrine.

24 "Yes, cold," the monk said. His teeth were black and his hair was cropped so close that his scalp appeared blue. He wore a white robe and sandals. Prayer beads hung from his wrist.

"This young man is from America," Mr. Ono said, gesturing to Lincoln, who was peeling off his backpack.

"Ah, America!"

"He is studying *kempō* while he's here."

"Ah, *kempō*!" the monk said, smiling. In Japanese, the monk told them he studied with Doshin Do, the founder of *shorinji kempō*. Mitsuo translated for Lincoln.

"You studied with the founder?" Lincoln asked in English. He was impressed.

25 The monk smiled and blushed faintly.

26 Mitsuo asked, "Will you please look at my father's arm? He's been bitten."

"Bitten? By an animal?" the monk asked.

"No, a spider," Mitsuo answered.

"It's nothing," Mr. Ono argued.

The monk, putting aside his broom, asked Mr. Ono to take off his shirt. Mr. Ono reluctantly agreed, peeling off his backpack. The monk took the arm into his thin hands and studied the wounds. He pressed the wounds until a squeak of pain escaped Mr. Ono. The bites had grown purplish and hard as tacks.

Mitsuo hovered over the arm. Lincoln stood back, watching the three of them. He knew now that Mr. Ono was seriously hurt.

The monk muttered and scolded Mr. Ono. He said that he should return immediately and seek a doctor. Mr. Ono protested, trying to laugh it off. The priest scolded him again and 27 turned to Mitsuo, warning him that if his father was not cared for he could die.

"Did you hear?" Mitsuo said to his father. "We must go back." He was worried, and so was Lincoln.

"Mitsuo, we should go back," Lincoln agreed. "Right away."

"You are right," Mr. Ono said after a moment. 28 "We should return. I am sorry to ruin our camping trip."

"Forget the camping," Lincoln said. He suddenly felt itchy, as if a spider had nestled under his shirt, puncturing his back with tiny holes. "We better hurry."

They thanked the monk, who bowed and 29 muttered a prayer. He gave them a stick of incense, which was extinguished by a cold wind within a few steps. When they were out of sight of the monk, they crushed it into the ground.

They walked quickly, with the father 30 between the two boys. The walk would take six

544 THE NOVEL

hours, but luckily it was not yet noon, so they could make it back to the car before nightfall.

"Look at me," the father said, chuckling to himself. "I'm being cared for by children."

"We're not children," Mitsuo said. "Quit joking."

The father offered each of the boys a stick of gum and, mimicking Lincoln, said, "Be cool, ése."

They talked about baseball for a while, then grew silent as they descended the path. They rested twice. By the third rest period, Mr. Ono was covered with sweat. He wanted to take off his jacket, but Mitsuo forced him to keep warm. Mr. Ono shed his backpack, leaving it propped against a rock. Although the boys were hungry, they had to leave the food, nineteen balls of rice in waxed paper.

They walked for three hours. Mr. Ono was now feverish, his armpit swollen as large as a softball. He was tired, and his breathing was shallow.

"Cut it," the father said when they stopped to rest at a small stream. He stripped off his jacket and shirt. "Open it up."

Lincoln and Mitsuo looked at each other. **31** They heard a bird cry in the distance and looked up at the trees. A warning? Lincoln wondered for a moment.

"You mean, cut it open?" Lincoln asked.

"Yes."

"I can't do it."

"I can't do it either," Mitsuo said, looking away. The bird they had heard swooped away with a lizard in its beak.

Lincoln hated the sight of blood. Once he had smashed his thumb in the car door and sprayed blood like a fountain pen. And there had been nosebleeds in playground fights. How many T-shirts had he ruined trying to be brave?

"Cut it!" the father scolded, handing Mitsuo a small knife with a white ivory handle.

32 Lincoln took the knife and said, "I'll do it." He remembered watching cowboy movies and how one of the snake-bitten cowboys would run a flame over the knife. Lincoln did the same with three matches bunched together. The blue flame licked the nickel-colored blade until it was black with soot. He wiped the soot off with a tissue.

Slowly Lincoln probed the first bite. He tightened his stomach and jaw as the tip of the blade slowly disappeared under the swollen skin. Yellowish blood began to run from the wound, and a small grunt issued from Mr. Ono's mouth. Mr. Ono was gripping a handful of earth, his brow tight from the pain.

33 "New experience," Mr. Ono said between clenched teeth.

"Don't joke," Mitsuo scolded.

Lincoln turned away, sick. His glance fell on the bird, which was blinking at him.

"Beat it!" Lincoln scolded. The bird flapped its wings and flew away.

34 Mitsuo took the knife from him and, almost crying, probed the second spider bite. His father watched him as liquid flooded from the wound. Mitsuo squeezed the wound, and more infected blood gushed out.

"Good, son," Mr. Ono said as he started to rise slowly to his feet. "Lincoln-kun, you are a brave boy."

Lincoln, sick with worry, sat on a rock. He didn't feel brave. He felt like he had the time he was jumped by three dudes after a school **35** dance. Scared.

"We should go," Mitsuo said.

Lincoln jumped up when he saw a long-legged spider at his feet. He stomped on the spider and yelled, "Man, they're ugly."

They wrapped the wounds and started off in a hurry. By the time they reached the car, two hours later, it was dusk. Mr. Ono's fever had returned. The boys, now stripped of backpacks, had to drag him between them on their

---

31
Foreshadowing. Bird again foreshadows an important task Lincoln will perform.

32
Lincoln overcomes his fear of blood and takes charge.

33
Even in pain Mr. Ono keeps his sense of humor.

34 Expressing an Opinion
Why does Mitsuo cut into second bite? Answers will vary. Perhaps Lincoln's example of bravery helps him overcome his fear. Perhaps he does not want Lincoln to help his father while he does nothing.

35 Finding Cause and Effect
Why does Lincoln feel scared? He is worried about Mr. Ono and is still thinking about what he has just done.

36
Lincoln once again rises to occasion and does something he has never done before.

37
Exaggeration. Narrator overstates effect of hitting pothole to make point that it causes a hard bump to passengers of car.

38
Simile. Compares driving to wrestling bull to make point it is difficult for Lincoln.

Chapter 13

1
Word Choice. Narrator calls sleep "hard" to mean it was deep and restful.

2
Tony's joke seems cruel, but he does not fully realize how scared Lincoln had been on camping trip.

3
Flashback. Narrator tells what happened during rest of trip.

---

shoulders. They were sweaty and tired, and hunger growled in their stomachs.

They unlocked the car door. Mitsuo looked at Lincoln and asked, "You know how to drive?"

"Me? Drive? I'm fourteen," Lincoln said. He **36** looked at the feverish Mr. Ono. "Yeah. I guess I can figure it out."

They put him in the backseat and wrapped him in a blanket.

Lincoln started the car and, muttering "Here goes," pressed on the gas pedal. The car lurched and slowly advanced from the side of the road onto the empty highway.

Mitsuo found an apple on the seat. He took a bite, and then Lincoln took a bite. "Man, I'm hungry," Lincoln said, his mouth rolling with apple pulp.

"Careful," Mitsuo warned. Lincoln swerved the car, nearly running into a fence. He looked down at the speedometer. He was going thirty-five. That's not too fast, he thought. He remembered going twenty-five on his skateboard, and nearly forty on a ten-speed bike. But he remembered he had crashed both times and skinned up his elbows and knees.

"We must get to that farm town," Mitsuo said, his voice urgent. "There will be a doctor there."

37 The car bounced when it hit a pothole, and the three of them nearly crashed their heads through the roof.

Mr. Ono muttered something, and Mitsuo lowered his ear to his father. "Quit joking!" Mitsuo exploded. "It's not funny!"

"What did your dad say?" Lincoln asked.

"He says he wants to hear rock music."

"That's what he's going to get," Lincoln said **38** as he flipped on the radio. He worked the steering wheel like the horns of a bull. It was ten miles to that town, and already dark in the unlit mountains where, at night, spiders took over.

13

Lincoln woke to see sunlight on the wall, not sure where he was. When he heard the squeak of the oven door in the kitchen, he knew he was back at his second home, the Onos'. He sighed **1** and smacked his lips, refreshed by a hard sleep that had left crust in his eyes. He yawned and opened his eyes wide to find himself face-to-face with a spider large as a black, evil flower. He screamed as he slapped it away, stood up, and whacked it with his jeans.

In the corner of the room, behind a wicker basket of clean clothes, Tony was laughing.
2 "*Carnal,* it's a plastic spider."

Lincoln looked down at the spider. Frowning, he rolled it over with his toe. Then he picked it up and flung it at Tony.

"I thought I would come see if you were dead or alive," Tony said, coming out from behind the basket.

"That's a dirty trick," Lincoln snapped. "You nearly scared me to death."

"It's a clean joke. A dirty joke would be if I brought you a real spider." Tony picked up Mitsuo's glove, opened it like a mouth, and pounded his fist into it. "I got the lowdown about Mr. Ono."

3 The lowdown was that Lincoln had driven the car down the narrow road at five thousand feet to a four-lane freeway at one thousand feet. And lived. Mr. Ono still lived, too. He had been unconscious by the time they pulled into Ina and took him to the hospital. There he was laid up in fresh sheets while the boys slept in the car. Mrs. Ono took the train to Ina the next day and brought the boys home, along with her husband, whose arm was in a white sling.

Lincoln put on his jeans and a clean San Francisco Giants T-shirt. He did a few deep knee bends and five push-ups.

"Step back," Tony warned playfully. He

bobbed and wove and threw a hook punch. "The *vato* is dangerous."

Mitsuo came into the bedroom and yelled, "Breakfast!" His hands were black and a smear darkened his nose. "How did you sleep, Linc?"

"Like a stone. What's that on your face?"

"Grease, I guess." He swiped at the grease on his nose with the back of his hand. "I took off the fender."

On the way down the mountain, Lincoln had run into a road sign, two fences, and a boulder that had fallen onto the road. He almost ran into a cow. The car was damaged, with one fender buckled beyond repair and the windshield cracked like lightning.

"The fender?"

"Yeah. Dad wants us to take it to the junkyard. He has another one on order."

The three went into the kitchen. Mrs. Ono was cooking eggs and potatoes. "Good morning, hero," she said. "I made something special for you." She peeled back a dish towel to reveal a small stack of steaming tortillas.

"Torts!" Lincoln and Tony shouted.

Mr. Ono came in from the *engawa*. Cigar smoke issued from his mouth in a big white O.

"You smoke cigars?" Lincoln said. He was already slashing a blade of butter across his tortilla.

"I'm celebrating my new life. I hear the spider bite was nothing compared to your crazy driving," he said jokingly.

Mrs. Ono set the plates at the kitchen counter. "I called your mother," she said. "You are lucky to have a nice mother."

"My mother?"

"Yes. I got the recipe for tortillas from your mother. She says everything is nice. And I spoke to your dog, Flaco."

"You spoke to him?"

"Yes. He barked and I barked back."

They laughed and pulled up their chairs. The tortillas disappeared in a hundred chomps.

After breakfast, Tony returned home, leaving Lincoln and Mitsuo to take off the cracked windshield. They raised screwdrivers and began working at the rubber seal, careful not to rip it.

Mr. Ono watched from the porch, basking in the rays of the morning sun. He drank iced tea, sipping its coolness slowly. He barked commands and chewed on his cigar, but not once did he get up to help. He was feeling as lazy as a cat stretched out in sunlight.

After twenty minutes of surgery, the windshield popped off. Mitsuo and Lincoln felt giddy. They wiped their sweaty faces and drank long and hard from the garden hose.

"I have a nice surprise for you when you two come back," Mr. Ono said, an unlit cigarette dangling from his mouth. "So hurry. The surprise starts at three."

Lincoln and Mitsuo tied a rope on the fender and placed the windshield on top of it. They dragged their improvised[1] sleigh of car parts up the street. Children followed them, begging for a ride. Dogs followed as well, and an old woman who came out of her house with her hands over her ears. She shouted that the noise of metal against asphalt was driving her crazy. She threw a small stone at the boys, but they only laughed and hurried away.

At the junkyard at the edge of town, Lincoln and Mitsuo nursed sodas, their shirts sticky with sweat, their arms sore, and their palms raw from the rope.

The owner came out from a shed and, eyeing the windshield and fender, muttered in Japanese that the stuff was junk and a tragedy for the environment.

"Junk? Yeah, but quality junk. It came off my dad's Honda," Mitsuo argued. He knew he

1. **improvised** (ĭm′prə-vīzd′): made up of available materials.

SPORTS LINK

Invite interested students to research popular Japanese sports described in the story, such as sumo wrestling and pachinko, as well as the martial arts, including judo and karate. Encourage students to create a poster or bulletin-board display showing the various belt colors in karate and their meanings. Extend this activity by inviting a martial-arts expert (or a student who studies the martial arts) to class to demonstrate some exercises.

---

13 Boys whistle pleasant tunes to disguise their fear of dog and to soothe dog so it will not bite them.

14 Lincoln means "heavy" in sense of "serious" or "important," but Mitsuo takes his statement literally.

15 Personification. In order to emphasize how hot it is in auditorium, narrator gives air conditioners human ability to strain.

16 Exaggeration. Overstates smallness of towels to emphasize size of wrestlers.

17 Simile. Compares fibers of muscle to steel cables to show how strong men are.

18 Lincoln's interest in martial arts probably makes him think in these terms.

19 Making Inferences
Why do wrestlers go through all of these motions? Answers will vary. Perhaps these are traditions. Perhaps they are designed to frighten each other.

20 Finding Details
What is main difference between sumo wrestling and American wrestling? Sumo wrestlers do not use their hands; American wrestlers do.

---

wasn't going to get much for the car parts, but it didn't hurt to play them up.

The owner waved Mitsuo off and opened his wallet, which was closed with rubber bands. He gave Mitsuo a handful of yen. Mitsuo was going to argue, but the owner's dog began to sniff their legs, growling and baring his fangs all the way to his pinkish gums.

"Nice doggie," Lincoln said as he stepped backward. "Be cool."

13 The boys backed out of the junkyard, whistling pleasant tunes.

They returned home and told Mitsuo's father that the junk man was cheap. Even his wallet was held together by rubber bands.

Mr. Ono was in the garden, playing a round of backyard golf. The golf club was rusty, and his single golf ball was chipped and yellow as an old tooth. "I'm on vacation. I can't worry about money," he said, concentrating on his putt and the dent in the earth twenty feet away. He swung the club, and the ball raced like a mouse under a cabbage leaf. He looked at the boys and said, "I need practice. Give me a couple of hours, and you'll see."

Mitsuo chased the ball for his father and returned it by rolling it back. Lincoln stopped the golf ball by trapping it under his shoe.

"You said you had a surprise for us," Mitsuo said.

"Yes, a surprise," Mr. Ono said. He brought out his wallet, which was also held closed together with rubber bands. He chuckled and said, "I am like the junk man."

He handed Lincoln and Mitsuo each a ticket.

"Sumo[2] wrestling, Lincoln-kun. It starts at three o'clock."

"Tough!" Lincoln said, studying the *kanji* on **14** the ticket. "Those dudes are heavy. Thanks."

"Four hundred pounds," Mitsuo said. "And sometimes even five hundred pounds."

---

2. **sumo** (soo′mō).

Lincoln and Mitsuo arrived at two-thirty at the city auditorium, where spectators, mostly **15** men, crowded for seats. The two overhead air conditioners strained to cool the room.

The spectators grunted and muttered when four sumo wrestlers came out wearing purple loincloths. Their hair was pulled back and knot- **16** ted into buns. Each wrestler had a towel that looked as small as a washcloth on his huge shoulders.

Lincoln was impressed. He could see that the wrestlers were strong and powerful. Their legs and bellies wiggled with fat, but Lincoln was **17** sure that underneath, muscle twisted like steel cables. And he was sure by the way they walked **18** that these men were warriors.

"The contest is short. Maybe a minute," Mitsuo explained. "The object is to push your opponent out of the ring."

The canvas ring was a circle, unroped, raised, and set under a tasseled canopy. A referee in a ceremonial kimono stepped into the ring and bowed deeply to the spectators. He was followed by two wrestlers, who stared at **19** each other, their eyes narrowed. They clapped their hands and slapped their thighs and stomachs. They feigned attacks. They stomped their bare feet. They threw a white powdery dust into the air and clapped at the dust.

The spectators grew restless with anticipation. The bout began with the wrestlers bowing to the audience and to each other. They stomped their feet, circled, and feinted.[3] Then **20** they were at each other, chest to sweating chest, knocking against each other so hard that their muscles quivered. And as soon as the bout began, it was over. The bigger of the two wrestlers was knocked out of the ring. He stepped off the platform, wiped his sweaty neck, and, Lincoln guessed, was relieved that he hadn't been crushed. The winning sumo wrestler

---

3. **feinted** (fānt′əd): pretended to attack.

bowed to the applauding crowd, some of whom were on their feet cheering.

"Man, that was quick," Lincoln said to Mitsuo. "It looks easy."

"But it's not."

Two other sumo wrestlers entered the ring and began pacing from one side of the ring to the other. They, too, clapped their hands and slapped their stomachs. As the anticipation rose, the crowd fanning itself into a sweaty storm of emotion, the referee bowed and introduced the "players." One was from Tokyo and the other from Osaka.

The sumo wrestlers bowed deeply and then circled each other. The player from Tokyo won in thirty-three seconds, or so Lincoln counted on his watch.

"Man, you can't blink," Lincoln said.

"If you blink, you lose," Mitsuo said.

"They're bad, but I'd hate to be that big. I'd have to shop at the Big and Tall shop."

"Yes, they are large. Too large. They say a sumo wrestler can eat twelve bowls of *rāmen* and still be hungry."

"That's a lot of noodles."

They watched four matches and started

21 Lincoln shows his inexperience with sumo wrestling by saying it looks easy.

22 Metaphor. Compares emotional reaction of crowd to storm.

23 Narrator uses quotation marks around *players* to indicate a figurative meaning, in this case ironic meaning.

Opening ceremony of sumo wrestling.

MATH LINK

Lincoln and Mitsuo took a 150-mile bullet train ride to Tokyo. Ask interested students to research Japan's high-speed bullet trains to learn how fast they go. Once students have gathered statistics on train speeds, encourage them to write challenging word problems, using the statistics, for the rest of the class to solve. Extend this activity by comparing and graphing the average train speeds in the United States and Japan.

24 Making Inferences
Why do Lincoln and Mitsuo wrestle sumo-style? Answers will vary. They may want to experiment with this form of wrestling.

25
Metaphor. Compares red marks on their arms to brightly colored flowers.

Chapter 14

1
To hold one's own means to not let someone get the better of you.

2 Analyzing
Why does Lincoln keep practicing kempō if it causes him so much pain? He really loves sport, and he realizes he has to suffer in order to get tough.

3
Simile. Compares swarm of flies to thick smoke that is hard to see through to emphasize how many flies there are.

4
Metaphor. Compares speed of train to speed of bullet.

5
Boys realize they are in for an adventure.

6 Drawing Conclusions
Why is Mr. Ono not concerned about boys' missing their connections? Answers will vary. Maybe he has faith in their ability to get around. Maybe he wants to teach boys to be responsible and self-reliant.

550

---

home, each with a bottle of soda and a comic book of sumo wrestlers autographed by one of the wrestlers who'd been thrown out of the ring.

At home, before dinner, Lincoln and Mitsuo 24 wrestled sumo-style, with their shirts off. They grunted and sweated and smashed against each 25 other's chests. Red welts blossomed on their arms. Toes were stepped on. Heads knocked.

Mr. Ono, shirt off, watched the boys from the *engawa* and waved away flies. "Cheap entertainment for a poor railroad man," he said, his cigarette glowing in the early dusk.

14

A week passed with Lincoln working hard at *kempō*. His test was six days away, just one day before he and Tony would board a jet and return to San Francisco. Oyama-*sensei* said that his skill had grown. He was as lean as a cat, and 1 fast. He could snap a kick, punch, and hold his own when he sparred with the black belts.

But his intense drills were not without pain. A bruise the color of an eggplant showed up on his shoulder. A toenail broke off, and a wiggle of blood splashed the grass as he jumped about on one leg, in pain. The middle finger on his left hand was hurt, and he strained his neck trying to break a choke hold. For two days he 2 walked around like Frankenstein,[1] unable to move his neck, and slept sitting up because it hurt when he lay down.

The days passed. The crops were in, and now Lincoln and Mitsuo were selling them in front of the house. They ate some of the vegetables, but mostly they haggled over the prices with housewives, who were tough customers.

One evening Mr. Ono returned from work and announced, "I have a test for you boys." He

---
1. **Frankenstein:** a reference to a monster often portrayed in the movies with a stiff and clumsy walk.

sucked long and hard on a soda.

They were lying down in the shade of the 3 porch, exhausted from the heat of the day. The flies were thick as smoke, now that some of the vegetables were spoiling.

Mitsuo looked up and asked, "A test?"

"Yes, a test. To see how fast you are. And if you're good listeners."

The boys sat up, curious. They slapped flies from their toes and listened to Mitsuo's father explain that he had hidden a note in Tokyo and that they were to fetch it for him. He said that they would take a train and that they would have to find the note, read it, and follow its instructions. They had to do this in one day and be home before he returned from work. Their reward would be a visit to the country with the boys driving.

Tokyo was 150 miles away from their own town. The distance wasn't a problem; they 4 would ride a bullet train. The problem was finding their way around Tokyo and through the hordes of workers. The problem was getting back on time.

5 The boys were excited. They punched each other in the stomach. Mitsuo swung a cupped hand at a fly and swatted the poor creature against the porch. The hurt fly buzzed in a circle, whirling its crushed wings.

"I've never been to Tokyo," Lincoln said. "Except the time you picked me up at the airport."

"I've been there plenty of times but never alone. What if we miss our connections back?" Mitsuo asked, somewhat worried.

Mr. Ono lit a cigarette. He inhaled, let out a stream of smoke from his mouth, and said, eyeing Lincoln, "How do you say the American 6 phrase 'That's too bad'?"

Mr. Ono laughed until he coughed. Lincoln and Mitsuo laughed and jumped up and down, wild at the thought of going to Tokyo by themselves.

550 THE NOVEL

"What does this note look like?" Mitsuo asked.

"A note folded into a boat," Mr. Ono replied like a prophet.

"Just a note? A paper boat?" Lincoln asked.

7 "That's it. Just a piece of paper. In a fern. In the Sumitomo Building in the Shinjuku district." Mr. Ono crushed his cigarette and started to leave; when Mitsuo asked him about the building, he waved them off. "Enough clues. We'll see how smart you two are."

Mitsuo knew the Sumitomo Building, a high rise with fifty-two floors. He knew the Shinjuku district. It was where there were small bars and restaurants, a hangout for young students and office workers.

"This is going to be fun," Lincoln said.

8 "I guess so," Mitsuo muttered, lost in thought. The fly that he'd swatted was now washing its face, apparently OK. "A paper boat in a fern. My dad's a character."

The next morning they woke before daybreak. They dressed quickly and ate a handful of rice balls on the run.

At 6:45 they arrived at the train station, where Mr. Ono worked as a mechanic. The bullet train was due to leave at 7:10; it was a late train that would stop only twice, to pick up commuters.

"Where are our tickets?" Mitsuo asked.

9 "You get no tickets. You boys get to ride with the mail and chickens."

"You mean in the back?" Mitsuo asked.

"I like it," Lincoln said, beaming. He had been on trains three times, but never in the mail compartment.

"But we won't be able to look out."

"Good, then you can close your eyes and go to sleep."

Mr. Ono scooted the boys to the cargo car. 10 He slid open the door to a mountain of bagged mail and stacks of newspapers.

"Welcome to your new home." He chuckled.

He gave the boys three thousand yen and handed them return tickets, warning them if they lost these then they would have to stay in Tokyo for good. They would have to work as dishwashers to get the money to come back.

Mitsuo hopped into the train and Lincoln 11 followed. Mr. Ono gave the boys a stiff salute and closed the door. Within minutes the train started, slowly at first, but then picking up speed until it jerked along at 110 miles per hour.

A small overhead light went on after the door was closed. The boys got comfortable and sat on 12 the bags, then opened one of them. They pulled out comic books. Lincoln liked the pictures of Japanese superheroes, all with cuts of muscle that would put Olympic athletes to shame.

For a second they thought of opening a package. They knew it was food, but they also knew it was a crime to open someone else's mail and they were scared of being arrested. So they only sniffed the package, Lincoln guessing that it held plums and Mitsuo guessing dried fish.

There was a small, greasy window high in a corner. Lincoln stacked a couple of mailbags against the wall and climbed up to the window. He stared out at farmland broken up with smoke. In the distance, he could see a mountain dotted with remnants of snow. And snow was what Lincoln was thinking about. The cargo car was heating up. The air grew thick and wet. The boys were sweating and dry-mouthed. Lincoln pulled a stick of gum out of his pocket and tore it in half to share.

"What do you think your father is hiding?" Lincoln asked, unbuttoning the front of his shirt.

"Probably money. He likes to give money away."

"I wish my mom was generous with money." Lincoln recalled being caught going through her coin purse. He recalled the race around the

---

7 Making Inferences
How does Mr. Ono know someone will not move or throw away note? Answers will vary. Maybe he does not and is just taking a chance. Maybe he has made special arrangements with someone in building to make sure note remains undisturbed.

8
Mitsuo is thinking about what note might say.

9
Exaggeration. There are no chickens. Mr. Ono exaggerates about where they will be riding to tease boys.

10
Exaggeration. Refers to stack of mail as mountain to emphasize large amount of mail in cargo car.

11 Drawing Conclusions
Why does Mr. Ono salute boys? Answers will vary. Maybe he is pretending to be doorman at hotel seeing guests off in the car.

12
Boys could probably get into trouble for opening mail bags, but they are full of mischief and do not think of this.

Pacific Crossing 551

Cultural Diversity

While Lincoln observes many similarities between Japanese culture and his own, he also takes note of some real differences. Invite the class to discuss these differences. Some examples include public bathing, eating habits, and the custom of bowing, as well as the respect for older people.

---

13 Irony. Lincoln steals money from his mother to buy her a present.

14 Lincoln and Mitsuo are alike in that they enjoy adventure.

15 Metaphor. Compares heat rising from asphalt to waves because heat makes asphalt appear to move.

16 Making Inferences
Why is cashier so abrupt with boys? Answers will vary. Maybe he is annoyed at them. Maybe he is tired of having to give directions.

17 Finding Cause and Effect
Why does driver want to put boys off bus? Answers will vary. Perhaps because Mitsuo was rude in way he spoke to him.

18 Lincoln is tempted to knock down driver using *kempō* skill.

19 Simile. Compares heat of day to heat coming from furnace to emphasize how hot it is in city.

---

living room and her yelling, "You little thief!" **13** Little did she know that he had been pinching $1.20 for a Mother's Day gift.

When the train pulled into Tokyo, they opened the cargo door and peeked out, scared that someone might scold them for going "baggage." There were enough witnesses: thousands of commuters hurrying to work.

"We could jump and run," Lincoln suggested.

14 "Why not?" Mitsuo agreed.

Counting, "*Ichi, ni, san, shi, go,*" they dropped to the platform, arms out like wings. A security guard turned when he heard their grunting fall. He shouted at them to stay, but the boys took off. The guard ran after them, weaving in and out of the crowd, but Lincoln and Mitsuo were too lean, too quick, too full of fear to let themselves get caught. They ran a half mile, stopped, and sat on a curb where a pigeon with a crooked beak was drinking from a small oily puddle.

"Let's get a Coke," Mitsuo suggested, breath-**15** ing hard. It was nine-thirty, and already the asphalt was wavering with the summer heat.

"Good idea," Lincoln said.

They bought sodas at a newsstand and drank slowly while looking at comic books. Finished, Mitsuo asked the cashier about the Sumitomo Building. The cashier waved his hand, mut-**16** tered in guttural Japanese, and shook his head at the boys for reading his comic books without buying one.

"Oh no." Mitsuo groaned. "We got off at the wrong stop. It's on the other side of the city!"

"The other side! What should we do?"

"Take a bus," Mitsuo suggested. "Let's go."

They boarded a bus, but it was going in the wrong direction, and they ended up traveling six blocks farther away from the Sumitomo Building. The ride cost them twenty minutes and two tokens.

"How come you didn't tell us?" Mitsuo yelled at the driver in Japanese.

17 The bus driver yelled at Mitsuo, telling him to get off the bus. Mitsuo answered back, and the bus driver picked up the telephone to call his station.

"What a slimeball," Lincoln muttered under **18** his breath. He wanted to drop the driver, but he knew better.

The boys started to get off the bus, but the driver cut the engine. The door wouldn't open. The air-conditioning groaned to a stop. All exits were blocked. The driver got out of his seat with an ugly sneer.

Lincoln spotted two policemen trying to cross against the traffic to their side of the street. They were wearing white gloves and looked very clean in spite of the heat—and very determined.

"Push, Mitsuo! ¡*La policía!*"[2] Lincoln yelled. Lincoln and Mitsuo heave-hoed, and the door sighed open just as the bus driver grabbed Mitsuo's sleeve.

Without thinking, Lincoln used a *kempō* technique to free Mitsuo, hitting a pressure point in the bus driver's forearm. The bus driver screamed in pain and dropped to his knees.

"Now I did it," Lincoln said. "¡*Ándale*,[3] Mitsuo!"

They darted from the bus, kicking their legs high and pumping their arms. When they looked back, the two cops were only a block behind. Lincoln and Mitsuo turned on the juice, their lungs sucking in Tokyo's heat.

The boys ducked into the subway and leaped onto a train that carried them, along with their worry, near the Sumitomo Building.

Once they left the subway and were at street **19** level, the heat blasted them like a furnace. The sharp sunlight hurt their eyes. Mitsuo asked for

---

2. *La policía* (lä pō-lē-sē′ä).
3. *Ándale* (än′dä-lā): Hurry up!

directions from a woman selling flowers under a striped awning. The roses seemed to gasp for air, and the daisies were hanging their heads, exhausted. She pointed to a nearby building, an unusual triangular building tall enough to block out the sun.

On their way the boys were ever watchful for police in blue uniforms. They seemed to be everywhere. Directing traffic at clogged intersections, standing before storefronts, peeking into alleys, and scolding kids crossing the street against red lights. When Lincoln and Mitsuo stopped to buy another soda, they turned to look directly into a policeman's eyes, and he seemed to know that Lincoln was a criminal, an American kid with brown skin who had pushed open a door to avoid an irate bus driver and then dropped him with a painful strike at a pressure point.

A lump of fear and some soda washed down Lincoln's throat when the policeman turned and walked away.

"Here we are," Mitsuo said.

They started to enter the lobby, but quickly backed out when a security guard looked at them hard. The building was all business, not a place for kids in sneakers, and especially not for teenagers who were going to rake their hands through a planter looking for a piece of paper folded into a boat.

"This is going to be difficult," Mitsuo said, looking back into the lobby. He spied four planters near the elevators.

"Yeah. How do we get in there?"

"I got it," Mitsuo said. "We just look like we belong to one of the people going in."

They turned and watched people entering the revolving doors: businessmen in heat-crumpled suits, office workers, and delivery people.

"There," Mitsuo said, pointing to an older woman. "We follow her in."

Mitsuo and Lincoln skipped into step behind the woman. Once they were in the lobby, Mitsuo struck up a conversation in rapid Japanese with her. He babbled on and on so that the security guard would not become suspicious. But he talked so much, so loudly, that the security guard looked over at them.

Mitsuo asked the woman about the fern in the nearest planter. She walked over to the fern and looked at it, puzzled, then looked at the boys. While she responded to Mitsuo's question, Mitsuo and Lincoln casually raked their hands over the soil: nothing. Mitsuo asked her about another fern, but she just gave him an odd look and started walking toward the elevator. Lincoln glanced at the security guard, who was tying his shoe and studying the three of them.

Mitsuo and Lincoln gave up on creating a distraction and rushed to the next fern. They plowed the earth with their fingers, coming up with leaves, rocks, and small pebbles, but no white paper boat. Mitsuo looked up to see the security guard walking toward them.

"Let's check the planter over there," Mitsuo said. They rushed over, raked the dirt, and searched among the leaves.

The guard was now hovering above them. Just as he started to question them, Lincoln parted a fan of leaves and screamed, "I got it!" He was staring at a piece of soggy paper shaped more like a hat than a boat.

He snatched it as they backed away from the guard, then darted for the exit, Lincoln first with Mitsuo at his heels.

The heat struck them as they raced away, the guard behind them, blowing his whistle and shouting for them to stop. Two cops eating *rāmen* at a stand-up eatery at the corner looked but didn't join the chase.

The boys ran three blocks, then stopped in an alley to catch their breath. Their shirts were soaked. The guard had been left far behind.

Mitsuo unfolded the piece of paper to find only an amateurish drawing of a clown. He

Cultural Diversity

Having a pen pal is a good way for students to learn about another culture. Have students establish a pen pal in another country by contacting student-exchange organizations, other youth groups, and language clubs. Also have students consider choosing a pen pal whose native language they are studying. In this way, they will have the opportunity to learn more about another culture, practice writing a foreign language, and discuss common interests such as baseball.

---

27 turned it over, at first baffled, then as mad as a cat dunked in water. There was nothing on the paper, except the clown with three large teeth.

"What kind of joke is this?" Lincoln asked.

Mitsuo tossed away the piece of paper, which appeared to laugh at them as it fell to the ground. "My father is a joker."

As they started down the street, they were spotted by the two policemen who had been eating *rāmen* outside the Sumitomo Building. **28** One pointed and shouted at them.

"Like heck," Lincoln said, fists doubled.

"Like heck," Mitsuo mimicked. "In your face!"

They outran the policemen and made their way to the subway that would take them to the train station. It was quarter to three. The train **29** ride would take an hour and a half, which would bring them back to Atami two hours before Mitsuo's father would get home from work. They would be glad to get out of Tokyo. The place was too dangerous, and they were exhausted.

They boarded the train, this time in the passenger section, and fell asleep ten minutes after it pulled out of the station.

At home, Mr. Ono was already on the *engawa*, nursing an iced tea. He had come home from work two hours early so that he would be sure **30** to beat the boys. "You two clowns look tired," he said as he rested his iced tea on his stomach.

"That was a terrible joke!" Mitsuo yelled as he closed the gate behind him. "A clown face."

"A clown face? What are you talking about?" Mr. Ono asked innocently. He fanned himself with a newspaper, holding back laughter.

"You know!" they both yelled. They threw themselves down on the steps. Their necks were sunburned and their heads hurt from too much sun.

"There must be a mistake. You did not find **31** my little note?" A wave of laughter broke from his throat. The iced tea jiggled and spilled on his stomach.

They ate dinner, and when the evening cooled, Mitsuo's father suggested that they go for a ride. Three miles outside of town, he pulled over and said, "You first, Mitsuo. Drive me around."

The boys were excited. Mitsuo started the car, revving the engine so that blue smoke stank up the air. He put the car into gear, and outside of town, out of view of his mother—and Lincoln's mother, and the police—they drove over the country road, utterly happy that they were fourteen.

15

After a two-hour practice, after a hundred kicks and punches, after the armlocks that sent pain shooting up to the elbows, after the rolls over the grass of the outdoor dojo, Oyama-*sensei* took Lincoln aside. She plucked at his hair and said, "It is too long again. Cut before you promote."

Lincoln touched his hair. It had grown in the six weeks he had been in Japan. The first week, Mrs. Ono had cut it so close that his scalp **1** showed. Now, in the middle of August, it was getting shaggy as a mop and nearly as stinky after a fierce workout.

Lincoln's promotion to *nikkyu*[1] would be **2** tomorrow evening. He was nervous. He knew the techniques, but he was still scared that he might disappoint his teacher. He was scared that he might do his *embu*,[2] his prearranged form, terribly wrong. And he was scared that he might lose his match. This promotion meant

---

1. *nikkyu* (nē-kē$\overline{oo}$): second rank.
2. *embu* (ĕm-b$\overline{oo}$).

27
Simile. Compares Mitsuo's anger to cat made angry by being dunked.

28
Police officers indicate they want boys to stop.

29
Boys will meet Mr. Ono's challenge if everything goes as planned.

30
Allusion. Mr. Ono refers to drawing of clown face boys found hidden in fern.

31 Analyzing
What effect does Mr. Ono's laugh have on boys? Answers will vary. It lets them know he played a joke on them. Perhaps his laughter also frustrates them a little at having been tricked.

Chapter 15

1
Simile. Compares Lincoln's hair to mop to indicate it is unruly and smells bad.

2
Lincoln has major achievement to accomplish before leaving Japan.

3 Drawing Conclusions
Why would Lincoln leave with his teeth in his pocket? They would have been knocked out by his sparring partner.

4 Drawing Conclusions
What does Oyama-sensei imply by her response? That she considers Lincoln ready.

5 Lincoln wants to spend as much of remaining time as possible with Mitsuo.

6 Imagery. Appeals to sense of smell.

he would have to spar, and there was no telling if he would leave Japan with his teeth in his pocket.

"Do you think I'm ready?" Lincoln asked.

"Don't talk like that. Be confident." Oyama-*sensei* walked away, untying her black belt. "Cut your hair by tomorrow." She disappeared into the house, leaving him in the yard, where he practiced his *embu* some more before dressing.

When he got home, Mitsuo was watching television. Bart Simpson was speaking Japanese. His duck lips seemed to sync up perfectly in his goofy tirade against his father.

"Where's your mom and dad?" Lincoln asked.

"They're at the movies," Mitsuo said, turning off the television. "Let's go for a walk."

Lincoln was tired, but he couldn't say no. He was going to miss Mitsuo, and he was going to miss Japan.

He felt better after a quick shower. Mitsuo was waiting for him on the *engawa*, and they left the yard and walked up the street. Atami, their farm town, smelled of harvest: cucumbers,

556 THE NOVEL

radishes, cabbage, tomatoes, and acres of rice sacked and ready for shipment.

"*Sushi o tabemashō*,"[3] Lincoln read from his secondhand book of Japanese as they walked. He wanted to learn as much Japanese as he could before he left. "Yeah, I wouldn't mind eating *sushi*." He looked down at the next sentence and whispered, "*Nani ō sashiagemasu ka?*[4] What should I give you?" Lincoln muttered his lessons, and now and then Mitsuo corrected him.

They passed the *sentō*. They could hear the spill of water from the faucets and men talking loudly about the day's work. They passed the bars, where men sipped sake and filled the air with cigarette smoke. They passed the *pachinko* palace, where the pinball-like game thundered with steel balls. They tried to sneak inside to play a game, but they were chased out by a man with tattoos running up and down his arms like snakes.

They crossed the street and walked up an alley. Near a Zen[5] temple, they saw a man trying to pry open the door of a bicycle shop. The man thought he was hidden by shadow, but he glowed fluorescent blue from the light of a nearby drugstore.

Lincoln and Mitsuo quietly watched as the man pried at the door, which was locked in three places. After each noisy try, the man paused, looked around, and then returned his attention to prying open the locks. He gave up when someone walked past, a man click-clacking in his *geta*. The would-be thief left, and Lincoln and Mitsuo followed him. They moved from car to car, car to tree, tree to building.

"This is cool," Lincoln said under his breath. "I feel like a detective."

"Like on 'Miami Vice,'"[6] Mitsuo agreed.

The man entered a bar where the entrance was covered with a bead curtain. Lincoln whispered, "Let's see what he's doing."

They crossed the street, looked in through the small window, and saw the bartender pouring sake into a white bowl.

Lincoln and Mitsuo jumped when they heard their names. They turned around and saw Mitsuo's parents, who were just returning home from the movie.

"What are you two doing?" Mrs. Ono asked. "Why are you looking in the bar?"

The boys' faces blazed with embarrassment. Neither could say anything for a moment.

"We were just looking," Lincoln finally said feebly.

"If you are so interested, we should go in," Mr. Ono said.

"But it's a bar," Mitsuo said. "We're not allowed."

"Then why are you looking in?" his mother scolded.

"I know the owner. He gets free train rides from me," Mr. Ono said. He entered, and the others followed, the beaded curtain clicking as they parted it.

The bar was smoky. Crates of beer and sake stood in the corner. An aquarium with gurgling green water but no fish stood near the cash register.

Mr. Ono greeted the owner with a smile, a short bow, and an explanation that Lincoln was from California and it was almost his last night in Japan. They were there to celebrate.

The owner bowed and showed them to a low table, where they were served drinks: sodas for the boys, tea for Mrs. Ono, and sake for Mr. Ono.

Lincoln and Mitsuo looked around. Two men

---

3. ***sushi o tabemashō*** (soo-shē ō tä-bē-mä-shō): Let's eat sushi.
4. ***Nani ō sashiagemasu ka?*** (nä-nē ō sä-shē-ä-gĕ-mäs kä).
5. **Zen** (zĕn): Zen Buddhism.

6. **Miami Vice:** an American television series in the mid-eighties dealing with undercover police officers in Miami, Florida.

7
Metaphor. Compares sound of steel balls to sound of thunder.

8
Simile. Compares tattoos to snakes to emphasize tattoos are all over arms.

9 Making Inferences
Why does thief leave? Answers will vary. Maybe he is scared he will get caught. Maybe he realizes he will not be able to get in.

10
Boys enjoy playing "cops and robbers" with a real potential robber.

11
Mrs. Ono demonstrates her command of logic.

12 Drawing Conclusions
What does Mr. Ono imply by this statement? That owner will not object to Mitsuo and Lincoln being in bar.

13
Lincoln treated like honored guest at bar.

14
Inference. Lincoln draws conclusion about two men based on how they act.

15
Exaggeration. Lincoln overstates his pain to emphasize that Mitsuo is hurting him.

16 Analyzing
Why are Lincoln and Mitsuo quiet? Answers will vary. They are sad because Lincoln will soon leave. They are thinking about fun they have had.

17
Lincoln feels his mother would honor request of a guest.

18
Personification. Ascribes life to activities around San Francisco.

19 Summarizing
Why do Mr. and Mrs. Ono want to go with Lincoln to kempō? They are proud of him and want to be there when he is promoted.

20 Making Inferences
Why does Lincoln say he is going to stink? Answers will vary. Maybe he really feels that way. Maybe he is just being modest. Maybe he is afraid he will fail and does not want to build up his hopes or anyone else's.

21
Sleeves snap because of rapid movement of his hands.

---

sat in the corner playing *go*. Others sat alone, nursing their drinks.

"Which one do you think he is?" Mitsuo asked in Lincoln's ear. Lincoln shrugged his shoulders and said, "Beats me." They felt giddy knowing they were sitting near a thief, or at least a potential thief.

13 They left the bar without paying, the owner insisting because it was the end of Lincoln's stay in Japan. Mr. Ono bowed, this time deeply, and Lincoln bowed as well and said, "*Arigatō* **14** *gozaimasu*."[7] He looked back at the two men sitting at the bar. Neither one smiled or bowed. One of them crushed his cigarette and immediately lit up another. Lincoln concluded that they were both thugs.

The next day, Lincoln woke up early. He practiced *kempō* in the yard, the kicks and punches, the armlocks and throws, and his *embu*.

Mrs. Ono washed Lincoln's clothes and packed them in his suitcase. The following morning, Saturday, he and Tony would be on a plane to San Francisco.

After lunch he let Mitsuo cut his hair. Mitsuo snipped and tugged and made Lincoln scream, **15** "You're killing me!"

Mr. Ono took over, and when he finished and whisked the snips of hair from Lincoln's shoulders, Lincoln's head was nearly as bald as a fist.

16 Lincoln and Mitsuo sat on the *engawa*, quiet. They knew they were about to leave each other, these brothers from different countries. A mosquito landed on Lincoln's arm, but instead of swatting it away, he let it drink. Tomorrow, when he was on the plane, he would look down at his arm and remember that mosquito and remember sitting with Mitsuo on the *engawa*.

"You'll have to come and visit us," Lincoln said.

---

7. **Arigatō gozaimasu** (ä-rē-gä-tō gō-zä-ē-mäs): Thank you very much.

Mitsuo agreed that the next time they would meet in California. He wanted to go to America's Disneyland, which he thought must be even better than Tokyo's Disneyland. Lincoln said that Disneyland was fine, but what he wanted to do with Mitsuo was go surfing in Santa Cruz. He had always wanted to try **17** surfing, but his mother wouldn't let him. If Mitsuo were with him, maybe she would break down and drive them to Santa Cruz.

"Yeah, you could cross the Pacific and see Tony and me," Lincoln said. He described the Mission District, Chinatown, Italian food, American cars, the Bay Bridge, the Golden **18** Gate Bridge, the 49ers, and the Giants—all the life that breathed around the San Francisco Bay.

After dinner, Lincoln excused himself and said that he was going to *kempō* practice. Mr. and Mrs. Ono wanted to go, knowing that **19** tonight he would test. But Lincoln was nervous and said that he didn't want them to see how terrible he was.

"You are a strong boy," Mrs. Ono said. She had washed and ironed his *gi*. It looked sharp as it lay on his bed.

"You will be bad." Mitsuo punched Lincoln in the arm, and Lincoln punched him back.

20 "Nah, I'm going to stink up the place, really."

Mr. Ono told him that he would do well. In the end, however, Lincoln persisted and they let him go alone.

They waved to Lincoln from the gate as he walked up the street. Sadness gathered in his throat. He wanted to run back and beg them, "Please, come and watch." But he couldn't. He kicked a rock, and it went flying.

At practice, Lincoln warmed up while Oyama-*sensei* stood watching. She called her students together. Three of them were being promoted: Lincoln and two boys about his age. The first part, the basic kicks and punches, **21** went well. He could hear his sleeve snap beautifully. He could feel his punch extend and recoil, his kick extend and recoil. He pictured himself: a brown boy in a white *gi*, five thousand miles from home.

Lincoln struggled some with the pins and armlocks, and had to repeat his *embu*. The first time, he had fallen face first into the grass. When he got up, bits of grass clung to his tongue. He swallowed and continued, less than perfect but good enough to make two black belts nod their heads approvingly.

Oyama-*sensei* asked them to put on their gloves. The picture of himself once again appeared in his mind's eye. He felt strong. Sweat blotted the back of his uniform. He saluted his opponent, a boy with shaved hair, and approached him carefully. Now is the time, Lincoln told himself. This is what you've practiced for.

Lincoln circled, and his first blow landed against his opponent's shoulder. Lincoln took a blow to his ear, and then they were on top of each other, kicking and punching. They broke and circled slowly. *Kempō* was lifelong. Lincoln knew this, and his opponent, who was bleeding from the nose, knew this. Why hurry?

16

Lincoln peered out of the small window that was flecked with drops of rain. The Pacific Ocean was thirty-five thousand feet down, flashing like a knife in the late-evening sun. He and Tony were seven hours into their return trip home. They had eaten twice and watched one movie, a comedy neither thought was funny.

Lincoln reclined his seat and looked at Tony, who was asleep with his mouth open and headphones on his ears. When Lincoln pulled off the headphones, Tony didn't even stir. He snored softly.

Lincoln recalled the sparring match with the boy his age, a boy whose hair, like Lincoln's, was cut so short that his scalp showed, a forest of bristles. Lincoln had passed to *nikkyu* rank, two steps from black belt. But he had been slammed around: his left eye was bruised, his lip was swollen, and a kick in the arm and one in the ribs had left him hurting. He had gotten his breath knocked out of him with a front snap kick. But on the lawn that was their dojo, in the

22
Lincoln likes having approval of two black belts because he knows they know what good *kempō* moves are like.

23
Pun. Sport is lifelong in sense that people can practice it their whole lives, not that a match takes a lifetime.

Chapter 16
1
Simile. Compares light reflected from water to flashes of light reflected from polished knife.

2
Metaphor. Compares boy's hair to forest and bristles to indicate density and amount of hair boy has.

The Wedded Rocks of the Ise-Shima National Park form a natural shrine to the gods Izanagi and Izanami. The rocks are joined by ropes of rice straw, which are replaced by Shinto priests every year.

Pacific Crossing **559**

presence of six black belts kneeling around the ring, and on his next-to-last day in Japan, Lincoln hadn't been able to double over and crumple to the grass. He was full of pride, Mexican pride. He wasn't going to be a pushover. So he took that kick, and the other blows. He took them and gave some back. The kid got a nosebleed and almost went down when Lincoln got him with a side kick. Only after the match did he find out the boy's name: Yoshi.

Lincoln had bowed deeply, and Yoshi had bowed back. "You will be very good one day," Yoshi said, breathing hard.

"You, too," Lincoln panted.

That was yesterday. Now he and Tony were returning home with gifts for their parents, and gifts for themselves. Lincoln's Japanese parents had given him a pair of *geta,* and Mitsuo had given him two bottles of *ramune,* which he had promised to save until Mitsuo visited San Francisco. They would toast themselves and toast their families—and then hit the streets of the Mission District.

Lincoln had been weak with sadness in the morning when he saw Mrs. Ono snap his suitcase closed, his suitcase that was bloated with clothes, gifts, and a new *kempō gi,* a gift from Oyama-*sensei.* He fought back tears as the Onos drove him and Tony to the airport, as the farmland gave way to houses and factories. At the airport he gave the Onos *abrazos,*[1] deep hugs of love, and promised them real Mexican food when they stepped onto the shores of California.

"Come back soon," Mrs. Ono cried. She eyed Lincoln's hair and combed it with her fingers. "Your hair grows like a bush, Lincoln-kun. What will your mother say if we send you back with hair to your feet?"

Lincoln smiled.

"Yes, come back and I will let you drive my car," Mr. Ono joked. "It will be a big American car—Cadillac."

Lincoln and Tony shook hands with Mitsuo *raza*-style, heaved their carry-on bags onto their shoulders, and departed through Gate 93.

Six weeks since he'd been home. Lincoln was thinking about his mother, a hard worker who kept him clothed and fed, and about his dog, Flaco. His Japanese parents were special, too, Mrs. Ono with her tenderness, Mr. Ono with his rough kindness and offbeat jokes. And now a brother, Mitsuo.

Lincoln looked out the window again. The sun had almost disappeared and far, far below was the Pacific Ocean. What life could be better than the one he was living?

1. *abrazos* (ä-brä′sōs).

Geta, high wooden clogs.

Cultural Diversity

After being selected as an exchange student, Lincoln tries to imagine what Japan will be like. After students finish reading the novel, invite them to discuss Lincoln's mistaken ideas about Japan and its culture. (He thought everyone in Japan was rich. He assumed all women would be wearing kimonos and men would be wearing wooden sandals. He believed most Japanese people were reserved and serious.) You may want to point out that, like Lincoln, all of us have ideas and beliefs about other cultures that may, in fact, be false.

Reading Check

1. How do Lincoln and Mitsuo help Mrs. Nakayama?
2. How do the boys help Oyama-*sensei*?
3. What foods do Lincoln and Tony serve their host families?
4. Where does Mr. Ono take the boys?
5. How is Mr. Ono injured?
6. What happens to Mr. Ono's car?
7. What surprise does Mr. Ono have for Mitsuo and Lincoln?
8. Why do the boys go to Tokyo?
9. Who is Yoshi?
10. At the end of the novel, how close is Lincoln to becoming a black belt?

For Study and Discussion

Analyzing and Interpreting the Novel

1. When Lincoln is asked to read his mother's letter aloud, he changes the contents. Why does he do that?

2. In this part of the novel, Lincoln faces several challenges. **a.** What are they? **b.** What does Lincoln learn from each challenge?

3. In many ways, Lincoln and Mitsuo are typical of young people their age, but in certain situations they prove themselves unusually mature and responsible. Choose some examples to support this statement.

4. Although Lincoln and Mitsuo are disappointed that Mr. Ono has not left a more valuable prize for them in the Sumitomo Building, why is the trip not a total failure and waste of time?

5a. Is it possible to say who won or lost the bout between Yoshi and Lincoln? **b.** Why does the author leave the results unclear?

Literary Elements

Understanding the Novel

Setting

1. Setting is an important aspect of *Pacific Crossing*. Lincoln must deal with many interesting situations for the first time. Identify four interesting places Lincoln discovers in Japan. What customs are associated with each one?

Character

2. When characters change or develop in a narrative, the changes in attitude or action have to be explained in some reasonable way. Describe the major events in the second half of the novel. How do these events contribute to a change in Lincoln's character?

Plot

3. The first two chapters function as flashbacks into Lincoln's past. On page 534 Mr. Ono's family history is discussed in another flashback. **a.** What do we learn about Mr. Ono's grandmother? **b.** What important information relating to Lincoln's stay is revealed by way of this flashback?

Point of View

4. Imagine this story told by one of the other characters or by an omniscient author. What would be the advantages and disadvantages of having either Mrs. Ono or Mitsuo tell the story?

Theme

5. **Theme** is the basic meaning of a literary work, the main idea it expresses about human nature. The central theme in this novel is about the experiences that change one boy's character. As Lincoln learns to cope with the uncertainties, responsibilities, and problems of the adult world, his attitude about himself and about life changes. Find a sentence or a passage in the book that comes close to stating the basic truth that Lincoln learns after his trip to Japan.

READING CHECK

1. Work in her field, weeding (p. 532).
2. By pointing out problems in her English translation of some Japanese poems (p. 537).
3. Frijoles, salsa, tortillas, ground beef (p. 538).
4. Camping in forest (p. 540).
5. Spider bites him (p. 543).
6. One fender buckles beyond repair, windshield is cracked (p. 547).
7. Tickets to sumo wrestling (p. 548).
8. To get note Mr. Ono has hidden there. It is test of speed and listening ability (p. 550).
9. Boy Lincoln fights in his promotion match (p. 559).
10. Two steps away (p. 559).

FOR STUDY AND DISCUSSION

1. Afraid Onos would not understand mother's tone.
2a, b. Challenges include getting letter (learns to translate American values into Japanese), helping with poetry (learns he knows something about English), cooking (learns to accept disappointment), helping save Mr. Ono (learns he can do what is necessary to help friend), going to Tokyo (learns he can get around on his own), passing *kempō* test (learns he is good at martial arts), and leaving Japan (learns how much he loves the Onos).
3. Examples include working in fields, saving Mr. Ono's life, and going to Tokyo.
4. They have fun and learn they are able to get around big city by themselves.
5a. No. Both seem to claim victory. **b.** Readers can decide for themselves.

Pacific Crossing **561**

TRANSPARENCY 43

Reader Response
Add Up the Ratings – asks students to evaluate and tally their responses to various aspects of a novel.

LITERARY ELEMENTS
1. Buddhist shrine: incense, monk in robes; Sumo wrestling arena: wrestlers' clothes, style; Tokyo: behavior of bus driver and police; bar: low tables, drinks served in bowls.
2. Lincoln grows in responsibility through events: field work, letter from mother, helping with poems, cooking, camping trip, going to Tokyo, passing kempō test.
3a. Died in atomic bombing of Hiroshima. **b.** As American exchange student, Lincoln is there to share himself with Onos.
4. Advantages: narrator could judge Lincoln's reactions from Japanese viewpoint; point out how Lincoln and Mitsuo differ. Disadvantages: readers would not know Lincoln's thoughts.
5. One possibility: "Lincoln was thinking about his mother, a hard worker who kept him clothed and fed. . . . His Japanese parents were special, too. . . . And now a brother, Mitsuo."

LANGUAGE AND VOCABULARY
Recognizing Idioms
1. Annoy someone. **2.** Start before time. **3.** Make someone lose interest. **4.** Not give someone enough credit. **5.** Not have good reasons for doing something. **6.** Detect villain. **7.** Frustrated to the point of not having enough energy to go on. **8.** Annoy someone. **9.** Take more to eat than one can hold. **10.** Brag. Person new to English might take statements literally.

Language and Vocabulary

Recognizing Idioms

An **idiom** is a specialized expression used by a group of people. In *Pacific Crossing* Mitsuo and his family, though quite fluent in English, are confused by Lincoln's idioms. In chapter 12, for example, Lincoln groans that he "has a frog in his stomach." Later, Lincoln tells Mitsuo that he "could eat a horse," to which Mitsuo replies, "Do Americans eat horses?" Below are several idiomatic expressions common to American English. Explain what they mean and comment how a nonnative speaker, new to the English language and culture, might misinterpret such an expression.

1 Drive someone up a wall
2 Jump the gun
3 Turn someone off
4 Sell someone short
5 Not have a leg to stand on
6 Smell a rat
7 At the end of one's rope
8 Get in someone's hair
9 Eyes are bigger than one's stomach
10 Toot one's own horn

Identifying Different Levels of Language

People use varying levels of formality in their speech depending on the situation and the people to whom they are speaking. In the following paragraph Mr. Ayala uses chiefly informal speech:

> "Your grades are crummy," Mr. Ayala said as he opened the folder that held Tony's school records. "But it could do you good to see another country. I want you to make us proud. ¿*Entiendes*?"

1 How is his speech appropriate to the situation, the person he is talking to, and the message he is trying to convey? Lincoln uses different levels of speech when talking to Tony, Mitsuo, and
2 adults like the Onos and Oyama-*sensei*. By using concrete examples, describe how Lincoln's speech varies when talking to each person.

Focus on Writing a Letter

Writing a Business Letter

A **business letter** is a letter addressed to a person or an organization for a specific purpose: for example, to order a product, to make a complaint, to express appreciation, or to ask for information. When you write a business letter, you should use standard English and a formal, polite tone.

A business letter has the following six parts:

heading	body
inside address	closing
salutation	signature

These parts are usually arranged in **block form,** as shown in the outline below:

Your Address (heading)
Today's Date

Name of the Person or (inside address)
Company You Are Writing

Dear _____ : (salutation)
_____ (body)
_____
_____
_____

Sincerely yours, (closing)
_____ (your signed name)
_____ (your typed or printed name)

Look through some magazines to find advertisements for pet foods and toys. Practice your letter-writing skills by composing a letter to one of the manufacturers of pet items. In your letter, request the company to send you a complete catalog that lists all the products the company makes. Save your writing.

About the Author

Gary Soto (1952–)

Soto says that even when writing about serious topics, he tries to see the world with the imagination of a child. He has many fond memories of his childhood. He describes himself as a "playground kid" who jumped at every chance to play any game that allowed him to compete. Soto also loved swimming in the public pool. His great dream, which came true when he was thirteen, was to toss himself head first into the ocean.

When he was in college Soto discovered poetry. His favorite writers were contemporary poets such as Pablo Neruda. Soto says, "I read everything I could get my hands on, and the love of reading made me want to try my hand at writing."

In addition to *Pacific Crossing*, he has written other prose works, including *Living up the Street* (1985), a book of autobiographical recollections. The stories, based on Soto's memories of a whimsical family of five children, won an American Book Award. *Baseball in April* (1990), another short-story collection, deals with young people in California's San Joaquin Valley. Soto has said of his writing, "I'm happy that the characters of my stories and poems are living in the hearts of young readers!" Soto has also begun producing several short films, including *The Pool Party*, which won the Andrew Carnegie Medal For Excellence in Children's Video.

Photo by Carolyn Soto

The Author Comments on His Novel

As a boy growing up in Fresno, California, I seldom went anywhere outside the confines of our neighborhood. Our family didn't ever plan vacations. We never went camping or to the beach. A big treat for us was to visit a nearby river or lake. Perhaps this is why I wrote *Pacific Crossing*—to exercise that longing for travel. Through Lincoln I could become an "exchange student" and travel to another part of the world. I used maps and books to help me understand Japan. I also practiced *shorinji kempo* and taught Madoka Ono, a thirteen-year old girl from Japan, to speak English. She loved the phrase, "Get real, Mom."

Connecting Cultures

Holidays

In *Pacific Crossing* Lincoln accompanies his homestay family on a pilgrimage to several Buddhist shrines to pay homage to ancestors. The Japanese do this formally on a holiday called *Obon,* which is held between August 13 and 15. The major holiday in Japan is *Shogatsu* or "New Year's." Friends and families exchange year-end gifts and large businesses hold *bonenkai*—"forgetting-the-year" parties. Many houses are decorated with pine branches set in bamboo baskets and tied with rice-straw rope. The pine represents health, strength, and a long life. The bamboo symbolizes strong character and rapid physical growth. At midnight on New Year's Eve, bells in Buddhist temples ring throughout the country. On New Year's day many families visit shrines.

Children's Festival.

Influences on Japanese Culture

Almost every aspect of Japan's intriguing culture owes its present form to either Shintoism or Buddhism—whether it is the evocative poetry of haiku, the artistic arrangement of nature in rock gardens, or the thrilling contest of strength and skill in sumo wrestling. Although Shintoism and Buddhism are distinct religions, most Japanese participate to some extent in the traditions of both.

Shintoism

Shinto—the way of *kami* or gods—is native to Japan and is its oldest religion. It arose almost two thousand years ago when the people of Japan shifted from hunting and gathering to agriculture. This prehistoric development led to the worship of *kami* for agricultural blessings. Prayers that exist from ancient Shinto times seek good rice harvests. Even today, the most important activities that take place at Shinto shrines occur in the spring—when rice is planted—and fall—when rice is harvested. And the momentous event of a new emperor's enthronement takes place in the fall when harvest festivals are traditionally celebrated. Early Shinto worship of natural phenomena—the sun, mountains, trees, water, rocks, and the fertility of life—partially explains the Japanese people's enduring love of nature and celebration of nature in art. Japanese legend has it that sumo wrestling, which dates back to the dawn of Japanese history, began when two *kami* struggled for possession of the country.

Shintoism has always placed great emphasis on purification and cleanliness. At Shinto shrines worshipers use water to purify their hands and mouths before entering the presence of *kami*. This Shinto practice is also important in sumo where the wrestler, before engaging

CLOSURE
Ask the class to create an outline of the main events of the **plot**. You can have a student record the events on the chalkboard as other students volunteer them. Formal outline form is not necessary, but correct order is.

EXTENSION AND ENRICHMENT
Students can learn much about Japanese life and culture through news and feature stories in newspapers and magazines. Ask the school librarian for recent back issues of periodicals that contain articles about Japan. Have students find an article, read it, and report to the class the article's contents. If articles can be clipped, have a group of students make a scrapbook for students to browse through when time permits.

---

his opponent, throws salt into the ring to purify it.

Shinto shrines throughout Japan continue to hold colorful and festive celebrations in honor of *kami*. The *matsuri*, or festival, designed to appease the *kami* in order to obtain abundant harvests or to drive evil spirits away, is an important feature in the social lives of the Japanese. In these festivals a *kami* is symbolically transported on a brightly decorated portable shrine throughout the village. A group of young men wearing traditional costumes carry the shrine, while shouting and rushing along the streets exuberantly. The mood is joyful and everyone derives great entertainment from the spectacle.

Buddhism

Buddhism, which originated in India, developed in Japan as a result of cultural exchanges with Korea and later, to an even greater degree, with China. In many ways Buddhism had the same influence on Japanese culture that Christianity had on Northern Europe. Like Christianity in Europe, Buddhism greatly influenced architecture, sculpture, and painting. In addition, martial arts, certain theater arts, flower-arranging arts, and the tea ceremony were brought to Japan by Buddhist priests and monks.

By the time Buddhism reached Japan in the sixth century A.D., it was already one thousand years old. The teachings of Buddha were based on a way of life that eliminated suffering and sought enlightenment—the realization of a higher peace. Japan first formally encountered Buddhism when a ruler from a Korean kingdom, having received military assistance, sent Buddhist writings and statues to Japan as a tribute for its help. But even before that event, Korean and Chinese Buddhist immigrants had been coming to Japan.

Most Japanese accepted both Shintoism and Buddhism. Shintoism embraced a simple love of nature whereas Buddhism, concerned with life's suffering, sought a path toward enlightenment. Today events that celebrate birth and marriage are Shinto; funerals and tributes to dead ancestors are generally Buddhist. Most people observe Buddhist traditions by paying tribute to family ancestors on holidays like *Obon* in August and visiting temples for various blessings at special times of the year.

Zen

Buddhism's early development in Japan was influenced by the arrival of several distinct sects that emphasized different aspects of Buddhist philosophy and practice. Perhaps the sect that had the greatest cultural influence in Japan was one called *Zen*. This Buddhist sect emphasizes meditation, simplicity, and a strong awareness and appreciation of nature. In formal meditation Zen monks sit in a special hall in their monasteries for several hours each day until each monk reaches enlightenment. An image often associated with Zen Buddhism is the lotus sitting position practiced during long periods of meditation.

Making Connections: Activities

1. The Japanese have two holidays in honor of children. They are called *Kodomo no hi*—"Children's Day"—and *Hinamatsuri*—"Doll's Festival." Find out how Japanese families and children celebrate these holidays and present your findings to the class. Include illustrations if possible.
2. Create a multicultural holiday and festival calendar that indicates major and unusual holidays celebrated around the world. For each month provide an illustration of something associated with a festival that occurs during that month. Find out about these holidays through library research and interviewing people from different cultural backgrounds.

Pacific Crossing **565**

CONNECTING CULTURES
1. You might want to have students stage for the class a typical family celebration from Japan. The staging could include special foods and games that are characteristic of Japanese celebrations.
2. Students can publish their calendars by giving a copy to the school library or to other classes in the school. One student can be responsible for watching the calendar and alerting the class of any upcoming holidays.

OBJECTIVES

The overall aim is for students to develop skills in critical thinking by using the techniques of analysis and synthesis.

PRESENTATION

The introduction to the use of analysis in examining the character development of *Pacific Crossing* encourages students to apply literary elements with which they are already familiar to their reading of the novel. Step-by-step instructions and specific examples help students see how the techniques of close analysis might be applied by a careful reader. Students are then given practice in synthesizing their ideas into a conclusion.

USING ANALYSIS AND SYNTHESIS

An alternate method of handling analysis of the book might be to use a line to represent major character developments in the novel, in this fashion:
1. Draw a straight line and label it **background information**. Below the line use a sequence of numbers that correspond to a legend on a loose-leaf page, containing short descriptive phrases which identify each personality characteristic of Lincoln or the chapters or the page numbers in the novel where this material can be found.
2. Extend a slanted line upwards from the straight line, and label it **character development**. Slash marks along this line can be used to mark the various changes which can be recorded in a numbered list.

FOCUS ON Reading and Critical Thinking

USING ANALYSIS AND SYNTHESIS

You have seen that different activities go on when you think: you make inferences; you compare and contrast; you draw conclusions; you evaluate. Two very important methods of reasoning are **analysis** and **synthesis**, which often go together. Analysis is a method of taking something apart to see how the individual parts function. Synthesis is a recombination of ideas to form something new. In the study of literature, the term *analysis* frequently stands for both thinking processes.

Suppose you were asked to analyze the development of Soto's main character in *Pacific Crossing*. One way to handle analysis is to ask questions and then answer them, in this fashion:

1. *What information do you have about the character of Lincoln Mendoza at the opening of the novel?* After moving from San Francisco, Lincoln has gone through a difficult period. Now that he is reunited with his friends and a familiar way of life, his schoolwork and his moods have improved.

2. *What forms the major action of the novel?* As an exchange student Lincoln must learn to understand and live within another culture. He comes to respect and enjoy aspects of Japanese culture, even as he shares aspects of American culture with his new Japanese friends.

3. *What are the major episodes that reveal Lincoln's development as a character?* He begins to accept customs that at first seem odd to him, such as the public bathhouse; he helps the Ono family work in the fields and assists a neighbor as well; he acts boldly to save Mr. Ono's life; he succeeds in becoming a skillful student of the martial arts.

4. *Are any changes evident by the end of the novel?* Lincoln's horizons have widened. Although he misses his home in San Francisco, he is sad to leave Japan and his new friends. He feels confident that he has done well in his training and has been passed to a rank two steps below black belt. He is filled with pride.

5. *Is the main character believable?* Lincoln talks and acts like a fourteen-year-old. He's not above pranks and gets into mischief when sent to Tokyo by Mr. Ono. He also has strengths. He perseveres and works hard at *kempo* even though he is often in pain.

After completing your analysis, proceed with the synthesis of your ideas. State your conclusion in one or two sentences:

> Lincoln Mendoza, the main character in *Pacific Crossing*, finds after spending six weeks in Japan that many American customs, as well as the English language, have already crossed the Pacific. He learns how to respond sensitively to the new people and traditions that he meets as the guest of a Japanese family.

Write a paragraph developing these sentences or write another statement of your conclusions. Develop a paragraph based on your ideas.

THE NOVEL

OBJECTIVES
The overall aim is for students to demonstrate the skills to write a personal letter or a business letter.

PRESENTATION
You may want to teach this material in conjunction with a particular issue, event, or unit of study. Students can compose letters for purposes related to what is being studied.

You can also coordinate the study of contemporary novels with this letter-writing unit. Students can write personal letters to friends and relatives and tell what they have learned from their reading, or they can write business letters to the authors about concerns they have. For more creative writing, students can write letters

HOLT WRITER'S WORKSHOP

This computer program provides help for all types of writing through guided instruction for each step of the writing process. (Program available separately.)

See *Elements of Writing, First Course,* Chapter 4, for more instruction on expressive writing.

FOCUS ON Writing

WRITING A LETTER

Communications technology may be changing rapidly, but letters are still an important part of our lives. As a letter writer you may have many purposes: for example, to thank someone for a gift, to send an invitation, to share news with a relative or a friend, or to request information about a product. In this assignment you will have the chance to write a letter of your own.

Prewriting

1. Depending on your **purpose** and **audience,** you will be writing either a personal letter or a business letter. In a **personal letter,** your purpose is usually to express yourself. You may want to share news or feelings, express your ideas, or thank someone.

In a **business letter,** your purpose may be to ask for information, order a product, complain about a product or service, or express your appreciation.

The chart below shows some of the important differences between a personal letter and a business letter:

Personal Letter	Business Letter
addressed to someone you know	addressed to a company or an individual in an organization
uses informal style and tone	uses standard English and a polite, formal tone
has a flexible format	has a specific format
is usually written by hand	is usually typewritten

2. What do you want to say in your letter? Write down your **main idea** in a sentence or two. This written statement of a main idea will help you to organize your letter. For example, your main idea might be to request information about a new pet collar, or you might want to tell a friend how much you liked a movie you saw recently.

Writing

1. When you draft a business letter, you will find these guidelines helpful:

- State the reason for your letter in the first paragraph.
- Include all the necessary information that your reader needs in order to answer your letter or handle your request. For example, if you are ordering a product, include a complete description. If you are complaining about poor service, be specific.
- Use standard English. Avoid contractions and slang.
- Remember to use a polite, respectful tone.

2. Business letters have six parts, as follows:
heading
inside address
salutation
body
closing
signature

WRITING A LETTER
Today, letter writing seems to be a lost art. Few people spend time or energy writing letters when the telephone is so accessible. Therefore, for many students letter writing is a new experience, but it can engage students in ways that other writing does not. Writing to a person who may actually read and respond can be a strong incentive to produce interesting, informative letters.

Prewriting
You might help students to brainstorm real-life situations for which they can write a personal letter or business letter. Students can develop lists for both purposes from which to choose an idea for writing.

Students can also work in small groups to create situations for which they might produce letters. For example, students may want to plan a career day. They can write business letters to potential speakers and personal letters describing the day to friends.

Writing
You may want to have students draft their letters independently either inside or outside class. Encourage students to write more than they think they might need and to write freely, not being overly concerned with form in their first drafts.

Focus on Writing

When you write a business letter, be sure to arrange the parts correctly on the page. Follow the **block form** outlined below:

```
Your Address   (heading)
Today's Date
Name of the Person or   (inside address)
Company You Are Writing

Dear _____ :  (salutation)
_____  (body)
_____
_____
_____

Sincerely yours,   (closing)
_____  (your signed name)
_____  (your typed or printed name)
```

[See **Focus** assignment on page 562.]

3. If you are writing a personal letter, you may use a more flexible format. Remember to include these parts:

- date
- salutation
- body
- closing
- signature

Besides sharing your news, feelings, and ideas, remember to show some interest in the person to whom you are writing. Ask questions about that person's recent activities, for example. [See **Focus** assignment on page 530.]

4. An **invitation** is a special kind of personal letter. If you are writing an invitation, remember to include specific information about the occasion such as the following:

- date, time, and place
- any other important details, such as style of dress, or whether people should bring food, or whether guests should bring a friend

Evaluating and Revising

1. When you have finished a first draft of your letter, review it to make sure that you have said what you wanted to say. If you have written a personal letter, check to see that you have expressed your main idea. If you have written a business letter, be sure that you have mentioned specific information that your reader needs.

2. You may find the following checklist helpful as you revise your letter.

Checklist for Evaluation and Revision

✓ Have I stated my message clearly?
✓ Have I used the proper format, style, and tone for a personal or business letter?
✓ Have I included all the necessary information?

568   THE NOVEL

Here is how one writer revised part of a business letter.

Writer's Model

72 Valley Road

St. Paul, MN 55107

May 22, 1996

Computnik Enterprises

One Computer Way

Austin, Texas 78746

Dear Sir or Madam:

Please send me information about your new computer product, "Creative Writer," specifically for writ- ers. I would like to know the manufacturer's recommended retail price, and whether or not this program includes a spelling checker and thesaurus.

Proofreading and Publishing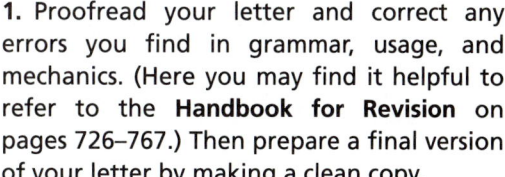

1. Proofread your letter and correct any errors you find in grammar, usage, and mechanics. (Here you may find it helpful to refer to the **Handbook for Revision** on pages 726–767.) Then prepare a final version of your letter by making a clean copy.

2. Publish your writing by addressing an envelope, adding postage, and mailing your letter!

Portfolio If your teacher approves, you may wish to keep a copy of your work in your writing folder or portfolio.

PART III

LITERARY HERITAGE

Unit Nine
CLASSICAL MYTHOLOGY
573

Unit Ten
NORSE MYTHOLOGY
635

Unit Eleven
FABLES
667

LITERARY HERITAGE
The three units in this section provide students with the background necessary to understand **allusions** that draw on the literature of ancient civilizations. The Classical Mythology unit offers stories about the Greek and Roman gods and goddesses, each one illustrating the values and beliefs of the ancients. Students will recognize some of these **heroes** and **heroines** but, perhaps, be surprised to discover the many ways in which the **myths** live on in today's world. The Norse Mythology unit provides yet another view of ancient cultural traditions that live on as a vital part of our literary heritage. The Fables unit includes selections from Aesop, favorites from the oral tradition of literature, selections of verse, and selections from James Thurber's humorous modern **fables**.

UNIT 9 • TEACHING GUIDE

LITERARY HERITAGE
CLASSICAL MYTHOLOGY

OVERVIEW OF THE UNIT

Although remote in time and place, the myths composing this unit take young people to the very fountainhead of their own culture. Here, students will encounter a timeless array of gods, goddesses, and heroes whose names have become part of the English language and whose deeds have been embedded in modern literature as allusions. This unit is directed toward helping students recognize Greek roots and interpret mythological allusions. More important, however, it is intended to provide an exciting introduction to mythological characters and to spark a lasting interest in their larger-than-life adventures.

OBJECTIVES OF THE UNIT

The aims of the unit are for the student:
- To demonstrate an understanding of the characteristics and cultural aspects of classical myths
- To identify specific details and cause-and-effect relationships in selections from classical mythology
- To draw conclusions about the relevance of myths to the Greek culture
- To use a dictionary for vocabulary development
- To focus on persuasive writing
- To write creative compositions
- To make connections between literature and sports, research, the arts, and cultures

CONCEPTS AND SKILLS

The following concepts and skills are treated in this unit:

LITERARY ELEMENTS/TERMS AND TECHNIQUES
Recognizing Gods and Goddesses by Their Titles   581

LANGUAGE AND VOCABULARY
Distinguishing Homophones   590
Learning Words from the Myths   611, 617, 628

WRITING OPPORTUNITIES
Creative Writing
Writing a Story About Metamorphosis   605
Writing a Television Script   628

Focus on Persuasive Writing
Choosing a Topic   582
Identifying Your Opinion   590
Thinking About Your Audience   612

FOR DRAMATIZATION
Dramatizing Scenes Based on a Myth   597

CONNECTIONS
Literature and Sports   582
Connecting Cultures   591, 632
Literature and Research   605, 619, 628
Literature and the Arts   617

TRANSPARENCIES

The following unit support materials with specific correlations to literature selections are available in the **Fine Art and Instructional Transparencies with Teacher's Notes and Blackline Masters** section of your *Audiovisual Resources Binder*.

FINE ART TRANSPARENCIES
Theme: Transformations That Teach a Lesson
46 *Apollo and Daphne*, Antonio Pollaiuolo

Theme: The Heroic Struggle
47 *Whaam!*, Roy Lichtenstein

READER RESPONSE
48 Breakfast of Role Models
49 Norse Notables

LITERARY ELEMENTS
50 Analyzing a Myth
51 Elements of Fables

WRITING PROCESS
52 Supporting an Opinion
53 Writing a Persuasive Paper

INTRODUCING THE UNIT

Display a large map of Greece, preferably a relief map, and ask students to identify major geographic features. If possible, show photographs of the rugged Greek landscape, perhaps including ruins of famous temples. Encourage speculation on how people might have lived in this land more than twenty-five hundred years ago. What natural disasters might they have experienced? Why would such phenomena as storms and volcanic eruptions have been even more terrifying than they are today? Explain that the Greeks, a highly rational people, often created myths to explain nature and thus impose order and predictability upon their world. As students read the myths in this unit, ask them to identify attempts to explain nature.

PLANNING GUIDE

FOR UNIT PLANNING
- Transparencies 46–53: *Audiovisual Resources Binder*
- Portfolio Assessment: *Professional Support Materials*
- Test Generator
- Mastery Tests: *Teaching Resources E,* pp. 107, 110
- Analogy Test: *Teaching Resources E,* p. 112
- Composition Test: *Teaching Resources E,* p. 113

SELECTION (Pupil's Page)	TEACHING RESOURCES E (page numbers shown below)							AV BINDER
	Teacher's Notes	Reading Check	Study Guide	Language Skills	Building Vocabulary	Selection Vocab. Test	Selection Test	Audio-cassette
CLASSICAL MYTHOLOGY *Introduction* (p. 573)	1							
Olivia Coolidge *The Gods and Godesses of Mount Olympus* (p. 575)	2	5	6	10	12			
Retold by Jeremy Ingalls *Prometheus the Fire-Bringer* (p. 583)	14		17		20	36	22	
Retold by Olivia Coolidge *The Origin of the Seasons* (p. 592)	24	28	29	33	35	36	37	TAPE 3 SIDE A
Retold by Rex Warner *Arachne* (p. 598)	39	51	41		45	59	46	
Retold by Sally Benson *The Reward of Baucis and Philemon* (p. 602)	48	51	52	54	57	59	60	
Retold by Edith Hamilton *Phaethon* (p. 608)	62	64	67		71	85	73	
Morris Bishop *Phaethon* (p. 613)	65		67		71		73	
Retold by Josephine Preston Peabody *Icarus and Daedalus* (p. 614)	75	76	79		83		86	TAPE 3 SIDE A
Anne Sexton *To a Friend Whose Work Has Come to Triumph* (p. 618)	77		79		83	85	86	
Retold by Edith Hamilton *The Adventure of Hercules* (p. 622)	88	91	93	97	101	103	104	

Student Learning Options

CLASSICAL MYTHOLOGY

1. Writing a Myth
Ask students to work with a partner to write brief, original myths to explain natural phenomena such as shorter winter days or leaves falling in autumn. They can choose one of the gods or goddesses in traditional Greek or Roman mythology, or they can make up a new god or goddess.

2. Making Spelling Audiotapes
Have small groups of students prepare spelling audiotapes for the class. Using the **Index of Names** on pp. 629–632, equally divide the names among the groups. Ask each group to check the pronunciation and spelling of each name before they make an audiotape, using the following steps: (1) Pronounce the name clearly. (2) Allow time for students to write the name. (3) Spell the name correctly. (4) Allow time for students to make corrections.

3. Acting Out a Myth
Have students work in groups to choose one of the myths (from the text or from another source) and plan a performance. You may want to have them perform for their own class and for other classes in school.

VISUAL CONNECTIONS

About the Artist
Church was interested in geology and history, and he believed that God was revealed in awesome displays of nature. Thus, many of his paintings show the march of time over a fixed site in the landscape.

About the Artwork
This painting exhibits many qualities typical of Church's style: an epic landscape, broad horizon, light, airy colors, and precise details. The light on the Parthenon, as if shining down from heaven, gives the painting the spiritual quality that Church wanted in his work.

Exploring the Subject
The Parthenon, the most famous temple of the ancient world, is a symbol, to many, of the Golden Age of Greece. It is the chief temple of Athens, the most important city-state during the Classical Period. The temple was named for an attribute of Athena, the namesake and patron goddess of Athens: she never married, remaining a maiden, *parthenos* (Greek for "virgin"). **Parthenon** thus means "temple of the maiden."

Ideas for Writing
Students might write about some landmark in their town as it will look 100 years into the future—the ruins of their school building, perhaps, or a recreational area. What remnants from the past would a visitor find? What conclusions would the visitor make about people from this generation?

CLASSICAL MYTHOLOGY

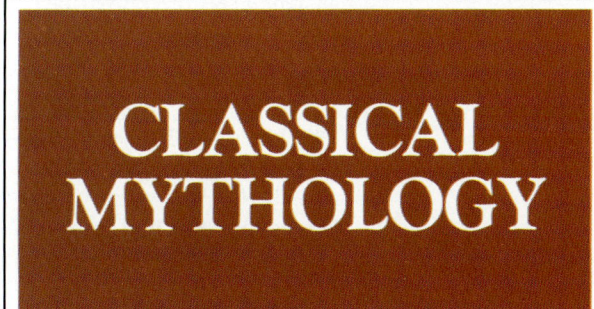

We now read the myths of ancient Greece as entertaining and instructive stories, but at one time the gods and goddesses of classical mythology were worshiped.

The Parthenon was built in the fifth century B.C. as a temple to house a statue of Athena Parthenos, the patron goddess of Athens. Even though what is left of the temple today is a ruin, the Parthenon is considered to be the finest example of ancient Greek architecture and one of the greatest buildings ever constructed.

What has the artist chosen to emphasize in his painting of this famous building? How does he use light to emphasize the magnificence of this ruin? Does this painting speak to you, in Poe's famous phrase, of the "glory that was Greece"?

The Parthenon by Frederic Edwin Church (1826–1920). Oil on canvas.

The Metropolitan Museum of Art, bequest of Maria De Witt Jessup, 1915. (15.30.67)

PRESENTATION
Before reading the introductory passage, ask students to give their own definitions of the word *myth*. Write some of the definitions on the board. Then ask students to supply names that are associated with mythology. Students will probably have heard names like *Apollo* and *Hercules*. Read the introductory passage aloud and discuss each of the four guidelines for reading myths, turning briefly to pp. 576 and 577 as the fourth one is discussed.

UNIT INTRODUCTION

1
Jupiter is derived from the words *Zeus pater,* which mean "Father Zeus."

2
Zeus means "bright sky."

3
Juno is wife of Jupiter just as Hera is wife of Zeus.

GUIDELINES FOR CLOSE READING
1. The entertaining "The Adventures of Hercules" shows the hero accomplishing twelve difficult labors; one **allusion** contributed to our language is the description of hard chores as "Herculean tasks."
2. Major figures are introduced in "The Gods and Goddesses of Mount Olympus." Different aspects of the gods are revealed in "The Reward of Baucis and Philemon," which shows Zeus as a rewarder of the deserving, in contrast to "Prometheus the Fire-Bringer," where he appears as a jealous guardian of his own power.
3. "The Origin of the Seasons" explains a complex natural process, while "Arachne" is a simple explanation of the spider's artistry in weaving an intricate web. Myths which highlight unacceptable behavior include "Phaethon" and "Icarus and Daedalus," both involving mortals who overstep their limits.
4. Characteristics valued by the ancients include the heroism and determination of Hercules and Prometheus as well as the piety and goodness of Baucis and Philemon.

Myths are stories that have come down to us from the distant past. They have survived for many centuries because they are appealing stories for old and young alike. The main characters in myths are generally gods and goddesses, but if you read carefully, you will find that myths have much to say about human nature.

Every people has its own body of myths, or *mythology*. Classical myths, the name given to the myths of the ancient Greeks and Romans, are the best-known myths in Western culture. These stories were first told by the ancient Greeks more than twenty-five hundred years ago. Later the stories were retold by the Romans, who substituted the names of their own gods and goddesses for those of the
1 Greeks. The Roman god Jupiter was identified with the Greek god
2 Zeus, the Roman goddess Juno with the Greek goddess Hera, and so
3 on. For this reason, many gods and goddesses in classical mythology are known by both Greek and Roman names.

Here are some guidelines to follow in reading the myths in this unit.

Guidelines for Close Reading

1. Read for enjoyment and for understanding. The myths are highly entertaining as literature. They also provide insight into universal human characteristics such as courage and honor. Moreover, they yield a good deal of information about words in our language and many aspects of our own culture.

2. Become familiar with the major figures in classical mythology. Many of the characters appear in various myths, and often in different roles. Apollo, for example, who is god of the sun, is also the god of youth, music, prophecy, archery, and healing. In the myth of Midas, he appears in his attribute or function as the god of music. In the myth of Niobe, he is an avenging archer. As you read the myths in this unit, you may want to refer to the chart on pages 576–577. For help with the pronunciation of names, see the *Index of Names* on pages 629–632.

3. Determine the function of individual myths. Some myths are attempts to explain natural phenomena like the seasons. Other myths are concerned with the proper relationship of mortals to the gods and goddesses, and offer lessons in acceptable and unacceptable behavior.

4. Note the individual characteristics valued by ancient Greeks and Romans. Determine which of these characteristics have value in our own society. For example, are there parallels for the Greek ideal of moderation in the contemporary world?

The Gods and Goddesses of Mount Olympus°

OLIVIA COOLIDGE

This selection will introduce you to the most important figures in classical mythology—Zeus and his family. What reasons does the author give for the continued popularity of this literature?

Greek legends have been favorite stories for many centuries. They are mentioned so often by famous writers that it has become impossible to read widely in English, or in many other literatures, without knowing what the best of these tales are about. Even though we no longer believe in the Greek gods, we enjoy hearing of them because they appeal to our imagination.

The Greeks thought all the forces of nature were spirits, so that the whole earth was filled with gods. Each river, each woodland, even each great tree had its own god or nymph.¹ In the woods lived the satyrs,² who had pointed ears and the shaggy legs of goats. In the sea danced more than three thousand green-haired, white-limbed maidens. In the air rode wind gods, cloud nymphs, and the golden chariot of the sun. All these spirits, like the

Head of Zeus. Roman copy of lost Greek original. Marble, fourth century B.C.
Pio Clementino Museum, Vatican Art Collection

° **Olympus** (ō-lĭm′pəs).
1. **nymph** (nĭmf): a goddess who inhabited a part of nature, such as a river, a mountain, or a tree.
2. **satyrs** (sā′tərz): woodland creatures who were part man and part goat.

PRESENTATION

This selection from Olivia Coolidge's *Greek Myths* tells how the second generation of gods differs from the monsters and giants that they overcame. Since this essay is filled with information that will be almost entirely new to most seventh graders, allow time for silent reading in class so that you may offer help as needed. If you have the essay read aloud, pause frequently for explanation. Immediate study of the chart on pp. 576–577 will clarify and reinforce identities of major gods and goddesses in the essay.

VISUAL CONNECTIONS

Exploring the Subject

The Greek gods were seen as being human, only better. They looked like humans (unlike the gods of Babylon and Egypt, who were depicted as being part animal, part human), but the Greeks believed the gods were more beautiful than any mortal. In Greek art, the gods are always shown as idealized, perfect. In addition, the gods were believed to possess certain skills that exceeded the most capable mortal's. Greeks believed that able mortals should use their talents to the fullest extent (wasting them would be shaming the god or goddess bestowing the abilities) and thus resemble the gods in creating something good and beautiful. However, accomplished humans were admonished not to think too highly of themselves, or else risk retribution from the gods for hubris (boastful pride).

Relating Expression Skills

Extend the textbook activity by dividing the class into teams for a contest in identifying gods and goddesses by titles.

Another way of helping students to remember the important names in Greek mythology is to create two sets of cards, one with names and the other with titles of gods and goddesses. Students might then play matching games or use the cards for an adaptation of the television game *Concentration*.

CLASSICAL GODS AND GODDESSES

GREEK	ROMAN	DESCRIPTION
Zeus	Jupiter, Jove	king of the gods; god of the sky and the weather
Hera	Juno	queen of the gods; goddess of marriage and childbirth
Poseidon	Neptune	god of the sea
Hades, Pluto	Pluto	god of the underworld
Demeter	Ceres	goddess of grain, plants, and fruit
Athena, Athene, or Pallas Athena	Minerva	goddess of wisdom, arts, crafts, and war; protector of Athens
Hephaestus	Vulcan	god of fire and metalworking
Aphrodite	Venus	goddess of love and beauty
Ares	Mars	god of war
Apollo, Phoebus Apollo	Apollo, Phoebus Apollo	god of youth, music, prophecy, archery, healing, and the sun

MEETING INDIVIDUAL NEEDS
Visual Learners • To help familiarize students with the names and descriptions of Greek gods and goddesses, you might have them copy the information from the chart in their own handwriting or on a computer program with chart-making capability. They could then add cutouts to depict notable traits and symbols associated with the gods and goddesses, using items cut from magazines or freehand paper cutouts. Students could use drawings from the textbook or mythology books as sources for symbols.

VISUAL CONNECTIONS
Exploring the Subject
The Greeks believed their gods and goddesses were involved in all aspects of human life—birth, marriage, childbirth, health or sickness, death—as well as events of nature—storms, earthquakes, growth of crops and livestock. As befits this concept of the omnipresent gods, Greeks painted, carved, or wove pictures of their gods and goddesses on many objects used in everyday life: tapestries, pottery, coins, jewelry, tilework on floors, paintings on ceilings. Statues were carved not just for decoration of temples but for ordinary homes and gardens.

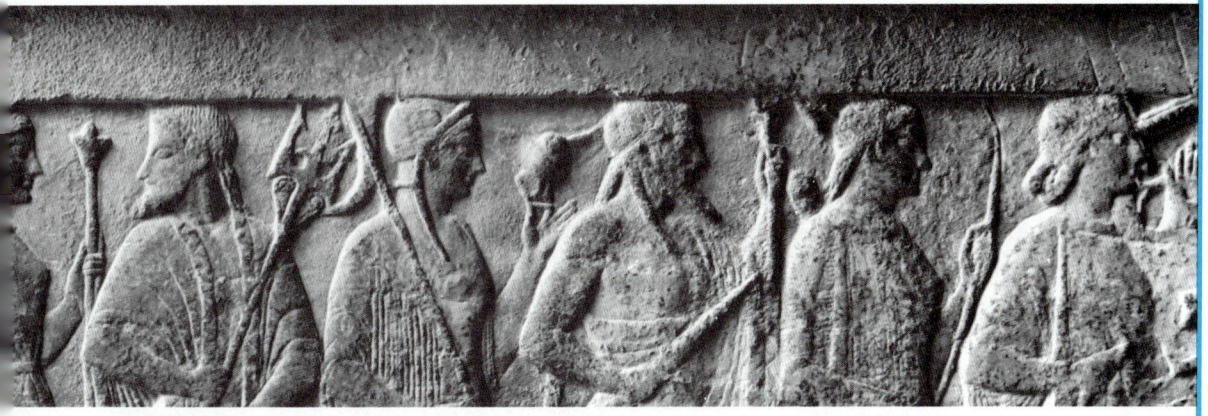

Procession of twelve gods and goddesses. From left: Persephone, Hermes, Aphrodite, Ares, Demeter, Hephaestus, Hera, Poseidon, Athena, Zeus, Artemis, Apollo. Marble relief.
Walters Art Gallery, Baltimore

GREEK	ROMAN	DESCRIPTION
Artemis	**Diana**	goddess of hunting, childbirth, wild animals, and the moon
Hermes	**Mercury**	messenger of the gods; god of travelers, merchants, and thieves
Persephone	**Proserpina**	goddess of spring and the underworld; Demeter's daughter
Dionysus, Bacchus	**Bacchus**	god of wine, fertility, and drama
Eros	**Cupid**	god of love; Aphrodite's son
Iris	**Iris**	goddess of the rainbow; messenger of the gods
Muses	**Muses**	nine goddesses who inspired artists
Fates	**Fates**	three goddesses who determined human destiny

Classical Gods and Goddesses

MEETING INDIVIDUAL NEEDS

Visual Learners • Students may not realize how many words in modern English are based on the names of Greek and Roman gods and goddesses. You might help students make associations by having them use a standard dictionary or an etymological dictionary to look up these and other words' meanings and determine their origin. Examples include: *jovial* (Jove), *cereal* (Ceres), *vulcanize* (Vulcan), *mercurial* (Mercury), *fatal* (the Fates), *iris* (Iris), *music*, *museum* (the Muses), *hero* (Hera), *mind* (Minerva), and *March* (Mars).

4
Greeks believed that gods were like them, with similar form, likes and dislikes, appetites, failings.

5
Imagery. Each god or goddess is associated with certain images that express his or her nature.

6
Twelve Titans in all, children of Mother Earth (Gaea) and the sky (Uranus).

7 Expressing an Opinion
Why do you think Apollo was more important than Artemis? Sun is necessary for life on earth; moon is not.

VISUAL CONNECTIONS
Exploring the Subject
Poseidon was the god of the seas, of great importance to the Greeks. Poseidon was believed to bestow favorable winds and friendly seas. No wide roads could be built across the mountainous Greek peninsula, and ancient trade and travel were carried out by sea.

Although Poseidon was also the god of horses, the Greeks considered this a lesser attribute. In a contest with Athena in which the god bestowing the most useful gift on mankind would become the patron of Athens, Athena's contribution—the olive tree—beat Poseidon's gift of the horse.

578

---

forces of nature, were beautiful and strong, but sometimes unreliable and unfair. Above **4** all, however, the Greeks felt that they were tremendously interested in mankind.

From very early times the Greeks began to invent stories to account for the things that went on—the change of seasons, the sudden storms, the good and bad fortune of the farmer's year. These tales were spread by travelers from one valley to another. They were put together and altered by poets and musicians, until at last a great body of legends arose from the whole of Greece. These did not agree with one another in details, but, on the whole, gave a clear picture of who the chief gods were, how men should behave to please them, and what their relationships had been with heroes of the past.

The ruler of all the gods was Zeus, the sky god, titled by courtesy "Father of gods and men." He lived in the clouds with most of the great gods in a palace on the top of Mount Olympus, the tallest mountain in Greece. **5** Lightning was the weapon of Zeus, thunder was the rolling of his chariot, and when he nodded his head, the whole earth shook.

Zeus, though the ruler of the world, was not the eldest of the gods. First had come a race of monsters with fifty heads and a hundred arms **6** each. Next followed elder gods called Titans, the leader of whom, Cronus, had reigned before Zeus. Then arose mighty Giants, and finally Zeus and the Olympians. Zeus in a series of wars succeeded in banishing the Titans and imprisoning the Giants in various ways. One huge monster, Typhon, lay imprisoned under the volcano of Aetna, which spouted fire when he struggled. Atlas, one of the Titans, was forced to stand holding the heavens on his shoulders so that they should not fall upon the earth.

Almost as powerful as Zeus were his two brothers, who did not live on Olympus: Poseidon,[3] ruler of the sea, and Hades,[4] gloomy king of the underworld, where the spirits of the dead belong. Queen of the gods was blue-eyed, majestic Hera. Aphrodite,[5] the laughing, sea-born goddess, was queen of love and most beautiful of all.

Apollo and Artemis were twins, god of the **7** sun and goddess of the moon. Apollo was the more important. Every day he rode the heavens in a golden chariot from dawn to sunset. The sun's rays could be gentle and healing, or they could be terrible. Apollo, therefore, was a great healer and the father of the god of medicine. At the same time he was a famous archer, and the arrows from his golden bow were arrows of infection and death. Apollo was also god of poetry and song; his instrument was a

Bust of Poseidon. Bronze.

The Athens Museum

---

3. **Poseidon** (pō-sī′dən).
4. **Hades** (hā′dēz).
5. **Aphrodite** (ăf′rə-dī′tē).

578 CLASSICAL MYTHOLOGY

GEOGRAPHY LINK
To help students see why the Greek and Roman gods are so closely associated in classical mythology, you might want to have students locate Greece and Italy on a map, preferably one which shows the geopolitical divisions of the classical period. You could point out names of places derived from gods' and goddesses' names, such as Apollonía and Artemón. You might also want to use a topographical map so that students notice the hilly terrain of Greece. Do students think the mountains had an effect on how the land was settled? Could sparse and separated settlements have contributed to the many variations in the myths?

(Right) Detail of statue of Apollo "Belvedere."
The Granger Collection, New York

(Below) Grand Artemis of Piraeus.
Copper and bronze.
Museum of Archaeology, Piraeus, Greece

8 golden lyre, and the nine Muses, goddesses of music and the arts, were his attendants. He was the ideal of young manhood and the patron of athletes.

9 Apollo was also god of prophecy. There were temples of Apollo, known as oracles, at which a man could ask questions about the future. The priestesses of Apollo, inspired by the god, gave him an answer, often in the form of a riddle which was hard to understand. Nevertheless, the Greeks believed that if a man could interpret the words of the oracle, he would find the answer to his problem.

Artemis, the silver moon goddess, was goddess of unmarried girls and a huntress of wild beasts in the mountains. She also could send deadly arrows from her silver bow.

Gray-eyed Athene,[6] the goddess of wisdom,

6. **Athene** (ə-thē′-nē): also called *Athena* (ə-thē′nə).

The Gods and Goddesses of Mount Olympus

VISUAL CONNECTIONS
Exploring the Subject
Artemis was patron goddess of the wilderness: she protected its wildlife as well as those who hunted there. Her devotees, male or female, who vowed perpetual chastity in honor of the goddess came under her special protection. When her brother Apollo became associated with the sun, she became associated with the moon, whose waxing and waning led to her association with childbirth.

Apollo was considered "the most Greek of all the gods." He represented the Greek ideal: the best attributes of mind and body, always with poise and never to excess. He was always shown as young, handsome, and athletic, but was also revered for being intelligent and skilled. He was patron of arts requiring skill as well as practice: poetry, music, medicine. He was often called *Phoebus Apollo* (Apollo the shining one), which led to his later association with the sun.

8 Summarizing
What did the Muses do for artists and poets? Inspired them to be imaginative or creative.

9
Delphi was the most famous and sacred of Apollo's oracles.

was patron of Athens. She was queen of the domestic arts, particularly spinning and weaving. Athene was warlike too; she wore helmet and breastplate, and carried a spear. Ares, however, was the real god of war, and the maker of weapons was Hephaestus,[7] the lame smith and metalworker.

One more god who lived on Olympus was Hermes, the messenger. He wore golden, winged sandals which carried him dry-shod over sea and land. He darted down from the peaks of Olympus like a kingfisher dropping to

7. **Hephaestus** (hĭ-fĕs′təs).

Athena. Roman copy of Greek original. Stone, fourth century B.C.

Hermes Running. Attributed to the Tithonos Painter. Red-figured vase, 480–475 B.C.

catch a fish, or came running down the sloping sunbeams bearing messages from Zeus to men. Mortal eyes were too weak to behold the dazzling beauty of the immortals; consequently the messages of Zeus usually came in dreams. Hermes was therefore also a god of sleep, and of thieves because they prowl by night. Healing was another of his powers. His rod, a staff entwined by two snakes, is commonly used as a symbol of medicine.

> **TRANSPARENCY 46**
> **Fine Art**
> Theme: *Transformations That Teach a Lesson* – highlights artwork that shows a magical change of a person or thing.

CLOSURE
Ask students to connect the second generation of gods headed by Zeus to the Titans who preceded them and to explain how Zeus came to power.

The Greeks have left us so many stories about their gods that it hardly would be possible for everyone to know them all. We can still enjoy them because they are good stories. In spite of their great age we can still understand them because they are about nature and about people. We still need them to enrich our
14 knowledge of our own language and of the great masterpieces of literature.

Reading Check

1. According to mythology, where did most of the Greek gods and goddesses live?
2. Who were the Titans?
3. Who kept the heavens from falling on the earth?
4. Where did Poseidon and Hades live?
5. Who were the Muses?
6. What did human beings learn from the oracles?
7. Why were the words of the oracles difficult to interpret?
8. Who was the messenger of the gods?
9. Which of the Olympians were twins?
10. Name two Olympians associated with war.

For Study and Discussion

Analyzing and Interpreting the Selection

1. The ancient Greeks believed that all of nature was ruled by divine beings. **a.** How did they explain lightning and thunder? **b.** What did they believe happened when Zeus nodded his head?

2. The ancient Greeks believed that each of the gods and goddesses had control over a special area of life. For example, Hephaestus was the god of fire and metalworking. Blacksmiths would have prayed to him to help them in their craft. To which god or goddess would the following persons have prayed for special help?

athletes   robbers   soldiers
hunters   sailors   weavers

3. Why do people still read stories about the ancient Greek gods and goddesses? Give two reasons stated by the author.

Literary Elements

Recognizing Gods and Goddesses by Their Titles

The gods and goddesses in classical mythology are often identified by their titles rather than by their names. Zeus is known by several titles: "the sky god," "father of gods and men," "king of the gods." Writers frequently refer to Apollo by one of his titles: "god of the sun," "god of poetry and song," "god of prophecy."

The gods and goddesses are also identified by certain of their physical characteristics. For example, Hera is often described as "the ox-eyed goddess." She is also described as "the goddess of the white arms." Athena is described as "gray-eyed" or "bright-eyed." Aphrodite is called "the pale-gold goddess." "Broad-browed" and "dark-misted" are often used to describe Zeus.

Sometimes the gods and goddesses are identified by their special powers. Zeus, for example, is referred to as "the summoner of clouds." Artemis is known as "goddess of wild things."

1 Which of the gods do you think is known as "the thunderer"?

14
Understanding literary allusions and their relevance to literature often depends on familiarity with myths.

READING CHECK
1. In a palace on top of Mount Olympus (p. 578).
2. Race of gods who preceded the Olympians (p. 578).
3. Atlas (p. 578).
4. Poseidon lived in the sea; Hades in the underworld (p. 578).
5. Goddesses of music and the arts (p. 579).
6. Learned about the future (p. 579).
7. Answers often in riddles (p. 579).
8. Hermes (p. 580).
9. Apollo and Artemis (p. 578).
10. Ares and Athene (p. 580).

FOR STUDY AND DISCUSSION
1a. Zeus used lightning as a weapon; thunder was caused by rolling of Zeus's chariot. **1b.** The world shook (earthquake).
2. Athletes to Apollo; hunters to Artemis; robbers to Hermes; sailors to Poseidon; soldiers to Ares; weavers to Athene.
3. Good stories that we can enjoy; we need to know about these mythical figures because language and literature allude to these myths.

LITERARY ELEMENTS
1. Zeus is known as "the thunderer" because the rolling of his chariot caused thunder.

The Gods and Goddesses of Mount Olympus

EXTENSION AND ENRICHMENT
Advanced students might explore further the Greek creation myth, perhaps by reading Chapter 3 of Edith Hamilton's *Mythology.*

Other students might identify gods and goddesses that could be used as symbols by producers of various goods and services:
- a telegraph company
- a munitions factory
- a solar energy firm
- a steamship line
- a computer dating service.

Students might then create logos or commercials incorporating mythological references.

The class might create a butcher-paper wall chart, outlining the genealogy of the gods. Work on this chart may continue throughout the unit.

---

2. Poseidon is called the "blue-maned" god because he ruled the sea.

3. Hephaestus is described as "strong-handed" because he would need strong hands to do a blacksmith's work.

To extend this exercise, you may wish to explain that words and phrases used to characterize people or things are called *epithets.* To fix the concept in their minds, students might take a few minutes to create epithets for characters in a well-known TV series.

FOCUS ON PERSUASIVE WRITING
You might want to have on hand some recent newspapers so students can peruse the editorial sections. Copies of your school newspaper might also help students to generate topics for persuasive writing.

ABOUT THE AUTHOR
Coolidge earned both her B.A. and M.A. degrees at Oxford University. In addition to the languages she taught—Latin, Greek, and English—she is proficient in German. After fifteen years of teaching, she devoted her life to writing. Students might find *The Golden Days of Greece* (1968) and *The Maid of Artemis* (1969) particularly interesting in their study of classical mythology.

LITERATURE AND SPORTS
As an alternative activity, have students work in small groups as planning committees for an Olympic festival to be held at their school. It is their committee's job to decide on the events that will be included. Would they include academic and musical contests along with physical games? In what order would they stage the events?

582

---

2 Why would Poseidon be called the "blue-maned" god?

3 Why would Hephaestus be described as "strong-handed"?

Focus on Persuasive Writing

Choosing a Topic

The ancient Greeks respected the power of persuasion so much that they personified it as a minor goddess, named Peitho. In **persuasive writing** you state an opinion on an issue and then support your view with information, reasons, and appeals to your audience's emotions. Your purpose in this type of writing is to persuade your audience to think or act in a certain way.

To choose a topic for persuasive writing, use these guidelines:

1. Find an issue that matters to you and to other people. For example, you could choose an issue in your school or neighborhood, such as a new dress code or a plan to close a park.
2. Choose an issue that is a matter of opinion, rather than a matter of fact. An *opinion* is a belief or an attitude; a *fact* is something that can be checked or proven true. Choose an issue about which people can and do disagree.

Join with a small group of classmates and brainstorm some topics for persuasive writing. Look through recent issues of magazines, and talk with your partners about school and neighborhood issues. Make notes on two topics that interest you. Save your notes.

582 CLASSICAL MYTHOLOGY

About the Author

Olivia Coolidge (1908–)

Olivia Coolidge is the author of twenty-seven books. She was born in London, England. She earned two degrees at Oxford University and then began her career as a teacher and writer. Her books include *Greek Myths* (1949), *The Trojan War* (1952), *Caesar's Gallic War* (1961), and *Lives of Famous Romans* (1965).

Literature and Sports

The Olympic Games

In classical times the Olympic Games were a festival held every four years at Olympia, a plain in the southern part of Greece, to honor Zeus. The festival was first celebrated in 776 B.C. and was discontinued in A.D. 394. Greek women did not participate in the Olympic Games but held games of their own called *Heraea,* in honor of the goddess Hera.

The Olympic Games consisted of contests not only in sports but also in poetry and music. The modern international revival of the Olympic Games began at Athens in 1896.

Making Connections: Activities

Choose one of these topics for research and present your findings in a short essay.

1. Find an illustration showing the Olympic symbol. Explain the significance of the interlocking rings and their colors.

2. Research the events of the Heraea.

3. Present to your class the story behind the Olympic Marathon footrace.

4. Report on one of the outstanding athletes in Olympic history.

OBJECTIVES
The overall aim is for students to discuss the myth of Prometheus as an explanation of how humans gained the secret of fire. For a complete list of objectives, see the **Teacher's Notes.**

VOCABULARY
The underlined words are in the Glossary. The **Language and Vocabulary** activity on p. 590 asks students to distinguish between the two homophones *councilor* and *counselor*.

FOCUS / MOTIVATION
Recall that the ancients once thought that there were four elements—earth, air, water, and fire. How does fire differ from the other three? Why did primitive people attach such importance to fire?

Prometheus° the Fire-Bringer

Retold by
JEREMY INGALLS

For people of early times, mythology was part of religion. The myths of gods, goddesses, and heroes were sacred stories. But mythology also served another function. Through myths these early people provided explanations for natural events that puzzled them.

The ancient Greeks believed that the secret of making fire once belonged only to the gods. As you read the following myth, ask yourself why the Greeks came to regard one of the Titans as their friend.

TEACHING RESOURCES E
Teacher's Notes, p. 14
Study Guide, p. 17
Building Vocabulary, p. 20
Selection Vocabulary Test, p. 36
Selection Test, p. 22

PREREADING FOCUS
Ask students to speculate on the reasons Zeus, king of the gods, was unwilling to give the Greek people the gift of fire.

Prometheus the Fire-Bringer

1
The first age of humanity was a "golden age," and each succeeding age was said to have been less illustrious.

2
Prometheus was a Titan, one of the huge beings who ruled before Zeus.

3
Description fits people from advanced cultures who have been treated like gods by people of simpler cultures.

4
Connotation. In this myth Arcadia is unpleasant before fire; modern connotation of Arcadia is of idyllic simplicity and contentment.

Fire itself, and the civilized life which fire makes possible—these were the gifts of Prometheus to the men of ancient times. Prometheus himself was not of the oldest race of men. He was not alive in the first age of mankind.

Ancient writers tell us there were three ages of men on earth before the fourth age, in which we are now living. Each of the previous ages ended in terrible disasters which destroyed a large part of the human race. A rag-
1 ing fire ended the first age of the world. At the end of the second age, vast floods engulfed plains and mountains. According to the oldest poets, these misfortunes were punishments the gods visited upon men for their wickedness and wrongdoing.

2 The story of Prometheus, remembered by the Greeks and set down in their books, tells of the days when Zeus was king of the world and Prometheus was his chief councilor. From their ancestors they and their companions upon Mount Olympus had inherited the secrets of fire, of rain, of farming and metalworking. This knowledge gave them a power
3 so great that they appeared as gods to the men who served them.

After the flood which destroyed many of the men of the second age, Zeus, with the help of Prometheus, had bred a new race of men in
4 Arcadia.¹ But Zeus did not find life on earth so simple for men and gods as it had been in earlier times.

When Cronus, the father of Zeus, had ruled the earth, summer had been the only season. Great land masses toward the north had barred all the icy winds. The age of Cronus

---
1. **Arcadia** (är-kā′dē-ə): a pleasant, mountainous district in Greece.

°**Prometheus** (prə-mē′thē-əs).

MOTIVATIONAL SUMMARY

Prometheus, one of the last of the Titans, serves as Zeus's councilor. He is distressed to learn that Zeus plans to destroy humankind. Prometheus argues that mankind can learn, if given a chance. Zeus disagrees. Prometheus foresees that someday humans will be able to break away from the domination of the gods and control their own destiny, but they need to have help in taking their first step toward independence: the gift of fire.

PRESENTATION

Call attention to the first sentence of the story and its assertion that fire makes civilized life possible. Ask students to explain this statement. Even today, for example, a wilderness camping trip would be less safe and less comfortable

VISUAL CONNECTIONS
Exploring the Subject

Zeus, as ruler of gods and people, had many demands on his attention in dealing with activities on Mt. Olympus as well as on earth. According to myth, he had a pet eagle who flew far and wide over the earth and reported the actions of people—both good and bad—to him. Zeus would then reward or punish the reported behavior of humans as he felt they deserved.

Zeus and His Eagle. Base of a Laconian cup, c. 550 B.C.
Louvre Museum

5
Most mythologies include references to a golden era in which humans lived in complete harmony with nature until displeasing the gods.

6
Having little knowledge, people are not much better off than beasts.

5 was an age of contentment. No man had needed to work for food or clothes or a house to shelter him.

After the first flood, the land masses were broken. Winter winds blew upon countries which before had known only summer.

The race of gods did not suffer. They warmed their houses, having the secret of fire. And the women of the race were weavers of cloth, so that the gods were clothed and defended from the north wind.

6 But winter was a harsh season for the men and women who did not live on the gods' mountain. Without defense from the cold,

584 CLASSICAL MYTHOLOGY

without fire. Why? Would human beings have been able to progress beyond the Stone Age without fire? Why? Suggest that the Greeks considered fire so important that they created a **myth** to explain its origin. Refer to the headnote. Because the action of this myth occurs after a fairly lengthy background, you may wish to read aloud through "Silently Prometheus turned away" (second column, p. 585). Students should then be able to finish on their own.

---

7 they huddled with the animals. They complained against the gods, whom they must serve for what little comfort they might find of food and warmth. They scarcely believed the stories which their ancestors had handed down to them of a time when men had lived in endless summer weather, when men were friends and favorites of the gods.

Men became rebels and grumblers. For this reason Zeus, seeing winter coming on again, determined to destroy the people of Arcadia. 8 Then Prometheus, his chief councilor, sought to save this third race of man from destruction.

9 "They quarrel among themselves," said Zeus angrily. "They start trouble in the fields. We must train up a new race of men who will learn more quickly what it means to serve the gods."

Zeus was walking across the bronze floor of his mountain palace. A tremendous, tall figure of a man he was, the king god Zeus. But he who stood beside him, Prometheus of the family of Titans, was even taller.

"Worthless," Zeus was saying as if to himself. "Worthless," he repeated again, "the whole race. They complain of the winters. They are too weak a race for the climate of these times. Why should we continue to struggle with them? Better to be rid of them, every man and woman of the troublesome tribe."

"And then?" inquired Prometheus. "What if you create a new race to provide manpower for the farms and the bigger buildings? That race, too, will rebel while they can see and envy our knowledge and our power."

"Even so, I will destroy these Arcadians," insisted Zeus stubbornly. "Men are our creatures. Let them learn to serve us, to do our will."

10 "Up here on your mountain," observed Prometheus thoughtfully, "you make men and destroy them. But what about the men themselves? How can they learn wisdom when, time after time, you visit them with destruction?"

11 "You have too much sympathy for them," answered Zeus in a sharp voice. "I believe you love these huddling, sheepish men."

"They have minds and hearts," replied Prometheus warmly, "and a courage that is worth admiring. They wish to live even as the gods wish to live. Don't we feed ourselves on nectar and ambrosia[2] every day to preserve our lives?"

Prometheus was speaking rapidly. His voice 12 was deep. "This is your way," he went on. "You won't look ahead. You won't be patient. You won't give men a chance to learn how to live. Over and over again, with floods or with cracking red thunderbolts, you destroy them."

"I have let you live, Prometheus," said Zeus in an ominous tone, "to advise me when you can. You are my cousin. But I am not your 13 child to be scolded." Zeus was smiling, but there was thunder behind the smile.

Silently Prometheus turned away. Leaving the marble-columned hall, he went out among the gardens of Olympus, the gods' mountain. The last roses were fading before the time of winter winds and rain.

This was not the first time Prometheus had heard thunder in the voice of Zeus. Prometheus knew that someday Zeus would turn against him, betray him, and punish him. Prometheus the Titan had the gift of reading the future. He could foresee the fate hidden and waiting for him and for others and even for Zeus himself.

Climbing among the upper gardens, Prometheus stopped at last beside an ancient, twisted ash tree. Leaning against its trunk, he looked toward the south. Beyond the last canal, the last steep sea wall, he could see the ocean. He

---

2. **nectar and ambrosia** (ăm-brō′zhə): the drink and food of the Olympian gods.

7
In myth, punishment always follows disrespect for the gods.

8 Summarizing
Why is Prometheus determined to save this race? He designed them himself, lovingly modeling them from clay; thus, his concern for humans' welfare.

9
Zeus, as ruler, is intolerant of disobedience.

10
Prometheus means "forethought." He believes in progress through teaching men to improve.

11
Characterization. Zeus is powerful but lacks empathy for human feelings.

12
Conflict. The central conflict of the story is between Zeus and Prometheus. Part of the conflict is that Zeus sees his role as a ruler; Prometheus sees his as a teacher.

13
Zeus is also god of thunder; he destroyed most of the other Titans, who rebelled against his rule.

TRANSPARENCY 48

Reader Response
Breakfast of Role Models – invites students to design a mock cereal box featuring a favorite hero.

---

14 Prometheus "looked far"—not only to distant landscape, but into future.

15 Simile. Convolutions of thought compared to coils of dragon.

16 Prometheus cannot help these friends now, but he can help humans.

17 Making Generalizations
Why is Zeus not content with what he has gained? Answers will vary. When the powerful fear losing their power, they sometimes lash out, causing unnecessary bloodshed.

18 Prometheus had hoped to teach and guide Zeus.

19 Zeus wants to punish humans for circumstances they cannot control.

20 Theme. This version of the story stresses the value of thought and approves the questioning of the gods.

---

14 looked far out toward that last shining circle of water. Then, with his head bent, he sat down on the tree roots bulging in thick knots above the ground.

It would be hard to tell you all the thoughts **15** in the mind of the Titan—thoughts that coiled and twined like a nest of dragons. In his mighty brain were long memories of the past and far-reaching prophecies of what was to come.

He thought most often of the future, but the talk with Zeus just now had brought the past before him once again. He remembered once more the terrible war in which Zeus had seized the kingship of the gods. He thought of the exile and imprisonment of Cronus, the father **16** of Zeus. He remembered the Titans, his people, now chained in the black pit of Tartarus.[3]

The great god Cronus himself, who had given peace to gods and men, where was he now? And the mighty-headed Titans, the magnificent engineers, builders of bridges and temples, where were they? All of them fallen, helpless, as good as dead.

Zeus had triumphed. Of the Titans, only two now walked the upper earth—he, Prometheus, and Epimetheus, his brother.

And now, even now, Zeus was not content. It was not enough for his glory, it seemed, to have dethroned his own father, not enough to have driven the race of Titans from the houses **17** of the gods. Now Zeus was plotting to kill the race of men.

Prometheus had endured the war against the Titans, his own people. He had even given help to Zeus. Having seen what was to come, **18** he had thought, "Since Zeus must win, I'll guide him. I'll control his fierce anger and his greed for power."

---

3. **Tartarus** (tär′tər-əs): a dark place below the underworld.

But Prometheus could not submit to this latest plot of Zeus. He would use all his wits to save the men of Arcadia from destruction.

19 Why were they to be destroyed? Because they were cold and full of fears, huddled together in caves like animals. It was well enough in the warm months. They worked willingly in the fields of the gods and reared the horses and bulls and guarded the sheep. But when the cold days came, they grumbled against Olympus. They grumbled because they must eat and hunt like the animals and had no hoof nor claw nor heavy fur for protection.

What did they need? What protection would be better than hoof or claw? Prometheus knew. It was fire they needed—fire to cook with, to warm them, to harden metal for weapons. With fire they could frighten the wolf and the bear and the mountain lion.

Why did they lack the gift of fire? Prometheus knew that too. He knew how jealously the gods sat guard about their flame.

More than once he had told Zeus the need men had of fire. He knew why Zeus would not consent to teach men this secret of the gods. The gift of fire to men would be a gift of power. Hardened in the fire, the spears which men might make to chase the mountain lion might also, in time, be hurled against the gods. With fire would come comfort and time to think while the flames leaped up the walls of **20** hidden caves. Men who had time to think would have time to question the laws of the gods. Among men who asked questions disorder might breed, and rebellion stronger than any mere squabble in the fields.

"But men are worth the gift of fire," thought Prometheus, sitting against the roots of his favorite ash tree. He could see ahead dimly into that time to come when gods would lose their power. And he, Prometheus, through his love for men, must help to bring on that time.

Prometheus did not hesitate. By the fall of

586 CLASSICAL MYTHOLOGY

night his plans were accomplished. As the sun went down, his tall figure appeared upon a sea beach. Above the sands a hundred caves, long ago deserted by the waters of the ocean, shel-
21 tered families of Arcadians. To them the Titan was bringing this very night the secret of the gods.

He came along the pebble line of high water. In his hand he carried a yellow reed.

This curious yellow stalk was made of metal, the most precious of the metals of the gods. From it the metalworkers molded rare and delicate shapes. From it they made the reedlike and hollow stalks which carried, in wisps of fennel[4] straw, coals from the gods' ever-burning fire. The gods who knew the sources of flame never built new fires in the sight of men. Going abroad on journeys, they took from their central hearth a smoldering coal.

Prometheus had left Olympus as one upon a journey. He alone knew he was not going to visit the home of Poseidon, Zeus's brother, lord of the sea—nor going into India, nor into the cold north. He was going only as far as the nearest sea beach.

22 He knew that, though he was going only to the sea beach, he was in truth starting upon a journey. He knew the hatred of Zeus would follow him. He knew that now he, Prometheus, could never return to the house of the gods. From this night he must live his life among the men he wished to save.

While the stars came out, bright as they are on nights when winter will soon come on, Prometheus gathered together a heap of driftwood. Opening the metal stalk, he set the flame of the gods in the waiting fuel.

Eating into the wood, the fire leaped up, fanned in the night breeze. Prometheus sat down beside the fire he had made. He was not long alone.

---

4. **fennel:** an herb.

Shadowy figures appeared at the mouths of caves. One by one, men, women, and children crept toward the blaze. The night was cold.
23 North winds had blown that day. The winds had blown on the lands of men, even as they had blown on the head of Zeus in his palace above them. Now in the night they came, the people of men, to the warmth of the beckoning fire.

Hundreds there were of them now. Those nearest the tall fire-bringer, the Titan, were talking with him. They knew him well. It was not the first time Prometheus had come to talk with them. But never before had he come late,
24 alone, and lighted a fire against the dark.

It was not the first time men had seen a fire or felt its warmth. More than once a god, walking the earth, had set a fire, lit from the coals he carried secretly. Men reverenced the slender magic wands with which, it seemed, the gods could call up flame. But never before had they stood so near a fire nor seen the firewand.

Now men might hold in their own hands the mysterious yellow rod. They said, "Look" and "See" and, fingering the metal, "How wonderfully the gods can mold what is hard in the hands."

For a while Prometheus let them talk. He watched with pleasure the gleam of firelight in their shining eyes. Then quietly he took the metal stalk from the man who held it. With a swift gesture he threw it into the heap of burning wood.

The people groaned. The fire-wrought metal crumpled against the heat. The metal which carried well a single coal melted in the blazing fire.

The people murmured among themselves, "Hasn't he taken away the secret now? Hasn't he destroyed before our eyes the source of fire?"

Patiently, silently they waited. A few asked

21
Prometheus' sacrifice two-fold: he gives up life he has known and brings about the fall of his own society.

22
Hero. The hero must often make a dangerous journey. For Prometheus, the danger lies not in the task he undertakes but in the consequences he must suffer.

23
The same cold wind blows on Zeus as on the men, yet Zeus will not share his fire (or power) because of his fear.

24
Fire lit against the dark; he literally gives light (knowledge) to their dark (primitive) lives.

25 Summarizing
What do the people think of fire? At first, fire is magical to them, beyond their understanding.

COOPERATIVE LEARNING

After students read this and other myths of explanation, have them work with a partner to write a myth to explain a phenomenon such as cities, nightmares, or the common cold. You could make up a list of possibilities and write the individual items on slips of paper for students to draw from.

Allow students time to write their myths and allow time for them to share their work. You might want to award prizes for the most imaginative stories or the most unusual explanations.

---

26 Drawing Conclusions
Why does Prometheus call aside men who had asked questions? These are the intellectually curious, who will best learn to use his gift.

27
Description. Detailed description of the making of the fire recreates the wonder of the moment.

28
Wood becomes warm due to friction; some scout groups still teach this fire-making technique.

29
Sorrow because of what he has left behind; pleasure because of his gift of fire to men.

30
It takes knowledge of science, not magic, to make fire.

31
Fire will not bring an end to the world but the end of total power of the gods.

32
Zeus, the powerful, can't imagine that Prometheus would willingly give up power.

33
Theme. The discovery of one's own power is a **theme** of the story, and the **hero** is one who brings about such discovery. Here "their own great power" refers to the power of men, as preceding paragraph clarifies.

34
The original myth continues with Zeus's punishment of Prometheus; here the **hero** is an outcast who suffers mentally but not physically.

588

---

questions but got no answers. The cold wind cut them as the last of the burning driftwood grayed and blackened in the sand.

While the embers crumbled away, Prometheus rose, calling with him a few of the men **26** who had asked him questions. Watching, they saw him scrape a hollow pit. Wondering, they followed his every movement, his hands holding a bronze knife, shaving chips of wood, taking from the fold of his cloak handfuls of bark and straw.

27 Next he set in his pit a chunk of ashwood, flat and firm, notched cleanly on one side. Beneath and around this notch he laid in bark and straw. Into the notch he set a pointed branch, slender, hard-tipped, and firm. Then slowly he swung the branch in his palms, twirled it in a steady rhythm, boring, drilling more and more rapidly with his skilled and powerful hands.

28 The wood grew warm. The dust ground from the ash block heated to smoldering. The straw caught. Light sputtered from the pit. Small sparks glowed, flew up, went out. Tugged by the night wind, smoke curled from the dry straw, from the bark, from the wood shavings fed gently from the heap Prometheus had made ready to his hand. At last, more suddenly than the eye could follow, out of the pit in the sand rose the living flame.

Deftly Prometheus removed the ash block, added heavier kindling. Last of all, the driftwood yielded to the strengthening fire. He knelt beside it awhile, breathing upon it, guarding, urging the blaze. At last he rose, **29** stood back, folded his arms. As if considering a thought, half sorrow, half pleasure, he looked up at the glare of fire invading the night sky.

Whispers and murmuring first, then cries, then shouting. Men ran to scoop new hollows in the sand. They begged Prometheus' knife. The children, running from the beach to the caves and fields, hurried back with fists crammed full of straw and withered leaves.

The people of the caves were breathless with excitement. Here was no secret. The fire-wand **30** did not breed the fire as they had thought. No nameless power of the gods bred the flame.

The hard, pale ashwood passed from hand to hand as men struggled to light their own fires. They despaired at first. New sparks flew up and died. Or the hands were weak, too weak to drill the flame. But at last came triumph. A dozen fires sprang up. Women and children ran with laden arms to feed each growing blaze.

The gods, from their distant houses, saw the glow. There to the south it shone, fighting **31** against the starlight, the glare in the sky. Was it the end of the world? Would the terrible fire consume the earth again?

Hermes, the messenger, came at last with an answer to all their questions.

"Great Zeus," said Hermes gravely in the assembly of the gods, "Prometheus, your cousin, stands in the midst of those rising fires. He took coals from the central hearth as for a journey."

"So?" asked Zeus, nodding his head. Then, **32** as if he were holding an argument with himself, he continued, saying, "But then? What then? The fire will die. It is not a crime for a god or for a Titan to light a fire for himself on a cold evening."

"But that fire will not die," interrupted Hermes. "That fire is not the fire of gods and Titans. Prometheus has taught men the source of fire. Those fires are their own, the fires of men. They've drilled flame out of hardwood with their own hands."

Then the gods knew the end of the world was not yet come upon them. But they knew, **33** and Zeus most of all, that it might be their own great power that was burning away in the fires **34** of men.

588 CLASSICAL MYTHOLOGY

MEETING INDIVIDUAL NEEDS
Visual Learners • You might assign each student a god or goddess and have them design a representation of this god or goddess on a piece of poster board. You might suggest that students first find as many illustrations as they can. They will probably want to make copies of the illustrations they find. Students might then use the illustrations they collect to make their own drawing of the god or goddess, using whatever style they prefer. Then, as you discuss the myths in this unit, you could post the appropriate illustrations of the gods or goddesses around the room to aid your discussion.

VISUAL CONNECTIONS
Exploring the Subject
Atlas and Prometheus, both Titans, giants who the Greeks believed once ruled earth violently, opposed Zeus's rule. Zeus defeated them and killed, imprisoned underground, or punished almost all the Titans. (Although this sounds cruel, some scholars see this myth as a Greek attempt to explain how massive land formations such as mountain ranges, peninsulas, and seas were formed: myths related that many of the giants had a hundred hands and loved to pile up boulders.)

Two famous Titans who survived the struggle were Atlas and Prometheus. Atlas held up the sky. Early Greeks believed the sky was a dome-shaped ceiling and the earth was a flat plate, with the Mediterranean Sea in the middle (*medi* = middle of; *terra* = earth). The Mediterranean was thought to be encircled by land and bordered on the outer rim by the great river Ocean.

Zeus punished Prometheus, after his gift of fire to man, by chaining him to a rock in the Caucasus Mountains. Every day, Zeus sent an eagle to feed on Prometheus' liver (shown in this illustration), but the organ would be magically restored overnight. Prometheus' punishment was thus cruel and long-lasting; fortunately, it did not last forever. Being able to see the future, Prometheus knew that one day Hercules would set him free.

Atlas and Prometheus. Attributed to the Arkesilias Painter. Base of a Laconian cup.
Vatican Art Collection

Prometheus the Fire-Bringer **589**

> **TRANSPARENCY 47**
> **Fine Art**
> Theme: *The Heroic Struggle* – invites students to analyze an artwork depicting an epic struggle of a hero.

CLOSURE
Ask students to explain how humans gained the use of fire. Tell students that this story has much in common with other Greek myths. Ask them to speculate on what the myths might have in common.

READING CHECK
1. Zeus's father (p. 583).
2. Nectar and ambrosia (p. 585).
3. Zeus chained them in Tartarus (p. 586).
4. Knew Zeus would win; hoped to guide Zeus (p. 586).
5. Believed it would give human beings power; they would learn to think and to rebel against tyranny (p. 586).

FOR STUDY AND DISCUSSION
1a. Always summer; no work necessary; clothing and shelter unneeded. **1b.** Flood caused destruction in North; winds brought harsh winter; people had no protection against cold.
2a. Believed them worthless, quarrelsome, and too weak to protect themselves. **2b.** That any new race would rebel eventually; that no race of humans could learn wisdom if Zeus kept destroying them; that this race of humans would eventually learn wisdom.
3a. Feared that humans would grow too powerful; they might begin to think and to question "laws of the gods." **3b.** He foresaw a time when humans would be as great as the gods. **3c.** Answers will vary. Students will probably see Prometheus' defiance of the gods as noble, heroic.
4. Zeus displays arrogance, temper, and shortsightedness, while Prometheus displays nobility, altruism, and wisdom.

LANGUAGE AND VOCABULARY
1. Counselor
2. Councilor

Reading Check

1. How was Cronus related to Zeus?
2. How did the gods and goddesses preserve their lives?
3. What had happened to the Titans?
4. Why had Prometheus helped Zeus in the war against the Titans?
5. Why did Prometheus choose fire as his gift to human beings?

For Study and Discussion

Analyzing and Interpreting the Myth

1. The reign of Cronus was known in Greek mythology as the Golden Age. **a.** How was life in that age different from life in later times? **b.** Why did this "age of contentment" end?

2a. Why did Zeus want to destroy the third race of humans? **b.** What objections did Prometheus raise? Summarize Prometheus' arguments in your own words.

3a. Why was Zeus unwilling to give mortals the gift of fire? **b.** Why did Prometheus deliberately disobey Zeus's wishes? **c.** Would you call Prometheus a hero? Why or why not?

4. What human characteristics are shown by Zeus and Prometheus in this myth?

Language and Vocabulary

Distinguishing Homophones

Prometheus, we are told, is Zeus's chief councilor. The word *councilor* means "a member of a council." This word is sometimes confused with its homophone *counselor*, which means "adviser." You have probably heard the word *counselor* used in reference to a lawyer, who gives counsel, or advice. It may help you to avoid confusing these two words if you remember that a *council* is an assembly of people created for a specific purpose, as a town council elected to manage the affairs of a town. The word *counsel* means "advice" or "opinion."

1. Which word—*councilor* or *counselor*—would be used for the person who acts as your program adviser in school?
2. Which word would be used for the delegate to a legislative body?

Focus on Persuasive Writing

Identifying Your Opinion

In an **opinion statement** you identify your topic and state what you believe about it. Writers often use the word *should* in an opinion statement. Read the following examples:

There should be a rating system for television programs.

Our school should offer more courses in music and art.

The seventh grade should organize a class picnic.

Choose one of the topics identified for the assignment on page 582 or select a new topic. Write a one-sentence opinion statement that sums up your position. Save your writing.

590 CLASSICAL MYTHOLOGY

EXTENSION AND ENRICHMENT
Some students might like to read other accounts of the Prometheus myth and tell the class how the great fire-bringer was punished. Others might compose and present a hypothetical **dialogue** between Pandora and Prometheus in which they compare notes on how each changed the world. Another possibility is to have students create and illustrate their own myths explaining how fire originated. The class might pretend to be ancient Greeks and plan a Prometheus Day, on which each student would pay tribute to this god for his contribution to humankind. Tributes might take the form of epithets, poems, speeches, and sketches of trophies or statues.

About the Author

Jeremy Ingalls (1911–)

Jeremy Ingalls was born in Gloucester, Massachusetts. She earned an A.B. and an A.M. from Tufts University and attended the Oriental Institute at the University of Chicago for advanced Chinese studies. She has taught English and Asian studies at many colleges and universities in the United States and has been a Fulbright professor and a Rockefeller Foundation lecturer in Japan. Her first book of poems, *The Metaphysical Sword,* won the prestigious Yale Younger Poets Prize in 1941. She has published many books of prose, poetry, and translations since then. Her poems have been set to music for a symphony orchestra and chorus and translated into Japanese, Korean, French, and Italian. Ingalls' most recent book of poetry is *This Stubborn Quantum: Sixty Poems* (1983).

Literature and Research

Sources of Information

The myth of Pandora is part of the Prometheus story. If you wished to learn about this myth, there are several sources you might consult. An encyclopedia is a useful place to start looking for information. There are dictionaries and encyclopedias of classical mythology. Your library might have a copy of the *Larousse Encyclopedia of Mythology* or *The Meridian Handbook of Classical Mythology.* You can also find retellings of the myths in special collections of mythology, such as *Mythology* by Edith Hamilton and *Gods, Heroes, and Men of Ancient Greece* by W.H.D. Rouse.

Making Connections: Activities

In one of the special reference books listed above or another source, look up the myth of Pandora. If there is no entry under "Pandora," what should you look under? Find the answers to these questions: How did Pandora get her name? What does the myth of Pandora explain? How is she connected to the Prometheus myth?

Connecting Cultures

Comparative Mythology

Many mythologies offer an explanation for the way human beings gained possession of fire. In American Indian mythology, where many of the chief figures are animals, such as Coyote or Raven, fire is obtained through the cunning of these trickster-heroes. In the mythology of the African people of the upper Nile, Dog is the hero who steals fire from the Rainbow and brings it to the human race.

Making Connections: Activities

In a collection of mythologies, locate one of the myths mentioned above or another myth telling how human beings obtained fire. Compare the details of that myth with those of the Prometheus myth. Write a brief essay telling what similarities and differences you have found in the stories.

FOCUS ON PERSUASIVE WRITING
Although an opinion statement presents a point of view rather than a fact, students should be able to support their point of view with reasons and evidence based on facts. When writing opinion statements, students should consider the kinds of information they will use as support. If they generate only more opinions, they should revise their statements.

ABOUT THE AUTHOR
After twenty years of teaching literature, Ingalls retired in 1960 to devote her time to writing. Her prose includes *A Book of Legends* (1941), *The Galilean Way* (1953), and *The Epic Tradition* (1964–65). Collections of her poems include *The Metaphysical Sword* (1941) and *Tahl* (1945). In addition to teaching and writing, she has given lectures on writing at colleges and universities in North America and Asia. She has also been a sponsor for many foreign-exchange students.

LITERATURE AND RESEARCH
1. "Greek Mythology" or "Prometheus."
2. All of the gods gave her gifts, so they called her *Pandora,* which means "the gift of all."
3. Two different versions: One explains the origin of the women, who are created as an evil to men. Other version explains how misfortunes such as sorrow and mischief, countered by hope, are unleashed into the world.
4. Prometheus has tricked Zeus, so Zeus creates Pandora as revenge.

CONNECTING CULTURES
As an alternative activity, have students work in groups to write their own myths about how human beings obtained fire. Before they begin writing, students might want to read some of the myths suggested in the activity.

OBJECTIVES
The overall aim is for students to demonstrate an understanding of the classical myth about Demeter. For a complete list of objectives, see the **Teacher's Notes**.

VOCABULARY
The underlined words are in the Glossary. You may want to prepare students by having them look up the words and write out definitions prior to reading the story.

FOCUS / MOTIVATION
Perhaps have a volunteer explain the cycle of seasons by using a globe and a flashlight. Remind students that such scientific understanding of the universe is a relatively recent development.

TEACHING RESOURCES E
Teacher's Notes, p. 24
Reading Check, p. 28
Study Guide, p. 29
Language Skills, p. 33
Building Vocabulary, p. 35
Selection Vocabulary Test, p. 36
Selection Test, p. 37

AV RESOURCES BINDER
Audiocassette 3, Side A

The Origin of the Seasons

1
Her appearance reflects her special domain; "ears" as in ears of corn, wheat, barley, etc.

2
First gathering of produce in harvest is offered as sacrifice of gratitude to goddess. *Reaping* is harvesting; *threshing* is separating grain from husks by beating; *winnowing* is separating it by sifting.

3 Summarizing
How does the "great mother" give gifts to farmers? Like Mother Earth, she makes things grow.

4
In the ancient manner of "arranged marriages," neither Persephone nor her mother is consulted about Hades' request or Zeus's agreement.

5
Marvelous in the sense of "amazing."

6
Persephone herself is as rare and unique as the flower.

7
Irony. Her youth and eagerness contribute to her downfall.

The Origin of the Seasons

Retold by
OLIVIA COOLIDGE

Like "Prometheus the Fire-Bringer," this is a myth explaining a natural phenomenon. How does the myth account for the cycle of the seasons?

Demeter,[1] the great earth mother, was goddess of the harvest. Tall and majestic was her appearance, and her hair was the color of ripe wheat. It was she who filled the ears with grain. In her honor white-robed women brought golden garlands of wheat as first fruits to the altar. Reaping, threshing, winnowing, and the long tables set in the shade for the harvesters' refreshment—all these were hers. Songs and feasting did her honor as the hard-working farmer gathered his abundant fruit. All the laws which the farmer knew came from her: the time for plowing, what land would best bear crops, which was fit for grapes, and which to leave for pasture. She was a goddess whom men called "the great mother" because of her generosity in giving. Her own special daughter in the family of the gods was named Persephone.[2]

Persephone was the spring maiden, young and full of joy. Sicily was her home, for it is a land where the spring is long and lovely, and where spring flowers are abundant. Here Persephone played with her maidens from day to day till the rocks and valleys rang with the sound of laughter, and gloomy Hades heard it as he sat on his throne in the dark land of the dead. Even his heart of stone was touched by her gay young beauty, so that he arose in his awful majesty and came up to Olympus to ask Zeus if he might have Persephone to wife. Zeus bowed his head in agreement, and mighty Olympus thundered as he promised.

Thus it came about that as Persephone was gathering flowers with her maidens in the vale of Enna, a marvelous thing happened. Enna was a beautiful valley in whose meadows all the most lovely flowers of the year grew at the same season. There were wild roses, purple crocuses, sweet-scented violets, tall irises, rich narcissus, and white lilies. All these the girl was gathering, yet fair as they were, Persephone herself was fairer far.

As the maidens went picking and calling to one another across the blossoming meadow, it happened that Persephone strayed apart from the rest. Then, as she looked a little ahead in the meadow, she suddenly beheld the marvelous thing. It was a flower so beautiful that none like it had ever been known. It seemed a kind of narcissus, purple and white, but from a single root there sprang a hundred blossoms, and at the sweet scent of it the very heavens and earth appeared to smile for joy. Without calling to the others, Persephone sprang forward to be the first to pick the precious bloom. As

1. **Demeter** (dĭ-mē′tər).
2. **Persephone** (pər-sĕf′ə-nē).

592 CLASSICAL MYTHOLOGY

MOTIVATIONAL SUMMARY
Demeter, the great earth mother, is very devoted to her daughter Persephone, the spring maiden. But one day, when Persephone and her friends are picking flowers in the meadow, Persephone disappears. Frantic, Demeter begs everyone for news and tries to determine what could have happened to her daughter. She disguises herself as an old woman and begins to search the earth to try to find her.

PRESENTATION
Demeter, sister of Zeus, was concerned with the sowing, cultivating, and harvesting of crops. Although she was considered to be "good" because of her vigilance over the crops, her moods sometimes resulted in terrible woes for

Persephone and Pluto. Relief, c. 500 B.C.

VISUAL CONNECTIONS
Exploring the Subject
In ancient Greece, Persephone was also called *kore,* or maiden. The word *kore* is also related to the word for corn, which in Europe means any grain-bearing plant (wheat, barley, oats, etc.). The story of Persephone's forced marriage served to explain not only the cycle of the seasons but also the life cycle of grain: the child of the grain (seed) is stolen from its mother (stalk) and hidden in the underworld (buried); it then reappears in the spring as new grain, continuing the cycle.

she stretched out her hand, the earth opened in front of her, and she found herself caught in a stranger's arms. Persephone shrieked aloud and struggled, while the armful of flowers cascaded down to earth. However, the dark-eyed Hades was far stronger than she. He swept her into his golden chariot, took the reins of his coal-black horses, and was gone amid the rumbling sound of the closing earth before the other girls in the valley could even come in sight of the spot. When they did get 8 there, nobody was visible. Only the roses and lilies of Persephone lay scattered in wild confusion over the grassy turf.

Bitter was the grief of Demeter when she heard the news of her daughter's mysterious fate. Veiling herself with a dark cloud she sped, swift as a wild bird, over land and ocean for nine days, searching everywhere and asking all she met if they had seen her daughter. Neither gods nor men had seen her. Even the birds could give no tidings, and Demeter in despair turned to Phoebus Apollo,[3] who sees all things from his chariot in the heavens.

"Yes, I have seen your daughter," said the god at last. "Hades has taken her with the consent of Zeus, that she may dwell in the land of mist and gloom as his queen. The girl struggled and was unwilling, but Hades is far stronger than she."

3. **Phoebus** (fē′bəs) **Apollo:** Apollo, god of the sun, was sometimes called *Phoebus,* which means "shining."

8
Imagery. "Wild confusion" of fallen flowers reflects disturbance of Persephone's former carefree life.

The Origin of the Seasons 593

human beings. When she was happy, humans had plenty to eat as summer crops flourished; when she was angry in winter, fields were barren and food was scarce.

Present "The Origin of the Seasons" as a retelling of an attempt by the early Greeks to explain the alternation of summer and winter. This myth is straightforward enough to be read independently, perhaps as homework.

9 Metamorphosis. The form she assumes reflects her sadness.

10 Her story of capture resembles Persephone's; story of escape reveals Demeter's deepest wish, for daughter's rescue.

11 Her goddesslike qualities cannot be completely hidden by her disguise.

12 Expressing an Opinion
Do you think her planning to take the boy away from his mother is as bad as Hades' taking her daughter? Answers will vary. Some might say that her intentions were better.

13 Ambrosia gives immortality to the gods; she also breathes immortality into him.

14 Fire purifies, purging boy of mortal flesh.

15 Expressing an Opinion
Do you think Metaneira would choose to have her son be immortal if it meant giving him up? Answers will vary. In Greek culture, this godlike quality was valued highly.

When she heard this, Demeter fell into deep despair, for she knew she could never rescue Persephone if Zeus and Hades had agreed. She did not care any more to enter the palace of Olympus, where the gods live in joy and feasting and where Apollo plays the lyre while **9** the Muses sing. She took on her the form of an old woman, worn but stately, and wandered about the earth, where there is much sorrow to be seen. At first she kept away from the homes of people, since the sight of little children and happy mothers gave her pain. One day, however, as she sat by the side of a well to rest her weary feet, four girls came down to draw water. They were kindhearted and charming as they talked with her and concerned themselves about the fate of the homeless stranger-woman who was sitting at their gates. To **10** account for herself, Demeter told them that she was a woman of good family from Crete across the sea, who had been captured by pirates and was to have been sold for a slave. She had escaped as they landed once to cook a meal on shore, and now she was wandering to find work.

11 The four girls listened to this story, much impressed by the stately manner of the strange woman. At last they said that their mother, Metaneira,[4] was looking for a nurse for their newborn brother, Demophoon.[5] Perhaps the stranger would come and talk with her. Demeter agreed, feeling a great longing to hold a baby once more, even if it were not her own. She went therefore to Metaneira, who was much struck with the quiet dignity of the goddess and glad to give her charge of her little son. For a while thereafter Demeter was nurse to Demophoon, and his smiles and babble consoled her in some part for her own darling daughter. She began to make plans for Demophoon: he should be a great hero; he **12** should become an immortal, so that when he grew up she could keep him with her.

Presently the whole household was amazed at how beautiful Demophoon was growing, the more so as they never saw the nurse feed him anything. Secretly Demeter would anoint him **13** with ambrosia, like the gods, and from her breath as he lay in her lap, he would draw his nourishment. When the night came, she would linger by the great fireside in the hall, rocking the child in her arms while the embers burned low and the people went off to sleep. Then when all was still, she would stoop quickly **14** down and put the baby into the fire itself. All night long the child would sleep in the red-hot ashes, while his earthly flesh and blood changed slowly into the substance of the immortals. In the morning when people came, the ashes were cold and dead, and by the hearth sat the stranger-woman, gently rocking and singing to the child.

Presently Metaneira became suspicious of the strangeness of it all. What did she know of this nurse but the story she had heard from her daughters? Perhaps the woman was a witch of some sort who wished to steal or transform the boy. In any case it was wise to be careful. One night, therefore, when she went up to her chamber, she set the door ajar and stood there in the crack silently watching the nurse at the fireside crooning over the child. The hall was very dark, so that it was hard to see clearly, but in a little while the mother beheld the dim figure bend forward. A log broke in the fireplace, a little flame shot up, and there clear in the light lay the baby on top of the fire.

Metaneira screamed loudly and lost no time in rushing forward, but it was Demeter who snatched up the baby. "Fool that you are," she said indignantly to Metaneira, "I would have made your son immortal, but that is now im- **15** possible. He shall be a great hero, but in the

---

4. **Metaneira** (mĕt′ə-nī′rə).
5. **Demophoon** (dī-mŏ′fō-ŏn′).

594 CLASSICAL MYTHOLOGY

end he will have to die. I, the goddess Demeter, promise it." With that, old age fell from her and she grew in stature. Golden hair spread down over her shoulders, so that the great hall was filled with light. She turned and went out of the doorway, leaving the baby on the ground and Metaneira too amazed and frightened even to take him up.

All the while that Demeter had been wandering, she had given no thought to her duties as the harvest goddess. Instead she was almost glad that others should suffer because she was suffering. In vain the oxen spent their strength in dragging the heavy plowshare through the soil. In vain did the sower with his bag of grain throw out the even handfuls of white barley in a wide arc as he strode. The greedy birds had a feast off the seed corn that season, or if it started to sprout, sun baked it and rains washed it away. Nothing would grow. As the gods looked down, they saw threatening the earth a famine such as never had been known. Even the offerings to the gods were neglected by despairing men who could no longer spare anything from their dwindling stores.

At last Zeus sent Iris, the Rainbow, to seek out Demeter and appeal to her to save mankind. Dazzling Iris swept down from Olympus swift as a ray of light and found Demeter sitting in her temple, the dark cloak still around her and her head bowed on her hand. Though Iris urged her with the messages of Zeus and offered beautiful gifts or whatever powers among the gods she chose, Demeter would not lift her head or listen. All she said was that she would neither set foot on Olympus nor let fruit grow on the earth until Persephone was restored to her from the kingdom of the dead.

At last Zeus saw that he must send Hermes of the golden sandals to bring back Persephone to the light. The messenger found dark-haired Hades sitting upon his throne with Persephone beside him, pale and sad. She had neither

Girl picking flowers. Roman wall painting from house in Stabiae, Italy, first century A.D.

eaten nor drunk since she had been in the land of the dead. She sprang up with joy at the message of Hermes, while the dark king looked gloomier than ever, for he really loved his queen. Though he could not disobey the command of Zeus, he was crafty, and he pressed Persephone to eat or drink with him as they parted. Now, with joy in her heart, she should not refuse all food. Persephone was eager to be gone; but since the king entreated her, she took a pomegranate[6] from him to avoid argument and delay. Giving in to his pleading, she

6. **pomegranate** (pŏm'grăn'ĭt): a reddish fruit containing many seeds.

The Origin of the Seasons 595

Cultural Diversity

Demeter disguises herself as an old woman, manifesting the grief she feels at losing Persephone. The use of disguise is a common theme in fairy tales and myths across cultures. Invite students to share stories from their own and other cultures in which the strategy of disguise plays an important part. Who assumes the disguise? What is the objective? Have students ever hidden their true identity from others? For what purpose? How successful were they?

21
Greeks believed Fates knew past and future and determined the length of a mortal's life; gods could not change any of their decisions.

22
Seven months reflect growing season of Greece; number would vary in different regions of world.

23
Personification. The skies smiling or weeping.

ate seven of the seeds. Then Hermes took her with him, and she came out into the upper air. **22**

When Demeter saw Hermes with her daughter, she started up, and Persephone too rushed forward with a glad cry and flung her arms about her mother's neck. For a long time the two caressed each other, but at last Demeter began to question the girl. "Did you eat or drink anything with Hades?" she asked her daughter anxiously, and the girl replied: "Nothing until Hermes released me. Then in my joy I took a pomegranate and ate seven of its seeds."

"Alas," said the goddess in dismay, "my **21** daughter, what have you done? The Fates have said that if you ate anything in the land of shadow, you must return to Hades and rule with him as his queen. However, you ate not the whole pomegranate, but only seven of the seeds. For seven months of the year, therefore, you must dwell in the underworld, and the remaining five you may live with me."

Thus the Fates had decreed, and even Zeus could not alter their law. For seven months of every year Persephone is lost to Demeter and rules pale and sad over the dead. At this time Demeter mourns, trees shed their leaves, cold comes, and the earth lies still and dead. But when in the eighth month Persephone returns, her mother is glad and the earth rejoices. The wheat springs up, bright, fresh, and green in the plowland. Flowers unfold, birds sing, and **23** young animals are born. Everywhere the heavens smile for joy or weep sudden showers of gladness upon the springing earth.

VISUAL CONNECTIONS
About the Artwork
The word *fresco* comes from the Italian word for "fresh." A fresco is a mural painted on a wall which has been freshly plastered; the paint is absorbed by and becomes bonded to the drying plaster. Frescos were popular wall treatments during the Roman Empire period: some popular topics were idealized scenes from nature (as shown), episodes from tales of gods or goddesses, or simple but colorful graphic designs such as top and bottom contrasting-color borders.

CLOSURE

Ask students to summarize the explanation for the origin of the seasons in classical mythology, relating the importance of the seasons to humans' need for food.

EXTENSION AND ENRICHMENT

Students might list images associated with the months of January, March, July, and October. These images might then be used to express the passing of a year—perhaps in a collage, a painting, a song, or a poem.

Have students find myths of other countries to explain cycles of day and night or summer and winter. These myths can then be shared with the class orally or summarized and illustrated for a bulletin-board display or a scrapbook.

Reading Check

1. Whose permission did Hades ask to kidnap Persephone?
2. What was Persephone doing when she was seized?
3. How did Demeter learn that her daughter had been taken to the underworld?
4. Why did Demeter wish to make Demophoon immortal?
5. How did Hades trick Persephone so that he could keep her in his kingdom?

Detail from a fresco, showing a garden from the house of Livia, Rome.

For Study and Discussion

Analyzing and Interpreting the Myth

1. Although the gods and goddesses had special powers denied to mortals, they often behaved like human beings. How was Demeter, goddess of the harvest, affected by her daughter's disappearance?
2. How was life on earth affected by Demeter's suffering? Why were the gods worried?
3a. Tell why Persephone was allowed to return to the earth.   b. Why couldn't she remain all year round?
4. What explanation of the cycle of the seasons is given in this myth?
5. Use the chart on page 576 to find the name of the Roman goddess associated with grains, plants, and fruit. What word do you know that comes from this goddess' name?

For Dramatization

Dramatizing Scenes Based on a Myth

Write a sequel to the story of Demeter, Persephone, and Hades in the form of a play. Begin the action of your play where the action of the myth ends. You might try writing some of the following scenes:

Demeter and Persephone say goodbye as winter approaches and it is time for Persephone to leave.
Hades welcomes Persephone as she arrives in the underworld.
Demeter complains to the other gods and goddesses on Mount Olympus that she does not like her son-in-law.
Persephone returns to the earth in spring.

READING CHECK
1. Zeus's (p. 593).
2. Gathering flowers (p. 593).
3. Apollo told her (p. 593).
4. Wanted a child (p. 594).
5. Persuaded her to eat pomegranate seeds (p. 595).

FOR STUDY AND DISCUSSION
1. Became grief-stricken, veiled herself, and searched for daughter; disguised herself as an old woman.
2. No one is able to harvest grain; seed corn eaten by birds, baked by sun, or washed away by rain. Gods worried about famine, that people would not make offerings of food.
3a. Demeter said she would not allow crops to grow until Persephone returned. 3b. Hades tricked her into eating seven pomegranate seeds; Fates decreed that if she ate anything in the underworld, she must return there.
4. For seven months, Demeter grieves for absent daughter, who is in the underworld; when Persephone returns, Demeter rejoices, and spring comes to earth.
5. *Cereal* comes from *Ceres*.

FOR DRAMATIZATION
In this assignment, students are asked to imagine an additional scene involving characters only sketchily developed in the myth. Before they begin to work—perhaps in small groups—suggest that students decide whether they want to treat their scenes seriously or humorously. Allow time for all scenes to be presented to the class.

The Origin of the Seasons

OBJECTIVES
The overall aim is for students to demonstrate an understanding of the **metamorphosis** of Arachne. For a complete list of objectives, see the **Teacher's Notes.**

VOCABULARY
The underlined words are in the Glossary. Many of the terms associated with weaving might be unfamiliar to students. A list of these words on the board, accompanied by definitions, would help students in their reading.

FOCUS / MOTIVATION
Ask students to recall what happened to the caterpillar in Robert Graves's poem "The Caterpillar" on p. 433. Ask them to give the word applied to what happened when the caterpillar emerged from his cocoon.

TEACHING RESOURCES E
Teacher's Notes, p. 39
Reading Check, p. 51
Study Guide, p. 41
Building Vocabulary, p. 45
Selection Vocabulary Test, p. 59
Selection Test, p. 46

PREREADING FOCUS
Inform students that the myth of Arachne offers an explanation for the characteristics of the spider. Ask students to describe the appearance and the behavior of a spider. Also, have students suggest the characteristics of a human that might have motivated a god or goddess to transform the human into a spider.

Arachne

1
Tmolus is a mountain god.

2
The sand of the river Pactolus turned to gold when King Midas bathed in it; the river freed him from his golden touch, a curse in disguise.

3
Minerva is Roman name for Athena.

4
Foreshadowing. Greeks considered boastful pride, or *hubris*, a fault that always led to tragedy.

5 Making Generalizations
Why does Arachne react angrily? Because of stubborn pride.

Arachne°

Retold by
REX WARNER

Through the power of a god or goddess, a human being could be changed into a plant, an animal, or a constellation. There are many stories of such transformations in classical mythology. The Greek word for "transformation" is metamorphosis, a word scientists now use to describe the changes during the life cycles of such creatures as the butterfly and the frog.

In mythology, metamorphosis is sudden and magical. In this myth, the metamorphosis explains how something in nature came to be.

Arachne was famous not for her birth or for her city, but only for her skill. Her father was a dyer of wool; her mother also was of no great family. She lived in a small village whose name is scarcely known. Yet her skill in weaving made her famous through all the great cities of Lydia. To see her wonderful work the nymphs 1 of Tmolus would leave their vineyards, the 2 nymphs of Pactolus would leave the golden waters of their river. It was a delight not only to see the cloth that she had woven, but to watch her at work, there was such beauty in the way she did it, whether she was winding the rough skeins into balls of wool, or smoothing it with her fingers, or drawing out the fleecy shiny wool into threads, or giving a twist to the spindle with her quick thumb, or putting in embroidery with her needle. You would think that 3 she had learned the art from Minerva herself, the goddess of weaving.

Arachne, however, when people said this, would be offended at the idea of having had 4 even so great a teacher as Minerva. "Let her come," she used to say, "and weave against me. If she won, she could do what she liked with me."

Minerva heard her words and put on the form of an old woman. She put false gray hair on her head, made her steps weak and tottering, and took a staff in her hand. Then she said to Arachne: "There are some advantages in old age. Long years bring experience. Do not, then, refuse my advice. Seek all the fame you like among men for your skill, but allow the goddess to take first place, and ask her forgiveness, you foolish girl, for the words which you have spoken. She will forgive you if you ask her."

5 Arachne dropped the threads from her hand and looked angrily at the old woman. She hardly kept her hands off her, and her face showed the anger that she felt. Then she spoke to the goddess in disguise: "Stupid old thing, what is wrong with you is that you have lived too long. Go and give advice to your daughters, if you have any. I am quite able to look

° **Arachne** (ə-răk′nē).

598 CLASSICAL MYTHOLOGY

MOTIVATIONAL SUMMARY

Arachne is a common girl who has one great talent: she can weave as if she were taught by the goddess Minerva herself. Rather than being grateful or gracious about her talent, however, she brags to an old woman that she is as good a weaver as the goddess. Imagine her surprise when the old woman throws off her disguise and reveals herself to be none other than the goddess Minerva! The goddess challenges Arachne to a contest to determine which of them is the better weaver.

PRESENTATION

Spark a discussion of characters who undergo dramatic changes—for example, Clark Kent / Superman, Dr. Jekyll / Mr. Hyde, and the fairy-tale prince who is reduced to an ugly frog. Observe that transformation stories, firmly rooted in clas-

VISUAL CONNECTIONS
Exploring the Subject

The culture of classical Greece was largely forgotten during the "Dark Ages," the centuries that followed the fall of the Roman Empire. The Renaissance was as much a rediscovery as a rebirth of interest in classical culture. Europeans began to incorporate classical **allusions** into art, music, and literature. In many cases, classical characters were depicted in clothing styles appropriate to the painter's era rather than to the myth's original time frame.

Detail from the *Month of March: The Triumph of Minerva* by Francesco del Cossa (1436–1478). Fresco. Palazzo Schiffanoia, Ferrara, Italy after myself. As for what you say, why does not the goddess come here herself? Why does she avoid a contest with me?"

"She has come," Minerva replied, and she put off the old woman's disguise, revealing herself in her true form. The nymphs bowed down to worship her, and the women also who were there. Arachne alone showed no fear. Nevertheless she started,[1] and a sudden blush came to her unwilling face and then faded away again, as the sky grows crimson at the moment of sunrise and then again grows pale. She persisted in what she had said already, and stupidly longing for the desired victory, rushed headlong to her fate.

Minerva no longer refused the contest and gave no further advice. At once they both set up their looms and stretched out on them the delicate warp. The web was fastened to the beam; reeds separated the threads and through the threads went the sharp shuttles which their quick fingers sped. Quickly they worked, with their clothes tucked up round their breasts, their skilled hands moving backward and forward like lightning, not feeling the work since they were both so good at it. In their weaving they used all the colors that are made by the merchants of Tyre—purple of the oyster and every other dye, each shading into each, so that the eye could scarcely tell the difference between the finer shades, though the extreme colors were clear enough. So, after a storm of rain, when a rainbow spans the sky, between each color there is a great difference, but still between each an insensible shading. And in their work they wove in stiff threads of gold, telling ancient stories by pictures.

Minerva, in her weaving, showed the ancient citadel of Athens and the story of the old quarrel between her and Neptune, god of the sea, over the naming of this famous land.[2] There you could see the twelve gods as witnesses, and there Neptune striking with his huge trident[3] the barren rock from which leaped a stream of sea water. And there was Minerva herself, with shield and spear and helmet. As she struck the rock there sprang up a green olive tree, and the victory was hers. Athens was her city, named from her other name, Athene.

As for Arachne, the pictures which she wove were of the deceitful loves of the gods. There was Europa, carried away by a bull over the sea. You would have thought it a real bull and real waves of water. Then she wove Jupiter coming to Danae in a golden shower, to Aegina as a flame, to Mnemosyne,[4] mother of the Muses, in the disguise of a shepherd. There was Neptune too, disguised as a dolphin, a horse, or a ram. Every scene was different, and each scene had the surroundings that it ought to have. Round the edge of the web ran a narrow border filled with designs of flowers and sprays of ivy intertwined.

Neither Minerva nor Envy itself could find any fault with Arachne's work. Furious at the success of the mortal girl, Minerva tore to pieces the gorgeous web with its stories of the crimes of the gods. With the hard boxwood spindle that she held, she struck Arachne on the head over and over again.

Arachne could not bear such treatment. In her injured pride she put a noose round her neck and hanged herself. As she hung from the rope, Minerva, in pity, lifted her body and said: "You may keep your life, you rude and arrogant girl, but you and all your descendants will still hang."

---

1. **started:** here, made a sudden movement from fear or surprise.
2. **the naming . . . land:** a reference to a contest that was held to see which god could give the better gift to the city and thus become its protector.
3. **trident** (trīd′ənt): a spear with three prongs.
4. **Europa** (yōō-rō′pə); **Danae** (dăn′ə-ē′); **Aegina** (ē-jī′nə); **Mnemosyne** (nĭ-mŏs′ə-nē): women loved by Jupiter. Danae was the mother of the hero Perseus.

12   Then, as she went out, she sprinkled over her some magic juices, and immediately her hair felt the poison it fell off; so did her nose and ears; her head became minute and all her body shrunk; her slender fingers were joined onto her body as legs; everything else was
13   stomach and now, turned into a spider, she still spins threads out of her own stomach and everywhere still exercises her old craft of weaving.

Reading Check

1. How did Minerva disguise herself to visit Arachne?
2. What advice did she give Arachne?
3. What quarrel did the goddess depict in her tapestry?
4. Which scenes did Arachne choose for her tapestry?
5. Why did Arachne hang herself?

For Study and Discussion

Analyzing and Interpreting the Myth

1. The ancient Greeks connected many things in nature with the actions of gods and mortals. How does the myth of Arachne explain the characteristics of the spider?

2. The myth of Arachne reveals that human beings could choose to please or offend the gods. What sin did Arachne commit?

3. What lesson do you think the ancient Greeks drew from the myth of Arachne?

About the Author

Rex Warner (1905–1986)

Rex Warner, an authority on classical literature, was born in England. He was educated at Oxford. Warner's books on the ancient world include *Pericles the Athenian*, *Imperial Caesar*, and *Men of Athens*. Warner also published many translations of classical works, including *Three Great Plays of Euripides*, *The Peloponnesian Wars* by Thucydides, and *Caesar's War Commentaries*. "Arachne" is from the collection of myths called *Men and Gods*.

OBJECTIVES
The overall aim is for students to demonstrate an understanding of how the Greeks used stories to teach proper behavior. For a complete list of objectives, see the **Teacher's Notes**.

VOCABULARY
The underlined words are in the Glossary. Students might familiarize themselves with words used to describe the old couple preparing the meal: *potherbs, flitch, beechen bowl, cornel berries,* etc.

FOCUS / MOTIVATION
Ask students to speculate on what their reactions might be if a stranger came to their door. Would they ask the stranger to come in and eat with them? How does today's society make such a possibility unlikely?

> **TEACHING RESOURCES E**
> Teacher's Notes, p. 48
> Reading Check, p. 51
> Study Guide, p. 52
> Language Skills, p. 54
> Building Vocabulary, p. 57
> Selection Vocabulary Test, p. 59
> Selection Test, p. 60

PREREADING FOCUS
Write *hospitality* on the board. Ask students to give examples that demonstrate hospitality. What part do qualities such as courtesy, respect, generosity, and friendliness play?

The Reward of Baucis and Philemon

1
Jupiter is Roman name for Zeus; *Mercury* is Roman name for Hermes, the messenger god.

2
Greeks and Romans valued hospitality; here the king of gods and his son test villagers' hospitality and find it lacking.

3
Characterization. Clearly the old couple is offering every available courtesy to guests.

4
"Scanty breath" and "trembling hands" show her old age.

5
Flitch is "a side or strip"; *beechen* means "made of beechwood."

6 Finding Details
What are some of the hosts' courtesies that honor the guests? Some responses may be the warm wash water, the special cloth, and the aromatic herbs.

7
Minerva (Athene) never married *(chaste);* she gave humans the olive tree.

602

The Reward of Baucis and Philemon°

Retold by
SALLY BENSON

In addition to being the ruler of the Olympians, Zeus was also the protector of guests. As you will see in this myth, inhospitality was considered an offense against the gods.

1   Once upon a time, Jupiter assumed human shape and taking his son Mercury journeyed to Phrygia.¹ Mercury had left his wings behind so that no one would know he was a god, and the two presented themselves from door to door as weary travelers, seeking rest and shelter. They found all doors closed to them as it was late, and the inhospitable inhabitants would not bother to let them in. At last, they came to a small thatched cottage where Baucis, a feeble old woman, and her husband, Philemon, lived. They were a kindly couple, not ashamed of their poverty, and when the two strangers knocked at their door, they bade them enter. The old man placed a seat, on which Baucis, bustling and attentive, spread a cloth, and begged his guests to sit down. Then Baucis raked out the coals from the ashes and kindled up a fire, fed it with leaves and dry bark, and with her scanty breath blew it into flames. She brought split sticks and dry branches out of a corner, broke them up, and placed them under a small kettle. Philemon collected some potherbs in the garden, and she shred them from the stalks and prepared them for the pot. He reached down with a forked stick a flitch of bacon hanging in the chimney, cut a small piece, and put it in the pot to boil with the herbs. A beechen bowl was filled with warm water, that their guests might wash. Host and visitors talked amicably together.

On the bench designed for the guests, a cushion stuffed with seaweed was laid; and a cloth, only produced on great occasions, was spread over that. The old lady, with her apron on, set the table with trembling hands. When the table was fixed, she rubbed it down with sweet-smelling herbs, and upon it she set some of chaste Minerva's olives, some cornel berries preserved in vinegar, and added radishes and cheese, with eggs lightly cooked in the ashes.

° **Baucis** (bô′sĭs); **Philemon** (fĭ-lē′mən).
1. **Phrygia** (frĭj′ē-ə): an ancient country in western Asia, now part of Turkey.

Philemon and Baucis (1658) by Rembrandt van Rijn (1606–1669). Oil on panel.
Widener Collection, © 1994 Board of Trustees, National Gallery of Art, Washington

602 CLASSICAL MYTHOLOGY

MOTIVATIONAL SUMMARY

Baucis and Philemon are an old, poor couple who live in a small thatched cottage. Late one night, there is a knock at their door, and they open it to find two richly dressed strangers. Remembering that one of Jupiter's particular concerns is hospitality to strangers, they invite the two travelers into their poor home and offer all they can of food and drink for their guests. But then strange things begin to happen.

PRESENTATION

The story of Baucis and Philemon, much like the story of Arachne, teaches a lesson through the idea of transformation. In the case of Baucis and Philemon, however, their transformations are a boon rather than a punishment. Baucis and Phi-

VISUAL CONNECTIONS
Exploring the Subject

This painting by Rembrandt, one of Europe's great masters, portrays the moment of Philemon and Baucis' recognition that the visitors to their humble home are actually Olympian gods. All of them are shown in contemporary attire: Jupiter and Mercury are dressed like nobles and the peasant couple is shown in rough farmers' clothing. The goose the two old people plan to offer for the gods' dinner is also shown in this painting, trying to escape from Baucis' grasp. Behind the two gods appears a radiance, as they reveal themselves in their immortal glory.

The **theme** of the myth appealed to people of Rembrandt's era for many of the same reasons as it appealed to the Greeks who first told it: the virtues emphasized—hospitality, humility, deference—were still as important in seventeenth-century Europe as they were in ancient Greece.

The Reward of Baucis and Philemon

lemon are rewarded for their hospitality toward the gods. If time permits, read the myth aloud to the class. Oral reading will ensure correct pronunciation of proper names and allow students to concentrate on the substance of the myth.

ART LINK
You might read the last paragraph of this myth aloud and have students interpret the end of the story with an illustration—in the style of a Greek fresco or Roman tapestry, for example. Have a collection of art materials available, such as chalk, pastels, pen and ink, crayon, tempera, or perhaps even finger paint. Students can either work in small groups or by themselves.

8
Sincerity of welcome is most important detail.

9
Characterization. Couple fears they have offended the strangers with their poverty.

10
Jupiter was guardian of hospitality; honor shown to stranger was thus duty performed to gods.

11
"Arrow's flight of the top" is distance arrow could fly between them and top of hill.

12
First wish honors gods; second wish honors each other.

13 Summarizing
How do the gods grant their second wish? By turning the couple into trees.

READING CHECK
1. When wine renewed itself in pitcher (p. 604).
2. To sacrifice their goose (p. 604).
3. Changed into temple (p. 604).
4. Their prayer to die together (p. 604).

604

Everything was served in earthenware dishes, and an earthenware pitcher with wooden cups stood beside them. When all was ready, the stew, smoking hot, was set on the table. Some wine, mild and sweet, was served, and for dessert they offered wild apples and honey. Over **8** and above all, there were the friendly faces and simple, hearty welcome of the old couple.

As the visitors ate and drank, Baucis and Philemon were astonished to see that the wine, as fast as it was poured out, renewed itself in **9** the pitcher. Struck with terror, they recognized their heavenly guests and, falling to their knees, implored forgiveness for the poor entertainment. They had an old goose which they kept as the guardian of their humble cottage and they decided to sacrifice him in honor of their illustrious visitors. But the goose was too nimble and eluded the elderly couple, and at last he took shelter between the gods themselves.

Jupiter and Mercury forbade it to be slain, **10** and spoke in these words: "We are gods. This inhospitable village shall pay the penalty of its impiety. You alone shall go free from the chastisement. Quit your house and come with us to the top of yonder hill."

Baucis and Philemon hastened to obey and labored up the steep ascent. They had reached **11** up to an arrow's flight of the top, when they beheld all the country they had left sunk into a lake, only their own house left standing. While they gazed with wonder at the sight, their house was changed into a temple. Columns took the place of the corner posts, the thatch grew yellow and turned to gold, the floors became marble, the doors were enriched with exquisite carvings and ornaments of gold.

Then Jupiter spoke to them kindly. "Excellent old man, and woman worthy of such a husband," he said, "speak! Tell us your wishes. What favor have you to ask us?"

12 Philemon whispered to his wife for a few minutes, and then declared to the gods their united wish. "We ask to be priests and guardians of this your temple. And since we have passed our lives in love and concord, we wish that one and the same hour may take us both from life, that I may not live to see her grave nor be laid in my own by her."

Their prayers were granted. They were keepers of the temple as long as they lived. When they were very old, as they stood one day before the steps of the sacred temple and were telling the story of the place to some visitors, Baucis saw Philemon begin to put forth leaves, and old Philemon saw Baucis changing in a like manner. And now a leafy crown had grown over their heads. As long as they could speak they exchanged parting words. "Farewell, dear spouse," they said together, as the **13** bark closed over their mouths.

Still on a certain hill in Phrygia, stand a linden tree and an oak enclosed by a low wall. Not far from the spot is a marsh, formerly good habitable land, but now dotted with pools, the haunt of fen birds and cormorants.[2] They are all that is left of the town and of Baucis and Philemon.

2. **fen birds and cormorants** (kôr′mər-ənts): birds that inhabit watery land.

> **Reading Check**
> 1. At what point did Baucis and Philemon realize that they had been entertaining gods?
> 2. How did Baucis and Philemon offer to honor their visitors?
> 3. How was their cottage transformed?
> 4. What favor did Jupiter grant?

604 CLASSICAL MYTHOLOGY

CLOSURE

Ask students to tell what lesson ancient Greeks might have learned from the story of Baucis and Philemon's reward. How do their transformations differ from Arachne's?

EXTENSION AND ENRICHMENT

Students might illustrate various myths of transformation by drawing before-and-after sketches of the characters they research for the **Literature and Research** exercise.

For Study and Discussion

Analyzing and Interpreting the Myth

1. Why did Jupiter and Mercury punish the inhabitants of Phrygia?

2. How was the metamorphosis of Baucis and Philemon a reward?

3. What lesson do you think was drawn from the myth of Baucis and Philemon?

Creative Writing

▶ **Writing a Story About Metamorphosis**

Choose some natural object, and write an original story explaining how and why someone was transformed into the object. Here are some suggestions:

a butterfly	an octopus
a diamond	a violet
a giraffe	a water lily
a lobster	a weeping willow
a mosquito	a whale

Decide which classical gods and goddesses might play a part in your story.

About the Author

Sally Benson (1900–1972)

Sally Benson wrote short stories for *The New Yorker* beginning in 1930. A collection of her short stories, *Junior Miss*, was published in 1941, and later became the basis for a comedy. She was the joint author of the screenplay for *Anna and the King of Siam*, and also wrote *The Young and the Beautiful*, a play based on F. Scott Fitzgerald's "Josephine" stories in the *Saturday Evening Post*, and *Seventeen*, a musical comedy based on Booth Tarkington's *Seventeen*. The selection in this anthology is from *Stories of the Gods and Heroes*.

Literature and Research

Entries in Reference Books

You may not always find the information you need listed in a dictionary or encyclopedia under the specific name or event you are researching. You may not find the reference you are looking for in the table of contents or the index. This does not mean, however, that the information is not available. You may need to check under a different or broader entry. For example, if you were looking for information about a minor character in classical mythology, you might not find an entry under that character's name. You would need to see if the character is mentioned in a general article on "Mythology" or "Greek Mythology" or "Classical Mythology."

Making Connections: Activities

Here are the names of some other figures in Greek mythology who were transformed by the gods:

Adonis	Daphne	Narcissus
Alcyone	Echo	Orion
Clytie	Hyacinthus	Scylla

1. Choose one of these characters and find out 1) why the person was transformed, 2) what the person was transformed into, and 3) which god or goddess was involved in the story. Then tell the story to the class in your own words.

▶ Before students begin this writing assignment, you may want to refer them to the **Practice in Reading and Writing** section on p. 139.

FOR STUDY AND DISCUSSION

1. Because of their inhospitality.
2. They were granted their wish of being taken from human life at the same time and allowed to be together as trees.
3. Cautions against inhospitality—even to strangers.

ABOUT THE AUTHOR

Other collections of Benson's short stories are *People Are Fascinating* (1936) and *Emily* (1938). Under the pen name of Esther Evarts, she contributed stories and reviews of stories to *The New Yorker* and other magazines. Other film scripts include *National Velvet* (1944), *The Farmer Takes a Wife* (1953), and *The Adventures of Huckleberry Finn* (1960). She received an Academy Award nomination for *Anna and the King of Siam* in 1946.

LITERATURE AND RESEARCH

1. **Adonis,** loved by Aphrodite, was changed into an anemone at death.
Alcyone, pitied by Hera, was changed into sea bird along with her drowned husband.
Clytie loved the Sun-god. As a sunflower, she continues to follow his movement.
Daphne was changed into a laurel tree by river-god Peneus to escape Apollo.
Echo, deprived of independent speech by Hera, pined for love of Narcissus until only her voice was left.
Hyacinthus was accidentally killed by Apollo, who changed him into a flower.
Narcissus, enchanted by Nemesis, fell in love with his own reflection. A flower grew where he died gazing at himself.
Orion was killed by Artemis, who placed him in heavens as a constellation.
Scylla, loved by sea-god Glaucus, was changed into a monster by enchantress Circe.

The Reward of Baucis and Philemon

OBJECTIVES
The overall aim is for students to demonstrate an understanding of the relationship of the zodiac to classical mythology.

PRESENTATION
Mention that the word *zodiac* comes from Greek words meaning "circle of carved figures," and then ask students to explain the image. Ready-made interest in signs of the zodiac should motivate students to apply reference skills and extend acquaintance with many of these mythological figures. Students will then easily relate the names of mythological figures to the names of constellations and of chemical elements.

Classical Mythology in Today's World

1. **Aries:** golden-fleeced ram rescued Phrixus and Helle, children threatened by wicked queen.
Cancer: crab Hera sent to attack Hercules while fighting Hydra.
Leo: Nemean lion slain by Hercules.
Sagittarius: probably, Chiron centaur who tutored Jason and other Greek heroes.
Capricorn: probably, goat Amalthea, who fed infant Zeus.
Pisces: Aphrodite and Eros used these fish shapes to escape from monster.

2. **Andromeda** was to be sacrificed to sea monster because of boast made by **Cassiopeia,** her mother. **Cepheus** was Andromeda's father; **Perseus** slew Medusa and used head to turn monster to stone, rescuing Andromeda.
Cygnus became a swan.
Pleiades were seven sisters pursued by Orion.
Ursa Major and **Ursa Minor,** once mother and son, were changed to big and little bears (*ursa* = bear).

3. Thanksgiving. **Cornucopia** means horn of plenty, named after horn of Amalthea, the goat that fed infant Zeus.

4. **Cerium,** named for Ceres, Roman goddess of harvest.
Helium for Helios, the sun.
Mercury, for swift messenger of gods.
Neptunium for Neptune, Roman sea god.
Plutonium for Pluto, god of underworld.
Selenium for Selene, goddess of moon.
Uranium for Uranus, god of heavens overthrown by Titans.

606

Classical Mythology in Today's World

The *zodiac* is an imaginary belt in the sky, divided into twelve parts called *signs* of the zodiac. Each of the signs is named for a different constellation. On its path through the sky, the sun passes through this imaginary circle, spending one month in each of the twelve parts.

The signs of the zodiac are shown on these pages. The first sign of the zodiac is *Aries,* "the ram." The second sign of the zodiac is *Taurus,* "the bull." The other signs, in order, are *Gemini,* "the twins"; *Cancer,* "the crab"; *Leo,* "the lion"; *Virgo,* "the maiden"; *Libra,* "the balance"; *Scorpio,* "the scorpion"; *Sagittarius,* "the archer"; *Capricorn,* "the horned goat"; *Aquarius,* "the water-bearer"; and *Pisces,* "the fish."

Each person has a sign determined by his or her date of birth. Find out what your sign is by looking up the entry for *zodiac* in a dictionary or an encyclopedia.

1 Find out how each of these signs is connected with classical mythology. (Consult the reference books listed on page 591.)

| Aries | Leo | Capricorn |
| Cancer | Sagittarius | Pisces |

2 Many of the constellations are named for figures in classical mythology. Locate, read, and summarize a myth associated with one of these constellations:

Andromeda	Perseus
Cassiopeia	Pleiades
Cepheus	Ursa Major (Big Dipper)
Cygnus	Ursa Minor (Little Dipper)

3 With what American holiday is the cornucopia associated? Find out why the cornucopia is associated with Zeus.

4 Seven of the chemical elements in this list are named for figures in classical mythology. Identify the seven elements and the figures for whom they are named.

antimony	helium	plutonium
californium	krypton	selenium
cerium	mercury	uranium
einsteinium	neptunium	yttrium

606 CLASSICAL MYTHOLOGY

CLOSURE
Ask students to explain briefly three ways that classical mythology is related to today's world.

Celestial globe with clockwork, supported by Pegasus (1566–1584) by Gerhard Emmoser. Silver, gilt, and brass.

Metropolitan Museum of Art, Gift of J. Pierpont Morgan, 1917. (17.190.636)

VISUAL CONNECTIONS
Exploring the Subject
Pegasus, the winged horse, has always been a popular figure. Greek myth says that Pegasus sprang from the body of Medusa when she was slain by Perseus. He then became the special favorite of Athena. Only once did Athena allow him to be ridden: she lent him to the hero Bellerophon, who needed the special advantage the aerial steed could give him in fighting a fire-breathing monster, the Chimera. Later, convinced that he deserved to join the company of the immortals on Mt. Olympus, Bellerophon attempted to fly there on Pegasus. The winged horse bucked him off in mid-air and flew alone to the abode of the gods. The Olympians set him among the stars (Pegasus is a constellation near the vernal equinox).

Classical Mythology in Today's World

Phaethon

Retold by EDITH HAMILTON

In classical mythology there are many stories of mortals who attempt too much, who try to rival the powers of the gods and goddesses. This is the story of a boy who for a few moments "felt himself the lord of the sky." How do you think Phaethon's adventure would have been viewed by the ancient Greeks—as an act of heroism or of arrogance?

The palace of the Sun was a radiant place. It shone with gold and gleamed with ivory and sparkled with jewels. Everything without and within flashed and glowed and glittered. It was always high noon there. Shadowy twilight never dimmed the brightness. Darkness and night were unknown. Few among mortals could have long endured that unchanging brilliancy of light, but few had ever found their way thither.

Nevertheless, one day a youth, mortal on his mother's side, dared to approach. Often he had to pause and clear his dazzled eyes, but the errand which had brought him was so urgent that his purpose held fast and he pressed on, up to the palace, through the burnished doors, and into the throne room where surrounded by a blinding, blazing splendor the sun god sat. There the lad was forced to halt. He could bear no more.

Nothing escapes the eyes of the Sun. He saw the boy instantly and he looked at him very kindly. "What brought you here?" he asked.

"I have come," the other answered boldly, "to find out if you are my father or not. My mother said you were, but the boys at school laugh when I tell them I am your son. They will not believe me. I told my mother and she said I had better go and ask you."

Smiling, the Sun took off his crown of burning light so that the lad could look at him without distress. "Come here, Phaethon," he said. "You are my son. Clymene[1] told you the truth. I expect you will not doubt my word too? But I will give you a proof. Ask anything you want of me and you shall have it. I call the Styx[2] to be witness to my promise, the river of the oath of the gods."

No doubt Phaethon had often watched the Sun riding through the heavens and had told himself with a feeling, half awe, half excitement, "It is my father up there." And then he would wonder what it would be like to be in that chariot, guiding the steeds along that dizzy course, giving light to the world. Now at his father's words this wild dream had become possi-

° **Phaethon** (fā′ə-thən).

1. **Clymene** (klĭm′ə-nē).
2. **Styx** (stĭks): one of the rivers in the underworld.

MOTIVATIONAL SUMMARY

Phaethon is a young man who has been told by his mother that his father is the god of the Sun. For years, he has endured the taunts of other boys who do not believe that his father is the Sun god, as Phaethon has told them. Braving many dangers, he travels far across the world to the palace of the Sun, intending to discover the truth of his parentage. Phaethon has thought of a way to prove—to everyone—that he is the son of the Sun.

PRESENTATION

Ask what picture of the sky has been suggested by the myths read so far in this unit. How scientifically accurate is this picture? Explain that "Phaethon" reflects an attempt to account for the daily journey of the sun across the heavens.

---

ble. Instantly he cried, "I choose to take your place, Father. That is the only thing I want. Just for a day, a single day, let me have your car to drive."

The Sun realized his own folly. Why had he taken that fatal oath and bound himself to give in to anything that happened to enter a boy's rash young head? "Dear lad," he said, "this is the only thing I would have refused you. I know I cannot refuse. I have sworn by the Styx. I must yield if you persist. But I do not believe you will. Listen while I tell you what this is you want. You are Clymene's son as well as mine. You are mortal and no mortal could drive my chariot. Indeed, no god except myself can do that. The ruler of the gods cannot. Consider the road. It rises up from the sea so steeply that the horses can hardly climb it, fresh though they are in the early morning. In midheaven it is so high that even I do not like to look down. Worst of all is the descent, so precipitous that the sea gods waiting to receive me wonder how I can avoid falling headlong. To guide the horses, too, is a perpetual struggle. Their fiery spirits grow hotter as they climb and they scarcely suffer³ my control. What would they do with you?

"Are you fancying that there are all sorts of wonders up there, cities of the gods full of beautiful things? Nothing of the kind. You will have to pass beasts, fierce beasts of prey, and they are all that you will see. The Bull, the Lion, the Scorpion, the great Crab, each will try to harm you. Be persuaded. Look around you. See all the goods the rich world holds. Choose from them your heart's desire and it shall be yours. If what you want is to be proved my son, my fears for you are proof enough that I am your father."

But none of all this wise talk meant anything to the boy. A glorious prospect opened before him. He saw himself proudly standing in that wondrous car, his hands triumphantly guiding those steeds which Jove himself could not master. He did not give a thought to the dangers his father detailed. He felt not a quiver of fear, not a doubt of his own powers. At last the Sun gave up trying to dissuade him. It was hopeless, as he saw. Besides, there was no time. The moment for starting was at hand. Already the gates of the east glowed purple, and Dawn had opened her courts full of rosy light. The stars were leaving the sky; even the lingering morning star was dim.

There was need for haste, but all was ready. The Seasons, the gatekeepers of Olympus, stood waiting to fling the doors wide. The horses had been bridled and yoked to the car. Proudly and joyously Phaethon mounted it and they were off. He had made his choice. Whatever came of it he could not change now. Not that he wanted to in that first exhilarating rush through the air, so swift that the East Wind was outstripped and left far behind. The horses' flying feet went through the low-banked clouds near the ocean as through a thin sea mist and then up and up in the clear air, climbing the height of heaven. For a few ecstatic moments Phaethon felt himself the lord of the sky. But suddenly there was a change. The chariot was swinging wildly to and fro; the pace was faster; he had lost control. Not he, but the horses were directing the course. That light weight in the car, those feeble hands clutching the reins, had told them their own driver was not there. They were the masters then. No one else could command them. They left the road and rushed where they chose, up, down, to the right, to the left. They nearly wrecked the chariot against the Scorpion; they brought up short and almost ran into the Crab. By this time the poor charioteer was half fainting with terror, and he let the reins fall.

3. **suffer:** here, bear.

---

9 "Fatal" refers to unbreakable nature of oath as well as to outcome of Phaethon's wild ride.

10 Helios' first reason: even other gods cannot drive chariot.

11 Finding Main Ideas
What is the road Helios describes? Path of sun.

12 Second reason: road is steep, and Phaethon cannot control horses.

13 Third reason: chariot must pass dangerous animals.

14 Conflict. The wisdom of the father loses to the foolishness of the son.

15 Jove is Roman variant of Jupiter.

16 As Helios warned, horses sense Phaethon's inexperience.

Phaethon **609**

VISUAL CONNECTIONS
Exploring the Subject
The story of Phaethon's ill-fated journey across the heavens not only provided a warning against youthful over-enthusiasm but also provided ancient Greeks with an explanation for certain natural phenomena. Phaethon's driving the sun chariot too far from the earth was used to explain the frozen arctic regions; his driving too close was used to explain the desert regions of North Africa as well as the dark (i.e., burned) skin of its inhabitants.

The Fall of Phaethon by Peter Paul Rubens (1577–1640). Watercolor drawing.

17 Dropping reins is another mistake; he now cannot even attempt to steer the chariot.

18 Muses were goddesses of music and art.

17 That was the signal for still more mad and reckless running. The horses soared up to the very top of the sky and then, plunging headlong down, they set the world on fire. The highest mountains were the first to burn, Ida
18 and Helicon, where the Muses dwell, Parnassus, and heaven-piercing Olympus. Down their slopes the flame ran to the low-lying valleys and the dark forest lands, until all things everywhere were ablaze. The springs turned into steam; the rivers shrank. It is said that it was then the Nile fled and hid his head, which still is hidden.

In the car Phaethon, hardly keeping his

PORTFOLIO ASSESSMENT

Pairs of students may want to write a ballad about the tragic story of Phaethon, put it to music, and audiotape or videotape it for inclusion in their portfolios. Suggest that student pairs use rhyming couplets as their line form and that they choose simple, easily rhymed words for the end of each line, such as *son, day, wish, mad, fire,* and *die.* Peer editors may suggest revisions for wording, rhythm, and rhyme. (See *Portfolio Assessment and Professional Support Materials* for additional information on student portfolios.)

---

place there, was wrapped in thick smoke and heat as if from a fiery furnace. He wanted nothing except to have this torment and terror ended. He would have welcomed death. Mother Earth, too, could bear no more. She uttered a great cry which reached up to the gods. Looking down from Olympus they saw that they must act quickly if the world was to be saved. Jove seized his thunderbolt and hurled it at the rash, repentant driver. It struck him dead, shattered the chariot, and made the maddened horses rush down into the sea.

Phaethon all on fire fell from the car through the air to the earth. The mysterious river Eridanus, which no mortal eyes have ever seen, received him and put out the flames and cooled the body. The naiads,[4] in pity for him, so bold and so young to die, buried him and carved upon the tomb:

> Here Phaethon lies who drove the sun
>   god's car.
> Greatly he failed, but he had greatly
>   dared.

His sisters, the Heliades, the daughters of Helios,[5] the Sun, came to his grave to mourn for him. There they were turned into poplar trees, on the bank of the Eridanus,

> Where sorrowing they weep into the
>   stream forever.
> And each tear as it falls shines in the water
> A glistening drop of amber.

---

4. **naiads** (nā′ădz): nymphs who lived in rivers, springs, and lakes.
5. **Helios** (hē′lē-ŏs′): an early Greek sun god, later identified with Apollo.

Reading Check

1. Why did the Sun take off his crown when Phaethon visited him?
2. What oath did the Sun take?
3. What favor did Phaethon ask?
4. What happened to the horses when Phaethon lost control?
5. How did Jove stop the runaway chariot?

For Study and Discussion

Analyzing and Interpreting the Myth

1. According to this myth, what explanation did the ancient Greeks have for the rising and setting of the sun?

2. Why did Phaethon want to drive his father's chariot?

3a. Why was Helios forced to keep his promise to Phaethon? **b.** What arguments did he use in an attempt to change his son's mind? **c.** Why was he unsuccessful?

4. What happened to the earth when Phaethon lost control of the chariot?

5. The inscription carved on Phaethon's tomb read: "Greatly he failed, but he had greatly dared." Was Phaethon's adventure an act of great daring or great folly? Explain your answer.

Language and Vocabulary

Learning Words from the Myths

Helios, the early sun god, has given his name to a number of English words. Whenever you see a word that begins with *helio-,* you can be sure that it has something to do with the sun.

19
Jove kills boy to save earth, not just to punish Phaethon.

20
Metamorphosis. Phaethon's sisters are turned into poplar trees, which weep for him by shedding their leaves into the river where he fell.

READING CHECK
1. Burning light hurt Phaethon's eyes (p. 608).
2. Called on river Styx to witness promise to grant son's request (p. 608).
3. To take his father's place for one day (p. 609).
4. Left path and began running recklessly (p. 609).
5. Hurled a thunderbolt and hit Phaethon (p. 611).

FOR STUDY AND DISCUSSION
1. Sun god's daily trip across the sky in a chariot.
2. For pride, to prove he was son of Helios.
3a. Had made oath to grant any request his son might make. 3b. Said no mortal could drive horses; that course was dangerous; that trip was full of dangerous beasts; that Phaethon did not have to make trip to prove he was Helios' son. 3c. Phaethon was rash that he didn't heed father's arguments.
4. Earth was set on fire.
5. Answers will vary. Some may admire Phaethon's boldness, ambition, and desire for glory. Others may think that he was arrogant and foolish for presuming to attempt what was beyond his powers.

CLOSURE
Ask students to summarize the story of Phaethon and tell what the **myth** explains. Ask them to relate explanation to scientific knowledge about relationship of sun to earth.

EXTENSION AND ENRICHMENT
Students might make collages, illustrating with contemporary images the inscription on Phaethon's tomb, "Greatly he failed, but he had greatly dared." As each student displays completed collage, other members of the class might interpret images and their composite effect.

LANGUAGE AND VOCABULARY
1. *Heliocentric* means having the sun as the center. "Our solar system is heliocentric because all the planets are in orbit around the sun."
A *heliograph* is a device that uses a mirror to send messages by flashing the sun's rays. "Ancient armies used to send messages by heliograph."
Heliotherapy is the use of sunlight (or artificial ultraviolet or infrared light) for healing purposes. "The doctor prescribed heliotherapy for my aunt."
Heliotropic refers to the tendency of plants and other organisms to turn toward the sun. "The sunflower is heliotropic."

FOCUS ON PERSUASIVE WRITING
To help students understand the idea of **audience,** you may want to choose a topic and show students how the information in the Audience Chart might change with two different audiences. As students fill out their own charts, suggest that they visualize a person they feel is representative of those to whom they are gearing their persuasive writing.

ABOUT THE AUTHOR
Hamilton received her B.A. and M.A. degrees in Greek and Latin from Bryn Mawr College in 1895. The following year she became headmistress of Bryn Mawr School, a post she held for over twenty-five years. She instilled in her students the belief that each person should be provided educational freedom to develop his or her specific talents. Upon retirement from the school, she began writing and translating full time. Her *Mythology* (1942) has become a standard resource in the study of classical myths.

612

---

1 Find the meanings of these words and use each one in a sentence:

heliocentric   heliotherapy
heliograph   heliotropic

Focus on Persuasive Writing

Thinking About Your Audience

Successful advertisers study their **audience**—the people they are trying to persuade to buy a product or service. In the same way, when you plan a piece of persuasive writing, you should consider the needs, interests, and concerns of your audience.

Here are some questions you can ask about the audience for a persuasive paper:

1. How much do they know already about the topic?
2. How do they feel about the topic?
3. What are their major interests and concerns?
4. What reasons might they have for opposing the view you support?

Choose one of the topics you have explored for earlier assignments in this unit. Fill out an **audience chart** like the one below. Save your notes.

```
┌─────────────────────────────────────────┐
│           Audience Chart                │
│ Topic: _____  │
│ Position/Opinion: _____  │
│ _____   │
│ Audience: _____  │
│ Interests and Concerns: _____  │
│ _____   │
│ Possible Opposing Opinions: _____  │
│ _____   │
│ Likely Reasons for Opposition: _____  │
│ _____   │
│ _____   │
└─────────────────────────────────────────┘
```

612 CLASSICAL MYTHOLOGY

About the Author

Edith Hamilton (1867–1963)

Edith Hamilton developed an interest in ancient Greek and Roman civilizations when she was very young. However, she did not begin writing about these ancient civilizations until she was sixty-three and had already had a career as the headmistress of a girls' school. One of her best-known works, *The Greek Way*, is a study of the life and thought of ancient Greece. She followed this book with *The Roman Way*, a study of ancient Roman civilization. *Mythology*, from which "Phaethon" is taken, contains retellings of Greek, Roman, and Norse myths. For her contributions to the study of ancient Greece, she was made an honorary citizen of Athens.

Phaethon

MORRIS BISHOP

What humorous parallel does this poem draw between the myth of Phaethon and modern youth?

1 Apollo through the heavens rode
         In glinting gold attire;
    His car was bright with chrysolite,°
         His horses snorted fire.
    He held them to their frantic course   5
         Across the blazing sky.
    His darling son was Phaethon,
         Who begged to have a try.

2 "The chargers are ambrosia-fed,
         They barely brook control;   10
    On high beware the Crab, the Bear,
         The Serpent round the Pole;
    Against the Archer and the Bull
         Thy form is all unsteeled!"°

3 But Phaethon could lay it on;   15
         Apollo had to yield.

    Out of the purple doors of dawn
         Phaethon drove the horses;
    They felt his hand could not command.
         They left their wonted° courses.   20
    And from the chariot Phaethon
         Plunged like a falling star—

4 And so, my boy, no, no, my boy,
5   You cannot take the car.

---

3. **chrysolite** (krĭs′ə-līt′): a greenish, transparent gem.
14. **unsteeled:** unprotected. 20. **wonted** (wôn′tĭd): habitual.

For Study and Discussion

Analyzing and Interpreting the Poem

1a. To whom is the speaker in this poem talking?   **b.** Why does he tell this person the story of Phaethon?

2. The Serpent in line 12 is the constellation Draco, which is also called the Dragon. Identify the Crab, Bear, Archer, and Bull mentioned in lines 11 and 13.

3. Morris Bishop's story differs from Edith Hamilton's retelling of the myth in certain details. What differences can you find?

About the Author

Morris Bishop   (1893–1973)

Morris Bishop was born in New York State and for many years was a professor of Romance languages at Cornell University. Bishop published several translations, histories, and a number of volumes of poetry. His books of verse include *Paramount Poems* (1929) and *A Bowl of Bishop* (1954).

Icarus and Daedalus°

Retold by
JOSEPHINE PRESTON PEABODY

Daedalus, we are told, was among the wisest of men, capable of reaching beyond even the laws of nature. What does this myth suggest about his kind of wisdom? How does Icarus' fate suggest the need for moderation?

Among all those mortals who grew so wise that they learned the secrets of the gods, none was more cunning than Daedalus.

He once built, for King Minos of Crete,[1] a wonderful Labyrinth[2] of winding ways so cunningly tangled up and twisted around that, once inside, you could never find your way out again without a magic clue.[3] But the King's favor veered with the wind, and one day he had his master architect imprisoned in a tower. Daedalus managed to escape from his cell; but it seemed impossible to leave the island, since every ship that came or went was well guarded by order of the King.

At length, watching the sea gulls in the air—the only creatures that were sure of liberty—he thought of a plan for himself and his young son Icarus, who was captive with him.

Little by little, he gathered a store of feathers great and small. He fastened these together with thread, molded them in with wax, and so fashioned two great wings like those of a bird. When they were done, Daedalus fitted them to his own shoulders, and after one or two efforts, he found that by waving his arms he could winnow[4] the air and cleave it, as a swimmer does the sea. He held himself aloft, wavered this way and that with the wind, and at last, like a great fledgling, he learned to fly.

Without delay, he fell to work on a pair of wings for the boy Icarus and taught him carefully how to use them, bidding him beware of rash adventures among the stars. "Remember," said the father, "never to fly very low or very high, for the fogs about the earth would weigh you down, but the blaze of the sun will surely melt your feathers apart if you go too near."

For Icarus, these cautions went in at one ear and out by the other. Who could remember to be careful when he was to fly for the first time? Are birds careful? Not they! And not an idea

---
° **Daedalus** (dĕd′l-əs).
1. **King Minos** (mī′nŏs′) **of Crete:** Minos was a son of Zeus. Crete is a large island southeast of the Greek mainland.
2. **Labyrinth** (lăb′ə-rĭnth).
3. **clue:** here, a ball of thread. Theseus, an Athenian hero, was able to escape by tying one end of the thread to the entrance, unwinding the ball as he went in, and rewinding it as he came out.
4. **winnow:** beat.

The Fall of Icarus by Bernard Picart. Eighteenth-century etching.

MOTIVATIONAL SUMMARY
Daedalus is the cleverest of men, capable of inventing many amazing things. He built the mazelike Labyrinth for King Minos of Crete, but the ungrateful king ordered Daedalus and his son Icarus to be imprisoned on a small island. Forced to think of a way for himself and his son to escape, Daedalus discovers the secret of flight. He builds mighty wings covered with feathers held in place by wax, and he and his son plan their daring escape.

PRESENTATION
Recall that Phaethon dared to brave the heavens. Explain that "Icarus and Daedalus" features another youth who reaches for the sky. Ask students to look for other similarities between these two stories.

VISUAL CONNECTIONS
Exploring the Subject
The story of Icarus' fall is a cautionary tale much like Phaethon's, but Icarus' demise was not used to explain any natural phenomena, as Phaethon's was. Perhaps because Icarus' story does not include such details of primitive scientific explanation, it appealed even more strongly to European artists and poets. In addition, Europeans in an era of rapid scientific development were drawn to the idea that Icarus, at least in part, was a youth whose exuberance was caused by his suddenly being enabled to fly—long an unattainable human desire but made possible for Icarus because of his father's technological wizardry. In Europe, as scientific advances made flight a more attainable possibility, the story of Icarus gained even more in appeal.

Harvey D. Parker Collection. Courtesy, Museum of Fine Arts, Boston

READING SKILLS PRACTICE
The underlined passage can be used to give students practice in the reading skill of identifying cause-and-effect relationships. Ask students to read the passage and choose the answer that expresses the most accurate description. **A.** The air is warm because he is moving his arms. (Not supported in the passage.) **B.** His arms relax because the air is warm. (Possibly true but not supported in the passage.) **C.** The feathers are falling because they are becoming snowflakes. (Incorrect detail.) **D.** He is falling from the sky because his wings are melting. (Correct.)

7
Daedalus tries to take precautions to protect Icarus.

8
Simile. Comparisons with bird and child reveal Icarus' sense of security and delight as he is uplifted by the wind.

9
Icarus loses caution in rapture of flight.

10
Too late, he remembers his father's warning.

11
Simile. Icarus is no longer borne up by the wind, but tossed down like a leaf.

READING CHECK
1. In a tower on Crete (p. 614).
2. Feathers, thread, and wax. (p. 614).
3. Not to fly too low or too high (p. 614).
4. He flew too close to sun, melted wax on his wings (p. 616).
5. Placed them in temple of Apollo in Sicily (p. 616).

---

remained in the boy's head but the one joy of escape.

The day came, and the fair wind that was to set them free. The father-bird put on his wings, and, while the light urged them to be

7 gone, he waited to see that all was well with Icarus, for the two could not fly hand in hand. Up they rose, the boy after his father. The hateful ground of Crete sank beneath them; and the country folk, who caught a glimpse of them when they were high above the treetops, took it for a vision of the gods—Apollo, perhaps, with Cupid after him.

At first there was a terror in the joy. The wide vacancy of the air dazed them—a glance downward made their brains reel. But when a

8 great wind filled their wings, and Icarus felt himself sustained, like a halcyon bird[5] in the hollow of a wave, like a child uplifted by his

9 mother, he forgot everything in the world but joy. He forgot Crete and the other islands that he had passed over: he saw but vaguely that winged thing in the distance before him that was his father Daedalus. He longed for one draft of flight to quench the thirst of his captivity: he stretched out his arms to the sky and made toward the highest heavens.

▶ Alas for him! Warmer and warmer grew the air. Those arms, that had seemed to uphold him, relaxed. His wings wavered, dropped. He fluttered his young hands vainly—he was

10 falling—and in that terror he remembered. The heat of the sun had melted the wax from his wings; the feathers were falling, one by one, like snowflakes; and there was none to help. ◀

11 He fell like a leaf tossed down by the wind, down, down, with one cry that overtook Daedalus far away. When he returned and sought high and low for the poor boy, he saw nothing but the birdlike feathers afloat on the water, and he knew that Icarus was drowned.

The nearest island he named Icaria, in memory of the child; but he, in heavy grief, went to the temple of Apollo in Sicily and there hung up his wings as an offering. Never again did he attempt to fly.

Reading Check
1. Where was Daedalus imprisoned by King Minos?
2. What did Daedalus use to make the wings?
3. What instructions did he give Icarus?
4. What caused Icarus' death?
5. What did Daedalus do with his wings?

For Study and Discussion

Analyzing and Interpreting the Myth

1. At the opening of the myth, you are told that Daedalus was so cunning that he learned the secrets of the gods. Do you think he was punished for his knowledge? Explain your answer.

2. Both Icarus and Phaethon fell from the sky to their deaths. Compare these young men. How are they alike, and how are they different?

3. Myths often show what attitudes and behavior were expected of human beings. **a.** What lesson might have been drawn from the myth of Icarus and Daedalus and about obedience to the laws of nature? **b.** What lesson might have been drawn about the obedience of young people to their elders?

---

5. **halcyon** (hăl'sē-ən) **bird:** a legendary bird, identified with the kingfisher, which supposedly had the power of calming the winter seas.

CLASSICAL MYTHOLOGY

> **TRANSPARENCY 50**
> **Literary Elements**
> *Analyzing a Myth* – invites students to explore a variety of elements commonly found in myths.

CLOSURE
Ask students to summarize "Icarus and Daedalus" and explain the lesson the story teaches.

EXTENSION AND ENRICHMENT
Students can enjoy a story better if they can identify with one of the characters. Ask them to pretend to be Daedalus or Icarus and to write a paragraph explaining what happened during the flight of escape.

Language and Vocabulary

Learning Words from the Myths

Daedalus built the original Labyrinth in Crete to house the Minotaur, a monster that was half man and half bull. King Minos ordered young men and women to be fed to the Minotaur. The Labyrinth kept them from escaping.

We now use the word *labyrinth* to mean any complicated system of passageways and dead ends. The word *labyrinth* may also be used for anything that is intricate or confusing. The poet Tennyson has referred to "the *labyrinth* of
1 the mind." What do you think the word means in this phrase?

About the Author

Josephine Preston Peabody (1874–1922)

Josephine Preston Peabody was best known as a poet and a playwright. The selection included in this anthology is from *Old Greek Folk Stories Told Anew*, a collection of stories that was written as a complement to Nathaniel Hawthorne's *Wonder Book* and *Tanglewood Tales*. Some of her works include *The Wolf of Gubbio*, a comedy; *The Wayfarers* and *Harvest Moon*, poetry; and *Fortune and Men's Eyes*, poems with a play.

Literature and the Arts

Interpretations of a Myth

The myth of Daedalus and Icarus has been interpreted by different artists, each of whom has given the myth a particular meaning. Some artists have chosen to focus on the figure of Icarus at the moment of his fall, whereas other artists have chosen to focus, not on Icarus, but rather on the reactions of onlookers.

Making Connections: Activities

1. Examine the illustration on page 615. Do you think the artist views Icarus as a noble, heroic figure whose fall is tragic, or as a boy whose terrible last moments are pitiful? Do you see another interpretation of the scene? Support your answer by referring to details in the illustration.
2. Locate a copy of *Jazz* by Henri Matisse and find the cut-out of Icarus. How has the artist reduced the story of the myth? What would you say is his focus?
3. Pieter Brueghel the Elder did a famous painting called *The Fall of Icarus*, in which Icarus has already plunged into the sea. Locate a copy of this work and compare it with the interpretation of the myth on page 615. What differences are there? Do you have a preference?

LANGUAGE AND VOCABULARY

The introductory illustration should spark immediate interest in exercise. Students might want to discuss how such mazes are used with laboratory animals and why. Reinforce exercise by having each student write two original sentences, using the word *labyrinth* in a different way.

1. Tennyson used *labyrinth* to suggest complexities of the human mind.

ABOUT THE AUTHOR

After graduating from Radcliffe College, Peabody published her first collection of poetry, *The Wayfarers*, in 1898. Other verse includes *The Singing Leaves* (1903) and *Harvest Moon* (1916). In 1910 she won the Stratford-on-Avon Prize for her play *The Piper*. Other plays include *Marlowe* (1901) and *Portrait of Mrs. W.* (1922).

Icarus and Daedalus

To a Friend Whose Work Has Come to Triumph

ANNE SEXTON

The title of this poem alludes, or refers, to the title of a poem by William Butler Yeats, "To a Friend Whose Work Has Come to Nothing." In that poem Yeats praises the efforts of a friend whose attempts to bring a collection of French art to Dublin had been thwarted by local officials.

Similarly, Sexton here is talking about triumph in defeat. In what way is Icarus' failure a great success?

Consider Icarus, pasting those sticky wings on,
testing that strange little tug at his shoulder blade,
and think of that first flawless moment over the lawn
of the labyrinth. Think of the difference it made!
There below are the trees, as awkward as camels;   5
and here are the shocked starlings pumping past
and think of innocent Icarus who is doing quite well:
larger than a sail, over the fog and the blast
of the plushy ocean, he goes. Admire his wings!
Feel the fire at his neck and see how casually   10
he glances up and is caught, wondrously tunneling
into that hot eye. Who cares that he fell back to the sea?
See him acclaiming the sun and come plunging down
while his sensible daddy goes straight into town.

For Study and Discussion

Analyzing and Interpreting the Poem

1. This poem is addressed to someone whose work has been unsuccessful in one sense, yet triumphant in another. **a.** Does the poet consider Icarus' death a defeat or a victory? **b.** Which lines support your answer?

2. The word *sensible* is used in line 14 to describe Daedalus. Do you think the author admires him for his caution? Explain your answer.

About the Author

Anne Sexton (1928–1974)

Anne Sexton, a native of Newton, Massachusetts, was, along with Sylvia Plath and others, one of the "confessional" poets. Under the influence of Robert Lowell, this group turned to the intimate details of their own lives and feelings for their subjects. Sexton once said that poetry "should be a shock to the senses. It should almost hurt." She received a Pulitzer Prize in 1967 for her volume of poetry *Live or Die*.

Literature and Research

Allusions to Mythology

The authors of the poems that appear on pages 613 and 618 expect their readers to recognize the characters and events in certain classical myths. If you know these myths, you can better understand and appreciate the poems.

Writers often use references to characters and events from classical mythology. In the following lines from *Childe Harold's Pilgrimage*, Byron, an English poet, compares the Rome of his day to Niobe, a character in mythology:

> The Niobe of nations! there she stands,
> Childless and crownless, in her voiceless woe.

Such a reference as this is known as an **allusion**. What does modern Rome, fallen from its past grandeur as a great empire, have in common with Niobe? In order to understand what Byron means, you need to research Niobe's story.

You might begin tracking down this allusion by looking in a dictionary:

> **Niobe** (nī′ō-bē), *n. Class. Myth.* the daughter of Tantalus and wife of Amphion of Thebes; her children were slain and Zeus turned her into stone, in which state she continued to weep over her loss.

This entry tells why Niobe was childless and why she was voiceless—she was turned to stone. But the entry does not tell why her children were slain or why Zeus turned her to stone. An encyclopedia might tell more of Niobe's story. Your best source, however, is a book of myths or a dictionary of mythology. Consult any of the sources suggested on page 591.

Making Connections: Activities

1. Find out what the expression "Achilles' heel" refers to. Locate the story of Achilles and tell how the expression came into being.
2. Find out what it means to be caught "between Scylla and Charybdis." Tell how these names figure in the story of Odysseus.
3. A Trojan Horse is the name given to a person or a device that is used for some subversive purpose. Find the story (sometimes called "The Wooden Horse") and explain how the phrase came to have its modern meaning.

OBJECTIVES

The overall aim is for students to demonstrate an understanding of English words derived from classical mythology.

PRESENTATION

To identify the words named for mythological characters as directed by the activities, each student or small group will need a dictionary to check etymology. You may need to review the conventions dictionaries use in citing etymologies. Major points might include that etymologies are usually placed in brackets and that the symbol <, meaning "from," is used for derivations. Also review the abbreviations used for languages, usually located in the introductory pages of a dictionary.

Classical Mythology in Today's World

1. **Hygeia:** hygiene ("habits of cleanliness"); hygienist.
Hypnos: hypnotize, hypnotist, hypnotic, hypnagogic ("causing sleep"), hypnotherapy, hypnology.
Oceanus: ocean, oceanography, oceanic, oceanaut, oceanology.
2. Jupiter, Neptune, Pluto, Venus, Mars, Mercury, Saturn (Zeus's father—called Cronos by Greeks), and Uranus (Zeus's grandfather).
3. June, January, March, May are named for Juno, Janus, Mars, Maia, respectively.
4. *Giant* comes from the Gigantes—huge, monstrous children of Gaea who were defeated by Olympians; *lethargic* comes from Lethe, underworld river of forgetfulness; *music* comes from Greek word mousa; *panic* comes from Pan, woodland god, who frightened travelers at night; *psychology* comes from psyche, the soul; *tantalize* comes from Tantalus, king who was punished tormentingly; *titanic* comes from Titans, a race of giant deities; *volcano* comes from Vulcan, Roman god of fire.
5. Atlas was condemned by Zeus to hold up skies; he thus had a view of the whole world. An *atlas* (book of maps) also gives a view of the world.

620

Classical Mythology in Today's World

Throughout this unit you have been learning about English words that come from the myths. Many more words and phrases can be traced to classical mythology. What words can you think of that come from the names of these figures?

Hygeia, a Greek goddess of health
Hypnos, a Greek god of sleep
Oceanus, a Titan who was the father of the river gods and sea nymphs

2 Which planets are named for gods and goddesses of classical mythology? Use a dictionary to check your answers.

3 Several of our months get their names from figures in classical mythology. Which months are they and for what figures are they named?

4 Use a dictionary to find the origin of these words:

giant	psychology
lethargic	tantalize
music	titanic
panic	volcano

5 A book of maps is called an *atlas*. The word comes from the name of a figure in classical mythology. Find out who Atlas was and explain his connection with maps.

Many towns and cities in the United States have been named for characters or places in classical mythology. Here are some of them:

Atlas (Illinois, Michigan)
Hercules (California)
Juno Beach (Florida)
Jupiter (North Carolina)
Mercury (Nevada, Texas)
Mount Olympus (Utah, Washington)
Olympia (California, Kentucky, Washington)
Venus (Florida, Nebraska, Pennsylvania, Texas)

CLOSURE
Ask students to give examples of English words derived from classical mythology. You may want to remind them to consider planets, months, towns, cities, and other place names.

Are the names of any towns or cities in your state derived from classical mythology? Consult an almanac or an atlas.

6. The city of *Carthage* figures in the story of Aeneas and Dido. Aeneas was a Trojan. When Troy fell to the Greeks at the end of the Trojan War, Aeneas and many of his people escaped and began searching for a new homeland. Find out how Aeneas came to Carthage and what happened to Dido after he left.

7. *Rome* is named for Romulus. Look up the myth of Romulus and Remus. Find out how Rome, the City of the Seven Hills, was founded.

8. *Sparta* is associated in mythology with King Menelaus, who was married to Helen, the most beautiful woman in the world. Find out how Helen is connected with the Trojan War.

9. The island of *Ithaca* was the home of Odysseus, or Ulysses, one of the Greek heroes who fought in the Trojan War. Find out how Odysseus was responsible for the fall of Troy and why he was forced to wander for ten years before he reached his home.

10. What relationship is there between these place names and the characters and events in classical mythology?

Atlantic Ocean   Hellespont
Europe   Icarian Sea

---

6. Aeneas escaped in a ship which was blown to coast of Africa; there he met Dido, queen of Carthage, who fell in love with him. When he left, she built a funeral pyre and threw herself into the flames, plunging a sword into her heart.
7. Romulus and Remus decided to found a new city in Italy. Requesting a sign of who should rule, Remus saw six vultures, while Romulus saw twelve. They quarreled. Remus was killed; Romulus became founder of Rome.
8. Paris, a guest of Menelaus, carried off Helen to Troy. Helen's former suitors came to Menelaus' aid and waged war against Troy for ten years.
9. Odysseus left a giant wooden horse outside walls of Troy. Trojans brought it in and, that night, Greeks hidden inside opened the gates, allowing army to attack and burn Troy. Heading home, Odysseus blinded Cyclops, Poseidon's son. Poseidon kept Odysseus from home for ten years.
10. *Atlantic Ocean,* named for Atlas; *Europe,* named after Europa, a Phoenician princess abducted by Zeus; *Hellespont,* strait named for Helle, who drowned there after rescue by flying ram with golden fleece; *Icarian Sea,* named after Icarus, who drowned there.

OBJECTIVES
The overall aim is for students to demonstrate an understanding of the characteristics and feats of the classical **hero** Hercules. For a complete list of objectives, see the **Teacher's Notes**.

VOCABULARY
The underlined words are in the Glossary. The **Language and Vocabulary** exercise on p. 628 will give students practice in finding the meanings of words for the Greek root *hydr–*.

FOCUS / MOTIVATION
Ask students to imagine a man who could be described as "the strongest man in the world." What might he look like? act like? What might his weaknesses be?

TEACHING RESOURCES E
Teacher's Notes, p. 88
Reading Check, p. 91
Study Guide, p. 93
Language Skills, p. 97
Building Vocabulary, p. 101
Selection Vocabulary Test, p. 103
Selection Test, p. 104

PREREADING FOCUS
The headnote suggests that Hercules' superhuman strength does not prevent him from having certain human weaknesses. Ask students to predict what these faults might be. Perhaps they can name some contemporary heroes who are less than perfect.

The Adventures of Hercules

1
Eurystheus—King of Mycenae; Hercules' cousin.

2
To atone for killing wife and children, Hercules was ordered by oracle of Delphi to perform whatever Eurystheus asked.

3
Offspring of Typhon and Echidna, two monsters sent by Mother Earth to fight Zeus when Zeus first overpowered Cronus.

4 Making Inferences
Why do you think Eurystheus will not let Hercules into the city? Perhaps he fears Hercules might seek vengeance.

5
Hydra: another one of Echidna's offspring; it emits poisonous fumes.

622

The Adventures of Hercules

Retold by
EDITH HAMILTON

The greatest hero in ancient Greece was Heracles, whose Roman name was Hercules. He was the strongest man on earth. Like many other heroes in classical mythology, he was the son of a god (Zeus) and a mortal (Alcmene). Throughout his life he suffered from fits of madness that the goddess Hera sent to plague him. In one of his fits, he killed his wife and children. In order to be purified of his crime, he sought the help of a priestess of Apollo, who brought him the message of the god: For twelve long years he was to serve as a slave, carrying out all-but-impossible labors.

As you read, determine which characteristics of Hercules show that despite his superhuman strength he had certain human weaknesses.

1 Eurystheus[1] was by no means stupid, but of a very ingenious turn of mind, and when the strongest man on earth came to him humbly prepared to be his slave, he devised a series of penances which from the point of view of difficulty and danger could not have been improved upon. It must be said, however, that he was helped and urged on by Hera. To the end of Hercules' life she never forgave him for being Zeus's son. The tasks Eurystheus gave him to do are called "the labors of Hercules." There were twelve of them and each one was all but impossible.

   The first was to kill the lion of Nemea, a beast no weapons could wound. That difficulty Hercules solved by choking the life out of him. Then he heaved the huge carcass up on his back and carried it into Mycenae.[2] After that, Eurystheus, a cautious man, would not let him inside the city. He gave him his orders from afar.

   The second labor was to go to Lerna and kill a creature with nine heads called the Hydra, which lived in a swamp there. This was exceedingly hard to do, because one of the heads was immortal and the others almost as bad, inasmuch as when Hercules chopped off one, two grew up instead. However, he was helped by his nephew Iolaus,[3] who brought him a burn-

1. **Eurystheus** (yoo-rĭs′thē-əs).
2. **Mycenae** (mī-sē′nē).
3. **Iolaus** (ī′ə-lā′əs).

622 CLASSICAL MYTHOLOGY

MOTIVATIONAL SUMMARY

Hercules is the strongest of classical heroes, but he is subject to terrible rages. In one of these bouts of madness, he kills his wife and children. When he emerges from his fit, he is horrified at his crime, and begs the gods to think of a punishment so that he can prove how sorry he is. He is assigned to serve King Eurystheus for twelve years and to do whatever he asks. Eurystheus is determined not to let Hercules off easy, and he orders Hercules to do twelve tasks: the Labors of Hercules.

PRESENTATION

Introduce the concept of the culture hero, a single exemplary individual who personifies all the traits most admired by a particular society. As an example, ask what values of the Age of Chivalry were embodied in King Arthur. What great

---

Hercules and the Nemean Lion. Black-figured terra cotta vase, c. 560 B.C.

The Metropolitan Museum of Art, Fletcher Fund, 1940. (40.11.20)

ing brand with which he seared the neck as he cut each head off so that it could not sprout again. When all had been chopped off he disposed of the one that was immortal by burying it securely under a great rock.

The third labor was to bring back alive a stag with horns of gold, sacred to Artemis, which lived in the forests of Cerynitia. He could have 6 killed it easily, but to take it alive was another matter and he hunted it a whole year before he succeeded.

The fourth labor was to capture a great boar which had its lair on Mount Erymanthus. He chased the beast from one place to another until it was exhausted; then he drove it into deep snow and trapped it.

The fifth labor was to clean the Augean stables in a single day. Augeas had thousands of cattle and their stalls had not been cleared out 7 for years. Hercules diverted the courses of two rivers and made them flow through the stables in a great flood that washed out the filth in no time at all.

8 The sixth labor was to drive away the Stymphalian birds, which were a plague to the people of Stymphalus because of their enormous numbers. He was helped by Athena to drive them out of their coverts, and as they flew up he shot them.

The seventh labor was to go to Crete and fetch from there the beautiful savage bull that Poseidon had given Minos. Hercules mastered him, put him in a boat and brought him to Eurystheus.

The eighth labor was to get the man-eating mares of King Diomedes of Thrace. Hercules 9 slew Diomedes first and then drove off the mares unopposed.

The ninth labor was to bring back the girdle[4] 10 of Hippolyta, the Queen of the Amazons. When Hercules arrived she met him kindly and told him she would give him the girdle, but Hera stirred up trouble. She made the Amazons think that Hercules was going to carry off their queen, and they charged down on his 11 ship. Hercules, without a thought of how kind Hippolyta had been, without any thought at all, instantly killed her, taking it for granted that she was responsible for the attack. He was able to fight off the others and get away with the girdle.

The tenth labor was to bring back the cattle 12 of Geryon, who was a monster with three bodies living on Erythia, a western island. On his

---

4. **girdle:** here, a belt.

VISUAL CONNECTIONS

Exploring the Subject

A lion's skin is Hercules' most characteristic garment. He is most frequently shown wearing the lion's skin with its head as a hood, the skin hanging cloaklike over his back and the feet dangling below his waist, emphasizing his thick, strong legs (another identifying heroic characteristic).

6 Summarizing
Why not just kill the stag? If he killed stag, Artemis would be angered.

7
Hero. Hercules has not only the brawn to divert the rivers but also the cleverness to think of the plan.

8
Their feathers are made of sharp brass and kill anyone they hit.

9
Mares eat dead king and are thereby subdued.

10
Amazons: tribe of warlike women.

11
Characterization. During fight, Hercules acts first and thinks later.

12
Geryon: monster with three bodies on top of one pair of legs.

The Adventures of Hercules

deeds of this hero demonstrated these traits? Would the traits of the twentieth-century American culture hero be the same? Ask students to recall the classical myths studied in this unit, focusing on characters' heroic traits. List those traits on the board. Explain that Hercules is one of the great culture heroes of the Greeks. As students read "The Adventures of Hercules" aloud in class, ask them to point out Greek values he personifies.

13
Only immortal can pick golden apples; mortal would die if he or she did so.

14
Hercules deserves more credit; he outwitted Atlas.

15
Inference. This incident leads reader to make inference about Hercules' compassion and willingness to fight for underdog.

16
Pluto: Roman name for Hades.

17
Antaeus' skull-roof warns of his winning record.

18
Antaeus possesses this kind of invincibility because he is one of Mother Earth's sons.

19
Characterization. Hercules is characterized directly as someone dominated by passion, not reason.

---

way there Hercules reached the land at the end of the Mediterranean and he set up as a memorial of his journey two great rocks, called the Pillars of Hercules (now Gibraltar and Ceuta). Then he got the oxen and took them to Mycenae.

13 The eleventh labor was the most difficult of all so far. It was to bring back the golden apples of the Hesperides,[5] and he did not know where they were to be found. Atlas, who bore the vault of heaven upon his shoulders, was the father of the Hesperides, so Hercules went to him and asked him to get the apples for him. He offered to take upon himself the burden of the sky while Atlas was away. Atlas, seeing a chance of being relieved forever from his heavy task, gladly agreed. He came back with the apples, but he did not give them to Hercules. He told Hercules he could keep on holding up the sky, for Atlas himself would take the apples to Eurystheus. On this occasion Hercules had only his wits to trust to; he had to give all his strength to supporting that mighty load.

14 He was successful, but because of Atlas' stupidity rather than his own cleverness. He agreed to Atlas' plan, but asked him to take the sky back for just a moment so that Hercules could put a pad on his shoulders to ease the pressure. Atlas did so, and Hercules picked up the apples and went off.

The twelfth labor was the worst of all. It took
15 him down to the lower world; and it was then that he freed Theseus from the Chair of Forgetfulness.[6] His task was to bring Cerberus, the
16 three-headed dog, up from Hades. Pluto gave him permission provided Hercules used no weapons to overcome him. He could use his hands only. Even so, he forced the terrible monster to submit to him. He lifted him and carried him all the way up to the earth and on to Mycenae. Eurystheus very sensibly did not want to keep him and made Hercules carry him back. This was his last labor.

When all were completed and full expiation made for the death of his wife and children, he would seem to have earned ease and tranquility for the rest of his life. But it was not so. He was never tranquil and at ease. An exploit quite as difficult as most of the labors was the conquest of Antaeus,[7] a Giant and a mighty wrestler who forced strangers to wrestle with
17 him on condition that if he was victor he should kill them. He was roofing a temple with the skulls of his victims. As long as he could
18 touch the earth he was invincible. If thrown to the ground he sprang up with renewed strength from the contact. Hercules lifted him up and holding him in the air strangled him.

Story after story is told of his adventures. He fought the river god Achelous[8] because Achelous was in love with the girl Hercules now wanted to marry. Like everyone else by this
19 time, Achelous had no desire to fight him and he tried to reason with him. But that never worked with Hercules. It only made him more angry. He said, "My hand is better than my tongue. Let me win fighting and you may win talking." Achelous took the form of a bull and attacked him fiercely, but Hercules was used to subduing bulls. He conquered him and broke off one of his horns. The cause of the contest, a young princess named Deianira,[9] became his wife.

He traveled to many lands and did many other great deeds. At Troy he rescued a maiden who was in the same plight as An-

---

5. **Hesperides** (hĕs-pĕr′ə-dēz′): sisters who guarded the golden apples belonging to Hera. These apples had been given to her as a wedding present by Gaea (jē′ə), an earth goddess.
6. **Chair of Forgetfulness:** Theseus, an Athenian hero and a cousin of Hercules, had been trapped in this chair when he accompanied a friend to Hades in order to kidnap Persephone.
7. **Antaeus** (ăn-tē′əs).
8. **Achelous** (ə-kĕl′ō-əs).
9. **Deianira** (dē′yə-nī′rə).

624 CLASSICAL MYTHOLOGY

dromeda,[10] waiting on the shore to be devoured by a sea monster which could be appeased in no other way. She was the daughter of King Laomedon, who had cheated Apollo and Poseidon of their wages after at Zeus's command they had built for the King the walls of Troy. In return Apollo sent a pestilence, and Poseidon the sea serpent. Hercules agreed to rescue the girl if her father would give him the horses Zeus had given his grandfather. Laomedon promised, but when Hercules had slain the monster the King refused to pay. Hercules captured the city, killed the King, and gave the maiden to his friend, Telamon of Salamis, who had helped him.

On his way to Atlas to ask him about the Golden Apples, Hercules came to the Caucasus, where he freed Prometheus,[11] slaying the eagle that preyed on him.

Along with these glorious deeds there were others not glorious. He killed with a careless thrust of his arm a lad who was serving him by pouring water on his hands before a feast. It was an accident and the boy's father forgave Hercules, but Hercules could not forgive himself and he went into exile for a time. Far worse was his deliberately slaying a good friend in order to avenge an insult offered him by the young man's father, King Eurytus.[12] For this base action Zeus himself punished him: he sent

10. **Andromeda** (ăn-dräm′ə-də): a princess rescued from a sea monster by Perseus, whom she later married.

11. **Prometheus:** See "Prometheus the Fire-Bringer," page 583. Zeus had punished Prometheus for his defiance by having him chained to a mountaintop and sending an eagle each day to devour his liver, which grew back each night.
12. **Eurytus** (yŏŏr′ĭ-təs).

20
The King still thinks he can get something for nothing, but Hercules' punishment is greater and faster than Zeus's.

21
Much of Hercules' behavior at this time results from Hera's causing him to go insane.

22
Hercules had won great glory for his twelve labors; Zeus decided this punishment would humiliate him.

VISUAL CONNECTIONS
Exploring the Subject
Cerberus was a three-headed dog with a serpent's tail which guarded the gates of the underworld. Only twice did he fail in his tasks, which included keeping the living from trespassing in the underworld. Once he was lulled to sleep by the irresistible music of Orpheus' lyre, and once Hercules choked each of his three heads sufficiently to cause Cerberus to submit to being carried to the upper world as the last of Hercules' twelve labors. Cerberus was then returned unharmed to his duties.

Detail from *Cerberus* by William Blake (1757–1827). Watercolor.
Tate Gallery, London

Art Link

Draw the outline of a tee shirt on the chalkboard and ask students what modern-day heroes are on tee shirts. Then ask students to design a tee shirt using Hercules (or another Greek hero) on the front of the shirt. Students might use large pieces of kraft paper or paper bags to make their tee shirt designs with markers. Other students might like to use fabric paints with inexpensive tee shirts to design their hero art.

VISUAL CONNECTIONS
Exploring the Subject
The ceaseless agony caused by the blood-daubed robe (shown as flames in this painting) prompted Hercules to perform self-cremation to escape his pain. After death, Hercules was brought to Mt. Olympus for a time. Later, the gods set him among the stars (Hercules is a large northern constellation).

23
Roles for men and women were clearly defined in Greece, thus accounting for his humiliation.

24
Hercules' uncontrollable angers are caused by Hera, who always hated Hercules because he was Zeus's son.

25
Conflict. Story of Hercules develops as a chain of conflict, in which revenge is prominent.

Hercules by Francisco de Zurbarán (1598–1664). Oil on canvas. Hercules is shown wearing the robe anointed with the blood of Nessus.
Prado Museum

him to Lydia to be a slave to the Queen, Omphale,[13] some say for a year, some for three years. She amused herself with him, making him at times dress up as a woman and do woman's work, weave or spin. He submitted patiently, as always, but he felt himself degraded by this servitude and with complete unreason blamed Eurytus for it and swore he would punish him to the utmost when he was freed.

As Hercules had sworn to do while he was Omphale's slave, no sooner was he free than he started to punish King Eurytus because he himself had been punished by Zeus for killing Eurytus' son. He collected an army, captured the King's city and put him to death. But Eurytus, too, was avenged, for indirectly this

13. **Omphale** (ŏm′fə-lē).

626 CLASSICAL MYTHOLOGY

victory was the cause of Hercules' own death.

Before he had quite completed the destruction of the city, he sent home—where Deianira, his devoted wife, was waiting for him to come back from Omphale in Lydia—a band of captive maidens, one of them especially beautiful, Iole, the King's daughter. The man who brought them to Deianira told her that Hercules was madly in love with this Princess. This news was not so hard for Deianira as might be expected, because she believed she had a powerful love-charm which she had kept for years against just such an evil, a woman in her own house preferred before her. Directly after her marriage, when Hercules was taking her home, they had reached a river where the centaur[14] Nessus acted as ferryman, carrying travelers over the water. He took Deianira on his back and in midstream insulted her. She shrieked and Hercules shot the beast as he reached the other bank. Before he died he told Deianira to take some of his blood and use it as a charm for Hercules if ever he loved another woman more than her. When she heard about Iole, it seemed to her the time had come, and she anointed a splendid robe with the blood and sent it to Hercules by the messenger.

As the hero put it on, the effect was the same as that of the robe Medea had sent her rival whom Jason was about to marry.[15] A fearful pain seized him, as though he were in a burning fire. In his first agony he turned on Deianira's messenger, who was, of course, completely innocent, seized him and hurled him down into the sea. He could still slay others, but it seemed that he himself could not die. The anguish he felt hardly weakened him. What had instantly killed the young Princess of Corinth could not kill Hercules. He was in torture, but he lived and they brought him home. Long before, Deianira had heard what her gift had done to him and had killed herself. In the end he did the same. Since death would not come to him, he would go to death. He ordered those around him to build a great pyre on Mount Oeta and carry him to it. When at last he reached it he knew that now he could die and he was glad. "This is rest," he said. "This is the end." And as they lifted him to the pyre he lay down on it as one who at a banquet table lies down upon his couch.

He asked his youthful follower, Philoctetes, to hold the torch to set the wood on fire; and he gave him his bow and arrows, which were to be far-famed in the young man's hands, too, at Troy. Then the flames rushed up and Hercules was seen no more on earth. He was taken to heaven, where he was reconciled to Hera and married her daughter Hebe, and where

> After his mighty labors he has rest.
> His choicest prize eternal peace
> Within the homes of blessedness.

But it is not easy to imagine him contentedly enjoying rest and peace, or allowing the blessed gods to do so, either.

Reading Check

1. Why was it difficult for Hercules to kill the Hydra?
2. How did Hercules manage to clean the Augean stables in a day?
3. Why was the twelfth labor the worst of all?
4. In what way did Hercules defeat Antaeus?
5. Why did Hercules' wife anoint a robe with the blood of Nessus?

---

14. **centaur** (sĕn′tôr′): one of a group of mountain creatures who were part man and part horse.
15. **the robe . . . marry:** Jason's intended bride, the Princess of Corinth, died in agony when she tried on the robe, which Medea had anointed with poison.

The Adventures of Hercules 627

CLOSURE
Ask students to list the characteristics of the classical **hero** Hercules and name the great feats he performed in "The Adventures of Hercules." Then have students contrast Hercules and Prometheus as heroes.

EXTENSION AND ENRICHMENT
Students might imagine that Hercules is alive today and that they are in charge of assigning him twelve all-but-impossible tasks. After making lists of the modern labors each would assign, have students compare and discuss these lists.

The twelve labors of Hercules provide an ideal subject for a butcher-paper mural.

FOR STUDY AND DISCUSSION
1. Killing Nemean lion—had to solve problem of killing animal no weapon could wound. Killing Hydra—had to solve problem of how to keep eight of Hydra's heads from growing back and how to dispose of ninth head, which was immortal. Cleaning Augean stables—had to figure out how to dispose of immense filth within single day. Securing Golden Apples—had to trick Atlas into retaking his burden of holding up sky.
2a. Killing Nemean lion, Hydra, boar, Stymphalian birds, man-eating mares, and Geryon; cleaning Augean stables. **2b.** Securing Golden Apples, girdle of Hippolyta, or Cerberus.
3. By immolation; climbed onto and lit funeral pyre.

LANGUAGE AND VOCABULARY
1. *hydrant:* fireplug, which provides water to put out fires.
hydraulic: operated or powered by movement of water
hydroelectric: refers to production of electricity by water power.
hydrophobia: fear of water; old name for rabies, characterized by inability to swallow liquids.

CREATIVE WRITING
Encourage students to think in visual terms, specifying camera shots when there is no dialogue, indicating close-ups, fade-ins, fade-outs, etc.

LITERATURE AND RESEARCH
1. **Chimera:** fire-breathing monster with lion's head, goat's body, serpent's tail.
Cyclopes: three sons of Uranus and Gaea, each with one eye in the middle of forehead.
Furies: three female spirits with snaky hair.
Gorgons: three female monsters with serpents for hair and staring eyes whose glance turned mortals into stone.

For Study and Discussion

Analyzing and Interpreting the Myth

1. All twelve labors required great strength, courage, and perseverance. Which labors required that Hercules also use his wits?

2a. Which labors were useful tasks that benefited humanity? **b.** Which were simply tests of strength and patience? Explain your answer.

3. Since Hercules had superhuman strength, he could not be killed by poison. How did he die?

Language and Vocabulary

Learning Words from the Myths

The Hydra was the nine-headed monster that Hercules killed in the second of his labors. The name *Hydra* comes from a Greek word meaning "water serpent." In English the root *hydro-* (or *hydr-*) means "water." Find the meaning of these words:

hydrant	hydroelectric
hydraulic	hydrophobia

Creative Writing

Writing a Television Script

Imagine that you are the creator of a new television series based on the adventures of Hercules. Choose one of the episodes in his life—one of the labors or one of his other feats—and plan a script for a half-hour show. You may want to work with three or four other students in planning and writing the script.

Before you begin to write, consider these questions:

How many characters will appear in the play?
What will be the main events in the plot?
Where will the action take place?
How many different scenes will there be?
What details will have to be invented?
What dialogue will have to be written?

Literature and Research

Mythological Monsters

Hercules fought and killed the Nemean lion, the nine-headed Hydra, and other fearsome monsters. Here are some other monsters from classical mythology:

Chimera	Gorgons	Python
Cyclopes	Harpies	Sphinx
Furies	Minotaur	Typhon

Making Connections: Activities

1. Choose several of the monsters listed here or others you know of. Consult one of the reference books suggested on page 591 and identify each creature in a sentence or two. If you like to draw, use your description to create an illustration of each monster.

628 CLASSICAL MYTHOLOGY

ART LINK
You might have students design a Greek or Italian postage stamp with a god, goddess, or mythological hero on it. If you have a student in your class who collects stamps, you could ask the student to bring a few examples to class for the group to examine. After students have had time to look at several examples, have them work either together or separately on a stamp. Ask them to use the correct currency notation for the stamps. They might want to use the Greek alphabet and the Greek term *Hellas* for the name of the country.

INDEX OF NAMES

Where a character is known by more than one name, a separate entry has been provided for each name. For example, you will find Zeus also listed under his Roman names, Jove and Jupiter.

Aphrodite (ăf′rə-dī′tē): Greek goddess of love and beauty. She was identified with the Roman goddess **Venus**.   578

Apollo (ə-pŏl′ō): Greek and Roman god of youth, music, prophecy, archery, healing, and the sun. He was also called **Phoebus** (fē′bəs) **Apollo**, from the Greek word for "shining." 578, 593, 613

Arachne (ə-răk′nē): an arrogant young woman who boasted of her skill in weaving to Minerva and challenged the goddess to a contest. She was transformed into a spider by Minerva. 598

Ares (âr′ēz): Greek god of war. He was identified with the Roman god **Mars**.   580

Artemis (är′tə-mĭs): Greek goddess of wild animals, hunting, childbirth, and the moon. She was identified with the Roman goddess **Diana**.   579

Athena (ə-thē′nə): Greek goddess of wisdom, arts, crafts, and war, and protector of the city of Athens. She was also called **Athene** (ə-thē′nē) and **Pallas** (păl′əs) **Athena**, and was identified with the Roman goddess **Minerva**. 579

Atlas (ăt′ləs): the Titan whom Zeus punished by making him hold up the sky on his shoulders.   578, 624

Bacchus. See **Dionysus.**

Baucis (bô′sĭs): a poor Phrygian peasant. She and her husband, **Philemon** (fĭ-lē′mən), gave shelter to Jupiter and Mercury when they visited Phrygia in disguise.   602

Centaurs (sĕn′tôrz′): a race of mountain creatures, part man and part horse.   627

Ceres (sîr′ēz): Roman goddess of agriculture. She was identified with the Greek goddess **Demeter.**

Cronus (krō′nəs): the Titan who ruled the universe until he was overthrown by his son Zeus. The reign of Cronus was known as the Golden Age. He was identified with the Roman god **Saturn**.   578, 583

Cupid (kyōō′pĭd): Roman god of love. He was identified with the Greek god **Eros**.   616

Sleeping Eros. Bronze, third century B.C.

Harpies: winged monsters with heads and trunks of women, and tails, legs, and talons of birds.
Minotaur: monster with man's body and bull's head.
Python: enormous serpent.
Sphinx: winged monster with lion's body and woman's head and chest.
Typhon: giant with hundred dragon heads and serpent-covered body.

VISUAL CONNECTIONS
Exploring the Subject
The Greek god Eros was different from the Roman god Cupid. Eros was usually depicted as a young man, Cupid as a baby (the bronze sculpture shown here was crafted during the Hellenistic period when Greek ideas were spread—and changed—by Roman colonization throughout the Middle East and Europe). The Roman concept of Cupid as the friendly, cuddly baby god inspiring warm, happy love by piercing reluctant human hearts with his golden arrows is a sharp contrast to the Greek idea of Eros as the god of unreasoning passion. To the Greeks, with their ideal of "nothing to excess," such uncontrolled and uncontrollable excess of emotion was not seen as attractive but as frightening. Homer, for example, speaks of Eros as making "wise men speak in the language of fools."

MEETING INDIVIDUAL NEEDS
Visual Learners • You might have students make a family tree for a group of gods. They could pick out an Olympian family and, using a branching tree, show the relationships of the members. Students could put their work together in an Olympian Family Album. To make sure all the possibilities for family trees are covered, you might want to assign families to students.

VISUAL CONNECTIONS
Exploring the Subject
The Roman goddess Diana was the counterpart of the Greek Artemis. As a mythological figure, she was always eclipsed by her enormously popular brother, Apollo. There was also some confusion about her particular attributes and interests. However, among the common people, Diana (Artemis) was popular as a protector of wild lands and an ensurer of fertility among wild game (much as Ceres [Demeter] ensured fertility and growth among growing things). In addition, although a determinedly virgin goddess herself, she was believed to be the protector of women during childbirth; offerings were made to her in behalf of women who wished to have short, uncomplicated labor.

Daedalus (dĕd′l-əs): an Athenian inventor and architect who built the Labyrinth for King Minos of Crete. He fashioned wings for himself and his son **Icarus** (ĭk′ə-rəs), who fell to his death when he flew too close to the sun. 614, 618

Demeter (dĭ-mē′tər): Greek goddess of agriculture and fertility. She was identified with the Roman goddess **Ceres**. 592

Diana (dī-ă′nə): Roman goddess of the moon and hunting. She was identified with the Greek goddess **Artemis**.

Diana the Huntress. Roman copy of Greek statue.

Louvre Museum

Dionysus (dī′ə-nī′səs): Greek god of wine, fertility, and drama. He was also called **Bacchus** (băk′əs) by the Greeks and the Romans.

Eros (îr′ŏs′): Greek god of love, Aphrodite's son. He was identified with the Roman god **Cupid**.

Fates: three goddesses who controlled human destiny and life. **Clotho** (klō′thō) spun the thread of each person's life, **Lachesis** (lăk′ə-sĭs) determined the length of each thread, and **Atropos** (ăt′rə-pŏs′) cut each thread. 596

Hades (hā′dēz): Greek god of the underworld, and husband of **Persephone**. He was also called **Pluto** (plōō′tō) by the Greeks and the Romans. 578, 592

Helios (hē′lē-ŏs′): early Greek god of the sun. He was later identified with **Apollo**. 608

Hephaestus (hĭ-fĕs′təs): Greek god of fire and metalworking. He was identified with the Roman god **Vulcan**. 580

Hera (hîr′ə): Greek goddess of marriage and childbirth, Zeus's wife, and queen of the gods of Olympus. She was identified with the Roman goddess **Juno**. 578, 622

Heracles (hĕr′ə-klēz′): a Greek hero, the son of Zeus and **Alcmene** (ălk-mē′nē). He was known as **Hercules** to the Romans. 622

Hercules. See **Heracles.**

Hermes (hûr′mēz): Greek god of travelers, merchants, and thieves, and messenger of the gods. He was identified with the Roman god **Mercury**. 580, 595

Icarus. See **Daedalus.**

Iris (ī′rĭs): goddess of the rainbow and messenger of the gods. 595

Jove. See **Jupiter.**

Juno (jōō′nō): Roman goddess of marriage and childbirth, Jupiter's wife, and the queen of the gods. She was identified with the Greek goddess **Hera**.

Jupiter (jōō′pə-tər): Roman god of the sky and the weather, and king of the gods. He was also called **Jove**, and was identified with the Greek god **Zeus**. 578

Mars (märz): Roman god of war. He was identified with the Greek god **Ares**.

Coin with the head of Mars, 280–276 B.C.

Mercury (mûr′kyə-rē): Roman god of business, science, and thieves, and messenger of the gods. He was identified with the Greek god **Hermes**. 580

Minerva (mĭ-nûr′və): Roman goddess of the arts and wisdom. She was identified with the Greek goddess **Athena**. 580, 598

Muses (myōō′zəz): nine sisters, daughters of Zeus and **Mnemosyne** (nĭ-mŏs′ə-nē), who were patronesses of the arts. Each Muse was associated with a different art: **Calliope** (kə-lī′ə-pē′), epic poetry; **Clio** (klī′ō), history; **Erato** (ĕr′ə-tō′), lyric poetry; **Euterpe** (yōō-tûr′pē), music; **Melpomene** (mĕl-pŏm′ə-nē), tragedy; **Polyhymnia** (pŏl′ē-hĭm′nē-ə), religious poetry; **Terpsichore** (tûrp-sĭk′ə-rē), dance; **Thalia** (thə-lī′ə), comedy; and **Urania** (yōō-rā′nē-ə), astronomy. 579, 610

Neptune (nĕp′tōōn′): Roman god of the sea. He was identified with the Greek god **Poseidon**.

Nymphs (nĭmfs): goddesses who inhabited parts of nature, such as rivers, mountains, and trees.

Pan: Greek god of woodlands, shepherds, and goatherds. He was often represented as having the head, chest, and arms of a man, and the legs, horns, and ears of a goat.

Persephone (pər-sĕf′ə-nē): Greek goddess of spring and the underworld, Demeter's daughter. The Romans called her **Proserpina** (prō-sûr′pə-nə). 592

Phaethon (fā′ə-thən): Helios' son. He was killed when he tried to drive the chariot of the Sun. 608

Philemon. See **Baucis**.

Pluto. See **Hades**.

Poseidon (pō-sī′dən): Greek god of the sea. He was identified with the Roman god **Neptune**. 578

Prometheus (prə-mē′thē-əs): the Titan who gave fire to mortals against the wishes of Zeus. 583

Proserpina. See **Persephone**.

Saturn (săt′ərn): Roman god of agriculture and fertility. He was identified with the Greek god **Cronus**.

Satyrs (sā′tərz): woodland creatures who were part human and part goat. They were followers of Dionysus. 575

Selene (sə-lē′nē): early Greek goddess of the moon. She was later identified with **Artemis**. 579

Index of Names

VISUAL CONNECTIONS
Exploring the Subject
Venus was also a more "friendly" goddess as seen by the Romans. The Greeks depicted Aphrodite as the goddess of beauty, but as being sometimes too proud and self-centered. The Romans were less equivocal: Venus represented all the womanly virtues (without the vices). She was beautiful but good-natured, a gentle goddess of springtime flowers and joy.

CONNECTING CULTURES
As an alternative activity, ask each student to choose a different country. Then ask students to locate a creation myth or explanation myth from that country. If none is available, they could try writing one that reflects the country's people and customs. Finally, have students share their myths, either by reading them aloud or by distributing written versions.

Titans (tīt′nz): a family of gods who ruled the universe before the Olympians.   578

Venus (vē′nəs): Roman goddess of gardens, spring, love, and beauty. She was identified with the Greek goddess **Aphrodite.**

Vulcan (vŭl′kən): Roman god of fire and metalworking. He was identified with the Greek god **Hephaestus.**

Zeus (zoōs): Greek god of the sky and the weather, and king of the gods of Olympus. He was identified with the Roman god **Jupiter**, also called **Jove.**   578, 583, 593

Louvre Museum

Detail from *Venus de Milo*. Marble statue, c. 150–100 B.C.

Connecting Cultures

Myths from Different Lands

Most myths fall into two categories—*creation myths* and *explanation myths.* Creation myths tell how the gods and goddesses were created, how the world came into being, and how human beings appeared on earth. Explanation myths chiefly tell about natural processes. In a number of mythologies, the deities have supernatural powers but resemble human beings in many ways. In other mythologies, such as that of the ancient Egyptians, the gods and goddesses resemble animals.

Making Connections: Activities

1. Using books in your local or school library, familiarize yourself with the mythologies of different people. Make a collection of myths that come from various cultures and that share a common subject. For example, look for myths that explain the origin of the seasons or myths that tell how human beings received the gift of fire. You can also look for myths in which people are transformed into animals or plants. Share these stories with the class.

2. Read about the major deities in several different mythologies. What are their characteristics? What part of nature are they identified with? What animals are associated with them? Compare them with the gods and goddesses of classical mythology.

OBJECTIVES
The overall aim is for students to develop skills in critical thinking by comparing and contrasting an American Indian myth with classical myths.

PRESENTATION
The brief myth "The Origin of Corn" and the questions that follow it challenge students to synthesize their reading of this unit to see similarities and differences among myths. Ask students to read "The Origin of Corn" silently while you read it aloud. Then have students answer the questions, comparing the Native American myth with classical and Norse myths they have read. Volunteers might share their responses with the class.

FOCUS ON Reading and Critical Thinking

USING METHODS OF COMPARISON AND CONTRAST

Myths in many different cultures offer explanations for the existence of natural phenomena. Often a god or some special human being is responsible for bringing an important gift, such as fire, to the people on earth. Seeing what different myths have in common can broaden your enjoyment and understanding of these stories.

Here is an American Indian myth about the origin of corn. As you read this myth, keep in mind the classical myths you have read in earlier units.

The Origin of Corn

A long time ago, when Indians were first made, there lived one alone, far, far from any others. He knew not of fire, and subsisted on roots, barks, and nuts. This Indian became very lonesome for company. He grew tired of digging roots, lost his appetite, and for several days lay dreaming in the sunshine; when he awoke he saw something standing near, at which, at first, he was very much frightened. But when it spoke, his heart was glad, for it was a beautiful woman with long *light* hair, very unlike any Indian. He asked her to come to him, but she would not, and if he tried to approach her she seemed to go farther away; he sang to her of his loneliness and besought her not to leave him; at last she told him, if he would do just as she should say, he would always have her with him. He promised that he would.

She led him to where there was some very dry grass, told him to get two very dry sticks, rub them together quickly, holding them in the grass. Soon a spark flew out; the grass caught it, and quick as an arrow the ground was burned over. Then she said, "When the sun sets, take me by the hair and drag me over the burned ground." He did not like to do this, but she told him that wherever he dragged her something like grass would spring up, and he would see her hair coming from between the leaves; then the seeds would be ready for his use. He did as she said, and to this day, when they see the silk (hair) on the cornstalk, the Indians know she has not forgotten them.

Using Methods of Comparison and Contrast

1. What natural phenomenon does this myth attempt to explain? Does this recall Greek myths you have read? Are the attitudes toward nature the same or are they different?

2. What part is played by magic or the supernatural in this myth? What similar magical events can you recall in other myths?

3. Are there important differences between this myth and the other myths you have read?

USING METHODS OF COMPARISON AND CONTRAST
Seeing patterns and relationships is one of the most natural ways to understand our world. We use this strategy in several ways: We define terms by how they are like and unlike other terms; we explain situations by comparing them to other situations; and we classify items based on their similarities and differences.

Answers
1. Attempts to explain how corn originated. It is similar to story of Prometheus in that a supernatural figure brings fire to people. Also similar to Demeter and Persephone in explanation of natural phenomena by association of goddess with growth and harvest. Attitudes toward nature differ; corn maiden promises to remain with him always. Nature in Greek myths is often unreliable and unfair.

2. Magical element is corn maiden who gives life to earth from her own body, transforming her hair into corn silk. Can be compared to transformation myths of Arachne (into spider), and Baucis and Philemon (into linden and oak trees).

3. In Greek myths, gods try selfishly to keep secrets of nature for themselves; in American Indian myth, corn maiden unselfishly shares secret of fire and corn.

Focus on Reading and Critical Thinking

UNIT 10 • TEACHING GUIDE

LITERARY HERITAGE
NORSE MYTHOLOGY

OVERVIEW OF THE UNIT

Although Greek mythology is more commonly taught, Norse mythology is a vital part of English and, ultimately, American heritage. The Norsemen or Vikings came from the coastal regions of Norway, Sweden, and Denmark. During their great period of adventure and conquest, they spread their customs, language, and stories to many countries of Northern Europe and the British Isles. In 793 the Vikings made their first attack on England's coast. The wave of succeeding attacks was interwoven with periods of settlement. The Vikings worshipped the warlike gods Odin and Thor in addition to gentler gods like their sun god Balder. These warriors believed that heroes who fell bravely in battle were welcomed into Valhalla, a special heavenly hall reserved for them.

The Vikings also brought with them an excellent system of law, a high regard for women (who were often leaders and chieftains), and an early jury system. They also bequeathed to us a wealth of stories. These myths show the tradition of heroism and courage that became part of the heritage of English-speaking peoples. This unit is intended to highlight the literary link that stretches between the Norsemen of yesterday and the Americans of today.

The unit opens with an overview of the setting and the principal characters of Norse mythology. In addition to introducing the gods and goddesses and the three levels of the Norse universe, this introductory section briefly contrasts the Norse deities with those of Greek mythology. A helpful chart identifying Norse names and providing their pronunciation is included.

OBJECTIVES OF THE UNIT

The aims of the unit are for the student:
- To identify specific details and cause-and-effect relationships in Norse mythology
- To demonstrate an understanding of the characteristics and cultural aspects of Norse myths
- To draw conclusions about the relevance of Norse myths to the Norse culture
- To use a dictionary to trace word origins
- To write analyses of aspects of Norse mythology
- To focus on persuasive writing

CONCEPTS AND SKILLS

The following concepts and skills are treated in this unit:

LANGUAGE AND VOCABULARY
Tracing the Origins of Calendar Names   643

WRITING OPPORTUNITIES

Writing About Literature
Explaining Characteristics of Odin   643
Analyzing the Image of the Wolf   647
Comparing Myths   652
Discussing Elements of Magic and Disguise   659
Analyzing a Character   662
Analyzing Heroic Characteristics   665

Focus on Persuasive Writing
Supporting Your Opinion   647
Using Appeals to the Emotions   652

TRANSPARENCIES

The following unit support materials with specific correlations to literature selections are available in the **Fine Art and Instructional Transparencies with Teacher's Notes and Blackline Masters** section of your *Audiovisual Resources Binder*.

FINE ART TRANSPARENCIES

Theme: Transformations That Teach a Lesson
46 *Apollo and Daphne*, Antonio Pollaiuolo

Theme: The Heroic Struggle
47 *Whaam!*, Roy Lichtenstein

READER RESPONSE
48 Breakfast of Role Models
49 Norse Notables

LITERARY ELEMENTS
50 Analyzing a Myth
51 Elements of Fables

WRITING PROCESS
52 Supporting an Opinion
53 Writing a Persuasive Paper

INTRODUCING THE UNIT

Before assigning any of the readings in this unit, you may wish to generate interest and build readiness by using one of the following approaches:

Display a large map (preferably a relief map) of the Scandinavian countries: Norway, Sweden, and Denmark. Ask students to identify major geographic features such as rugged mountains, rivers and seas, lakes and fjords. Point out that parts of Scandinavia are within the Arctic Circle. Ask the students to imagine what life must have

PLANNING GUIDE

For Unit Planning
- Transparencies 46–53: *Audiovisual Resources Binder*
- Portfolio Assessment: *Professional Support Material*
- Test Generator
- Mastery Test: Teaching Resources E, p. 182
- Analogy Test: Teaching Resources E, p. 184
- Composition Test: Teaching Resources E, p. 185

SELECTION (Pupil's Page)	TEACHING RESOURCES E (page numbers shown below)							AV BINDER
	Teacher's Notes	Reading Check	Study Guide	Language Skills	Building Vocabulary	Selection Vocab. Test	Selection Test	Audio-cassette
NORSE MYTHOLOGY *Introduction* (p. 635)	115							
Barbara Leonie Picard *The Norse Gods and Goddesses* (p. 640)	116	127	118		121		123	TAPE 3 SIDE B
Retold by Olivia Coolidge *The Fenris Wolf* (p. 644)	125	127	128		131		132	
Retold by Hamilton Wright Mabie *How Thor Found His Hammer* (p. 648)	133	148	135	138	141		143	
Retold by Olivia Coolidge *Thor and the Giant King* (p. 653)	145	148	149		153	168	155	
Retold by Edith Hamilton *The Death of Balder* (p. 660)	157	172	160	163	166	168	169	TAPE 3 SIDE B
Barbara Leonie Picard *The End of All Things* (p. 663)	170	172	173		176		178	

been like for Scandinavian peoples in the first century. Provide pictures of Vikings and Viking ships. Lead the students to understand that because life was a struggle in the Far North, the people literally waged a daily battle to survive. Help the students understand the importance of traits such as courage, loyalty, and perseverance as they read the selections in this unit.

Explain that "Old English" is the ancient version of English spoken by the Angles and Saxons, Norse peoples who invaded, conquered, and settled what was then called Britain (a former Roman province). Write on the board *Angle-land* and explain to students that this was the origin of the name England. Help the students understand that the coming of the Norsemen to Britain created a mixture of culture and languages: Old English is basically a Germanic language which, during its "Middle" period, was powerfully influenced by Latin (Roman) culture and vocabulary, as represented by the Norman French. List on the chalkboard modern English words that can be traced back to Old English: *ice, snow, fight, sword, boat.* Suggest that the class make a collection of words that have come down to Americans from Old English as they read the Norse myths in this unit. (Hint: think of one-syllable, common nouns and verbs. Words of three syllables or more tend to be French or Latin.) Reserve a special part of the class bulletin board to include these words.

Student Learning Options

NORSE MYTHOLOGY
1. Making Comic Books
After dividing the class into groups, ask students to create comic strips telling one of the Norse myths. You may want to have them read their comic books to younger students, showing the pictures as they read.

2. Discussing American Myths
After students have read the Norse myths, ask them to think of people that have become part of an American myth. Guide them to discover what these myths tell us about American culture. Examples for starting the discussion could be Paul Bunyan and Johnny Appleseed. The discussion might also include real people whose lives approach myth because many stories have been made up about them.

3. Making Models
Have students make models, perhaps in shoe boxes, of the settings and characters in the myths they read. They can get help from resource books to see how the Norse dressed and what their land looked like.

VISUAL CONNECTIONS

Exploring the Subject

The sea was the Norsemen's primary highway and their most dependable food source. The North Sea is known for sudden, freezing squalls and huge icebergs that can sink a ship in seconds. If a ship went down in these subarctic waters, there were rarely survivors. To those awaiting a missing ship's return, it seemed as though the sea simply swallowed it up. It is little wonder that the Norsemen believed the sea was the home of sea serpents, including the earth serpent (Midgard-Serpent), a monster so huge it encircled the earth and fastened its jaws onto its own tail.

About the Artist

American-born, Elihu Vedder settled in Rome in 1865. He was interested in religions, especially Buddhism. In his paintings, he tried to make statements about human existence by adding images of mysticism and unreality to realistic scenes.

About the Artwork

Vedder worked in the "visionary tradition." Aloof from any artistic movement or group, he followed his own artistic way. Vedder once explained that he wandered through nature and through the world of his imagination, using his paintings as a mirror to reflect what he saw. This painting shows one such "wandering," the setting real, the serpent a fantasy.

The Lair of the Sea Serpent by Elihu Vedder (1836–1923). Oil on canvas.
The Metropolitan Museum of Art, gift of Mrs. Harold G. Henderson, 1976. (1976.106.1)

NORSE MYTHOLOGY

NORSE MYTHOLOGY

Norse mythology, like most other mythologies and folklores, began as a body of spoken stories passed down through the generations. Writing was introduced to Scandinavia after the establishment of Christianity (about 1000), and this great collection of tales was not written down until after 1100. Two Icelandic books are the source of our present knowledge of the world view of the ancient Norsemen. The first, the Poetic Edda, is a collection of alliterative verse written down sometime between the tenth and thirteenth centuries. The second, the Prose Edda, is a collection of myths and tales written down by Snorri Sturluson about 1200.

The Norse gods and goddesses are more compassionate toward human beings than their Greek and Roman counterparts. They principally value honor, justice, and wisdom. In fact, the well-being of the world tree, Yggdrasill (ĭg' drə sĭl'), depends on the gods' maintaining these virtues. The roots of this great ash tree reach down beneath the earth; its branches spread out over Midgard, the earth; and its topmost limbs hold the sky. When Yggdrasill dies, the rule of the Aesir will end as all evil—including the frost giants, the trolls, and the Fenris Wolf—rises one last time to battle the forces for good—the Aesir, the Vanir (nature gods), and spirits of human heroes. The Norse believed that after this fearsome last battle, a new, gentler, and better world would arise.

OBJECTIVES
The overall aim is for students to demonstrate an understanding of the gods and goddesses of Norse mythology as contrasted with the gods and goddesses of classical mythology.

PRESENTATION
In this introduction, three major contrasts are drawn between the gods of Greek mythology and those of Norse mythology. Following this comparison is an overview of the Norse cosmos, consisting of Asgard (heavens), Midgard (earth), and Niflheim (underworld). A list of names from Norse mythology is included on pp. 636–639. You may want to go over in class the pronunciations of the names found on the chart.

This introduction is not difficult, but it does contain some critical material. Be sure the stu-

UNIT INTRODUCTION

1
Classical: of the Greek and Roman period.

2
Olympians were dwellers of Mt. Olympus—the gods and goddesses of Greek mythology.

3
In Norse mythology, three mysterious women, the Norns, determined at birth the fate of every child.

4
As translates as "god," *gard* as "enclosure" (found as root of modern English "yard" and "garden").

NAMES IN NORSE MYTHOLOGY
Students should be able to use this guide as a reference to pronunciation and identification of names in Norse mythology as well as a description of significant attributes. The names are alphabetized to allow students to return to these pages as a quick reference while covering material in the unit.

---

1 Norse mythology consists of the myths of ancient Scandinavia and Germany. Norse mythology is very different from classical mythol-
2 ogy. Unlike the Olympians, the gods and goddesses in Norse mythology are not all-powerful. Although they rule the worlds of humans,
3 giants, and dwarfs, they themselves are ruled by fate and cannot change their destiny. They do not have the gift of eternal youth: in order to remain young, they must eat the apples of Idun every day. Furthermore, they are not immortal. They await a great final battle, called Ragnarok (răg′nə-räk′), which is to be fought between the gods and goddesses and their enemies, the giants. In this battle, all will perish and the earth will be destroyed. Then a new race of gods and goddesses will be reborn and a new world re-created for the human race.

There are three separate levels in the universe of Norse mythology.
4 At the first level, there is Asgard (ăs′gärd, äz′), the world of the gods and goddesses. At the middle level, there is Midgard (mĭd′gärd′), where human beings, dwarfs, and giants dwell. At the bottom level, there is Niflheim (nĭv′əl-hām′), the world of the dead. All three levels are held together by the roots and branches of a mighty ash tree.

In this unit you will meet the major figures in Norse mythology and read some of the best stories ever told. As you read the myths in this unit, you may want to refer to this chart. Note that some names may be spelled in more than one way.

NAME	DESCRIPTION
Aesir (ă′sîr, ē′sîr)	warrior gods of Norse mythology
Asgard (ăs′gärd′, äz′)	home of the Aesir and slain heroes
Balder (bôl′dər)	god of daylight; wisest and most beautiful of the gods
Bifrost (bēf′räst)	rainbow bridge connecting Asgard and Midgard
Bragi (brä′gē)	god of poetry
Fenris (Fenrir) (fĕn′rĭs)	Wolf, the son of Loki
Frey (frā)	god of plenty

Dragon Ship by John Taylor Arms. Aquatint.

dents can picture the three separate levels—held together by the roots and branches of a mighty ash tree—of the Norse universe.

VISUAL CONNECTIONS
Exploring the Subject
In Old Norse, the verb *vik* means "to raid." The Vikings were preeminently sea raiders.

Their ships were marvels of engineering. The hull of a Viking ship was constructed of narrow planks, lapped on the upper edges and well-caulked on the inside. This gave the ship a light, flexible shape which allowed it to ride high in the water and to endure brutally stormy seas that would have crushed a heavier or less maneuverable ship. In addition, little breeze was needed to propel it, and it could sail or be rowed in very shallow waters.

Although Viking ships were graceful and well-built, they were not particularly comfortable: there was little shelter from the cold and the damp for the men who sailed in them. As shown here, a Viking ship often had a tentlike arrangement on the deck, but this was intended to keep provisions dry, not the men. Norsemen usually hung their round battle shields on the outer railings to lessen the amount of sea water sloshing over the sides and also to provide some protection against the projectile weapons of their enemies. The "dragon" on the prow gave the ship balance when sailing, but its ferocious expression also served to terrify those being raided.

NAMES IN NORSE MYTHOLOGY

Students may find the Norse names difficult at first. Reading through this list with the class should help them to feel more comfortable with the pronunciation. Also, students perusing this list of names and attributes will quickly notice parallels between Norse gods and goddesses and those of classical mythology. The recognition of many such similarities usually encourages students who might otherwise be intimidated by unfamiliar and complex-looking Norse names.

Students may enjoy studying the Norse gods and goddesses as a game. Placing the name on one side of an index card and the description on the reverse side, make the information in the chart into a whole deck of index cards. Individual students or student teams can quiz one another so that, given the description of a person, place, or thing in Norse mythology, they can supply the name, or given the name they can supply a description.

NAME	DESCRIPTION
Freya (Freyja) (frā′ə)	goddess of love and beauty
Frig (Frigg, Frigga) (frĭg)	goddess of the heavens; Odin's wife
Heimdall (hām′däl′)	watchman of the rainbow bridge
Hel (Hela) (hĕl)	goddess of the underworld
Hermod	Odin's messenger
Hod (Hoder)	blind god of night
Honir	shining god
Idun (Iduna) (ē′do͞on)	goddess responsible for the apples of youth
Jotunheim (Iotunheim) (yô′to͞on-hām′, yō′-)	world of the giants
Loki (lō′kē)	god of fire; trickster and sky traveler
Midgard (mĭd′gärd′)	middle world inhabited by human beings
Mimir (mē′mîr)	guardian of the well of wisdom
Mjolnir (Miollnir, Mjollnir)	Thor's hammer
Niflheim (Nifelheim) (nĭv′əl-hām′)	world of the dead
Njord (Niord, Njorth) (nyôth)	wind god
Norns (nôrns)	three goddesses of destiny
Odin (ō′dĭn)	king of the gods and goddesses; god of war, wisdom, and art
Ragnarok (răg′nə-räk′)	final battle between gods and human beings, giants, and monsters
Thor (thôr)	lord of thunder
Tyr (tîr)	bravest of Aesir gods

CLOSURE
Ask students to identify three major differences between the gods and goddesses of Norse mythology and the gods and goddesses of classical mythology.

Raging Wotan Rides to the Rock! (1910) by Arthur Rackham (1867–1939). In German mythology, Odin is sometimes called Wodan or Wotan.

VISUAL CONNECTIONS
Exploring the Subject

Odin's name was *Odin* in Scandinavian languages, *Wotan* in German, and *Woden* in Old English. He was the god of wisdom, and he paid dearly to gain his knowledge (see pp. 641–642). He also suffered in order to learn the art of poetry which, according to Norse belief, he then bestowed on poets and minstrels (*skalds*) who told heroic tales.

However, these "refinements" are considered by some scholars to have been later developments as Norse culture became more sophisticated. As the chief god of a fierce warrior people, Odin's original character may have been that of a god of war. Even in the later period of Norse culture, one of Odin's chief concerns was the recruitment of slain heroes to help fight alongside the gods during Ragnarok. One warrior tradition was that of the *berserkers*. The name comes from the Old Norse for "bear coat" and refers to the belief that these men, dedicated to Odin, could take on the character as well as the shape of a fierce fighting animal—usually a bear but sometimes a wolf, bull, or eagle.

NAME	DESCRIPTION
Utgard (o͞ot′gärd′)	citadel of giants in Jotunheim
Valhalla (Valhall) (văl-hăl′ə)	huge hall in Asgard where slain warriors are brought and feasted
Valkyrie (Valkyr) (văl-kîr′ē, văl′kîr-ē)	warrior-maiden who carries slain warriors to Valhalla
Vanir (vä′nîr)	nature gods and goddesses who live in Asgard
Yggdrasill (ĭg′drə-sĭl, üg′-)	ash tree that supports all levels of the Norse universe

Names in Norse Mythology

Bronze statue of Odin.
Ny Carlsberg Glyptotek, Copenhagen

The Norse Gods and Goddesses

BARBARA LEONIE PICARD

In this selection you will meet some of the most important figures in Norse mythology. As you read, see if you can find any parallels to the Olympians in classical mythology.

The gods of the Norsemen were the Aesir and the Vanir. The Vanir were the gods of nature: Niord, the god of the shore and the shallow summer sea; and his son and daughter, Frey and Freya, Frey who ruled over the elves of light and Freya the goddess of love and beauty; and Aegir,[1] the lord of the deep and stormy seas, with Ran his wife, who caught sailors in her net and drowned them. Aegir and Ran were not truly of the kindly Vanir, for they were cruel and more akin to the giants, but like the Vanir, they ruled over nature and were on good terms with all the other gods.

The Aesir were the gods who cared for men; Odin the Allfather, king of all the gods, wise and just and understanding; and Frigg, his

1. **Aegir** (ăg′ər).

PRESENTATION

"The Norse Gods and Goddesses" is an overview of the figures of Norse mythology. Chief among these are the Aesir, the gods and goddesses whose special province includes the affairs of mortals, and the Vanir, the gods of nature. Of the Aesir, the most important is Odin, king of all the gods. In addition to a description of Odin's three palaces in Asgard, Odin's character is revealed through the sacrificial act in which he exchanges his own eye for wisdom and understanding. A peculiar Norse character is cunning Loki, god of fire, a trickster who is a troubling mixture of good and evil.

Tell students that these tales are some of the most interesting of the Norse myths, tales which feature bold adventure, humor, cleverness, and—especially—bravery despite adversity.

---

queen, who presided over human marriages; Honir, Odin's brother, the shining god, who lived among the Vanir; large, noisy Thor, the god of thunder, Odin's son, who always had a special corner in his heart for the peasants and 4 the poor and the dispossessed; Tyr, the brave god of war; Balder and Hod, the twin sons of Odin and Frigg, Balder the god of daylight, who was the most beautiful of all the gods, and Hod who was blind and ruled over the hours of darkness; Hermod, Odin's messenger; and Heimdall, the divine watchman who kept guard over Bifrost, the bridge between Asgard and the world.

And lastly there was Loki, who was neither of the Aesir nor of the Vanir, nor yet of the 5 giant race; crafty red-haired Loki, quick to laugh and quick to change his shape, the god of the fire that burns on the hearth, good and kindly when it wishes, but a merciless destroyer when it leaves its proper place. From the earliest days Odin and Loki had sworn an oath of brotherhood; and it was this which so often saved Loki in later times, when his cunning tricks so much displeased the other gods.

In Asgard Odin had three palaces; in one the gods met in council; and in another stood his throne, Hlidskialf,[2] which served him as a watchtower from where he might see all that 6 passed not only in Asgard, but in Midgard and Iotunheim, and even in the depths of dark Niflheim, the home of mist, as well. Here would he sit with his two ravens perched upon his shoulders. Each day he sent these birds flying forth across the world and each evening they returned to tell him of the happenings of the day. At his feet would lie his two wolves who followed him like hounds wherever he went in Asgard, and at the feasting would eat the meat that was set before him; for the Allfather lived on mead[3] alone, and no food passed his lips so long as he was among the gods, though when he traveled through Midgard, he lived like other men.

Odin's third palace was called Valhall and was set in the midst of a grove of trees whose leaves were gleaming gold. This palace had five hundred and forty doors, and its walls were made of glittering spears and its roof of 7 golden shields. To this hall came all those warriors who had died in battle, when death had passed away from them as a dream, to feast and tell tales of their deeds as living men, and to test their fighting skill on one another with weapons and armor made of imperishable gold. For the Norsemen were great warriors, and they believed that when a battle raged, Odin would send out his warrior-maidens, the Valkyrs, to ride across the sky and fetch the slain to Valhall, where they would be with Odin himself, and feast upon the flesh of the boar Saehrimnir,[4] which, though slaughtered and roasted each day, came back to life each night, and drink of the mead provided by the goat Heidrun.[5] Thus every Norseman longed, when the time came, to die in battle; and his 8 greatest fear was that he should suffer a straw-death, and die in bed, lying on his straw-stuffed mattress. For the spirits of all those who did not die fighting went down to dark Niflheim.

9 Odin sought knowledge and wisdom, that he might use them to the good of both gods and men; and one day he went to Mimir's well, the fount of wisdom and understanding, which 10 flowed by that root of the ash tree Yggdrasill which grew in Midgard, and asked the giant Mimir to let him drink of the magic waters.

Mimir looked long at Odin before he an-

---

2. **Hlidskialf** (lĭd'skē-ălf): "Hill-Opening."
3. **mead** (mēd): a drink made from fermented honey and water.
4. **Saehrimnir** (sā'rĭm-nīr).
5. **Heidrun** (hā'drŭn).

4
Tyr is somewhat similar to Ares, Balder to Apollo, and Hermod to Hermes.

5
Description. Loki's appearance resembles fire (color of flames); his personality resembles fire in quickness, form changing, and frequent laughter (resembles fire's crackle). Fire and Loki both have potential for great help or great harm.

6
Midgard, the "middle-earth" dwelling of humans, also encompassed homes of dwarfs, elves, and giants.

7
Odin gathers fighters in preparation for the cataclysmic battle between the Aesir and their enemies.

8
Highest regard was given to warriors in Norse culture.

9
Characterization. Explains Odin's motives, actions. (Odin's self-sacrifice contrasts with Zeus's selfishness.)

10
The world tree with top branches stretching to Asgard, trunk in Midgard, roots in Niflheim.

The Norse Gods and Goddesses

MEETING INDIVIDUAL NEEDS
Visual Learners • Have students draw a picture or diagram of the Norse universe composed of three separate levels held together by the roots and branches of a mighty ash tree. Have them label each of the three levels and tell who lives there.

PORTFOLIO ASSESSMENT
Students may be interested in comparing a Norse mythological character and a similar Greek mythological character, such as Aphrodite and Freya, the Fates and the Norns, or Zeus and Odin. Suggest that students research the characters they want to compare to find out more about them than is revealed by the selections in these units. Comparisons may take the form of paragraphs or charts listing similarities and differences in character.

VISUAL CONNECTIONS
Ideas for Writing
Valkyrie means "chooser of the slain." The Valkyrie were battle-maidens who served Odin, flying on winged horses to the scene of a battle and transporting a selected few who died a heroic death to Valhalla to feast with Odin.

As a class activity, play Richard Wagner's "Ride of the Valkyrie" and ask students to write a paragraph describing their impressions of the music, or of the attitude of the Valkyrie to their task as expressed in the music. The musical passage is from Act II of the second opera of Wagner's four-opera Ring Cycle series. It can often be found in lending libraries, perhaps in recorded collections of passages from famous operas.

The Ride of the Valkyries (1910) by Arthur Rackham.

11
Norse mythology has many instances of "paying"; if goal is worthy, Norse hero must make any sacrifice, without complaint.

12
Hero. Odin exhibits heroic characteristics: goodness, strength, bravery, intelligence. "Good will" shown in Odin's sacrifice to gain knowledge of last battle, in which all Aesir (including Odin) and most Vanir will die fighting; major beneficiaries of the gods' ultimate sacrifice will be humankind.

642

11 swered, and then he said, "Even the gods must pay for knowledge."

"And what is the price of wisdom?" asked Odin.

"Give me one of your eyes as a pledge," said Mimir.

12 Unhesitatingly, Odin plucked out one of his eyes and gave it to Mimir, and Mimir let him drink from the well, and straightway Odin was filled with the knowledge of all things past and present, and even into the future could he look. And though his new knowledge gave him joy, it brought sorrow to him also, for he could now tell not only what was past, but also the grief that was to come. Yet he returned to Asgard to use his knowledge to help the other gods and those men who sought his aid.

And Mimir dropped Odin's eye into his well, and it lay there evermore, shining below the water, a proof of Odin's love of wisdom and his good will towards mankind.

642   NORSE MYTHOLOGY

CLOSURE

Ask students to name the most important Norse gods and goddesses and to list the values reflected in Norse mythology.

EXTENSION AND ENRICHMENT

Have students begin a Who's Who mural of the characters of Norse mythology, drawing pictures and giving brief descriptions of them. They can begin with Odin, whose hair, hat, or cloak usually covered the wound left when he sacrificed an eye. Use pictures in library books for ideas. For example, the gods and goddesses are pictured on the title page of D'Aulaires' *Norse Gods and Giants* (1986).

Reading Check

1. In Norse mythology the Aesir ruled over human beings. What did the Vanir do?
2. How was Loki different from the other gods?
3. How was Asgard, the realm of the gods, connected to the earth?
4. What different functions were served by Odin's three palaces?
5. How did Odin obtain wisdom?

For Study and Discussion

Analyzing and Interpreting the Selection

1. The Norse Universe consists of three levels. Briefly describe each one.
2. Odin, the Allfather, occupies the central role in Norse mythology as Zeus does in classical mythology. Yet he is a very different figure. How is this difference shown in his attitude toward human beings?
3. In Norse mythology Loki is the Trickster god. He is sly and he enjoys making mischief. In what way are these characteristics appropriate for the god of fire?
4. How does Norse mythology reflect the importance of physical courage and military glory in the culture of the Norse people?

Language and Vocabulary

Tracing the Origins of Calendar Names

Several of our weekdays are named for Old English gods who trace their ancestry to the gods of Norse mythology. Here is an etymological entry for the word *Thursday*:

> [Middle English *thur(e)sday*, Old English *thur(e)s dâeg* (influenced by Old Norse *thōrsdagr*, "Thor's day"), from earlier *thunresdâeg*, "Thor's day" (translation of Late Latin *Jovis diēs*, "Jupiter's day"): *thunres*, genitive of *thunor*, THUNDER + *dâeg*, DAY.]

This entry tells you that our word *Thursday* appeared in Middle English (between 1100 and 1500) as *thuresday*. This word had come from Old English words (between 400 and 1100), which were influenced by the Old Norse word meaning "Thor's day." The Old Norse word, in turn, had been a translation of the Latin words meaning "Jupiter's day." Like the Roman god Jupiter, Thor was associated with thunder, as the last item of the etymological entry shows.

1. Use a college or unabridged dictionary to find the etymology of each of these calendar names:

   Tuesday   Wednesday   Friday

Writing About Literature

▶ Explaining Characteristics of Odin

Although Tyr is identified as the brave god of war, Odin also has characteristics of a war god. In a paragraph explain Odin's role as god of battle.

▶ Before students begin this writing assignment, you may want to refer them to the **Writing About Literature** section on p. 688.

READING CHECK
1. Ruled nature (p. 640).
2. Was crafty and could be merciless destroyer (p. 641).
3. Bifrost bridge (p. 641).
4. Meeting place, watchtower, hall of heroes (p. 641).
5. Exchanged eye for drink from Mimir's well (p. 642).

FOR STUDY AND DISCUSSION
1. *Asgard:* home of gods and goddesses. *Midgard:* home of people, dwarfs, and giants. *Niflheim:* home of unheroic dead.
2. Odin cares about humans; he is wise, just, and understanding.
3. Fire provides needed warmth but can cause grief and destruction if uncontrolled.
4. In emphasis on privileged afterlife awaiting heroes slain in battle.

LANGUAGE AND VOCABULARY
1. *Tuesday:* Middle English *tiwesday, tuesdai,* Old English *tiwesdaeg,* "day of Tiu": Tiw, Tiu day. *Tiw* or *Tiu* was Old English for Norse god Tyr.
Wednesday: Middle English *Wodnesday, Wednesday,* Old English *Wonesdag,* "Woden's day" (translation of Latin *Mercurii dies,* "day of Mercury"). *Woden* is Old English for Norse god Odin.
Friday: Middle English *fridai,* Old English *frigedaeg.* Old Norse *Frigg,* goddess of love, wife of Odin, *frijedagaz,* "day of Frigg" (translation of Latin *Veneris dies,* "Venus' day"), in Old English *frigedaeg,* Friday.

WRITING ABOUT LITERATURE
Have students go back to the unit introduction and "The Norse Gods and Goddesses" to make prewriting notes about Odin's warlike characteristics. Then, from these notes, students can write the first draft of their paragraph.

OBJECTIVES
The overall aim is for students to describe the characteristics of the Fenris Wolf and to explain the techniques used by the gods to subdue him. For a complete list of objectives, see the **Teacher's Notes**.

> **TEACHING RESOURCES E**
> Teacher's Notes, p. 125
> Reading Check, p. 127
> Study Guide, p. 128
> Building Vocabulary, p. 131
> Selection Test, p. 132

PREREADING FOCUS
The headnote introduces the Fenris Wolf, a particularly fierce Norse monster. Ask students why monsters are common in mythology and what forces they might represent to primitive people.

The Fenris Wolf

1
Characterization. Clever, evil and handsome: first sentence sums up Loki's character. Like most mythological characters, he has a set nature.

2
Loki is one of the most troublesome characters in all mythology, yet Odin protected him. Some myths say Odin foresaw all, allowed Loki's "tricks" in order to bide time, preparing for last battle when Loki would be powerful, evil enemy.

3
English word *hell* derived from her name; her "grisly" appearance included having half her face a lovely woman's, half a rotting corpse's (or, in some versions, a skeleton's).

4 Drawing Conclusions
Norse monsters (world serpent, wolf, giants) tend to be enormous and ferocious. What Norse fear might this tendency reflect? Their fear of dangerous natural forces.

5
In Norse myth, sun and moon are eternally chased by giant wolves; in last battle, they are swallowed up; thus their reaction to wolf howl is foreboding.

The Fenris Wolf

Retold by
OLIVIA COOLIDGE

In Norse mythology, as in classical mythology, there are many fearsome monsters, none perhaps more terrifying than the Fenris Wolf. How would the gods subdue him?

1 Though Loki, the fire god, was handsome and ready-witted, his nature was really evil. He was, indeed, the cause of most of the misfortunes which befell the gods. He was constantly 2 in trouble, yet often forgiven because the gods valued his cleverness. It was he who found ways out of difficulty for them, so that for a long time they felt that they could not do without him.

In the early days Loki, though a god, had wedded a monstrous giantess, and the union of these two evil beings produced a fearful brood. The first was the great world serpent, whom Odin cast into the sea, and who became so large that he completely encircled the earth, his tail touching his mouth. The second was 3 Hel, the grisly goddess of the underworld, who reigned in the horrible land of the dead. The third was the most dreadful of all, a huge monster called the Fenris Wolf.

When the gods first saw the Fenris Wolf, he was so young that they thought they could tame him. They took him to Asgard, therefore, and brave Tyr undertook to feed and train him. Presently, however, the black monster grew so enormous that his open jaws 4 would stretch from heaven to earth, showing teeth as large as the trunks of oak trees and as sharply pointed as knives. The howls of the beast were so dreadful as he tore his vast meals of raw meat that the gods, save for Tyr, dared not go near him, lest he devour them.

At last all were agreed that the Fenris Wolf must be fettered if they were to save their very lives, for the monster grew more ferocious towards them every day. They forged a huge chain, but since none was strong enough to bind him, they challenged him to a trial of strength. "Let us tie you with this to see if you can snap the links," said they.

The Fenris Wolf took a look at the chain and showed all his huge white teeth in a dreadful grin. "Bind me if you wish," he growled, and he actually shut his eyes as he lay down at ease to let them put it on.

The gods stepped back, and the wolf gave a little shake. There was a loud cracking sound, and the heavy links lay scattered around him in 5 pieces. The wolf howled in triumph until the sun and moon in heaven trembled at the noise.

Thor, the smith, called other gods to his aid, and they labored day and night at a second

644 NORSE MYTHOLOGY

MOTIVATIONAL SUMMARY
The Fenris Wolf—offspring of Loki, the fire god—is allowed to live in Asgard. However, when he grows fierce and huge, the gods realize that he must be chained up. They make the heaviest chains they can, but the wolf breaks them. Finally, they ask the dwarfs for help, and the dwarfs give the gods a little silken rope. When the wolf sees it, he suspects a trick.

PRESENTATION
Loki, the god of fire, and his wife, a monstrous giantess, had three terrible children: the world serpent; Hel, the goddess of the underworld; and the Fenris Wolf, the most dreadful of all. Emphasize to students that the Fenris Wolf will

chain. This was half as strong again as the first, and so heavy that no one of the gods could drag it across the ground. "This is by far the largest chain that was ever made," said they. "Even the Fenris Wolf will not be able to snap fetters such as these."

Once more they brought the chain to the wolf, and he let them put it on, though this

6
The Norse gods are not all-powerful; their courage is more remarkable because of their limitations.

VISUAL CONNECTIONS
Ideas for Writing
Discuss this illustration with students after they have read the selection. It shows the Fenris Wolf, after the gods have twice attempted to bind him with heavy chains, being held by the magical cord Gleipnir, which was crafted by the dwarfs.

As a class activity, you might ask students to write a short myth using "The Fenris Wolf" as a model. Imagine that there is a specific monster, evil person, or imminent catastrophe that the gods wish to control, prevent from creating harm, or destroy by means of a magical device which is crafted by the dwarfs. Describe the danger presented by the situation and give details of the ingredients used in the "magic" formula of the device created to avert catastrophe.

The Binding of Fenris by Dorothy Hardy.

The Fenris Wolf

be a very important enemy of the gods at the time of Ragnarok. As students read, they should pay attention to how this myth foreshadows the end of all things when the Fenris Wolf will break his bonds and devour Odin. Remind them that just as the gods struggle and sacrifice to chain the awful wolf, so in the last battle they will fight with great bravery and determination.

> **TRANSPARENCY 52**
> **Writing Process**
> *Supporting an Opinion* – helps students to identify, analyze, and organize support for a statement of opinion.

7
Description. Burning eyes show wolf's heritage (father is Loki). Bristling hair, gnashing teeth express wild nature of Fenris Wolf.

8 Comparing/Contrasting
How powerful are the Norse gods in comparison to the Greek and Roman gods? Gods' inability to bind wolf reflects their humanlike limitations; contrasts with magical, limitless powers of classical gods.

9
This list of "ingredients" fits into the Norse folk tradition of riddles and puzzles.

10
Tyr's sacrifice reflects concern for others; trait not found in his classical counterpart Ares.

11
The Norse Fates, called the Norns, make decisions about the future that even the gods cannot change.

12
Thus, according to Norse mythology, evil is not vanquished but only restrained.

READING CHECK
1. Great world serpent; Hel; Fenris Wolf (p. 644).
2. Tyr (p. 644).
3. The wolf continued to grow more ferocious and dangerous (p. 644).
4. Dwarfs (p. 646).
5. Fenris Wolf bit it off (p. 646).

646

time it was clear that he somewhat doubted his strength. When they had chained him, he shook himself violently, but the fetters held. **7** His great, red eyes burned with fury, the black hair bristled on his back, and he gnashed his teeth until the foam flew. He strained heavily against the iron until the vast links flattened and lengthened, but did not break. Finally with a great bound and a howl he dashed himself against the ground, and suddenly the chain sprang apart so violently that broken pieces were hurled about the heads of the watching gods.

8 Now the gods realized in despair that all their strength and skill would not avail to bind the wolf. Therefore Odin sent a messenger to the dwarf people under the earth, bidding them forge him a chain. The messenger returned with a little rope, smooth and soft as a silken string, which was hammered on dwarfish anvils out of strange materials which have never been seen or heard. The sound of a cat's **9** footfall, the breath of a fish, the flowing beard of a woman, and the roots of a mountain made the metal from which it was forged.

The gods took the little rope to the Fenris Wolf. "See what an easy task we have for you this time," they said.

"Why should I bother myself with a silken string?" asked the wolf sullenly. "I have broken your mightiest chain. What use is this foolish thing?"

"The rope is stronger than it looks," answered they. "We are not able to break it, but it will be a small matter to you."

"If this rope is strong by enchantment," said the wolf in slow suspicion, "how can I tell that you will loosen me if I cannot snap it after all? On one condition you may bind me: you must give me a hostage from among yourselves."

"How can we do this?" they asked.

The Fenris Wolf stretched himself and yawned until the sun hid behind clouds at the sight of his great, red throat. "I will let you bind me with this rope," he said, "if one of you gods will hold his hand between my teeth while I do it."

The gods looked at one another in silence. The wolf grinned from ear to ear. Without a word Tyr walked forward and laid his bare hand inside the open mouth.

The gods bound the great wolf, and he stretched himself and heaved as before. This time, however, he did not break his bonds. He gnashed his jaws together, and Tyr cried out in **10** pain as he lost his hand. Nevertheless, the great black wolf lay howling and writhing and helplessly biting the ground. There he lay in the bonds of the silken rope as long as the **11** reign of Odin endured. The Fates[1] declared, however, that in the last days,[2] when the demons of ice and fire should come marching against the gods to the battlefield, the great sea **12** would give up the serpent, and the Fenris Wolf would break his bonds. The wolf would swallow Odin, and the gods would go down in defeat. Sun and moon would be devoured, and the whole earth would perish utterly.

1. **Fates:** the three goddesses of destiny.
2. **last days:** In Norse mythology, there is to be a final battle called Ragnarok, in which almost all life is destroyed.

> **Reading Check**
> 1. Who were the three monstrous children born to Loki and the giantess?
> 2. Which god was responsible for feeding and training the Fenris Wolf?
> 3. Why was it necessary for the gods to bind the Fenris Wolf?
> 4. Who made the silken rope to bind the monster?
> 5. How did Tyr lose his hand?

646 NORSE MYTHOLOGY

CLOSURE
Ask students to tell in their own words the story of how the Norse gods restrain the terrible Fenris Wolf.

EXTENSION AND ENRICHMENT
Some students might use other sources to find out more about Loki, his background and his family. Have them discover the answers to these questions: Who were Loki's parents? Did he have other brothers and sisters? What are Loki's nicknames? Who was Loki's wife in Asgard? How did Odin keep Loki's monstrous child, the world serpent, from growing any more? Ask them to prepare a special report on Loki.

Other students might work together to prepare a dramatization of "The Fenris Wolf."

For Study and Discussion

Analyzing and Interpreting the Myth

1. What makes the Fenris Wolf such a terrible threat to the gods?

2. Which characteristics does the Fenris Wolf appear to have inherited from his father, Loki?

3. In Norse mythology the dwarfs, who live under Midgard, are credited with great cunning and skill. **a.** What is the silken rope made of? **b.** What do all these things have in common?

4. In order to overcome the Fenris Wolf, the gods have to make a terrible sacrifice. What significance can you see in the bravest of the gods losing his right hand?

Writing About Literature

▶ **Analyzing the Image of the Wolf**

In Norse mythology the Fenris Wolf represents the fearsome enemy of the gods, who will eventually swallow Odin. In literature the wolf is often depicted as a frightening and fierce enemy to human beings. We even use the expression "wolf down" for someone who devours food greedily. Think of the character of the wolf in fairy tales like "The Three Little Pigs" and "Little Red Ridinghood."

In other stories, however, the wolf is depicted as befriending human beings. The Roman myth of Romulus and Remus tells how twin boys are raised by a she-wolf.

Choose four different selections you have read in which a wolf appears. In a paragraph analyze the image of the wolf as enemy, as friend, or as both.

▶ Before students begin this writing assignment, you may wish to refer them to the **Writing About Literature** section on p. 688.

Focus on Persuasive Writing

Supporting Your Opinion

When you try to persuade an audience to agree with your opinion about an issue, your argument will be stronger if you develop **support** for your view. Here are some types of support you can use:

Reasons tell why; facts are items of information that can be checked; expert knowledge comes from people who have experience with an issue or situation.

Choose a position you would like to support in a persuasive speech to your classmates. For example, you might want to support a candidate in a class election, or you might want to persuade your listeners to start a class newspaper. Write a one-sentence opinion statement on the issue. Then list as many reasons, facts, and expert opinions as you can to support your view. Save your notes.

FOR STUDY AND DISCUSSION
1. He is a huge, devouring creature, cunning and very ferocious.
2. Tendencies to be sly, cunning, evil, and destructive.
3a. The sound of a cat's footfall, the breath of a fish, the flowing beard of a woman, the roots of a mountain. 3b. They are made of things unseen, unheard.
4. For bravest of gods to sacrifice hand shows how deadly dangerous he felt wolf to be; for Tyr—a warrior-god, who grips sword with right hand—it is a catastrophe.

WRITING ABOUT LITERATURE
For prewriting, have students make a list of at least four stories about wolves and include the following for each: name of story, characteristics of wolf, example of wolf's behavior. If students choose to focus on the image of the wolf as enemy or as friend, the topic sentence may state the characteristics of a good or bad wolf. Remind students that when they analyze something, they break it into smaller parts and consider how these parts are related.

Students who choose to discuss both images of wolves need to think in terms of comparison as well as analysis. After giving examples of each type of wolf, they might offer an opinion about which image is more common and why or speculate about why wolves are viewed in such different ways.

The Fenris Wolf

OBJECTIVES

The overall aim is for students to demonstrate an understanding of the importance of Thor in Norse mythology as represented in "How Thor Found His Hammer." For a complete list of objectives, see the **Teacher's Notes**.

VOCABULARY

The underlined words are in the Glossary. The Norse word for "giant" was *jotun*; *Jotunheim* means "home of the giants."

FOCUS/MOTIVATION

Ask students to name stories involving disguises, and tell why a disguise is used in each. In the following myth, two of the main characters are disguised. Who are they, and why are they disguised?

TEACHING RESOURCES E
Teacher's Notes, p. 133
Reading Check, p. 148
Study Guide, p. 135
Language Skills, p. 138
Building Vocabulary, p. 141
Selection Test, p. 143

How Thor Found His Hammer

1
Characterization. Frost Giants detest beauty and nature; these feelings provide motivation for their actions in this selection. The giants symbolize life-threatening cold.

2
Miolnir, like Fenris Wolf's rope, was made by dwarf craftsmanship; it always hit whatever Thor threw it at and then returned to Thor's hand.

3
Thor was thunder-god; thrown hammer caused thunder, lightning.

4
Thor and Loki often share adventures in Norse tales. Thor's strength keeps Loki from pushing him too far; Loki's quick thinking complements Thor's tendency to act without thinking.

5
Freyja, goddess of love and beauty, was basically a fertility goddess. In different regions, she was paired with other partners, but here she is apparently distraught over absence of Frey, god of fertility, who leaves the North in the cold season.

648

How Thor Found His Hammer

Retold by
HAMILTON WRIGHT MABIE

Thor, the mighty god of thunder, is a key figure in several of the best-known Norse myths. In reading this myth, can you see the reasons for his popularity?

The Frost Giants[1] were always trying to get into Asgard. For more than half the year they held the world in their grasp, locking up the streams in their rocky beds, hushing their music and the music of the birds as well, and leaving nothing but a wild waste of desolation under the cold sky. They hated the warm sunshine which stirred the wildflowers out of their sleep, and clothed the steep mountains with verdure, and set all the birds a-singing in the swaying treetops. They hated the beautiful god, Balder, with whose presence summer came back to the ice-bound earth, and, above all, they hated Thor, whose flashing hammer drove them back into Jotunheim and guarded the summer sky with its sudden gleamings of power. So long as Thor had his hammer, Asgard was safe against the giants.

One morning Thor started up out of a long, deep sleep and put out his hand for the hammer; but no hammer was there. Not a sign of it could be found anywhere, although Thor anxiously searched for it. Then a thought of the giants came suddenly in his mind, and his anger rose till his eyes flashed like great fires and his red beard trembled with wrath.

"Look, now, Loki," he shouted, "they have stolen Miolnir[2] by enchantment, and no one on earth or in heaven knows where they have hidden it."

"We will get Freyja's falcon-guise[3] and search for it," answered Loki, who was always quick to get into trouble or to get out of it again. So they went quickly to Folkvang[4] and found Freyja surrounded by her maidens and weeping tears of pure gold, as she had always done since her husband went on his long journey.

"The hammer has been stolen by enchantment," said Thor. "Will you lend me the falcon-guise that I may search for it?"

---

1. **Frost Giants:** In Norse mythology, the Frost Giants, who represent the cold Northern winter, are the enemies of the gods.
2. **Miolnir** (myəl′nər). Thor's hammer. Also spelled *Mjolnir*.
3. **falcon-guise:** a magic disguise that allowed Freyja to fly like a falcon, a small, swift hawk.
4. **Folkvang** (fōlk′vǎng): "Field of Folk," Freyja's home.

648 NORSE MYTHOLOGY

MOTIVATIONAL SUMMARY
Thor's hammer is an important weapon in defense of Asgard, but one morning Thor awakes to find it missing. Loki borrows a falcon disguise and searches for Thor's hammer. He discovers that a giant, Thrym, has stolen and hidden the hammer, demanding the goddess Freyja as his bride before he will return Thor's weapon. Freyja refuses to marry the giant, and Thor is forced to disguise himself as a most unusual bride, with Loki as his servant-maid, to get the hammer back.

PRESENTATION
The Frost Giants hate Thor, god of thunder and the greatest fighter among the Aesir. The Norse believed that, with his magic hammer Miolnir, Thor drove these giants back to Jotunheim each year so that summer could come. No wonder

Marble statue of Thor by B. E. Fogelberg.

"If it were silver, or even gold, you should have it and welcome," answered Freyja, glad to help Thor find the wonderful hammer that
6 kept them all safe from the hands of the Frost Giants.

So the falcon-guise was brought, and Loki put it on and flew swiftly out of Asgard to the home of the giants. His great wings made broad shadows over the ripe fields as he swept along, and the reapers, looking up from their work, wondered what mighty bird was flying seaward. At last he reached Jotunheim, and no sooner had he touched ground and taken off the falcon-guise than he came upon the giant Thrym,[5] sitting on a hill twisting golden collars for his dogs and stroking the long manes of his horses.

"Welcome, Loki," said the giant. "How fares it with the gods and the elves, and what has brought you to Jotunheim?"

"It fares ill with both gods and elves since
7 you stole Thor's hammer," replied Loki, guessing quickly that Thrym was the thief, "and I have come to find where you have hidden it."

Thrym laughed as only a giant can when he knows he has made trouble for somebody.
8 "You won't find it," he said at last. "I have buried it eight miles underground, and no one shall take it away unless he gets Freyja for me as my wife."

The giant looked as if he meant what he said, and Loki, seeing no other way of finding the hammer, put on his falcon-guise and flew back to Asgard. Thor was waiting to hear what news he brought, and both were soon at the great doors of Folkvang.
9 "Put on your bridal dress, Freyja," said Thor bluntly, after his fashion, "and we will ride swiftly to Jotunheim."

But Freyja had no idea of marrying a giant just to please Thor, and, in fact, that Thor

5. **Thrym** (thrīm).

VISUAL CONNECTIONS
Exploring the Subject
Thor had all the qualities that Norsemen admired most. He was a mighty and fearless fighter and an enjoyable companion. Thor had a great love of humor, adventure, good food, and drink. Although Thor's usual weapon was his magic hammer Miolnir, he was sometimes depicted as having a double-bladed axe. Warriors often wore amulets in the shape of a hammer or an axe, supposed to bestow on the wearer some of Thor's strength.

6
Freyja's generosity here contrasts with her later refusal to marry giant to ransom hammer.

7 Summarizing
How is Loki able to identify the thief? Thrym's effort to appear innocently busy, greeting him pleasantly as if expecting a visitor, makes the quick-witted Loki suspicious.

8
Plot. The story takes an interesting turn when Thrym demands Freyja's hand in marriage in exchange for hammer. Giants always wanted Freyja (representing spring, warmth, beauty) for their bride.

9
Characterization. Thor is a warrior, not a diplomat; he usually says exactly what he thinks.

How Thor Found His Hammer

that when Thor awakens one day to find that Miolnir has been stolen, he trembles with wrath.

Read aloud with the students the first paragraph, which lays the foundation for the Aesir gods' anxiety over the missing hammer. Rather than a grim or somber tale, however, this story turns into a rollicking, humorous adventure in which Thor must resort to a ridiculous disguise to retrieve his hammer.

10
Norse believed Milky Way was Freyja's necklace, made by magic of gnomes.

11
Freyja's willingness to help does not include sacrifice of her own happiness.

12
Irony. Of all the gods, the gruff and burly Thor is least likely to be disguised as a feminine, dainty bride.

13
A housewife's keys were badge of authority; she doled out supplies as needed in household tasks; the more keys, the richer the household.

14
A warrior's only fear: that he will be mocked.

15 Finding Details
What does the dim-witted giant fail to notice? Clues of Thor's presence—thunder, earth blazing and smoking.

16
Luckily, Thrym is a simpleton; otherwise, Thor's insatiable appetite would ruin his disguise, leaving him and Loki in great danger.

---

should ask her to do such a thing threw her into such a rage that the floor shook under her **10** angry tread and her necklace snapped in pieces.

"Do you think I am a weak lovesick girl, to follow you to Jotunheim and marry Thrym?" she cried indignantly.

11 Finding they could do nothing with Freyja, Thor and Loki called all the gods together to talk over the matter and decide what should be done to get back the hammer. The gods were very much alarmed, because they knew the Frost Giants would come upon Asgard as soon as they knew the hammer was gone. They said little, for they did not waste time with idle words, but they thought long and earnestly, and still they could find no way of getting hold of Miolnir once more. At last Heimdall, who had once been a Van,[6] and could therefore look into the future, said: "We must have the **12** hammer at once or Asgard will be in danger. If Freyja will not go, let Thor be dressed up and **13** go in her place. Let keys jingle from his waist and a woman's dress fall about his feet. Put precious stones upon his breast, braid his hair like a woman's, hang the necklace around his neck, and bind the bridal veil around his head."

14 Thor frowned angrily. "If I dress like a woman," he said, "you will jeer at me."

"Don't talk of jeers," retorted Loki; "unless that hammer is brought back quickly, the giants will rule in our places."

Thor said no more, but allowed himself to be dressed like a bride, and soon drove off to Jotunheim with Loki beside him disguised as a servant-maid. There was never such a wedding journey before. They rode in Thor's chariot and the goats drew them, plunging swiftly along the way, thunder pealing through the mountains and the frightened earth blazing and smoking as they passed. When Thrym saw **15** the bridal party coming, he was filled with delight.

"Stand up, you giants," he shouted to his companions; "spread cushions upon the benches and bring in Freyja, my bride. My yards are full of golden-horned cows, black oxen please my gaze whichever way I look, great wealth and many treasures are mine, and Freyja is all I lack."

It was evening when the bride came driving into the giant's court in her blazing chariot. The feast was already spread against her coming, and with her veil modestly covering her face she was seated at the great table, Thrym fairly beside himself with delight. It wasn't every giant who could marry a goddess!

If the bridal journey had been so strange that anyone but a foolish giant would have hesitated to marry a wife who came in such a turmoil of fire and storm, her conduct at the table ought certainly to have put Thrym on his guard; for never had bride such an appetite before. The great tables groaned under the load of good things, but they were quickly relieved of their burden by the voracious[7] bride. **16** She ate a whole ox before the astonished giant had fairly begun to enjoy his meal. Then she devoured eight large salmon, one after the other, without stopping to take breath; and having eaten up the part of the feast specially prepared for the hungry men, she turned upon the delicacies which had been made for the women, and especially for her own fastidious[8] appetite.

Thrym looked on with wondering eyes, and at last, when she had added to these solid foods three whole barrels of mead, his amazement was so great that, his astonishment getting the better of his politeness, he called out, "Did

---

6. **Van:** one of the Vanir.

7. **voracious** (vô-rā′shəs, vō-, və): greedy in eating.
8. **fastidious** (fă-stĭd′ē-əs, fə-): delicate.

NORSE MYTHOLOGY

17 anyone ever see such an appetite in a bride before, or know a maid who could drink so much mead?"

Then Loki, who was playing the part of a serving-maid, thinking that the giant might 18 have some suspicions, whispered to him, "Freyja was so happy in the thought of coming here that she has eaten nothing for eight whole days."

Thrym was so pleased at this evidence of affection that he leaned forward and raised the veil as gently as a giant could, but he instantly dropped it and sprang back the whole length of the hall before the bride's terrible eyes.

"Why are Freyja's eyes so sharp?" he called to Loki. "They burn me like fire."

19 "Oh," said the cunning serving-maid, "she has not slept for a week, so anxious has she been to come here, and that is why her eyes are so fiery."

Everybody looked at the bride and nobody envied Thrym. They thought it was too much like marrying a thunderstorm.

The giant's sister came into the hall just then and, seeing the veiled form of the bride sitting there, went up to her and asked for a bridal gift. "If you would have my love and friendship, give me those rings of gold upon your fingers."

20 But the bride sat perfectly silent. No one had yet seen her face or heard her voice.

21 Thrym became very impatient. "Bring in the hammer," he shouted, "that the bride may be consecrated, and wed us in the name of Var."[9]

If the giant could have seen the bride's eyes when she heard these words, he would have sent her home as quickly as possible and looked somewhere else for a wife.

The hammer was brought and placed in the bride's lap, and everybody looked to see the marriage ceremony; but the wedding was more strange and terrible than the bridal jour- 22 ney had been. No sooner did the bride's fingers close round the handle of Miolnir than the veil which covered her face was torn off and there stood Thor, the giant-queller, his terrible eyes blazing with wrath. The giants shuddered and shrank away from those flaming eyes, the sight of which they dreaded more than anything else in all the worlds; but there was no chance of escape. Thor swung the hammer round his head and the great house rocked on its foundations. There was a vivid flash of lightning, an awful crash of thunder, and the burning roof and walls buried the whole company in one common ruin.

Thrym was punished for stealing the hammer, his wedding guests got crushing blows instead of bridal gifts, and Thor and Loki went back to Asgard, where the presence of Miolnir made the gods safe once more.

---

9. **Var** (vär): goddess who hears marriage oaths.

Reading Check

1. Why do the Frost Giants hate Balder?
2. How does Thor defend Asgard from the Frost Giants?
3. Why does Loki borrow the falcon-guise?
4. Whose idea is it to send Thor in Freyja's place?
5. How does Thor keep his identity a secret?

How Thor Found His Hammer 651

CLOSURE

Ask students to tell in their own words the story of Thor's hammer as represented in "How Thor Found His Hammer" and tell reasons why Thor is such an important figure in the Norse myths.

EXTENSION AND ENRICHMENT

Some students might research the myth concerning Thor's wife Sif's golden hair. This myth gives the background of how Thor's hammer was created. Have them present the myth to the class, preferably as a dramatization.

Other students might plan and prepare a bulletin board display illustrating summer and winter as depicted in Norse mythology. Summer could show Balder and Thor; winter could show the fierce Frost Giants with heads of stone and feet of ice.

FOR STUDY AND DISCUSSION

1. Frost Giants want to get into Asgard. They hate sunshine, flowers, and birds of summer that are brought by Balder. As long as summer comes, giants cannot get into Asgard.
2. Like Thor, it is quick, flashing, and powerful.
3. Disguising himself as a servant-maid, Loki quickly and cleverly explains why Thrym's "bride" eats and drinks so much and has such fiery eyes.
4. Kindness to their animals, hospitality to friends, gullibility, and foolishness. Also seem to appreciate feminine beauty and desire to own beautiful things.
5. Responses will vary. Thor's disguise as a blushing bride.

WRITING ABOUT LITERATURE

Before students begin this assignment, review the classical myth "The Origin of the Seasons" and help students identify points of comparison to use in their essays. They might begin with similarities: Balder is like Persephone in that his presence inspires the return of spring, and Freyja, like Demeter, is a fertility goddess who makes green plants grow. Then students can explore significant differences. Norse myths about the seasons, reflecting the harsh North climate, depict struggle and envision the end of the world. Thor and his hammer are necessary to keep the Frost Giants at bay. Greek myths, in contrast, depict a rather benign cycle of death and rebirth.

FOCUS ON PERSUASIVE WRITING

Remind students to keep their audience in mind when they consider opinion statements and **emotional appeals.** You may want to model for students how an opinion statement and emotional appeals can change when the audience changes, even though the topic remains the same.

For Study and Discussion

Analyzing and Interpreting the Myth

1. The conflict of the gods and the giants is a dominating theme in the Norse myths. What explanation is given for this antagonism at the opening of the myth?

2. In what way is Thor's hammer a symbol of the god's strength?

3. This myth shows a more attractive side of Loki, as Sky Traveler and as the Sly One. How does he outwit Thrym?

4. The Frost Giants are usually shown as evil and destructive. What characteristics are emphasized in this myth?

5. What do you think contributes most to the humor of this myth?

Writing About Literature

▶ **Comparing Myths**

Write a short essay comparing the Norse explanation of the seasons with that of the classical myth "The Origin of the Seasons" (page 592).

Focus On Persuasive Writing

Using Appeals to the Emotions

Besides using reasons and facts, you can also support your argument in a persuasive paper by using **emotional appeals.** To convince an audience to donate money to the local animal shelter, for example, you could describe how abandoned pets face starvation in winter.

Write a one-sentence opinion statement on an issue you care about. Make notes about one or two emotional appeals you could use in a paper or speech about this issue. When you have finished, hold a conference with a partner and discuss each other's ideas. Save your notes.

▶ Before students begin this writing assignment, you may wish to refer them to the **Writing About Literature** section on p. 688.

Thor and the Giant King

Retold by
OLIVIA COOLIDGE

Magic and illusion are important elements in Norse mythology. As you read, note how the gods themselves can be deceived by appearances.

Thor and Loki in a goat-drawn chariot rumbled through the air faster than wind. As night was falling, they neared the great sea which surrounds the earth. "I see a small farmhouse," said Loki peering through the dusk. "Let us go there for shelter."

"We will descend to the earth," answered Thor, "lest we frighten the peasants here."

The great forms of the gods shrank to mortal size, and the goats trotted over the pasture with their chariot bumping behind.

Pine torches were already lit in the peasant's rude cottage. He himself was by the fireside whittling a plow handle. The son of the house was out feeding the oxen, but the peasant's wife sat sewing, while the daughter stirred a porridge of water and meal, which was all the supper they had.

"Welcome, strangers!" cried the master of the house. "You are in time to share our supper, poor though it is. Beds we have none, but Thjalfe,[1] my son, shall fetch you an armful of dry, fresh rushes. Wife, bring our guests some ale."

The old woman offered thin beer in rude,

---
1. **Thjalfe** (thē-ăl′fē): Also spelled *Thialfi*.

wooden cups. Thor and Loki sat down on the bench beside the fire. Presently above the smells of damp clothes and wood smoke which pervaded the air, Thor's nose detected the scent of the porridge which the daughter still stirred in the iron pot. His face went blank with disgust. "Is this all you have to set before us?" he inquired.

"We are no lords that we should eat meat every day," answered the peasant.

"Thjalfe," cried Thor, turning to the son, who had just come in, "take my two goats and kill them for supper. Only before you put them in the pot, bring me their skins."

Thjalfe hastened to do his bidding, and presently the whole family was seated around an appetizing meal. First, however, Thor spread the goatskins in a corner. "Cast all the bones in these skins," he commanded, "and be careful to break none." He did not notice that Thjalfe had broken a thigh bone before he threw it in the corner with the rest.

The next morning Thor tapped the bones of his goats with his hammer and made them arise again younger and stronger than ever, save that one was now lame. When Thor be-

Thor and the Giant King 653

MOTIVATIONAL SUMMARY
In search of adventure, Thor and Loki stop at a farm cottage. Their hosts, a peasant couple, have very little food, but Thor instructs their son Thjalfe to kill and cook his two magic goats. Despite instruction, the boy breaks one of the goats' bones. When Thor restores them to life the next morning, one is lame. Thjalfe offers himself as servant to appease the god's wrath. Thor, Loki, and Thjalfe travel to Giantland, where they take shelter inside an odd hall with several inner chambers. This is only the first of many things they meet up with on this adventure that is not quite what it first appears to be.

6 Though generally compassionate, Thor has a lightning-quick temper.

7 Thor is also fair and quick to forgive.

8 Setting. Scene shifts; characters enter forbidding territory of giants.

9 Giantland: Literal translation of *Jotunheim*.

10 Giant's comparing Thor's voice to a mouse's squeak makes the mighty Thor seem small.

11 Apparently, this warning is meant to demoralize Thor before he reaches Utgard (literally: "outland").

12 Vivid example of great size difference between giant and the three tiny travelers.

13 Finding Details
What characteristic of Thor adds humor to his predicament? This hearty eater doesn't like missing a meal.

14 Note that they can't see giant clearly.

held this and knew that he had been disobeyed, he was terribly angry. His great red eyebrows came down over his eyes, and he **6** gripped his huge hammer with such force that his knuckles turned white. The unfortunate peasant and his family sank to their knees imploring his mercy.

"Spare at least my parents," pleaded Thjalfe, "for they are not at fault. As for me, I will go with you to be your servant if you will but grant me my life."

7 Thor's frown relaxed, and he nodded, appeased. "That is good," said he. "Thjalfe shall become my servant, and I will leave my goats here in his father's care until the broken leg is **8** healed." Thus the two gods and their new servant set out on foot, Thjalfe carrying a bag of provisions. Across the great sea they traveled, **9** to Giantland, a trackless country of great forests and barren heaths, where they wandered for a long time without seeing giant or dwelling.

At last as dark approached, they came to a strange hall with no doors or windows, but a great, irregular opening at one end. Inside, it was dark and empty, but since the wind blew chill, the three travelers were glad enough to sleep there on the floor.

They were awakened in the middle of the night by a terrible noise and an earthquake. Loki and Thjalfe felt their way into one of a row of small inner chambers which opened from the hall, and lay there huddled together, trying not to listen to the dreadful sounds. Thor took his hammer in his hands and sat in the great hall until daylight, when he crawled out to find the source of the fearsome roaring.

A man the size of a mountain was lying snoring across their path. The earth shook as his chest rose and fell. He was so huge that as he lay, Thor could only just reach up to shout in his ear.

10 "Hey! Hallo! What's that? What squeaked?" said the giant, sitting up and rubbing his eyes. "Well, little fellow, what do you want? Hey! Get out of my glove!" He picked up the strange-looking hall in which they had spent the night and fitted it on his hand.

"We are traveling in Giantland," shouted Thor. "We come in peace."

"Oho! Doubtless King Utgard-Loke[2] will be glad to hear that," laughed the giant. "You think a good deal of yourself, I see, but I warn you that at the king's court, I am not particu- **11** larly large. Unless I am much mistaken, you will not be greatly regarded there."

"Where is the king's court?" asked Thor.

"To the North. I am going that way, but I am in no hurry. If you start out over the hill, I will overtake you and put you on the road."

Thjalfe shouldered his sack in haste, and the three companions set out as fast as their legs would carry them. The giant ate, slept, and waited until noon. Then in three strides he was up with the gods, who were toiling, hungry **12** and thirsty, over a dusty plain. "I see I must carry your sack," said he good-naturedly. "Let me put it in mine. I will give it back this evening when the time comes to make a meal." He scooped up the sack of provisions from Thjalfe and was out of sight in three strides.

Thor looked grimly at his companions. "If **13** we are to eat, we must catch up with this giant," said he. The three hastened over the hills until **14** sunset. When it was almost dark, they made out the huge form in the distance and quickened their flagging steps.

"Here you are at last!" cried the giant. "I thought you were never coming. Take my sack

2. **Utgard-Loke** (o͞ot'gärd' lō'kē): Utgard, the home of Utgard-Loke, is also known as Jotunheim.

Thor and the Mountain by J. C. Dollman.

PRESENTATION

You may wish to explain that Norse culture revered hospitality. A person was required always to keep his doors open to a traveler. In the cold, bitter northern climate, travelers constantly needed a place by the fire where they could dry their clothes. In addition, the host was expected to provide good food. This was no easy task with Thor, who had an enormous appetite.

Under the following headings, students might keep a chart of the action of the story: "Appearance," "Opponents," "Reality." The first entries might be the following: *caves, gods vs. giant, glove*.

VISUAL CONNECTIONS
Exploring the Subject

Explain this illustration to students after they have completed the story. It shows Thor, holding his mighty hammer (here depicted as giant-sized) and being shown, by the giant king Utgard-Loke, the true results of the humiliating tricks played on Thor and his companions by the giants. The reason Thor's hammer seemed not to have any effect when he struck the sleeping giant three times is because he was tricked into hitting a range of hills instead. The mighty blows of Thor's hammer have split the hills from top to bottom, leaving huge clefts.

READING SKILLS PRACTICE
The underlined passage can be used to give students practice in the reading skill of identifying specific details. Ask students to read the passage and choose the answer that most clearly answers the question. What part of the citadel is intended to keep travelers out, but is so large that Thor and his companions can walk right through? **A.** The gate's bars. **B.** The towering wall. **C.** The huge gate. **D.** The tower. **E.** The lock on the gate. (Answer: A)

---

15 Giant-versions of "strings" are probably size of ship's cables.

16 Thor's hammer is famous for destroying what it hits.

17 Expressing an Opinion
How do you think Thor felt when his hammer had no effect? Answers will vary. Possibly sheepish, puzzled.

18 Thor's hammer was also famous for its accuracy.

19 Giant's belittling description makes Thor's blows sound like minor annoyances.

20 Again, note low visibility.

21 Another remark meant to undermine Thor's confidence.

22 Irony. As it turns out, Utgard-Loke is (or has been) near.

---

and open it, for I have eaten and am ready for sleep." He tossed over his sack and lay down. Presently the whole place resounded with snores.

"I cannot open this sack," said Thjalfe.

"Let Thor try," said Loki wearily. "He is the strongest, and I am too hungry to wait any more."

15 Thor took the sack and tugged at the strings, but try as he would, he could neither loosen or break them. "Wake up!" he yelled to the giant, but his voice was drowned in the noise of snoring.

The three companions looked at one another in despair. "Wait a moment," said Thor between his teeth. "I have something with me that can make even giants pay attention." He took out his hammer and strode up to the **16** monstrous head. Drawing himself up to his full height, he whirled his weapon and brought it down on the giant's forehead with the full strength of both arms.

"Ugh!" said the giant thickly. He put up a hand and turned over. "What tickled?" he asked sleepily. "Did a leaf fall out of the tree?"

Thor put up his hammer completely crest-**17** fallen. "We shall have to eat in the morning," said he to his companions with as much authority as he could muster. "You had better go to sleep."

"I am far too hungry," grumbled Loki. "Besides, he makes such an earthshaking noise!"

All three lay down, but while the snoring went on, sleep was impossible. The more Thor thought of his blow, the more certain he felt that he must have missed the giant altogether **18** in the darkness. "Unlikely though that may seem," he said to himself, "it is less incredible than that he should not have felt Mjolnir, the mightiest weapon on earth."

Presently his fury at hunger and sleeplessness got the better of him, and he crept out to try again. He took care this time to find his way to a rock where he stood right over the giant and could feel his beard fluttering in the fierce wind of the monster's breath. He whirled the hammer three times, brought it down, and felt it sink into something yielding.

19 "What is the matter with this tree?" said the giant sitting up crossly. "There must be birds in it. They are throwing down twigs in my face." He lay down once more.

"I cannot believe it," said Thor grimly to himself. "I felt my hammer sink in. I must try again when it is light."

The gray light of morning dawned at last on a miserable trio, cold, sleepless, and hungry, regarding the giant with furious eyes. "Just let him wait until I can see him," said Thor at intervals all night long. "He will notice Mjolnir this time, I can promise."

20 By the faint light the giant's face, though indistinct, was clear enough. With a terrible blow Thor buried his hammer, head and handle, deep in the mighty forehead.

"Agh!" said the giant this time. "Those birds!" he complained. "I hope you slept out in the open. They keep throwing down moss in my face." He looked around. "Why, you are awake and ready to go. You are in a great **21** hurry, though I fear King Utgard-Loke will not think you very important. Still, his citadel lies but a short distance ahead. My way now takes me elsewhere." With that he got up, lifted his sack, and was gone in three strides.

22 "There goes our breakfast," said Loki. "I hope Utgard-Loke is near!"

▶ It was not long until they saw the giant king's citadel, but it was many hours before they came close to it. It towered so huge in front of them that, though they craned their necks, they could not see the top of the wall. The great, locked gate had bars the thickness of oak trees, but the spaces between them were so wide that the gods could easily creep through. ◀

656 NORSE MYTHOLOGY

MEETING INDIVIDUAL NEEDS
ESL/LEP • The story contains several idiomatic expressions that require explanation. Here are some examples from pp. 657–658.
". . . and he was still somewhat **cast down**. . . ." (depressed; discouraged) (p. 657)

"My young men empty this **at a draft**." (in one drink) (p. 657)
". . . yet I dare not **set you** a hard task. . . ." (assign) (p. 658)
". . . for now **my blood is up**." (I am angry) (p. 658)

". . . and early next morning they **took their leave**." (said goodbye) (p. 658)

King Utgard-Loke sat in his hall amid a company of mountainous giants. "Who are you, little fellows?" asked he, looking down on the gods.

"I am Thor," answered the god, "and these are Loki and my servant. We have traveled hither to visit the king of Giantland."

23 "You are welcome, little gods," said the king. "I had not expected that you would be so small. Nevertheless, if you are indeed Thor and Loki, you should be able to show us some
24 feats, for it is our custom to prove our guests before we sit down to the feast. Tell us, therefore, what you will do."

25 "I," said Loki immediately, "will eat more and faster than anyone in your company."

"That is a fine wager," said the king laughing. "Loge³ here is considered a fast eater among us, but no doubt he is outclassed by you. We will put a trough of meat between you and let one start at each end. We shall soon see who is the better."

Loki was ravenous with hunger. Even Thor marveled at his appetite. Yet fast as he ate, Loge did equally well. When the two met finally in the middle of the trough, Loki had eaten all the meat, but Loge had eaten meat, bones, and the trough itself. He was therefore adjudged the winner. "Never mind," whis-
26 pered Loki to Thor. "At least I have had my fill!"

"Loki is not very impressive," remarked the giant king. "What now will you show us?"

"I will run a race with anyone you care to put forward," cried Thjalfe, who was the swiftest of mankind.

"Come with us, Huge,"⁴ said the giant king. "Let us go out to the race course."

Huge and Thjalfe were set to race, and though Thjalfe ran like the wind, Huge touched the goal and turned to face his rival

3. **Loge** (lōg′ē).
4. **Huge** (yōō′gē).

before Thjalfe could come up with him. The
27 second time they ran, there was a long bolt shot between them. The third time, Huge turned back from the winning post to meet Thjalfe still only halfway along the course.

"I do not think Thjalfe has brought you much credit," said the king, "but now that we come to Thor himself, the tale is bound to be different. Tell us, great Thor, what will you do?"

Thor was angered at the mockery of the king's tone, and he was still somewhat cast
28 down by his failure of the night before. Therefore he refrained from trials of strength and said sulkily, "I am called a deep drinker. Perhaps I can astonish you with that."

"Bring here my horn," cried the king. "My young men empty this at a draft. A poor drinker takes two, but I have never yet known one who could not empty it in three."

29 The horn seemed very long to Thor, but it was not wide. He put his lips down to the brim, lest he spill it, but as he drank more deeply, he tried to tilt it to his mouth. To his surprise, the horn would not move, and he was forced to bend over it. At last he straightened up exhausted and saw in astonishment that it was almost impossible to tell whether it were emptier than before.

"That is not much of a draft," said the king, "but perhaps you are saving your strength for your second one."

Thor bent down angrily, but the second time that he stopped for breath, he had only emptied the horn enough for it to be carried without spilling.

30 "I do not think your feats are as great as your reputation," remarked the king. "You have left a great deal for your last draft."

Thor bent down again and drank with all his might, but though this was the mightiest draft he had ever taken, he could not empty the horn. Its contents were visibly less, but that was

Thor and the Giant King **657**

23
Dialogue. Words reveal characters' personality: king expresses haughty hospitality, expects to be honored; Loki brags smugly.

24
Prove, in this context, means "to put to a test."

25
Clever Loki thinks of a way to be sure he gets a meal.

26 Making Generalizations
What does this comment reveal about Loki's character? He is more concerned with own needs than team's honor.

27
Bolt is an arrow or similar airborne projectile; thus, "bolt shot" is length a bolt would travel when shot.

28
Apparently, giants' continual belittling has begun to shake Thor's confidence; now hesitates to test strength.

29
Odd details—horn's being so long, not moving, not decreasing in volume—hint at hidden trick; Thor too angry to suspect.

30
Giant apparently enjoying opportunity to belittle Thor.

all. He pushed it away sullenly. "Let me try something else," said he.

"I have heard much of your strength," answered the king, "and I would gladly see something of it, yet I dare not set you a hard task, since I perceive you are not such a hero as I had thought. Will you try to lift my cat from the floor?"

A huge, gray cat sprang forward. Thor put his shoulders under its middle, but the cat only arched its back, and he could not lift it an inch. At last he got both hands under one paw, and by tugging and straining managed to raise it a little.

"Let be," said the king. "Every child among us could do that feat."

"I will wrestle with anyone and beat him," cried Thor, "for now my blood is up."

"I do not think I can ask my young men to wrestle with you," answered the king. "It seems hardly worth their while. Nevertheless, you may try a fall with my old nurse, Elle,⁵ if you wish."

Thor advanced upon the old woman in anger, but though he put forth all his strength, he could not budge her. After a while she in her turn tightened her grasp. Thor's footing failed him, and after hard struggles he was forced down on one knee.

"That is enough," said the king. "It is not worth contesting with you. Sit down and take your supper, but in future let other people boast."

The three companions ate their meal in silence, and early next morning they took their leave. King Utgard-Loke himself went out to say farewell to them and to ask when they were likely to return.

"When I can avenge my disgrace," answered Thor sulkily.

Utgard-Loke laughed. "You are not disgraced, but rather covered with glory," he replied. "If you will promise to visit me no more, I will tell you how that is so."

"I will gladly promise," cried Thor, "if you can convince me of this."

"Know then," said Utgard-Loke, "that I was the giant you met in the forest, and that my size, which seemed so great to you, was but an illusion of magic. Do you see those hills over there?"

Thor nodded.

"That range of hills I brought between my forehead and your hammer as I lay pretending to sleep. See the three great notches you have made in them by blows such as I would have thought incredible, had I not beheld them."

"I knew you must notice Mjolnir," said Thor with a grim laugh.

"For two days I kept you without food and sleep," said the king. "I hoped that you would be discouraged and return to the earth; but if not, at least I might expect that when you came to my court, your strength would be somewhat lessened. Alas, it was not so!"

"I had not thought any of us had shown great prowess," replied Thor.

"You did not think so, but we who beheld you were frightened and amazed. First, Loki had an eating match with Loge, who is fire itself. No wonder Loge burned through bones and trough, and yet Loki ate as much meat as he, after all. As for Thjalfe, he was matched against Huge, who is my thought. It is clear that he had no chance, and yet the first time he ran, he came within an arm's length!"

"What of me, then?"

"The end of the horn that you drank from lay in the sea. When you come to the shore, you will see how greatly the water has ebbed. We all held our breath for a moment and thought that, though it was clearly impossible, you might actually drink the ocean dry. The cat in turn was none other than the serpent

---

5. **Elle** (ĕl′ē).

CLOSURE

Ask students to tell the story of Thor and the giant king in their own words, including the use of magic and illusion by the giant in tricking Thor and rigging the contests.

EXTENSION AND ENRICHMENT

Some students might read other stories involving Thor and his adventures among the giants, including "Thor and the Jotun Geirrod," "Thor and the Jotun Rungnir," and "Thor and the Jotun Aegir." Have them take notes about these stories and present them orally to the rest of the class.

Other students might prepare either a series of pictures in a mural or a comic strip illustrating the contests in which Utgard-Loke tricked the three travelers.

---

who lies stretched around the sea, his tail meeting his mouth. When you raised the monster's back to the sky, you appeared about to tear it from its resting place. When you actually lifted it a little, we feared lest the Day of Doom was upon us!"

38

"I have fought with the serpent before," said Thor. "I wish I had known the creature again, for this time it would not have escaped me."

"Last of all, you wrestled with Elle, who is Old Age. None may ever get the better of her!"

"I see you have thoroughly fooled us," said Thor, "but it is now my turn." With that he lifted his hammer, but the great form of the giant dissolved into wavering mist before his eyes. A mocking laugh sounded near him. Thor whirled in fury and beheld the outlines of the citadel and all that it contained grow dim. In another second they too had scattered into air.

"Remember your promise," said the voice. "Never again!"

"I suppose not," answered Thor glumly. "Nevertheless, should I meet you some time by chance, beware!"

"I will not leave that to chance," answered the voice. "Farewell."

Thor shouldered his weapon and set out with his companions across the long, dusty plains to the sea.

Reading Check

1. Why does one of Thor's goats become lame?
2. Who are Thor's companions on his journey to the land of the giants?
3. How does Thor try to awaken the sleeping giant?
4. What three "tests" does Thor fail?
5. What promise does Thor make to Utgard-Loke?

▶ Before students begin this writing assignment, you may want to refer them to the **Writing About Literature** section on p. 688.

For Study and Discussion

Analyzing and Interpreting the Myth

1. A number of Norse myths tell of conflicts between the gods and the giants. This myth might be viewed as a comic battle between the two sides. In what way are the giants the winners and the gods the losers in this encounter?

2. Thor's hammer is an important weapon which he uses to keep law and order and to protect the gods from the giants. Why does it fail him in this myth?

3. How are Loki, Thjalfe, and Thor tricked by Utgard-Loke?

4. Consider the importance of magic and illusion in this myth. How do both Thor and Utgard-Loke make use of magic and illusion?

Writing About Literature

▶ **Discussing Elements of Magic and Disguise**

In classical mythology, disguise and magic are important elements. In the myth of "Arachne" (page 598), Minerva visits Arachne in the guise of an old woman. In "The Reward of Baucis and Philemon" (page 602), Jupiter and Mercury assume human shape to travel the earth. In "The Origin of the Seasons" (page 592), the goddess Demeter uses magic to make the baby Demophoon immortal.

These elements are important in Norse mythology as well. In a brief essay, discuss the role of magic and disguise in the three myths read so far: "The Fenris Wolf" (page 644); "How Thor Found His Hammer" (page 648); and "Thor and the Giant King."

Thor and the Giant King   659

38
When last battle begins, Midgard Serpent will uncoil from sea floor. If Thor had pulled the serpent loose, doomsday would have begun.

READING CHECK
1. Thjalfe breaks a thigh bone (p. 653).
2. Loki and Thjalfe (p. 654).
3. Hitting him with hammer (p. 656).
4. Drinking from horn, lifting cat, wrestling with old woman (p. 657–658).
5. Not to return to Giantland (p. 658).

FOR STUDY AND DISCUSSION
1. Gods are humiliated by defeats, and Thor is tricked into promising never to return.
2. Hammer is really striking a range of hills, not giant.
3. In eating contest, Loki is actually competing against fire; Thjalfe races thought; Thor tries to drain horn which is pipeline to sea; cat he tries to lift is actually earth serpent; Thor actually wrestles Old Age.
4. Thor brings slaughtered goats back to life; his hammer is magic. Utgard-Loke makes hills appear to be giant's forehead, fire to be Loge, thought to be Huge, horn attached to sea appear as ordinary drinking horn, earth serpent as cat, Old Age as old woman; he disappears into mist.

WRITING ABOUT LITERATURE
This assignment requires students to synthesize their thinking about the role of magic and disguise in three different myths. Remind them that the word *discuss* means to examine in detail. For prewriting, they should review each myth to select the pertinent details for their composition.

OBJECTIVES
The overall aim is for students to demonstrate an understanding of the **irony** in the story of the Norse god Balder. For a complete list of objectives, see the **Teacher's Notes**.

VOCABULARY
The underlined words are in the Glossary. Ask students to review the names of the Norse gods on the chart on pp. 636–639 before reading the selection, paying close attention to the pronunciation keys.

FOCUS / MOTIVATION
Ask students to recall Zeus's punishment of Prometheus for disobeying his commands. Tell them that in this myth, the tricky Loki finally commits a deed so terrible that the gods assign him an awful punishment.

TEACHING RESOURCES E
Teacher's Notes, p. 157
Reading Check, p. 172
Study Guide, p. 160
Language Skills, p. 163
Building Vocabulary, p. 166
Selection Vocabulary Test, p. 168
Selection Test, p. 169

AV RESOURCES BINDER
Audiocassette 3, Side B

The Death of Balder

1 These disasters eventually lead to Ragnarok.

2 Odin fears because nothing can prevent a death the Norns (fates) decree.

3 All-wise Odin doesn't interfere; knows that stopping game won't save Balder.

4 Joy in game lies in Balder's apparent invincibility, not in any malice on the gods' part.

5 **Conflict.** Loki's malice increases as the reign of the Aesir approaches its end.

6 Other mythological examples of incomplete invulnerability include dragon with one weak spot in scales and "impregnable" castles with one hidden entrance. Point is that no protection is perfect; fate (death) cannot be avoided.

7 In some versions, Loki uses fire to harden the mistletoe twig into sharp dart.

The Death of Balder

Retold by
EDITH HAMILTON

In Norse mythology, the most beautiful of all the gods is Balder, the god of sunlight. His twin brother, the god of darkness, is Hoder (or Hod), who is blind. Here is a tragic and ironic story about these brothers.

Balder was the most beloved of the gods, on earth as in heaven. His death was the first of **1** the disasters which fell upon the gods. One night he was troubled with dreams which seemed to foretell some great danger to him. When his mother, Frigga, the wife of Odin, heard this she determined to protect him from the least chance of danger. She went through the world and exacted an oath from everything, all things with life and without life, **2** never to do him harm. But Odin still feared. He rode down to Niflheim, the world of the dead, where he found the dwelling of Hela, or Hel, the goddess of the dead, all decked out in festal array. A wise woman told him for whom the house had been made ready:

The mead has been brewed for Balder.
The hope of the high gods has gone.

Odin knew then that Balder must die, but the **3** other gods believed that Frigga had made him safe. They played a game accordingly which gave them much pleasure. They would try to hit Balder, to throw a stone at him or hurl a dart or shoot an arrow or strike him with a sword, but always the weapons fell short of him or rolled harmlessly away. Nothing would hurt **4** Balder. He seemed raised above them by this strange exemption and all honored him for it, except one only, Loki. He was not a god, but the son of a giant, and wherever he came trouble followed. He continually involved the gods in difficulties and dangers, but he was allowed to come freely to Asgard because for some reason never explained Odin had sworn brotherhood with him. **5** He always hated the good, and he was jealous of Balder. He determined to do his best to find some way of injuring him. He went to Frigga disguised as a woman and entered into talk with her. Frigga told him of her journey to ensure Balder's safety and how everything had sworn to do him no harm. Ex**6** cept for one little shrub, she said, the mistletoe, so insignificant she had passed it by.

That was enough for Loki. He got the mistletoe and went with it to where the gods were amusing themselves. Hoder, Balder's brother, who was blind, sat apart. "Why not join in the game?" asked Loki. "Blind as I am?" said Hoder. "And with nothing to throw at Balder, either?" "Oh, do your part," Loki said. "Here is a twig. Throw it and I will direct your aim." **7** Hoder took the mistletoe and hurled it with all his strength. Under Loki's guidance it sped to

660 NORSE MYTHOLOGY

MOTIVATIONAL SUMMARY
Balder, most beloved of the gods, dreams one night of deadly danger. In an effort to protect him, his mother Frigga requires every living thing and every object on earth to promise to do no harm to her son—except one.

PRESENTATION
A large amount of material is compressed into this one myth. There are four major parts: (1) The prophecy of Balder's death; (2) Loki's role in Balder's death; (3) Hermod's journey to Hel to seek Balder's release; and (4) Loki's punishment. With the death of Balder, the world lost gentleness, kindness, and forgiveness.

The Death of Balder by Peter Cramer (1726–1782). Oil on canvas.
National Museum of Art, Copenhagen

VISUAL CONNECTIONS
Exploring the Subject
According to Norse myth, the death of Balder was the first in a series of disasters that would lead inevitably to Ragnarok. Some scholars see Balder as representative of a later, more sophisticated hero in Norse culture. Unlike Thor or Tyr, Balder is not warlike. He is described as pure and good and represents all that is joyous in life: laughter, good cheer, happiness.

Loki, often shown as being merely mischievous in Norse myths, is here branded as truly evil and punished by the gods because of his complicity in Balder's death. He becomes an enemy of the gods, intending them harm when his chains are broken on the last day.

Yet even the Norse myth of this final awful battle was not without hope: the Norse believed that after the end of all things, Balder would return from the underworld and reign over a better, happier world.

8 Balder and pierced his heart. Balder fell to the ground dead.

His mother refused even then to give up hope. Frigga cried out to the gods for a volunteer to go down to Hela and try to ransom Balder. Hermod, one of her sons, offered himself. Odin gave him his horse Sleipnir[1] and he sped down to Niflheim.

The others prepared the funeral. They built

9 a lofty pyre on a great ship, and there they laid Balder's body. Nanna, his wife, went to look at it for the last time; her heart broke and she fell to the deck dead. Her body was placed beside his. Then the pyre was kindled and the ship pushed from the shore. As it sailed out to sea, the flames leaped up and wrapped it in fire.

When Hermod reached Hela with the gods' petition, she answered that she would give Balder back if it were proved to her that all everywhere mourned for him. But if one thing or

1. **Sleipnir** (slāp′nĭr): Odin's eight-legged horse.

8 Analyzing
What is ironic about the manner of Balder's death? A friendly game and Balder's dear brother cause the beloved god's death.

9
Pyre: a heap of combustible materials upon which dead body is placed for cremation.

The Death of Balder

CLOSURE

Ask students to tell the story of the Norse god Balder, identifying the four major parts of the narrative. Ask them to explain the significance of Loki's actions and why the gods decide that he must be punished.

EXTENSION AND ENRICHMENT

Some students might explore how the Greek Achilles' supposed invulnerability failed to prevent his death. Have them compare and contrast the Achilles myth with Balder's story.

10
In some versions, giantess is Loki in disguise.

11
Plot. Resolution of conflict comes with acceptance of Balder's death and punishment of Loki.

12
Sigyn is honor-bound to do duty for husband.

13
At Ragnarok, Loki's chains break and he fights gods.

READING CHECK
1. Obtains oath from all things not to harm him (p. 660).
2. Hates good, is jealous of Balder (p. 660).
3. Loki helps Hoder throw mistletoe at him (p. 660).
4. Everything must weep for him (p. 661).
5. Binding him in cavern with serpent dripping painful venom on him (p. 662).

FOR STUDY AND DISCUSSION
1. In attempting to protect Balder's life, Frigga ignores lowly mistletoe and doesn't demand its oath. She reveals only thing that can harm Balder to disguised foe. Seemingly innocent game results in Balder's death by hand of beloved brother.
2. Providing weapon; persuading Hoder to throw it, guiding it at Balder's heart with force enough to kill.
3. Balder is fated to die. No precautions can protect him.

WRITING ABOUT LITERATURE
Before students begin, encourage them to discuss the meaning of the adjective *complex* (involved, complicated, interconnected, intricate). Suggest that students make prewriting notes about Loki's behavior as shown in each myth.

---

one living creature refused to weep for him she would keep him. The gods dispatched messengers everywhere to ask all creation to shed tears so that Balder could be redeemed from death. They met with no refusal. Heaven and earth and everything therein wept willingly for the beloved god. The messengers rejoicing started back to carry the news to the gods. Then, almost at the end of their journey, *10* they came upon a giantess—and all the sorrow of the world was turned to futility, for she refused to weep. "Only dry tears will you get from me," she said mockingly. "I had no good from Balder, nor will I give him good." So Hela kept her dead.

11 Loki was punished. The gods seized him and bound him in a deep cavern. Above his head a serpent was placed so that its venom fell upon his face, causing him unutterable pain. But his *12* wife, Sigyn, came to help him. She took her place at his side and caught the venom in a cup. Even so, whenever she had to empty the cup and the poison fell on him, though but for a moment, his agony was so intense that his *13* convulsions shook the earth.

Reading Check

1. How does Frigga try to protect Balder?
2. Why does Loki wish to harm Balder?
3. How is Balder killed?
4. Hela offers to return Balder on one condition. What is it?
5. How do the gods punish Loki?

For Study and Discussion

Analyzing and Interpreting the Myth

1. Irony occurs when events take a surprising or unexpected turn. In what way are the circumstances of Balder's death ironic?

2. In this myth Loki again appears as an evil, treacherous enemy of the gods. How does he cause the death of Balder?

3. The Norsemen believed that the fates of gods as well as human beings were determined by the goddesses of destiny and were impossible to escape. How is this fatalism reflected in the myth of Balder's death?

Writing About Literature

▶ **Analyzing a Character**

Loki is the most complex figure in the Norse myths. In a paragraph analyze the aspects of his character revealed in the myths you have read. If you wish, use the first sentence of this paragraph as your thesis sentence.

▶ Before students begin this writing assignment, you may want to refer them to the **Writing About Literature** section on p. 688.

NORSE MYTHOLOGY

OBJECTIVES	VOCABULARY	FOCUS / MOTIVATION
The overall aim is for students to demonstrate an understanding of the Norse explanation for the end of all things. For a complete list of objectives, see the **Teacher's Notes**.	The underlined words are in the Glossary. Review names: Skoll and Hati (wolves that chase sun and moon); Gleipnir (magic cord—binds Fenris Wolf); Garm (Hel's hound); Skirnir (Frey's servant); Vidar (son of Odin).	Ask students to imagine the Norse gods that they have read about all taking part in the battle against evil on the day of doom. In this next section, students will discover how the Norse envisioned it.

The End of All Things

BARBARA LEONIE PICARD

The Norse gods and goddesses knew that their own end was foretold by the death of Balder. Here is the dramatic conclusion of their story.

> **TEACHING RESOURCES E**
> Teacher's Notes, p. 170
> Reading Check, p. 172
> Study Guide, p. 173
> Building Vocabulary, p. 176
> Selection Test, p. 178

PREREADING FOCUS
The headnote introduces the end of the story of the Norse gods. This final tale incorporates details and events from other Norse myths. Ask students to remember what they have learned of Norse mythology as they read the selection and to note how parts of other stories fit into this one.

The End of All Things

1
Inversion. Author writes, "First would there be," rather than "First there would be," setting a tone of stateliness and giving the passage an ancient, timeless feeling. Device is used throughout the selection.

The Norsemen believed that, as Odin had foreseen, the gods were doomed one day to perish, and this is how they told that it would come to pass.

1 First would there be three winters more terrible than any that had ever gone before, with
2 snow and ice and biting winds and no power in the sun; and no summers to divide this cruel season and make it bearable, but only one long wintertime with never a respite. And at the end of that winter, Skoll,¹ the wolf who had ever
3 pursued the sun, would leap upon it and devour it, and likewise would Hati² with the moon. And the stars which had been sparks from Muspellheim³ would flicker and go out,
4 so that there would be darkness in the world.

The mountains would shake and tremble, and the rocks would be torn from the earth; and the sea would wash over the fields and the forests as Iormungand,⁴ the Midgard-Serpent, raised himself out of the water to advance on the land. And at that moment all chains would be sundered and all prisoners released; Fenris Wolf would break free from Gleipnir,⁵ and Loki rise up from his prison under the ground. Out of fiery Muspellheim would come Surt the giant with his flaming sword; and out of her house would come Hel, with Garm⁶ the hound at her side, to join with her father, Loki. And all the frost and storm giants would gather together to follow them.

5 From Bifrost, Heimdall, with his sharp eyes, would see them come, and know that the moment which the gods had feared was at hand, and he would blow his horn to summon them to defend the universe. Then the Aesir and the Vanir would put on their armor, and the spirits of the dead warriors that were feasting in Valhall take up their swords, and with Odin at their head in his golden helmet, ride forth to
6 give battle to the enemies of good.

And in the mighty conflict which would follow, all the earth, all Asgard, even Niflheim itself, would shake with the clang and cry of war. Odin would fight against huge Fenris Wolf, and hard would be the struggle they would have. Thor, with Miolnir, would kill the

---
1. **Skoll** (skōl).
2. **Hati** (hä′tē).
3. **Muspellheim** (mŭs′pĕl-hām): the realm of fire. Muspell was guarded by a giant named Surt.
4. **Iormungand** (yôr′mŭn-gănd): the offspring of Loki and a giantess. See page 644.
5. **Gleipnir** (glāp′nîr): the silken rope forged by the dwarfs.
6. **Garm** (gärm).

2
To Norsemen, life was always a struggle against the cold; thus, extra long and cold winter is particularly frightening idea.

3
Another fear was that the sun and moon would perish and the stars be extinguished.

4
Reign of darkness suggests evil's rise to power.

5
Heimdall, the guardian of the Bifrost rainbow bridge to middle earth, rallies the forces of good with a warning on his horn.

6 Summarizing
What are the two sides in the conflict? The forces of good (all the gods except Loki) versus the forces of evil (Loki, monsters, and giants).

The End of All Things 663

PRESENTATION

This myth explains what the Norsemen believed would come to pass at the end of all things. After Ragnarok, however, a new world would arise with happiness for all.

Before students read, you may wish to assign individual students to identify the fate of a character. Tell them to look carefully at what happens to that character so they can inform the class after the reading what his or her fate was. Remind students to watch for what happens in the myth *after* everything is destroyed.

TRANSPARENCY 49

Reader Response
Norse Notables – asks students to choose a character and identify specific attributes they admire.

7
In many stories, Thor has attempted to fight this monster; he finally succeeds, but is mortally wounded.

8
Frey, sitting on Odin's throne from which all things can be seen, saw and loved Gerd. Frey gave Skirnir his sword as payment for arranging for his marriage to Gerd.

VISUAL CONNECTIONS
Exploring the Subject
This illustration shows Odin, mounted on his faithful steed Sleipnir, fighting the Fenris Wolf, whose magic bindings have ceased to restrain him as the last battle begins. The Norse believed that Odin would fight bravely but would be slain by the awful wolf, which would then be killed by Odin's son Vidar. Other opponents who would slay each other in the battle were Loki and Heimdall (the guardian of the Bifrost Bridge), and Thor and the Midgard-Serpent. The cataclysm was not to be absolute, however, and a better world would arise from the ashes of the old.

---

7 Midgard-Serpent, as had ever been his wish to do; but he would not long survive his victory, for he would fall dead from the dying monster's poisonous breath.

Tyr and Hel's hound, Garm, would rush at each other and close to fight, and with his good left hand, brave Tyr would hew down the mighty beast; but in its last struggles it would tear the god to pieces, and so would they perish both.

Surt with his flaming sword would bear down on Frey, but Frey had given his own 8 sword to Skirnir,[7] and as Loki had foretold, bitterly would he regret it, for he would have no more than the antler of a deer with which to defend himself. Yet would he not perish without a struggle.

As they had met and fought once before, over Freya's necklace,[8] so Loki and Heimdall would come together in battle once again, and Loki would laugh as he strove with his one-

---

7. **Skirnir** (skîr′nîr): Frey's messenger.
8. **necklace:** In one of the myths, Freya's necklace is stolen by Loki.

Odin and Fenris by Dorothy Hardy.

time friend. And in the same moment, each would strike the other a deadly blow, and both alike fall dead.

Though Odin would fight long and bravely with Fenris Wolf, in the end that mighty monster would be too strong for him, and the wolf with his gaping jaws would devour the father of the gods, and then perish at the hands of Vidar[9] the silent.

Then fire from Muspellheim would sweep over all, and thus would everything be destroyed; and it would indeed be the end of all things.

But the Norsemen believed that one day, out of the sea that had engulfed it, and out of the ruins, the world would grow again, fresh and green and beautiful; with fair people dwelling on it, born from Lifthrasir and Lif,[10] the only man and woman to escape the fire. And they believed that out of the ashes of old Asgard would arise another home for the gods, where would live in joy and peace the younger gods, who had not perished; the two sons of Odin, Vidar the silent god, and Vali[11] the son of Rind. And with them would be Magni,[12] the strong son of Thor, mightier even than his father; while out from the house of Hel, at last, would come Balder, and Hod, his brother. And everywhere would be happiness.

9. **Vidar** (vē′där): a son of Odin.
10. **Lifthrasir** (lĭft′rä-sîr); **Lif** (lĭf).
11. **Vali** (vä′lē): son of Odin and the goddess Rind.
12. **Magni** (măg′nē).

Reading Check

1. In Norse mythology, what supposedly will happen to the sun and moon on the day of doom?
2. What will happen to the monsters that the gods had imprisoned or chained?
3. Who will follow Odin into battle?
4. How will the earth be destroyed?
5. Which of the gods will be restored to life?

For Study and Discussion

Analyzing and Interpreting the Myth

1. What natural disasters will accompany the struggles of the gods and their enemies?

2. In what way is the ending of the gods a new beginning?

3. How will the earth be purified by the great destruction called Ragnarok?

Writing About Literature

▶ Analyzing Heroic Characteristics

In the Norse myths the gods and goddesses are depicted as heroic figures, grander and larger than life. Analyze the heroic characteristics shown by the gods during their last battle.

▶Before students begin this writing assignment, you may want to refer them to the **Writing About Literature** section on p. 688.

The End of All Things 665

UNIT 11 ◆ TEACHING GUIDE

LITERARY HERITAGE
FABLES

OVERVIEW OF THE UNIT

This unit features a brief look at three kinds of fables. The first section begins with traditional favorites by Aesop—"Belling the Cat," "The Town Mouse and the Country Mouse," "The Ant and the Grasshopper," and "The Fox and the Crow." The next selections are verse fables—John Godfrey Saxe's "The Blind Men and the Elephant" and Marie de France's "The Wolf and the Dog." The unit closes with a sampling of James Thurber's *Fables for Our Times,* all with a humorous twist.

Related activities reinforce recognition of allusions, challenge students to analyze morals, and develop understanding of proverbs. **Focus on Reading and Critical Thinking** gives students practice in distinguishing facts from opinions. Finally, **Focus on Writing** guides students through the process of writing a persuasive paper.

OBJECTIVES OF THE UNIT

The aims of the unit are for the student:
◆ To interpret the morals of fables
◆ To write a fable including a moral
◆ To write analyses of the morals of various fables
◆ To write a persuasive paper

CONCEPTS AND SKILLS

The following concepts and skills are treated in this unit:

LITERARY ELEMENTS/TERMS AND TECHNIQUES
Recognizing Allusions   674
Understanding Proverbs   678

WRITING OPPORTUNITIES
Writing About Literature
Analyzing the Moral of a Fable   678
Creative Writing
Writing a Fable   684
Focus on Persuasive Writing
Evaluating Reasoning   674
Organizing a Persuasive Paper   684
Writing a Persuasive Paper   686

FOCUS ON READING
Expressing a Moral   684

FOCUS ON READING AND CRITICAL THINKING
Distinguishing Between Facts and Opinions   685

TRANSPARENCIES

The following unit support materials with specific correlations to literature selections are available in the **Fine Art and Instructional Transparencies with Teacher's Notes and Blackline Masters** section of your *Audiovisual Resources Binder.*

FINE ART TRANSPARENCIES
Theme: Transformations That Teach a Lesson
46 *Apollo and Daphne,* Antonio Pollaiuolo
Theme: The Heroic Struggle
47 *Whaam!,* Roy Lichtenstein

READER RESPONSE
48 Breakfast of Role Models
49 Norse Notables

LITERARY ELEMENTS
50 Analyzing a Myth
51 Elements of Fables

WRITING PROCESS
52 Supporting an Opinion
53 Writing a Persuasive Paper

INTRODUCING THE UNIT

This unit features both traditional and modern fables—brief tales written in prose or verse, whose main characters are usually animals that possess human attributes. By contrasting both appropriate and improper behavior, most often in a humorous tone, a fable conveys a moral, a statement of universal truth or useful advice about life. For example, "Look before you leap" suggests that one should exercise sound judgment or prudence in unfamiliar situations. Meaningful and entertaining, the fable is a unique literary art form enjoyed by readers of all ages.

PORTFOLIO ASSESSMENT

Suggestions for use of portfolios as support for this unit are described in the *Portfolio Assessment and Professional Support Materials* booklet accompanying this program. Specific suggestions are provided for a variety of student projects that may be suitable for inclusion in a portfolio. In addition, copying masters are provided for guides that may be used for evaluation and assessment of student projects.

665A

PLANNING GUIDE

FOR UNIT PLANNING
- Transparencies 46–53: *Audiovisual Resources Binder*
- Portfolio Assessment: *Professional Support Materials*
- Test Generator
- Mastery Tests: Teaching Resources E, pp. 221, 223
- Composition Test: Teaching Resources E, p. 225

SELECTION (Pupil's Page)	TEACHING RESOURCES E (page numbers shown below)							AV BINDER
	Teacher's Notes	Reading Check	Study Guide	Language Skills	Building Vocabulary	Selection Vocab. Test	Selection Test	Audio-cassette
FABLES Introduction (p. 667)	187							
Fables By Aesop Retold by Joseph Jacobs Belling the Cat (p. 669)	188	190	191		206	217	194	
Fables By Aesop Retold by Joseph Jacobs The Town Mouse and the Country Mouse (p. 670)	188	190	191		206	217	194	TAPE 3 SIDE B
Fables By Aesop Retold by Joseph Jacobs The Ant and the Grasshopper (p. 672)	188	190	191		206	217	194	TAPE 3 SIDE B
Fables By Aesop Retold by Joseph Jacobs The Fox and the Crow (p. 673)	188	190	191		206	217	194	
John Godfrey Saxe The Blind Men and the Elephant (p. 675)	196		200	204	206	217	218	TAPE 3 SIDE B
Marie de France The Wolf and the Dog (p. 677)	196	199	201				208, 218	
Fables by James Thurber The Fairly Intelligent Fly (p. 679)	209	212	213			217	218	TAPE 3 SIDE B
Fables by James Thurber What Happened to Charles (p. 680)	209	212	213		216	217	218	TAPE 3 SIDE B
Fables by James Thurber The Fox and the Crow (p. 682)	209	212	213		216	217	218	

Student Learning Options

FABLES

1. Naming Characteristics of Animals
Lead a discussion on what different animals have come to stand for as stereotypes. Examples might include fox=tricky, snake=evil, bird=nervous, bull=angry, and monkey=funny. Then ask students to name examples of fables that draw on these generalizations about different animals.

2. Drawing Illustrations
Ask students to draw a picture to illustrate each fable they read. Encourage them to notice details in the fable to make the picture more accurate.

3. Acting Out Fables
Divide the class into pairs of students. Ask each pair to choose one fable to act out. The students need not write a script; they just need to plan carefully what they will say and do. They can also use props and sound effects when they perform before the entire class.

VISUAL CONNECTIONS

About the Artwork
The hares in this gothic manuscript illumination reflect an anthropomorphized view of the animal kingdom similar to that found in fables. The hares look as though they could be speaking to one another, and, in a characteristically Gothic use of proportion, they are depicted as being as large as the trees. This manuscript page also shows the influence of stained glass on Gothic manuscript illumination. The brilliant colors, particularly the blue, imitate the colors characteristic of stained glass, and the border strips imitate the partitions made by leading. The emphasis is on color and the impression of things rather than on three-dimensional form. The Gothic love of ornament is shown by the ornately decorated backdrop.

Exploring the Subject
At the time this illumination was painted, the Middle Ages were coming to a close. Free cities dominated commerce, producing the wealth necessary for secular patronage of the arts. However, the social structure of the Middle Ages still existed, with guilds organizing middle-class life. Manuscript illumination, no longer confined to monasteries, was often done in guild workshops. For the masters, guilds obtained commissions and ensured proper payment. For the patrons, guilds ensured quality of craftsmanship and materials.

Relating Expression Skills
Students might discuss the role of animals in stories and fairy tales. Why do they suppose the characters are animals instead of people? Would the stories be as effective if all the characters were human?

FABLES

Certain animal characters are well-known figures in folk tales and fables of different cultures. The hare is probably best known for the race he loses against the tortoise because of his overconfidence. What stories do you know in which a hare or a rabbit is an important player? What stories do you know that feature a fox? a crow? a cat? a lion? What characteristics of each animal are emphasized in these stories?

Make up a tale about the animals shown in this illuminated manuscript. If you wish, introduce other animal characters into your story. Give your characters names and invent dialogue for them.

"Hares" from an illuminated manuscript, *Livre de la Chasse (Book of the Chase)*, by Gaston Phebus (M. 1044, f. 15v), Paris, c. 1410.
The Pierpont Morgan Library, bequest of Miss Clara S. Peck

PRESENTATION

You may begin by defining **fable** and providing brief background information about Aesop, who is given credit for creating the fable form. The **Guidelines for Close Reading** will help students develop skills in reading and analyzing a fable. You may want to go over each guideline before beginning the unit and then return to the guidelines after each of the three sections of the unit. Combining a review of the reading guidelines with the **For Study and Discussion** questions at the end of each section will give students experience in following the guidelines as they read.

UNIT INTRODUCTION

1
Fables, from the Latin *fabula,* meaning "a thing said," usually have animals as characters and, although they impart practical wisdom, often have a magical or fantastic quality (an ant chiding a grasshopper, for example).

2
Many fables are attributed to Aesop, who is said to have been a deformed slave living in Asia Minor in the sixth century B.C. Though Aesop probably did exist, no one can be sure how many of the fables were actually written by him since they were not compiled until the late 1400s.

GUIDELINES FOR CLOSE READING

1. Students should enjoy these short, humorous selections since they are fun to read and easy to understand.
2. Students should look for characteristics the fables consistently ridicule and those they commend.
3. In the unit, "The Blind Men and the Elephant" is the only fable without a clearly stated moral. For this fable, have students suggest one.
4. Often, students can apply fables' morals to their own lives.

---

1 Fables are brief tales that combine common sense with entertainment. The stories are fun to read. At the same time, they teach useful lessons about human behavior. The characters in fables are usually animals who speak and act like human beings. The meaning of a fable is often summed up in its *moral,* a statement of the lesson to be learned, such as *Do not trust flatterers.*

No one knows when fables were first told. Some say that the credit
2 for creating the fable form belongs to Aesop, a Greek who probably lived around the sixth century B.C. Not much is known about Aesop, but his fables have remained popular for centuries. You will find several examples of his work in this unit.

In addition to the fables by Aesop, you will find modern retellings of well-known fables. Two examples, in verse, will show you how poets have adapted the fable form to their own needs. In the fables by James Thurber, one of America's most humorous writers, you will see that the old form has been given a new twist.

Guidelines for Close Reading

1. Read for pleasure and understanding. Fables often teach their lessons through humor or through irony.
2. Look for qualities or traits that the characters represent. In many fables the characters stand for characteristics like industriousness or indolence.
3. Determine the moral if it is not stated explicitly.
4. Try to restate the moral of the fable in your own words. Ask yourself if the moral of the fable applies to modern-day situations.

Fables by Aesop

Retold by JOSEPH JACOBS

Belling the Cat

Long ago, the mice had a general council to consider what measures they could take to outwit their common enemy, the Cat. Some said this, and some said that; but at last a Young Mouse got up and said he had a proposal to make which he thought would meet the case. "You will all agree," said he, "that our chief danger consists in the sly and treacherous manner in which the enemy approaches us. Now, if we could receive some signal of her approach, we could easily escape from her. I venture, therefore, to propose that a small bell be procured and attached by a ribbon round the neck of the Cat. By this means we should always know when she was about and could easily retire while she was in the neighborhood."

This proposal met with general applause, until an Old Mouse got up and said, "That is all very well, but who is to bell the Cat?" The mice looked at one another and nobody spoke. Then the Old Mouse said:

"It is easy to propose impossible remedies."

"Lion, King of the Beasts" from an illuminated manuscript, *Der Renner (The Racer)*, by Hugo von Trimberg (M. 763, f. 29v), Austria, fifteenth century.
The Pierpont Morgan Library

The Town Mouse and the Country Mouse

Now you must know that a Town Mouse once upon a time went on a visit to his cousin in the country. He was rough and ready, this cousin, but he loved his town friend and made him heartily welcome. Beans and bacon, cheese and bread, were all he had to offer, but he offered them freely.

The Town Mouse rather turned up his long nose at this country fare, and said: "I cannot understand, Cousin, how you can put up with such poor food as this, but of course you cannot expect anything better in the country; come you with me and I will show you how to live. When you have been in town a week you will wonder how you could ever have stood a country life."

No sooner said than done: the two mice set off for the town and arrived at the Town Mouse's residence late at night. "You will want some refreshment after our long journey," said the polite Town Mouse, and took his friend into the grand dining room. There they found the remains of a fine feast, and soon the two mice were eating up jellies and cakes and all that was nice. Suddenly they heard growling and barking.

"What is that?" said the Country Mouse.

"It is only the dogs of the house," answered the other.

"Only!" said the Country Mouse. "I do not like that music at my dinner."

Just at that moment the door flew open, in came two huge mastiffs,[1] and the two mice had to scamper down and run off. "Goodbye, Cousin," said the Country Mouse.

"What! going so soon?" said the other.

"Yes," he replied:

"Better beans and bacon in peace than cakes and ale in fear."

---

1. **mastiffs:** a breed of dogs used for hunting and as watchdogs.

"The Town Rat and the Country Rat," an illustration by Gustave Doré (1832–1883) for the *Fables of La Fontaine*, c. 1860.

PORTFOLIO ASSESSMENT
Small groups of students may want to perform dramatizations of some of the fables in this unit. Suggest that students assign parts, rehearse stage movements, and recite lines with expression and emotion. Actors may wish to make and use simple masks that represent the animals. Performances may be videotaped for peer review later. Ask students to write a paragraph evaluating their own participation in the performance for inclusion in their portfolios. (See *Portfolio Assessment and Professional Support Materials* for additional information on student portfolios.)

VISUAL CONNECTIONS
Ideas for Writing
This picture of mice, apparently taking great risks for their feast, scampering across expensive table settings might serve (along with the fable) as a springboard for student writing about priorities. Students might consider what rewards attract people to high-risk professions such as being a soldier, police officer, or firefighter, or they might write about someone they know (or have heard about) who does not make a great deal of money but who seems to lead a simple, happy life.

The Town Mouse and the Country Mouse

READING SKILLS PRACTICE
The underlined passage can be used to give students practice in the reading skill of determining the sequence of events. Ask students to read the passage, paying attention to the events that occur. Then ask students to answer the following question. What happens after the Grasshopper sees the Ant eating every day? **A.** The Ant continues working. (Contradicted in the passage.) **B.** The Grasshopper learns that one should prepare for the future. (Correct.) **C.** Winter comes. (Contradicted in the passage.) **D.** The Grasshopper dies of hunger. (Unsupported by the passage.)

TEACHING RESOURCES E
Teacher's Notes, p. 188
Reading Check, p. 190
Study Guide, p. 191
Building Vocabulary, p. 206
Selection Vocabulary Test, p. 217
Selection Test, p. 194

AV RESOURCES BINDER
Audiocassette 3, Side B

The Ant and the Grasshopper

1
Characterization. Difference between Ant and Grasshopper is presented through two sharply contrasted activities.

2 Making Generalizations
What does the Grasshopper ask the Ant to do? What characteristic of the Grasshopper is suggested by his request? To stop working and chat. Request implies Grasshopper's laziness and impracticality.

VISUAL CONNECTIONS
Ideas for Writing
Sanders' painting of the grasshopper and ants, along with the fable, might be used as the basis for a persuasive paragraph. Students might imagine themselves as either the grasshopper or the ant and imagine that they must persuade the other to adopt their point of view. What arguments would they use? What would be the most effective ways to express their arguments?

672

The Ant and the Grasshopper

1 In a field one summer's day a Grasshopper was hopping about, chirping and singing to its heart's content. An Ant passed by, bearing along with great toil an ear of corn he was taking to the nest.

"Why not come and chat with me," said the
2 Grasshopper, "instead of toiling and moiling in that way?"

"I am helping to lay up food for the winter," said the Ant, "and recommend you to do the same."

"Why bother about winter?" said the Grasshopper; "we have got plenty of food at present."

▶ But the Ant went on its way and continued its toil. When the winter came the Grasshopper had no food, and found itself dying of hunger, while it saw the ants distributing every day corn and grain from the stores they had collected in the summer. Then the Grasshopper knew:

It is best to prepare for the days of necessity. ◀

▶Reading Skills Objective: Identifying Sequence of Events

The Ant and the Grasshopper by Christopher Sanders. Watercolor.
The Granger Collection, New York

672 FABLES

The Fox and the Crow

A Fox once saw a Crow fly off with a piece of cheese in its beak and settle on a branch of a tree. "That's for me, as I am a Fox," said Master Reynard, and he walked up to the foot of the tree.

"Good day, Mistress Crow," he cried. "How well you are looking today: how glossy your feathers; how bright your eye. I feel sure your voice must surpass that of other birds, just as your figure does. Let me hear but one song from you, that I may greet you as the Queen of Birds."

The Crow lifted up her head and began to caw her best, but the moment she opened her mouth, the piece of cheese fell to the ground, only to be snapped up by Master Fox.

"That will do," said he. "That was all I wanted. In exchange for your cheese I will give you a piece of advice for the future:

" 'Do not trust flatterers.' "

For Study and Discussion

Analyzing and Interpreting the Fables

1. The animals in a fable often show contrasting traits of character. For example, in "Belling the Cat," the Young Mouse is inexperienced and foolish; the Old Mouse is experienced and wise. What contrasts in character do you find in the other fables?

2. It is possible to state the moral of a fable in different ways. The moral of "The Town Mouse and the Country Mouse" might be stated in this way: *It is better to live humbly in peace than to live luxuriously in fear.* Restate the moral of "Belling the Cat" in your own words.

3. A fable expresses a general truth or gives practical advice about life and behavior. To what modern-day situations could you apply the moral of "The Ant and the Grasshopper"?

4a. What kinds of behavior do these fables support or praise? b. What kinds of behavior do they ridicule or condemn?

5. Aesop's fables were first told more than two thousand years ago, yet we continue to enjoy them today. Why do you think these fables still appeal to readers?

CLOSURE
Ask students to identify the different animals used as characters in Aesop's fables and to offer reasons why he chose these animals to play these roles.

EXTENSION AND ENRICHMENT
Have students write alternate morals for each fable. Some students might prefer to read additional fables by Aesop and share their favorites with the class.

Supply a list of aphorisms for students to use in writing original fables:
Love sees no faults.
A stumble may prevent a fall.
A stitch in time saves nine.
No pain, no gain.

LITERARY ELEMENTS
1. Danny's "race" is intellectual and academic.
2. *Lion's share:* largest or best portion; derived from fable where animals go hunting and lion takes all the spoils. *Sour grapes:* tendency to belittle something one cannot have; derived from fable where fox tries unsuccessfully to reach grapes and concludes that they are too sour to enjoy.

FOCUS ON PERSUASIVE WRITING
Specific examples might help students locate misleading emotional appeals in newspapers and magazines. You could share the following examples:
1. **False Cause and Effect:** If four students become ill after football practice, one could wrongly assume that the practice session was the cause.
2. **Attacking the Person:** A political candidate might call public attention to an opponent's physical appearance rather than to the opponent's views on issues.
3. **Bandwagon:** A student votes for a student body president because all of his friends are voting for her; however, no one mentions why the candidate is worth supporting.

Literary Elements
Recognizing Allusions

In one of Aesop's fables, there is a race between a tortoise and a hare. The hare, certain of an easy victory, becomes overconfident. Midway through the race, he decides to take a rest. As a result, he loses the race to the tortoise, who slowly but surely overtakes him. The fable makes this point: *Slow and steady wins the race.*

A number of expressions that we use in speaking and writing are **allusions**, or references, to Aesop's fables. People often use the moral *Slow and steady wins the race* when they wish to point out the rewards of perseverance and effort. In the following sentence, what kind of "race" has been run?

> Everyone was surprised when Danny won the scholarship, but Danny has always believed that *slow and steady wins the race.*

Each italicized expression in the sentences below refers to a fable by Aesop. Which of these expressions have you read or heard before?

> Whenever it comes to dividing a cake, Sylvia always takes the *lion's share.*

> Reynaldo says that he wouldn't have attended the party even if he had been invited, but I think it's a case of *sour grapes.*

To find the meanings of the italicized expressions, look them up in a dictionary. If your library has a collection of Aesop's fables, locate "The Lion's Share" and "The Fox and the Grapes," and tell the fables to the class.

Focus on Persuasive Writing
Evaluating Reasoning

In "The Fox and the Crow" the fox uses flattery to persuade the crow to sing. If the crow had been wiser, however, she would not have been tricked into dropping the piece of cheese.

Flattery is one of several emotional appeals that are really tricks, not truth. When you write a persuasive paper, **evaluate** your reasoning to avoid statements that masquerade as reasons. Here are some examples of misleading support that you should avoid:

1. **False Cause and Effect:** assuming that one event caused another just because it came before the other
2. **Attacking the Person:** ignoring the issue by attacking the person instead of the person's view on the topic
3. **Bandwagon:** asking people to believe or do something just because many other people do so

Look through some recent issues of newspapers and magazines and study the ads and the letters to the editor. See if you can find some examples of misleading emotional appeals like the ones listed above. Make notes on your findings, and save your writing.

Fables in Verse

The Blind Men and the Elephant

JOHN GODFREY SAXE

This fable comes from India. Like most fables, it points up a human weakness. Are these men blind in more than one way?

It was six men of Indostan°
   To learning much inclined,
Who went to see the Elephant
   (Though all of them were blind),
That each by observation   5
   Might satisfy his mind.

The *First* approached the Elephant,
   And happening to fall
Against his broad and sturdy side,
   At once began to bawl: 10
"God bless me! but the Elephant
   Is very like a wall!"

The *Second*, feeling of the tusk,
   Cried, "Ho! what have we here
So very round and smooth and sharp?   15
   To me 'tis mighty clear
This wonder of an Elephant
   Is very like a spear!"

The *Third* approached the animal,
   And happening to take   20
The squirming trunk within his hands,
   Thus boldly up and spake:
"I see," quoth he, "the Elephant
   Is very like a snake!"

The *Fourth* reached out an eager hand,   25
   And felt about the knee.
"What most this wondrous beast is like
   Is mighty plain," quoth he;
"'Tis clear enough the Elephant
   Is very like a tree!"   30

The *Fifth*, who chanced to touch the ear,
   Said: "E'en the blindest man
Can tell what this resembles most;
   Deny the fact who can,
This marvel of an Elephant   35
   Is very like a fan!"

---

1. **Indostan** (ĭn′dō-stăn′): Hindustan, an old name for India.

PRESENTATION

The succinct nature of the **fable** is well suited for the confines of a poem. Like **poetry**, the fable relies on **connotation**, **inference**, concrete **imagery**, and other literary devices to express the ideas the writer wishes to convey. Ask students to look for these devices as they read the fables.

In "The Blind Men and the Elephant" and "The Wolf and the Dog," **rhyme** and **rhythm** enhance the humor of the fables. Thus the fables should be read aloud to be fully appreciated. In the first poem, Saxe describes how six blind men "see" an elephant. Each man touches only a part of the elephant and then concludes that he knows all there is to know about the animal. In the second poem, de France tells about a wolf who realizes freedom is more important than a comfortable life in chains.

5
Connotation. Suggests narrow-mindedness.

6
Alliteration. Repetition of several initial letters in ll. 44–46 adds to sing-song nature of the rhyme and humorously deflates characters.

7
Possible moral: Get the big picture before coming to conclusions.

VISUAL CONNECTIONS
About the Artist
Hokusai was a master printmaker of the *Ukiyo-e* school (pictures of the "floating world"): the world of the theater and passing amusements. However, this print comes from a different tradition which was also very popular: illustrations of well-loved fables. Before his death at the age of 89, Hokusai wrote that it was not until he was 73 that he came to understand something of the true nature of the living things he painted.

Ideas for Writing
Students might write their own version of "The Blind Men and the Elephant," describing another unusually shaped animal such as a giraffe or a camel.

The *Sixth* no sooner had begun
   About the beast to grope,
Than, seizing on the swinging tail
5 That fell within his scope,   40
"I see," quoth he, "the Elephant
   Is very like a rope!"

And so these men of Indostan
6 Disputed loud and long,
Each in his own opinion   45
   Exceeding stiff and strong,
7 Though each was partly in the right,
   And all were in the wrong!

The Blind Men and the Elephant (1817) by Katsushika Hokusai (1760–1849). Japanese woodblock print.

676 FABLES

The Wolf and the Dog

MARIE DE FRANCE

Marie de France, who lived sometime during the end of the twelfth century, was probably the first woman to compose poems in French. Does this fable remind you of other fables you have read?

A wolf and dog met on the way
While passing through the woods one day.
The wolf looked closely at the dog,
And then began this dialogue:
1 "Brother," he said, "you look so fine!   5
And oh, such fur! How it does shine!"
The dog replied, "That's very true;
I eat quite well, a great deal, too.
Each day I make my cozy seat
While resting at my master's feet   10
Where daily I gnaw bones, and that
Is what makes me so big and fat.
If you would like to come with me,
If to obey him you'll agree—
And act like me—you'll have from this   15
More food than you could ever wish."
"I'll do that! Sure!" the wolf replied.
2 Together off they went, allied.
Before they'd at the town arrived,
The wolf looked at the dog and eyed   20
3 The way the dog a collar wore
And how a dragging chain he bore.
"Brother," he said, "how odd is that
Thing 'round your neck—I know not what."
4 "That's my chain-leash," the dog replied,   25
"With which all through the week I'm tied;
For his possessions I would chew on,
And many items I would ruin.
My master wants them all protected,
And that's why I'm tied and restricted.   30
At night, around the house I peer
And make sure that no thieves draw near."
"What!" cried the wolf. "By this you mean
You can't go out except with him!
Well, you can stay! I won't remain.   35
I'll never choose to wear a chain!
I'd rather live as a wolf, free,
Than on a chain in luxury.
I still can make a choice, and so
You fare to town; to woods I'll go."   40
5 A chain thus brought the termination
Of friendship and fraternization.°

---

42. **fraternization** (frăt′ər-nĭ-zā′shən): friendly association.

CLOSURE

Ask students to interpret the moral of "The Blind Men and the Elephant" and "The Wolf and the Dog." Also, ask students to define and give examples of **proverbs**.

EXTENSION AND ENRICHMENT

For a week, have students keep logs of proverbs seen or heard. Possible sources include conversations, books, magazines, newspapers, radio, and television.

Some students might want to work individually or in small groups to write verse fables based on selections from Aesop.

Some students might like to create cartoons illustrating a proverb or a fable.

FOR STUDY AND DISCUSSION

The Blind Men and the Elephant
1. Each man assumes he can infer what the entire animal looks like based on the feel of one part of its body.
2. Possible morals are *Do not jump to conclusions* or *Each of us knows only part of the truth.*

The Wolf and the Dog
3. Both the dog and the town mouse brag about the lives they lead. They have an abundance of food, but they depend on human beings for it; both the wolf and the country mouse live meagerly and are attracted by the possibility of comfort and abundance. Both realize their independence is far more important than food and comfort.
4. Possible moral: *Beware of the chains of luxury.*

LITERARY ELEMENTS

1a. Eager, industrious people who do not waste time will win over competitors who do.
1b. A person who leads an unsettled life will not acquire close associations.

WRITING ABOUT LITERATURE

Student analyses of the moral will differ, but most will recognize that the physical blindness of the men represents their blindness to truth. The men cannot "see" because they refuse to look beyond their own pride and ignorance. Stopping their search too soon, the men jump to the wrong conclusion. They could have avoided their error if they had compiled more evidence by searching further themselves or by listening to the evidence of others.

678

For Study and Discussion

Analyzing and Interpreting the Poems

The Blind Men and the Elephant

1. Each blind man makes the same mistake in deciding what the Elephant is like. What is the mistake?

2. How would you state the moral of "The Blind Men and the Elephant"?

The Wolf and the Dog

3. Compare this fable with Aesop's fable of the town mouse and the country mouse (page 670). How are the dog and the town mouse alike? the wolf and the country mouse?

4. Write the moral that might accompany this fable.

Literary Elements

Understanding Proverbs

The moral of a fable generally gives some practical advice or warning that is intended to guide our behavior. A similar kind of common sense is contained in the sayings known as **proverbs**.

Proverbs are brief and to the point. They are often expressed in a catchy way that makes them easy to remember:

A fool and his money are soon parted.
Haste makes waste.
He who laughs last laughs best.
Better late than never.
Where there's a will, there's a way.

Some proverbs are metaphors. "A stitch in time saves nine" tells us that we can prevent a tear or a hole from growing by catching it early with a single stitch. By extension, the proverb means that we can avoid some future difficulty or problem by acting early enough to prevent it.

1 Explain these proverbs in your own words.
a The early bird catches the worm.
b A rolling stone gathers no moss.

Collect some proverbs that you like. Ask the older members of your family if they remember sayings or proverbs they heard when they were children.

Writing About Literature

▶ **Analyzing the Moral of a Fable**

In "The Blind Men and the Elephant," Saxe uses the men who are physically blind to point up another kind of blindness in human nature. How would you describe this kind of blindness? Why do the blind men jump to the wrong conclusions? How could they have avoided their error? In a short paper, analyze the moral of the fable.

About the Author

John Godfrey Saxe (1816–1887)

John Godfrey Saxe was born in Vermont and graduated from Middlebury College. He was a lawyer, a politician, and an editor of several newspapers. Saxe is best known as a writer of humorous and satirical verse, including *Progress: A Satire*. "The Blind Men and the Elephant," a modern fable in verse, is one of his most popular pieces.

▶ Before students begin this writing assignment, you may want to refer them to the *Writing About Literature* section on p. 688.

678 FABLES

Fables by James Thurber

In these modern fables, Thurber enjoys giving a new twist to the conventional form of the fable.

The Fairly Intelligent Fly

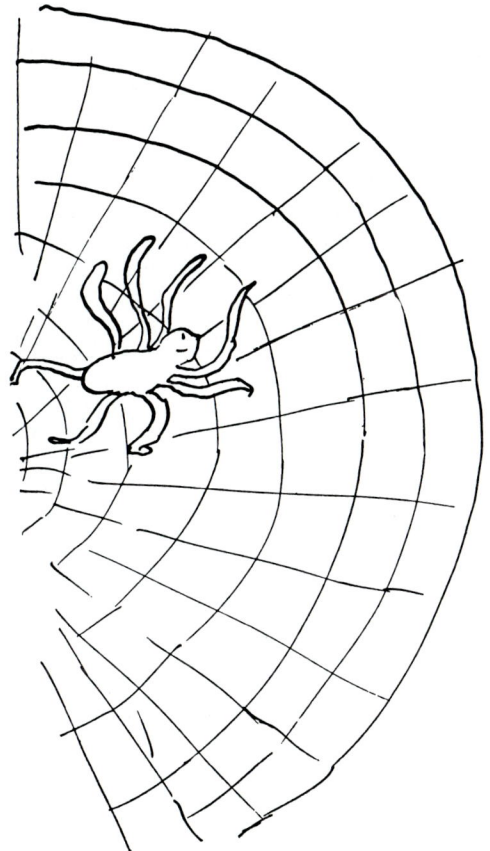

A large spider in an old house built a beautiful web in which to catch flies. Every time a fly landed on the web and was entangled in it the spider devoured him, so that when another fly came along he would think the web was a safe and quiet place in which to rest. One day a *fairly intelligent fly* buzzed around above the web so long without lighting that the spider appeared and said, "Come on down." But the fly was too clever for him and said, "I never light where I don't see other flies and I don't see any other flies in your house." So he flew away until he came to a place where there were a great many other flies. He was about to settle down among them when a bee buzzed up and said, "Hold it, stupid, that's flypaper. All those flies are trapped." "Don't be silly," said the fly, "they're dancing." So he settled down and became stuck to the flypaper with all the other flies.

Moral: There is no safety in numbers, or in anything else.

From *Fables for Our Time* by James Thurber, © 1940 by James Thurber, © 1968 Helen Thurber. Harper & Row, New York

What Happened to Charles

A farm horse named Charles was led to town one day by his owner, to be shod. He would have been shod and brought back home without incident if it hadn't been for Eva, a duck, who was always hanging about the kitchen door of the farmhouse, eavesdropping, and never got anything quite right. Her farmmates said of her that she had two mouths but only one ear.

On the day that Charles was led away to the smithy, Eva went quacking about the farm, excitedly telling the other animals that Charles had been taken to town to be shot.

"They're executing an innocent horse!" cried Eva. "He's a hero! He's a martyr! He died to make us free!"

"He was the greatest horse in the world," sobbed a sentimental hen.

"He just seemed like old Charley to me," said a realistic cow. "Let's not get into a moony mood."

"He was wonderful!" cried a gullible goose.

"What did he ever do?" asked a goat.

Eva, who was as inventive as she was inaccurate, turned on her lively imagination. "It was butchers who led him off to be shot!" she

From *Further Fables for Our Time* by James Thurber, Simon and Schuster, New York, © 1956 by James Thurber, © 1987 by Helen Thurber.

town to be "shod." Eavesdropping at the farmhouse, the duck Eva misunderstands and announces that poor Charles is to be "shot." What does Eva learn from her mistake? The third fable varies the story of the Fox and the Crow. Trying the old trick of flattery to get a crow to drop his cheese, the fox is foiled by the crow, who thinks himself unique. How does the fox react? Tell students to expect surprises as they read these fables.

shrieked. "They would have cut our throats while we slept if it hadn't been for Charles!"

"I didn't see any butchers, and I can see a burnt-out firefly on a moonless night," said a barn owl. "I didn't hear any butchers, and I can hear a mouse walk across moss."

"We must build a memorial to Charles the Great, who saved our lives," quacked Eva. And all the birds and beasts in the barnyard except the wise owl, the skeptical goat, and the realistic cow set about building a memorial.

Just then the farmer appeared in the lane, leading Charles, whose new shoes glinted in the sunlight.

It was lucky that Charles was not alone, for the memorial-builders might have set upon

8 him with clubs and stones for replacing their hero with just plain old Charley. It was lucky, too, that they could not reach the barn owl, who quickly perched upon the weather vane of

9 the barn, for none is so exasperating as he who is right. The sentimental hen and the gullible goose were the ones who finally called attention to the true culprit—Eva, the one-eared duck with two mouths. The others set upon

10 her and tarred and unfeathered her, for none

11 is more unpopular than the bearer of sad tidings that turn out to be false.

12 *Moral: Get it right or let it alone. The conclusion you jump to may be your own.*

VISUAL CONNECTIONS
About the Artwork
Thurber has drawn Charles the farm horse with a large head and strong neck. The horse has a resigned expression and conveys a plodding quality. Thurber's drawing of Eva the duck emphasizes her flapping mouth.

Relating Expression Skills
Artistically inclined students might enjoy drawing their own illustrations for Thurber's fables.

8
They resent losing their illusions and would rather have their fancy memorial than real horse.

9
Comment on human behavior: Those proved wrong often resent those who were right from beginning.

10
Play on "tarred and feathered"; here duck is plucked.

11
Reference to custom in ancient times when bearer of bad news would be killed.

12
This moral would fit story "Chicken Little," in which everyone is convinced the sky is falling.

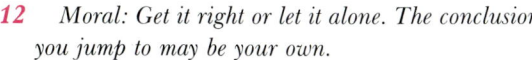

The Fox and the Crow

A crow, perched in a tree with a piece of cheese in his beak, attracted the eye and nose of a fox. "If you can sing as prettily as you sit," said the fox, "then you are the prettiest singer within my scent and sight." The fox had read somewhere, and somewhere, and somewhere else, that praising the voice of a crow with a cheese in his beak would make him drop the cheese and sing. But this is not what happened to this particular crow in this particular case.

"They say you are sly and they say you are crazy," said the crow, having carefully removed the cheese from his beak with the claws of one foot, "but you must be nearsighted as well. Warblers wear gay hats and colored jackets and bright vests, and they are a dollar a hundred. I wear black and I am unique." He began nibbling the cheese, dropping not a single crumb.

"I am sure you are," said the fox, who was neither crazy nor nearsighted, but sly. "I recognize you, now that I look more closely, as the most famed and talented of all birds, and I fain would hear you tell about yourself, but I am hungry and must go."

"Tarry awhile," said the crow quickly, "and

From *Further Fables for Our Time* by James Thurber, Simon and Schuster, New York, © 1956 by James Thurber, © 1987 by Helen Thurber.

MEETING INDIVIDUAL NEEDS
Visual Learners • Have students compare and contrast the two versions of "The Fox and the Crow" by using a Venn diagram to show the similarities and differences. Encourage them to think creatively and critically about the ways the fables are alike and different. Allow time for them to share their work with the class.

---

share my lunch with me." Whereupon he tossed the cunning fox the lion's share of the cheese and began to tell about himself. "A ship
4 that sails without a crow's-nest sails to doom," he said. "Bars may come and bars may go, but crowbars last forever. I am the pioneer of flight, I am the map maker. Last, but never
5 least, my flight is known to scientists and engineers, geometrists and scholars, as the shortest distance between two points.¹ Any two points," he concluded arrogantly.

1. **my flight . . . two points:** A crow is said to fly in a straight line, which is the shortest distance between two points.

"Oh, every two points, I am sure," said the fox. "And thank you for the lion's share of what I know you could not spare." And with this he trotted away into the woods, his appetite appeased, leaving the hungry crow perched forlornly in the tree.

6 *Moral: 'Twas true in Aesop's time, and La Fontaine's,² and now, no one else can praise thee quite so well as thou.*

2. **La Fontaine** (lä fŏn-tän'): Jean la Fontaine, a seventeenth-century French poet who wrote verse fables that criticized the French court.

For Study and Discussion

Analyzing and Interpreting the Fables

The Fairly Intelligent Fly
1. The familiar moral Thurber alludes to in this fable is *There is safety in numbers.* **a.** What happens to the fly when he puts his faith in this old moral? **b.** Explain Thurber's new moral in your own words.

2a. Why do you think the fly is described as "fairly intelligent"? **b.** How might the fly have behaved if he had been "very intelligent"?

What Happened to Charles
3. What mistake does Eva, the duck, make after hearing the word *shod*?

4. In Aesop's fables the animals often reveal contrasting traits of character. **a.** Which characters in Thurber's fable are shown to be foolish or hasty? **b.** Which are shown to be wise or cautious?

5. The moral is not the only message in this fable. **a.** Find two statements that are direct comments on human behavior. **b.** What kinds of behavior is Thurber criticizing in this fable?

The Fox and the Crow
6. You have read two versions of "The Fox and the Crow," Aesop's version on page 673 and Thurber's version on page 682. Both fables have a clever fox and a vain crow. How is Thurber's crow different in character from Aesop's?

7. In Aesop's fable the fox uses flattery and succeeds in outwitting the crow. Thurber's fox also uses flattery to trick the crow. What difference is there in his approach?

8. Thurber's crow attaches a great deal of importance to words that carry his name. **a.** How do you think *crow's-nest* got its name? **b.** What does a crow have to do with a *crowbar*?

9. Compare the morals in the fables by Aesop and Thurber. What new advice does Thurber offer on the subject of flattery?

4
Crow's-nest: perch on ship for seeing long distances; *crowbar:* tool for prying heavy objects.

5
Refers to common phrase "as the crow flies," meaning straight line.

6
When we praise ourselves, we can stretch the truth to include honors we wish we had gotten or achievements we wish we had made.

FOR STUDY AND DISCUSSION
The Fairly Intelligent Fly
1a. He sees number of flies stuck to flypaper, joins them, and becomes stuck himself. **1b.** Possibly, never rely totally on any saying as guide to action.
2a. It makes him just like the majority of readers. **2b.** Fly would have realized there is not always safety in numbers and heeded bee's advice.
What Happened to Charles
3. She mistakes *shod* for *shot*.
4a. Eva (duck), hen, and goose.
4b. Owl, goat, and cow.
5a. "None is so exasperating as he who is right" and "none is more unpopular than the bearer of sad tidings that turn out to be false." **5b.** Criticizing mob behavior, blind to reason, quick to turn on false leaders. There is also an implied criticism of hypocrisy and self-dramatization.
The Fox and the Crow
6. Thurber's crow is vain about his importance, not his appearance or voice.
7. His flattery is more subtle and slipped in as a regret.
8a. Answers will vary. Crow's-nest is a lookout point on ship; its great height led to its name. **8b.** Thin end of bar resembles crow's beak.
9. Beware of self-flattery.

CLOSURE
Ask students to give examples of the conceit shown by the animals in Thurber's fables. Discuss how their conceit causes their downfall.

EXTENSION AND ENRICHMENT
Have students write an essay relating one of the fables and its moral to an experience in their own lives.

Provide students with several morals of Aesop's fables, and ask them to write modern fables in a humorous style similar to that of Thurber.

Encourage students to compile a book of fables, illustrating either favorite fables from their reading or fables they have written themselves.

FOCUS ON READING
Possible moral: Greed often leads to destruction.

CREATIVE WRITING
Help students to brainstorm before they begin writing their fables. You might lead the entire class in brainstorming about each situation, or you might divide the class into groups and have each group brainstorm about one situation. The brainstorming should elicit a list of animals that might cause their own misfortune (geese, ducks, chickens, cows), clever persons or animals as opposed to foolish ones (owl versus goose, horse versus cow, cat versus dog, mouse versus cat), and strong persons or animals as opposed to weak ones (lion versus rabbit, elephant versus mouse, ox versus dog). Remind students that animals should represent characteristics appropriate to their size and abilities but that one kind of animal need not always represent the same trait. (For example, the cow is wise in Thurber's fable, but cows may be portrayed as foolish in other fables.)

FOCUS ON PERSUASIVE WRITING
Students might get a better understanding of the purpose of an **outline** by comparing the outline in their textbooks with a finished essay or speech that follows the outline's structure. Locate such an essay, distribute copies to students, and point out how the essay follows the format of the outline.

Focus on Reading

Expressing a Moral

As you have seen in this unit, the meaning of a fable is often summed up in its moral. Read the following Eskimo fable and write a moral that expresses its meaning.

The Owl and the Two Rabbits

An Owl spotted two Rabbits playing close together and seized them, one clutched in each foot. But they were too strong for him and ran away, sliding the Owl along the ice. The Owl's wife shouted to him, "Let one of them go and kill the other!"

But he replied, "The moon will soon disappear, and then we shall be hungry. We need both of them."

The Rabbits ran on; and when they came to a boulder, one ran to the right side of it, the other to the left. The Owl did not let go quick enough, and was torn in two.

Creative Writing

Writing a Fable

A fable, as you have seen, has certain characteristics. It is brief, it has a few characters, and it teaches some lesson and about human behavior. It generally ends with a moral.

Here are some common situations in fables:

A person or animal is the cause of his or her own misfortune.
A clever person or animal outwits a foolish one.
A strong person or animal preys upon a weaker one.

Write a fable of your own in prose or verse based on one of these situations. Use a moral that appears in this unit, some common saying, or an original moral of your own.

Focus on Persuasive Writing

Organizing a Persuasive Paper

When you write a persuasive paper or speech, you may find it helpful to use an **outline** like the one below:

I. Introduction
   A. Attention-grabbing statement
   B. Opinion statement
II. Body
   A. Information and emotional appeal
   B. More support if necessary
III. Conclusion
   A. Restatement of opinion/summary of reasons
   B. Call to action (if appropriate)

Choose a topic for a persuasive paper. Following the model above, write an outline for your paper. Then exchange outlines with a partner and offer each other suggestions for making your papers clearer and more convincing. Save your writing.

OBJECTIVES
The overall aim is for students to analyze a passage to distinguish **facts** from **opinions**.

PRESENTATION
To emphasize the introductory information, you might want to read aloud the first two paragraphs. Then ask for a volunteer to read aloud the Hamilton passage. Next, have students analyze the passage in small groups, using the questions that follow. Group leaders can share their group's responses with the class.

FOCUS ON Reading and Critical Thinking

DISTINGUISHING BETWEEN FACTS AND OPINIONS

A **fact** is something that has happened or is true. An **opinion** is a statement that represents a belief or attitude and that cannot be proved. For example, the statement that New York is the largest city in the United States is a fact. The statement that more New Yorkers should take mass transit to work is an opinion. Even though many people will agree that the second statement is based on sound facts, it is an assertion that cannot be proved.

As a reader and as a listener, you need to know whether the information you receive is fact or opinion. Read the passage by Edith Hamilton below. Then use a separate sheet of paper to answer the questions that follow.

The world of Norse mythology is a strange world. Asgard, the home of the gods, is unlike any other heaven men have dreamed of. No radiancy of joy is in it, no assurance of bliss. It is a grave and solemn place, over which hangs the threat of an inevitable doom. The gods know that a day will come when they will be destroyed. Sometime they will meet their enemies and go down beneath them to defeat and death. Asgard will fall in ruins. The cause the forces of good are fighting to defend against the forces of evil is hopeless. Nevertheless, the gods will fight for it to the end.

Necessarily the same is true of humanity. If the gods are finally helpless before evil, men and women must be more so. The heroes and heroines of the early stories face disaster. They know that they cannot save themselves, not by any courage or endurance or great deed. Even so, they do not yield. They die resisting. A brave death entitles them—at least the heroes—to a seat in Valhalla, one of the halls in Asgard, but there too they must look forward to final defeat and destruction. In the last battle between good and evil they will fight on the side of the gods and die with them.

Distinguishing Between Facts and Opinions

1. What opinion does Hamilton express about Norse mythology?

2. List three facts about Norse mythology that Hamilton uses to support her opinion.

3. What other opinions about Norse mythology do you have, based on the selections you have read in Unit 10? How would you support your views?

DISTINGUISHING BETWEEN FACTS AND OPINIONS
The distinction between **fact** and **opinion** may not always be clear, for a statement may include both fact and opinion. For example, consider the statement "When Ernest Hemingway died in 1961, he was America's most popular writer." That Hemingway died in 1961 is a **fact**. That he was America's most popular writer is an **opinion**. Yet because the first part of the statement is true, careless readers may also accept the second part of the statement as fact. Therefore, distinguishing between fact and opinion requires close analysis and sound reasoning.

Answers
1. Hamilton says that the Norse world of mythology is strange.
2. She says that Asgard is not like other heavens men have dreamed of. The gods know that they and Asgard will be destroyed. The gods will fight against the forces of evil until the end.
3. Answers may vary. Students might mention that Norse myths reflect a world that is often a threat to human survival. The stories are populated with evil giants and monsters that heroes—both divine and mortal—combat. Fate plays an unrelenting part. Norse gods possess human personalities, and they interact with one another and with giants, but they do not often involve themselves with human beings. A recurrent conflict is the forces of good against the forces of evil. The gods reflect the nature and values of the people who worshipped them—courage, dignity, generosity, humor, wit, loyalty, and honor.

OBJECTIVES
The overall aim is for students to apply the key elements of persuasion in a written **persuasive** paper.

PRESENTATION
To motivate students for **persuasive writing**, begin by discussing how persuasion affects their everyday lives. Ask students some of these questions and discuss their responses: (1) What is the last product you bought because of a commercial? What in the commercial attracted you to that product? (2) How would you convince your parents to give you a special privilege? (3) Think about the last school election. How would you evaluate the speeches of students running for student government?

HOLT WRITER'S WORKSHOP

This computer program provides help for all types of writing through guided instruction for each step of the writing process. (Program available separately.)

See *Elements of Writing, First Course,* Chapter 8, for more instruction on persuasive writing.

WRITING A PERSUASIVE PAPER
Persuasion is the art of getting others to do something or believe something. In almost any human activity we rely on our ability to persuade each other—something is or is not good, should or should not be done. To persuade, however, means more than just winning an argument; it means changing the other person's mind and convincing him or her to agree with you. To persuade requires that the other person stop arguing and respond with "I guess you're right" or "I never thought of it that way."

Prewriting
After students have chosen topics, encourage them to spend time analyzing their audiences. Remind them that the clearer the picture they have of their audiences, the more they can tailor their writing for those people and bring about the desired results.

Students might find that creating a pro and con chart will help them as they develop their arguments. This process often forces writers to think through their own arguments more carefully as they consider the other sides to their positions, thus eliminating fallacies or weak support.

FOCUS ON Writing

WRITING A PERSUASIVE PAPER

Persuasive writing has many different forms. Its purpose is usually the same: to get the reader or listener to think or act in a certain way. Now that you have learned about some of the key elements of persuasion, you will have a chance to write a persuasive paper of your own.

Prewriting

1. Begin by thinking about issues that matter to you. List some topics on which you have an opinion. The topic you choose should be a subject about which people can and do disagree—that is, it should be a matter of opinion, not a question of fact.
   - A **fact** is something that has happened or is true.
   - An **opinion** is a statement of belief or judgment.

[See **Focus** assignment on page 582.]

2. Write a one-sentence **opinion statement** on the issue you choose. This statement will serve as the **main idea** for your paper.

[See **Focus** assignment on page 590.]

3. Think about the interests, concerns, and opinions of your **audience**. You may want to make an **audience chart** like the one below:

Audience Chart
Topic: _____
Position/Opinion: _____
Audience: _____
Audience's Knowledge About Topic: _____

[See **Focus** assignment on page 612.]

4. Find information to support your opinion. Here are some kinds of support to use:
   - facts
   - reasons
   - examples
   - expert knowledge
   - appeals to emotions
   - personal experiences

[See **Focus** assignments on pages 647 and 652.]

5. Evaluate your reasoning. Here are three misleading types of support to avoid:
   - **False Cause and Effect:** assuming that one event caused another just because it came before the other
   - **Attacking the Person:** ignoring the issue by attacking the person instead of the person's view on the topic
   - **Bandwagon:** asking people to believe or do something just because many others do so

[See **Focus** assignment on page 674.]

Writing

1. Follow an **outline** like the one below as you write your first draft:
   I. Introduction
      A. Attention-grabbing statement
      B. Opinion statement
   II. Body
      A. Information and emotional appeal
      B. More support if necessary
   III. Conclusion
      A. Restatement of opinion/summary of reasons
      B. Call to action (if appropriate)

[See **Focus** assignment on page 684.]

686 LITERARY HERITAGE

As students share their experiences, you might point out that most persuasion is meant to bring about change—change in attitude or behavior. To be convincing, a person needs strong, well-developed arguments that are often laced with emotional appeals.

CLOSURE
Ask students to list the basic elements of **persuasion** and to identify the fallacies they should avoid when developing an argument.

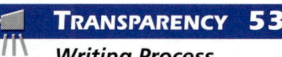

Writing Process
Writing a Persuasive Paper – helps students to plan and write an effective persuasive paper.

Writing
Remind students that they do not have to start their writing with their introductory paragraphs; instead, they might want to write the body of their paper first. Encourage students to include plenty of illustrations, examples, details—anything that will allow their readers to identify with the situation and to see what the writer sees.

Then students can experiment with their introductions and conclusions. You might want to brainstorm with students some of the ways they can grab the audience's attention and develop strong endings.

2. Remember to use **transitional words and phrases** in your paper to make the relationship of ideas clear. Some helpful transitions are *also*, *another*, *because*, *but*, *finally*, *first*, *however*, *last*, *likewise*, *most important*, *then*, and *therefore*.

Evaluating and Revising

1. Look over your first draft critically. Pay special attention to making your reasons as specific as possible. Here is an example of one writer's revision of a paragraph in a persuasive paper.

2. You may find the following checklist helpful as you revise your paper.

Checklist for Evaluation and Revision
- ✓ Do I grab the reader's attention?
- ✓ Do I clearly state my opinion on the issue?
- ✓ Is there enough support to convince the audience?
- ✓ Is my reasoning sound?
- ✓ Do I end with a strong conclusion?

Proofreading and Publishing

1. Proofread your persuasive paper and correct any errors you find in grammar, usage, and mechanics. (Here you may find it helpful to refer to the **Handbook for Revision** on pages 726–767.) Then prepare a final version of your paper by making a clean copy.

2. Consider some of the following ways to share your paper:
- join with some classmates to make a bulletin board display
- send your writing to a newspaper as a letter to the editor
- use your paper as the basis for a debate with a classmate who takes an opposing view on the same issue

Portfolio If your teacher approves, you may wish to keep a copy of your work in your writing folder or portfolio.

Evaluating and Revising
Students should read their drafts to a small group. The listeners can use the questions in the **Checklist for Evaluation and Revision** to take notes as the writers speak. Then the listeners should share their responses. For self-evaluation purposes, students might use the **Checklist for Evaluation and Revision** to label the margins of their drafts with the corresponding terminology—attention grabber, opinion statement, support, information, and strong conclusion. Then students can revise any weakness they or their listeners have noted.

Proofreading and Publishing
Remind students that an important aspect of persuasion is correctness, not only in its logical and emotional development, but also in its external appearance. They may want to spend extra time with spelling, punctuation, capitalization, and verb and pronoun usage.

OBJECTIVES
The overall aim is for students to understand how to use the writing process in developing essays about literature and in answering essay questions.

PRESENTATION
Before students read **Developing Skills in Critical Thinking,** determine informally how much experience they have had in writing essays about literature. You might ask them to cite the writing assignments they have had. If students are not familiar with **Literary Terms and Techniques** (p. 706), you might have students look up any of the terms mentioned (**plot, climax,** and so on).

When presenting **The Writing Process,** stress three important points about the stages that fol-

WRITING ABOUT LITERATURE

Developing Skills in Critical Thinking

Many of the compositions you will be asked to write in English class will be about the literature you read. The writing may be in response to an examination question, a homework assignment, or a research
1 project. At times you may be given a topic to work on; at other times you may have to choose your own subject for a paper.

In writing about literature, you generally focus on some aspect of a work. For example, you may give your impression of a character in a short story; you may discuss the suspense that is developed in a play;
2 you may explain the main idea of a poem. Such writing assignments are an important part of literary study, which aims at greater understanding and appreciation of the works you read.

Writing about a literary work is a way of getting to know it better. Before you write a composition about a story, a poem, or a play, you
3 must study the selection carefully. You must sort out your thoughts and reach conclusions. In putting your thoughts down on paper, you become more fully involved with the work.

Throughout your studies you will become familiar with a great
4 many elements that are useful in analyzing literary works. When you refer to the sequence of events in a short story or play, for instance,
5 you may use such terms as *plot, climax,* and *resolution* in describing the action. You may concern yourself with the *conflict,* or struggle, that a *character* faces. In discussing the meaning of a poem, you may refer to its *imagery* or *figurative language.* These words are part of a common vocabulary used in writing about literature. You can assume that your readers will understand what you mean when you write about such el-

DEVELOPING SKILLS IN CRITICAL THINKING

1 Expressing an Opinion
Do you prefer to choose your own topic or to be given a topic? Why? Responses will vary.

2 Comparing/Contrasting
How do these assignments differ from book reports? Require writer to analyze one aspect of work; are not summaries or overall impressions.

3
In any kind of writing, knowing subject well is essential.

4
Considering relationship of elements or parts to work as a whole is purpose of literary analyses.

5 Finding Details
Which of these terms do you recognize? Answers will vary.

688

688 WRITING ABOUT LITERATURE

low writing a draft: writers must *evaluate* a draft, identifying its strengths and weaknesses, before they make improvements; writers can *revise* a draft by adding, cutting, reordering, and replacing words, phrases, and sentences; *revising* and *proofreading* differ in intent—revising focuses on substantive changes while proofreading concentrates on surface errors.

Answering Examination Questions treats nine methods of developing essays. The list is not exhaustive and you may wish to expand it. Tell students that methods frequently overlap and that a combination of methods is often effective.

When discussing **Writing on a Topic of Your Own**, you may introduce other strategies for choosing and limiting topics, including brainstorming, cubing, and the 5W-How approach.

ements. (See *Literary Terms and Techniques,* page 706.)

The material on the following pages offers help in planning and writing papers about literature. Here you will find suggestions for answering examination questions, choosing topics, gathering evidence, organizing essays, and writing, evaluating, and revising papers. Also included are several model essays.

The Writing Process

1 We often refer to writing an essay as a *process,* which consists of several key stages or phrases: **prewriting, writing a first draft, evaluating and revising,** and **proofreading and publishing.** In this process, much of the critical work—the thinking and planning—comes before the actual writing of the paper.

2 In the **prewriting** stage, the writer makes decisions about what to say
3 and how to say it. Prewriting activities include choosing a topic; consid-
4 ering purpose, audience, and tone; gathering ideas and organizing them; and developing a *thesis*—the controlling idea for the paper. In **writing a first draft,** the writer uses the working plan to get ideas down
5 on paper. In the **evaluating and revising** stage, the writer judges the first draft to identify strengths and weaknesses in content, organization, and style. The writer then makes changes to eliminate the weaknesses identified through evaluating. The writer can revise by adding, cutting, reordering, or replacing ideas and details. In the **proofreading and publishing** stage, the writer checks the revised draft to correct errors in grammar, usage, and mechanics. The writer then prepares a
6 clean copy and proofreads the work before sharing it with others.

The stages of the writing process are related. For this reason, there is usually a "back and forth" movement among the stages. Few writers finish one stage completely before they move on to the next one. At the same time, few writers move in a straight line from one stage to the next. For example, the writer might think up new ideas as he or she is writing a first draft. This would probably require going "back"
7 to prewriting to restate the thesis or to locate new supporting evidence. This movement among the stages of the writing process is a natural part of writing—for all writers.

The amount of time devoted to each stage will vary with individual assignments. During a classroom examination, you will have limited time to plan your essay and to proofread your paper. For a term paper, you may have weeks or months to prepare your essay.

On the following pages the steps in this process are illustrated through the development of several model essays.

THE WRITING PROCESS

1
Writing is a process because a series of steps is involved, as in other processes such as cooking, sewing, building a house.

2
Some people attempt to save time by skipping prewriting stage; usually results in wasting time because writing becomes disorganized, unfocused.

3
Prewriting strategies may include writers asking and answering questions about the topic.

4
Plan might be formal outline or simple list.

5
Revising means re-seeing; involves rethinking, reconsidering.

6
Clean copy is indication that writer cares about the paper and reader.

7 Finding Details
What constitutes evidence when writing about literature? Answers will vary. May include narrator's comments, character's speech, imagery, sensory details.

Answering Examination Questions

ANSWERING EXAMINATION QUESTIONS

1 Taking careful notes while reading is good preparation for essay exams. Recalling class discussion is also helpful, as is considering and developing answers to kinds of questions likely to be asked.

2 To be relevant, answer must directly relate to question. Purpose of answering question is to prove understanding of concept, not to demonstrate vague awareness of topic.

3 Expert test-takers ask themselves "Why do I say this?" and then provide answer for person evaluating test.

4 Usually, at least two pieces of evidence should be given to support each point.

5 When answering essay questions, many writers find that asking themselves additional questions is a good prewriting strategy. Verb in test question determines what additional questions to ask.

6 First answering the question "What are the parts?" is helpful in planning answer to analysis question.

---

1 Often you may be asked to show your understanding of a literary work or topic by writing a short essay in class. Usually, your teacher will give you a specific question to answer. How well you do will depend not only on how carefully you have read and mastered the material, but on how carefully you read and interpret the essay question.

2 Before you begin to write, be sure you understand what the question calls for. If a question requires that you give three reasons for a character's actions, and you supply only two, your answer will be incomplete. If the question asks you to *contrast* two settings, be sure that you point out their differences, not their similarities. Don't use essays or short stories if the question calls for poetry. Always take some time to read the essay question carefully in order to determine how it should be answered.

3 Remember that you are expected to demonstrate specific knowledge of the literature. Any general statement should be supported by evidence. If you wish to show that a character changes, for example, you should refer to specific actions, dialogue, thoughts and feelings, or direct comments by the author, in order to illustrate your point. If you are allowed to use your textbook during the examination, you may occasionally quote short passages or refer to a specific page in order to provide supporting evidence.

4 At the start, it may be helpful to jot down some notes to guide you in writing your essay. If you have four main points to make, you may then decide what the most effective order of presentation will be. You might build up to your strongest point, or you might present your points to develop a striking contrast. Aim for a logical organization.

Also remember that length alone is not satisfactory. Your answer must be clearly related to the question, and it must be presented in acceptable, correct English. Always take some time to proofread your paper.

5 The key word in examination questions is the *verb*. Let us look briefly at some common instructions used in examinations.

ANALYSIS

6 A question may ask you to *analyze* some aspect of a literary work. When you analyze something, you take it apart to see how each part works. In literary analysis you generally focus on some limited aspect of a work in order to better understand and appreciate the work as a whole. For example, you might analyze the technique of suspense in

"The Tiger's Heart" (page 170); you might analyze the role of moonlight in "The Highwayman" (page 468); you might analyze Thurber's use of exaggeration in "The Night the Bed Fell" (page 133).

COMPARISON CONTRAST

7 A question may ask that you *compare* (or *contrast*) two characters, two settings, two ideas. When you *compare*, you point out likenesses; when you *contrast*, you point out differences. Sometimes you will be asked to *compare and contrast*. In that event, you will be expected to deal with similarities and differences. You might, for instance, compare and contrast the characters of Ruth and Eileen McKenney in "Guinea Pig" (page 41). You might compare and contrast two versions of a fable, "The Fox and the Crow," by Aesop (page 673), and by Thurber (page 682). Sometimes, the word *compare* is used to include both comparison and contrast. Always check with your teacher to make sure that you understand how the term *compare* is being used.

DEFINITION

A question may ask you to *define* a literary term—to answer the question "What is it?" To define a term, first place it in a large group. Then discuss the features or characteristics that make it different from other members of the same group. You should also include a specific example to illustrate the term. For example, if asked to define the term *irony*, you would first say it is an element of literature (large group) in which there is a contrast between what is expected to happen and what actually happens (feature). For example, in the story "You Can't Take It with You" (page 264), Uncle Basil's relatives expect him to leave his money behind. Instead he actually takes it with him by using it to line his coffin.

8

DESCRIPTION

9 If a question asks you to *describe* a setting or a character, you are expected to give a picture in words. In describing a setting, include not only details that establish the historical period and locale, but also details that evoke a mood. In describing a character, you should deal with methods of direct and indirect characterization (see pages 707–708). You might describe the scene in "Stopping by Woods on a Snowy Evening" (page 455); you might describe each of the Christmas spirits in "A Christmas Carol" (page 276).

DISCUSSION

10 The word *discuss* in a question is much more general than the other words we've looked at. When you are asked to discuss something, you are expected to examine it in detail. If you are asked to discuss the images in a poem, for example, you must deal with all major images; if asked to discuss the use of dialect in a story or poem, you must be sure to cover all significant examples. Suppose your assignment asked you

7
When planning an answer to comparison/contrast question, ask "How are these things alike?" and "How are they different?"

8
Specific example is given to illustrate the term *irony*.

9
When answering questions that call for description, test-takers should keep in mind purpose for describing, not merely repeat information from selection. Purpose is usually to convey dominant impression created by **setting** or character. Question might be "What dominant impression is created?"

10
A good way to plan answer to discussion question is to ask "What major points could I make about this topic?" and "How are these points related?"

to discuss Charles Dickens' characterization of Ebenezer Scrooge in "A Christmas Carol" (page 276). In your answer you would have to examine and provide examples of Dickens' methods of indirect and direct characterization.

EVALUATION

11 To plan an evaluative answer, test-taker must first ask "What are the criteria for making a judgment?"

If a question asks you to *evaluate* a literary work, you are expected to show whether an author has achieved his or her purpose. To evaluate, you must apply standards of judgment that relate to both literary content and form. For example, you might be asked to evaluate how well Kipling has succeeded in giving distinctive personalities to his characters in "Rikki-tikki-tavi" (page 229) or how effectively Frost uses rhyme scheme to reinforce meaning in "Stopping by Woods on a Snowy Evening" (page 455).

EXPLANATION

12 Before beginning answer to question calling for explanation, test-taker might ask "How many reasons can I think of?"

A question may ask you to *explain* something. When you explain, you give reasons for something being the way it is. You make clear a character's actions, or you show how something has come about. For example, you might explain what happens to the *Hesperus* and its crew (page 164); you might explain Holmes's plan for recovering the Mazarin Stone (page 318).

ILLUSTRATION

13 Illustration requires test-takers to plan answer by recalling as many examples as they can.

The word *illustrate, demonstrate,* or *show* asks that you provide examples to support a point. You might be asked to give examples of musical devices in "Annabel Lee" (page 460). You might be asked to illustrate characteristics of the chimpanzees in Jane Goodall's *In the Shadow of Man* (page 386). You might be asked to select and demonstrate instances of natural dialogue in *The Governess* (page 343).

INTERPRETATION

14 Question test-taker must ask is "What does this mean?"

The word *interpret* in a question asks that you give the meaning or significance of something. You might, for example, be asked to interpret "The Listeners" (page 457), a poem that is famous for its mysterious meaning.

15 Effective test-takers usually incorporate purpose in thesis statement.

At times it will be useful to combine approaches. In discussing a subject, you may draw upon illustration, explanation, or analysis. In comparing or contrasting two works, you may rely on description or interpretation. However, an examination question generally will have a central purpose, and you should focus on this purpose in preparing your answer.

Using the Writing Process to Answer an Essay Question

The following suggestions show how you can use the writing process to answer an essay examination question efficiently. As you write, plan your time—decide how long you can work on each stage and stick to your schedule.

PREWRITING

In an essay examination, the question itself gives a narrow topic. Its key verb also suggests a way to answer the question. Several prewriting steps remain:

1. *Write a thesis statement.* A thesis statement gives the main idea of your essay. It should appear at the beginning of your essay.
2. *Develop points to support, or explain, the thesis.* The main idea should be supported by at least two main points. In a short essay all the points may be discussed in a single paragraph. In a longer essay each point may be discussed in a separate paragraph. Each point must clearly support the main idea of the essay.
3. *Locate supporting evidence from the literary work(s).* Evidence can include specific details, direct quotations, incidents, or images. This evidence should support or explain each main point you are discussing.
4. *Organize the main points and evidence.* You should arrange your ideas and details into a logical order—one that your reader can follow easily. By arranging your ideas, you will develop a plan that you can use to write your essay. This plan should include an introduction, a body, and a conclusion for your essay.

WRITING A FIRST DRAFT

Write your essay, following the plan you made in prewriting. In the introduction, state the title of the literary work and your thesis. In the body, present the main points and the supporting evidence. In the conclusion, state your thesis again or summarize your main points. Be sure to use language that is serious enough for your purpose (to convey ideas) and for your audience (your teacher, in most cases). Also use transitional expressions (words or phrases that connect ideas, such as *first*, *then*, and *finally*) to make it clear how ideas are related.

EVALUATING AND REVISING

Quickly evaluate, or judge, your essay by answering the following questions:

USING THE WRITING PROCESS TO ANSWER AN ESSAY QUESTION

1 Prewriting starter can be series of quick notes jotted on separate piece of paper.

2 Thesis statement is controlling plan for essay, gives writer direction about how to proceed.

3 Each point will probably require at least one specific example or piece of evidence from text.

4 Good writers give as much evidence as possible.

5 Many writers believe that saving strongest point for last is most effective method of organization.

6 Brief introductions and conclusions are acceptable when answering essay questions.

7 Some test-takers find it useful to pretend that teacher is only vaguely familiar with material they are discussing. Pretense forces them to explain clearly.

Purpose	1. Have I answered the specific question given?
Introduction	2. Have I included a thesis statement that expresses the main idea of my essay?
Body	3. Have I included at least two main points that support the thesis statement?
	4. Have I included evidence from the literary work to support each main point?
	5. Is the order of ideas clear and logical?
Conclusion	6. Have I included a conclusion that states the main idea again or that summarizes the main points?

8
This process is easier if the writer has skipped every other line to provide space for revision.

9
One effective method of proofreading is to begin with last sentence and read backwards through essay before reading essay in normal order.

8 Using your evaluation, improve your essay by *adding, cutting, reordering,* or *replacing* words.

PROOFREADING AND PUBLISHING

9 Read your essay to locate and correct any mistakes in grammar, usage, and mechanics. You can make a clean copy of your essay if your teacher says you have time to do so. If so, proofread again to catch any mistakes made in copying.

Sample Examination Questions and Answers

On the following pages you will find some sample examination questions and answers for study and discussion. Note that the assignments (shown in italics) may be phrased as direct questions or as essay topics.

I

QUESTION

The boy in Ernest Hemingway's story "A Day's Wait" (page 242) mistakenly believes that he is going to die. Why is he confused? Explain in a single paragraph.

SAMPLE EXAMINATION QUESTIONS AND ANSWERS

1 Analyzing
Why isn't the list a sufficient answer to the question? Provides only a few details. Does not explain.

2 Analyzing
Why is it a good idea to restate key words of question in thesis? Makes purpose of answer clear to reader; helps writer hold to purpose.

DEVELOPING AN ANSWER

This question calls for reasons. Before writing, jot down some notes to guide you:

1 The boy is familiar with the Celsius scale.
The doctor uses a Fahrenheit thermometer.
Boy has a temperature of 102°.
On the Celsius thermometer, a temperature of 44° would be fatal.

2 In the opening sentence of your answer, state your *thesis*, your main point, wording it in such a way that you restate the key words of the question. Here is a model paragraph based on the writer's notes.

694 WRITING ABOUT LITERATURE

WRITING AN ANSWER   **Main Idea**

Supporting Statements

3 **The boy in Hemingway's "A Day's Wait" is confused about two systems of temperature measurement.** Because he has gone to school in France, he is familiar with the Celsius scale of temperature. The normal temperature on the Celsius scale is 37°. A temperature as high as 44° would be fatal. The doctor who examines the boy uses a Fahrenheit thermometer on which the normal reading is 98.6°. The boy thinks that the doctor has used a Celsius thermometer. When he learns that his temperature is 102°, he assumes he is going to die.

Length: 93 words

3
Writer develops list with further details, clear cause-and-effect relationships.

II

QUESTION

In *Pacific Crossing* (page 503), Lincoln Mendoza visits Japan as an exchange student. What new experiences does he have? Refer to specific episodes in the novel.

DEVELOPING AN ANSWER

Begin by recalling major scenes or episodes. Select several of the most memorable or unusual things Lincoln finds. Jot down notes you can refer to when you write your answer to the question.

WRITING AN ANSWER

Here is a model answer that includes a summary of several episodes in the novel.

Main Idea
Supporting Evidence

4 **Lincoln Mendoza, the main character in *Pacific Crossing*, learns a great deal about Japanese people and their culture during his sum-**
5 **mer in Japan.** On his first day in Atami, he gets to visit a public bath house called a *sentō*, where people relax in a large communal tub after having themselves soaped and scrubbed. When he attends his first *kempō* class, he is surprised to find that his *sensei*, or teacher, is a woman and that instead of practicing on tatami mats, the students work out on a lawn. During a pilgrimage to Buddhist shrines, he learns that it is the custom to fast—he eats only rice balls—and to camp out in the open. Perhaps the most surprising thing Lincoln learns is that many Japanese people, like his friend Matsuo, are enthusiastic about baseball and American music.

Length: 140 words

4
Main idea refers clearly to question.

5
Paragraph gives specific examples in chronological order.

III

QUESTION What makes T. J. a natural leader of the boys in "Antaeus" (page 187)? Discuss his qualities of leadership, using specific references to the story.

DEVELOPING AN ANSWER Begin by skimming the story to locate examples of T. J.'s leadership abilities. Take notes as you read, jotting down the page number of each piece of evidence you locate. Here is a list of prewriting notes that one writer developed.

6 Notes

T. J. had a slow, gentle voice, but he was no sissy (page 187).
He was not insecure with strangers; he reserved his opinions (page 187).
He was not ashamed of being different (page 188).
He was self-assured, not easily bullied (page 188).
He had pride in his accomplishments (page 189).
Boys were attracted to his "stolid sense of rightness and belonging" (page 189).
His imagination excited other boys (page 189).
T. J. persisted in his project, keeping others interested (page 190).
He was intelligent (page 191).
He made others share his goal (page 191).
He knew when to compromise (page 191).

There is a great deal of information to organize here. You might try grouping the prewriting notes so that you can present the evidence under three categories: perhaps self-confidence, imagination, and persistence.

WRITING AN ANSWER Here is a model essay that builds on the writer's notes. Notice how 7 each of T. J.'s qualities is discussed in a separate paragraph.

Main Idea 8 T. J., a character in "Antaeus," is a natural leader because of his self-confidence, imagination, and persistence. **Although he is a stranger, he is**
First Quality **not ashamed of being different.** He feels secure about himself. He does not get upset or angry when the boys in the gang begin to tease
Supporting Statements him. When Blackie laughs at him because he comes from Alabama, T. J. remains calm and assured. When Charley kids him about his
9 name, T. J. replies without hesitation or shame. He doesn't allow himself to be bullied, and he doesn't lose his temper because he has a "stolid sense of rightness and belonging."

Second Quality **T. J. has imagination, and his ideas appeal to the other boys.** He
10 starts them thinking about a roof garden, and whenever their enthusiasm begins to wane, he renews their interest in the project. He talks to them about raising watermelons, flowers, grass, and trees. Because
Supporting Statements he is intelligent, he knows when to give in. Although he wants to grow

---

6 Good notes, but need organizing principle.

7 Separate paragraphs necessary because essay is lengthy.

8 Question is incorporated in thesis statement.

9 Details not in notes included ("he doesn't lose his temper"); necessary for clarity and support of thesis.

10 Again details from the story are added.

696 WRITING ABOUT LITERATURE

corn and vegetables, he compromises on his dream and agrees to grow a grass lawn.

Third Quality

Supporting Statements

11

T. J. perseveres throughout the winter. He gives the boys direction and organization. Even though the others become distracted, T. J. persists in carrying earth up to the roof. He works harder than any of the other boys to fulfill their mutual goal, and he inspires the others by his example.

Length: 230 words

Writing on a Topic of Your Own

Prewriting: Choosing a Topic

1 At times you may be asked to choose a topic of your own. Often it will be necessary to read a work more than once before a suitable topic presents itself.

2 A topic may focus on one element or technique in a work. If you are writing about fiction, you might concentrate on some aspect of plot, such as conflict. Or you might concentrate on character, setting, or theme. If you are writing about poetry, you might choose to analyze imagery or figurative language. A topic may deal with more than one aspect of a work. You might, for example, discuss several elements of a short story in order to show how an idea or theme is developed.

3 Above all, be sure to limit a broad subject to a manageable topic—one that is sufficiently narrow. A narrow topic is one you can discuss in the time and space you have for the essay. Once you have a topic in mind, your object is to form it into a *thesis*, a controlling idea that represents the conclusion of your findings. You would then need to present the evidence supporting your position. It may be necessary to read a work several times before you can formulate a thesis. Here are some examples:

"Guinea Pig" (page 41) and "The Night the Bed Fell" (page 133)

Topic Comparing the humor in these essays
Thesis *4* In both essays, humor results from situations in which people's intentions misfire.

"Last Cover" (page 153)

Topic Contrasting attitudes toward nature of Colin and his father
Thesis Although Colin and his father both love nature, Colin shows a greater instinct for understanding the woods and wild things.

---

11 Drawing Conclusions
Why are some ideas in notes (such as his "slow, gentle voice") not included in essay? Not relevant to characteristics writer chose to discuss in essay.

CHOOSING A TOPIC

1
If class has read work together, writer might choose topic from issues raised in class discussion. Questions at end of selection in text may suggest topic.

2
To choose topics, writers might ask themselves questions about elements of work. Possible questions include the following: What kind of person is a particular character? What changes occur in a particular character? What is function of **setting** in work? How should work be interpreted—i.e., what does it mean? What is relationship between two elements in work? How is the work similar to (or different from) another work?

3
Writer might brainstorm or list ideas, and then consider how much time and space would be required to develop each topic. If broad topic is particularly interesting, writer could narrow by choosing one aspect of topic.

4 Finding Details
If this thesis statement were to be the first sentence of the essay, what changes would the writer need to make? Add titles and authors.

5 Analyzing
For what length essay is this thesis appropriate and why? Short. Requires development of only one major point.

6 Analyzing
For what length essay is this thesis appropriate and why? Longer essay. Will require discussion of insights gained from visits of three spirits.

GATHERING EVIDENCE / DEVELOPING MAJOR POINTS

1
Thinking Models in **Close Reading** sections (pp. 2–7, 202–207, 308–317, 382–385, 430–432) provide examples of kinds of notes to take during first reading. On second reading, notes can be amplified.

2
Important step. Putting ideas in own words helps writer clarify thoughts.

3
When citing fewer than three lines, no need to separate quoted material from main text.

"You Can't Take It with You" (page 264)

Topic 5 Explaining the significance of a title
Thesis The old saying about money is disproved with an ironic twist.

"Rip Van Winkle" (page 247)

Topic Comparing the characters of Rip and Dame Van Winkle
Thesis Both Rip and Dame Van Winkle are treated as comic stereotypes.

"A Christmas Carol" (page 276)

Topic 6 Analyzing the change in Scrooge's character
Thesis During the visit of each Christmas spirit, Scrooge gets valuable insights into his own character, which help to change him from a hardhearted miser into a kind and charitable man.

"Zlateh the Goat" (page 270)

Topic Interpreting the theme of "Zlateh the Goat"
Thesis The statement "We must accept all that God gives us—heat, cold, hunger, satisfaction, light, and darkness" may be taken as the theme, or underlying meaning, of the work.

Gathering Evidence/Developing Major Points

1 It is a good idea to take notes as you read, even if you do not yet have a topic in mind. Later on, when you have settled on a topic, you can discard any notes that are not relevant. Some people prefer a worksheet, others index cards. In the beginning, you should record all your reactions. A topic may emerge during this early stage. As you continue to read, you will shape your topic into a rough thesis.

2 When you take notes, make an effort to state ideas in your own words. If a specific phrase or line is so important that it deserves to be quoted directly, be sure to enclose the words in quotation marks. When you transfer your notes to your final paper, be sure to copy quotations exactly.

In working with a short poem, you may cite phrases and lines without identifying the quotations by line numbers. If you cite lines in a long poem, you should enclose the line numbers in parentheses fol-
3 lowing the quotation. The following note, which is for Longfellow's poem "The Wreck of the *Hesperus*" (page 164), shows you how to do this:

> When the *Hesperus* struck the breakers, the rocks "gored her side/ Like the horns of an angry bull" (lines 71–72).

The slash (/) shows the reader where line 71 ends and line 72 begins.

4   If you cite three or more lines of a poem, you should separate the quotation from your own text in this way.

> Longfellow compares the *Hesperus* to a frightened horse that trembles, then springs from the ground when the storm strikes:
>
> > Down came the storm, and smote amain
> >   The vessel in its strength;
> > She shuddered and paused, like a frighted steed,
> >   Then leaped her cable's length.
> >
> > (lines 25–28)

5   Let us suppose you have chosen to compare the following poems:

The Wind   JAMES STEPHENS

The wind stood up, and gave a shout;
He whistled on his fingers, and

Kicked the withered leaves about,
And thumped the branches with his hand,

And said he'd kill, and kill, and kill;
And so he will! And so he will!

The Wind Tapped like a Tired Man
EMILY DICKINSON

The wind tapped like a tired man,
And like a host, "Come in,"
I boldly answered; entered then
My residence within

A rapid, footless guest,   5
To offer whom a chair
Were as impossible as hand
A sofa to the air.

No bone had he to bind him,
His speech was like the push   10
Of numerous hummingbirds at once
From a superior° bush.

12. **superior:** here, high up.

---

4 When quoted material is separated from text, quotation marks are not used.

5 To compare, writer will concentrate on similarities.

6 Careful reader will note **repetition** in last **stanza**; will check to see if similar repetition occurs in second poem. Even if checking does not provide useful ideas, it is important to careful reading.

AV RESOURCES BINDER
Audiocassette 3, Side B

7 Careful reader will check to see if previous poem also contains **simile**.

8 In both poems, wind is male.

9 "Push" refers to the rush of air from many wings.

10
Billow: wave.

11
Careful reader might note similarity in **alliteration**. Both poets repeat *d* and *s* sounds.

12
Although differences outnumber similarities, writer chooses to focus on how poems are alike.

13
Assigning human characteristics to inanimate objects or to abstractions is called **personification**.

---

10 His countenance° a billow,
　　His fingers, as he passed,
　　Let go a music, as of tunes　　15
　　Blown tremulous° in glass.

　　He visited, still flitting;
　　Then, like a timid man,
　　Again he tapped—'twas flurriedly°—
　　And I became alone.　　20

13. **countenance** (koun′tə-nəns): face, expression.

16. **tremulous** (trĕm′yə-ləs): vibrating, quivering.

19. **flurriedly** (flûr′ē-əd′lē): excitedly.

11 As your reading shows, there is common ground for comparison of these poems. You might work out a chart of this kind for taking notes, letting the letter A stand for "The Wind," and B for "The Wind Tapped like a Tired Man":

12 *Similarities*

The subject of both poems is the wind.

The poets compare the wind to a person.

Both poems describe the wind in terms of human feelings and characteristics.

Differences

In A, the wind is a strong gale. The "withered leaves" suggest autumn. In B, the wind is a gentle breeze.

In A, the poet describes the wind as a furious man.
In B, the poet describes the wind as a shy visitor.

In A, the wind is angry and violent. It shouts and whistles. It kicks the leaves and thumps the branches. It is determined to kill.

In B, the wind is timid. Its movements are light and rapid. It flits and taps timidly, "like a tired man." It has no visible form—no feet ("footless") and no bones, yet has speech, a face, and fingers. Its speech is like the sound of hummingbirds. Its face ("countenance") is a billow. Its fingers produce music like the sound that comes from a reed instrument. It is shy, "like a timid man," and taps "flurriedly."

13 Both poems suggest that nature has something in common with human beings.

700　WRITING ABOUT LITERATURE

14 You might find at this point that a thesis statement has begun to emerge. *Although the poems are quite different in their treatment of the wind, both convey the special character of the wind by representing it as having human qualities.* You would continue to study the poems, gathering additional evidence, developing major points, and refining your thesis statement. The next step is organizing your ideas.

Organizing Ideas

1 Before you begin writing, organize your main ideas to provide for an introduction, a body, and a conclusion. The introduction should identify the author(s), the work(s), or the problem that is under study. It should contain a statement of your thesis as well. The body of your *2* paper should present the evidence supporting your thesis. The conclusion should bring together your main ideas.

3 This is one kind of plan you might use for a short paper. It indicates the main idea of each paragraph.

INTRODUCTION

Paragraph 1 *Thesis* Although the poets describe different aspects of the wind, both choose to convey the special character of the wind by representing it as having human qualities.

BODY

Paragraph 2 Stephens' poem represents the wind as an angry, violent man, whose object is destruction.

Paragraph 3 Dickinson's poem represents the wind as a visitor with a gentle, shy temperament.

CONCLUSION

Paragraph 4 In treating the wind in terms of human feelings and characteristics, the poets make us aware of certain resemblances between nature and human beings.

14
Thesis suggests body of paper will focus on human attributes of wind in both poems.

ORGANIZING IDEAS

1
An essay should usually have a paragraph of introduction and one of conclusion.

2
Body paragraphs should contain sentence that both states main idea of paragraph and establishes relationship of paragraph to thesis; usually first sentence in paragraph.

3
Plan is like blueprint for paper, provides overall structure.

WRITING THE ESSAY

1 **Making Generalizations**
What kind of language should you avoid? Answers will vary. Students should know to avoid slang, nonstandard usages, colloquialisms.

2 **Finding Details**
What are some more examples of transitional expressions? Answers will vary. Possible answers: *Also, another, for example, in addition, on the other hand.*

3
The preferred title form for an essay about literature states authors and works to be discussed.

4
Stating authors and works in first paragraph of essay is required when writing about literature.

5 **Analyzing**
How does the main idea of paragraph relate to thesis statement? States human qualities of wind.

6
Words taken directly from poem are enclosed in quotation marks.

7
When writing about literature, writer usually uses present tense verbs.

Writing the Essay

1 As you write your essay, you should use language that is serious enough for your purpose and audience. Remember that your purpose is to convey ideas clearly, and that you are writing for your teachers or, occasionally, for your classmates. Use transitional expressions ***2*** (words like *then, second,* and *therefore*) to make the order of ideas clear.

Here is a model essay developing the thesis statement. Notice how the essay follows the writer's notes.

TITLE ***3***
A COMPARISON OF JAMES STEPHENS' "THE WIND" AND EMILY DICKINSON'S "THE WIND TAPPED LIKE A TIRED MAN"

INTRODUCTION ***4***
Identify works and authors.

"The Wind" by James Stephens and "The Wind Tapped like a Tired Man" by Emily Dickinson deal with very different types of wind. Stephens' wind is a strong blast, perhaps a gale; Dickinson's wind is a light, gentle breeze. *Although the poets describe different aspects of the wind, both choose to convey the special character of the wind by representing it as having human qualities.*

Thesis

BODY/Main Idea ***5***
6

Stephens' wind is a violent, raging figure. From the reference to "the withered leaves" in line 3, we can infer that it is late autumn, when powerful gusts are common. Stephens treats the characteristics of the wind—its sounds and its movements—as if they were produced by a human voice, human limbs, and human feelings. The "shout" is the sudden roar of the wind as it sweeps over the land. As it moves, it makes a high, shrill sound, its "whistle." The wind appears to be act- ***7*** ing in fury as it lifts and scatters the leaves and pounds the branches of the trees. The wind's rage mounts as it builds to gale proportions. The repetition of the words *kill* and *will* in the concluding lines of the poem emphasizes the destructive intent of the storm.

Main Idea/Transition

While Stephens presents his wind as a threatening figure that shouts, whistles, kicks, and thumps, Dickinson gives us a gentle ghost of a wind. This wind is timid: it taps softly, "like a tired man." It has no visible form. Since it is "footless" and has no "bone," or skeleton, it cannot be seated. Its speech is a low, continuous humming, like that produced by the vibration of hummingbirds' wings. Its face ("countenance") is a great swelling or surging of air. The sound the breeze makes is attributed to the fingers of the wind, making music like that produced by glass reeds that vibrate when air is blown over them. The wind's movements are light and rapid; it flits, and shyly, "like a timid man," taps "flurriedly" and leaves.

Give evidence of close reading.

CONCLUSION 8 By choosing to describe the wind in terms of human feelings and characteristics, the poets seem to be saying that nature has a great deal in common with human beings. The poets make us conscious of similarities we might never have discovered for ourselves.

Length: 374 words

8
In this example, conclusion is not restatement of major points, but evaluation of effect of poems.

Evaluating and Revising Papers

1 When you write an essay in class, you have a limited amount of time to plan and develop your essay. Nevertheless, you should save a few minutes to read over your work and make necessary corrections.

2 When an essay is assigned as homework, you have more time to prepare it carefully. Get into the habit of revising your work. A first draft of an essay should be treated as a rough copy of your manuscript. Chances are that reworking your first draft will result in a clearer and stronger paper.

3 To evaluate an essay, you judge its content, organization, and style. Your aim is to decide what the strong points and weak points are in your essay. You can then make the changes that will improve your essay. To evaluate your essay, answer the following questions:

EVALUATING AND REVISING PAPERS

1
All professional writers evaluate and rewrite constantly. If experienced writers must use the process to achieve good work, then, logically, so must inexperienced writers.

2
One step in process might be to share draft with other writers and ask for feedback.

3
Learning to evaluate work of others by participating in peer-group evaluation can help writers learn to evaluate own work more effectively. By answering these questions about someone else's work, writers can learn to apply guidelines to themselves.

Guidelines for Evaluating a Paper

Introduction
1. Have I included an introduction that identifies the title and author of the literary work(s)?
2. Have I included a thesis statement that gives the main idea of the essay?

Body
3. Have I included at least two main points that support the thesis statement?
4. Have I included evidence from the literary work to support each main point?

Conclusion
5. Have I included a conclusion that brings together the main points?

Coherence
6. Does the order of ideas make sense?

Style
7. Do the sentences differ in length and in the way they begin?

Word Choice
8. Is the language serious enough for the purpose and audience?
9. Have I defined unfamiliar words for the audience?
10. Have I used vivid and specific words?

Writing on a Topic of Your Own

4
Writers can also add evidence, cut unnecessary words from sentences, replace unclear ideas with clear ones, reorder words in sentences for clarity.

5 Summarizing
What does "conciseness" mean? Absence of superfluous ideas, details, or words.

6
The addition of titles tells the reader which poems the essay discusses.

7
"Types of wind" is more specific than "forces of nature."

8
Reordering places sentences in a logical order.

9
Sentence combining and the use of phrases instead of clauses improve conciseness and fluency.

Using your evaluation, you can revise your essay. Writers revise by using four basic techniques: *adding, cutting, reordering,* or *replacing.* For example, if the order of ideas is not clear, you can *add* words like *first, second,* and *finally.* If your language is not serious enough, you can *replace* slang and contractions with formal language. You can *cut* evidence that does not explain a main point, and you can *reorder* ideas that are difficult to follow.

On the following pages you will find a revised draft of the essay that appears on page 702. The notes in the margin show which revision technique the writer used. Study the two versions of the essay. As you do so, notice how the writer has revised for greater clarity, accuracy, and conciseness.

replace; add 6 ~~In their poems,~~ "The Wind" by James Stephens and "The Wind Tapped Like a Tired Man" by Emily Dickinson deal with very different

replace; cut; cut; add 7 types of wind. ~~forces of nature.~~ In Stephens' poem, ~~the~~ wind is a strong blast, perhaps a gale; Dickinson's wind

replace; replace; add is a light, gentle breeze. Although the poets describe ~~poems deal with~~ different aspects the ~~kinds of winds,~~

cut both ~~poets~~ choose to convey the special character of the wind by representing it

as having human qualities.

reorder Stephens' wind is a violent, raging figure. Stephens treats the characteristics

8 of the wind—its sounds and its movements—as if they were produced by a human

replace voice, human limbs, and human feelings. From the reference to "the withered leaves" in line 3, we can infer that it ~~The season~~ is late autumn, when pow-

add; cut erful gusts are common. The "shout" is the sudden roar of the wind ~~As it sweeps over the land, the wind roars. This is its~~

replace; replace 9 ~~shout.~~ As it moves, it makes a ~~Its "whistle" is the~~ high, shrill sound its "whistle." ~~it makes as it moves.~~ The wind ap-

reorder; cut pears to be acting in fury as it lifts the leaves and scatters ~~them,~~ and pounds the

704 WRITING ABOUT LITERATURE

CLOSURE

Ask students to name the steps in the writing process. Ask them to explain how the writing process can be used to answer essay questions and to develop essays.

---

reorder 10 branches of the trees. The repetition of the words <u>kill</u> and <u>will</u> in the concluding

replace; replace 11 lines of the poem emphasizes the ~~fury~~ *destructive intent* of the storm. The wind's ~~fury~~ *rage* mounts as it builds to gale proportions.

add 12 *While Stephens presents his wind as a threatening figure that shouts, whistles, kicks and thumps,* Dickinson gives us a gentle ghost of a wind. This wind is timid: it taps softly,

add 13 "like a tired man." *Since it is "footless" and has no "bone" or skeleton,* It has no visible form. It cannot be seated. Its speech is a

add low, continuous humming, like that produced by *the vibration of* hummingbirds' wings. Its face

add ("countenance") is a great swelling or surging of air. The sound is attributed to *the breeze makes*

add the fingers of the wind, making music like that produced by glass reeds *that vibrate* when air

cut is blown over them. The wind's movements are light and rapid; it flits and ~~leaves~~

add 14 shyly. *"like a timid man," taps "flurriedly" and leaves.*

By choosing to describe the wind in terms of human feelings and characteristics, the poets seem to be saying that nature has a great deal in common with

replace 15 human beings. ~~We become~~ *The poets make us* conscious of similarities we might never have discovered for ourselves.

10 Reordering places sentences in a logical order.

11 Use of "destructive intent" and "rage" avoids repetition of word *fury*.

12 Addition provides a transition between paragraphs.

13 Quotations from poem add evidence.

14 Addition quotes relevant descriptions.

15 This revision clarifies who makes us conscious.

Proofreading and Publishing

1 After you revise, you should proofread your essay to correct any mistakes in grammar, usage, and mechanics. Pay special attention to the correct capitalization and punctuation of any direct quotations you use as supporting evidence. Then make a final copy of your essay by using correct manuscript form or your teacher's instructions. After writing this clean copy, proofread again to catch any mistakes made in copying. Share your essay with others.

PROOFREADING AND PUBLISHING

1 After reading through essay backward, some writers then read through forward, placing left index finger on first word of first sentence and right index finger on punctuation mark that ends sentence, and then reading the sentence to check for coherence, clarity, and correctness. They repeat the process with every sentence in the essay.

Literary Terms and Techniques

ALLITERATION *The repetition of a sound in a group of words usually related in meaning.* Alliteration occurs in many common phrases and expressions: "*w*ild and *w*ooly *W*est," "*b*rown as a *b*erry," and so on. Alliteration is usually confined to consonants, but vowels are sometimes alliterated too. Most alliteration occurs at the beginning of words, but sometimes writers like to alliterate in the middle and at the end of words as well.

One of the uses of alliteration seems to be to gain emphasis and to make a group of words meaningful to us. This is why many advertising jingles depend on alliteration. Manufacturers use alliteration in naming their products as an aid to memory.

Politicians often use alliteration. When we are asked to put up with hardship, we are asked to "*T*igh*t*en our bel*t*s," or to "*B*ite the *b*ullet." Abraham Lincoln once said, "Among free men there can be no successful appeal from the *b*al*l*ot to the *b*ullet."

Poets use alliteration to the most obvious and memorable effect. Some examples of alliteration in poetry are:

> Blue were her eyes as the *f*airy *f*lax,
> Her cheeks like the *d*awn of *d*ay, . . .
> Henry Wadsworth Longfellow
> "The Wreck of the *Hesperus*"

> The angels, not *h*alf so *h*appy in *H*eaven,
> Went envying *h*er and me:
> Edgar Allan Poe
> "Annabel Lee"

> I *r*emembe*r*, I *r*emembe*r*
> The *r*oses, *r*ed and white
> The vio*l*ets and the *l*i*l*y cup—
> Those *f*lowers made of *l*ight!
> Thomas Hood
> "I Remember, I Remember"

These are serious examples, but sometimes alliteration is used simply for fun. One poet, Algernon Charles Swinburne, actually wrote a poem that made fun of his own style. He had been criticized for using too much alliteration. So he composed "Nephelidia" (little clouds), which is complicated and funny nonsense. It starts this way:

> From the *d*epth of the *d*reamy *d*ecline of the *d*awn through a *n*otable *n*imbus of *n*ebulous *n*oonshine,
> *P*allid and *p*ink as the *p*alm of the *f*lag-*f*lower that *f*lickers with *f*ear of the *f*lies as they *f*loat, . . .

Swinburne makes the point that heavily alliterated poetry can seem to mean more than it does.

Prose writers use alliteration, too, but they have to be careful not to sound too artificial. Some of the most memorable expressions from the King James translation of the Bible are alliterated: "*L*et there be *l*ight: and there was *l*ight" (Genesis). Even the famous quotation from Ecclesiastes uses alliteration: "There is *n*o *n*ew thi*n*g u*n*der the su*n*."

> See **Repetition**.
> See also page 466.

ALLUSION *A reference in one work of literature to another work of literature or to a well-known event, person, or place.* Allusion can be used equally well in prose or poetry. It is used to best effect when the reference calls up appropriate associations.

Literature contains many allusions to the Bible. Characters will sometimes be described as having the patience of Job, who was noted for his patience. When Henry James called one of his stories "The Tree of Knowledge," he expected his readers to recognize the allusion to the tree that grew in the Garden of Eden. He also expected his readers to associate the word *knowledge* with a specific context—the knowledge of good and evil.

Allusions to the literature of ancient Greece and Rome are also common in literature. The great writers of years past were carefully trained to read both Latin and Greek. We do not study these languages or their literature as intensely nowadays, so we miss many of the allusions that such writers as William Shakespeare, John Milton, William Wordsworth, and Alfred, Lord Tennyson took for granted.

Often literature makes allusions to famous events. When someone points out that a character has "met his Waterloo," the allusion is to the battle at which Napoleon was finally defeated by the English. Allusions to battlefields are common because much of history was decided by the outcome of battles. Therefore, references to Gettysburg, for the American Civil War; Flanders, for World War I; and the beaches of Normandy, for World War II, occur frequently. "Black Monday" is a reference to the day the stock market on Wall Street collapsed—referred to universally as "The Crash"—and all the world was plunged into the Great Depression of the 1930s.

Allusions to the media are growing more and more common, though these are not as lasting as allusions to the Bible and classical literature.

See pages 619, 674.

ANECDOTE *A very short story with a simple, usually amusing point.* Many jokes are anecdotes. Often short stories are expanded anecdotes. In "Guinea Pig," Ruth McKenney recalls several anecdotes having to do with lifesaving.

ATMOSPHERE *The general feeling or mood established in a work of literature.* In literature atmosphere is most often established by description. Landscapes lend themselves to creating atmosphere. Washington Irving's description of the Hudson Valley at the opening of "Rip Van Winkle" creates a magical quality. Later in the story, Irving creates an eerie feeling when Rip wanders over the mountains just before evening.

See pages 98, 247.

BALLAD *A story told in verse and usually meant to be sung.* Ballads use regular patterns of rhythm and strong rhymes. A common element is the **refrain.** Most ballads are full of adventure, action, and romance. The earliest ballads, known as **folk ballads,** were composed anonymously and transmitted orally for generations before they were written down. A popular ballad like "Bonny Barbara Allan" has many different versions, since the story changed as it was passed down through the years. **Literary ballads** are composed by known writers who imitate the folk ballad.

See **Refrain.**
See also pages 474, 477.

BIOGRAPHY *The story of a person's life.* When a person writes his or her own biography, it is called an **autobiography.** Biography and autobiography are two of the most popular forms of **nonfiction,** and most libraries have a section set aside for these books. Almost every famous person has been the subject of a biography. One of the greatest biographies ever written is *The Life of Samuel Johnson* by James Boswell. Another is Carl Sandburg's six-volume biography of Abraham Lincoln. Well-known autobiographies include *The Story of My Life* by Helen Keller, *The Autobiography of Lincoln Steffens,* and *The Autobiography of Mark Twain.*

See pages 403, 404, 414.

CHARACTERIZATION *The methods used to present the personality of a character in a narrative.* A writer can create a character by: (1) giving a physical description of the character; (2) showing the character's actions and letting the character speak; (3) revealing the character's

Characterization: See Character, Transparency 10.

Conflict: See Transparency 28.

Literary Terms and Techniques

thoughts and feelings; (4) revealing what others think of the character; and (5) commenting directly on the character. The first four methods are **indirect** methods of characterization. The writer shows or dramatizes the character and allows you to draw your own conclusions. The last method is **direct** characterization. The writer tells you directly what a character is like.

In "Rip Van Winkle," Washington Irving develops Rip's character through direct and indirect means. In this passage, for example, the author first comments on Rip's character and then lets Rip reveal himself through his actions.

> Rip Van Winkle, however, was one of those happy mortals, of foolish, well-oiled dispositions, who take the world easy, eat white bread or brown, whichever can be got with least thought or trouble, and would rather starve on a penny than work for a pound. If left to himself, he would have whistled life away in perfect contentment; but his wife kept continually dinning in his ears about his idleness, his carelessness, and the ruin he was bringing on his family. Morning, noon, and night, her tongue was incessantly going, and everything he said or did was sure to produce a torrent of household eloquence. Rip had but one way of replying to all lectures of the kind, and that, by frequent use, had grown into a habit. He shrugged his shoulders, shook his head, cast up his eyes, but said nothing. This, however, always provoked a fresh volley from his wife; so that he would take to the outside of the house—the only side which, in truth, belongs to a henpecked husband.

Animals can be characterized through the same techniques. Here is a description of Wolf, Rip's dog:

> True it is, in all points of spirit befitting an honorable dog, he was as courageous an animal as ever scoured the woods—but what courage can withstand the terrors of a woman's tongue? The moment Wolf entered the house his crest fell, his tail drooped to the ground, or curled between his legs, he sneaked about with a gallows air, casting many a sidelong glance at Dame Van Winkle, and at the least flourish of a broomstick or ladle, he would fly to the door, yelping.

Characterization can be sketchy, particularly if the character does not play an important role in the piece. Or, it can be extraordinarily full, as when the character is the main focus of a piece.

We often describe characters as being "flat" or "round." A "flat" character is merely sketched out for us. There is no full development. Dame Van Winkle in "Rip Van Winkle" is a flat character because she is represented as a shrew. She is never really given a chance to speak for herself or to be further characterized.

"Flat" characters are often **stereotypes**. Harry Thorburn, in "The Erne from the Coast," is an example of a "round" character, since we see him under many different circumstances and we watch him grow and change.

See **Description, Narration, Point of View.** See also pages 240, 261.

COMEDY *A literary work with a generally happy ending. A comedy may be funny and still carry a serious theme.* Any narrative can be a comedy—a short story, novel, play, or narrative poem. The term, however, is most often applied to plays. *The Governess* is a one-scene dramatic comedy that has a serious underlying idea. A typical plot of comedies involves young lovers who almost don't end up together.

CONFLICT *The struggle that takes place between two opposing forces.* A conflict can be between a character and a natural force, like a bear or a hurricane; between two characters; or between opposing views held by separate characters or groups of characters. Such conflicts are **external conflicts**. Conflict can also be **internal**—it can exist within a character and be a psychological conflict.

Usually a conflict arises from a blocking of desires. In "The Highwayman," King George's men intend to kill the highwayman when he comes to visit his sweetheart. They literally block him from achieving his goal.

There may be more than one conflict in a work.

See **Plot**.
See also page 218.

CONNOTATION *All the emotions and associations that a word or phrase arouses.* Connotation is different from **denotation**, which is the strict literal (or "dictionary") definition of a word. For example, the word *springtime* literally means "the season of the year between the vernal equinox and the summer solstice." But *springtime* usually makes most people think of love, rebirth, youth, and romance.

Poets are especially sensitive to the connotations of words. For example, Walter de la Mare uses the words *moonlight* and *moonbeams* in "The Listeners." The two words literally mean light reflected from the moon. But *moonlight* and *moonbeams* have certain connotations associated with things mysterious and ghostly that help create the poem's eerie mood. You can imagine how different the poem would be if you substituted the word "sunshine" for *moonlight* or *moonbeam*.

See page 487.

DESCRIPTION *Any careful detailing of a person, place, thing, or event.* We associate the term with prose, both fiction and nonfiction, but poems also use description, if a bit more economically.

Description appeals to the senses. In this passage from Charles Dickens' "A Christmas Carol," note how the description of the Christmas pudding appeals to both smell and sight:

> Hallo! A great deal of steam! The pudding was out of the copper. A smell like a washing day! That was the cloth. A smell like an eating house and a pastry cook's next door to each other, with a laundress' next door to that! That was the pudding! In half a minute Mrs. Cratchit entered—flushed but smiling proudly—with the pudding, like a speckled cannonball, so hard and firm, blazing in half of half a quartern of ignited brandy and bedight with Christmas holly stuck into the top.

Some description is simple, direct, and factual. But more often, description is used to establish a mood or stir an emotion. When Dickens describes the Ghost of Christmas Yet to Come, he emphasizes the shadowy and frightening appearance of the phantom:

> The phantom slowly, gravely, silently approached. When it came near him, Scrooge bent down upon his knee; for in the air through which this spirit moved it seemed to scatter gloom and mystery.
> It was shrouded in a deep black garment, which concealed its head, its face, its form, and left nothing of it visible save one outstretched hand.

See **Mood**.

DIALECT *A representation of the speech patterns of a particular region or social group.* Dialect often is used to establish local color. Some of the regional dialects in America are the Down-East dialect of Maine, the Cajun dialect of Louisiana, the Southern and Western dialects, and, in some of the writings of the early twentieth century, a city-slang.

Mark Twain often has his characters speak in dialect. This line of dialogue appears in *Adventures of Huckleberry Finn*, which is set in a region

Dialect: See Evaluating Short Stories, Transparency 21. See also Analyzing and Evaluating a Novel, Transparency 44, and Character, Transparency 10.

Dialogue: See Character, Transparency 10.

of the Mississippi River more than a hundred years ago:

> "I've seed a raft act so before, along here . . . 'pears to me the current has most quit above the head of this bend durin' the last two years."

Twain increases local color by having his character speak ungrammatically (by traditional grammar standards) and clip the "g's" off some of his words.

See **Dialogue**.
See also pages 218, 444.

DIALOGUE *Talk or conversation between two or more characters.* Dialogue usually attempts to present the speech of characters in a realistic fashion. It is used in almost all literary forms: biography, essays, fiction, poetry, and drama. Dialogue is especially important in drama, where it forwards all the action of the play. Dialogue must move the plot, set up the action, reveal the characters, and even help establish some of the mood.

When dialogue appears in a play, there are no quotation marks to set it apart, since—besides stage directions—there is nothing but dialogue. When dialogue appears in a prose work or in a poem, it is customary to set it apart with quotation marks.

Biographies often include dialogue. In most cases the dialogue is imagined and presented as it would have sounded if it really had been delivered. Biographers take many such liberties because the use of dialogue helps to liven up their presentations.

The use of dialogue in fiction is one of the ways a writer makes a story come alive. A short story that uses dialogue extensively will seem more realistic. The following passage was written by Sarah Orne Jewett, an American writer well known in the late 1800s. It is part of a story called "A White Heron":

> "So Sylvy knows all about birds, does she?" he exclaimed, as he looked round at the little girl who sat, very demure but increasingly sleepy, in the moonlight. "I am making a collection of birds myself. I have been at it ever since I was a boy." (Mrs. Tilley smiled.) "There are two or three very rare ones I have been hunting for these five years. I mean to get them on my own ground if they can be found."
>
> "Do you cage 'em up?" asked Mrs. Tilley doubtfully, in response to this enthusiastic announcement.
>
> "Oh no, they're stuffed and preserved, dozens and dozens of them," said the ornithologist, "and I have shot or snared every one myself. I caught a glimpse of a white heron a few miles from here on Saturday, and I have followed it in this direction. They have never been found in this district at all."

The author is able, in this brief piece of dialogue, to clarify character, set the stage for the next action, and to build suspense.

See **Dialect**.

DRAMA *A story acted out, usually on a stage, by actors and actresses who take the parts of specific characters.* The word *drama* comes from a Greek word meaning "act." In reading a drama it is best to try to imagine real actors as they would play their parts onstage. We usually think of two main kinds of drama: **tragedies,** serious plays generally ending in suffering and death, like William Shakespeare's *Macbeth;* and **comedies,** lighter plays that are often funny, like Shakespeare's *Twelfth Night.*

Drama involves the use of **plot,** the sequence of related events that make up the story. The plot pits characters against one another or against forces that are powerful and sometimes greater than they are. The characters carry forward the plot by means of **dialogue.**

Most playwrights include **stage directions,**

710 LITERARY TERMS AND TECHNIQUES

which tell the actors and actresses what to do or how to feel when certain lines are spoken. The stage directions are useful to the director, who must help the actors and actresses interpret their lines correctly. The director decides such things as the timing of a line, the speed of delivery, the way the players stand or move when speaking their lines, and what they do when they are not speaking their lines. In many productions the director is as important as the author of the play.

Most plays are presented on stages with **sets.** A set is a realistic representation of the room, landscape, or locale in which the play takes place. **Props** (short for *properties*) are representations of important items in the drama, such as telephones, radios, flashlights, working automobiles, or other objects that figure in the action. **Lighting** helps to establish the desired moods. Or, instead of establishing mood, lighting can help establish the time of day or the season.

A drama usually begins with **exposition,** which explains the action that has already occurred. It then introduces the **conflict** or difficulties that the characters must overcome. All this happens at the same time the audience is getting to know the characters. Each act may be composed of several scenes. The end of each act often includes a **climax,** which is designed to keep the audience in suspense so it will come back after the intermission. The final act of the drama usually builds to a climax or crisis greater than any that has gone before. The end of the drama involves the **resolution** of the climax, usually by death in a tragedy or by marriage in a comedy.

See **Dialogue, Plot.**
See also pages 333, 334.

ESSAY *A piece of prose writing that discusses a subject in a limited way and that usually expresses a particular point of view.* The word *essay* means "an evaluation or consideration of something." Therefore, most essays tend to be thoughtful observations about a subject of interest to the author. Most essays are *expository* in nature, which means simply that they explain a situation, circumstance, or process. They often go on to consider the results or consequences of what they have explained. Essays are often divided into two types—formal and informal. J. Frank Dobie's "When I Was a Boy on the Ranch" is an example of an autobiographical essay.

See **Exposition.**
See also page 382.

EXPOSITION *A kind of writing that explains something or gives information about something.* Exposition can be used in fiction as well as in nonfiction. The most familiar form it takes is in **essays.** A typical piece of exposition is this passage from Henry David Thoreau's *Walden:* "It is not all books that are as dull as their readers. There are probably words addressed to our condition exactly, which, if we could really hear and understand, would be more salutary than the morning or the spring to our lives, and possibly put a new aspect on the face of things for us. How many a man has dated a new era in his life from the reading of a book." Exposition is also that part of a play in which important background information is revealed to the audience. At the opening of *The Mazarin Stone,* Holmes provides the audience with essential information when he tells Watson his plan for recovering the diamond.

See **Essay.**

FABLE *A brief story with a moral, written in prose or poetry.* The characters in fables are often animals who speak and act like human beings. The most famous fables are those of Aesop, who was supposed to have lived around the sixth century B.C. Almost as famous are the fables of the seventeenth-century French writer Jean de La Fontaine (là fôn-těn′).

A typical fable is Aesop's "The Wind and the Sun," in which the Wind and the Sun quarrel about which is the stronger. When they see a

---

Essay: See Evaluating Nonfiction, Transparency 33.

Exposition: See Evaluating Nonfiction, Transparency 33.

Fable: See Elements of Fables, Transparency 51.

traveler coming down the road, they propose to settle the dispute in this way: Whichever causes the traveler to take off his coat will be considered the stronger. The Wind blows as hard as he can, but this causes the traveler to wrap himself up in his cloak. The Sun then shines down upon the traveler and causes him to remove his cloak. The moral of the story is "Kindness can achieve more than harshness."

See page 668.

FANTASY *A form of fiction, poetry, or drama that takes place in an imaginary world and makes use of unrealistic elements.* It involves combinations of an impossible sort—animals that think and talk like people, plants that move or think, or circumstances that are highly fanciful, like worlds and societies beneath the sea. Fantasy has been popular in almost all ages and among people of most cultures.

Time travel is one of the favorite themes in fantasy. In Mark Twain's novel *A Connecticut Yankee in King Arthur's Court,* a man from the nineteenth century suddenly finds himself back in the Middle Ages. In H. G. Wells's *The Time Machine,* a man builds a machine that can take him into the past and into the future.

FICTION *A prose account that is invented and not a record of things as they actually happened.* Much fiction is based on personal experience, but involves invented characters, settings, or other details that exist for the sake of the story itself. Fiction generally refers to short stories and novels.

FIGURATIVE LANGUAGE *Any language that is not intended to be interpreted in a strict literal sense.* When we call a car a "lemon," we do not mean it is a citrus fruit, but that its performance is "sour," or defective. When we hear someone refer to another person as a clown, a brick, a prince, or an angel, we can be sure that the person is none of those things. Instead, we understand that the person shares some quality with those other things. Figurative language always makes use of comparisons between different things.

The main form of figurative language used in literature is **metaphor.** Metaphor draws a comparison between two unlike things. Metaphor never uses any special language to establish a comparison. The opening stanza of "The Highwayman" contains a number of metaphors. The road is called "a ribbon of moonlight"; the moon "a ghostly galleon"; the sky is referred to as "cloudy seas." Longfellow compares himself to a castle in "The Children's Hour" and expresses his affection for his daughters through the metaphor of imprisonment:

I have you fast in my fortress,
   And will not let you depart,
But put you down into the dungeon
   In the round tower of my heart.

Similes are easier to recognize than metaphors because they do have a special language to set them off. That language is *like, as, as if, than, such as,* and other words that make an explicit comparison. When Robert Burns says, "My love is like a red, red rose," he is using a simile. Like metaphor, the simile does not use all the points of comparison for its force. It uses only some. For instance, the comparison of "my love" to a rose does not necessarily mean that the loved one is thorny, nor that she lives in a garden, nor that she has a green neck. Rather, it means that "my love" is delicate, fragrant, and beautiful as the flower is.

Similes in everyday language are common: "He was mad as a hornet"; "He roared like a bull when I told him"; "Louie laughed like a hyena"; "Float like a butterfly, sting like a bee"; "Be as firm as Gibraltar and as cool as a cucumber"; "She's like Wonder Woman"; "She sang like a bird."

See **Metaphor, Simile, Personification.**
See also pages 450, 451, 489.

FLASHBACK *An interruption of the sequence of a narrative to relate an action that happened at an earlier point in time.* The flashback is an effective technique because it is usually unexpected. A plot generally moves in chronological order: it starts at a given moment, progresses through time, and ends. A flashback interrupts that flow by suddenly shifting to past time and narrating important incidents that make the present action more intelligible.

See pages 30, 160.

FOLK TALE *A story that was not originally written down, but was passed on orally from one storyteller to another.* Folk tales often exist in several forms because they are carried by storytellers to different parts of the world. Many fairy tales, such as the story of Cinderella, are folk tales that originated in Europe, and versions of them later appeared in the Appalachian Mountains of the New World. Folk tales often involve unreal creatures, like dragons, giants, and talking animals. In the United States, folk tales have grown up about such figures as the lumberjack Paul Bunyan, the riverboatman Mike Fink, and the frontiersman Davy Crockett.

Here is a folk tale from Nigeria. In folk tales of certain cultures, the characters are animals. This particular tale shows that inhospitality is a shameful act.

How Ijapa°, Who Was Short, Became Long
Retold by Harold Courlander

Ijapa the tortoise was on a journey. He was tired and hungry, for he had been walking a long time. He came to the village where Ojola[1] the boa lived, and he stopped there, thinking, "Ojola will surely feed me, for I am famished."

Ijapa went to Ojola's house. Ojola greeted him, saying, "Enter my house and cool yourself in the shade, for I can see you have been on the trail."

Ijapa entered. They sat and talked. Ijapa smelled food cooking over the fire. He groaned with hunger, for when Ijapa was hungry he was more hungry than anyone else. Ojola said politely: "Surely the smell of my food does not cause you pain?"

Ijapa said: "Surely not, my friend. It only made me think that if I were at home now, my wife would be cooking likewise."

Ojola said: "Let us prepare ourselves. Then we shall eat together."

Ijapa went outside. He washed himself in a bowl of water. When he came in again he saw the food in the middle of the room and smelled its odors. But Ojola the boa was coiled around the food. There was no way to get to it. Ijapa walked around and around, trying to find an opening through which he could approach the waiting meal. But Ojola's body was long, and his coils lay one atop the other, and there was no entrance through them. Ijapa's hunger was intense.

Ojola said: "Come, do not be restless. Sit down. Let us eat."

Ijapa said: "I would be glad to sit with you. But you, why do you surround the dinner?"

Ojola said: "This is our custom. When my people eat, they always sit this way. Do not hesitate any longer." The boa went on eating while Ijapa again went around and around trying to find a way to the food. At last he gave up. Ojola finished eating. He said: "What a pleasure it is to eat dinner with a friend."

Ijapa left Ojola's house hungrier than he had come. He returned to his own village. There he ate. He brooded on his experience with Ojola. He decided that he would return the courtesy by inviting Ojola to his house to

---
° **Ijapa** (ē-jä′pä).
1. **Ojola** (ō-jō′lä).

From *Olode the Hunter and Other Tales from Nigeria* by Harold Courlander with Ezekiel A. Eshugbayi. Copyright © 1968 by Harold Courlander. Reprinted by permission of Harold Courlander.

Literary Terms and Techniques

Hero/Heroine: See Character, Transparency 10.

Imagery: See Transparency 15.

Literary Terms and Techniques

eat with him. He told his wife to prepare a meal for a certain festival day. And he began to weave a long tail out of grass. He spent many days weaving the tail. When it was finished, he fastened it to himself with tree gum.

On the festival day, Ojola arrived. They greeted each other at the door, Ijapa saying, "You have been on a long journey. You are hungry. You are tired. Refresh yourself at the spring. Then we shall eat."

Ojola was glad. He went to the spring to wash. When he returned, he found Ijapa already eating. Ijapa's grass tail was coiled several times around the food. Ojola could not get close to the dinner. Ijapa ate with enthusiasm. He stopped sometimes to say: "Do not hesitate, friend Ojola. Do not be shy. Good food does not last forever."

Ojola went around and around. It was useless. At last he said: "Ijapa, how did it happen that once you were quite short but now you are very long?"

Ijapa said: "One person learns from another about such things." Ojola then remembered the time Ijapa had been his guest. He was ashamed. He went away. It was from Ijapa that came the proverb:

"The lesson that a man should be short came from his fellow man.
The lesson that a man should be tall also came from his fellow man."

FORESHADOWING *The use of hints or clues in a narrative to suggest what action is to come.* Foreshadowing helps to build **suspense** because it alerts the reader to what is about to happen. It also helps the reader savor all the details of the buildup. Of drama, it is often said that if a loaded gun is presented in Act One, it should go off before Act Five. In other words, presenting a loaded gun or a potentially dangerous or interesting opportunity early in a literary work is an effective kind of foreshadowing.

See **Plot**.
See also page 227.

GENRE *A literary type.* Included in this textbook are the following genres: short story, nonfiction, drama, poetry, novel, mythology, and folklore.

HAIKU *A three-line poem with five syllables in the first line, seven syllables in the second line, and five syllables in the third line.*

See pages 491, 492.

HERO/HEROINE *The chief character in a story.* In older heroic stories, the hero or heroine often embodies the best or most desirable qualities of the society for which the story was written. The hero or heroine in such stories is usually physically strong, courageous, and intelligent. Often the conflict involves the hero or heroine with a monster or with a force that threatens the entire social group. Nowadays, we use the term **hero** or **heroine** simply to mean the main character in any narrative.

IMAGERY *A description that appeals to any one or any combination of the five senses.* Most images tend to be visual in nature, but they may also suggest the way things sound, smell, taste, or feel to the touch. In "A Christmas Carol," Charles Dickens associates the Ghost of Christmas Present with images that appeal not only to the visual sense but also to the sense of taste: "Heaped upon the floor, to form a kind of throne, were turkeys, geese, game, brawn, great joints of meat, suckling pigs, long wreaths of sausages, mince pies, plum puddings, barrels of oysters, red-hot chestnuts, cherry-cheeked apples, juicy oranges, luscious pears, immense twelfth-cakes, and great bowls of punch." Dickens heralds the entrance of Marley's ghost with images of noise. First Scrooge hears every bell in the house ringing. Then he hears "a clanking noise, deep down below, as if some person were dragging a heavy chain over the casks in the wine merchant's cellar."

Good images involve our sensory awareness

and help us be more responsive readers.

See pages 113, 446.

INFERENCE *A reasonable conclusion about something based on certain clues or facts.* Often the author of a literary work does not tell us everything there is to tell, but gives us the pleasure of drawing an inference about the characters, the situation, or the meaning of the work. The process of drawing an inference is pleasurable because we are actually making a discovery on our own.

In "Rip Van Winkle," Washington Irving expects his readers to grasp the truth about his hero's long sleep before it becomes evident to Rip. When Rip awakens, he is puzzled by what he finds, but the reader can infer what has happened from different clues:

> He looked round for his gun, but in place of the clean, well-oiled fowling piece, he found an old firelock lying by him, the barrel incrusted with rust, the lock falling off, and the stock worm-eaten.
>
> As he rose to walk, he found himself stiff in the joints.
>
> As he approached the village, he met a number of people, but none whom he knew, which somewhat surprised him, for he had thought himself acquainted with everyone in the country round. Their dress, too, was of a different fashion from that to which he was accustomed. They all stared at him with equal marks of surprise, and whenever they cast their eyes upon him, invariably stroked their chins. The recurrence of this gesture induced Rip to do the same, when, to his astonishment, he found his beard had grown a foot long!

See pages 86, 110, 121, 129.

INVERSION *A reversal of the usual order of words to achieve some kind of emphasis.* For example, in this line from "The Pied Piper of Hamelin," Robert Browning inverts the subject and object: "To blow the pipe his lips he wrinkled." The device usually appears in poetry, but it occurs in prose and in speech as well. Its effect is to give special importance to a phrase or thought.

Sometimes it is not just the order of words but the actual sequence of events which is inverted. One of the most common uses of this kind of inversion in everyday language occurs in the expression, "Wait until I put on my shoes and socks." We all know that socks go on first—then come the shoes! But it is not only more effective to invert the order, but for many people more natural. We do not think of the sequence as an inversion.

A more usual kind of inversion is that which appears in Alfred, Lord Tennyson's poem "Sir Galahad":

> When down the stormy crescent goes,
> A light before me swims,
> Between dark stems the forest glows,
> I hear a noise of hymns.

It would be more normal to write: "When the stormy crescent goes down, a light swims before me; the forest glows between dark stems, and I hear a noise of hymns." But Tennyson liked the stateliness, the slightly unexpected quality he achieved by inverting these lines. The inversion is also designed to produce effective rhyme.

See page 442.

IRONY *A contrast between what is stated and what is really meant, or between what is expected to happen and what actually does happen.* Irony is used in literature for different effects, from humor to serious comments on the unpredictable nature of life. A good example of irony is found in the short story "The Landlady." Impressed by appearances, Billy Weaver thinks he has found a cheap, attractive place to live in,

Literary Terms and Techniques 715

Legend: For Elements of Fables, see Transparency 51.

Limerick: See Sound Effects in Poetry, Transparency 39.

whereas he is actually in grave danger.

See page 268.

LEGEND *A story handed down from the past. Legends seem to have some basis in history.* A legend usually centers on some historical incident, such as a battle or a journey in search of a treasure or the founding of a city or nation. A legend usually features a great hero or heroine who struggles against some powerful force to achieve the desired goal. Most legends were passed on orally long before they were written down, so that the characters became larger than life, and their actions became fantastic and unbelievable. Browning's poem "The Pied Piper of Hamelin" is based on a well-known legend about events that occurred in the town of Hamelin in 1284.

LIMERICK *A comic poem written in three long and two short lines, rhymed in the pattern aabba.* No one knows if the limerick was actually invented in Limerick, Ireland, but the form of the poem is very popular throughout that country. Writing limericks is also a popular pastime in our country. Much of the fun comes in using the name of a place or person. Limericks often begin in this fashion: "There was a young girl (boy) from St. Paul." What comes later is up to the writer.

Sometimes writers twist the spellings of rhyme words to build more humor into limericks. The following Irish limerick plays on the spelling of a town south of Dublin: *Dun Laoghaire,* pronounced "dun leery."

> An ancient old man of Dun Laoghaire
> Said, "Of pleasure and joy I've grown
>   waoghaire.
>   The life that is pure,
>   Will suit me I'm sure,
> It's healthy and noble though draoghaire."

Perhaps a more typical limerick is this one, also Irish:

> There was an old man of Tralee,
> Who was bothered and bit by a flea,
>   So he put out the light,
>   Saying, "Now he can't bite,
> For he'll never be able to see."

The pattern of rhythm for lines 1, 2, and 5 is the same:

The pattern for lines 3 and 4 is also the same:

See page 496.

METAMORPHOSIS *A change, mainly of shape or form.* In literature, it usually involves the miraculous change of a human or god into an animal or tree or flower. The most famous examples of metamorphosis are found in classical myths. In the myth of Arachne, the goddess Minerva transforms Arachne into a spider. In the myth of Daphne and Apollo, Daphne is transformed into a laurel tree, which thereafter becomes sacred to Apollo. Classical myths often employ metamorphosis to suggest a close relationship among gods, humans, and the world of nature. The goddess Aphrodite, for instance, sprang from the foam of the sea. The goddess Athene appeared to the Greek hero Odysseus in the form of a mist. She also assumed the form of an owl when it suited her. In the myths metamorphosis reflects a sense of wonder about the nature of the world: the shapes of things are not necessarily reliable indications of what the things are. If an owl could be a goddess, then it was only wise for a Greek to be cautious of the owl and to respect it. Such respect typifies other mythologies as well: American Indian myths express the same kind of respect for the natural world.

Metamorphosis is found in many popular European folk tales. In "The Princess and the Frog," the frog metamorphoses into a handsome prince, and in "Beauty and the Beast," a prince is metamorphosed into an animal.

See pages 598, 605.

Myth: See Analyzing a Myth, Transparency 50.

METAPHOR *A comparison between two unlike things with the intent of giving added meaning to one of them.* A metaphor is one of the most important forms of **figurative language.** It is used in virtually all forms of language, from everyday speech to formal prose and all forms of fiction and poetry.

When one says, "He was a gem to help me like that," the metaphor lies in calling a person a gem. Gems are stones; they glisten; they are usually quite small. But these are not the qualities that the metaphor above wants us to consider. The metaphor relies on our understanding that it is the person's gemlike or jewel-like value that is referred to. Thus, we see that metaphors use selected points of comparison that are supplied by the context.

Should we say, "The miser had a heart of flint," we do not mean that his heart is small, black, bloodless, and nonfunctioning. Rather, we mean he has no capacity to feel emotionally for someone else.

Unlike a **simile,** a metaphor does not use a specific word to state a comparison. The difference is illustrated in this pair of sentences. The first expresses a simile, the second a metaphor.

Life is like a dream.
Life is a dream.

See **Figurative Language, Simile.**
See also page 451.

MOOD *The emotional situation that a piece of literature tries to establish.* Mood is very closely related to atmosphere because certain kinds of atmosphere will create moods of different sorts. The mood of a piece of literature might be described in a single word: somber, gay, strange, comfortable, easy, happy, hopeful, or reflective. But more often the mood of a piece will not be easily described in a single word. More complex moods, such as those of apprehension, fear, and excitement—in combinations that resist such simple definition—will be harder to describe.

Mood is apparent in all forms of literature: fiction, nonfiction, poetry, and drama. It is achieved often by description. But it can be achieved by skillful **dialogue** as well. The uses of **foreshadowing** and of **suspense** can help establish a variety of moods.

Edgar Allan Poe, a master of mood in poetry, establishes an unforgettable mood in his poem "To Helen." He uses vowel sounds such as the open **o** sound and the long **e** sound to set the mood. He then uses an unusual amount of **alliteration.** His intention is to connect Helen with the beauties of classical Greece by using language that is musical in sound. He also describes classical beauty by referring to classical ships (Nicaean barks):

Helen, thy beauty is to me
　Like those Nicaean barks of yore,
That gently, o'er a perfumed sea,
　The weary wayworn wanderer bore
　To his own native shore.

On desperate seas long wont to roam,
　Thy hyacinth hair, thy classic face,
Thy naiad airs have brought me home
　To the glory that was Greece,
　And the grandeur that was Rome.

See **Atmosphere, Foreshadowing, Suspense.**

MYTH *An ancient story often serving to explain a natural phenomenon and generally involving supernatural beings.* Sometimes myth, like legend, seems to have a general rooting in some historical event, but, unlike legend, myth concentrates far less on history than it does on stories that include supernatural elements. Myths explaining the origin of specific events, such as the ways in which the seas or the mountains came into being, exist in almost every culture. Likewise, almost every culture has myths that explain the beginnings of the world.

Classical mythology is the name given to the

Narration: See Story Map, Transparency 22.

Nonfiction: See Evaluating Nonfiction, Transparency 33.

Novel: See Analyzing and Evaluating a Novel, Transparency 44.

Onomatopoeia: See Sound Effects in Poetry, Transparency 39.

Literary Terms and Techniques

myths developed by the ancient Greeks and the Romans. Most classical myths are about the gods and goddesses of Olympus. Norse mythology consists of myths of ancient Scandinavia and Germany.

See pages 574, 636.

NARRATION *The kind of writing or speaking that tells a story (a narrative).* Any narrative must be delivered by a narrator, whether it is the author or a character created by the author. The narrator's **point of view** can sometimes color the narration. In one famous mystery story by Agatha Christie, the reader does not realize until the last page that the narrator is the murderer. And the narrator's point of view is such that he thinks of himself as innocent.

See **Point of View.**
See also page 245.

NONFICTION *Any prose narrative that tells about things as they actually happened or that presents factual information about something.* One of the chief kinds of nonfiction is a history of someone's life. When a person writes his or her own life story, we call it **autobiography.** When someone else writes a person's life story, we call it **biography.** In each case, the purpose of the writing is to give an accounting of a person's life. Presumably, it is a true and accurate accounting. When someone writes about personal observations on some subject—as Julia Alvarez does in "Names/Nombres"—the result is an **essay.** Essays are among the most common forms of nonfiction and appear in most of the magazines we see on the newsstands. Another kind of nonfiction is also to be found on newsstands: the newspaper itself. News stories, editorials, the letters to the editor, and feature stories of all kinds are forms of nonfiction. Travel stories, personal journals, and diaries are also forms of nonfiction.

See **Biography, Essay.**
See also page 381.

NOVEL *A fictional narrative in prose, generally longer than a short story.* The novel allows for greater complexity of character and plot development than the short story. The forms the novel may take cover a wide range. For example, there are the **historical novel,** in which historical characters, settings, and periods are drawn in detail; the **picaresque novel,** presenting the adventures of a rogue; and the **psychological novel,** which focuses on characters' emotions and thoughts. Other forms of the novel include the detective story, the spy thriller, and the science-fiction novel.

See page 502.

ONOMATOPOEIA *The use of a word whose sound in some degree imitates or suggests its meaning.* The names of some birds are onomatopoetic, imitating the cries of the birds named: *cuckoo, whippoorwill, owl, crow, towhee, bobwhite.* Some onomatopoetic words are *hiss, clang, rustle,* and *snap.* In these lines from Edgar Allan Poe's poem "The Bells," the word *tintinnabulation* is onomatopoetic:

> Keeping time, time, time
> In a sort of Runic rhyme,
> To the *tintinnabulation* that so musically wells
> From the bells, bells, bells, bells
> Bells, bells, bells—

See pages 300, 466, 468, 472.

PARAPHRASE *A summary or recapitulation of a piece of literature.* A paraphrase does not add anything to our enjoyment of a literary work. It merely tells in the simplest form what happened. A paraphrase of "The Highwayman" might go this way.

> The highwayman tells his sweetheart Bess that he will return to her with the gold he plans to steal that very night. Tim, a stableman who is in love with Bess, overhears this conversation and tells the British soldiers of the lovers' plan. A troop of soldiers comes to the inn and waits for the highwayman to return. Bess is gagged and bound to her bed,

but she is able to reach the trigger of a musket. When she hears the sound of horse hoofs in the distance, she pulls the trigger and warns the highwayman with her death. After he learns how Bess has died, the highwayman rides back for revenge, and is shot down on the highway. There is a legend that the lovers can still be seen and heard at the old inn on winter nights.

This summary gives us some essential information and is useful for checking to see just what did happen. But it is also clear that such a paraphrase is no substitute for the charm and beauty of the original poem.

See page 442.

PERSONIFICATION *A figure of speech in which something nonhuman is given human qualities.* In these lines from "Blow, Blow, Thou Winter Wind," William Shakespeare personifies the wind. He addresses it as if it were a person who could consciously act with kindness or unkindness. He also gives it teeth and breath.

> Blow, blow, thou winter wind,
> Thou art not so unkind
>   As man's ingratitude.
> Thy tooth is not so keen,
> Because thou art not seen,
>   Although thy breath be rude.

See page 489.

PLOT *The sequence of events or happenings in a literary work.* We generally associate plot with short stories, novels, and drama. Plot differs from narrative in that it is not merely a record of events as they happen, but an ordering of events in such a fashion as to bring them to a strongly satisfying conclusion. The use of **foreshadowing**, surprise, **suspense**, and carefully worked out **conflict** produces a tight pattern of action. Plot implies a step-by-step working out of events, in which each step takes us perceptibly closer to the unraveling of the action.

The major element in plot is **conflict**, or struggle of some kind. Sometimes the conflict is **external**: it takes place between characters and their environment—whether that be nature, the gods, or other characters. Often, the conflict is **internal**, or within the character's own mind. A plot will slowly reveal the nature of the conflict, the source of the conflict, illustrate its effects on the characters, and then show us how the conflict is resolved. If the conflict is not resolved, the plot will point toward changes in the lives of the characters that will be necessary to accommodate the conflict.

In most plots there is a point at which the intensity of the action rises to such a height we must consider it a point of **climax.** In Charles Dickens' "A Christmas Carol," the point of climax comes when Scrooge sees a vision of a tombstone bearing his name, and resolves to become a better man.

The **resolution** is the moment in the plot when the conflict ends. Not all plots have a resolution as such. In older stories, there generally is a resolution. In "A Christmas Carol," the conflict is resolved when Scrooge changes from a hardhearted miser to a warm and generous man. But many modern stories end without a resolution. They provide us with enough information so that we may draw our own inferences as to how the conflict will be resolved.

See pages 218, 333.

POETRY *Traditional poetry is language arranged in lines, with a regular rhythm and often a definite rhyme scheme. Nontraditional poetry does away with regular rhythm and rhyme, although it usually is set up in lines.* There is no satisfactory way of defining poetry, although most people have little trouble knowing when they read it. Some definitions offered by those concerned with it may help us. The English poet William Wordsworth called it "the spontaneous overflow of powerful feelings." He also called it "wisdom married to immortal verse." Matthew Arnold, an English writer and poet of the nineteenth century, defined it in this fashion:

Plot: See Transparency 4. For Plot in fiction, see Transparencies 21 and 22.

Poetry: For Sound Effects in Poetry, see Transparency 39.

Point of View: For point of view in fiction, see Story Map, Transparency 22. See also Evaluating Short Stories, Transparency 21.

Literary Terms and Techniques

"Poetry is simply the most beautiful, impressive, and widely effective mode of saying things."

Poetry often employs lines set up in **stanza** form. It uses **rhyme** in order to build the musicality of the language or to emphasize certain moods or effects. It uses **imagery** and **figurative language** widely. Techniques like **alliteration, repetition,** and **inversion** are often considered specifically poetic. Poetry depends heavily on strong **rhythms,** even when they are not regular.

A **narrative poem** tells a story, and like a story, it has characters, a setting, and action. A **lyric** expresses personal thoughts and feelings; it is usually brief. **Dramatic poetry** presents characters who speak to other characters or to some unidentified listener.

See the terms noted above.
See also pages 429, 430, 440, 474, 488, 493.

POINT OF VIEW *The vantage point from which a work is told.* Writers may choose a totally unlimited point of view or a narrow, limited one. In some cases the point of view will be of great importance, since we will be expected to draw inferences about the nature of the narrator. In other cases, the point of view will be of less importance, since it will have been chosen only to give us all the details of the story in the most direct way possible.

In the **third-person point of view,** the story is told by an outside observer. In the following passage, we are told that a character, Hester Martin, has made a decision. She is referred to in the third person ("she"), which is how this point of view gets its name:

> Hester Martin could let the insult get her down. She could reply rudely or call for the man's manager and make a formal complaint. But she decided against both courses. Instead, she took the man aside and explained to him what it felt like to have someone who was a total stranger say something cruel, even if the man did not intend to be insulting. Whether he intended to be insulting or not, once Hester told him how she felt, he changed his manner entirely. She had done the right thing. She had educated him.

This is an example of the **omniscient, or all-knowing, point of view.** The author tells us things that Hester Martin does not directly think or observe. The author speculates on whether the man was consciously rude, just as the author ultimately tells us that Hester made the right decision. She does not know whether it was right or not. The author tells us so.

A **limited third-person** narrative tells only what one character sees, feels, and thinks. The same scene written from a limited third-person point of view might go this way:

> Hester Martin felt her face flush. Did he notice it, too? Should she go to his manager? Should she insult him back? She took a moment to bring her emotions back under control, but when she collected herself she drew the man aside and lectured him carefully and patiently on the subject of insulting a patron. His apologies and his extraordinary politeness and caution gave her a small measure of satisfaction.

The **first-person point of view** tells everything from the "I" vantage point. Like the third-person limited point of view, this point of view tells only what the narrator knows and feels. We cannot be told what any other character thinks, except when the narrator may speculate about the character's feelings or thoughts. It is a very limited point of view, but its popularity is secure since we all identify with "I" in a story. The scene above, in the first-person narrative, might go this way:

> I felt my face burn with the insult. I wondered if he noticed it. Should I go to his manager? No, I thought. And I won't stoop to his level and return the comment. When I thought I could control myself, I took the

man aside and I told him in no uncertain terms that I did not like being insulted by a stranger. The only satisfaction I got was watching him try to squirm out of it, telling me he didn't mean it as an insult. But at least I got him to admit he was wrong. Maybe he learned a lesson.

See **Narration.**
See also pages 245, 275.

PROVERB *A wise saying, usually quite old and usually of folk origin.* Proverbs are related to **morals,** the concluding lessons that are often attached to fables. A proverb like "A stitch in time saves nine," "A rolling stone gathers no moss," or "A new broom sweeps clean" could easily be the moral tag on a fable. Benjamin Franklin was one of the most prolific of modern proverb writers. His publication *Poor Richard's Almanac* always included at least one proverb per issue. One of Franklin's most famous sayings is, "A penny saved is a penny earned."

See page 678.

QUATRAIN *A four-line stanza, usually rhymed.* Sometimes an entire poem will be in the form of a quatrain, while at other times the poem will be broken up into stanzas of quatrain length. One of the most famous quatrains in poetry is that of Edward Fitzgerald in his translation of Omar Khayám's *The Rubáiyát*:

A book of verses underneath the bough,
A jug of wine, a loaf of bread—and thou
　Beside me singing in the wilderness—
O, Wilderness were paradise enow!

REFRAIN *A word, phrase, line, or group of lines that is repeated regularly in a poem or song, usually at the end of each stanza.* One of the delights in refrains is in anticipating their return. Many ballads use refrains. Sometimes the refrain is repeated exactly the same way and sometimes it is varied slightly for effect.

See pages 163, 465, 477.

REPETITION *The return of a word, phrase, stanza form, or effect in any form of literature.* Repetition in all its forms is probably the most dependably used literary device. **Alliteration,** repeating sounds at the beginning, middle, or end of words, is one of the most common kinds of repetition in poetry. **Rhyme** is also a form of repetition. The **refrain** in ballads and songs is a form of repetition. Once we realize that these are forms of repetition, we can begin to appreciate how important the device is. We do not wholly understand how it affects us, since the device is very complex. We do know that a stanza such as the opening quatrain in Lewis Carroll's "Jabberwocky" reads at first as if it were a foreign language:

'Twas brillig, and the slithy toves
　Did gyre and gimble in the wabe;
All mimsy were the borogoves,
　And the mome raths outgrabe.

After the entire story of the boy's adventurous slaying of the Jabberwock is told, the stanza is repeated. Then it seems much clearer and much easier to read. It also takes on the odd quality of being comforting to us.

One of the great masters of repetition is Edgar Allan Poe. He actually worked out theories of how poetry affects a reader. His conclusion was that simple repetition was one of the most important and functional devices a poet could use. His poem "Annabel Lee" is filled with repetitive references to her name, since it was for him an immensely musical name. He also repeats in its entirety the phrase "kingdom by the sea." Such repetitions are not only pleasurable—they also build emotional tension in his poems. In one of his poems, "Annie," Poe tries to build a sense of feverish intensity. The subject of the poem is Annie's death. In one stanza, Poe repeats himself almost nervously:

A holier odor
　About it, of pansies—

A rosemary odor,
　Commingled with pansies—

Repetition: See Sound Effects in Poetry, Transparency 39.

Literary Terms and Techniques

Rhyme: See Sound Effects in Poetry, Transparency 39.

With rue and the beautiful
   Puritan pansies.

Sometimes a poet will repeat a formula line with slight differences each time. Christina Georgina Rossetti, an English poet of the nineteenth century, wrote this stanza in her poem "A Birthday":

My heart is like a singing bird
   Whose nest is in a watered shoot;
My heart is like an apple tree
   Whose boughs are bent with thick-set
      fruit;
My heart is like a rainbow shell
   That paddles in a halcyon sea;
My heart is gladder than all these,
   Because my love is come to me.

      See **Alliteration, Refrain, Rhyme.**
      See also pages 460, 463.

RHYME *The repetition of sounds in words, usually, but not exclusively, at the ends of lines of poetry.* One of the primary uses of rhyme is as an aid to memory. Rhyme is used for this purpose in certain rules, such as: "Thirty days hath September, April, June, and November," and *"I before e except after c."*

The most familiar form of rhyme is the **end rhyme.** This simply means the rhymes come at the end of the lines. The following passage is from a long poem on the muse of music by the English poet Alexander Pope. He is trying to re-create the sounds of the underworld when Orpheus sang there in order to rescue his beloved wife, Eurydice:

What sounds were heard,
What scenes appeared,
  O'er all the dreary coasts!
    Dreadful gleams,
    Dismal screams,

    Fires that glow,
    Shrieks of woe,
    Sullen moans,
    Hollow groans,
And cries of tortured ghosts!

Each of these rhymes was an **exact rhyme** for Pope, although we now pronounce *heard* differently from *appeared.* (We call this a **partial rhyme**—the final consonant sounds are the same, but the vowel sounds are different.) The rhyme of *coasts* and *ghosts,* separated by six lines, is a marvelous example of **distant rhyme.**

Exact rhyme insists that the two words rhymed sound exactly the same. The most common form of exact rhyme is **strong rhyme.** Strong rhyme refers to words of one syllable that rhyme: *place/space.* It also refers to words of more than one syllable where the rhyme occurs on the stressed syllable: *approve/remove.* In **weak rhyme,** there are two or more syllables that rhyme, but the accent does not fall on the last syllable: *sínging/clínging: wéarily/dréarily.* The terms *strong* and *weak* do not have anything to do with the qualities of the sounds themselves. The first two rhymes in John Gay's poem "Song" are weak. The next two are strong:

O ruddier than the cherry!
O sweeter than the berry!
  O nymph more bright
  Than the moonshine night.

Rhyme that occurs within a line is called **internal rhyme.** Usually, the rhyme word appears in the middle of a line and rhymes with an end rhyme from the line above or from its own line. One of the masters of this technique is Edgar Allan Poe, who begins the first line of "The Raven" with the internal weak rhyme *eerie:* "Once upon a midnight dreary, while I pondered, weak and weary." Clearly, the reasons for rhyming in these poems go far beyond a simple memory device.

Rhymes in the work of Pope, Poe, or any other careful poet serve many purposes. One is to increase the musicality of the poem. Rhyme appeals to the ear. Another purpose is to give delight by rewarding our anticipation of a returning sound, such as the *coasts/ghosts* rhyme in Pope's poem. There is also the purpose of humor. Limericks, for instance, would not be half so funny if they did not rhyme—particularly when the rhymes are strained for comic effect.

See **Poetry, Repetition.**
See also pages 460, 463.

RHYTHM *The pattern of stressed and unstressed sounds in a line of poetry.* All language has rhythm of some sort or another, but rhythm is most important in poetry, where it is carefully controlled for effect.

The effects of rhythm are several. Rhythm contributes to the musical quality of a poem, which gives the reader or listener pleasure. Rhythm can also be used to imitate the action being described in the poem. In Robert Browning's poem "How They Brought the Good News from Ghent to Aix," the lines actually imitate the galloping rhythm of horses' hoofs:

> And there was my Roland to bear the
>   whole weight,
> Of the news which alone could save Aix
>   from her fate,
> With his nostrils like pits full of blood to the
>   brim,
> And with circles of red for his eye sockets'
>   rim.

Scanning the lines—examining them for the stressed and unstressed syllables—is not easy. It requires practice. One thing to remember is that good poets usually put stress on the most important words in the line. If you say the line to yourself in a natural voice, you will hear that the most important words demand the stress.

Browning uses techniques other than just stressed and unstressed syllables to intensify his rhythm. The lines above are all one sentence and must be read in a single breath, thus building a feeling of constant motion. Even the internal rhyme of *there* and *bear* in the first line builds rhythmic intensity, since the stresses fall on those words. In the last two lines, stressed words are accented by having them also alliterate: *b*lood/*b*rim; *r*ed/*r*im. Such devices help build even more rhythmic pressure in a poem that depends heavily on rhythm for its effect.

Rhyme also contributes to rhythm in poetry, since it causes us to feel that a passage has come to an end. When rhymes fall close together, we have the feeling that we must pause in our reading of the lines. An extreme example is from "Endymion," a long poem by John Keats:

> O sorrow!
> Why dost borrow
> The natural hue of health, from vermeil
>   lips?—
>   To give maiden blushes
>   To the white rose bushes?
> Or is it the dewy hand the daisy tips?

In addition to the rhymes, Keats uses another technique that many poets like to employ: that of asking questions in the poem. Any question has a natural rhythm of its own, so poets can capitalize on this fact and use it to their own purposes. Here, Keats is trying to have us read rhythmically in order to build in us a questioning sense of the meaning of things. He is asking in these lines why sorrow takes the healthy redness from some people's lips. Perhaps, he asks, it is to give the redness to the roses and the daisies.

One of the most powerful means of building rhythm in poetry is through repetition. Consider this passage, the last lines from Edgar Allan Poe's "The Bells":

> Keeping time, time, time,
> In a sort of Runic rhyme,
>   To the throbbing of the bells—
> Of the bells, bells, bells—
>   To the sobbing of the bells;
> Keeping time, time, time,
>   As he knells, knells, knells.
> In a happy Runic rhyme,

Rhythm: See Sound Effects in Poetry, Transparency 39.

Setting: For setting in fiction, see Story Map, Transparency 22.

> To the rolling of the bells—
> Of the bells, bells, bells:—
> To the tolling of the bells—
> Of the bells, bells, bells, bells,
> Bells, bells, bells—
> To the moaning and the groaning of the bells.

The repetition of the words *bells, knells,* and *time* builds up a rhythm that suggests the repeated ringing of bells.

See **Alliteration, Repetition, Rhyme.**
See also pages 468, 473.

SETTING *The time and place of action.* In short stories and novels, the setting is generally established by description. Setting can be important in poetry and nonfiction as well, and the means of establishing setting is through description, as in fiction. In dramas, the setting is usually established by stage directions and then reinforced in dialogue. Since a drama normally has sets that appear before an audience, elaborate descriptions of setting are unnecessary.

In the first sentence of "The Legend of Sleepy Hollow" Washington Irving establishes the setting of the story:

> In the bosom of one of those spacious coves which indent the eastern shore of the Hudson, at that broad expansion of the river named by the ancient Dutch navigators the Tappan Zee, there lies a small market town or rural port, which by some is called Greensburgh, but which is more generally and properly known by the name of Tarrytown.

The setting establishes not only the physical locale (Tarrytown) but also something of historical moment as well. This tells us right away that history may have something to do with the story.

Setting can be of great importance in establishing mood or building emotional intensity. Here is the famous opening passage from "The Fall of the House of Usher" by Edgar Allan Poe. Note how the italicized words help to build an atmosphere of gloom:

> During the whole of a *dull, dark,* and *soundless* day in the autumn of the year, when the clouds hung *oppressively low* in the heavens, I had been passing alone, on horseback, through a *singularly dreary* tract of country, and at length found myself, as the shades of the evening drew on, within view of the *melancholy* House of Usher.

In "The Wreck of the *Hesperus,*" Henry Wadsworth Longfellow describes the setting in highly emotional terms. Longfellow uses figurative language to intensify his description of a storm at sea:

> Colder and louder blew the wind,
>   A gale from the Northeast,
> The snow fell hissing in the brine,
>   And the billows frothed like yeast.
>
>   . . .
>
> And fast through the midnight dark and
>   drear,
>   Through the whistling sleet and snow,
> Like a sheeted ghost, the vessel swept
>   Toward the reef of Norman's Woe.

See pages 176, 260.

SIMILE *A comparison between two unlike things, using* like, as, *and similar words of comparison.* Similes are **figures of speech** and are common in everyday language and in most forms of literature. We use simile when we say: "He fought like a tiger"; "He was as mild as a dove"; and "She was cooler than a cucumber." A more poetic use of simile is this, from Lord Byron's "Stanzas for Music":

> There will be none of Beauty's daughters
>   With a magic like thee;
> And like music on the waters
>   Is thy sweet voice to me.

See **Figurative Language.**
See also pages 168, 451.

STANZA *A group of lines forming a unit in a poem.* Some poems have a single stanza. Other poems are divided into several stanzas, each of which has the same number of lines and the same rhyme scheme. Some poems do not repeat the same structure in each stanza, yet each group of lines is still referred to as a stanza. "The Broncho That Would Not Be Broken" by Vachel Lindsay has a regular pattern of five stanzas, each containing eight lines. "Annabel Lee" by Edgar Allan Poe has six stanzas. Three of the stanzas have six lines, one has seven lines, and two have eight lines.

See **Poetry**.

SUSPENSE *That quality in a literary work that makes the reader or audience uncertain or tense about what is to come next.* Suspense is a kind of "suspending" of our emotions. We know something is about to happen, and the longer the writer can keep us anticipating what will happen, the greater the suspense. The device is popular in all kinds of literature that involve plot, whether nonfiction, short stories, drama, or poetry. Suspense is possible even when the reader knows the outcome. At the opening of "Guinea Pig," Ruth McKenney tells us that she was almost drowned by a Red Cross Lifesaving Examiner and that she received a black eye in the cause of serving others. Although we know what to expect, we are still eager to find out what has led to these circumstances. Holding the reader off for as long as possible is part of the strategy of building suspense. Some writers feel it works even better when we know what is coming, so they let us know through **foreshadowing**.

See **Plot**.

See also page 227.

THEME *The main idea or the basic meaning of a literary work.* Not all literary works can be said to have a theme. Some stories are told chiefly for entertainment and have little to say about life or about human nature. But in those stories that try to make a comment on the human condition, theme is of great importance.

Theme: For theme in fiction, see Story Map, Transparency 22.

Because theme in fiction is rarely expressed directly, it is not always obvious to every reader. Theme is one of those qualities of a piece of literature that must be dug out and thought about. The reason for this is that writers develop their themes for thoughtful people. They expect that one of the rewards of reading for such people is the pleasure of inferring the theme on their own.

Usually, however, careful writers set up their stories so that one can pick out passages here and there that focus on the theme. Such "key passages" point in the right direction so that we are not totally unaided in coming to understand the theme. Key passages are recognizable because they seem to speak directly to us as readers. They also make direct statements of a philosophical nature, discussing the meaning of the action and the lessons the characters may have learned. In "A Christmas Carol," one key passage that points toward the theme of the story is this speech by Marley's ghost, warning Scrooge to change his ways before it is too late:

> "Mankind was my business. The common welfare was my business; charity, mercy, forbearance, benevolence, were all my business. The dealings of my trade were but a drop of water in the comprehensive ocean of my business!"

Some simple themes can be stated in a single sentence. Sometimes a literary work is rich and complex, and a paragraph or essay is needed to state the theme. When deciding upon what we think the theme of a story is, we must be careful to doublecheck our ideas against the action of the story. We must test our sense of theme to be sure the actions of the main characters are consistent with our conclusions. If their actions contradict the theme we have arrived at, we must go back, reread the story, and see if we have made a mistake, or if the author has used the contradiction to some literary purpose.

See page 274.

WRITING PROCESS TRANSPARENCIES

In the *Audiovisual Resources Binder,* you will find **Writing Process** transparencies with accompanying **Teacher's Notes** and student activity pages. You may want to use these audiovisual materials when discussing specific aspects of the writing process or of particular types of writing.

HANDBOOK FOR *Revision*

Contents

Part 1: **MODEL ESSAYS 727**
- Persuasive Essay
- Informative Essay

Part 2: **SENTENCE STRUCTURE 738**
- Sentence Fragments
- Run-On Sentences
- Comparisons

Part 3: **PRONOUNS 739**
- Pronoun-Antecedent Agreement
- Case Forms of Personal Pronouns

Part 4: **VERBS 740**
- Missing or Incorrect Verb Endings
- Subject-Verb Agreement
- Sequence of Tenses

Part 5: **WORD ORDER 744**
- Misplaced Modifiers
- Dangling Modifiers

Part 6: **COMMA USAGE 744**
- Compound Structure
- Items in a Series
- Two or More Adjectives
- Nonessential Elements
- Introductory Elements
- Interrupters

Part 7: **STYLE 746**
- Sentence Variety
- Stringy Sentences
- Overwriting
- Creative Use of Synonyms
- Vivid Words
- Clichés
- Levels of Language

Part 8: **GLOSSARY OF USAGE 749**

Part 9: **GRAMMAR REFERENCE GUIDE 757**

Part 10: **MECHANICS 760**
- Capitalization
- Punctuation

Part 1: Model Essays

■ Persuasive Essay   ■ Informative Essay

The essays on the following pages are shown in two versions: a rough draft and a final copy. In the draft, the writer has examined and revised the essay for logic, clarity, style, and supporting information. The writer has also proofread the essay for errors in grammar, usage, punctuation, spelling, and capitalization. The writer's corrections are shown on the draft. The reasons for many of the revisions and corrections are shown in the margin. Marginal notes in the final copy identify important parts of each essay.

Symbols for Revising and Proofreading

Symbol	Example	Meaning of Symbol
≡	Bay avenue	Capitalize a lowercase letter.
/	Rick's Father	Lowercase a capital letter.
/	fortun*a*tely	Change a letter.
∧	the gym*n*asium	Insert a missing word, letter, or punctuation mark.
⌒	I am am sure.	Delete a word, letter, or punctuation mark.
⌒	Where is my pen?	Delete and close up.
tr	Can you give us some help and our neighbors?	Transfer the circled material.
¶	"Hi," he said.	Begin a new paragraph.
⊙	Open the door⊙	Add a period.
∧	Well I think you're wrong.	Add a comma.
∨	Juanitas coat	Add an apostrophe.
⊙	as follows	Add a colon.
∧	Ed Dowell, Sr. Jo Chen, A.S.I.D.	Add a semicolon.

Model Essays 727

WRITING PROCESS TRANSPARENCIES

In the *Audiovisual Resources Binder,* you will find **Writing Process** transparencies with accompanying **Teacher's Notes** and student activity pages. You may want to use these audiovisual materials when discussing specific aspects of the writing process or of particular types of writing, such as the transparencies listed below.

Writing a Persuasive Paper: See Transparency 53.

MODEL 1: A PERSUASIVE ESSAY
Rough Draft

OUR SCHOOLS AND THE COMMUNITY

Which public buildings in our community are used for only seven hours a day and lie vacant for more ~~longer~~ than two months a year? If you guessed that these buildings are our schools, ~~your~~ you're right. We ~~can~~ should expand the usage of our school buildings by designing programs for schools as community centers. ~~A~~ The most important benifit/benefit this change would bring is that it would make our schools magnets for people of all ages. If our school buildings ~~was~~ were open eighteen or even twenty-four hours a day, they could serve the community in creative, new ways. Many adults, for example, want to learn a new skill or brush up on a subject. Programs in continuing education might be offered for these people. Such programs might appeal as well to young people ~~which~~ who have recently graduated and need special kinds of vocational training. Charging a small, afordable/affordable fee for these courses would help to pay the maintenance costs of keeping school buildings open beyond regular hours.

Revision marks:
- Double comparison
- Usage
- Transition/Spelling
- Subject-verb agreement
- Commas with interrupter
- Pronoun usage
- Spelling

728 HANDBOOK FOR REVISION

MODEL 1: A PERSUASIVE ESSAY
Final Copy

OUR SCHOOLS AND THE COMMUNITY | **Title**

    Which public buildings in our community are used for only seven hours a day and lie vacant for more than two months a year? If you guessed that these buildings are our schools, you're right. We should expand the usage of our school buildings by designing programs for schools as community centers.

    The most important benefit this change would bring is that it would make our schools magnets for people of all ages. If our school buildings were open eighteen or even twenty-four hours a day, they could serve the community in creative, new ways. Many adults, for example, want to learn a new skill or brush up on a subject. Programs in continuing education might be offered for these people. Such programs might appeal as well to young people who have recently graduated and need special kinds of vocational training. Charging a small, affordable fee for these courses would help to pay the maintenance costs of keeping school buildings open beyond regular hours.

Introduction

Opinion statement

Body

Supporting reasons

Handbook for Revision

Model Essays 729

Transition	Our school buildings might <ins>also</ins> be used to assist with the problems of the homeless. Setting up a food pantry and
Sentence fragment	organizing a soup kitchen are examples of activities<ins>, that</ins> ~~W~~would give students a chance to perform community service. It is true that
Spelling	some churches and munici~~j~~pal organizations are active in these
Pronoun-antecedent agreement	areas, but ~~its~~ <ins>their</ins> efforts have not succeeded in meeting the need completely.
	A third use for our school buildings might be for
Commas with series/Spelling	community events such as book fairs<ins>,</ins> art ex~~i~~<ins>h</ins>ibits<ins>,</ins> and issue forums. At present, we have no building to serve as a
Run-on sentence	community-wide culture center<ins>. W</ins>~~w~~hy not use one or more of our schools for this purpose?
Subject-verb agreement	Putting our tax-supported school buildings to work for us
Comma after introductory element	around the clock make<ins>s</ins> economic sense. Even more important<ins>,</ins> this program would put the schools back where they belong: right in the mainstream of community life. If you support this program,
Spelling	write the City Council today in fav~~e~~<ins>o</ins>r of schools as community centers.

730   HANDBOOK FOR REVISION

Our school buildings might also be used to assist with the problems of the homeless. Setting up a food pantry and organizing a soup kitchen are examples of activities that would give students a chance to perform community service. It is true that some churches and municipal organizations are active in these areas, but their efforts have not succeeded in meeting the need completely.

A third use for our school buildings might be for community events such as book fairs, art exhibits, and issue forums. At present, we have no building to serve as a community-wide culture center. Why not use one or more of our schools for this purpose?

Putting our tax-supported school buildings to work for us around the clock makes economic sense. Even more important, this program would put the schools back where they belong: right in the mainstream of community life. If you support this program, write the City Council today in favor of schools as community centers.

Additional support	
Additional support	
Emotional appeal	
Conclusion	

WRITING PROCESS TRANSPARENCIES

In the *Audiovisual Resources Binder,* you will find **Writing Process** transparencies with accompanying **Teacher's Notes** and student activity pages. You may want to use these audiovisual materials when discussing specific aspects of the writing process or of particular types of writing, such as the transparencies listed below.

Writing an Informative Paper: See Transparency 16.

MODEL 2: AN EXPOSITORY ESSAY
Rough Draft

CELEBRATING KWANZAA

One of the oldest holidays in Africa is one of the newest in America. Kwanzaa⁁, the traditional African celebration of the harvest⁁, is observed from December 26 to January 1. This holiday has grown steadily in pop*u*larity since 1966, when Dr. Maulana Karenga, a California professor, ~~brung~~ *brought* the festival to this country.

Kwanzaa comes from a Swahili word that means "first fruits." To celebrate the holiday, you need only a few materials: a straw placemat, some ears of corn, a few fresh fruits and veg*e*tables, a wooden candle holder called the <u>kinara</u>, and seven candles. Best of all, adults and children should have some <u>zawadi</u>, or Kwanzaa gifts, to give each other during the holiday.

At the begi*n*ning of the holiday, the family decorates the home with symbols of Kwanzaa. The straw placemat, or <u>mkeka</u>, is ~~lain~~ *laid* on a table, and one ear of corn is placed on the

Margin annotations:
- Commas with appositive phrase
- Spelling
- Verb form
- Spelling
- Spelling
- Verb form

Handbook for Revision

MODEL 2: AN EXPOSITORY ESSAY
Final Copy

CELEBRATING KWANZAA | **Title**

One of the oldest holidays in Africa is one of the newest in | **Introduction**
America. Kwanzaa, the traditional African celebration of the harvest, is observed from December 26 to January 1. This holiday has grown steadily in popularity since 1966, when Dr. Maulana Karenga, a California professor, brought the festival to this country.

Kwanzaa comes from a Swahili word that means "first | **Body**
fruits." To celebrate the holiday, you need only a few materials: a | **Materials**
straw placemat, some ears of corn, a few fresh fruits and vegetables, a wooden candle holder called the <u>kinara</u>, and seven | **Definition of terms**
candles. Best of all, adults and children should have some <u>zawadi</u>, or Kwanzaa gifts, to give each other during the holiday.

At the beginning of the holiday, the family decorates the home with symbols of Kwanzaa. The straw placemat, or | **Description of process**
<u>mkeka</u>, is laid on a table, and one ear of corn is placed on the

Sentence fragment	mat for each child in the family. Vegetables, fruits, yams, and nuts may also be placed on the <u>mkeka</u>. As symbols of the earth's fruitfulness.
Capitalization	Starting on december 26, a candle is lighted on each day
Subject-verb agreement/ Spelling	of the holiday. These candles symbolize the seven principles of Kwanzaa: unity, self-determination, responsibility, economic cooperation, purpose, creativity, and faith. On each day, the
Usage/Spelling	family tries to live up to these principles in a spirit of
Commas with series	togetherness. Family activities include dancing, telling traditional stories, doing a chore together, and buying a gift that the whole family can share.
Run-on sentence	The high point of Kwanzaa is on the seventh day. This is the day of the <u>karamu</u>, the family feast. After a wonderful meal,
Spelling	families celebrate with music, singing, and dancing. The calendar page reads January 1: a time for new beginnings.
Spelling	As the seven principles show, the African American holiday of Kwanzaa celebrates universal ideals and values.

734 HANDBOOK FOR REVISION

mat for each child in the family. Vegetables, fruits, yams, and nuts may also be placed on the <u>mkeka</u> as symbols of the earth's fruitfulness.

Starting on December 26, a candle is lighted on each day of the holiday. These candles symbolize the seven principles of Kwanzaa: unity, self-determination, responsibility, economic cooperation, purpose, creativity, and faith. On each day, the family tries to live up to these principles in a spirit of togetherness. Family activities include dancing, telling traditional stories, doing a chore together, and buying a gift that the whole family can share.

The high point of Kwanzaa is on the seventh day. This is the day of the <u>karamu</u>, the family feast. After a wonderful meal, families celebrate with music, singing, and dancing. The calendar page reads January 1: a time for new beginnings.

As the seven principles show, the African American holiday of Kwanzaa celebrates universal ideals and values.

Verb usage	Kwanzaa can ^be^ a holiday for all peoples. So, next year, on the day
Capitalization	after Christmas, celebrate an old-and-new tradition. ring out the old year and ring in the new with Kwanzaa!

Kwanzaa can be a holiday for all peoples. So, next year, on the day after Christmas, celebrate an old-and-new tradition. Ring out the old year and ring in the new with Kwanzaa!

LANGUAGE SKILLS WORKSHEETS

In the *Teaching Resources* booklets, you will find **Language Skills** worksheets that address specific grammar, usage, and mechanics skills and show how these are applied by the writers of particular literary selections. The topics discussed and the **Language Skills** worksheets that discuss them are indicated on the pages that follow.

Sentence Fragments: See Sentence Completeness, *Teaching Resources A,* page 35. For practice with independent and subordinate clauses, see *Teaching Resources A,* page 23.

For definitions of grammatical terms, see The Grammar Reference Guide on pages 757–760.

Part 2: Sentence Structure
- Sentence Fragments
- Run-on Sentences
- Comparisons

SENTENCE FRAGMENTS

A **sentence** is a group of words that expresses a complete thought. A sentence has a subject and a predicate. A group of words that looks like a sentence but that doesn't make sense by itself is a **sentence fragment**.

1. **Correct a fragment by adding the necessary sentence parts. Usually you will need to add a verb, a subject, or both.**

   Fragment
   During the chase, the claim jumpers following Walt. [verb missing: what about the claim jumpers, or what did they do?]

   Sentence
   During a chase, the claim jumpers following Walt **shoot** the lead dog.

   Fragment
   Is embarrassed by Grandpa's traditional ways. [subject missing: who is embarrassed?]

   Sentence
   Martin is embarrassed by Grandpa's ways.

   Fragment
   Later that night, still angry with his sister. [subject and verb missing]

   Sentence
   Later that night, still angry with his sister, **Joey offers** to let her ride the broken sled.

2. **Correct a fragment by connecting it to an independent clause.**

   Fragment
   When the Fenris Wolf gnashes his teeth together. The god Tyr loses his hand.

   Sentence
   When the Fenris Wolf gnashes his teeth together**, the** god Tyr loses his hand.

RUN-ON SENTENCES

A **run-on sentence** consists of two complete sentences run together as if they were one sentence. Most run-ons are *comma splices*—or two complete thoughts separated only by a comma. Other run-ons are *fused sentences*—two complete thoughts separated by no punctuation.

1. **Correct a run-on sentence by using a period to form two complete sentences.**

   Run-on
   Dobie begins his essay by describing how he and the other children played then he tells about some of his favorite pets.

   Corrected
   Dobie begins his essay by describing how he and the other children played**. Then** he tells about some of his favorite pets.

2. **Correct a run-on by using a comma and a coordinating conjunction (such as *and, but,* or *yet*) to create a compound sentence.**

   Run-on
   Uncle Basil's relatives follow his orders to cremate him they do not know that a fortune in cash is also in the coffin.

   Corrected
   Uncle Basil's relatives follow his orders to cremate him**, but** they do not know that a fortune in cash is also in the coffin.

HANDBOOK FOR REVISION

COMPARISONS

1. Avoid incomplete comparisons.

Incomplete
The weather is colder today. [colder than what?]

Complete
The weather is colder today **than it was yesterday.**

2. Avoid double comparisons.

Nonstandard
At the end of Victor's first day in class, he is **more surer** of himself than at the beginning.

Standard
At the end of Victor's first day in class, he is **more sure** of himself than at the beginning.

Nonstandard
Chimpanzees are some of the **most smartest** of all animals.

Standard
Chimpanzees are some of the **smartest** of all animals.

Part 3: Pronouns
- Pronoun-Antecedent Agreement
- Case Forms of Personal Pronouns

PRONOUN-ANTECEDENT AGREEMENT

The noun or pronoun to which a pronoun refers is called its **antecedent.**

1. A pronoun must agree with its antecedent in number and in gender.

Example
Rikki-tikki fights **Nag** and kills **him.**

2. Use a singular pronoun to refer to an antecedent that is a singular indefinite pronoun. Use a plural pronoun to refer to an antecedent that is a plural indefinite pronoun.

Examples
Each of the daughters has **her** own room.

Many of these writers use striking sound effects in **their** poems.

3. When the antecedent may be either masculine or feminine, rephrase the sentence to avoid an awkward construction, or use both the masculine and the feminine forms.

Standard
All the ancient Olympians have **their** special powers.

Standard
Each of the ancient Olympians has **his** or **her** special powers.

4. Use a plural pronoun to refer to two or more antecedents joined by *and*.

Nonstandard
Serafín Quintero and his **brother** Joaquín were still teenagers when **his** first play was produced.

Standard
Serafín Quintero and his **brother** Joaquín were still teenagers when **their** first play was produced.

5. Use a singular pronoun to refer to two or more singular antecedents joined by *or* or *nor*.

Nonstandard
Neither **Browning** nor **Longfellow** wrote **their** poems in the twentieth century.

Pronoun-Antecedent Agreement: See Pronouns, *Teaching Resources B,* page 182. See also Pronoun Agreement, *Teaching Resources B,* page 153.

Case Forms of Personal Pronouns: See Pronoun Case, *Teaching Resources B,* page 194. See also Possessive Case, *Teaching Resources C,* page 22.

Standard

Neither **Browning** nor **Longfellow** wrote **his** poems in the twentieth century.

Sentences of this type can sound awkward if the antecedents are of different genders. If a sentence sounds awkward, revise it to avoid the problem.

Awkward

Each of the main characters in *A Sunny Morning* wishes to keep **his or her** identity a secret from the other.

Revised

Both of the main characters in *A Sunny Morning* wish to keep **their** identity a secret from the other.

CASE FORMS OF PERSONAL PRONOUNS

Be sure to use the correct case for personal pronouns that are part of compound constructions. To choose the right form, try each pronoun of the compound separately.

Nonstandard

Scout says that **her** and Jem thought that Atticus was feeble. [object form used for subject]

Standard

Scout says that **she** and Jem thought that Atticus was feeble.

Nonstandard

Did Ms. Kumar ask you and **she** to read "Annabel Lee" aloud? [subject form used for direct object]

Standard

Did Ms. Kumar ask you and **her** to read "Annabel Lee" aloud?

Nonstandard

Between you and **I,** did you understand all the words in "Rip Van Winkle"? [subject form used for object of preposition]

Standard

Between you and **me,** did you understand all the words in "Rip Van Winkle"?

Part 4: Verbs

- Missing or Incorrect Verb Endings
- Subject-Verb Agreement
- Sequence of Tenses

MISSING OR INCORRECT VERB ENDINGS

1. **A *regular verb* forms the past and past participle by adding *-d* or *-ed* to the infinitive form. Don't make the mistake of leaving off or doubling the *-d* or *-ed* ending.**

Nonstandard

In "The Erne from the Coast," Harry was **suppose** to care for the sick lamb.

Standard

In "The Erne from the Coast," Harry was **supposed** to care for the sick lamb.

Nonstandard

The captain **drownded** because he did not heed the warning of the old sailor.

Standard

The captain **drowned** because he did not heed the warning of the old sailor.

2. An *irregular verb* forms the past and past participle in some other way than by adding *-d* or *-ed* to the infinitive form. Irregular verbs form their past and past participle by

- changing a vowel
- changing consonants
- adding *-en*
- making no change at all

Examples

Infinitive	Past	Past Participle
stand	stood	(have) stood
throw	threw	(have) thrown
give	gave	(have) given
hurt	hurt	(have) hurt

When you proofread your writing, check your sentences to determine which form—past or past participle—is called for. Remember that many nonstandard verb forms sound quite natural. Keep a dictionary handy to check any verb forms you're not sure about.

Nonstandard
Colin and his brother thought that Bandit **had went** away for good.

Standard
Colin and his brother thought that Bandit **had gone** away for good.

Nonstandard
Billy **seen** the sign and a vase of yellow flowers in the window.

Standard
Billy **saw** the sign and a vase of yellow flowers in the window.

Nonstandard
In James Thurber's story, the loud crash of the bed falling **throwed** the family into confusion.

Standard
In James Thurber's story, the loud crash of the bed falling **threw** the family into confusion.

SUBJECT-VERB AGREEMENT

1. **A verb must agree with its subject in number—either singular or plural.**

   Nonstandard
   As we see in "The Circuit," migrant worker **families moves** often.

   Standard
   As we see in "The Circuit," migrant worker **families move** often.

2. **When a sentence contains a verb phrase, the first helping verb in the verb phrase agrees with the subject.**

   Nonstandard
   The **students has** rehearsed that scene several times already.

   Standard
   The **students have** rehearsed that scene several times already.

3. **The number of a subject is not changed by a phrase or clause coming between the subject and the verb.**

   Nonstandard
   The **characters** in that play **is** uninteresting.

   Standard
   The **characters** in that play **are** uninteresting.

4. **Use a singular verb to agree with the following singular indefinite pronouns:** *anybody, anyone, each, either, everybody, everyone, neither, nobody, no one, one, somebody,* **and** *someone.*

   Nonstandard
   Everyone in "The Night the Bed Fell" **draw** mistaken conclusions.

   Standard
   Everyone in "The Night the Bed Fell" **draws** mistaken conclusions.

   Nonstandard
   Val likes those stories because **each** of them **have** a surprise ending.

Standard
Val likes those stories because **each** of them **has** a surprise ending.

5. **Use a plural verb to agree with the following plural indefinite pronouns:** *both, few, many,* **and** *several.*

   Nonstandard
   Many of Ogden Nash's poems **has** comic rhymes and unusual spellings.

   Standard
   Many of Ogden Nash's poems **have** comic rhymes and unusual spellings.

   Nonstandard
   Several of the students in our class **has** seen movies based on Sherlock Holmes's adventures.

   Standard
   Several of the students in our class **have** seen movies based on Sherlock Holmes's adventures.

6. **The following indefinite pronouns are singular when they refer to singular words and plural when they refer to plural words:** *all, any, most, none,* **and** *some.*

   Nonstandard
   Some of the play **are** difficult to read.

   Standard
   Some of the play **is** difficult to read.

   Nonstandard
   Some of the scenes in the play **is** funny.

   Standard
   Some of the scenes in the play **are** funny.

7. **Subjects joined by** *and* **usually take a plural verb.**

   Nonstandard
   Martin and his **friends gathers** around Grandpa.

   Standard
   Martin and his **friends gather** around Grandpa.

When the elements of a compound subject joined by *and* may be considered a single item or refer to the same thing, the compound subject takes a singular verb.

Example
A famous **poet** and **playwright is** coming to speak at our school. [One person is meant.]

8. **Singular subjects joined by** *or* **or** *nor* **take a singular verb.**

   Nonstandard
   Neither **Merle Hodge** nor **Roald Dahl are** an American writer.

   Standard
   Neither **Merle Hodge** nor **Roald Dahl is** an American writer.

9. **When a singular subject and a plural subject are joined by** *or* **or** *nor,* **the verb agrees with the subject nearer the verb.**

   Nonstandard
   In Gwendolyn Brooks's story "Home," neither **Mama** nor the other family **members thinks** that Papa will succeed in getting an extension from the Home Owners' Loan.

   Standard
   In Gwendolyn Brooks's story "Home," neither **Mama** nor the other family **members think** that Papa will succeed in getting an extension from the Home Owners' Loan.

10. **When the subject follows the verb, as in questions and in sentences beginning with** *here* **and** *there,* **identify the subject and make sure that the verb agrees with it.**

    Nonstandard
    Here **are** a **list** of some poems by Henry Wadsworth Longfellow.

    Standard
    Here **is** a **list** of some poems by Henry Wadsworth Longfellow.

    Nonstandard
    When **does** play **rehearsals** begin?

Standard
When **do** play **rehearsals** begin?

11. **A collective noun takes a singular verb when the noun refers to the group as a unit. A collective noun takes a plural verb when the noun refers to the individual parts or members of the group.**

    Examples
    In "The Erne from the Coast," the **herd** of sheep **is** terrified by the eagle.

    The **class were** divided in their opinions of that story.

12. **A verb should always agree with its subject, not with its predicate nominative.**

    Nonstandard
    Hercules' **labors was** a great challenge.

    Standard
    Hercules' **labors were** a great challenge.

13. **The contractions *don't* and *doesn't* must agree with their subjects.**

    Examples
    According to Jane Goodall, most wild **animals don't** use objects as tools.

    In "The Tiger's Heart," **Pepe doesn't** want the villagers to know that he killed the jaguar with a machete.

14. **Words stating amounts are usually singular.**

    Example
    Seventy-five **cents is** Luke Baldwin's weekly salary for rounding up Mr. Kemp's cows.

15. **The title of a book, or the name of an organization or a country, even when plural in form, usually takes a singular verb.**

    Examples
    Sound-Shadows of the New World **is** an autobiographical narrative by Ved Mehta.

    The **Seychelles is** an island nation in the Indian Ocean.

16. **A few nouns, though plural in form, take a singular verb.**

    Examples
    Anita thinks that **mathematics is** an easy subject.

SEQUENCE OF TENSES

1. **Changing verb tense in mid-sentence or from sentence to sentence without good reason creates awkwardness and confusion. Be sure that the verb tenses in a single sentence or in a group of related sentences are consistent.**

    Awkward
    As darkness **fell,** the narrator **lights** a fire to make the room more cheerful.

    Better
    As darkness **fell,** the narrator **lit** a fire to make the room more cheerful.

2. **The past perfect tense with *had* is used to express an action that was completed before another action in the past.**

    Nonstandard
    The speaker's grandmother **told** him about things she **saw** during her girlhood in Mexico.

    Standard
    The speaker's grandmother **told** him about things she **had seen** during her girlhood in Mexico.

Sequence of Tenses: See Past Perfect Tense, *Teaching Resources B,* page 48.

Handbook for Revision

Verbs

Misplaced Modifiers: See Careful Placement of Modifiers, *Teaching Resources C,* page 143.

Compound Structure: See Compound Sentences, *Teaching Resources A,* page 143.

Items in a Series: See Punctuating Items in a Series, *Teaching Resources D,* page 179.

Part 5: Word Order
- Misplaced Modifiers
- Dangling Modifiers

MISPLACED MODIFIERS

Avoid a *misplaced modifier,* which is a modifying phrase or clause that is placed too far from the word it sensibly modifies.

Misplaced
Aunt Polly gave Tom the water treatment **concerned about her nephew.**

Clear
Concerned about her nephew, Aunt Polly gave Tom the water treatment.

Misplaced
Pepe killed the jaguar with a machete, **whose gun misfired.**

Clear
Pepe, **whose gun misfired,** killed the jaguar with a machete.

DANGLING MODIFIERS

Avoid *dangling modifiers,* which are phrases or clauses that do not sensibly modify any word or group of words in the sentence.

Dangling
Working carefully and steadily, a garden was made.

Clear
Working carefully and steadily, the boys made a garden.

Part 6: Comma Usage
- Compound Structure
- Items in a Series
- Two or More Adjectives
- Nonessential Elements
- Introductory Elements
- Interrupters

COMPOUND STRUCTURE

Use a comma before a coordinating conjunction (*and, but, or, nor, for, so,* and *yet*) that joins two independent clauses. If the clauses are very short, you may omit the comma.

Examples
Grandpa relaxed**, and** between sips of soup he told us of his journey.
   —Sneve, "The Medicine Bag" (p. 35)

The jaguar sprang **and** Pepe quickly swerved aside.

But Luke was frightened**, for** he knew what his uncle was like.
   —Callaghan, "Luke Baldwin's Vow" (p. 80)

I was at the trolley stop**, but** it was so pleasant that I decided to continue walking and explore the route.
   —Mehta, from *Sound-Shadows of the New World* (p. 409)

Ever since I was ten I'd been allowed to hunt with Father**, so** I was good at reading signs.
   —Annixter, "Last Cover" (p. 156)

ITEMS IN A SERIES

Use commas to separate words, phrases, and clauses in a series.

Examples
Mama, Maud Martha, and Helen rocked slowly in their rocking chairs . . . . [series of nouns]
   —Brooks, "Home" (p. 127)

Scrooge was **his sole executor, his sole administrator, his sole assign, his sole residuary legatee, his sole friend, his sole mourner.** [series of phrases]
—Dickens, "A Christmas Carol" (p. 276)

The air was crystal, the sky was aquamarine, and the far horizon of palms and oaks lay against the sky. [series of clauses]
—Rawlings, "Rattlesnake Hunt" (p. 400)

TWO OR MORE ADJECTIVES

Use a comma to separate two or more adjectives preceding a noun. However, do not use a comma before the final adjective in a series if the adjective is thought of as being part of a noun. Determine if the adjective and noun form a unit by inserting the word *and* between the adjectives. If *and* fits sensibly, use a comma.

Examples
He was a **stocky, robust** kid with a shock of white hair . . . . [stocky *and* robust; comma needed]
—Deal, "Antaeus" (p. 187)

Just outside town, they hopped a ride on the back of a produce truck, and **three dusty** miles later they jumped off when the truck slowed at a railroad crossing. [*and* sounds awkward]
—Soto, *Pacific Crossing* (p. 522)

NONESSENTIAL ELEMENTS

A *nonessential* (or *nonrestrictive*) clause or participial phrase contains information that is not necessary to the meaning of the sentence. Use commas to set off nonessential clauses and nonessential participial phrases. An *essential* (or *restrictive*) clause or participial phrase is not set off by commas, because it contains information that is necessary to the meaning of the sentence.

Nonessential Clause
Those arms**, that had seemed to uphold him,** relaxed. [The clause can be omitted without changing the main idea.]
—Peabody, "Icarus and Daedalus" (p. 616)

Essential Clause
The house of our own construction **that we enjoyed most** was in a tree. [The clause is necessary to identify which house is meant.]
—Dobie, "When I Was a Boy on the Ranch" (p. 420)

Nonessential Phrase
That story**, written by Harper Lee,** comes from the novel *To Kill a Mockingbird*.

Essential Phrase
The story **written by Harper Lee** comes from her novel *To Kill a Mockingbird*.

INTRODUCTORY ELEMENTS

Use a comma after *yes*, *no*, or any exclamation at the beginning of a sentence. Also use a comma after an introductory participial phrase, after two or more introductory prepositional phrases, and after an introductory adverb clause.

Examples
"**Yeah,** you're right," Tony agreed.
—Soto, *Pacific Crossing* (p. 508)

Climbing among the upper gardens, Prometheus stopped at last beside an ancient, twisted ash tree. [introductory participial phrase]
—Ingalls, "Prometheus the Fire-Bringer" (p. 585)

In a long ramble of the kind on a fine autumnal day, Rip had unconsciously scrambled to one of the highest parts of the Catskill Mountains. [introductory prepositional phrases]
—Irving, "Rip Van Winkle" (p. 251)

When he woke, the car was pulling into a driveway. [introductory adverb clause]
—Soto, *Pacific Crossing* (p. 511)

INTERRUPTERS

1. **Nonessential appositives and appositive phrases are usually set off by commas.**

   Mr. Lema**, the sixth-grade teacher,** greeted me and assigned me a desk.
   —Jiménez, "The Circuit" (p. 75)

Interrupters: See Appositives, *Teaching Resources C,* page 131.

Sentence Variety: See *Teaching Resources E,* page 138. See also Kinds of Sentence Structure, *Teaching Resources A,* page 197.

Leah**, his mother,** wiped the tears from her eyes when she heard the news.
—Singer, "Zlateh the Goat" (p. 270)

2. **Words used in direct address are set off by commas.**

Examples

"**Nephew,** keep Christmas in your own way, and let me keep it in mine."
—Dickens, "A Christmas Carol" (p. 277)

"What's the matter with you**, boy,** can't you talk?" said Mr. Tate, grinning at Jem.
—Lee, "One-Shot Finch" (p. 108)

"What's the matter**, Schatz**?"
—Hemingway, "A Day's Wait" (p. 242)

3. **Use commas to set off parenthetical expressions.**

Examples

Father**, however,** loved to fish, even if he didn't catch a single fish in three weeks, which on this trip he didn't.
—McKenney, "Guinea Pig" (p. 41)

It happened**, then,** that my father had decided to sleep in the attic one night, to be away where he could think.
—Thurber, "The Night the Bed Fell" (p. 133)

We didn't really know what he was talking about, so we were more puzzled than angry; otherwise**, I guess,** we'd have chased him off the roof and wouldn't let him be part of our gang.
—Deal, "Antaeus" (p. 189)

Part 7: Style

- Sentence Variety
- Stringy Sentences
- Overwriting
- Creative Use of Synonyms
- Vivid Words
- Clichés
- Levels of Language

SENTENCE VARIETY

1. **Create sentence variety in length and rhythm by using different kinds of clauses, as well as simple sentences.**

Little Variation

In "The Medicine Bag" by Virginia Driving Hawk Sneve, Grandpa comes to visit Martin's family. Martin is embarrassed by Grandpa. He does not want his friends to meet him. Martin's friends learn that Grandpa is in the house. They decide to visit. They have not been invited. They are very impressed by Grandpa.

More Variation

In "The Medicine Bag" by Virginia Driving Hawk Sneve, Martin is embarrassed when Grandpa comes to visit the family. He does not want his friends to meet Grandpa. However, after Martin's friends learn that Grandpa is in the house, they decide to visit, even though they have not been invited. They are very impressed by Grandpa.

2. **Expand short, choppy sentences by adding details.**

Choppy

Jack London was born in 1876. His family was very poor. He did not receive much education. He worked as a longshoreman and as a seaman. Then he studied for a while. Then he left California and went to hunt for gold in the Klondike.

More Detailed

Jack London was born in San Francisco in 1876. Since his family was desperately poor, he received little education. When he was in his teens, he worked as a longshoreman, as an oyster pirate, and as a seaman. When he was nineteen, he studied for a year to finish high school. In 1897, he abandoned his studies, however, and set out for the Klondike in search of gold.

3. **Vary sentence openers by using appositives, single-word modifiers, phrase modifiers, clause modifiers, and transitional words.**

   ### Little Variation
   Scout and Jem think that Atticus is dull. He doesn't seem to "do" anything. The children's opinion of their father changes, though. The dog Tim Johnson contracts rabies. It must be shot. Sheriff Tate asks Atticus to shoot it. There is one quick motion. Atticus lifts the rifle to his shoulder. He brings the dog down with a single shot. The children learn that the whole town knows their father to be an expert marksman.

   ### More Variation
   Because Atticus doesn't seem to "do" anything, Scout and Jem think he is dull. **When the dog Tim Johnson contracts rabies,** though, the children's opinion of their father changes. **Deciding that the dog must be shot,** Sheriff Tate asks Atticus to do the job. **With one quick motion,** Atticus lifts the rifle to his shoulder **and** brings the dog down with a single shot. **Later,** the children learn that the whole town knows their father to be an expert marksman.

STRINGY SENTENCES

Simplify stringy sentences by writing as concisely as you can. Cut down your use of prepositional phrases. Reduce clauses to phrases, if possible. If you can, reduce clauses and phrases to single words.

Stringy
Ruth and her sister Eileen visit a fishing camp in Michigan and they begin rocking their rowboat, with the result that Ruth falls into the water, and Eileen tries to rescue her but hits her twice with the oar instead and she nearly drowns.

Better
On a visit to a fishing camp in Michigan, Ruth and her sister Eileen begin rocking their rowboat. Ruth falls into the water. When Eileen tries to rescue her, she hits her twice with the oar instead, and Ruth nearly drowns.

OVERWRITING

1. **Eliminate unnecessary words.**

   ### Wordy
   The **climax and high point** of "A Christmas Carol" is Scrooge's vision of the tombstone.

   ### Better
   The **climax** of "A Christmas Carol" is Scrooge's vision of the tombstone.

   ### Wordy
   Kipling describes Rikki-tikki as a **brave and courageous** mongoose.

   ### Better
   Kipling describes Rikki-tikki as a **brave** mongoose.

2. **Avoid pretentious, complicated words where plain, simple ones will do.**

   ### Pretentious
   Robert P. Tristram Coffin **utilizes** a simile in line 15 of "The Spider."

   ### Simpler
   Robert P. Tristram Coffin **uses** a simile in line 15 of "The Spider."

CREATIVE USE OF SYNONYMS

Avoid awkward repetition by using synonyms creatively.

Awkward
As Pepe studies the **tiger,** he sees that the **tiger's** right front foot is swollen.

Better
As Pepe studies the **tiger,** he sees that the **big cat's** right front foot is swollen.

Stringy Sentences: For practice in changing clauses to phrases, see *Teaching Resources C,* page 94.

Vivid Words: See Vivid, Precise Nouns, *Teaching Resources C*, page 46. See also Using Vivid Verbs, *Teaching Resources B*, page 142.

Handbook for Revision

VIVID WORDS

1. Whenever possible, replace vague words with specific ones.

Vague
I was roaming around, not paying attention to anything, when I became aware of some noises up ahead.

Specific
I was blundering about in the Sonoran hills, daydreaming as usual, when I gradually became aware of a snorting, snuffling sound ahead, accompanied by the shuffle of many active hoofs.

—Abbey, "Desert Creatures" (p. 149)

2. Replace abstract words with vivid, concrete words that appeal to the senses.

Abstract
Atami's main street had heavy traffic and many tall, modern buildings. Pedestrians had to exercise care to avoid the bicycles.

Concrete/Sensory
Today Atami's main street was choked with cars and gleaming with tall glass buildings. Bicycles came rattling down the narrow streets and pushed pedestrians against the walls.

—Soto, *Pacific Crossing* (p. 516)

CLICHÉS

A *cliché* is a tired expression. Replace clichés in your writing with fresh, vivid expressions.

Cliché
Tom was **red as a beet**.

Vivid
Tom's cheeks burned. He gathered himself up and sneaked off, crushed and crestfallen.

—Twain, "The Cat and the Pain Killer" (p. 52)

LEVELS OF LANGUAGE

Depending on your purpose, audience, and form of writing, you should use an appropriate level of language. For example, *formal English* is appropriate for serious essays, reports, and speeches on solemn occasions. *Informal English* is suitable for personal letters, journal entries, and many articles. The following chart gives an outline of formal and informal levels of language.

	Formal	Informal
WORDS	longer, rare, specialized	shorter, colloquial
SPELLING	in full	contractions
GRAMMAR	complex, complete	compound, fragmentary

Formal English usually creates a serious tone. Informal English tends to have a friendlier, more personal tone.

Formal
The great error in Rip's character was an insuperable dislike of all kinds of profitable labor.

—Irving, "Rip Van Winkle" (p. 249)

Informal
"That's what I said, Jem Finch. Guess you'll change *your* tune now. The very idea, didn't you know his nickname was Ol' One-Shot when he was a boy? Why, down at the Landing when he was coming up, if he shot fifteen times and hit fourteen doves he'd complain about wasting ammunition."

—Lee, "One-Shot Finch" (p. 109)

Part 8: Glossary of Usage

a, an Use the indefinite article *a* before words beginning with a consonant sound. Use the indefinite article *an* before words beginning with a vowel sound.

Examples
Grandpa wants to give Martin *a* medicine bag.

Trinidad is *an* island off the coast of South America.

It took *an* hour to find *a* hotel.

accept, except *Accept* is a verb meaning "to receive." *Except* may be either a verb or a preposition. As a verb, *except* means "to leave out." As a preposition, *except* means "excluding."

Examples
In Ruskin Bond's story, Ranji *accepts* the challenge of Suraj to fight.

In James Thurber's story, the crash of the bed falling awakens everybody *except* the narrator. [preposition]

None of the ship's crew was *excepted* from the storm's fury. [verb]

adapt, adopt *Adapt* means "to change or adjust something in order to make it fit or to make it suitable." *Adopt* means "to take something and make it one's own."

Examples
Many films have been *adapted* from Dickens' story "A Christmas Carol."

When young Ved Mehta set out for Little Rock, he *adopted* an independent attitude and threw away his cane.

affect, effect *Affect* is a verb meaning "to influence." As a verb, *effect* means "to bring about" or "to accomplish." As a noun, *effect* means "the result of an action."

Examples
How did reading the classical myth "Arachne" *affect* your opinion of the goddess Minerva?

Tom claimed that the pain killer *effected* some remarkable changes in the cat Peter's behavior. [verb]

At the end of "The Circuit," the need for his family to move again must have had a depressing *effect* on the narrator. [noun]

all, all of The word *of* can usually be omitted, except before some pronouns.

Examples
All my friends liked reading "The King of Mazy May." [preferable to *all of*]

All of us wanted to learn more about Sherlock Holmes. [*of* is necessary]

allusion, illusion An *allusion* is an indirect reference to something. An *illusion* is a mistaken idea or a misleading appearance.

Examples
The title of Morley Callaghan's story is an *allusion* to the promise Luke makes to himself.

Did Scrooge really see the ghosts, or were they merely *illusions*?

among, between Use *between* when you are referring to two things at a time, or to more than two when one item is being compared individually with each of the others.

Examples
Denzel couldn't decide *between* "The Highwayman" and "The Pied Piper of Hamelin" as the subject for his report.

In her report, Farah discussed differences *between* lyric poetry, narrative poetry, and dramatic poetry.

Use *among* when you are referring to more than two items.

Example

Among the myths we have read, which one was your favorite?

Notices about the book sale were distributed *among* the class.

amount, number Use *amount* to refer to a singular word. Use *number* to refer to a plural word.

Examples

The speaker in Edna St. Vincent Millay's poem envies the *amount* of courage that her mother had.

Greek mythology contains a large *number* of stories about the hero Hercules.

anxious, eager *Anxious* means "worried" or "uneasy." *Eager* means "feeling keen desire or strong interest."

Examples

In "Luke Baldwin's Vow," Luke becomes *anxious* about his uncle's decision to get rid of the dog.

Lisa is *eager* to read more stories by Gary Soto.

as, like *Like* is a preposition. In formal situations, do not use *like* for the conjunction *as* to introduce a subordinate clause.

Examples

Writers *like* Gwendolyn Brooks have explored the experiences of African Americans.

Did the story "You Can't Take It with You" end *as* you expected it would?

assure, ensure *Assure* means "to give confidence to" or "promise." *Ensure* means "to make sure" or "to guarantee."

Examples

In "A Day's Wait," the father *assures* his son that the fever is not fatal.

To *ensure* that the villagers continue to respect him, Pepe shoots the tiger after he has killed the animal with his machete.

awhile, a while *Awhile* is an adverb meaning "for a short time." *A while* is made up of an article and a noun and means "a period or space of time." *Awhile* is never preceded by a preposition such as *for*.

Examples

Carlos and Gloria studied *awhile* in the library.

Jack London worked for *a while* as a longshoreman.

bad, badly *Bad* is an adjective. *Badly* is an adverb. In standard English, only the adjective form should follow a sense verb, such as *feel, see, hear, taste, look*, or other linking verb.

Examples

In "Sled" by Thomas E. Adams, Joey played a *bad* trick on his sister.

Do you think that the owner of the building in Borden Deal's "Antaeus" treated the boys *badly*?

At first, Martin feels *bad* about Grandpa's visit.

because In formal situations, do not use the construction *reason . . . because*. Instead, use *reason . . . that*.

Informal

The reason Bandit disappeared was *because* he was looking for a mate.

Formal

The reason Bandit disappeared was *that* he was looking for a mate.

beside, besides *Beside* is a preposition meaning "by the side of" or "next to." *Besides* may be used as either a preposition or an adverb. As a preposition, *besides* means "in addition to" or "also." As an adverb, *besides* means "moreover" or "furthermore."

Examples

Who sat *beside* you on the school bus this morning?

Besides "Zlateh the Goat," which other stories featured important animal characters? [preposition]

James Thurber was a brilliant essayist; he was an outstanding cartoonist, *besides*. [adverb]

between See **among, between.**

bring, take *Bring* means "to come carrying something." *Take* means "to go carrying something."

Examples

Please *bring* copies of "A Christmas Carol" to class tomorrow.

Please *take* these reports to Mr. Swenson in Room 118.

bust, busted Do not use these words as verbs. Use a form of *break* or *burst*.

Examples

The softball sailed out of the lot and *broke* a neighbor's window.

After the temperature fell below freezing, the pipes *burst*.

compare to, compare with Use *compare to* when you want to stress either the similarities or the differences between two things. Use *compare with* when you wish to stress both similarities and differences.

Examples

The metaphor in Carl Sandburg's poem *compares* the fog *to* a cat.

Karl's report *compared* the myth of Phaethon *with* the story of Icarus and Daedalus.

connote, denote *Connote* means "to suggest or imply." *Denote* means "to indicate or signify explicitly."

Examples

To many people, the title "A Christmas Carol" *connotes* pleasant images of an old-fashioned Christmas.

In the dialect of the British sheep country, the expression "aw reet" *denotes* "all right."

convince, persuade *Convince* means "to win someone over through argument." *Convince* is usually followed by *that* and a subordinate clause. *Persuade* means to move someone to act in a certain way. *Persuade* is often followed by *to*.

Examples

At the end of "The Bracelet," the narrator's mother *convinces* her *that* the loss of Laurie's gift is not so serious after all.

Sheriff Heck Tate *persuades* Atticus *to* shoot the rabid dog.

could of Do not write *of* with the helping verb *could*. Write *could have*. Also avoid *had of, ought to of, should of, would of, might of,* and *must of*.

Example

The narrator realizes that no one except T. J. *could have* [not *of*] organized the effort to create the garden.

different from, different than Use *different from*, not *different than*.

Example

Nonfiction is *different from* fiction because nonfiction deals with events from real life.

doesn't, don't *Doesn't* is the contraction of *does not*. *Don't* is the contraction of *do not*. Use *doesn't*, not *don't*, with *he, she, it, this, that,* and singular nouns.

Examples

Holmes *doesn't* hesitate to play a practical joke on Lord Cantlemere.

At the end of the story, the villagers *don't* recognize Rip Van Winkle.

Glossary of Usage

due to the fact that Replace this wordy phrase with *because*.

Wordy
Due to the fact that the Fenris Wolf has grown so fierce, the gods of Asgard must find a way to restrain him.

Better
Because the Fenris Wolf has grown so fierce, the gods of Asgard must find a way to restrain him.

eager See **anxious, eager.**

effect See **affect, effect.**

emigrate, immigrate *Emigrate* means "to leave a country or a region to settle elsewhere." *Immigrate* means "to come into a country or region to settle there." *Emigrate* is used with *from; immigrate* is used with *to*.

Examples
The writer Isaac Bashevis Singer *emigrated from* his native Poland in 1935 and settled in New York City.

Monica Sone's parents, who *immigrated to* America, were known as Issei.

ensure See **assure, ensure.**

everyday, every day *Everyday* is an adjective meaning "daily" or "common." *Every day* is an adverbial phrase meaning "each day."

Examples
Myths and legends do not usually tell about *everyday* events.

Every day of the children's life on the ranch brought them a new adventure.

everyone, every one *Everyone* is an indefinite pronoun. *Every one* consists of an adjective and a pronoun and means "every person or thing of those named."

Examples
Everyone in class wants to see the new movie based on Hercules' adventures.

Hector wants to read *every one* of Edgar Allan Poe's stories.

except See **accept, except.**

farther, further Although *farther* and *further* are used interchangeably by some writers, in current usage there is a distinction in meaning. *Farther* refers to geographical distance. *Further* means "in addition to" or "to a greater degree."

Examples
The *farther* Walt traveled, the more nervous he became about the poor lead dog.

At the end of his essay, Edward Abbey describes the javelina *further* by explaining how the animal eats its favorite vegetable, the barrel cactus.

fewer, less Use *fewer*, which tells "how many," to modify a plural noun. Use *less*, which tells "how much," to modify a singular noun.

Examples
With each accounting, the rubles that the mistress says she will pay Julia become *fewer* and *fewer*.

At first, Sumter thinks that Colin should spend *less* time drawing.

good, well *Good* is an adjective. *Well* may be used as an adjective or an adverb. The expressions *feel good* and *feel well* mean different things. *Feel good* means "to feel happy or pleased." *Feel well* means "to feel healthy."

Examples
At the end of "The Medicine Bag," Martin feels *good* about Grandpa.

In "Stolen Day," the narrator pretends that he does not feel *well*.

Avoid using *good* to modify an action verb. Instead, use *well* as an adverb meaning "capably" or "satisfactorily."

Nonstandard
Roald Dahl uses suspense *good* in "The Landlady."

Standard
Roald Dahl uses suspense *well* in "The Landlady."

had of See **could of.**

had ought, hadn't ought Do not use *had* or *hadn't* with *ought*.

Examples
We *ought* [not *had ought*] to have returned the books to the library yesterday.

We *ought not* [not *hadn't ought*] leave the lunch trays on the table.

hardly, scarcely The words *hardly* and *scarcely* convey negative meanings. They should never be used with another negative word.

Example
Ruth *can* [not *can't*] *hardly* pull the middy off, and she almost drowns.

At the beginning of "Seventh Grade," Victor *has* [not *hasn't*] *scarcely* enough nerve to talk to Teresa.

he, she, they Do not use an unnecessary pronoun after the subject of a clause or a sentence. This error is called the *double subject*.

Nonstandard
In Harper Lee's story, Atticus Finch *he* turns out to be a crack shot.

Standard
In Harper Lee's story, Atticus Finch turns out to be a crack shot.

historic, historical *Historic* means "crucial" or "especially important." *Historical* means "concerned or connected with history."

Examples
Jane Goodall tells about a *historic* discovery that involves chimpanzees and toolmaking.

The story "Rip Van Winkle" includes references to *historical* characters and events.

how come In informal situations, *how come* is often used instead of *why*. In formal situations, *why* should always be used.

Informal
I don't know *how come* we left so early.

Formal
I don't know *why* we left so early.

illusion See **allusion, illusion.**

imply, infer *Imply* means "to suggest something indirectly." *Infer* means "to interpret" or "to get a certain meaning from a remark or an action."

Examples
Many writers *imply* rather than directly state the theme of a literary work.

At the end of Roald Dahl's story, we *infer* that Billy will die of poison.

in, into, in to *In* means "within." *Into* means "from the outside to the inside." *In to* refers to motion with a purpose.

Examples
Rudyard Kipling is an English writer who was born *in* India.

Aaron and Zlateh crawled *into* the haystack, where it was warm.

During earth science class, Mr. Rubinstein came *in to* make an announcement.

its, it's *Its* is a possessive pronoun. *It's* is the contraction for *it is* or *it has*.

Examples
The story "Guinea Pig" is notable for *its* use of humor and exaggeration.

Glossary of Usage

It's clear from his essay that the young Ved Mehta enjoyed confronting challenges.

kind(s), sort(s), type(s) With the singular form of each of these nouns, use *this* or *that*. With the plural form, use *these* or *those*.

Examples

Do you like *this type* of essay?

Those kinds of myths are about the creation of the world.

lay, lie The verb *lay* means "to put (something) in a place." *Lay* usually takes an object. The past tense of *lay* is *laid*. The verb *lie* means "to rest" or "to stay, to recline, or to remain in a certain state or position." *Lie* never takes an object. The past tense of *lie* is *lay*.

Examples

Please *lay* those magazines on the table.

After the narrator *lies* down to sleep, his bed collapses.

learn, teach *Learn* means "to obtain knowledge" or "find out." *Teach* means "to show how" or "to give instruction."

Examples

Maria decided to *learn* some Czech phrases before visiting her uncle in Prague.

She *taught* her cousins how to count to a hundred in English.

leave, let *Leave* means "to go away." *Let* means "to permit" or "to allow." Avoid using *leave* for *let*.

Nonstandard
Please *leave* us stay up to watch the fireworks!

Standard
Please *let* us stay up to watch the fireworks!

Standard
The train was supposed to *leave* at 7:30 P.M.

less See **fewer, less.**

might of, must of See **could of.**

number See **amount, number.**

on, onto, on to *On* refers to position and means "upon," "in contact with," or "supported by." *Onto* implies motion and means "to a position on." Do not confuse *onto* with *on to*.

Examples

In "The Listeners," the Traveler is *on* horseback.

Please don't come *onto* the stage before the cue for your entrance.

In "The Wind and the Mountains," Nina Otero tells first about a shepherd gathering his flock together; she then goes *on* *to* describe the storm's fury during the night.

or, nor Use *or* with *either*. Use *nor* with *neither*.

Examples

Eddie's report will focus *either* on Gary Soto *or* on Julia Alvarez.

Neither Rudyard Kipling *nor* Robert Graves was an American writer.

ought to of See **could of.**

principal, principle *Principal* is an adjective meaning "first" or "main." It can also be a noun meaning the head of a school. *Principle* is a noun meaning "rule of conduct" or "a fact or general truth."

Examples

The *principal* characters in Gary Soto's novel are Lincoln and Mitsuo.

Harriet Tubman fought hard for the *principles* of freedom and equality.

real In informal situations, *real* is often used as an adverb meaning "very" or "extremely." In formal situations, *very* or *extremely* is preferred.

Informal
Pepe came *real* close to being killed by the tiger.

Formal
Pepe came *very* close to being killed by the tiger.

relation, relationship *Relation* refers to a person connected to another by kinship. *Relation* also means as association or connection. *Relationship* refers to a connection between thoughts or meanings. The word *relationship* also refers to an involvement between individuals.

> **Examples**
> Do your friends and *relations* like detective stories?
>
> Studies have shown that there is a strong *relation* between diet and heart disease.
>
> What is the *relationship* between setting and mood in "Rip Van Winkle"?
>
> Because Rolando was raised by his aunt and uncle, he has a close *relationship* with his cousins.

respectfully, respectively *Respectfully* means "with respect" or "full of respect." *Respectively* means "each in the order indicated."

> **Examples**
> As Monica Sone shows, Japanese children are taught to treat their parents and elders very *respectfully*.
>
> Robert Browning and Emily Dickinson are the authors of "The Pied Piper of Hamelin" and "I'm Nobody," *respectively*.

rise, raise *Rise* means "to go up" or "to get up." *Rise* never takes an object. The past tense of *rise* is *rose*. *Raise* means "to cause (something) to rise" or "to lift up." *Raise* usually takes an object. The past tense of *raise* is *raised*.

> **Examples**
> Papa, Roberto, and the narrator *rose* early to get to the vineyard.
>
> The cobra Nag *raises* his head and speaks scornfully to Rikki-tikki.

scarcely, hardly See **hardly, scarcely.**

should of See **could of.**

sit, set *Sit* means "to rest in an upright, seated position." *Sit* seldom takes an object. The past tense of *sit* is *sat*. *Set* means "to put (something) in a place." *Set* usually takes an object. The past tense of *set* is *set*.

> **Examples**
> Mama, Maud Martha, and Helen *sat* in their rocking chairs on the porch.
>
> Harry *set* the dead erne at his father's feet.

some, somewhat In writing, do not use *some* for *somewhat* as an adverb.

> **Nonstandard**
> Lord Cantlemere was surprised *some* to find the Mazarin Stone in the pocket of his own overcoat.
>
> **Standard**
> Lord Cantlemere was surprised *somewhat* to find the Mazarin Stone in the pocket of his own overcoat.

than, then *Than* is a conjunction used in comparisons. *Then* is an adverb telling *when*.

> **Examples**
> Hercules was stronger *than* any of the other Greek heroes.
>
> First, Bruton tried the obstacle course; *then*, it was Branch's turn.

that See **who, which, that.**

their, there, they're *Their* is the possessive form of *they*. *There* means "in that place." *There* is often used at the opening of a sentence in which the subject follows the verb. *They're* is a contraction of *they are*.

> **Examples**
> They carried *their* costumes to the party.
>
> You'll find your name tag over *there*.
>
> *There* were more than fifty students on line.
>
> *They're* checking the facts in an almanac.

Glossary of Usage

this here, that there The words *here* and *there* are unnecessary after *this* and *that*.

Example
This [not *this here*] story is a myth, but *that* [not *that there*] tale is a fable.

try and In informal situations, *try and* is often used instead of *try to*. In formal situations, *try to* should be used.

Informal
Try and stress the rhythm when you read this poem aloud.

Formal
Try to stress the rhythm when you read this poem aloud.

use to, used to Be sure to add the *d* to *use*.

Example
Many people *used to* [not *use to*] read Charles Dickens' stories around the family fireside.

well See **good, well**.

when, where Do not use *when* or *where* to begin a definition.

Nonstandard
Figurative language is *when* you use language that is not meant to be interpreted literally.

Standard
Figurative language is language that is not meant to be interpreted literally.

Nonstandard
A fable is *where* a brief story gives a moral.

Standard
A fable is a brief story with a moral.

where Do not use *where* for *that*.

Nonstandard
Angie read *where* Morely Callaghan was born in Toronto, Canada.

Standard
Angie read *that* Morley Callaghan was born in Toronto, Canada.

who, which, that *Who* refers to persons only. *Which* refers to things only. *That* may refer to either persons or things.

Examples
The poet *who* wrote "A Parrot" was May Sarton.

The ranch where J. Frank Dobie grew up, *which* is located in Texas, offered the children in his family many interesting activities.

A poet *that* Jill liked a lot was Lucille Clifton.

One story *that* uses irony skillfully is "You Can't Take It with You."

who, whom *Who* is used as the subject of a verb or as a predicate nominative. *Whom* is used as an object of a verb or as an object of a preposition. The use of *who* or *whom* in a subordinate clause depends on how the pronoun functions within the clause.

Examples
Who is the author of the poem "Full Fathom Five"?

Stan, *who* is Colin's older brother, searches for Bandit.

The poet *whom* Samantha liked best was Amy Ling.

To *whom* did Monica's family pay a visit on New Year's?

whose, who's *Whose* is the possessive form of *who*. *Who's* is a contraction for *who is* or *who has*.

Examples
In "The Highwayman," *whose* daughter is Bess?

Who's familiar with the myths about Thor?

without, unless Do not use the preposition *without* in place of the conjunction *unless*.

Example
In "The Pied Piper of Hamelin," the people threaten to send the mayor packing *unless* [not *without*] he does something about the plague of rats.

would of See **could of**.

your, you're *Your* is the possessive form of *you*. *You're* is the contraction of *you are*.

Examples

Is *your* team practicing this afternoon?

You're in Ms. Ortega's class, aren't you?

Part 9: Grammar Reference Guide

SUBJECT-VERB AGREEMENT

A verb should agree with its subject in number—singular or plural.

> The **javelina** also **fancies** the barrel cactus.
> —Abbey, "Desert Creatures" (p. 151)

> **Everything was** packed except Mama's pot.
> —Jiménez, "The Circuit" (p. 72)

> When the **weather is** fair and settled, **they are** clothed in blue and purple, and **print** their bold outlines on the clear evening sky.
> —Irving, "Rip Van Winkle" (p. 247)

NOUNS

A **noun** is a word used to name a person, place, thing, or idea. Nouns can function in sentences as subjects, direct objects, indirect objects, objects of prepositions, predicate nominatives, and appositives.

> **Billy Weaver** had traveled down from **London** on the slow afternoon **train**, with a **change** at **Reading** on the **way**.
> —Dahl, "The Landlady" (p. 220)

> **Dandy** was a black **horse** of thoroughbred trotting **stock**.
> —Dobie, "When I Was a Boy on the Ranch" (p. 417)

> **Count Sylvius** is about to give **Merton** the **diamond** when **Holmes** snatches it out of his **hand**.

> **Heck Tate**, the **sheriff**, asks **Atticus** for **help**.

PRONOUNS

A **pronoun** is a word used in place of a noun or of more than one noun. **Personal pronouns** refer to the person speaking (first person), the person spoken to (second person), or the person, place, or thing spoken about (third person).

Singular

	Subject Form	Object Form	Possessive Form
First Person	I	me	my, mine
Second Person	you	you	your, yours
Third Person	he	him	his
	she	her	her, hers
	it	it	its

Plural

	Subject Form	Object Form	Possessive Form
First Person	we	us	our, ours
Second Person	you	you	your, yours
Third Person	they	them	their, theirs

> **His** mind told **him** that Paddy was right, but somehow **he** couldn't give in to **it** and **he** replied: "**She**'ll not forsake **it**! **She**'ll not! I know **she**'ll not!"
> —McLaverty, "The Wild Duck's Nest" (p. 182)

> **He** nearly drowned himself in the bathtubs: put **his** nose into the ink on a writing table, and burned **it** on the end of the big man's cigar. . . .
> —Kipling, "Rikki-tikki-tavi" (p. 230)

Subject-Verb Agreement: See *Teaching Resources B,* page 83.

Nouns: For review of parts of speech, see *Teaching Resources A,* page 18. See Vivid, Precise Nouns, *Teaching Resources C,* page 46. See also Proper Nouns, *Teaching Resources B,* page 165.

Pronouns: See *Teaching Resources B,* page 182.

Verbs: For review of Parts of Speech, see *Teaching Resources A,* page 18. For practice with action verbs and linking verbs, see *Teaching Resources B,* page 16.

Adjectives: See Adjective Clauses, *Teaching Resources A,* page 58, and Adjectives Derived from Verbs, *Teaching Resources D,* page 7.

Handbook for Revision

A **reflexive pronoun** ends in *-self* or *-selves* and refers back to the subject of a verb.

Putting his head down on the dog's neck, he vowed to **himself** fervently that he would always have some money on hand . . . .

—Callaghan, "Luke Baldwin's Vow" (p. 85)

An **intensive pronoun** ends in *-self* or *-selves* and adds emphasis to a noun or pronoun in the same sentence.

The landlady **herself** answered the door when Billy rang the bell.

A **relative pronoun** is used to introduce adjective and noun clauses.

In his village, the man **who** owned a rifle must remain supreme.

—Kjelgaard, "The Tiger's Heart" (p. 175)

The metal **which** carried well a single coal melted in the blazing fire.

—Ingalls, "Prometheus the Fire-Bringer" (p. 587)

Gently he tapped her on the side and reluctantly she went towards the brown-mudded path **that** led out of the valley.

—McLaverty, "The Wild Duck's Nest" (p. 181)

It would have been in vain for Scrooge to plead **that** the weather and the hour were not adapted to pedestrian purposes.

—Dickens, "A Christmas Carol" (p. 282)

An **interrogative pronoun** is used to begin questions.

Who could have thought, considering the way we treated him, that the old man had such a kindly heart!

—Henshaw, *The Jewels of the Shrine* (p. 367)

A **demonstrative pronoun** is used to point out a specific person or thing.

What had been wanted was **this** always, **this** always to last . . . .

—Brooks, "Home" (p. 127)

An **indefinite pronoun** is used to refer to people or things in general.

Anybody can copy echoes I make.

—Berry, "One" (p. 10)

VERBS

A **verb** is a word that expresses action or a state of being. An **action verb** tells what action someone or something is performing.

His knowing, crafty mask **blended** perfectly with the shadows and a mass of drift and branches that **had collected** by the bank of the pool.

—Annixter, "Last Cover" (p. 158)

A **linking verb** helps to make a statement by serving as a link between two words (for example, subject with predicate nominative or predicate adjective). The most commonly used linking verbs are forms of the verb *be*.

His voice **was** resolute with the knowledge of his rightness . . . .

—Deal, "Antaeus" (p. 188)

What **seemed** particularly odd to Rip **was** that, though these folks **were** evidently amusing themselves, yet they maintained the gravest faces, the most mysterious silence, and **were** the most melancholy party of pleasure he had ever witnessed.

—Irving, "Rip Van Winkle" (p. 253)

A **helping verb** is a verb that can be added to another verb to make a verb phrase.

Mama, my sister Keiko and I **were being sent** from our home, and out of Berkeley, and eventually, out of California.

—Uchida, "The Bracelet" (p. 64)

ADJECTIVES

An **adjective** is a word used to modify a noun or pronoun. Adjectives tell *what kind, which one,* or *how many.*

The wind was a torrent of darkness among the **gusty** trees,

The moon was a **ghostly** galleon tossed upon **cloudy** seas.

—Noyes, "The Highwayman" (p. 468)

The articles *the, a,* and *an* are adjectives. *An* is

used before a word beginning with a vowel sound or with an unsounded *h.*

ADVERBS

An **adverb** is a word used to modify a verb, an adjective, or another adverb. Adverbs tell *how, when, where,* and *to what extent.*

> "You are old, Father William," the young man said,
> "And your hair has become **very** white;
> And yet you **incessantly** stand on your head—
> Do you think, at your age, it is right?"
> —Carroll, "Father William" (p. 493)

PREPOSITIONS

A **preposition** is a word that shows the relationship of a noun or a pronoun to some other word in the sentence. Prepositions are almost always followed by nouns or pronouns. A group of words that begins with a preposition and ends with a noun or pronoun is called a **prepositional phrase.**

> Once more he stepped **into the street.**
> And **to his lips** again
> Laid his long pipe **of smooth straight cane.**
> —Browning, "The Pied Piper of Hamelin" (p. 483)

> **In fifty years of official life** I cannot recall such a liberty being taken! I am a busy man, engaged **upon important affairs,** and I have neither time nor taste **for foolish jokes.** [four prepositional phrases]
> —Michael and Molly Hardwick, *The Mazarin Stone* (p. 331)

CONJUNCTIONS

A **conjunction** is a word used to join words or groups of words. **Coordinating conjunctions** join equal parts of a sentence or similar groups of words.

> For Reuven the furrier it was a bad year, **and** after long hesitation he decided to sell Zlateh the goat.
> —Singer, "Zlateh the Goat" (p. 270)

Correlative conjunctions are used in pairs to join similar words or groups of words.

> **Both** Athena **and** Aphrodite are goddesses in Greek mythology.

A **subordinating conjunction** is used to introduce a clause that has less importance than the main clause in a sentence.

> Ranji had been less than a month in Rajpur **when** he discovered the pool in the forest.
> —Bond, "The Fight" (p. 56)

A **conjunctive adverb** is an adverb used as a conjunction to connect ideas.

> Walt was worried, **however**; the claim was liable to be jumped at any moment because of this delay . . . .
> —London, "The King of Mazy May" (p. 20)

INTERJECTIONS

An **interjection** is a word that expresses emotion and has no grammatical relation to other words in the sentence.

> "**Ah!** Bed curtains! Don't drop that oil upon the blankets, now."
> —Dickens, "A Christmas Carol" (p. 293)

PHRASES

A **phrase** is a group of words that does not contain a subject and a verb.

A **prepositional phrase** is a group of words that begins with a preposition and ends with a noun or pronoun.

> **from** the street   **over** the hill
> **inside** the bus   **with** us

An **appositive** is a noun or pronoun placed beside another noun or pronoun to identify or explain it. An **appositive phrase** is made up of an appositive and its modifiers.

> That was when his sister asked him to take on Verner, **her somewhat slow-witted eldest son.**
> —Wuorio, "You Can't Take It with You" (p. 265)

Adverbs: See Adverb Clauses, *Teaching Resources A,* page 119.

Prepositions: See Prepositions and Prepositional Phrases, *Teaching Resources C,* page 59. See also Phrases, *Teaching Resources A,* page 248.

Conjunctions: See Connecting Ideas Through Word Choice, *Teaching Resources E,* page 33.

Handbook for Revision

Grammar Reference Guide

Clauses: See Independent and Subordinate Clauses, *Teaching Resources A,* page 23.

A **participial phrase** consists of a participle and its complements or modifiers. The entire participial phrase acts as an adjective.

> Then the collie, **thrusting his legs out stiffly,** tried to hoist himself up, staggered, tried again, then stood there in a stupor.
> —Callaghan, "Luke Baldwin's Vow" (p. 82)

> It was leaning against the wall, its varnished wood **glistening in the moonlight.**
> —Adams, "Sled" (p. 115)

> It was six men of Indostan
> **To learning much inclined,**
> Who went to see the Elephant
> (Though all of them were blind).
> —Saxe, "The Blind Men and the Elephant" (p. 675)

> In midmorning he stopped short, dropped his stick, and brought up a five-foot rattlesnake **draped limply over the steel L.**
> —Rawlings, "Rattlesnake Hunt" (p. 398)

An **infinitive phrase** consists of an infinitive together with its modifiers and complements. The entire phrase can be used as a noun, an adjective, or an adverb.

> And trees put forth
> New leaves **to sing**
> **In joy beneath the sky**

[infinitive phrase used as an adjective modifying *leaves*]
> —Hughes, "In Time of Silver Rain" (p. 162)

CLAUSES

A **clause** is a group of words that has a subject and a verb. An **independent clause** expresses a complete thought and can stand by itself as a sentence.

> Three days later Mr. Thorburn took Harry, still stiff and bandaged, down to the village inn.
> —Beachcroft, "The Erne from the Coast" (p. 217)

A **subordinate clause** does not express a complete thought and cannot stand alone.

> Persephone shrieked aloud and struggled, **while the armful of flowers cascaded down to earth.**
> —Coolidge, "The Origin of the Seasons" (p. 593)

Part 10: Mechanics
■ Capitalization ■ Punctuation

CAPITALIZATION

1. FIRST WORDS

■ **Capitalize the first word of every sentence.**

Example
He showed Luke that nothing of value was ever wasted around the mill.
—Callaghan, "Luke Baldwin's Vow" (p. 77)

■ **Capitalize the first word of a direct quotation when the word begins with a capital letter in the original. If the original writer has not used a capital letter, do not capitalize the first word of the quotation.**

Examples
And then the words he didn't want to hear rushed from Paddy in a mocking chant. **"You** had it in your hand! . . . She'll forsake it!"
—McLaverty, "The Wild Duck's Nest" (p. 182)

"You can't go out," his mother said, **"until** you learn how to act like a gentleman."
—Adams, "Sled" (p. 114)

"Cal," said Jem, **"can** you come down the sidewalk a minute?"
—Lee, "One-Shot Finch" (p. 105)

■ **Traditionally, the first word in a line of poetry is capitalized, although some writers do not follow this rule for reasons of style.**

Examples

In the harbor, in the island, in the Spanish Seas,
Are the tiny white houses and the orange trees.
—Masefield, "Trade Winds" (p. 447)

If you dig that hole deep enough,
you'll reach China, they used to tell me,
a child in a backyard in Pennsylvania.
—Ling, "Grandma Ling" (p. 131)

2. THE PRONOUN *I* AND THE INTERJECTION *O*

▍ **Capitalize the pronoun *I* and the interjection *O*.**

Examples

When **I**'m old, tired, melancholy,
I'll build a leaf-green mausoleum.
—Graves, "The Caterpillar" (p. 433)

"What is it, **O** Killer of the terrible Nag?"
—Kipling, "Rikki-tikki-tavi" (p. 236)

3. PROPER NOUNS AND PROPER ADJECTIVES

▍ **A *proper noun* names a particular person, place, or thing. A *proper adjective* is formed from a proper noun. Capitalize proper nouns and proper adjectives.**

Examples

Haiti	Nigeria	Vietnam	Peru
Haitian	Nigerian	Vietnamese	Peruvian

▍ **In proper nouns consisting of two or more words, do not capitalize articles (*a, an, the*), short prepositions (those with fewer than five letters, such as *at, of, for, with*), and coordinating conjunctions (*and, but, for, nor, or, so, yet*).**

Examples

Kansas City	Governor Dix	President Taft
Indian Ocean	Isle of Pines	Oahu

If you are not sure whether to capitalize a word, check in an up-to-date dictionary.

4. NAMES OF PEOPLE

▍ **Capitalize the names of people. Note that some names may contain more than one capital letter.**

Examples

Ruth McKenney	Yoshiko Uchida
Eva-Lis Wuorio	T. O. Beachcroft
J. Frank Dobie	Joseph Bruchac

5. GEOGRAPHICAL NAMES

▍ **Capitalize geographical names, such as towns, cities, counties, townships, states, regions, countries, continents, islands, mountains, bodies of water, parks, roads, highways, and streets.**

Examples

Los Angeles	Puget Sound	Marin County
Antarctica	Block Island	Fifth Avenue
Panama Canal	Lake Ontario	El Salvador
Indiana	Route 278	Interstate 10

▍ **Note that words such as *south*, *east*, and *northwest* are not capitalized when they indicate direction.**

Examples

east of the Mississippi   southwest of town

6. ORGANIZATIONS

▍ **Capitalize the names of organizations, teams, businesses, institutions, buildings, and government bodies.**

Examples

National Hockey League	General Motors
Johnson High School	Ramada Inn
Miami Dolphins	State Department

7. HISTORICAL EVENTS

▍ **Capitalize the names of historical events and periods, special events, and calendar items.**

Examples

Civil War	Texas State Fair	New Year's Day
Middle Ages	Thursday	Special Olympics
Thanksgiving Day	Super Bowl	World War I

Mechanics

8. NATIONALITIES, RACES, AND RELIGIONS

▎ Capitalize the names of nationalities, races, and peoples.

Examples

Korean	Yoruba	Israeli
Maya	Hmong	Sioux
Antiguan	Hispanic American	Puerto Rican

▎ Capitalize the names of religions and their followers, holy days, sacred writings, and specific deities.

Examples

Hinduism	Yom Kippur	Advent
Unitarian	Palm Sunday	the Koran
Judaism	Vishnu	Holy Spirit
Easter	Allah	the Torah
Ramadan	the Bible	Episcopalian

9. BRAND NAMES

▎ Capitalize the brand names of business products. Do not capitalize the noun that often follows a brand name.

Examples

Ford trucks	Nike shoes
Tide detergent	Tropicana juice

10. PARTICULAR PLACES, THINGS, AND EVENTS

▎ Capitalize the names of ships, trains, airplanes, spacecraft, monuments, buildings, awards, planets, and any other particular places, things, or events.

Examples

Titanic	*Super Chief*	*Air Force One*
Saturn	London Bridge	*Challenger*
Room 505	Pulitzer Prize	Sears Tower

11. SPECIFIC COURSES, LANGUAGES

▎ Do *not* capitalize the names of school subjects, except for languages and for course names followed by a number.

Examples

physics	history	statistics
biology	Russian	Chemistry 101

12. TITLES OF PEOPLE

▎ Capitalize a title belonging to a particular person when it comes before a person's name.

Examples

President Yeltsin	Professor Fong
Principal Shuster	Dr. Desai
General Bradley	Ms. Graziano

▎ Do *not* capitalize a title used alone or following a person's name, especially if the title is preceded by *a* or *the*.

Examples

Donna Archabal, mayor of Rochester
the governor's schedule
an earl's castle

▎ Capitalize a word showing a family relationship when the word is used with a person's name but *not* when it is preceded by a possessive.

Examples

Aunt Cassie	Uncle Henry	his uncle Henry

13. TITLES OF LITERARY AND OTHER CREATIVE WORKS

▎ Capitalize the first and last words and all important words in titles of books, magazines, newspapers, short poems, stories, historical documents, movies, television programs, works of art, and musical compositions.

Unimportant words within titles are articles (*a, an, the*), short prepositions (fewer than five letters, such as *at, of, for, to, from, with*) and coordinating conjunctions (*and, but, for, nor, or, so, yet*).

Examples
Pacific Crossing
"When I Was a Boy on the Ranch"
"The Night the Bed Fell"
The Pelican Brief
The Jewels of the Shrine
Jungle Tales
The Price Is Right
"Scarborough Fair"
"Icarus and Daedalus"
"Zlateh the Goat"

▍ The word *the* written before a title is capitalized only when it is the first word of a title.

Examples
"The Cat and the Pain Killer"
"The Origin of the Seasons"
"The Wreck of the *Hesperus*"
"Belling the Cat"

PUNCTUATION

1. END MARKS

▍ End marks—*periods, questions marks,* and *exclamation points*—are used to indicate the purpose of a sentence. (A period is also used at the end of many abbreviations.)

Use a period to end a statement (or declarative sentence).

Example
As I got off the bus, my little brothers and sisters ran up to meet me.
—Jiménez, "The Circuit" (p. 75)

▍ A question (or interrogative sentence) is followed by a question mark.

Examples
Did you fix it again, Harriet?
—Childress, *When the Rattlesnake Sounds* (p. 349)

Indeed? Pray, what is this missing fact?
—Michael and Molly Hardwick, *The Mazarin Stone* (p. 325)

▍ Use an exclamation point to end an exclamation.

Examples
"I saw that, One-Shot Finch!"
—Lee, "One-Shot Finch" (p. 108)

"O father ! I see a gleaming light;
  Oh, say, what may it be?"
—Longfellow, "The Wreck of the *Hesperus*" (p. 166)

"Oh! that flagon! that wicked flagon!" thought Rip—"what excuse shall I make to Dame Van Winkle?"
—Irving, "Rip Van Winkle" (p. 254)

▍ An imperative sentence may be followed by either a period or an exclamation point.

Examples
Take it in your hands.
—Rawlings, "Rattlesnake Hunt" (p. 400)

Shut up, Sam! Let me think!
—Michael and Molly Hardwick, *The Mazarin Stone* (p. 327)

▍ Use a period after an abbreviation.

Examples
Personal Names: Thomas E. Adams
Titles Used with Names: Dr., Gen., Ms., Rev.
States: N.J., N.D., Mich.
Time of Day: A.M., P.M.
Years: B.C., A.D.
Addresses: St., Ave., Blvd.
Organizations and Companies: Co., Corp., Inc.
Units of Measure: lb., oz., in., ft., yd., mi.

▍ No periods are used in abbreviations with states when the zip code is included: NY 11963.

▍ Abbreviations in the metric system are often written without periods: for example, km for kilometer, kg for kilogram, ml for milliliter. Abbreviations for government agencies and international organizations and some other frequently used abbreviations are written without periods: for example, FBI, PTA, PBS, VHF.

Commas: Conventional Uses: See Punctuating Items in a Series, *Teaching Resources D,* page 179. See also Punctuating Clauses, *Teaching Resources A,* page 210.

Semicolons: See Punctuating Clauses, *Teaching Resources A,* page 210.

2. COMMAS: CONVENTIONAL USES

▪ **Use a comma to separate items in dates and addresses.**

Examples

I wrote to Sally on April 14, 1995.

I sent the letter to 8 Oak Dr., South Hadley, MA 01075.

▪ **Notice that a comma also separates the final item in a date and in an address from the words that follow it. A comma does *not* separate the month from the day, the house number from the street name, or the state name from the ZIP code.**

▪ **Use a comma after the salutation of a friendly letter and after the closing of any letter.**

Examples

Dear Dr. Tanzio,   My dear Pru,
Sincerely yours,   Yours truly,

For other uses of commas, see pages 744–746.

3. SEMICOLONS

▪ **Use a semicolon between independent clauses that are closely related in thought and that are not joined by *and, but, or, nor, for, so,* or *yet*.**

Example

Aaron's mother and sisters cried for him; his father remained silent and gloomy.

—Singer, "Zlateh the Goat" (p. 273)

▪ **Use a semicolon (rather than a comma) before a coordinating conjunction to join independent clauses that contain commas.**

Example

During the whole time Rip and his companion had labored on in silence; for though Rip marveled greatly what could be the object of carrying a keg of liquor up this wild mountain, yet there was something strange and incomprehensible about the unknown, that inspired awe and checked familiarity.

—Irving, "Rip Van Winkle" (p. 252)

4. COLONS

▪ **Use a colon before a list of items, especially after expressions like *as follows* and *the following*.**

Example

Gerry's favorite writers were the following: Nina Otero, Gwendolyn Brooks, Mark Twain, and Roald Dahl.

▪ **Use a colon in certain conventional situations: between the hour and the minute, between chapter and verse in a biblical citation, and after the salutation of a business letter.**

Examples

9:05 A.M.   Luke 2:1   Dear Rev. Foster:

5. ITALICS

▪ **When writing or typing, indicate italics by underlining. Use italics for titles of books, plays, periodicals, works of art, films, television programs, long musical compositions, ships, aircraft, and spacecraft.**

Examples

BOOK: *The Family Moskat*
PLAY: *The Governess*
PERIODICAL: *Time*
WORK OF ART: *Sunset on the Sea*
FILM: *Send Me No Flowers*
TELEVISION PROGRAM: *Nightline*
LONG MUSICAL COMPOSITION: *An American in Paris*
SHIP: *Pequod*
AIRCRAFT: *Hindenburg*
SPACECRAFT: *Atlantis*

▪ **Use italics for words, letters, and figures referred to as such.**

Examples

Except may be a preposition or a verb.

Double the *n* to form the present participle of *win*.

Is *3* your lucky number?

6. QUOTATION MARKS

▮ **Use quotation marks to enclose a direct quotation—a person's exact words.**

Example
"Yes," she agreed with a sigh. "You make Grandpa comfortable, Martin."
—Sneve, "The Medicine Bag" (p. 35)

▮ **Do *not* use quotation marks to enclose an indirect quotation—a rewording of a direct quotation.**

Example
I thought maybe by some miracle, a messenger from the government might be standing there, tall and proper and buttoned into a uniform, come to tell us it was all a terrible mistake; that we wouldn't have to leave after all.
—Uchida, "The Bracelet" (p. 64)

▮ **Begin a direct quotation with a capital letter.**

Example
She took a tiny, birdlike sip and said, "My husband thinks that he likes foreign food."
—Soto, *Pacific Crossing* (p. 538)

▮ **When an expression identifying the speaker interrupts a quoted sentence, the second part of the quotation begins with a small letter.**

Example
"It should be Christmas Day, I am sure," said she, "on which one drinks the health of such an odious, stingy, hard, unfeeling man as Mr. Scrooge."
—Dickens, "A Christmas Carol" (p. 289)

▮ **A direct quotation is set off from the rest of the sentence by commas or by a question mark or an exclamation point.**

Examples
"That dog can't see any more," Uncle Henry said.
—Callaghan, "Luke Baldwin's Vow" (p. 79)

"Did you go up in the foothills?" Mom asked.
—Annixter, "Last Cover" (p. 153)

"Get me out of this!" I bawled.
—Thurber, "The Night the Bed Fell" (p. 136)

▮ **Commas and periods are always placed inside closing quotation marks.**

Examples
"It's our earth," T. J. said desperately.
—Deal, "Antaeus" (p. 192)

"Many can't go there; and many would rather die."
—Dickens, "A Christmas Carol" (p. 278)

▮ **Question marks and exclamation points are placed inside closing quotation marks if the quotation is a question or an exclamation. Otherwise, they are placed outside.**

Examples
"Can I speak to Ana?" I asked, pronouncing her name the American way.
—Alvarez, "Names/Nombres" (p. 395)

"Right, Ma—Josephine!"
—Hodge, from *Crick Crack, Monkey* (p. 94)

Did you enjoy May Sarton's poem "A Parrot"?

Let's all read "When the Frost Is on the Punkin"!

▮ **When both the sentence and the quotation at the end of the sentence are questions (or exclamations), only one question mark (or exclamation point) is used. It is placed inside the closing quotation marks.**

Example
Have you ever read Frank R. Stockton's short story, "The Lady, or the Tiger?"

▮ **When you write dialogue (conversation), begin a new paragraph every time the speaker changes, and enclose each speaker's words in quotation marks.**

Examples
"Don't kill me," said Chuchundra, almost weeping. "Rikki-tikki, don't kill me!"

"Do you think a snake-killer kills muskrats?" said Rikki-tikki scornfully.

Apostrophes: See *Teaching Resources D,* page 102.

"Those who kill snakes get killed by snakes," said Chuchundra, more sorrowfully than ever.
—Kipling, "Rikki-tikki-tavi" (p. 234)

▌ **When a quotation consists of several sentences, place quotation marks at the beginning and at the end of the whole quotation.**

Example

"Nor do I expect you to. Even a tiger will not eat an entire goat, and you are sure to find what is left of my favorite nanny. Whatever the tiger has not eaten, you may have for your pay."
—Kjelgaard, "The Tiger's Heart" (p. 172)

▌ **Use single quotation marks to enclose a quotation within a quotation.**

Example

"I think the little fellow's afraid of the snow.
He isn't winter-broken. It isn't play
With the little fellow at all. He's running away.
I doubt if even his mother could tell him,
  'Sakes,
It's only weather.' He'd think she didn't know!
Where is his mother? He can't be out alone!"
—Frost, "The Runaway" (p. 178)

▌ **Use quotation marks to enclose titles of short works, such as short stories, short poems, articles, songs, episodes of television programs, and chapters and other parts of books.**

Examples

SHORT STORY: "Seventh Grade"
SHORT POEM: "Trade Winds"
ARTICLE: "V-Mail Trouble"
SONG: "Go Down, Moses"
TV EPISODE: "Growing Up Hispanic"
CHAPTER: "Roman Myths"

7. APOSTROPHES
POSSESSIVE CASE

▌ **To form the possessive of a singular noun, add an apostrophe and an *s*. Add only the apostrophe to a proper noun ending in an *s* sound if the addition of *'s* would make the name awkward to pronounce.**

Examples

the **moon's** light   Ms. **Sanchez'** office
a **child's** portion   **Hercules'** adventures

▌ **To form the possessive of a plural noun that does not end in *s*, add an apostrophe and an *s*.**

the **mice's** whiskers   **women's** clothes

▌ **To form the possessive of a plural noun ending in *s*, add only the apostrophe.**

Examples

the **dancers'** movements
the **students'** books

▌ **Do not use an apostrophe with possessive personal pronouns.**

Incorrect
I believe this coat is **your's**.

Correct
I believe this coat is **yours**.

▌ **To form the possessive of some indefinite pronouns, add an apostrophe and an *s*.**

Examples

Jose is **everyone's** choice for captain.

Somebody's gloves are on the desk.

CONTRACTIONS

▌ **Use an apostrophe to show where letters or numerals have been left out in a contraction.**

Examples

I'm here. [I am]   **We're** home! [We are]
Let's eat. [Let us]   **Where'll** I go? [Where will]
in the **'80s** [1980s]   **You'd** left. [You had]

PLURALS

▌ **Use an apostrophe and an *s* to form the plurals of letters, numerals, signs, and of words referred to as words.**

Examples

That word has three *a*'s.

Pronounce your *d*'s and *t*'s more clearly, please.

766 HANDBOOK FOR REVISION

Include the $'s in that invoice.

Be careful where you place the *only*'s in that paragraph!

8. HYPHENS

▌ **Use a hyphen to divide a word at the end of a line.**

Example
Lucille Clifton has written children's **fiction**.

▌ **Divide a word only between syllables.**

Incorrect
Stage directions appear without **parentheses.**

Correct
Stage directions appear without **parentheses.**

▌ **Do not divide a one-syllable word.**

Incorrect
Mood is the emotional situation that a work **tries** to establish.

Correct
Mood is the emotional situation that a work **tries** to establish.

▌ **Do not divide a word so that one letter stands alone.**

Incorrect
Suspense makes the reader uncertain **about** what is to come next.

Correct
Suspense makes the reader uncertain **about** what is to come next.

▌ **Use a hyphen with compound numbers from** *twenty-one* **to** *ninety-nine* **and with fractions used as modifiers.**

Examples
twenty-two players   a **three-fifths** majority

9. DASHES

▌ **Use a dash to indicate an abrupt break in thought or speech.**

Examples
But I must say Providence was kind enough to burn down that old mausoleum of mine, I'm too old to keep it up—maybe you're right, Jean Louise, this is a settled neighborhood.
—Lee, "One-Shot Finch" (p. 103)

He plodded down the alley, thrilling in the cold white silence—the snow was thick.
—Adams, "Sled" (p. 116)

10. PARENTHESES

▌ **Use parentheses to enclose material that is added to a sentence but is not considered of major importance.**

Examples
He was an old male—perhaps between thirty and forty years of age (chimpanzees in captivity can live more than fifty years).
—Goodall, from *In the Shadow of Man* (p. 386)

He strode up to Ranji, who still sat on the rock and, planting his broad feet firmly on the sand, said (as though this would settle the matter once and for all), "Don't you know I am a Punjabi? I do not take replies from villagers like you!"
—Bond, "The Fight" (p. 57)

Hyphens: See *Teaching Resources D,* page 63.

Glossary

The words listed in the glossary in the following pages are found in the selections in this textbook. You can use this glossary as you would a dictionary—to look up words that are unfamiliar to you. Strictly speaking, the word *glossary* means a collection of technical, obscure, or foreign words found in a certain field of work. Of course, the words in this glossary are not "technical, obscure, or foreign," but are those that might present difficulty as you read the selections in this textbook.

Many words in the English language have several meanings. In this glossary, the meanings given are the ones that apply to the words as they are used in the selections in the textbook. Words closely related in form and meaning are generally listed together in one entry (**immobile** and **immobility**), and the definition is given for the first form. Regular adverbs (ending in *-ly*) are defined in their adjective form, with the adverb form shown at the end of the definition.

The following abbreviations are used:
    adj., adjective   *n.*, noun
    adv., adverb   *v.*, verb

For more information about the words in this glossary, consult a dictionary.

A

abash (ə-băsh′) *v.* To embarrass.—**abashed** *adj.*
abate (ə-bāt′) *v.* To lessen.
abet (ə-bĕt′) *v.* To encourage.
abnormal (ăb-nôr′məl) *adj.* Not normal; strange.—**abnormally** *adv.*
abode (ə-bōd′) *n.* A home.
abrupt (ə-brŭpt′) *adj.* Sudden.—**abruptly** *adv.*
abundant (ə-bŭn′dənt) *adj.* Plentiful.
acclaim (ə-klām′) *v.* To greet; salute.
accommodate (ə-kŏm′ə-dāt′) *v.* To serve; oblige.
accomplice (ə-kŏm′plĭs) *n.* A partner in an activity, especially in a crime.
accost (ə-kôst′, ə-kŏst′) *v.* To meet and speak to first, often in an aggressive way.
acknowledgment (ăk-nŏl′ĭj-mənt) *n.* **1.** An admission. **2.** A sign of recognition.
acquiesce (ăk′wē-ĕs′) *v.* To agree without protest but without enthusiasm.
adept (ə-dĕpt′) *adj.* Expert.

adhesive (ăd-hē′sĭv, zĭv) *adj.* Sticky.
adjoining (ə-joi′nĭng) *adj.* Next to; neighboring.
adjudge (ə-jŭj′) *v.* To determine or declare.
admonish (ăd-mŏn′ĭsh) *v.* To correct someone in a kindly manner.
adobe (ə-dō′bē) *adj.* Made of sun-dried bricks of clay and straw.
adversary (ăd′vər-sĕr′ē) *n.* An enemy or opponent.
aesthetic (ĕs-thĕt′ĭk) *adj.* Relating to principles of beauty.—**aesthetically** *adv.*
affect (ə-fĕkt′) *v.* To put on; pretend.
afflict (ə-flĭkt′) *v.* To cause to suffer.—**afflicted** *adj.*
afford (ə-fôrd′, ə-fōrd′) *v.* To provide.
aggravate (ăg′-rə-vāt′) *v.* To irritate; annoy.
aghast (ə-găst′, ə-gäst′) *adj.* Shocked; horrified.
agitation (ăj′ə-tā′shən) *n.* Emotional upset.
airs (ârs) *n.* Affectation.
ajar (ə-jär′) *adj.* Slightly open.
alcove (ăl′kōv′) *n.* A recessed area in a room.
alienate (āl′yən-āt′, ā′lē-ən-) *v.* **1.** To make unfriendly. **2.** To turn away.
alight (ə-līt′) *v.* To come down and settle on after flight.
alist (ə-lĭst′) *adj.* Tilted.
allay (ə-lā′) *v.* To soothe; calm.
allege (ə-lĕj′) *v.* To declare or affirm.
alleged (ə-lĕjd′) *adj.* Supposed.
alloy (ə-loi′, ăl′oi′) *v.* To lessen or mar.
allurement (ə-lōōr′mənt) *n.* A temptation.
aloof (ə-lōōf′) *adj.* Unfriendly; cold.
amble (ăm′bəl) *v.* To walk in a leisurely way.
amiable (ā′mē-ə-bəl) *adj.* Friendly; agreeable.
ample (ăm′pəl) *adj.* Large; spacious.
analogous (ə-năl′ə-gəs) *adj.* Similar.
anesthetic (ăn′ĭs-thĕt′ĭk) *n.* Something that deadens physical sensations.
anguish (ăng′gwĭsh) *n.* Great suffering.
animated (ăn′ə-mā′tĭd) *adj.* Lively.—**animatedly** *adv.*
annihilate (ə-nī′ə-lāt′) *v.* To demolish; destroy completely.
anoint (ə-noint′) *v.* To rub the body with oil.
anonymous (ə-nŏn′ə-məs) *adj.* Without a name; not identified.
anticipation (ăn-tĭs′ə-pā′shən) *n.* An expectation.
antiquity (ăn-tĭk′wə-tē) *n.* The quality of being old or ancient.

anvil (ăn′vĭl) *n.* A heavy iron or steel block, smooth on top, on which metal is shaped and hammered into objects.
anxiety (ăng-zī′ə-tē) *n.* Worry.
apparition (ăp′ə-rĭsh′ən) *n.* A ghost or phantom.
appease (ə-pēz′) *v.* To satisfy.—**appeased** *adj.*
appendage (ə-pĕn′dĭj) *n.* An attachment.
appendix (ə-pĕn′dĭks) *n.* Something added on.
appraise (ə-prāz′) *v.* To judge the value of.—**appraising** *adj.*
apprehension (ăp′rĭ-hĕn′shən) *n.* Fear.
apprehensive (ăp′rĭ-hĕn′sĭv) *adj.* Uneasy; fearful.
approbation (ap′rə-bā′shən) *n.* Approval.
aquamarine (ăk′wə-mə-rēn′, ăk′wə-) *adj.* Pale blue-green.
aquiline (ăk′wə-līn′, -lĭn) *adj.* Curved like an eagle's beak.
ardent (är′dənt) *adj.* Enthusiastic; intense.
areaway (âr′ē-ə-wā′) *n.* A passageway between buildings.
arid (ăr′ĭd) *adj.* Very dry.
aristocracy (ăr′ĭs-tŏk′rə-sē) *n.* The upper class.
aristocrat (ə-rĭs′tə-krăt′, ăr′ĭs-tə-) *n.* A member of the nobility; an upper-class person.
array (ə-rā′) *n.* A large display.
arresting (ə-rĕs′tĭng) *adj.* Attracting attention.
arrogant (ăr′ə-gənt) *adj.* Excessively proud; self-important.
articulate (är-tĭk′yə-lĭt) *adj.* Able to speak clearly.
asbestos (ăs-bĕs′təs, ăz-) *adj.* Made of asbestos, which is fire-resistant.
ascent (ə-sĕnt′) *n.* An upward slope.
askance (ə-skăns′) *adv.* With a side glance.
aspen (ăs′pən) *n.* A kind of poplar tree.
aspiration (ăs′pə-rā′shən) *n.* High ambition or desire.
assail (ə-sāl′) *v.* To attack.—**assailant** *n.*
assault (ə-sôlt′) *n.* An attack.
assess (ə-sĕs′) *v.* To determine the value of.
asset (ăs′ĕt′) *n.* An advantage.
astride (ə-strīd′) *adj.* With one leg on each side of.
atmosphere (ăt′mə-sfîr′) *n.* The air surrounding the earth.
atonement (ə-tōn′mənt) *n.* Satisfaction or amends for wrongdoing.
atrocious (ə-trō′shəs) *adj.* Monstrous, extremely bad.
attitude (ăt′ə-tōōd′, -tyōōd′) *n.* A position of the body expressing some action or emotion.
attribute (ăt′rə-byōōt′) *n.* A quality or characteristic.
atypical (ā-tĭp′ĭ-kəl) *adj.* Unusual.
aura (ôr′ə) *n.* **1.** An air or quality that seems to surround a person. **2.** An aroma or vapor.
avail (ə-vāl′) *v.* To be of help or use.
avaricious (ăv′ə-rĭsh′əs) *adj.* Greedy.—**avariciously** *adv.*
avenge (ə-vĕnj′) *v.* To take revenge.
avert (ə-vûrt′) *v.* To prevent.
avowed (ə-voud′) *adj.* Confessed; admitted.
awe (ô) *n.* A feeling of great reverence for someone or something.—**awed** *adj.*
azure (ăzh′ər) *adj.* Sky-blue.

B

bafflement (băf′əl-mənt) *n.* Bewilderment; state of being confused.—**baffle** *v.*
balk (bôk) *v.* To stop and refuse to go on.
bandanna (băn-dăn′ə) *n.* A large, brightly colored handkerchief, usually figured or patterned.
banish (băn′ĭsh) *v.* To force to leave.
bankrupt (băngk′rŭpt′, -rəpt) *v.* To ruin financially.
banter (băn′tər) *v.* To tease in a good-humored way.
barrette (bə-rĕt′, bä-) *n.* A clip for holding the hair in place.
bay (bā) *v.* To bark or howl.
bayonet (bā′ə-nĭt, -nĕt′, bā′ə-nĕt′) *n.* A daggerlike blade attached to a rifle.
bazaar (bə-zär′) *n.* A street lined with stalls and shops.
beaker (bē′kər) *n.* A large container for liquids.
beckon (bĕk′ən) *v.* To motion to come forward.—**beckoning** *adj.*
begrudge (bĭ-grŭj′) *v.* To resent.
behest (bĭ-hĕst′) *n.* Request.
belligerent (bə-lĭj′ər-ənt) *adj.* Displaying a willingness to quarrel or fight.
benevolence (bə-nĕv′ə-ləns) *n.* Good will.
bewilderment (bĭ-wĭl′dər-mənt) *n.* Puzzlement; confusion.
billow (bĭl′ō) *n.* A large wave.

ă p**a**t/ā p**ay**/âr c**are**/ä f**a**ther/b **b**i**b**/ch **ch**ur**ch**/d **d**ee**d**/ĕ p**e**t/ē **be**/f **f**i**fe**/g **g**a**g**/h **h**at/hw **wh**ich/ĭ p**i**t/ī p**ie**/îr p**ier**/j **j**u**dge**/k **k**ic**k**/
l **l**i**d**, **need**le/m **m**u**m**/n **n**o, sudde**n**/ng thi**ng**/ŏ p**o**t/ō **toe**/ô p**aw**, f**or**/oi n**oi**se/ou **ou**t/ōō t**oo**k/ōō b**oo**t/p **p**o**p**/r **r**oa**r**/s **s**auce/
sh **sh**ip, di**sh**/t **t**igh**t**/th **th**in, pa**th**/th **th**is, ba**the**/ŭ c**u**t/ûr **ur**ge/v **v**al**ve**/w **w**ith/y **y**es/z **z**ebra, si**z**e/zh vi**si**on/ə **a**bout, **i**tem, ed**i**ble, gall**o**p, circ**u**s/ä *Fr.* **a**mi/œ *Fr.* **feu**, *Ger.* sch**ö**n/ü *Fr.* t**u**, *Ger.* **ü**ber/KH *Ger.* i**ch**, *Scot.* lo**ch**/N *Fr.* bo**n**.

blare (blâr) *n.* A loud, brassy sound.
bleak (blēk) *adj.* Cheerless.
blemish (blĕm´ĭsh) *n.* A slight defect.
blimp (blĭmp) *n.* **1.** A light, buoyant, nonrigid aircraft. **2.** Something swelled and inflated by air so that it resembles a blimp.
bloat (blōt) *v.* To swell up.
bloated (blōt´əd) *adj.* Swollen.
bloom (blo͞om) *v.* To grow; flourish.
bloomers (blo͞o´mərs) *n.* Baggy trousers once worn by women for athletics.
blunt (blŭnt) *adj.* Frank and abrupt.
bootleg (bo͞ot´lĕg´) *v.* To produce or sell something, such as liquor, illegally.—**bootlegger** *n.*
boudoir (bo͞o´dwär´, -dwôr´) *n.* A woman's bedroom.
bough (bou) *n.* A branch of a tree.
bound (bound) *v.* To leap up or forward.
bow (bou) *n.* The front of a ship.
brand (brănd) *n.* A piece of burning wood or a hot iron.
brandish (brăn´dĭsh) *v.* To wave in a threatening way.
bravado (brə-vä´dō) *n.* False courage.
breaker (brā´kər) *n.* A wave as it breaks, especially against the shore.
bridle (brīd´l) *v.* To put a harness on a horse.—**bridled** *adj.*
brine (brīn) *n.* The sea.
brisk (brĭsk) *adj.* Lively.—**briskly** *adv.*
bristle (brĭs´əl) *v.* To react angrily.
brood (bro͞od) *n.* The young of a family.
brook (bro͝ok) *v.* To put up with; permit.
brusque (brŭsk) *adj.* Rude.—**brusquely** *adv.*
buffet (bŭf´ĭt) *v.* Hit.—**buffeted** *adj.*
bulbous (bŭl´bəs) *adj.* Rounded or swollen into a bulb shape.
burden (bûrd´n) *n.* A heavy weight.
burly (bûr´lē) *adj.* Husky.
burnish (bûr´nĭsh) *v.* To polish.—**burnished** *adj.*
butte (byo͞ot) *n.* A hill with steep sides.

C

cable (kā´bəl) *n.* A heavy rope or chain.
calamity (kə-lăm´ə-tē) *n.* A disaster.
calculate (kăl´kyə-lāt´) *v.* To figure out; guess.
caliber (kăl´ə-bər) *n.* Quality or worth of a person or thing.
calico (kăl´ĭ-kō) *n.* A spotted cat.
camaraderie (kä´mə-rä´də-rē, kăm´ə-) *n.* A friendly feeling among people in a group.
camisole (kăm´ə-sōl´) *n.* A woman's waist-length sleeveless undergarment.
camouflage (kăm´ə-fläzh´, -fläj´) *v.* To conceal; disguise.—**camouflaged** *adj.*
canopy (kăn´ə-pē) *n.* A covering.
canter (kăn´tər) *v.* To move at an easy pace.
capacious (kə-pā´shəs) *adj.* Able to hold a large quantity; roomy.
caper (kā´pər) *v.* To leap playfully.—**capering** *n.*
capital (kăp´ə-təl) *adj.* Excellent.
capsize (kăp´sīz´, kăp-sīz´) *v.* To turn over.
capsule (kăp´səl, -syo͞ol) *n.* A small container of medicine.
caravel (kăr´ə-vĕl´) *n.* A sailing ship used in the fifteenth and sixteenth centuries.
carcass (kär´kəs) *n.* The dead body of an animal.
cardinal (kär´dn-əl, kärd´nəl) *adj.* Chief; most serious.
careen (kə-rēn´) *v.* To move rapidly, out of control.
caress (kə-rĕs´) *v.* To touch someone lovingly.
carrion (kăr´ē-ən) *n.* Dead, decaying flesh.
cascade (kăs-kād´) *v.* To fall in great amounts.
catapult (kăt´ə-pŭlt) *v.* To leap.
catechism (kăt´ĭ-kĭz´əm) *n.* The teaching of religious doctrine through a series of questions and answers.
cathedral (kə-thē´drəl) *n.* A large, impressive church, often the official seat of a bishop.
caustic (kôs´tĭk) *adj.* Sharp in speech.
cavernous (kăv´ər-nəs) *adj.* **1.** Like a cave. **2.** Empty; hollow.
celebrity (sə-lĕb´rə-tē) *n.* A famous person.
celluloid (sĕl´yə-loid´) *n.* A substance used for toys, film, and toilet articles.
chaff (chăf) *n.* The waste part of grain.
chagrin (shə-grĭn´) *n.* A feeling of annoyance and embarrassment.
chamois (shăm´ē) *adj.* Referring to a soft leather made from the hide of the chamois, a small antelope, or from the skin of sheep, deer, or goats.
champ (chămp) *v.* To chew on.
chaos (kā´ŏs´) *n.* Extreme confusion.—**chaotic** *adj.*
char (chär) *v.* To burn; scorch; blacken by burning.
charger (chär´jər) *n.* A horse trained for battle or parade.
chasm (kăz´əm) *n.* A deep opening in the earth's surface.
chaste (chāst) *adj.* Pure.
chastisement (chăs-tīz´mənt, chăs´tĭz-mənt) *n.* Punishment.

chivalrous (shĭv′əl-rəs) *adj.* Showing the gallantry and courtesy of a knight.
chops (chŏps) *n.* The mouth, the jaws.
churl (chûrl) *n.* A miser.
churn (chûrn) *v.* To move or shake vigorously.
citadel (sĭt′ə-dəl, -dĕl′) *n.* A fort that protects a city.
civic (sĭv′ĭk) *adj.* Referring to a city or to a citizen.
clamber (klăm′ər, klăm′bər) *v.* To climb clumsily or with difficulty, usually on hands and knees.
clamor (klăm′ər) *n.* A loud noise. *v.* To make a loud, continuous noise.—**clamorous** *adj.*
cleave (klēv) *v.* To cut.
clientele (klī′ən-tĕl′) *n.* Customers.
clutch (klŭch) *v.* To hold tightly.
cobble (kŏb′əl) *n.* A stone used to pave streets.
colleague (kŏl′ēg′) *n.* A co-worker; associate.
colossal (kə-lŏs′əl) *adj.* Gigantic.
combatant (kəm-băt′nt, kŏm′bə-tnt) *n.* Fighter.
commencement (kə-mĕns′mənt) *n.* Ceremony at which academic diplomas are conferred.
commission (kə-mĭsh′ən) *n.* A fee or percentage paid to another for doing something.
commit (kə-mĭt′) *v.* To bind by promise; pledge.—**committed** *adj.*
commotion (kə-mō′shən) *n.* A minor upset or disturbance; confusion.
commute (kə-myōōt′) *v.* To travel back and forth regularly, as from one city to another.
compel (kŏm-pĕl′) *v.* To force.
competent (kŏm′pə-tənt) *adj.* Skillful.
compost (kŏm′pōst) *n.* Decaying vegetable matter used as fertilizer.
compound (kŏm-pound′, kəm-) *v.* To mix.— (kŏm′pound) *n.* A mixture.—**compounded** *adj.*
compressor (kəm-prĕs′ər) *n.* A machine for increasing the pressure of gases.
compulsion (kəm-pŭl′shən) *n.* A force; an irresistable urge.
concede (kən-sēd′) *v.* To admit.
conceivable (kən-sēv′ə-bəl) *adj.* Imaginable.
concerto (kən-chĕr′tō) *n.* A kind of musical composition.
concoct (kən-kŏkt′) *v.* To prepare by combining various ingredients.
concord (kŏn′kôrd, kŏng′-) *n.* Peace.

confound (kən-found′, kŏn-) *v.* To surprise and confuse.—**confounded** *adj.*
confront (kən-frŭnt′) *v.* To meet someone face to face, often in an unfriendly way.
congeal (kən-jēl′) *v.* To become solid; jell.
congenial (kən-jēn′yəl) *adj.* Pleasant; agreeable.
conjure (kŏn′jər, kŏn-jōōr′) *v.* To call upon; bring to mind.
conquest (kŏn′kwĕst, kŏng′-) *n.* A victory.
conservatory (kən-sûr′və-tôr′ē, -tōr′ē) *n.* A school of music.
consolation (kŏn′sə-lā′shən) *n.* A comfort.
console (kən-sōl′) *v.* To comfort.—**consoled** *adj.*
conspicuous (kən-spĭk′yōō-əs) *adj.* Easily seen; obvious.
conspire (kən-spīr′) *v.* To act or plan together in secret.
constrain (kən-strān′) *v.* To check; control.—**constrained** *adj.*
consume (kən-sōōm′, -syōōm′) *v.* To destroy.
consumption (kən-sŭmp′shən) *n.* Using up.
contemplate (kŏn′təm-plāt′) *v.* To look at thoughtfully.
contemplation (kŏn′təm-plā′shən) *n.* Meditation; deep thought.
contemporary (kən-tĕm′pə-rĕr′ē) *n.* A person of about the same age as another.
contempt (kən-tĕmpt′) *n.* Scorn.
contemptuous (kən-tĕmp′chōō-əs) *adj.* Scornful.—**contemptuously** *adv.*
contort (kən-tôrt′) *v.* To twist into unusual shapes.
contrive (kən-trīv′) *v.* **1.** To manage to do something. **2.** To scheme or plan.—**contrivance** *n.*
contuse (kən-tōōz′, -tyōōz′) *v.* To bruise.—**contusion** *n.*
conventional (kən-vĕn′shən-əl) *adj.* Usual; ordinary.
converge (kən-vûrj′) *v.* To move toward one point; to come together.
convert (kən-vûrt′) *v.* To change.
conviction (kən-vĭk′shən) *n.* Assurance of being believable.
convivial (kən-vĭv′ē-əl) *adj.* Good-humored; sociable.—**conviviality** *n.*
convoluted (kŏn′və-lōō′tĭd) *adj.* Involved; complicated.

ă p**a**t/ā p**ay**/âr c**are**/ä f**a**ther/b **b**i**b**/ch **ch**ur**ch**/d **d**ee**d**/ĕ p**e**t/ē b**e**/f **f**i**f**e/g **g**a**g**/h **h**at/hw **wh**ich/ĭ p**i**t/ī p**ie**/îr p**ier**/j **j**u**dg**e/k **k**ic**k**/ l **l**id, need**l**e/m **m**u**m**/n **n**o, sudde**n**/ng thi**ng**/ŏ p**o**t/ō t**o**e/ô p**aw**, f**o**r/oi n**oi**se/ou **ou**t/ŏŏ t**oo**k/ōō b**oo**t/p **p**o**p**/r **r**oa**r**/s **s**auce/ sh **sh**ip, di**sh**/t **t**i**gh**t/th **th**in, pa**th**/*th* **th**is, ba**th**e/ŭ c**u**t/ûr **ur**ge/v **v**al**v**e/w **w**ith/y **y**es/z **z**ebra, si**z**e/zh vi**s**ion/ə **a**bout, **i**tem, ed**i**ble, gall**o**p, circ**u**s/ȧ *Fr.* **a**mi/œ *Fr.* f**eu**, *Ger.* sch**ö**n/ü *Fr.* t**u**, *Ger.* **ü**ber/ᴋʜ *Ger.* i**ch**, *Scot.* lo**ch**/ɴ *Fr.* bo**n**.

convulsive (kən-vŭl′sĭv) *adj.* Jerky.
coral (kôr′əl, kŏr′əl) *n.* A stonelike substance used in jewelry and other ornaments.
corroborate (kə-rŏb′ə-rāt′) *v.* To confirm.
countenance (koun′tə-nəns) *n.* The face.
counter (koun′tər) *v.* To oppose; retaliate.
countinghouse (koun′tĭng-hous′) *n.* A place where accounting and other business operations take place.
covert (kŭv′ərt, kō′vərt) *n.* A hiding place.
covetous (kŭv′ə-təs) *adj.* Greedy.
covey (kŭv′ē) *n.* A small flock.
crack (krăk) *adj.* First-rate.
crafty (krăf′tē, krăf′-) *adj.* Shrewd; deceitful.
crane (krān) *v.* To stretch.
cranny (krăn′ē) *n.* A crack in a wall.
cremation (krĭ-mā′shən) *n.* The incineration of a body.
crescendo (krə-shĕn′dō) *n.* A gradual increase in loudness.
crestfallen (krĕst′fô′lən) *adj.* Low in spirits; depressed.
crevasse (krə-văs′) *n.* A deep crack in the earth.
crimson (krĭm′zən) *adj.* Deep red.
croon (kroōn) *v.* To sing softly.
croupier (kroō′pē-ər, -pē-ā′) *n.* A person who takes in and pays out money at a gambling table.
crucial (kroō′shəl) *adj.* Decisive.
crux (krŭks, kroōks) *n.* The most important part.
culprit (kŭl′prĭt) *n.* A guilty person.
cumbersome (kŭm′bər-səm) *adj.* Heavy and awkward.
curator (kyoō-rā′tər, kyoōr′ə-tər) *n.* A person in charge of a museum, library, or exhibit.
cutlass (kŭt′ləs) *n.* A short, curved sword with a single cutting edge.
cynical (sĭn′ĭ-kəl) *adj.* Sneering; sarcastic.

D

dappled (dăp′əld) *adj.* Spotted.
decamp (dĭ-kămp′) *v.* To leave.
deceitful (dĭ-sēt′fəl) *adj.* Not honest.
decipher (dĭ-sī′fər) *v.* To figure out.
declamation (dĕk′lə-mā′shən) *n.* A long, pompous speech.
decline (dĭ-klīn′) *v.* To turn down; refuse.
deform (dĭ-fôrm′) *v.* To cause to be misshapen; disfigure.
deformed (dĭ-fôrmd′) *adj.* Misshapen.
deft (dĕft) *adj.* Skillful.—**deftly** *adv.*

deliberate (dĭ-lĭb′ə-rāt′) *v.* To think about carefully.—(dĭ-lĭb′ər-ĭt) *adj.* Intentional.—**deliberately** *adv.*
deluge (dĕl′yoōj) *v.* To flood. *n.* A flood.
delve (dĕlv) *v.* To study something deeply.
deportment (dĭ-pôrt′mənt, dĭ-pōrt′-) *n.* Behavior.
depressed (dĭ-prĕst′) *adj.* Sad.
descendant (dĭ-sĕn′dənt) *n.* The offspring of a particular ancestor, family, or ethnic group.
desolate (dĕs′ə-lĭt) *adj.* Deserted.—**desolateness** *n.*
desolation (dĕs′ə-lā′shən) *n.* Ruin; emptiness.
despondency (dĭ-spŏn′dən-sē) *n.* Hopelessness.
despotism (dĕs′pə-tĭz′əm) *n.* Tyranny; dictatorship.
destitute (dĕs′tĭ-toōt′, -tyoōt′) *adj.* Extremely poor; abandoned; forsaken.
desultory (dĕs′əl-tôr′ē, -tōr′ē) *adj.* Aimless.
detect (dĭ-tĕkt′) *v.* To discover.
detonate (dĕt′n-āt′) *v.* To make explode.—**detonation** *n.*
devise (dĭ-vīz′) *v.* To plan.
devoid (dĭ-void′) *adj.* Completely without.
dexterity (dĕk-stĕr′-ə-tē) *n.* Skill in using the hands.
diameter (dī-ăm′ĭ-tər) *n.* **1.** Width. **2.** A straight line through the center of a circle.
dilapidated (dĭ-lăp′ə-dā′tĭd) *adj.* In very bad condition.
dilate (dī-lāt′, dī′lāt′, dĭ-lāt′) *v.* To become larger.—**dilated** *adj.*
dimension (dĭ-mĕn′shən) *n.* Size; scope.
diminish (dĭ-mĭn′ĭsh) *v.* To reduce.
dingy (dĭn′jē) *adj.* Dirty; dull.
dire (dīr) *adj.* Frightening.
disability (dĭs′ə-bĭl′ə-tē) *n.* **1.** A condition that prevents someone from working. **2.** A disadvantage.
discard (dĭs-kärd′) *v.* To throw away.
discharge (dĭs-chärj′) *v.* To dismiss.
disclose (dĭs-klōz′) *v.* To reveal; to make known.
discriminate (dĭs-krĭm′ə-nāt′) *v.* **1.** To show prejudice. **2.** To draw fine distinctions.
discriminating (dĭs-krĭm′ə-nā′tĭng) *adj.* **1.** Making fine distinctions. **2.** Selective.
disengage (dĭs′ĭn-gāj′) *v.* To release or get free.
dishearten (dĭs-härt′n) *v.* To discourage; depress.—**disheartened** *adj.*
dislodge (dĭs-lŏj′) *v.* To force from a position.
dismay (dĭs-mā′) *v.* To fill with alarm.—**dismayed** *adj.*
dismount (dĭs-mount′) *v.* To get down from a horse.
dispatch (dĭs-păch′) *v.* To send off.
dispense (dĭs-pĕns′) *v.* To give out; distribute.

disposition (dĭs′pə-zĭsh′ən) *n.* **1.** Personality; temperament. **2.** The manner in which something is arranged or settled.
dispute (dĭs-pyo͞ot′) *v.* To argue.
disreputable (dĭs-rĕp′yə-tə-bəl) *adj.* Not respectable; disgraceful.
dissuade (dĭ-swād′) *v.* To persuade someone not to do something.
distract (dĭs-trăkt′) *v.* To turn one's attention elsewhere.—**distracted** *adj.*
distraction (dĭs-trăk′shən) *n.* Anything that draws attention from an original focus of interest.
distress (dĭs-trĕs′) *n.* Discomfort.
divert (dĭ-vûrt′, dī-) *v.* To turn aside.—**diverted** *adj.*
divine (dĭ-vīn′) *v.* To guess; to know by intuition.
domain (dō-mān′) *n.* Territory.
domestic (də-mĕs′tĭk) *adj.* Having to do with the home.
dour (do͞or, dour) *adj.* Gloomy.
draggle (drăg′əl) *v.* To make dirty.—**draggled** *adj.*
dram (drăm) *n.* A small amount of something.
drench (drĕnch) *v.* To wet thoroughly.
drivel (drĭv′əl) *n.* Stupid talk.
duly (do͞o′le, dyo͞o′-) *adv.* Properly.
dun (dŭn) *adj.* Grayish brown.
duplicate (do͞o′plĭ-kĭt, dyo͞o′-) *n.* An exact copy.

E

ebb (ĕb) *v.* To diminish; weaken.
eccentric (ĕk-sĕn′trĭk, ĭk-) *adj.* Peculiar; odd.
eccentricity (ĕk′sĕn-trĭs′ə-tē) *n.* Peculiarity.
ecstatic (ĕk-stăt′ĭk) *adj.* Very joyful.
eddy (ĕd′ē) *n.* A current moving against another current, usually in a swirling motion.
edification (ĕd′ə-fə-kā′shən) *n.* Moral improvement or instruction.
eerie (îr′ē) *adj.* Weird.
efficiency (ĭ-fĭsh′ən-sē) *n.* Ability to get things done with little effort.
elaborate (ĭ-lăb′ər-ĭt) *adj.* Complicated.
elective (ĭ-lĕk′tĭv) *n.* An academic course selected by choice, as opposed to one that is required.
elicit (ĭ-lĭs′ĭt) *v.* To draw out.
elocution (ĕl′ə-kyo͞o′shən) *n.* The art of speaking well.
eloquence (ĕl′ə-kwəns) *n.* Forceful or persuasive speech.
eloquent (el′ə-kwənt) *adj.* Expressive.
elude (ĭ-lo͞od′) *v.* To escape from.
emanate (ĕm′ə-nāt′) *v.* To flow out; issue.
embed (ĕm-bĕd′, ĭm-) *v.* To fix firmly in something.
ember (ĕm′bər) *n.* A glowing piece of coal or wood from a dying fire.
emblem (ĕm′bləm) *n.* A badge.
embolden (ĕm-bōl′dən) *v.* To make bold or courageous.—**emboldened** *adj.*
emerge (ĭ-mûrj′) *v.* To appear.
emery (ĕm′ə-rē, ĕm′rē) *n.* A substance used for grinding and polishing.
emissary (ĕm′ə-sĕr′ē) *n.* Messenger or representative.
emphatic (ĕm-făt′ĭk) *adj.* Definite.—**emphatically** *adv.*
endear (ĕn-dîr′, ĭn-) *v.* To make dear or beloved.
endeavor (ĕn-dĕv′ər, ĭn-) *n.* An attempt.
engage (ĕn-gāj′, ĭn-) *v.* To employ.
engulf (ĕn-gŭlf′, ĭn-) *v.* To submerge; overwhelm.
enhance (ĕn-hăns′, -häns′, ĭn-) *v.* To make better.
enterprise (ĕn′tər-prīz′) *n.* An undertaking.
enthrall (ĕn-thrôl′, ĭn-) *v.* To hold as in a spell.—**enthralled** *adj.*
entreat (ĕn-trēt′, ĭn-) *v.* To beg.
entreaty (ĕn-trē′tē, ĭn-) *n.* A plea.
entwine (ĕn-twīn′, ĭn-) *v.* To twist around.
enumerate (ĭ-no͞o′mə-rāt′, ĭ-nyo͞o′-) *v.* To list.
enumeration (ĭ-no͞o′mə-rā′shən, ĭ-nyo͞o′-) *n.* A list of items.
envelop (ĕn-vĕl′əp, ĭn-) *v.* To cover completely.
enviable (ĕn′vē-ə-bəl) *adj.* Desirable.
envision (ĕn-vĭzh′ən) *v.* To imagine something that has not yet happened.
epidemic (ĕp′ə-dĕm′ĭk) *n.* A rapid spread of a disease.
equity (ĕk′wə-tē) *n.* Justice; fairness.
erect (ĭ-rĕkt′) *adj.* Upright; not bent or leaning.
erratic (ĭ-răt′ĭk) *adj.* Irregular.—**erratically** *adv.*
essence (ĕs′əns) *n.* The essential nature of a person or a thing.
ethnicity (ĕth-nĭs′ĭ-tē) *n.* Affiliation with a particular ethnic group.

ă p**a**t/ā p**ay**/âr c**are**/ä f**a**ther/b **b**i**b**/ch **ch**ur**ch**/d **d**ee**d**/ĕ p**e**t/ē b**e**/f **f**i**f**e/g **g**a**g**/h **h**at/hw **wh**ich/ĭ p**i**t/ī p**ie**/îr p**ier**/j **j**u**dg**e/k **k**i**ck**/l **l**i**d**, need**l**e/m **m**u**m**/n **n**o, sudde**n**/ng thi**ng**/ŏ p**o**t/ō t**o**e/ô p**aw**, f**o**r/oi n**oi**se/ou **ou**t/o͝o t**oo**k/o͞o b**oo**t/p **p**o**p**/r **r**oa**r**/s **s**au**ce**/sh **sh**ip, di**sh**/t **t**igh**t**/th **th**in, pa**th**/*th* **th**is, ba**th**e/ŭ c**u**t/ûr **ur**ge/v **v**al**v**e/w **w**ith/y **y**es/z **z**ebra, si**z**e/zh vi**si**on/ə **a**bout, **i**tem, ed**i**ble, gall**o**p, circ**u**s/á *Fr.* **a**mi/œ *Fr.* f**eu**, *Ger.* sch**ö**n/ü *Fr.* t**u**, *Ger.* **ü**ber/ᴋʜ *Ger.* i**ch**, *Scot.* lo**ch**/ɴ *Fr.* bo**n**.

Glossary 773

evolve (ĭ-vŏlv′) *v.* To develop gradually.
exact (ĕg-zăkt′, ĭg-) *v.* To demand; force.
exalt (ĕg-zôlt′, ĭg-) *v.* To raise to a high position.—**exalted** *adj.*
exasperate (ĕg-zăs′pə-rāt, ĭg-) *v.* To make angry.—**exasperating** *adj.*
exceedingly (ĕk-sē′dĭng-lē, ĭk-) *adv.* Extremely.
excel (ĕk-sĕl′, ĭk-) *v.* To do better than others.
exemption (ĕg-zĕmp′shən) *n.* Release from obligation.
exhale (ĕks-hāl′, ĕk-sāl′, ĭk-sāl′) *v.* To breathe out.
exhilarate (ĕg-zĭl′ə-rāt′, ĭg-) *v.* To excite.—**exhilarating** *adj.*
exile (ĕg′zīl′, ĕk′sīl′) *n.* Separation from one's country.
exotic (ĕg-zŏt′ĭk, ĭg-) *adj.* Unusual and fascinating.
expectant (ĕk-spĕk′tənt, ĭk-) *adj.* Waiting for something to happen.
expiation (ĕk′spē-ā′shən) *n.* The act of making amends.
exploit (ĕks′ploit′) *n.* A daring act.
exposure (ĕk-spō′zhər, ĭk-) *n.* Being without protection from natural forces.
exquisite (ĕks′kwĭ-zĭt) *adj.* Extremely beautiful.—**exquisitely** *adv.*
extemporize (ĕk-stĕm′pə-rīz′, ĭk-) *v.* To improvise; to prepare something for temporary use.
extension (ĕk-stĕn′shən, ĭk-) *n.* An extra period of time allowed for payment of a debt.
extract (ĕk-străkt′, ĭk-) *v.* To pull out.
extricate (ĕk′strĭ-kāt′) *v.* To set free.
exude (ĕg-zōōd′, ĭg-, ĕk-sōōd′, ĭk-) *v.* To give off.
exultant (ĕg-zŭl′tənt, ĭg-) *adj.* Joyful.—**exultantly** *adv.*
exultation (ĕg′zŭl-tā′shən) *n.* Great joyfulness; triumph.

F

façade (fə-säd′) *n.* The front of a building.
fain (fān) *adv.* Willingly.
falter (fôl′tər) *v.* To show uncertainty.
famine (făm′ĭn) *n.* A severe and widespread shortage of food.
fancy (făn′sē) *v.* To imagine. *n.* Imagination; invention.
fathom (făth′əm) *v.* **1.** To measure the depth of. **2.** To understand thoroughly. *n.* A unit of measurement equal to six feet.
feat (fēt) *n.* An act of great skill or courage.
feign (fān) *v.* To pretend.
fend (fĕnd) *v.* To ward off; resist.

ferocity (fə-rŏs′ə-tē) *n.* Fierceness.
fervent (fûr′vənt) *adj.* Very enthusiastic; intense.
festal (fĕs′təl) *adj.* Joyous; merry.
festive (fĕs′tĭv) *adj.* Merry.
fetter (fĕt′ər) *v.* To put in chains. *n.* A chain.
feud (fyōōd) *n.* A bitter, prolonged quarrel between two individuals or families.
flabbergast (flăb′ər-găst′) *v.* To shock and surprise.—**flabbergasted** *adj.*
flagging (flăg′ĭng) *adj.* Weakening.
flail (flāl) *v.* To move one's arms about vigorously.
flank (flăngk) *v.* To be on either side of. *n.* The side of something.—**flanked** *adj.*
flaw (flô) *n.* A defect.—**flawless** *adj.*
flax (flăks) *n.* A plant with delicate blue flowers.
fleck (flĕk) *n.* A spot.—**flecked** *adj.*
fledgling (flĕj′lĭng) *n.* A young bird.
flexible (flĕk′sə-bəl) *adj.* Capable of being bent.
flicker (flĭk′ər) *v.* To burn unsteadily.
flinch (flĭnch) *v.* To draw away; wince.
florid (flôr′ĭd, flŏr′-) *adj.* Ornate; flowery.
flouncy (flouns′ē) *adj.* Decorated with wide, ornamental ruffles.
flounder (floun′dər) *v.* To struggle clumsily.
fluorescent (flōō′rĕs′ənt, flô-, flō-) *adj.* Exhibiting electromagnetic radiation of visible light.
flush (flŭsh) *v.* To frighten out of a hiding place.
flustered (flŭs′tərd) *adj.* Upset; confused.
foible (foi′bəl) *n.* Weakness in character.
folly (fŏl′ē) *n.* Foolishness.
foolhardy (fōōl′här′dē) *adj.* Rash; foolishly daring.
forage (fôr′ĭj, fŏr′-) *n.* Food for domestic animals such as cattle, sheep, and horses.
foray (fôr′ā′) *n.* A surprise attack or raid.
forbearance (fôr-bâr′əns) *n.* Patience; self-control.
forlorn (fôr-lôrn′, fər-) *adj.* Deserted.—**forlornly** *adv.*
forsaken (fôr-sāk′ən) *adj.* Deserted.
fortitude (fôr′tə-tōōd′, -tyōōd′) *n.* Courage.
foul (foul) *adj.* Disgusting.
fount (fount) *n.* A source.
frantic (frăn′tĭk) *adj.* Wild.—**frantically** *adv.*
fraudulent (frô′jə-lənt) *adj.* Deceitful.
fray (frā) *n.* A fight.
frenzy (frĕn′zē) *n.* Violent activity.
fretful (frĕt′fəl) *adj.* Complaining; discontented.
fringe (frĭnj) *v.* To grow along the edge of.
frothing (frôth′ĭng, frŏth-) *n.* Enthusiasm.
fumble (fŭm′bəl) *v.* To grope about clumsily or unskillfully.
functional (fŭngk′shən-əl) *adj.* Practical; usable.

furtive (fûr′tĭv) *adj.* Sneaky; sly.—**furtively** *adv.*
futility (fyoo-tĭl′ə-tē) *n.* Uselessness.
futuristic (fyoo′chər-ĭs-tĭk) *adj.* Having to do with the future.

G

gait (gāt) *n.* A manner of walking.
gall (gôl) *v.* To irritate.
garble (gär′bəl) *v.* To mix up; confuse.—**garbled** *adj.*
garland (gär′lənd) *n.* A wreath.
gaudy (gô′dē) *adj.* Flashy; lacking taste.
gazebo (gə-zē′bō, -zā′bō) *n.* A roofed structure serving as a shelter.
gesticulate (jĕ-stĭk′yə-lāt′) *v.* To use gestures in place of speech.
giddy (gĭd′ē) *adj.* Dizzy; dazed.
gingerly (jĭn′jər-lē) *adv.* Carefully.
girth (gûrth) *n.* A strap that goes under the belly of an animal to secure a saddle or a pack.
glade (glād) *n.* An open area in a forest.
glaze (glāz) *v.* To apply a shiny coating.—**glazing** *adj.*
glower (glou′ər) *v.* To stare in an angry or ill-humored way.
glum (glŭm) *adj.* Gloomy; in low spirits.—**glumly** *adv.*
glutton (glŭt′n) *n.* One who overeats.
gouge (gouj) *v.* To scoop or force out.
greatcoat (grāt′kōt′) *n.* A heavy overcoat.
greenhouse (grēn′hous′) *n.* A glass-enclosed structure where plants are grown.
grim (grĭm) *adj.* Stern; unfriendly.—**grimly** *adv.*
grimace (grĭ-mās′, grĭm′ĭs) *v.* To twist or distort the face.
grisly (grĭz′lē) *adj.* Horrifying.
grizzle (grĭz′əl) *v.* To become gray.—**grizzled** *adj.*
grope (grōp) *v.* To feel one's way.
gross (grōs) *adj.* Referring to total income before deductions are made.
gruel (groo′əl) *n.* Thin, watery porridge, usually made of oatmeal.
grueling (groo′ə-ling) *adj.* Harsh; extremely difficult.
guffaw (gə-fô′) *n.* A loud burst of laughter.
gullible (gŭl′ə-bəl) *adj.* Easily deceived or cheated.
gust (gŭst) *n.* A rush of wind.—**gusty** *adj.*
gut (gŭt) *v.* **1.** To destroy the insides of. **2.** To take out the inner organs.—**gutted** *adj.*
guttural (gŭt′ər-əl) *adj.* Coming from the throat.

H

habitable (hăb′ə-tə-bəl) *adj.* Able to be lived in.
haggle (hăg′əl) *v.* To bargain; argue about prices.
hamstring (hăm′strĭng′) *v.* To cripple by cutting the tendons in the hind legs.
hapless (hăp′lĭs) *adj.* Unlucky.
hark (härk) *v.* To listen.
harry (hăr′ē) *v.* To annoy constantly.—**harried** *adj.*
haughty (hô′tē) *adj.* Proud; arrogant.
havoc (hăv′ək) *n.* Extreme disorder.
headland (hĕd′lənd, -lănd′) *n.* A point of land that juts out into the water.
hearken (här′kən) *v.* To listen carefully.
heath (hēth) *n.* An open, uncultivated area; a moor.
heifer (hĕf′ər) *n.* A young cow.
heirloom (âr′loom′) *n.* A prized family possession that is handed down from generation to generation.
helm (hĕlm) *n.* The steering wheel of a ship.
hemorrhage (hĕm′ə-rĭj) *n.* A heavy flow of blood.
hideous (hĭd′ē-əs) *adj.* Ugly.
hoard (hôrd, hōrd) *v.* To store up or hide.
hobble (hob′əl) *v.* To limp; walk awkwardly.
hobnail (hŏb′nāl) *n.* A nail put on the soles of shoes to keep them from wearing or slipping.
hoist (hoist) *v.* To lift.
homage (hŏm′ĭj, ŏm′-) *n.* Honor; respect.
horde (hôrd, hōrd) *n.* A large, disorderly group.
hospitable (hŏs′pə-tə-bəl) *adj.* Friendly toward visitors.
hostile (hŏs′təl) *adj.* Unfriendly.
hover (hŭv′ər, hŏv′-) *v.* To remain suspended in one place in the air.
hummock (hŭm′ək) *n.* A small hill.
hunker (hŭng′kər) *v.* To crouch; squat.
hurl (hûrl) *v.* To throw vigorously.
hurtle (hûrt′l) *v.* To move with great speed.
hysteria (hĭ-stĕr′ē-ə) *n.* Uncontrolled emotion.
hysterical (hĭ-stĕr′ĭ-kəl) *adj.* Wildly emotional.

I

ignite (ĭg-nīt′) *v.* To set on fire.—**ignited** *adj.*

illuminate (ĭ-lōō′mə-nāt′) v. To light up.
immobile (ĭ-mō′bəl, -bēl′) adj. Not moving.—**immobility** n.
immortal (ĭ-môrt′l) n. One who will never die.—adj. Living forever.
impact (ĭm′păkt′) n. A forceful strike.
impasse (ĭm′păs′) n. A situation from which there seems to be no escape or solution.
impediment (ĭm-pĕd′ə-mənt) n. A hindrance.
imperceptible (ĭm′pər-sĕp′tə-bəl) adj. Barely noticeable.—**imperceptibly** adv.
imperial (ĭm-pîr′ē-əl) adj. 1. Of superior size or quality. 2. Majestic.
imperishable (ĭm-pĕr′ĭ-shə-bəl) adj. Not likely to be destroyed.
impiety (ĭm-pī′ə-tē) n. Lack of reverence for God; disrespect.
impish (ĭm′pĭsh) adj. Playful.
implore (ĭm-plôr′, -plōr′) v. To beg.
imposing (ĭm-pō′zĭng) adj. Impressive.
impressive (ĭm-prĕs′ĭv) adj. Creating a strong effect or impression.
improbable (ĭm-prŏb′ə-bəl) adj. Not likely.
impudent (ĭm′pyə-dənt) adj. Disrespectful; insolent.—**impudently** adv.
inaudible (ĭn-ô′də-bəl) adj. Not able to be heard.
inaugurate (ĭn-ô′gyə-rāt′) v. To start officially.
incantation (ĭn-kăn-tā′shən) n. The chanting of words to cast a magic spell.
incarnate (ĭn-kär′nĭt) adj. In the flesh; embodied.
incessant (ĭn-sĕs′ənt) adj. Continuing without interruption.—**incessantly** adv.
incompetent (ĭn-kŏm′pə-tənt) adj. Lacking needed abilities; not capable.
incomprehensible (ĭn′kŏm-prĭ-hĕn′sə-bəl, ĭn-kŏm′-) adj. Unable to be understood; baffling.
inconspicuous (ĭn′kən-spĭk′yōō-əs) adj. Attracting little notice.
incredulous (ĭn-krĕj′ə-ləs) adj. Unwilling or unable to believe.
indifference (ĭn-dĭf′ər-əns) n. A lack of concern.—**indifferent** adj.—**indifferently** adv.
indignant (ĭn-dĭg′nənt) adj. Angry, especially at an injustice.—**indignantly** adv.
indignation (ĭn′dĭg-nā′shən) n. Anger, especially at an injustice.
indispensable (ĭn′dĭs-pĕn′sə-bəl) adj. Absolutely essential.
induce (ĭn-dōōs′, -dyōōs′) v. To persuade.
inert (ĭn-ûrt′) adj. Inactive.

inevitable (ĭn-ĕv′ə-tə-bəl) adj. Unavoidable.—**inevitably** adv.
inexplicable (ĭn-ĕk′splĭ-kə-bəl, ĭn′ĭk-splik′ə-bəl) adj. Not able to be explained.
infamous (ĭn′fə-məs) adj. Outrageous.
infatuated (ĭn-făch′ōō-ā′tĭd) adj. Characterized by a foolish attraction to someone or something.
inflated (ĭn-flā′tĭd) adj. Expanded; puffed up.
infringe (ĭn-frĭnj′) v. To trespass; violate. *Infringe on* or *upon.*
infuriate (ĭn-fyōōr′ē-āt′) v. To make very angry; enrage.
ingenious (ĭn-jēn′yəs) adj. Very clever.
inhospitable (ĭn-hŏs′pĭ-tə-bəl, ĭn′hŏ-spĭt′ə-bəl) adj. Unfriendly toward visitors.
initiative (ĭ-nĭsh′ə-tĭv) n. The first step toward changing a situation.
insensible (ĭn-sĕn′sə-bəl) adj. So small as to be hardly noticeable.
insolent (ĭn′sə-lənt) adj. Insulting.
insulation (ĭn′sə-lā′shən, ĭns′yə-) n. Something that prevents or reduces the passage of heat, electricity, sound, etc., in or out.
insuperable (ĭn-sōō′pər-ə-bəl) adj. Unable to be overcome.
intact (ĭn-tăkt′) adj. Whole; complete.
intercept (ĭn′tər-sĕpt′) v. To seize or stop on the way; cut off.
interlude (ĭn′tər-lōōd′) n. An intervening period of time.
interminable (ĭn-tûr′mə-nə-bəl) adj. Endless or seeming to be endless.—**interminably** adv.
intermittent (ĭn′tər-mĭt′ənt) adj. Stopping from time to time; not continuous.—**intermittently** adv.
intimate (ĭn′tə-māt′) v. To hint.—**intimation** n.
intolerable (ĭn-tŏl′ər-ə-bəl) adj. Unbearable; too painful to be endured.
intrude (ĭn-trōōd′) n. To enter without being welcome; to force one's way in.—**intruder** n.
invariable (ĭn-vâr′ē-ə-bəl) adj. Unchanging.—**invariably** adv.
invective (ĭn-vĕk′tĭv) n. Insulting or abusive language.
invincible (ĭn-vĭn′sə-bəl) adj. Not able to be conquered.
involuntary (ĭn-vŏl′ən-tĕr′ē) adj. Done without choice or intention.—**involuntarily** adv.
irate (ī-rāt′, ī′rāt′) adj. Very angry.
ironic (ī-rŏn′ĭk) adj. Opposite to what might be expected.—**ironically** adv.

irresolute (ĭ-rĕz′ə-lo͞ot′) *adj.* Undecided.
irrevocable (ĭ-rĕv′ə-kə-bəl) *adj.* Not able to be undone or recalled.
islet (ī′lĭt) *n.* A small island.
isolation (ī′sə-lā′shən) *n.* Aloneness.

J

jar (jär) *v.* To bump.
jaunty (jôn′tē, jän′-) *adj.* Gay.—**jauntily** *adv.*
jeer (jîr) *v.* To make fun of.
jetty (jĕt′ē) *n.* A pier, a landing place for ships.
jolt (jōlt) *v.* To shake about; bump into.
jovial (jō′vē-əl) *adj.* Merry; jolly.
jubilant (jo͞o′bə-lənt) *adj.* Showing great joy.—**jubilantly** *adv.*
judicious (jo͞o-dĭsh′əs) *adj.* Wise.—**judiciously** *adv.*
juncture (jŭngk′chər) *n.* A point in time.
justify (jŭs′tə-fī′) *v.* To defend.

K

kiln (kĭl, kĭln) *n.* An oven for baking or firing substances, especially pottery.
knoll (nōl) *n.* A small hill.

L

lacerate (lăs′ə-rāt) *v.* To tear.—**laceration** *n.*
lament (lə-mĕnt′) *v.* To grieve; mourn.
lance (lăns, läns) *n.* A weapon with a long shaft and a pointed tip.
languid (lăng′gwĭd) *adj.* Without energy or enthusiasm.—**languidly** *adv.*
larceny (lär′sə-nē) *n.* Theft.
lash (lăsh) *v.* To tie securely.
launch (lônch, länch) *n.* A large, open motorboat.
lavish (lăv′ĭsh) *adj.* Generous.—**lavishly** *adv.*
lax (lăks) *adj.* Not strict; negligent.
lethal (lē′thəl) *adj.* Deadly.
lethargic (li-thär′jik) *adj.* Listless; drowsy.
level (lĕv′əl) *v.* To knock down.
liability (lī′ə-bĭl′ə-tē) *n.* A disadvantage.
limber (lĭm′bər) *adj.* Supple; lithe.
limpid (lĭm′pĭd) *adj.* Clear; transparent.
lineage (lĭn′ē-ĭj) *n.* Family background.
linger (lĭng′gər) *v.* To continue to stay.
linnet (lĭn′ĭt) *n.* A small songbird.
listless (lĭst′lĭs) *adj.* Showing no energy or interest.—**listlessly** *adv.*
lithe (līth) *adj.* Graceful.
loincloth (loin′klôth′, -kläth′) *n.* A strip of cloth worn about the hips and lower abdomen.
loiter (loi′tər) *v.* To stand around idly or aimlessly.
lollop (lŏl′əp) *v.* To move in bounds or leaps.—**lolloping** *adj.*
loom (lo͞om) *v.* To come into sight, as something fearful.—**loomed** *adj.*
lope (lōp) *v.* To move with an easy, bounding gait.
lucent (lo͞o′sənt) *adj.* Glowing; luminous.
lumber (lŭm′bər) *v.* To walk with a heavy, awkward step.
luminous (lo͞o′mə-nəs) *adj.* Able to glow in the dark.
lunge (lŭnj) *n.* A sudden forward movement.
lurch (lûrch) *v.* To stagger.
lurid (lo͝or′ĭd) *adj.* Glowing or shining fiery red.

M

majestic (mə-jĕs′tĭk) *adj.* Grand; stately.—**majestically** *adv.*
malevolence (mə-lĕv′ə-ləns) *n.* Ill will.
malice (măl′ĭs) *n.* Intention to harm another person.
mania (mā′nē-ə, mān′yə) *n.* Excessive fondness; craze.
manifest (măn′ə-fĕst′) *v.* To become evident.
martial (mär′shəl) *adj.* Eager to fight; warlike.
martyr (mär′tər) *n.* One who suffers or dies for something he or she believes in.
massive (măs′ĭv) *adj.* Huge.
mast (măst, mäst) *n.* A pole used to support the sails and rigging of a ship.
materialize (mə-tîr′ē-əl-īz′) *v.* To take shape.
materially (mə-tîr′ē-əl-ē) *adv.* Significantly.
mausoleum (mô′sə-lē′əm, mô′zə-) *n.* A large, grand tomb.
mawkish (mô′kĭsh) *adj.* Overly emotional.
maze (māz) *n.* **1.** A network of paths used in a laboratory to test animals. **2.** A puzzle; something that is confusing.
meander (mē-ăn′dər) *v.* To wander aimlessly.
meditation (mĕd′ĭ-tā′shən) *n.* Deep thought; solemn reflection.

ă pat/ā pay/âr care/ä father/b bib/ch church/d deed/ĕ pet/ē be/f fife/g gag/h hat/hw which/ĭ pit/ī pie/îr pier/j judge/k kick/l lid, needle/m mum/n no, sudden/ng thing/ŏ pot/ō toe/ô paw, for/oi noise/ou out/o͝o took/o͞o boot/p pop/r roar/s sauce/sh ship, dish/t tight/th thin, path/*th* this, bathe/ŭ cut/ûr urge/v valve/w with/y yes/z zebra, size/zh vision/ə about, item, edible, gallop, circus/ä *Fr.* ami/œ *Fr.* feu, *Ger.* schön/ü *Fr.* tu, *Ger.* über/KH *Ger.* ich, *Scot.* loch/N *Fr.* bon.

megaphone (mĕg′ə-fōn′) *n.* A cone-shaped device to make the voice louder.
melancholy (mĕl′ən-kŏl′ē) *adj.* Sad; gloomy.
memorial (mə-môr′ē-əl, mə-mōr′-) *n.* Something, such as a monument or holiday, intended as a reminder of some person or event.
menagerie (mə-năj′ə-rē, mə-năzh′-) *n.* A zoo.
mesa (mā′sə) *n.* An elevation having steep sides and a flat top, usually found in the southwestern United States.
metabolism (mə-tăb′ə-lĭz′əm) *n.* The processes by which the body uses food or breaks it down into waste matter.
metropolis (mə-trŏp′ə-lĭs) *n.* A large city.
mettle (mĕt′l) *n.* Courage; worth.
microbe (mī′krōb′) *n.* A germ.
misjudge (mĭs-jŭj′) *v.* To judge wrongly.
mobility (mō-bĭl′ə-tē) *n.* Ability to move.
mockery (mŏk′ər-ē) *n.* Derision; ridicule.
moil (moil) *v.* To work hard.
molder (mōl′dər) *v.* To decay.—**moldering** *adj.*
molest (mə-lĕst′) *v.* To annoy.
monotonous (mə-nŏt′n-əs) *adj.* Lacking variety; dull because repetitious.
moony (mōō′nē) *adj.* Dreamy.
moor (moor) *n.* A stretch of open land, often swampy.
morality (mə-răl′ə-tē, mô-) *n.* Principles of right and wrong conduct.
mortal (môrt′l) *adj.* Subject to death.
mortgage (môr′gĭj) *v.* To pledge something valuable in return for a loan.
mosaic (mō-zā′ĭk) *n.* A picture or design made from small pieces of colored material such as stone or glass.
motivate (mō′tə-vāt′) *v.* To move to action.—**motivated** *adj.*
motive (mō′tĭv) *adj.* Causing motion.
mottle (mŏt′l) *v.* To mark with spots of various colors and shapes.—**mottled** *adj.*
mournful (môrn′fəl, mōrn′-) *adj.* Extremely sad; melancholy.
mucilage (myōō′sə-lĭj) *n.* A type of glue.
multitude (mŭl′tĭ-tōōd′, -tyōōd′) *n.* A large number of persons gathered together as a group.
musket (mŭs′kĭt) *n.* A shoulder gun used before the rifle was invented.
muster (mŭs′tər) *v.* To summon up; collect or gather.
myriad (mîr′ē-əd) *n.* A vast number.

N

network (nĕt′wôrk′) *n.* A structure made up of intersecting threads.
nominal (nŏm′ə-nəl) *adj.* Of minimal value.
nonchalance (nŏn′shə-läns′) *n.* A lack of concern.
notion (nō′shən) *n.* An idea.
nuptial (nŭp′shəl, -chəl) *adj.* Pertaining to mating.
nurture (nûr′chər) *v.* To rear; to care for.

O

obeisance (ō-bā′səns, ō-bē′-) *n.* An act of respect, such as bowing.
oblique (ō-blēk′, ə-) *adj.* At an angle; not straight.—**obliquely** *adv.*
obliterate (ə-blĭt′ə-rāt′) *v.* To remove completely; erase.—**obliterated** *adj.*
oblivious (ə-blĭv′ē-əs) *adj.* Unmindful; unaware.
obnoxious (ŏb-nŏk′shəs, əb-) *adj.* Hateful.
obscure (ŏb-skyoor′, əb-) *adj.* Unclear.
obstinate (ŏb′stə-nĭt) *adj.* Stubborn.
ochre (ō′kər) *n.* A yellowish- or reddish-brown color.
odious (ō′dē-əs) *adj.* Hateful.
ogre (ō′gər) *n.* A monster.
ointment (oint′mənt) *n.* A salve; something that soothes.
ominous (ŏm′ə-nəs) *adj.* Sinister; threatening.
omnivorous (ŏm-nĭv′ər-əs) *adj.* Eating every kind of food.
onyx (ŏn′ĭks) *n.* A semiprecious stone used in jewelry and other ornaments.
opaque (ō-pāk′) *adj.* Not permitting light to go through.
opportune (ŏp′ər-tōōn′, -tyōōn′) *adj.* Well-timed.
oppress (ə-prĕs′) *v.* To weigh down.—**oppressed** *adj.* Depressed or burdened.
option (ŏp′shən) *n.* A choice.
ordeal (ôr-dēl′) *n.* A difficult experience.
orientation (ôr′ē-ĕn-tā′shən, -ən-, ōr′-) *n.* Instruction about a new place or situation.
ornate (ôr-nāt′) *adj.* Very fancy.

P

pandemonium (păn′də-mō′nē-əm) *n.* Noisy confusion.
parade (pə-rād′) *v.* To show off; make a display of.
parasol (păr′ə-sôl′, -sŏl′) *n.* A small umbrella used for protection from the sun.
passel (păs′əl) *n.* A large number.
passionate (păsh′ən-ĭt) *adj.* Very affectionate.
passive (păs′ĭv) *adj.* Not participating.

pathetic (pə-thĕt′ĭk) *adj.* Pitifully ineffective or unsuccessful.—**pathetically** *adv.*
patron (pā′trən) *n.* **1.** A customer. **2.** In ancient times, the god or goddess who protected a city.
patronize (pā′trə-nīz′, păt′rə-) *v.* To be a regular customer.
pauper (pô′pər) *n.* A person who is extremely poor.
peaked (pēkt, pē′-kĭd) *adj.* Pale.
peasant (pĕz′ənt) *n.* Someone who works the land; a country person of humble birth.
pedagogy (pĕd′ə-gō′jē, -gŏj′ē) *n.* Teaching.
pedestrian (pə-dĕs′trē-ən) *adj.* Walking.—*n.* A walker.
pedigree (pĕd′ə-grē′) *n.* **1.** Ancestry. **2.** A record of descent, particularly of purebred animals.
peer (pîr) *n.* An equal.
pelt (pĕlt) *v.* To run rapidly.
penance (pĕn′əns) *n.* Self-punishment for a sin or wrongdoing.
penetrate (pĕn′ə-trāt′) *v.* To go through or into.
peninsula (pə-nĭn′syə-lə, -sə-lə) *n.* A land area almost completely surrounded by water.
perceive (pər-sēv′) *v.* **1.** To become aware of. **2.** To understand. **3.** To notice or observe.
perceptible (pər-sĕp′tə-bəl) *adj.* Noticeable.
peril (pĕr′əl) *n.* Danger.—**perilous** *adj.*
perimeter (pə-rĭm′ə-tər) *n.* Limits; boundary.
periodic (pîr′ē-ŏd′ĭk) *adj.* At regular intervals—**periodically** *adv.*
perpendicular (pûr′pən-dĭk′yə-lər) *adj.* Upright; vertical.
perpetual (pər-pĕch′ōō-əl) *adj.* Lasting forever or for an unlimited time.
perplex (pər-plĕks′) *v.* To confuse.
perplexed (pər-plĕkst′) *adj.* Confused; puzzled.
persevere (pûr′sə-vîr′) *v.* To continue in some line of action or thought despite obstacles.
persist (pər-sĭst′, -zĭst′) *v.* To continue to do something with great determination.
pervade (pər-vād′) *v.* To spread through; extend all over.
perverted (pər-vûr′tĭd) *adj.* Misdirected; not used properly.
pestilence (pĕs′tə-ləns) *n.* A widely spread disease.
phantom (făn′təm) *n.* A ghost.

phenomenon (fĭ-nŏm′ə-nŏn′) *n.* An unusual happening.
philosophical (fĭl′ə-sŏf′ĭ-kəl) *adj.* Wise—**philosophically** *adv.*
philter (fĭl′tər) *n.* A magic potion or charm.
pilfer (pĭl′fər) *v.* To steal small amounts of money or objects of little value.
pilgrimage (pĭl′grə-mĭj) *n.* A journey to a holy place or shrine.
pillar (pĭl′ər) *n.* A column.
pillbox (pĭl′bŏks′) *adj.* Shaped like a small, round box.
pine (pīn) *v.* To yearn for.
pique (pēk) *v.* To arouse.
pivot (pĭv′ət) *v.* To turn like a wheel.
placid (plăs′ĭd) *adj.* Peaceful.
plague (plāg) *n.* A highly contagious, epidemic disease.
plaintive (plān′tĭv) *adj.* Sad.
pledge (plĕj) *n.* A token of a promise.
pliant (plī′ənt) *adj.* Easily bent; flexible.
plight (plīt) *n.* A difficult situation.
plowshare (plou′shâr′) *n.* The cutting blade of a plow.
plump (plŭmp) *v.* To fall heavily.
poise (poiz) *v.* To balance or steady.—**poised** *adj.*
ponder (pŏn′dər) *v.* To think carefully about.
ponderous (pŏn′dər-əs) *adj.* **1.** Very heavy. **2.** Dull.—**ponderously** *adv.*
populous (pŏp′yə-ləs) *adj.* Having many people.
porcelain (pôrs′lĭn, pōrs′-, pōr′sə-lĭn) *n.* A hard, white, translucent earthenware, used for china, vases, and figurines.
portly (pôrt′lē, pōrt′-) *adj.* Large and heavy in a dignified or imposing way.
potential (pə-tĕn′shəl) *adj.* Possible but not yet realized. *n.* An ability capable of development.
potter (pŏt′ər) *v. Chiefly British.* To putter; dawdle.
poultice (pōl′tĭs) *n.* A hot pack applied to a sore part of the body.
pounce (pouns) *v.* To spring on something.
practitioner (prăk-tĭsh′ə-nər) *n.* One who practices a technique or profession.
prance (prăns, präns) *v.* To rise up on the hind legs and spring forward, as a horse.

ă p**a**t/ā p**ay**/âr c**are**/ä f**a**ther/b **b**i**b**/ch **ch**ur**ch**/d **d**ee**d**/ĕ p**e**t/ē b**e**/f **f**i**f**e/g **g**a**g**/h **h**at/hw **wh**ich/ĭ p**i**t/ī p**ie**/îr p**ier**/j **j**u**dg**e/k **k**ic**k**/ l l**i**d, need**l**e/m **m**u**m**/n **n**o, sudde**n**/ng thi**ng**/ŏ p**o**t/ō t**oe**/ô p**aw**, f**o**r/oi n**oi**se/ou **ou**t/ŏŏ t**oo**k/ōō b**oo**t/p **p**o**p**/r **r**oa**r**/s **s**auce/ sh **sh**ip, di**sh**/t **t**igh**t**/th **th**in, pa**th**/*th* **th**is, ba**th**e/ŭ c**u**t/ûr **ur**ge/v **v**al**v**e/w **w**ith/y **y**es/z **z**ebra, si**z**e/zh vi**s**ion/ə **a**bout, **i**tem, edi**b**le, gall**o**p, circ**u**s/ä *Fr.* **a**mi/œ *Fr.* f**eu**, *Ger.* sch**ö**n/ü *Fr.* t**u**, *Ger.* **ü**ber/ᴋʜ *Ger.* i**ch**, *Scot.* lo**ch**/ɴ *Fr.* bo**n**.

precaution (prĭ-kô′shən) *n.* Care taken in advance, as a safeguard.
precedent (prĕs′ə-dənt) *n.* An act or decision used as an example in dealing with later cases.
precipice (prĕs′ə-pĭs) *n.* A steep cliff.
precipitous (prĭ-sĭp′ə-təs) *adj.* Steep.
preliminary (prĭ-lĭm′ə-nĕr′ē) *n.* Something that comes before the main action or business.
prelude (prĕl′yōōd′, prē′lōōd′) *n.* An introductory event.
premature (prē′mə-chōōr′, -tōōr′, -tyōōr′) *adj.* Happening too early; too hasty.
premonition (prē′mə-nĭsh′ən, prĕm′ə-) *n.* A feeling that something bad will happen.
preoccupied (prē-ŏk′yə-pīd′) *adj.* Already occupied or busy; engrossed.
preside (prĭ-zīd′) *v.* To be in control.
presume (prĭ-zōōm′) *v.* To take for granted.
prevalent (prĕv′ə-lənt) *adj.* Widespread.
prig (prĭg) *n.* A smug, pompous person.
prim (prĭm) *adj.* Formal.—**primly** *adv.*
prime (prīm) *v.* To get a gun ready for firing.
priming (prīm′ĭng) *n.* Powder or other explosive material used to set off a charge in a gun.
primitive (prĭm′ə-tĭv) *adj.* Belonging to earliest times.
probe (prōb) *v.* To investigate; examine.
proclaim (prō-klām′, prə-) *v.* To declare publicly.
procure (prō-kyōōr′, prə-) *v.* To get; obtain.
prod (prŏd) *v.* To incite to action.
profess (prə-fĕs′, prō-) *v.* To claim; declare.—**professing** *n.*
proffer (prŏf′ər) *v.* To offer.
profusion (prə-fyōō′zhən, prō-) *n.* A large amount.
projection (prə-jĕk′shən) *n.* Something that sticks out.
prolific (prō-lĭf′ĭk) *adj.* Abundant.
propel (prə-pĕl′) *v.* To push forward; cause to move.
prophecy (prŏf′ə-sē) *n.* A prediction.
prophet (prŏf′ĭt) *n.* One who predicts future events.
prospector (prŏs′pĕk′tər) *n.* Someone who looks for oil or mineral deposits.
protest (prə-tĕst′, prō-, prō′tĕst′) *v.* To object to; disagree with.
protrude (prō-trōōd′) *v.* To stick out.
providence (prŏv′ə-dəns, -dĕns′) *n.* **1.** The care and control exercised by God over the universe. **2.** (**P-**) God.
province (prŏv′ĭns) *n.* An area of duties and responsibilities.

provoke (prə-vōk′) *v.* To stir up.—**provoking** *adj.*
prowess (prou′ĭs) *n.* Great ability or skill; strength.
pry (prī) *v.* To open something with difficulty.
puberty (pyōō′bər-tē′) *n.* The stage of development between childhood and adulthood.
pulsate (pŭl′sāt′) *v.* To throb or beat rhythmically, as the heart does.
pungent (pŭn′jənt) *adj.* Sharp-smelling.
puny (pyōō′nē) *adj.* Weak; undersized.
purgative (pûr′gə-tĭv) *n.* A laxative.
pyre (pīr) *n.* A funeral pile on which a dead body is burned.

Q

quack (kwăk) *adj.* Referring to someone or something that pretends to have power to cure disease.
quail (kwāl) *v.* To cower or cringe in fear.
quarters (kwôr′tərz) *n.* The place where one lives.
quell (kwĕl) *v.* To put down; quiet.
quench (kwĕnch) *v.* **1.** To put an end to. **2.** To cool by plunging into water.
quest (kwĕst) *n.* A search.
quiver (kwĭv′ər) *v.* To tremble.—**quivering** *adj.*

R

racy (rā′sē) *adj.* Daring.—**racily** *adv.*
radiant (rā′dē-ənt) *adj.* Bright; glowing.
radiate (rā′dē-āt′) *v.* To send out rays of light or heat.
rake (rāk) *v.* To search through carefully.
rampage (răm′pāj′) *v.* To behave in a wild or violent manner.
ramshackle (răm′shăk′əl) *adj.* Rickety; likely to fall apart.
rapture (răp′chər) *n.* A feeling of great joy.
ravenous (răv′ən-əs) *adj.* Extremely hungry.
ready (rĕd′ē) *v.* To prepare.
recitation (rĕs′ə-tā′shən) *n.* Something that is told aloud from memory.
reckon (rĕk′ən) *v.* To guess.
recoil (rĭ′koil′) *v.* To spring back.
recollect (rĕk′ə-lĕkt′) *v.* To remember.
recommend (rĕk′ə-mĕnd′) *v.* To advise.
recompense (rĕk′əm-pĕns′) *v.* To reward.
redeem (rĭ-dēm′) *v.* To recover.
redress (rĭ-drĕs′) *v.* To make up for.
reek (rēk) *v.* To give off a strong smell.
reel (rēl) *v.* To sway; stagger.
reflect (rĭ-flĕkt′) *v.* To think about seriously.
refrain (rĭ-frān′) *n.* A part of a poem or song that is regularly repeated. *v.* To hold back.

refuge (rĕf′yōōj) *n.* Shelter.
refugee (rĕf′yōō-jē′) *n.* A person who flees from danger to a safe place.
rehabilitation (rē′hə-bĭl′ə-tā′shən) *n.* Concern with using education or therapy to help someone to a former state.
rehash (rē-hăsh′) *v.* To retell or repeat over and over.
rejoin (rĭ-join′) *v.* To return to a group after being away.
reluctant (rĭ-lŭk′tənt) *adj.* Unwilling.—**reluctantly** *adv.*
reminiscent (rĕm′ə-nĭs′ənt) *adj.* Recalling some memory.
remnant (rĕm-nənt) *n.* Leftover trace of something.
remote (rĭ-mōt′) *adj.* Distant; aloof.
repast (rĭ-păst′, -päst′) *n.* A meal.
repentance (rĭ-pĕn′təns) *n.* Sorrow for wrongdoing.
repentant (rĭ-pĕn′tənt) *adj.* Showing remorse or sorrow for one's sins.
replenish (rĭ-plĕn′ĭsh) *v.* To fill again.
replica (rĕp′lə-kə) *n.* A copy.
reprimand (rĕp′rə-mănd′, -mänd′) *n.* A severe scolding.
repository (rĭ-pŏz′ĭ-tôr′ē, -tōr′ē) *n.* A place in which to store things.
reproachful (rĭ-prōch′fəl) *adj.* Expressing blame or censure.
reputed (rĭ-pyōō′tĭd) *adj.* Generally thought or considered.
residential (rĕz′ə-dĕn′shəl) *adj.* Referring to the place where one lives.
resign (rĭ-zīn′) *n.* To give over; consent.
resolute (rĕz′ə-lōōt′) *adj.* Determined; unyielding.
resolution (rĕz′ə-lōō′shən) *n.* A decision or determination to do something.
resolve (rĭ-zŏlv′) *v.* To make a decision.
resound (rĭ-zound′) *v.* **1.** To echo back. **2.** To make a loud noise.
resourceful (rĭ-sôrs′fəl, rĭ-sōrs′-, rĭ-zôrs′-, rĕ-zōrs′-) *adj.* Clever in finding ways to handle problems.—**resourcefulness** *n.*
respite (rĕs′pĭt) *n.* An interval of rest.
restive (rĕs′tĭv) *adj.* Restless.
retort (rĭ-tôrt′) *v.* To answer in a sharp or witty way.

revere (rĭ-vîr′) *v.* To show deep respect toward someone or something.—**revered** *adj.*
reverence (rĕv′ər-əns) *v.* To honor.
ricochet (rĭk′ə-shā′, -shĕt′) *v.* To skip off a surface after striking it at an angle.
riled (rīld) *adj.* Annoyed; angered.
riotous (rī′ət-əs) *adj.* Abundant; lush.
rite (rīt) *n.* A ceremonial act.
ritual (rĭch′ōō-əl) *n.* A ceremony.
rivulet (rĭv′yə-lĭt) *n.* A small stream.
roan (rōn) *adj.* Reddish brown speckled with white or gray.
robust (rō-bŭst′, rō′bŭst) *adj.* Healthy and strong.
rogue (rōg) *n.* A playful person; rascal.
roguish (rō′gĭsh) *adj.* Mischievous.
root (rōōt, rŏŏt) *v.* To dig in the earth with the snout.
rout (rout) *v.* To drive out.
rowdy (rou′dē) *adj.* Rough.
rude (rōōd) *adj.* Crude; rough.
rudiment (rōō′də-mənt) *n.* A basic principle. (Often used in the plural.)
rummage (rŭm′ĭj) *v.* To search through a collection of objects.—**rummaging** *n.*

S

sable (sā′bəl) *adj.* Black or dark brown in color.
saffron (săf′rən) *adj.* Orange-yellow.
sagacious (sə-gā′shəs) *adj.* Wise.
sage (sāj) *n.* A wise person.
salamander (săl′ə-măn′dər) *n.* A lizardlike creature with four legs and a soft, moist skin.
salute (sə-lōōt′) *v.* To greet in a friendly manner.
sanction (săngk′shən) *v.* To approve.
sanctuary (săngk′chōō-ĕr′ē) *n.* A safe place.
sanitarium (săn′ə-târ′ē-əm) *n.* A place where one may go to rest or to recover from an illness.
saucy (sô′sē) *adj.* Pert; bold.
saunter (sôn′tər) *v.* To walk slowly.
scabbard (skăb′ərd) *n.* A holder for a dagger or sword.
scepter (sĕp′tər) *n.* A staff a king or queen holds as a sign of authority.
schooner (skōō′nər) *n.* A kind of sailing ship having two or more masts.

ă p**a**t/ā p**ay**/âr c**are**/ä f**a**ther/b **b**i**b**/ch **ch**ur**ch**/d **d**ee**d**/ĕ p**e**t/ē b**e**/f **f**i**fe**/g **g**a**g**/h **h**at/hw **wh**ich/ĭ p**i**t/ī p**ie**/îr p**ier**/j **j**u**dge**/k **k**i**ck**/ l **l**i**d**, need**l**e/m **m**u**mm**/n **n**o, sudde**n**/ng thi**ng**/ŏ p**o**t/ō t**oe**/ô p**aw**, f**or**/oi n**oi**se/ou **ou**t/ŏŏ t**oo**k/ōō b**oo**t/p **p**o**p**/r **r**oa**r**/s **s**au**ce**/ sh **sh**ip, di**sh**/t **t**igh**t**/th **th**in, pa**th**/*th* **th**is, ba**the**/ŭ c**u**t/ûr **ur**ge/v **v**al**ve**/w **w**ith/y **y**es/z **z**ebra, si**z**e/zh vi**si**on/ə **a**bout, **i**tem, ed**i**ble, gall**o**p, circ**u**s/á *Fr.* **a**mi/œ *Fr.* f**eu**, *Ger.* sch**ö**n/ü *Fr.* t**u**, *Ger.* **ü**ber/KH *Ger.* **ich**, *Scot.* lo**ch**/N *Fr.* bo**n**.

scope (skōp) *n.* Reach.
scorch (skôrch) *v.* To burn.
score (skôr, skōr) *n.* A group of twenty.
scourge (skûrj) *v.* To whip.
scowl (scoul) *v.* To express anger or disapproval by wrinkling the brow and lowering the corners of the mouth.
scrawny (skrô′nē) *adj.* Skinny.
scroll (skrōl) *n.* A roll of paper or other writing material.
scuffle (skŭf′əl) *n.* A fight.
scurry (skûr′ē) *v.* To hurry. *n.* **scurry, scurrying.**
scurvy (skûr′vē) *adj.* Vile; contemptible.
scuttle (skŭt′l) *v.* To move hastily. *n.* A container for coal.
sear (sîr) *v.* To burn the surface of something.—**searing** *adj.*
senile (sē′nīl, sĕn′īl) *adj.* Exhibiting marked deterioration as a result of old age.
sensuous (sĕn′shoō-əs) *adj.* Pleasing to the senses.
sentiment (sĕn′tə-mənt) *n.* A feeling; emotion.
sentimental (sĕn′tə-mĕnt′l) *adj.* Acting from feeling rather than from reason.
servitude (sûr′və-toōd′, -tyoōd′) *n.* Slavery.
shaft (shăft, shäft) *n.* A ray of light.
shallow (shăl′ō) *adj.* Not deep.
shamble (shăm′bəl) *v.* To shuffle; to walk in an unsteady manner.
sheepish (shēp′ĭsh) *adj.* Embarrassed.—**sheepishly** *adv.*
shiftless (shĭft′lĭs) *adj.* Lazy.
shimmer (shĭm′ər) *v.* To shine.
shoat (shōt) *n.* A young pig.
shorn (shôrn, shōrn) *adj.* Deprived.
shrine (shrīn) *n.* A place or structure used in the worship of a deity.
shroud (shroud) *v.* To wrap in a burial garment.
shuttle (shŭt′l) *n.* A device used in weaving.
sidle (sīd′l) *v.* To move sideways cautiously or stealthily.
silhouette (sĭl′oō-ĕt′) *v.* To outline.—**silhouetted** *adj.*
simultaneous (sī′məl-tā′nē-əs, sĭm′əl-) *adj.* Happening at the same time.—**simultaneously** *adv.*
sinister (sĭn′ĭ-stər) *adj.* Threatening.
skein (skān) *n.* A length of yarn wound in a coil.
skeptical (skĕp′tĭ-kəl) *adj.* Doubting; questioning; not easily convinced.
skinflint (skĭn′flĭnt′) *n.* A miser.
skirt (skûrt) *v.* To go around; avoid.
skitter (skĭt′ər) *v.* To move quickly over water.

skulk (skŭlk) *v.* To move in a quiet, fearful way.
slack (slăk) *adj.* **1.** Weak. **2.** Loose.
slacken (slăk′ən) *v.* To slow down.
slander (slăn′dər) *n.* Spoken statements damaging to another person's character or reputation.
slither (slĭth′ər) *v.* To slide.
slobber (slŏb′ər) *v.* To drool.
sluice (sloōs) *n.* An artificial channel for water.
smolder (smōl′dər) *v.* To burn without a flame.—**smoldering** *adj.*
snappish (snăp′ĭsh) *adj.* Irritable; apt to speak sharply.
snigger (snĭg′ər) *v.* To laugh in a sneaky way. Same as *snicker.*
sober (sō′bər) *adj.* Serious.
socket (sŏk′ĭt) *n.* An opening into which something can fit.
sodden (sŏd′n) *adj.* Thoroughly soaked.
solace (sŏl′ĭs) *n.* Something that affords relief from discomfort or unhappiness.
solarium (sō-lâr′ē-əm) *n.* A glassed-in room which receives sunlight.
solder (sŏd′ər, sôd′-) *v.* To mend with solder, a metal alloy, which when melted can be used to connect metal parts.—**soldered** *adj.*
solemn (sŏl′əm) *adj.* Serious; grave.—**solemnly** *adv.*
souse (sous) *n.* Pickled pork.
sow (sō) *v.* To plant seeds.—**sower** *n.*
span (spăn) *v.* To stretch across.
spar (spär) *n.* A pole used to support a ship's sail.
spasm (spăz′əm) *n.* A fit.
specter (spĕk′tər) *n.* A ghost.
spindle (spĭnd′l) *v.* To send out thin threads.
spineless (spīn′lĭs) *adj.* Without courage; weak-willed.
splice (splīs) *v.* To join by twisting or interweaving.
splotch (splŏch) *n.* A stain or spot.
splutter (splŭt′ər) *v.* To speak in an excited, confused way.
spontaneous (spŏn-tā′nē-əs) *adj.* Not planned.
spouse (spous, spouz) *n.* A husband or wife.
sprint (sprĭnt) *v.* To run quickly. *n.* A short run or dash.
spume (spyoōm) *n.* Foam; froth.
spur (spûr) *v.* To urge a horse forward by using spurs. *n.* Pointed devices attached to a rider's boots.
squeamish (skwē′mĭsh) *adj.* Easily sickened or disgusted.
squelch (skwĕlch) *v.* To move heavily, as through

mud, with a sucking or squishing sound.
staccato (stə-kä′tō) *adj.* Abrupt and emphatic.
stagger (stăg′ər) *v.* To sway, reel, or move unsteadily.
stark (stärk) *adj.* Rigid.
stately (stāt′lē) *adj.* Dignified.
steed (stēd) *n.* A high-spirited horse.
sterile (stĕr′əl) *adj.* Barren.—**sterility** *n.*
stevedore (stē′və-dôr, -dōr′) *n.* Someone who loads or unloads a ship.
stigma (stĭg′mə) *n.* A mark of disgrace.
stipulate (stĭp′yə-lāt′) *v.* To state the conditions of an agreement.—**stipulated** *adj.*
stolid (stŏl′ĭd) *adj.* Unemotional.
straggle (străg′əl) *v.* To wander or ramble over a wide area.
stratagem (străt′ə-jəm) *n.* A trick or scheme.
strategic (strə-tē′jĭk) *adj.* Important to the strategy, or plan of action.—**strategically** *adv.*
strive (strīv) *v.* To try hard; struggle.
stubble (stŭb′əl) *n.* The stumps of crops remaining after a harvest.
stucco (stŭk′ō) *n.* A covering used for building surfaces, made of cement and other materials.
stupendous (stoo-pĕn′dəs, styoo-) *adj.* Overwhelming.
stupor (stoo′pər, styoo′-) *n.* A confused state; daze.
subdue (səb-doo′, -dyoo′) *v.* To bring under control.
submerge (səb-mûrj′) *v.* To put under water.—**submerged** *adj.*
subsequent (sŭb′sə-kwənt) *adj.* Succeeding.
subside (səb-sīd′) *v.* To settle down.
subsist (səb-sĭst′) *v.* To live.
succulent (sŭk′yə-lənt) *adj.* Juicy.
suet (soo′ĭt) *n.* Fatty tissue used in cooking.
sulky (sŭl′kē) *adj.* Slow-moving; sluggish.—**sulkily** *adv.*
sullen (sŭl′ən) *adj.* Gloomy; ill-humored.—**sullenly** *adv.*
sultry (sŭl′trē) *adj.* Hot and humid.
summerhouse (sŭm′ər-hous′) *n.* A small open structure in a garden.
sumptuous (sŭmp′choo-əs) *adj.* Extravagant; luxurious.
sunder (sŭn′dər) *v.* To sever or break something apart.
supple (sŭp′əl) *adj.* Flexible; limber.
supplicate (sŭp′lĭ-kāt′) *v.* To beg.—**supplication** *n.*
supposition (sŭp′ə-zĭsh′ən) *n.* Something thought to be true.
surfeit (sûr′fĭt) *v.* To overfeed.—**surfeited** *adj.*
surge (sûrj) *v.* **1.** To rise up or swell. **2.** To increase suddenly.
surly (sûr′lē) *adj.* Bad-tempered; rude.
surname (sûr′nām′) *n.* A person's family name or last name, as distinguished from a given name.
surmount (sər-mount′) *v.* **1.** To climb up and over. **2.** To be at the top of.
suspend (sə-spĕnd′) *v.* To hang.
sustain (sə-stān′) *v.* To support.—**sustained** *adj.*
swagger (swăg′ər) *v.* To walk in a bold, self-important manner.

T

tableau (tăb′lō′, tă-blō′) *n.* A striking scene.
tactful (tăkt′fəl) *adj.* Showing sensitivity to another's feelings.
talon (tăl′ən) *n.* The claw of a bird or other animal.
tantalize (tăn′tə-līz′) *v.* To tease by offering something and then withdrawing it.—**tantalizing** *adj.*
tarry (tăr′ē) *v.* To linger.
tart (tärt) *adj.* **1.** Sharp. **2.** Sarcastic.—**tartly** *adv.*
taunt (tônt) *v.* To make fun of.
taut (tôt) *adj.* Pulled tight.
tauten (tôt′n) *v.* To pull tight.—**tautened** *adj.*
tawny (tô′nē) *adj.* Tan; brownish-yellow.
teeter (tē′tər) *v.* To step or walk uncertainly.
tend (tĕnd) *v.* To look after.
terrarium (tə-râr′ē-əm) *n.* An enclosed container in which small plants or animals are kept.
terse (tûrs) *adj.* Brief; to the point.—**tersely** *adv.*
testy (tĕs′tē) *adj.* Touchy; irritable.—**testily** *adv.*
tether (tĕth′ər) *v.* To confine an animal's movements to a limited area by tying it to a rope or chain.
thatch (thăch) *n.* A roof covering made of straw or leaves.
thong (thông, thŏng) *n.* A leather cord.
thresh (thrĕsh) *v.* To separate grain from straw.—**threshing** *adj.*
threshold (thrĕsh′ōld′, thrĕsh′hōld′) *n.* A doorway.
throng (thrŏng) *n.* A great number of people.

ă pat/ā pay/âr care/ä father/b bib/ch church/d deed/ĕ pet/ē be/f fife/g gag/h hat/hw which/ĭ pit/ī pie/îr pier/j judge/k kick/ l lid, needle/m mum/n no, sudden/ng thing/ŏ pot/ō toe/ô paw, for/oi noise/ou out/oo took/oo boot/p pop/r roar/s sauce/ sh ship, dish/t tight/th thin, path/*th* this, bathe/ŭ cut/ûr urge/v valve/w with/y yes/z zebra, size/zh vision/ə about, item, edible, gallop, circus/ă *Fr.* ami/œ *Fr.* feu, *Ger.* schön/ü *Fr.* tu, *Ger.* über/ᴋʜ *Ger.* ich, *Scot.* loch/ɴ *Fr.* bon.

timorous (tĭm′ər-əs) *adj.* Timid.
tirade (tī′rād′, tī-rād′) *n.* A long, angry speech.
toil (toil) *v.* To work hard.
tolerate (tŏl′ə-rāt′) *v.* To put up with or permit.
topple (tŏp′əl) *v.* To fall over.
torrent (tôr′ənt, tŏr′-) *n.* **1.** A fast-moving stream. **2.** An abundant or violent flow.
torso (tôr′sō) *n.* A human body without the head or limbs.
totter (tŏt′ər) *v.* To move unsteadily.—**tottering** *adj.*
trace (trās) *n.* One of the chains that connect an animal to the wagon it is pulling.
trackless (trăk′lĭs) *adj.* Unmarked; without paths or trails.
tradition (trə-dĭsh′ən) *n.* A longstanding custom or practice.
train (trān) *n.* That part of a gown that trails on the ground.
trample (trăm′pəl) *v.* To crush with the feet.
trance (trăns) *n.* A dreamlike state.
tranquil (trăn′kwəl) *adj.* Calm.—**tranquilly** *adv.*
tranquillity (trăn-kwĭl′ə-tē) *n.* Peacefulness; serenity.
transaction (trăn-săk′shən, -zăk′shən) *n.* A business dealing.
transcend (trăn-sĕnd′) *v.* To rise above.
transfix (trăns-fĭks′) *v.* To make motionless.
transient (trăn′shənt, -zhənt, -zē-ənt) *adj.* Staying only briefly.
translucent (trăns-lōō′sənt, trănz′-) *adj.* Allowing light to shine through but not allowing a clear view of anything beyond.—**translucency** *n.*
transparent (trăns-pâr′ənt, -păr′ənt) *adj.* Able to be seen through.
transplant (trăns-plănt′, -plănt′) *v.* To dig up and replant in another place.
transpose (trăns-pōz′) *v.* To change a piece of music from one key to another.
tremor (trĕm′ər) *n.* A trembling movement.
tremulous (trĕm′yə-ləs) *adj.* Trembling.
trespass (trĕs′pəs, -păs′) *n.* Violation of a law or duty.
trifle (trī′fəl) *v.* To treat lightly, as if unimportant.
trivial (trĭv′ē-əl) *adj.* Of little value or importance.
troll (trōl) *v.* To fish by dragging a line through water.
trough (trôf, trŏf) *n.* A long, narrow container that holds water or feed for animals.
trudge (trŭj) *v.* To walk in a plodding, heavy-footed way.
turf (tûrf) *n.* Grass-covered soil.
turmoil (tûr′moil) *n.* Confusion.
turret (tûr′ĭt) *n.* A small tower.
tutor (tōō′tər, tyōō′-) *n.* A private teacher.
twine (twīn) *v.* To twist.

U

unanimous (yōō-năn′ə-məs) *adj.* Of one mind.
uncanny (ŭn′kăn′ē) *adj.* Strange.
uncommon (ŭn′kŏm′ən) *adj.* Unusual.—**uncommonly** *adv.*
understate (ŭn′dər-stāt′) *v.* To express in a restrained way.—**understated** *adj.*
unearth (ŭn-ûrth′) *v.* To dig up.
unflinching (ŭn-flĭn′chĭng) *adj.* Resolute; steadfast; not betraying fear.
unimpaired (ŭn′ĭm-pârd′) *adj.* Not damaged or lessened.
unique (yōō-nēk′) *adj.* **1.** Having no equal. **2.** One and only.
unison (yōō′nĭ′sən, -zən) *n.* **1.** Several voices speaking or singing together in harmony. **2.** A group acting or behaving as a unit.
unutterable (ŭn′ŭt′ər-ə-bəl) *adj.* Not capable of being expressed or described.
upsurge (ŭp′sûrj′) *v.* To rise up.—**upsurgence** *n.*
urchin (ûr′chĭn) *n.* A mischievous youngster.
usurer (yōō′zhər-ər) *n.* Someone who lends money at a very high rate of interest.

V

vale (vāl) *n.* A valley.
vandalism (vănd′l-ĭz′əm) *n.* Intentional destruction of property, especially beautiful property.
vapor (vā′pər) *n.* A mist.
vault (vôlt) *n.* **1.** An arched structure. **2.** The sky.
veer (vîr) *v.* To change direction.—**veering** *adj.*
vehement (vē′ə-mənt) *adj.* Showing great force or feeling.—**vehemently** *adv.*
veneration (vĕn′ə-rā′shən) *n.* Great respect or reverence.
venison (vĕn′ə-sən, -zən) *n.* The flesh of deer used as food.
venom (vĕn′əm) *n.* **1.** Poison. **2.** Evil; malice.—**venomous** *adj.*
venture (vĕn′chər) *v.* To risk danger.
veranda (və-răn′də) *n.* A porch.
verdure (vûr′jər) *n.* Flourishing vegetation.
vermilion (vər-mĭl′yən) *adj.* Of a vivid-red color.
vestige (vĕs′tĭj) *n.* A trace of something that once existed.
vex (vĕks) *v.* To annoy.—**vexed** *adj.*

vexation (vĕk-sā′shən) *n.* Annoyance.
vicious (vĭsh′əs) *adj.* Dangerous; violent.
vigil (vĭj′əl) *n.* A period of watchfulness.
vigilance (vĭj′ə-ləns) *n.* Alertness.
vigorous (vĭg′ər-əs) *adj.* Energetic; powerful.—**vigorously** *adv.*—**vigor** *n.*
villa (vĭl′ə) *n.* A country home.
vindictive (vĭn-dĭk′tĭv) *adj.* Revengeful.
virtually (vûr′chōō-ə-lē) *adv.* In effect; practically.
visceral (vĭs′ər-əl) *adj.* Very emotional.
vogue (vōg) *n.* Fashion.
vow (vou) *v.* To promise solemnly.

W

wager (wā′jər) *n.* A bet.
waggish (wăg′ĭsh) *adj.* Playful.
waistcoat (wĕs′kĭt, wāst′kōt) *n.* A vest.
wallow (wŏl′ō) *v.* To roll about.
wan (wŏn) *adj.* Weak; pale.—**wanly** *adv.*
warp (wôrp) *n.* The threads in a fabric that run lengthwise.
wary (wâr′ē) *adj.* Cautious.—**warily** *adv.*
wash (wŏsh, wôsh) *n.* The dry bed of a stream.
waver (wā′vər) *v.* To hesitate; be unsteady.—**wavering** *adj.*
wend (wĕnd) *v.* To go.

wharf (hwôrf) *n.* A place where ships are loaded and unloaded; dock.
wheel (hwēl) *v.* **1.** To turn around quickly. **2.** To fly in a circular path.
wheeze (hwēz) *n.* A whistling sound made when breathing is difficult.
whet (hwĕt) *v.* To stimulate or sharpen.
whimper (hwĭm′pər) *v.* To sob softly. *n.* A low whining sound.—**whimpering** *adj.*
whimsical (hwĭm′zĭ-kəl) *adj.* Unpredictable; odd.
whimsy (hwĭm′zē) *n.* Strange or fanciful humor.
whittle (hwĭt′l, wĭt′l) *v.* To pare thin shavings from a piece of wood.
wickerwork (wĭk′ər-wûrk′) *adj.* Made of wicker—twigs or sticks woven together for furniture or baskets.
wicket (wĭk′ĭt) *n.* A door or gate.
wily (wī′lē) *adj.* Sly; tricky.
wince (wĭns) *v.* To make a face as in pain or embarrassment.
winnow (wĭn′ō) *v.* To blow husks away from the grain.
wobbly (wŏb′lē) *adj.* Unsteady; shaky.
writhe (rīth) *v.* To twist or turn; squirm.
wrought (rôt) *adj.* Done.

ă pat/ā pay/âr care/ä father/b bib/ch church/d deed/ĕ pet/ē be/f fife/g gag/h hat/hw which/ĭ pit/ī pie/îr pier/j judge/k kick/l lid, needle/m mum/n no, sudden/ng thing/ŏ pot/ō toe/ô paw, for/oi noise/ou out/ōō took/ōō boot/p pop/r roar/s sauce/sh ship, dish/t tight/th thin, path/*th* this, bathe/ŭ cut/ûr urge/v valve/w with/y yes/z zebra, size/zh vision/ə about, item, edible, gallop, circus/ă *Fr.* ami/œ *Fr.* feu, *Ger.* schön/ü *Fr.* tu, *Ger.* über/KH *Ger.* ich, *Scot.* loch/N *Fr.* bon.

Outline of Concepts and Skills

Page numbers in italics refer to entries in Literary Terms and Techniques.

READING/LITERARY SKILLS

Alliteration *706*
   Understanding How Sounds Convey Feeling 466
Allusion *706*
   Recognizing Allusions 396, 674
   Allusions to Mythology 619
Anecdote 47, 413, *707*
Atmosphere *707*
Ballad 474, *707*
   Analyzing Ballad Characteristics 477
Biography *707*
Characterization *707*
   Understanding Methods of Characterization (direct and indirect) 240
   Understanding Character Types 261
   Discussing Stock Characters 269
Comedy *708*
Conflict *708*
   Understanding Conflict and Plot 218
Connotation 437, 487, *709*
Denotation 437, 487
Description *709*
Dialect 218, 443, 444, *709*
   Recognizing Cockney Speech 334
   Understanding the Role of Dialect 444
Dialogue *710*
Diction 437
   Understanding the Role of Diction 438
Drama *710*
   Close Reading of a Play 308
   Imagining a Play in Performance 333
Essay *711*
   Close Reading of an Essay 382
Exposition *711*
Fable 668, *711*
Fantasy *712*
Fiction *712*
Figurative Language 450, 451, *712*
   Understanding Similes 168
   Understanding Figurative Language (Metaphor, Simile) 451
Flashback *713*
   Recognizing and Understanding Flashback 30
   Following the Order of Events 160
Folk Tale *713*

Foreshadowing *714*
   Understanding Suspense and Foreshadowing 227
Genre *714*
Haiku 491, *714*
   Understanding Haiku 492
Hero/Heroine *714*
Humor
   Recognizing Humor in Situations 46
Imagery 446, *714*
Inference *715*
   Drawing Conclusions 86, 129
   Noting Details That Reveal Character 110
   Inferring Character from Thoughts and Feelings 121
Inversion *715*
   Understanding the Purpose of Inversion 442
Irony *715*
   Recognizing Irony 268
Legend *716*
Limerick 496, *716*
Main Idea
   Finding the Main Idea of a Paragraph 391
Metamorphosis 598, 605, *716*
Metaphor 451, *712*, *717*
Mood *717*
Motivation 27
Myth 574, 636, *717*
   Recognizing Gods and Goddesses by Their Titles 581
Narration 245, *718*
   Understanding the Narrator's Point of View 245
Nonfiction 381, *718*
Novel 502, *718*
   Understanding the Novel 529, 561
Onomatopoeia 468, *718*
   Recognizing Onomatopoeia 300
   Understanding How Sounds Convey Feeling 466
   Understanding How Sound Imitates Action 472
Paraphrase *718*
   Paraphrasing a Poem 442
Personification *719*
   Recognizing Personification 489
Plot *719*
   Understanding Conflict and Plot 218
   Understanding Plot (in Drama) 333
Poetry 429, 474, 488, 493, *719*
   Close Reading of a Poem 430
   Understanding the Purpose of Poetic License 440

Point of View *720*
   Understanding the Narrator's Point of View   245
   Understanding Point of View   275
Proverb *721*
   Understanding Proverbs   678
Quatrain *721*
Refrain   163, 477, *721*
   Understanding the Refrain   465
Repetition   460, 477, *721*
   Understanding Repetition in Poetry   463
Research
   Classical Mythology in Today's World   606, 620–621
Rhyme   460, *722*
   Understanding Repetition in Poetry   463
Rhythm   468, *723*
   Responding to Rhythm   473
Setting *724*
   Focusing on Details of Background   176
   Focusing on Setting   260
Simile   451, *712*, *724*
   Understanding Similes   168
Stage Directions
   Imagining a Play in Performance   333
Stanza   *725*
Suspense   *725*
   Understanding Suspense and Foreshadowing   227
Theme   455, *725*
   Interpreting Theme   274

LANGUAGE/VOCABULARY SKILLS

Analogies
Recognizing Analogies   301
Connotation and Denotation
Recognizing Denotative and Connotative Meanings   487
Context
Getting Meaning from Context   52
Using Context Clues   121, 194, 412
Finding the Appropriate Meaning   129, 177
Dialect
Recognizing Cockney Speech   334
Understanding Dialect   98, 218
Glossary
Using the Glossary   25
Homophones
Distinguishing Homophones   590
Multiple Meanings of Words
Recognizing Special Uses of a Word   76
Finding the Appropriate Meaning   177
Recognizing Shades of Meaning   262
Determining Exact Meanings   268

Names
Identifying Animal Names   160
Prefixes
Analyzing Words with *dis-*   46
Adding Different Meanings with *in-*   110
Roots
Analyzing Words with *-phobia* and *philo-*   137
Analyzing Words with the Same Combining Form   392
Sensory Details
Recognizing Sensory Details   151
Special Vocabularies
Recognizing Ranch Terms   423
Recognizing Idioms   562
Suffixes
Forming Modifiers with *-ly*   86
Forming Adverbs from Adjectives (*-ly*)   184
Forming Words with *-logy*   403
Synonyms
Determining Exact Meanings   11
Usage
Recognizing Informal Language   31
Using Vivid Verbs   184
Recognizing Formal Speech   382
Identifying Different Levels of Language   562
Word Origins
Tracing Origins of Words   17
Learning Word Origins   146
Recognizing Words from Other Languages   530
Learning Words from the Myths   606, 611, 617, 620, 628
Tracing the Origins of Calendar Names   643

FOCUS ON READING

Evaluating a Character's Behavior   17
Recognizing Humor in Situations   46
Drawing Inferences   61
Drawing Conclusions   86
Noting Details that Reveal Character   110
Inferring Character from Thoughts and Feelings   121
Drawing Conclusions   129
Following the Order of Events   160
Focusing on Details of Background   176
Imagining a Play in Performance   333
Finding the Main Idea of a Paragraph   391
Expressing a Moral   684

FOR SPEAKING AND LISTENING

For Oral Reading
Preparing a Reading of the Poem   70
Reciting the Story   138

Preparing a Presentation   169
Avoiding Singsong   463
Presenting a Choral Reading   473
Illustrating Characters in Myths   632

For Dramatization
Assembling a Director's Notebook   355
Dramatizing Scenes Based on a Myth   597

FOCUS ON READING AND CRITICAL THINKING

Making Generalizations About Theme   88
Evaluating Short Stories   303
Drawing Inferences   376
Understanding Cause and Effect   424
Relating Sound to Meaning   497
Using Analysis and Synthesis   566
Using Methods of Comparison and Contrast   633
Distinguishing Between Facts and Opinions   685

WRITING ABOUT LITERATURE

Interpreting a Poem   54
Supporting a Statement of Theme   87
Showing How Conflict Is Developed and Resolved   219
Analyzing Methods of Characterization   240
Explaining the Function of Setting   262
Discussing Stock Characters   269
Analyzing Character   342
Describing the Narrator   413
Paraphrasing a Poem   442
Interpreting a Poem   459
Analyzing Ballad Characteristics   477
Analyzing Character   530
Explaining Characteristics of Odin   643
Analyzing the Image of the Wolf   647
Comparing Myths   652
Discussing Elements of Magic and Disguise   659
Analyzing a Character   662
Analyzing Heroic Characteristics   665
Analyzing the Moral of a Fable   678

CREATIVE WRITING

Writing About Characters in Action   240
Assuming Another Identity   435
Composing a Haiku   492
Writing a Limerick   496
Writing a Story About Metamorphosis   605
Writing a Television Script   628
Writing a Fable   684

FOCUS ON WRITING

Focus on Personal Narrative
Choosing a Topic   18
Gathering Details   31
Focusing on Your Senses   40
Telling an Anecdote   47
Using Vivid Action Verbs   53
Using Chronological Order   62
Reflecting on Meanings   67
Writing a Personal Narrative   89

Focus on Descriptive Writing
Finding a Focus   98
Identifying Your Purpose   111
Using Specific Details   113
Using Sensory Details   121
Using Exact Words   126
Organizing Descriptive Details   130
Using Figures of Speech   138
Writing a Description   139

Focus on Informative Writing
Choosing a Process to Explain   146
Gathering Details to Explain a Process   152
Organizing Information   161
Exploring Cause and Effect   177
Using Transitional Expressions   185
Preparing an Oral Report   195
Writing an Informative Paper   196

Focus on Writing a Short Story
Finding a Story Idea   219
Building a Plot   228
Creating Characters   241
Exploring Point of View   246
Listing Details of Setting   262
Experimenting with Irony   269
Exploring a Theme   275
Making a Story Map   301
Writing a Short Story   304

Focus on Writing a Scene
Using Improvisation to Explore a Scene   334
Creating Dialogue   355
Visualizing a Scene for Stage Directions   371
Writing a Scene   377

Focus on Biographical Report
Choosing a Subject   392
Identifying a Main Idea   403
Using Anecdotes   413
Organizing a Report   423
Writing a Biographical Report   425

Focus on Writing a Poem
Choosing a Subject   436
Experimenting with Imagery   442
Listing Sensory Details   449
Experimenting with Sound Effects   463
Writing a Poem   498

Focus on Writing a Letter
Writing a Personal Letter   530
Writing a Business Letter   562
Writing a Letter   567

Focus on Persuasive Writing
Choosing a Topic   582
Identifying Your Opinion   590
Thinking About Your Audience   612
Supporting Your Opinion   647
Using Appeals to the Emotions   652
Evaluating Reasoning   674
Organizing a Persuasive Paper   684
Writing a Persuasive Paper   686

LITERATURE AND THE ARTS

Illustrated Editions   263
Adaptations of "A Christmas Carol"   302
Interpretations of a Myth   617

LITERATURE AND HISTORY

The Internment of Japanese Americans   68

LITERATURE AND MATHEMATICS

Learning Prefixes Used in Measurement   246

LITERATURE AND RESEARCH

Sources of Information   591
Entries in Reference Books   605
Allusions to Mythology   619
Mythological Monsters   628

LITERATURE AND SCIENCE

Protective Coloration   161

LITERATURE AND SPORTS

The Olympic Games   582

CONNECTING CULTURES

The Influence of American Indian Languages   40
Bazaars   62
Trickster Heroes   99
Words of Indian Origin   241
The Trickster in Folk Tales   372
Games from Around the World   530
International Exchange   530
Holidays   564
Japanese Culture   564
Comparative Mythology   591
Myths from Different Lands   632

INDEX OF FINE ART TRANSPARENCIES BY TYPE

In the *Audiovisual Resources Binder*, you will find **Fine Art** transparencies that relate to the literature units in the textbook. Each **Fine Art** transparency is accompanied by **Teacher's Notes** and student activity pages. Although these **Fine Art** transparencies are arranged in unit order, you may want to relate them to a variety of selections by literary type, such as those listed below.

Myths, Fables, Folk Tales: For characters from mythology and folklore, see Transparencies 46 and 47.

Index of Contents by Types

Myths, Fables, Folk Tales

Adventures of Hercules, The, retold by Edith Hamilton, 622
Ant and the Grasshopper, The, an Aesop fable retold by Joseph Jacobs, 672
Arachne, retold by Rex Warner, 598
Belling the Cat, an Aesop fable retold by Joseph Jacobs, 669
Blind Men and the Elephant, The, John Godfrey Saxe, 675
Death of Balder, The, retold by Edith Hamilton, 660
End of All Things, The, Barbara Leonie Picard, 663
Fables by Aesop, 669
Fables by James Thurber, 679
Fairly Intelligent Fly, The, James Thurber, 679
Fenris Wolf, The, retold by Olivia Coolidge, 644
Fox and the Crow, The, an Aesop fable retold by Joseph Jacobs, 673
Fox and the Crow, The, James Thurber, 682
Gods and Goddesses of Mount Olympus, The, Olivia Coolidge, 575
How Ijapa, Who Was Short, Became Long, a Nigerian folk tale retold by Harold Courlander, 713
How Thor Found His Hammer, retold by Hamilton Wright Mabie, 648
Icarus and Daedalus, retold by Josephine Preston Peabody, 614
Norse Gods and Goddesses, The, Barbara Leonie Picard, 640
Origin of Seasons, The, retold by Olivia Coolidge, 592
Owl and the Two Rabbits, The, an Eskimo fable, 684
Phaethon, retold by Edith Hamilton, 608
Prometheus the Fire-Bringer, retold by Jeremy Ingalls, 583
Reward of Baucis and Philemon, The, retold by Sally Benson, 602
Thor and the Giant King, retold by Olivia Coolidge, 653
Town Mouse and the Country Mouse, The, an Aesop fable retold by Joseph Jacobs, 670

Nonfiction: For artwork featuring an authentic event or person, see Transparencies 30 and 31.

The Novel: For depiction of personal reflections or purposeful interaction, see Transparencies 2, 41, and 42.

Plays: For a view of dramatic presence and artistic talent, see Transparencies 24 and 25.

Poetry: For a variety of artwork depicting everyday life and nature, see Transparencies 2, 6, 7, 12, 13, 35, 36, 41, and 42.

Short Stories: For a view of different cultures, traditions, and relationships, see Transparencies 1, 6, 7, 17, 18, and 42.

What Happened to Charles, James Thurber, 680
Wolf and the Dog, The, Marie de France, 677

Nonfiction

Desert Creatures, Edward Abbey, 147
Guinea Pig, from *My Sister Eileen,* Ruth McKenney, 41
Hidden Life of Dogs, The, from Elizabeth Marshall Thomas, 424
In the Shadow of Man, from, Jane Goodall, 386
Names/Nombres, Julia Alvarez, 393
Night the Bed Fell, The, from *My Life and Hard Times,* James Thurber, 133
Nisei Daughter, from, Monica Sone, 122
One Writer's Beginnings, from, Eudora Welty, 3
Rattlesnake Hunt, from *Cross Creek,* Marjorie Kinnan Rawlings, 398
River Notes, from, Barry Holstun Lopez, 383
Sound-Shadows of the New World, from, Ved Mehta, 404
When I Was a Boy on the Ranch, J. Frank Dobie, 414
Wind in the Mountains, The, Nina Otero, 144

The Novel

Cat and the Pain Killer, The, from *The Adventures of Tom Sawyer,* Mark Twain, 48
Crick Crack, Monkey, from, Merle Hodge, 94
Home, from *Maud Martha,* Gwendolyn Brooks, 127
One-Shot Finch, from *To Kill a Mockingbird,* Harper Lee, 102
Pacific Crossing, Gary Soto, 503

Plays

Governess, The, Neil Simon, 343
In the Fog, Milton Geiger, 309
Jewels of the Shrine, The, James Ene Henshaw, 357
Mazarin Stone, The, Michael and Molly Hardwick, from a story by Sir Arthur Conan Doyle, 318
Sunny Morning, A, Joaquín and Serafín Quintero, 335
When the Rattlesnake Sounds, Alice Childress, 347

Poetry

Annabel Lee, Edgar Allan Poe, 460
Bearded Man, The, Edward Lear, 496
Birdfoot's Grampa, Joseph Bruchac, 186
Blind Men and the Elephant, The, John Godfrey Saxe, 675
Broncho That Would Not Be Broken, The, Vachel Lindsay, 464
Caterpillar, The, Robert Graves, 433
Chipmunk's Day, The, Randall Jarrell, 441
Courage That My Mother Had, The, Edna St. Vincent Millay, 100
Father William, Lewis Carroll, 493
Fog, Carl Sandburg, 437
Full Fathom Five, William Shakespeare, 466
Golden Vanity, The, Anonymous, 475

Grandma Ling, Amy Ling, 131
Haiku, 491
Highwayman, The, Alfred Noyes, 468
I'm Nobody, Emily Dickinson, 490
in Just-, E. E. Cummings, 439
In Time of Silver Rain, Langston Hughes, 162
Lama, The, Ogden Nash, 496
Listeners, The, Walter de la Mare, 457
Little Things, James Stephens, 490
Living Tenderly, May Swenson, 450
maggie and milly and molly and may, E. E. Cummings, 69
May Day, Sara Teasdale, 431
My Father's Song, Simon J. Ortiz, 497
One, James Berry, 10
One of the Seven Has Somewhat to Say, Sara Henderson Hay, 435
Parrot, A, May Sarton, 448
Phaethon, Morris Bishop, 613
Pied Piper of Hamelin, The, Robert Browning, 478
Runaway, The, Robert Frost, 178
Snowflakes, Henry Wadsworth Longfellow, 488
Spider, The, Robert P. Tristram Coffin, 452
Stopping by Woods on a Snowy Evening, Robert Frost, 455
Tableau, Countee Cullen, 54
The 1st, Lucille Clifton, 438
Those Winter Sundays, Robert Hayden, 112
To a Friend Whose Work Has Come to Triumph, Anne Sexton, 618
Trade Winds, John Masefield, 447
Tutor, A, Carolyn Wells, 496
When the Frost Is on the Punkin, James Whitcomb Riley, 443
Wind, The, James Stephens, 699
Wind Tapped like a Tired Man, The, Emily Dickinson, 699
Wolf and the Dog, The, Marie de France, 677
Wreck of the Hesperus, The, Henry Wadsworth Longfellow, 164

Short Stories

Antaeus, Borden Deal, 187
Bracelet, The, Yoshiko Uchida, 63
Christmas Carol, A, Charles Dickens, 276
Circuit, The, Francisco Jiménez, 71
Day's Wait, A, Ernest Hemingway, 242
Dinner Party, The, Mona Gardner, 204
Erne from the Coast, The, T. O. Beachcroft, 208
Fight, The, Ruskin Bond, 56
King of Mazy May, The, Jack London, 19
Landlady, The, Roald Dahl, 220
Last Cover, Paul Annixter, 153
Luke Baldwin's Vow, Morley Callaghan, 77
Medicine Bag, The, Virginia Driving Hawk Sneve, 32
Rikki-tikki-tavi, Rudyard Kipling, 229
Rip Van Winkle, Washington Irving, 247
Seventh Grade, Gary Soto, 13
Sled, Thomas E. Adams, 114
Stolen Day, Sherwood Anderson, 27
Tiger's Heart, The, Jim Kjelgaard, 170
Wild Duck's Nest, The, Michael McLaverty, 180
You Can't Take It with You, Eva-Lis Wuorio, 264
Zlateh the Goat, Isaac Bashevis Singer, 270

Index of Fine Art and Illustrations

Adventures of Tom Sawyer, The, illustration from, 52
Apollo "Belvedere," statue (detail), 579
Arm ornament in the form of a lion, 358
Arms, John Taylor, *Dragon Ship,* 637
Athena, statue, 580
Atlas and Prometheus, cup, 589

Beaux, Cecilia, *New England Woman,* 101
Blake, William, *Cerberus* (detail), 625
Buddha, sculpture, 537

Chase, William Merritt, *Mrs. Chase in Prospect Park,* 8–9
Church, Frederic Edwin, *The Parthenon,* 572–573
Court sword of Kazadachi, Japan, 527
Cramer, Peter, *The Death of Balder,* 661

Darley, Felix O. C., illustrations for the 1848 edition of *Rip Van Winkle,* 247, 248, 250, 253, 255, 259
Del Cossa, Francesco, *The Month of March: The Triumph of Minerva,* 599
Diana the Huntress, statue, 630
Dollman, J. C., *Thor and the Mountain,* 655
Doré, Gustave, "The Town Rat and the Country Rat," an illustration for the *Fables of La Fontaine,* 671

Emmoser, Gerhard, *Celestial Globe with Clockwork,* 607

Fogelberg, B. E., marble statue of Thor, 649
Frescoes, Indian, details of, 57, 60

Garden, detail from a Roman fresco, 596–597
Girl picking flowers, wall painting, 595
Grand Artemis of Piraeus, statue, 579
Great Wave of Kanagawa, The, from *Thirty-six Views of Fuji,* woodblock print, 64
Greene, Walter L., *A National Institution,* 5

Hardy, Dorothy, *The Binding of Fenris,* 645
Odin and Fenris, 664
Henri, Robert, *Pepita of Santa Fe,* 394
Hercules and the Nemean Lion, vase, 623
Hermes Running, vase, 580
Hip pendant showing an Oba, bronze, 369
Hokusai, Katsushika, *The Blind Men and the Elephant,* 676
Homer, Winslow, *The Pumpkin Patch* (detail), 92–93

Kantor, Morris, *The Wreck,* 164
Kensett, John Frederick, *Sunset on the Sea,* 142–143
Kimono detail showing chrysanthemums, 63

Larson, Frank, *Mark Twain,* 53
Leech, John, illustrations for 1846 edition of *A Christmas Carol,* 280, 283, 286, 294, 298
Lee-Smith, Hughie, *The Wall,* 55

Manet, Édouard, *The Balcony* (detail), 339
Mars, head of, coin, 631
Menzel, Adolph Von, *Theatre du Gymnase in Paris,* 306–307

Oba, An (Benin king), head of, 365
Oba with mud-fish legs, bronze plaque, 370
Odin, bronze statue, 640

Peacock, mosaic, Jaipur, India, 206
Persephone and Pluto, relief, 593
Phebus, Gaston, "Hares" from *Livre de la Chasse,* 666–667
Picart, Bernard, *The Fall of Icarus,* 615
Pied Piper of Hamelin, The, 484
Pindell, Howardena, *Autobiography: Water/Ancestors/Middle Passage/Family Ghosts,* 353
Portuguese carracks. Detail from a fifteenth-century painting, 476–477
Poseidon, bust of, 578
Procession of twelve gods and goddesses, fresco, 576–577

Rackham, Arthur, *Raging Wotan Rides to the Rock!,* 639
Ride of the Valkyries, The, 642
Rembrandt van Rijn, *Philemon and Baucis,* 603
Rockwell, Norman, a scene from *The Adventures of Tom Sawyer,* 49
Roesen, Severin, *Still Life: Flowers and Fruit,* 428–429
Rubens, Peter Paul, *The Fall of Phaethon,* 610

Sanders, Christopher, *The Ant and the Grasshopper,* 672
Sendak, Maurice, illustration for *Zlateh the Goat and Other Stories,* 271
Shannon, James Jebusa, *Jungle Tales (Contes de la Jungle),* 200-201
Sioux bandolier bag, 37
Sioux beaded buffalo robe, 33
Sleeping Eros, bronze, 629

Taylor, W. L., *Annabel Lee,* 462
Tenniel, John, illustrations for *Father William,* 493–495
Terracotta statue with three-colored glaze, Tang Dynasty, 131
Thurber, James, illustration from *Fables for Our Time,* 679
Illustrations from *Further Fables for Our Time,* 680–682
Illustrations from *My Life and Hard Times,* 134, 135
Toyo, Seshu, *Flowers and Birds,* 491
Trimberg, Hugo von, "Lion, King of the Beasts," from *Der Renner (The Racer),* an illuminated manuscript, 669

Underground Railroad, quilt, 356

Vedder, Elihu, *The Lair of the Sea Serpent,* 634–635
Venus de Milo (detail), statue, 632

Wiggins, Guy C., *Metropolitan Tower,* 380–381

Zeus, head of, 575
Zeus and His Eagle, cup, 584
Zurbarán, Francisco de, *Hercules,* 626

Photo Credits

Abbreviations: AA—Animals, Animals; AR—Art Resource, Inc.; BA—The Bettmann Archive; BCI—Bruce Coleman, Inc; BS—Black Star; CP—Culver Pictures, Inc.; GC—The Granger Collection, New York; MP—Magnum Photos, Inc.; PR—Photo Researchers; SM—The Stock Market; TIB—The Image Bank; TSI—Tony Stone Images; IW—Image Works.

Title Page, Back Cover; William S. Nawrocki/Nawrocki Stock Photo; vi, Giraudon/AR; vii, S. Zeiberg; viii, National Museum of American Art, Smithsonian/AR; ix, Werner Forman Archive, British Museum, London/AR; x, Joel Greenstein/Omni-Photo Communications, Inc.; xi, Pamela Zilly/TIB; xiii, Scala/AR; xiv, Walters Art Gallery (detail of Procession of Twelve Gods and Goddesses; xv (both) AR.

1(t), The Metropolitan Museum of Art, The Chester Dale Collection; (c), The Mead Art Museum, Amherst College; (b), The Metropolitan Museum of Art, gift of Thomas Kensett; 2, Sam Dudgeon/HRW Photo; 6, Gregg Adams/Allstock; 11(t), Courtesy Harper Collins; (b), Lou Jawitz/TIB; 12, Elyse Lewin/TIB; 15, Maria Taglienti/TIB; 18, Carolyn Soto; 19, Oregon Historical Society, OrHi 70669; 21, GC; 23, New York Public Library Picture Collection; 26, Robert Lebeck/BS; 28, Philip Jon Bailey/SB; 31, GC; 33, Denver Art Museum; 34, Richard Erdoes; 42, Jack Spratt/IW; 49, Courtesy Mark Twain House and Museum, Hannibal, MO. © 1936, 1964 The Heritage Press, Inc.; 52, CP; 53, Painting by Frank Larson/National Portrait Gallery/ Smithsonian Institution/AR, NY; 55(b), BA; 57, Lindsay Hebberd/Woodfin Camp & Associates; 59, Ken Heyman/ Woodfin Camp & Associates; 60, Lindsay Hebberd/Woodfin Camp & Associates; 62, Courtesy Ruskin Bond; 63, Werner Forman/AR; 64, AR; 68, Scribner Book Co., Inc.; 69, Stephen Krasemann/Peter Arnold; 70, GC; 71, 74-75, L.L.T. Rhodes; 76, Glenn Matsumara/Santa Clara University; 78, W. Metzen/H. Armstrong Roberts; 80, Uniphoto; 87, Archive Photos; 95, Luis Villota/SM; 96, Seale Graphics/TIB; 100, GC; 103, Museum of Modern Art; 106, Springer/Bettmann Archive; 111, R. Owen/BS; 112, Donald Specker/Earth Scenes; 113, Courtesy October House, Inc.; 114, Larry Mulvehil/PR; 116-117, William Johnson/SM; 123, Michal Heron/Monkmeyer; 127, S. Zeiberg; 130, GC; 131, Erich Lessing/AR/National Museum, Beijing, China; 132, Lynn Levy/University of Wisconsin Photo Media Center; 138, Henri Cartier-Bresson/MP; 144, Harvey Lloyd/SM; 147, Katherine S. Thomas; 148, Bob & Clara Calhoun/BC; 149, George Kelley/PR; 150, George Kelley/PR; 152, Cynthia Farah; 153, Robert Sottlemeyer/ International Stock Photograph; 156, Brian Parker/Tom Stack & Associates; 157, Nicholas De Vore III/BC; 161, Jane Sturzel; 162-3(tc), Carson Baldwin/Earth Scenes; 163(r), Edward Weston/National Portrait Gallery, Center for Creative Photography; 164, AR; 166-67, National Maritime Museum, San Francisco; 169, GC; 170, G. I. Bernard/Earth Scenes; 172, Erwin & Peggy Bauer/BC; 175, L.L.T. Rhodes/International Stock Photograph/Telegraph Colour Library; 177, Courtesy Holiday House, Inc.; 178, Dodo Knight; 179, Kosti Rudhomaa/BS; 180-1, Cary Wolinski/SB; 183, Aaron Klein; 186, Patti Murray/AA; 188, Barry O'Rourke/SM; 199(tl), The Metropolitan Museum of Art, Arthur Hoppock Hearn Fund; 199(tr), Nationalgalerie Staatliche Museen Preussischer Kulturbesitz, Berlin; 199(cl), The Metropolitan Museum of Art, George A. Hearn Fund; 199(bl), © Mike Yamashita/Woodfin Camp & Associates; 199(br), The Metropolitan Museum of Art; 202, Sam Dudgeon/HRW Photo; 203, Thomas Ives/SM; 205, Luis Villota/SM; 206, Lindsay Hebberd/Woodfin Camp & Associates; 209, Leo de Wys; 210; Mike & Barbara Reed/AA; 216, Russ Kinne/Comstock; 221, Larry Doell/SM; 228, Davey/Camera Press/Photo Trends; 229, Warren & Jenny Garst/Tom Stack & Associates; 231, Z. Leszczynski/AA; 233, E.R. Degginger/AA; 241, Bassano/Camera Press/Photo Trends; 243, Phoebe Dunn/DPI; 245, Robert Capa/MP; 246, Malmberg/BS; 247-59, Historic Hudson Valley, Tarrytown, New York; 263, GC; 271, By permission of Harper & Row Publishers, Inc.; 275, M. Carlebach/BS; 280-298, Dan McCoy/Rainbow; 302, GC; 308, Sam Dudgeon/HRW Photo; 311, Harry Gruyaert/MP; 316, Guido Alberto Rossi/TIB; 321-334, CP; 346, C. Brownie Harris/BS; 351, Seale Graphics/TIB; 356(l), Jerry Bauer/Coward, McCann & Geohegan; 358, Werner Forman/AR; 365, 369-370, Werner Forman/AR; 373(t), Susan McCartney/PR; 373(b), Joan Marcus/Marc Bryan-Brown/Walt Disney Theatrical Productions.; 374(tl), Ben Simmons/SM; 374(tr), R. Ian Lloyd/SM; 374(b), Luca Gavagna/PR; 375(t), Sylvain Grandadam/PR; 375(bl), Gary Lewis/SM; 375(br), David Ball/SM; 382, Sam Dudgeon/HRW Photo; 383, Tom Marschal/TIB; 384, Scott McKiernan/BS; 387, Michael K. Nichols/MP; 388-390, Chris Steel-Perkins/MP Perkins/MP; 392, AP/Wide World Photos; 397, Bill Eichner/ Susan Bergholz; 399, Z. Leszczynski/Earth Scenes; 401, M. P. Kahl/BC; 403, CP; 405, Arkansas School for the Blind; 413, Wide World Photos; 415, Richard Rowan/PR; 417, Mimi Forsyth/Monkmeyer; 418-419, Mimi Forsyth/ Monkmeyer; 421, Paul Conklin/Monkmeyer; 423, UPI/ Bettmann Archive; 430, Sam Dudgeon/HRW Photo; 432, Pamela Zilly/TIB; 434, Ron Goor/BCI; 436(t), Archive Photos; 436(b), University of Arkansas Press; 438, Robert Tultin/ International Stock Photograph; 440, Joel Greenstein/Omni-Photo Communications, Inc.; 441, John Gerlach/AA; 445(tl), Robert Phillips/BS; 445(bl), University of Massachusettes Press; 445(br), CP; 448, Tom McHugh/PR; 449(t), GC; 449(b), Lotte Jacobi/Courtesy W.W. Norton and Co.; 453, Leo de Wys; 454(t), LaVerne H. Clark; 454(b), CP; 456, Sigurd Owens/International Stock Photograph; 457, Akuma Takegami/International Stock Photograph; 462, Copyright Curtis Publishing Co./New York Public Library Picture Collection; 464, Mark Newman/Tom Stack & Associates; 466, Ralph Oberlander/SB; 467(tl)(tr), GC; 467(br), CP; 473, GC; 484, GC; 487, National Portrait Gallery; 489, John Gerard/ Uniphoto; 491, Freer Gallery of Art, Smithsonian Institution, Washington, D.C.; 492(t),; 492(b), GC; 493-495(t) John

Tenniel; 495(b) GC; 500–501, Mike Yamashita/Woodfin Camp & Associates, Inc.; 505, Phillip Wallick/SM; 508-509, Tom Wagner/Odyssey Productions; 516, Mike Yamashita/Woodfin Camp & Associates, Inc.; 527, Werner Forman/AR; 531, Ken Straiton/SM; 535, Alan Oddie/PhotoEdit; 537, Rich Iwasaki/AllStock; 541, James H. Carmichael, Jr./TIB; 549, Chad Ehlers/AllStock; 554, Keyphotos/SM; 556, Phil Shermeister/AllStock; 559, Steve Krongard/TIB; 560, Gary A Conner/PhotoEdit; 563, Carolyn Soto; 564, David Ball/SM; 571(tl), The Metropolitan Museum of Art, bequest of Maria DeWitt Jessup, 1915; 571(cr), The Metropolitan Museum of Art, gift of Mrs. Harold G. Henderson; 571(bl), The Pierpont Morgan Library, bequest of Miss Clara S. Peck; 575, AR; 578, AR; 579(l), Scala/AR; 579(r), GC; 580(l), AR; 582 Courtesy Houghton, Mifflin and Company; 584, Giraudon/AR; 589, Giraudon/AR; 591, Jeremy Ingalls; 593-599, AR; 601, Jerry Bauer; 605, CP; 610, GC; 612, Historical Picture Service; 615, Harvey D. Parker Collection. Courtesy, Museum of Fine Arts, Boston; 619, UPI/Bettmann Archive; 625, AR; 626, Prado Museum, Reproducciones MAS; 630, AR; 631, GC; 632, AR; 637, National Museum of American Art, Smithsonian Institution; 639; AR; 640, Ny Carlsberg Glyptotek, Copenhagen; 642, AR; 645-55 George Harrap & Co., London, 1914; 664, George Harrap & Co., London, 1914; 672, GC; 676, GC; 679-82, Harper & Row, New York.

Index of Authors and Titles

The page numbers in italics indicate where a brief biography of the author is located.

Abbey, Edward, 147, *152*
Adams, Thomas E., 114, *121*
Adventures of Hercules, The, 622
Aesop, 669
Alvarez, Julia, 393, *397*
Anderson, Sherwood, 27, *31*
Annabel Lee, 460
Annixter, Paul, 153, *161*
Ant and the Grasshopper, The, 672
Antaeus, 187
Arachne, 598

Bashō, Matsuo, 491
Beachcroft, T. O., 208, *219*
Bearded Man, The, 496
Belling the Cat, 669
Benson, Sally, 602, *605*
Berry, James, 10, *11*
Birdfoot's Grampa, 186
Bishop, Morris, 613, *613*
Blind Men and the Elephant, The, 675
Bond, Ruskin, 56, *62*
Bracelet, The, 63
Broncho That Would Not Be Broken, The, 464
Brooks, Gwendolyn, 127, *130*
Browning, Robert, 478, *487*
Bruchac, Joseph, 186, *186*

Callaghan, Morley, 77, *87*
Carroll, Lewis, 493, *495*
Cat and the Pain Killer, The, 48
Caterpillar, The, 433
Childress, Alice, 347, *356*
Chipmunk's Day, The, 441
Chiyo, 491
Chosu, 491
Christmas Carol, A, 276
Circuit, The, 71
Clifton, Lucille, 438, *445*
Coffin, Robert P. Tristram, 452, *454*
Coolidge, Olivia, 575, *582*, 592, 644, 653
Courage That My Mother Had, The, 100
Courlander, Harold, 713
Cullen, Countee, 54, *55*
Crick Crack, Monkey, 94
Cummings, E. E., 69, *70*, 439

Dahl, Roald, 220, *228*
Day's Wait, A, 242
De la Mare, Walter, 457, *459*
Deal, Borden, 187, *195*
Death of Balder, The, 660
Desert Creatures, 147

Dickens, Charles, 276, *302*
Dickinson, Emily, 490, *492*, 699
Dinner Party, The, 204
Dobie, J. Frank, 414, *423*
Doyle, Sir Arthur Conan, 318, *334*

End of All Things, The, 663
Erne from the Coast, The, 208

Fables by Aesop, 669
Fables by James Thurber, 679
Fairly Intelligent Fly, The, 679
Father William, 493
Fenris Wolf, The, 644
Fight, The, 56
Fog, 437
Fox and the Crow, The (Aesop), 673
Fox and the Crow, The (Thurber), 682
France, Marie de, 677
Frost, Robert, 178, *179*, 455
Full Fathom Five, 466

Gardner, Mona, 204
Geiger, Milton, 309
Gods and Goddesses of Mount Olympus, The, 575
Golden Vanity, The, 475
Goodall, Jane, 386, *392*
Governess, The, 343
Grandma Ling, 131
Graves, Robert, 433, *436*
Guinea Pig, 41

Haiku, 491
Hamilton, Edith, 608, *612*, 622, 660, 685
Hardwick, Michael, 318
Hardwick, Molly, 318
Hay, Sara Henderson, 435, *436*
Hayden, Robert, 112, *113*
Hemingway, Ernest, 242, *246*
Henshaw, James Ene, 357, *372*
Hidden Life of Dogs, The, from, 424
Highwayman, The, 468
Hodge, Merle, 94, *99*
Home, 127
How Ijapa, Who Was Short, Became Long, 713
How Thor Found His Hammer, 648
Hughes, Langston, 162, *163*

Icarus and Daedalus, 614
I'm Nobody, 490
in Just-, 439
In the Fog, 309
In the Shadow of Man, 386
In Time of Silver Rain, 162
Ingalls, Jeremy, 583, *591*
Irving, Washington, 247, *263*

Jacobs, Joseph, 669
Jarrell, Randall, 441, *445*
Jewels of the Shrine, The, 357
Jiménez, Francisco, 71, *76*

King of Mazy May, The, 19
Kipling, Rudyard, 229, *241*
Kjelgaard, Jim, 170, *177*

Lama, The, 496
Landlady, The, 220
Last Cover, 153
Lear, Edward, 496
Lee, Harper, 102, *111*
Lindsay, Vachel, 464, *467*
Ling, Amy, 131, *132*
Listeners, The, 457
Little Things, 490
Living Tenderly, 450
London, Jack, 19, *26*
Longfellow, Henry Wadsworth, 164, *169*, 488
Lopez, Barry Holstun, 383
Luke Baldwin's Vow, 77

Mabie, Hamilton Wright, 648
maggie and milly and molly and may, 69
Masefield, John, 447, *449*
May Day, 431
Mazarin Stone, The, 318
McKenney, Ruth, 41, *47*
McLaverty, Michael, 180, *185*
Medicine Bag, The, 32
Mehta, Ved, 404, *413*
Millay, Edna St. Vincent, 100, *100*

Names/Nombres, 393
Nash, Ogden, 496
Night the Bed Fell, The, 133
Nisei Daughter, from, 122
Norse Gods and Goddesses, The, 640
Noyes, Alfred, 468, *473*

One, 10
One of the Seven Has Somewhat to Say, 435
One Writer's Beginnings, from, 3
One-Shot Finch, 102
Origin of the Seasons, The, 592
Otero, Nina, 144, *146*
Owl and the Two Rabbits, The, 684

Pacific Crossing, 503
Parrot, A, 448
Peabody, Josephine Preston, 614, *617*
Phaethon (Bishop), 613
Phaethon (Hamilton), 608
Picard, Barbara Leonie, 640, 663
Pied Piper of Hamelin, The, 478
Poe, Edgar Allan, 460, *467*
Prometheus the Fire-Bringer, 583

Quintero, Joaquín, 335, *342*

Quintero, Serafín, 335, *342*

Rattlesnake Hunt, 398
Rawlings, Marjorie Kinnan, 398, *403*
Reward of Baucis and Philemon, The, 602
Rikki-tikki-tavi, 229
Riley, James Whitcomb, 443, *445*
Rip Van Winkle, 247
River Notes, from, 383
Runaway, The, 178

Sandburg, Carl, 437, *445*
Sarton, May, 448, *449*
Saxe, John Godfrey, 675, *678*
Seventh Grade, 13
Sexton, Anne, 618, *619*
Shakespeare, William, 466, *467*
Simon, Neil, 343, *346*
Singer, Isaac Bashevis, 270, *275*
Sled, 114
Sneve, Virginia Driving Hawk, 32, *40*
Snowflakes, 488
Sone, Monica, 122, *126*
Soto, Gary, 13, *18*, 503, *563*
Sound-Shadows of the New World, from, 404
Spider, The, 452
Stephens, James, 490, *492*, 699
Stolen Day, 27
Stopping by Woods on a Snowy Evening, 455
Sunny Morning, A, 335
Swenson, May, 450, *454*

Tableau, 54
Teasdale, Sara, 431
The 1st, 438
Thomas, Elizabeth Marshall, 424
Thor and the Giant King, 653
Those Winter Sundays, 112
Thurber, James, 133, *138*, 679, 680, 682
Tiger's Heart, The, 170
To a Friend Whose Work Has Come to Triumph, 618
Town Mouse and the Country Mouse, The, 670
Trade Winds, 447
Tutor, A, 496
Twain, Mark, 48, *53*

Uchida, Yoshiko, 63, *68*

Warner, Rex, 598, *601*
Wells, Carolyn, 496
Welty, Eudora, 3
What Happened to Charles, 680
When I Was a Boy on the Ranch, 414
When the Frost Is on the Punkin, 443
When the Rattlesnake Sounds, 347
Wild Duck's Nest, The, 180
Wind in the Mountains, The, 144
Wind, The, 699
Wind Tapped like a Tired Man, The, 699
Wolf and the Dog, The, 677

Wreck of the Hesperus, *The,* 164
Wuorio, Eva-Lis, 264, *269*

You Can't Take It with You, 264

Zlateh the Goat, 270

AUDIO-VISUAL CENTER
MISSOURI SOUTHERN STATE COLLEGE